EXAMPLES&EXPLANATIONS

Contracts

Contracts

Sixth Edition

Brian A. Blum
Professor of Law
Lewis & Clark Law School

Wolters Kluwer
Law & Business

About Wolters Kluwer Law & Business

Wolters Kluwer Law & Business is a leading global provider of intelligent information and digital solutions for legal and business professionals in key specialty areas, and respected educational resources for professors and law students. Wolters Kluwer Law & Business connects legal and business professionals as well as those in the education market with timely, specialized authoritative content and information-enabled solutions to support success through productivity, accuracy and mobility.

Serving customers worldwide, Wolters Kluwer Law & Business products include those under the Aspen Publishers, CCH, Kluwer Law International, Loislaw, Best Case, ftwilliam.com and MediRegs family of products.

CCH products have been a trusted resource since 1913, and are highly regarded resources for legal, securities, antitrust and trade regulation, government contracting, banking, pension, payroll, employment and labor, and healthcare reimbursement and compliance professionals.

Aspen Publishers products provide essential information to attorneys, business professionals and law students. Written by preeminent authorities, the product line offers analytical and practical information in a range of specialty practice areas from securities law and intellectual property to mergers and acquisitions and pension/benefits. Aspen's trusted legal education resources provide professors and students with high-quality, up-to-date and effective resources for successful instruction and study in all areas of the law.

Kluwer Law International products provide the global business community with reliable international legal information in English. Legal practitioners, corporate counsel and business executives around the world rely on Kluwer Law journals, looseleafs, books, and electronic products for comprehensive information in many areas of international legal practice.

Loislaw is a comprehensive online legal research product providing legal content to law firm practitioners of various specializations. Loislaw provides attorneys with the ability to quickly and efficiently find the necessary legal information they need, when and where they need it, by facilitating access to primary law as well as state-specific law, records, forms and treatises.

Best Case Solutions is the leading bankruptcy software product to the bankruptcy industry. It provides software and workflow tools to flawlessly streamline petition preparation and the electronic filing process, while timely incorporating ever-changing court requirements.

ftwilliam.com offers employee benefits professionals the highest quality plan documents (retirement, welfare and non-qualified) and government forms (5500/PBGC, 1099 and IRS) software at highly competitive prices.

MediRegs products provide integrated health care compliance content and software solutions for professionals in healthcare, higher education and life sciences, including professionals in accounting, law and consulting.

Wolters Kluwer Law & Business, a division of Wolters Kluwer, is headquartered in New York. Wolters Kluwer is a market-leading global information services company focused on professionals.

To Bryce, Kylie, William,

Lexie, and Katherine with love

Summary of Contents

Summary of Contents

Contents

Contents

Chapter 3   The Doctrine of Precedent and a Contract Case Analysis   41

Chapter 4   The Objective Test and Basic Principles of Offer and Acceptance   59

Contents

Chapter 7   Consideration   177

Chapter 9   Unjust Enrichment, Restitution, and "Moral Obligation"   269

Contents

Chapter 10 Interpretation and Construction: Resolving Meaning and Dealing with Uncertainty in Agreements — 305

Contents

Chapter 12 The Parol Evidence Rule   385

Chapter 14   Incapacity   497

Chapter 15   Mistake, Impracticability, and Frustration of Purpose   521

Contents

Chapter 19   Assignment, Delegation, and Third-Party Beneficiaries   753

Contents

Preface

I expect that most readers of this book will be first-year law students who will use it as a resource to assist in learning and understanding the law of contracts — to prepare for class, to unravel and supplement class materials and discussion, and to review and prepare for exams. In deciding on the scope, depth, and approach of the book's coverage, I have aimed at their needs. My focus has been on what is likely to be most appropriate and helpful to a person who approaches contract law as a novice and is trying to assimilate and understand not only the details but also the larger issues of this complex subject.

Changes in the Sixth Edition

In revising this book for the sixth edition, I have retained the scope, approach, and most of the material in the fifth edition, including the expanded treatment of standard contracts and contracts formed through electronic media, and the notes on the transnational perspective of contract law. I have not changed the overall organization of the book, but have made changes in the internal reorganization of some chapters to improve clarity. In my revisions for the sixth edition, I have continued my efforts to provide an accessible and helpful treatment of the law of contracts. I have concentrated on matters of detail, altering text and diagrams to the extent necessary to update and clarify textual materials, adding new cases, and refining the examples and explanations by adding new ones and changing or eliminating some of the older ones.

The sixth edition continues to have the comprehensive index and glossary at the end of the book. In response to suggestions by users, I have added tables of cases and statutes.

The Treatment of the Sale of Goods in the Sixth Edition

Article 2 of the Uniform Commercial Code (UCC), which governs contracts for the sale of goods, forms part of most contracts courses. Coverage of Article 2 is supplemented by those provisions of Article 1 (the general article of the UCC) that contain general principles and definitions applicable to Article 2. The provisions of UCC Articles 1 and 2 are dealt with throughout this book, to the extent that these provisions are relevant to the contracts course. I use the Official Text of Article 1, as revised in 2001, and adopted by most states. I use the Official Text of Article 2, as currently enacted in most states. In prior editions of the book, I gave some attention to the revision of Article 2 that had been proposed in 2003. However, the revision was never adopted by states, and has been abandoned. (This is explained in Chapter 2.) Therefore, this edition refers only occasionally to the proposed 2003 revisions, usually in the footnotes, where reference to the proposed changes casts light on the existing provision of article 2.

The Style, Approach, and Purpose of This Book

Like many other law school courses, contract law is typically taught by means of discussing and debating cases and other materials that have been assigned for reading in advance of the class session. A terrible flood of information is unleashed by this process, and it is difficult for a student to assimilate and appreciate it all by studying the casebook and working through the materials in class. Supplementary reading is very helpful to understanding and digesting what is covered in class. To be most useful, such a supplementary text should be written with an awareness of the coverage, depth, and scope of most contracts courses, and with a sense of what students are likely to need by way of additional reading. In writing this book, I have tried to keep that goal in mind. Relying on my own experience as a teacher of contract law, and on the content of casebooks, I have tried to maintain the discussion in this book at the level that may be expected in a typical contracts class.

To achieve this purpose, it is not enough to outline legal rules or to state doctrine. Although it is surely one of the aims of a contracts class to teach the current rules of law governing contracts, a knowledge of current legal rules is only one of the components of an adequate understanding of contract law. Students are also expected to learn the derivation and development of the rules, their historical and contemporary rationale, the public policies that they are meant to serve, and the way in which they coalesce to form a coherent body of law. Because neither rules nor their underlying policies are static, and are often unsettled and the subject of controversy, students must also be exposed to the uncertainties of the law and must learn to develop the ability to evaluate critically and to form judgments. In addition, like so many other courses in law school, a contracts course serves the goal of exposing students to broader issues of legal process, legal analysis, dispute resolution, and lawyering skills such as drafting, advising, and evaluating the strength of a case. This book attempts to encompass this range of learning. Its principal aim is the clear and accessible explanation of the fundamentals of the law, with a particular concentration on what information is likely to be helpful to a student who approaches the subject for the first time

As part of the effort to clarify legal principles and the relationships between contracting parties, I have used diagrams extensively. I believe that visual representations can be a great help in clarifying and reinforcing verbal exposition.

The Use of Examples and Explanations

Concrete examples place doctrine and abstract principles in context and show how they operate to affect behavior and resolve disputes. Examples and the facts of selected cases are therefore used extensively in the text itself to illustrate concepts under discussion. In addition, a distinctive feature of this book is the "examples and explanations," which take up a substantial part of each chapter. Their purpose is not only to provide further illustration and discussion of the subject matter of the text but also to give students a means of self-testing on the topics covered. The examples pose questions based on hypothetical facts, and the explanations analyze and offer a resolution to the problems. As a general rule, the examples and explanations do more than simply provide a means of reviewing what has been stated in the text. To resolve them adequately, one must use reasoned argument and must thoughtfully apply the principles set out in the text. You will therefore benefit the most from them if you do not merely read through them but rather take the time to formulate your own answer to an example before reading its explanation. This will allow you to test your knowledge and understanding of the material, to practice identifying issues, and to develop skills in composing and organizing answers to the kind of questions commonly found in exams.

The Organization of This Book in Relation to Your Contracts Course

There are a number of different ways to organize a contracts course, and the casebooks reflect quite a diverse approach to the sequence in which material may be covered in class. It is therefore quite possible that your contracts course will not follow the same sequence as the chapters in this book. (For example, some courses begin with remedies for breach of contract, which is not covered here until Chapter 18, and some begin with consideration doctrine, which is not reached until Chapter 7.) This book has been written with an eye on the divergent ways in which the topics of contract law are presented in different classes, so a student should have no trouble reading chapters out of order. To use this book in the same sequence as your contracts course, simply refer to the table of contents, to find the part of the book that deals with the subject under discussion in class. (The index, table of cases, and table of statutes are also helpful in identifying those sections and examples in the book that correspond to what you are studying in class.) Cross-references are included in each chapter to help give you an idea of where to find allied topics or further reference to the subject under discussion.

A Recommendation About Chapters 1 Through 3 and the Glossary

Irrespective of the organization of your class, I do recommend, however, that you read Chapters 1, 2, and 3 as soon as possible. These short chapters are intended as an introduction to some of the root principles of contract law and legal analysis. They contain basic information and guidance on core concepts, terminology, and case analysis that may not be articulated fully or at all in your class materials or discussion. A little time spent in working through these chapters at the beginning of the semester may save you needless puzzlement and confusion. Also, you should refer to the glossary at the end of the book for short definitions of terms that may be unfamiliar to you.

The Use and Citation of Authority in This Book

To make this book as readable and accessible as possible, I have kept citation of authority to a minimum. You will not find detailed footnotes and citations that you would expect in a treatise or law review article. However, some sources of authority are such an integral part of the process of learning contract law that to omit them would impede understanding. These sources are referred to constantly throughout the book. They are:

1) The Restatement (Second) of Contracts (referred to in the book in abbreviated form as Restatement, Second), a compendious and highly influential formulation of the rules of contract law.
2) Articles 1 and 2 of the Uniform Commercial Code (UCC). Article 2 governs contracts for the sale of goods and is the principal focus of our study of the UCC. Article 1 is supplementary to Article 2. It has general provisions applicable to all Articles of the UCC, including Article 2.
3) Caselaw. Court opinions are a vital source of law in our system. I discuss cases selectively but regularly in the text and also, to a lesser extent, in the explanations. I do not use cases merely as authority for legal rules but as factual illustrations and as a means of highlighting legal principles, argument, and reasoning. I selected many of the

cases in this book because of their interesting or even entertaining facts. I have tried to use recent cases wherever possible to reflect the law in its contemporary state. However, there are many important or well-known older cases that are taught in almost every contracts course, and I have included those, too. I have also kept an eye on the content of casebooks and have made a point of mentioning some of the cases that have been chosen by casebook authors. You should therefore find that at least some of the cases discussed here are familiar from class.

Brian A. Blum
April 2013

Acknowledgments

I owe thanks to many people who have helped me with successive editions of this book. I have had able research assistance from a number of Lewis & Clark Law School students for each edition of this book. I have also benefitted from the guidance and careful editorial work of several members of the staff of Wolters Kluwer Law & Business. Finally, I am grateful to the many students and professors who have used this book and who have offered comments and suggestions.

Contracts

1

The Meaning of "Contract" and the Basic Attributes of the Contractual Relationship

§1.1 INTRODUCTION

Some contracts courses may begin with material that provides students with background information on the law of contracts. Others may launch immediately into the study of substantive principles of contract law. Whatever form your contracts course takes, you may find it helpful to read the first three chapters of this book right at the beginning of your course. They introduce and articulate basic concepts about contract law and our legal system that you will find very helpful as you begin your studies. Many of the principles and concepts introduced in these three initial chapters will appear frequently throughout the book, so this will not be the only time that you read about them. However, this first encounter will set the stage for your studies and will enable you to begin to understand legal analysis and identify themes that run through contract law. You will find immediately that the discussion goes well beyond the exposition of rules of law. Even if one assumes that it is possible to articulate a clear and settled body of rules (an assumption that you will quickly find to be false), the rules are just one component of what needs to be studied in learning the law. Rules do not exist in a vacuum, but must be understood in light of historical perspective, public policy, legal theory, and the legal process.

We begin our introductory survey in this chapter by defining what is meant by a contract. This discussion gives you a brief overview of a number of the central themes of contract law and it broadly sketches the contractual relationship. Chapter 2 describes some of the fundamental concepts and distinctions that are essential to a comprehension of contract law in the context of our legal system as a whole. It explains the importance of historical perspective and legal theory, describes the nature of our common law system, and introduces the crucial distinction between judge-made law and statutory law, with particular reference to the statute that pervades contract law, Article 2 of the Uniform Commercial Code (UCC). Chapter 3 concentrates on the nature and composition of judicial opinions and on the method of analyzing and gleaning legal rules from them. Its primary purpose is to explain the doctrine of precedent as it applies in contract law and in our legal system as a whole. The Examples in Chapter 3 offer a specimen opinion, constructed to provide an exercise in reading, understanding, and applying the precedent of a judicial decision. Because contract law is commonly taught through the study of court decisions, you will become familiar with the methodology of case analysis as you use it throughout the contracts course. However, Chapter 3 provides an early opportunity for you to focus on and to begin to understand how to approach caselaw and case analysis.

§1.2 THE LEGAL MEANING OF "CONTRACT"

By the time they reach law school, most people have a good idea of what a contract is. Nevertheless, lay usage of a legal term such as "contract" is likely to be less exacting than the legal definition, and so we must begin by defining and describing the elements of contract. It is not easy to provide a simple and accurate definition of a legal relationship as complex as contract, and the following definition is necessarily an oversimplification. However, it serves as a starting point for discussion and allows us to focus on the crucial elements of the relationship.

A contract may be defined as an exchange relationship created by oral or written agreement between two or more persons, containing at least one promise, and recognized in law as enforceable. This definition reflects several essential elements:

1. An oral or written agreement between two or more persons
2. An exchange relationship
3. At least one promise
4. Enforceability

The central concept of each of these elements is introduced below and will be returned to in greater detail later in the book.

§1.2.1 An Oral or Written Agreement Between Two or More Persons

Probably the most important attribute of contract is that it is a voluntary, consensual relationship. There need only be two parties to a contract, but there is no limit on the number of parties that could be involved in the transaction. A contract is created only because the parties, acting with free will and intent to be bound, reach agreement on the essential terms of their relationship. It is the element of agreement that distinguishes contractual obligation from many other kinds of legal duty (such as the obligation to compensate for negligent injury or to pay taxes) that arise by operation of law from some act or event, without the need for assent.

Although voluntary agreement between the parties is essential to the creation of contract, "agreement" in the legal sense is subject to an important qualification. The law does not require that the parties reach true agreement, in a subjective sense — that their minds are in accord. It is enough that the words and conduct of a party, evaluated on an objective standard, would lead the other party reasonably to understand that agreement was reached. (The reason for using this objective standard is explained in sections 1.4.3 and 4.1.) Also, volition should not be taken too literally. We assume that a party may not be acting with completely free will in entering into a contract. He may feel some compulsion to make the contract as a result of market forces, the persuasiveness of the other party, necessity, or the lack of a more attractive alternative. However, volition does at least mean that a party cannot be improperly coerced or tricked into making a contract, and the law has principles and standards (covered in Chapter 13) to distinguish when pressure to make a contract is no longer acceptable, and has so undermined the party's will as to defeat his volition.

Note that our definition refers to an oral or written agreement. In common terminology, people often use the word "contract" to refer to a written document that records the parties' agreement. However, it is important to understand that "contract" describes a relationship that may or may not be recorded in a document. As a general rule, a contract does not have to be in writing to be a binding and enforceable legal obligation. (Under a legal rule called the statute of frauds, there are some types of contract that must be recorded in a signed writing to be enforceable. This is discussed in Chapter 11. However, most contracts are not covered by the statute of frauds, and are binding as soon as oral agreement has been reached.) Of course, it may be harder to prove an oral contract than one that has been recorded in writing, but do not confuse problems of proof with the more fundamental question of enforceability.

Although contract requires a voluntary agreement between the parties, this does not mean that all voluntary agreements are contracts. People make all kinds of agreements that do not rise to the level of contract. For example, social agreements (the acceptance of a dinner invitation or a commitment to go together to see a movie), a politician's campaign promises, or a spouse's promise to clean out the attic next weekend. Courts sometimes describe promises of this kind as moral or ethical obligations, rather than legal ones. The distinction between a legally binding contractual obligation and moral obligation is not always easy to draw, but often this question is settled by determining the intent of the parties (measured objectively). In some cases there may be other indications that the agreement creates only a moral obligation. For example, the requirement of exchange, discussed in section 1.2.2, may be missing. For this reason (as explained in Chapter 7), a promise to give a gift or to make a contribution to charity may create a moral obligation, but it does not qualify as a legally binding contractual obligation.

§1.2.2 An Exchange Relationship

As mentioned earlier, a contract is a relationship. By entering into the agreement, the parties bind themselves to each other for the common purpose of the contract. Some contractual relationships last only a short time and require minimal interaction. For example, a contract for a haircut involves a fairly quick performance by the hairdresser, followed by the fulfillment of the customer's payment obligation. Other contractual relationships, such as leases, construction contracts, or long-term employment contracts, could span many years and require constant dealings between the parties, regulated by detailed provisions in the agreement.

The essential purpose of the contract relationship is exchange. The trade in property, services, and intangible rights is fundamental to our economy and society, and the primary function of contract is to facilitate and regulate these exchanges. The concept of exchange (discussed more fully in Chapter 7) means that the very essence of contract is a reciprocal relationship in which each party gives up something to get something. These "somethings" are as varied as one could imagine: The owner of a car could sell it for cash or barter it for other goods; a celebrity's butler may promise to reveal his employer's dark secrets to a tabloid for cold hard cash; an inventor may trade the rights to her idea for a promise by a manufacturer to develop the idea for mutual profit; a fond uncle may promise his nephew money in exchange for an undertaking not to drink, smoke, and gamble. These situations vary greatly. Some involve tangible things, others intangible rights. Some of the promises have economic value, others do not. Yet their basic format is the same — a bargain has been reached leading to a reciprocal exchange for the betterment (real or perceived) of both parties.

As discussed in Chapters 7, 8, and 9, the modern concept of contract embraces some transactions in which exchange in the traditional sense is tenuous. Nevertheless, exchange continues to be the principal motivation for contracting and the guiding rationale for the rules of contract law.

§1.2.3 Promise

A contract is a relationship that can be enforced by legal process. Therefore, if the parties simply enter into an instantaneous exchange (say, an exchange of goods for cash, without any warranty relating to the goods) neither makes any commitment, and there is no role for contract law to play in enforcing the exchange. It is therefore usually said that there must be some promise made by at least one of the parties for a contract to exist.

The concept of promise or commitment needs explanation and refinement. A promise is an undertaking to act or refrain from acting in a specified way at some future time. This promise may be made in clear and express words, or it could be implied — that is, inferred from conduct or from the circumstances of the transaction. A contractual promise is sometimes called a covenant. However, "promise" is the more common word and is less subject to confusion because "covenant" is sometimes used as a synonym for "contract."

Notice that the definition of "contract" indicates that only one promise needs to be made for an enforceable contract to come into existence. This concept may be puzzling at first impression because the definition also characterizes contract as an exchange relationship, so one would expect reciprocal promises. In most cases, contracts do contain reciprocal promises — the parties exchange promises, so that each makes a promise to the other. However, an exchange relationship also exists if one of the parties makes a promise of future action in exchange for an instantaneous performance by the other.[1]

The following illustration shows the distinction between an instantaneous exchange (also called an executed exchange) and a contractual obligation: Rocky Rapids decided to sell his kayak. He placed it on the sidewalk in front of his house with a sign that read "For sale, without any warranties. $400."[2] Eddy Undertow saw the sign and decided to buy the kayak. He handed over $400 in cash to Rocky and took the kayak away. This is an

---

1. Where at the instance of contracting, promises remain outstanding on both sides, the contract is called bilateral. If one of the parties has already fully performed at the instant of contracting, and all that remains is a promise by the other, the contract is called unilateral. Do not worry about this distinction now. It is explored in section 4.12.

2. For this example to work, you must assume that the disclaimer of warranties is completely effective to eliminate all warranties, so that Rocky makes no promises as to the condition and quality of and title to the goods. We will not examine whether such a disclaimer is effective — the complexities relating to the creation and disclaimer of warranties are beyond our scope.

instantaneous exchange and therefore not a contract. Eddy paid cash and made no promise to do anything else. Rocky's legal obligation was completely performed as soon as he let Eddy take the kayak. He also made no promises.

However, the transaction would have been a contract either if Eddy had given a check to Rocky for $400 instead of cash, or if Rocky had not sold the kayak "as is," but had instead assured Eddy that it was in good condition and watertight. In each of these situations, at least one of the parties would have made a promise. Eddy's check would be a promise because a check is not an immediate payment, but a short-term credit transaction in which Eddy, in effect, promises Rocky that his bank will pay Rocky the $400 on presentation of the check. Likewise, had Rocky given a warranty, he would have made a future commitment relating to the kayak.

§1.2.4 Legal Recognition of Enforceability

Once the parties have entered into an exchange relationship that qualifies as a contract, they commit themselves to perform the promises that they have made in the contract. Contracting is often described as an act of private lawmaking by which the parties create a kind of personalized "statute" that governs their transaction. The law so created by the terms of the contract is binding on the parties. It is a hallmark of a contractual promise that if it is broken, the party to whom the promise was made can enforce it by initiating suit in court, thereby invoking the power of the government to uphold the other party's commitments. This does not mean that every breach of contract will end up in litigation. In most cases the parties have strong incentives to avoid a lawsuit. Litigation is expensive and time-consuming, and legal action might damage the parties' long-term commercial relationship as well as tarnish the breaching party's business reputation. Therefore, if there is a reasonable prospect of persuading the breaching party to perform or of otherwise settling the contractual claim informally, the parties are likely to pursue that avenue before resorting to litigation. Even where the parties cannot resolve their dispute by negotiation, their agreement may preclude litigation in court by binding them to resolve the dispute by arbitration. Arbitration provisions are included in many contracts and are generally upheld. Although a contractual claim may not reach the stage of formal resolution by a court or arbitrator, the power to use a binding legal process to enforce the contract gives the parties confidence in their contractual relationship, provides a deterrence to breach, and assures a means of compelling performance or recovering compensation for failure of performance.

Although a detailed discussion of the process of enforcement of a contract through litigation is beyond the scope of this book, it is helpful to outline the procedure that a party must follow to assert a contractual claim in court. The victim of the breach institutes action in court by filing a summons and a complaint. If the other party defends the suit, it will file an answer. Various other pleadings and processes follow as the parties prepare for trial. It often happens that the case is settled or disposed of by a summary process before it reaches trial. If not, the case proceeds to trial. Unless the parties have elected a trial by judge alone, factual questions are usually decided by a jury, and legal issues are decided by the judge. In the first instance, the role of the court is to adjudicate any questions concerning the existence of a valid contract and to resolve any disputes over its terms and their breach. Once it is established that a contract was entered into and breached, the court will enforce it by giving a remedy for the breach.

The most obvious form of remedy may seem to be for the court to force the breacher to do what was promised. For example, say that Rocky and Eddy entered into a contract under which Rocky agreed to sell the kayak to Eddy for $400. The contract provided that Rocky would deliver the kayak to Eddy the next day in exchange for $400 in cash. The next day, when Eddy arrived with the $400 in hand, Rocky said he had changed his mind and refused to go through with the sale. This is a breach of the contract. If Eddy sued Rocky, one might assume that the primary mode of legal enforcement of the contract would be a court order compelling Rocky to hand over the kayak against payment of the $400.

However, it is a firm principle of contract law (for reasons explained in Chapter 18) that the primary remedy for breach of contract is not such specific enforcement of the promise. An order compelling performance is available in only exceptional situations. Rather, it is a judgment awarding compensatory damages to the disappointed party. That is, the disappointed party must prove that the breach caused financial loss, and the court will award judgment against the breacher to compensate for that financial loss. Thus, Eddy would have to show that he had lost money or suffered some other kind of quantifiable economic harm as a result of the breach. For example, he may testify that following Rocky's refusal to deliver, he sought to buy another kayak of a similar type and condition, and could not find one of equivalent quality for less than $450. Eddy's damages are $50. The court will award him a money judgment in this amount. If Rocky fails to pay the judgment voluntarily, Eddy will attempt to recover the debt through a process called execution. Under this procedure, a court official (usually called a sheriff) is commanded by the court (in a document called a writ) to try to seize property of Rocky's and to sell it at public auction to raise the money needed to satisfy the judgment. If the sheriff is unable to find any property, the judgment debt remains unsatisfied. There is little further that can be done.

The purpose of sketching this enforcement process here is to make the point that legal enforcement seldom entails judicial compulsion of performance. In most cases, the plaintiff's victory in court is nothing more than a determination that the defendant owes him a stated amount of money. This does not end the matter because the plaintiff now has to collect the debt. If the breacher has no means of paying the judgment, the process of trying to enforce the contract could involve additional cost and inconvenience, and still end in frustration. This is an important perspective to take with you as you begin to study the law of contracts.

Finally, on the subject of legal enforcement, it is helpful to outline the arbitration process that is alluded to above. As noted earlier, many contracts provide that any disputes arising out of the contract must be resolved by arbitration or by some other process of extra-judicial dispute resolution. Arbitration is a means of enforcing the contract by a less formal and speedier means than litigation. The case is heard and disposed of by an arbitrator (or panel of arbitrators), a private person (or persons) selected by the parties. Although an arbitrator's decision may be appealable to a court on narrow grounds, the arbitrator's determination is usually final and binding on the parties and may be enforced in the same way as a judgment of a court. The law generally favors arbitration provided that it is voluntarily agreed. Therefore, if a party who is bound by a valid arbitration agreement commences suit in court, the court will compel arbitration and will dismiss or stay the lawsuit.

§1.3 CONTRACT AS A GENERAL BODY OF LAW APPLICABLE TO DIVERSE TRANSACTIONS

Contract law covers a wide range of very different transactions — leases and sales of real and personal property, employment, credit, insurance, construction, and so on. These many and diverse types of contract each have their own attributes and concerns, so it stands to reason that there cannot be a single and uniform body of legal rules that applies to all of them. With each type of contract, special rules develop to respond to distinct features of the transaction or particular needs or issues in the commercial context. For example, a whole body of law has developed to protect consumers who purchase goods or seek credit and is not applicable when the purchaser or borrower is a commercial entity; employment contracts are subject to rules designed to regulate the employment relationship, and many of them focus on the protection of employees; a construction or procurement contract with the government is subject to regulations not found elsewhere; insurance and banking contracts are also controlled by specific regulations. This recital could continue for some length. Although each of these categories of contract has its specialized rules, they all share common ground and are based on similar general principles that are encompassed within a general law of contracts.

The law of contracts is the common core of rules and principles applicable to all contracts and it governs except to the extent that it has been varied by laws specific to the transaction. This specific law may have been created by statute or by judicial decision, or both. You will therefore find, as you read through this book and your class materials, that all kinds of different contracts are considered. In most cases, because we are considering this common core of rules and principles, the type of contract involved is not of overwhelming significance. The law discussed is usually relevant to other types of contract. However, this is not always so, and one must always be on the lookout for variations, whether statutory or judge-made, based upon the particular features of the contract in issue.

§1.4 THE FUNDAMENTAL POLICIES AND VALUES OF CONTRACT LAW

Although contract law is not usually at the center of political debate and contracts professors are almost never invited to discuss their work on talk shows, it would be a mistake to think of it as purely technical and bloodless. There are a number of strongly held ideological values at the bottom of contract law and its rules are motivated by conscious and deliberate public policy. Some aspects of the ideology and policy of contract law have already been intimated in section 1.2 and they will be raised throughout the book. An understanding of the law's basic goals and assumptions is essential to a full appreciation of legal rules and so it is useful to identify and articulate significant policy themes from the outset. This section introduces them briefly.

§1.4.1 Freedom of Contract

a. Individual Autonomy

The consensual and voluntary nature of contract was stressed in section 1.3. The power to enter contracts and to formulate the terms of the contractual relationship is regarded in our legal system as an exercise of individual autonomy — an integral part of personal liberty. The converse is also true: Because contracting is an exercise of personal liberty, no one may be bound in contract in the absence of that person's assent. In the United States, the power of contracting has been elevated to a status higher than that accorded it under English common law because it is guaranteed by the

Constitution. (The due process clause, U.S. Const. amends. V and XIV, and the contracts clause, U.S. Const. art. 1 §10, provide the constitutional safeguards of liberty of contract.)

Liberty of contract is augmented by another right protected by the due process clause — the right to hold and deal with property. Contracts involve the exchange of economic values, whether in the form of tangible property, services, or intangible rights. These are property rights and the power to use or dispose of them, or to choose not to do so necessarily brings into play their constitutional protection. Furthermore, where the contract involves the rendition of personal services by an individual, that person's right to dispose of her labor or to withhold it unless she wishes to dispose of it is protected by the prohibition on involuntary servitude in the Thirteenth Amendment. The ideological basis of contract freedom is reinforced by the pragmatic consideration that economic intercourse is most efficient when its participants desire it and are free to bargain with each other to reach mutually desirable terms.

Although freedom of contract is an important value, it is not the only value that courts seek to uphold in adjudicating contract disputes. Where other public policies are implicated in the contract dispute, the court must take them into account and must balance them against the policy of protecting freedom of contract. For example, policies prohibiting criminal enterprise, protecting the environment, or forbidding anticompetitive behavior may restrict the right to make certain contracts, or may prohibit certain terms in a contract. Once again, these issues will be discussed in detail later. For the present it is enough to note that while contract liberty is an important value, it is subject to a variety of limitations that are justified either by the protection of corresponding rights in other persons or by the demands of other public interests.

b. Imbalance of Bargaining Power and Adhesion

While freedom of contract is a fundamental value, the exercise of this freedom by one person cannot be untrammelled. Like other liberties, it is delimited by corresponding rights held by other persons, and by the state's legitimate interest in appropriate regulation. In an ideal situation, a contractual relationship involves an equal exercise of autonomy by both parties. Each enters the transaction voluntarily and has the knowledge and ability to negotiate its terms. However, in many transactions, this equality does not exist. One of the parties has greater sophistication and bargaining power than the other. In some cases this imbalance of bargaining power is so great that the stronger party is able to insist that it will only contract on its own terms. If the other party wants the contract, it has no choice but to accept the terms, even if they are one-sided and drafted to favor the interests of the dominant party. For example, a consumer who buys an insurance policy, an airline ticket, or a software program may have some limited ability to select among alternative terms, but is otherwise unable to negotiate much of the content of the standard contract used by the dominant party; a small business that buys inventory from a large supplier may have insufficient market power to insist on a change to terms that the supplier has chosen to include in its standard contract.

Contracts of this kind, proffered on a "take-it-or-leave-it" basis, are known as contracts of adhesion because the less powerful party has no choice but to adhere to the proffered terms. (Contracts of adhesion are discussed more fully in Chapter 13.) Although significant imbalance in bargaining power does diminish the contractual autonomy of the weaker party, the general approach of the law is to recognize that such an imbalance is an inevitable feature of a market economy, and that it precludes the exercise of a pure and unrestricted freedom of contract by both parties in many transactions. The general policy of contract law is therefore not to interfere with contracts merely because one party had the power to formulate and impose its terms on the other. However, to prevent the abuse of this power, contract law contains many doctrines, some developed by courts and others enacted by legislation, that regulate it and allow judicial intervention when a party's conduct or the imposition exceeds the bounds of hard bargaining and becomes unfair bargaining or improper imposition. You will find these doctrines referred to in many parts of this book, but we focus on them in Chapter 13.

§1.4.2 The Morality of Promise — *Pacta Sunt Servanda*

The Latin maxim *pacta sunt servanda* (agreements must be kept) comes from Canon law.[3] It reflects a longstanding moral dimension of contract in our law — that there is an ethical as well as a legal obligation to keep one's contractual promises. Contracts should be honored not only because reliability is necessary to foster economic interaction, as discussed in section 1.4.3, but simply because it is morally wrong to break them. The role that this basic moral value plays in contract law is subtle. You will see later that courts and scholars often underplay the moral aspect of keeping promises and deal with breach of contract in purely economic terms. It is often suggested, for example, that breach of contract is an acceptable economic

---

3. Canon law is a system of ecclesiastical law developed from Roman law by the medieval Catholic church. Although it is not part of the English common law, it existed as a parallel system in England, governing matters within the Church's jurisdiction, until the English Church broke away from Rome. As a result of their long period of co-existence, many principles of Canon law influenced the common law.

choice, provided that the breacher pays monetary compensation. Nevertheless, it would be a mistake to assume that society or courts are indifferent to the ethical implications of dishonoring contracts. Where a party has breached a contract deliberately, unethically, or in bad faith, this may have an impact on the disposition of the case or the remedy. In some cases, the court expresses its disapproval of the conduct and its adverse consequences. However, even where moral condemnation is not articulated, the choice of applicable rules sometimes reflects disapprobation of wrongful conduct. Outside of the realm of litigation, social pressure and business relationships frequently provide disincentives to treat contractual undertakings in a cavalier fashion.

§1.4.3 Accountability for Conduct and Reliance

The objective test of assent was introduced in section 1.2. In determining whether or not a person agreed to a contract or specific contractual terms, the person's manifested conduct by words or action is given more weight than her testimony about her actual intentions. An emphasis on the objective appearance of assent is important not only because of evidentiary considerations (that is, it is easier to prove because it is observable) but also because one of the fundamental values of contract law is that a person should be held accountable for words or acts reasonably manifesting intent to contract, and that the other party, acting reasonably, should be entitled to rely on that manifestation of assent. (Note that the perception of the conduct by the other party is also subject to an objective test of reasonableness. Contract law does not seek to protect the unreasonable reliance of a party who places an idiosyncratic or irrational interpretation on conduct.) Thus, the principles of accountability and reliance qualify the value of voluntariness — volition is not measured by the true and actual state of mind of a party, but by that state of mind as made apparent to the other contracting party. Even if a person does not really wish to enter a contract, if she behaves as if the contract is desired and intended, that conduct is binding, and evidence of any mental reservation is likely to be disregarded. (Of course, this rule is not absolute. As we see later, where the manifestation of assent is induced by trickery, coercion, or other illegitimate means, there are grounds for going behind it.)

The value of protecting reasonable reliance is pervasive in contract law. It has both a specific and a general aspect. It is specific in that a person who has entered a contract has the right to rely on the undertakings that have been given. If they are breached, the law must enforce them. It is general because when parties in numerous specific situations feel secure in relying on promises, the expectation arises in society as a whole that contracts can be relied on, and that legal recourse is available for breach. This general sense of reliance, sometimes called "security of contracts" or "security of transactions," is indispensable to economic interaction. If it did not exist, there would be little incentive to make contracts.

In summary, accountability for conduct that induces reasonable reliance is a vital goal of contract law. This is tempered by the consideration that in some cases manifested conduct is induced by illegitimate means, and one who uses such means cannot truly be regarded as having relied on the apparent assent.

§1.4.4 Commercial and Social Values

Because most contracts are concerned with economic exchanges, contract law is quintessentially economic in its purpose. Its goal is to facilitate trade and commerce, to regulate the manner in which people deal with each other in the marketplace, and to enforce commercial obligations. Contract law reflects the prevailing economic philosophy of the United States, which is capitalist and oriented toward a market economy. However, there is an ongoing debate among scholars, reflected also in differences in the judicial philosophy of judges, over the extent to which the rules of contract law should emphasize economic or commercial considerations at the expense of other important social values. At one pole of this debate, it is argued that the role of contract law is to facilitate transactions on a free market. In this view, great store must be placed in free market mechanisms; the law should facilitate, rather than regulate, market activity; and economic efficiency should be the most important goal of contract law. That is, the rules of contract law should aim to encourage commercial interaction that creates the greatest economic value for the parties and society. At the other pole, it is argued that an important function of contract law is to regulate free market forces to promote other values such as fairness in transactions and the protection of weaker parties.[4] Most courts hover somewhere between these two poles, and as you read contracts cases, you will find many in which the court articulates the economic basis of contract law. In other cases, you will find that the court seeks to achieve a result that advances other values such as fairness in contract terms, doing justice between the parties, avoiding undue hardship to one of the parties, or furthering the public interest. In some of these cases, the court will deliberately weigh and balance economic and social values. You should be aware at all times that contract law is not merely a set of rules but is an instrumentality for achieving social policy.

---

4. The various philosophical views of the role of contract law are discussed further in section 2.3.

Examples

1. Liquidators, Inc., held a liquidation sale of the inventory of a furniture store that had gone out of business.[5] Employees of Liquidators, Inc., placed price tags on all the items offered for sale and posted a large sign on the premises that stated "Liquidation sale! All sales are final. All items sold without any warranty." The sign was prominent and was undisputedly seen and understood by all buyers before they made their purchases. At the sale, a customer bought a sofa priced at $400. He gave Liquidators, Inc., $400 in cash, loaded the sofa onto his pickup, and drove away. Did Liquidators, Inc., enter a contract with the customer?

2. Would the answer to Example 1 change if the customer had given Liquidators, Inc., a check for $400 rather than cash?

3. Another customer at the liquidation sale wished to buy a dining room suite for $2,000. She had no means of transporting the suite herself, so she agreed with Liquidators, Inc. that it would deliver the suite to her home the next day and would collect payment on delivery. Liquidators, Inc. filled out an invoice form with a price and description of the suite and the customer's name and delivery address. The customer signed the invoice. Do the parties have a contract?

4. Maggie Zine owns a newsstand. She needed to visit the dentist one morning. On the night before, she asked her brother if he would take care of the stand during the morning. Her brother agreed to do it if Maggie paid him $50 in advance. She agreed and gave him $50 in cash. Did Maggie and her brother enter into a contract that evening?

5. In March Harry asked Tom, his oldest friend, to be his best man at his wedding on June 1. Harry told Tom that if he would agree to be his best man, Harry would buy him a new suit to wear at the wedding. Tom agreed. On May 25, Tom told Harry that he had decided to leave on a two-week vacation the next day, so he would not be able to attend Harry's wedding or to be his best man. Is Tom's commitment to Harry contractual? If it is, can Harry obtain an order of specific performance, compelling Tom to be his best man?

6. May LaDroit was browsing through an antique store. Prominent signs were posted in several places throughout the store: "Please be careful in handling the merchandise. If you damage merchandise, you will be responsible to pay for it." May picked up a porcelain figurine to examine

---

5. This transaction involves a sale of goods. It would therefore be subject to Article 2 of the Uniform Commercial Code. This statute is introduced in section 2.7 and will be referred to frequently throughout the book. However, you do not need to apply it or to know about it to answer this Example or any other Example in this set that involves a sale of goods.

it. The figurine slipped out of her fingers and smashed into pieces on the floor. It bore a price tag of $1,500. Does May have a contract with the store under which she is committed to pay it $1,500?

Explanations

1. Both the customer and Liquidators, Inc., have performed instantaneously — delivery of the goods was exchanged for payment of the cash. Because there are no outstanding obligations at the time of agreement, there is nothing to enforce as a contract. (Liquidators, Inc., would have assumed an obligation if it had warranted the sofa or had given any other undertaking. However, the sign on the premises made it clear that Liquidators, Inc. did not undertake any such future commitment.[6]

2. The answer would change if the customer had paid by check. Unlike cash, a check is not a completed act of payment but merely an instruction by the customer to his bank to pay Liquidators, Inc., upon presentation of the check. In other words, although people may think of payment by check as a form of cash transaction, Liquidators, Inc. is actually giving the customer short-term credit. The customer's check constitutes a promise by him that the check will be paid by the bank when it is deposited. The customer has therefore made a future commitment, which makes this a contract.

3. Liquidators, Inc., entered into an agreement with the customer for the sale of the dining room suite, and this agreement is recorded in the invoice. Under the agreement, both parties have made promises that will be performed in the future, so this agreement does qualify as a contract. (Although a written record of agreement is not a prerequisite for validity of most contracts, it is required for a sale of goods over $500. This is known as a statute of frauds, and is discussed in Chapter 11. The signed invoice does satisfy the requirements of the statute of frauds.)

4. Maggie's agreement with her brother satisfies all the attributes of a contract: They agreed to enter into a commercial relationship under which Maggie exchanged money for her brother's promise to provide services the next day. It does not matter that they are family members, nor is it necessary that the arrangement comply with any formalities. (Unlike the sale of goods in Example 3, there is no statute of frauds that governs this transaction, so an oral contract is enforceable.) Although Maggie's

---

6. The possibility of a warranty and its disclaimer was also raised in the illustration in section 1.2.3 involving Rocky's sale of his kayak to Eddy. Assume here, as you did there, that the disclaimer effectively excluded any warranty.

performance appears complete, her brother has a promise outstanding at the time of the agreement.

5. When Tom accepted Harry's invitation to be his best man, they made an agreement under which they exchanged promises — Tom promised to perform the duties of best man, and Harry promised him a new suit. (These are the principal promises. There were probably others implied in the relationship as well.) This may therefore appear to have the hallmarks of a contract. However, where the commitments are social in nature, a court is likely to find that they are not contractual because the parties did not reasonably intend them to be so. This distinction does not mean that a contract must necessarily have a commercial purpose. It is possible for parties to make a contract that does not have a commercial goal. However, the lack of a commercial purpose, the presence of apparent non-commercial motives for the agreement, and the general societal expectation that promises of this kind do not create legal relationships, are strong indictors that the parties did not intend to enter into a legally enforceable relationship. Although Tom's breach of his commitment was morally reprehensible, he will not be held to account by the legal system. This answer disposes of the second part of the question. However, even if a court had found a breach of contract here, it would not have issued an order of specific performance, compelling Tom to perform his duties as best man. The remedy of specific performance is not readily granted, especially where the performance would involve the rendition of personal services by an individual.

6. The first lesson introduced by this Example is that a contract can arise by implication from conduct, and it need not be spelled out in express terms. The second point to note is that terms of a contract do not necessarily have to be contained in a document or spoken. A contract could include terms that are posted or otherwise made conspicuously part of the contract at the time that the contract is entered. (A similar situation occurred in Example 1. There we accepted that the sign stating that the goods were sold "as is" was effective, which led to the conclusion that the seller made no warranties and the transaction was therefore an instantaneous exchange.) It is therefore possible that a contract was created under which the store allowed May to handle the merchandise in exchange for her promise to pay for anything that she broke. Another point introduced by this Example is that one should always be on the lookout for alternative theories under which to claim relief. Even if the store cannot establish a contract here, it may be able to claim damages from May in tort because her negligence resulted in damage to the store's property.

Facets of the Law of Contract and the Source of Its Rules, Processes, and Traditions

§2.1 THE PURPOSE OF THIS CHAPTER

Chapter 1 introduced the legal concept of contract and outlined the policies and values of contract law. This chapter covers some more fundamentals. Although much of what is said here will slowly become apparent as you study contracts, it is very helpful to have these basics explained before you begin to encounter them in cases and other materials. The chapter begins in sections 2.2 and 2.3 with a little history and theory. Sections 2.4, 2.5, and 2.6 have a brief discussion of the source of contract law and some of the structural and conceptual aspects of the legal system of which it forms part. Section 2.7 introduces Article 2 of the Uniform Commercial Code (UCC), a statute that governs contracts for the sale of goods. Sales of goods are very common contracts, so Article 2 will come up constantly in the rest of this book. Section 2.8 introduces and explains the role of the Restatement, Second, of Contracts, an influential compilation of the rules of contract law that have been generally applied by courts. Section 2.9 is one of many similar sections that you will find in most chapters of this book. It introduces a transnational perspective on contract law. Although the focus of the contracts course and this book is on domestic (that is, American) contract law, these brief notes on the transnational perspective have the modest aim of giving you some idea of how the concepts and principles of our law of contracts might comport with or differ from those that might be found in other legal systems.

§2.2 THE HISTORICAL PERSPECTIVE OF CONTRACT LAW

The primary purpose of the contracts course is to teach you the contemporary law of contract. However, you cannot fully appreciate the current law without some sense of its history. Indeed, the very process by which the law is decided involves some degree of historical analysis, as the discussion of precedent in Chapter 3 shows. Most of the rules and principles of contract law were developed in the past. Some of them have remained relatively unchanged while others have been adapted or overruled as they have become superannuated. These changes tend to be evolutionary and incremental, built upon a traditional framework that is still apparent. In this respect, contract law is like a great and ancient cathedral, whose contemporary appearance reflects millennia of building, destruction, rebuilding, and addition.

Therefore, although the contracts course is not a course in legal history, modern doctrine must be studied and evaluated in its historical perspective. It is only in this way that current law can be fully understood, and a reasonably reliable prediction of the future course of the law can be made. Because a lawyer's work often centers on a prediction of how a court may decide an issue that could arise in the transaction, the ability to gauge the direction of the law is invaluable.

Although an understanding of the substantive law is one of the principal purposes of studying cases through the historical spectrum, this is not the only insight to be gained. The historical progression of caselaw is at the very heart of our common law system of jurisprudence. By tracing the development of legal rules over time, the student learns about the process of legal evolution. Familiarity with this process is essential to the analysis of court opinions and other legal materials. The common law and its rulemaking process are examined in section 2.4 and Chapter 3.

§2.3 CLASSICAL AND CONTEMPORARY CONTRACT LAW

§2.3.1 Classical Contract Law

Although the common law of contracts is many centuries old, it did not become a systematic, interwoven body of doctrine until relatively recently. Prior to the eighteenth century the law of contracts was seen not so much as a cohesive system of rules, linked by general principles, but as a collection of discrete rules, each specifically applicable to various particular types of trans-actions. From the eighteenth century, English legal scholars began to think of contract law in more systematic terms. They began to recognize that the specific rules reflected a general approach to contracts that could be identified and formulated as broader doctrine. This trend developed further in both England and America during the nineteenth century, at a time when economic and industrial expansion called for a more sophisticated and comprehensive system of contract law. It reached its zenith in what is referred to as the classical period. While one could quibble about the exact dates, the classical period can be thought of as spanning the last decades of the nineteenth century and the beginning of the twentieth. The Restatement, Contracts, published in the 1930s (introduced in section 2.8) reflects the mature think-ing of the classical school, but by that stage the classical conception had already begun the process of change that leads into the contemporary period.

To find a general doctrine of contract, the classicists examined decided cases, extracting from them a set of coherent and well-defined rules, which they then used as the basis for constructing more abstract general principles. The general principles formed a framework for organizing and linking the rules into a body of doctrine. Some classicists went so far as to conceive of law as a science in which certain and consistent results could be achieved in the resolution of cases by the rather mechanical process of selecting the right rule from the body of doctrine and applying it to the facts.

The classical school reflects the priorities of its age, which greatly valued free enterprise, private autonomy, and a laissez-faire approach to economic activity. Classical theory therefore stressed the facilitation of contractual relationships and favored a strictly objective approach. If parties manifested contractual intent, the classicists favored enforcement of the transaction. They were not inclined to probe the actual state of understanding of either party. This meant that they were not especially sensitive to the impact that enforcement of an apparent contract might have on a party whose exercise of free will may have been impaired by economic impotence or lack of sophistication.

The classical approach was also heavily influenced by the legal philosophy of positivism, which stressed the primacy of legal rules and considered the court's principal role to be finding and applying those rules to the facts of individual cases. Because of its emphasis on clear rules and its belief in a scientific approach to adjudication, classicism tends to be relatively formalistic and rigid, which has led to an alternative label for the approach — formalism.

§2.3.2 Contemporary Contract Law

By the late nineteenth century, some legal scholars began to challenge the formalism and rule orientation of the classical approach. As the twentieth century wore on, the classical conception of contract law eroded further. Enthusiasm for the free market was tempered by a growing recognition of the need to regulate the freedom of powerful contractors, to safeguard the rights of weaker parties, and to affect social policy concerning matters such as consumer protection, employee rights, and business ethics. The formalism of the classical approach came to be perceived as too rigid and too heavily biased in favor of dominant contracting parties. The idea that law could be treated as a science sounded more and more naive as insight into human interaction grew, and it was realized that the creation and resolution of contract relationships is too complex and variable to admit of "scientific" determination.

Succeeding schools of legal philosophy turned away from heavy reliance on rules, which may create the illusion of certainty, but do not in fact adequately reflect what really occurs in the resolution of cases. Instead, law came to be studied in a multidisciplinary way, taking into account its social context and the actual workings of the legal system. While many different approaches to contract law can be identified during this century, the two most influential schools were the sociological jurisprudents, who studied the relationship between law and society, and the legal realists, who stressed the dynamics of the legal process, challenged the preeminence of rules, and advocated a looser, more flexible approach to legal analysis. Many of the once-radical ideas of the legal realist movement have become widely accepted and commonplace today. For example, law should reflect social policy, it should evolve as society evolves, and it should be grounded on the factual investigation of practices in the marketplace.

Today, legal realism (also called neoclassicism) is the prevalent legal philosophy. In fact, it is conventional enough that it is sometimes labeled as traditionalist. We have become used to thinking about law in a broader context and to considering not merely what the doctrine says, but also how it actually works in light of such factors as the makeup and philosophy of the judiciary, the use of legal tactics, and the social goals to be achieved. In this, we are indebted to the insights of the legal realists who forever changed our way of thinking about law. Although legal realism permeates the current approach to the law, other schools of thought continue to evolve as scholars and judges build on or challenge the realist tradition. It is not possible, in this short introduction, to identify and describe all the strains of modern contract theory. However, it is at least worth mentioning some of the jurisprudential writing that has made an impact on the way in which we think of contract law. The promissory theory of contracts emphasizes the morality of keeping promises and argues that the sanctity of promise is the core justification of contract law. The consent theory of contract focuses on the assent of the parties as the primary value to be served and protected by the rules of contract law. The relational theory criticizes traditional contract theory for not sufficiently taking into account that many contracts involve ongoing relationships between the parties, which affect their contractual behavior and expectations. The critical legal studies movement explores the doctrines of contract law from the perspective of groups that have historically been excluded from power, and criticizes traditional contract rules as instruments of the dominant economic class. This movement argues, in essence, that although rules may appear to be neutral, they have come about as a result of political choices, made by persons who hold political power to serve the interests of their class. The critical legal studies movement has generated other movements that explore this theme in relation to particular groups, such racial minorities and women. Perhaps the most influential of the post-realist philosophical trends has been the Law and Economics movement. Although the movement consists of scholars who have differing views, the common thread of the scholarship is to examine law from the perspective of economic principles, and to be concerned with the economic efficiency of legal rules. Commonly, those who advocate the economic analysis of law urge that laws should be primarily concerned with the facilitation of exchanges on the free market, and should not seek to regulate conduct as a means of social engineering. Particularly in recent times, and in part as a reaction to the economic modeling of the law and economics movement, a number of scholars have applied principles of behavioral economics to the study of contract law. These scholars examine the psychological reaction to legal rules and the interaction between the law and the behavior and perceptions of the persons affected by it. Finally, some scholars and judges adopt an approach that has been described as neoformalist. They believe that the law has drifted too far away from the rule-orientation of the classical period, so that judges have too much discretion and the law has become too uncertain and unpredictable. They advocate a stronger emphasis on rules and at least a partial return to a more formalistic approach to the application of legal rules.

In sum, we are left with a contemporary contract law that is a mix of doctrine, policy, and process, at a stage of sophistication that goes beyond that of the classicists. Nevertheless, one must acknowledge the importance of the classical period. The classicists' quest for a comprehensive body of clear and certain rules was a milestone in the evolution of contract law. Many of our current rules and principles were formulated during the classical period and modern developments have proceeded from that base. Our law still reflects the tension between the classicists' desire for certainty and formality (an orientation toward clear rules) and the need to understand the legal process and to develop flexible rules that accommodate and correctly describe that process.

§2.4 THE MEANING OF "COMMON LAW"

The "common law" is often referred to in legal writing. This term is confusing to the uninitiated because its meaning varies depending on the context in which it is used.

§2.4.1 "Common Law" Used to Designate Our Legal System as a Whole

In early times, much of English law was based on local custom, applied in local courts. As the centralized Royal Courts began to increase in importance, their decisions formed the basis of a national law that gradually overshadowed local law. This national law, common to all of England,[1] came to be called the "common law." When Britain established colonies around the world the settlers transplanted English law into these foreign territories. In most of the ex-colonies, including those that became the United States, the common law of England has remained the basic legal system. Therefore, the term "common law" used in the broadest international sense, designates a country whose legal system is based on the common law of England. These countries share a legal heritage and an approach to legal analysis even though they may have widely different political, economic, and social structures and may have diverged in their rules of substantive law.

Most other countries in the world have legal systems derived from Roman law, as developed in continental Europe. Because the source of Roman law was the *Corpus Juris Civilis* of the emperor Justinian, these systems are called civilian. Cross-pollination and the unifying pressure of international commerce have reduced the differences between the civil law and the common law, but each system continues to have a distinctive approach to legal analysis. In the present context, probably the most striking difference is that civilian systems have a long tradition of comprehensive codification and tend to focus on their codes and scholarly commentary as a source of law. By contrast, common law systems tend to emphasize more strongly the role of the judge in the development of the law.

---

1. Note that the text refers to English, not British, common law. The United Kingdom does not have a unitary legal system. English common law applies in England and Wales. Northern Ireland's law is based on English law, but has its own variants. Scots law is quite distinct from English law. It draws its legal tradition from both English and Civil law.

§2.4.2 "Common Law" Used to Denote the Judge-Made Component of Our Legal System

When the focus moves from the international (i.e., characterizing the legal system as a whole) to the domestic (i.e., examining the components of the system), "common law" takes on a different meaning. It refers to those portions of our law based upon decisions of the courts, as distinct from those created by legislation. Contracts is described as a common law subject because most of its rules have been developed over the years by judges rather than by legislators. (This process of development is described in Chapter 3.)

This does not mean that there is no statute law governing contracts. Even in early times, the English parliament enacted some law concerning contracts which became part of the received common law. In the modern period, legislative action has increased considerably, and there are many areas of contract law that have been legislated upon. Some of these statutes codify the common law. That is, they take rules and principles already developed by judges and put them into statutory form. The purpose of this may be to reinforce or clarify the law or to make it more accessible. A statute may do more than codify, though. It may reform, alter, or modernize common law rules, it may intervene to hasten or mold the development of doctrine, or it may be enacted with the express purpose of changing legal rules developed by courts, or it may create new rules designed to deal with a problem not yet addressed by courts. As noted in section 1.3, some statutes are confined to particular contracts while others are of general application. Because contracts are governed by state law, as explained in section 2.6, some states have more extensive statutory treatment of contract than others. Although legislatures have, over the years, enacted many laws that relate to contracts, the field is still regarded as part of the common law, because judge-made rules continue to predominate.

§2.4.3 "Common Law" Used to Denote a Process or Approach to Legal Analysis

The prior two meanings of "common law" are relatively easy to spot, but the term is also used in a more subtle sense. It is sometimes used to describe the mode of legal thinking and the process of judicial development inherent in a common law system.

As mentioned before, the common law develops through the decisions of judges in actual cases. Whether a rule's origin is the common law or statute, it will ultimately be applied by a judge in a specific case. In deciding the case, the judge interprets and may embellish the rule. Over time, as courts apply the rule in more and more cases, it acquires a judicial gloss that becomes part of the law. Therefore, in using patterns of thinking and modes of analysis molded by the common law tradition, judges continue to develop the law, even if the source of law is statutory. This process is as much part of the common law as the judicial creation of rules. In a civilian jurisdiction, by contrast, the judicial application of statutory rules tends to be more confined to the case under decision, and is less likely to be influential in the development of legal doctrine.

§2.5 THE DISTINCTION BETWEEN LAW AND EQUITY

The distinction between law and equity permeates the common law system, and you will find discussion of it throughout this book. An early explanation will help you to understand the distinction when you encounter it. In everyday usage, "equity" simply means fairness. In law, it is sometimes used this way as well. However, it also has a more technical meaning.

Sections 2.4.1 and 3.2 briefly discuss the way in which the Royal Courts developed the common law. As practiced in the Royal Courts during its formative period, the common law was a rigid system. It was based on forms of action called writs. A litigant seeking a remedy applied to court for a writ (a written order calling on someone to do something) compelling the performance claimed. The writs were narrow, specific, and formalistic. Although new writs were developed as the need arose, it often happened that a person who needed relief could not fit the case into a recognized writ, and could therefore not obtain relief at law. The Monarch had the prerogative to do justice between his or her subjects, and if the court could not give a remedy, the Monarch had the power to intervene. The Monarch did not deal with these matters personally but delegated them to the chancellor, the highest royal officer. Over time, the chancellor had more and more of these cases in which relief was given on the basis of fairness (equity in the usual sense) in the absence of a remedy at law. This eventually led to the growth of a court of chancery, which had jurisdiction over all those claims for relief that were equitable in nature. The court of chancery developed its own rules and principles and became something of a competitor of the courts of law.

This dual system of jurisdiction lasted for many centuries. Over time, it became a matter of established practice that certain claims and remedies were legal in nature and others were equitable. For example, a claim for damages for breach of contract was within the jurisdiction of the law courts, but law courts had no power to order a party to perform the contract. Therefore, a claim for specific performance of a contract or for an injunction prohibiting breach could only be granted by the equity court. Furthermore, the equity court would not assume jurisdiction unless the plaintiff could show that the legal remedy of damages was not an adequate remedy under all the circumstances of the case. Thus, the common law system, in its broad sense, incorporated a jurisdictional division between the courts of common law (used here in a narrower sense) and equity. This dual system was part of the common law of England adopted by American jurisdictions, and so it entered our legal system. It is even embodied in the U.S. Constitution. For example, Art. III §2 extends the judicial power of the United States to all cases in law and equity arising under the Constitution or the laws of the United States. Amendment VII preserves the right to a jury trial in suits at common law, but does not mention equitable suits because courts of equity did not have juries when the Constitution was drafted.

Since the nineteenth century the distinction between law and equity has been eroding both in England and in the United States. Separate courts of equity have been abolished in the federal system and in most states. Courts of general jurisdiction now hear both legal and equitable suits. Also, the substantive distinction between law and equity is fading as many principles of equity gradually become incorporated into the law as legal principles. However, the distinction is not entirely dead, and it has an impact in many areas. For example, the availability of remedies is still influenced by the rule that a party who claims equitable relief must show that the legal remedy is inadequate; the right to a jury trial is confined to actions at law and is not available in equity suits; an appellate court has a much wider scope of review in an equity suit; and some courts still confine equitable defenses and doctrines to suits in equity and do not recognize them in actions at law. Again, it must be stressed that none of these distinctions are applied with the same rigor as they used to be, and there are many cases in which courts have moved away from them. Nevertheless, the tradition is strong and its breakdown is gradual and uneven, so it must be taken into account even in modern cases. We will return to the law-equity distinction periodically as it comes up in different areas of contract law.

§2.6 STATE LAW GOVERNS CONTRACTS

The common law of contract (as well as much of the statutory law governing contracts) is state law. Although there is some federal law applicable to contracts, it is limited to federal concerns such as the regulation of interstate commerce or to contracts entered into by the federal government. Because contracts are within the realm of state law, most contracts cases are decided by state courts. However, because federal courts sometimes acquire jurisdiction over cases that involve issues of state contract law (for example, because there is diversity of citizenship, or because the contract dispute may arise in a bankruptcy case under federal law), it is not uncommon to find a federal court deciding a state law contracts issue. Where a federal court hears a state law contracts case, it applies the law of the state whose law governs the transaction, and is bound by state law precedents. (*See* section 3.2.2.)

It is therefore not, strictly speaking, correct to talk of the law of contracts. There are in fact 50 different bodies of state contract law in this country, as well as those in U.S. Territories and the District of Columbia. Each one of the states, except Louisiana, has adopted the common law of England as its basic legal system. (Louisiana adopted the civilian system, in the form of the French Code Napoleon during the short period that it was a French possession.) However, although each state has its own contract law, there is a significant degree of similarity in the laws of the states. Not only does the law of every state (except Louisiana) derive from the common law, but also, as the law develops state courts and legislatures are influenced by each other. This makes it possible to study a generalized law of contract in law schools, and to select cases based not on the state from which they emanate, but on the quality of their facts and legal exposition. Therefore, while you should always bear in mind that a particular rule of law may not be followed in every state, you can be confident that you are studying broadly accepted principles and are learning the reasoning and analytical skills that will enable you to find the answer to a legal question wherever you end up practicing.

You will find that it is sometimes convenient, particularly when comparing our law to that of another country, to use the term "American law of contract." This term is awkward because it inaccurately suggests that the law of contract in the United States is a single body of law.[2] Nevertheless, it is sometimes the easiest and crispest way to refer to the general principles of contract law that are widely recognized in the many state jurisdictions within the United States.

§2.7 THE UNIFORM COMMERCIAL CODE (UCC)

§2.7.1 The UCC as a Uniform Model Statute and State Legislation

a. The Creation and Purpose of the UCC

As mentioned earlier, contracts are generally governed by common law except to the extent that legislation has been enacted to codify, change, or add to it. The UCC is such a statute. Although all of contract law is, in

---

2. Also, it is awkward to equate "American" with "United States" because there are so many other nations on the American continents. Nevertheless, this is a common usage, and it is followed in this book for convenience where a general comment is made about contract law in the United States.

a sense, commercial, the UCC is not applicable to all contracts. It covers only certain specific types of commercial transactions. Each type of transaction is provided for in a separate article of the UCC. In the contracts course, we are concerned with only one of the types of transactions covered by the UCC — sales of goods, governed by UCC Article 2. We also deal with some of the provisions of UCC Article 1, which contains general provisions that apply to all articles of the UCC, including Article 2. Most contracts courses cover basic principles of the sale of goods because sales of goods are such commonplace contracts, and because there is a close relationship between Article 2 and the development of the common law. The other types of commercial transaction, covered by the remaining articles of the UCC (as well as some of the more specialized and complex principles regarding sales of goods) are left for courses on commercial law.

The UCC was promulgated in the mid-twentieth century. Some of its provisions were innovative, but others were based on earlier statutes or on principles and rules that were already established in common law. That is, the purpose of the UCC was in part to modernize the law and to bring it into accord with contemporary commercial practice, and in part to codify and clarify existing legal doctrine. Apart from codifying and reforming commercial law, the other goal of the UCC is to unify it throughout the country. Like the law of contracts generally, commercial law is state law. There is, therefore, no national legislature that can enact a single commercial statute with nationwide application.[3] The only way to create uniform commercial law among the states is to draft a model statute and to persuade the legislature of each state to enact it. This task was undertaken jointly by two very influential national law reform organizations, the National Conference of Commissioners on Uniform State Laws (NCCUSL) and the American Law Institute (ALI). Their work resulted in the completion of a model code during the 1950s. (The model code as promulgated by NCCUSL and ALI is called the "Official Text.") The aim of having this model code adopted by state legislatures was fully successful, and it has been enacted in every state except Louisiana. (As noted in section 2.6, Louisiana has a civilian system, and the enactment of the UCC as a whole was not appropriate. Louisiana has enacted some portions of the UCC.) Of course, the law of the states can never be entirely uniform. Some states have made legislative variations from the standard model provisions. Even when states have enacted the same uniform provisions, courts in different states often reach divergent interpretations of the code provisions.

---

3. Of course, Congress has enacted a considerable amount of commercial legislation under the commerce clause (U.S. Const. art. 1 §8 cl. 3), which gives Congress power over interstate commerce. However, Congress has not sought to enact a federal statute governing general commercial law. It has treated general commercial law as the law of a particular jurisdiction, which is reserved to the states under the Constitution.

b. Revisions of the UCC

The process of reform and updating did not end with the enactment of the original draft of the Code. Shortly after the completion of the model code, a Permanent Editorial Board was set up to review the Code and propose amendments. The process of amendment is slow because the drafters take many years to develop recommendations for change, and after the proposed changes are promulgated by NCCUSL and ALI, they still have to be adopted by state legislatures. Nevertheless, since the enactment of the UCC, changes have been proposed by NCCUSL and ALI to various Articles of the UCC, and those revisions have generally been adopted by state legislatures.

Articles 1 and 2 have been reviewed periodically since their original enactment. Most recently, NCCUSL and ALI completed a revision of Article 1 in 2001 and (after more than a decade of effort and debate) a revision of Article 2 in 2003. As noted above, the promulgation of a revised official text of a Code Article by NCCUSL and ALI does not make it law. Each state legislature must enact it for the changes to take effect as the law of that state.[4] The 2001 revision of Article 1 has been widely enacted by the states, so the 2001 version of the Official Text of Article 1 can be used reliably as representative of state law. However, the 2003 revision of Article 2 was not received well. Although the revision included some sensible and useful reforms and clarifications, it also contained some controversial provisions that engendered strong resistance to it. As a result, NCUSSL and ALI were unable to get the 2003 revision enacted in any state, and in 2011 those bodies conceded its failure by withdrawing their support of it. Therefore the pre-2003 Official Text of Article 2 remains the law, and that is the version of Article 2 referred to in this book.[5]

c. Citations to the UCC

When the UCC is cited in this book and in other texts (including your casebook), the citation is to the model code, that is, to the Official Text as promulgated by NCCUSL and ALI. For example, section 102 of Article 2 is cited as §2.102. However, when a UCC section is cited in a case, the court

---

4. As you may realize on reading this, where some, but not all, states adopt the revision of an article, the UCC's goal of uniformity is placed under great strain because there are two versions of the uniform law. NCCUSL and ALI therefore endanger uniformity when they promulgate a new official text. But if they fail to update the law, they run the risk that individual states will make their own amendments, which could be even more destructive of uniformity.

5. The reforms proposed by the failed 2003 revision are occasionally mentioned in footnotes where the proposed solution to an issue is helpful to the discussion of the current law.

usually cites the state statute in which the Code was enacted in the court's jurisdiction. For example, a Connecticut court would cite section 102 of Article 2 as General Statutes §42a-2-102, and an Oregon court would cite it as ORS §72-1020. As you can see, it is usually not that difficult to identify the model code section because it is incorporated into the statutory citation. As noted before, most sections of the UCC have been enacted by states in exactly the same form as they appear in the Official Text. However, it occasionally happens that a state deviates from the Official Text in enacting a particular provision. This occurrence is not of concern to us, and you can assume that the Official Text reliably represents the actual law as enacted by the states. Of course, a practitioner in a state that has made a nonuniform change must be aware of that change because the language enacted by the state legislature, not the Official Text, is the law in that state.

d. The Official Comments to the UCC

When NCCUSL and ALI drafted the original Code (and also when they drafted revisions) they included a commentary after each section to explain and expand upon the provisions of the section. This commentary, called the Official Comments, is typically not part of the statute as enacted by the states. It is therefore not binding law, as the text of the actual enacted section is. However, the commentary is very important because it reflects the intentions of the drafters. Courts treat the Official Comments as highly influential and often rely on them in interpreting the Code. You will frequently see them mentioned in cases.

§2.7.2 The Use and Application of UCC Article 2

As mentioned already, the UCC covers a variety of different types of commercial transactions, and each type of transaction is contained in a separate, self-contained Article. The only articles that concern us in the contracts course are Article 2, governing the sale of goods, and Article 1, which has general provisions applicable in all articles, including Article 2.

a. The Scope of Article 2: When Does It Apply?

UCC §2.102 states that Article 2 applies to "transactions in goods." Although the word "transaction" is broader than the word "sale," you should not be concerned about this. You can assume for all purposes in the contracts course that if the contract is a sale of goods, Article 2 governs and must be applied. This is an important point that often confuses students, so it is worth emphasizing strongly. When you are dealing with a contracts issue, the first thing you should do is determine whether or not the transaction is a sale of goods. If it is, you must apply Article 2, which is the governing law. If it is not, you must not apply Article 2, but must apply principles of common law. (But see section 2.7.3 for an explanation of how Article 2 may be used indirectly as persuasive authority in a common law case.)

Although Article 2 must be applied to a sale of goods, this does not mean that Article 2 comprehensively contains every rule of law that may be applicable to the transaction. There are many issues that could arise in a sale of goods that are not covered by the provisions of Article 2. Where those issues arise, UCC §1.103(b) states that unless the Code displaces them, principles of law and equity supplement the provisions of the Code. The Code was drafted with the intention that common law principles will complement the Code provisions and will be used in conjunction with them to cover any areas that are not provided for in the Code. As the contracts course proceeds, you will see many areas of contract law in which Article 2 does not have specific provisions, so that UCC §1.103(b) incorporates common law rules and makes them applicable to the sale of goods.

b. What Is a Sale?

UCC §2.106(1) states that "a sale consists in the passing of title from the seller to the buyer for a price." As this definition indicates, there are two essential characteristics of a sale. One is that title (ownership of the goods) must pass from the seller to the buyer, and the other is that the buyer must pay for them. The price paid for the goods is usually money, but it need not be. UCC §2.304 states that the price may be payable in money or otherwise.

Because the passage of title is an element of a sale, Article 2 does not apply to a transaction in which the owner of property merely leases it for a period of time. In a lease, the owner retains title of the leased goods, which must be returned at the end of the lease period. (Leases of goods are dealt with separately in the UCC, by Article 2A. Article 2A is not covered in the typical contracts course and is not mentioned again in this book.) Likewise, if the owner of property donates it to another person, the gift is not a sale of the goods, so it is governed by common law, not Article 2.

The grant of the right to use intellectual property, such as software, is difficult to characterize, both because it is not clear whether software is goods (as discussed below) and because it is not clear if a software license is a sale. The copyright in the software is held by its creator, and when the creator "sells" the software to a user, she does not transfer title to the software or the copyright. The holder keeps the copyright and merely conveys to the user a right to use the software (a license). A number of courts have recognized the ambiguity of transactions involving the grant of a license to use intellectual property, and have struggled with both the questions of whether a sale has occurred and whether the object of the sale is goods.

c. What Are Goods?

Goods are defined in UCC §2.105(1) as movable things, including manufactured goods, livestock, and growing crops. The definition expressly excludes money and various intangible rights. In many cases, it is relatively easy to tell whether a contract involves a sale of goods. For example, a customer's purchase of clothing from a department store is obviously a sale of goods. Conversely, a contract with a laundry to clean clothes, while relating to goods, is for the provision of a service. Similarly, the purchase of a house, while a sale transaction, involves real property, not goods. The purchase of shares in a corporation or of coverage under a life insurance policy is likewise a sale, but the subject of the sale is intangible rights, not goods.

Transactions involving the sale of copyrighted creative work embodied in a physical form, such as a painting, a book, a music CD, or a DVD, are sales of goods, even though the real value of the object is in its content, and even though the creator's copyright may restrict the use of the object. However, the proper characterization of sales of this kind of intellectual property is less clear where the intellectual property is purchased on the Internet without any physical object changing hands. Where music, books, movies, and games are sold online and downloaded directly from the seller's website to the buyer's computer, it is more difficult to conclude with confidence that the transaction is a sale of goods, and it could be seen as a sale of intangible rights or the licensing of rights to intellectual property.

As mentioned above, the licensing of software and similar intellectual property is ambiguous in relation to both the question of whether the transaction is a sale, and the question of whether intellectual property qualifies as goods. The issue of whether licensing is a sale of anything at all is discussed in (b) above. Even if it is a sale, software may or may not properly be characterized as goods. By "buying" the software, the buyer gains the right to access and use its content, which remains the intellectual property of the creator. It therefore could be argued that the transaction really involves the transfer of an intangible right, rather than a physical object. Nevertheless, where the software has been incorporated into a physical medium that is sold as a tangible object (such as a disk), some courts treat the sale of the object as a sale of goods, even though its real value is not in the physical item itself, but in its content. (In this respect it may be seen as analogous to the purchase of a book or CD.) However, where the software is downloaded from the Internet, without any physical object changing hands, the characterization of the software as goods is more tenuous. There is no general agreement among courts as to whether such transactions should be treated as sales of goods.[6] In *Conwell v. Gray Loon Outdoor Marketing Group, Inc.*, 906 N.E. 2d 805 (Ind. 2009), the court rejected the notion that the means of delivering software — whether by tangible medium or electronically — should make a difference to its characterization as goods or an intangible right.

d. What Law Applies to Hybrid Transactions?

It is quite common to have a hybrid transaction that includes both a sale of goods and a component that is not a sale of goods. For example, a contract to repair a car may include both the supply of parts (a sale of goods) and the provision of labor. When such a hybrid transaction is in issue, most courts use a "predominant purpose" or "predominant factor" test to decide whether to apply Article 2. If the sale of goods is the more significant aspect of the transaction, and the nonsale component is incidental to the sale, Article 2 applies. However, if the sale of goods is ancillary, and the other component is predominant, Article 2 does not apply and the transaction is governed by common law. Some courts favor a different approach, known as the "gravamen" test. Under this test the court does not attempt to classify the contract as a whole one way or the other, but applies Article 2 if the controversy in question relates to the sales component, and applies common law if the issue arises out of the services component. The problem with the gravamen test (and the reason why most courts do not follow it) is that it is often problematic, and sometimes even impossible, to divide a contract into different components and to apply different legal rules to its different parts. For example, say that a homeowner buys a carpet from a store. As part of the deal, the store undertakes to deliver and install the carpet on April 15. Assume that the predominant purpose of the contract is a sale of the carpet, and that delivery and installation are incidental. The store fails to deliver and install the carpet on April 15, but its workers arrive with the carpet a day later, on April 16. If the common law applies to the transaction, the buyer is obliged to accept the late delivery unless she can show that delivery on April 15 is a material (important and central) term of the contract, so that

---

6. In drafting the failed 2003 revision of Article 2, NCCUSL and ALI sought to tackle this question by amending the definition of goods to specifically exclude "information." The Official Comment to the revised definition distinguished the transfer of "information" (such as computer software) that is not associated with goods from "information" that is a component of goods (such as a computerized component of a car or appliance). This revision would have made Article 2 inapplicable to a sale of software on its own, whether in tangible or electronic form, but applicable where the software is a component of the goods, designed to make them operate. Although this revision never became law, it does indicate how ALI and NCUSSL thought this question should be resolved.

the delay in delivery is more than a trivial breach. However, if Article 2 applies, the buyer may reject the carpet, even without showing that the breach is material.[7] Under the predominant purpose test, because the sale of goods predominates, Article 2 applies, and the buyer can reject on the grounds of late delivery without showing that the breach was material. However, the gravamen test would be difficult to apply because it would provide conflicting resolutions: Article 2 would allow the buyer to reject the carpet, even if late delivery is not material. But the common law would require the buyer to show materiality to refuse its installation.

e. What Is the Importance of Deciding the Question of Scope Correctly?

I mentioned earlier that many provisions of Article 2 are codifications of common law — that is, they did not change the common law rule, but merely reduced it to statutory form. In addition, I explained earlier that because Article 2 is not comprehensive, UCC §1.103(b) incorporates many principles of common law to supplement the provisions of the Code. Because there is so much congruence between Article 2 and the common law, there are many issues that would be answered the same way, irrespective of whether one applied Article 2 or the common law. That is, there are certainly many situations in which a struggle with the question of scope is just not practically significant, because the decision on whether Article 2 should or should not be used makes no difference to the end result. Notwithstanding this, there are also many situations in which Article 2 and the common law diverge, so deciding whether Article 2 applies is crucial. One example was given above. A few further examples illustrate other situations in which scope may be important: an implied warranty may exist if the transaction is a sale of goods, but may not exist if it is not; the contract may have to be recorded in a signed writing if it is a sale of goods, but may not need to be if it is not; and the statute of limitations (the period within which a party must commence suit) may differ depending on whether the transaction is a sale of goods. These are just a few examples. You will encounter other situations in which the legal rules applicable to a sale of goods differ from those under common law.

---

7. The principles relating to breach and the concept of material breach are commonly not covered until near the end of the contracts course, and are dealt with in Chapter 17. For now, just accept that the common law and Article 2 have these different approaches, so that deciding which applies has a significant result.

f. Must the Parties Be Merchants for Article 2 to Apply?

This question is intended to raise and clarify a perennial source of confusion to students. The simple answer is that if the contract is a sale of goods, Article 2 applies, irrespective of who the parties to the contract may be. It is the nature of the transaction, not the attributes or occupation of the parties, that is determinative. However, the confusion arises because there are some provisions of Article 2 that have special rules that apply to parties that satisfy Article 2's definition of a "merchant." This term is defined in UCC §2.104(1) to include persons who deal in goods of the kind involved in the transaction, or who, by their occupation, have knowledge or skill relating to the practices or goods involved in the transaction. In short, a merchant is an experienced professional buyer or seller, rather than a casual or occasional buyer or seller. As you proceed through the contracts course, you will encounter some of the Article 2 provisions that contain special rules for merchants. The important point to note, for now, is that Article 2 applies to everyone who enters into a contract for the sale of goods. It is only in those narrow situations that specifically impose different rules for merchants that the question of whether a party meets the definition of merchant is relevant. Do not make the mistake of thinking that Article 2 does not apply unless the parties are merchants.

§2.7.3 The Influence of Article 2 in Cases Involving Contracts Other Than Sales of Goods

After Article 2 was enacted in the mid-twentieth century, it had a significant impact on the development of the common law, beyond transactions involving the sale of goods. Of course, it is not directly applicable outside sales of goods. However, it was a modern, reform-minded statute, and its provisions relating to sales of goods have often been seen by courts as worth adopting in the development of the general common law of contract. Courts have therefore tended to consult Article 2 as a resource for resolving analogous questions in other contracts. The result of this trend is that in many areas, differences between Article 2 and the common law have diminished over the years. This trend was reinforced by the Restatement (Second) of Contracts, which deliberately adopted many provisions of Article 2 in formulating its rules of the common law of contracts. This does not mean that one can ignore the distinction between the common law and Article 2. There are still many Article 2 provisions that have not been generalized into common law. However, these differences are not as widespread as they were when Article 2 was first adopted.

§2.8 WHAT IS THE RESTATEMENT (SECOND) OF CONTRACTS?

You will find constant reference in this book, in other contract texts, and in cases, to the Restatement (Second) of Contracts (referred to from now on as Restatement, Second). The Restatement, Second, looks like a statute. It has numbered sections that set out rules in statutory style, followed by comments and illustrations. However, unlike the UCC, the Restatement, Second, is not a statute. It is a secondary authority[8] — a textbook setting out the rules of the common law of contract as its drafters find them to be, or sometimes, would like them to be. It is created by the American Law Institute (which, as you may recall from section 2.7.1 is one of the organizations involved in drafting the UCC).

As its title suggests, the Restatement, Second, is the second edition of the Restatement of Contracts to be published. The original was produced in the 1930s. It was the first thorough systematization of American contract law and the first comprehensive attempt to give coherent form to American contract doctrine. As such, it was immensely important in the development of the modern common law of contracts. As mentioned in section 2.3.1, it was strongly influenced by classical thinking, and reflects the formalism and objectivism of the classical school. However, legal realism was becoming influential at that time and also had an impact on the drafting. By the 1960s, the Restatement had become outdated, and a revision was begun, culminating in the Restatement, Second, published in final form during the 1980s. The Restatement, Second, reflects the post-classicist thinking described in section 2.3.2, and is also heavily influenced by the UCC, which had been enacted by the time that work was begun on the Restatement, Second. As mentioned before, its adoption of rules and concepts from Article 2 has helped to generalize the innovations of that statute.

The rules in the Restatement, Second, are largely extracted from cases that had been decided at the time that it was drafted, but this does not mean that they actually represent what the majority of courts had held. Despite its name, the Restatement, Second, does not necessarily "restate" the settled law. Indeed, given the number of jurisdictions involved, it is often not possible to find a settled law. Also, because it seeks to offer guidance on the direction that its drafters believed the law should take, it sometimes favors a legal rule that had only minimal acceptance in decided cases. The Restatement, Second, is now about 30 years old, so there have

---

8. The term "secondary authority" refers to legal writings like textbooks, law review articles, and commentaries that lack the binding force of official sources of law — such as statutes and court decisions (called "primary authority"). To the extent that a secondary authority is reliable and persuasive, it could be influential, but it never binds a court.

been many cases decided since its publication. As a general matter, courts have embraced the rules as articulated in the Restatement, Second, thereby reinforcing the drafter's exposition of the law. However, there are some rules set out in the Restatement, Second, that have not gained widespread judicial recognition, so that its account of those rules is not a reliable indicator of the law. Therefore, the best approach to the Restatement, Second, is to recognize that it is a very important and influential account of the law, frequently relied on by courts, but not binding on courts, and not necessarily a reflection of what courts in a particular jurisdiction may have decided.

§2.9 A TRANSNATIONAL PERSPECTIVE ON CONTRACT LAW

The contracts course focuses on domestic contract law (that is, the law applicable within the United States to contracts entered into in the United States). However, many contracts are entered into between parties in the United States and parties in foreign countries. Although it is beyond the scope of a first-year contracts course to delve into issues of transnational contracts, many professors feel that it is important for students to at least have some sense of what may lie beyond the borders of domestic law. To that end, most chapters of this book include a brief transnational perspective. The purpose of these notes is not to present detailed or comprehensive information on foreign or transnational contract law, but merely to keep you mindful of the fact that other legal systems may sometimes have rules that are similar to those of American domestic law, but may sometimes approach issues quite differently.

Commonly, the law applicable to contracts across national boundaries is the domestic law of one of the countries whose citizen or resident is a party to the contract or the domestic law of the place where the contract was formed. This is because the parties may select the law of that jurisdiction as the law governing their contract, or because international rules of choice of law determine that it is the applicable law. It is therefore possible that one would find, for example, that New York law governs a contract entered into in New York between a U.S. company and a German company. Where the law of a foreign country governs the transaction, one may expect to find that law to have some similarities to our domestic law of contracts (many basic principles of contract law are quite universal), but also to have some notable differences. Just to give one example: The distinction between law and equity, described in section 2.5, is a creation of English law and is not found in countries that have a civilian legal system. As a result, the preference for damages over specific performance, described in section 1.2.4, which is based on the law-equity distinction, is not typically found in civilian systems.

The term comparative law is used to describe a comparative study of the law of two nations (for example, a study of American and French law relating to the formation of contract). Comparative law is distinct from international law, which is the law governing the relationship between nations and, in some situations, applicable to citizens of nations in the international sphere. For the most part, comparative law — the comparison of our system to that of other countries — is of greatest interest and relevance in the field of contracts. However, the examination of the laws of multiple nations would be difficult and exhausting. Therefore, where contracts courses offer a transnational perspective, they do so by referring to two documents that provide a reasonable insight into principles of transnational law. One is the UNIDROIT Principles of International Commercial Contracts (UNIDROIT Principles), and the other is the United Nations Convention on Contracts for the International Sale of Goods (CISG).

The UNIDROIT Principles are a set of principles first promulgated in 1994 and updated in 2004 and 2010. This document is not a treaty, but a compilation of general rules that are recommended as applicable to transnational commercial transactions. The status of this document is similar to that of the Restatement, Second: It is not binding law, but is an influential scholarly publication. The authors studied the law of many countries and sought to distill them into a set of broadly accepted common principles. Although the UNIDROIT Principles are not binding rules, parties can adopt them in a contract, or they could have persuasive force in the adjudication of transnational contracts.

The CISG is a treaty. It has been ratified by the United States (as well as about 70 other countries), so it is binding law in transactions that fall within its scope. As its title indicates, it applies to sales of goods, so, you can think of it as a kind of international version of Article 2. Like Article 2, its scope is confined to sales of goods, but its applicability is more restricted than Article 2. Under CISG Article 1, it applies only if both parties' places of business are in signatory states, the transaction is not a consumer sale, and the parties have not excluded its application in their contract.

Examples

1. As mentioned in section 2.7, UCC Article 2 is directly applicable only to sales of goods, even though it may have persuasive influence in cases involving other contracts. Students studying contract law often overlook this and become muddled, forgetting about Article 2 when the contract is a sale of goods or citing it as the governing law when the contract does

not involve a sale of goods. These simple questions on the scope of Article 2 are included early in the book to emphasize the distinction between sales and other contracts. Which of the following contracts would be governed by Article 2?

a. The sale of a condominium.

b. A contract to employ someone as a sales clerk in a department store.

c. The sale of a cow.

d. The sale of food in a restaurant.

2. Buyer bought a mePhone (a state-of-the-art "smart" phone) by going to the manufacturer's website and ordering it online. The mePhone performs multiple functions such as phone, text, e-mail, Internet browser, camera, and game player. Its electronic innards are encased in a small rectangular plastic box with a screen in the front. The mePhone sells for $300. The physical product costs $40 to make, and the value of the instrument lies in its electronic functioning. Is the purchase of the mePhone a sale of goods?

3. Mark N. Tile is a wealthy merchant. He recently discovered that St. Francis of Assisi is the patron saint of merchants, so he decided to honor the saint by placing a large sculpture of him in the lobby of his building. He entered into a contract with Chip Chisel, a sculptor, under which Chip agreed to carve a 15-foot-high marble sculpture of St. Francis for a price of $100,000. (The piece of marble cost Chip $15,000. The rest of the price for the sculpture represents his labor in executing the sculpture.) Is this a sale of goods? Would your answer change if Mark, not Chip, supplied the piece of marble?

4. Sally bought a new car, so she advertised her old car for sale. Ben responded to the advertisement, and on May 1, Sally and Ben made an oral agreement that Ben would buy the car for $6,000. The parties arranged that delivery and payment would take place on May 5. On May 3, Sally called Ben and cancelled the sale. This is a breach of contract, and Ben has suffered damages of $500 (the additional cost of buying an equivalent car on the market.) If Article 2 applies, Ben cannot sue Sally because under the Article 2 statute of frauds, the oral contract is unenforceable. However, if Article 2 does not apply, Ben can enforce the contract, because the common law does not have a statute of frauds applicable under these circumstances. Ben argues that Article 2 does not apply because neither he nor Sally is a merchant. Is he right? Would he be right if Sally was a used car dealer?

Explanations

1. a. Although this is a sale, a condominium is not goods but real property. The concept of movability distinguishes tangible personal property that is capable of being moved (even if machinery is needed to move it) from land and structures on land that are so incorporated into the land as to become united with it. Article 2 does not govern the sale.

   b. Although the clerk will be selling goods in the course of his employment, the contract to employ him is not a sale of goods but a contract for labor (services).

   c. Although the cow is a living animal, not an inanimate object, it still qualifies as goods. Livestock and crops (including unborn animals and growing crops) are clearly included within the definition of goods in UCC §2.105.

   d. The sale of food in a supermarket is a sale of goods subject to Article 2. However, a restaurant meal involves both the sale of the food and the provision of services associated with it, such as cooking it; serving it; and providing a table, silverware, and all those other little touches that enhance the dining experience. To establish whether Article 2 applies to this hybrid transaction, one must apply either the gravamen test or the more widely used predominant purpose test. Under the gravamen test, the question would be whether the issue in the case related to the food itself or the service aspect of the meal. Under the predominant purpose test, the court evaluates what the predominant purpose of the contract is. In making this decision, it looks at all the circumstances of the transaction. The relative value of the sale and nonsale aspects of the contract is important, but the court also takes into account other factors, such as the language used by the parties in the agreement and their reasonable expectations based on the nature of the transaction and the commercial context.

2. The purchase of the mePhone is a sale of goods. The device is a moveable physical object. It does not matter that the ability to use it is dependent on software that itself may not be goods. Although the purchase and downloading of software from the Internet may not qualify as a sale of goods, this is not what occurred here. The buyer bought the mePhone, and the software incorporated into it is an integral component of the phone and is necessary to enable it to function. The fact that the buyer bought the phone from the manufacturer's website is not relevant to its classification. (In Chapter 5 we will discuss contracts entered into on the Internet.)

3. Although the sculpture is large and probably needs heavy machinery to move it, it is tangible, movable property, and therefore goods. You may be tempted to characterize this as a hybrid transaction, and to apply the predominant purpose test. That would likely lead you to the conclusion

that the predominant purpose of the transaction is the work of executing the sculpture, and that the goods component — the marble — is incidental to that purpose. You would therefore conclude that this is not a sale of goods. However, this would be wrong. It is not enough merely to evaluate the relative cost of the materials and labor that go into the fabrication of goods. If this was the approach, a vast percentage of the sales of manufactured goods would not fall within UCC Article 2 because most goods have to be fabricated or processed before they are sold. Remember that a sale involves transfer of title from the seller to the buyer, so the correct approach is to ask whether the end product, on which the labor has been expended, is the object of the transfer of title. If it is, the transaction is a sale of goods, even though the process of manufacture involves labor as well as materials, and even if the value of the labor greatly exceeds that of the materials. Therefore, if the seller's labor is entirely employed in the creation of the tangible, movable end-product that is sold, the transaction is properly treated as a sale of goods.

The answer would change if Mark supplied the marble because Chip would then be supplying no goods at all and there is no transfer of title to the physical object, which was owned by Mark at all times. Chip would therefore be performing labor on Mark's chunk of marble. The transaction would not be governed by Article 2.

4. Ben would be wrong in both cases. This Example is intended to emphasize what was said in section 2.7.2(f): Article 2 applies if the transaction qualifies as a sale of goods, which this does. It applies to all sales of goods irrespective of whether one or both parties are merchants. Although there are some provisions of Article 2 that are expressly stated to be applicable only if one or both parties are merchants, the absence or presence of this status makes no difference in the rest of Article 2. Ben cannot enforce the oral contract against Sally because it is subject to Article 2 and the statute of frauds applies.

CHAPTER 3

The Doctrine of Precedent and a Contract Case Analysis

§3.1 STUDYING CONTRACT LAW THROUGH APPELLATE CASES

This chapter is primarily concerned with case analysis and the doctrine of precedent. Because the analysis of cases is so central to the study of contract law, it is worth spending some time at the outset on the techniques and principles of reading, understanding, and applying caselaw. It is likely that you will receive instruction on this skill in your legal writing and research class, and you will also begin to develop it as you proceed through your contracts course and other substantive law courses. This chapter, which ends with an Example based on a fictional court opinion in a contract dispute, should help you to gain some early insight into the process of working with caselaw.

The study of case reports has been the standard teaching methodology in law schools since the latter part of the nineteenth century. In its initial use, the casebook reflected the classical conception described in section 2.3. It was thought that students could "find" the law in the cases, using the scientific approach to the study of law. While the focus of casebooks has changed to reflect the broader and more flexible post-classical view of law, case analysis is still largely used in teaching contracts. This is appropriate because case analysis is an important skill for lawyers, and the study of cases allows exposure to the common law method described in section 2.4.3. Case reports also serve as illustration of what would otherwise be abstract principles. Some casebook authors love to throw in weird cases or mis-guided opinions to challenge the students' critical faculties or to provoke debate.

As valuable as this learning process is, it is helpful to approach it with a recognition of some of its shortcomings. First, a collection of cases seldom produces a nice, concise and organized discourse on the law. That is why books like this one are needed. Second, the emphasis on caselaw gives students a rather skewed perspective because they are constantly exposed to transactions that have gone wrong — indeed, so irreconcilably wrong that the parties have felt it necessary to litigate, usually all the way to the appellate level, rather than to compromise. It is important to remember that only a fraction of contracts end up in litigation and fewer still reach the highest courts without being settled along the way. A related problem with the case method is that it focuses too strongly on contractual disputes at the expense of other lawyering skills such as counseling, drafting, and negoti-ation. Although there is an unavoidable emphasis on litigation when law is studied through cases, this problem can be ameliorated by paying attention to formation and negotiation issues whenever they are raised in the cases.

State court cases in casebooks are mostly decisions of appellate courts. In fact, trial court opinions are not binding precedent, and only a few states publish them.[1] States typically have two levels of appellate courts. Appeal from the trial court is usually made first to an intermediate court of appeals. Thereafter, there is the possibility of a further appeal to the state's supreme court. Unlike trial courts, which consist of a single judge (with or without a jury), an appellate court sits in panels consisting of several judges. The exact size of the panel varies from one jurisdiction to another. If all the judges on the panel agree on the result and its rationale, the court is able to render a unanimous decision. However, it is common for members of an appellate panel to disagree on the proper disposition of the case. When that happens, the decision of the court is that adopted by the majority of judges on the panel. (The majority opinion is written by one of them and is joined by the other judges who support it.) A judge who disagrees with the reasoning of the majority but agrees with the result writes a concurring opinion (or, if more than one judge concurs, they may join in a concurring opinion or write separate concurring opinions). A judge who disagrees with the resol-ution reached by the majority writes a dissenting opinion (or, if there is more than one dissenting judge, they may join in a dissenting opinion or write separate dissenting opinions). Sometimes a panel is so badly divided that no majority of its judges sign onto any opinion. In that case, the opinion with the most votes becomes the plurality opinion of the court.

---

1. As noted in section 2.6, federal courts do sometimes deal with contracts cases. In the federal system, trial court decisions are published and are often included in casebooks.

§3.2 HOW JUDGES MAKE CONTRACT LAW: JUDICIAL PRECEDENT

§3.2.1 What Is Precedent?

As mentioned in section 2.4.1, the common law developed in the Royal Courts of England. Although the Monarch was the font of justice, he or she could not deal personally with disputes between subjects, so this task was delegated to judges. As these judges decided cases over time, they recognized the value of deciding similar cases in the same way. This allows for efficiency in the administration of justice, it enables people to predict case outcomes more accurately, and it serves one of our fundamental conceptions of justice: the equal treatment of people in like situations. As the common law developed, it became established practice for court decisions to be recorded so that they could be used as the basis of resolving later cases. This meant that a decision no longer only settled the dispute between the immediate parties. It formed a rule to be followed in the next case involving similar facts. As the number of recorded decisions grew to cover a greater variety of cases, the collection of legal rules expanded to create a compendious body of law. The principle that a judicial decision creates a rule of law, binding upon later cases with similar facts, is known as the doctrine of precedent or, in Latin, *stare decisis* (roughly translated, "the decision stands").

§3.2.2 Who Is Bound by Precedent?

Obviously, the parties to a case are bound by the judicial determination of their suit. However, the doctrine of precedent deals with the binding effect of the decision beyond the parties, on later cases between other litigants. The first general rule of the doctrine has already been alluded to: The rule of a case is only binding on later cases with substantially similar facts. If there is a material factual difference between the cases, the earlier decision is not on point. You will often see passages in opinions in which the court declines to follow a case cited as precedent by one of the parties, on the grounds that the facts of the prior case are distinguishable. Of course, no two cases are likely to have exactly the same facts, so the issue is one of substantial similarity — are the crucial factual elements sufficiently similar that the second case comes within the rule of the first. Even when there are notable factual differences, the later court may find the circumstances of the cases to be analogous, so that the rule may be treated as governing the second case as well.

The factual similarity between the current and earlier case is an important factor in deciding whether the prior case binds the court as a precedent.

43

This can be a subtle and difficult enquiry. However, it is not the only consideration. The precedential weight of the prior case may be affected by other factors, such as the procedural context in which the court rendered its decision or the court's purpose in dealing with that point of law. Quite apart from this, judicial opinions are not always completely clear and unambiguous, so a later court may have to interpret the prior opinion to decide on its scope and meaning. As a result, the precedential value of a prior opinion could be unclear and disputed, giving the court some flexibility in deciding whether to apply or distinguish it. If the court does not agree with the disposition in an earlier case, there are often distinguishing features that allow the court to find the decision in the earlier case inapplicable. Conversely, if the court favors the earlier decision, there are often ways to find the facts to be close enough or analogous. Precedents are not universally binding on every court. The binding force of a precedent depends on the seniority of the court and the jurisdiction in which it sits. The court that decided the case should follow its own precedents. This is true even where the membership of the court changes, so that different judges hear the later case. Therefore, for example, the state supreme court will usually consider itself bound by a precedent that it set in an earlier case. However, a court cannot be absolutely bound by its own precedents, and may depart from them where the court concludes that the precedent is wrong or no longer tenable. A court's decision to overrule its own precedent is not taken lightly. The court weighs the need for flexibility and development in the law against the policies of predictability and fairness that motivate the doctrine of precedent.

A precedent is absolutely binding on courts of inferior rank in the same judicial hierarchy. Unlike the court that decided the prior case, a lower court cannot simply refuse to follow a precedent because it considers it to be wrong. (However, as noted above, the lower court may find a basis for distinguishing a prior case if it wants to avoid following the precedent.) As explained in section 2.6, the judicial hierarchy that usually deals with contract cases is the state court system. Therefore, if the state supreme court decides a case, the rule of that case binds every other court in that state. If a case is not appealed to the state supreme court, the intermediate appellate court makes the final decision in the case. Its decision binds all courts in the state except for the supreme court, which is senior in the judicial hierarchy. If, later on, a different case with substantially similar facts does reach the supreme court, the court may find the earlier decision of the intermediate appellate court persuasive, and may decide to adopt it. However, it is not bound to do so. A case decided, even by the highest court, in one judicial hierarchy (that is, the supreme court of one state) is of no binding force on any court in another judicial hierarchy (another state). Again however, it could be of persuasive weight because courts often look to the cases decided in other states for guidance in resolving issues of first impression in their own jurisdictions.

The relationship between state and federal courts is too complex for discussion in any depth here. As a broad rule, when a federal court decides a matter of state law, it must follow precedents established by the courts of that state. If the superior courts of the state have not yet had occasion to decide the particular legal issue, the federal court must try to determine from analogous or related caselaw how the state courts would decide the matter if presented with it. Because a federal court is outside the state's judicial hierarchy, its decision on a matter of state law does not absolutely bind the courts of the state, but it is persuasive authority.

Finally, it is important to recognize the relationship between judge-made law and legislation. Unless the court has pronounced on a matter of constitutional interpretation that cannot be overturned by legislation, the legislature may enact a statute that overrides a judicial precedent, even by the state's highest court.

§3.2.3 The Drawbacks of the System of Precedent

The advantages of the system of precedent — efficiency, predictability, and fairness — have already been alluded to. The system also has some drawbacks. First, it can perpetuate unsound or unfair rules when a later court is bound by a poor or outdated earlier decision. As just mentioned, there are means of avoiding this problem by making factual distinctions when possible, by overruling if the court is of sufficient rank, or by legislation. However, the inertia inherent in both the legislative and judicial processes often allows unsatisfactory rules to remain in force.

Second, rulemaking through court decisions tends to be sporadic and disorganized. When a legislature decides to enact a law, it can proceed in an orderly way to address the problem comprehensively. It can hold hearings, order staff research, and engage in debate. A statute can then be fashioned that is designed to deal with all the issues involved and to set out all the applicable rules. Caselaw develops more spasmodically. Courts have no control over the order in which cases arise, and they can respond only to the immediate issues involved in each case. They cannot legislate broadly but must confine themselves to resolving the dispute at hand. The rules that they create are very specifically tied to the facts in the case. As a result, judicial development of doctrine is haphazard. Some areas of law may be covered thoroughly because they are litigated frequently, while others may languish for decades. Some areas of the law may thus be regularly refined and updated while others are neglected. It sometimes happens that a major issue remains unresolved for years, because no party has wished to pursue it to the point of a definitive appellate pronouncement. Again, sometimes these gaps may be filled by legislative action, but they often are not.

Third, it is often harder to find the legal rule in a judicial opinion than in a statute. Statutes usually simply state their rules. Judge-made rules are contained in opinions, which can be dense, detailed, and lengthy pieces of writing. An opinion sets out the facts of the case, contains an often extended dissertation on the law, and finally reaches a decision or judgment resolving the issues between the parties. Somewhere in this body of writing, there are legal rules that serve as precedent. It is not always obvious what these rules are. To find them, the lawyer must study and interpret the case. To make matters worse, if the case has been decided by a divided appellate court, it can be harder still to determine the precedential weight of a majority or plurality opinion, called into question by concurrence or dissent.

§3.3 THE ANATOMY OF A JUDICIAL OPINION

§3.3.1 *Ratio Decidendi* (Rule or Holding) and *Obiter Dictum*

As mentioned before, the opinion states the facts of the case, as determined by the factfinder (the jury, or in non-jury cases, the judge) after weighing the evidence and resolving conflicts in testimony. The factual conclusions reached at trial are not disturbed on appeal unless they are so unreasonable that no support can be found for them in the evidence. Therefore, the recital of facts in an appellate opinion is based on the findings at trial. As the previous discussion indicates, the factual basis of the opinion is very important because the rule of the case can only be determined with reference to it.

Having laid the factual foundation for its decision, the court proceeds to resolve the legal issues. The judge could simply state the rule to be applied and give judgment. However, in most cases that involve significant legal issues, the judge justifies and articulates the rationale for the rule and its application in the case. The statement of the rule and its reasoning are the portion of the case that constitutes the precedent. This part of the opinion is called the rule or the holding or, in Latin, the *ratio decidendi* (roughly translated as "reasoning for the decision").

Frequently, the opinion does not confine itself to matter that is directly related to the resolution of the dispute before the court, but ranges beyond this to deal with ancillary or collateral matters on which the judge considers it necessary to express a view. These collateral discussions may be included, for example, to further explain and qualify the holding or to give guidance in future cases on how this court will view variations of the factual circumstances. This collateral matter is called *obiter dictum* ("said in passing") or simply dictum. As stated before, because it is not necessary to the disposition of the case, it is not binding precedent and has only persuasive value. Its persuasive value depends on the seniority of the court that issued the opinion. For example, a dictum in a unanimous supreme court opinion strongly signals how the court will likely decide that question, so it is highly influential to a lower court. A simple exercise in identifying the rule of a case and distinguishing it from dictum can be found in the Examples.

§3.3.2 The Process of Inductive and Deductive Reasoning in the Creation and Application of Legal Rules

When a general rule is applied to a particular case, a process of deductive reasoning is followed. The general rule, accepted as true, serves as the major premise. The particular facts to which it will be applied are the minor premise. Provided that there is a necessary connection between these two premises, a conclusion is produced that must also be true. For example:

Major premise (the generally applicable rule of law): The contract of a minor is voidable at the instance of the minor.

Minor premise (the particular facts): June Nior is a minor who entered a contract and now seeks to avoid it.

Conclusion: June has the right to avoid the contract.

Deductive reasoning, therefore, allows a rule of law to be applied in a particular case.

But where did this major premise, the rule of law, come from? In the common law, it has been created by precedent through a process opposite from deductive reasoning: The ruling in a particular case is generalized to create a rule of law applicable beyond the case. This is called inductive reasoning. In an earlier case another minor, Joe Venile, had entered into a contract with May Jore that he sought to avoid. In that case the court ruled that Joe, as a minor, had the power to avoid the contract. This rule then becomes generalized by the doctrine of precedent, so that it declares that not simply Joe, but all minors, may avoid contracts. The next time a minor, such as June, seeks to avoid a contract in a case with substantially similar facts, the general rule is applied by deductive reasoning to resolve it.

It must be stressed again that the pertinent facts in the subsequent case (the minor premise[2]) must be substantially the same as in the prior case,

---

2. This is not a pun.

otherwise there is no connection between the major and minor premise necessary to reach a conclusion. As stated earlier, material rather than absolute similarity is required. But even when there is a notable difference in the facts, the rule could serve as persuasive precedent and could be applied by analogy if the rationale motivating the first decision is equally applicable in the second. For example, say in the next case the issue arises whether a mentally impaired adult has the power to avoid a contract. The rationale for the decision in the first case was that when a person requires protection from bad judgment and exploitation resulting from youth, the values of freedom of contract and the protection of reasonable reliance in the marketplace must be weighed against the need to protect the minor. The court in the second case may find that the rule should be applied to a mentally impaired adult too, because this rationale is equally compelling in this case.

§3.3.3 The Use of Authority and Supporting Rationale in Judicial Opinions

Much has been said already on the use of precedent and legal exposition to justify the court's conclusion. The strength and extent of precedential authority and the force of the court's reasoning must be evaluated critically by one who wishes to interpret the opinion and to evaluate its worth as precedent. It is therefore useful to take a little more time to point out some of the elements that constitute the rationale in an opinion.

When the decision is based on a prior case that serves as precedent, the earlier case is cited with some explanation of why it is controlling. The same is true if a rule of statute law is applicable. In some cases, this citation of authority may be the only justification advanced by the court for the rule. That is, in deciding in a particular way, the court may rely solely on an established rule and advance no explanation of its own. For example: "The contract of a minor is avoidable at the instance of the minor. See *Joe Venile v. May Jore.*"

However, if there is no controlling precedent or statutory provision, the court cannot simply rely on some authoritative source for its rule. It has to develop the rule itself and must explain why it does so. Even when there is authority, the court may consider it useful to bolster that citation to authority by explaining why the rule makes sense. Most policy rationales for a rule fit into one or more of the three related but distinct classes listed below. As you read opinions, take note of their structure. You will find that one or more of these justifications appears in most of them.

1. A rule may be justified on the basis of public policy goals. The court feels that some particular social, economic, or political policy is

served by the rule. For example, the court may discuss how it balanced countervailing public policies where the policies of freedom of contract and the protection of reliance have to be weighed against the policy of protection of a minor.

2. A rule may be grounded in ethics or fairness. For example, the court may justify the minor's power of avoidance by arguing that an adult should not contract with a minor, because this is exploitive. It may also focus on the injustice of holding a person of tender years to a contractual commitment. The unfairness to the minor, combined with the unethical conduct of the major party and the likelihood that that party could tell by appearances that the other was under age, justifies the minor's power of avoidance.

3. Courts sometimes rationalize results on the basis of institutional efficiency. For example, the court may concede that some minors are more sophisticated than others, so that some may indeed be able to make a mature judgment. However, the court may conclude that a clear rule setting a definite age for contractual capacity is efficient because it is certain and avoids litigation over the question of actual competence.

§3.4 A TRANSNATIONAL PERSPECTIVE ON THE DOCTRINE OF PRECEDENT

The doctrine of precedent is a central feature of the common law system, but court decisions do not carry the same weight in civilian systems. Although civilian systems accord some weight to judicial precedent, they rely primarily on comprehensive codes and scholarly commentary as the source of legal rules. Civilians typically see the role of courts as dispute resolution, not lawmaking — the court's job is to apply the law to the facts of the case for the purpose of settling the immediate dispute between the parties, and not to establish legal rules that will be applicable to later cases. With the exception of certain high courts and constitutional tribunals, court decisions in civilian countries are short, not very analytical, and fact-based.

Examples

1. This Example provides a simple illustration of case analysis and the operation of the doctrine of precedent. It is based on an opinion in a fictitious case involving a minor's contract. Although the substantive law of contractual capacity is not discussed until Chapter 14, the principles of substantive law are not difficult to grasp and the focus is on the analysis

in the opinion rather than on the rules of law. The case is decided by the Supreme Court of Savannah, which consists of nine justices. Seven joined the majority opinion, one concurred, and one dissented. Read the opinions and consider the questions that follow them.

Supreme Court of Savannah, 2012

LORNA GREEN, Plaintiff

v.

MO MEADOWS, Defendant

VERDANT, Chief Justice, delivered the opinion of the court.

Plaintiff, Lorna Green, owns a golf practice putting course. On February 1, 2010, she entered into an agreement with defendant, Mo Meadows, doing business under the name "Mo's Mowing Services." In terms of the agreement, defendant agreed to mow the plaintiff's course bi-weekly during the period March 1 to October 31, 2010, for a total price of $20,000, payable in weekly installments. At the time of the agreement, defendant was 17 years old and just 2 weeks short of his 18th birthday. Plaintiff did not know or even think about his age. He was of mature appearance, operated his own business, and approached plaintiff to solicit the work. Although plaintiff was unaware of defendant's domestic circumstances, he had in fact been living on his own for some time and was financially independent of his parents. Two days after entering into the agreement with plaintiff, defendant accepted a more lucrative business opportunity that precluded him from performing the mowing services for plaintiff. He therefore called plaintiff and told her that he was no longer able to mow her course. At this stage the contract was fully executory — that is, no services had been performed under the contract, and no payments had been made.

After trying in vain to persuade defendant to honor his undertaking, plaintiff made inquiries and found another person to perform the same services for a fee of $30,000. This was the cheapest substitute available. Plaintiff then sued defendant for $10,000, the difference between what the services would have cost her under her contract with defendant and what they cost under the substitute transaction. This is the correct measure of damages because it compensates plaintiff for her disappointed expectation and places her in the position that she would have been in had the contract been performed. However, these damages are only recoverable if defendant's refusal to perform was an actionable breach of contract.

None of the above facts were disputed at trial. Defendant admitted entering into and subsequently refusing to perform the contract. The sole defense that he raised was that he was a minor at the time of contracting and therefore had the right to avoid the contract, which he did a couple of days later. The trial court found in favor of defendant on this issue of law and granted judgment in his favor, dismissing plaintiff's claim. The court of appeals affirmed.

On appeal to this court, plaintiff concedes that defendant was a minor both when entering and terminating the contract. However, plaintiff urges us to hold defendant bound to the contract under the circumstances of the case: Defendant was almost 18, operated his own business, looked mature, lived independently of his parents, and fully understood the nature of the transaction. Plaintiff dealt fairly with defendant and had no knowledge of his age. In effect, while plaintiff acknowledges that a minor's contract is normally avoidable, she contends that the application of that rule in the present case would be highly technical and unfair. While this argument has some appeal, it is contrary to the law and policy of this state and must fail.

At common law, a person attained the age of majority at 21. However, in 1960 the legislature of this state changed the age of majority to 18. The statute expressly states that "until midnight on the day preceding a person's 18th birthday, that person shall be a minor for all purposes in law." Clearly, then, defendant was a minor both when he contracted and disaffirmed his contract.

The law of this state on minors' contracts was first pronounced on by this court in *Senex v. Youngblood*, 50 Savannah Reports 100 (1908), in which we held that a contract entered into by a minor may be avoided by the minor, either expressly or by implication, at any time before attaining majority or within a reasonable time thereafter. As we explained in *Senex*, this rule is intended to protect minors from improvidence and bad judgment and to prevent advantage-taking by adults. This rationale is as applicable today as it was when first advanced, and the rule has been followed consistently ever since. Plaintiff refers us to *Teenbride v. Groanup*, 150 Savannah Reports 200 (1945), in which we recognized an exception to the rule where a minor had become fully emancipated from her parents as a result of marrying and setting up her own home. However, the marital status of the minor was a material element of that case and distinguishes it from the situation before us today. Given the law's purpose of affording protection to minors, we are not inclined to broaden the rule in *Teenbride*.

It may be true, as plaintiff argues, that it is technical and unfair to allow an independent and mature minor to avoid a contract entered into so close to majority. However, this argument invites the court to abandon a clear and definite rule in favor of a case-by-case investigation into the minor's circumstances. While it may be arbitrary to fix contractual capacity as arising at a precise hour on a person's 18th birthday, this rule is at least predictable and easy to apply. A fact-based analysis of a minor's actual ability to use mature judgment would create uncertainty in the law and would surely encourage litigation. The arbitrary rule does not really impose great hardship on the major party who has the opportunity to demand proof of age whenever dealing with a person of youthful appearance. In any event, even if plaintiff's argument has merit, it is better addressed to the legislature than to the courts, because the legislature has spoken on this matter and we have no authority to disregard a clear statutory provision.

Finally, we note in passing that plaintiff has referred us to several decisions from other states in which it has been held that a minor loses the right to disaffirm a contract where he or she has misrepresented his or her age. The wisdom of such decisions may be called into question, given the policy of protecting minors from improvident and irresponsible behavior. Nevertheless, we need not pass on this question here, because there is no evidence that defendant affirmatively misrepresented his age. It is not enough to constitute a misrepresentation that a minor simply appears to be over 18 and says nothing to counter that impression.

We find, therefore, that the courts below did not err in giving judgment for the defendant and we affirm.

TURF, Justice, concurring.

I agree with the conclusion reached by the court on the facts of this case. However, I write separately to emphasize that I take the majority's opinion to be confined to a wholly executory contract. Had the contract been performed in whole or in part, it would have been appropriate for the court to take this into account in deciding whether to exercise its discretion to enforce the contract. In this respect, I take a more expansive view of the court's discretion than the majority seems to assert.

WEED, Justice, dissenting.

In allowing defendant to avoid this contract, the majority adopts an absurdly rigid approach. While it is true that minors need protection from improvident action and exploitation by adults, there is no evidence in this case to suggest that any such factors were present. Rather, defendant unscrupulously and cold-bloodedly reneged on his contractual promise purely for the sake of exploiting more profitable economic opportunities. Given the age and independence of defendant, he was in fact emancipated. His situation is really indistinguishable from that of the married minor in Teenbride, and the rule in that case should have been followed. By refusing to extend that rule and narrowly confining the Teenbride decision, the majority allows defendant to escape his undertaking with impunity and teaches young people a very poor lesson on business ethics. The advantage of legal certainty is greatly outweighed by the need to do justice between the parties in specific cases.

Furthermore, the majority's claim that its hands are tied by statute is misconceived. The statute simply fixes the age of majority. It says nothing of the court's power at common law to recognize appropriate exceptions to the general rule concerning the avoidability of minors' contracts. Indeed, the rule in *Teenbride* was already in existence at the time that the statute was enacted, and no one has suggested that the statute was intended to overrule it.

For the above reason, I dissent from the majority opinion and would reverse the decision of the lower courts, awarding judgment to plaintiff.

Consider the following questions based on this opinion:
a. What is the holding of the case?
b. What nonbinding dicta can you find in the majority opinion?
c. What is the precedential effect of the dissenting opinion?
d. It is easy to see why a judge who disagrees with the majority's disposition would be motivated to write a dissenting opinion. But why would a judge who agrees with the majority's conclusion feel the need to write a concurring opinion? What purpose does the concurring opinion serve in this case?
e. Bearing in mind the discussion of judicial rationale in section 3.3.3, identify the rationales used to support the majority opinion and the dissent.
f. Consider the differing treatment of the *Teenbride* decision in the majority and dissenting opinions. What does this tell you about the process of following precedent?
g. What lessons do the majority and dissenting opinions teach on the role of courts and the relationship between judicial and legislative rulemaking?

2. After *Green v. Meadows* was decided, the supreme court of another state has to resolve a case with substantially similar facts. The case is one of first impression in this other jurisdiction (that is, there is no judicial precedent in the state on this issue). What impact will the *Green* decision have in the resolution of this subsequent case?

3. After *Green v. Meadows*, a trial court in Savannah is dealing with a case in which a minor deliberately and expressly misrepresented to the major party that she was 20 years old and bolstered this misrepresentation by producing a forged driver's license. Is *Green* binding authority in this case? If not, does it offer the court any guidance on how to dispose of the case?

4. In another subsequent case before a trial court in Savannah, the facts are almost identical to those in *Green v. Meadows*. The only material difference is that the contract was entered into three days before the minor's 18th birthday. One week after his birthday, before the services had been

delivered or paid for, the minor disaffirmed the contract. How does *Green* affect the disposition of this case?

Explanations

1. a. The holding of the case is the legal rule of the case that becomes binding precedent. It is narrowly confined to those pronouncements of law necessary to resolve the factual issues in the case. The rule in this case may be formulated as follows: A person is a minor until midnight of the day before his or her 18th birthday. A wholly executory contract[3] entered into by a minor at any time before reaching majority is avoidable by the minor if expressly disaffirmed by the minor prior to majority. This right of avoidance continues to exist even if the minor lives apart from and is financially independent of his or her parents. A minor has no duty to disclose his or her age, and the minor's physical appearance and the major party's lack of knowledge of the minor's age are not relevant to the right of avoidance.

   Notice that the holding is considerably narrower than the court's discourse on the law. For example, although the court says disaffirmance can occur expressly or by implication, before or within a reasonable time after reaching majority, the facts in the case are that disaffirmance was express and occurred before majority. Therefore, the court's recognition of implied and post-majority disaffirmance are dicta, not part of the holding. Also, it is a significant fact that the contract was wholly executory, so this should be reflected in the formulation of the holding. The absolute tone of the opinion suggests that the same rule may apply even if one or both parties had performed wholly or in part. However, this is dictum at best, and may not even rise to that level because the opinion does not address the question of whether the result might have been different had there been some performance. The concurring judge focuses on the fact that the contract is executory, and she makes it clear that her judgment is based on that fact.

   b. There are a number of dicta in the majority opinion. Remember that a dictum is a statement on the law that is not necessary for the resolution of the case but is pronounced on by the court in passing. A dictum is not binding precedent, but it has persuasive value. It allows the court to expound on legal doctrine and policy and provides guidance on how the court would be likely to deal with a later case that presents the issue covered by the dictum. Apart from the two dicta mentioned in

---

3. As explained in the majority opinion, a wholly executory contract is one in which neither party has begun to perform its obligations under the contract.

Explanation 1(a) concerning implied and post-majority disaffirmance, the majority opinion contains the following dicta:

i. The discussion of plaintiff's damages is dictum because plaintiff lost the case on the issue of capacity, making the issue of remedy moot.

ii. The court's recognition of the exception regarding emancipation in the *Teenbride* case is dictum because the defendant in this case was not married. Note, however, that the court hints that it is not particularly well-disposed to the precedent, and this may undermine its value, as discussed in 1(f) below.

iii. The discussion of misrepresentation of age is holding to the extent that the court states that physical appearance combined with nondisclosure does not constitute misrepresentation. This aspect of the opinion does address facts in issue in the case. The remainder of the court's observations on this question are dicta at best. Their import is discussed in Example 3.

c. The dissenting opinion is merely the view of this individual judge. No part of it, whether directly related to the facts or not, is the holding of the case. It is not binding precedent. However, a dissent can be influential, particularly when it is the well-reasoned opinion of a respected jurist. When a court in another jurisdiction seeks persuasive authority, a dissenting opinion may be preferred to the majority approach. Even in this jurisdiction, the dissent may in time persuade the majority of the court to move away from the position adopted in this case. Alternatively, as the court's composition changes, successors to the current majority may be more sympathetic to the dissent's view. Dissents do not always have these beneficial effects. Sometimes the existence of dissent on the court can undermine the force of the majority opinion or cause confusion for lawyers trying to interpret the case.

d. Most commonly, a judge is motivated to write a concurring opinion when she agrees with the judgment of the court (so she does not dissent), but reaches the conclusion on a different basis. A judge may also decide to write a concurring opinion when, as here, the judge feels that the majority opinion should express a qualification or limitation that the majority has declined to articulate. Although the majority mentions in passing that the contract was wholly executory, its opinion does not expressly indicate if it considered this fact significant, or if it might have decided the case differently had the contract been performed fully or in part. The concurring judge therefore feels the need to articulate that she considers this to be a pertinent fact, relevant to her decision to affirm the lower courts' judgment. The concurring judge also makes a point of distancing herself from the majority's suggestion that courts have no discretion to depart from the clear language of the statute.

e. The majority opinion uses all the elements referred to in section 3.3.3. The authoritative basis for the decision is the *Senex* case and the state statute. This recourse to authority is bolstered by rationale based on public policy, fairness, and institutional efficiency: The protection of minors from improvidence and exploitation serves both the ends of public policy and fairness; the preference for the arbitrary but certain rule is justified with reference to the goal of institutional efficiency; and the court's deference to the legislature is based on both policy and institutional grounds.

As the dissent shows, the court is not unanimous in the perception of how these different rationales come into play. The dissenting opinion finds the *Teenbride* case to be applicable authority and the statute not to be on point. It considers that the majority opinion does not serve the goals of public policy and fairness, and finds the goal of institutional efficiency to be outweighed by the policy of fairness.

f. The treatment of the *Teenbride* case in the majority and dissenting opinions highlights the point that a precedent is binding only when the facts of the cases are substantially similar. It seldom happens that a later case is identical to an earlier one, and it is often difficult to know whether factual differences between them are material enough to disqualify the earlier case as binding precedent. Sometimes the court's view of this issue is colored by its desire to follow or depart from the earlier decision. The majority apparently does not like the rule in *Teenbride* and does not wish to use it, so it finds the case distinguishable on the ground that the minor in the earlier case was married. The dissent feels that the independence, not necessarily marriage, of the minor is the crucial consideration and therefore feels that *Teenbride* should be followed. The dissenting judge therefore refuses to find the fact of marriage to be a material difference between the cases.

g. One of the perpetual issues confronting courts is the relationship between the judicial and the legislative role. While judges clearly do make law through the common law process, this function is circumscribed by the predominant lawmaking authority of the elected legislature. Therefore, if a statute deals with an issue, the judge must apply the statute and not disregard it. In this case there is a statute prescribing the age of minority. The difference between the majority and dissenting opinions reflects a different view on the scope and intended meaning of the statute. The majority interprets it as providing authority for a rigid rule on contractual capacity; the dissent sees it merely as altering a common law rule on age, while preserving judicial discretion to deal with the actual effect of minors' contracts.

The issue of statutory interpretation can be difficult, and the extent to which the court is willing to defer to perceived legislative intent is often influenced by the judge's broad or narrow view of the court's rulemaking function.

2. This decision is not binding precedent in another judicial hierarchy. When a court deals with an issue of first impression in its jurisdiction, it is likely to seek guidance by consulting the decisions in other jurisdictions and will be influenced by the persuasiveness of supporting rationales in decided cases which should have been brought to its attention by one or the other party during the course of argument. Because the court of another state is not bound by the majority opinion, it could find the qualification in the concurring opinion or the different approach of the dissent to be more compelling and may decide to use it as persuasive authority.

3. As noted in Explanation 1(b), *Green* is only of binding authority in its holding that physical appearance plus nondisclosure is not misrepresentation. Beyond that, the court's observations on misrepresentation are no more than dictum. In fact, the court does not even provide clear dictum on this question. It merely refers to decisions in other states that recognize an exception for misrepresentation and then calls into question the wisdom of those decisions. Therefore, although the decision does not give clear guidance to the trial court in the later case, it does hint that if the judge recognizes the misrepresentation exception, the decision may be overturned on appeal. This signals to the judge (and to the attorneys in the case) that some careful and thorough argument should be prepared if reliance is to be placed on the misrepresentation.

4. As noted in Explanations 1(a) and (b), the holding of *Green* is confined to disaffirmance by the minor before reaching majority. In the later case, disaffirmance occurred after the age of majority, so it is not within the rule of *Green*. However, *Green* has a very clear dictum that post-majority disaffirmance is also effective if within a reasonable time. (The earlier case of *Senex* said the same thing, but we do not know if it was dictum or holding in that case. If it was holding, that case is binding precedent. If it was dictum, the fact that it was reinforced by later dictum in *Green* strengthens its persuasive force.) Therefore the trial court should take the pronouncement in *Green* very seriously. Of course, *Green* does not say what a reasonable time after majority would be, and the trial court will have to resolve that issue.

4

The Objective Test and Basic Principles of Offer and Acceptance

§4.1 INTERPRETATION AND THE OBJECTIVE TEST

§4.1.1 Introduction

For a contract to be formed, the parties must intend to enter a contractual relationship, and the terms of the contract are those on which they have mutually agreed. This sounds simple and straightforward, but it is complicated by the fact that the parties must communicate their intentions to each other, and this communication could be poorly expressed or incorrectly understood. Where a dispute arises between the parties over whether they entered a contract at all, or over the terms that they agreed to, their communications must be interpreted to resolve this dispute. Interpretation of the parties' words and actions is therefore a pervasive theme in the area of contract formation, as it is throughout contract law. One of the fundamental principles of modern contract law is that where a court seeks to ascertain the intent of the parties, it does not focus on what each party may have thought or believed he was agreeing to (that is, his subjective intent) but on the reasonable perception of that intent, as conveyed by his words or actions (his objective intent).

§4.1.2 The Communication of Contractual Intent

Mutual assent is the basis of contract. This means that each party must intend to enter the contract and must agree with the other to do so on mutually acceptable terms. Courts often describe this mutual assent by using the well-worn term "meeting of the minds." However, it would be a mistake to understand this to mean that the true assent of the parties is needed for the formation of a contract. Agreement requires communication — the intent to enter into the contract must be signaled by each of the parties through words and actions that are observed and given meaning — that is, interpreted — by the other. Often, this interaction does lead to true assent on a subjective level. Each party uses clear and unambiguous signals that accurately convey intent, and these signals are fully and correctly understood by the other. Where this happens, there really is a "meeting of the minds" in which perceived intent corresponds to what each party had in mind. But this is not always so. Communication can be fouled by so many different causes: A poor choice of words or actions may obscure intent; a manifestation of intent may be perceived differently or misconstrued by the person to whom it is addressed; or secret reservations or deviousness may result in deliberate obfuscation. In addition, in so many transactions, the one party manifests assent to standard terms presented by the other. It is quite common, in these standard transactions, for the nondrafting party to signify assent without reading or fully understanding the standard term. Therefore, while contracts are consensual relationships and in many contracts there is a genuine "meeting of the minds," some transactions end up in litigation because it turns out that the minds of parties were not in true accord, even though their manifestations of assent appear to be congruent.

§4.1.3 Assent and Accountability: Subjective and Objective Tests of Assent

When imperfect communication leads to a dispute about the existence or terms of a contract, two fundamental contract policies must be accommodated. The assent policy dictates that contractual obligation should not be imposed on a person who did not in fact agree to be bound. However, if the need for true assent is too heavily stressed, the policy of protecting reliance is undermined. If no one could rely on words or conduct that indicate assent, it would be difficult for anyone to have confidence in the system of commercial exchange. Therefore, the assent policy must be tempered by the goal of protecting the expectations of one who reasonably relied on the appearance of assent. A person must be held accountable for behavior that signifies assent.

4. The Objective Test and Basic Principles of Offer and Acceptance

Court opinions prior to the classical period[1] suggest that contract was seen as requiring a real "meeting of the minds," in the sense that there could be no contract unless the parties' subjective intent coincided on the creation and terms of the relationship. Classicists felt that a subjective approach was wrong in principle because it made transacting less dependable. It was also not workable because it placed too much store on obviously unreliable (and not easily rebuttable) self-serving testimony of actual intent. Classical contract law therefore moved toward the opposite pole, refusing to see any relevance in the subjective state of mind of the parties and employing a strict objective or external test for assent. If agreement was apparent from the manifestations of assent, reasonably interpreted, a contract had been formed on the terms reflected in the manifestation. It was neither necessary nor permissible to receive testimony on what either party actually thought or believed.

A complete disregard of the actual state of mind of the parties gives too little weight to the assent policy and could lead to injustice where subjective evidence could cast some light on the meaning of a manifestation. For example, evidence of a party's subjective understanding could provide an alternative explanation of the meaning of words or actions, or it could indicate justifiable misapprehension induced by the other party's unfair bargaining methods. Recognizing this, modern law has moved away from the strict objectivist approach of the classical period, and is not as absolute in its focus on the manifestation of assent. It is now accepted that evidence of a party's state of mind may sometimes be helpful in interpreting or giving a context to words or conduct, provided that the subjective evidence is credible and compatible with the overt behavior. Although less rigid than it used to be, the objective test is firmly established and a subjective "meeting of the minds" is not required for contract formation. In the absence of compelling contrary indications, assent is legally sufficient if each party, by the deliberate use of words or conduct, manifested agreement to be contractually bound.

The contemporary approach is reflected in several sections of the Restatement, Second. In defining a promise, §2 speaks of a manifestation of intent by the promisor that justifies the promisee in understanding that a commitment has been made; §3 describes "agreement" as a manifestation of mutual assent; §§19 and 20 stress the accountability principle by holding a party liable for deliberate manifestations by words or conduct, made with reason to know that they will create a reasonable impression of assent. UCC Article 2 does not specifically address the objective test, which is therefore governed by the general principles of common law by virtue of §1.103(b).[2]

---

1. The classical period is described in section 2.3.1. Classical contract theory was dominant from about the late nineteenth to the early twentieth century.
2. As explained in section 2.7.2, §1.103(b) adopts the general principles of common law to the extent that they are not displaced by the particular provisions of the UCC.

§4.1.4 The Substantive and Evidentiary Aspects of the Objective Test

Having introduced the objective test, we now look more carefully at its operation and implications. The test may be thought of as having both a substantive aspect (that is, it prescribes a legal standard for determining assent) and an evidentiary aspect (that is, it regulates what evidence is admissible to prove intent). Although these aspects are closely interrelated, it aids understanding of the objective test to articulate and describe them separately.

Manifestations of assent are interpreted, not in light of what the utterer actually meant or the other party actually understood, but from the standpoint of what that utterance reasonably meant in the entire context of the transaction. That is, we ask not what the words or actions actually meant to either party, but how they should have been meant and understood if interpreted reasonably under the circumstances of the transaction. The reason for this, of course, is that the objective test is aimed at balancing the requirement of assent with the protection of reasonable reliance. It is therefore not concerned with any actual perception of meaning that may form in the mind of either party, but with the rational meaning that should have been placed on it by the parties. How do we find this reasonable person? In essence, this is a construct meant to represent the community standard, as identified by the trier of fact.

An example may help to illustrate the way in which the "reasonable person" construct focuses the inquiry: Lender lent Borrower $10,000. Under the loan agreement, Borrower promised to repay the loan "with interest at the market rate within one year of the date of receiving the advance." At the time that the contract was executed, the market interest rate was 4 percent. Two months later, it rose to 5 percent. This led to a dispute between Lender and Borrower about the meaning of "interest at the market rate." Lender contends that the market rate is a variable rate that increases or decreases from month to month during the period of the loan. Borrower contends that it is fixed at the rate prevailing at the time the loan was made. To establish the meaning of "market rate," the factfinder is not so much concerned about what either Lender or Borrower thought it meant. Rather, it will seek to determine what reasonable people in their position would have understood the term to mean under all the circumstances of the transaction. To make this determination the factfinder must focus on objective evidence — that is, observable significations of intent — to establish contractual intent. This evidence consists of the language used by the parties in the agreement, as well as any other communications between them, or any other overt behavior. It also covers any custom or usage in the marketplace, as well as any generally accepted meaning of the language used in the parties' communications.

4. The Objective Test and Basic Principles of Offer and Acceptance

A rigid objective test would confine evidence to these objective sources, and would treat as irrelevant any subjective evidence of what either party may have thought the words meant. This approach is summed up by a famous passage from the opinion of Judge Learned Hand in *Hotchkiss v. National City Bank of New York*, 200 F 287, 293 (S.D.N.Y. 1911):

> . . . A contract has, strictly speaking, nothing to do with the personal or individual intent of the parties. A contract is an obligation attached by mere force of law to certain acts of the parties, usually words, which ordinarily accompany and represent a known intent. If, however, it were proved by twenty bishops that either party, when he used the words, intended something else than the usual meaning which the law imposes upon them, he would still be held, unless there were some mutual mistake, or something else of the sort[3] . . . ,

Modern courts are not generally as rigid as this about the absolute exclusion of subjective evidence. Although they focus strongly on objective manifestations of intent, they are usually willing to admit subjective evidence of what a party thought or intended to the extent that this evidence is congruent with the objective manifestations of intent and it is relevant to provide insight into those manifestations. Therefore, in our example, evidence of each of the parties' actual understanding of "interest at the market rate" should be admissible, merely as pieces of relevant evidence. To the extent that the subjective understanding of a party is plausible and consistent with the objective evidence, it may reinforce the court's determination of the reasonable meaning of the language. Even on this more tolerant approach to subjective evidence, a court is not likely to admit evidence of a party's intent that is implausible and not reconcilable with the objective indicia of assent. For example, a claim by Borrower that she understood that the loan was to be interest-free could not be squared with her manifestation of intent to pay interest at the market rate.

A modern court's approach to the admission of subjective evidence under the objective test is well illustrated by *SR International Business Insurance Co., Ltd. v. World Trade Center Properties, LLC.*, 467 F.3d 107 (2d Cir. 2006). Various insurance companies had issued binders (commitments to insure pending the execution of a final insurance policy) on the World Trade

---

3. Judge Hand's reference to "mutual mistake, or something else of the sort" points to an important qualification of the objective test, that was mentioned earlier: A court will look behind a party's manifestation of assent if it appears that assent is not genuine because of some defect in the bargaining process, such as a mistake of fact or the other party's improper or unfair bargaining practices. For example, a person may not be held to a manifestation of assent if the other party coerced her into signifying assent, or she was acting in reliance on a fraudulent misrepresentation by the other party. This issue is just noted here. The doctrines governing improper bargaining are discussed in Chapter 13, and mistake is discussed in Chapter 15.

Center. The binders provided for coverage of $3.5 billion "per occurrence." The question of interpretation in dispute was whether the terrorist attack on the twin towers on September 11, 2001, in which two planes were crashed into the towers, constituted a single occurrence, for which total indemnification under the policies would be $3.5 billion, or two occurrences, which would increase the maximum coverage amount to $7 billion. The trial court admitted testimony of the insurers' witnesses about what they thought the policies meant. On appeal, the insured parties argued that the trial court should have excluded this subjective evidence. The court of appeals found no error in the admission of the evidence. It expressed the established principle that a contract must be interpreted objectively, based on the parties' manifested intent, rather than their actual intent. Therefore, although uncommunicated subjective intent cannot supply the meaning of a contract, it could be relevant and admissible to cast light on the meaning of the objective manifestations. This is particularly true where there is some ambiguity or lack of clarity in the objective manifestations.

§4.1.5 The Duty to Read

Because the objective test binds a party to his manifestation of assent, he is accountable for reading and understanding the terms of a contract before he signifies assent to them. If he fails to do that, he will not likely succeed in arguing that he is not bound to the contract because he did not actually agree to it. That is, under the objective test, a party is bound by his objective indication of assent to a contract despite a lack of subjective agreement caused by his failure to read and understand its terms. Courts often express this approach by saying that a party has a duty to read a document before signifying assent to it.

The problem of a party not being fully aware of the terms to which he indicated assent arises most commonly with standard contracts drafted by the other party. People presented with standard contracts quite commonly do not read them well or at all before indicating agreement to them by signing the form or clicking an "I agree" button on a website. A person who does that may find that he has manifested agreement to terms that he did not expect and that are contrary to his interests. However, in most cases, unless the terms are unusually harsh and one-sided, or they were unfairly inconspicuous, the manifestation of assent binds the party and precludes an argument that he did not actually agree to them.

We will return to the duty to read in Chapter 5, in the context of standard contracts entered into in writing or via an electronic medium. However, it is helpful to anticipate that discussion here by using a couple of examples involving standard form contracts to illustrate the duty to read. In *Morales v. Sun Constructors, Inc.*, 541 F.3d 218 (3rd Cir. 2008), the court held that an employee was bound to his manifested assent to a standard arbitration agreement even though it was clear that he did not read or understand what he was signing. At the time that he was hired Morales, a Spanish-speaking employee, was required to attend an employee orientation, during which he signed a standard employment agreement containing an arbitration provision. The orientation was conducted in English and the agreement was written in English, which Morales did not understand. The employer knew this and asked another new employee, who was bilingual, to translate what was said at the orientation and to help Morales with the agreement form. However, this employee did not explain the agreement form, and Morales did not ask about it. Morales later sought to sue the employer for wrongful termination and claimed that he was not bound to the arbitration clause because he did not actually agree to it. The court of appeals rejected that argument and found that Morales had bound himself to arbitrate the dispute. It held that under the objective test, Morales had the obligation to ensure that he read and understood what he was signing. If he could not understand English, he should have made sure that someone translated the agreement form for him. This result may seem harsh, but the case does show just how difficult it can be for a person to overcome the duty to read.

Morales involved a standard agreement printed on paper, but much standard contracting is conducted on the Internet. The same principle applies to electronic significations of assent. Consider the following familiar situation: Don Loader visits the website of SoftWary.com and decides to buy a video game, to be downloaded onto his computer. He places the game in his virtual shopping cart and proceeds to order it. Just before he submits his order, a box appears on his computer screen headed "Terms and Conditions of Sale." The box contains several pages of standard terms that can be read by scrolling down the text in the box. Don cannot be bothered to read all that stuff, so he just clicks the "I accept" button at the bottom of the box. Even though Don has no idea what he agreed to, the objective test binds him to his signification of assent.[4]

§4.1.6 Lack of Serious Intent: Jokes and Bluffs

As mentioned in section 4.1.2, miscommunication of intent can result from many different causes. Most commonly, the problem is inadvertent failure to express intent clearly. However, there are some cases in which a party who claims lack of contractual intent alleges that he was not serious about making a contract, but was joking or bluffing, and that the other party

---

4. Again, this assertion should be qualified by noting that in some cases, a court may not bind a party to a standard term that is unconscionable or unfairly inconspicuous.

should have realized it. Although this does not happen very often, there are a few well-loved cases that involve this situation, and that serve as good examples of the application of the objective test.

One of these is *Lucy v. Zehmer*, 84 S.E.2d 516 (Va. 1954). Zehmer, the owner of property, contended that his offer to sell it to Lucy was a bluff. The alleged contract was made under most unbusinesslike circumstances while the parties sat drinking one evening in a restaurant operated by Zehmer. The memorial of the alleged contract was written in very sketchy terms on the reverse side of a restaurant guest check. When Lucy sought to enforce the sale, Zehmer claimed that it was not intended seriously. He testified that he and Lucy had been drinking too much, and he was just calling Lucy's bluff because he did not believe that Lucy had the money to buy the property. Whatever Zehmer's actual intent may have been, the court found that Lucy was in earnest and under the objective test, had no reason to believe that Zehmer was not. (The court also declined to allow Zehmer to avoid the contract on grounds of mental disability caused by intoxication because it did not believe that Zehmer was drunk enough.)

More recently, in the rather wacky case of *Leonard v. PepsiCo, Inc.*, 88 F. Supp. 2d 116 (S.D.N.Y. 1999), aff'd 210 F.3d 88 (2d Cir. 2000), the court found that an alleged offer really should have been reasonably understood as a joke. Pepsi conducted a promotional campaign in which buyers of Pepsi products could earn "Pepsi points" that could be redeemed for prizes listed in a catalog. The points did not all have to be earned by consuming soft drinks. As long as 15 actual points were submitted with the redemption form, the remaining points required for the prize could be purchased for ten cents a point. The TV commercial advertising the promotion showed various prizes that could be won (such as t-shirts and sunglasses) and the number of points needed to win them. The commercial ended with a teenager landing a Harrier jet on the grounds of his high school. As he emerged from the jet, the words "Harrier fighter, 7,000,000 points" appeared on the screen. Leonard submitted a redemption form claiming the jet. He included the 15 original Pepsi points and a check for just under $700,000 to buy the balance of the 7 million points needed. Pepsi refused to award the jet to him on a number of theories. One of them was that the jet was used in the commercial merely for humor and entertainment, and could not reasonably have been understood as a real prize. (The other theories are discussed in Example 10.) The court agreed. It found that no reasonable person could have understood the commercial to be a serious offer of a jet, but would have realized that the use of the jet was just to add an absurd comic touch and to exaggerate the excitement of the drink. Furthermore, the fact that a Harrier is a fierce war machine unsuitable for consumer use and costing some $23 million would alert the reasonable viewer that it could not possibly be offered in exchange for about $700,000.

§4.2 THE PURPOSE AND APPLICATION OF THE RULES OF OFFER AND ACCEPTANCE

§4.2.1 Introduction

The formation of the contract is the beginning of the parties' legal relationship, but it is also the culmination of a process of bargaining. This is reflected in the expression that parties "conclude a contract," which means, not that they have finished performing, but that they have completed the interaction leading up to the execution of a contract.

In some cases, a deal may be struck very quickly, with a minimum of bargaining: One party may make a proposal that is accepted without qualification by the other. In other cases the path to contract formation may be long and arduous. Initial proposals may lead to counterproposals, negotiations, and compromise. If the transaction is complex, each step in the process may require consultation with different corporate departments, technical experts, and attorneys. In either event, where this interaction is successful, there comes a time when the parties reach agreement and bind themselves to the relationship — a contract comes into being.

Sometimes the creation of a contract is marked by the signing of a written memorial of the agreement.[5] When this happens, it is relatively easy to fix the time of formation and the exact terms of the contract. However, this helpful indicator of formation is not always present because the parties may have formed a contract without recording it in a formal comprehensive writing. A contract could be contained in a series of correspondence or in some other collection of interrelated documents; it could have been made orally with the intention of later drafting and signing a written memorial or it may be partly written and partly oral or entirely oral.[6] Such circumstances may create uncertainty and disputes over the question of whether a contract was formed at all, and if so, whether certain terms became part of it. The rules of offer and acceptance provide a framework for resolving these questions.

The offer and acceptance model conceives of a process of bargaining between the parties that leads to the formation of a contract. It developed in

---

5. In colloquial speech, people often talk of "signing a contract." Strictly speaking, this is inaccurate terminology. The contract is the legal relationship between the parties, and the document that is signed is actually the record or memorial of that contract.

6. Under the statute of frauds (see Chapter 11), certain types of contracts are not enforceable unless their essential terms are recorded in a signed writing. However, many contracts are not subject to this rule and are fully valid and enforceable in oral form. This does not mean that it is a good idea to dispense with a written memorial, even where the law does not require writing. It is harder to prove the existence and terms of an oral contract.

the context of person-to-person interaction in which the parties dicker over the terms of their relationship. It is sometimes said that this model is too old-fashioned and rudimentary to be helpful in an age in which so much contracting is done on standard terms, or through electronic media. However, the model has proven to be remarkably durable, and courts continue to apply the well-established rules, sometimes with an adjustment or modification, to transactions that were not conceived of when the rules were first developed. (We deal specifically with standard forms and contracting via electronic media in Chapter 5).

§4.2.2 When Are Offer and Acceptance Issues Presented?

Upon learning the rules of offer and acceptance, an inexperienced student may be tempted to waste time and effort in trying to unravel the sequence of offer and acceptance in every case or problem. However, not every contract dispute raises formation issues, because the parties may not be in disagreement over the facts of formation. The rules of offer and acceptance tend to be relevant in three types of dispute:

First, the rules of offer and acceptance may be used to determine if a contract came into existence at all where the parties dispute whether their communications resulted in the formation of a contract. Second, even if it is settled that a contract was formed, a determination of which communication constituted the offer, and which was the acceptance, can resolve a dispute about the content of the contract. Third, the rules of offer and acceptance can be relevant to the determination of which state's law governs the contract or which state's courts have jurisdiction to hear a dispute over the contract. This issue may arise where the parties are located in different jurisdictions and communicate across state lines, so that the point of contract formation becomes relevant to choice of law and jurisdiction. This third situation is merely noted here and is not discussed further. The remainder of this chapter is confined to the application of offer and acceptance rules to resolve questions about the existence and terms of the contract.

§4.2.3 The Basic Offer and Acceptance Model at Common Law

The rules of offer and acceptance are based on a particular conception of how contracts are formed. In the simplest terms, they envisage that one person (called the offeror) makes an offer to another person (the offeree) to enter into a contract on specified terms. (Note that the legal meaning of the word "person" includes not only individuals, but also incorporated organizations such as corporations, partnerships, associations, and government bodies. When an organization contracts, it is represented by an authorized officer who acts as its agent.)

The offer creates a power of acceptance in the offeree so that she can bring the contract into existence by signifying acceptance of the transaction on the proposed terms. If the offeree rejects the offer either expressly or simply by not accepting it within a particular time, the offer lapses and no contract arises. If the offeree is interested in forming a contract, but not on the exact terms proposed, the offeree may respond by making a counter-offer, which has the effect of terminating the original offer and reversing the process: The original offeror now becomes the offeree with the power of acceptance. This could go on several more times until the parties reach accord or tire of trying. There are some variations and complications that could arise, as the following sections will show.

Diagram 4A

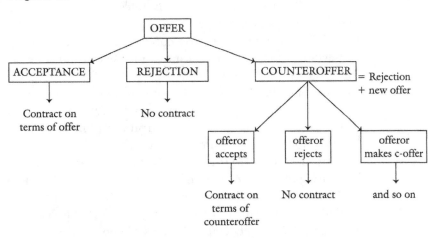

When you first approach the subject of offer and acceptance, you may have the impression that it consists of a set of firm, even technical rules that can be applied quite mechanically. This may create a sense of certainty and order that can be deceiving. As usual, courts do not completely agree on what the rules are. Even where courts apply the same rule, factual circumstances, considerations of fairness, and issues of interpretation often lead to variations in result. In addition, as pointed out in section 4.3, modern courts generally disfavor a rigid and technical approach to offer and acceptance and try to give effect to commercial practice and the reasonable intent of the parties. The discussion in this chapter is centered on the offer and acceptance rules formulated in the Restatement, Second. Remember, however, that while the Restatement, Second's formulation of the rules is persuasive and generally representative of the caselaw, it does not bind courts and is not always followed by them.

§4.3 THE RULES OF OFFER AND ACCEPTANCE APPLICABLE IN SALES OF GOODS UNDER UCC ARTICLE 2

Recall from section 2.7.2 that where a transaction is a sale of goods, Uniform Commercial Code (UCC) Article 2 governs and must be applied. Recall, also, that §2.105(1) defines goods to include movable things other than money and various intangible rights; under §2.106(1) a sale consists of the passing of title from the seller to the buyer for a price; and under §2.304, the price paid for the goods may be payable in money or otherwise.

Because Article 2 must be applied to a sale of goods, it is important to determine, before proceeding to analyze the legal issues raised by a transaction, whether the transaction constitutes a sale of goods. In the area of offer and acceptance, there are some questions that Article 2 resolves differently from common law,[7] so a correct determination of the nature of the transaction could have significant consequences. However, for the most part, you will find that the same rules apply to common law transactions and sales of goods. This is because Article 2 has very few specific provisions that cover offer and acceptance principles, so that most offer and acceptance issues in sales of goods are resolved under principles of common law. The basis for applying common law rules where Article 2 does not provide its own rules is §1.103(b), which states that unless they are displaced by particular provisions of the Code, the general principles of common law apply to transactions governed by the Code. Therefore, as you read about the common law principles of contract formation in this chapter, you should assume that they apply equally to sales of goods unless stated otherwise.

While Article 2 defers to the common law on most offer and acceptance issues, it does strongly encourage courts to be realistic and to keep an eye on business practice in resolving formation disputes. When Article 2 was first enacted in the 1950s, this flexible approach was a notable difference from the common law. However, during the years since it was enacted, it has influenced courts to adopt the same attitude toward contracts under

---

7. For example, Article 2 differs from the common law in its treatment of irrevocable offers, as discussed in section 4.13.4, and it diverges from the common law in its approach to resolving disparities between writings exchanged by the parties, as discussed in Chapter 6. Also, a sale of goods for a price of $500 or more must be sufficiently recorded and signed to comply with Article 2's statute of frauds, discussed in Chapter 11.

common law, and is now generally reflected in the modern common law approach to offer and acceptance as well.

The two Code sections that most directly address general formation issues are §§2.204 and 2.206. The fundamental point made by §2.204 is that the court should focus on the existence of agreement between the parties, whether shown by words or conduct, and if agreement is apparent, the court should not be concerned about technicalities but should do what it can to uphold and enforce the contract. Section 2.206 eschews technical rules on the manner and medium of acceptance and emphasizes that an offer should be interpreted as inviting acceptance by any reasonable mode unless the offer or circumstances make it clear that the mode is restricted.

§4.4 THE NATURE OF AN OFFER, AS DISTINCT FROM A PRELIMINARY PROPOSAL

Restatement, Second, §24 describes an offer as a ". . . manifestation of willingness to enter into a bargain, so made as to justify another person in understanding that his assent to that bargain is invited and will conclude it." This definition identifies the hallmarks of an offer. The offer must contain these elements either expressly or by implication:

1. Because an offer must be manifested, it must necessarily be communicated to the person to whom it is addressed.
2. The offer must indicate a desire to enter into a contract. To do this it has to specify the performances to be exchanged and the terms that will govern the relationship. It is important to remember that as the creator of the offer, the offeror has control over what its terms will be. (The traditional maxim is that the offeror is "master of the offer.") In addition to proposing the terms of the exchange, the offer may also prescribe the manner and time for an effective acceptance.
3. The offer must be directed at some person or group of persons. Although an offer is usually addressed to a specific person, it is legally possible to make an offer to a defined or undefined group. Where this happens, it is a question of interpretation if it contemplates multiple acceptances or may be accepted only by the first person to reply.
4. The offer must invite acceptance. It may or may not indicate how and by what time this acceptance is to be communicated. If a mode and time for acceptance are prescribed, they must be followed. If these are not set out in the offer, the court must decide whether the acceptance was reasonable and timely.

5. The offer must engender the reasonable understanding that acceptance will create the contract. That is, upon acceptance, a contract will arise without any further approval being required from the offeror.

The last hallmark distinguishes an offer from a proposal intended as nothing more than an overture; that is, a tentative expression of interest in transacting, an invitation to make an offer, or a request for information that may lead to an offer. To be an offer, the communication must convey the reasonable understanding (note the objective standard) that the offeror intends a contract to arise and expects to be committed upon acceptance. The offeror thus confers on the offeree the power to decide whether or not a contract will come into being. (As mentioned earlier, this is known as the power of acceptance.) If the proposal reserves to the proponent the final say on whether to be bound, it is not an offer but merely a preliminary communication.

Of course, it is up to the person initiating contractual negotiations to choose whether the communication is to be an offer or merely a preliminary nonbinding proposal, and careful choice of language eliminates or at least reduces the risk that the communication may be misunderstood. However, when intent is not clearly expressed, the communication must be interpreted objectively. The question is whether, taking into account the entire context of the communication, the addressee was justified in understanding that the proponent intended to be bound on acceptance.

For example, if the owner of property wishes to make an offer to a prospective buyer, she may write:

> I offer to sell you my farm "Bleakacre" for $2 million cash. If you wish to buy this property you must deliver your written acceptance to me by midnight on Wednesday, October 13, 2012.

The strong wording (including the use of the terms "offer" and "acceptance") leave little doubt that an offer is intended. If, on the other hand, the owner wanted to make it clear that this is not an offer, she may couch the letter something like this:

> I wish to sell my farm "Bleakacre" and will consider an offer of not less than $2 million. I invite you to make an offer if you are interested in purchasing it.

However, if the owner is less precise in her choice of language, she may come up with something like this:

> I am willing to sell my farm "Bleakacre" to you, but will not accept less than $2 million cash. Let me have your reply as soon as possible.

This flabby language does not make the offeror's intention clear. It could lead the addressee to understand the communication to be an offer, whether or not the owner meant it as such. The ambiguity could keep a couple of lawyers happily employed for some time as the parties litigate over its meaning.

One cannot be sure who will win the last "Bleakacre" dispute because I have not provided any contextual information that may clarify the ambiguity in the owner's letter. In trying to resolve disputes like this, one must weigh all the facts of the case. Courts have identified some general indicia that help to distinguish an offer from a preliminary proposal:

1. The words used in the communication are always the primary indicators of what was intended. Even where the language of the communication does not make its import absolutely clear, clues to reasonable meaning may be found in what was said. The use of terms of art, such as "offer," "quote," or "proposal," may be helpful but are not conclusive if the context indicates that they were not used in their legal sense. (For example, signs erected on real property sometimes announce that the property is "offered for sale," yet no one would seriously argue that the seller thereby makes an offer in the legal sense.)

2. Because an offer is intended to form a contract upon acceptance (and as discussed below, an offeree is not usually permitted to accept in terms that go beyond the offer), a communication that omits significant terms is less likely to be an offer. Therefore, the comprehensiveness and specificity of the terms in the communication are an important clue to its intent.

3. The relationship of the parties, any previous dealings between them, and any prior communications in this transaction may cast light on how the recipient reasonably should have understood the communication.

4. Where parties are members of the same community or trade, they are or should be aware of any common practices or trade usages, so these are taken into account in determining reasonable understanding of a communication.

It must be stressed that these are just factors to be considered. This is not a list of firm rules and it is not exhaustive. The facts of each case must be evaluated to decide on the reasonable meaning of a communication.

In most transactions, a proposal to make a contract is directed to a specific, identified person. This is what happened in all the "Bleakacre" examples. However, an offeror could communicate a desire to enter a contract with multiple persons. The addressees could be a defined group or the public at large. Most commonly, this occurs where a person places an advertisement in a newspaper, catalog, website, or other medium of mass communication. The question of whether an advertisement is an offer or merely an invitation to make an offer must be resolved by the usual process of interpreting its apparent reasonable intent in light of its language in context. If it is an offer, the advertiser is bound to a recipient of the communication as soon as that recipient signifies his assent to its terms. If it is not an offer, but merely a solicitation, a recipient makes an offer by responding and the advertiser has the discretion to accept or reject that offer. Therefore, the question of whether or not an advertisement is an offer can have serious consequences if the advertiser did not expect to be committed to multiple contracts. In most situations, common practice in the marketplace would lead a reasonable person to understand that an advertisement or other generally disseminated proposal is not an offer, but merely a solicitation. However, this is just a general assumption. It can be overturned by the advertiser's choice of language or by proof that commercial practice does support the reasonable understanding that an offer was made.

One of the best-known cases that found an advertisement to be an offer is *Lefkowitz v. Great Minneapolis Surplus store*, 86 N.W.2d 689 (Minn. 1957). The store published a newspaper advertisement that read "Saturday 9 A.M. Sharp 3 Brand New Fur Coats Worth to $100 First Come First Served $1 Each" (lack of punctuation in the original). Although the plaintiff was the first person at the store on Saturday morning and he tendered the $1, the store refused to sell a coat to him on the grounds that it was a "house rule" that the offer was intended for women only. The next week the store placed a similar advertisement in the newspaper in which 3 items were listed for $1 each, "First Come First Served." One of the items was a "Black Lapin Stole Beautiful, worth $139.50." The plaintiff was again the first to show up at the store, but his tender of the $1 was again refused. The plaintiff sued for damages for breach of contract based on the difference between the value of the garments and the $1 price. The store contended that the advertisements were not offers, but merely invitations to the public to make offers to the store. The plaintiff made an offer which it declined. The court agreed that this may often be true, but the legal effect of the advertisement depends on its apparent intent as reasonably understood by the plaintiff. The terms of the advertisements were clear, definite, explicit, and left nothing open for negotiation. They therefore qualified as offers. The store's "house rule" did not restrict the power of acceptance to women because it was not expressed in the offer.[8]

---

8. Of course, the plaintiff had been told of the "house rule" before he accepted the second offer, but the court did not address this. Although the court found that both advertisements led to binding contracts, it only gave the plaintiff damages for the second contract, measured as the difference between the price of $1 and the advertised value of the stole, $139.50. The court said that damages under the first contract were too speculative because the advertisement stated only that the coat was worth "to $100," and it did not state a precise value. This seems unduly strict because the court could have used the maximum value asserted by the store as the best evidence of the coat's worth.

§4.5 THE EXPIRY OF THE OFFER BY PASSAGE OF TIME

§4.5.1 The Specified or Reasonable Duration of the Offer

An offer does not last forever. It has a limited duration and lapses if not accepted in time. As the creator of the offer, the offeror is entitled to specify the time within which the acceptance must be made. If the offeror does not state the duration of the offer, it must be accepted within a reasonable time. The offeror takes a risk by not specifying a time for acceptance because the question of what period is reasonable for acceptance may be unclear until settled by litigation. To decide what is a reasonable time, the factfinder must ask what amount of time would be needed to receive, consider, and reply to the offer under all the circumstances of the transaction. As a rough guide, it is usually assumed that if the parties are in each other's presence, the reasonable time for acceptance concludes when they part company, but if they communicate at a distance by mail or similar noninstantaneous means, the time for transmission must be taken into account. Other factors relevant to this question include the nature of the transaction; the relationship of the parties; any course of dealing, custom, or trade usage; the means of communication used; and the stability of the market.

An offeror may not entirely eliminate the risk of uncertainty by stating a time for acceptance, if the time specified is ambiguous. For example, if the offer requires acceptance by 5 P.M. Pacific Daylight Time on Friday, October 15, 2012, there can be no doubt as to the exact time that the power of acceptance ends. However, an acceptance required "within five days" is ambiguous because it does not indicate if the five-day period runs from the date of the writing or receipt of the offer, or whether the offer can be accepted after business hours on that final day.

§4.5.2 The Effect of a Late Attempt to Accept

If the offeree attempts to accept the offer after the period for acceptance has expired, the legal effect of this late communication may be difficult to decide and depends on the circumstances and the language used. It could be a legally meaningless act. Alternatively, the course of dealings between the parties and the language of the late acceptance could create the reasonable understanding that it is a new offer by the former offeree, creating a power of acceptance in the original offeror. In some cases, especially where there is doubt about the exact duration of the offer, the offeror's failure to object to a late acceptance may suggest either that it was not late at all, or even if it was late, that the offeror acquiesced in the delay, making the acceptance effective despite its tardiness. There is thus no hard-and-fast rule on the treatment of a late acceptance, and its effect must be determined on the facts of each case.

§4.6 TERMINATION OF THE OFFER FOR REASONS OTHER THAN EXPIRY BY LAPSE OF TIME

The stated or reasonable duration should be thought of as the longest period that an offer could remain open. It may terminate even before that under four circumstances identified in Restatement, Second, §36:

§4.6.1 Rejection

The offeree does not have to take positive action to reject an offer. Except in unusual circumstances (discussed in section 4.10.2), an offeror cannot set up an offer so that the offeree is deemed to accept it by failing to respond. That is, in most situations, silence or inaction cannot constitute acceptance. Therefore, rejection occurs as a matter of course simply if the offeree fails to respond to the offer before it expires. However, an offeree may choose to communicate rejection of the offer before it expires by lapse of time, and if she does so, the offer lapses immediately on communication. Once rejection has been communicated, the offeree cannot recant the rejection and accept, because the offer has come to an end. A purported acceptance after rejection could, of course, qualify as a new offer by the former offeree.

§4.6.2 Counteroffer

An offeree may wish to enter the transaction proposed by the offeror, but on terms different from those set out in the offer. To qualify as an acceptance, the response to an offer must agree to the offeror's terms. If it expresses agreement to the transaction, subject to some change in the terms, it is not an acceptance, but a counteroffer. A counteroffer is defined in Restatement, Second, §39 as an offer by the offeree to the offeror, relating to the same matter as the original offer and proposing a different substitute bargain. The counteroffer is therefore both a rejection of the offer and a new offer by the former offeree for a contract on different terms. It thus terminates the original offer and creates a power of acceptance of the counteroffer in the original offeror. Because the counteroffer is a rejection of the original offer, the offeree loses the power to accept the original offer once he has made the counteroffer. He cannot go back to it and accept it if the original offeror rejects the counteroffer. In some cases it is obvious that a response is a counteroffer, but in others, the meaning of language used by the offeree in response to an offer may be less clear and harder to determine. This is discussed in section 4.8.

§4.6.3 The Offeror's Death or Mental Disability

If the offeror dies before the offer is accepted, the offer lapses automatically, even if the offeree did not know about the offeror's death at the time of attempted acceptance. Despite the fact that the rationale for the rule appears to be subjectivist (there can be no "meeting of the minds" if death intervenes before acceptance) the rule is still generally followed. Note that it applies only when the death occurs before acceptance. Once a contract has been formed, the supervening death of a party does not terminate it unless the contract expressly or impliedly contemplates that the death of a party will terminate it. The rights and obligations under the contract pass to the deceased party's estate.

The mental disability of the offeror is treated by §36 in the same way as death, so that if the offeror becomes mentally incompetent between the time of making the offer and the time of acceptance, the offer lapses. But if the mental disability arises after acceptance, it does not affect the formation of the contract. Note, however, that the offeror's mental incapacity before the time of acceptance could be analyzed on a different basis. Instead of treating it as a lapse of the offer (resulting in no contract), it could be seen as creating a contract by a mentally incompetent person. As will be explained in Chapter 14, the effect of this is to create a voidable contract (one that exists but can be voided by the offeror) rather than to preclude formation at all.

§4.6.4 Revocation

Unless the offer qualifies as an option or as a firm offer under UCC Article 2 (discussed in section 4.13), an undertaking to keep it open for a particular period is not binding on the offeror. The offeror therefore has the power to revoke the offer at any time before its acceptance, whether or not the offer states that it will be held open for a stated time.

Revocation only becomes effective when it is communicated to the offeree. This usually means either that the offeree has received notice of revocation from the offeror or that the offeree has learned from other reliable sources that the offer has been withdrawn. The offeror therefore bears the risk that the offeree may have accepted the offer, thereby creating a contract, before receiving notice of revocation. (The mechanics of acceptance are explained later. For now, merely take note that it is possible for an acceptance to take effect even before the offeror hears about it.) The effect of this is that the offeror has the responsibility to withdraw the manifestation of contractual intent created by the offer, and until he does so must assume that it could still be acted upon. The distinction between direct and indirect revocation requires some expansion:

As indicated above, revocation can take effect either where the offeree receives notice of revocation from the offeror (called direct revocation) or where the offeree has learned indirectly of the withdrawal of the offer. For direct revocation to be effective, the offeree must receive notice of revocation that clearly indicates on a reasonable interpretation that the offeror is no longer willing to enter the contract. As with other communications, obscure or ambiguous language could give rise to a dispute over meaning and to interpretational difficulties.

The legal concept of receipt requires that the notice becomes available to the offeree so that if acting reasonably, the offeree would be aware of its contents. The nature of an effective receipt depends on the circumstances of the offer. For example, if a written offer was made to a specific offeree, a written notice of revocation is deemed to be received when the writing is delivered into the possession of the offeree or his authorized representative or it is deposited in an authorized place, even if the offeree fails to handle it physically or to read it. By contrast, if the offer was made to multiple persons in some publication, a revocation published in the same way as the offer is effective, whether or not a particular offeree actually read it.

Although the offeror may have failed to give direct notice of revocation, or something may have gone wrong with the communication, an offer is nevertheless revoked indirectly if the offeror takes action clearly inconsistent with the continued intent to enter a contract, and the offeree obtains reliable information of this action. For example, the offeree would be taken to know that the offer to sell "Bleakacre" has been revoked if, while considering the offer, the offeree learns reliably that the property has been sold to someone else. This conclusion would not be reached if the information is uncertain (for example, the offeree had merely heard rumors to this effect), or the action is not clearly inconsistent with the continued existence of the offer (for example, if the offeree was aware that the offeror was negotiating the sale but had not yet committed to sell to someone else).

The classic case establishing the principle of indirect revocation, decided by the Chancery Division of the English Court of Appeal, is *Dickenson v. Dodds* 2 Ch. D. 463 (1876). Dodds made an offer to sell real property to Dickenson. The offer specified that it was open for acceptance until Friday 9 A.M. On Thursday, Dickenson heard from a third party that Dodds had been "offering or agreeing to sell" the property to someone else. Immediately after hearing this, and before the deadline, Dickenson communicated his acceptance to Dodds. Dodds declined it, saying that it was too late because he had already

sold the property. The court found that although Dodds had not communicated his revocation, Dickenson had indirectly obtained information that
he no longer intended to sell the property to him. The court expressed its
opinion in subjectivist terms, saying that as Dodds had changed his mind
before Dickenson accepted, there could be no meeting of the parties' minds.
However, the case can be reconciled with the objective test because Dickenson reasonably knew that Dodds had changed his mind.[9]

§4.7 THE NATURE AND EFFECT OF ACCEPTANCE

Acceptance is the offeree's manifestation of assent to the offer. It is the event
that brings the contract into existence because, as noted before, the offer
necessarily contemplates that the parties will become bound immediately
upon the offeree's exercise of the power of acceptance.

Acceptance must be a volitional act, performed freely, deliberately, and
with the intent to enter a contract on the terms of the offer. Like the intent to
make an offer, intent to accept is determined objectively. The question is not
whether the offeree actually intended to accept, but whether a reasonable
person in the offeror's position would have understood the manifestation as
an acceptance. As always, the objective standard is not rigid, so that a manifestation of acceptance does not bind the offeree if coerced or induced by
fraud. Similarly, as discussed in section 4.10.2, the offeror cannot structure
the offer in a way that traps the offeree into inadvertent acceptance.

Only the offeree may accept the offer. The offeree is, of course, the
person whose acceptance is invited by the offer. This is most commonly a
single specific person, but an offer could be made to several identified
persons or even to a broad or unidentified group. Unless the offer indicates
otherwise, or is clearly open to anyone who sees it, it is regarded as personal
to, and can only be accepted by, the person or persons to whom it is
addressed. An identified offeree cannot transfer the power of acceptance.[10]

As stated earlier, the offeror, as the proponent of the transaction, has the
power to set out not only the terms of the proposed contract itself but also
the requirements for an effective acceptance. To validly accept the offer, the
offeree must acquiesce in the offeror's terms and must manifest this agreement in the manner and within the time prescribed. If either of these two

---

9. *Dickenson v. Dodds* also stands for the rule that a promise to hold open an offer for a stated time
does not bind the offeror unless consideration is given for that promise. This is dealt with in
section 4.13.
10. This rule only applies to offers. Once a contract has been formed, a party is normally
allowed to transfer (assign) his or her rights under the contract. Assignment is discussed in
Chapter 19.

conditions are not satisfied, the attempted acceptance may be ineffective. Time for acceptance has already been discussed. We now examine the content and mode of acceptance.

§4.8 THE EFFECT OF INCONSISTENCY BETWEEN THE OFFER AND THE RESPONSE: COUNTEROFFER

To be an acceptance, the response to the offer must conform to the offer. An acceptance cannot qualify or change the offer or add new terms. If the response to the offer does this, it is not an acceptance, but a counteroffer. As noted in section 4.6.2, a counteroffer is a response that indicates interest in the transaction, but proposes a contract on terms different from those in the offer. If there are significant differences between the offer and response, the response cannot be an acceptance. If the response proposes to enter a contract on the offeree's terms, it will be a counteroffer. However, minor differences may not disqualify the response as an acceptance. The attitude of courts to such small inconsistencies between the offer and acceptance has changed over the years. Under classical common law, the acceptance must correspond exactly with the offer. This is sometimes called the "mirror image" or "ribbon matching" rule. A response is not an acceptance if the offeree imposes any conditions on the acceptance or seeks to change or qualify the terms of the offer in any way. Any variation in the response to an offer disqualifies it as an acceptance. Although some courts still apply the "mirror image" rule, modern courts tend to be somewhat more flexible and treat a response as a counteroffer only if it has a material discrepancy from the offer. This approach has the disadvantage of adding the complication of trying to distinguish material and trivial alterations, but it has the benefit of enabling the court to find a contract despite a trivial or technical variation between the offer and response. If the court does find that a response with minor changes is an acceptance, this does not mean that the offeree's changes become part of the contract. The common law rule is that the response is treated as an acceptance on the offeror's terms. The variations from the offer in the response do not become part of the contract, and simply fall away.[11]

Sometimes it is clear that the offeree's response to an offer is a counteroffer, but sometimes a response is ambiguous. It is clearly not an acceptance, but it may not be a counteroffer either. A few examples illustrate this

---

11. When we deal with UCC §2.207 in Chapter 6, you will see that Article 2 has a special rule for handling discrepancies between the offer and the response where the parties exchange writings.

issue of interpretation: The owner of "Bleakacre" offers to sell it to the offeree for $2 million. The offeree responds, "Thanks for your offer. I am interested in buying 'Bleakacre'; however, your asking price is too high. I will pay you $1.8 million for the property." This is clearly a counteroffer because it indicates interest in the transaction but proposes a different price (surely a material variation from the offer) and signifies intent to enter the contract if the original offeror agrees to that price. The response therefore rejects the original offer and substitutes a new offer to the former offeror. However, say that the response stated, "Thanks for your offer. Although I am interested in buying 'Bleakacre,' I cannot accept your offer because your asking price is too high." This cannot be a counteroffer because it does not propose a new price. However, it also indicates that the offeree does not intend to enter the transaction on the terms proposed by the offeror. It must therefore be reasonably understood as rejection with an explanation. Its legal effect is simply to terminate the offer. The effect of the offeree's response is even more ambiguous if he says, "Thanks for your offer. Would you accept $1.9 million?" This is not an acceptance, but it may not be a counteroffer either, which would terminate the buyer's power of acceptance. It may be merely a request for modification of terms, intended to keep alive the buyer's opportunity to accept the offer if the offeror sticks to the asking price.

In some cases, a response may seem to be a counteroffer, but the terms of the offer and response must be interpreted to ascertain whether it really is. For example, the response may seem to add terms that are not expressed in the offer but are implicit in the offer or would be incorporated into the offer by law or usage. If so, the response may appear superficially to be a counteroffer, but it is in fact an unqualified acceptance, because it merely articulates what was inherent in the offer. For example, the owner of "Bleakacre" offers to sell the property to a prospective buyer for $2 million. The offeree responds, "I accept your offer, subject to your proof of clear title, payment to be placed in escrow and made to you against transfer of the deed." The offer is silent on these points. It did not warrant good title and said nothing about payment being concurrent with transfer of the deed. However, common usage and accepted legal practice implies these terms in a contract for the sale of land, so they were part of the offer in the absence of language clearly excluding them. Articulating them in the acceptance does not harm its effectiveness.

§4.9 THE MODE OF ACCEPTANCE

An acceptance must be manifested and communicated. The offeror has control over the manner of acceptance, and, in addition to stipulating the terms of the proposed contract, the offeror may specify what the offeree must do to accept. To be an effective acceptance, the offeree's response must be in conformity with these instructions. However, if the offer does not require acceptance to take a particular form, no special formalities are required for effective acceptance.[12] It may be signified in any manner reasonable under the circumstances, including spoken or written words or conduct, and conveyed by any reasonable means of communication. As explained in section 4.12, the acceptance may be a promise to perform the requested exchange or the actual performance of the offeree's consideration.

To avoid confusion, it is important to distinguish the substantive terms of the offer (that is, the terms of the proposed contract itself) from the instructions concerning acceptance (that is, the procedure that must be followed by the offeree to accept). The substantive terms are central — they go to the very heart of the relationship and are the offeror's dominant concern. The instructions for acceptance are ancillary to the offeror's principal purpose of securing a contract. They are concerned only with the way in which the offeree communicates assent and are aimed at a communication process that the offeror considers most convenient and efficacious. Although the manner of acceptance is ancillary to the goal of making a contract, the offeror may not be indifferent to controlling it. If the offeror is concerned about knowing of the acceptance as soon as it takes effect and of having written proof of it, the offer should prescribe an exclusive mode of acceptance that ensures acceptance only takes effect upon the offeror's personal receipt of a signed letter of acceptance. If the offeror does not care about the mode of acceptance and is willing to assume any risk of late or undelivered notice of acceptance,[13] the offeror may not specify a mode at all or may indicate a permissible but not exclusive mode. Factors such as the desire to accommodate the offeree's convenience, to encourage acceptance, or to maintain good relations with the offeree, may outweigh the offeror's desire for certainty and may dissuade the offeror from making too fine a point of the procedure for accepting. Taking this into account, the usual assumption of the law is that unless the offer clearly

---

12. Subject to the qualification that if the statute of frauds applies, as discussed in Chapter 11, its requirements of writing and signature must be satisfied.

13. For example, under the "mailbox" rule, discussed in section 4.11, if it is reasonable to accept through the mail or a similar medium, the acceptance takes effect as soon as properly deposited in the post or introduced by the offeree into whatever other appropriate delivery system is used. It is therefore possible that the offeror will not know of the acceptance until some time after it occurred, and bears the risk of the acceptance never arriving. If the offeror does not wish to take this risk, the offer should either stipulate that acceptance is effective only on receipt, or exclude this mode of acceptance in favor of one (such as personal delivery by hand) that will ensure instantaneous knowledge of acceptance.

indicates otherwise, the offeror is more interested in attracting the acceptance than in being punctilious about the mode of acceptance.

In summary, the rules governing mode of acceptance are:

1. When the offer clearly manifests the intention that a prescribed mode of acceptance is mandatory and exclusive, the offeror's intent must be deferred to, and that particular manner of acceptance must be complied with exactly.

2. If a manner of acceptance is specified, but it does not reasonably appear intended as exclusive, any reasonable method of acceptance is effective provided that it is consistent with the prescribed mode and provides protection to the offeror equal to that of the stated mode. As always, the wording and circumstances of the offer must be interpreted to decide if a mode of acceptance is exclusive and, if not, whether the mode used is reasonably consistent with that specified.

   For example, say the offer states, "Please signify your acceptance by mailing your written and signed acceptance. . . ." The offer does not make it clear that mail is the only acceptable medium, so a written, signed acceptance by private courier is probably just as good. However, a faxed acceptance may not be, because the communication would be a copy rather than an original signature and possibly less verifiable as genuine.

3. If the offer does not specify any mode of acceptance, the test for the appropriateness of the communication is even less stringent. The offeree may use the same mode as used by the offeror, or any other method of communication that is customary for transactions of that kind or is reasonable under the circumstances. For example, in *Ellefson v. Megadeth, Inc.*, 2005 WL 82022 (S.D.N.Y. 2005), the parties (a heavy metal rock band and one of its original members) entered into lengthy negotiations to settle various disputes. Much of the negotiation was by e-mail, culminating in a final version of the offered contract sent by fax. The offeree accepted by signing the offer and returning it by mail. After the acceptance was mailed, but before it was received, the offeror revoked the offer by e-mail. If mail was an effective means of acceptance, the acceptance took effect under the mailbox rule as soon as the acceptance was mailed. (*See* section 4.11.) The court rejected the offeror's argument that the offer had been revoked before effective acceptance because the use of regular mail was not a permissible mode of acceptance. It held that the use of e-mail and fax during the negotiations and leading up to the offer did not preclude acceptance by mail, because there were no express restrictions on the mode of acceptance and regular mail was a reasonable method of communication under the circumstances.

§4.10 INADVERTENT ACCEPTANCE AND SILENCE OR INACTION AS ACCEPTANCE

§4.10.1 Inadvertent Acceptance

Although the objective test is used to determine intent to accept, the offeree must at least know about the offer to accept it. To this narrow extent, the subjective state of mind of the offeree could take precedence over his apparent intention. It does not happen too often that an offeree inadvertently manifests intent to accept an offer that he does not know exists. However, this has come up in cases in which the offer is not communicated to the offeree, but the offeree's subsequent conduct creates the impression of acceptance. The best-known case involving such a situation is *Glover v. Jewish War Veterans of the U.S.* 68 A.2d 233 (D.C. 1949). The association published an offer of reward for information leading to the arrest and conviction of the murderer of one of its members. On being questioned by the police, the mother of the girlfriend of one of the culprits furnished information that led to his apprehension and ultimate conviction of the murder. The act of providing the information would have been the acceptance of the offer of reward.[14] However, when she gave the information to the police, she did not know of the reward, and only found out about it afterwards. The court held that she was not entitled to the reward. She could not have intended to accept an offer of which she was unaware.

The result of the case seems harsh and contrary to the purpose of the rule. The reason for requiring knowledge of the offer is to protect the offeree from being held to an inadvertent manifestation of acceptance, so this rationale does not apply when the offeree desires the acceptance to be effective. However, the result may be justified on a different ground — because the offeree did not know about the offer, she was not induced by it to furnish the information, and the court's refusal to find a contract did not defeat any reliance interest that she might have had. This argument did not persuade the court in *Anderson v. Douglas Lomason Co.*, 540 N.W.2d 277 (Iowa 1995). The Court had to decide whether an employee was protected by a provision in the employees' handbook that required progressive discipline and precluded summary dismissal. When an employer adds provision to a handbook, this is treated as an offer which the employee accepts by continuing in employment. However, the employee in this case had not read the

---

14. As explained in section 4.12, the offer in this case is for a unilateral contract, and so the giving of the information is both the act of acceptance and the performance required under the contract. That is, the only way that the offeree can accept is to render the requested performance.

handbook and did not know of the provision. Therefore, if knowledge of the offer is required for an effective acceptance, this employee would not have been protected by the provision in the handbook barring summary dismissal. The court refused to follow the rule requiring knowledge of the offer for effective acceptance. It reasoned that a strong policy of treating employees evenhandedly would be defeated by distinguishing employees who had read the handbook from those who had not. In a subsequent case in Iowa (the same jurisdiction) involving a handbook that had not been read by the employee, the Iowa Court of Appeals distinguished *Anderson* and refused to find a contract. In *Poeckes v. City of Orange City* 707 N.W.2d 336 (Iowa App. 2005) the court noted that *Anderson* had created a narrow exception to the usual rule that an offeree must have knowledge of an offer to accept it. However, the court found a significant factual difference in the cases. In *Anderson* the employer actually gave the handbook to the employee, while in this case, the employer, although it never officially rescinded the handbook, had discontinued using and distributing it. The employee had simply found it in her desk drawer. (That is, this seems to be a case in which both the offer and the acceptance were inadvertent.)

§4.10.2 Acceptance by Silence or Inaction

The offeror cannot impose a duty on the offeree to take some affirmative step to reject the offer, making failure to act an acceptance. For example, the offer cannot impose a duty on the offeree to speak by stating "... if you do not wish to accept this offer, you must deliver notice of rejection to me by Friday, failing which you are deemed to have accepted."

To illustrate further, in *Pride v. Lewis*, 179 S.W.3d 375 (Mo. App. 2005) a potential buyer of real property made a written offer to purchase it from the owner. The owner signed and returned the offer, signifying intent to accept it, but changed the closing date on the offer from May 15 to June 1. The court, applying the "mirror image" rule, found that the alteration of the closing date made the owner's response into a counteroffer. The buyer did not respond to the counteroffer, did not attend the closing, and never requested the return of his earnest money. The issue in the case was whether the buyer could be taken to have accepted the counteroffer by failing to object to the change in the closing date (of which he was aware) or to claim return of his earnest money. The court held that silence or inaction could not be an acceptance except in narrow circumstances where there is a duty to speak. Although it would have been courteous for the buyer to tell the owner that he rejected the counteroffer, there was nothing in the relationship that required him to notify the owner. Furthermore, there was no explanation on record of the buyer's failure to request the return of his earnest money, and that alone was not enough to signify assent to the counteroffer.

The rule that silence does not constitute acceptance is intended to protect the offeree from imposition. It therefore does not apply if the offeree does intend her silence to constitute acceptance. She may rely on the offeror's authorization of silence as a mode of acceptance, and the offeror cannot argue that this method of acceptance is ineffective. Therefore, an offeror who invites acceptance by silence assumes a risk of uncertainty. The meaning of the silence depends on the offeree's subjective intent, and the offeror cannot be sure if the failure to reject is an acceptance.

There are two situations in which silence binds the offeree, even in the absence of intent to accept. First, silence operates as acceptance if the offeror proffers property or services with the offer, and the offeree, having a reasonable opportunity to return or refuse them, exercises ownership rights over the property or accepts the benefit of the service. For example, to promote a new wine, a local wine shop leaves a case of wine on the offeree's doorstep with an offer to sell the wine for $200. The offer ends with the statement, "You may refuse this offer by returning the wine to us within 24 hours of delivery. If you do not return it, you have accepted this offer and must mail your check to us within a week." The offeree is not required to return the wine, or to communicate with the offeror in any way to reject the offer. He can simply ignore the wine. However, if he drinks it or pours it down the sink, he does accept the offer.[15] (If the offeree does not want the wine on his doorstep indefinitely, he can call on the offeror to remove it, and if the offeror fails to do so within a reasonable time, the offeree can then dispose of it.)

Second, silence may operate as acceptance if prior dealings between the parties or other circumstances make it reasonable for the offeror to expect the offeree to give notice of rejection. For example, say that the offeree was a longstanding customer of the wine shop, which had regularly delivered cases of wine to the offeree whenever it had a new wine to promote. On receiving wine on previous occasions, the offeree had either returned the cases or paid for them.

Acceptance need not always be explicit, so there are some situations in which an offeree does not respond to an offer, but ongoing conduct is enough to signify acceptance. It can be difficult to know when conduct alone, without any expression of assent, constitutes acceptance. For example, in *Morvant v. P. F. Chang's China Bistro, Inc.*, 2012 WL 1604851 (N.D. Cal. 2012), P. F. Chang (the employer) implemented an arbitration policy in 2006, after Morvant had already started working for it. P. F. Chang gave copies of the agreement to its employees with a cover letter setting out the effective date of the policy and

---

15. To protect people from this kind of marketing practice, and to discourage merchants from using it, federal legislation varies this common law rule if the merchandise is sent through the mail. The recipient may keep and use the unsolicited goods without becoming obliged to pay for them. States may have similar laws relating to merchandise delivered otherwise than through the mail.

stating that "this policy applies to you." Morvant received but did not sign the agreement or otherwise indicate assent to it, but continued working for P. F. Chang for a few months. When Morvant later sued P. F. Chang over alleged breaches of the conditions of employment, P. F. Chang moved to compel arbitration. The court denied the motion on the grounds that Morvant had never signified assent to the agreement. The court characterized the new arbitration policy as an offer, which Morvant did not accept merely by continuing to work for P. F. Chang. However, the court noted (distinguishing other cases) that it would have reached the opposite result if the arbitration agreement or cover letter had specified that continued employment would constitute acceptance of the terms of the arbitration policy.

§4.11 THE EFFECTIVE DATE OF ACCEPTANCE AND THE "MAILBOX" RULE

§4.11.1 The Traditional Rule

The question of when acceptance takes effect is linked to but distinct from the method of acceptance. Where the parties are negotiating face to face or are otherwise in instantaneous communication and are able to hear or observe each other's manifestations immediately. There is no temporal separation between the offeror's expression of acceptance and its communication to the offeree, so there is no need to decide whether acceptance takes effect when it is uttered or when it is heard. Acceptance occurs as soon as it is manifested.

However, where the parties are at a distance and the means of communication entail a delay between the manifestation and the offeror's knowledge of it, there are two possible points at which we could treat the acceptance as becoming effective. It could take effect immediately upon its being dispatched, or only upon its being received by the offeror. As with the mode of acceptance, the offeror has the right to specify when acceptance becomes effective. In many situations if a mode of acceptance is prescribed, this also implicitly establishes the effective point of the acceptance. For example, if the offeror requires acceptance to be only by the personal delivery of a signed, written acceptance, this covers both the mode of acceptance and the event (delivery) that brings it into effect. However, the offeror may not have specified a mode of acceptance or, even if having done so, may not fix the point at which the acceptance takes effect. For example, the offer may state that acceptance must be by mail, but may not make it clear if a contract comes into being upon the acceptance being mailed or only upon its being received by the offeror.

In the absence of specification in the offer, the acceptance takes effect as soon as it is put out of the offeree's possession, provided that the acceptance is made in a manner and via a medium expressly or impliedly authorized by the offer. Therefore, if acceptance by mail is permissible, acceptance occurs as soon as the offeree deposits a properly stamped and addressed acceptance in the mailbox. This is known as the "mailbox" rule or "deposited acceptance" rule. Because acceptance takes effect on depositing the acceptance in the mail, it does not matter if it was received after the offer terminated or was never received at all. The burden is on the offeree to prove proper dispatch, so the offeree should make a good record of the mailing to avoid evidentiary problems. The offeree must also ensure that the letter is correctly addressed, stamped, and otherwise properly prepared for delivery. This concept is illustrated by *Casto v. State Farm Mutual Automobile Insurance Co.*, 594 N.E.2d 1004 (Ohio App. 1991), in which an insurance company mailed an offer to the insured to renew a car insurance policy. The insured sought to accept the offer by mailing a check for the premium but forgot to put a stamp on the envelope. The post office therefore did not deliver the letter and the premium payment was never received. The insured did not discover this problem until the unstamped letter was returned by the post office. In the interim, the car had been damaged in an accident. The court found that although acceptance by mail was authorized, so that the mailbox rule would have applied to make acceptance effective on mailing the check, the mailbox rule cannot be applied where the offeree cannot show proper mailing.

There have been a number of rationales advanced for the "mailbox" rule. The most convincing is that the offeror could have allocated the risk of uncertainty, delay, or nonreceipt to the offeree. Because he did not do this, he assumes this risk, and the offeree gains the benefit of a reliable basis for establishing effective acceptance.

The "mailbox" rule does not apply if the acceptance follows a counteroffer or rejection — that is, the offeree initially mails a rejection and then changes her mind and mails an acceptance. To protect the offeror, who might receive the rejection before the acceptance, the acceptance only takes effect on receipt. Therefore, if it arrives before the rejection, the offer is accepted, and if it arrives afterwards, it is ineffective.[16]

If the "mailbox" rule does not apply, acceptance takes effect only on receipt — the writing must come into the possession of the addressee or his authorized representative, or must be deposited in an authorized place. (Provided this has happened, the addressee does not actually have to read it.) It is important to remember that the "mailbox" rule applies only to acceptances. A rejection or counteroffer sent by the offeree, and a revocation sent by the offeror, are effective only on receipt.

---

16. Section 4.13 deals with irrevocable offers (options). If an offer is irrevocable, some courts hold that the mailbox rule does not apply and acceptance is effective only on receipt unless the offer specifies otherwise. The reason for this variation is explained in section 4.13.

§4.11.2 Application of the Rule to Electronic Media

The mailbox rule is so called because it was established to deal with acceptance through the medium of the mail. However, today, offer and acceptance are commonly conducted via electronic media such as phone, e-mail, fax, or the Internet. Some forms of electronic communication are clearly instantaneous, so that even though the parties are not physically in each other's presence, there is no delay between the articulation and receipt of acceptance. Where this is so, the general rule, articulated in Restatement, Second, §64 is that acceptance "by telephone or other medium of substantially instantaneous two-way communication" is treated the same as if the parties are physically in each other's presence.

However, some forms of electronic communication are not substantially instantaneous, so that their use is more analogous to mailing. Matters are further complicated by the fact that, unlike mail, some of these forms of communication are sometimes instantaneous, and sometimes not. For example, a fax or e-mail must travel through a medium from the sender to the recipient, and the message may or may not be received immediately. There is also the possibility of significant disruption or delay in the transmission. Where there is a delay in delivery or service is disrupted so that the acceptance is not delivered at all, it may be important to decide whether the mailbox rule applies to make the communication effective on sending or receipt. The answer is not easy or obvious. There are a few cases in which the court has applied the mailbox rule to acceptance by fax. For example, in *Trinity Homes, L.L.C. v. Fang*, 2003 WL 22699791 (Va. Cir. Ct. 2003), the court said that the essence of substantially instantaneous communication is that transmission occurs within a minute or two at most so that the parties are able to determine readily that their communications are going through and the offeror will know exactly when the offeree has accepted. This was not how the fax transmission was set up in this case, so the court found that the mailbox rule applied. (The offeree nevertheless lost because his machine did not have a log and he could not prove when he sent the fax.)

§4.12 ACCEPTANCE BY PROMISE OR PERFORMANCE: BILATERAL AND UNILATERAL CONTRACTS

§4.12.1 The Distinction in Perspective

Students are often perplexed by the distinction between unilateral and bilateral contracts. A note on perspective may therefore be helpful before we become involved in the details of the distinction: Bear two things in mind. First, the bilateral-unilateral distinction is nothing more than a particular application of the general principles governing the proper mode of acceptance. Second, the distinction does not come up often because most contracts are clearly bilateral.

§4.12.2 The Offer for a Bilateral Contract

As stressed in sections 4.5, 4.9, and 4.11, the offeror has the power to prescribe the time, effective date, and method of acceptance. Included in this power is not only the ability to authorize or require a particular medium of acceptance (such as the mails, telephone, or personal delivery) but also a particular action to manifest acceptance. The most common action used to signify acceptance is the use of words, oral or written, to express assent. When words are used to accept, the acceptance invariably constitutes a promise of future performance. For example, if the owner of "Bleakacre" offers to sell it for $2 million and the offeree replies by expressing acceptance, a contract is created under which both the parties make promises of future performance: The offeror promises to convey the farm and the offeree promises to pay the price. Because, at the point of contract formation, both parties have outstanding promises to be performed in the future, the contract is said to be bilateral. This is represented in Diagram 4B.

Diagram 4B

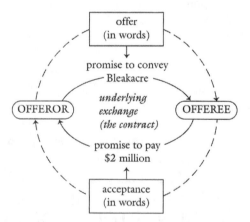

Instead of authorizing acceptance in the form of words, the offeror could demand a nonverbal signification of acceptance. The offer could state, for example, "I offer to sell you 'Bleakacre' for $2 million. If you wish to accept this offer, you must stand in your underwear at the corner of Main and Broadway at 2 P.M. today. This is the only way that you may accept this offer." If the offeree complies with this request, the offer is accepted. At that point a contract comes into being under which the offeror promises to convey "Bleakacre" and the offeree promises to pay $2 million. Although this offer required the offeree's assent to be signified by conduct instead of words, this is still a bilateral contract. The prescribed act of acceptance has exactly the same legal effect as the delivery of a piece of paper on which the words "I accept" are written. By performing the act, the offeree signifies assent and impliedly promises to perform the consideration (payment of $2 million) demanded in the offer. This is represented in Diagram 4C.

Diagram 4C

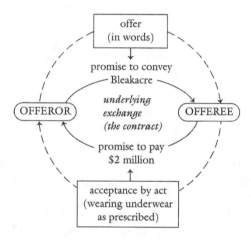

§4.12.3 The Offer for a Unilateral Contract

In the last example, the prescribed act of acceptance was merely intended to symbolize assent to the offer. It is nothing more than a mode of acceptance and has nothing to do with the actual performance—the exchange of detriments—called for by the contract. However, the offeror could have structured the offer so that the act of acceptance is not merely symbolical, but is at the same time also the performance of the offeree's side of the contract. For example, the offer could have stated: "I offer to sell you 'Bleakacre' for $2 million. To accept this offer you must come to my office today at 2 P.M. and pay me $2 million in cash. This is the only way that you may accept this offer." The act of acceptance is also the complete act of performance. The offeree's consideration under the contract is furnished in full immediately upon acceptance, and the offeree has no further duty under the contract. All that remains is for the offeror to perform the promise in the offer and to transfer title and possession of "Bleakacre." Because, at the moment of formation, only one of the parties has a promise outstanding, the contract is said to be unilateral. This is represented in Diagram 4D.

Diagram 4D

Note, therefore, that "unilateral" does not mean one-sided, in the sense that only one party has given or done something. As explained in Chapter 7, a transaction in which one of the parties has made a promise and the other has given or promised nothing in return lacks consideration and is not a valid and enforceable contract. Rather, the word "unilateral" signifies that although both parties have given consideration, only one of them has made a promise as consideration. The other has furnished consideration by rendering the required exchange performance at the very point of contract formation.

§4.12.4 When the Offer Does Not Clearly Prescribe Promise or Performance as the Exclusive Mode of Acceptance

In the last example, the offeror made it clear that acceptance could only be made by performance of the offeree's consideration, so there is no doubt that a unilateral contract was called for. Similarly, the offer could use clear language that makes promise the only permissible means of acceptance. An offeror who really cares about prescribing either a promise or performance as the exclusive mode of acceptance should use clear language to this effect in the offer to remove any doubt as to her intent. However, even in the absence of such clear language, the nature of the contract itself may lead to the conclusion that acceptance has to be only by promise, or only by performance. In most contracts, the performance is to take place some time after the prescribed or reasonable time for acceptance, so acceptance by promise is the only permissible mode. For example, an offer of employment, made on May 1, calls for the employee to begin work on June 1, but requires acceptance by May 7. In some cases, even in the absence of express language limiting acceptance to performance, the nature of the transaction makes it clear that the offer may be accepted only by performance. For example, a sign posted on a fence around a construction site reads, "$1,000 reward to anyone who reports theft of equipment or materials from this site." It is obvious that this offer does not contemplate formation of a contract by a promise to report theft, but may be accepted only by the actual performance of reporting a theft.

However, there are situations in which neither the language of the offer nor its nature and circumstances clearly require either promise or performance to be the exclusive mode of acceptance. If the offer appears to be ambivalent on this question and acceptance by either promise or performance is feasible, the general approach, as reflected in Restatement, Second, §32 and UCC §2.206 (and discussed in section 4.9) applies: The preferred interpretation of the offer is that the offeree may choose to accept either by promise or by performance.

For example, the offeror delivers an offer to the offeree on Monday stating, "I offer to sell you 'Bleakacre' for $2 million. If you wish to buy it, you must pay me $2 million in cash at my office on Friday at 2 P.M." Clearly, it is a term of the proposed contract that the buyer's performance — the delivery of her consideration under the contract — must take place on Friday at 2 P.M. at the seller's office. However, although the offer is clear on the due date of the cash payment, it does not actually say that the only way that the offeree can accept is by making the cash payment on Friday at 2 P.M. The absence of clear language to this effect would likely be interpreted as giving the offeree the choice of accepting either by payment Friday at 2 P.M., (creating a unilateral contract) or by making a promise of payment at some time before Friday at 2 P.M. (creating a bilateral contract in which the acceptance is by promise to pay the $2 million by Friday at 2 P.M.) Therefore, if the offeree is anxious to close the deal immediately and to bind the offeror before Friday at 2 P.M., she could write to the offeror on Monday, stating "I accept." A contract immediately comes into existence on dispatch of the letter. The offeree has accepted by making a promise on Monday to perform as required on Friday, and the offeror's offer immediately becomes a promise to convey the property at some future (unspecified but reasonable) time. The early acceptance by promise creates a bilateral contract that binds both parties. The importance of this is that the offer has now become a contract, so the offeror is bound and has lost the right to revoke the offer. Alternatively, if the offeree chooses not to accept by promise before Friday at 2 P.M., she could show up at that time with the money and accept by performance. Diagrams 4E and 4F represent these alternative choices of acceptance. Diagram 4E represents the offeree's election to accept by promise on Monday, and Diagram 4F shows his election to accept by performance on Friday.

Diagram 4E. Acceptance by Promise on Monday

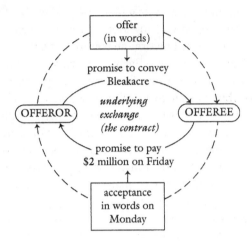

Diagram 4F. Acceptance by Performance on Friday

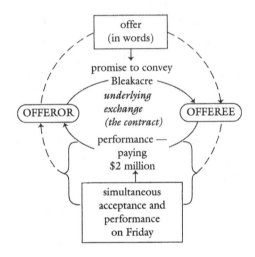

§4.12.5 Acceptance by a Performance That Cannot Be Accomplished Instantly

In the examples concerning the offer to sell "Bleakacre," the offeree's contractual performance was cash payment, a single, relatively instantaneous act. However, some performances cannot be accomplished in one stroke. For example, "Bleakacre" is run-down and overgrown. The owner writes to her nephew, "If you come down and clean up the property for me this summer, I will pay you $2,000 when the work is complete. You need not make a decision now. If you wish to accept my offer, just come down this summer and do the work."

If the nephew did respond early by making a promise, and the aunt thereafter revoked before the summer, we would have to decide if the offer called for acceptance only by performance. We would probably conclude that it did not, because neither the language used nor the circumstances reasonably indicate that performance was intended as the exclusive mode of acceptance. However, assume that the nephew did not make an early promissory reply and that the aunt did not revoke before the summer. The nephew came down in early summer and began the work of clearing the property. Before he completed the task, the aunt changed her mind about cleaning up the property and revoked her offer.

If acceptance only takes place on completion of performance, the nephew risks revocation while he is in the process of performing. To protect him from this risk, Restatement, Second, §§62 and 45 give legal effect to the commencement of performance. Section 62 applies where the offer does not mandate acceptance by performance, so that it can be accepted either by performance or promise. The commencement or tender[17] of performance constitutes an implied promise to complete the performance within the time called for by the offer. Therefore, the commencement or tender of the performance is, in effect, an acceptance by promise creating a bilateral contract. In the present example, as soon as the nephew began work, a bilateral contract came into being under which he was committed to complete the work by the end of summer, and the aunt was committed to pay him $2,000 on completion. The creation of an implied promise by beginning performance is represented in Diagram 4G.

Diagram 4G

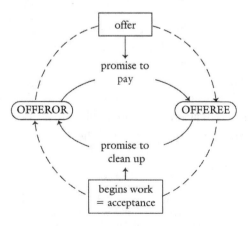

---

17. A tender is an offer of performance by a party who is willing and able to begin it.

Restatement, Second, §45 applies where the offer calls for performance as the exclusive mode of acceptance (that is, it is clearly an offer only for a unilateral contract), so that the commencement of performance cannot be an acceptance by promise, because such an acceptance is not authorized. Restatement, Second, §45 treats the beginning or tender of performance as creating an option in favor of the offeree, so that the offeror loses the right to revoke once performance has been tendered or begun. To exercise the option, the offeree must complete the performance in the required time. If he fails to do so, the option is not taken up and the offer lapses. This means that the offeror is discharged from her own performance under the offer, so the offeree receives no contractual payment[18] for the incomplete work. The creation of an option by beginning performance is represented by Diagram 4H.

Diagram 4H

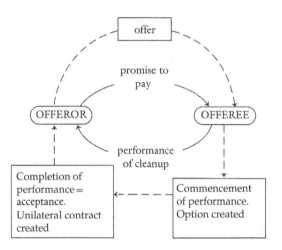

From the offeree's point of view, it is more advantageous to have commencement of performance treated as creating an option instead of an acceptance by implied promise. The latter approach brings the contract into existence as soon as performance begins, so the offeree is bound to complete the work and failure to do so not only precludes his contractual recovery but also makes him liable for damages for breach of contract. This is why the more favorable option approach is confined to the rarer cases where the offeror actually forecloses promissory acceptance.

---

18. Because the nephew's work may have resulted in an unpaid-for benefit to his aunt, he may be entitled to recover the value of this benefit on the ground that it would unjustly enrich his aunt to allow her to enjoy the benefit of his work without paying for it. That is, he may be entitled to restitutionary relief under the theory of unjust enrichment — a basis of relief distinct from contract. We do not consider this here, but defer discussion of unjust enrichment to Chapter 9.

The comments to Restatement, Second, §§45 and 62 emphasize that neither the promise nor the option arises merely when preparation for performance starts. The actual performance must be begun or tendered. In some situations it may be relatively clear where the dividing line between preparation and performance is to be drawn, but in others the line could be fuzzy. For example, when the nephew packs his belongings in his car and sets off for the property this is probably preparation, but when he buys necessary tools and equipment for the specific task of clearing the property, this may be closely enough linked to his contract obligation to be actual performance.

§4.12.6 Notice When an Offer Is Accepted by Performance

As we have seen, when an offer is accepted by a promise, the offeree must communicate acceptance to the offeror. If an offer is accepted by performance, the acceptance normally comes to the offeror's attention as a matter of course, because the offeror receives the performance. Unless the offer requires notice of performance, the offeree ordinarily has no duty to take action to notify the offeror of acceptance. However, the offeree does have a duty of notification if the performance in question is not rendered directly to or in the presence of the offeror and the offeror has no reasonably prompt and reliable means of learning of it.

Say, for example, that the owner of "Bleakacre" does not live on the land but resides in a distant state. She has no contacts in the area and is not likely to visit the property because she is elderly and in poor health. If her nephew responds to her offer not by promise, but by commencing the clearing work, she is not likely to learn of his acceptance unless he tells her. Therefore, although the nephew may accept by performance and need not communicate with the aunt to accept, he is required to notify her within a reasonable time after commencing performance if he knows or should know that she has no means of learning of his acceptance with reasonable speed and certainty. This notice is not itself the acceptance, which occurred as soon as performance began, but if it is not given (and the aunt does not otherwise hear of the performance) within a reasonable time, the acceptance becomes ineffective and the aunt's contractual duty is discharged.

§4.12.7 Reverse Unilateral Contracts

A reverse unilateral contract comes about when the offeree accepts by promise, but the offeror's performance occurs and is completed at the instant of contract formation. This is also a unilateral contract because only one party — the offeree in this case — has a promise outstanding at the point of contracting. For example, hearing that his friend is in financial difficulty, the offeror approaches the friend and holds out ten crisp $100 bills, saying "Here, I'll lend this to you for a year at 6 percent interest." If the offeree accepts by taking the money, he thereby promises to repay the loan on the offeror's terms. However, the offeror has no outstanding obligation because his performance was completed immediately upon acceptance.

§4.13 IRREVOCABLE OFFERS: OPTIONS AND FIRM OFFERS

§4.13.1 Introduction

It was noted in section 4.6.4 that an offer is revocable, even if it states that it will be held open for a stated term, unless it meets the legal requirements for an option under common law or a firm offer under UCC Article 2. We now look at these legal requirements. To understand options and firm offers, you need to know something about consideration doctrine, which is covered fully in Chapter 7. In the interim, the brief explanation of consideration doctrine in section 4.13.2 will provide enough background to enable you to understand options and firm offers.[19]

§4.13.2 Options and Consideration

An option is a promise to keep an offer open for a stated period of time. By granting a valid option, the offeror makes a binding commitment not to revoke the offer for a specified period, so that the offeree is assured of a set time to consider and respond to the proposal without the risk of its being withdrawn before the expiry date. As we saw in section 4.6.4, under common law a promise to keep an offer open for a stated time is not binding on the offeror unless the offeree has given consideration for that promise. Recall that in *Dickenson v. Dodds*, 2 Ch. D. 463 (Court of Appeals, Chancery Division, 1876), the court held that Dodds was legally entitled to revoke his offer before its expiry date because Dickenson had not given consideration for Dodds's promise to keep the offer open. As you will see in Chapter 7, the question of what constitutes consideration is complex. However, for present purposes, it is enough to understand that in exchange for the grant of an

---

19. Some contracts courses defer coverage of options and firm offers until after consideration doctrine has been studied. If your course is structured in this way, you should return here when you reach this subject in class.

option (the offeror's promise to keep the offer open and not revoke it for a designated period of time), the offeree has to give something to the offeror.

The most obvious "something" would be a cash payment or a promise to pay a specific sum of money for the option. But consideration for the option need not be in money. It could also be property or the relinquishment of some legal right. Whatever form the consideration takes, the basic legal requirement is that the grantee must "pay" for the option by transferring or promising money or other property or by sacrificing a legal right in exchange for the promise to keep the option open.

Because an option is a form of offer, it necessarily contemplates that, if accepted, a contract will come into existence involving the exchange of performances contemplated by the offer. For example, if the offeror writes to the offeree offering to sell "Bleakacre" to her for $2 million, and giving her until next Friday to accept, the offeror contemplates an exchange of the farm for $2 million. Upon acceptance of the offer, the offeree promises to pay the $2 million, and that payment is surely consideration given in exchange for the farm. However, this consideration, exchanged under the contract proposed in the offer, is distinct from and does not also support the option itself. To be valid, the option must have its own separate consideration—the offeree must, in effect, purchase the option by providing an additional consideration, tied to the promise not to revoke. In the above example, if at the time of receiving the offer the offeree had paid the offeror $100 in exchange for the promise to keep the offer open until Friday, the promise not to revoke would have qualified as a valid and binding option. Diagram 4I represents the distinction between the consideration for the option and the consideration under the underlying contract.

Diagram 4I

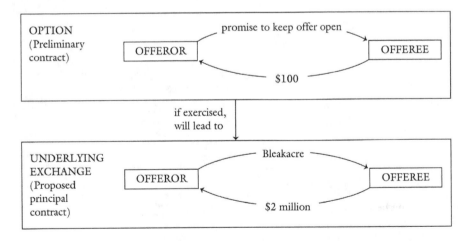

This rule requiring separate consideration for an option applies only in relation to the formation of a new contract — that is, when the option is a promise not to revoke an offer to enter into a contract. If an option is granted within an existing contract, it is part of the bundle of rights exchanged in the contract and is supported by the grantee's contractual consideration.

For example, no separate consideration would be required if Buyer is the tenant of "Bleakacre" under an existing lease, and the lease contains a term granting Buyer the option of purchasing the property for $2 million at any time before expiry of the lease. This option is simply one of the rights purchased by the lessee under the lease and is supported by the consideration given by the lessee under the lease (such as the payment of rental). It does not need separate consideration to bind the lessor. This distinction is shown in Diagram 4J.

Diagram 4J

OPTION IN THE FORMATION OF A NEW CONTRACT

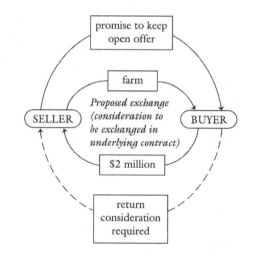

OPTION AS PART OF THE DETRIMENT EXCHANGED
IN AN EXISTING CONTRACT

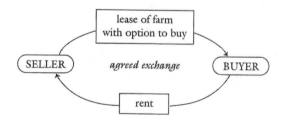

As explained more fully in Chapter 7, one of the principal aims of consideration doctrine is to confine legal enforcement to those transactions in which the parties have actually exchanged promises or performances. It refuses legal enforcement of a gratuitous promise — one that is given as a gift without any return benefit. Options are not usually motivated by gratuitous intent. Their common purpose is commercial — by committing to give the offeree an irrevocable opportunity to accept, the offeror hopes to facilitate a desired economic exchange. For this reason, courts usually try to uphold an option if there is any basis for finding consideration for it. As long as the option has been obtained by fair means, the length of the period for acceptance is not unduly long, and the parties have taken the trouble to formalize the grant in a writing that recites that consideration was given, a court is likely to uphold the option. Therefore, courts often accept nominal consideration (that is, a small payment or minimal performance that is patently not equivalent to the actual commercial value of the option) or even sham consideration (that is, consideration that is recited in the grant of the option purely for the sake of formality, but not actually given). This approach is reflected in Restatement, Second, §87(1)(a), which says that the grant of an option is valid if it is in writing, is signed by the grantor, recites a purported consideration for the offer, and proposes an exchange on fair terms within a reasonable time. (Of course, not all courts adopt this flexible attitude, and some may refuse to find an option to be valid if the consideration is nominal or a sham.)

§4.13.3 The Effect of an Option

As stated already, the principal effect of a valid option is to bind the offeror to keep the offer open for the stated period. The offeree's power of acceptance does not expire until the end of that period and is generally not cut short by action that would terminate an ordinary offer. Most importantly, this means that the offeror cannot lawfully revoke the option prior to its expiration. It also means, at least in cases when the offeree has given valuable consideration for the option (as opposed to nominal or sham consideration), that the option does not come to an end if the offeree rejects it (or makes a counteroffer, which is effectively the same as a rejection) before the end of the option period. If the offeree changes her mind she is able to countermand the rejection by communicating acceptance before the end of the period. This rule is based on the premise that the grantee has paid consideration to acquire the effective option, which is a valid contract in itself. If so, rejection before the end of the option period amounts to a waiver of contract rights by the optionee, and such a waiver is unenforceable if the optionee did not receive new consideration for it. (This principle is expanded on in sections 7.5 and 13.9, where modifications to an existing contract are discussed.) This rule is subject to a qualification: Although waiver needs consideration, the doctrine of estoppel may protect the offeror who reasonably relied on the rejection to his prejudice. Therefore, if the offeror has taken substantially detrimental action in reliance on a rejection (such as contracting with someone else for the same performance), the offeree may not reverse the rejection by later acceptance.

To accept an irrevocable offer, the offeree must communicate acceptance to the offeror within the option period. This usually requires that the offeror actually receives the acceptance. Restatement, Second, §63(b) says that the "mailbox" rule does not apply to acceptance of a valid option, so that acceptance is effective only on receipt. Comment f to §63 justifies this distinction on the basis that irrevocability sufficiently protects the offeree, so the "mailbox" rule is not needed to safeguard the offeree's interests or to provide a dependable basis for knowing that the acceptance has occurred. Some courts are unconvinced by this reasoning and see greater merit in having a standard, predictable rule for all acceptances.

§4.13.4 Firm Offers Under UCC §2.205

In a sale of goods, §2.205 dispenses with the need for consideration to validate an option (called a "firm offer" in the section) under defined circumstances. The section applies only when all of its prerequisites are satisfied, namely:

1. The offer to buy or sell goods must be made by a merchant. The merchant status under Article 2 was introduced in section 2.7.2. Recall that §2.104(1) defines a merchant as one who deals in goods of the kind involved in the transaction or who otherwise, by trade or profession, represents that he has skill or knowledge in regard to the goods or the transaction. In essence, a merchant, as distinct from one whose dealings in the goods is casual or inexpert, is a person who trades professionally in goods of that kind, either as seller or buyer. Although Article 2 does not in all cases provide different rules for merchants and casual buyers and sellers, there are some sections — §2.205 being one of them — that are applicable only to merchants or have stricter standards for them. Some of these sections are applicable only in transactions "between merchants" — that is, if both parties to the transaction are merchants — but others apply if only one of them is. Section 2.205 fits into the latter category. For the rule validating firm offers to apply, only the offeror need be a merchant.

2. The offer must be in a signed writing. Although §2.205 refers to a writing, modern courts readily recognize that "writing" is not

confined to hard copy on a tangible document, but also extends to recording in electronic form.

3. It must give an assurance to the offeree that it will be held open.
4. If the assurance is contained on a form supplied by the offeree, the offeror must sign the assurance separately. The purpose of this is to ensure that the offeror was aware of the term and is not bound by an assurance of irrevocability hidden in the offeree's standard terms.

If all these conditions are satisfied, consideration is not needed to make the offer irrevocable for the time stated, or for a reasonable time if no expiry date is specified. Section 2.205 limits the period of irrevocability to a maximum of three months, so that neither a stated time nor a reasonable time can exceed that period. Therefore, if the option is intended to last more than three months, the offeree must give consideration to validate it beyond the three-month period.

§4.14 A TRANSNATIONAL PERSPECTIVE ON OFFER AND ACCEPTANCE

This brief note on perspective is not comprehensive. Its purpose is just to give you a flavor of how the formation of a contract might be approached in a transnational contract. It merely identifies some of the similarities in general approach and some of the differences between domestic American law and general principles of transnational law, as reflected in the UNIDROIT Principles and the CISG. (*See* section 2.9 for an explanation of the scope and purpose of the UNIDROIT Principles and the CISG.)

Broad general principles of offer and acceptance are expressed in both the UNIDROIT Principles and the CISG in a manner that would sound familiar to an American lawyer. (Remember that the UNIDROIT Principles are not binding law in any country, but rather set out a set of widely accepted general principles applicable to international contracts. In contrast, the CISG is a treaty, and is hence binding law in international sales of goods that fall within its scope, provided that the parties have not excluded its application.) Both the UNIDROIT Principles and the CISG provide for the fundamentals of offer and acceptance in general terms and contain few specific or detailed rules.

Both the CISG and the UNIDROIT Principles adopt the kind of flexible, nontechnical approach to offer and acceptance that we find in UCC §§2.204 and 2.206: To constitute an offer, a proposal must be sufficiently definite and must indicate the offeror's intent to be bound upon acceptance. Acceptance is a statement or conduct indicating intent to assent to the offer. There are some differences from common law principles as well. For example, neither the CISG nor the UNIDROIT Principles recognize the "mailbox" rule, so acceptance is effective only on receipt unless the offer provides otherwise. Because consideration doctrine is confined to the common law (as explained in Chapter 7), it is not a prerequisite for the validity of an option in either the CISG or the UNIDROIT Principles. Instead, they recognize the validity of a promise not to revoke an offer if it expresses the offeror's intent to make it irrevocable.

Examples

1. Joe Kerr owns and lives in a handsome Victorian house that has been in his family for over 100 years. Every time that his friend Hume Orless has visited him, Hume has said, "Joe, I love your house. Please sell it to me right now." Joe has consistently answered, "Never!" After this had been going on for many years, Joe became irritated with it. As far as he knew, Hume had no money and had never been serious in his request to buy the house. It was simply mindless prattle. Joe decided to put an end to the annoying routine by shaming Hume into silence. He prepared a deed of sale that he placed in a drawer. The deed was on a real legal form that Joe had purchased from a stationer. He fully filled out all the blanks, included a price somewhat exceeding the market value of the house, and signed it. The next time Hume was at the house and urged Joe to sell it to him, Joe whipped the deed out of the drawer and exclaimed, "Okay, Hume. Put up or shut up! Sign this and the house is yours."

   Instead of reacting with embarrassment and confusion, as Joe expected, Hume coolly read the deed, expressed satisfaction, and signed it. At first, Joe thought that Hume was playing along with him, but it is now clear that he did not see the bluff, took the offer seriously, and does have the financial means of buying the house. Hume insists that the transfer proceed. Joe is sick with grief at the prospect of parting with his beloved family homestead. Is he bound?

2. Professor Ivor E. Tower has spent the last three years working on his book entitled *Foolproof Contracting — A Lay Person's Guide to Effective Dealmaking*. On completing the book, Ivor set about getting it published. On July 1, he sent an identical letter and a copy of the manuscript to several publishers. The letter read: "I submit the enclosed manuscript for your consideration. If you would like to publish it, let me know by July 30. I want the book published as soon as possible, at least within this year. If you are willing to commit to this, I would be willing to give it to you on the customary terms, and expect the usual royalty of 15 percent of sales."

   One of the publishers to whom he sent the book was Sel Phelp & Company, Inc. The editors at Sel Phelp read the book, which was a real page-turner. They decided that they would like to publish it. On July 24, Sel Phelp mailed a letter to Ivor, in which it accepted the book for publication, committed to have it published within the year, and enclosed its standard contract for Ivor to sign. The terms in the standard contract are those generally found in publishing contracts, and included a royalty of 15 percent of sales. On July 25, before receiving Sel Phelp's letter, Ivor signed a contract with one of its competitors for the book's publication, and he immediately faxed a letter to Sel Phelp telling them that the book had been given to another publisher and was no longer available for publication by them. Ivor received Sel Phelp's letter later that day. Is Ivor now in the uncomfortable position of having made two contracts for the same book?

3. Ann Teek is an antique dealer. Art Deco collects tableware from the 1920s and '30s. He visited Ann's store and saw a richly decorated platter made in 1935. It was marked with a $450 price tag. Art told Ann that he was interested in buying it but would like to take it home to see if it fitted in with his collection. Ann agreed to let him take it home for a day on the understanding that if he did not want it, he would return it the next day. Ann took Art's credit card information so that if he decided to keep the platter, he could just call her and she would charge the price of the platter to his card.

Ann had misgivings about selling the platter because she also collected tableware from that period and it was a very attractive piece. She therefore decided, later that day, to call Art and to tell him that she had changed her mind and wanted the platter back. Ann called and Art answered the phone. As soon as he heard that it was Ann calling, and before Ann could tell him that she wanted him to return the platter, Art said, "Hi, Ann. I have decided to take the platter. Debit my card." Has Ann sold the platter to Art?

4. Kay Nine was going on an overseas trip for the month of July. She knew that her neighbor would keep an eye on her house and take care of her dog, Pettodor, but she preferred having someone live in the house. She had a cousin, Doug Sitter, who attended college in another city and would probably enjoy having a house to live in for part of the summer. On June 10, Kay wrote the following letter to Doug:

Dear Doug,
I am going to be away from July 1 to July 30. I had planned to have my neighbor take care of Pettodor, but it occurs to me that you may be free during July and may enjoy staying at my house for the month. You will just have to take care of Pettodor and keep an eye on things. In return, you will have free accommodation. Also, when I return from vacation, I will pay for your food and other expenses for the month of July. I don't need to hear from you right away. If you would like to spend July here, just come down on June

29. If you are not here by the end of that day, I will assume that you cannot do it and I will make arrangements with my neighbor to take care of the house and the dog.

Best wishes,

Kay

Doug received Kay's letter on June 12. He had nothing to do during July and liked the idea of an all-expenses-paid month in Kay's house. He wrote back immediately telling her that he would be down on June 29. Doug mailed the letter on June 13, but he wrote the wrong zip code on the envelope. The post office was able to deliver it anyhow, but it was considerably delayed and Kay received it on June 20. In the interim, Kay had remembered that Doug was a real slob, and she had changed her mind about having him live in her house. On June 21, she wrote back to him, telling him that she had made other arrangements and no longer needed him. Doug received the letter on June 23. Doug feels aggrieved because he believes that Kay cannot simply back out of their arrangement. Is he right?

5. Change the facts of Example 4: Doug did not write back to Kay. Instead, he arrived at her house on June 29. Kay had not made other arrangements, and she was happy to see him. Doug moved in and Kay left on her vacation on July 1. However, she got bored within a week and returned home on July 7. She wants Doug to leave and does not wish to pay his expenses for more than a week. May she revoke her offer?

6. Art Walls owns a building whose exterior has been spraypainted by vandals with infuriating regularity. In an attempt to put an end to this expensive nuisance, he placed an advertisement in the newspaper on January 15, offering a reward of $1,000 to ". . . anyone who furnishes information leading to the conviction of those guilty of defacing the walls . . ." of his building. On January 16, the police arrested Fresco Furtive, a young man who was caught in the act of spraypainting another building in the neighborhood. Fresco seemed to be quite proud of his handiwork, and upon being caught, he freely recounted his exploits to the police, detailing all the buildings he had sprayed, including Art's building. He was tried for all these acts of vandalism, convicted, and placed on probation.

Although Fresco was not aware of the reward offer at the time of his confession, he found out about it later that day. He claims the reward. Upon hearing this, Art is outraged. He says that he never intended to pay the culprit himself, and in any event, when he said "conviction," he had a stiff jail term in mind and not some wimpy probationary sentence. Is Fresco entitled to the reward?

7. Assume that the police obtained no confession from Fresco Furtive. However, Fresco's nocturnal artistry had been observed by N. Former and I. Witness, two denizens of Art Wall's neighborhood who happened to be lurking separately in the area that night. Although neither of them are public-spirited enough to expose Fresco for free, they both happened to read Art's reward offer on January 15, and independently contacted Art to tell him who had vandalized his building. N. Former told him on the morning of January 16, and I. Witness told him that afternoon. As a result, Art filed charges and Fresco was arrested and tried. He was convicted of the offense and was sentenced to five years on a chain gang. Being completely delighted with this result, Art is happy to pay the reward. The problem is that both N. Former and I. Witness claim it. Art refuses to pay it twice and does not know who should receive the $1,000. To whom is he liable and for how much?

8. Last August, a country club held a golf tournament to raise funds for an organization called "Youth Golf America" that arranges and funds golf camps for troubled children. To support the charity tournament, the Caddy-Lack Golf Cart Co. donated one of its luxurious electric golf carts to be used as a prize for anyone who hit a hole-in-one during the tournament. Just before the tournament, the cart was displayed in front of the clubhouse with a sign that stated:

HIT A HOLE-IN-ONE
AND WIN THIS FABULOUS GOLF CART

by
CADDY-LACK

Courtesy of Caddy-Lack, "The Cadillac of Golf Carts"
Caddy-Lack is a proud sponsor of Youth Golf America. Thank you for supporting our children.

The charity tournament took place on Sunday, and no one qualified for the prize by hitting a hole-in-one. Caddy-Lack did not get around to removing its display until Monday at 5 P.M. On that Monday afternoon, Jock Awesome passed the display as he set out for his weekly golf game. He read the very obvious large print as he walked by, but did not stop to read the smaller print at the bottom of the sign referring to the sponsorship of the youth organization. He did not know that there had been a tournament on the day before and did not realize that the display was intended to be applicable only during the tournament. As luck would have it, at 5:15 P.M. he hit a hole-in-one at the 17th hole.

As he hurried back to the clubhouse to claim his prize at the pro shop (which was the official Caddy-Lack representative at the club), he was puzzled to notice that the cart and sign had been removed. It was only when he claimed the prize that he discovered that the offer was confined to the tournament. Nevertheless, he says that he is entitled to the cart. Caddy-Lack refuses to give it to him. Who is right?

9. On April 10, Maggie Cumlaude, a bright and enterprising law student, wrote a note to one of her professors, Prof. Minnie Wage, and slipped the note under her door. The note stated: "I would love to be your research assistant this summer. I will be available to work 40 hours per week from June 10 through August 15 and would like to be paid $12 per hour. Please reply by April 16 if you are interested."

   On April 13, Minnie replied, stating "I would like to have you work for me this summer, but $12 seems a little steep. I usually pay my research assistants $8 per hour. Tell me as soon as possible how you feel about this." She got Maggie's home address from the registrar and put the letter in the mailbox on her way home from work on April 13. Maggie received it the next day.

   When Minnie was sitting in the faculty lounge on the morning of April 16, her insufferable colleague, Prof. Max E. Molument sidled up to her and gloated: "Your cheapness lost you a good research assistant. When Maggie Cumlaude told me a couple of days ago that you would only pay her $8 an hour, I outbid you and hired her for $10."

   Minnie rushed to her office and wrote another note to Maggie that read "On thinking about this matter further, I have decided that $12 per hour is a fair rate, so I agree to pay what you ask. I look forward to having you work for me. I will be away at a conference until June 12. Please come to my office on June 13 to get instructions on your assignment."

   She mailed the note on April 16, and Maggie received it on April 17. Do Maggie and Minnie have a contract?

10. Flaky Cereal Co. manufactures "Flaky's Frosties" sugar-coated cornflakes. The logo for this product is a cute cartoon leopard named "Frosty Fangs." To promote the sale of its cornflakes, Flaky ran a competition, which it announced on the back of the cereal boxes. The competition was initiated in May 2012. Its simple point was that people could win various prizes by sending in the tops of cereal boxes accompanied by a form printed on the back of the box. The more tops that were collected, the bigger the prize. The box listed four categories of prizes: Four box tops earned a plastic "Frosty Fangs" pin, 10 earned a cuddly "Frosty Fangs" stuffed toy, 20 earned a "Frosty Fangs" watch, and 1,000 earned a real leopard cub. Each of the prizes was illustrated by a color photograph. The back of the cereal box proclaimed: "Boys and Girls, collect your box tops now and send them in by January 1, 2013, to claim your prizes! (Prizes limited to quantities on hand, so don't delay.)"

Manny Eater owns "Carnivore Campground," a safari park. He had been trying to obtain a leopard for some time, but leopards are very expensive (a good specimen can cost up to $500,000) and hard to get. Manny happened to buy a box of "Flaky's Frosties" (his favorite cereal) in early June. When he read the back of the box at breakfast the next day, he had a brilliant idea. He went from one supermarket to another until he had bought 1,000 boxes of "Flaky's Frosties." (At an average of $4 a box, this cost him $4,000.) In mid-June 2012, he mailed the box tops to Flaky with the properly completed form and claimed his prize of a leopard cub.

Flaky refused to deliver a leopard club to Manny on several grounds. Consider each of these grounds and decide if any of them justify Flaky's refusal to award the prize to Manny:

a. Flaky denied that it had any legal obligation to Manny because the back of the cereal box was merely an invitation to consumers to claim prizes, and not an offer. Therefore, by submitting the box tops and form Manny made the offer, which Flaky rejected.

b. Even if Flaky did make an offer on its cereal boxes, the offer was open only to "boys and girls," not to grown men. Manny therefore had no power of acceptance.

c. The leopard club obviously was not intended as a prize but was just a bit of hyperbole to attract attention to the competition. This was obvious to any reasonable person because leopards do not make good pets, no consumer could reasonably be expected to consume 1,000 boxes of cereal in the few months before the expiry date of the competition, and no reasonable person would believe that a rare and expensive animal could be won for the cost of 1,000 boxes of cereal.

d. Even if Flaky did make an offer, it expressly stated that prizes were limited to quantities on hand, and Flaky never had a leopard cub.

11. Shelly Shally had been negotiating with Ray Vocator for the purchase of "Blandacre," an old farm now engulfed by suburban sprawl and zoned for housing development. By May 1, 2012, they had reached agreement in principle on the price and the other important terms on which the sale would be made, but Shelly could not decide if she really wanted the property. Ray agreed to give her a few days to make up her mind, and on May 1, Ray gave Shelly the following document:

> I offer to sell my farm "Blandacre" to Shelly Shally for $500,000, subject to the following terms . . . [the note then set out the material terms of the sale]. If Shelly wishes to accept my offer, she must deliver her written acceptance to me by 5 P.M. on May 3, 2012. I undertake not to withdraw this offer before that date. (Signed) Ray Vocator.

a. On May 2, Shelly decided that she would accept the offer. However, before she could let Ray know, she received a note from Ray withdrawing the offer. Did Ray have the legal right to withdraw the offer?

109

b. Would the result be different if the last sentence of Ray's offer had instead stated, "In consideration for $1.00 received, I undertake not to withdraw this offer before that date," and after receiving the document, Shelly handed a dollar bill to Ray?

12. John Dear had leased his farm "Blightacre" to Al Falfa for the period of one year at a monthly rent of $1,000. One of the terms in the lease gave Al the option to purchase the property for $500,000. To exercise the option, Al had to ". . . give written notice to John, to be received no later than 30 days before the expiry of the lease period."

   On the fortieth day before the expiry of the lease, Al wrote to John stating that he did not intend to exercise the option. John received that letter two days later and immediately replied, acknowledging receipt and confirming that the option had lapsed. Al received that reply the following day. Later on that same day, Al changed his mind and decided that he did want to buy the property. He wrote a second letter to John, countermanding the first and exercising his right to purchase the property. John received that letter thirty-four days before expiry of the lease. Has Al bought the property?

13. John Dear owned a tractor. Because he had leased his farm, he no longer needed the tractor, so he advertised it for sale. Harv Ester responded to the ad and came to see the tractor on May 1. He wanted a few days to decide whether to buy it, and John agreed. John gave Harv a signed note that stated, "To Harv Ester: I agree to sell you my tractor for $5,000 cash. If you decide to buy it, you must notify me in writing by 5 P.M. on May 4, 2012. I will not withdraw this offer before that date. (Signed) John Dear." On May 2, John sold the tractor to someone else and notified Harv that he withdrew his offer. Can Harv refuse to recognize the revocation and accept the offer, thereby creating a binding contract?

Explanations

1. Under the objective test it is not enough for Joe to assert that he did not actually intend to sell his house. He is accountable for his apparent intent, as reasonably interpreted by Hume from his words and actions. We do not judge Joe's manifestation purely on the basis of Hume's subjective interpretation, nor do we look at it from the perspective of reasonableness in the abstract. The proper test is whether a reasonable person in Hume's position would have understood Joe as manifesting contractual intent. That is, was Hume, under all the circumstances of their relationship, and knowing what he did about Joe, justified in concluding that the offer was serious? Joe apparently took great trouble

to make his bluff credible, and there seems to be nothing that could have reasonably indicated to Hume that Joe was fooling around.

This Example is based on *Lucy v. Zehmer*, 84 S.E.2d 516 (Va. 1954), discussed in section 4.1.6. Like Mr. Zehmer the joke was on Joe.

2. If Ivor's letter of July 1 was an offer, Sel Phelp's reply of July 24 could constitute an effective acceptance, as discussed below. If it was not an offer, but merely an invitation to deal, Sel Phelp's letter of July 24 was itself an offer which was not accepted. A communication is an offer if it manifests the maker's intent to invite acceptance and conveys the reasonable understanding to the addressee that, upon acceptance, the maker expects to be committed to a contract without any opportunity for further approval. The test of intent is objective, focusing on what Ivor apparently intended, as perceived by a reasonable person in Sel Phelp's position. The language of the offer is the most important indication of apparent intent, but the context of the transaction — including any prior dealings between the parties, usages that are or should be familiar to them, or other circumstances relevant to the transaction — can cast light on what must reasonably have been intended. No such contextual evidence is set out in the facts of this Example. (Ivor's reference to customary terms suggests that there are probably usages regarding book publication, but no usage is revealed relating to contract formation.)

The language of Ivor's letter does not solidly convey his intent one way or the other. There are aspects of it that quite strongly suggest an offer: He provides for a specific date for response, he states that he "would be willing" to give the book to Sel Phelp in exchange for the publication commitment, and he does set out the essential terms on which he would like to contract. The rather vague reference to "customary" terms may suggest that further negotiation is contemplated, but if publication contracts tend to follow a common and well-accepted format, even these terms may be sufficiently certain to be ascertainable. Had the letter indicated that the manuscript had been sent to several publishers, this would have given some indication to Sel Phelp that it may not have been intended as an offer. However, the letter gives no hint that it has been sent to multiple parties. Where a communication is phrased in the unclear way that Ivor has chosen, it is quite hard to predict how a court will decide what was intended. A person who does not clearly express intent in negotiations runs the risk of being held to an offer when none may actually have been intended.

A couple of cases illustrate the disparate situations in which a communication must be interpreted to decide if it is an offer, and what considerations a court may take into account in deciding whether a communication may reasonably be understood as an offer. In *Bourque v.*

Federal Deposit Insurance Corp., 42 F.3d 704 (5th Cir. 1994) the FDIC was liquidating a failed savings bank and selling its assets, including a piece of real property that Bourque wanted to buy. Bourque made the original offer to buy the property for $105,500, which the FDIC rejected in a letter stating "FDIC's counteroffer is $130,000. All offers are subject to approval by the appropriate FDIC delegated authority. FDIC has the right to accept or reject any and all offers." Bourque replied, agreeing to buy the property at this price but the FDIC sold it to someone else. Bourque claimed that the FDIC made a counteroffer which he accepted. However, the court found that FDIC's letter was not a counteroffer. Even though it used the word "counteroffer" and specified clear terms, it was qualified by the language that made it clear that the FDIC retained the final say in deciding whether to form the contract.

In *Barnum v. Review Board of Indiana Employment Security Division*, 478 N.E.2d. 1243 (Ind. App. 1985) the court had to decide if a laid-off employee was disqualified from unemployment benefits on the grounds that he had refused an offer of suitable employment. When layoffs were imminent, the employer had employees fill out a "recall choice form" which allowed the employee to state if he would prefer to be laid off or employed in a reduced position. The employee indicated a preference for layoff. The Review Board concluded that this was the refusal of an offer of employment which disqualified him from benefits. The court disagreed. It held that the form could not qualify as an offer under Restatement, Second, §24 because it provided no specifics about what the reduced position would be, and did not commit the employer to re-employ the worker. It did nothing more than indicate the possibility of re-employment and gave the employee an opportunity to express interest.

If Ivor did make an offer, Sel Phelp's response is likely to qualify as an acceptance. By leaving it to Sel Phelp to formulate terms in accordance with custom, Ivor implies into his offer an intent to contract on terms that are standard and usual in the trade. Provided that the terms in Sel Phelp's standard contract are indeed customary, they would not conflict with or add to his offer. The response is entirely in accord with Ivor's proposal with regard to the publication date and royalties. Ivor did not stipulate a mode of acceptance and transmitted his offer by mail. Sel Phelp's response by mail was therefore authorized, and the mailbox rule would apply, making the acceptance effective upon mailing. As a result, the revocation of July 25 was too late.

3. This is clearly a sale of goods, so UCC Article 2 applies. Article 2 has very few specific offer and acceptance rules, and except to the extent that they are displaced by provisions of the Code, general principles of common law are applicable. UCC §2.204(1) and (3) provide a flexible

test for deciding whether a contract was formed: It may be made in any manner sufficient to show agreement, including conduct. If the parties intended to contract, missing terms do not cause it to fail for indefiniteness if the court can find a reasonably certain basis for giving a remedy.

The issue is whether Ann has made an oral contract with Art under which she has committed to sell the platter to him. Article 2 has a statute of frauds (§2.201, discussed in Chapter 11) that requires an agreement for the sale of goods to be in writing where the price of the goods is $500 or more. However, as the price of the platter is under $500, the statute of frauds does not apply and will not preclude enforcement of the transaction merely on the grounds that there was no written and signed record of it. Ann's conduct in allowing Art to take the platter home is ambiguous. It could be an offer or merely an invitation to Art to make an offer. It is an offer if Art would be justified in understanding that his assent would conclude the bargain, without any need for further assent by Ann. It has sufficiently definite terms to qualify as an offer. The subject matter of the sale and the price are clear: Delivery is to be accomplished by Art retaining the plate, and payment is to occur upon delivery through a credit card debit. If Ann made an offer, §2.206 dispenses with technicality in the mode of acceptance. It presumes that unless a particular manner and medium of acceptance is clearly required, acceptance may be by any means reasonable in the circumstances, and may be either by promise or performance. The parties did contemplate acceptance by telephone as a permissive (although not exclusive mode), and this is how it occurred.

Although Ann called Art with the intent of revoking, revocation only takes effect when that intent is manifested to the offeree. Art accepted before Ann could express the revocation. Therefore, if Ann's conduct constituted an offer (which I think it does), Art accepted it and Ann is committed to the sale. (Of course, if Ann's conduct is not an offer, Art's words on the phone would be the offer, and Ann did not accept.)

4. Doug is probably right. Kay's letter is surely an offer. It sets out the terms of the proposed transaction and gives the reasonable impression that Doug's acceptance will create a binding contract. The question is whether the offer was for a unilateral contract prescribing that the rendition of performance was the exclusive mode of acceptance. If it was, Doug's letter was not an effective acceptance, and Kay's revocation was communicated to him before he had a chance to accept. Courts do not readily assume that an offer calls for performance as the exclusive means of acceptance. Therefore, unless an offer clearly prescribes performance as the exclusive mode of acceptance, a promise is permissible.

There is no language in Kay's letter to signify that Doug can accept only by showing up at the house on June 29. In fact, the very nature of a unilateral contract is inconsistent with her apparent intent. As she will be relying on Doug to care for the house and the dog, she could not reasonably have intended that his commencement of performance would merely give him an option, and would create no promise by him to continue to perform until her return.

As Kay's offer did not require performance as the exclusive mode of acceptance, Doug's promise in his letter of June suffices as an acceptance. Because Kay made the offer through the mail, an acceptance via the same channel of communication is authorized, and the "mailbox" rule would apply, provided that the mailing was proper. However, the mailbox rule presupposes proper mailing and does not apply if the acceptance is improperly mailed. Because Doug misaddressed the letter, the mailing was deficient and receipt was delayed, which deprives Doug of the protection of the "mailbox" rule. However, if a wrongly mailed acceptance does in fact reach the offeror, it is effective upon receipt. Kay received the offer before she communicated her intent to revoke, so the revocation is too late. A contract has been concluded, and Doug is justified in feeling aggrieved.

5. Where an offer requires or permits acceptance by performance, and the act of performance is instantaneous, acceptance occurs immediately upon performance of the act. However, where performance cannot be instantaneous, but will take time — as in this case, where it spans a full month — acceptance is not complete until the performance is finished (on July 30). In the interim, the offeree is protected from having his reliance on the offer defeated by a revocation. The nature of the protection depends on whether performance was the exclusive mode or a permissible mode of acceptance. If performance is the exclusive mode of acceptance, an option would have been created in law as soon as Doug showed up at Kay's house on June 29. If performance is not the exclusive mode of acceptance (as we concluded in Explanation 4), the commencement of performance constitutes an implied promise by Doug to complete performance, so a bilateral contract is created immediately on the beginning of performance on June 29. In either event, Doug is protected from revocation, either because he has an option or a contract. The difference between the option and the implied promise is that the implication of a promise binds both parties to a bilateral contract, so that Doug is obliged to complete performance. However, an option would not have bound Doug, who would have had the right to cease performance at any time, thus terminating his act of acceptance and precluding the formation of a contract.

6. The advertisement clearly appears intended as an offer, so this issue does not require discussion. The most reasonable interpretation of public offers of reward is that they require acceptance, not by promise but by performance of the consideration called for — in this case, the furnishing of the information. If the confession qualified as an acceptance, it would have created a unilateral contract under which the only outstanding promise is Art's commitment to pay $1,000. As no time for acceptance was stated, the offer had to be accepted within a reasonable time. The amount of time reasonable for acceptance is a factual question, to be decided under all the circumstances of the case. A factfinder would surely find acceptance on the day after the offer to be within a reasonable time. It seems clear that by confessing, Fresco did furnish information that led to his conviction for defacing Art's walls. However, there are three arguments against treating the confession as a valid acceptance of Art's offer.

First, Fresco was not aware of the offer when he provided the information. Even under the objective test, apparent acceptance cannot be treated as acceptance unless deliberate and made with knowledge of the offer. In this respect, Fresco's situation is similar to that of the plaintiff in the *Glover* case discussed in section 4.10. As noted in section 4.10, the rule requiring knowledge of the offer is intended to protect the offeree from being held to an inadvertent manifestation of assent. This rationale does not apply here because, like the plaintiff in *Glover*, Fresco desires the acceptance to be effective. Nevertheless, there may still be a good policy reason for applying the rule because Fresco's ignorance of the offer means that he has no reliance interest to protect.

Second, even if Fresco made the confession with knowledge of the offer and intent to accept it, he has no power of acceptance unless the offer was addressed to him. The offer is addressed to "anyone" and is apparently aimed at the public at large, so on its face it is open for acceptance by any person who reads it and performs the requested act of furnishing the information. However, even though the offer expresses no restriction excluding the culprit as a possible offeree, the context of the offer may lead to the reasonable construction that this restriction was implied. This argument might be bolstered by the public policy of not permitting a criminal to gain from his crime. (But it could be argued that considerations of public interest point in the opposite direction. The reward is for the information, not the crime, and it may encourage confessions.)

Third, Art's argument that "conviction" requires a prison sentence is unconvincing. In the absence of evidence of some special usage, language is interpreted in accordance with its plain meaning. The conviction of a criminal is the determination of guilt in a court proceeding, and is distinct from sentencing.

7. There are three possible resolutions of this issue: Both informants accepted the offer and Art is liable to each of them for $1,000; both informants accepted and must share the reward; or the reward is due to N. Former only, because the offer was no longer open when I. Witness sought to accept. Art's offer is not clear on what happens if more than one person seeks to accept, so its reasonable intent must be ascertained by interpretation.

   A person could make an offer in a way that permits multiple acceptances and thus many contracts. However, where it is clear from the offer that a single performance is all that the offeror needs, the more reasonable inference is that the offer is open to the first person who accepts by rendering the performance requested. Once that performance is given, the object of identifying and prosecuting the criminal is achieved, and it is no longer possible for another to give information that accomplishes the stated goal. If the condition of expiry is implicit in the offer, it is not necessary for the offeror to publish notice of revocation. Therefore, the best resolution is that the $1,000 must be paid to N. Former. The possibility of sharing may have been presented if each of the witnesses provided only part of the information needed to identify Fresco, but that did not happen here. Also, it does not matter if the testimony of both witnesses led to Fresco's conviction. The reward was for the information, not for the testimony.

8. This transaction could be classified as a sale of goods, which is defined in UCC §2.106(1) to consist of the passing of title to goods for a price. The golf cart is goods, and because §2.304(1) makes it clear that the price of goods need not be in money, it could be argued that the act of hitting the hole-in-one constitutes the price. However, even if this is classified as a sale of goods, the application of Article 2 would make no difference to the resolution of the case, which would be decided under principles of common law under §1.103(b).

   There are more hole-in-one cases than one might expect. For example, in *Cobaugh v. Klick-Lewis, Inc.*, 561 A.2d 1248 (Pa. 1989), a car dealer set up a display offering the prize of a free car for a hole-in-one hit during a charity tournament and failed to remove it when the tournament ended. A golfer who hit a hole-in-one after the tournament demanded the prize. The court found that the display was an offer, reasonably understood by a person seeing it as being open for acceptance by anyone who performed by hitting a hole-in-one. Upon accomplishing this feat, the golfer accepted the offer and was entitled to the car. The offer is for a unilateral contract because the dealer does not conceivably contemplate acceptance by promise. The same conclusion was reached in *Harms v. Northland Ford Dealers*, 602 N.W.2d 58 (S.D. 1999), in which the court held that the golfer's act of hitting a hole-in-one was acceptance of a car dealer's offer of a car prize. (Unlike in *Cobaugh*, the golfer in *Harms* was playing in the tournament for which the prize had been offered. The problem was that the tournament organizers had failed to inform participants that the rules of the competition required women golfers to hit the ball from the men's tee. Ms. Harms hit the ball from the women's tee, and the dealer disqualified her from the prize. The court held that the dealer was bound by the terms manifested to participants and could not impose an unexpressed condition on the plaintiff.)

In *Cobaugh* there was no language in the display that suggested that it related to a tournament, and the display had not been removed before the golfer claimed the prize. The removal of the display before Jock claimed the prize is not legally relevant. Although it could be seen as an attempt to revoke the offer, it came too late because the display was removed only after Jock had accepted the offer by hitting the hole-in-one. However, the language in the offer could be legally significant, and the existence of the small print at the bottom of the sign could distinguish Jock's case from *Cobaugh* if it would signal to a reasonable reader that the offer had lapsed at the end of the prior day's tournament. The language on the sign is not as clear as it could be. It does not expressly identify the tournament or confine the offer to it, but it does raise the possibility that the offer related to some charity event. If the print was reasonably visible to a passing golfer, and a reasonable golfer, knowing the usual custom of offering prizes and promotions in connection with such tournaments, would have taken note of it and realized that the offer was no longer open for acceptance, Jock would have no claim.

9. If Maggie's initial note is not an offer, there is clearly no contract because Minnie's responses would themselves be nothing more than unaccepted offers. However, Maggie's letter can reasonably be interpreted as an offer. It contains a specific proposal and appears to contemplate that a positive response by April 16 would conclude a contract.

Minnie's first response could be a counteroffer. If it is, it operates as a rejection, and the offer lapses so that there cannot be a later acceptance. However, the wording used by Minnie suggests that she did not intend an unequivocal rejection and counteroffer, but rather that she wished to explore the possibility of a change in terms. She appears to be negotiating an alternative while holding open the possibility of acceptance if Maggie refuses to budge on her initial demands. This being so, it would have been possible for Minnie to abandon her effort at securing more favorable terms and to accept the offer on April 16. Acceptance by mail would likely have been permissible because Maggie did not prescribe an exclusive medium of acceptance, and acceptance may be by any reasonable means. Also, as Maggie did not specify that acceptance would only be effective on receipt, the "deposited acceptance" or "mailbox" rule applies. The acceptance would have taken effect on April 16, as soon as Minnie deposited it in the mailbox, correctly addressed and stamped.

However, there are two reasons why Minnie's letter of April 16 does not qualify as an effective acceptance. First, it may not be an acceptance at all because it still does not completely correspond with the offer. It calls for Maggie to begin work two days after the date specified in the offer. Although this may be a minor variation, a strict application of the "mirror image" rule disqualifies it as an acceptance. The variation is less likely to be a problem if the less rigid "materiality" standard is used, because the change in dates may be too insignificant to be a material alteration of the offer's terms. (I stress the word "may" because it is a question of fact whether the change in dates would be a material departure from the terms of the offer.)[20] The problem created by the change in dates could also be overcome by interpreting the offer as impliedly authorizing Minnie to make minor adjustments in the dates.

A more serious problem is that the offer had been revoked before Minnie accepted it. Revocation is only effective when communicated to the offeree. However, even if, as happened here, the offeror fails to communicate the revocation to the offeree, the offer may be indirectly revoked when the offeree obtains definite and unambiguous information from a reliable source that the offer is no longer open for acceptance. (See *Dickenson v. Dodds* discussed in section 4.6.4.) Minnie did receive apparently reliable information from Max that Maggie has agreed to work for him and was no longer able to do research for Minnie. (There is no suggestion that Maggie has time to work for both of them.) Therefore, even if Minnie's response to Maggie on April 16 qualified as an acceptance, it was too late because it occurred after the offer had been revoked indirectly.

10. Like Example 8, this transaction could qualify as a sale of goods even though no money was exchanged for the prize. The prizes offered (including the leopard cub) qualify as goods, and the exchange of the box tops could constitute a price. As in Example 8, regardless of whether this is a sale of goods, the issues in this Example would be resolved under principles of common law, which are not displaced by any Code provisions. Flaky's arguments should be resolved as follows:

a. *The argument that the cereal box was a solicitation, not an offer.* The usual assumption is that advertisements (including competitions designed

---

20. The concept of materiality is introduced more fully in section 6.5.2.

to promote products) are not offers but merely solicitations for offers from the public. On this assumption, when a member of the public responds affirmatively to the advertisement, this is usually the offer, which the advertiser can accept or reject. Although this is what ordinarily should be understood, it does not mean that an advertisement can never be an offer. Like any other communication, its reasonable intent must be determined by interpretation. Therefore, as the *Lefkowitz* case in section 4.4 shows, an advertisement could qualify as an offer if it is clear, definite, and explicit; leaves nothing open for negotiation; and makes it apparent to a reasonable person that a commitment is intended without further action by the advertiser. (*See* Restatement, Second, §26, Comment *b*.)

Although *Lefkowitz* is an old case, it continues to be influential. It was used by the court in *Harris v. Time, Inc.*, 191 Cal. App. 3d 449 (1987) to support the court's finding that Time made an offer to all recipients of a mailer that promised a free calculator watch "just for opening this envelope." (Time did not actually mean to offer the watch merely for opening the envelope, and the full text of the sentence made it clear that the recipient had to subscribe to *Fortune* magazine to get the watch. However, the first part of the sentence showed through the window in the envelope, and the qualification in the remainder of the sentence did not.) The court held the text of the mailer, as revealed through the envelope window, did constitute an offer to give a watch to the recipient for opening the envelope. Like the advertisement in *Lefkowitz*, it was clear in its terms, called for a specific act of acceptance (opening the envelope), and left nothing for further negotiation. The offer was therefore accepted by opening the envelope.[21]

Although cases like *Lefkowitz* and *Harris* are resolved by application of the mechanics of offer and acceptance, the opinions indicate that the courts were really motivated by the concern that advertisers should be held accountable for what they appear to promise.

Lefkowitz was also cited but distinguished by the court in *Leonard v. PepsiCo* (discussed in section 4.1.6 in relation to the objective test). Recall that one of the grounds for not finding a contract in *Leonard* was that the advertisement for the Harrier jet was a joke. However, the court also held that even had the TV commercial not been a joke, it

---

21. The suit was a class action that claimed significant compensatory and punitive damages on behalf of all recipients of the mailer. Although the court found the existence of a contract, and hence potential liability for damages, it dismissed the case on the maxim "de minimis non curat lex" — the law is not concerned with trifles. The court felt that the harm suffered by the recipients was trivial and did not merit a lawsuit. However, its finding that Time's promotion was an offer recognized the important principle that advertisements of this type could be interpreted as offers.

would still not have been an offer because it was not specific or detailed enough. The catalog published by Pepsi, listing the prizes and setting out the procedure for redeeming them could clearly not be an offer of a Harrier jet, because the jet was not listed as a prize in the catalog. However, the court went further and held that the catalog was also not an offer of the other prizes that it did list, because the catalog lacked words of limitation such as the phrase "first come, first served" used by the store in *Lefkowitz*, and no reasonable customer could have believed that PepsiCo intended to risk exposure to an unlimited number of acceptances. Note that this conclusion is not inevitable. If the prize offerings are specific, and nothing is left for negotiation, a catalog like this could be interpreted as an offer unless the catalog includes specific language stating that it is not an offer.

How should Flaky's promotion be interpreted in light of these cases? The cases show that in interpreting advertisements courts weigh two factors: On one side is the usual market expectation that few advertisements are intended to give members of the public the power to bind the advertiser simply by responding to the advertisement. However, if an advertiser uses language that reasonably indicates a willingness to give potential customers the last word on forming a contract, it could be bound immediately upon the customer's response. The crucial indicators of such an intent are clarity and completeness in the proposed terms of the transaction, and the absence of any language or circumstances that may suggest a reservation of the right to retain control over the process of contract formation. In addition, courts are mindful of the need to hold advertisers responsible to the public for promises made in their advertisements. Although false advertising is statutorily regulated, contract law can also serve as a means of policing misleading or extravagant assertions and imposing liability on those who make them.

Flaky's promotion is fully set out on the backs of its cereal boxes, which seem to describe the prizes with particularity (including an illustration) and to set out in detail the mode of responding and the performance required in exchange for the prizes. The boxes also specify an expiry date for responses and contain a limitation to protect Flaky from having to award more prizes than it has on hand. There seems to be nothing left for future resolution, so all that is called for is a response in the proper form. This may indeed be a case in which a court could find that Flaky's choice of language and format belies the normal expectation of a solicitation and creates an offer.

b. *Even if the box created an offer, it was open only to* "boys and girls." This is a better argument than the store's assertion in *Lefkowitz* that its undisclosed house rule was that the offer was open only to women. Here, Flaky at least has some basis for claiming that the limitation was expressed in the offer. However, even if "boys and girls" can be interpreted to mean "children," there is no language that restricts the offer to them or clearly excludes adults from claiming the prizes.

c. *A reasonable person would understand that the leopard cub was not a real prize, but just a bit of hyperbole.* This argument is based on several grounds: the unsuitability of leopards as pets, the high number of box tops needed, and the huge discrepancy between the value of the cub and the cost of 1,000 boxes of cereal. These rationales are similar to those advanced by the court in *Leonard v. PepsiCo* to support the conclusion that the TV commercial could not reasonably have been understood as serious.

Flaky's joke may be more apparent than that of Joe or Mr. Zehmer in Example 1, but it is not as clearly tongue-in-cheek as PepsiCo's Harrier jet commercial. It could be that a reasonable cereal box reader would have understood that the leopard cub was not seriously intended as a prize, but Flaky took a risk in using deadpan humor that did not make its joke glaringly obvious. (Of course, even if Flaky is held to have made a serious offer, which Manny accepted, it would not necessarily have to deliver the cub to him.[22] However, it would be liable to him for damages measured as the difference between the value of the cub and the contract price.)

d. *Even if Flaky made an offer, prizes were limited to quantities on hand, and Flaky never had a leopard cub.* This interpretation of the qualification gives it an evasive meaning that the advertiser should not be allowed to advance. A more reasonable understanding of the qualification is that Flaky has stocks of all prizes, based on a fair expectation of responses, but that it will be released from supplying prizes once demand for an item exceeds these expectations. To allow Flaky to claim that the language permits it to begin with no prizes of a particular kind would be to condone deceptive advertising. As noted in the discussion of argument (a) above, courts are mindful of this issue when interpreting advertisements.

11. a. Ray's note is clearly an offer to sell the property to Shelly. He expressly states that it is an offer, it sets out all the material terms on which he intends to enter the contract, and it requires nothing more than a proper signification of acceptance to create a binding relationship. The offer contains an unequivocal promise that it will

---

22. As explained briefly in sections 1.2.4 and 2.5, and more fully in section 18.10, the common remedy for breach of contract is damages, and a plaintiff has to make a special showing to obtain a court order granting specific performance of a contract.

not be revoked. The problem is that Shelly has given no consideration to Ray for the promise to keep the offer open. A promise not to revoke an offer is treated as distinct from the underlying contract that would come into existence upon valid acceptance, so it needs its own separate consideration to qualify as a binding option — the $500,000 to be paid for the farm, had a contract arisen, cannot serve as consideration for the promise not to revoke. Therefore, Ray is not legally bound by his promise not to revoke, and he effectively revoked the offer when Shelly received notice of his intent to revoke before she had communicated her intent to accept.

b. In this changed form, the grant of the option now records that consideration was given for it. We have no indication of what the actual economic worth may be of a three-day option to buy a piece of property for $500,000, but it is probably fair to assume that $1.00 does not and is not intended to bear any relationship to the option's actual value. Rather, it is inserted in the grant purely for the sake of formality. The parties know that consideration is required to validate the option, so they provide for it in a nominal amount for the purpose of showing their intent to create a legally binding promise. As you will see in Chapter 7, it is a general principle of consideration doctrine that as long as some consideration is given for a promise, a court will generally not inquire into the question of whether the consideration is equivalent or adequate. However, a court may not be willing to treat something as consideration if it is clearly nominal or a sham. Where options are concerned, courts are more likely to find token consideration to be legally sufficient to bind the offeror to the promise not to revoke.

Note that Shelly did actually pay the $1.00 to Ray. Had she not done so, it is possible that a court would find a lack of consideration because the recited payment was not even nominal, but was a complete sham. However, even under those circumstances, a court that wishes to enforce the option could find an implied promise by the offeree to pay the $1.00 or estop the offeree from denying payment.

12. Here the option is not a self-standing promise by John to keep an offer open. Rather, it is one of the obligations he has assumed under the lease in exchange for Al's consideration under the lease — his promise to pay the monthly rent. It is part of the collection of rights that Al has purchased under the lease and is enforceable like any other term of the contract. It needs no separate consideration.

In terms of the lease, Al had until 30 days before the expiry of the lease term to exercise his option. Ten days before this deadline, he sent a letter informing John that he did not intend to buy the property — in effect, rejecting the offer. John received the rejection and acknowledged it in writing. Had this been an ordinary offer, it would have been effectively terminated before Al changed his mind and decided to accept. However, when a grantee has purchased a valid option by giving consideration for it, the option qualifies as a contract in itself. Because it is a contract, the grantee's relinquishment of rights under it is valid only if the grantee receives consideration for giving up the rights, or the grantor takes detrimental action in reliance on the grantee's assertion that he will not exercise the option. If this sounds a bit complicated, do not worry about it for now. It is explained in sections 7.5 and 13.9. The simple point, for present purposes, is that because Al received no consideration for giving up his option, and John did not act in reliance on Al's rejection, Al is not bound by his notice that he does not plan to exercise the option. Therefore, he may still change his mind and accept the offer before the expiry of the option. His subsequent letter was an effective exercise of the option. Recall that some courts do not apply the "mailbox" rule to the acceptance of an option, but this does not matter on our facts because John received the letter exercising the option before the end of the option period.

13. Harv gave no consideration to John for John's promise to hold the offer open, so if this was a contract at common law, John's promise not to revoke would not bind him, and his revocation would be effective upon Harv's receipt of it. However, this is a sale of goods, so if the requirements of UCC §2.205 are satisfied, the promise is binding as a firm offer despite the lack of consideration.

    Section 2.205 only applies if the offeror is a merchant. (It is not necessary that the offeree be a merchant as well.) There may be a basis for finding that John is a merchant with regard to the tractor sale, but whether he has sufficient work-related expertise in transactions of this kind to qualify as a merchant under §1.104(1) is a question of fact that cannot be finally decided on the scanty information furnished here. He had apparently been farming at some time in the past and had used the tractor for that activity. A farmer (even one who is disposing of the farm and its equipment) may qualify as a merchant with regard to farming implements, not necessarily because he deals in goods of that kind with any frequency, but because, by his occupation, he holds himself out as having knowledge or skill in relation to the goods or the transaction. The issue, in essence, is whether John has sufficient sophistication and knowledge in relation to the transaction to be subject to Article 2's more exacting rules for "professionals."

    If John does satisfy the definition of a merchant, the offer is binding on him as a firm offer until its stated expiry time of 5 P.M. on May 4, because it meets the other requirements of §2.205: It is in a writing signed by John, and it gives assurance that it will be held open for a stated time, not exceeding three months. Harv may therefore ignore the attempted revocation and accept the offer before the time for acceptance lapses. This will create a binding contract. (Although Harv will probably not be able to compel John to deliver the tractor, he will be able to claim any money damages suffered as a result of the breach.)

CHAPTER 5

Standard Form Contracts and Contracts Through Electronic Media

§5.1 INTRODUCTION

While some contracts consist of terms that are drafted for the particular transaction, many are based, in whole or in part, on standard terms that have been drafted in advance of the transaction and are incorporated into the offer (or the counteroffer). The use of standard terms in contracts is so widespread that it is surely the norm in modern contracting. This practice is efficient and sensible because most contracts involve commonplace exchanges, and there is no reason to take the trouble to draft individualized terms for each transaction. In some cases, particularly where the offeror engages in many transactions of the same kind, the offeror may have drafted its own standard terms. For example, an insurer, an airline, or a credit card issuer provides its service subject to a standard set of terms that it has drafted to cover all contracts of that kind. In other cases, the offeror may employ standard terms drafted by someone else. For example, the seller of a home may use a standard contract drafted by an association of real estate brokers, or a building contractor may use one drafted by a builder's trade association. In some cases, the entire contract is in a standard form, with blanks to accommodate matters such as the date of the transaction, the names of the parties and the description of the goods or services sold (that is, it is fully a standard form contract). Even where the whole contract is not on standard terms, an offeror may select individual terms from a form book or a previous transaction. Standard language that is used routinely in many contracts is referred to as boilerplate.

Although the objective test and the rules of offer and acceptance were not originally developed with standard form contracts in mind, there is no reason why they should not apply where all or some of the terms in the offer or counteroffer are standard. You should therefore assume that the same rules generally apply, whether the terms have been individually crafted or are standard. However, in some situations, the use of standard terms can raise questions about whether a contract was formed, or, if it was, whether particular terms actually became part of the contract. This chapter focuses on those issues. This is not the only place in the book in which standard terms or standard form contracts are discussed. They arise in many contexts. For example, the issues discussed in Chapter 6 on the "battle of the forms" often involve standard terms, and standard terms quite commonly give rise to claims of unconscionability, introduced in section 5.4 and discussed more fully in section 13.11.

The objective test and the rules of offer and acceptance were developed long before the invention of the technology that is widely used today. The availability of modern means of communication has significantly changed business practices and has created new opportunities for efficient contracting. As new technology has changed business practices, the law has had to adapt by adjusting old rules to new situations. This is not a new phenomenon. In the early twentieth century the rules of offer and acceptance had to accommodate the advances in communications via telegraph, telephone, or teleprinter. More recently, the rules have had to take account of faxes, e-mails, the Internet, and other forms of electronic communication. Of these, e-mail and the Internet and the development of paperless recording have probably caused the most profound change in contracting practices. Many, but not all, electronic transactions also implicate standard terms, so that they raise not only new questions of how to treat the communication, but also the older questions mentioned in the previous paragraph: Was a contract formed, and if so, what terms did it incorporate? Again, it is important to stress that we do not have a separate body of formation rules that apply where technology is used in creating a contract. The general principles of offer and acceptance apply, with some adaptation to take account of the new means of communication.

§5.2 THE PROCESS AND TERMINOLOGY OF STANDARD CONTRACTING

Consider a routine transaction: The buyer, a consumer, decides to buy a new digital camera. She goes into a photographic store, selects the camera, and takes it to the cashier. Just before the buyer pays for the camera, the cashier prints out and gives the buyer a piece of paper headed "Invoice." The invoice has a description of the camera and the price and contains the following language, printed in bold letters at the foot of the page: "Return Policy: This camera may be returned for replacement within 10 days of purchase only if defective. The buyer's remedy is confined to replacement of the defective product. The buyer is not entitled to return this camera for other reasons, and is not entitled to a refund of the price." The cashier has the buyer sign the invoice in a blank space provided. Based on the rules discussed in Chapter 4, we can conclude that there is a contract for the sale of the camera that incorporates the return policy. There are different ways that we can characterize the parties' conduct. For example, it could be that the buyer made the initial offer by taking the camera to the checkout counter, the cashier then made a counteroffer by proffering the invoice with the return policy, and the buyer accepted the counteroffer by completing the purchase. Alternatively, it may be that the buyer merely solicited an offer by taking the camera to the checkout counter, the cashier then made an offer, which the buyer accepted.[1] As discussed in section 4.1 on the objective test, the buyer has a duty to read the terms presented to her and will likely be bound by her manifestation of assent, even if she did not pay attention to the standard printed language on the invoice. (However, see sections 5.3 and 5.4 for qualifications on this conclusion.)

a. Box-top Terms

Change the facts slightly: The cashier does not print out an invoice. Instead, the shrinkwrapped box containing the camera has a bright orange sticker with bold black print that sets out the return policy in the language quoted above. Again, the most sensible conclusion is that a contract was entered at the point of sale. Because the sticker was on the exterior of the box, we do not even have to include the step in which the store made a counteroffer. On picking up the box, the buyer saw or reasonably should have seen the return policy. Therefore, by taking the box to the cashier, the buyer actually manifests intent to contract subject to the return policy, which is incorporated into her offer. Where standard terms are placed on the packaging by the seller, so that they are discernable to the buyer on the box itself, they are called box-top terms.

---

1. A third possibility is that the store made the offer by displaying the camera and the buyer accepted it by taking it up to the cashier's counter. However, this seems like a less likely description of what occurred. A store's display of merchandise is more likely to be nothing more than a solicitation, so that the actual contracting comes about at the point of sale.

b. Shrinkwrap Terms

Change the facts again: There is no invoice and no sticker on the box. When the buyer gets the camera home and opens the box, she finds a piece of paper in the box that sets out the return policy. This is called a shrinkwrap term because it is included in the box or container and not likely to be seen by the buyer until after he has bought the goods, torn the inevitable protective shrinkwrap off the box, and opened it. Including a term in the box with the goods presents problems that are not present in the first two illustrations because the term was not made known to the buyer at the time of contracting. The general rule is that once a contract has been concluded, one of the parties cannot unilaterally add terms to or change the terms of the contract. Any change in terms must be agreed to by both parties in a valid modification. However, this general rule applies only if the shrinkwrap term is in fact a modification. It may happen that the shrinkwrap term merely expresses what was impliedly agreed to by the parties when they entered the contract. This could occur where the buyer knows that the contract was subject to a standard term of the kind, or even where the buyer should reasonably have expected the contract to be subject to such a term. This can be a difficult question, which is discussed in section 5.5. This situation must be distinguished from cases involving rolling contracts in which offer and acceptance does not occur at the point of purchase. Rolling contracts are also discussed in section 5.5.

c. Clickwrap Terms

Change the facts of the illustration once again: The buyer does not go into a store to buy the camera. Instead, she buys it online. She visits the seller's website, selects the camera from the products shown on the website, places it in the virtual shopping cart, and proceeds to the virtual checkout. Before she completes the purchase, the website refers her to the seller's standard terms, which contain the return policy. The terms may be set out on the web page itself, or they may be accessible by clicking on a link, or they may appear in a pop-up window. Before submitting the order, the buyer must click on a button that indicates acceptance of the standard terms. This situation is analogous to a buyer signing a written standard form contract. The terms are available at the time of contracting, and the buyer has a duty to read them. If the buyer manifests assent without reading them, the buyer cannot later claim that she did not know what they were and did not intend to be bound by them. Where a party is called on to indicate assent to a term by clicking on a box or button on a website, the term is called a clickwrap term.

A clickwrap term may also be embedded in software that the buyer has purchased, either by downloading it or by buying a disk containing it. If the clickwrap term is in the software itself, the term may not have been available to the buyer at the time of sale. If that is so, it is similar in character to, and should be approached in the same way as a shrinkwrap term. This is discussed in section 5.3.

d. Browsewrap Terms

Like a clickwrap term, a browsewrap term is set out on a website and is available to be read by the user of the website before submitting her order for the service or product purchased. However, a browsewrap term is different from a clickwrap term in that the user does not have to indicate assent to it by affirmative conduct, such as clicking on an "I accept" button. Because the user does not have to take deliberate action to manifest assent to the term, the conclusion that the user did assent to the term is not as compelling as it is with a clickwrap term, and issues of conspicuousness and notice may arise, as discussed in section 5.3.

§5.3 CONSPICUOUSNESS, NOTICE, AND REASONABLE EXPECTATIONS

a. Reasonable Expectations

Because standard form contracting is so prevalent, reasonable people have come to expect that many contracts will have standard terms. Experience and general knowledge of the marketplace will usually also give them a good idea of what those terms are likely to be. For example, if you buy an airline ticket, you should expect that the contract has terms specifying what happens if you wish to cancel or change your flight, what baggage you may carry without extra charge, and what responsibility the airline has if your flight is canceled or delayed or if your luggage is lost. If you buy an insurance policy, you should expect that the contract has terms excluding certain losses from the coverage, providing for a deductible, and specifying the claim procedure to be followed. Because arbitration provisions have become so commonplace, you should expect that almost any contract you enter could have a provision requiring disputes to be arbitrated. However, you may not expect in these contracts that the airline disclaims all liability for losing your luggage, or that the insurer can refuse to pay out on the policy unless you prostrate yourself before the claims adjuster. The concept of reasonable expectations runs throughout this chapter (and surfaces elsewhere in the book). As a general rule, courts are more likely to enforce standard terms if they are fair and reasonably expected.

b. Conspicuousness and Notice

Courts also often make a point of stressing the importance of setting out standard terms in a clear, conspicuous, and intelligible form, whether the terms are contained in a written paper contract or in electronic form, such as a website or software. Where the nondrafting party did not actually know of the term, a court may refuse to find that the nondrafting party had a duty to read and should have known of the term if the term is not apparent or comprehensible to a reasonably conscientious person. That is, in the absence of actual notice of a term, the court will not deem a person to have notice of it, and therefore to have assented to it, if the term is not apparent to a reasonable person (for example, it is buried in fine-print boilerplate) or is written in language that is difficult for a lay person to understand. This is particularly true where the term is not one that would obviously be found in such a contract (and therefore not reasonably expected). Where the nondrafting party is a consumer or is commercially unsophisticated, courts are especially solicitous of protecting her from the imposition of terms that are unfair, unexpected, or insufficiently clear and obvious from the writing.

Two contrasting cases illustrate the important role that notice of terms and conspicuousness play in the decision to enforce standard terms. Both cases involve standard terms on a website, and in both the courts made it clear that they resolved the question of reasonable notice of the web-based standard terms by applying general principles of common law that had long been recognized in relation to paper contracts: Where a party has reasonable notice of intelligible terms, she has a duty to read the terms, and her manifestation of assent binds her, even if she failed to read them.

In *Specht v. Netscape Communications Corporation*, 306 F.3d 17 (2d Cir. 2002), the court refused to uphold a browsewrap arbitration provision on the grounds that it was not sufficiently brought to the notice of the offeree. (The court treated Netscape as the offeror and the users as the offerees.) The Netscape website allowed users to download free software, subject to the terms of a license that contained the arbitration clause. The problem was that Netscape did not use the clickwrap technique of displaying the license agreement on the download page or in a pop-up box requiring the user to click an "I accept" button before downloading. Instead, the user had to scroll down beyond the "Download" button to find a link to a separate web page that had the license terms. The court recognized a general duty to read standard terms and applied a test of reasonable notice that is well established in the context of paper contracts: A reasonably prudent person would have been alerted to the terms. On the basis of this test, it rejected Netscape's argument that a reasonably prudent person should have known to scroll down beyond the "Download" button to find the terms and had both the time and the opportunity to discover the terms. The court held that because the offer was for free software, offerees may not have realized that they were making a contract at all, and there was just not enough warning to offerees to look for the terms. It could be argued that the court was too forgiving of the offerees' lack of attentiveness — after all, it seems that a reasonable offeree should know that there are usually standard terms applicable to such transactions, and could have found them without too much trouble. Nevertheless, Netscape made the mistake of structuring its website in a way that did not require the offeree to specifically manifest assent to the terms or that presented the terms in a way in which they could not be overlooked by a reasonable offeree.

By contrast, in *Feldman v. Google, Inc.*, 513 F. Supp.2d 229 (E. D. Pa 2007), Google had structured its website to minimize the risk of a successful argument of lack of notice and allowed the court to distinguish *Specht* and uphold a clickwrap forum selection clause.[2] The clause was a standard term included by Google in its online contracts for the purchase of advertising on its site. The person purchasing the advertising was presented with Google's standard terms in a prominent scrollable window, headed by language in boldface type that stated, "**Carefully read the following terms and conditions**. If you agree with these terms, indicate your assent below." The window also contained a printer-friendly version of the terms, and the advertiser could not complete his order for the advertising without clicking an "I agree" button at the bottom of the web page. The court held that the terms were clear and conspicuous and presented in a way that would alert a reasonably prudent Internet user to the existence of the terms before manifesting assent by clicking the "I agree" button. They therefore bound the advertiser.

Subject to the possible problem of unconscionability, discussed in section 5.4, courts generally uphold clickwrap terms. Because the customer must deliberately signify assent by clicking an "I agree" button, she cannot claim a lack of notice and assent. In addition, because clickwrap terms are usually nonnegotiable, the customer cannot vary them by communicating disagreement to the owner of the website. This concept is illustrated by *A.V. v. Iparadigms*, L.L.C., 544 F. Supp.2d 473 (E.D. Va. 2008). Iparadigms operated a website that checked written work for plagiarism by comparing submitted work to content available on the Internet. The plaintiffs were students at a school that required them to submit work to Iparadigms for a plagiarism check. The students had to register on the Iparadigms website to use its services and in so doing, had to consent to a clickwrap standard user agreement. The standard user agreement authorized Iparadigm to archive work submitted for checking, and it specifically stated that its services were conditional on the user's acceptance of the standard terms without modification. Notwithstanding that they clicked the "I agree" button on the

---

2. Forum selection clauses are explained below.

website, the students included a notice on the submitted papers stating that they did not consent to the archiving of their works. The court held that the students were bound by the clickwrap agreement, and the attempt to modify the standard terms was ineffective. Users had a simple choice to agree and accept the benefits of the contract, or to disagree and decline them. They had no option to accept on terms other than those offered.[3]

Although a clickwrap term provides the strongest proof of agreement, this does not mean that a browsewrap term is fatally defective, merely because it lacks the feature of a clickwrap term that requires the user to take an affirmative step to signal assent. The crucial issue is whether the user had actual notice of the term or, if not, whether the term was set out on the website in a way that afforded reasonable notice. For example, in *Southwest Airlines Co. v. Boardfirst, L.L.C.*, 2007 WL 4823761 (N.D. Tex. 2007), the court distinguished *Specht* in holding that a browsewrap term on the Southwest website bound Boardfirst because it had actual knowledge of the term. The court indicated that even if it had not known of the term, it would have been bound provided that the website provided adequate notice of the term.

c. Standard Arbitration and Forum Selection Provisions

i. *Arbitration Clauses*

Because arbitration and forum selection provisions are such common terms in both negotiated and standard contracts they are worth highlighting. You may recall that an arbitration clause was involved in the *Morales* case, discussed in section 4.1.5 as an illustration of the duty to read. An arbitration provision was also in issue in *Specht*, and you will come across many other cases that involve challenges to the validity of a standard arbitration clause. The process of arbitration as a means of enforcing a contract is introduced in section 1.2.4. As explained there, where parties agree to arbitrate any disputes arising out of their contract, they forgo the right to litigate disputes in court and must instead have the dispute resolved by arbitration. The arbitration is conducted by a private person or panel designated in the agreement. The arbitrator's decision binds the parties and cannot be reviewed by a court except on limited grounds. Therefore, by entering an arbitration agreement, a party abandons her fundamental right to have a court resolve a dispute relating to the contract. Because arbitration provisions are so commonly found in standard contracts, there is justification for the concern that the parties who have the

---

3. The case also concerned issues of copyright law, which were the subject of an appeal. See *A.V. v. Iparadigms, LLC*, 562 F.3d 630 (4th Cir. 2009). The district court's resolution of the contract formation issue was not challenged on appeal.

power and sophistication to set the terms of those contracts are routinely imposing the obligation to arbitrate on their customers.

Notwithstanding, courts generally uphold arbitration agreements, even where they are contained in standard contracts. In fact, there is a widely recognized policy in favor of arbitration in both state and federal law. The policy is justified on the grounds that court dockets are crowded, litigation is slow, and arbitration can be a more efficient and less expensive means of settling disputes. The federal policy in favor of arbitration is given legislative form in the Federal Arbitration Act, 9 USC §§1-16 (FAA), which expressly recognizes the validity of an agreement to arbitrate, unless there are grounds to invalidate it under principles of contract law. Many states have similar legislation and state courts generally follow the same approach.

A party who has signified assent to a standard arbitration provision may decide, after the dispute has arisen, that her interests would be better served by litigating the dispute. To overturn the arbitration agreement, she must show that it has some defect that makes it unenforceable or invalid as a contract. The most common grounds on which to challenge the agreement are either that the party did not actually assent to it because she was unaware of it and it was not adequately brought to her attention, or because it is unconscionable. Because of the general policy in favor of arbitration, most courts require a strong showing of these grounds.

For example, in *D'Antuono v. Service Road Corp.*, 789 F. Supp. 2d 308 (2011) exotic dancers challenged an arbitration agreement in an "entertainment lease" under which the dancers performed at clubs operated by Service Road. (The contract was structured as a lease of performance space, rather than an employment contract.) The standard lease was presented to the dancers, who signed it immediately, apparently without reading it. The arbitration clause was set out on the last page of the four-page lease, just above the signatures. Most of it was in underlined capital letters. The court rejected the dancers' argument that they had not assented to the lease. They had a duty to read it, the clause was clearly apparent, and there had been no conduct by the club to dissuade them from reading it or to put them off their guard. As discussed in section 5.4, the court also held that the clause was not unconscionable.

ii. *Forum Selection Clauses*

A forum selection clause is a term in a contract under which the parties agree to litigate disputes in the courts of a specified jurisdiction. That is, the parties agree in advance to submit any disputes to the jurisdiction of the selected court. Like arbitration clauses, forum selection clauses are commonly found in standard agreements and usually designate the jurisdiction most convenient to the party who drafted the contract. When a dispute arises, the other party may discover that she manifested agreement to an inconvenient jurisdiction, and may challenge the clause. As with arbitration clauses, this challenge is not likely to succeed unless the party can show circumstances that excuse the duty to read or that demonstrate that the selected forum is inappropriate and unfair.

§5.4 THE PROBLEM OF ADHESION AND UNCONSCIONABILITY IN STANDARD CONTRACTS

The concepts of adhesion and unconscionability are discussed in section 13.11 and are applied specifically to standard form contracts in section 13.12. However, because these concepts are so closely associated with standard contracts, it is helpful to introduce them here and to explain briefly how they affect the discussion in this chapter. A party who drafts standard terms may be expected to create terms that best serve its own interests. For the most part, the drafting party has every right to favor its own interests and has no duty to be altruistic or evenhanded. However, where the drafting party's terms are harsh or unfairly one-sided, and it has enough market power to make those terms nonnegotiable, a court may refuse to enforce the terms.

Where standard terms are proffered on a take-it-or-leave-it basis by a party with the market power to refuse to contract except on the standard terms, the resulting agreement is called a contract of adhesion: The nondrafting party has no choice but to adhere to the nonnegotiable terms.[4] Adhesion is even more apparent where the nondrafting party has little or no alternative but to enter into this contract. This may occur, for example, where the product or service is not merely a luxury and there is no competing provider with whom to contract on different terms. Contracts with nonnegotiable standard terms are commonplace. For example, a passenger usually does not have any ability to negotiate the standard terms and conditions to which travel is subject, the purchaser of software cannot usually negotiate the standard terms of the license, and a patient cannot usually negotiate the hospital's standard conditions of admission and treatment. As a general matter, a nondrafting party who assents to an adhesive contract cannot challenge its terms merely because they were nonnegotiable. However, courts recognize that there may not be true assent to adhesive terms, so that if the terms are harsh, oppressive, or unexpected, a court may decline to enforce them. The question of whether the nondrafting party had reasonable notice of the term, discussed in section 5.3, is relevant to its

---

4. Even in a contract of adhesion, a party can usually negotiate some of the terms. However, it is the nonnegotiable terms that raise the issue of adhesion.

enforceability. However, apart from that, if the imposition of the standard term is an abuse of the drafter's dominant market power, the court may refuse to enforce it even if the nondrafting party had adequate notice of it. In this respect, the concept of adhesion is closely tied to the doctrine of unconscionability.

In short, a contract or term of a contract is unconscionable if the contract or term is imposed on the party by unfair means (called "procedural unconscionability") and the term itself is unfair or unduly harsh or one-sided (called "substantive unconscionability"). We will examine the details of unconscionability doctrine in sections 13.11 and 13.12, but a couple of brief examples here illustrate how adhesion and unconscionability may come into play in the context of standard contracting.

Ad Here.com operates an online advertising agency that places advertisements on websites. Potential advertisers buy advertising space through a contract on Ad Here's website. Before placing the order for the advertising, the advertiser is presented with a clickwrap agreement setting out Ad Here's standard contract terms. The advertiser cannot submit the order until it clicks a box that records its acceptance of the standard terms. One of the standard terms states that Ad Here is not responsible for any damages suffered by the advertiser as a result of errors in the content or placement of advertisement, resulting from any cause, including Ad Here's negligence. We saw in sections 5.2 and 5.3 that by manifesting assent to the clickwrap terms, with reasonable notice of their existence and an opportunity to read them, the advertiser has formed a contract with Ad Here subject to the clickwrap terms. However, even though the formation issue is clear, there is room for an inquiry into whether the disputed nonnegotiable term (the advertiser's waiver of its right to claim damages for breach of the contract) is unconscionable. As we will see in sections 13.11 and 13.12, it is not enough, for unconscionability, that the term was nonnegotiable and favorable to the interests of Ad Here. There must be a finding that the term is both[5] procedurally unconscionable (that is, there has been some kind of improper conduct in the way that Ad Here secured the advertiser's manifestation of assent) and substantively unconscionable (that is, the term is so unfair or one-sided that it shocks the conscience of the court). There appears to be little that was procedurally improper about the way that Ad Here obtained the manifestation of assent. The terms were not concealed or obscure (as you can see, the issue of notice and conspicuousness is a consideration here), and there was no other improper bargaining such as high-pressure selling techniques. The question of whether a term is substantively unconscionable involves a complex set of considerations that call for an

---

5. As you will see in section 13.11, it is not always necessary to show both procedural and substantive unconscionability. Some courts may dispense with the need to satisfy both the procedural and substantive elements where one of them is particularly egregious.

examination of the contract as a whole in its commercial context, in light of commercial practices and mores. It may well be that a provision insulating a contracting party from damages for negligence may not be substantively unfair under all the circumstances of the case.

The *D'Antuono* case, described in section 5.3, provides a second example. The court noted the distinction between the formation issue (whether the dancers agreed to the clause) and the validity issue (whether the clause is valid and effective). The duty to read is pertinent to the formation issue, but unconscionability doctrine is concerned with the validity of what was agreed. (Of course, because procedural unconscionability is concerned with the circumstances under which the manifestation was made, there is some overlap between these issues.) After finding that the dancers were bound by their manifestation of assent to the arbitration clause, the court went on to decide if the arbitration provision was unconscionable. Because of the general policy in favor of arbitration, it is most unlikely that a court will find an agreement to arbitrate, in itself, to be unconscionable. There must be something in both the manner that the agreement was reached and in the terms of the arbitration that is procedurally and substantively unfair. As noted in section 5.3, the court found no impropriety in the manner in which the standard contract was presented to the dancers. There was no attempt to conceal its content or to prevent the dancers from reading it or getting legal advice on its terms. The fact that the contract was presented on a take-it-or-leave-it basis (that it was adhesive) was not enough, on its own, to make the arbitration provision procedurally unconscionable. The dancers argued that the terms of the arbitration provision were substantively unconscionable. They based this argument on three features of the arbitration: (1) It waived the right to collective and class actions,[6] (2) it provided for cost and fee shifting (the losing party would pay the costs of the arbitration and the attorney's fees of the prevailing party), and (3) it required claims to be made within six months (which shortened the usual statute of limitations—the time within which a claim may be brought).[7] After an extensive discussion of these features of the agreement, the court concluded that they were not sufficiently draconian to overcome the advantages of

---

6. A class action is a suit by a small group of named plaintiffs in which the named plaintiffs bring the suit for the benefit of a larger class of similarly situated persons. Members of the class are not joined in the suit, but are entitled to share in any remedy that the court grants if the suit is successful. The ability to initiate a class action can be very beneficial where the claims of individual plaintiffs are too small to merit litigation, but the total amount of claims by the whole class is significant. Some state courts have found waivers of the right to bring a class action to be unconscionable, but in *AT&T Mobility LLC v. Concepcion*, 131 S. Ct. 1740 (2011) the U.S. Supreme Court held that the policy in favor of arbitration preempts state law that disallows a waiver of class actions.

7. At the time of the suit, the club had waived the last two features (the cost- and fee-shifting provision and the truncated statute of limitations). However, the court analyzed the agreement for unconscionability as if all three features were present.

speed and informality that would be achieved by arbitration and they therefore did not render the agreement substantively unconscionable.

§5.5 "CASH NOW, TERMS LATER": DEFERRED COMMUNICATION OF TERMS AND ROLLING CONTRACTS

§5.5.1 Deferred Communication of Terms

The rules of offer and acceptance require that the offer set out all the terms of the contract. This does not always mean that all the terms are expressly articulated in the offer. It could be that terms exist even though they are not actually mentioned in the offer, because they are implied by law or usage. For example, an offer for the sale of property (whether real property or goods) may not specify the date on which and the manner in which payment of the price and transfer of the land or goods is to occur, but usage or default rules of law may fill the gap by requiring transfer of title and payment within a reasonable time, to be conducted simultaneously; a sale of goods may not specify whether the seller must ship the goods to the buyer, or whether the buyer or seller is responsible for the shipping costs, but usage or default rules of law may fill this gap by making the buyer responsible for collecting the goods or paying for their shipment.[8]

Apart from terms that may be implied by usage or law, one of the parties may have drafted standard terms intended to cover the transaction, which are not made available to the other at the time of contracting, but are revealed only after the offer has been accepted. This situation commonly occurs where the party who drafted the terms enters into many similar transactions and intends all of them to be subject to the same standard terms. For example, a person calls an airline or theater box office to book an air ticket or a concert ticket. Conventional offer and acceptance analysis usually treats the offer and acceptance as occurring at the time of booking. In requesting the booking, the buyer invites an offer. The airline or box office offers the buyer an available booking, and the buyer then accepts by agreeing to take it. Some time after the booking, the buyer receives the ticket in the mail. It contains standard terms that were not discussed at the time of booking. A similar situation could occur, for example, where a person calls an insurance agent to buy an insurance policy, or a person buys a product at

---

8. The discussion of counteroffers in section 4.8 provides another example of a term that is implicit as a result of common practice. Implied terms are covered more fully in sections 10.6. to 10.9.

a store that has standard shrinkwrap terms (such as a warranty or a license agreement) printed on a piece of paper in the sealed carton. Where terms are revealed to the offeree only after she has bought the goods or services, she may argue that the standardized terms never became part of the contract. In some cases, this argument succeeds: The court holds that the drafting party cannot bind the other party to standard terms that were not brought to her attention at the time of contracting. However, if a court finds the standard terms to be reasonable and reasonably expected, it may conclude that they were part of the contract despite the late communication. It is more likely to reach this conclusion where a transaction of that kind is commonly subject to standard terms and the nondrafting party had reason to know this and should have ascertained what they were. If she failed to acquaint herself with reasonably expected terms, she did not fulfill her duty to read and cannot disavow her manifestation of assent.

§5.5.2 Rolling Contracts

The discussion in section 5.5.1 is based on the conclusion that offer and acceptance occurred at the point of purchase of the goods or services and that the standard terms were made available only after the contract had been formed. However, in some situations, the facts may indicate that the transaction is a rolling contract — final assent to the contract is deferred until after the nondrafting party has an opportunity to read the terms. That is, no final contract is made at the point of purchase, but the delivery of the standard terms (which occurs upon delivery of the ticket, policy, or goods containing notice of the terms) is an offer. The buyer accepts the offer if she does not reject it within a reasonable time by declining the benefit of the contract. This imposes a duty to read at the time of delivery and gives the buyer the opportunity to refuse to contract on the offeror's standard terms.

One of the best known cases in which a rolling contract occurred is *ProCD, Inc. v. Zeidenberg*, 86 F.3d 1447 (7th Cir. 1996). A buyer bought software at a retail store. The software was sold in two versions, one for commercial use and the other for personal use. The program itself was the same in both versions, but the cheaper version contained a restriction in the license that prohibited its commercial use. Zeidenberg bought the cheaper version but used it for commercial purposes. ProCD sought an injunction to enforce the restriction.[9] The problem was that the buyer was not specifically told of the restriction on use of the software at the time that he bought the software. Instead, it was packaged inside the box

---

9. An injunction is a court order compelling or prohibiting the defendant from taking specified action. In this case, ProCD was asking the court to prohibit Zeidenberg from using the software commercially.

containing the disk and was set out in the users' manual and on the disk. The term appeared on the computer screen when the disk was inserted, and the user could not proceed to use the software without indicating assent to the terms. The license expressly gave the buyer the right to return the software for a refund if the license terms were unacceptable and treated the buyer as having accepted the terms if he continued to use the software and did not return it. The trial court held that offer and acceptance occurred at the retail store. Therefore, because the term restricting use of the software was made known to the buyer only after contracting, it was not part of the contract and did not bind the buyer. The court of appeals disagreed. Because the terms gave the buyer the right to return the software if the terms were unacceptable, the court found that ProCD made an offer by supplying the software with the license, and the buyer accepted by failing to return the software and using it.

There are two facts that seem crucial to the court's decision that offer and acceptance occurred at the time that Zeidenberg loaded the software. First, ProCD did not sell the program to Zeidenberg. He bought it at a retail store. Therefore, there does not appear to have been any contract between ProCD and Zeidenberg at the point of purchase. Second, the fact that the buyer had the right to reject the terms after opening the box justifies the conclusion that the buyer had a power of acceptance or rejection at that stage. The court would have had much more difficulty finding offer and acceptance at this stage had the buyer had no power to return the software after an opportunity to read the terms. This does not mean that this particular court would not have found some means to uphold the term, even in the absence of a right to return the software. The court did indicate that it strongly favored upholding the restriction in the license as a matter of policy because mass vendors of goods and services need standard terms to protect their rights, and it would often be impractical and burdensome to require them to articulate these terms in detail at the time of sale. The court therefore suggested that even in the absence of a right of rejection, the term should be upheld if it was fair and reasonably expected. In this case, the court felt that the term was legitimate because the restriction on the use of the software was directly related to the reduced price of the software sold for private use. ProCD is an influential but controversial decision, and it troubles those who believe that vendors should not be able to impose its standard terms without giving the purchaser proper notice of those terms at the time of sale.

Casavant v. Norwegian Cruise Line Ltd, 829 N.E.2d 1171 (Mass. App. 2005) provides a different perspective on this issue. In October 2000, the Casavants booked a roundtrip Boston-to-Bermuda cruise aboard a Norwegian Cruise Lines ship. The cruise was to depart on September 16, 2001. They paid a deposit at the time of booking and paid the balance of the total ticket price by July 2001. It was only upon receiving the tickets at the beginning of September 2001 that the Casavants were given the standard terms of the contract. One of the standard terms placed all risks of travel on the passenger. Another was a forum selection clause that required all disputes under the contract to be commenced and litigated in Florida. As you can see from the dates, the Casavants received the tickets just a few days before the terrorist attacks of September 11, 2001, and the cruise was scheduled to leave a few days afterward. The Casavants were frightened to board a cruise ship (especially one that left from Boston, from which two of the hijacked planes originated), so they sought to postpone or cancel their cruise booking. Norwegian refused to reschedule or to cancel and refund the ticket price on the basis that the contract allocated any risk of travel to the passenger. The Casavants sued Norwegian in Massachusetts, their home state, for refund of the ticket price. The sole issue to be decided was whether the trial court was correct in dismissing their case because they had agreed to litigate any dispute in Florida. The court of appeals reversed the dismissal, holding that the forum selection clause did not bind the Casavants. The court was vague on exactly when the contract came into being, so it is not clear whether it saw the offer and acceptance as having occurred at the time of booking or only when the standard terms were delivered with the ticket. (However, language in the opinion seems to suggest that the court considered contract formation to have been deferred until the latter event.) The court concluded that because the Casavants did not have sufficient time to reject the terms of the contract without sacrificing their payment, the forum selection clause was unfairly imposed and unenforceable.[10] (The issue of unfair imposition of standard terms is taken up more fully in section 13.12.)

§5.6 MODIFICATION OF STANDARD TERMS

Many standard contracts provide for a future modification of the standard terms during the course of the relationship. For example, a credit card issuer's standard terms, or the web-based standard terms of a service provider, may provide that the drafter of the terms has the right to modify the terms at its discretion at any time in the future. The term allowing for modification may further provide that the customer accepts any such modification by continuing to use the drafter's services following the

---

10. After the court invalidated the forum selection clause, the case proceeded on the merits in the Massachusetts courts. The Casavants' right to a refund of the price became moot because Norwegian gave them a refund, so the subsequent litigation concerned the issue of whether Norwegian's failure to disclose its refund policy violated deceptive trade practices law. The court held that it did, and that the Casavants were entitled to damages. *Casavant v. Norwegian Cruise Line Ltd*, 460 Mass. 500, 952 N.E.2d 908 (2011).

modification. Like other standard terms, a provision giving the drafter the right to modify its terms is a binding part of the agreement if the customer can be held to have manifested assent to it at the time of entering the contract. As discussed previously, this manifestation may be by signing a written contract, clicking on an "I accept" button, or otherwise engaging in conduct that signals assent to properly noticed or reasonably expected terms.

However, a provision allowing for the drafter to modify terms in the future creates an additional complication: Is it appropriate to treat the customer as having assented to the modification by continuing to use the services? This question was addressed in *Douglas v. U.S. District Court for the Central District of California*, 495 F.3d 1062 (9th Cir. 2007). Douglas contracted with America Online for long distance telephone service. AOL was bought by another company that made changes to the standard provisions of the service contract. It posted the changes on its website but never notified subscribers of the changes. Douglas, unaware of the changes, continued to use its services. The district court held that posting of the notice on the website was sufficient, but the court of appeals disagreed. The court pointed out that the modification of a contract is itself a contract — the drafter proposes the modification, which must be accepted by the other party. It held that assent cannot be deemed to have occurred through the continued use of the services unless the subscriber had reasonable notice of the proposed modification. Because the subscriber had no obligation to visit the website or to check for changes, the mere posting of changes on the website was not enough. Even had the subscriber looked at the website, the changes would not be apparent unless he checked them against an earlier version of the terms. In short, the court concluded that a subscriber must receive clear and separate notice before assent to the changes could be attributed to him as a result of continued use of the services.

§5.7 STATUTORY RECOGNITION OF ELECTRONIC CONTRACTING

There are both federal and state statutes that recognize the formation of contracts through electronic means. In 1999, the National Conference of Commissioners on Uniform State Laws (NCCUSL)[11] promulgated the Uniform Electronic Transactions Act (UETA), which, like the UCC, is a

---

11. NCCUSL is one of the two bodies that was responsible for drafting the Official Text of the UCC. *See* section 2.7.1.

uniform model law that must be enacted by state legislatures to become effective. It has been enacted by almost every state. In 2000, Congress enacted the Electronic Signatures in Global and National Commerce Act (E-SIGN). These state and federal statutes are similar in scope and language, and E-SIGN defers to state law provided that the state has enacted UETA or an equivalent statute. The statutes have a narrow focus: Their goal is to ensure that general principles of contract formation and validity are applied to electronic transactions. They validate electronic signatures[12] and electronic records (the computerized equivalent of writing) and generally remove legal barriers to the recognition and enforcement of electronic commerce. The statutes do not deal with substantive principles of contract law, which are left to the common law or, in a sale of goods, to UCC Article 2.

§5.8 CONTRACTING BY AUTOMATED MEANS

One or both parties may use technology designed to execute transactions automatically. For example, a seller of goods, services, or software may create a website that automatically accepts orders, without the involvement of a human operator, or a buyer may use an automated system to order inventory from designated suppliers when its stock falls below a specified level. Where a party uses an automated means of making or accepting an offer, he is not actually involved in the transaction at the time that the contract is concluded. However, under the objective test, he has manifested contractual intent by setting up a process for an automated manifestation of assent. Both UETA and E-SIGN recognize this by treating the computer program as the electronic agent of the party who employs it. UETA §2(6) and E-SIGN §7006(3) define an electronic agent as "a computer program or an electronic or other automated means used independently to initiate an action or respond to electronic records or performances in whole or in part without review or action by an individual." UETA §14 and E-SIGN §7001(h) recognize that a contract can be formed by an electronic agent used by one or both parties, even if no human reviews or approves the resulting agreement.

---

12. An electronic signature is the computer equivalent of a signature on paper — some kind of recognizable symbol associated with a party and executed or adopted by the party to validate a writing or record. Signatures, in both traditional and electronic form, are discussed in section 11.3.3 in relation to the statue of frauds.

§5.9 ONLINE AUCTIONS

Many websites (such as eBay) provide a means for users to sell goods or services by auction. The websites require users to consent to a clickwrap or browsewrap agreement that governs the use of the website's services, and likely also provides standard terms that are applicable to transactions on the website. The general rules of contract formation are applicable to online auctions and can be used to determine when an offer was made, what its terms were, and whether and when acceptance occurred.

Examples

1. Spammer's Seaside Resort sent an e-mail to Annette X. Plorer, in which it stated, "Take advantage of our off-season rates! Spend a week at the beach for as little as $1,000! This is a limited-time offer, so visit our website and book now!" Annette visited Spammer's website. After viewing what was available and the prices of various room options, she filled in the appropriate boxes on the website, selecting an arrival and departure date and a seafront room. The website showed that the price of the room for the period was $1,500. Annette clicked on the "Book now" button. Another page appeared, where she filled out her name, address, and credit card information. She then clicked on the "Submit booking" button. A message appeared that set out the particulars of her booking and stated, "Thanks for your booking. Your confirmation number is 100889456. Please print out this page for your records." The next day Annette changed her mind and no longer wished to spend a week at Spammer's Seaside Resort. Has she committed herself to a contract?

2. Dotty Tureed lives in Iowa. She noticed termites in her house. She called in Standard Termite Controls, Inc., a large pest control company with branches across the country. Its local representative visited her home and offered to rid the house of termites for $600. Dotty agreed, and the representative presented her with a document headed "Contract." The document was a single page, printed on both sides. The front page had blanks for the customer information and a description of the work and the price. At the foot of the front page there was a blank for the customer's signature immediately below a sentence in normal, 12-point type that read, "I have read and agree to the terms of this contract, including the terms printed on the reverse side of this page." The reverse side of the page contained 15 numbered paragraphs in normal 12-point type. Dotty signed the front page of the document without turning it around and reading the writing on the reverse. After the work was done, Dotty claimed that the chemical used by

Standard Termite to kill the termites was toxic to humans and had made her ill. She sued Standard Termite for damages in an Iowa court. Standard Termite has moved to dismiss the suit on the grounds that clause 13 on the reverse side of its contract form specifies that all disputes must be resolved in the courts of California, where Standard Termite is headquartered. Is the forum selection clause part of the contract?

3. Standard Terminals, Inc. operates a parking structure. Parker Carr drove his car into the structure. At the entrance, he encountered a ticket dispenser and a boom. When Parker pressed a button on the dispenser, it issued a ticket, which Parker took and put into his pocket. The boom then opened, and Parker drove up to the first place that he found, on the second floor of the structure. He parked his car and left the structure. Had Parker looked at the ticket, he would have seen printed language at the back of the ticket that read, "Floors 1 though 5 of this garage are reserved for holders of monthly parking passes. General public parking is confined to the 6th and 7th floors. Cars parked on floors 1 through 5 without a monthly parking sticker will be towed and released only upon payment of a $200 fine." At the entrance of floors 1 though 5, there is a large sign that reads, "Monthly passes only on this floor. For general parking go to floors 6 and 7. Unauthorized vehicles subject to towing and a $200 fine." Parker does not have a monthly parking pass, but because he did not notice the signs or read his ticket, he did not know that he was not allowed to park on the second floor. Standard Terminals towed his car and refuses to release it unless Parker pays the fine. Is this within Standard Terminals' contractual rights?

4. Fanny Fervent was a devoted fan of the rock group Rolling Rockers, who were scheduled to perform a concert in her city on June 1. On April 1, Fanny visited the website of Ticketmaker.com to buy tickets to the concert. To buy tickets on the website, Fanny had to click on the "Look for tickets" link, printed in blue and underlined. Immediately above the link, there was a sentence in bold print that read, "By clicking on the 'Look for tickets' link, you agree to Ticketmaker's standard terms of use". The words "terms of use" were in blue print and underlined, indicating that they were also a link. Clicking on them would open a page containing the terms of use. One of the terms stated, in capital letters, "DATE AND TIME ARE SUBJECT TO CHANGE. TICKETS MAY BE EXCHANGED FOR A RESCHEDULED PERFORMANCE, BUT IN NO EVENT IS THE CUSTOMER ENTITLED TO A REFUND." Fanny did not click on the "Terms of use" link, but she did click on the "Look for tickets" link and bought tickets for the concert. In late May, the Rolling Rockers cancelled the performance for June 1 and rescheduled it for June 15, a date on which Fanny will be out of town on business and cannot attend. Does Fanny have the right to claim a refund from Ticketmaker?

5. Meg O'Pixel is an amateur photographer. She decided to buy a program to edit and manipulate the photographs taken on her digital camera. She visited a retail store operated by Hard Driver, Inc., a large producer of software, and selected Hard Driver's Fotofabulous program. The program was contained on a disk packaged in a box. The box was adorned by the product's name in a colorful and attractive graphic design. At the back of the box, the following language appeared in the smallest print possible: "©Hard Driver, Inc. All rights reserved. This program is sold subject to the license terms enclosed." Apart from this, there was no mention of license or contract terms on the box. They were also not mentioned by the sales clerk or on the sales receipt.

Meg bought the program, took it home, and inserted the disk into her computer. An installation window appeared that stated: "You are about to install Fotofabulous. The use of this program is subject to license terms. By installing the program, you agree to these terms. Click here to view the terms." The "Click here" was a link to the terms. The window did not give the user any means of proceeding further with the installation without clicking on the link. Meg therefore clicked on it, and a window appeared with a page of terms, preceded by the following boldface language: **"Please read these terms carefully. By clicking on the 'Install' button at the bottom of this page, you indicate your acceptance of these terms and are bound by them."**

Meg did not read the license terms. She just scrolled down to the "Install" button and clicked on it. One of the license terms was a choice of forum clause that required all litigation concerning the contract to be before the courts of California, Hard Driver's home state. A few months after installing the software, Meg claimed that it was defective and unusable. She claims that Hard Driver misrepresented the features and qualities of the program and that it committed a fraud on the public by marketing the program, knowing that it would not work properly. Meg plans to commence a class action suit against Hard Driver. Is she obliged to commence the suit in a California court?

Explanations

1. Section 5.1 noted that the traditional rules of offer and acceptance, formulated on the assumption that the parties actually engage in active bargaining in person, are adaptable enough to be applied to standard form contracting, even when part of the process is automated.

    Spammer's initial e-mail cannot reasonably be interpreted as an offer even though it uses the words "limited-time offer." It proffers the accommodation and its minimum cost ("as little as $1,000") in a general way, without any specific proposal that could be accepted by simple assent to its terms. Such specificity is achieved once Annette has made the selections on the website. It is therefore possible that Spammer makes an offer on its website by showing the selected rooms, prices, and dates as available for booking on the website. (Despite the reference to "as little as $1,000" in the promotional e-mail, the actual offer for the accommodation is $1,500.) If it is an offer, Annette manifests assent to it and accepts by clicking the "Submit booking" button. The listing of products or services on a website may not generally be seen as an offer (in this respect they are similar to advertisements or catalogs), but this is just a usual assumption, not a hard-and-fast rule. The listing on the website must be interpreted in context to determine whether it could reasonably be understood by the customer to be an offer. Marketplace usage and general expectations could play a significant role in deciding whether a customer might reasonably understand the website to be making an offer. If there is any question about the legal effect of inviting customers to enter transactions on a website, the owner of the site can avoid uncertainty on this issue by making it clear on the website whether the customer's submission of the order will conclude a contract. There is no indication in the facts that Spammer did this.

If Spammer's listing of the property on its site is not an offer, Annette's clicking on the "Submit booking" button seems to meet all the criteria of an offer to take the accommodation at a price of $1,500. The window that appeared immediately afterward could be an acceptance. Clearly, the window was generated automatically, so Spammer had no conscious and deliberate intent to accept at the time that the response was sent. However, a party can set up an electronic response in a way that will allow the law to treat the automatic response as an effective acceptance. Modern law has come to recognize that a party can, in effect, create an "electronic agent" to act on its behalf by accepting an offer that the program identifies as meeting predetermined standards. It therefore seems quite likely that Annette has committed herself to a contract.

2. In *Specht v. Netscape Communications* the court felt that a reasonable Internet user would not expect to find terms by scrolling down beyond the "Download" button to a second Web page with a link to the terms. It may be that the court was correct in finding that the website was not structured to provide reasonable notice of the terms to a prudent offeree. However, this does not mean that, by analogy, a person presented with a paper contract has no duty to read terms on the reverse side of the page. The reasonableness of notice and conspicuousness are factual questions, dependent on the context and nature of the transaction. In *Specht*, the court applied a standard of reasonable notice drawn from paper contracting and observed that a person has a duty to read readily available terms of which there is reasonable notice. A set of terms printed in

normal-sized print on the second page of a two-page contract, and referred to just above the signature line on the first page is highly likely to come to the attention of a reasonably prudent offeree. The forum selection clause is therefore likely to be part of the contract.

3. Standard Terminals probably does have the contractual right to tow Parker's car and refuse to release it unless the fine is paid. A contract came into being when Parker drove his car into the structure after taking the ticket. In offer and acceptance terms, Standard, using the dispenser as its electronic agent, made an offer on the terms set out in the ticket. Parker manifested acceptance by proceeding into the garage after receiving the ticket. Parker did not read the ticket, so he did not know what he agreed to, but he will be bound nevertheless if he had a duty to read the ticket before entering the garage, or if he reasonably should have expected to find the term on the ticket. One does not normally expect a driver to pause at the entrance to a parking structure to read the print on the ticket, and such conduct would surely be rewarded by impatient horn honking from vehicles behind him. The unlikelihood that a driver would be able to read the terms on the ticket raises the possibility that Standard did not provide adequate notice of the term. We cannot be sure that a court would reach this conclusion, but it certainly seems like a good argument for Parker to make. Even if Parker did not receive notice of the term set out on the ticket, there were signs to the same effect posted in the garage itself. Again, Parker was not aware of them. It could be that a reasonable person should have seen them, depending on how prominent they were and whether a prudent person would take note of signs as he is navigating the ramps in a garage. Note, also, that even if the signs do provide sufficient notice of the term, they are seen by the driver after the contract is entered into and will therefore not be part of the contract unless the driver should have known of the term at the time of contracting. Standard would have had a stronger assurance of binding Parker if a sign containing the term was in full view as the driver pulled up to the ticket dispenser.

4. This Example is based on *Druyan v. Jagger*, 508 F. Supp. 2d. 228 (S.D.N.Y. 2007). Druyan had bought a ticket to a Rolling Stones concert in Atlantic City through the Ticketmaster website. A while before the concert, Mick Jagger contracted a sore throat, and the Rolling Stones decided to reschedule the show. Ticket holders were told of the rescheduling at 4 P.M. on the day of the concert. Ticketmaster offered to refund the price of the tickets or to exchange them for the rescheduled show, but Druyan declined and commenced a class action[13] in which she sued Mick Jagger,

---

13. *See* footnote 6 for an explanation of class actions. In this case, the class of plaintiffs represented were the holders of tickets to the concert.

the Rolling Stones, Ticketmaster, and others on a number of theories, including breach of contract. She claimed that the defendants had a duty to give her adequate notice of the cancellation and that the late notice had caused her and other members of the class to suffer damages in the form of wasted travel and hotel expenses incurred to attend the concert in Atlantic City. Unfortunately for Druyan, the Ticketmaster website was set up in much the same way as the Ticketmaker website described in the Example: It had a prominent notice that the user agrees to Ticketmaster's terms of use by clicking on the "Look for tickets" button. The notice had a link to the terms of use, which included a term that made it clear that Ticketmaster did not have an obligation to notify ticketholders of cancellations and precluded suit against Ticketmaster for damages. The court dismissed the breach of contract claim against Ticketmaster, holding that regardless of whether Druyan actually read the terms of use, she was bound by them because they were sufficiently conspicuous. (The court also dismissed all her other claims against all the defendants.)

5. Hard Driver's process for binding buyers to its license terms has some similarity to that used by ProCD (*see* section 5.5.2) in that the license terms are not readily apparent when the software is purchased, but are brought to the buyer's attention only when the software is about to be used. However, there are important differences: Unlike ProCD, Hard Driver is itself the seller of the software; there was apparently no reference to the license terms on ProCD's box, but Hard Copy's box does mention the license, albeit in very small print that is not easily noticed; ProCD gave the buyer the right to return the software if the terms were unacceptable, but Hard Driver does not. The term in issue in ProCD related directly to the use of the software, and the restriction was justified by a lower price. The term in issue here is a forum selection clause that is unrelated to the use of the software.

These are important factual differences and could lead to a different result from that reached in *ProCD*. As noted in section 5.5.2, the conclusion in that case is justifiable because ProCD was not the seller of the software and it does not seem to have had any contractual relationship with Zeidenberg at the time that the software was purchased. It was therefore deemed to make an offer by setting out its terms in the manual and the software, and Zeidenberg plausibly accepted the offer by not taking advantage of the right to return the software. The fact that ProCD had charged a lower price for the software to be used for noncommercial purposes also meant that the restriction was necessary to ensure that a buyer did not buy the cheaper consumer package and use it for commercial purposes. Because of these differences, the better analysis is to find that Hard Driver and Meg entered into a contract at the time that Meg bought the software. As a result, Hard Driver cannot unilaterally impose the standard license terms on her after contract formation, so the terms, including the forum selection clause, are not part of the contract unless she knew of them when contracting or had reasonable notice or expectation of them, so that she is deemed to know of them. The tiny print on the box is likely insufficient to alert her to the existence of the standard terms. However, a reasonable buyer of software should expect that the software is subject to terms of use and may have a duty to enquire about them. Even if this is so, it does not necessarily mean that she would be bound by a forum selection clause, which is unrelated to the actual use of the software. A court might hold her to the term if it considers the term fair and reasonably expected, but it might refuse to treat the term as part of the contract if it is not.

6

Mismatching Standard Terms: The "Battle of the Forms" Under UCC §2.207

§6.1 THE SCOPE AND PURPOSE OF UCC §2.207

§6.1.1 The Basic Purpose and Drafting Inadequacies of §2.207

Like all provisions of Article 2, §2.207 applies only where the agreement qualifies as a sale of goods.[1] When it was originally drafted in the mid-twentieth century, §2.207 was a revolutionary provision. It was aimed at reforming the law relating to the sale of goods by eliminating and replacing certain common law offer and acceptance rules (described in section 6.2), which the drafters considered formalistic and inconsistent with commercial practice. Although §2.207 has been partially successful in its goal of bringing the rules of offer and acceptance more into accord with commercial practice, the section is not very well conceived and is poorly drafted. As a result, it has created interpretational difficulties and replaced the formalism of the common law rules with a new set of formalistic problems. In dealing with §2.207 over a period of about 60 years, courts have developed a means of working with it, but it has always been messy, convoluted, and, for the beginner, difficult to penetrate. The revision of Article 2 proposed in 2003 attempted to cure these longstanding problems by completely redrafting §2.207 and simplifying it. However, because the attempt to revise Article 2

---

1. See section 2.7.2 for a discussion of the scope of Article 2.

in 2003 failed,[2] we are stuck with the awkward language of the original version of §2.207, as judicially interpreted.

§6.1.2 The Two Distinct Issues Covered by §2.207: Formation and Confirmation

Section 2.207 was enacted long before the advent of widespread electronic communications, so it is focused on the exchange of paper documents, such as purchase orders, order acknowledgements, and invoices. The key factor that brings §2.207 into force is that there is a conflict or disparity in the terms contained in the written communications used by the parties in the process of forming an agreement for the sale of goods. For example, say that Boilerplate Contractors, Inc., a boilermaker located in Alabama, sends a purchase order form to Ironclad Steelworks, Inc., a steel manufacturer in Pennsylvania, ordering two tons of steel. Boilerplate's order form contains a standard printed clause that states that all disputes arising under the transaction must be resolved by arbitration. Ironclad receives the order and sends an order acknowledgment in which it accepts the order. However, Ironclad's acknowledgement contains a standard printed forum selection clause that states that all disputes under the contract must be litigated in the courts of Pennsylvania. As a result, although the order and acknowledgement are in agreement on the core terms of the sale itself, they have conflicting provisions relating to the resolution of any dispute that may arise in the transaction. (In many cases, at the time that the forms are exchanged, the parties do not realize that there is a conflict in the standard terms because they have not read each other's printed terms.) The purpose of §2.207 is to resolve the question of whether a contract was formed despite this disparity in the offer and response, and, if a contract was formed, which of the conflicting terms became part of the contract. The manner in which §2.207 deals with these matters is discussed in section 6.3.

Although §2.207 is principally involved with the offer and acceptance questions described in the previous paragraph, it also applies in a completely different situation: There is no issue of offer and acceptance because it is clear that a contract has been formed (say, by oral communication). However, one or both of the parties subsequently send a written confirmation of the contract that either adds to or contradicts terms that were agreed to. For example, Boilerplate orders the steel by phone, and Ironclad accepts the order during the phone call. The parties do not discuss the question of how disputes under the agreement will be resolved. Following the phone conversation, Ironclad sends an acknowledgment of the contract to

---

2. See section 2.7.1 for an explanation of the unsuccessful attempt to revise Article 2 in 2003.

Boilerplate in which the printed forum selection clause is included. Here the purpose of §2.207 is not to decide whether a contract was formed through offer and acceptance—the formation occurred during the phone call.[3] Rather, its role is to determine whether the forum selection clause in the acknowledgment became part of the contract. This function of §2.207 is dealt with in section 6.4.

If you study the text of §2.207(1) you may be able to discern that it covers these two separate issues of formation (offer and acceptance) and written confirmation of an oral agreement. This is suggested by reference in §2.207(1) to both an "expression of acceptance" and a "written confirmation." However, the section is poorly drafted, and so it hints at the distinction rather than clearly spelling it out. We will look more closely at the language relating to each of these separate aspects of §2.207 in sections 6.3 and 6.4.

In the illustrations used above, the conflicting terms were preprinted standard terms. Because the use of preprinted standard terms is common, §2.207 usually applies where there is disagreement between the standard terms set out in the parties' paperwork, which explains its nickname, "battle of the forms." However, there is nothing in the language of §2.207 that confines it to situations in which standard terms are used, so it could apply where the conflict or difference arises in transactions that do not involve forms. However, this situation is much less common, and §2.207 cases typically do involve conflicting forms.

§6.1.3 The Application of §2.207 to Electronic Communications

Although §2.207 was drafted with paper documents in mind, there is nothing in its language that precludes its application to electronic communications, such as e-mail. Although the section uses the words "written" and "writings," it is clear in modern law that these words encompass forms of electronic recording. Therefore, had Boilerplate ordered the steel by an e-mail message containing an arbitration clause, and Ironclad had responded by an e-mail message containing a forum selection clause, §2.207 would be

---

3. In some cases, an oral agreement is not enforceable. As discussed in Chapter 11, a sale of goods for a price of $500 or more is subject to the statute of frauds provided for in §2.201. That is, the sales agreement must be memorialized in a writing or electronic record signed by the party against whom it is to be enforced. Therefore, when such a contract is made orally, it exists but cannot be enforced. However, once a written confirmation is sent, the contract becomes enforceable, at least against the sender, if the confirmation meets the requirements of the statute of frauds.

applicable to decide whether a contract had been formed, and if so, which of the conflicting terms was part of the contract.

Note, however, that §2.207 is not normally pertinent where contract formation takes place through the website of one of the parties, because the owner of the website can set up the formation process to avoid a nonconforming response. A clickwrap transaction usually requires the other party to signify assent to the terms provided on the website without any opportunity to proffer its own terms during the contracting process. For example, Boilerplate visits Ironclad's website to order the steel. The website sets out Ironclad's standard terms, including the forum selection clause, and Boilerplate cannot complete its order until it has clicked an "I accept" button on the website. The contract is complete once Boilerplate has done this, and Boilerplate never has the opportunity to proffer its arbitration clause as part of its offer. It cannot effectively add the arbitration clause by sending a standard form after completing its order, because contract formation has already occurred, and the effect of the subsequent communication can be nothing more than a proposal to modify the contract, which Ironclad can ignore or decline without jeopardizing contract formation. Although a browsewrap transaction does not require signification of assent to the standard terms before the order is placed, browsewrap terms usually bind the party submitting the order, and therefore also become part of the contract, provided that the link to them is readily apparent. Therefore, to the extent that web-based contracting replaces contracting by the exchange of forms, §2.207 is implicated in fewer transactions and declines in importance.

§6.2 THE PROBLEM TACKLED BY §2.207: THE COMMON LAW "MIRROR IMAGE" AND "LAST SHOT" RULES

Consider how the traditional rules of offer and acceptance would have resolved the transaction in which Boilerplate sent an order form to Ironclad ordering two tons of steel, and including the printed arbitration clause. Ironclad received and sought to accept the order by sending Boilerplate its standard order acknowledgment. The acknowledgement accords with the order in all respects, except that it includes the forum selection clause that conflicts with the arbitration clause. The parties may not have read each other's forms, and may not have noticed the conflict, so that they thought that they had a contract. However, no contract was formed by the exchange of documents under traditional common law principles, because Ironclad's nonconforming response would be treated as a counteroffer, which Boilerplate never accepted. The drafters of Article 2 considered this result wrong.

They felt that the common law rule that required the acceptance to match the offer exactly (the so-called "mirror image" rule[4]) was too formalistic. The parties did in fact intend a contract, and contract formation should not be precluded simply because there was a discrepancy in the standard terms printed in the offer and acceptance. To allow this preclusion simply aids the party who subsequently looks for a technicality to renege on the contract. Section 2.207 was therefore drafted to eliminate the "mirror image" rule and to allow a court to find a contract if Ironclad's response constituted a definite expression of acceptance, despite the conflicting term. Section 2.207 then contains rules on how the conflicting terms should be handled. As we will discuss in section 6.3, except in limited circumstances, the result is usually that the conflicting term in the acceptance falls away, and the contract is on the offeror's terms.

In the example above neither party had performed under the contract before the formation of contract was challenged. However, if, after the exchange of forms, Ironclad shipped the steel and Boilerplate accepted it, there would no longer be a basis for arguing that no contract was formed. The parties' conduct proves that they both intended to contract. Because traditional common law rules treat the order as the offer and the non-conforming acknowledgment as a counteroffer, Boilerplate's acceptance of the goods becomes its acceptance of the counteroffer by conduct. As a result, a contract is formed on Ironclad's terms, so that the arbitration clause in its original offer falls away, and the parties are deemed to have agreed to the forum selection clause. Because common law tends to find a contract on the terms of the party who sent the last communication before performance, this result is known as the "last shot" rule. The drafters of Article 2 considered the "last shot" rule to be random and formalistic, especially where standard terms are involved. They therefore drafted §2.207 to replace this rule by a different test for deciding whether Ironclad's or Boilerplate's terms should be part of the contract. As explained in section 6.3, there are two alternative resolutions of this situation: If Ironclad's response is an acceptance, the conflicting term in the acceptance enters the contract only in limited circumstances. More likely, it simply falls away, and the contract is on the offeror's terms. If it is not an acceptance, but a counteroffer, the conflicting terms in both parties' forms fall away and are replaced by a gap filler that is supplied by law.

As intimated already, although §2.207 did succeed in eliminating the "mirror image" and "last shot" rules in transactions such as these, it is generally acknowledged to be poorly drafted, difficult to apply, and capable

---

4. As explained in section 4.8, even at common law, many modern courts do not strictly apply the "mirror image" rule, but treat a response as a counteroffer only if it materially varies the terms of the offer.

of leading to results no less arbitrary than those under traditional common law rules.

§6.3 OFFER AND ACCEPTANCE UNDER §2.207

§6.3.1 Section 2.207(1): Acceptance, Rejection, and Counteroffer

The language of §2.207(1), relating to offer and acceptance, may be charted as shown in Diagram 6A.

Diagram 6A

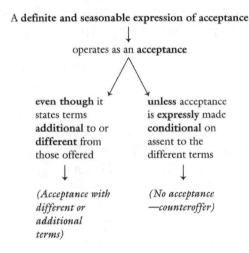

A definite and seasonable expression of acceptance
↓
operates as an **acceptance**

even though it states terms **additional** to or **different** from those offered
↓
(Acceptance with different or additional terms)

unless acceptance is **expressly** made **conditional** on assent to the different terms
↓
(No acceptance —counteroffer)

a. The Offer

Section 2.207(1) provides no guidance on whether the initial communication qualifies as an offer. This question must be resolved under the general common law principles set out in section 4.4. Once an offer is established under common law, §2.207(1) concentrates on the question of whether or not the response is an acceptance. It abolishes the "mirror image" rule, so the response to the offer need not match it exactly to be an acceptance. Instead, a fact-based approach is adopted to distinguish a reply that is clearly not an acceptance (so it can fairly be interpreted at best only as a counteroffer) from a reply that really is an acceptance with terms at variance with the offer. Diagram 6B illustrates this dichotomy.

6. Mismatching Standard Terms

Diagram 6B

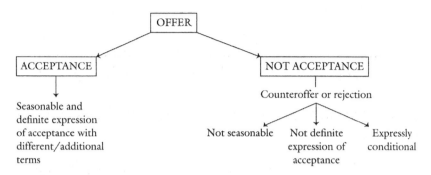

b. Replies That Are Not an Acceptance

If the response is clearly not a definite expression of acceptance or if it is sent after the offer has lapsed (that is, it is not "seasonable") or if it expressly states that acceptance is conditional on assent to its new terms, then it is a rejection or counteroffer.

For example, On June 1, Boilerplate sends a purchase order to Ironclad in which it orders two tons of steel at a stated price, to be delivered by July 1 and paid for on delivery. The offer has no term providing for arbitration, forum selection, or dispute resolution, and it states that it must be accepted by June 5. If Ironclad accepts on June 7, the acceptance is not seasonable and hence ineffective. Similarly, there is no acceptance, even if Ironclad responds in time, if the response states "Thank you for your order. Unfortunately we cannot deliver by July 1, but will make delivery on July 10." Most courts would regard this alteration in the delivery date — one of the transaction-specific terms specified in the offer — to be a counteroffer rather than a definite expression of acceptance.

Even where the variation does not relate to a transaction-specific term and is not central to the performance requested in the offer, the response is not an acceptance if it specifies that acceptance is conditional on the offeror's assent to some new or altered term. So Ironclad makes a counteroffer if it returns a timely acknowledgement in accord with all Boilerplate's proposed terms, but with the added provision: "Your order is accepted on condition that you agree to the following term: Any dispute or claim under this contract shall be litigated in the courts of the state of Pennsylvania. No court of any other state shall have jurisdiction over disputes or claims arising under this contract." This expressly conditional assent could be contained in preprinted standard language. Even if it is, §2.207(1) gives effect to the form of words used in the boilerplate by treating the response as a counteroffer. This is ironical because the purpose of §2.207 is to underplay the effect of boilerplate. As mentioned in section 6.3.2, this is not the only instance in which §2.207 can be interpreted as adopting an inconsistent approach to standard terms.

c. The Result When a Reply Is Not an Acceptance

If the response is not an acceptance, it is either a rejection, which terminates the negotiations, or a counteroffer. As under the common law, a counteroffer terminates the offeree's power of acceptance and creates a new power of acceptance in the former offeror. If the offeror elects to exercise that power, it can accept the counteroffer, creating a contract on the offeree's terms. If not, no contract comes into being unless the parties go ahead and perform. As noted in section 6.2, when such performance follows a counteroffer, §2.207 departs from the common law. Unlike the common law, it does not assume that acceptance of the counteroffer can be inferred merely because the offeror subsequently proceeds with performance of the transaction. The counteroffer is accepted only if it is clear that the offeror was aware of the alteration in terms and manifested assent to it by unambiguous words or action. If there is no such clear acceptance, a contract is recognized by virtue of the performance, but its terms are resolved under §2.207(3), as explained in section 6.3.3.

This may be represented as shown in Diagram 6C.

Diagram 6C

d. A Response That Is an Acceptance with Additional or Different Terms

If the response is a definite and seasonable expression of acceptance, and it is not expressly conditional on assent to any new terms, it is an acceptance even though it states terms different from or additional to those in the offer.

For example, say that Ironclad's response in the last illustration had no language making the acceptance expressly conditional on Boilerplate's assent to the forum selection clause but had simply contained preprinted language stating, "Any dispute or claim under this contract shall be litigated in the courts of the state of Pennsylvania. No court of any other state shall have jurisdiction over disputes or claims arising under this contract." Assume that in the absence of this term, the courts of Alabama (Boilerplate's state) would have had jurisdiction to deal with disputes under the contract. The response is likely to be an acceptance despite the new term. The fact that Ironclad expressed agreement with all the central terms of the offer and that the forum selection clause is set out in a printed standard term gives rise zto the reasonable interpretation that Ironclad's primary focus was on making the sale, and its intent was to accept. A contract is therefore formed, and the question of whether the forum selection clause becomes part of it is dealt with in §2.207(2), discussed below.

Note that §2.207(1) covers both "additional" and "different" terms — a distinction that creates problems discussed in section 6.3.2c. It is not always easy to decide if a term is "additional" or "different," and this depends on the interpretation of the offer and the response. As a rough guideline, a term is different if it varies or contradicts something provided for in the offer, but it is additional if it adds new matter not covered in the offer. Although this guideline is of some help, it may not always easily resolve the ambiguity, as illustrated by the forum selection clause in the above example: Had Boilerplate's order contained an arbitration clause, it would have been quite easy to conclude that the forum selection clause is in conflict and hence "different." However, Boilerplate's order form did not have an arbitration clause and made no mention of dispute resolution or forum selection. In this case, one could characterize Ironclad's forum selection clause as additional because it seems to add a new term that is not covered in the offer. However, the absence of any dispute resolution or forum selection clause in Boilerplate's order would usually be interpreted by implication to allow suit in the courts of an appropriate state other than Pennsylvania. This would mean that the forum selection clause actually conflicts with an implied term in the purchase order, and is therefore "different," rather than "additional."

§6.3.2 Section 2.207(2): The Treatment of Proposals in an Acceptance

The language of §2.207(2) may be charted as shown in Diagram 6D.

6. Mismatching Standard Terms

Diagram 6D

The **additional** terms are construed as **proposals** for addition to the contract.
↓
Between **merchants**

such terms become **part of the contract**
↓
unless:
(a) the **offer expressly limits** acceptance;
(b) they **materially alter** it; or
(c) notification of **objection** to them has already been given or is given within a reasonable time after notice of them is received.

a. The Scope and Basic Purpose of §2.207(2)

Section 2.207(2) only applies if the response to an offer is found to be an acceptance. It does not apply to a counteroffer, which only leads to a contract if accepted or if performance occurs as contemplated by §2.207(3). Because §2.207(1) contemplates that a contract exists despite a variance between the terms of the offer and acceptance, §2.207(2) treats any such additional terms as proposals that do not become part of the contract unless the conditions in the subsection are satisfied.

b. The Grounds for Excluding Proposals from the Contract

Section 2.207(2) is couched in deceptively positive terms. It says that the additional terms enter the contract *unless* one of the stated exceptions apply, but this is a very big "unless." The exceptions leave the rule applicable only to relatively unimportant terms in a small range of cases. In most situations, the offeree does not succeed in adding terms in the acceptance, and the general impact of §2.207(2) is to exclude most proposed additions. We now examine each of the exclusions. Note that they do not all have to be satisfied for the term to be excluded. If any one applies, the term does not enter the contract.

i. Additional Terms Do Not Become Part of the Contract Unless Both Parties Are Merchants

The concept of a merchant in Article 2 was introduced in section 2.7.2. The definition of "merchant" in §2.104(1) is much broader than in common usage. It includes not only a person who deals in goods of that kind, but also one who, by following a particular occupation, has or represents having knowledge or skill concerning the goods. Therefore, as

6. Mismatching Standard Terms

Comment 1[5] to §2.104 points out, even a person that does not trade in the goods could be a merchant if that person is a "professional" user of the goods, as opposed to a "casual or inexperienced seller or buyer." Section 2.207(2) requires that the transaction be "between merchants." They must both be merchants, and if either of them is not a merchant, this ends the matter. The proposals do not become part of the contract, even if none of the other exclusions apply.

ii. The Term Does Not Enter the Contract If It Materially Alters It

Materiality is a complex issue, to be discussed more fully in section 17.3. Simply speaking, a term is material if it provides for an important aspect of the contractual performance. That is, it is a significant element of the exchange bargained for by a party. Although some terms are more obviously important than others, one can seldom decide materiality in the abstract. The contract must be interpreted in context to decide if the provision in question did occupy this central role in the bargain. This concept is expressed in the context of proposals under §2.207(2) by Comment 4 to §2.207. It says that a proposed alteration in an acceptance is material and does not enter the contract if it would result in "surprise or hardship" to the other party.

"Surprise" is determined with reference to reasonable expectations in light of common practice and usage. If a particular term is widely used, the party has reason to assume that it would be part of the contract, and its inclusion should be no surprise. (Of course if it is that common, it may be implied in the oral agreement or offer in any event.) "Hardship" means that the term imposes an unbargained-for burden (financial or otherwise) on, or detracts significantly from, the reasonable expectations of the other party. The concept of hardship does not do much to help resolve the question of whether an alteration is material, because it begs the question of materiality rather than helping to answer it: A material alteration causes hardship, therefore it is material.

The Comment's use of the disjunctive "or" is misleading because the concepts of surprise and hardship are usually both elements of materiality and, in most cases, must both be satisfied to some degree. That is, even an important alteration may not be material if its inclusion should be fully expected, and a trivial alteration should not be treated as material, even if it is unexpected. The basic point of the exclusion is this: Even if the sale is between merchants, a proposed term does not enter the contract if it has more than a minimal impact on the exchange, and it is not sufficiently

---

5. Section 2.7.1 introduced the role and effect of comments to the UCC. They are the drafter's explanation of the intent and purpose of code sections. They are very influential but are not part of the statute.

common to be expected. If you apply this principle to the forum selection clause in Ironclad's response to Boilerplate's offer, you can see how tricky the question of materiality may be. Although the forum selection clause does not relate to a central aspect of the transaction, such as the nature of the goods sold, the price, payment terms, or delivery terms, the waiver of the right to sue in a court other than in Pennsylvania may or may not be material. This is not a question that can be decided without reference to all the facts of the transaction and its context.

In *Rocheux International of N.J., Inc. v. U.S. Merchants Financial Group*, 741 F. Supp. 2d 651 (D. N.J. 2010), the court considered the concept of materiality in relation to §2.207(2). The case involved multiple disputes arising out of the sale of a large quantity of raw plastic from Rocheux to U.S. Merchants. One of the issues in the case was whether the parties' contract contained a term that obligated the buyer to pay a service charge on outstanding balances plus collection costs and attorney's fees. The seller contended that this term became part of the contract because it was included in the standard order confirmations that it sent to the buyer following each of the buyer's orders. Both parties were merchants, so the crucial issue was whether the term materially altered the contract. The court noted that the determination of materiality involves a complex inquiry including both legal and factual elements, encompassed within the "surprise or hardship" standard set out in Comment 4. A term is unreasonably surprising if, under all the circumstances (including such factors as the prominence of the term in the writing, industry custom, and any course of dealings between the parties) it cannot be presumed that a reasonable merchant would have expected or consented to the term. The court found that the buyer could not claim unfair surprise because the term was prominently displayed in multiple acknowledgments sent to the buyer over an extensive course of dealings and was not an uncommon provision in transactions of this kind. Although the total amount due for interest and attorney's fees would be substantial — about $3 million — this did not, in itself, impose unfair hardship on the buyer because the inclusion of the term was not an unfair surprise, and the amount of the liability was within the range of commercial practice.

iii. The Term Does Not Enter the Contract If the Offer Limits Acceptance to Its Terms

Even if the parties are merchants and the term is not material, it does not become part of the contract if there is language in the offer expressly limiting acceptance to its terms. This means that an offeror can simply eliminate the possibility of proposals entering the contract by putting appropriate standard language in the offer. This again raises the issue noted in the discussion of preprinted "expressly conditional" language in a purported acceptance. By giving effect to standardized exclusions or conditions, §2.207 breaks faith with its avowed purpose of disregarding boilerplate.

iv. The Term Does Not Enter the Contract If the Offeror Objects

If the offer did not limit acceptance to its terms, the offeror still has an opportunity to eliminate the proposal by subsequent objection, either in anticipation of the proposal or within a reasonable time of acquiring notice of it. This appears to contemplate not only a deliberate objection but also a standard objection issued by the offeror as a matter of course. This again raises the inconsistency displayed by §2.207 in its reaction to boilerplate.

c. The Omission of "Different" Terms from the Text of §2.207(2)

As noted in section 6.3.1, §2.207(1) refers to "additional" and "different" terms, while §2.207(2) only mentions "additional" terms. This has created two problems. First (as stated in section 6.3.1) it is not always easy to tell if a term is "additional" or "different." Second, it is not clear if the omission of "different" terms in §2.207(2) was really intended or was just an oversight. The failure to include "different" terms in §2.207(2) has led courts to adopt divergent approaches to the treatment of terms found to be "different."

Some courts have treated the omission as inadvertent and have applied the subsection irrespective of whether the term may be classified as "additional" or "different." This approach has some support in Comment 3, which seems to assume that both fall within §2.207(2). (The Comment is not entirely clear on this point because it makes this remark in relation to confirmations, not acceptances.) It also has the obvious advantage of eliminating the problem of struggling to distinguish them.

Other courts have taken §2.207(2) literally and have held that because "different" terms are not in the subsection, they must simply be disregarded. Once it is held that the response is an acceptance, there is no basis in principle for allowing this unilateral proposal for a "different" term to slip into the contract, and it must be excluded. The fact that "different" terms are not mentioned in §2.207(2) suggests not that they be treated more favorably than "additional" terms, but that they be treated less so. In other words, the "different" term can never become part of the contract, even if it meets all the tests for inclusion in §2.207(2).

A third approach is to treat the conflicting terms as cancelling each other out. Some courts have reasoned that if the purpose of §2.207 is to take boilerplate less seriously, it makes no sense to prefer one party's "different" term over that of the other. Therefore, they should both fall away and be replaced by whatever term the law would supply in the absence of agreement. (This has been called the "knockout" rule.) Although this approach seems to accord with the spirit of §2.207, there is no basis for it in the express provisions of the section. It sounds a little like the solution prescribed in §2.207(3), but that provision applies only where the parties perform despite their failure to conclude a contract. It is not directly on point and is at best justified by analogy when the offer has been accepted and the issue is whether a proposed "different" term in the acceptance is included in the contract.

§6.3.3 Section 2.207(3): The Effect of Mutual Performance When No Contract Is Formed by the Parties' Writings

The language of §2.207(3) may be charted as shown in Diagram 6E.

Diagram 6E

Conduct by both parties
that recognizes the existence of a contract
is **sufficient to establish a contract** for sale
↓
although
the writings of the parties do not otherwise establish a contract.
↓
In such a case
the terms of the particular contract consist of
those terms on which the **writings** of the parties **agree**
together with
any **supplementary terms** incorporated under any other provisions of this Act

Section 2.207(3) only applies when there is no contract formed by the writings — typically because the offeree's response is not an acceptance with additional or different terms but a counteroffer which has never been deliberately accepted. As noted earlier, the common law "last shot" rule treated the offeror's performance as an acceptance by conduct of the counteroffer, thereby imposing the risk of inadvertent assent to the offeree's variation in terms.

Section 2.207(3) seeks to avoid this unfair imposition. If no contract was formed by the writings of the parties, but their conduct (typically in the form of tendering and accepting performance) shows that they intend a contract, the contract is recognized as existing. However, its terms are not simply those contained in the last communication. The contract includes only those terms on which the parties' writings agree, and all conflicting terms fall away. Any gaps in the contract are filled by supplementary terms recognized by the UCC. If there is any applicable trade usage or course of dealing or performance between the parties, the missing terms can be supplied as a matter of factual implication.[6] Failing that, Article 2 itself provides a number of standard terms (known as "gap fillers") that are implied as a matter of law into all sales of goods unless excluded by the contract. (For example, unless the parties agree otherwise, §2.308 states that delivery must take place at the seller's premises; §2.310 requires payment on delivery; and §§2.314 and 2.315 provide for minimum warranties.) If Article 2 does not have a gap filler that covers the particular gap in question, there may be a default term recognized by common law that can be used to fill the gap.

To illustrate the operation of §2.207(3) reconsider the example in section 6.3.1b in which Boilerplate ordered two tons of steel. The offer did not have an arbitration provision and made no reference to dispute resolution or forum selection. Ironclad responded by accepting the order expressly on the condition that Boilerplate agree to Ironclad's standard forum selection clause. It was noted in section 6.3.1b that the expressly conditional language makes the response a counteroffer. Boilerplate never communicates assent to this condition. In fact, having not read the reply, Boilerplate is not even aware of the term. Ironclad ships the steel and it is accepted by Boilerplate. Some time later, Boilerplate has a dispute with Ironclad over the quality of the steel, and sues Ironclad in Alabama, Boilerplate's home state. In the absence of the forum selection clause, the Alabama court would have jurisdiction over the litigation, but Ironclad insists that Boilerplate has agreed to sue only in Pennsylvania. Under common law, Boilerplate's conduct in accepting the delivery would be deemed an acceptance of the counteroffer, making Ironclad's forum selection clause part of the contract. Under §2.207(3), however, a contract is recognized only on the terms on which the writings agree (description, quantity, price, delivery, and payment) and the forum selection clause falls away. The resulting gap may be filled by trade usage, if any such usage exists and is applicable. If not, it is filled by a gap filler supplied by Article 2, or, if Article 2 does not address that issue, by a general principle of common law. Article 2 does not address questions of jurisdiction, so this question must be settled by common law principles. The general principle under common law is that in the absence of a forum selection clause, suit may be brought in any court that has jurisdiction over the litigation. Therefore, in this case, the result under §2.207(3) happens to favor Boilerplate by upholding the dispute resolution provision that the law implies into its offer. By contrast, say that Boilerplate's original offer contained the arbitration clause. Under

---

6. The role of trade usage, course of dealing, and course of performance in the interpretation of contractual intent is discussed in section 10.6.2. For the present, it is enough to understand in general terms that the context in which the parties made their contract often provides much useful information on what they must have intended their contract terms to be.

§2.207(3), both Boilerplate's arbitration clause and Ironclad's forum selection clause would be knocked out, and the resulting gap in contract would be filled by the general principle that disputes must be resolved by lawsuit, and that Boilerplate, as plaintiff, may select any forum that has jurisdiction over the litigation. Here, the general rule of law provides a neutral result that is different from both parties' conflicting terms.

§6.4 WRITTEN CONFIRMATION FOLLOWING AN ORAL OR INFORMAL CONTRACT UNDER §2.207(1) AND (2)

It is impossible to decipher the provisions of §2.207(1) with regard to written confirmations. The subsection seems to say that ". . . a written confirmation that is sent within a reasonable time operates as an acceptance even though it states terms additional to or different from those . . . agreed upon, unless acceptance is expressly made conditional on assent to the additional or different terms."

However, this makes no sense. The written confirmation apparently follows an agreement. Although §2.207(1) does not say what this agreement might be, Comment 1 indicates that the drafters contemplated a situation in which an oral or informal agreement is followed by written confirmations. Presumably, this means that the parties have actually made a contract already. If so, the subsequent writing cannot be an acceptance, conditional or otherwise. The process of offer and acceptance has already been concluded.[7] If a contract already exists, the purpose of any confirmations is, of course, to confirm what has been agreed. This may be motivated by a need to satisfy the statute of frauds or simply by a desire to create a written record of the transaction.

Therefore, the references to acceptance in §2.207(1) are inappropriate in the context of confirmations and should be disregarded. This leaves us with just a few snippets of disjointed statutory language to interpret. What it seems to be trying to say is:

1. If an oral or informal contract is formed,
2. and if one or both parties thereafter send written confirmations,
3. and one or both confirmations go beyond or vary what was agreed orally or informally,

---

7. As mentioned in footnote 3, the contract is fully enforceable in its oral form unless the price of the goods is $500 or more, in which case it does not become enforceable until reduced to writing sufficient to comply with the statute of frauds.

4. any terms that add to or differ from the oral contract cannot simply become part of the contract,
5. but must be treated as proposals in the same way as proposals in an acceptance.

This leads to the conclusion that where confirming memoranda are involved, the only issue is whether the additional or different terms in a confirmation become part of the contract. This question is decided using the same analysis, set out in section 6.3.2, as would be used if the additional or different term were contained in an acceptance. The one difference, of course, is that one is not so much concerned with a clash between conflicting writings (in fact, only one party may have sent a confirmation) but between one or more writings and the original oral or informal agreement.

Section 2.207(3) states that it governs where conduct establishes contractual intent but "... the writings of the parties do not otherwise establish a contract." If mutual performance occurs after a confirmation, a literal reading of §2.207(3) suggests that it is applicable. The contract arises, not from the writings but from the earlier oral agreement. This is surely not the intent. Section 2.207(3) is meant to deal with situations in which no contract would exist in the absence of performance and not where an oral contract has been concluded. Remember, however, that although §2.207(3) is not directly applicable, some courts have followed its spirit by adopting the "knockout" rule when a confirmation has terms "different" from the oral contract.

§6.5 A TRANSNATIONAL PERSPECTIVE ON THE "BATTLE OF THE FORMS"

Both the UNIDRIOT Principles and the CISG contain general principles of acceptance that can be used to address conflicts between terms in an offer and acceptance.

Article 2.1.11 of the UNIDROIT Principles sets out the broad general principle relating to all forms of acceptance: A response to an offer is a counteroffer if its terms digress materially from the offer, but a response with nonmaterial alterations qualifies as an acceptance unless the offeror objects. In the absence of objection, the terms in the acceptance become part of the contract. Article 2.1.12 adopts a similar approach to additional or different terms in a confirmation, which become part of the contract unless they are material or are objected to. Where standard forms are used by the parties, Article 2.1.22 specifically addresses the "battle of the forms" and provides for a form of knockout rule: Where the parties use standard forms and reach agreement except on the standard terms, the contract consists of those terms on which the writings agree, including the standard terms that are essentially the same. One-sided standard terms fall away. However, both parties have the ability to reject the contract by notice.

The CISG does not have a provision that deals specifically with "battle of the forms" situations, so its general principles of acceptance apply where a conflict arises in the exchange of forms. CISG Article 19(1) treats a response to an offer as a counteroffer if it contains modifications of the offer, but Article 19(2) relaxes this "mirror image" approach by recognizing the response as an acceptance if the modifications are nonmaterial. They become part of the contract unless the offeror objects to them without delay. Article 19(3) contains a list of examples of material alterations, which includes price, payment, quantity, delivery, and dispute resolution terms.

Examples

1. Carr Buff's hobby is restoring vintage cars. After working on it for many years, he just completed the restoration of a 1957 Ford. On December 15, he parked the car in the parking lot of a shopping mall. When he returned to it, he found a note stuck under the windshield wiper that read: "Dear owner of 1957 Ford: I love this car and would like to buy it from you. I offer to pay you $100,000 for it, which I will pay on delivery of the car and its title papers. If you would like to sell the car to me, please reply to the address below as soon as possible, but not later than December 20. On your acceptance, we will arrange a date to complete this transaction before Christmas." The note was signed by Rod Hott, and contained a street address.

    After thinking about the offer for a couple of days, Carr decided to accept it. On December 18 he mailed a letter to Rod in which he said, "I agree to sell the Ford to you for $100,000. Please note that payment must be in cash or by cashier's check. Call me as soon as you get this letter to arrange the time for delivery. Note, however, that I sell the car to you on condition that you agree to return it to me for one day on February 15 next year, because I have already entered it in an antique car exhibition on that day." Rod received the letter on December 21.

    a. Do Rod and Carr have a contract on December 21?

    b. If so, what are its terms?

    c. Assume that after Rod received Carr's letter on December 21, he called Carr and they arranged for delivery on December 24. Carr delivered the Ford and the title to Rod, who handed Carr a cashier's check for $100,000. Neither party said anything about Carr borrowing the Ford for the exhibition on February 15. On February 10, Carr called Rod to arrange to collect the car for the exhibition, but Rod refused to give it to him, claiming that he had no contractual obligation to do so. Is Rod correct?

2. Ballet de la Forms, Inc., a manufacturer of dance apparel, needed to replenish its stock of fabric. It submitted a written purchase order to Material Alterations, Inc., a fabric manufacturer, in which it specified the description, quantity, and price of the fabric ordered as well as the delivery date and payment terms. Ballet's order form contained a pre-printed term that stated, "Ballet de la Forms shall have the right to return unused goods to the seller within 60 days of delivery of the goods under this order. Acceptance of this offer is limited to the terms stated in this purchase order." Material Alterations received the order on the next day and immediately mailed its order acknowledgment to Ballet. Unquestionably, the response was mailed and received in good time and before the offer had lapsed. The acknowledgment expressed assent to the order and accorded in all respects with the order, except that it contained a printed term that stated: "Return Policy: Goods may be returned only if defective. No returns will be accepted for any other reason." Material Alterations has not yet shipped the goods. Do the parties have a contract? If so, what is the contract's term relating to return of the goods?

3. Tutu O'Severn decided to take up dance lessons. She needed a tutu, so she searched the web and found the website of Ballet de la Forms, Inc., a supplier of dance apparel. She selected a tutu for $150, clicked on it to place it in her virtual "shopping cart," and filled out the online order form in which she inserted her name, e-mail address, shipment and billing address, and credit card particulars. In the box called "delivery options," she selected "standard, 1 to 2 weeks delivery." She clicked the "submit" button. A couple of seconds later, an automated response headed "Order Confirmation" appeared on the screen. It set out a confirmation number, the details of the order as submitted by Tutu, and instructions on how she could track the progress of the shipment.

Two days later, Tutu received an e-mail from Ballet, which stated, "Thank you for your order. Regrettably we are out of stock of the item that you ordered. We expect new supplies shortly and will ship as soon as possible. Please allow 4 to 6 weeks for delivery." Tutu was disappointed, but resigned herself to wait for the tutu.

Three weeks later, Tutu received another e-mail from Ballet, which said, "We are pleased to inform you that the tutu that you ordered is now in stock. Unfortunately, the manufacturer has increased the price since you placed your order, and the tutu now costs $250. If you would still like to buy the tutu at the new price, please resubmit your order." Tutu insists that she had already bought the tutu at the original price and that Ballet is obliged to deliver it to her at that price. Is she correct?

4. In addition to a tutu, Tutu needed tights for her dance lessons. She called Leo Tard, a specialist in dancing attire, and ordered three pairs of tights for a total of $350. She arranged with Leo that the tights would be delivered C.O.D. within a week. Leo immediately shipped the tights to Tutu, accompanied by his standard invoice. The invoice stated "For sanitary reasons, we cannot accept the return of clothing delivered to a customer. All sales are final once the clothing leaves our premises." By the time that Tutu received the tights, a week later, she had changed her mind about taking dancing lessons and no longer wants the tights. Leo insists that she has bought them and cannot return them. Is he right?

5. Ballet de la Forms, Inc., a retailer of dance apparel, sent an e-mail to Formfitting Fashion Fabricators, Inc., in which it ordered 1,000 pairs of tights. The order simply contained the quantity, price, and description of the goods and the particulars relating to payment and delivery. Formfitting responded by e-mail on the same day, acknowledging the order and agreeing to supply the tights on the terms set out in Ballet's e-mail. Formfitting's e-mail contained a standard term, automatically included in all its order acknowledgements, stating that any dispute arising out of the sale would be resolved by final and binding arbitration under the rules of the American Arbitration Association and the Federal Arbitration Act. The goods were shipped and accepted, but a dispute has arisen about their quality. The parties concede that they are both merchants, that Formfitting's e-mail was an acceptance of Ballet's offer, and that the arbitration provision is an additional term in the acceptance, to be dealt with under §2.207(2). However, they disagree on whether the arbitration provision should fall away as a material alteration of the contract. How can you tell if it is a material alteration?

Explanations

1. a. This is a sale of goods, so §2.207 applies. Although it is nicknamed the "battle of the forms," §2.207 is not confined to transactions in which forms are used. Article 2 does not deal with the question of whether a communication qualifies as an offer, so general common law principles apply. Rod's letter appears to qualify as an offer. It sets out the terms on which he proposes to buy the car, and can be reasonably understood to confer a power of acceptance on the offeree. Although Rod does not know who the owner of the car is, he has addressed the offer to the owner, an identifiable person.

Carr intends to accept. Unless the offer clearly prescribes a particular mode of acceptance, §2.206 permits acceptance in any manner and medium reasonable under the circumstances. Rod included his address on the offer, and did not specify a method of acceptance. Therefore, a response by mail is authorized because Rod has furnished his street address, and there is nothing to indicate that mail would not be a reasonable mode of acceptance. As Rod invites response by mail, the "mailbox" rule applies. Therefore, assuming that Carr properly stamped and addressed the letter, his acceptance took effect on December 18 before the offer lapsed, even though Rod only received the letter on December 21.

Under §2.207(1), a response qualifies as an acceptance if it is a definite and seasonable expression of acceptance. We have determined that it was seasonable (that is, timely). It is more difficult to decide if Carr's letter was a definite expression of acceptance. His response does not exactly accord with the offer. His statement that the price must be paid in cash or by cashier's check does not deviate from the offer because payment in cash on delivery is implied in the offer. (Rod's letter is silent on the method of payment, and in the absence of agreement to the contrary this is the payment term implied by §2.310.) Carr's condition about borrowing the Ford on February 15 does go beyond the terms of the offer. He says that he sells the car to Rod "on condition that you agree to return it to me for one day on February 15." This conditional language appears to qualify Carr's assent to the contract, and could be interpreted as making his acceptance expressly conditional on assent to the new term. If so, the statutory qualification in §2.207(1) applies and the section treats the letter as a counteroffer. It is therefore not a definite expression of acceptance. Courts tend to interpret the "expressly conditional" element of §2.207(1) narrowly, so it is conceivable that a court may find that the borrowing of the car is merely a proposal for a term in the contract, and not a condition of acceptance. (To reach this result, a court would have to strain against the rather clear language of Carr's letter.) If Carr's letter is a counteroffer, the parties never reached agreement because Rod did not accept it, and the parties have no contract on December 21. If the term about borrowing the Ford does not make Carr's response expressly conditional, Carr's letter otherwise indicates a desire to accept the offer, so it could qualify as a definite expression of acceptance, which would result in the parties having made a contract on December 21. Question (b) deals with the content of the contract.

b. If we assume that Carr's response was an acceptance rather than a counteroffer, the term becomes a proposal for addition to the contract. A proposal for a new term in the acceptance does not normally become part of the contract, but §2.207(2) creates a narrow exception to this rule. Section 2.207(2) does not apply unless both parties are merchants. The facts do not indicate what Rod does for a living. He may be a dealer in antique cars, or may just be a consumer who liked the Ford and wanted it for personal use. Carr restores old cars as a hobby, but that does not in itself make him a merchant. To qualify as a merchant under §2.104(1), Carr would have to deal in antique cars or hold himself out, by virtue of his occupation, "as having knowledge or skill peculiar to the practices or goods involved in the transaction." This language is not broad enough to cover a hobbyist who may make the occasional, isolated sale of a car that he has restored. If we conclude that either party is not a merchant, §2.207(2) does not apply. Therefore, although a contract is formed under §2.207(1), there is no provision in §2.207 that tells us what to do with the additional term. Therefore, the common law rule applies, and the additional term is nothing more than a proposal for a post-formation modification. Because Rod never agreed to the modification, Carr has no contractual right to have the car returned for the purpose of the exhibition. If both parties were merchants, §2.207(2) would apply. (There is an interpretational difficulty relating to the omission of the word "different" in §2.207(2), as explained in section 6.3.2. On our facts, we can probably skirt that difficulty because the proposed term relating to Carr's use of the Ford on February 15 seems to be additional rather than different. As a general rule of thumb, we can consider a term additional if it adds to rather than contradicts the offer.) As the offer did not expressly limit acceptance to its terms, and Rod did not give notification of objection to the term, §2.207(2) will incorporate the term into the contract unless it materially alters it. Materiality is a question of interpretation, to be decided by determining the parties' reasonable intent in light of the circumstances of the transaction and the parties' reasonable expectations. We cannot answer the question of materiality without a further exploration of these matters, but it may be that an obligation to lend the car to the seller for one day for purposes of exhibition may not constitute a material alteration of the offer. If so, the term would become part of the contract if both parties are merchants. If not, it falls away.

c. The parties have now proceeded with performance of the contract, so there is no longer any question of whether a contract exists. If Carr's response was an acceptance with a proposal for an additional term, the fact that the parties have performed the exchange would not be significant. The analysis to decide if the proposal became part of the contract would be the same as in question (b): If the parties were both merchants and the term was not a material alteration of the offer, it would have entered the contract under §2.207(2) and Rod would be obliged to lend the Ford to Carr on February 15. Otherwise, the term did not become part of the contract, and Carr has no right to borrow the Ford.

However, if Carr's response was not an acceptance but a counteroffer, the parties' subsequent performance is important because it would create a contract under §2.207(3). Section 2.207(3) applies where the conduct of both parties recognizes the existence of a contract, even though their writings do not otherwise do so. The resulting contract is on the terms on which the writings agree, supplemented by Article 2 gap fillers. Because the term relating to Carr's use of the Ford on February 15 is not one on which the writings agree, and there is no default rule under Article 2 that allows a seller to regain temporary possession of the goods for exhibition purposes, Carr has no right to demand the Ford.

2. It seems clear that Ballet's order form was an offer. The question is therefore whether Material Alterations' acknowledgment with the conflicting term on return of the goods was an acceptance and, if it was, whether Ballet's or Material Alterations' term became part of the contract. Under the traditional common law "mirror image" rule, the conflicting term in the acknowledgment relating to return of the goods would make it a counteroffer. However, Material Alterations' acknowledgment, which expresses agreement on all the transaction-specific terms and conflicts with the offer only in the boilerplate, seems to be exactly the kind of response that §2.207(1) would treat as a definite and seasonable expression of acceptance, rather than a counteroffer.

This being so, there is a contract, and the question to be resolved is which of the conflicting terms becomes part of it. Section 2.207(2) is designed to deal with this issue, but it only applies if both parties are merchants. In this case, both do clearly qualify as merchants, so it would seem that §2.207(2) will resolve this question except for one other twist: Material Alterations' term directly conflicts with Ballet's term, and so it is better characterized as "different" rather than "additional." Some courts decline to apply §2.207(2) to "different" terms because the subsection refers only to "additional" terms. A court that adopts this approach will find that as there is nothing in §2.207 that allows the term to enter the contract, it simply falls away. On this analysis, the contract is on Ballet's terms.

Other courts treat the omission of "different" from §2.207(2) as inadvertent and apply it irrespective of whether the term is "different" or "additional." On this analysis, Material Alterations' term enters the contract only if none of the barriers in §2.207(2) apply. We probably have to go no further than §2.207(2)(a), which excludes the proposal for an addition to the contract if the offer expressly limits acceptance to the terms of the offer. Ballet included such language in its order form, so Material Alterations' term cannot enter the contract, and we do not need to agonize over whether it is material.

Although there is no statutory language authorizing it, some courts adopt a third approach to "different" terms, under which they use a knockout rule to resolve the conflict. On this approach, both terms relating to return of the goods are eliminated, and the question of whether Ballet can return unsold goods must be resolved by trade usage or, if none exists, by a gap filler. Article 2 makes no provision for the return of goods in the absence of a defect, so the neutral principles of article 2 would favor Material Alterations in this situation.

3. Ballet could have set up its website differently so that a contract would have been formed upon Tutu's order submission. However, it has chosen not to do business in this way. Note, also, that there is no question here of whether Tutu is bound through clickwrap or browsewrap assent to any standard terms proffered by Ballet. The question simply involves an analysis of offer and acceptance principles to determine whether the parties made a contract through their communication.

Unless the language or the circumstances strongly indicate otherwise, the usual assumption is that the proffering of goods on a website, catalog, or advertisement is not an offer, but a solicitation for offers from the public. We are not told exactly what the website said, but we will assume that there was nothing in its language to overturn the usual assumption. Tutu's order was made on an electronic form supplied by Ballet, but this does not detract from the order's qualities as an offer, and it can reasonably be interpreted as such. It sets out the terms of the proposed transaction with particularity and reasonably appears to invite acceptance by shipment or promise to ship the goods. Ballet's immediate automated response might conceivably be seen as an acceptance, but this is not likely. It has no language that signifies assent to the order, and seems to do no more than confirm that the order was received.[8]

Ballet's e-mail a couple of days later could qualify as an acceptance, but it changes one of the terms of the offer — the time of delivery. We must therefore decide if this makes the e-mail a counteroffer or a response with a proposal for a different term. Ballet's e-mail does have some indication of assent to the offer — it seems to accede to the order and undertakes to ship as soon as possible. However, it also makes it clear that it cannot ship by the date specified in the offer. To treat it as an acceptance with a proposal for change would place Ballet in the risky position of simultaneously accepting and repudiating the terms of the offer. It is therefore more reasonable to interpret Ballet's response as a counteroffer, which will not bind it to a contract unless Tutu agrees to the new delivery term. If that is so, Tutu apparently did agree subjectively,

---

8. If the automated response had been an acceptance, it would bind Ballet because the software program running its website would constitute its electronic agent, as explained in section 5.8. However, the question of electronic agency does not arise because the automated response was not an acceptance.

even though she did not manifest this agreement expressly. Silence is not normally regarded as effective assent under common law, and this is even more so under §2.207, which operates on the assumption that people do not read forms, and requires an articulated expression of assent to bind a party. Notwithstanding, because it serves Tutu's interests to treat her silence as acquiescence, the need to protect her from inadvertent acceptance of the counteroffer falls away. A court may therefore hold Ballet to the counteroffer on the grounds that Tutu did assent to it, and Ballet, by saying that it would ship as soon as possible, impliedly dispensed with the need to communicate assent. If we find either that Ballet's response was an acceptance with a proposed different term,[9] or a counteroffer that was accepted by Tutu, Ballet is bound to deliver the tutu at the original price.

4. The facts make it clear that Tutu and Leo made an oral contract on the phone. Because an enforceable contract came into existence at the time of the telephone call,[10] there are no offer and acceptance issues implicated in Leo's response. The only question to be decided is if Leo's "no return" term was part of the contract. The garbled language of §2.207(1) muddles the very different situations that occur when the additional or different terms are in a confirmation rather than an acceptance. However, where a post-contractual confirmation is concerned, the purpose of the section is not to raise an offer and acceptance issue, but simply to provide the same rule for confirmations as applies to additional or different terms in an acceptance. That is, they only become part of the contract if both parties are merchants and none of the three other barriers to entry in §2.207(2) apply. Because Tutu is not a merchant, the answer is simple: an additional or different term in the confirmation does not become part of the contract. The twist here is that Leo's term may not actually be additional or different on the facts of the case. It may have been if, for example, the question was whether it precluded the return of defective goods, because it would then have conflicted with the warranty of merchantability that would have been implied in Tutu's offer. However, the issue here is whether Tutu can reject goods that are in conformity with the contract, purely on the ground that she no longer wants them. In the

---

9. Even if we decided that the response was an acceptance with a different term, we would not have to go through the agony of determining if the later delivery date became part of the contract, because that is not in issue. However, it is worth noting, just for the sake of exercise, that if this had been an issue, the term would not have entered the contract under §2.207(2) because Tutu is not a merchant. In any event, as the term is "different" rather than additional, some courts would not apply §2.207(2), even in a sale between merchants.

10. The price of the goods is less than $500, so the sale is not subject to the statute of frauds and the oral agreement is enforceable. Had the price been $500 or more, the oral agreement would not have been enforceable on its own, so the subsequent written confirmation would have had to be a writing sufficient to satisfy the statute of frauds.

absence of a term in her offer that gives her this right (whether express or implied by clear and accepted usage), she cannot simply change her mind and refuse to accept the goods. Therefore, on these particular facts (and assuming the absence of an established usage), Leo's term does not add anything that would not already be implied as a matter of law in the offer.

5. Ballet's order was silent on the means of dispute resolution, and Formfitting's acknowledgement includes a standard arbitration provision. Because the parties have conceded all other issues arising out of §§2.207(1) and (2), the only question raised by this Example is whether the additional arbitration provision in the acceptance falls away as a material alteration of the contract. Materiality cannot be decided in the abstract, but requires an interpretation of the language of the contract in context. The test for materiality set out in Comment 4 to §2.207 is that the term would result in "surprise or hardship" to the offeror. As explained in Section 6.3.2b, despite the Comment's use of the word "or," these two elements must both be present and are considered in combination. Because arbitration provisions are so commonly included in boilerplate language, the problem of deciding the impact of such a provision in an acceptance comes up periodically. For example, in *Shaney Co., Ltd. v. Crain Walnut Shelling, Inc.*, 2012 WL 1979244 (E.D. Cal. 2012) an arbitration provision was included in the seller's order confirmation relating to the sale of walnuts. The issue was whether the arbitration provision materially altered the contract. One might think that a provision that precludes the buyer from resorting to litigation to enforce its rights under the contract would be important enough to qualify as material. However, the court held that the buyer had not made an adequate showing of surprise and hardship. Even though there was no course of dealings or discussion in negotiations that would have alerted the buyer to the presence of an arbitration provision, such provisions were sufficiently common in the industry to preclude an argument of surprise and hardship. We do not have enough facts about the commercial context of the contract between Ballet and Formfitting to know if it would point to the same conclusion, but the general prevalence of standard arbitration provisions may make it difficult for an offeror to claim the degree of reasonable surprise and hardship that would make such a term a material alteration of the contract.

CHAPTER 7

Consideration

§7.1 CONSIDERATION AS THE BASIS OF CONTRACT OBLIGATION

Consideration can be fun.[1] It has a network of interlocking rules that can be applied to all kinds of silly cases featuring beneficent aunts, sanctimonious uncles, hypothetical tramps, mysteriously illusory promises, and detriments that are actually beneficial. Yet at the same time, consideration doctrine can be a huge pain in the neck. How often have poor students (and poor professors) cursed the quirk of history[2] that left us with so sad a legacy. It is not that the basic rules of consideration are difficult, arcane, or unfathomable. The real problem lies in rationalizing these rules, understanding how courts are likely to use them, and justifying them in light of the policies of contract law.

Consideration doctrine is not static, but has gradually changed over many years. It has evolved away from the more rigid and certain classical form. Courts have long recognized that an inflexible insistence on doctrinaire rules can undermine freedom of contract by precluding the enforcement of serious promises, fairly and voluntarily made. As a result,

---

1. Obviously, depending on your idea of fun. It does help to be deranged.
2. It is beyond our scope to delve into the history of consideration doctrine, but its origins are mentioned briefly in section 7.2. As section 7.4.1 explains, the doctrine is peculiar to common law and does not exist in civilian jurisdictions. (See section 2.4.1 for an explanation of the distinction between common law and civil law.)

they have manipulated the rules, created exceptions and legal fictions, and have recognized alternative theories for enforcing promises that lack consideration. It is therefore not enough simply to learn the rules of consideration and to attempt to apply them mechanically to a set of facts. Consideration must be studied with an awareness of the purpose of these rules, a focus on their impact in each transaction, and an understanding of the way in which consideration doctrine fits in with the broader principles and policies of contract law. You will not be fully able to appreciate this complex interaction between consideration and other elements of contract law just yet, but it will become more apparent as your study of contract law proceeds. At this stage it may be helpful to alert you to some themes that you will begin to see.

Often you will find that although consideration doctrine is the basis of a decision, the court is really concerned with the legitimacy of the transaction in issue and is in fact using the doctrine to achieve an appropriate result in the case. Therefore, a court may stretch to find consideration when the promise appears to be seriously intended and fairly obtained, but may more readily apply the doctrine to invalidate a promise that appears to have resulted from advantage-taking or unfair dealing. In this respect, consideration often serves a purpose parallel to other doctrines such as fraud, duress, or unconscionability (discussed in Chapter 13) in the policing of bargaining behavior.

Consideration is an essential element of contract, and a promise is not recognized or enforced as contractual unless consideration has been given for it. However, an obligation assumed without consideration may be enforceable under an alternative theory such as promissory estoppel, restitution, or moral obligation, discussed in Chapters 8 and 9. Therefore, although we may decide in this chapter that a promise or assumption of duty is not a contract because of lack of consideration, this may not mean that the person to whom it is owed is without remedy. Under appropriate circumstances there may be grounds for full or partial relief under one of those other theories, developed to avoid the injustice of turning away an obligee[3] empty-handed where the lack of consideration precludes contractual liability.

§7.2 THE ESSENCE AND SCOPE OF CONSIDERATION

When "consideration" entered the legal lexicon many centuries ago, its usage by lawyers was apparently close to its lay meaning of "reflection,"

---

3. An obligee is a person to whom an obligation is owed.

"contemplation," or "thinking." It was a vague concept that probably did no more than assert the general principle that a promise must be seriously contemplated and deliberately intended to be legally binding. As courts expounded on this principle over the years, they gradually embellished it so that it came to require something more than a serious and deliberate intent to be bound. It demanded, in addition, that some quid pro quo be given for the promise by the promisee (that is, the person to whom it was made).[4] In other words, a purely gratuitous promise — one that is not "paid for" in some way — cannot be enforced as a contract. This is the essence of consideration doctrine. From this, we can draw some initial inferences about the scope of our subject.

We are concerned with the validity of promises. Consideration is only an issue when there is an outstanding promise to be enforced, and it does not affect the validity of an executed performance — that is, one that has already been completed. Therefore, even if a donor gives property or services to another as a gift, once the transfer is completed, it is an executed gift and it is too late to claim that no consideration was received.

Although consideration issues may potentially arise in connection with any unexecuted promise, there are two types of cases in which it presents no problems, simply because its absence or presence is so obvious. At the one end of the scale, we have the unquestionable donative promise, in which the promisor, motivated by kinship, friendship, generosity, or charity, unconditionally undertakes to make a future gift and asks for and receives nothing in return. There is no point in agonizing over consideration here because it is obviously absent, and the promise is not legally binding. For example, following his 300th nosedive into the snow, Al Pine has become terminally frustrated with the sport of skiing. He decides to give his skis to his friend Buster Legg and promises to drop them off at Buster's home as soon as he gets out of traction. Until the skis are handed over to Buster, this is simply an unexecuted promise. There is no suggestion that Buster gave Al any quid pro quo for the promise, which is purely gratuitous. On these facts, consideration is not in issue because it is so obviously absent. If Al changes his mind and fails to deliver the skis, Buster can sulk or pout or even have a massive tantrum, but he has no legal recourse.

---

4. In discussions of consideration, the person who makes the promise is called the promisor and the person to whom it is made, the promisee. This terminology is clear where only one party has made a promise, and the issue is whether some immediate performance of the other is consideration. However, in many contracts, both parties make promises and each is therefore both promisee and promisor. In such a case, common usage is that the word "promisor" denotes the person whose promise is sought to be enforced, and "promisee" refers to the recipient of that promise whose return promise is challenged as insufficient to constitute consideration.

At the other end of the scale, we have the straightforward commercial exchange in which the promise is clearly purchased for an economically equivalent price, so that there is no plausible argument that consideration was lacking. For example, instead of promising to donate the skis to Buster, Al agrees to sell them to him for $100, their market value. Buster pays Al $100 in cash immediately, and Al promises to deliver the skis as soon as he leaves the hospital. On these facts, there is no issue that Al's promise was not paid for.

Between these two obvious cases is the happy hunting ground of consideration doctrine, in which apparently commercial promises are made for an unclear or questionable exchange, and apparently gratuitous promises have strings attached to them. Unless you are using very boring class materials, most of the consideration cases that you study will fall within this range.

§7.3 THE ELEMENTS OF CONSIDERATION: DETRIMENT, BENEFIT, AND BARGAINED-FOR EXCHANGE

The broad statement was made above that a promise must be paid for to be contractually binding. As you will soon see, "payment" for the promise is much more complicated than you might first have suspected. Especially in older cases (but one still finds this language in modern cases) consideration is commonly described in the alternative as either a detriment to the promisee or a benefit to the promisor. The idea here is that if the promisee suffers a detriment by giving up property, money, or some legal right, the receipt of that detriment translates into a benefit to the promisor. We should therefore be able to identify consideration either by looking for a detriment to the promisee or a benefit to the promisor. However, although this definition is quite commonly found, it not the best formulation, and can be misleading if taken literally. Its shortcoming is that it does not clearly articulate the relationship between the promisee's detriment and the promisor's benefit. Some courts began to recognize, beginning in the late nineteenth century, that it is not accurate simply to look for detriment or benefit. It also had to be apparent that the promisee's detriment was suffered in exchange for the promise: The parties must have bargained for (that is, agreed to) an exchange of the promise for the detriment, so that each induces the other. This became known as the "bargain theory" of consideration.[5]

---

5. Justice O. W. Holmes is credited with being primarily responsible for articulating the bargain theory, but it has been plausibly argued that he simply recognized what was already happening in the cases, rather than created a new requirement for consideration.

Because benefit to the promisor is simply a natural consequence of having the promisee suffer whatever detriment was sought in the exchange (that is, the benefit is simply getting what was bargained for), the bargain theory obviates any need to focus on benefit to the promisor as a distinct element of consideration. (As explained in section 7.3.2, the fact that some tangible benefit was received may have evidentiary value in showing that an exchange was intended.)

So far, the words "detriment," "benefit," and "bargained-for exchange" have been used in an abstract way. These are terms of art that can easily be misinterpreted. We now explore their scope and meaning.

§7.3.1 What Is a "Detriment"?

A legal detriment is any relinquishment of a legal right. In the context of consideration doctrine, "detriment" does not mean that the person has suffered some horrible harm, loss, or injury. In fact, a detriment could even be something that benefits or advances the interests of the sufferer. The important element is not harm but the yielding of a legal right. It could take the form of an immediate act (that is, doing or giving something), a forbearance (refraining from something), or the partial or complete abandonment of an intangible right.

Consideration may be found either in the action of incurring the detriment or in the promise to perform (to act or forbear) in the future. That is, provided that an immediate performance is a detriment, a promise of that performance creates a future liability to perform, which is also a detriment. (Stated differently, a promise to do something in the future is an abandonment of the legal right not to do it, and is therefore consideration.) To be a promise, and hence a detriment, the undertaking must be a genuine commitment. If it is too vague, too discretionary, or too qualified, it may not qualify as a promise. This is discussed in section 7.9.

In the example of the sale of skis by Al to Buster for $100, Buster's payment of $100 was an act constituting his detriment. It would equally have been a detriment if, instead of paying the money, Buster had promised to pay $100 to Al on delivery of the skis. As the act of payment is consideration, the promise to perform that act is also consideration. (Al's detriment is, of course, the promise to deliver the skis. Buster's promise to pay $100 makes this a standard bilateral contract, in which the promise by each party is exchanged for and induces the promise by the other.)

If instead of paying or promising to pay $100, Buster had accepted the promise of the skis in settlement of a prior overdue claim of $100 that he had against Al, Buster's detriment would be the abandonment of his right to sue on the claim, or stated differently, his forbearance from exercising that right.

7. Consideration

Diagram 7A illustrates the exchange of Buster's detriment for Al's promise in these examples.

Diagram 7A

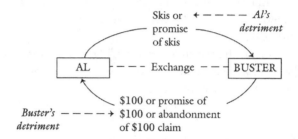

Because both the skis and the money (or the claim for money) have economic value, it is not hard to see that each party suffers a detriment by giving them up. If instead of asking for $100 for the skis, Al had agreed to give them to Buster in exchange for Buster's promise to quit smoking, the detriment to Buster is less obvious. Unanimous medical opinion is that giving up smoking is decidedly not detrimental but is beneficial. Notwithstanding, because Buster has the legal right to smoke, his promise to refrain from doing so (forbearance) is a legal detriment and can qualify as consideration for Al's promise of the skis. Restatement, Second, §79(a) reflects this principle by stating that if the requirement of consideration is met, there is no additional requirement of loss or disadvantage to the promisee.

One of the best-loved cases illustrating the meaning of detriment is *Hamer v. Sidway*, 124 N.Y. 538 (1891), in which sanctimonious Uncle William Story promised $5,000 to his nephew, William II, if the nephew refrained from drinking, using tobacco, swearing, and playing cards or billiards for money until he reached the age of 21. Young Willie complied but had not been paid by the time that his uncle died. The court enforced Willie's claim against the uncle's estate. It rejected the estate's argument that Willie had not given consideration for his uncle's promise. Defining consideration as either a benefit to the promisor or a detriment to the promisee, the court found that Willie's abstention from the stated activities pursuant to the promise was sufficient detriment, because it was the abandonment of his legal right to engage in them. The legal benefit to the uncle did not need to be economic. His benefit lay in having his expressed desire fulfilled. Although the court in *Hamer* used the older definition of consideration, the result is consistent with the bargain theory in that the parties manifested the intent to exchange Willie's conduct for Uncle William's promise.

This concludes our first look at the concept of detriment. Specific applications of this subject are discussed below.

§7.3.2 How Does Benefit to the Promisor Fit In?

Benefit to the promisor is even more prone to misunderstanding than detriment to the promisee. As stated earlier, it is sometimes expressed as one of the alternative tests for consideration, but under the bargain theory, it plays only an evidentiary role. In many cases, the promisee's detriment translates easily into a benefit to the promisor. In the exchange of the promise of skis for money, the detriment to Buster (a loss of $100) is obviously a benefit to Al (a gain of $100). By contrast, when Al's promise of skis is exchanged for Buster's promise to quit smoking, it is not as clear that Buster's detriment of giving up the legal right to smoke translates into any benefit to Al. However, in the same way as "detriment" has a very broad meaning, "benefit" is seen as meaning simply that Al got what he bargained for. As *Hamer v. Sidway* shows, it need not be established that Al received any tangible or economically valuable gain. Restatement, Second, §79(a) states that a gain or advantage to the promisor is not a requirement for consideration. This is illustrated by Diagram 7B.

Diagram 7B

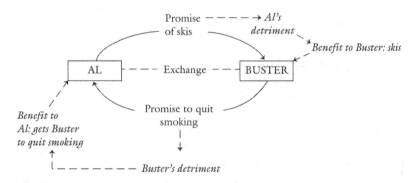

Thus, we need not ask why Al wished for Buster to quit smoking, nor need we speculate what is in it for him. His motive in making the exchange is not of central concern, as long as it is apparent that he intended to exchange his promise of skis for the promise to quit. This does not mean that Al's motive is entirely irrelevant, because it could be evidence of his intent to make the exchange. If a gain or advantage to Al can be identified, this bolsters the argument that he did in fact bargain for the detriment suffered by Buster. This issue is discussed further in the next section.

§7.3.3 The Bargained-For Exchange

As stated earlier, the bargain theory was formulated around the end of the nineteenth century and it is now thoroughly well-established in our law. It is reflected in Restatement, Second, §71, which requires that a performance or return promise must be bargained for to constitute consideration. That is, the performances or promises of the parties must induce each other: The promisee's performance or promise must be sought by the promisor and given by the promisee in exchange for the promise. Section 33 reinforces this by defining a bargain as an agreement (in turn defined as a manifestation of mutual assent) to exchange promises, performances, or promise for performance. The bargain theory recognizes that contracts are voluntary exchange relationships involving reciprocal promises or performances. It means nothing if a party suffers a legal detriment unless the parties agree that it is the price for the promise.

Be careful not to get too carried away by all this talk of bargain and inducement. "Bargain" simply means "agreement" and does not suggest that the parties have to dicker back and forth or to negotiate at length. If each agrees to a performance desired by the other, the bargain can be struck instantly without any fuss. Also, the objective test (discussed in section 4.1) applies to the determination of contractual intent, so "inducement" is gleaned from the manifestation of intent rather than from a probing of the party's actual state of mind. The motive for the transaction is therefore the apparent motive, as evidenced by the nature of the exchange in context.

§7.3.4 The Distinction Between Bargained-For and Incidental Detriment

In the example of the sale of the skis for $100, the fact that Al and Buster had agreed to an exchange seems obvious. In most commercial transactions the existence of a bargained-for exchange is not in question. Exchange also seems to be quite clear in the case of the promise of skis for the promise to quit smoking. Even though the motivation is apparently not commercial, we can still understand an incentive for the exchange based on friendship. However, what if Al had said to Buster, "If you walk over to my car, I will give you the skis that I have on my rack." Under the broad concept of legal detriment, Buster's act of walking to the car is a detriment: He gave up his legal right to remain where he was and undertook the perambulation across the parking lot. However, this detriment seems incidental to Al's promise. Common experience suggests that the parties did not see it as the price for the skis but simply as the act needed to take delivery of the gift. This conclusion is based, not on a probing of Al's innermost thoughts but on the apparent purpose of his request, based on our understanding of human motivation. There is no evidence from which one could reasonably understand that Al was so desirous of having Buster walk across the lot, that he felt it was worth promising him skis to induce him to do it. This is shown in Diagram 7C.

7. Consideration

Diagram 7C

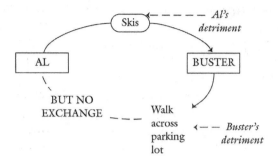

The same conclusion would follow if Al had said to Buster, "Put out your hand, and I will place a $10 bill in it." It would be hard to argue with a straight face that the act of extending the hand was bargained for as the exchange for the money. Al's apparent purpose is to give a gift to Buster, and the request to position the hand is merely intended as a means of its efficient delivery — better than cramming it in his ear or casting it on the ground.

However, there may be some additional evidence that makes this conclusion less obvious, so that under all the circumstances, Buster may reasonably understand from Al's words and conduct that the extension of his hand was a bargained-for detriment. (Note the objective test used here: It is not what Buster in fact understood, but what he has reasonably understood. We measure Buster's interpretation of Al's words and conduct from the perspective of a reasonable person in Buster's position.) Say, for example, that Buster was one of those sidewalk performers who strikes a pose and tries to stand dead-still like a statue. Al's offer of money may well be in exchange for the hand movement, because Buster could reasonably infer that Al is bargaining for the pleasure of seeing Buster abandon his art for filthy lucre. (Is that pleasure worth $10? We do not usually need to inquire. As discussed in section 7.7, once exchange is determined, it is not necessary to evaluate the adequacy of consideration.)

This example again confronts the awkward fit between benefit to the promisor, motive, and the objective test of intent. When no benefit to Al was evident, we concluded that the detriment was not bargained for. When additional facts were supplied that suggested a motive, albeit not an economic one, the conclusion was that the detriment was bargained for. Yet we did not try to seek Al's actual motive for the exchange, but rather his apparent motive. The benefit to the promisor, measured objectively, is purely the satisfaction of having his apparent desire fulfilled. This is sufficient to support a finding of exchange. (As we will see later in this chapter, the exchange requirement has many facets.)

§7.3.5 The Distinction Between a Detriment and a Condition of Gift

One of the most elusive distinctions in consideration doctrine is that between an act or promise that is a legal detriment, and one that merely relates to the manner in which a gift is to be used. For example, Al Umnus promises to donate $10,000 to his alma mater and specifies that the gift is to be allocated to the college's scholarship program. The college accepts the promise and agrees to use the funds as specified by Al. The college has made a promise to Al in return for his promise of $10,000, but is that promise consideration? As a doctrinal matter, there is a good argument that it is not, because the college's promise is not a legal detriment. At the time of the promise, Al has not handed over the money to the college, and the college has no right to spend Al's money. Therefore when it makes the promise to use Al's prospective payment in a specified way, it does not forbear from any legal right that it has at the time that it makes the promise. On this reasoning, there is no contract. Al has simply made a gift to the college with a condition attached. Some courts will follow this approach, but others will not, especially if the court believes that as a matter of policy, the public interest is best served by the enforcement of charitable promises whenever there is a plausible rationale for doing so.

The case would be a bit easier, and a finding of detriment in exchange for Al's promise would be more justifiable on doctrinal grounds, if the college's undertaking included any promise that went beyond the simple promise to use the gift for its intended purpose. Say, for example, Al and the college had agreed not only that the promised funds would be used for the scholarship program, but also that the college would include Al's name on a donor's list published in its alumni magazine. The college's promise to publicize the gift goes beyond the use of the money, so it can constitute a legal detriment. To be sure, it is a small detriment, and the idea that it was exchanged for (that is, induced) the promise is quite artificial, but it is likely enough to qualify as consideration. As discussed in section 7.7, the court does not enquire into the adequacy of consideration.

A few cases illustrate the subtlety of the distinction between a detriment and a promise to use a gift as required by the donor. In *King v. Trustees of Boston University*, 420 Mass. 52 (1995) the estate of Dr. Martin Luther King Jr. sued the university to recover papers that Dr. King had deposited with the university library. The estate claimed that Dr. King gave the university only temporary custody of his papers, but the university asserted that he had transferred ownership of them. At the time of handing over the papers, Dr. King had written a letter to the university reserving ownership of the papers until his death, but stating that they would become the property of the university when he died. The question was whether this promise to transfer ownership of the papers was merely an unenforceable gift, or a contract for which the university had given consideration.[6] The court upheld the jury's finding that the university gave consideration to Dr. King. When accepting the papers, the university had undertaken to index them, to take care of them, and to make them available to researchers. The court found that these duties went beyond a mere promise to use the gift as instructed by the donor. Recognize that the court could easily have reached the opposite conclusion. There is a good argument that these duties were nothing more than conditions imposed by Dr. King on the use of the gift.

In *Massachusetts Eye and Ear Infirmary v. Eugene B. Casey Foundation*, 417 F. Supp. 2d 192 (D. Mass. 2006) the foundation pledged to give $2 million to the infirmary to be used for a voice restoration research program. When the foundation terminated its pledge, the infirmary sued it for breach of contract. The foundation moved to dismiss the case on several grounds, one of which was that the infirmary gave no consideration to the foundation for its promise. The court refused to dismiss the case because it considered that there was a colorable argument that the infirmary gave consideration for the pledge by committing to use the funds only for the express purpose of supporting the voice restoration program, and by undertaking to submit biannual reports to the foundation. Again, the decision could have been opposite — the infirmary's undertakings can be seen as no more than conditions of the gift. The court, citing the *King* case, revealed the policy rationale for its decision. It observed, quite obliquely, that the public interest in protecting and supporting charitable subscriptions calls for a different standard to decide on the existence of consideration in relation to charitable pledges.[7]

Sometimes this distinction comes up in cases that do not involve charitable gifts. For example, in *Bono v. McCutcheon*, 824 N.E.2d 1013 (Ohio App. 2005) the parties entered into an agreement under which McCutcheon gave Bono possession of a whippet puppy named Doozie. Bono paid no money for Doozie, but the agreement required her to keep the dog in good condition, to show her, to breed her, to give McCutcheon a puppy from her first litter, and to allow McCutcheon to take and breed her for one litter. At some time later, McCutcheon regained possession of Doozie and refused to return her. Bono sued for conversion and breach of contract. McCutcheon moved to dismiss the suit, claiming that there was

---

6. You may be wondering if it could not have been argued that Dr. King's deposit of his papers with the university was an executed gift, making consideration doctrine irrelevant. Although the university had possession of the papers, it held them only as bailee. The promise that required consideration was Dr. King's promise to transfer ownership of the papers to the university.

7. In both *King* and *Massachusetts Eye and Ear Infirmary*, the court also discussed the issue of whether the promise would be enforceable had there been no consideration, but the donee had acted in reliance on the promise. In such a situation, the doctrine of promissory estoppel may provide relief. We will cover this issue in Chapter 8.

no contract because Bono had not paid anything for the dog.[8] The issue was whether Bono's undertakings were consideration for the dog or just conditions of gift. The trial court found no consideration and granted the motion to dismiss but the court of appeals took the opposite view and reversed. Again, it is hard to be sure that the court of appeals was right and the trial court was wrong.

§7.4 THE PURPOSE AND FUNCTION OF CONSIDERATION DOCTRINE

§7.4.1 Consideration Doctrine in Common Law and Its Absence in Civil Law

Having identified the basic principles of consideration doctrine, it is helpful to consider the policy justifications for the doctrine. There has been much written over the years in an effort to explain why the doctrine arose in the common law, and why it has survived. A plausible argument can be made that there really is no coherent and persuasive policy basis for the continued existence of the doctrine, which is nothing more than an historical relic that has survived in our law because of inertia and tradition. Indeed, the various policy justifications that have been advanced by courts and scholars over the years seem to be quite dubious and not very convincing. Whatever the rationale for the continued vitality of the doctrine, it unquestionably remains part of our law, and courts routinely assert that the presence of consideration is one of the crucial elements of a valid contract. Of course, that does not mean that courts apply the doctrine with an unflinching rigor. As courts have worked with it over time, they have developed a variety of principles, distinctions, and qualifications that allow some flexibility in applying it, and have recognized alternative bases of enforcing promises under some circumstances where consideration is absent.

Civilian jurisdictions have never had a similar doctrine, and simply operate under the general principle that a contract must be founded on just cause, which is constituted by a serious and deliberate intent to be bound. The UNIDROIT Principles expressly adopt the civilian position by stating, in Article 3.2, that a contract is concluded by the mere agreement of the parties, without any further requirement. (The CISG does not directly address consideration doctrine and largely defers, in Article 4, to domestic

---

8. Contrary to the *King* case, it seems that the argument could have been made here that even if Doozie was a gift, the gift had been executed when McCutcheon originally gave possession of the dog to Bono, so there was no need to find consideration. This issue was not raised in the opinion.

law on issues relating to the validity of a contract.) We therefore know that it is possible for a legal system to operate without the doctrine and that many of the functions that it serves could be accomplished by the use of other doctrines of contract law.

§7.4.2 The Formal and Substantive Basis for the Doctrine in Relation to Gratuitous Promises

Probably the most influential and enduring justification of consideration doctrine is Professor Lon Fuller's 1941 article, *Consideration and Form* (41 Colum. L. Rev. 799). Fuller identified both formal and substantive bases for consideration. He identified three formal functions of consideration, which he called "evidentiary," "cautionary," and "channeling." In essence, he argued that by requiring consideration, the law gives courts some evidentiary indication that a contract was intended, allows them to distinguish between contractual commitments and mere informal or tentative expressions of intent, and makes the promisor aware that she has made a serious legal commitment. Since Fuller wrote his article there has been much scholarly discussion of his identification and characterization of the formal functions of consideration. Some of the discussion reinforces his views, and some refutes them. Nevertheless, Fuller's analysis is still widely cited, and the comment to Restatement, Second, §72 adopts it.

Fuller recognized that the formal functions of consideration do not fully justify the doctrine's continued vitality in our law. If its role was purely formal, it could easily be dispensed with because these formal functions could be accomplished simply by having a rule that upholds written, signed promises. Our law does not have such a rule.[9] In fact, as section 7.7.3 explains, the parties cannot usually circumvent the requirement of consideration by using sham or nominal consideration purely for the purpose of validating the promise. Fuller therefore also identified a substantive (policy-based) justification for the doctrine. The doctrine's substantive function may better explain its durability.

---

9. In this respect, modern law has moved away from older common law, which did have a formal device — the seal — that could be used to make a promise binding without consideration. The promisor could create a binding gratuitous promise by sealing the document. Originally, the seal was made by dripping sealing wax on the document and impressing the hot wax with a signet ring. In time it became acceptable simply to append the letters "L.S." (*locus sigilli* — meaning "in place of a seal") to a signature. The seal did not develop as an exception to consideration doctrine but predates the doctrine, which applied only to "informal" (i.e., unsealed) promises. Today, the seal has been abolished or given only residual evidentiary effect in most jurisdictions. In only a few states has the formal device of the seal been replaced by a statutory method of formally validating a gift promise.

The substantive basis of consideration lies in the policy that the law should not hold a person to a promise that was made gratuitously. The point here is that the law should be concerned only with the enforcement of exchanges, and should not hold a promisee to a promise motivated by affection, generosity, or altruism, and lacking in any return benefit. Because the promisor has received nothing in exchange for the promise, and the promisee loses nothing by nonenforcement except the prospect of a gift, the promisor should be able to recant without legal liability. This policy protects the donor from improvidence. It also indirectly protects her heirs and creditors by ensuring that their claims against her assets will not be defeated by her promise to donate them. Of course, there is a contrary policy argument, especially where charitable promises are made: Charitable organizations serve a crucial role in our society, and important public interests are served by the sustenance and support of these organizations. Nevertheless, in the absence of consideration, the prevailing principle is that these promises are not to be enforced. (We will see later in this chapter that in some cases courts are able to uphold these promises by a manipulation of bargained-for detriment. In addition, we will see in Chapter 9 that there is an alternative basis for enforcing charitable promises if the promisee has acted in reliance on the promise and can establish the elements of promissory estoppel.)

§7.4.3 Consideration Doctrine in the Commercial Context

So far, this discussion of the function of the doctrine has focused on gratuitous promises, and if consideration doctrine were strictly confined to promises of gifts, its operation would be relatively straightforward. However, as you will find as you proceed through this chapter, the doctrine often arises in transactions that are not motivated by generosity, charity, or altruism, but have a commercial purpose. A commercial promise without consideration may sound like a contradiction in terms because the purpose of a commercial transaction is usually exchange. Nevertheless, you will see many situations in this chapter in which consideration issues do arise in commercial transactions because there is some problem with the apparent consideration that is claimed to support the promise. For example, apparent consideration in the form of a promise may be illusory or unenforceable, or it may not qualify as an exchanged detriment because of its timing. In a commercial transaction, in which there is no charitable or donative intent, the rationale relating to the nonenforcement of gifts is inapplicable. The usual justification for not enforcing the promise is that the lack of consideration shows that the parties did not have the legal intent to create a binding contractual relationship.

§7.4.4 The Flexibility of Consideration Concepts and the Use of the Doctrine for Policing Purposes

It has already been intimated, and will become even more apparent as you read this chapter, that concepts such as detriment and exchange are quite open-ended. In all but the most clear-cut cases, this allows courts considerable flexibility in deciding whether to find that purported consideration actually qualifies as such. Courts seldom apply consideration doctrine mechanically in cases that are not clear cut and use flexibility in the doctrine to achieve a result that seems best to serve the policies of contract law. That is, a court will likely try to find the existence of consideration if it believes that the promise should be enforced and will likely refuse to find consideration it if believes that the promisor should not be bound. One of the reasons why a court may decline to bind the promisor is because it concludes that there is something unfair or improper in the way in which the promise was exacted (for example, that the promisor was taken advantage of or was coerced or tricked into making the promise). There are several doctrines, discussed in Chapter 13, that are available to prevent the enforcement of a promise induced by fraud, duress, or other unfair means. However, consideration doctrine can also sometimes be used by a court as a tool to protect a promisor from an ill-advised or improperly obtained promise.

§7.5 DETRIMENT AND "PRE-EXISTING DUTY"

§7.5.1 The Basic Rule

If a detriment is the relinquishment of a right, it follows that one does not suffer a detriment by doing or promising to do something that one is already obliged to do or by forbearing to do something that is already forbidden. Therefore, the rule is often stated that the performance of, or promise to perform, a pre-existing duty is not consideration. For example, say that Al Pine owns a ski lodge. He entered into a contract with Buster Legg under which he sold the lodge to Buster for $400,000. Before the sale closed, Al realized that he had underpriced the lodge, which is worth at least $450,000. He approached Buster and asked him to agree to change the price to $450,000. Buster believed that he did underpay and felt that the lodge was still a good buy at $450,000. Not wishing to take advantage of Al's mistake, he agreed to pay the extra amount, and the parties amended their written contract. An agreement to modify an existing contract is itself a contract, and needs new consideration, separate from the consideration given under the original contract. Therefore, the agreement to modify the contract by increasing the price is not a valid contract because Al gave Buster no consideration for his promise to pay $50,000 more. Al already had a duty to transfer the lodge under the original contract, and he neither gave nor promised anything new. It cannot be a legal detriment to promise what he is already obliged to do. Because Buster's second promise is not binding, he can refuse to perform it and can insist on transfer of the lodge for the original price of $400,000. This is shown in Diagram 7D.

Diagram 7D

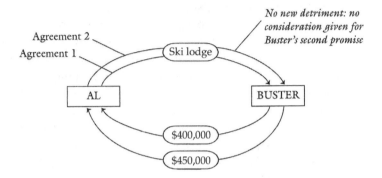

The pre-existing duty rule only applies if the performance of the promisee is completely encompassed by the pre-existing duty. Therefore, if Al had in any way added to his performance or obligation as an apparent incentive to Buster's agreement to pay more (for example, Al offered to include a snowplow in the sale), this new increase in his detriment would be sufficient to constitute consideration for Buster's promise of more money. It would not matter if the snow plow was worth much less than $50,000 because, as explained in section 7.7, economic equivalence is not normally required in the exchange. *See* Diagram 7E.

Diagram 7E

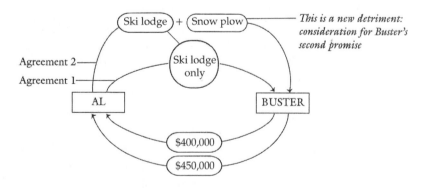

§7.5.2 The Justification for the Rule Where the Duty Is Owed to the Promisor: Coerced Modifications

It is quite easy to express the pre-existing duty rule in its basic form, but application of the rule is seldom this simple. In some cases, the problem may be factual. For example, it may be unclear if a pre-existing duty exists or if the detriment in the later agreement really is coextensive with this duty. However, the bigger problem is a conceptual one. Why have the rule at all? True, it is consistent with and simply a specific application of the concept of detriment, so the rule is doctrinally justifiable. But what policy does it serve?

The rule makes most sense when, after a contract has been made, one of the parties takes advantage of the other's dependence on his performance, by threatening to breach the contract unless the other promises to increase her payment or other return performance. When a modification of an existing contract has been coerced in this way, the court can employ the pre-existing duty rule to void the unfair modification. Although we will return to the subject of contract modification in section 13.9 in connection with a broader study of the doctrines governing unfair bargaining, we must deal with it here as well, because it has a significant connection to consideration doctrine. To illustrate, say that a traveler, on arriving at the airport of a large city, contracts with a cab driver to pay him $85 to take her to a hotel on the other side of town. Halfway through the journey, as they are driving through a dark and frightening part of town, the cab driver jams on the brakes, turns to the passenger, and says, "Sorry, but unless you agree to pay me $150 for my fare, I am going to dump you off here." Of course the passenger agrees to this modification of the contract. However, the cab driver had a pre-existing duty to complete the trip. He has therefore given the passenger nothing more than what he originally promised — transport to the hotel. Because he has suffered no further detriment in exchange for the passenger's promise to pay another $65, this promise of additional payment lacks consideration and the passenger can refuse to pay any more than $85 when they reach the hotel.[10]

Although the justification of the rule is the prevention of this kind of coerced modification, the rule has two serious shortcomings. First, a promisee who knows of the rule can evade it simply by agreeing to add some minor new detriment to his side of the exchange. Because the courts do not generally inquire into adequacy of consideration, the new detriment does not have to be economically equivalent to the additional performance exacted from the promisor. For example, the cab driver would have made it harder for his passenger to challenge the modification on grounds of lack of consideration if he had promised in exchange for the increase in

---

10. Furthermore, she need not tip him, either.

fare, to hum soothing melodies during the remainder of the journey. Second, the rule covers all modifications, even those, such as the genuinely consensual increase in the price of the ski lodge in the contract between Al and Buster. In these circumstances (unless the parties know the rule and provide for some new detriment by the promisee), application of the rule precludes parties from making a binding agreement to modify the obligations of one of them, even when circumstances justify a modification and the promisor genuinely agreed to it without unfair pressure. Such an unquestioning use of the rule undermines freedom of contract and has led many commentators and courts to believe that the rule is unnecessary and undesirable.

In response to this concern, some courts do take into account whether the modification was fairly agreed to and justifiable. If a court is persuaded that the modification was legitimate, it will probably do what it can to find some new detriment incurred by the promise to support it. However, this only works if there is some colorable basis for finding a detriment. Conversely, if a party seeks to validate a coerced modification by providing some purely technical form of detriment, a court will likely try to find that the purported exchange did not really constitute consideration. Notwithstanding, there is a better way to distinguish legitimate and improper modifications. Doctrines such as duress, fraud, and unconscionability and the general obligation of good faith provide a more direct way of policing for unfair modification, and unless the modification has been unfairly obtained, there is no good policy reason for refusing to enforce it. The drafters of Article 2 have recognized this, as explained in section 7.5.3, but the complications of using consideration doctrine to police modifications still encumber the common law.

§7.5.3 The Abolition of the Pre-Existing Duty Rule in Relation to Modifications Under Article 2

Although the pre-existing duty rule precluded the enforcement of Al's promise to pay more for real property (the ski lodge), the result would have been different if the contract involved a sale of goods. Say, for example, that Al and Buster contracted for the sale of Al's skis to Buster for $100, and the parties later agreed to increase the price to $150. UCC §2.209(1) states that an agreement modifying a sale of goods needs no consideration to be binding. Instead, the Official Comment to §2.209 explains that all that is required to validate the modification is that it meets Article 2's test of good faith. In essence, an extorted modification would not satisfy that test, but a modification that is fairly agreed to and justified by a legitimate business reason is valid even in the absence of consideration. This is discussed more fully in section 13.9.

§7.5.4 Modifications in Light of Supervening Difficulty

The requirement that contract modification requires consideration is not applied where the modification was motivated by supervening difficulties that materially affect the basic assumption under which the contract was made. The underlying rationale for this exception is that a modification to take account of an unexpected burden on the promisee is less likely to be coercive. Of course, the exception can only be used where the facts support it. The promisee must be able to show that such an unforeseen difficulty did arise in the course of performance and did motivate the modification.

§7.5.5 Pre-Existing Duty to a Third Party

So far, we have talked only about a pre-existing duty owed by the promisee to the promisor. What if the duty is owed to someone else? For example, Al contracted to sell his ski lodge to Buster for $400,000. Buster has promised Ava Lanche that when he takes over the ski lodge, he will grant her a concession to run the snack bar in the lodge. Ava is most anxious for the sale to go through, so to give Al an additional incentive to complete his contract with Buster, Ava promises Al that if he completes the sale to Buster, she will pay him $1,000. Because Al has already contracted with Buster to transfer the lodge, he has a pre-existing legal duty to perform that promise. It would therefore seem that he has not incurred any new legal detriment by making the same promise to Ava. This is illustrated by Diagram 7F.

Diagram 7F

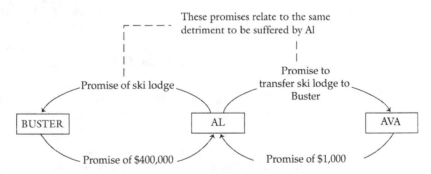

However, the concern about extorted contract modification is not present in a case like this, so this justification for the pre-existing duty rule is not applicable. Some courts (and Restatement, Second, §73) simply confine the pre-existing duty rule to cases in which the duty is owed to the promisor. An alternate way of looking at the situation is to say that Al does incur a detriment in that he forbears from the right to negotiate with Buster for the cancellation of the contract to sell the lodge to him.[11] A pre-existing duty may be owed, not to the promisor or a third party, but to the state or the public. This type of duty presents slightly different policy concerns because the public interest may demand that external incentives to obey that duty must be discouraged. This is particularly so when the promisee is a public official, and an additional reward for performing the public duty may create the danger of corruption or favoritism. For example, a police officer has a pre-existing duty to apprehend criminals. Therefore, if the owner of a store promises a police officer a reward for catching the robber who robbed the store, the court is likely to invalidate this promise on the basis of the pre-existing duty rule. However, the true basis for refusing to recognize a contract is not some technical approach to consideration doctrine, but the public policy that a member of the public should not be able to influence the police officer's priorities in performing his duties.

§7.6 CONSIDERATION IN AN AGREEMENT TO SETTLE A DISPUTED CLAIM OR DEFENSE

As we have seen, under the pre-existing duty rule, a party suffers no legal detriment by performing or promising to perform something that she already is legally obliged to do. Under this principle, a creditor who agrees to accept partial payment of a debt, or to extend the payment period of an undisputed debt, is not bound by that promise. This is because the debtor already owes the undisputed debt, and a new promise by the debtor to pay in part or after due date is nothing more than a promise to pay what is already owed. For example, say a borrower owes $20,000 to a lender, payable on August 1. He fails to pay and the lender sues him to recover the debt. Upon receiving the summons, the borrower contacts the lender and explains that he has severe financial difficulty and cannot pay the $20,000 in full. He offers to settle the lawsuit by paying the lender $10,000 in cash within one week in full settlement of the claim. The lender accepts because she decides that it is better to receive $10,000 within a week than to struggle, possibly unsuccessfully, to recover the full $20,000. Clearly, the lender has suffered a detriment by forgiving half of her claim and agreeing not to continue her suit. However, unless the borrower undertook some new detriment in addition to the promise to pay a portion

---

11. Al also forbears from the power to breach his contract with Buster. However, this should not constitute consideration for Ava's promise because Al has no legal right to breach that contract. Accordingly, he does not suffer a legal detriment by giving up that power.

of the debt, he is doing no more than what he was obliged to do under the original contract, so that his promise to pay is a pre-existing duty, rather than a legal detriment. The lender is therefore not bound by her promise to settle the claim for half its value.

The pre-existing duty rule applies only where the debt is undisputed. If there is a dispute over the debt, an agreement between the parties is supported by consideration because, by compromising the dispute, each of them gives up a right: The creditor party forbears from asserting her full claim, and the debtor party forbears from asserting his defense to the claim. For example, Sue Permodel attended a gala reception at a hotel. She wore a breathtakingly tight-fitting evening gown and inconceivably high heels, which badly restricted her agility. As a result, when she stepped onto the highly-polished marble floor of the hotel lobby, she slipped and injured herself. She sued the hotel for $500,000 damages for medical expenses, pain and suffering, and public humiliation, on the grounds that the hotel was negligent in having such a slippery floor in its lobby. The hotel defended the suit, denying liability on the basis that the floor was not unduly slippery, and that Sue's restrictive attire caused her to slip. Just before the trial, the hotel offered to settle the suit by paying Sue $10,000. Sue was relieved at being spared the further mortification of a trial and accepted the offer. Although the injury occurred before the settlement, and the hotel may have already incurred the duty to compensate Sue for her injury, the fact and extent of liability is uncertain. Therefore, this agreement to compromise the disputed and uncertain claim is very different from the settlement of the loan debt in the previous example. There is no consideration problem here. Because Sue's claim is disputed and the outcome of the litigation is uncertain, each party gives up something: Sue's detriment is her agreement to accept less than she claimed and to forbear from pursuing her suit against the hotel. The hotel's detriment, exchanged for Sue's, is its promise to pay Sue $10,000 and its forbearance from asserting its defense to liability. Because a jury could have found that the hotel had no liability, or lesser liability to Sue, the hotel's uncertain debt is not treated as a pre-existing duty to pay Sue $10,000, or any other amount. This result is not only in accordance with consideration principles, but it is also good public policy. There is a strong public interest in the settlement of disputes by agreement, and the law should therefore encourage and uphold honest and legitimate compromise agreements.

The words "honest and legitimate" indicate an important qualification: While genuine compromises should be encouraged, the law should not be used as a means of extorting payment or evading obligations through spurious or vexatious claims or defenses. Say, for example, that Sue did not slip on the hotel floor. However, she dishonestly claims that she did, and the hotel cannot prove otherwise. She sues the hotel, which agrees to settle the claim for $10,000, just to avoid the cost and publicity of a trial. Before paying, the hotel discovers that Sue's claim is false. Sue cannot claim that she gave consideration by settling her claim because she had no right to assert a false claim.[12] The same principle applies to a vexatious defense: A party who defends a claim without having a genuine basis for disputing it cannot claim that he gave consideration by giving up the defense.

Sue's trumped-up claim is clearly spurious, but in some cases it is harder to decide whether the claim or defense is genuine. In any claim that is litigated, the jury will ultimately find in favor of one of the parties. Therefore, to establish that the claim or defense was legitimate, the party does not need to show that he would ultimately have prevailed in the litigation.

Rather, the test for legitimacy is based on the existence of enough doubt about the claim or defense to make the dispute genuine. Restatement, Second, §74 adopts a test that measures legitimacy on, alternatively, an objective or subjective standard. Either the claim or defense must be objectively reasonable (that it is subject to reasonable doubt because of uncertainty in fact or law), or the party asserting the claim or defense must have an honest belief in its merits (that is, he is subjectively in good faith). Some courts are stricter and require the claim and defense to satisfy both the objective and subjective standards — that it has a colorable legal basis, and also that it is asserted in good faith. Some courts do not enquire into the objective plausibility of the claim or defense, but require only an examination of the good faith of the party asserting it. In many cases, the outcome of these tests may amount to the same thing because it may be hard to convince a jury that a party had a genuine belief in the validity of a claim or defense that has no objective basis of support. However, the subjective test does allow the court to take account of honest ignorance. Whatever test is used, the legitimacy of the claim must be determined as at the date of the agreement, not in light of later events.

For an example of a case in which the court required only a good faith belief in the merits of the claim, see *Denburg v. Parker, Chapin, Flattau, & Klimpl*, 604 N.Y.S.2d 900 (1993). A law firm's partnership agreement contained a clause that created financial disincentives for a partner to leave the firm and practice in competition with it. Provisions of this kind are void as against public policy because, by discouraging a partner from setting up a competing practice upon leaving the firm, they inhibit his clients' right to maintain access to the attorney of their choice. The firm sought to enforce the provision against a partner who left the firm and the partner challenged its right to do so. The parties then settled the dispute by agreement. Thereafter, the ex-partner claimed that the settlement agreement lacked consideration because it compromised an invalid claim. The court upheld the

---

12. In addition to challenging Sue's consideration, the hotel has grounds for avoiding the agreement for fraud. (Fraud is discussed in section 13.6.) Sue's fraud is also a criminal offence.

settlement. Although the partnership's claim was not legally tenable, the firm believed in good faith that it was viable. This was enough to validate the firm's forbearance as consideration.

§7.7 THE MEASUREMENT OF DETRIMENT: ADEQUACY OF CONSIDERATION

§7.7.1 The General Rule: Courts Are Not Concerned with Adequacy of Consideration

Recall the illustrations in section 7.3.1 involving Al's promise to sell his skis to Buster. In one of the illustrations, Buster's consideration was the payment of, or promise to pay, $100 to Al in exchange for the skis. In another example, Buster's consideration was his promise to quit smoking. When skis are exchanged for money, items of ascertainable economic worth are involved, so it is usually not difficult to determine if there has been equivalence in the exchange. It is a lot harder to value the right given up by Buster in promising to quit smoking. However, this generally does not matter, because consideration doctrine does not require that the performances or promises exchanged be of equal value. As long as a legal detriment has been suffered in exchange for the promise, consideration is present, and the court will not invalidate the contract (or make an adjustment to the contract terms) on the ground that the consideration given for a promise is inadequate in relation to the value of the promise. (Restatement, Second, §79(b).) A related principle is that there does not have to be an equivalence in the number of promises or performances provided by each party. One party can exchange a single promise or performance for multiple promises and performances by the other. For example, Al could have given Buster the skis in exchange for Buster's payment of $100 plus his promise to stop smoking and his forbearance from asserting a claim that he has against Al. For the purposes of finding consideration, we need not worry that Buster has given up three rights to one of Al's, nor need we fret about whether the promise of the skis is worth more or less than Buster's detriment.

The rule that the court will not inquire into adequacy of consideration is based on the policy of enforcing the voluntary exchange on the terms agreed by the parties. As long as consideration has been found to exist, the court should not second-guess the value placed on the exchange by the parties at the time of contracting, even if one of the parties subsequently seeks to overturn the transaction because the other received a great bargain at his expense. The disparity in value may be the result of many and varied factors such as poor judgment, inaccurate cost calculations, bad luck in market predictions, or even deliberate underpricing. Whatever the reason, the party who fairly agreed to take less than the value of his performance has no basis to complain after entering the contract. Therefore, if Al's skis are actually worth $500, and he agreed to sell them to Buster for $100, the court should not allow him to escape the contract and disappoint Buster's expectations. This argument has even more force when the economic value of one of the performances is hard to determine (or was so at the time of contracting). For example, one really cannot place an economic value on Buster's promise to stop smoking, so one cannot even be sure that this promise was an inadequate exchange for the skis. (Some may think that $100 is overpayment for taking the sensible action of overcoming a dangerous addiction, while others may think it is a measly reward for the agony of withdrawal.)

§7.7.2 Inadequacy of Consideration as the Result of Unfair Bargaining

The general rule that the court will not inquire into the adequacy of consideration cannot be applied blindly, and courts do examine the adequacy of consideration where the disparity in the exchange results from oppressive or underhanded bargaining or justifiable mistake. In such cases, a court may find that the promisee's performance is so lacking in value that it cannot count as consideration at all. If so, the court may invalidate the transaction on the grounds of lack of consideration. More commonly, however, courts employ other doctrines, such as fraud, duress, or unconscionability (dealt with in Chapter 13) or mistake (dealt with in Chapter 15) to give relief to the party who is the victim of the unfair bargaining or the error. In some cases, the appropriate relief under these doctrines is the avoidance of the contract, but in other situations, the more fitting remedy may be an adjustment of the terms of the exchange to make it fairer.

§7.7.3 Sham or Nominal Consideration

The rule that a court will not inquire into adequacy of consideration may not apply where it is clear that the purported consideration is so inadequate that it cannot be said that it really amounts to consideration at all. Where the parties intend a promise to be gratuitous, they may seek to make the promise binding by creating an apparent consideration. They may do this by falsely reciting that the promisee did give consideration (that is, create a sham consideration) or may provide for the promisee to suffer some nominal detriment in apparent exchange for the promise. For example, a donor agrees to pledge $100,000 to a charitable organization. The pledge is recorded in writing, is signed by the donor, and states that it is given for consideration received, even though no consideration was actually given to the donor. Here, the recital of consideration for the $100,000 pledge is a sham. Alternatively, the pledge may state that the promise is given in consideration for a coffee mug bearing the organization's logo. If the coffee mug is in fact given to the promisor, the purported consideration for the pledge is not a sham, but it is nominal. In both these cases, the pretense of consideration is not really given in exchange for the promise, but simply serves the purpose of establishing an apparent exchange to validate the promise.

There is a convincing policy argument that the parties should be able to use the device of recited or nominal consideration to validate a gratuitous promise, provided that the pretense at consideration is not designed to defraud a third party and the promisor has not been tricked or coerced into making the promise. However, Restatement, Second, does not take this approach. While it asserts the general rule that courts should not inquire into adequacy of consideration, it states several times that the pretense of a bargain does not satisfy the exchange element. It does not treat as sufficient consideration a false detriment that cannot reasonably be conceived as inducing the return promise. (See §71, Comment b; §72, Comment c; §79, Comment d; and §81, Comment b.)

Sham or nominal consideration satisfies the formal functions of consideration doctrine: The parties' effort to go through the formality of constructing apparent consideration provides evidence of their serious intent to be bound, cautions the promisor that she has made a binding commitment, and allows the court to distinguish this as such. Therefore, any justification for the Restatement, Second's position must lie in the substantive function of the doctrine: It is contrary to the public interest for courts to become involved in the enforcement of gratuitous promises. Sometimes the circumstances may suggest that the goal of protecting against generosity outweighs the policy of upholding private autonomy, but in other situations, despite what the Restatement, Second, says, the better approach may be to treat the apparent consideration as sufficient where the formal functions of consideration are fully satisfied by a clear document, there is no suggestion of advantage taking or underhanded conduct by the promisee, and no indication that the promisor acted impulsively and with immediate regret.

In some cases, courts adopt the position of the Restatement, Second, and refuse to recognize consideration when it is clearly nominal or false. In others, courts have been willing to give effect to the parties' effort to validate the promise and have upheld promises that were really gratuitous, but were supported by recited or nominal consideration. They have recognized nominal consideration on the basis of the general principle that a court will not inquire into adequacy of consideration, and they have upheld a false recital of consideration either by interpreting the recital as an implied promise to provide the stated act or forbearance at some future time, or by estopping[13] the promisor from denying receipt of recited consideration. For many courts, the decision to validate recited or nominal consideration depends on the court being satisfied that the equities do not favor protecting the promisor for ill-considered generosity or unfair imposition.

§7.7.4 Nominal Consideration in Options

Recall, from section 4.13 that an option (a promise not to revoke an offer for a stated period) does not bind the offeror unless the offeree has given consideration to the offeror in exchange for that promise.[14] The consideration given by the offeree to support the option is distinct from the consideration that the offeree would provide under the underlying contract if he accepts the offer. However, in relation to options, Restatement, Second, adopts a more lenient attitude to purely formal consideration. The justification for this is that an offeror who grants an option does not typically have gratuitous motives. Rather, she has decided to grant the option in the hope of inducing the grantee to enter the underlying contract. Therefore, there is less concern about protecting a grantor from generosity and not intervening to impose legal liability for the promise of a gift. Many courts that follow the stricter attitude toward nominal consideration in other situations are willing to follow the Restatement, Second, and adopt a more flexible approach to options. Similarly, if the consideration recited in an offer is a sham, the court will more readily interpret the recital as a promise to furnish the consideration or will more easily estop the grantor from asserting that the recital was a sham.

§7.8 PAST PERFORMANCE

Because exchange is the basis of consideration, each party's detriment must induce and be induced by the other's. Therefore, if the promisee suffered the detriment before the promise was made, it cannot be said that the detriment was exchanged for the promise. Although the detriment may have induced the promise, it was not itself induced by the promise which had not yet been

---

13. Estoppel is explained in section 8.4. In short, its impact in this context is that because the promisor has participated in setting up the pretense of consideration, he or she cannot now deny that consideration was given. The promisor's earlier conduct induced the promisee reasonably to rely on the validity of the promise, and the promisor is therefore held accountable for that conduct and is precluded from asserting that the consideration is a sham.
14. As explained in section 4.13.4, UCC §2.205 creates an exception to this rule for sales of goods by dispensing with consideration for a firm offer that satisfies its requirements.

made. This means that if a person makes a promise to compensate another for some prior performance, that prior detriment cannot be consideration for the promise. The promise is seen as gratuitous and nonbinding, even if it was seriously and freely made, and even if the prior detriment conferred a valuable benefit on the promisor. For example, in January, Buster lent Al his car for a week so that Al could use it to go on a skiing vacation. At the time, Buster did not ask Al for anything in return for lending him the car. In March, Al decided to give up skiing. Remembering Buster's kindness to him in January, Al promised to give the skis to Buster, stating that he was doing so in consideration for Buster's loan of the car in January. Buster did suffer a legal detriment in lending his car to Al. However, even though Al has described this detriment as consideration, it cannot be. It was suffered prior to the promise and not in exchange for it. This kind of prior detriment is sometimes referred to as "past consideration," but this is a misnomer because it is not consideration at all.

§7.9 THE QUALITY OF A PROMISE AS CONSIDERATION: "MUTUALITY OF OBLIGATION," ILLUSORY, CONDITIONAL, AND ALTERNATIVE PROMISES

§7.9.1 Mutuality and Illusory Promises

The requirement of mutuality of obligation is expressed in the old maxim "both parties must be bound, or neither is bound." Taken too literally, the concept of mutuality can be confusing and misleading, because it seems to suggest that one could never have a unilateral contract, or a contract in which one of the parties has the legal right to escape liability. Yet, both types of contract are well recognized in law. It has been explained in section 4.12 that a promise can be exchanged for an immediate performance, resulting in a unilateral contract in which only the promisor has an outstanding obligation at the instant of contract formation. Elsewhere in this book many other situations are described in which only one of the parties is bound because the other has the right to end the contractual relationship. This is true, for example, in an option contract (see section 4.13) or a contract that is voidable by one party on such grounds as minority (see section 14.2.1), incapacity (see section 14.3.3), bargaining impropriety (see section 13.3), or mistake (see section 15.5). It is also quite valid to provide in a contract for a party to have the right to terminate the contract by giving notice.

Therefore, in modern law, "mutuality" does not mean that both parties must make a future commitment or, if they do, that each must be bound with the same degree of firmness. It also does not mean that the parties must have equal and coextensive obligations under the contract. Because there need not be economic equivalence in the exchange, it is permissible and common for one party to incur far more numerous, extensive, or onerous obligations than the other.[15]

If "mutuality" does not carry any of these implications, what does it mean? In modern law, it is nothing more than a specific application of the general principle of consideration: When consideration consists of the exchange of mutual promises, the undertakings on both sides must be real and meaningful. If the promise of one party has qualifications or limitations so strong that they negate it, it is really no commitment at all. Because it does not bind that party, this lack of consideration voids the apparent contract, so neither party is bound. For example, Buster promises to buy Al's skis for $100, and Al promises to sell them to Buster unless Al changes his mind. This qualification reserves such unlimited discretion to Al that he has really promised nothing. His apparent promise is said to be illusory and hence cannot be consideration. *See* Diagram 7G.

Diagram 7G

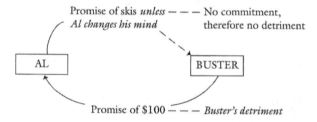

Using the language of mutuality, we could say that because Al is not bound, Buster is not bound either. However, we do not need to formulate it this way. The real problem is that Al has suffered no detriment because he has neither given nor actually promised anything to Buster. Therefore, Buster's return promise is not supported by consideration and is not binding. Because "mutuality" is redundant and misleading, Restatement, Second, §79(c) and Comment f disavow the concept and stress that it should not be thought of as a separate or additional requirement for consideration.

In the above example, Al may have thought that he was being very clever in getting a promise from Buster while keeping his own options open, but his lack of commitment removes binding force from Buster's promise as

---

15. If the imbalance in commitments has been caused by unfair bargaining, the doctrine of unconscionability (*see* section 13.12) may be used to address the problem of unfair imposition.

well, so Al cannot hold Buster to his promise if Al decides to exercise his discretion to go through with the sale. This is a mistake sometimes made in commercial contracts by a party that uses its dominant bargaining power to retain its freedom of action while trying to firmly bind the other party. For example, in *Harris v. Blockbuster, Inc.*, 622 F. Supp. 2d 396 (N.D. Tex. 2009), a subscriber to Blockbuster's online video rental program sued it, claiming that it had violated a federal statute protecting the subscriber's privacy. Blockbuster sought to invoke an arbitration provision in its standard terms, to which the subscriber had signified assent at the time of subscribing by clicking an "I agree" box on Blockbuster's website. (That is, the subscriber bound himself to Blockbuster's standard terms through a clickwrap agreement, as discussed in sections 5.2 and 5.3.) Notwithstanding the subscriber's signification of assent, Blockbuster was not able to enforce the arbitration clause because the court found that it lacked consideration. In its standard terms, Blockbuster had reserved the right to modify the terms, including the arbitration clause, at its discretion. It had no duty to notify its subscribers of the modification, which would take effect immediately, and which would be deemed assented to if the subscriber continued to use the service following the modification. Furthermore, modifications were not stated to be prospective, which meant that changes relating to the arbitration provision could affect disputes that had arisen prior to the modification. The court held that by retaining such broad power to change the terms, Blockbuster had in fact not committed itself to anything, so that any apparent promise that it made was illusory. *See also Hooters of America, Inc. v. Phillips*, 39 F. Supp. 2d 582 (D.S.C. 1998),[16] in which the court held that an arbitration agreement between Hooters and its employee lacked consideration because Hooters' promise was illusory. The agreement was structured to absolutely bind the employee to arbitrate but left Hooters with the discretion to terminate the agreement on notice and to change the arbitration rules and procedures without notice.

The example and cases in the previous paragraph illustrate situations in which a promise is illusory because the party retained unlimited discretion to perform. This is possibly the most obvious illustration of an illusory promise. However, a promise could also be illusory for other reasons. For example, it is also an illusion to promise something based on a condition that cannot occur — say that Al gives his skis to Buster in return for Buster's promise to pay $100 for them if, by the end of the week, Elvis is returned to earth by the aliens who stole him.[17]

---

16. Affirmed without discussion of the consideration question at 173 F.3d 933 (4th Cir. 1999).
17. Of course, some people do not believe this to be an impossible condition.

§7.9.2 Interpretation and the Use of Implied Terms to Cure an Apparently Illusory Promise

The examples given so far try to provide obvious illustrations of the absence or presence of commitment. It is not always this easy to tell if a qualification so eviscerates a promise as to make it illusory: The promise could be subject to some degree of discretion that may not be broad enough to negate commitment. For example, Al and Buster agree that Buster will buy Al's skis for $100 C.O.D. next Monday on condition that Buster can obtain a loan of $100 by then. Al's promise to sell the skis is firm, but Buster's promise to buy is subject to a condition. It could be argued that Buster has made no real commitment. He can prevent fulfillment of the condition simply by not trying to borrow the money. However, if we imply into Buster's undertaking a promise to use best efforts to secure a loan, we impose a detriment upon him and cure the lack of commitment. This promise to make best efforts is not the same as a promise to buy the skis, so that Buster has no obligation to consummate the sale if he tries conscientiously but unsuccessfully to secure the loan. But if he makes no effort at all, he is liable for breach of contract. *See* Diagram 7H.

Diagram 7H

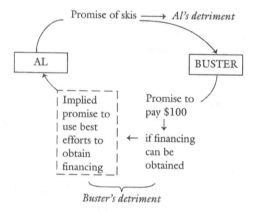

This brings to mind one of the most cherished cases in the contracts repertoire — *Wood v. Lucy, Lady Duff-Gordon*, 222 N.Y. 88 (1917) — in which Judge Cardozo implied an obligation to use best efforts to validate an exclusive dealing contract between Lucy, a fashion maven of her time, and Wood, her business agent. Wood had agreed to pay Lucy half the profits earned from placing her endorsements and selling her designs, but had not, in so many words, promised to promote her wares. When Lucy breached the exclusive agency by endorsing products on her own and keeping all the profits for herself, Wood sued for his share. Lucy argued that there was no contract: Although Wood had undertaken to pay half the profits to her, he had not actually promised to do anything to earn those profits. In light of the obviously commercial intent of the agreement, the court concluded that Lucy's grant of an exclusive agency necessarily gave rise to the implication that Wood was obliged to use best efforts in generating profits. UCC §2.306(2) follows this approach by implying an obligation of best efforts in exclusive dealing contracts involving goods.

We look more closely at the principles of interpretation — including the implication of terms by a court — in Chapter 10. The point to note here is that in most transactions with a commercial purpose, apparently discretionary promises can fairly be interpreted as subject to some implied limitation. When contracting, the parties usually intend their promises to be meaningful, and a later assertion that one of them is illusory is probably just a pretext to escape a bargain that is no longer desired. The process of implying terms to give content to apparently vacuous language comes up in many types of cases, and you will find many examples of this as you read through this book. However, there are some situations in which absolute discretion is exactly what was intended, because one of the parties takes the gamble that the attractiveness of the product or service will be enough to motivate the other to exercise discretion favorably. In such a case, if a court imposes unintended limitations on that discretion, it creates a contract out of an informal relationship that was not intended to be one.

§7.9.3 "Mutuality" in Requirements and Output Contracts Under UCC §2.306

Most sales contracts involve a single item or a specified quantity of goods. In some situations, however, it may suit the parties to leave the quantity of goods open-ended on the understanding that the quantity to be supplied under the contract will be determined either by the buyer's requirements or by the seller's output. The parties are likely to find a requirements contract most desirable if the seller is confident that it can produce enough to satisfy the buyer's demands, and the buyer is unsure of its exact needs and wishes to avoid the risk of ordering a specified quantity which may turn out to be short or excessive. An output contract suits the parties when the seller wishes to dispose of its full production in one transaction, and the buyer is confident that it can use all that the seller can supply.

For example, assume that the seller is a vineyard and the buyer is a winery. The buyer is not exactly sure what quantity of grapes it will need next year because it only buys grapes to supplement what it produces on its own vines. The quantity it needs will depend on its own crop yield. The winery therefore does not want to try to predict its needs in advance by contracting for a set quantity of grapes because this could lead to waste if its own grapes are plentiful, and a shortfall if they are scarce. The buyer therefore makes a requirements contract with the seller under which the buyer promises to buy and the seller to supply the buyer's total demand for grapes during a specific period. By contrast, an output contract better suits the parties' needs if the buyer knows that it can use everything that the seller produces — it can never grow enough of its own grapes to satisfy its needs, and it has enough capacity to use all its own grapes plus all the grapes that the seller can produce. The seller is happy to sell its entire crop to the buyer, because this saves the costs of multiple transactions with different buyers. The parties therefore enter an output contract under which the seller promises to sell and the buyer to take all the grapes grown by the seller during a specified period.

Some earlier cases refused to uphold requirements and output contracts because the flexible quantity term was regarded as too vague and also because such contracts lacked "mutuality." That is, the broad discretion given to the party who determined quantity made that party's promise illusory because a requirements buyer could elect to have no requirements and an output seller could decide to produce no goods. In time, it came to be generally accepted that requirements and output contracts served a valuable commercial purpose, and that this approach was untenable. The problems of vagueness and lack of mutuality were solved by recognizing that even if the contract did not say so expressly, the discretion to determine quantity is limited by an implied obligation of good faith or reasonableness, and by an implied obligation of exclusive dealing.

The obligation of exclusive dealing is essential for an arrangement to qualify as a requirements or output contract. The promise to buy requirements or to sell output is meaningless if the party with the discretion could simply manipulate the extent of the requirements or output by buying or selling elsewhere.[18] As noted above, even if there is no express promise of exclusive dealing, it is often possible to imply it from the language of the contract in context. *See*, for example *Essco Geometric v. Harvard Industries*, 46 F.3d 718 (8th Cir. 1995). However, sometimes the language used in the agreement or the context may preclude such an interpretation. For example, in *Brooklyn Bagel Boys, Inc. v. Earthgrains Refrigerated Dough Products, Inc.*, 212 F.3d 373 (7th Cir. 2000) the court could not find any basis for interpreting the contract to require the buyer to buy all its bagel requirements exclusively

---

18. The obligation for exclusive dealing need not necessarily relate to the party's entire requirements or output of a product. It is permissible to confine it to a defined portion of the requirements or output, provided that the scope of the exclusive dealing is clear and identifiable. For example, a seller of corn could agree to commit only the output from particular fields, or a buyer of office stationery could commit to take only its requirements of copier paper from the seller.

from the seller, so it found the arrangement to be merely a "buyer's option" under which the seller made an ongoing offer to sell bagels at a stated price, accepted by the buyer each time it placed an order. This means that there was no requirements contract, but rather a series of discrete contracts which imposed no ongoing obligation on the buyer to buy bagels.

The relationship between a buyer and seller in a requirements contract is illustrated by Diagram 7I. (In an output contract, the discretionary performance would be on the seller's side of the exchange.)

Diagram 7I

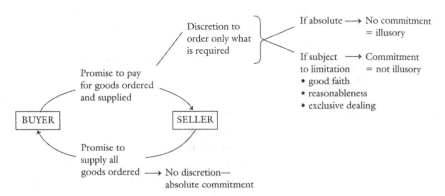

This approach forms the basis of UCC §2.306(1) that implicitly recognizes the exclusive dealing obligation and imposes both a good faith and a reasonable expectations test on the party who determines quantity. It states that when a contract measures quantity by the seller's output or the buyer's requirements, this means the actual output or requirements as may occur in good faith. In addition, it provides that the quantity tendered or demanded may not be disproportionate to any estimate, or if no estimate was stated, to any normal or otherwise comparable output or requirements. This language sets out two tests: The disproportionality standard is an objective measure that prevents the buyer in a requirements contract or the seller in an output contract from demanding or tendering a quantity of the goods that is disproportionate to an estimated or historic requirement or output. In essence, the purpose of this standard is to protect the output buyer or requirements seller by pegging the quantity of goods at a level approximate to what might reasonably be expected, based on an estimate or on prior dealings under the contract. The disproportionality standard does not apply in every case. It is relevant only where the parties have stated an estimate or where prior dealings under the contract have established a comparable prior quantity. Also, a number of courts have interpreted §2.306 as applicable only to increases in demand or output, so it is not helpful where a disproportionally small quantity is demanded or tendered.

7. Consideration

By contrast, the good faith test applies in all situations and is therefore the broader and more important test. In addition, because good faith is such an open-ended and relative standard, courts often struggle to decide whether particular conduct crosses the line that separates acceptable self-interest from bad faith. The good faith standard therefore merits special attention.[19]

"Good faith" is defined in both Articles 1 and 2. The definitions used to be different. The Article 1 definition (§1.201(19)) used a purely subjective standard, "honesty in fact in the conduct or transaction concerned," which applied generally. However, the Article 2 definition (§2.103(b)) had a stricter standard that combined an objective and subjective element. It required both "honesty in fact" and "the observance of reasonable commercial standards of fair dealing in the trade." The Article 2 definition applied only to merchants. Therefore, prior to the revision of Article 1, the good faith of a buyer or seller who qualified as a merchant was determined under the combined subjective-objective standard, while the good faith of a nonmerchant was tested purely on the basis of subjective honesty.

In revising Article 1, the drafters felt that the general definition of good faith, requiring only subjective honesty, was too weak, so they changed it to conform to the definition in §2.103(b). (In the revision, the numbering of the section was changed from §1.201(19) to §1.201(20)). Therefore, except in the few states that have not adopted the new definition of good faith in revised Article 1, there is now only one definition of good faith, applicable to all parties, regardless of whether they are merchants. It requires both the subjective "honesty in fact" and the objective "observance of reasonable commercial standards of fair dealing."

One of the principal problems in enforcing the obligation of good faith is that honesty and fair dealing are such elastic and relative standards. It is therefore difficult to apply those broad standards to particular conduct and to predict whether a court will find that conduct to satisfy or fall short of them. To decide whether action is honestly motivated and commercially reasonable, the court must evaluate all the circumstances under which the contract was made and the requirements or output were determined. Clearly, the very fact that the parties have made a requirements or output contract means that they must contemplate that the buyer or seller is not bound to fixed quantities, and that it may make a decision that significantly changes its requirements or output. The crucial question is therefore to determine if that decision was made in good faith. *Empire Gas Corp. v. American Bakeries Co.*, 840 F.2d 1333 (7th Cir. 1988) is one of the leading cases on this issue. The court said that it would clearly not be good faith for a buyer

---

19. In addition to the discussion in this section, the good faith standard is also raised in section 10.8.2.

to reduce its requirements by buying the goods from another seller, or to reduce orders simply because it has second thoughts about the contract or because the contract is not as advantageous as it had hoped. However, a buyer may be in good faith in reducing its requirements for legitimate and compelling business reasons, such as technological advances that change fundamental needs or dramatic changes in market demand for the buyer's products. In a more recent case, *Wiseco, Inc. v. Johnson Controls, Inc.* 155 Fed. Appx. 815 (6th Cir. 2005), the buyer entered into a requirements contract with the seller to buy components used by the buyer to make headrests for Jeeps. The buyer's orders for the parts dropped dramatically when Jeep changed the headrest design, making the particular components supplied under the requirements contract inappropriate. The court applied the good faith test and concluded that the buyer had legitimate business reasons for its reduced requirements. It no longer needed the parts because its customer had changed the design of the headrest. The seller bore the burden of proving that the buyer's reduction in requirements was in bad faith, and it had not sustained that burden.

§7.9.4 Conditional Promises

In the example in which Buster promised to pay for the skis if Elvis is returned by the aliens, the promise was illusory because it was conditional on an event that could not occur. However, a promise is not illusory merely because it is conditional. A qualified or conditional promise is good consideration provided that the contingency is genuine. That is, it is an uncertain future event within the realm of possibility and outside the complete and discretionary control of the promisor. If these requirements are satisfied, the conditional promise is a commitment. A legal detriment is suffered, even though the obligation to perform the promise only comes into effect upon fulfillment of the condition. For example, Al and Buster make an agreement under which Al promises to give his skis to Buster, and Buster promises to pay $100 for them on condition that he win this week's state lottery, in which he has already bought a ticket. If Buster does not win the lottery, the parties agree that he need not pay anything for the skis. Although Al's promise to give the skis to Buster is absolute, Buster's return promise is conditional. If he wins, he must pay. If not, he gets the skis free. The contingent nature of his promise does not prevent it from being consideration, because he suffers the detriment of binding himself to pay on the happening of an uncertain future event outside his control. This is a real contingency (unlike the return of Elvis), and its occurrence is not within Buster's control.

A type of conditional promise that appears to involve very wide discretion is a condition of satisfaction. This is a condition that allows one of the parties to reject a performance by the other (and to refuse to perform his own undertaking) if he is not satisfied with it.[20] For example, on February 1, Al and Buster enter an agreement under which Al sells his skis to Buster for $100. The agreement provides that Al will deliver the skis to Buster on February 15 and Buster will pay for them in installments of $10 per month for ten months, beginning on March 1. The agreement authorizes Al to examine Buster's credit record and to cancel the contract by February 14 if the credit report is not satisfactory to him. Such a condition might appear to render Al's promise illusory because he could simply negate his promise to sell the skis by declaring himself dissatisfied with Buster's credit record. However, unless the only plausible interpretation of the agreement is that the parties intended to give unrestrained discretion to the party making the judgment of satisfaction, a court will imply a term that limits the discretion enough to avoid the problem of illusory promise. Therefore, even if the contract does not expressly say so, the party who determines satisfaction is obliged to exercise his judgment either in good faith or reasonably.

To decide whether to apply the subjective good faith standard or the objective reasonableness standard, the court looks at all the circumstances of the transaction. The rule of thumb is that dissatisfaction must be in good faith where the performance involves a matter of personal taste, but it must be reasonable where the performance is of a technical, mechanical, or commercial nature. Stated differently, a court may conclude that the parties contemplated good faith subjective judgment where the performance involves a matter of personal taste. However, the party whose performance is to be judged would not reasonably expect such an idiosyncratic standard to be applied to a commercial or technical performance. (Of course, parties who want to avoid the uncertainty of allowing the court to decide on the proper standard can simply express in the contract which standard is to be used.)

The evaluation of a person's creditworthiness is a matter of commercial judgment, which means that an objective approach would usually be more appropriate. However, the particular circumstances of this case, involving a consumer-to-consumer sale and a creditor who is not in the business of extending credit, may call for a more subjective test based on good faith satisfaction. Whatever test is used, the point for present purposes is that the implication of a standard to control Al's judgment prevents his promise from being illusory.

§7.9.5 Promises of Alternative Performances

A form of discretionary promise is one involving alternative performances. For example, Al promises to sell his skis to Buster in exchange for Buster's

---

20. Conditions of satisfaction are discussed further in section 16.8.2.

promise, in his discretion, to pay $100 or to mow Al's lawn for two months. Provided that each of the promises, on its own, would be consideration, there is nothing objectionable in permitting a party to select between alternative promises. This is illustrated by Diagram 7J.

Diagram 7J

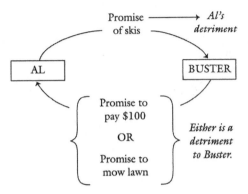

The case is more difficult if one of the alternatives imposes so small a burden on the party who has the choice that it would not likely have induced the promise on its own. For example, Buster may make the alternative promises either to buy the skis for $100 or to give Al notice of cancellation of the sale. The purpose of this is to give Buster the discretion to escape the contract if he so desires, and he is really no more firmly bound than if he promised to buy the skis if he feels like it. Although the obligation to give notice is a detriment, it is such a slight detriment that it would not on its own be likely to have induced Al to commit himself to sell the skis. Nevertheless, seen as a package with the more burdensome alternative, one can understand that the parties could have been satisfied with the commercial utility of this arrangement, and Al may have bargained for the chance that Buster would exercise his discretion in favor of completing the sale. By refusing to inquire into the adequacy of Buster's alternative detriment of giving notice, a court can uphold the transaction. This may seem like the exultation of form over substance when compared to the invalid purely discretionary promise, but the provision of notice gives the court a basis for validation, if it deems the agreement to have been fairly bargained for.[21]

---

21. For example, in *Johnson Lakes Development, Inc. v. Central Nebraska Pub. Power & Irrigation Dist.* 576 N.W.2d 806 (Neb. 1998) the court held that an obligation to give advance notice of termination was enough to prevent a party's promise from being illusory, provided that the party was irrevocably bound for an appreciable period of time or otherwise rendered some performance that would qualify as consideration.

Examples

1. Penny Less entered college two years ago at the age of 22. At the time, her Uncle Rich, concerned about reports of excessive drinking by college students, promised her that if she did not drink any alcoholic beverages in her first year of college, he would give her $5,000 at the end of that year. Penny thanked Uncle Rich, stating that it would be easy money because she hated the taste of alcohol.

   Penny did not consume any alcohol during her first year of college. When she reported this to Uncle Rich at the end of the year and asked for her reward, he said, "I have changed my mind about giving you the money. Don't be disappointed. Sobriety is its own reward." Was Uncle Rich free to change his mind?

2. Would your answer to Example 1 change if Penny was 19 years old at the time that she made her agreement with Uncle Rich? At that time she was old enough to be a major for the purposes of contracting. However, state law prohibits a person below the age of 21 years from consuming alcohol and provides for penalties to be imposed on a minor who violates the prohibition.

3. In January 2011, Dotty Com borrowed $500,000 from Angel Investor to finance her new startup business. The loan bore 6 percent interest and was due for repayment on June 1, 2012. In late May 2012 Dotty told Angel that the business was struggling and she did not have the cash to repay the loan. She believed, however, that if her creditors would give her a break she could save the business, but if they refused to cooperate, she would have to liquidate it. Because the business was presently insolvent, creditors would receive only about 50 percent of their claims on liquidation. Dotty asked Angel to accept 80 percent of the debt in full settlement, and to wait six months for payment. Dotty told Angel that she planned to ask all her other creditors for the same concession. Angel agreed and the parties executed a written agreement reflecting that Dotty would pay Angel $400,000 in full settlement of the debt, with interest at 6 percent, by no later than December 1, 2012. Did Angel receive consideration for this agreement?

4. When Chevy K. Marro was 29 years old, his Aunt Charity expressed the intention of buying him a new car for his thirtieth birthday. Chevy knew that Aunt Charity always talked big but never did what she promised, so he suggested that if Charity really meant what she said, she would write out the promise and sign it. Charity agreed, and Chevy (known for his shrewd business sense) drew up the document. It stated that Charity, "in consideration for value received" from Chevy, undertook to deliver the car (which was specifically described by make,

model, and year) to Chevy on his thirtieth birthday. Charity and Chevy signed the writing. True to form, Aunt Charity gave Chevy a sweater for his thirtieth birthday and did not deliver the car.

a. Is Aunt Charity obligated by her promise of the car?

b. Change the facts to the following extent: The writing stated that Charity undertook to deliver the car "in consideration for a cheeseburger, which Chevy delivered to Charity upon signing this agreement." Chevy did in fact deliver the cheeseburger to Charity. Is she obligated by her promise of the car?

c. When Chevy threatened to sue her for the car, Aunt Charity became very annoyed. She demands that he return the sweater that she gave him as a thirtieth birthday present on the basis that Chevy gave her no consideration for it. Does she have the right to reclaim it?

5. Hunter Fortune used to work as a gardener on the country estate of Buck Plentiful, a billionaire. After Hunter was discharged by the groundskeeper for incompetence, he sued Buck for $1 million, alleging that he was sexually harassed and emotionally abused by the groundskeeper while in Buck's employ. Buck believed that the claim was without substance but did not want any scandal in his household, so he offered to settle the claim out of court for $10,000. Hunter accepted, and a settlement agreement was executed. After the agreement, Buck had second thoughts and refused to pay Hunter. Does Hunter have a valid claim arising from the agreement?

6. Ivor E. Keyes is a gifted pianist. On hearing him play, his beloved Aunt Charity determined to do something to help him advance his career. Ivor told her that he needed to get some training from a really fine pianist to improve his interpretation and style. He had contacted the celebrated Maestro Molto Bravissimo but had not engaged him as a teacher because he could not afford his fee of $150 an hour. Aunt Charity declared: "You shall have him as your teacher. I will send you a check for $15,000 tomorrow. That should cover 100 lessons." Ivor thanked her and said, "Auntie, if I ever make it to Carnegie Hall, I will get you the best seat in the house." She replied, "Yes, that will be nice, dear. I'll hold you to it." Do Ivor and Aunt Charity have a contract?

7. Save Our Slugs (SOS) is a nonprofit organization formed to advance the interests of common garden slugs and to lobby for legislation to prevent assault on their natural habitat. One evening an articulate and persuasive fundraiser for the organization called on E.Z. Tutch to solicit a contribution. The fundraiser's impassioned and heart-rending plea for support convinced E.Z. Tutch that the poor creatures were under siege, and that urgent action was needed to save them from extinction. He therefore signed the following pledge card. (Portions of the card

were preprinted. E.Z. Tutch's handwritten portions are in italics and underlined.)

> In consideration of my love of all earth's defenseless creatures, and in consideration for the promise of SOS to use my contribution to advance the cause for which it was constituted, I, *E.Z. Tutch*, hereby pledge the sum of *$500.00* to SOS, payable in *10* equal monthly installments, beginning on *December 1, 2012*. I understand that this contribution is tax deductible.
>
> Signed: *E.Z. Tutch* Date: *November 30, 2011*.

The next day, E. Z. Tutch realized that he had been overcome by his emotions the prior evening and had acted thoughtlessly. He has had many large expenses lately and really cannot afford the amount pledged. He regrets his decision to make the pledge and wishes to cancel it. May he do so without incurring legal liability?

8. Gutter Press, Inc., is a publisher of paperback books. Bonzo Steele, a famous bodybuilder and action-movie hero, was recently indicted for the gruesome murder of his agent, and the case has attracted enthusiastic public attention. Gutter Press plans to publish a book on Bonzo's seamy past and on the events that led to his present predicament. It wishes to produce the book as quickly as possible so that it hits the stands at supermarket checkouts before the inevitable lapse of the public attention span.

   Gutter Press engaged Tabb Lloyd, a journalist, to write the book. The parties signed a written agreement which included the following terms:
   a. Tabb promised to submit a completed manuscript within four weeks.
   b. Gutter Press promised to publish the manuscript provided that it found it to be satisfactory.
   c. If the manuscript was published, Gutter Press would pay Tabb a royalty of 15 percent of gross receipts.
   d. During the first week following execution of the agreement, Gutter Press had the right, for any reason, to cancel it by delivering written notice of termination to Tabb. After the first week, Gutter Press could cancel at any time before completion of the manuscript by delivering the notice to Tabb and paying him a fee of $1,000 for all work done up to that time.

   The day after signing the agreement, Tabb told his friends about it. They were disgusted and accused him of selling out and perverting his art for the sake of a quick and dirty buck. This so shamed Tabb that he no longer wishes to write the book. Can he escape his commitment to Gutter Press?

9. Constance De Votion decided to retire after working for the Turn Coat Corporation for 40 years. On her last day of work, the president of the

company called her into his office and presented her with the following letter, signed by all the members of the board of directors:

> In recognition of your long and faithful service to this company, we are honored to give you an all-expenses-paid, two-week vacation at the hotel of your choice anywhere on the North American continent. When you have decided on your destination, please call the company's travel agent to make the arrangements. We hope that this vacation will be a joyful beginning to your richly-deserved retirement.

Constance spent a happy couple of weeks planning her vacation and settled on a lavish coastal resort. When she called the travel agent, he denied any knowledge of this arrangement and said that he had not been authorized by Turn Coat to book a trip for her. Constance called the president of Turn Coat, who told her with obvious discomfort that, a few days after the letter was given to Constance, the board had to approve cutbacks in spending because of a downturn in the company's profits. One of the savings approved was the withdrawal of its promise to her. Can Constance hold Turn Coat to its promise?

10. Gerry Atrick, another employee of the Turn Coat Corporation, had worked for it for 35 years. Although he used to be a superb worker, he had recently become absentminded and slow. His work was incompetent and had to be redone by others. Gerry was an employee at will, which meant that he could be summarily dismissed. The president was going to fire him, but the president's secretary dissuaded her from doing so by pointing out that the dismissal of such an old and loyal employee would be cruel and would upset and demoralize his coworkers. The president therefore offered Gerry a year's pay if he would retire. Gerry accepted and submitted his resignation. That night, as the president was thinking about the events of her day, she suddenly realized that she did not really care if the staff was upset and she would now have to justify this decision to the tightfisted Board. The next day, she called Gerry into her office, revoked the promise, and dismissed him. Is Turn Coat's promise binding?

11. Peters Pickled Peppers manufactures pickled peppers. Last fall it made an agreement with Hal Apeno, a farmer, under which Hal undertook to supply all the peppers Peters would need for its bottling operations next season. During negotiations preceding the agreement, Peters told Hal that its average needs in the last five years had been between seven and ten tons of peppers. Hal was satisfied that he could grow sufficient quantities to meet this range of demand. This range of expected requirements was recorded as an estimate in the written contract.

A short time later, Peters' Board met to discuss disappointing sales in the prior year. Studies showed that new and aggressive competitors had gained the lion's share of the pickled pepper market, and all indications were that next year would be even worse. The Board decided to switch from peppers to persimmons, for which there was very little competition. Peters' existing plant was suitable for the processing of persimmons, so the conversion could be achieved at small cost.

Because of this decision, Peters had no need for peppers, and it wrote to Hal telling him so. Hal sued Peters for breach of contract and Peters defended the suit on the basis that it had the right under the contract to order no pickles if it had no requirements. The trial court granted summary judgment to Peters on the theory that there was no contract because the transaction lacks mutuality of obligation. Is the judge right?

Explanations

1. This Example pays homage to cases such as *Hamer v. Sidway*, discussed in section 7.3.1, in which a well-to-do family member promises some reward for specified behavior. Like Willie, the nephew in *Hamer*, Penny's detriment is not "detrimental" in the usual sense because it is really in her best interests. In fact (apparently unlike Willie) she does not even "suffer" in the usual sense because she has no desire to engage in the activity. Notwithstanding, she suffers a legal detriment simply by forgoing something that she is entitled to do. She exchanges this for Uncle Rich's promise of payment, providing him with a noneconomic but identifiable benefit.

   Because the benefit to Uncle Rich has no commercial purpose and is apparently motivated by his concern for Penny's well-being, one may be tempted to see his promise as the promise of a conditional gift. However, Penny's promise is not related to the manner in which the gift is to be used nor is it a means of taking delivery of the gift. Even a noncommercial promise may be bargained for if it reasonably appears intended to induce particular action desired by the promisor.

   Another factor that may make Uncle Rich's promise appear to be a conditional gift is that it is hard to imagine that he could sue Penny to enforce her obligation not to drink. However, this can be explained if we recognize that Uncle Rich's offer proposed a unilateral contract, in which Penny gave no undertaking but accepted Uncle Rich's offer by rendering the performance, which was not complete until the end of the semester.[22]

2. If Penny had the legal right to drink alcohol, her forbearance from drinking it would be consideration. However, because the state prohibits her from consuming alcohol, she does not actually give up any legal right, and hence does not suffer a legal detriment, by promising to abstain. In fact, she has a pre-existing duty to the state not to drink. Of course, Penny could disobey the law, so the question is whether it is good consideration to forbear from unlawful activity. As a matter of both doctrine and policy, the law could justify holding that Penny's forbearance from violating the law is not a legal detriment, and therefore not consideration for Uncle Rich's promise.[23]

    However, there is an argument for finding consideration: There is value to Uncle Rich in Penny's obedience to the law, so, despite what is said above, she may be able to persuade a court to treat her desisting from the power to drink as a legal detriment. In addition, there is a basis for not applying the pre-existing duty rule where the duty is not owed to the promisor. Unless an agreement may risk the corruption of a public official (such as an official's promise to perform his job in exchange for a promise of additional reward) or is otherwise a violation of public policy, the public interest is not necessarily harmed by upholding a promise meant to give a person an added incentive to comply with the law.

3. The principal focus of this Example is the application of the pre-existing duty rule to contract modification.[24] The general rule is that a creditor's promise to accept less than the amount owing on an admitted debt or to extend the due date of the debt is not binding, because the debtor incurs no legal detriment in exchange for that promise. (*See* Restatement, Second, §73.) The debtor had a pre-existing duty to pay the debt when it fell due on June 1, and her promise to pay it over time after that date adds nothing to that duty.[25] As noted in sections 7.5.2 and 7.6, if the agreement to reduce and extend the debt was fairly bargained, it is

---

22. The acceptance of an offer for a unilateral contract is explained in section 4.12. In short, if Uncle Rich's offer could be accepted only by the completion of Penny's performance (forbearing from drinking for the entire semester), no contract comes into existence until completion of Penny's performance. Once the performance is complete, a unilateral contract arises in which only Uncle Rich's obligation remains outstanding. If Penny does not perform, she never accepts the offer, and Uncle Rich has no contractual right to enforce. To protect Penny from having the offer revoked after she has begun her performance in reliance on it, the law deems the offer irrevocable as soon as Penny begins her performance.

23. This issue did not come up in the *Hamer* case.

24. In addition to the discussion in this chapter, contract modification is dealt with in section 13.9.

25. Had the debt been disputed, an agreement to compromise the dispute would likely be supported by consideration, as discussed in section 7.6 and Example 5.

hard to justify the policy of invalidating the agreement under the pre-existing duty rule. However, a strict application of doctrine will invalidate it unless the court can find that Dotty incurred some new detriment in exchange for Angel's promise to reduce and extend the debt.

It is not easy to find any new detriment on Dotty's part. Her undertaking to pay interest at 6 percent is not a new detriment because she was already obliged to pay interest at that rate under the original contract. Dotty's statement that she intended to approach other creditors with the same proposal could be a detriment if she made a promise to do that. However, as described in the facts, this seems more a statement of intent than a commitment. Finally, a promise not to liquidate a business could be consideration provided that the business is truly in financial trouble and Dotty had the legal right to liquidate it. The liquidation must be a legitimate solution to the financial problems, and not suggested in bad faith as a form of blackmail. However, again, Dotty's vague reference to the possibility of liquidation does not seem to rise to the level of a promise.

The common law recognizes a narrow exception to the requirement that a modification must be supported by consideration: It dispenses with the need for consideration if the modification is in response to unforeseen difficulties that have imposed an unexpected burden on the promisee. However, financial adversity is usually not unforeseen in a new business venture unless Dotty can establish some significant and unexpected external cause for the difficulty.

4. a. Chevy has given no consideration to Aunt Charity for her promise, which is clearly intended as a gift, not an exchange. The parties have attempted to validate the transaction by reciting that an unspecified consideration has been given. Restatement, Second, §71, comment b, regards such a false recital as ineffective. Some courts may be more sympathetic to this kind of effort at satisfying the formal function of consideration, but other courts will only uphold a formal recitation of consideration if a promise to furnish the recited consideration can be implied (which cannot be done when the recital does not specify what the purported consideration is), or the promisee's reliance on the promise creates grounds for estopping the promisor from denying the receipt of consideration.

   b. There is obviously a huge disparity in value between a new car and a cheeseburger. However, the cheeseburger could qualify as consideration if the court adopts the approach of refusing to inquire into the adequacy of consideration. The court applied this principle in *Harris v. Time, Inc.* 191 Cal. App. 3d 449 (1987). Recall that this case was discussed in Explanation 10(a) of Chapter 4 in relation to the question of whether an advertisement could constitute an offer.

The court decided that Time did make an offer by stating on the mailer envelope that it would give the recipient a calculator watch "just for opening this envelope." In addition to the offer and acceptance issue, the court considered whether the recipient of the mailer had given consideration for the promise of the calculator watch. Time argued that the mere act of opening an envelope was too slight and valueless to constitute a bargained-for detriment. The court disagreed — Time obviously attached some value to enticing the recipient to open the envelope and, in any event, the court would not enquire into the adequacy of consideration.

If we assume that the calculator watch in *Harris* was a cheap trinket, the disparity between the value of the detriment of opening an envelope and the value of a promise of the watch may not be that great. By contrast, the value difference between the cheeseburger and the new car is monumental. In the absence of evidence that Aunt Charity had some special reason for craving the burger, we have to assume that it was exchanged simply as a formality, in an attempt to validate her promise of a gift. Some courts respect the parties' use of this formal device and decline to enquire into the adequacy of the exchange. Others refuse to employ the rule against measuring the adequacy of consideration where the consideration is so slight as to be nominal.

c. The gift of the sweater has already been given, and there is no longer a promise to be enforced. Although the absence of consideration precludes enforcement of a promise, it is not grounds for recovering an executed gift. (We need not concern ourselves with any grounds outside of contract law for reclaiming a gift.)

5. Unlike the agreement between Dotty and Angel in Example 3, this settlement agreement compromises a claim disputed on the merits and unliquidated in amount.[26] An agreement to settle a disputed claim is supported by consideration because each party forbears from persisting in the full claim and defense. However, as discussed in section 7.6, for consideration to exist the dispute must be genuine. A person has no legal right to assert a bogus claim or defense, so forbearing from that right is not a legal detriment. This technical explanation accords with a more compelling public policy concern: A person should not be allowed to assert a vexatious claim or defense and then to argue that he gave consideration by settling it. Restatement, Second, §74 applies an alternative objective or subjective test to decide if a dispute is genuine.

---

26. A claim is unliquidated where its amount is uncertain and cannot be determined by simple arithmetic means. The only way that the amount of Hunter's damages can be determined is by a trial.

Either the claim or defense must be reasonably tenable because of uncertainty in law or fact, or the party asserting it must have a good faith belief in its merits. Some courts require both these standards to be met, and some focus only on subjective good faith.

The Example is deliberately ambiguous on Hunter's claim. The claim appears to be based on alleged sexual harassment, the intentional infliction of emotional distress, and possibly wrongful discharge. If the wrongful acts were committed by Buck's agent, he could be liable for damages. There is, doubtless, a plausible basis in law to make the claim for damages. The crucial question is whether there is a genuine dispute on the facts. If Hunter was in fact discharged for incompetence and his claim is fabricated for revenge or to extort a nuisance payment from his wealthy ex-employer, his forbearance from asserting this bogus claim cannot furnish consideration for the settlement on either a good faith or a reasonableness test.

6. Aunt Charity clearly has suffered a detriment in promising to pay $15,000 to Ivor. However, this is nothing more than a gratuitous promise, like her promise to Chevy in Example 4, unless Ivor has given consideration in exchange for it. The only undertaking that could conceivably qualify as consideration is his assertion that he will get her the best seat in the house if he ever makes it to Carnegie Hall. (His implicit undertaking to use the money for piano instruction is best treated as nothing more than a condition of the gift and should not qualify as consideration.)

It is not clear that Ivor's statement was really a serious promise at all. The context in which it was made and its tone suggest that it may have been nothing more than an expression of gratitude and hope for spectacular success. Even if it is a real promise, it has several problems. First, it is very vague. It does not make it clear what is meant by the "best seat," nor does it specify the concert or concerts for which it will be obtained. Second, it is contingent on a very uncertain future event. A conditional promise could qualify as consideration provided that the fulfillment of the condition is not entirely at the will of the promisor, and the contingency is not so remote as to make it unlikely that the event would occur. (A promise subject to such a remote contingency would be nothing more than a sham.) Third, unless Ivor can be interpreted to have promised a large number of free concerts, the value of his apparent consideration is disproportionately small in relation to Aunt Charity's promise. (It is worth even less than the face amount of a ticket because its value must be discounted to take account of the uncertainty of the condition occurring.) Courts normally do not evaluate the adequacy of consideration, and a court may decline to do so in this case. However, sometimes (especially when there are other indications of gratuitous intent) a court could take a significant discrepancy in values into account, and may find that the transaction is really not an exchange but a gift formalized by a nominal return.

Finally, even if Ivor did make a promise and Aunt Charity accepted it by her response, it does not seem that his promise was in exchange for Aunt Charity's promise. He made it after she had already told him she would give him $15,000, so it cannot be said to have induced her promise.

The basis for holding that Ivor gave consideration for Aunt Charity's promise is therefore quite thin, and the transaction really seems to be nothing more than a promise of a gift. An argument for consideration is not inconceivable, but it is shaky.

7. The pledge suggests three forms of purported consideration, but none of them likely qualifies as consideration.

First, the pledge form recites that the pledge is in consideration for E.Z. Tutch's love of defenseless creatures. This love may have motivated him to make the pledge (and even this is suspect, given that it is a standard recitation on the pledge form), but motive must be distinguished from consideration that must consist of a legal detriment suffered by SOS in exchange for his promise.

Second, the pledge form recites as consideration SOS's promise to use the contribution to further the purpose for which it was established. Even if the commitment by SOS is a promise, given in exchange for E.Z. Tutch's promise to donate money, SOS's promise may not qualify as a detriment to it for two reasons. One is that SOS may have a pre-existing duty, under its charter as a nonprofit organization, to use donated funds to further the purpose for which it is established. This duty likely is owed not only to the state, but also to the public, including contributors. The other is that to suffer a detriment, SOS must have had the legal right not to use the funds for the promised purpose. However, at the time of making the promise, and until E.Z. Tutch actually gives the funds to SOS, it has no legal right to use them at all. Therefore, its undertaking to use them for the purpose specified by E.Z. Tutch seems more in the nature of an undertaking to use a gift for the purpose designated by the donor. As noted in section 7.3.5, it can be very tricky to distinguish a promise that is a legal detriment from one that is merely a condition of gift. A court may underplay this distinction so that it can validate a charitable promise. The task of finding consideration for a rather obvious gift is made easier if the donee makes a commitment that extends even slightly beyond the mere promise to use the gift as specified. That small additional detriment could qualify as consideration, even if it is implausible that it really induced the promise. In this case, no such additional detriment is apparent.

Third, the pledge form indicates that the contribution is tax deductible, which may suggest that E.Z. Tutch receives consideration for his pledge in the form of the benefit of a tax deduction. However, it is important to remember that a benefit to the promisor is not enough for consideration. The benefit must be linked to a detriment suffered by the promisee. The benefit of a reduction in taxes, gained from the government, does not translate into a legal detriment suffered by SOS.

It would be a stretch to find that SOS gave consideration for E.Z. Tutch's pledge. If the pledge is not supported by consideration, he can cancel it without liability. Consideration doctrine has fulfilled its cautionary function by enabling the donor to escape his generous impulse and allocate his income to the payment of his creditors.

8. Gutter Press and Tabb have exchanged promises. The issue is whether Gutter Press's discretion to escape its commitment to publish the book and to pay royalties is so wide as to make its promise illusory. The agreement gives Gutter Press two grounds for escaping its commitment. First, it can refuse to publish the manuscript if it finds it unsatisfactory. Second, it has the absolute right to terminate the agreement by giving notice in the first week, and thereafter by giving notice and paying Buck $1,000.

Conditions of satisfaction were explained in section 7.9.4. Unless the contract made it clear that Gutter Press would have unbridled discretion to be dissatisfied (which it does not) the satisfaction clause obliges Gutter Press to exercise its discretion either in good faith or reasonably. Even if this commitment is not expressed in the agreement, it is readily implied. If the agreement does not specify the standard (as this agreement does not), the court determines whether it is subjective or objective. The rule of thumb is that a subjective standard is used if the purpose of the contract is to serve the party's personal taste, but an objective test is used if the satisfaction clause relates to matters of technical or commercial utility. Subjective satisfaction might be appropriate if Tabb's contract was with an individual who planned to use the manuscript for his personal enjoyment. However, this is a commercial venture, and Tabb surely would not reasonably expect that the publisher could reject the manuscript on the basis for purely subjective reasons. The proper enquiry is whether a reasonable publisher would find the book up to standard and capable of gainful exploitation. Undoubtedly, the writing of literature is not a purely technical matter, so some element of taste (even if that is bad taste) must come in to the evaluation, but the focus is on generally acceptable standards in the trade, rather than the idiosyncratic tastes of this publisher. Of course, the question of whether to imply an objective or subjective standard would become important if Gutter Press had rejected the manuscript and we had to decide if it was justified in doing so. However, at this stage, we are concerned only with the question of whether the satisfaction clause gives it such wide discretion as to make its promise illusory. The implication of either a good faith or a reasonableness standard cures that problem.

An unfettered termination right removes all commitment and makes the promise illusory. However, if Gutter Press undertakes to incur any detriment in terminating, consideration is present. The agreement may be viewed as giving Gutter Press the right to choose between alternative performances, and as long as each one would be consideration on its own, this right to select between alternatives does not negate consideration.

Is each consideration on its own? There can be little doubt that the promise to publish and pay royalties and the promise to pay $1,000 are detriments. The termination on notice in the first week may seem to be an unbridled right to escape the contract, but courts usually uphold agreements subject to such termination provisions provided that notice of termination must be given. The provision of notice is essential and the right to terminate without notice makes the promise illusory. (Even where there is no express requirement of notice, a court may have the basis to imply a promise of reasonable notice if the implication is consistent with the express language of the agreement and supported by the context in which the agreement was made.) The giving of the notice is regarded as a detriment because it is a new duty assumed under the agreement. This may sound a little flimsy and Tabb surely would not have bargained for this as the exclusive consideration for his promise. However, courts are disinclined to inquire into adequacy of consideration unless it clearly appears to be sham or there is some indication that the disparity resulted from deceit or coercion.

In this contract, only Gutter Press has the right to terminate and Tabb has no equivalent right. As a general rule, this does not cause a consideration problem because the parties' obligations do not have to be coextensive. "Mutuality" in that sense is not required, and as long as each party has given consideration in some form, it does not matter that one of them has greater rights under the contract.

In short, neither the satisfaction clause nor the termination provisions should invalidate the contract and Tabb cannot escape his commitment to Gutter Press.

9. The relationship between Constance and Turn Coat is commercial, and Turn Coat's promise is in recognition of valuable work. However, Constance's services were rendered prior to the promise, and not in

exchange for it. Her work preceding the promise is "past consider-ation," and she suffers no new detriment to support the promise.

Because Turn Coat has breached its faith to Constance, the court may make great effort to find some new detriment on her part, however slight, to validate the promise. However, this would be a real strain on the present facts. Her assent to call the agent is some detriment, but it is obviously nothing more than a means of receiving the gift rather than bargained for as the price of the promise. If Constance had taken any action in reliance on the promise, the doctrine of promissory estoppel could afford a remedy, as discussed in Chapter 8, but no such action is suggested here. (In *Feinberg v. Pfeiffer*, 322 S.W.2d 163 (Mo. 1959), the court found no consideration for the promise of a pension made by the employer after years of service. However, it did apply promissory estoppel to enforce the promise because the employee had relied on the promise to her detriment. This aspect of the case is discussed in Example 3 of Chapter 8.)

10. The fact that Turn Coat contemplated some benefit — worker morale — from the resignation is not in itself consideration. This is merely the motive for the promise. However, the fact that some benefit would be gained by the company does serve as evidence that the resignation was bargained for in exchange for the promise. The issue in this case is whether the resignation was a legal detriment to Gerry. If Turn Coat could fire him at will, it could be argued that Gerry gave up no legal right by retiring because he had no right to continued employment. However, he did have the right to stay on the job until dismissed. Although this is not a very valuable right, equivalence in consideration is not required, and his sacrifice of the right should be sufficient to support the promise. As noted already, there is a reasonable basis for finding that the company did bargain for the advantage of not having to exercise its power to dismiss him.

   In *Katz v. Danny Dare, Inc.*, 610 S.W.2d 121 (Mo. 1980), a longstand-ing employee suffered a head injury in trying to stop a thief who had stolen money from his employer. The injury impaired his ability to work competently, and the president of the employer (who also hap-pened to be the employee's brother-in-law) tried to persuade the employee to retire by offering him a pension. The employee eventually agreed and left the company with the Board's promise of a life pension. Like Gerry, the employee could have been dismissed at will. A dispute later developed over the employer's obligation to continue paying the pension. Contrary to the resolution that I suggest above, the court held that an employee-at-will gives up no legal right by retiring. This seems to be an unduly narrow view, especially given the obvious desire of the employer to avoid the embarrassment of firing an old employee, injured in the line of duty, and related to the president. Nevertheless, the case turned out satisfactorily, because the court found that the employee had relied on the promise, and it enforced the promise under the doctrine of promissory estoppel. Again, this aspect of the case is taken up in Example 3 of Chapter 8.

11. Shame on the judge for using that naughty phrase that is so easily misunderstood. What the court means, of course, is that it considers Peters' promise to be illusory because Peters has the discretion to have no requirements for peppers. In this too, the judge betrays a sadly old-fashioned state of mind. Many years ago, some courts did take this approach to requirements and output contracts, but this view died out as it became accepted that contracts for flexible quantities have commercial utility and should not be found to lack consideration. Since the enactment of UCC §2.306, this matter is beyond doubt because the section limits the discretion of the buyer in a requirements contract and the seller in an output contract. Peters' requirements must be its actual requirements as may occur in good faith. Furthermore, as there is a stated estimate, this sets the range of permissible variation. (Even had there not been an estimate, any normal or prior comparable requirements that Peters may have had would set the range.)

For §2.306 to apply, the contract must in fact be intended by the parties to be a requirements contract. If the buyer does not agree to buy its requirements only from the seller, leaving the buyer free to buy from other parties, there is no restriction on the buyer's discretion and its promise is illusory. That is, although §2.306(1) does not say so expressly, one of the hallmarks of a requirements contract is that the buyer must commit to fill those requirements exclusively from the seller. The description of the transaction in the facts does not indicate if Peters did make this commitment of exclusive dealing in the contract. However, even if it did not do so expressly, the intent to deal exclusively with Hal could be implied from the language of the contract and the context.

Assuming that a promise of exclusive dealing can be implied, the next question is whether Peters breached the requirements contract by deciding to eliminate its requirement for Peppers. The fact that an estimate has been made may suggest that this case can simply be resolved on the disproportionality test. However, most courts have said that the disproportionality test applies only to increases in demand and not to decreases.

Therefore, Peters' elimination of its requirements must be measured on the good faith standard, which imposes a test of both subjective honesty in fact and the observance of commercially reasonable standards of fair dealing.[27] Is Peters' decision, based on a business judgment to discontinue production of pickled peppers, in good faith? Comment 2 to UCC §2.306 indicates that the good faith standard permits an honest discontinuance of requirements resulting from lack of demand. It draws a distinction between the justifiable shutdown of the buyer's plant for lack of orders, and an impermissible shutdown merely to curtail losses. This suggests that the good faith standard is not satisfied merely because Peters has made a sensible business judgment based on profitability. There must be hardship serious enough to overcome Peters' duty to honor Hal's reasonable expectations. This seems to be a matter of degree, and it is not clear from the facts whether the threat of competition is so severe as to necessitate the change in product line as a matter of survival.

27. As explained in section 7.9.3, prior to the 2001 revision of Article 1, the objective standard of good faith would have applied only if Peters qualified as a merchant (which it does). However, the inquiry into Peters' status as a merchant is not necessary under the revised Article 1 because §1.201(20) has now adopted the mixed subjective-objective test as the general test of good faith.

Promissory Estoppel as the Basis for Enforcing Promises

CHAPTER

8

§8.1 INTRODUCTION

As Chapter 7 shows, consideration is a prerequisite to a valid contract. A promise that has not been bargained for in exchange for some detriment cannot be enforced as a contract. Of course, as we have seen, consideration doctrine has a degree of flexibility that enables courts to stretch the concept of bargained-for exchange to accommodate some deserving cases. But this only works up to a point. Sometimes the facts are such that no manipulation of consideration doctrine could produce a realistic argument that consideration was given for a promise. In many cases the resulting nonenforcement of the promise is an appropriate consequence, but this result can be unfair when the promisee incurred some loss in relying justifiably on the promise. Promissory estoppel has developed to provide relief in such cases. When all its elements are satisfied, a promisor may be held accountable for a promise without consideration, and the court may enforce it either to the same extent as if a contract was made, or to the extent necessary to remedy the unfair result of reliance on it.

Promissory estoppel was first articulated as a distinct basis of liability in §90 of the First Restatement. The original formulation, with subtle revisions, survives in §90 of Restatement, Second. Although the Restatement section does not itself call the doctrine promissory estoppel, this name is firmly established by long usage.

Several factors must be considered in deciding whether promissory estoppel relief is appropriate, as will be discussed shortly. However, its

229

essential elements can be stated simply: A promise coupled with detrimental reliance on that promise. Although these two prerequisites do not always receive the same emphasis, a combination of them must be present for relief to be granted.

In this chapter, we discuss the general principles of promissory estoppel and also look at some specific applications of the doctrine in various contexts such as charitable pledges (section 8.8), negotiations (section 8.9), and options (section 8.11). In addition, promissory estoppel comes up again in other contexts later in the book, for example, in relation to the statute of frauds (section 11.4) and contract modifications (section 13.9).

§8.2 THE NATURE OF PROMISSORY ESTOPPEL AS AN INDEPENDENT BASIS OF RELIEF OR AS A CONSIDERATION SUBSTITUTE

Promissory estoppel has grown in importance as a doctrine, and there are many cases in which it is used as a basis for upholding promises that do not qualify as contractual. However, it is important to understand that promissory estoppel is an ancillary basis for relief. It is not needed where the promise is supported by consideration and there are no other problems that prevent the promise from being enforced as contractual. When analyzing a problem, it is therefore logical to first consider if a contract has been formed and to turn to promissory estoppel only if that question is answered negatively.

Because it allows for the enforcement of a promise without consideration, promissory estoppel is sometimes called a substitute for consideration. One must approach this phrase carefully, because there is disagreement among both courts and commentators over the categorization of promissory estoppel and its relationship to contract. This debate is partly philosophical, reflecting contrasting opinions on the way that the law should be conceived, and partly empirical, based on different interpretations of how the courts actually treat promissory estoppel. If promissory estoppel is classified as a contractual cause of action, the promise would be enforced as a contractual undertaking once the elements of promissory estoppel are satisfied. That is, promissory estoppel is treated as an alternative basis for finding contractual liability where consideration is lacking or there is some other defect in the formation process. Comment d to Restatement, Second, §90 suggests that the drafters favor this approach by stating that a promise binding under §90 is a contract.

The opposing view is that promissory estoppel does not result in enforcement of the promise as a contract but is an alternative and independent basis for enforcing the promises — a separate theory of obligation, based not on bargain but on accountability for conduct that induces reliance. This conception of promissory estoppel emphasizes its affinity to tort and to equitable estoppel (explained in section 8.4) and sees it more as a redress for injury suffered in reliance than as a contract-like relationship.

The characterization of promissory estoppel is not just a matter of theory, but can have significant practical consequences. As explained in sections 8.3 and 8.7, it has an impact on the remedy awarded to the promisee. Apart from the question of relief, the nature of promissory estoppel could give rise to other legal consequences. For example, if promissory estoppel is classified as a contractual cause of action, it is likely subject to the statute of limitations[1] applicable to contract suits, which is commonly six years. However, if it is classified as a tort-based cause of action, the shorter statute of limitations for tort actions (typically two years) could apply. *Matarazzo v. Millers Mutual Group, Inc.*, 927 A.2d 689 (Pa. Cmwlth 2007) provides a second example of a practical consequence of classification. The Matarazzos sued a municipality for damage caused to a vacant property by the municipality's failure to turn off the water supply to the property. They sued on the basis of promissory estoppel, not contract, claiming that they had relied to their detriment on the municipality's promise to turn off the water. The municipality argued that the suit was really just a disguised tort suit, and it sought to dismiss the suit on the basis of the doctrine of sovereign immunity. (This doctrine precludes a tort action against a governmental authority without its consent, and it applies only to tort claims, not to contractual claims.) The majority of the court recognized that promissory estoppel sounds in contract, and that a governmental unit would not be immune from a promissory estoppel claim. However, it concluded that the underlying basis of the claims in this case was not that the municipality had made a promise, but rather that it had been negligent in failing to turn off the water. The court therefore concluded that the claim was actually in tort and therefore barred.

§8.3 THE DIFFERENCE IN REMEDIAL EMPHASIS BETWEEN CONTRACT AND PROMISSORY ESTOPPEL

The way in which promissory estoppel is characterized — as a contract-based doctrine or an independent tort-like theory — has a bearing on the question of its most appropriate remedial goal. As discussed more fully in section 8.7, if promissory estoppel creates contractual liability, the normal

---

1. A statute of limitations specifies the period within which a person must commence suit on a claim. If suit is not initiated within that period, it is barred.

relief for promissory estoppel should be the full enforcement of the promise, and it is only appropriate to limit relief under special circumstances. Conversely, if one focuses on the protection of reliance, the remedy should usually be confined to reimbursement of actual loss, with fuller enforcement reserved for cases when justice so demands. This could make a substantial difference in recovery: Expectation damages, the primary form of contract damages, look toward the future and aim to place the promisee in the position he would have been in had the contract been honored. Their goal is to give the promisee the benefit of the bargain by awarding the money equivalent of what the promisee would have gained as a result of the contract.[2] On the other hand, if the principal focus of promissory estoppel is merely to reimburse for loss caused by reliance, the most appropriate form of relief is an award of damages that looks toward the past and aims to restore the promisee to the position he was in before the promise was made. Damages that reimburse loss or expense incurred in reliance on a promise are called reliance damages. The aim of reliance damages is similar to that of tort damages, which also aim to restore the victim to the position he was in before the tort was committed.

§8.4 AN INTRODUCTION TO EQUITABLE ESTOPPEL AND ITS LINK TO PROMISSORY ESTOPPEL

As intimated above, the essential function of promissory estoppel is to provide relief for justifiable reliance on a promise given without consideration. Promissory estoppel derives from the much older principle of equitable estoppel, also known as estoppel in pais. It is therefore helpful to understand the basic idea of equitable estoppel. Equity was introduced in section 2.5. Because a court of equity exercises its discretion to do justice between the parties, it is a general principle of equity that the litigants must themselves behave equitably in seeking the court's assistance. Relief that may otherwise be available is barred by the claimant's unworthy conduct.

Equitable estoppel reflects this principle. Its basic purpose is to preclude (i.e., "estop") a person from asserting a right when, by deliberate words or conduct, he or she has misled the other party into the justifiable belief that the right does not exist or would not be asserted. Like many equitable

---

2. As mentioned in section 1.2.4 and discussed more fully in section 18.10, expectation damages are the usual form of relief for breach of contract. In some situations, it is possible for the victim of a breach to obtain the relief of specific performance — a court order compelling the breacher to perform. However, courts do not award specific performance as a matter of course, and confine that relief to situations where the equities favor it and an award of damages would not adequately compensate for the breach.

doctrines, estoppel involves a balancing of the equities between the parties and a comparative evaluation of the fault and responsibility of the parties. Therefore, it generally only bars relief when the party asserting the rights deliberately engaged in the misleading behavior with knowledge or reason to know it could be misleading and could induce reliance by the other. In addition, the other, unaware of the true facts, must have relied on the apparent facts in a way that would result in some loss or prejudice if the claimant is permitted to assert the right.

For example, the syllabus for Professor Punctilio's law school class on equitable remedies states that students will be evaluated in the class by four short written papers, to be assigned during the course of the semester. The syllabus declares, in bold print, that all assignments must be submitted by the due date and that the professor will refuse to accept a late submission and will record a failing grade for it. Di Latory struggled with the first assignment and could not finish it on time. Although it was two days late, she put it in the box outside Professor Punctilio's office and hoped for the best. The professor did not reject it and later returned it with a B grade. Di was delayed in completing her second paper by trouble with her computer. She placed the second paper in the box three days late. Again, the paper was returned a short while later with an A- grade. When it was time for the submission of the third paper, Di did not worry about getting it in exactly by the due date, and she submitted it two days late. Professor Punctilio returned it the next day with a note stating "Rejected as untimely. Grade: F." When Di goes to Professor Punctilio's office to confront him over the failing grade, she should be able to persuade him, as a scholar of equitable remedies, that he is estopped from rejecting her third paper on grounds of tardiness: She suffered prejudice by submitting the third paper late in reasonable reliance on his deliberate conduct. It does not matter that Professor Punctilio did not intend his conduct to mislead Di. Estoppel is not based on fraud, but on accountability for deliberate words or conduct that induced reliance and consequent detriment.

This is a case of equitable, not promissory, estoppel, because Professor Punctilio did not promise Di that he would accept her late paper. However, equitable estoppel is the doctrine from which promissory estoppel developed. Courts originally refused to apply estoppel to promises and confined it to conduct or factual speech that was not promissory in nature. However, during the nineteenth century (and possibly even before that) some courts began to recognize that reliance on a promise was just as worthy of protection as reliance on a factual assertion, and they began to apply equitable estoppel to promises. The theory of these cases was that the promisor was estopped from asserting a lack of consideration for the promise, hence consideration was deemed to be present. Therefore the early cases did treat estoppel as a consideration substitute. Not all courts followed this approach. Some refused relief despite reliance if consideration was absent, and others sought to protect reliance indirectly by bending over backwards to find consideration in the most tenuous of detriments.

By the time of the drafting of the First Restatement, there was enough caselaw to support the inclusion of a new doctrine that came to be called promissory estoppel. The Restatement's formulation (in §90) did not treat the promise as estopping the denial of consideration, but simply recognized detrimental reliance on the promise as a basis of enforcing it. Therefore, while the drafters of the Restatement did not necessarily conceive of promissory estoppel as a theory of liability separate from contract, they planted the seeds of this idea. Following publication of the Restatement, the judicial recognition of promissory estoppel grew, and the doctrine has become well established, even though courts differ on its scope and range. Its formulation in Restatement, Second, §90 follows that of the original Restatement quite closely but makes changes to reflect its development over the intervening years.

§8.5 THE RANGE OF PROMISSORY ESTOPPEL: GIFTS AND COMMERCIAL TRANSACTIONS

When promissory estoppel first developed, it was primarily used to validate gratuitous promises such as family gifts and charitable donations. It was not thought to be applicable to promises made during the course of commercial interaction. It continues to have application to donative promises, but the tendency has been to expand it. Promissory estoppel is now commonly invoked as a basis for enforcing a commercial promise in appropriate circumstances. Of course, promissory estoppel has no role in most commercial transactions. No gift is intended and once agreement is reached, consideration is present. However, we have already seen that consideration problems do sometimes arise in the commercial setting, or other factors may prevent a promise from being enforceable as a contract.

There are at least three broad types of situation in which promissory estoppel may be applicable to a commercial promise. Although these situations technically involve a lack of consideration, the real reason for the absence of contractual liability is usually something else, and the real issue is whether it is appropriate to enforce the noncontractual promises.

1. A promise made for good consideration is not enforceable because of noncompliance with legal formality such as the statute of frauds. Promissory estoppel may permit the enforcement of the informal promise when fairness demands that the promisor not be allowed to escape liability. Discussion of this ground is deferred to section

11.4 where it is treated in conjunction with the statute of frauds. (Although it could technically be argued that consideration is absent here because an unenforceable informal promise is not a legal detriment, the real issue is whether a promise should be enforced despite the failure to comply with required formalities.)

2. Promissory estoppel may be used to hold a party to a promise made during negotiations for an abortive contract. When parties negotiate, they may make tentative commitments, not intended to bind unless and until final agreement is reached. Therefore, as a general rule, statements of intent made during negotiations are not treated as promises, and a party who incurs expense or relinquishes an opportunity on the strength of such a statement usually assumes the risk of loss if no contract comes about. Sometimes, however, a precontractual statement may reasonably be intended as a binding commitment, justifying reliance and attracting liability if not honored. The situations in which this might happen are discussed in section 8.9.

3. Promissory estoppel may afford relief for reliance on a promise that falls short of becoming contractual because of some defect or omission in the agreement formed by the parties. For example, there may be a fatal vagueness in the terms of the putative contract, or it may have an escape clause that negates commitment, yet there is enough of a commitment to justify reliance. One could say that this is also a consideration issue, and that the vague or discretionary promise is not consideration. However, the real issue is whether fairness demands accountability even in the absence of a binding contract. In short, the role of promissory estoppel goes beyond the enforcement of gift promises and covers a variety of promises that do not qualify as contractual, either because they lack consideration or because of some other deficiency or missing element in the process of contract formation.

§8.6 THE ELEMENTS OF PROMISSORY ESTOPPEL

§8.6.1 Introduction and Overview of the Elements

Assume that Uncle Rich says to his niece, Penny Less, "I think it is very important for you to get a college education, and I would like to help you do that. If you enroll in college, I will pay you $40,000 to help cover the costs of tuition." On the strength of this promise, Penny enrolls in college, committing herself to the payment of $40,000 tuition for her first year, but Uncle Rich fails to honor his promise to her. It is plausible to argue that the parties have entered into a contract. Penny's enrollment in college appears to have been bargained for in exchange for the promise and, as she had no legal obligation to enroll, this is a legal detriment. Penny could therefore seek enforcement of the promise as a contractual obligation. However, she may not succeed on that ground. As we have seen, in family transactions it is sometimes difficult to distinguish a bargained-for exchange from a gift given subject to conditions as to its use. A court could conclude that Uncle Rich merely promised a gift of money to be used for a specified purpose. On these facts, while Penny may ultimately be found not to have given consideration, she does at least have some basis for arguing that she did. However, in many family transactions, there is no basis at all for finding consideration. For example, if Uncle Rich simply promised to give Penny an unconditional gift of $40,000, and if she decided, on the strength of the promise, to enroll in college, she would have no grounds for asserting that Uncle Rich had bargained for anything in return.

Once consideration is lacking, the promise cannot be enforced as a contract, yet in both these examples Penny has relied on it by incurring a debt for tuition. Promissory estoppel developed as a response to situations like this and affords relief to the promisee when the equities favor holding the promisor accountable for the promise.

The elements for promissory estoppel, set out in Restatement, Second, §90, center around the promise and detrimental reliance on it. In short, §90 calls for the following factors to be taken into account in deciding whether and to what extent a promise without consideration should be binding:

1. A promise was made by the promisor with the reasonable expectation that the promisee would rely on it. (This element focuses on the promisor's conduct and evaluates his intent objectively.)
2. The promise did in fact induce the promisee's action or forbearance. Although §90 does not say so expressly, this reliance must be justified. (This element focuses on the promisee's reaction and evaluates his reliance largely on an objective standard.)
3. The enforcement of the promise is necessary to avoid injustice. (This element focuses on the consequence of reliance. Although §90 does not refer expressly to the detriment — that is, harm or loss — suffered by the promise as a result of reliance, this is a crucial factor.)
4. The remedy may be limited as justice requires. (This focuses on the appropriate form of relief. The nature and extent of the promisee's detriment is relevant here too.)

As this suggests, the decision to enforce a promise involves an evaluation of the conduct and reasonable understanding of each party and the fairness of holding the promisor accountable for a promise that would not otherwise be binding in contract law. While separate elements can be identified, their nature is such that they flow into and affect each other. Thus, for example, if the promise is clear and express, it is easier to infer intent to induce reliance and to justify reliance, and enforcement is more likely to be needed to avert injustice. Conversely, if there is doubt about the apparent promise, it is harder to show these other elements convincingly. We now survey each of the factors outlined above.

§8.6.2 A Promise Must Have Been Made

Section 1.2.3 introduced the meaning of promise and pointed out that not every assertion or statement of intent qualifies as a promise. Unless clear language of commitment is used, it can be difficult to decide if a promise has been made. Words and conduct must be interpreted in all the relevant circumstances of the case to determine if the alleged promisor manifested an intent to commit to a particular performance or course of action. Norton v. McOsker, 407 F.3d 501 (5th Cir. 2005) illustrates some of the issues that can arise in deciding if a promise was made. A woman had been involved in a 23-year adulterous relationship with a married man. When he ended the relationship, she sued him under various theories. Her promissory estoppel claim was based on the grounds that he had frequently promised during the relationship to divorce his wife and marry her, and also that, both during and at the end of the relationship, he had promised to support her for life. The court of appeals upheld the trial court's grant of summary judgment against the woman. Neither of the alleged undertakings established an enforceable promise. The man's promise to divorce his wife and marry the woman was void as against public policy. His undertaking of lifetime support was too general and nonspecific to qualify as an enforceable promise.

Note that it is manifested, rather than actual, intent that is determinative. As in contract, intent for the purpose of promissory estoppel is gauged by an objective test. The question is not what the promisor actually intended, but what the promisee was justified in understanding that intent to be, based on the promisor's utterances and conduct. This could not be otherwise because promissory estoppel aims to protect reliance that necessarily is based on a reasonable perception of exhibited intent rather than on the undisclosed thoughts and beliefs of the promisor. The objective evaluation of whether a promise was intended can sometimes trap a party into a promise that was never actually meant to be a commitment. In East Providence Credit Union v. Geremia, 239 A.2d 725 (R.I. 1968) the credit union financed a car purchase and took a security interest in the car to secure the debt. The credit agreement obliged the borrower to keep the car insured and provided that if he failed to do so, the credit union could pay the insurance premium and add the payment and interest to the balance of the loan. When the borrower failed to pay the insurance premium, the credit union notified him that it would exercise its right to pay it and add the cost of the insurance to the debt. The borrower did not respond to the notice. Notwithstanding its notice, the credit union did not pay the premium and the policy lapsed. The car was later stolen. The court found that the credit union's notice constituted a promise to pay the premium. The case was resolved on the basis of consideration doctrine because the court held that the borrower's undertaking to pay interest was consideration for the promise. As a result the credit union was liable for the loss of the car.[3] The court went on to discuss promissory estoppel in dictum as an alternative basis for enforcement and found that all its elements were satisfied, which would have permitted enforcement of the promise under this theory as well. The credit union surely did not think that it was making a promise when it provided in the contract for the right to pay the premium and when it sent the notice. The credit union's contractual right to pay the insurance premium was not for the borrower's benefit, but was designed to protect the credit union's interest in its collateral, and the notice was more in the nature of a threat than a promise.

The objective determination of intent in this context is subject to the same qualification that applies in deciding upon contractual intent — the promise must have been voluntarily and deliberately made. Therefore, as in contract, doctrines such as fraud, duress, and mistake (covered in Chapters 13 and 15) may be used to go behind the objective appearance of a promise. In addition to affecting the quality of the promise, any improper conduct by the promisee would also, of course, impact his justifiable reliance.

Also bear in mind the evidentiary, cautionary, and channeling functions served by consideration doctrine. The fact that consideration was not given for the promise means that these functions are not fulfilled by any act of exchange. Therefore, a court must exercise particular care before finding a promise when there is little or no formality in its execution or the circumstances suggest that the promisor may have acted on impulse or with rash generosity.

§8.6.3 The Promisor Should Reasonably Have Expected the Promise to Induce Action or Forbearance by the Promisee

This element is so closely connected to the inquiry into promise that it is a little artificial to treat it separately. However, it is helpful to split the

---

3. The value of the car was not actually paid to the borrower, but was used to offset the balance due to the credit union, thereby eliminating its claim against the borrower.

evaluation of promisor accountability into two issues for the purpose of building a framework for analysis. Because the promisor is accountable only for a deliberate and voluntary promise, one must go beyond simply interpreting the meaning of the manifestation and must also evaluate the promisor's justifiable understanding of the likely impact of the promise. The circumstances must be such as to warrant holding the promisor accountable for creating the situation leading to reliance and the resulting loss.

This means that the promisor knew or reasonably should have realized that the promisee would likely understand that a promise had been made and would thereby be induced to take or refrain from action of the kind that occurred. (Thus, not only the likelihood of reliance but also the general nature and extent of the response must have been reasonably foreseeable by the promisor.) Again, an objective standard is used, so the promisor is held to a standard of reasonableness, whether or not he actually intended the promise to be relied on.

§8.6.4 The Promise Must Have Induced Justifiable Action or Forbearance by the Promisee

We now move from the promisor's accountability to the promisee's reliance. In dealing with inducement, the text of §90 does not expressly require the reliance to be justifiable, but this principle is referred to in the comments and is inherent in the purpose of promissory estoppel. To decide if the promisee justifiably relied on the promise, we must ask two questions. First, we must ask if the promise did in fact induce the promisee's action or forbearance. There must have been a cause and effect between the promise and the conduct, so there is no inducement if the promisee would have incurred the loss or expense even had the promise not been made, or incurred it before the promise was made.

Second, even if the promise did induce the promisee's conduct, he should not be given relief unless his particular response was a justifiable reaction to the promise. Justification is evaluated under a largely objective standard with some subjective aspects. It allows weight to be given to the personal attributes and situation of the promisee. The essential question is whether a reasonable person in the promisee's position would have so acted or refrained from acting as a result of the promise. Because the promissor's liability under promissory estoppel is based on a noncontractual promise, the justifiability standard is an essential safeguard. It protects the promisor from being held accountable for consequences caused by a promisee's reaction that could not have been anticipated fairly because it was rash, quirky, or unreasonable. If the promisee behaves in this way, he should bear the risk of having made the judgment to incur loss or expense in the absence of a contract.

As you can see, the inquiry into the nature and strength of the promise, the promisor's reasonable expectation of reliance on it, and the promisee's justification in relying on it tend to meld together. They are frequently just different aspects of the same overall pattern: The stronger the sense of commitment, the greater the likelihood of a reasonable expectation of inducement and, consequently, of justifiable reliance. For example, in the *Norton* case, discussed in section 8.6.2, the court found that the man had made no enforceable promise to marry or to support the woman during or at the end of their 23-year affair. The court also noted that even had his undertakings qualified as promises, the woman would not have been justified in relying on them. His promise of lifelong support was too vague to induce reliance. She could not have had any reliance on his promises to leave his wife and marry her because he had made and broken that promise countless times over the 23 years of their relationship.

Section 90 dispenses with proof of reliance for charitable pledges and marriage settlements. (Marriage settlements are beyond our scope and are not discussed here.) A few courts have followed this rule and have upheld promises of charitable contributions, even where reliance cannot be established. However, most courts have not adopted the Restatement, Second's position and still require charitable organizations to show justifiable reliance on the gratuitous promise. (This serves as a reminder that the Restatement, Second, although highly influential, is just secondary authority that may sometimes reflect what the drafters feel the law should be, rather than what it is.) Of course, even those courts that disavow the Restatement, Second's exception are sometimes able to give promissory estoppel relief by stretching the facts to find justifiable reliance.

§8.6.5 The Promise Is Binding If Injustice Can Be Avoided Only by Its Enforcement

This element reflects the total balance that the court must draw after evaluating the equities, so that its decision achieves a fair result in all the circumstances. (This balancing is an aspect of the equitable roots of promissory estoppel.) It takes into account not only the issues of promise and reliance discussed above, but also any other factors that bear upon the appropriateness of enforcing the promise.

The most significant of these is the detriment or harm suffered by the promisee in relying on the promise. Because the protection of reliance is the fundamental purpose of promissory estoppel, it is not enough that the promisee had merely a generalized expectation of gain which has been disappointed. The promisee must have suffered some actual harm by relying on the promise. Therefore, "detriment" in this context is usually not used in the attenuated sense associated with consideration doctrine but describes a real economic loss such as an expenditure, a sacrificed opportunity, a commitment or some other prejudice of a substantial kind. While some courts may accept less, especially if the other equities strongly favor enforcement, the need to avert injustice by enforcement of the promise is not very strong if there is no loss that needs redress and the only effect of nonenforcement is the failure to receive the promised benefit.

Another important factor that weighs in the balance was mentioned earlier in connection with the promise in section 8.6.2, but should be reemphasized here in dealing with the general equities of enforcement. Comment b to §90 stresses that the promisor needs protection from an ill-considered promise or a bogus claim of promise. Because consideration is absent, its safeguards — the channeling, cautionary, and evidentiary functions — are missing. The court should therefore weigh the lack or presence of formality and the apparent deliberateness of the commitment in deciding whether the equities favor enforcement, and if so, to what extent.

§8.7 THE REMEDY WHEN PROMISSORY ESTOPPEL IS APPLIED

Restatement, Second, §90 states that the remedy for breach of the promise may be limited as justice requires. Although Comment d to that section says that a promise binding under the section is a contract, this limitation of remedy means that the promisee is not necessarily entitled to full contractual relief. That is, the court could grant the promisee full contractual relief, which typically takes the form of expectation damages, designed to compensate for loss of gains resulting from the breach, and to place the promisee in the position he would have been in had the promise been performed. However, it has the discretion to provide a lesser remedy. Typically, this lesser remedy takes the form of reliance damages, which focus on the reimbursement of the actual loss or expense incurred in reliance on the promise.

Although §90 suggests a range of damages and makes it clear that the balance of the equities affects the extent of relief, there is some debate on the correct emphasis to be placed on the choice of remedy. If the role of promissory estoppel is to estop the promisor from denying the existence of a contract, it follows that the law treats the promise as if it was a contract, and the remedy for breach of contract (usually expectation damages) should be the normal measure of relief. The lesser remedy, restricting relief to the reimbursement of reliance losses, would therefore be appropriate only in exceptional cases. However, if promissory estoppel is an independent tort-like theory of liability, reimbursement of actual reliance losses should be the normal relief, with full enforcement confined to cases in which the lesser remedy is clearly inadequate. Some studies suggest that courts do in fact incline to full enforcement except when there is some problem in proving expectation damages. In short, it is difficult to say for sure where the primary focus is, given the spectrum of damages available to courts. It is important to recognize, however, that courts have a discretionary range of relief. Some of the factors that a court may consider in exercising this discretion are illustrated by *Tynan v. JBVBB, LLC,* 743 N.W. 2d 730 (Wis. App. 2007). Tynan began working for the defendant as a consultant before the parties had settled the terms of an employment contract. The parties never reached agreement on the terms of the employment contract, and Tynan's consultancy was eventually terminated. He sued the defendant for specific performance of promises to pay various bonuses to him.[4] The jury found that the promises had been made and that Tynan had relied on them. However, the court refused to award expectation relief to him and confined his relief to reliance losses. The court acknowledged that it had the discretion to award expectation relief but declined to do so because it found that the promises were somewhat vague, Tynan had not been employed as a consultant for very long, and the defendant had not acted unfairly. The court then gave Tynan the opportunity to prove reliance damages. He tried to show that he had lost opportunities for employment in reliance on the promise, but he could not prove this with sufficient certainty, and ended up with no award of damages.

As a further illustration of the possible range of remedies for promissory estoppel and the distinction between full contractual damages and reliance recovery, consider Penny's enrollment in college on the strength of Uncle Rich's promise to give her $40,000 to pay for tuition if she enrolled in college: Penny's expectation is $40,000, and full contractual enforcement would give her this amount. By contrast, reliance damages would depend on the extent of her actual loss or prejudice. Therefore, if she enrolled in college on the strength of Uncle Rich's promise and committed herself to pay $40,000 for her first year's tuition, injustice might be averted only by full enforcement of the promise. However, say that Penny received a scholarship so that her annual tuition is only $10,000 and Penny is committed for only one year's tuition. Enforcement to the extent of $10,000 may be enough to prevent injustice. Although Penny, in a sense, may have relied on having the balance of $30,000 to pay for future years' tuition, the broken promise of future funding disappoints her expectation but does not

---

4. As mentioned in section 8.3, an order of specific performance is a form of expectation relief under which the court orders the breaching party to render the performance promised under the contract.

constitute an actual out-of-pocket loss. The facts become more complicated if, in addition to committing herself for $10,000 tuition, she gave up a job to attend college, because her sacrificed earnings are also a reliance loss and should be taken into account in deciding her recovery. The court's ability to award reliance damages where full enforcement of the promise would be excessive gives the court the flexibility to avoid an "all or nothing" resolution. This allows some measure of relief to a promisee who can show losses resulting from reliance but cannot justify enforcement of the promise as if it was a contract.

Penny Less is not the only person to be disappointed by the breach of a promise to pay tuition. In *Conrad v. Fields*, 2007 WL 2106302 (Minn. App. 2007) Walter Fields, a wealthy man, encouraged his friend, Marjorie Conrad, to attend law school and promised to pay her tuition. Conrad enrolled in law school on the basis of this promise, giving up a job that paid her an annual salary of $45,000. Fields made a relatively small tuition payment immediately after Conrad entered law school, but then claimed temporary financial difficulties, and made no further payments. However, he did say that he would pay Conrad's tuition after she graduated and passed the bar. She did graduate and pass the bar, but Fields refused to pay. Conrad sued him on a theory of promissory estoppel for reimbursement of $87,314 that she had paid for her tuition. (She did not claim loss of the earnings.) The trial court found that all the elements of promissory estoppel were satisfied, and awarded her the damages claimed. It concluded that Fields made the promise to Conrad intending her to rely on it. He knew that she would have to quit her job to attend law school and that she could not afford to pay for law school herself. Conrad knew that Fields was wealthy and generous and she trusted him. On the faith of his promise, she did stop working and enroll in law school. The court of appeals affirmed. Because Fields had told Conrad that his financial difficulties were temporary and he would pay her tuition after she graduated, the court was not persuaded by his argument that Conrad was not justified in relying on his promise when she continued to incur tuition expenses after he stopped paying. The court also noted that the $87,314 was a reimbursement of actual reliance losses, and was therefore an appropriate promissory estoppel award. It rejected Field's argument that Conrad suffered no real detriment because she received a valuable law degree: Although the degree was beneficial to her, her detriment was the debt that she incurred in acquiring it. Note that the $87,314 qualifies as reliance damages because it is an actual expense incurred in reliance on the promise. However, in this case, the reliance damages are in fact equivalent to Conrad's full expectation. If the situation had been different — say that Fields clearly repudiated his promise during Conrad's first year, and she sued him then — her actual reliance damages (her tuition payments up to the time of repudiation) would have been considerably less than her expectation damages. Under those circumstances, the court may have considered it appropriate to confine her recovery to that lesser amount.

§8.8 CHARITABLE PLEDGES AND PROMISSORY ESTOPPEL

Section 7.3.5 raises the sometimes difficult and subtle distinction between an act or promise that constitutes bargained-for exchange, and one that would merely be an incident of receiving the gift, or an undertaking to use the gift for the purposes for which it was given. Sometimes a court may resolve this ambiguity by finding that the promisee did suffer some detriment, so that the promise can be enforced as a contract. However, where there is no basis for finding consideration, the pledge or promise of a gift may still be enforced under the doctrine of promissory estoppel, provided that the donee can establish that the elements of promissory estoppel are satisfied.[5]

Allegheny College v. National Chautauqua County Bank, 159 N.E. 173 (N.Y. 1927) illustrates well the interplay between consideration doctrine and promissory estoppel where a donee gives undertakings in return for a pledge. Mary Yates Johnston pledged $5,000 to be paid to the college on her death. The pledge required the money to be used to educate students preparing for the ministry. It also stipulated that the fund would be known as the "Mary Yates Johnston Memorial Fund." She paid $1,000 of this amount while she was alive and the college set it aside for a scholarship fund as stipulated, but did nothing further in reliance on the pledge. The donor repudiated the pledge before her death. After she died, the college sued her estate for the balance of the pledged amount. Judge Cardozo found that the college had given consideration for the pledge because the college, by accepting the $1,000, impliedly promised to memorialize the donor's name. (He did not rely on the college's implied promise to use the fund for the purpose stipulated, possibly because that seems too clearly to be a condition of the gift.) Because he found consideration for the promise, Judge Cardozo did not have to deal with promissory estoppel. However, he suggested in dictum that promissory estoppel could have been used as an alternative basis for enforcing the gift. It is clear from the opinion that the underlying motivation for the court's conclusion was its belief that the charitable pledge should be upheld as a matter of public

---

5. As stated in section 8.6.4, most courts require all the elements, including justifiable reliance, to be satisfied even where the gift is a charitable gift. They have not adopted the approach of Restatement, Second, §90(2), which treats a charitable pledge as binding even in the absence of reliance.

policy. To get this result, the court strained to fit the facts into a theory of recovery, but those facts do not provide much support for either basis of relief. The legal detriment found by the court is quite flimsy, and it is difficult to see grounds for promissory estoppel. There is no indication that the donor reasonably intended to induce reliance until the money was paid out on her death, or that the college took any action in reliance on the pledge. The mere banking of the money cannot really be seen as the kind of detrimental reliance that would support a claim of promissory estoppel.

King v. Trustees of Boston University, 420 Mass. 52 (1995) similarly found that a promise could be enforced under both consideration and promissory estoppel theories where the circumstances were ambiguous enough to support the contrary conclusion that the donor had promised a gift subject to conditions. This case was discussed in connection with consideration doctrine in section 7.3.5. It was noted there that the court found that by undertaking to index and care for Dr. King's papers and to make them available to researchers, the university had given consideration for Dr. King's promise to transfer ownership of his papers. Although the court disposed of the case on consideration grounds, it also addressed the university's alternative claim based on promissory estoppel. The court stressed that despite Restatement, Second, §90(2), it did require a charitable organization to show justifiable reliance for promissory estoppel relief. However, that reliance was apparent in the actions that the university took (indexing and taking care of the papers and making them available for research) beyond just retaining custody of the papers.

By contrast, in *Congregation Kadimah Toras-Moshe v. DeLeo*, 540 N.E.2d 691 (Mass. 1989) the court adopted a purely doctrinal approach. The donor had promised $25,000 to the synagogue. The synagogue planned to use the money to convert a storage room into a library to be named for the donor. However, there was no indication that the donor had attached any conditions to his promise, or that the synagogue had promised to use the money for this purpose or to name the library for the donor. The donor died without paying and the synagogue sued his estate. The court found no consideration because the synagogue had not made any promise or suffered any other detriment in exchange for the promise. It also found no basis for enforcing the donor's promise under the doctrine of promissory estoppel because the synagogue had not yet begun the renovation or taken any other action in reliance on the promise. It had merely allocated the fund to the library renovation in its budget, which was nothing more than an accounting entry with no prejudicial effect.

Because *Allegheny College* and *King* both found consideration, they fully enforced the promises as contracts. Had they not found consideration, but had given relief on the basis of promissory estoppel, the remedy may have been the same if the court decided that nothing short of full enforcement would prevent injustice. However, the court would have had the option of awarding the lesser relief of reimbursing reliance costs. For many courts, the lesser remedy is more appropriate unless the detriment to the promisee cannot be undone except by full enforcement. *Estate Timco v. Oral Roberts Evangelical Ass'n.*, 215 N.W.2d 750 (Mi. 1974) is an example of a case in which the court found full enforcement of the promise to be necessary to avert injustice. The court awarded judgment to the promisee for the balance of the price of a building where the promisor, as a member of the association's board, proposed and collaborated in the purchase and induced the association to buy the building by undertaking to pay the balance of the price.

§8.9 PROMISSORY ESTOPPEL AS A MEANS OF ENFORCING PROMISES MADE IN NEGOTIATIONS

Section 8.5 introduced the idea that promissory estoppel may sometimes provide relief for promises made during negotiations. It must be stressed that it is rarely appropriate to apply promissory estoppel to any statement made while the parties are working toward the formation of a contract. In most situations, negotiating parties understand or reasonably should understand that nothing said in negotiations is to be taken as a promise, and no commitment is made until a contract is formed. Even though a statement made during negotiations may sound like a promise, a reasonable party should normally realize that it is nothing more than an expression of intention or a proposal for a term that will become an undertaking in the contract if the negotiations culminate in final agreement. Therefore, if a party takes action on an apparent promise made during negotiations, the usual assumption, in the absence of clear understanding to the contrary, is that she bears the cost and risk of acting. For example, a buyer and seller are negotiating the sale of a business. They have agreed on the price of $10 million, but the buyer does not have enough cash to pay the price. He therefore suggests that the seller sell the business to him on credit, and that he will pay the price over a two-year period from profits gained from operating the business. After considering this proposal the seller tells the buyer that she will not give him credit for the full $10 million price, but if he can find an investor who can provide half the price, she will be amenable to a credit sale for the balance. The buyer makes great efforts to find an investor. In doing so he incurs considerable expense in researching prospects, seeking legal advice on how to set up the investment, and preparing materials to show potential investors. While he is in the process of doing this, the seller notifies him that she has found another buyer for the business and is terminating the negotiations. Because the parties had not yet concluded a contract, the buyer has no claim against the seller for breach of contract. He should not have a promissory estoppel claim either. In the negotiating phase, unless the seller has clearly committed to do so, the buyer is not usually justified in expecting that the seller will pay the buyer's expenses in trying to secure investors. Nor can the buyer use promissory estoppel to enforce the seller's nonbinding expression of intent to proceed with the sale if the buyer does find investors. Although it may be reasonable, in a business sense, for the buyer to rely on this statement of intention by making efforts to find the financing, he should understand that in the absence of a contractual commitment, he bears the risk that he will incur expenses in trying to set up the deal and may not secure the contract in the end.

Although apparent promises during negotiations are not typically enforceable under the doctrine of promissory estoppel, there are some situations in which a party really does make a precontractual commitment on which the other party reasonably places compensable reliance. One of the best-known cases to apply promissory estoppel to uphold a promise made in the course of negotiations is *Hoffman v. Red Owl Stores, Inc.*, 133 N.W.2d 267 (Wisc. 1965). Hoffman approached Red Owl to set him up with a Red Owl grocery store franchise. After reviewing and approving his proposed financial arrangements, Red Owl encouraged Hoffman to take a series of actions to prepare to open a store. Hoffman conscientiously followed Red Owl's guidance, incurring expenses in the process. After some considerable time, negotiations eventually collapsed, primarily because Red Owl had not been entirely straight with Hoffman about the financing of the business. The parties had not yet made a contract, and Red Owl had never expressly promised Hoffman that he would receive a franchise. Nevertheless, the court awarded Hoffman his wasted reliance expenses on the basis of promissory estoppel. (The court made it clear that relief was confined to the recovery of wasted expenses, and could not include any claim for lost profits.) The court found that Hoffman had placed faith in Red Owl's expertise and good faith, and it had been careless of his interests. Red Owl's indifference to Hoffman's welfare outweighed his naiveté in unquestioningly following its advice. *Hoffman* is distinguishable from the usual negotiation situation because Red Owl so strongly influenced Hoffman's actions that a relationship of trust was created that is not normally present where parties approach each other as adversaries in negotiations. Indeed, the underlying rationale of *Hoffman* and the more recent cases discussed below is that the promisor had violated a duty to bargain in good faith. These cases have an affinity with other cases on this principle that you will encounter in section 10.11.

Pop's Cones, Inc. v. Resorts International Hotel, Inc., 307 N.J. Super. 461 (1998), and *Carey v. FedEx Ground Package System, Inc.*, 321 F. Supp. 902 (S.D. Ohio 2004) are more recent cases in which the dominant negotiating party was able to induce the other party's detrimental reliance on its precontractual promises.

In both cases, the court refused to grant the promisor's motion for summary judgment and allowed the promisee to proceed to trial on a claim of promissory estoppel. *Pop's Cones* involved negotiations for a lease. Pop's operated a frozen yogurt store in a town near Atlantic City. It entered into negotiations with Resorts International (RI) to move the store into RI's casino in Atlantic City. Pop's told RI on several occasions during their protracted negotiations that the time for it to renew the lease on its current premises was approaching. RI assured Pop's that it would obtain a lease in the casino and that completion of the transaction was no more than a formality. On the strength of that, Pop's gave up its current lease. In the end, RI failed to follow through with the transaction and negotiations terminated. Pop's sued RI for damages, and the court held, on the motion for summary judgment, that Pop's allegations made out a case for relief on grounds of promissory estoppel.

Carey is a mind-boggling example of a runaround that makes Red Owl's conduct seem mild by comparison. Carey had approached FedEx in January 2001 in the hope of acquiring a FedEx delivery route. For a period of almost two years, FedEx led him on with assurances that he would receive the route. Carey was in constant contact with FedEx. He followed its many suggestions and directions to qualify as a carrier, and was repeatedly told that he would get a route when it became available. During this period, FedEx induced Carey to buy a truck (which was ultimately repossessed because Carey could not afford payments on it without the income from a delivery route). In addition, to the knowledge of FedEx, Carey's wife gave up her job in reliance on the prospective extra income that Carey would earn once he had the route. When routes did become available, FedEx gave them to other drivers, while reassuring Carey that he was in line for the next route to become available. In the end, Carey never received the route and he sued FedEx on several theories[6] including promissory estoppel. The court denied summary judgment to FedEx on these claims. As to promissory estoppel, the court said that on the facts alleged, a jury could find that Carey had justifiably relied on FedEx's precontractual promise that he would get a route. The court stressed that relief would be confined to reimbursement for Carey's reasonable reliance losses, and would not cover any profits he might have lost as a result of not obtaining the route. Lost profits are contractual expectation damages, which would not be appropriately awarded for reliance on promises made at the stage of negotiations.

---

6. It is worth mentioning the other causes of action because they add to the sense of bad faith dealing and show why this case, like *Hoffman*, is concerned with the duty to bargain in good faith. One of the causes of action was race discrimination. Carey was African-American and the facts suggested that FedEx's actions in giving other drivers routes before Carey could have been racially motivated. The other was fraud. There were indications that FedEx may have led Carey on because he was doing temporary driving work while he waited for his route and FedEx found it convenient to keep him on hand as long as possible as a temporary driver.

§8.10 PROMISSORY ESTOPPEL AND AT-WILL EMPLOYMENT AGREEMENTS

Employment is at will if either party can terminate the employment at any time for any reason. The default rule under common law is that employment is at will unless the parties agree to employment for a definite term, or agree that employment cannot be terminated except for cause or following a specified period of notice.[7] At-will employment agreements present particular problems of both consideration and promissory estoppel during the period after the employment agreement has been made, but before the employee begins work. Even where employment has been offered and accepted, courts commonly hold that before the employment actually begins, there is no contract because consideration is absent.[8] They reason that since both parties have complete discretion to terminate an at-will employment agreement, neither party makes any future commitment.

In addition, many courts hold that the at-will nature of the prospective employment precludes promissory estoppel relief for the reimbursement of loss for actions taken in reliance on the promise to employ. Although it is readily apparent that an employee is likely to incur some detriment in reliance on a promise of at-will employment, such as leaving an existing job, moving to the location of the new job, or forgoing other opportunities, these courts hold that the employee must bear the risk of this reliance because he has no assurance of job security. *See*, for example, *Leonardi v. City of Hollywood*, 715 So. 2d 1007 (Fla. App. 1998).

Other courts, for example, *Grouse v. Group Health Plan, Inc.*, 306 N.W.2d 114 (Minn. 1981) find this approach unduly harsh and have been more sympathetic to the disappointed employee. In *Grouse*, a pharmacist gave notice to his current employer and declined another offer of employment on the strength of the health plan's promise of employment. Before he began work, the health plan withdrew its commitment to hire him. Although the court found that the pharmacist had no contractual cause of

---

7. Many employment agreements do eliminate the default rule of employment at will, either by the express terms of the contract itself, or by virtue of rules in an employee handbook published by the employer, or by collective bargaining agreements, or by implication from usage or conduct. Statutes have also made inroads into the at-will doctrine.

8. This discussion is confined to the period before employment has begun and does not deal with the issue of whether it is easier to find consideration or reliance once the employment has commenced. The problem is that even after the employee starts work, both parties continue to have the discretion to terminate at-will employment, and the employee has no promise of continued employment on which he can rely. Some courts hold that the same principles apply before and after the employment has begun. Other courts do distinguish between promises made before and after the employee has started working, and may find consideration or reliance as a result of conduct or promises made during the course of employment.

action because the employment could be terminated at will, the health plan had at least committed itself to allow the pharmacist an opportunity to begin, which induced him to take the detrimental action. He was therefore entitled to promissory estoppel relief.

Even where a court applies promissory estoppel in this context, the relief is likely to be modest. The employee cannot get damages based on his expected salary because he could be terminated at will. Damages such as opportunity losses are usually difficult to prove, and damages for giving up the prior employment may be nonexistent if it was also at will. Therefore, relief is likely to be confined to actual out-of-pocket losses such as wasted moving expenses.

§8.11 RELIANCE ON AN OPTION WITHOUT CONSIDERATION: THE APPLICATION OF PROMISSORY ESTOPPEL TO PROMISES OF IRREVOCABILITY

We have already seen one situation in which reliance on a revocable offer has created an option: Section 4.12.5 explains how the commencement of a noninstantaneous performance creates an option in favor of the offeree when the offer is for a unilateral contract. (That is, the offer requires performance as the exclusive mode of acceptance.) Although no consideration was given for this option (and indeed, there may not even have been an express promise to keep the offer open), an option is created by law to protect the reliance of the offeree in beginning the combined act of acceptance and performance.

Quite apart from this type of case, the doctrine of promissory estoppel can sometimes be used to create an enforceable option, even though no consideration was given for the promise of irrevocability. The circumstances under which a court will uphold an option on the basis of promissory estoppel are narrow, because in most cases the absence of consideration for the promise of irrevocability means that the offeror should not reasonably be held to have induced reliance, and the offeree should not be treated as having relied justifiably on the promise. For example, the seller offers to sell her farm "Bleakacre" to the buyer for $2 million and undertakes to hold the offer open until Friday. The promise not to revoke the offer until Friday is not a binding option because the buyer has given no consideration for it. The buyer intends to accept the offer by Friday. On Tuesday, believing he still has time to accept, he quits his job in the city so that he can devote full attention to his new farm. On Wednesday, before the buyer has had the chance to communicate his acceptance, the seller revokes the offer.

The buyer disregards the revocation and accepts the offer on Thursday morning. He asserts that the acceptance is effective because the seller could not revoke the offer. Although he gave no consideration for the promise not to revoke, he argues that it should be enforceable on grounds of promissory estoppel because he detrimentally relied on it. Restatement, Second, §87(2) recognizes the possibility of applying promissory estoppel in this kind of situation. It sets forth requirements modeled on §90. It states that an offer is binding as an option to the extent necessary to avoid injustice if the offeror "should reasonably expect to induce action or forbearance of a substantial character on the part of the offeree before acceptance and which does induce such action or forbearance." Although he has suffered prejudice in reliance on the promise, the buyer will likely not succeed in satisfying the elements of §87(2) because he was probably not justified in quitting his job in reliance on a promise of irrevocability for which he had paid or given nothing.

The issue of applying promissory estoppel to create an option has come up periodically in cases involving subcontractor bids. Although there is some variation in the facts of these cases, this is their typical pattern: Reliant Contracting Co., a prime contractor, plans to bid on contract to build an apartment building for City Housing Corp. Reliant needs subcontractors to perform many aspects of the project, so on June 1 it calls for subcontractor bids for various parts of the work, to be submitted by June 15. One of the jobs to be subcontracted is the supply and installation of a central heating system. Several heating companies submit bids for this aspect of the construction. One of them, Lobidder Heating Co., submits a bid for $2.5 million on June 14. This is the lowest bid for the heating, and it is $200,000 less than the next lowest bid. On June 16, Reliant uses Lobidder's bid in formulating its own bid to City Housing. On June 25, Reliant is awarded the contract to build the building. On June 26, Lobidder discovers that it made an error in calculating its bid, which should really have been $2.9 million. On that same day, Lobidder tells Reliant of the error. It withdraws its bid and refuses to perform the work for less than $2.9 million. This places Reliant in a very difficult position. It is now committed to its contract price with City Housing, but it has to pay $200,000 more to the next highest bidder for the heating work. There are a few possible arguments that Reliant could make in claiming damages from Lobidder.

Breach of Contract Reliant might argue that Lobidder's bid was an offer, which Reliant accepted by using the bid in making its own bid. The problem with this argument is that even if Lobidder's bid was an offer, Reliant did not communicate acceptance of it before Lobidder revoked it. Communication of acceptance is required unless the offeror dispensed with it either expressly or by implication. In the absence of such a waiver of communication, use of the bid on its own is not enough to constitute acceptance.

Actual Option   Reliant might argue that Lobidder impliedly promised that it would not revoke the bid until Reliant had a reasonable time to accept it after the award of the prime contract. The problem with this argument is, first, that there would need to be some factual basis to imply such a promise. Second, even if it could be implied, Reliant would have trouble showing that it gave Lobidder the consideration necessary to validate it. The best argument for consideration is that Reliant made an implied promise that if it used the bid, it would be committed to accept it. However, Reliant probably did not consider itself bound by use of the bid, and unless usage or other circumstances show otherwise, it would be difficult to imply such a promise.

Promissory Estoppel   The argument that has been most successful in cases like this is that although there is no contract or option, the promise to hold open the offer should be enforced under the doctrine of promissory estoppel, which, in effect, serves as a substitute for consideration in creating an enforceable option. To enforce the option under promissory estoppel, Reliant must establish that all of its elements are satisfied: First, Lobidder must have made a promise. There is no express promise here, but all the circumstances could give rise to an implied promise by Lobidder to keep its bid open for a reasonable time to enable Reliant to accept it expeditiously as soon as it is awarded the construction contract. Second, Lobidder must reasonably have expected that Reliant would rely on its promise. Reasonable expectations are based on the entire context in which the promise was made, including not only the language and apparent firmness of the promise, but also the prevailing practices in the industry and any prior relationship that the parties may have had. Reliant must establish that, under all these circumstances, a reasonable person in Lobidder's position would have realized that Reliant might rely on its bid in formulating the bid to City Housing. Third, Reliant must have relied justifiably on this promise. This requirement not only examines the question of whether there were reasonable grounds for Reliant to believe that a serious promise was made and could be relied upon, but it also requires consideration of the nature and justification of the action taken in reliance. It precludes recovery if Reliance reasonably should have realized, in comparing Lobidder's bid with others, that Lobidder likely made an error. Fourth, enforcement of the promise must be necessary to avoid injustice. This element is usually satisfied if all the other elements are present and the prime contractor suffers the significant detriment of being bound to the owner for a price based on the subcontractor's bid. However, it also takes other equities into account, such as whether Reliant acted in good faith in accepting the bid as soon as possible, and did not try to speculate at Lobidder's expense, say, by bid shopping (that is, using the bid to shop around for a lower bid from competing subcontractors).

If all these elements are satisfied, the remedy is the enforcement of the promise not to revoke the offer. Because the offer is treated as a valid option, Lobidder's attempt to revoke failed. Reliant is therefore still able to accept the bid, even after Lobidder's attempted revocation on June 26. However, Reliant must actually take the step of accepting the offer, and must do so within a reasonable time after June 26. It may sound pointless to accept an offer after the offeror has made it clear that it will not perform at the bid price, but the formal act of acceptance is legally required to create a contract for the performance of the work at the price bid. If Reliant does not accept within a reasonable time, its claim for damages will fail because promissory estoppel is used here only to validate the option — it does not validate the underlying contract, which must be created by acceptance of the offer. As noted above, if Reliant delays beyond a reasonable time in accepting, or if it acts in bad faith by bid shopping, it will not benefit from the option that was created by promissory estoppel.

Two famous cases, separated in time by about 25 years, are usually used to contrast the differing approaches that courts may take in resolving a situation like this. The facts of the cases were similar to those outlined above, and in both the courts found that there was no basis for finding an accepted offer and no consideration for a valid option. They differed on the propriety of using promissory estoppel to validate the option. In *James Baird Co. v. Gimbel Bros., Inc.*, 64 F.2d 344 (2d Cir. 1933), the court refused to adopt a promissory estoppel theory to make the subcontractor's bid irrevocable. In part, this approach can be explained by the fact that the promissory estoppel doctrine was much less developed at the time and had been largely confined to situations in which a donee had taken action in reliance on a promise to make a gift. The court was reluctant to extend it to the commercial context. However, even if it was appropriate to use the doctrine in a commercial case, the court felt that the contractor was not justified in relying on an unaccepted offer. If it wanted to bind the offeree to the offer, it should have purchased an option. As it did not do this, it assumed the risk of committing itself before securing its subcontract.

By contrast, in *Drennan v. Star Paving*, 333 P.2d 757 (Cal. 1958), the court did apply promissory estoppel doctrine to hold the subcontractor to an implied promise not to revoke its bid. The court saw no reason to confine the doctrine to donative promises, but recognized the protection of justifiable reliance as a general value of the law. (This position has since become well accepted.) The court saw the creation of an option in this situation as analogous to the legal recognition of an option to protect an offeree who begins to accept a unilateral offer by commencing a noninstantaneous performance. (*See* section 4.12.5.) The court held that in the commercial context, the subcontractor must have understood that the prime contractor might use its bid in calculating the bid for the prime contract. The prime contractor did rely justifiably on the bid.

The discrepancy between the bid of this subcontractor and others did not alert the prime contractor to the possibility of a mistake. The court made it clear that the doctrine should be applied carefully and selectively in the precontractual context because promises are not normally made during negotiations prior to making a contract, and a party is not normally justified in acting in reliance until the contract is concluded. The court also stressed that the prime contractor must attempt to accept the bid within a reasonable time of being awarded the prime contract.

There are a number of more recent decisions that have followed the approach in *Drennan*. In *Pavel Enterprises, Inc. v. A.S. Johnson & Co., Inc.*, 674 A.2d 521 (Md. App 1996), the court accepted that where usage creates an expectation that a general contractor will rely on a subcontractor's bid in formulating its own bid, promissory estoppel can be used to validate the option without consideration. The court stressed that the general contractor must behave fairly to merit the protection of promissory estoppel. Any manipulation such as bid shopping[9] will defeat reasonable reliance. In *Deide Construction v. Monterey Mechanical Co.*, 22 Cal. Rptr. 3d 763 (Cal. App. 2005), the court of appeals found the doctrine of promissory estoppel to be applicable where the prime contractor had committed itself to the property owner on the basis of the subcontractor's bid. The trial court had held that when the prime contractor discovered the error in the subcontractor's bid, it should have asked the owner to release it from its contract. The court of appeals disagreed. It would be unjust to require the prime contractor to sacrifice its profit and reputation. However, because the variance between the bids of the subcontractor and its next lowest competitor was $425,000, the court remanded the case for a determination of whether the prime contractor was reasonable in relying on such a low bid. In *I&R Mechanical, Inc. v. Hazelton Mfg. Co.*, 817 N.E.2d 799 (Mass. App. 2004), the court found that the elements of promissory estoppel were not satisfied. Applying offer and acceptance principles, the court found that the subcontractor's bid did not amount to an offer, but merely solicited an offer from the prime contractor. This in itself precluded the use of promissory estoppel because there was no promise. Even if promissory estoppel was applicable, the discrepancy between the subcontractor's price and other bids was so great that it should have alerted the contractor to an error. In addition, the contractor had also engaged in bid shopping, which was inequitable and indicated that it was not relying on the bid.

---

9. As explained earlier, bid shopping occurs where the prime contractor does not wish to award the subcontract to the bidder, but instead uses the bid as a means of persuading a competing bidder to reduce its bid, with the intention of awarding the job to the competitor.

§8.12 A TRANSNATIONAL PERSPECTIVE ON PROMISSORY ESTOPPEL

Because civilian legal systems do not require consideration for contract formation, they have no need for a doctrine like promissory estoppel to enforce promises that lack consideration. However, there may be other reasons why a promise does not qualify as contractual, so an equivalent doctrine does have some role to play. In civilian jurisdictions, this doctrine does not derive from equitable estoppel. As explained in section 2.5, the distinction between law and equity is peculiar to the common law and has its origins in the particular historical circumstances under which English courts developed. Nevertheless, civil law recognizes a principle similar to estoppel under which a person is held accountable for conduct and cannot claim to enforce a right that is asserted in contradiction of that conduct. Under this principle, detrimental reliance on a promise can give rise to liability to honor the promise.

Although neither the CISG nor the UNIDROIT Principles articulate a general doctrine of detrimental reliance, equivalent to Restatement, Second, §90, they do contain a number of provisions that protect reliance on conduct or promise in specific situations. For example, CISG Article 16(2)(b) makes an offer irrevocable if the offeree acted in reasonable reliance on its irrevocability. Article 2.1.4(2)(b) of the UNIDROIT Principles is to the same effect. CISG Article 29 provides that where a contract has a provision requiring modifications to be in writing, a party is precluded from enforcing that provision where its conduct led the other party to reasonably rely on the effectiveness of an oral modification. Article 2.1.15 of the UNIDROIT Principles recognizes a principle similar to that articulated in Hoffman v. Red Owl Stores (see section 8.9) by providing that a party may be held liable for losses resulting from the bad faith termination of negotiations.

Examples

1. Aunt Jenny Rouse was very fond of her nephew, Juan El. After Juan graduated from college, he took a job as a sales representative. He earned well, but did not think of this as a permanent career. He really wanted to become a lawyer. Juan told Aunt Jenny that he wanted to quit his job and go to law school, but he was worried about the huge debt that he would have to incur to pay tuition and living expenses for the three years. During this conversation, Aunt Jenny was very sympathetic and told Juan that she wanted to think about what she could do to help. About a week later, Aunt Jenny wrote a letter to Juan in which she said, "I have been thinking about your ambition to become a lawyer and would love to see you achieve what you want. I realize that you will not be able to

work while studying and that the cost of a legal education is high. There-fore, if you do decide to go to law school, I will give you $20,000 toward your first-year tuition and living expenses, which I will pay to you when you begin law school."

After receiving this letter, Juan immediately applied for admission to law school, paying the required nonrefundable $100 application fee. In April he was offered admission for the next academic year, beginning at the end of August. Juan told Aunt Jenny about the offer and said he was going to accept it. She was delighted and reaffirmed her intention to pay him $20,000 when he began school. A week later, Juan accepted the law school's offer and paid a nonrefundable $500 deposit. He planned to work until the end of July, and did not yet resign from his job. In May, Aunt Jenny died. In June, the executor of Aunt Jenny's estate told Juan that because Aunt' Jenny's promise of $20,000 was gratuitous, the estate would not honor it. Notwithstanding, Juan quit his job in July and entered law school at the end of August. He then sued the estate to enforce the promise. Will he likely succeed?

2. Faith Reliance owns a motorbike, which she has kept comprehensively insured. However, she recently lost her job and cannot afford to pay the insurance premium due on August 1. On July 20, she asked her father to help her by paying the premium. He agreed and took the policy renewal notice from her, promising to pay it the next day. Sadly, it is well known in the family that Faith's father is a big talker, but he almost never does what he promises. True to form, he did not pay the premium on July 21 and Faith received a final warning from the insurer on July 25 that the policy would lapse if the premium was not paid by August 1. When she showed it to her father, he apologized for forgetting to pay it and assured her that he would mail the check to the insurer the next morning. Hearing nothing further from the insurer, Faith assumed that matters had been taken care of. A couple of weeks later, the bike was stolen. Faith then discovered that her father had never paid the premium. Can Faith recover anything from her father? If so, what is she entitled to claim?

3. Examples 9 and 10 of Chapter 7 identified a consideration problem in which promises of reward for long service were made to retirees at the point of retirement. Under the "past consideration" rule, prior service is not consideration because it has already occurred and is not therefore bargained for in exchange for the promise. Both cases involved the fickle and ungrateful company, Turn Coat Corporation. In summary, the facts were:

In Example 9, when Constance De Votion retired after working for Turn Coat for 40 years, the company promised her an all-expenses-paid vacation in recognition of her faithful service. She planned the vacation, but when she tried to book it, she discovered that the company had revoked its promise as part of an economy drive. She could not enforce the promise under consideration doctrine because she had suffered no new detriment in exchange for it.

In Example 10, Gerry Atrick was a longstanding employee who had become incompetent. Although he could have been summarily dismissed as an employee at will, the company decided that worker morale would best be served if he could be persuaded to retire. The company offered and he accepted the promise of a year's wages in exchange for his voluntary retirement. The company then changed its mind and fired him. It is arguable that his agreement to retire is sufficient legal detriment to be consideration for the promise of a year's wages. However, the contrary argument could be made that an employee at will gives up no legal right in agreeing to resign because the company can dismiss him summarily.

Assuming that the court finds no consideration for the company's promises to these employees, do these facts support recovery under promissory estoppel?

4. Since graduating from the Elmo Mater College a few years ago, Al Lumnis has been very successful in business. Toward the end of the financial year, he decided to share a little of his wealth with his old college. As he thought back to his days on campus, he remembered how difficult it had been to find a good cup of coffee. The bilge in the cafeteria was undrinkable, and the closest source of espresso was ten blocks away. He therefore decided that his gift to the college would be a fully equipped espresso bar. He wrote a letter to the president in which he stated: "In consideration of my desire to enhance and ennoble the quality of campus life at the Elmo Mater College, I hereby pledge to the College the sum of $40,000 to be paid as soon as the College submits plans to me for the construction of a fully equipped espresso bar in the Student Union building. The bar shall be known as the 'Al Lumnis Mochamorial.'"

The president of the college wrote back, thanking Al for the pledge and undertaking to begin work immediately on planning the coffee bar. The president appointed a joint faculty-student committee to consult with architects. She also instructed the editor of the alumni magazine to prepare a flattering article on Al and his gift for the next edition of the magazine.

It is now a couple of weeks later. The committee has met a couple of times and has had one consultation with an architect. Copy has been written for the magazine which has not yet been published. The president has just received another letter from Al which states: "My offer to fund an espresso bar was a bad idea. The trouble with kids today is that life is too easy. My character was built by trudging through the snow to get my cappuccino. This hardship gave me the resilience to succeed in business. Please disregard my last letter. I withdraw my pledge."

Can the College hold Al to his pledge?

5. Chilly Winters lives in Rustburg, a cold and congested northern city. Sonny Climes, his college roommate, moved south a few years ago and lives in Tropicana, a balmy southwestern metropolis. Sonny had established a flourishing high-tech business and often told Chilly that if he ever decided to escape the snow and smog, a job would be waiting for him at Sonny's company. After suffering through a particularly harsh winter, Chilly decided that it was time to move south. He called Sonny and asked if a job was still available. Sonny responded, "You bet! Get down here as soon as you can and I'll put you to work. I can start you off as a trainee at a salary of $40,000 a year. Your salary will increase as you become more experienced and assume more responsibility." Chilly agreed and told Sonny that he would give notice to his present employer and would be in Tropicana in a month.

Chilly immediately gave notice to his employer and his landlord and bought a one-way air ticket to Tropicana. When he called Sonny a week later to tell him his exact time of arrival, he received an unpleasant surprise. Sonny told him that he had just received an offer for the sale of his business that was too good to resist. He had accepted it and planned to retire. He was sorry, but he could no longer employ Chilly.

As Chilly no longer had any employment prospects in Tropicana, he decided to remain in Rustburg. He tried to retract his notice to his employer and his landlord, but his employer had already hired a replacement and his apartment had been relet. Chilly found a new apartment at a higher rental. After two months searching, he found a new job that paid the same salary as the old one. He cannot obtain a refund of his airfare, but airline policy allows him to cancel his booking and to use the ticket for travel within the U.S.A. at any time within the next year.

What recourse, if any, does Chilly have against Sonny?

6. In August, Primo Contracting Co., a building contractor, was invited by a developer to submit a bid for the construction of a new building. Primo was given until September 15 to submit the bid. To produce an accurate bid, Primo needed to know what it would have to pay plumbers, electricians, and other specialists to whom work would be subcontracted. On September 1, Primo sent the building specifications to a number of potential subcontractors and invited them to submit bids by September 13, explaining that it required the bids by that time to enable it to submit its own bid for the whole project on time.

Lois Bidder was one of the electricians invited to bid on the electrical work. After studying the specifications, Lois calculated the amount of material and labor required and submitted a written bid to Primo for

$100,000. The bid stated: "This bid is open for your acceptance within a reasonable time after you have been awarded the prime contract."

Upon receiving the bid on September 13, Primo compared it to others received and saw that it was $20,000 cheaper than the next lowest bid. It therefore decided to use Lois for the electrical work and included her figure in the bid to the owner. Primo submitted its bid on September 14, and the owner accepted it on September 15.

Primo immediately prepared letters to all the selected subcontractors, notifying them that their bids had been successful and that the project would proceed. On September 16, just before the letters were mailed, Primo received a fax from Lois, stating that on checking her calculations after submitting her bid, she had discovered that she had mistakenly overlooked the cost of some of the materials that would be required. As a result, she had underestimated her costs by $30,000, and she could not profitably perform the work for the bid price. Lois apologized for the error, which resulted from having to get her bid ready in a rush, and regretted that she must withdraw her previous bid. She was willing, however, to perform the work for $130,000.

On September 16, Primo faxed back, informing Lois that it had already committed to the owner on the basis of electrical subcontracting costs of $100,000 and it considered Lois bound by her original bid. Immediately after sending the fax, Primo mailed the letter of acceptance to Lois.

Is Lois bound to Primo by her bid?

Explanations

1. Aunt Jenny undoubtedly made a promise to Juan. The promise was expressed clearly and definitely in writing after Aunt Jenny had time to think about it carefully, but Juan would be hard-pressed to argue that he entered a contract with Aunt Jenny because he gave no consideration for the promise. Quitting a job and enrolling in law school could qualify as a detriment for consideration purposes, but this was not bargained for in exchange for Aunt Jenny's promise. Although Aunt Jenny's promised performance was conditional on Juan going to law school, this is more properly interpreted as a condition of the gift.

If Aunt Jenny's promise was gratuitous, Juan's only basis for relief is promissory estoppel. Judged on an objective standard, Aunt Jenny, in making a clear promise, must reasonably have expected that it would induce Juan's reliance. This expectation is reinforced by her reaffirmation of the promise when Juan told her he had been offered admission to law school. The more difficult question is whether Juan's conduct was induced by the promise and was justifiable. The fact of inducement and the justification for inducement tend to flow together on these facts. In deciding on whether these elements are satisfied, we have to consider separately each action taken by Juan after the promise, because he may have taken some, but not others in justifiable reliance on the promise. Juan's actions before Aunt Jenny's death — his application to law school, his acceptance of the law school's offer of admission, and his payment of the nonrefundable fee and deposit — are causally linked to the promise and are justifiable. Aunt Jenny's promise was clear, carefully considered, and reaffirmed before Juan accepted the law school's offer. He had no reason to doubt that he could take the action that the letter encouraged.

Juan's further action — resigning from his job at the end of July and entering law school at the end of August — were taken after Aunt Jenny had died and her executor had made it clear that the estate would not honor her promise. If Aunt Jenny's promise was not binding because it was gratuitous, the estate had the legal right to refuse payment, thereby breaking the causal link between the promise and Juan's actions, and removing his justification for relying on the promise.

This being so, his claim for promissory estoppel should be confined to the detriment incurred before Aunt Jenny died. At that stage, Juan had done nothing more than complete the law school application process and pay the fee and deposit. Nothing in the facts indicates that he was committed to the law school beyond the forfeiture of the nonrefundable fee and deposit. However, on the facts of this case, even these expenses may not be recoverable because Juan did ultimately enroll in law school, and they were therefore not wasted. True, he lost the hope and expectation of receiving help toward his tuition, but this is in the nature of an expectation interest, more properly confined to a case in which a contract is established. Given that Juan incurred only a modest financial expense and could have avoided any further economic detriment, this does not seem to be a case in which injustice can be averted only by enforcing the promise to its full extent. (It is conceivable that a court that treats promissory estoppel as a consideration substitute may take a different view. That is, it could hold that Aunt Jenny became contractually bound to pay the $20,000 once Juan took action in reliance on her promise by accepting the offer of admission. On this theory, a contract was formed at that time, and the estate's subsequent action in reneging on the promise is merely a breach of that contract.)

This Example is inspired by *Alden v. Presley*, 637 S.W.2d. 862 (Tenn. 1982). The Presley in this case was none other than the King and the plaintiff was his fiancée's mother. When the plaintiff decided to divorce her husband, Elvis undertook to pay the expenses of her divorce, to pay out her husband's share of their house, and to pay off the mortgage so she would own the house free and clear. Elvis died after the divorce proceedings had begun, but before the divorce settlement had become legally binding. His estate notified the plaintiff that it would not honor Elvis's promise to pay off the mortgage. Notwithstanding, the plaintiff committed herself to the divorce settlement that released her husband from the mortgage. The court refused to enforce the promise to pay off the mortgage. It was gratuitous, so it was not a contract. It was also not enforceable on grounds of promissory estoppel because the plaintiff was no longer justified in finalizing the settlement in reliance on the promise once she knew that the estate would not honor it.

2. Faith gave no consideration for her father's undertaking to pay the premium. It was simply a gift promise motivated by family relationship and cannot be enforced as a contract. Promissory estoppel was developed to provide a basis for enforcing this kind of gratuitous promise, relied on by the promisee to her detriment.

Are the elements of promissory estoppel satisfied? Whether or not Faith's father subjectively intended to honor his undertaking, his words, interpreted objectively, convey a clear commitment to pay the premium. There can be little doubt that he did or reasonably should have expected Faith to rely on it. It was an unequivocal response to her need for financial assistance, made with knowledge of her circumstances and reiterated when the cancellation warning was received.

The promise apparently induced forbearance on Faith's part in that she did not pay the premium herself. There is a suggestion that financial difficulty may have compelled Faith to let the comprehensive coverage lapse had her father not undertaken to help. If that is so, it can be argued that she did not forbear in reliance on the promise because she did not have the financial ability to take the action of renewing the policy. However, we cannot be sure of this. She may have been able to find the money to pay the premium by some other means.

Faith's reliance must have been justified. A daughter would usually be justified in relying on her father's clear and unequivocal promise, made with apparently serious intent. However, she knew that her father had a record of breaking his promises. This could mean that Faith may not have been entirely justified in relying unquestioningly on his word without checking to see if he had made the payment. This point was made in the *Norton* case mentioned in sections 8.6.2 and 8.6.4. While blind faith on the promise of a person known to be unreliable may weaken the promisee's case, it may not be fatal. After all, the promisor is not likely to motivate a court to balance the equities in his favor by arguing, in effect, that although he made a promise, he should not be held to it because he is untrustworthy.

Although Faith may have difficulty establishing the elements of promissory estoppel, if they are satisfied the remaining task is to select the proper remedy. There are no wasted out-of-pocket costs in this case, so reimbursement of reliance expenses is not a meaningful alternative. Even full enforcement of the promise would not cover Faith's loss because that would simply be an award of the cost of the unpaid premium, which is much less than Faith's loss of the entire value of the bike. To decide if the full recovery of the value of the bike is appropriate, the court must weigh all the equities. It must consider the extent to which the elements of promissory estoppel have been established (here, a strong and unequivocal, albeit oral, promise, but a possibly unjustified reliance). It must also balance the harm Faith will suffer if it refuses enforcement against the hardship to her father if it enforces the promise. It is difficult to predict how a court may strike this balance, but the equities seem to tilt in Faith's favor, so the court could well hold her father liable for the value of the bike. (Faith's case has some similarity to the *Geremia* case discussed in section 8.6.2, in that it was not clear that the borrower would have been able to pay the premium himself. The court indicated that had it not found consideration for the credit union's promise to pay the borrower's insurance premium, it would have considered an award of the value of the car appropriate relief under a theory of promissory estoppel.)

3. There have been a number of cases in which courts have used promissory estoppel to validate a promise of retirement benefits when the promise was found to lack consideration under the "past consideration" rule. This happened in both cases cited in Examples 9 and 10 of Chapter 7, *Feinberg v. Pfeiffer Co.*, 322 S.W.2d 163 (Mo. 1959), and *Katz v. Danny Dare Inc.*, 610 S.W.2d 121 (Mo. 1980). In each of those cases, the court found that a promise had been made with the intention of inducing reliance, that the promisee acted detrimentally in reliance, and that full enforcement of the promise was necessary to prevent injustice.

In *Feinberg*, the employer promised the employee a life pension when she retired. This promise was made about 18 months before her retirement, as a reward for 37 years of service. The employer paid the pension for a few years until its management changed. The new management reduced the amount of the pension. Although the court found that the employee had given no consideration for the promise of the pension, it enforced the promise on the basis of promissory estoppel. The court found that the employer had made the promise with intent to induce reliance, and that the employee had suffered irreversible detriment by retiring on the strength of it. By the time the promise was revoked, she had become too old and too ill to find other employment. The court treated promissory estoppel as a consideration substitute and fully enforced the promise as if it was a contract. Similarly, in *Katz* the court found no consideration for the promise of a pension because the employment was at will and the employee could have been summarily dismissed. Because he had no right to continued employment, he suffered no legal detriment by retiring. However, the court fully enforced the promise on the basis of promissory estoppel. This seems inconsistent because, as an at-will employee, Katz did not suffer much of a detriment in retiring in reliance on the promise, since the employer could simply have dismissed him at any time. Nevertheless, the result is fair, and shows that sometimes a court can use the doctrine of promissory estoppel to do justice where it feels constrained to apply consideration doctrine strictly.

Employees do not invariably succeed in enforcing pension promises under the doctrine of promissory estoppel. For example, in *Hayes v. Plantation Steele Co.*, 438 A.2d 1091 (R.I. 1982) an ex-employee was promised that the company "would take care of him" when he retired following 51 years of service. The company paid the employee $5,000 per year for several years and then ceased payments. The court refused to enforce the promise because the undertaking was too vague to be a promise, and also because the undertaking was given after the employee's retirement so he did not retire in reliance on it.

Under these principles Constance probably cannot recover. She retired before the promise, so it did not induce that decision. Her only other action was planning her vacation and communicating with the travel agent. Apart from wasting some of her free time, she incurred no loss or expense. Unquestionably, her expectation of a vacation has been dashed by her ingrate ex-employer, but if promissory estoppel is aimed at protecting reliance, the enforcement of this expectation interest is beyond the scope of the doctrine. A gratuitous promise was made, and in the absence of detrimental reliance, it simply fails because consideration is lacking. This unpleasant result could be avoided by underplaying the element of detriment in promissory estoppel. However, the real policy question is whether the "past consideration" rule has any justification at all in a case like this.

Turn Coat Corporation did make a definite promise to Gerry with the clear intent to induce action. Gerry relied on it, suffering the detriment of giving up his job. His actual loss is very small because he had no right to long-term employment. Because substantial actual loss is a significant factor in weighing the justice of enforcement, the lack of detriment for consideration purposes could also make the harm too trivial to support promissory estoppel. Nevertheless, as the *Katz* case shows, a court that is literal-minded in applying consideration doctrine may take a more equitable view in relation to promissory estoppel.

4. Again, this problem treads that uncertain line between a promise with consideration and a gift made subject to instructions on its use, but it more likely falls on the latter side of the line. The recited "consideration" is not consideration at all but merely expresses Al's purpose in giving the

donation. Although the president replies by promising to use the fund for this purpose, as a matter of strict doctrine, the college suffers no legal detriment in undertaking to use a gift for its designated purpose. It had no right to the money in the absence of the gift, and hence gives up no legal right by promising to use it in a particular way. The publication of the flattering article in the alumni magazine could have been consideration, had it been bargained for in exchange for the promise. However, Al's letter does not mention the article or any other form of recognition, apart from the naming of the espresso bar. The naming of the bar could itself be consideration because the naming may be far enough removed from the actual use of the funds to be a detriment. This is quite flimsy, but may provide a means of finding consideration for a court sympathetic to the college's claim.

This Example raises the different approaches to these ambiguous transactions raised in section 8.8, where *Allegheny College* and *King* found a basis of enforcement either under consideration doctrine or on grounds of promissory estoppel, while *DeLeo* did not. The facts here seem more strongly to point to some degree of reliance than those in *DeLeo* or even *Allegheny College*. Al stipulated that the planning must occur before payment, and the college did begin the planning process in reliance on the promise. However, the reliance had not extended beyond this by the time that Al revoked his promise. This leads to the question of remedy.

Although the court could fully enforce Al's promise to pay the $40,000 under promissory estoppel, it also has the option of providing lesser relief aimed at reimbursing the college's reliance costs. The college should at least be able to recover the fee paid to the architect. It could possibly also receive reimbursement for the value of the time spent by committee members in planning (to the extent that the time of faculty and students has any value at all).[10] If it was reasonably foreseeable that the donation would generate an article in the alumni magazine, the cost of the wasted production effort may also be claimable. Even if all these expenses are awarded, this recovery cannot be more than a fraction of the $40,000 promised.

5. Although the parties were friends at the time of contracting, this is a purely commercial transaction. Sonny appears to have made an offer to Chilly which he accepted. The offer could have been fuller and more precise in setting out the terms of the employment, but there is probably enough specificity to avoid problems of indefiniteness. The agreement does not provide otherwise, so the employment is deemed to be at will, as explained in section 8.10. As noted there, it can be difficult to persuade a court that there is consideration for a promise of at-will employment,

---

10. Just kidding, of course.

even after offer and acceptance has occurred. A court may find that consideration is lacking as a result of the parties' discretion to terminate at will. Even if consideration is found, expectation damages are likely to be small where the employer has the right to terminate the employment at will.

In the absence of a viable claim on contract, the question is whether promissory estoppel would be a more advantageous basis of recovery. Sonny did promise Chilly a job. His intent was clearly expressed, and because Chilly told him that he was going to quit his job and move, he must have realized that Chilly planned to act in reliance on the promise. Chilly did rely on the promise, but the difficult question is whether this reliance was justified. As discussed in section 8.10, some courts hold that while it may be rational for a promisee to take detrimental action in reliance on a promise of at-will employment, this action does not provide grounds for actionable reliance for promissory estoppel purposes. That is, the employee cannot shift the risk of his reliance to the employer, because he should understand that he is incurring loss or expense without any promise of job security. Other courts consider this approach too harsh, and are willing to give relief, especially where the promise and intent to induce reliance is clear and there are no specific facts that would make the reliance unreasonable.

However, even if the court grants relief, it is likely to be limited. Chilly could possibly recover the two months' lost salary, but only if he had some security of employment at his old job. If he was an at-will employee in that job, he may not be able to show that loss with reasonable certainty. In addition, Chilly's delay in finding a replacement job would have to be reasonable. If he did not make a reasonably diligent effort in seeking new employment, he cannot hold Sonny accountable for loss that he could have prevented. (This is the principle of mitigation of damages, discussed in section 18.6.3.) Chilly may also be able to claim any increase in rent as a result of having ended his apartment lease in reliance on the promise. Again, he would have to show that he would have had a right to retain his old apartment and that the substitute was reasonable. Chilly might have been able to claim the wasted expense of the air ticket, but because the ticket is salvageable, he has probably not suffered a loss unless he can show that it would not be possible for him to use it within the year or to sell it.

6. By soliciting bids, Primo was inviting subcontractors to make offers. The language used by Lois in her bid creates the reasonable understanding that she intended it as an offer with a promise of irrevocability for a reasonable time after the prime contract was awarded. The undertaking not to revoke does not bind Lois, however, because she received no consideration for it. (There could have been

consideration if Primo had bound itself, expressly or impliedly, to use the lowest bid, but there is no indication of such a commitment.) Although Primo used Lois's offer in calculating its own bid, there is no evidence of circumstances that would make this an acceptance of the offer. Lois revoked the offer before Primo had the chance to communicate its acceptance, and there is no indication in the bid that Lois waived communication of acceptance. Because there is no consideration to validate the promise not to revoke, Primo can hold Lois to her promise of irrevocability only if it can validate that promise on grounds of promissory estoppel. As the discussion in section 8.11 indicates, the availability of promissory estoppel in this context is now well established.

The question is therefore whether the facts satisfy the elements of promissory estoppel. Lois made an express promise of irrevocability, so the element of promise is easily established. It is likely that this promise was made with the reasonable understanding that Primo would rely on it if Primo used Lois's bid. In *Drennan*, the court emphasized that the expectation of reliance is a factual question, to be decided under all the circumstances, including common practice in the industry. We do not have any information about industry practice. If it is a general practice in the industry for subcontractors to protect contractors who use their bids as the basis of bidding on prime contracts, there is a strong likelihood of a reasonable expectation of reliance. Even in the absence of such a clear practice, the language Lois used in her bid suggests a reasonable expectation of reliance — it recognizes that her bid might be used and that Primo needed time to accept after it was awarded the contract.

There are two factors to be considered in deciding whether Primo's reliance was justified. First, was Primo reasonable in understanding that a promise was made on which it could rely? This question parallels the above analysis, now examined from the perspective of a reasonable person in Primo's position, and there is no reason to reach a different answer. Second, should Primo have suspected an error when it saw that there was a $20,000 discrepancy between Lois's price and the next lowest bid? Even if it did not know for sure that Lois must have made a mistake, it had a duty to enquire if the low price looked wrong, and it cannot just jump at the bargain. Of course, there could be many explanations for variations in price, so the question is whether, under all the circumstances, Primo was reasonable in not questioning it.

Promissory estoppel relief must be necessary to prevent injustice. This element calls on the court to weigh all the equities of the situation, including the strength of the elements discussed above. A predominant issue here is the degree of detriment that will be suffered by Primo if the promise to hold the offer open is not enforced. As in most of the bid cases, this detriment is an increase in the costs of the job and a corresponding loss of profit. The more dramatic this loss is, and the fewer the reasonable alternatives for averting it, the stronger the injustice. Other factors also enter the determination of injustice. Several of the cases discussed in section 8.11 examined the conduct of the prime contractor in the way it used the bid. An unreasonable delay in acceptance after the award of the prime contract, or any kind of manipulation such as bid shopping, could tip the balance against the grant of relief. In this case, Primo was not guilty of any such misconduct. It accepted the bid the day after being awarded the prime contract and just three days after the bid was submitted.

The appropriate remedy in a case like this is to enforce the promise to keep the bid open so that Primo's acceptance is effective, even though it was made after attempted revocation. Because the acceptance is effective, a contract was created. If Lois failed to perform it, Primo can claim damages measured by the difference between Lois's price and the higher price that Primo reasonably had to pay to another subcontractor for the work.

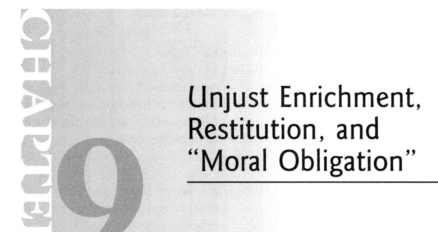

Unjust Enrichment, Restitution, and "Moral Obligation"

§9.1 INTRODUCTION

Chapter 8 explained how promissory estoppel can sometimes be used to ameliorate the harsh consequences of consideration doctrine by enforcing a promise that induced justifiable reliance. Although the remedy of restitution is available in a variety of different situations, both within the bounds of contract law and beyond them, in one of its aspects it serves a purpose similar to promissory estoppel by allowing for the enforcement of obligations that do not qualify as contractual. Having drawn this general parallel, it must be stressed that restitution and promissory estoppel have very different conceptual bases. Restitution is not predicated on accountability for promise. In fact, its usefulness is greatest when no promise has been made. Its purpose is the restoration of an unfair gain. Its focus is on cases in which one party has obtained a benefit at the expense of another under circumstances that make it unfair for the recipient to retain the benefit without paying for it.

§9.2 UNJUST ENRICHMENT, THE BASIS FOR RESTITUTION

It is common to confuse restitution, a remedy, with unjust enrichment, the cause of action that gives rise to the remedy. Restitution is the act of restoring something or its value. When a court grants restitution, it adjudges that the recipient of a benefit is obliged to give back that benefit or to pay its value to the person who conferred it. The basis of this judgment is that the recipient has been unjustly enriched at the expense of grantor. That is, there is no legal justification for retention of the benefit without pay. In short, when the elements of the cause of action, unjust enrichment, are satisfied, the remedy of restitution is the relief awarded. (Courts and commentators do not always observe this distinction in terminology between the cause of action and the remedy, so it is quite common to find the word "restitution" used in reference to both the cause of action and the remedy.)

Unjust enrichment is not a subcategory of contract law. It is a distinct and independent basis of obligation, occupying a place alongside contract, promissory estoppel,[1] and tort. Diagram 9A charts this relationship between different causes of action and remedies.

Diagram 9A

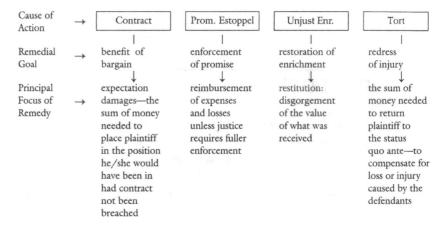

Cause of Action	→	Contract	Prom. Estoppel	Unjust Enr.	Tort
Remedial Goal	→	benefit of bargain	enforcement of promise	restoration of enrichment	redress of injury
Principal Focus of Remedy	→	expectation damages—the sum of money needed to place plaintiff in the position he/she would have been in had contract not been breached	reimbursement of expenses and losses unless justice requires fuller enforcement	restitution: disgorgement of the value of what was received	the sum of money needed to return plaintiff to the status quo ante—to compensate for loss or injury caused by the defendants

§9.3 THE RELATIONSHIP BETWEEN UNJUST ENRICHMENT AND CONTRACT

Unjust enrichment is a complex field, covering many situations that have nothing to do with contract. It falls within our scope in two broad areas. These two different roles of unjust enrichment in the contractual context must be distinguished to prevent confusion. Diagram 9B charts the role of

---

1. But remember that one view of promissory estoppel is that it is not an independent theory of liability but a subcategory of contract law. *See* section 8.2.

restitution in contract and unjust enrichment. The diagram is followed by a brief general description and explanatory illustrations.

Diagram 9B

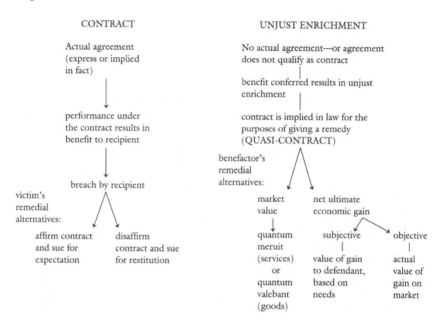

Unjust enrichment serves as an independent theory of liability in cases when no contract has come into existence, either because something went wrong or failed to happen in the process of formation, or because the parties simply did not attempt to make a contract. Yet they had some interaction that resulted in the one party obtaining a gain from the other. In situations like this, there is no basis for contractual relief, but unjust enrichment permits restitutionary recovery. The link to contract could be close here because there could be strong contractual elements in the interaction. However, some of these situations have only a marginal relationship to contract, based on the legal fiction called "quasi-contract" explained in section 9.4. This chapter is concerned with cases like these, when no contract exists and unjust enrichment is the basis of obligation.

Unjust enrichment also plays an important role when a valid contract was created, but it has been breached, or it has been rescinded. In the case of breach, unjust enrichment — and its remedy of restitution — may be used as an alternative to expectation damages. One of the parties may have conferred a benefit on the other in the course of performing the contract before its breach, and restitution of that benefit may be a better option than enforcement of the contract. (In some cases it may be the only option because, for example, contractual expectation damages cannot be proved.) Even though there is a valid contract, the plaintiff may elect to forego contractual relief in favor of restitution. This role of restitution is an issue of damages for breach of contract. Apart from this brief mention of it and the illustration below, this question is deferred to the discussion of remedies for breach in section 18.9. Where a contract has been created but is later rescinded (avoided) because there was a defect in the bargaining process (such as fraud or mistake), the remedy of restitution, based on the theory of unjust enrichment, is available to a party who rendered performance under the contract before its avoidance. This use of restitution is discussed in Chapters 13, 14, and 15.

The following examples illustrate the range of the restitutionary remedy by showing its application in a number of situations. The first involves restitution when a valid contract exists, the next two show the use of restitution when the parties aimed to enter a contract but their dealings did not result in a valid contract, the fourth illustrates the use of restitution where a contract is rescinded, and the fifth demonstrates the use of restitution when there has been no contractual interaction between the parties.

Illustration 1.   *Restitution as an alternative remedy when a valid contract has been breached*

Buyer and Seller made a contract for the sale of Seller's house. Buyer paid a deposit of $5,000 to Seller. Seller later reneged on the contract and refused to close. Because a valid contract exists, Buyer has the right to claim expectation damages for breach of contract that would place her in the position she would have been in had the contract been performed. If the price under this contract is less than the cost of buying an equivalent house on the market, Buyer's expectation damages would be the difference between the contract price and what she would have to pay for a substitute.[2] However, assume that Seller's house was overpriced, and it turns out that Buyer can purchase an equivalent house for less on the market. Expectation damages are zero because Buyer has suffered no economic loss as a result of Seller's breach. However, Buyer has enriched Seller by the $5,000 down payment that Seller no longer has any right to keep. His enrichment is unjust, and if he fails to repay, the remedy of restitution is available to Buyer to recover the down payment.

Illustration 2.   *Restitution when a benefit is conferred pursuant to an invalid or unenforceable contract*

Assume that the parties in the above illustration had made an oral agreement for the sale of the house. Under the statute of frauds, a sale of real

---

2. The measure of expectation damages is fully discussed in section 18.3.

property must be in writing and the oral agreement is unenforceable as a contract.[3] Therefore, if Seller reneges, Buyer does not have the option of suing for enforcement of the contract. But because Seller no longer has any right to keep the money, Buyer can, nevertheless, obtain restitution of the down payment on the theory of unjust enrichment. Restitution is also available as a remedy where the parties reach an understanding that is too vague to qualify as a contract, but one of the parties performs under the arrangement. For example, in *Schepperley v. DePinna*, 2009 WL 765524 (Conn. Super. 2009), a mother and daughter agreed orally that the mother would pay for the construction of an "in-law apartment" in the basement of the daughter's house, and in return, would live in the apartment. The agreement was too vague to qualify as a contract because the parties had not settled crucial terms such as the exact amount of the mother's contribution, the details of the construction, the term of the mother's residence in the apartment, or the extent and nature of any future obligations that she may have. The mother moved in and lived in the apartment for about six months. She then left following a disagreement with her daughter and sued her daughter and son-in-law for return of the funds that she had paid to construct the apartment. Although the court found no enforceable contract between the parties, it awarded restitution to the mother on the basis of unjust enrichment: The apartment was a capital improvement to the house, and the mother was entitled to reimbursement of what she paid for the construction.

Illustration 3. *Restitution when a benefit is conferred on the strength of a promise without consideration*

The principle of Illustration 2 applies in other situations when no valid contract came into existence. For example, say that Owner made a written promise to donate her house to Charity, a nonprofit organization that provides shelter for victims of abuse. Before taking transfer of the house, Charity obtained Owner's permission to build a wall around the house and to install a security system. After Charity had done this work, Owner reneged on the promise and refused to transfer the house. Charity's enhancement of the property was obviously not intended as consideration for the promise of the house and was not bargained for by or owed to Owner. It was simply done to enable Charity to make proper use of the gift. Because the promise is not supported by consideration, Charity cannot enforce it as a contract. But it has improved the house that now remains Owner's property. This unjustly enriches Owner, so Charity can obtain restitution for the value of the wall and security systems.

---

3. *See* section 11.2.

This illustration raises a number of points that will be discussed later:

1. Unlike the prior illustrations, it involves not the restoration of a fixed sum of money but the value of labor and materials. This is common. When the value of a benefit is not fixed and certain, evidence of value is required as discussed in section 9.6.

2. Owner may not particularly want a security system and wall on the property, but because he changed his mind about giving the house to Charity, he is stuck with paying for them. Under the circumstances, this result is justifiable because Owner authorized the work. However, principles of unjust enrichment ensure that this will not happen when a benefit is imposed on a recipient without consent.

3. These facts appear to support recovery under promissory estoppel: Acting in reliance on the promised donation, Charity incurred a loss in installing the security system and wall on the property. Injustice may be averted only by enforcing the promise, if not in full, at least to the extent of the costs incurred in supplying the materials and doing the work. Although it does not always happen that the same circumstances support relief either in restitution or in promissory estoppel, this is not an uncommon situation. When facts support alternative causes of action with different remedies, the claimant may choose which of them to pursue. The selection between them is based on factors such as ease of proof and extent of recovery. The elements of one cause of action may be easier to establish than the other. In addition, the relief for each may be quite different, because restitution focuses on the restoration of the value of the benefit conferred, while promissory estoppel is more concerned with the costs incurred by the claimant.

Illustration 4. *Restitution where a contract is rescinded*

Buyer and Seller entered into a contract for the sale of a plot of land. Based on a geological survey, both parties believed that there were no valuable mineral deposits under the surface of the land. Subsequent to executing the contract, they discovered that the survey was wrong, and there are significant gold deposits under the land. Under the doctrine of mistake, discussed in Chapter 15, Seller probably has grounds to avoid the contract because of the error. However, if Seller succeeds in avoiding the contract, Buyer is entitled to restitution of the price that he paid to Seller under principles of unjust enrichment.

Illustration 5. *Restitution in cases when no contractual interaction occurred*

Victim slipped on a banana peel and fell down a flight of stairs. Doctor, a stranger who happened to be walking by, administered emergency treatment to unconscious Victim. Doctor never entered into a contract with Victim, who could not consent to treatment because he was unconscious. The only basis on which Doctor could recover a fee for her services is unjust enrichment, on the theory that Victim would have had to pay for them in the marketplace, and it is unjust that he should receive them for free. (The merits of this argument will shortly be explored in more detail.) Although this is not a contract case, it is historically linked to contract law through a quaint legal fiction known as "quasi-contract."

§9.4 THE MEANING OF "QUASI-CONTRACT"

§9.4.1 Quasi-Contract — A Contract "Implied in Law"

Where a claim is not based on contract but is premised solely on the grounds of unjust enrichment, our legal tradition has created a peculiar fiction that makes the case sound as if it has something to do with contract. In early common law, courts were bound by a rigid set of writs called "forms of action." To obtain relief, the plaintiff had to fit his or her claim into one of these recognized categories of suit. There was no writ for unjust enrichment, so the court needed to fit enrichment claims into some other writ. It chose the contract writ of assumpsit, and squeezed enrichment into a contractual form by pretending that the benefit was conferred on the recipient pursuant to a contract with the grantor. Thus, to use Illustration 5 as an example, the court would act as if Victim had asked Doctor to treat his injuries, so that Doctor could recover the value of her services under the writ of assumpsit. Claims for unjust enrichment based on this fictional contract were said to arise *quasi ex contractu*, and the restitutionary remedy based on this fiction has come to be called quasi-contract, or contract implied in law. It is easy to be confused by this terminology, so it is important to remember that a quasi-contract or a contract implied in law is not a real contract. Legal implication is a fiction created for remedial purposes. It must be distinguished from a contract implied in fact, which is explained in section 9.4.2.

To put all this terminology together, we can describe the general principle of unjust enrichment as follows: When a benefit has been conferred on a recipient under circumstances in which it is unfair to permit him to retain it without payment, the cause of action of unjust enrichment is available to the person who conferred the benefit. Using this cause of action, the conferrer can claim the remedy of restitution, under which the court will restore the benefit or its value to her. To fit this newly recognized cause of action into existing legal forms, earlier common law courts used various legal fictions. The one that we are concerned with here (there are others that are beyond the scope of a contracts course, but are commonly covered in Remedies courses) was based on the fiction that the benefit had been contracted for. That is, the court implied a contract in law, even though no contractual relationship actually existed between the conferrer and the beneficiary. Restitutionary recovery based on unjust enrichment was therefore described as "quasi ex contractu," and the term "quasi-contract" has come down to us as an alternative name for this form of relief.

When it comes to enforcement of the obligation, relief for unjust enrichment (quasi-contractual relief) can be very different from that for contract. For example, if Doctor had made a real contract with Victim, she could enforce its actual terms and could recover whatever fee was agreed on for the treatment. As no contract was made and the cause of action is a quasi-contract, there cannot be an agreed fee, so recovery is based on the value of the benefit, typically determined by market value as discussed in section 9.6. Latin terms are commonly used to denote market value. Quantum meruit ("as much as deserved") is used to indicate the market value of services, and quantum valebant ("as much as they are worth") indicates the market value of goods. Sometimes there may be no difference between market value and contract price, but the difference could be significant.

§9.4.2 Quasi-Contract Distinguished from a Contract Implied in Fact

As noted in section 9.4.1, a quasi-contract (or contract implied in law) is not a contract at all, but merely a legal fiction. By contrast, a contract implied in fact is an actual contract. There is no difference in the legal nature or effect of an express contract and a contract implied in fact. The only difference is in the manner and evidence of contract formation. The parties create an express contract by articulating their agreement in written or oral words. A contract is implied in fact where the parties do not express agreement in words, but it is apparent from a reasonable interpretation of their conduct, viewed in context, that they intended to make a contract.[4] A variation of the facts of

---

4. The distinction between implication in law and in fact is also made where the issue is not whether a contract was formed, but whether it contains a particular disputed term. A term might be implied into a contract in fact, based on evidence that the parties intended it to be part of the contract even though they did not express it. Sometimes, even in the absence of such evidence of agreement on the term, the court might construe a term — that is, imply the term as a matter of law — because the term should be in the contract. This is discussed in section 10.4.

illustration 5 shows the distinction between quasi-contract and contract implied in fact. Victim slipped and fell down the stairs. Although he was injured, he was fully conscious, and his ability to make a contract was not impaired. He used his cell phone to call an ambulance, which took him to a hospital. Victim had no discussion with the dispatcher or the paramedics in the ambulance about payment for the service. Even though no words of agreement passed between Victim and employees of the ambulance company, there is surely a contract implied in fact under which Victim is responsible for paying a fee for the ambulance service. Given the general understanding that ambulances do not operate for free, both Victim and the ambulance company must reasonably have understood that Victim would be responsible for paying for the service. Because the parties did not discuss the fee, there is no agreed price for the service. Where parties make an actual contract (whether express or implied in fact) but do not specify the price, the tacit contract must be interpreted in context to decide how to determine the price. A court may conclude that Victim implicitly agreed to pay the ambulance service's usual or customary fee. Alternatively, if there is no usual or customary fee, or if it is not clear if the parties intended that fee to apply, the court may determine the fee with reference to the market value of the service — that is, it may use the quantum meruit measure. Therefore, although quantum meruit is commonly associated with quasi contract, there are circumstances in which it may be used to fix compensation for a service in an actual contract implied in fact, where there is no other means of determining an agreed price.

Where performance is rendered by one party to another in the absence of express agreement, it can be difficult to tell whether acceptance of the benefit of the performance created an actual contract, implied in fact, or gave rise to enrichment to be remedied by the device of quasi contract. The distinction often turns on whether there is sufficient usage and context on which to base the implication of an actual contract. In some cases, there may be no practical significance in the distinction, especially where the price under any implied-in-fact contract would have to be determined by quantum meruit. In other cases, the remedy available for an actual contract could be significantly different from that for unjust enrichment. This was intimated in the above example involving the ambulance. If there was a contract implied in fact, Victim would likely have been bound to the usual or customary charge for the service, which might be higher or lower than the market price of the service.

Contractual liability, based on intent (albeit implied) to enter a contract, has a different factual basis from unjust enrichment, which is founded on the injustice of permitting the beneficiary to retain a benefit without paying for it. It is therefore possible that the facts of the case will support recovery on one theory, but not the other. Illustration 5 in section 9.3, involving the rendition of medical services to an unconscious patient is an example of a case in which the facts provide no basis for finding an actual contract. By contrast, the facts of the example involving the ambulance are ambiguous — there could be a contract implied in fact or, if not, a basis for claiming that Victim would be unjustly enriched if he failed to pay the value of the service. *Contship Containerlines, Inc. v. Howard Industries, Inc.*, 309 F.3d 910 (6th Cir. 2002), provides an example of a situation in which the facts may not have supported recovery in contract, but did give rise to a claim in quasi contract. A shipper contracted with a freight forwarder to book its cargo onto a ship. The shipper paid the freight forwarder for the entire cost of the shipping. The shipper then delivered the cargo to the ship, and it was shipped to its destination. The freight forwarder never transmitted payment for the freight charges to the carrier (that is, the ship owner). The carrier sought to obtain payment from the shipper on the basis of contract implied in fact, alternatively, unjust enrichment. In response to the carrier's motion for summary judgment, the court held that there was a genuine dispute of fact on the question of a contract implied in fact, so the issue must go to trial. The shipper had delivered the cargo to the carrier, knowing that the carrier was not performing the service for free. This could provide a basis for implying an actual contract. However, the contrary argument could be made that a contract implied in fact must be based on agreement and the shipper did not reasonably intend to make a contract with the carrier. It had contracted with and had paid the freight forwarder and had never had any contact with the carrier except for the delivery of the cargo. Although the shipper overcame summary judgment on the contract claim, the court did grant summary judgment to the carrier on the unjust enrichment claim. This may seem surprising because the shipper had not actually been enriched at all — it had in fact paid the shipping costs to the freight forwarder. The court found that this was no defense to the carrier's restitution claim because the shipper, by paying a third-party intermediary, assumed the risk that payment would not be transmitted to the carrier. That is, the court was faced with the task of allocating the loss between two innocent parties — the shipper who had already paid someone else for the service and was not actually enriched, and the carrier who had not been paid for the service. The court allocated the risk to the shipper because it had been the one to cause this problem by entrusting the funds to the third party.

Courts will not usually imply a contract where the parties already have an express contract, especially if the implied contract is inconsistent with the terms of the express contract. For example, in *Yarde Metals, Inc. v. New England Patriots L.P.*, 834 N.E.2d 1233 (Mass. App. 2005), the holder of a season ticket argued that the Patriots were bound by an implied contract to give it the opportunity to renew the subscription. It based this claim on the fact that over the past 20 years, the Patriots had consistently offered it the opportunity to renew the subscription. The court held that this conduct did not give rise to an implied contract because such an implication contradicted the terms printed on the ticket, which stated that the ticket was a revocable license that gave the purchaser no renewal rights for a subsequent year. The court also found that implication of a contract would be inconsistent with common practice and would confer a right on the ticket holder far more valuable than the price paid for the tickets.

§9.5 THE ELEMENTS OF UNJUST ENRICHMENT

As stated earlier, the remedy of restitution is aimed at restoring money, property, or the value of property or services when it would be unjust to permit the recipient to retain what was received without paying for it. As its name suggests, unjust enrichment is predicated on two elements: The recipient must have been enriched at the expense of the claimant, and the circumstances must be such as to make this enrichment unjust. This is represented in Diagram 9C.

Diagram 9C

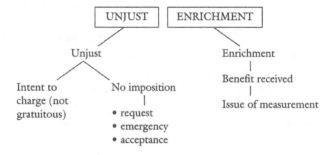

§9.5.1 Enrichment

Enrichment is an economic benefit. When a person receives and retains money or property, it is easy to see that the recipient has been enriched to the extent of the payment or the value of the property because the recipient's net worth has been increased by that amount. However, a person could also be enriched by consuming goods or receiving intangible services that result in no long-term financial advantage. One is not obviously made wealthier by consuming a free bag of pretzels or getting a free haircut, but one has saved the cost of buying these items in the marketplace. Naturally, the existence or absence of lasting economic advantage and its extent are factors taken into account in deciding on relief, as discussed in section 9.6.

However, it is necessary to recognize the general principle that enrichment occurs whenever something of value is received, even if it does not enlarge the recipient's net worth.

Usually, enrichment results only where the benefit passes directly from benefactor to the beneficiary, but sometimes a person is indirectly enriched by a benefit conferred on a third party. For example, in *Emergency Physicians Integrated v. Salt Lake County*, 167 P.3d. 1080 (Utah 2007), the physicians group sued the county for the market value of medical services rendered to county inmates. The county had a constitutional duty to provide medical services to the inmates and had made some payment to the physicians, based on a statutory fee schedule. However, the physicians argued that they were entitled to receive a higher rate of pay based on the market value of their services. The county countered that the benefit of the medical services went to the inmates and that it was only incidentally benefitted by the services. The court rejected the county's argument. It said that it did not matter that the patients also benefitted from the service. The county received the benefit of having the physicians fulfill its constitutional duty to the inmates.

Although a benefit may be conferred indirectly, the person seeking restitution must show a link between its actions and the recipient's benefit. In *Ashley County, Arkansas v. Pfizer, Inc.*, 552 F.3d 659 (8th Cir. 2009), the county came up with a novel but unsuccessful argument for claiming that Pfizer and other drug company defendants had been enriched at its expense and owed it restitution. The county's theory was that the drug companies had declined to cooperate in imposing controls on cold and allergy medications that could be used in the manufacture of methamphetamine. As a result, the companies had made handsome profits by selling the medications, many of which were bought for the illegal purpose of making methamphetamine. The county argued that this enrichment came at its expense in that it had to provide services to deal with the methamphetamine epidemic. The court rejected the county's argument on the basis that there was no link between the services rendered by the county and the drug companies' profits.

§9.5.2 When Is Enrichment Unjust?

To receive restitution, it is not enough that the claimant has conferred an uncompensated benefit on the recipient, because it is not always unjust for a person to receive a benefit without paying for it. Justice is only offended if the conferral of the enrichment meets two criteria: The claimant must not have intended to confer the benefit gratuitously and must not have imposed it on the recipient.

a. Gratuitous Intent

Enrichment is not unjust if the benefit was conferred with gratuitous intent. It is not unfair to allow a donee to keep a gift.[5] Quite the contrary, it would unfairly disrupt the donee's reasonable expectations by allowing the donor to demand payment for something originally given for free. A person who confers a benefit gratuitously is sometimes called a "volunteer." In the context of unjust enrichment, this word carries more than its common meaning. It connotes not only that something was done or given by free choice, but also with the intent not to seek compensation.

As usual, intent is not measured subjectively but is based upon apparent intent, as manifested by the conduct of the person conferring the benefit in light of all the circumstances. An objective test is used, not only because it is difficult to divine a person's true state of mind, but also because the recipient's reasonable expectations should be protected. Therefore, if a reasonable person in the recipient's position would perceive the grantor as not expecting compensation, the intent is gratuitous, no matter what the grantor claims to have been thinking.

Benefits are sometimes conferred in an emergency when it is unlikely that the benefactor was thinking about compensation at all when taking the beneficial action, so it is sometimes artificial to talk of intent. Therefore, intent is likely to be determined by inference from the circumstances. One of the significant considerations in deciding whether or not the benefit was conferred with gratuitous intent is the relationship of the benefit to the trade or profession of the conferrer. For example, think back to the doctor who gave emergency treatment to the unconscious patient in illustration 5 in section 9.3. Unless she is particularly crass and cold-blooded, a doctor probably does not think of her fee as she is administering emergency aid to a victim. Nevertheless, if the general expectation is that a doctor would charge for services in these circumstances, intent to charge is attributed to her. Because the doctor rendered professional services, it is conceivable that she had a reasonable expectation of payment. The reasonableness of this expectation would have been even stronger if the doctor was not a passer-by but attended to the victim after he was rushed, unconscious, into her consulting rooms for emergency treatment. Some courts go so far as to say that where services are rendered by a professional, there is a presumption that they were not intended to be gratuitous. By recognizing this presumption, the court places the burden on the beneficiary to prove gratuitous intent.

By contrast, if the aid was provided by a lay person, the general expectation is likely to be that there was no intent to charge. We normally think of nonprofessional emergency intervention as public spirited and gratuitous.

---

5. As explained in section 7.2, there is no consideration issue once the donation has been given. Consideration doctrine only applies to the enforcement of unexecuted promises.

There is a difficult policy question to be considered when deciding whether services rendered by a nonprofessional should be presumed as gratuitous: We should expect people to respond to crises altruistically without expectation of reward. But a strict presumption of voluntarism could be unfair and could discourage intervention in emergencies, especially if loss or injury was suffered in the course of conferring the benefit.

Sometimes, although there was an intent to charge for the benefit, the intent may not have been to charge the recipient. If so, from the recipient's perspective, the benefit is gratuitous. For example, say a suitor orders flowers on credit for his paramour. If the suitor fails to pay after the florist has delivered them, the florist cannot claim that the recipient was unjustly enriched. Although it had intended to charge for the flowers, it had never intended to charge her.

b. Imposition

If restitution was available for any benefit conferred with intent to charge, this would open the way for all kinds of imposition from busybodies and sleazy operators. Imagine how a homeowner would feel if, upon returning from work one day, she found that her overgrown yard had been weeded and trimmed without her knowledge. On the front door was a note that read:

> Your yard was a mess, so we cleaned it up for you. Our charge is $300. Please send a check right away.
> Your friendly neighbors,
> O. Fishus
> N. Termeddler

Alternatively, it may not be the neighbors who did the yard work, but some roving landscaper who makes a living by seeking out unkempt yards, beautifying them without permission, and then demanding payment. In either case, the law treats these claimants as undeserving of compensation. Even though they did not intend to confer the benefit gratuitously, they were not justified in imposing a benefit on someone without asking first, so they are not entitled to restitution. The term "officious intermeddler" is commonly used to describe a person who unjustifiably imposes a benefit.

Although the above examples are obvious, it is not always so easy to decide if a benefit was conferred officiously. In the clearest case, a benefit is not officious if it was requested by the recipient.[6] When the benefit has not

---

6. Where the benefit was requested, an actual contract may have been created, but if the request falls short of a contractual commitment, unjust enrichment is the basis of obligation.

been requested by the recipient, it is likely to be officious unless there was a good justification for conferring the unasked-for benefit. This is usually satisfied only when an emergency has arisen and three conditions are satisfied: First, immediate action is required; second, advance assent is impracticable; and third, the claimant has no reason to believe that the recipient would not wish for the action to be taken.

The greater the urgency and the more at stake, the more likely that unrequested action will be justified. Threats to life or health are generally regarded as giving good cause for unsolicited action. Thus, the doctor in the earlier example is likely to obtain restitution. Not only was she not a volunteer, she was also not an officious intermeddler. Although the protection of the person of the beneficiary is the strongest justification for unrequested emergency action, an emergency response to avert harm to property is also of value to the property owner and to society. Therefore, if a person, in response to an immediate threat, takes lawful and appropriate action to save or preserve the property, he is not likely to be treated as an officious intermeddler.

Even if a benefit is imposed on the recipient, restitution may still be appropriate if, being able to reject it and return the benefit, the recipient accepts it. In the yardwork example, the owner of the unkempt yard cannot return the benefit, even if undesired, because it is incorporated into the land. To deem acceptance would eviscerate the rule against intermeddling because there is no means of rejection. However, some benefits can be easily returned. For example, if instead of weeding and trimming, the neighbors beautified the yard by installing a garden gnome, it would be a simple matter for the homeowner to reject the gnome and to allow the neighbors to remove it. If the owner chooses to keep the gnome, acceptance of the unrequested benefit justifies compensation.

§9.6 MEASUREMENT OF BENEFIT

§9.6.1 The Remedial Aim of Restitution

As noted in section 9.2, the remedial focus of restitution is different from contract. Contractual damages are based on the breach victim's expected gains under the contract and are calculated to approximate the monetary value of the benefit that he or she would have realized had the contract not been breached. By contrast, the primary focus of restitutionary damages is not the grantor's loss of expectation, but the recipient's gain. They are calculated to approximate the monetary value of what has been given to the recipient. Damages for breach of contract and the distinction between contractual expectation damages and restitution are dealt with in some detail in Chapter 18. However, because restitutionary relief is so tied into the subject matter of this chapter, it is convenient and logical to deal with the nature and measurement of restitution here.

§9.6.2 Alternative Methods for Measuring Enrichment

The following illustration suggests the two principal ways in which enrichment can be measured:

Maggie Zine owns a newsstand in an office lobby. As she was opening the booth early one morning, she fainted and was rushed to the hospital. She spent the day there for observation and tests and was discharged that evening. Sam Aratan, Maggie's friend, happened to be in the lobby coffee bar when he heard that Maggie had been taken away in the ambulance. As he had the day off, he decided to help Maggie by keeping her booth open. He ran the booth the whole day, making $600 in sales, of which $200 is profit. The going wage for a kiosk clerk is $7 per hour. Sam ran the newsstand for ten hours.

Assume that Sam is neither a volunteer nor an intermeddler, so that he should receive restitution for his services. There are two alternative means of calculating Maggie's enrichment:

1. The market value of Sam's service, represented by the going wage of kiosk clerks, $70, or
2. Maggie's net economic gain — her profit for the day, $200. (Not her net sales, of course, because she had to buy $400 worth of goods to generate the $600 income.)

Market value of the benefit and the recipient's ultimate net fiscal gain are the two alternative choices for measuring enrichment. Market value tends to be the standard measure, but net gain is used when the circumstances make recovery of market value either excessive or inadequate. If net gain is the basis of measurement, the gain could be valued differently depending on whether it is measured objectively — that is, in the abstract (what it is reasonably worth in general) or subjectively — with regard to the beneficiary's particular circumstances. This breakdown may be represented as shown in Diagram 9D.

Diagram 9D

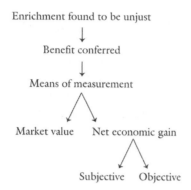

We will now look more closely at each of these means of measurement.

§9.6.3 Market Value

When the benefit is the payment of money, value is readily apparent, but if the benefit consists of the receipt of property or services, their value must be established by evidence of their price on the market. As noted in section 9.4.1, Latin terms are commonly used to express market value. Quantum meruit expresses the market value of services and quantum valebant expresses the market value of goods.[7] Market value is most reliably determined by testimony of an expert who is familiar with the market and can provide objective information about customary pricing. However, if such evidence is not available, the plaintiff may be able to make a prima facie showing of value by providing evidence of his own usual price. This is not the most convincing evidence, but if the defendant offers nothing to rebut it, and the plaintiff's basis for calculating it appears reasonable, it may be sufficient. If there is no evidence of either the objective market value or the plaintiff's usual price, evidence of the plaintiff's costs in providing the property or services may be accepted as the best evidence of value, provided that it appears that the plaintiff acted efficiently and that costs were not higher than they should be. (Of course, the reimbursement of cost is likely to be a less attractive basis of recovery for the plaintiff, because market price usually consists of cost plus profit.)

---

7. This terminology is not confined to restitution, but is also used in connection with contracts in which the parties have left the price open. In fact, the terms derive from contract law and enter the language of restitution through the fiction of quasi-contract.

§9.6.4 The Recipient's Net Gain

As you will see in section 9.6.5, market value is most commonly used to measure benefit, and restitution based on the recipient's net gain is a less common means of measurement, used only where the equities call for it. The net actual enrichment of the recipient—that is, the actual amount by which the recipient's wealth is increased—could be more or less than the market value of the services. For example, although the market value of hiring Sam was $70, Maggie actually gained $200 from his services. Conversely, had it been a slow day, her takings from the booth could have been less than $70.

In this example, net gain is relatively easy to determine. This is not always true. Net gain could be speculative or difficult to quantify. Consider the example of the doctor who came to the aid of the victim in an emergency. Say that the customary fee for the doctor's services is $200. If, as a result of her prompt efforts, the victim was saved from death or crippling injury, this is surely worth more than $200 but it is difficult to value the gain. If restitution were to be based on the victim's net gain, testimony would have to be given on the monetary value of his life and health. Conversely, if despite the doctor's valiant effort the victim died soon after the fall, he received no ultimate benefit and has no net gain. This illustration is used merely to illustrate the difference between market value and net gain, and is not meant to suggest that it would be appropriate to measure the benefit in this example by net gain. Where medical services are rendered, market value is the proper measure. (This is explained in section 9.6.5.)

A further problem with net gain is that it can be perceived in two different ways. If it is determined subjectively, it is measured with reference to the actual recipient, taking into account the recipient's needs, circumstances, and intentions. Objective valuation is based on the worth of the benefit in market terms. (This is not the same as market value of the service, because it is the ultimate gain that is measured by the market standard.) For example, Contractor builds a patio on Owner's property without authorization, but under circumstances that make contractor neither an intermeddler nor a volunteer. The market value of the work is $1,000. The patio enhances the value of the house by $400. However, Owner has no intention of selling the house, and she hates sitting outside, so she has no use for the patio. Owner has received labor and materials worth $1,000 on the market, but her objective net gain is $400 and her subjective net gain is zero.

§9.6.5 Choosing Among Market Value, Objective, or Subjective Net Gain

As the above illustrations show, the means of measuring the benefit can make quite a difference to recovery. The selection of the most appropriate measure is within the court's discretion, exercised to achieve a result that is fair under all the circumstances. The goal is to reach a figure that neither overcompensates nor undercompensates the claimant while imposing liability on the recipient that is realistic and not excessive. While one cannot state hard-and-fast rules in an area involving discretion, there are some guidelines that are commonly followed:

1. *Market value is the preferred measure of recovery.* Market value is likely to be the fairest and most balanced basis of compensating the conferrer at a rate that could reasonably be expected by the beneficiary. Also, because quantum meruit (or quantum valebant) approximates what the contract price would have been, had the parties made a contract for the services or property, it is conceptually most consistent with the underlying theory of quasi-contractual recovery, which is based on a fictional contract. This basis of calculation is therefore particularly appropriate when the benefit had been requested (even though there is no contract), or circumstances indicate that it likely would have been had the beneficiary had the opportunity to do so.

   Maggie would thus be liable to Sam for the $70 reasonable wage, rather than the $200 profit, and the victim would have to pay the doctor $200 for the successful treatment, rather than the value of life and health.

2. *The court may select the lowest measure of relief where there is some fault on the part of the conferrer.* If there is some fault or impropriety in the conduct of the person who conferred the benefit that is not serious enough to preclude relief, the court may award the lowest measure of relief. For example, when a party materially breaches a contract after having partially performed, the breacher cannot recover under the contract but can obtain restitution for what has been given. Because the breacher is at fault for breaking the contract, restitutionary recovery is limited to the smaller of the market value of what was done or the portion of the price allocated to the performance under the contract. For example, say that a builder wrongfully abandons work after erecting part of a building. The market value of what has been done before abandonment is $5,000, but because the builder underbid, the amount of the contract price attributable to that work is only $4,000. The builder cannot recover more than $4,000, and that amount may be further reduced if the owner has suffered damages as a result of the breach. (This is discussed more fully in connection with material breach in section 17.6.2.)

3. *Disproportionality.* Even in the absence of imposition or fault, if one measure is disproportionately large or small, fairness or reasonable community expectations may require that it not be selected. For example, irrespective of the concern for imposition, there

would never be any basis for awarding the doctor the value of the victim's life. Not only could this be a gargantuan recovery, imposing great hardship on the victim and grossly overcompensating the doctor for her work, but it is not customary for doctors to be rewarded for services in this way.

4. *Dishonest or improper conduct by the beneficiary.* If the recipient has been guilty of dishonest or improper conduct, the highest measure is likely to be used. To illustrate, recall the example in which Sam managed Maggie's kiosk after she fainted. Instead of paying over the $600 proceeds to Maggie, Sam used it to buy lottery tickets and won $100,000. Sam is now the recipient of enrichment by using Maggie's property without authority, and his wrongful act in misappropriating it justifies holding him liable for the full extent of his gain. That is, he is treated in law as having won the $100,000 on Maggie's behalf so that he has to disgorge the full amount of his winnings. If he won nothing in the lottery, so that he has no ultimate gain, the value of what he took, $600, is the higher measure and the most appropriate one to be used.

5. *Agreed compensation for a requested benefit.* If the benefit was requested (that is, when there is a contract, but the conferrer elects restitution, or the request does not qualify as a contract), any price agreed to by the parties is probative evidence of value and may be used in preference over other measures.

6. *Discretionary measurement of benefit.* In some cases, none of the more common bases of measurement work at all, and the court may have to use its discretion to make an award more in keeping with the circumstances. For example, say that a climber is stranded on a cliff. A passerby sees this and climbs the cliff and rescues the climber. In doing so, the rescuer falls and is injured. She does not claim a fee for the rescue (which she most likely will not get for reasons stated in section 9.5.2), but she does claim reimbursement of her medical expenses on the theory that it would unjustly enrich the climber if he did not pay them. Although it is possible that the rescuer would be held to have been performed with gratuitous intent, a court may feel that it would be unjust to deny relief altogether. However, the medical expenses do not fit into any of the categories mentioned — they are not the market value of the service, nor the net enrichment of the climber, objectively or subjectively determined. To give relief, the court would have to use its discretion to create a remedy based on plaintiff's post-benefit medical expenditure. This resolution may be fair if the medical expenses are not too high, but if they are substantial, the concern is raised about imposing massive liability on the climber.

§9.7 "MORAL OBLIGATION" AND THE MATERIAL BENEFIT RULE

§9.7.1 Introduction

As we have seen, restitution is not dependent on the obligor having made any promise. It is predicated on unjust enrichment rather than commitment. The doctrine traditionally known as "moral obligation" is something of a hybrid, in that it covers situations in which the facts do not fully support restitutionary recovery, but the justification for giving relief is bolstered by a promise made after receipt of the benefit. In other words, it blends restitutionary concepts and promise.

To illustrate, add a fact to the example of the busybody neighbors, O. Fishus and N. Termeddler, who cleaned up the unkempt yard while the owner was at work and left a bill for $300. As officious intermeddlers, they are not entitled to restitution. However, instead of tossing the bill in the garbage, the homeowner wrote back to them thanking them for their effort and promising to pay the $300 at the end of the month. This promise is not contractual because the neighbors' detriment was "past consideration." It was not exchanged for, but preceded, the promise. Similarly, the sequence of action followed by promise precludes promissory estoppel relief because the neighbors' action was not induced by the homeowner's promise. *See* Diagram 9E.

Diagram 9E

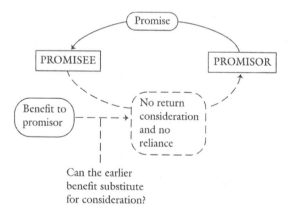

Can the earlier
benefit substitute
for consideration?

The question addressed in this section is whether the prior benefit plus the later promise should create a ground for enforcing the promise independent of consideration, restitution, and promissory estoppel.

§9.7.2 The Role of the Doctrine of "Moral Obligation" and the Development of the Material Benefit Rule

Under the influence of Lord Mansfield, the great English jurist, a movement grew in eighteenth-century English courts to enforce promises without consideration, purely on the basis that they were morally binding. As Chapter 7 amply demonstrates, this trend did not take root. In the absence of consideration, an obligation cannot be enforced as a contract even if it is morally binding. Relief under promissory estoppel and restitution likewise require more than moral obligation. Indeed, when people say that an obligation is morally binding, they usually mean that the obligor should honor it despite the lack of legal duty to do so.

Notwithstanding this general sense in which "moral obligation" is understood, it has also come to be used as a term of art to describe a particular doctrine under which a promise without consideration may be enforced in a narrow range of circumstances. It is important not to confuse this technical use of "moral obligation" with its wider and more general meaning. Although promises are not enforced simply because they are morally binding, a promise that satisfies the prerequisites of the doctrine of "moral obligation" is enforceable despite the absence of consideration. There are two aspects of the doctrine. One of them, the traditional doctrine of "moral obligation," is widely accepted by courts. The other, an expansion from the traditional doctrine, is commonly known as the "material benefit rule." It is recognized by Restatement, Second (which does not call it the "material benefit rule," but uses the term "promise for benefit received") but has not been widely adopted by courts.

Although both the traditional rule and its extension are aimed at the enforcement of a promise for "past consideration," the link between these doctrines and unjust enrichment is strong. The underlying rationale for enforcing the later promise is that the promisor had previously been enriched by the benefit that motivates the promise. This is made particularly clear in the elements of the material benefit rule, which incorporate principles of unjust enrichment.

§9.7.3 The Traditional Scope of the Doctrine of "Moral Obligation"

Although Lord Mansfield's efforts did not lead to the general substitution of moral obligation for consideration as the basis of contract, some vestiges of this idea remain in our law in the form of narrow exceptions to consideration doctrine. These exceptions apply only to a small number of specific situations in which a debtor makes a promise to pay an earlier unenforceable debt. Although the later promise lacks consideration, the moral obligation to pay the pre-existing unenforceable debt is treated as sufficient to make the promise enforceable. The three specific situations in which courts have traditionally applied the doctrine of "moral obligation" are described below.

A Debt Barred by the Statute of Limitations   Because witnesses disappear and memories fade over time, and because claims should not be allowed to fester indefinitely, all claims are subject to a time bar called a statute of limitations. The claimant must initiate suit before the expiration of a specified period after it arises, failing which the right to sue is lost. The legal effect of expiry of the limitation period is not elimination of the claim, but only of the right to sue on it. For most purposes, this distinction does not mean much, but the vestigial obligation is enough to support a later promise by the obligor to pay the debt.

Say, for example, that Debtor borrowed $5,000 from Creditor seven years ago. The loan should have been repaid six months later, but Debtor never paid and Creditor never got around to suing for recovery of the money. The statute of limitations for contractual claims is typically six years, so the claim is now barred. Upon realizing that the limitation period had run, Debtor was at first jubilant, but then his conscience troubled him. He therefore wrote to Creditor and promised to pay the old loan. Although there was no new consideration given by Creditor for this promise, the pre-existing valid but barred debt is recognized as furnishing a "moral obligation" sufficient to dispense with the need for new consideration. The new promise is therefore binding on the debtor and can be enforced if he declines to perform it. *See* Diagram 9F.

Diagram 9F

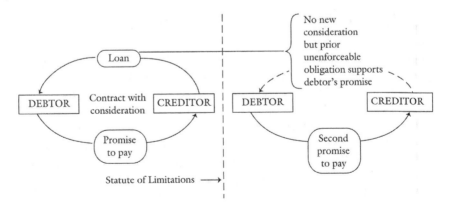

291

A Debt Discharged in Bankruptcy   When a debtor becomes bankrupt, her prebankruptcy debts are usually paid only in part by a distribution from the bankrupt estate. The balance is discharged and creditors are forbidden by law to take any steps to try to collect it. However, the doctrine of "moral obligation" validates a later promise by the debtor to pay the discharged debt. (This common law rule is now heavily regulated by statute. To prevent creditors from undermining the discharge, federal bankruptcy law imposes a strict procedure for reaffirmation of discharged debts that includes a variety of safeguards to protect the debtor from agreeing to a reaffirmation that is not in his interests.)

A Voidable Debt   A voidable debt is one that can be avoided by the debtor because of some defect in formation such as fraud or mistake, or lack of contractual capacity. A voidable obligation must be distinguished from a void one. When a putative contract is void (as happens when consideration is lacking), it is a legal nullity and neither party can enforce it. However, if a contract is voidable by one of the parties, that party has the choice of treating the contract as fully valid and enforceable, or relying on the defect to escape the contractual relationship.[8] Under the doctrine of "moral obligation," if the party with the right of avoidance ratifies the contract by a second promise after becoming aware of the defect or after the basis for contractual incapacity has ended, the later promise is binding despite the lack of new consideration.

These discrete situations form the core of the traditional doctrine of "moral obligation," and have become well-accepted exceptions to the "past consideration" rule. The difficult question is whether the doctrine should be broadened beyond this narrow range to create a more general basis for enforcing promises motivated by prior benefits.

§9.7.4 The Broad "Material Benefit" Rule

In *Webb v. McGowin*, 168 So. 196 (Ala. 1935) the court, by manipulating consideration doctrine, took the bold step of extending the "moral obligation" doctrine beyond its well-accepted confines. Webb, working on the upper floor of a mill, was in the process of dropping a large wooden block to the ground when he noticed that McGowin was in the path of its fall. To divert the block from crushing McGowin, Webb held onto it and fell with it. He thereby saved McGowin from death or severe injury at the cost of serious and disabling injury to himself. In gratitude, McGowin promised a life pension to Webb which he paid for several years until his death. His

---

8. We return to the distinctions between void and voidable obligations in section 13.3.

estate discontinued payment. The "past consideration" rule precluded enforcement of the promise as a contract because Webb's detriment preceded and was not exchanged for the promise. However, the court recognized that application of the "past consideration" rule would be very unjust in the circumstances, so it used a legal fiction to overcome it — the court deemed the detriment to have been contemporaneous with the promise. In justifying this resolution, the court drew analogies to restitution cases and to the situations described above in which courts had enforced promises to pay prior unenforceable legal obligations. The court considered that McGowin's moral obligation to honor his promise justified expanding those principles.

Webb's broader "moral obligation" doctrine has not been widely accepted by other courts. However, Restatement, Second, §86 does adopt it. Section 86 does not employ the legal fiction used in *Webb*. Instead, it formulates the doctrine as a distinct cause of action under which a promise to pay for a previous benefit may be enforced despite the lack of consideration. Section 86 sets forth the following requirements:

1. The promisor has been unjustly enriched by a benefit previously received from the promisee.
2. The benefit was not given as a gift. (However, according to Comment d, the later promise shifts the burden of showing gratuitous intent to the recipient. The effect of this is that in ambiguous circumstances, where it is not clear if there was gratuitous intent, the benefit will not be treated as a gift, unless the recipient (promisor) can prove that it was so intended.)
3. The promisor subsequently makes a promise in recognition of the benefit.
4. The promise is not binding to the extent that its value is disproportionate to the benefit.
5. If these requirements are satisfied, the promise is binding to the extent necessary to prevent injustice.

The elements set out in §86 make it clear that although the material benefit rule provides for the enforcement of a promise, its focus is very different from contract and promissory estoppel. It does not enforce the promise to protect a contractual expectation or reliance interest, but to rectify a situation in which the promisor had been unjustly enriched. The first two elements mirror those for restitutionary relief, and the fourth makes it clear that a court should not enforce the promise to the extent that it is disproportionate in value to the benefit that was received. Even if a nongratuitous benefit was received, if the reward subsequently promised is too generous, the court can reduce the award to correspond to actual enrichment. Beyond this, the general discretion to prevent injustice allows the court to weigh whatever other factors bear upon the appropriate extent of relief.

To illustrate how this doctrine may work, return to the example of the neighbors' claim for the yardwork in which the homeowner made a subsequent promise to pay the $300 bill: The making of the subsequent promise could remove the objection that the neighbors were officious intermeddlers. The comments to Restatement, Second, §86 say that a clear, well-considered, and uncoerced subsequent promise to make restitution lessens the concern about imposition by demonstrating the utility of the benefit. Thus, clear and voluntary ratification of the benefit acts as a counterweight to the meddling and changes the equities in favor of enforcement. The facts indicate that the other prerequisites for relief, a prior benefit, enrichment, and an intent to charge are satisfied, so we turn to the question of relief.

The market value of the yardwork is not stated, so we do not know if $300 is disproportionate to the value of the benefit. If it is, the court may reduce recovery. Therefore, although a valuation issue arises here, as it does in a restitutionary claim based on unjust enrichment, the existence of a promise changes the dynamics of the valuation issue. The promise is at least evidence of what the promisor considered the worth of the benefit to be, and evidence of market value is relegated to a subsidiary role of policing the promise to ensure that it is not too generous. Proportionality is a rough equivalence between the amount promised and the value of the benefit, and does not require an exact match. The proportionality requirement is congruent with the goal of restoring only the enrichment gained by the promisor. It is also related to the cautionary function of consideration doctrine, in that it protects the promisor from a promise that is too generous or rash.

In addition to ensuring proportionality, the court exercises a broad discretion (similar to the overall balancing employed in promissory estoppel cases) to evaluate all the circumstances of the case to decide what must be done to achieve justice. The nature and circumstances of the enrichment and the quality of the promise must both be taken into account. In a case like this one, in which the original imposition was outrageous, the promise must be looked at carefully to ensure that it was a voluntary commitment, unaffected by the manipulations of the intermeddler. The degree to which the promise satisfies the evidentiary and cautionary functions of legal formality is relevant here. In addition, the court must take into account the danger of reinforcing meddlesome behavior and may conclude that even a subsequent promise should not validate the actions of the neighbors.

Although a broad principle of restitution based on a subsequent promise is advocated by Restatement, Second, there are very few cases that have applied the material benefit rule, and most courts that have considered the question have refused to follow the lead of Restatement, Second, in extending the "moral obligation" doctrine beyond the few narrow situations involving prior unenforceable legal obligations.

Examples

1. Consider whether the following transactions gave rise to a contract implied in fact, and if not, whether they create grounds for finding a contract implied in law by establishing grounds for relief on the basis of unjust enrichment:

   a. Sara Nade is a violinist who makes her living as a street musician. When she plays, she places a hat on the sidewalk in front of her, with a note attached to it reading "thanks." One afternoon, while she was playing on a street corner, Mel Odious walked up to her and stood near her, listening to her play. When she finished, he applauded and asked her to play another tune, which she did. He applauded again and then began to walk away. Sara called out to him, "Hey, you have to put some money in my hat!" He replied, "No, I don't."

   b. Change the facts of Example a: Mel was enjoying a picnic with friends in a nearby park when he heard Sara playing on the street corner. He thought that she played beautifully, but it was hard to hear her well over the traffic noise. He therefore went up to her and said "I enjoy your playing very much. Would you come and stand near us in the park and play while we have our picnic so that we can hear you better?" Sara agreed. She played for Mel and his friends until their picnic was over, about 30 minutes later. At the end of the picnic, as Mel was packing up and getting ready to leave, Sara said "That will be $200."

   c. Kwazi Contracting Co. entered into a contract with Flyby Nightwatch, Inc. under which Flyby agreed to provide nighttime security services for Kwazi's office premises for a monthly price of $5,000. Flyby had undertaken too many contracts and did not have the staff to perform all of them. It therefore made a contract with one of its competitors, Beneficial Security, Inc. under which Beneficial provided the security officers to patrol Kwazi's offices. Beneficial charged Flyby a monthly fee of $2,000 for this service. The arrangement worked for two months, but ended when Flyby became insolvent and went out of business. At that time, Kwazi had paid Flyby the full $10,000 due for two months' services, but Flyby had not made any payments to Beneficial. During the two months that the services were performed, Kwazi's executives had noticed that the premises were being patrolled by security guards who wore Beneficial arm patches. They thought nothing of this and assumed that Flyby and Beneficial were associated. Because it cannot recover anything from Flyby, Beneficial claims that Kwazi owes it $4,000.

    d. Quantum Merriment Co., Inc. was planning to build a theme park. It needed to develop some preliminary plans for the park so that its board of directors could make a decision on the feasibility and rough cost of the resort. The president of Quantum approached Ben E. Factor, a designer of amusement parks, and asked him to draw some preliminary plans. Quantum's president made it clear to Ben that he would be doing the work "on spec," which meant that he would only be paid for it if the board decided to go ahead with the development of the park. Ben drew the plans and the board reviewed them. It ultimately decided not to proceed with the development.

2. Benny Fishery has been involved in a longstanding feud with his neighbor, Sam Aratin, arising out of the alleged excretory habits of Sam's dog. Matters have become so bad that Benny has purchased a shotgun and vows to use it on Sam or his dog if either sets foot on his property.

    Last Saturday, Benny locked up his house and left on a two-week camping trip in the wilderness. On Saturday evening a faulty appliance caused a fire to break out in his kitchen. Sam saw the fire through the kitchen window. Having seen Benny set off that morning with his camping gear, Sam realized that immediate action was called for. He grabbed his disposable fire extinguisher, smashed the window, and discharged its contents into the flames, dousing the fire. Afterwards he made inquiries and ascertained that Benny was incommunicado for the next two weeks. Sam was concerned that a burglar could easily enter the vacant house through the broken window, so he hired a contractor to replace the broken glass for $200. Sam had to pay the contractor because he insisted on cash and refused to wait for his money until Benny returned.

    Sam left a note on Benny's charred kitchen counter, telling him what had happened and asking for payment of $300, made up as follows:

a. Cost of the disposable fire extinguisher, $30.

b. $200 paid for the window.

c. Sam's fee for services rendered, $70.

    On his return from vacation, Benny sent back Sam's note, having scrawled on it an unpleasant suggestion on what Sam should do with it. Should Sam follow this suggestion, or does he have a right to payment?

3. Change the facts in Example 2 as follows: The extinguisher did not completely douse the fire, so Sam entered the kitchen through the broken window and stamped out the remaining flames. He burned his legs in the process. As a result, he incurred $4,000 in medical expenses and had to take three weeks unpaid sick leave, losing an additional $2,000. He has no medical or disability insurance. Apart from the financial loss, he has suffered excruciating pain.

    When Benny returned from vacation and heard of Sam's sacrifice, he was overcome with gratitude and felt deep remorse for his hostile attitude to Sam's dog. He visited Sam in the hospital and tearfully promised to pay Sam $200 per month for the next three years to compensate Sam for the medical expenses, loss of earnings, and pain. Sam accepted this offer in an emotional display of reconciliation.

Benny paid installments for two months until, looking out of his window one morning, he saw Sam's dog busy decorating his lawn. This rekindled the old feud, and Benny refuses to pay another cent to Sam. Is his promise enforceable?

4. Rhoda Hogg began hearing noises from her car when she accelerated beyond 85 m.p.h. on the freeway. She took the car to Mark Price, a mechanic, to have the trouble determined and repaired. She told Mark that he was to call her for authorization if the repair would cost more than $200. Mark neglected to communicate this instruction to his assistant, who completed an expensive repair without checking with Rhoda. When Rhoda was presented with a bill for $650, she refused to pay it, and insists that she is liable for no more than $200. Mark admits his mistake, but argues that the repair was necessary and $650 is a fair charge for the parts and labor. This is in fact true. Is Rhoda obligated to pay the $650?

5. Val Unteer and Justin Richmond entered into a contract of sale under which Val purchased Justin's house. The contract was conditional on Val obtaining a mortgage loan to finance the purchase. Justin knew that Val had a poor credit record and did not qualify for a loan, so he encouraged her to apply to a particular lender that had a reputation for lenience in evaluating borrower qualifications.

Val applied for the loan. While she was waiting to hear the decision on her application, she began to plan her move. One of the items that had to be moved to her new house was a hot tub. As the house had no suitable firm area on which to place it, Val realized that a concrete slab would have to be built on which to install it. She had ascertained from the moving company that she would save considerable costs if the tub could be moved and installed in one operation, because this would eliminate moving the tub to storage and then transporting it and setting it up on site. Because she was anxious to have the slab in place by closing, Val felt that she could not wait for the decision on the loan application. She discussed the matter with Justin, who expressed confidence that Val would get the loan and told her that he would have no objection if she laid the slab immediately. The parties did not discuss what would happen if the loan was refused.

Val's cousin is a contractor and he agreed to build the slab for her for the special price of $1,000. (His normal charge would be $2,000.) A few days after the slab was completed, Val was notified by the loan company that her application had been rejected. As there were no other prospects for financing, the sale fell through.

Justin now has a slab on his property at Val's expense. He has no use for it and it does not enhance the value of his house. Val would like to be reimbursed for the slab. Can she recover? If so, how much?

Explanations

1. a. Sara and Mel made no express contract because no words of agreement were uttered or articulated. They may have entered into a contract implied in fact, under which Mel agreed to pay for Sara's services, provided that such a contract could be inferred from their conduct, reasonably interpreted in context. Mel clearly did take the benefit Sara's playing and even asked her to play an encore. However, if there is no general expectation in the community that street musicians are paid for their services, an agreement to pay cannot be inferred. Instead, we must conclude that Sara provided the entertainment for free, and her hat on the sidewalk merely invited members of the public to show their appreciation by giving her a gratuity. The fact that Sara did not have a reasonable expectation of payment also precludes a claim for unjust enrichment because she conferred the benefit on Mel as a volunteer.

   b. Mel has now asked Sara to come and play at his picnic and she has done so. Although the usual expectation may be that street musicians perform gratuitously, this expectation could change when Mel specifically asks Sara to come into the park and to play for him and his friends. If these circumstances do give rise to a reasonable expectation of payment, the parties may have entered into a contract implied in fact, under which Mel is liable to pay Sara for her services. Because the parties did not agree to a fee, the amount due to Sara in contract would be her customary fee, or a fee based on the market value (quantum meruit) of her services. Alternatively, even if there is no factually implied contract, Sara may be able to get relief in quasi contract, provided that she did not intend her performance to be gratuitous. She should be able to recover the value of her services on the basis of unjust enrichment, measured here too on the quantum meruit standard. We do not know how she arrived at the $200 that she claims, so we cannot say if this is the appropriate amount of her recovery.

   c. Beneficial should not be able to recover from Kwazi either on grounds of contract or unjust enrichment. The parties never dealt with each other at all, and certainly never made an express contract. The facts do not support the factual implication of a contract either. A party can be held to an implied contract if it voluntarily accepts services without objection on the reasonable understanding that the services are not rendered gratuitously. However, there is nothing in these facts to indicate such assent or reasonable expectation on Kwazi's part. A contract can only be implied in fact if there is some conduct from which agreement can be inferred. Kwazi's conduct does not give rise to this inference. As far it was concerned, its contract was with Flyby. Nothing alerted it to the possibility that Beneficial might look to it for payment, and it had no involvement or interest in any arrangements that Flyby might make to find the staff to perform its obligations under the contract.

Beneficial's claim also does not satisfy the elements of unjust enrichment. Kwazi paid for the services, so it received no free benefit. In addition, because Beneficial provided the services under a contract with Flyby, it had no expectation of compensation directly from Kwazi and never asked Kwazi to guarantee Flyby's payment obligation. Therefore, as far as Kwazi is concerned, Beneficial is in the position of a volunteer in that it conferred the benefit without intent to receive compensation from Kwazi. It would also be an unfair imposition to allow Beneficial to hold Kwazi liable for services rendered where Beneficial could have, but failed to demand a guarantee of payment before rendering the services. Like *Contship Containerlines* described in section 9.4.2, this case involves the allocation of loss between two innocent parties. However, unlike the carrier in *Contship Containerlines* the loss here should rest with Beneficial. The shipper in *Contship Containerlines* was saddled with the loss because it bore the risk of paying a third-party intermediary who failed to transmit the funds to the carrier. The situation here is quite different. Only Beneficial dealt with Flyby and gave it credit. Flyby was not an intermediary for Kwazi, which did not even have reason to know of the transaction between Flyby and Beneficial.

d. Ben has no right to payment in contract. Normally, where a person requests another to perform a service in the course of business, we would readily find a contract. Even if payment is not discussed, there would be a reasonable expectation that the services are not to be rendered gratuitously, and must be paid for at the customary rate or the market rate (quantum meruit). However, the parties here expressly agreed that Ben's services would be "on spec." Although the parties may have had a contract in which Ben's services were exchanged for the commitment to make a good faith decision about developing the park, this contract contained a contingent payment term, and the condition of payment was not satisfied. The agreement that Ben would not be entitled to a fee unless the board decided to proceed with the development also means that he has no claim for unjust enrichment. In the absence of fulfillment of the condition, he agreed to perform the services gratuitously. (*See Forrest Associates v.*

Passamaquoddy Tribe, 760 A.2d 1041 (Me. 2000). The plaintiff conducted a market assessment for the tribe's possible development of a high-stakes bingo operation. His work was done "on spec," subject to the understanding that he would not be paid unless the tribe went ahead with the development. The tribe did not proceed with the project, and the court held that the plaintiff was not entitled to recover for the value of its work, either in contract or in unjust enrichment.)

2. Unlike in Example 1, there is no question here that Sam and Benny have a contract implied in fact. Any relief awarded to Sam would have to be on the basis of unjust enrichment. Sam's actions can be divided into two stages. In the first, he acted on the spur of the moment to extinguish the fire. In the second, he made the considered decision to replace the window glass. These two stages present different considerations, so they are analyzed separately.

To receive compensation for the emergency response, Sam must have conferred a benefit on Benny and must be neither a volunteer nor an intermeddler. Clearly, Sam's successful action in extinguishing the fire benefited Benny by saving his property. Sam should not be treated as an officious intermeddler. A person is generally not justified in imposing an unrequested benefit, but in an emergency situation, where the harm of inaction would be serious, there is no opportunity to get authorization, and no reason to believe that the beneficiary would object, the intervention is not intermeddling. This was an emergency in which no advance authorization was possible and although Benny had told Sam that he did not want Sam on his property, it is reasonable to assume that this ban would not apply where Sam entered the property to prevent its destruction. It is not clear whether Sam had gratuitous intent in dousing the fire. Gratuitous intent is objectively determined based on Sam's reasonable expectations, and it does not matter whether or not he was actually thinking of compensation as he rushed out to fight the fire. It is reasonable to attribute to Sam the intent to claim reimbursement for the extinguisher. However, his claim for the services is another matter. A professional person who renders services for which he customarily charges, usually has a reasonable expectation of compensation, but a neighbor's emergency intervention is more likely intended as altruistic and gratuitous. Therefore, Sam should be reimbursed for the market value of the fire extinguisher, but not for the value of his services.

The replacement of the window glass is also clearly a benefit to Benny. Sam is not a volunteer with regard to the glass replacement because he did intend to claim reimbursement for it. However, Sam has a more difficult case to show that this action was not officious intermeddling.[9] There was no great urgency to replace the window glass. Sam could have secured the house by boarding up the window until Benny's return. Benny apparently did accept the benefit of the new window glass. (The facts do not indicate that he demanded its removal.) Acceptance of the benefit could cure the problem of intermeddling, but only if it is possible to return the benefit. Therefore, unless it is physically impossible to undo the repair, Benny's retention of the window glass would make him liable for the market value of the window repair. The cost to Sam is probative but not conclusive evidence of market value.

3. This Example is inspired by *Webb v. McGowin*, discussed in section 9.7.4. This case is distinguishable from *Webb* in that Sam was injured saving Benny's property, not his person. Although rescue from personal injury or death provides the strongest equities in favor of enforcing the beneficiary's later promise, there is also moral value in upholding a promise in recognition of property preservation.

Sam would have trouble enforcing Benny's promise as a contract because of the "past consideration" rule. Although it is conceivable that a court would award relief on a theory of unjust enrichment, Sam's claim is an awkward fit for restitutionary recovery. The question of whether Sam acted with gratuitous intent could create a problem for a person who responds altruistically in an emergency situation. In addition, restitution focuses on the benefit to Benny, which does not bear a relationship to Sam's loss.

However, because Benny made the promise in recognition of Sam's prior service, the material benefit rule of Restatement, Second, §86 provides a much more satisfactory basis for relief.[10] The premise of §86 is that Benny's subsequent ratifying promise shifts the equities in Sam's favor by recognizing and placing a value on the benefit and creating the presumption that it was not conferred with gratuitous intent. The disproportionality principle assures that the promise is not too generous in relation to the value of the benefit. However, where the focus is not on the value of the benefit, but on the relationship between the promise and the injury, it seems fair to measure proportionality in reference to the injury, not the benefit.

A court that applies §86 must also take care that the promise was made under fair circumstances, and that it was not induced by coercion or motivated by impulsive generosity. There is no hint that Sam put any pressure on Benny to make the promise. The fact that he made it tearfully

---

9. Assume that Sam was justified in breaking the window in the first place to extinguish the fire. If he was not, he would be liable for improper damage to Benny's property, and he would certainly not be able to make a claim for reimbursement.
10. As noted in section 9.7.4, only a few courts have been willing to recognize the broad material benefit rule advocated by §86.

in Sam's hospital room soon after the incident could give pause. (The cautionary function of consideration doctrine plays a role here.) However, this concern is alleviated by the fact that Benny continued to make payments for some time after this emotionally charged moment.

4. In contrast to Examples 2 and 3, there is a contract in this case under which services were requested by Rhoda. The problem is that Mark negligently exceeded his authority under the contract. As the repair was necessary and reasonably priced, refusal to award its value would enrich Rhoda by giving her a $650 repair for $200.

   If asked, Rhoda may have authorized the repair, but she was given no opportunity to exercise this choice and had the repair imposed on her. She cannot return it because it is incorporated into her property. This imposition makes Mark an intermeddler as much as if he had made the repair without any request. Rhoda's enrichment is not unjust, and Mark is not entitled to quantum meruit relief. He is bound by the maximum price settled by the contract, $200.

   In *Deck v. Jim Harris Chevrolet-Buick*, 386 N.E.2d 714 (Ind. 1979), the case on which this Example is based, the court reached this conclusion. Although the mistake may have been honest, the repairer was in a better position than the customer to prevent it and must take responsibility for the negligence that led to the customer's enrichment.

5. The principal purpose of this Example is to emphasize the point, made in section 9.3, that some facts may give rise to alternative theories of liability. This case invites consideration of possible recovery under contract, promissory estoppel, or unjust enrichment, and a comparison of the remedies under each theory. Unfortunately for Val, her prospects for relief are not good under any of them.

   Contract. The claim for contractual relief is tenuous at best. The parties had a contract for the sale of the house, but made no express contract concerning the slab. Val clearly intended it for her own benefit and made no commitment to Justin to build it. If she had changed her mind and had not laid the slab, Justin could not have claimed that he had breached any obligation to him. Because the parties apparently did not contemplate failure of the sale, they made no agreement on what would happen in that event. There is no evidence from which to infer a commitment by Justin to pay for the slab if the property remained his.

   Promissory estoppel. Val's claim for relief on the basis of promissory estoppel runs into difficulty on the issues of both promise and justifiable reliance. Justin's only express promise, to transfer title to the house, was discharged because Val could not satisfy the condition of financing. While there is some hint that Val relied on Justin's recommendation of a lender and his permission to build the slab, there is not enough here to support a finding that Justin promised that Val would be able to make use of the slab or that he reasonably intended to induce her to build it. By laying the slab in anticipation of a successful loan application, without resolving liability if the sale fell through, Val assumed the risk of wasting her money. In the absence of a clear promise of reimbursement or of circumstances that impose some special duty of care on Justin, Val must take responsibility for poor judgment in the precontractual period.

Unjust enrichment. Although Justin has been enriched by the building of a slab on his property, this enrichment is not unjust, and Val should not be able to receive restitution. Justin's grant of permission to build was not a request for this benefit. Had he been told that he would have to pay for the slab if the sale fell through, he may well have refused permission. To treat his permission as a request would unfairly impose on him a useless concrete slab that adds no value to his property. Val's failure to resolve his liability in the event of the sale's failure makes her a volunteer. She assumed the risk that if the sale collapsed, she would have conferred a gratuitous benefit on Justin.

The different forms of relief under these theories. Although Val has had no luck under any theory of liability, it is a useful exercise to consider briefly the different forms of relief that would have been available to her under each theory: If a contract had been established, she would have been entitled to enforce it and to recover the agreed price of the slab. If no price had been agreed, she would be entitled to a reasonable price based on quantum meruit. If the contractor's normal price reflects market value, the market price is $2,000, and the fact that Val obtained the work for $1,000 because of family connections does not detract from the market value. She is entitled to retain this profit unless it could also be implied that she undertook to furnish the slab at her cost. Promissory estoppel would aim primarily at reimbursing Val for her expenditure in reliance, the actual cost of $1,000. Restitution is based on Justin's enrichment, which is normally measured on the basis of quantum meruit in the same way as it would be under a contract with an open price term. It could be as high as $2,000 if that is the true market value of the construction work. But if the slab did not add a full $2,000 value to the property, the award may be reduced to the extent of Justin's actual economic gain. Because he had no use for the slab and it added no value to his property, his ultimate gain is zero, whether measured subjectively or objectively.

Interpretation and Construction: Resolving Meaning and Dealing with Uncertainty in Agreements

§10.1 ASCERTAINING THE MEANING OF AN AGREEMENT: INTERPRETATION AND CONSTRUCTION

§10.1.1 Introduction to the Process of Interpretation and Construction

The processes of interpretation (inferring meaning from facts) and construction (inferring meaning as a matter of law) have been alluded to in earlier chapters.[1] If you have read them already, the basic point of the present discussion will not be entirely unfamiliar. This section more closely examines and differentiates the methods and uses of the related, but separate, functions of interpretation and construction. To begin, a broad distinction may be drawn:

Restatement, Second, §200 describes interpretation as the ascertainment of the meaning of a promise or agreement. It is an evaluation of facts (that is, evidence of what the parties said and did and the circumstances

---

1. For example, section 7.9.2 discusses the implication of a promise to use best efforts or to exercise reasonable judgment as a means of giving content to an apparently illusory promise, and section 4.1 discusses the interpretation of objective manifestations of assent in the context of offer and acceptance. This is not a definitive list. The issue of interpretation comes up often.

surrounding their communications) for the purpose of deciding their mutual intent. The word "construction" is sometimes used interchangeably with "interpretation," but properly speaking, it does have a different meaning. Construction is the implication of a term in law. It usually occurs where it appears that the parties did not actually deal with a particular issue in their contract, and there is no factual evidence to establish how they intended that issue to be handled. That is, although it is clear that the parties did make a contract, they just did not address this particular issue. The court may therefore determine, based on what it knows of the contract and its context, how the parties would have dealt with this issue had they thought of it. Stated differently, a court will use the process of construction only when the existing evidence supports the reasonable conclusion (based on objective manifestations of assent) that the parties did intend to make a contract, but there is little or no evidence from which a factual inference can be drawn on their intent regarding a particular aspect of that contract. In seeking to effectuate the parties' intent, the court builds on what it knows of the transaction to interpolate from that a meaning that the parties probably would have agreed upon, had they focused on the issue. Although courts are wary of devising an agreement that the parties did not actually make, it is sometimes preferable to do this instead of defeating contractual expectations by demanding clear proof of intent for every gap and uncertainty.

The difference between interpretation and construction can be subtle. *Wood v. Lucy, Lady Duff-Gordon*, 222 N.Y. 88 (1917), discussed in section 7.9.2 in relation to illusory promises, may be used as an illustration. Lucy, a well-known fashion designer, appointed Wood as her exclusive agent to sell her designs and place her endorsements on the designs of others. Under their agreement, Wood was to pay Lucy half the profits generated by the sales and endorsements. However, Wood did not actually promise in the agreement that he would do anything to promote her designs and endorsements. Lucy endorsed products on her own and kept all the proceeds. When Wood sued her for his share of this income, she argued that they had no valid contract because Wood had given her no consideration. Even though he promised to share any profits that he generated, he made no promise to do anything to earn those profits. In a famous opinion by Judge Cardozo, the court rejected that argument on the basis that Lucy's grant of an exclusive agency to Wood, under circumstances in which the parties clearly intended a serious commercial relationship, gave rise to the implication that Wood had obligated himself to use best efforts to earn profits. If the court's recognition of Wood's promise to use best efforts was based on evidence of intent, such as discussions in negotiations, a course of performance by the parties after the agreement had been made, or prevailing usage in the trade, the court would have reached its conclusion as a matter of interpretation. However, if there was no such evidence, the court's implication of the obligation to use best efforts is construction — the court finds that term based on what the parties would rationally have agreed had the question been presented to them at the time that they made the agreement.

As this shows, there is often a fine dividing line between interpretation and construction. In addition, in most cases the distinction is not of great practical significance because the end result — the establishment of meaning — is the same. However, the distinction is important to an understanding of the process by which courts resolve disputes over the meaning and scope of contract terms.

§10.1.2 Interpretation as a Question of Fact or Law

There is some confusion over the proper roles of the judge and jury in deciding the meaning of agreements, and cases offer conflicting views on whether the ascertainment of meaning is a matter of fact or law. Where interpretation involves the determination of meaning by the evaluation of evidence, it is most appropriately performed by the finder of fact — the jury, unless the case is being tried without one. However, if interpretation merely involves the ascertainment of the plain or ordinary meaning of words, and there is no factual dispute requiring an assessment of credibility, or where meaning must be construed based on what the parties must have intended, the determination of meaning is a legal question for the judge. This dichotomy is not always carefully observed by courts, and the fact-law distinction sometimes becomes blurred. This is particularly so where meaning is based on a combination of the grammatical meaning of words, contextual evidence, and legal implication. In such cases, it can be very difficult to unravel the proper roles of judge and jury, and concern about control over decisionmaking tends to push in the direction of the judge assuming the function of weighing the relative probity of these different elements.

Apart from the question of who decides meaning, the fact-law distinction has significance beyond the trial phase of the case. If meaning is determined as a matter of law, it can be reversed on appeal on the standard of review for legal questions: that the judge erred in the application of the law. However, if the determination is a question of fact, it can be reversed only if it satisfies a much stricter standard: The evidence must provide no reasonable basis for supporting the factfinder's conclusions. Also, a legal determination has weight as precedent, but a factual one does not.

§10.1.3 The Sources of Evidence Used in Interpretation

The process of interpretation was introduced in section 4.1 on the objective test, where it was noted that agreement is manifested by the use of outward signals: words — whether written or spoken; actions; and, in appropriate situations, a failure to speak or act. As the parties move toward developing consensus in the process of contract formation, intent thus communicated by each party is necessarily interpreted by the other. If a dispute later arises about whether consensus was reached or about what was agreed, the communications of the parties must again be interpreted — this time in court — to determine which party's interpretation is correct. Under the objective test, meaning is based on how words and actions reasonably would be perceived by the party to whom they were manifested. The subjective understanding of the parties may have some relevance to the inquiry to the extent that it is consistent with, and may help to explain, the meaning of the manifestation.

This section looks more closely at the process of interpretation and examines the type of evidence that may be available to cast light on the meaning of manifestations of apparent intent. Interpretation first focuses on the normal, accepted meaning of the words used by the parties. However, words are never spoken in a vacuum, so there is always some context in which the words were used. To the extent that this context provides information of what the words might mean, the process of interpretation goes beyond the language used by the parties to take this context into account.

Of course, context does not always provide information that may be relevant to the meaning of a term in dispute, so neither party may be able to offer contextual evidence that bears on what the parties must have meant. Where the court has no evidence of meaning extrinsic to the bare language of the agreement, it is necessarily confined to interpreting that language to ascertain its meaning. However, where a party does seek to prove contextual evidence pertinent to meaning, that evidence should be considered and given appropriate weight. The degree to which it is persuasive often depends on the clarity of the contractual language. Where the contract expresses the disputed term in apparently clear and unambiguous language, extrinsic evidence as to its meaning is treated with caution.[2] Some courts are quite strongly resistant to considering extrinsic evidence if the language used in the contract is clear on its face. (This strict "four corners" approach

---

2. Where the agreement is recorded in writing, a party's ability to offer evidence of context is much more heavily restricted because of the parol evidence rule, discussed in Chapter 12. In this chapter, we focus on the sources of evidence available to interpret language in the agreement, and are not concerned with the parol evidence rule. In Chapter 12 we will examine barriers to admissibility of contextual evidence created by the rule.

is more common in older cases.) Other courts are more receptive to extrinsic evidence because they recognize that words do not have a constant and immutable meaning and can be colored by context. Because interpretation aims at ascertaining the intended meaning of words, those courts consider it important to hear available contextual evidence in trying to decide what meaning the parties intended.

Where contextual evidence is available and pertinent, the interpretation of a contract involves five principal areas of factual inquiry. At the center of the inquiry are the actual words used by the parties in the agreement. Even where there is contextual evidence, the language of the agreement is the starting point and the primary source of meaning. The wording of the very term in dispute is the central focus of the interpretation effort, but it cannot be read in isolation from the rest of the agreement and must be interpreted in light of the document (or oral agreement) as a whole. Beyond the language of the agreement, the inquiry spreads to its context. This context includes the discussions and conduct of the parties when they negotiated the contract, their conduct in performing the contract after it was formed (course of performance), their conduct in prior comparable transactions with each other (course of dealing), and the customs and usages of the market in which they are dealing with each other (trade usage). (*See* Diagram 10A.)

Diagram 10A

The Environment for Contractual Interpretation

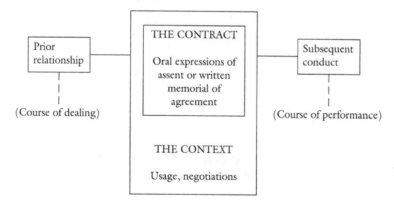

Notice that in each of these five areas we are concerned with objective evidence, in the form of words or conduct manifested by the parties, or verifiable facts in the contractual environment. The evidence of one party concerning what she may have thought or believed is only marginally helpful or relevant. Obviously, not all of these components are present in every transaction. However, the more that exist in a transaction, the richer the background from which meaning can be ascertained. In a fortunate case, all the evidence drawn from these different aspects of the context will point to the same meaning. If they conflict, the general rule (reflected in UCC §§1.303(e) and 2.208(2) and in Restatement, Second, §203(b)) is to give greatest weight to the express terms of the parties, followed in order by any course of performance, course of dealing, and usage.

We will look more closely at these indicators of intent in the rest of this section. Before doing so, it is enlightening to see how they were used by the court in one of the best illustrative cases on this subject, *Frigaliment Importing Co. v. B.N.S. International Sales Corp.*, 190 F. Supp. 116 (S.D.N.Y. 1960). The buyer, a Swiss importer, ordered a large quantity of chicken from the seller. The contract called for "U.S. fresh frozen chicken, grade A" of two different sizes. The agreement reflected a lower price per pound for the larger chickens than the smaller ones. When the seller delivered the chickens, the buyer protested that the larger, cheaper ones were not in accordance with the contract because they were stewing chickens, not suitable for frying. The buyer claimed that the word "chicken" used in the contract meant frying chicken so that all chicken delivered had to be of this quality. The seller denied that it had breached the contract by delivering stewing chickens. It contended that the word "chicken" was a generic term for both frying and stewing chickens and that the price difference in the contract made it clear that the cheaper birds would be stewing chickens.

The subsequent litigation centered on the meaning of the word "chicken" as used in the contract. The definition of "chicken" in dictionaries and U.S.D.A regulations did not exclude either party's meaning. The court's examination of the terms of the contract document as a whole was somewhat more helpful in casting light on the meaning of "chicken." The price term supported the seller's contention that two different types of chicken were contemplated because the price of the larger birds was below the market price for fryers. The court moved beyond the written agreement to explore the entire context of the transaction in an attempt to decide if "chicken" should be understood in the narrower or wider sense. Several experts testified as to the meaning of "chicken" in the trade, but the expert testimony was in conflict and did not clearly support the position of either party. Finally, the court considered evidence of the parties' course of performance to see if it cast any light on what they may have meant. The course of performance did not show a common intention because the buyer protested about the stewing chickens immediately on delivery. In the end, despite these efforts, the court was not able to establish what the parties meant by the use of the word "chicken" in the contract, so the case was resolved on the basis of the burden of proof. The buyer lost because it failed to prove that the word was used in the narrow sense that it alleged.

We now move to a more detailed consideration of each of the indicators of intent sketched above.

a. The Express Words Used by the Parties

The ordinary meaning of words used by the parties in formulating their rights and obligations is always the primary indicator of what they intended. Restatement, Second, §203(b) and UCC §§1.303(e) and 2.208 give greatest weight to express terms. These express terms might be oral, written, or otherwise recorded.[3] As noted above, although the language of the disputed term is at the center of the court's examination of the express terms, the court does not look at that language in isolation, but reads it in light of the agreement as a whole — it reads all the terms of the written agreement or considers the entire oral contract. Often (as illustrated by *Frigaliment*, above), terms in one part of a contract cast light on terms in another.

Of course, interpretation of the ordinary meaning of the parties' language is not always a simple and mechanical matter, and different judges could find different meanings in the same words. For example, in *Breeding v. Kye's, Inc.*, 831 N.E.2d 188 (Ind. App. 2005), Breeding reserved Kye's hall for her wedding. The written agreement stated that $600 of the fee for the facility was for the services of a disc jockey. The agreement also made it clear that the client had no choice of disc jockey because Kye had granted an exclusive license to Sounds Unlimited Productions to provide disc jockey services for all events at the hall. (This suited Breeding well because the owners of Sounds Unlimited were friends of her family and she wanted Sounds Unlimited as the disc jockey at her wedding. In fact, this was apparently why she selected Kye's venue.) About three months before the wedding, Kye notified Breeding that its license arrangement with Sounds Unlimited had terminated, and it would not permit Sounds Unlimited to work in its hall. Kye would not budge in its refusal to allow Sounds Unlimited onto its premises, even though Breeding was willing to hire Sounds Unlimited herself. Breeding sued Kye for breach of contract and return of her deposit on the basis that Kye had broken its undertaking to provide disc jockey services by Sounds Unlimited. Kye defended the suit on the basis that the contract was merely for the hire of the hall and contained no promise to use Sounds Unlimited. The majority of the court of appeals found that the provisions in the contract relating to disc jockey services clearly and

---

3. An oral agreement is legally binding and enforceable unless the statute of frauds, discussed in Chapter 11, requires it to be written (or recorded). However, even if valid, an oral agreement presents problems of proof that are obviated or reduced by recording the agreement. If there is a dispute over the exact language used by the parties in an oral agreement, the actual words used must be proved as a fact before they can be interpreted. Also, where the agreement is written or recorded, the parol evidence rule (*see* Chapter 12) may preclude evidence of alleged oral terms that were not included in the writing or record.

unambiguously constituted a commitment by Kye to provide the services of Sounds Unlimited. Despite the majority's confidence in this clarity, the dissent read the contract terms differently and reached the opposite conclusion. It disagreed that the provisions relating to the disc jockey were a promise to Breeding that Sounds Unlimited would provide the services. Rather, they merely limited the client's choice of disc jockey. (The dissent noted that under the objective test, the express terms of the contract were not affected by Breeding's subjective motivation in selecting the hall because of the disc jockey.)

b. Discussions and Conduct of the Parties During Negotiations

Apart from the actual words spoken or written to express agreement, there may be a history of communication and negotiation leading up to the execution of the contract. Evidence of what was expressed by the parties during the period leading up to contract formation could be useful and relevant to establish the meaning of what was ultimately provided for in the agreement.[4]

c. Course of Performance: Conduct by the Parties in the Course of Performing Under the Agreement

If the parties have begun to perform the contract before the uncertainty to be resolved by interpretation becomes an issue, their conduct in proffering and accepting, or otherwise reacting to performance may provide evidence of what was intended by an indefinite term. This postformation behavior is called the "course of performance" and its relevance to interpretation is based on the assumption that the actual performance tendered and accepted without objection is a strong indicator of what must have been intended. The evidentiary value of the course of performance is recognized by UCC §§1.303(e) and 2.208, mimicked by Restatement, Second, §202(4).

For example, a lease provides that "dogs, cats, and other animals may not be kept on the premises." Lessee owns a pet duck that he thinks of as a bird, not an animal. Dictionaries offer alternative definitions of "animal." One includes all breathing creatures, and the other confines it to four-legged land creatures, excluding birds and fish. Lessee has kept the duck on the premises for several months. Lessor has seen it on several occasions and has never complained. The mutual conduct of the parties creates the fair inference that they were in agreement that "animals" does not include ducks.

Not all postformation conduct necessarily reflects what the parties intended at the time of contracting. The conduct may simply not be

---

4. Again, if the agreement is written or recorded, the parol evidence rule may restrict the admission of this evidence. *See* Chapter 12.

pertinent to the meaning of the term in issue, or, even if it is, it may reflect a subsequent change of mind or a disinclination to enforce rights under the contract.[5] Therefore, it is possible to draw the wrong inference from behavior that is ambiguous or does not really have a bearing on the term in issue. There are several guidelines that help to avoid misconstruing conduct as a course of performance:

1. For a course of performance to be valid as a source of interpretation, it must be pertinent to the meaning of the term in controversy. For example, if the term in dispute concerned the date on which the rent payments were due, lessor's tolerance of the duck does nothing to clarify the uncertainty.
2. The conduct must show that the party performed or accepted performance without a protest or reservation of rights. Therefore, if on each occasion that Lessor saw the duck, she protested that it was not allowed, Lessor's failure to take stronger action does not support the conclusion that the parties intended "animals" not to include ducks.
3. Conduct by only one of the parties, not known and acquiesced in by the other (for example, if Lessee kept the duck inside and Lessor never saw it or knew about it), may show what the performing party understood the agreement to be, but does not prove that the other party shared this view.
4. The more extensive or repetitious the conduct, the stronger the inference that it does reflect what was intended by the parties. By contrast, isolated or single instances of conduct are more ambiguous and could simply be a waiver of, or disinclination to enforce, rights on a particular occasion. For example, merely because Lessor sees the duck on one occasion and does nothing about it, does not necessarily show that she shares Lessee's view of the meaning of "animals."

d. Course of Dealing: Prior Dealings Between the Parties in Similar or Analogous Contractual Relationships

While "course of performance" means the parties' postcontractual relationship, the term "course of dealing" refers to any relationship they may have had in the period before the transaction in question. The parties may have

---

5. It can be difficult to distinguish a course of performance, which casts light on what the parties meant at the time of contracting, from postformation conduct that is either a waiver of rights or a modification of the contract. For example, the lessor's failure to complain about the duck could indicate that the parties did not include it in the definition. However, it could mean instead that the lessor has simply chosen not to enforce the ban on ducks, or that the parties have implicitly agreed by conduct to eliminate the restriction on animals. If it is not a course of performance but a waiver or modification, it is subject to different rules, which are discussed in sections 13.9 and 16.10.2.

dealt with each other on prior occasions, and the current transaction may be the latest in a series of similar ones that have taken place over a period of time. If so, the parties' conduct in prior dealings may provide information that helps to interpret a term that has generated a dispute in the present transaction. This is recognized by UCC §1.303(b) and Restatement, Second, §§202 and 203.

For example, Lessee previously rented premises from Lessor under a lease that had the identical clause forbidding animals. During the prior lease term, Lessor discovered the duck and told Lessee to get rid of it or face eviction. He sadly obeyed and boarded it with his mother. When the parties enter into a new lease with the same term, it is reasonable to infer that they intend its wording to have the meaning established under the prior relationship. If they intend otherwise, they must make this clear in the new lease. If they do not, Lessee cannot claim that the parties intend that "animals," as used in the new lease, does not include ducks.

A course of dealing is only pertinent if the earlier relationship is comparable or analogous. The transactions must be substantially similar, the term in controversy must have been present in the earlier dealings, and past conduct must be relevant to the meaning in issue. As with course of performance, repetition strengthens the inference, so multiple transactions with consistent, pertinent behavior more clearly establish intended meaning.

e. Trade Usage, Common Usage, or Custom That Is Reasonably Applicable to the Parties' Dealings

Although the ordinary or general sense of words must be the starting point in any exercise of interpretation, UCC §1.303(c) and Restatement, Second, §§202(5) and 222 emphasize the significant impact of trade usage on the meaning of language. Parties usually deal with each other in the context of a larger community. This may be a particular market (whether international, national, or more local), or it may be a specialized trade or industry. If the market has a well-accepted custom or practice that explains language or supplements an omission in an agreement, this customary usage is of value in ascertaining the parties' intent. Although UCC §1.303 and Restatement, Second, §§202(5) and 222 use the term "usage of trade," this does not mean that custom or usage is only pertinent where the parties are members of a particular vocation, industry, or profession. Rather, "usage of trade" must be understood to encompass any applicable commercial custom, whether it derives from a specific trade or from a broader market in which the parties are involved. (UCC §1.303(c) and Restatement, Second, §222 recognize this by defining "usage of trade" to include any regular practice or method of dealing in a place, vocation, or trade.)

Wolf v. Superior Court of Los Angeles, 8 Cal. Rptr. 3d 649 (Cal. App. 2004), illustrates the role that evidence of trade usage could play in interpreting an agreement. The dispute in that case involved the royalties payable by Walt Disney Pictures and Television to the author of the book on which the movie *Who Framed Roger Rabbit* was based. The agreement between Disney and the author provided that the author would receive a royalty of 5 percent of "gross receipts." The dispute was whether this term meant only cash receipts, or also included the value of other consideration Disney had received from licenses granted for the use of the characters in the movie. The meaning of the term "gross receipts" had to be determined to resolve this dispute. None of the parties to the negotiations had any recollection of ever discussing the meaning of the term. The plain meaning of the words, read in relation to other language in the written contract, suggested that royalties might be confined to cash receipts. However, the author sought to introduce the testimony of an expert that "gross receipts" was generally understood in the movie industry to include noncash consideration, and the court of appeals held that the trial court had erred in refusing to admit the evidence of usage. (The expert did subsequently testify on remand but apparently did not persuade the jury to interpret the term in light of the alleged usage. This case, like *Frigaliment* shows that even if evidence of usage is offered, its probative weight is ultimately decided by the factfinder.)

Older common law did not recognize any practice as a usage unless it was so firmly established as to be notorious, universal, and ancient. The modern approach is more flexible. Official Comment 4 to UCC §1.303 and Comment *b* to Restatement, Second, §222 explicitly reject any requirement of great longevity and universality and admit the possibility of new usages. The UCC test is simply whether the usage is "currently observed by the great majority of decent dealers." In common law transactions, while some courts may still apply the stricter test, modern common law tends to follow the broader recognition of usage advanced by the UCC and Restatement, Second.

A party who alleges that a usage explains or supplements an agreement must (1) define the trade or market with which the transaction is associated and show the parties' connection to it, (2) prove (usually by expert testimony) that the usage actually exists in the applicable trade or market, (3) show that the usage is pertinent to the dispute in that it relates to the matter on which the parties disagree, and (4) show that the usage is consistent with the express terms of the agreement and has not been excluded by them.

The initial issue of defining the trade or market and showing the relationship of the transaction to that trade or market can be crucial. The determination of the market is sometimes, but not always, straightforward. For example, say the dispute arises from a transaction between a manufacturer of television sets and one of its distributors. Is the relevant market confined to the distribution market for televisions, or is it broader — say the distribution market for home electronics, or for all electronics? Or is the appropriate market wider still, covering the electronics industry as a whole? The choice of the market could be crucial because the existence and nature of usage could be different, or relatively stronger or weaker, if the market is defined more broadly or narrowly.

One of the key factors in defining the trade or market is the parties' relationship to it. If both parties are active participants in the market or trade, usages in that market or trade are readily attributable to their contract, except to the extent that the contract clearly excludes a usage. However, if one of the parties is not involved in the market or trade, its usages should not be relevant to the contract unless the nonmember party knew of the usage and the circumstances show that the parties reasonably expected it to apply to the transaction. As usual, the objective standard is used to decide if a party should be subject to a usage. We are not concerned about whether the party actually knew of and expected the usage to apply, but whether he reasonably should have done so.[6]

Nanakuli Paving and Rock Co. v. Shell Oil Co., 664 F.2d 772 (9th Cir. 1991), illustrates the inquiry into the appropriate market.[7] The case involved a contract between Shell and Nanakuli under which Shell supplied asphalt for Nanakuli's use in paving projects on the island of Oahu. The contract did not have a fixed price term, but provided that the price would be Shell's "posted price at time of delivery." Despite this, Nanakuli claimed that usage in the Oahu paving trade required Shell to "price protect" Nanakuli. That is, where Nanakuli had committed itself to the customer based on a lower posted price at the time of its bid, Shell would charge Nanakuli that price, even if the posted price at the time of delivery was higher. The court defined the scope of the paving trade broadly to include not only paving contractors but also asphalt suppliers because the suppliers had a close relationship with the pavers and had reason to know of the usage. *Nanakuli* also addressed the issue of whether the alleged usage was consistent with the express terms of the contract. This is important because usage should not be employed to interpret the contract if the parties have indicated the intention to exclude it. If the usage cannot be reconciled with the express terms of the contract, this strongly indicates that the parties did not intend to follow the usage. Because established and applicable usage is such a strong indication of intent, courts usually require the term excluding usage to be very clear and unequivocal. In *Nanakuli*, the court did not find the price protection usage to be inconsistent with the contract's express term

---

6. Note that the focus is on presumed knowledge rather than actual knowledge of usage. The effect of this is that usage sometimes enters a contract as a matter of construction, not interpretation. This reinforces the point made in section 10.1.1 that the dividing line between these processes is often blurred.

7. This case is discussed further in relation to the parol evidence rule in section 12.10.

that the price was to be Shell's posted price at the time of delivery. Although it is difficult to reconcile these terms, the court found no clear indication that the parties did not intend price protection to qualify the express language of the contract.

§10.1.4 Some General Rules of Interpretation and Construction

When a term is omitted or its meaning is uncertain, this indefiniteness can often be resolved by having recourse to one of a variety of general principles that have been developed by courts as guidelines in the ascertainment of reasonable but unexpressed intent. Many of these rules are based on commonsense inferences, but some are dictated by policy or a perception of fairness. These rules are sometimes called rules of interpretation and sometimes rules of construction — again reflecting the subtle distinction mentioned before. The important point, from a practical standpoint, is that they are guides to enable the court to draw the proper inferences of meaning from whatever facts may be available. Typically, they are used only when there is some uncertainty in the intent of the agreement. They should not be applied mechanically and must take into account the reasonable expectations of the parties and the underlying purpose of the agreement.

There are many rules of interpretation. They are not all of equal strength, and some are more compelling than others. Obviously, they are not all relevant to every case. Although several of the common ones are included here, no attempt is made to catalog them all. These examples sufficiently illustrate the range and kind of rules covered under this category:

1. If possible, the court should try to interpret an agreement in a way that gives effect to all its terms.
2. Unless the context indicates otherwise, words used in a contract should be given their ordinary, general, or lay meaning rather than a specialized or technical meaning. For example, in *E.M.M.I., Inc. v. Zurich American Insurance Co.*, 9 Cal. Rptr. 3d 701 (2004), a jeweler's insurance policy excluded coverage where jewelry was stolen from a vehicle unless the jeweler's representative was "in or upon the vehicle" at the time of the theft. The jewelry was stolen from the car while the salesman was checking the car's tailpipe. The insurer argued that the term "in or upon" was used in a technical sense to mean that the insured must actually be in the vehicle, not just next to it. The court disagreed. If the insurer intended to use a term in a technical sense, it should so indicate, say by defining the term in the policy. Because the term "upon" was ambiguous, it should be

interpreted in a sense that accords with the insured's reasonable expectation that the exclusion applies only where the car is unattended. *Meridian Leasing, Inc. v. Associated Aviation Underwriters*, 409 F.3d 342 (6th Cir. 2005), followed the same approach in finding that an insurance policy on an aircraft covered damage to the engine when it caught fire upon being started. The insurance policy excluded damage caused by "wear and tear" and the insurer argued that the exclusion for "wear and tear" should be broadly understood to restrict coverage to damage from an accident and to exclude damage resulting from a mechanical problem. The court disagreed. The policy had no technical definition of "wear and tear." In ordinary usage, a fire caused by mechanical fault is not "wear and tear," which means deterioration resulting from the ongoing operation of the plane.

3. *Ut res magis valeat quam pereat*, "The thing should rather have effect than be destroyed." If one interpretation would make the contract invalid and another would validate it, the court should favor the meaning that validates the contract. In the same spirit, there are allied rules that prefer an interpretation that would make a term reasonable and lawful over one that would have the opposite effect, and an interpretation that positively rather than negatively impacts public policy or the public interest. For example, say that a partnership agreement, entered into in New York City, contains a covenant not to compete. This covenant states that a partner will not engage in a competing business "in New York" for a period of two years after leaving the partnership. Agreements that stifle competition and restrict a person's ability to earn a living are unenforceable as against public policy unless they are reasonable in scope.[8] A partner leaves the partnership and sets up a competing business a few blocks away. She claims that the covenant is unenforceable because it is overbroad and unreasonably extends to the entire state of New York. The partnership contends that it is not unreasonable because it is intended to cover only to the city of New York, There is no extrinsic evidence from which the court can determine the intended meaning of "New York." Therefore, if the more restrictive meaning would save the covenant from invalidity, the court will favor that meaning.

4. Specific or precise provisions should be given greater weight than general provisions. For example, one clause in a lease says "no pets may be kept on the premises." However, there is another provision in the lease that says "guide or service dogs shall be kept on leashes at

---

8. *See* section 13.13.4 for a further discussion of the public policy concerns relating to covenants not to compete.

all times in the public areas of the building." The specific provision concerning guide and service dogs makes it clear that the general rule on keeping pets on the premises does not apply to them.

5. Where an agreement consists of both standardized and negotiated terms (or preprinted and handwritten or typed terms), any conflict between them should be resolved in favor of the negotiated, hand-written, or typed terms.

6. *Ejusdem generis*, "of the same kind." When specific and general words are connected, the general word is limited by the specific one, so that it is deemed to refer to things of the same kind. For example, a lease states that "skateboards, roller skates, rollerblades, and other means of locomotion are prohibited in common areas and hallways." The common denominator here is that all these items make use of wheels under the feet. On this reasoning, the general words "other means of locomotion" do not include wheelchairs or motorbikes. However, if the common denominator is taken to be wheels, these two items would be included in the general language, but a camel would not be.

7. *Noscitur a sociis*, "known from its associates." This rule is similar to *ejusdem generis*, but is not confined to linked general and specific words. Whenever a series of words is used together, the meaning of each word in the series affects the meaning of others. For example, if a term in a lease provides that "no dogs, cats, or primates may be kept on the premises," the meaning of "primates" is qualified by the others. It would therefore cover only primates in the sense of apes and monkeys, and would not forbid the lessee from having his uncle, a bishop, move in with him.

8. *Expressio unius est exclusio alterius*, "The expression of one thing excludes another." This is in some sense the opposite of the *ejusdem generis* rule. When a thing or list of things is specifically mentioned without being followed by a general term, the implication is that other things of the same kind are excluded. For example, a term that prohibits "dogs, cats, and primates" impliedly does not prohibit ducks.

9. *Contra proferentum* (or stated in full, *omnia praesumuntur contra proferentum*), "All things are presumed against the proponent." When one party has drafted or selected the language of an unclear provision, the meaning is preferred that favors the other party. This rule is often said to be a tie breaker, in that it should be used as a last resort when no more direct and pertinent guide to meaning is applicable. It is not always used as a last resort, however, and tends to be much favored when the proponent of the terms is a party with relatively strong bargaining power who has produced a preprinted standard form for the other's signature. The E.M.M.I and *Meridian Leasing* cases in item 2 above both demonstrate this approach to the interpretation of an

insurance policy. Insurance policies are prime examples of standard form contracts that are fertile ground for application of the *contra proferentum* rule.

§10.2 GAP FILLERS USED TO EFFECTUATE THE PARTIES' REASONABLE INTENT

§10.2.1 Introduction

A gap filler is a provision legally implied into a contract to supplement or clarify its express language. As its name suggests, the principal purpose of a gap filler is to supply a logically inferable contract term when it is clear that the parties intended a contract, but have failed to provide adequately or at all for the question in issue. Of course, some apparent gaps in an express agreement could be filled by contextual evidence, so a legally implied gap filler is usually used only when no pertinent contextual evidence is available to establish the existence of a term as a matter of fact. Gap fillers are therefore standard terms supplied by law. Some have been developed by courts and others are provided by legislation. Courts and legislatures do not pick them out of the air but base them on common expectations, commercial practice, and public policy. For this reason, standard terms supplied by law are meant to reflect what the parties likely would have agreed had they discussed the issue. As this description indicates, when a court resorts to legally implied gap fillers, it is usually engaged in construction, rather than fact-based interpretation.

For example, Buyer agrees to buy Seller's house, subject to Buyer being able to secure the necessary financing. Nothing is said in the written agreement or in the negotiations about Buyer having the duty to make a conscientious effort to obtain the financing. If Buyer does nothing to seek financing, he will likely be held to have breached a legally implied promise to make reasonable efforts to apply for and secure the financing. The implication of such a promise is a logical extension of the express provisions of the agreement and gives effect to the presumed intent of the parties. It recognizes that they probably did not contemplate that Buyer could slip out of his obligations simply by not bothering to apply for a loan. In this way, the implied term constructs what the parties must have intended, had they been acting fairly and reasonably, and it gives effect to their reasonable expectations and to the underlying purpose of the agreement. Because legally implied terms are derived from and known in the market, there is commonly an affinity between legally implied terms and usage. Therefore, this same term requiring best efforts in seeking a loan could probably have been established by evidence of the customary practices pertaining to the sale of a home subject to the contingency of financing. However, the difference is that if a usage is so well established that it has reached the point of being recognized as a legal standard term, it becomes part of the contract as a matter of law, not of fact. It is therefore not necessary to establish it by evidence.

Some gap fillers are well established and others have been recognized more recently. Additional ones will continue to develop in the future as new legal implications are drawn from changing market expectations. Of course, there cannot be standard terms for every conceivable gap, so there are some omissions that cannot be cured by legal implication. Some gap fillers supply generalized obligations that are likely to be implied in all kinds of contracts, and some are very specific, relating to particular types of term in specialized contracts. The following samples of general and specific gap fillers illustrate their range and nature.

§10.2.2 Gap Fillers That Supply General Obligations

When a contract does not clearly specify a level of performance but it is clear that the parties' purpose can be achieved only if the obligor puts some energy and dedication into the performance, the law implies an obligation to make best efforts or reasonable efforts[9] to effect the contract's purpose. The above example of the house sale subject to financing illustrates this. Another illustration is provided by *Wood v. Lucy, Lady Duff-Gordon*, 222 N.Y. 88 (1917), discussed in sections 10.1.1 and 7.9.2, in which the court found that an exclusive distributorship contract impliedly required the distributor to make best efforts to sell the product. This general principle is likely to apply in any type of contract under which the grantor of a license, distributorship, or dealership relies on the conscientiousness of the grantee to market a product effectively. The facts and resolution of *B. Lewis Productions, Inc. v. Angelou*, 2005 WL 1138474 (S.D.N.Y. 2005), are strikingly similar to *Wood*. The poet Maya Angelou entered into a written agreement with Lewis under which she granted him the exclusive right to represent her in placing her work in greeting cards, calendars, and other stationery items. Lewis agreed to contribute "all the capital necessary" and Angelou agreed to contribute "original literary works." The agreement did not particularize

---

9. There may be a difference between "reasonable efforts," which appears strongly objective, and "best efforts," which suggests some blend of subjective and objective standards. However, the distinction is probably not substantial. Whichever term is used, the decision on what constitutes an acceptable effort should take into account both the objective market standards and the subjective honesty and particular circumstances of the party who is to exert the effort.

Lewis's duties, but it did provide that the parties would share the net profits of the venture after revenue had been applied to the repayment of Lewis's capital contribution and expenses. Lewis began work immediately. Just over two years after the agreement was entered, and when Lewis was close to executing a licensing agreement with Hallmark cards, the personal relationship between the parties soured, and Angelou terminated the agreement. Shortly thereafter, Angelou entered into a licensing agreement with Hallmark on her own. Protracted litigation followed in which Lewis sued Angelou for breach of contract. The court, quoting from *Wood* at length, noted that like Wood and Duff-Gordon, Lewis and Angelou unquestionably intended to form a business relationship in which each party assumed obligations. Rather than defeat this intent by declaring the contract to be too indefinite to enforce, the court followed the approach of *Wood* and supplied an obligation of good faith and fair dealing to give content to the vaguely expressed undertakings of the parties.

The problem with the legal implication of broad, generalized obligations is that they are vague in themselves. Therefore, although they may go part of the way in curing a vagueness or omission in the agreement, they may not settle the scope and content of the obligation. That is, a concept such as "best efforts" is mushy and nonspecific, so that it is not enough simply to imply the obligation. The further step must be taken to determine with some precision what degree of effort is required by the obligation. It may be easy to find a breach when no effort is made at all, but more clarity is needed to decide if some greater degree of effort is an adequate performance. To define the obligation more acutely, a further inquiry must be made into the underlying purpose of the contract and the reasonable expectations of the parties.

§10.2.3 Gap Fillers That Supply More Specific Rights and Duties

Both the UCC and the common law supply gap fillers that relate to specific aspects of particular kinds of contracts. Some of these are concrete and precise, but others include generalized concepts, such as reasonableness, that present interpretational problems similar to those discussed above. The following selection illustrates the kind of supplementary terms available to fill gaps left by the parties. These are merely random examples. No attempt is made to be comprehensive. Remember, they are used only if the contract has a gap or uncertainty that has not been resolved by contextual evidence.

The common law has developed many gap fillers through the process of judicial decision. Three examples, discussed elsewhere in this book, are enough to illustrate this point. First, if the parties to an employment contract do not specify its duration, it is deemed to be terminable at will. (*See* section 8.10.) Second, if the parties do not state that rights under a contract are personal to the obligee, the obligee may transfer (assign) those rights to another person. (*See* sections 12.9 and 19.3.3.) Third, if the contract does not provide for the sequence of performance, it is presumed that when both performances are a single instantaneous act, they must be made concurrently. But if one performance is instantaneous and the other needs time to perform, it is presumed that the longer performance must take place first. Therefore, in the sale of a house, unless otherwise stated in the contract, it is implied that transfer of title and payment occur at the same time, but in a contract to build a house, the builder must complete the construction before the owner has to pay. (*See* section 16.8.4.)

UCC Article 2 also has a number of gap fillers. Because they are set out in the statute, they are easier to find than those provided by common law. For example: Unless the agreement expresses otherwise, §§2.312, 2.314, and 2.315 imply certain minimum warranties that a seller makes under defined circumstances regarding the title to and quality of the goods; if the parties do not specify the price of the goods, §2.305 infers that they agreed to a reasonable price unless the apparent intent of the agreement is otherwise; if payment terms are not expressed, §§2.307 and 2.310 assume that payment must be made upon delivery of the goods; §§2.307, 2.308, and 2.309 require that the goods be delivered in a single lot at the seller's place of business within a reasonable time; in a requirements or output contract,[10] §2.306(1) implies both a good faith and a reasonableness obligation on the party who is to determine the quantity of goods ordered or supplied; and §2.306(2) implies an obligation of best efforts on both parties when the contract imposes an obligation on one of them to deal exclusively with the other.

§10.3 TERMS CONSTRUED AS A MATTER OF POLICY

§10.3.1 Supplementary Terms That Cannot Be Excluded by Agreement

There is an exception to the general rule, stated in section 10.2, that terms supplied by law are intended to bring out the perceived reasonable intent of the parties and will not be included in the contract unless consistent with that intent. Some legally implied obligations are so fundamental to

---

10. *See* section 7.9.3 for an explanation of this type of contract.

fair dealing or so strongly demanded by public policy that they are mandatory and are part of the contract irrespective of the parties' actual intent. Even if they wish to, the parties cannot effectively agree to exclude such a term.

Construed terms of this kind are not properly called gap fillers. They are not default rules, but enter the contract whether or not there is a gap or uncertainty about the parties' intent. Although such strongly construed terms are raised here as part of the discussion of the process of finding meaning in agreement, they are more a matter of regulation than of seeking intent. The law's true purpose in such a firm imposition of standard terms is not so much to ascertain what the parties reasonably must have intended, but to limit contractual autonomy in the interest of public policy. Sometimes the policy in question is not directly related to contract law, but is concerned with the undesirable effect of particular contract terms on some other field, such as tort, antitrust, or criminal law. Often, however, the underlying public policy is that of protecting a weaker party from one-sided and unfair terms. In this respect, mandatory construed terms are part of the broader subject of regulating the formation and content of contracts, discussed in Chapter 13.

§10.3.2 The General Obligation of Good Faith and Fair Dealing

One of the most important and pervasive mandatory construed terms is the general obligation of good faith and fair dealing that the law imposes on both parties in the performance and enforcement of the contract. Whether or not the agreement expressly articulates this obligation, and even if it expressly excludes it, the law implies it into every contract.[11] This duty is recognized in both UCC §1.304 and Restatement, Second, §205.

It is one thing to recognize a general obligation of good faith and fair dealing, but quite another to give specific content to these broad and abstract concepts when one of the parties claims that the other's conduct breached the obligation. We encountered this question in section 7.9.3 when discussing the obligation of good faith imposed by UCC §2.306 on buyers and sellers in output and requirements contracts. We saw there that the determination of whether a party acted in good faith must be made with reference to the reasonable expectations of the parties in the context of

---

11. There is a link between this principle and the second rule of construction mentioned in section 10.1.4, which favors a reasonable, effective, and lawful interpretation of unclear provisions. However, it goes even further than that rule by imposing a duty of fair dealing on the parties.

the transaction. Even narrowing the concept to the reasonable expectations of the parties does not make it easy to apply, and the question of whether some conduct violated the obligation can be difficult and a matter of strong disagreement.

For example, in *United Airlines, Inc. v. Good Taste, Inc.* 982 P.2d 1259 (Alaska 1999) United entered into an in-flight catering contract with Good Taste. To perform the contract, Good Taste had to expand its capacity extensively, incurring $1 million in costs to enlarge its operation. The period of the contract was three years, but the contract provided that either party could terminate it on 90 days' notice. After about one year, United exercised its right to terminate the contract by giving the 90 days' notice. The reason it terminated was because it had decided to use another company for its in-flight catering. Good Taste claimed that United had violated its obligation of good faith by terminating the contract. It contended that it would not have spent the money to expand its operations had it not had a reasonable assurance of a three-year contract, and that United's representative had told it that United would not use the termination provision unless it stopped flying to Alaska. Because the termination provision had no qualification, the majority of the court interpreted it as allowing termination at will, without any requirement of cause. The majority recognized that this contract, like every contract, contained an implied covenant of good faith and fair dealing. However, it granted summary judgment to United because it refused to find that United had violated this obligation merely by exercising a clear and unambiguous termination right. The obligation of good faith precludes a party from opportunistic advantage-taking and actions motivated by malicious or improper motives (such as the intent to drive the party out of business). However, where the contract contains an at-will termination clause, the obligation of good faith and fair dealing does not preclude exercise of that right to terminate, even if motivated by the purpose of getting a better deal elsewhere. To so hold would convert the contract's clear at-will termination right into one that required cause for termination. A dissenting justice argued that the termination clause did not expressly state that United could terminate at will, but was silent on the question of whether United needed to show cause for cancellation. Therefore, the termination clause must be read in light of the obligation of good faith, to be determined in light of the parties' reasonable expectations. The parties understood that Good Taste would not have made a significant investment in its facilities unless it had some assurance that United would not simply terminate the contract if a better deal came along. United's termination without cause violated Good Taste's reasonable expectations, and the case should go to trial so that a jury could decide if this constituted a violation of United's obligation of good faith.

§10.3.3 Construed Terms That Can Be Excluded Only by Express or Specific Language

Below the level of absolute legal implication, there are construed terms that are important enough to be more strongly implied than other gap fillers. Although public policy does not preclude the parties from contracting out of them, it requires the intent to exclude them to be clearly expressed. Stated differently, while most gap fillers enter the contract only when necessary to resolve an uncertainty or omission, there are some that are so strongly implied as a matter of policy that they become part of the contract unless its express terms clearly exclude them. In some cases, even a clear exclusion is not good enough unless it complies with specified rules that may prescribe the use of particular language or format.

For example, UCC Article 2 has a policy in favor of providing warranties in certain types of sales of goods. Therefore, although §2.316(2) allows the seller to contract out of them, it recognizes a warranty disclaimer as effective only if it satisfies certain formalities. To disclaim the merchant[12] seller's warranty of merchantability (that is, that the goods meet minimum trade standards), the sales contract must mention "merchantability" and, if in writing, the disclaimer must be conspicuous. When goods are sold for a particular purpose, the seller gives an implied warranty of fitness for that purpose unless it is disclaimed conspicuously in writing. The goal of these rules is to make it more likely that the buyer notices the disclaimer, and to prevent the seller from hiding it in a mass of boilerplate.

§10.4 THE PROBLEM OF INDEFINITENESS IN AN AGREEMENT

If the terms of an agreement are expressed clearly and comprehensively, the fact of contract formation and the extent of each party's commitment can be ascertained with relative ease by the interpretation of their language in context. However, parties sometimes fail to express their assent adequately because they have left a material aspect of their agreement vague or ambiguous, or they have failed to resolve it or to provide for it at all. When the agreement suffers from this kind of uncertainty, it is said to be indefinite.

There could be many different causes of indefiniteness. For example, the parties may not take the trouble of discussing all aspects of the proposed relationship, they may not give enough attention to detail, they may be unclear in their thinking or articulation of what is expected, or they may

---

12. *See* sections 2.7.2 and 6.3.2 for the definition of "merchant."

avoid confronting thorny issues that threaten to collapse the deal. Sometimes it is clear that the parties genuinely intended a contract despite the indefiniteness, but in other cases the lack of resolution means that they had not yet achieved consensus.

The general rule is that no contract comes into being if a material aspect of the agreement is left indefinite by the parties and the uncertainty cannot be resolved by the process of interpretation or construction. The existence of such an irresoluble key aspect of the relationship means that the parties never reached sufficient consensus to conclude an enforceable contract, and the court should not try to concoct a contract for them.

This statement of the general rule suggests two central issues that must be confronted in dealing with problems of indefiniteness: First, for an apparent contract to fail for indefiniteness, there must be an incurable uncertainty about what the parties agreed to, so that their intent to enter a contract is in doubt, or the court is at a loss in establishing a basis for enforcing what was agreed. This first issue involves many considerations that form the basis of the remainder of this chapter. Second, the uncertainty must relate to a material aspect of the relationship. Although an indefinite nonmaterial term does need to be settled by the court if it is relevant to the dispute, the uncertainty does not preclude contract formation.

A term is material if it is an important component of the contract. It is so central to the values exchanged under the contract that it is a fundamental basis of the bargain.[13] Although materiality is sometimes obvious, it is not always easy to decide because the significance of a term in any particular relationship can be gauged only by interpreting the agreement in context to uncover the reasonable expectations of the parties.

Although a court should not find a contract where indefiniteness is severe enough to indicate a lack of assent to its material terms, this does not mean that the court should refuse contractual enforcement unless every material term of the agreement has been expressed with piercing clarity. Such a rigorous standard would err in the opposite direction by failing to recognize a contract when the evidence suggests that the parties reasonably expected to be bound, did intend to enter a contract despite the indefiniteness, and had relied on the existence of a contract.

The balance between these poles results in a general principle that tolerates some degree of indefiniteness provided the evidence indicates that the parties did intend a contract, and there is some means of resolving the uncertainty, so that a breach can be identified and a remedy provided. Both UCC §2.204(3) and Restatement, Second, §33(2) adopt this approach by emphasizing that a contract should be treated as reasonably certain if the

---

13. This broad definition of materiality is sufficient for present purposes. Materiality was also discussed in section 6.3.2 in connection with the battle of the forms, and is examined in greater detail in section 17.3 in relation to breach of contract.

language of agreement, interpreted in context and in light of applicable legal rules, provides enough content to establish an intent to contract, a basis for finding breach, and a means of providing a remedy.

Although remedies are not discussed until Chapter 18, it is useful to focus on the relationship between definiteness and remedy suggested by Article 2 and Restatement, Second. Definiteness is not absolute but relative, and the degree of certainty required may be different depending on the nature of the controversy and the relief claimed. For example, if the plaintiff claims enforcement of a clear obligation due by the defendant, and the defendant contends that the contract is too indefinite because of vagueness in the plaintiff's obligation, the court does not have to establish the plaintiff's obligation with as much certainty as it would have to do if that was the obligation in issue. Similarly, if the plaintiff is claiming damages for the breach of an unclear obligation of the defendant, the court needs just enough information to determine a monetary award. However, if the plaintiff was seeking specific performance of the obligation (that is, a court order compelling the defendant to perform the contract), the court would need a greater degree of certainty to grant the order because the court must be able to define the obligation clearly if it is going to order its performance.

Although it is relatively easy to identify the general range of appropriate judicial intervention to cure indefiniteness, it is much more difficult to know if an individual case falls within that range — that is, whether the indefiniteness is properly remediable or should preclude contractual enforcement. As in so many other situations, the answer can be reached only by finding the mutual intent of the parties through the process of interpretation and construction.

§10.5 DIFFERENT CAUSES AND FORMS OF INDEFINITENESS

Indefiniteness in an agreement could be caused by vagueness, ambiguity, omission, or irresolution. These different shortcomings have much in common, but they may raise different concerns that call for separate treatment. It is therefore useful to begin by articulating this distinction.

§10.5.1 Unclear Terms: Vagueness and Ambiguity

a. Vague Terms

A term is vague (or uncertain) if it is stated so obscurely or in such general language that one cannot reasonably determine what it means. For example,

Lessor agrees to let certain business premises to Lessee for one year in exchange for "a periodic rental payment based on a fair percentage of Lessee's earnings." One cannot determine on the face of this language the amount and the due date of the rent. The wording fails to convey a certain and concrete meaning. *Baer v. Chase*, 392 F.3d 609 (3d Cir. 2004) provides another illustration of incurable vagueness. Baer, an ex-prosecutor and would-be screenwriter, assisted Chase, the creator of the hugely successful series, *The Sopranos*, by helping him with background information on the New Jersey mob and by reading and commenting on his draft script. Baer asserted that Chase had agreed orally that if the show became a success, he would "take care" of him and would reward him "in a manner commensurate with the true value" of his services. The court of appeals affirmed the trial court's grant of summary judgment against Baer on the contract claim. It held that even if such a promise was made, these terms were too indefinite to enable the court to ascertain with reasonable certainty what performance was to be rendered by Chase. The court acknowledged that indefiniteness can sometimes be resolved by the implication of a term, such as a reasonable price. However, the vagueness in this undertaking was beyond cure.[14]

By contrast, the court did not find indefiniteness to be fatal in *B. Lewis Productions, Inc. v. Angelou*, discussed in section 10.2.2. Recall that Maya Angelou granted to Lewis the exclusive right to represent her in placing her work in greeting cards, calendars, and other stationery items. Lewis agreed to contribute "all the capital necessary" and Angelou agreed to contribute "original literary works." The agreement did not set out Lewis's duties, but it did provide that the parties would share the net profits of the venture. About two years after the agreement was made, and just as Lewis was about to secure a licensing agreement with Hallmark cards, Angelou terminated the agreement because of personal differences with Lewis. Angelou ultimately entered into a licensing agreement with Hallmark on her own. Lewis sued Angelou for breach of contract.[15] Angelou moved for summary judgment on the ground that the agreement was too indefinite to be enforced as a contract. The court denied her motion. It noted that the court's role was not to make a contract for the parties, and it would not enforce an agreement whose terms are so indefinite that the parties' intentions cannot be ascertained with reasonable certainty. However, it observed that courts are

---

14. As an alternative to his contract claim, Baer sought relief in restitution, claiming that Chase had been unjustly enriched by Baer's services. The trial court initially dismissed this claim on the ground that the statute of limitations had run. Dismissal on that ground was reversed on appeal, and the trial court ultimately awarded Baer restitutionary damages. However, because the court found the market value of Baer's services to be modest, the amount of his recovery was small. *Baer v. Chase*, 2007 WL 1237850 (D.N.J. 2007).

15. He also sued Hallmark for tortious interference with contract on the grounds that it induced Angelou's breach by contracting directly with her knowing that Lewis had been negotiating with Hallmark on her behalf.

reluctant to strike down contracts for indefiniteness and cautioned that courts should not turn the search for certainty into a "fetish." Some degree of indefiniteness can be found in most contracts. The court recognized that the parties did intend to form a business relationship, and it felt that all of the open-ended terms could be given adequate content by supplying a standard of reasonableness and good faith to the parties' undertakings.

b. Ambiguity

A term is ambiguous if it is capable of more than one meaning. Ambiguity can lie in a word itself or in the structure of a sentence. Ambiguity in a word may be illustrated by a term in a lease that confines the use of the premises to "the purpose of conducting a bookmaking business." The word "bookmaking" could refer either to the manufacture of books or to the making and placing of bets on horses and sporting events. Ambiguity can also result from inept sentence construction. For example, although the lease makes it clear that "bookmaking" is used in the latter sense, it goes on to provide that Lessor "shall be entitled to ten percent of Lessee's profits from all gambling activities that shall be lawfully conducted on the premises." The clumsy sentence construction may mean that Lessor is entitled to ten percent of all profits earned by Lessee from gambling, and that Lessee is obliged to conduct only lawful activity on the premises, or it may mean that Lessor is entitled to ten percent of the profits from lawful gambling but gets no share of illegal gambling proceeds.

Ambiguity in language must be distinguished from a dispute over the application of unambiguous language to a particular set of facts. The court made this distinction in *Psenicska v. Twentieth Century Fox Film Corp.* 2008 WL 4185752 (S.D.N.Y. 2008), aff'd 409 Fed. Appx. 368 (2d Cir. 2008). The case involved the movie *Borat*, in which the character, a fictional Kazakh television reporter, tours America with the apparent purpose of making a documentary on American life. The movie is a comedy, and its particular brand of humor (described by the court as "childish and vulgar") is to dupe ordinary people (that is, members of the public who are not actors) into believing that they are participating in a documentary film. As the filming proceeds, the documentary character of the film deteriorates into chaos as the Borat character engages in surprising, outrageous, and offensive conduct. Several of the people set up in this way sued the studio for damages for the use of their images in the movie. Each had signed an agreement consenting to appear in a "documentary-style motion picture," and the studio therefore moved to dismiss their suits on the basis of this consent. The plaintiffs argued that dismissal was not appropriate because the term "documentary-style motion picture" was ambiguous. The court disagreed. The dictionary definition of the words "documentary" and "style" make it clear a "documentary-style movie" is "a work displaying the characteristics of a film that provides a factual record or report." None of the parties challenged this dictionary-based definition, and the dispute related more to the question of whether *Borat* fit that definition. The court held that it did, and dismissed the suits.

c. Curing Vagueness or Ambiguity with Contextual Evidence

A term that is not readily comprehensible on its face may not be incurably vague or ambiguous, because it may become clear if interpreted in context. Evidence of what the parties said or did in negotiations, correspondence, or dealings prior to the agreement or during the period following it may help to clarify what they meant by the language used. In addition, clarity may be supplied by a custom or usage in the commercial environment in which the parties made the agreement, or by standardized terms recognized by law. We will shortly turn to these matters in detail. For the present, simply note that language that seems vague or ambiguous in isolation may become more certain if interpreted in the wider environment of the transaction. In the first example above, the vague rental provision may not be as unclear as it sounds if its meaning is embellished by facts in the context. Say, for example, that these clauses are regularly used in the commercial real property market, in which "fair rental" is widely understood to be based on an index published by an association of landlords, and rent is customarily paid monthly in advance. Similarly, the ambiguous word "bookmaking," while unclear in isolation, may become more definite if other provisions in the lease, discussions during negotiations, or other facts are available to show what the parties meant.

But contextual evidence cannot always save a vague or ambiguous term. Sometimes unclear language defies interpretation, even in context, because the circumstances of the transaction are devoid of helpful indicators of meaning. If a central component of an apparent agreement suffers from this degree of incurable indefiniteness, one can only conclude either that no contract was intended or, if it was, that the parties failed to form a clear intent or failed to communicate it well enough to create an enforceable relationship.

d. Plain-meaning or Contextual Ambiguity

While an unclear term can be clarified by contextual evidence, the opposite may also be true: A term that seems clear on its face may turn out to be ambiguous if viewed in the context of the transaction. If the plain meaning of words is clear at face value, some courts, particularly in older cases, refuse to go behind that plain meaning to examine contextual evidence that may undermine the plain meaning. This is called a "four corners" approach because the court looks for meaning within the four corners of the document. However, most modern courts recognize that words do not always have a single, fixed meaning. To base interpretation of the parties' intent on nothing more than the apparent meaning of words is too rigid and may lead the court to a literal interpretation that the parties did not intend. Therefore, if extrinsic evidence is available to cast light on the meaning of language, most modern courts are willing to take it into account in determining what the parties intended. This is known as the contextual approach to interpretation. This does not mean that the court will ignore the plain meaning of the parties' language or that it will ultimately be persuaded to reach an interpretation contrary to the evident plain meaning of the language. The probity of contextual evidence is dependent on the clarity with which the parties have chosen to express their intentions and the degree to which the meaning suggested by the context is consistent with the language used by the parties.

Pacific Gas and Electric Co. v. G. W. Thomas Drayage & Rigging Co., 442 P.2d 641 (Cal. 1968) is a landmark in the development of the principle that the words used by the parties must be interpreted, not at face value, but within the entire context of the transaction. A provision in a contract to repair machinery provided that the repairer would "indemnify" the owner "against all loss, damage, expense, and liability resulting from . . . injury to property" arising in the performance of the contract. The repairer damaged property belonging to the owner. The owner claimed that the indemnity made the contractor liable for this damage, but the contractor argued that the provision was intended to apply only to damage to property of third parties. The trial court interpreted the language of the provision solely at its face value and concluded that its plain meaning did not restrict the repairer's liability to damage to the property of third parties. The Supreme Court reversed the trial court's decision because the trial court had refused to admit extrinsic evidence offered by the repairer (such as evidence of admissions by the owner and prior practices of the parties) that allegedly showed that the parties intended the indemnity clause to apply only to damage to the property of third parties. The court emphasized that the purpose of interpretation is to determine the intent of the parties, which cannot be done if the court refuses to look beyond the meaning of the words as the judge understands them. Words are just symbols of thought, and the context in which they are used can affect their meaning.

The court applied the principles set out in Pacific Gas in Wolf v. Superior Court of Los Angeles County, discussed in section 10.1.3. Recall that the case involved a dispute over royalties between Walt Disney Pictures and Television and the author of the book on which the movie Who Framed Roger Rabbit was based. The agreement under which Disney had bought the rights to the book provided that the author would receive a royalty of 5 percent of "gross receipts." The author claimed that "gross receipts" included the value of consideration, other than cash, that Disney had received from licenses granted for the use of the characters in the movie. The author sought to admit the testimony of an expert that trade usage in the movie industry supported the broader interpretation, but the trial court refused to admit the evidence on the ground that the term (interpreted in light of the writing as a whole) was unambiguous on its face and covered only cash receipts. On the basis of this conclusion, the trial court granted Disney's motion for summary judgment. Citing *Pacific Gas*, the court of appeals reversed the summary judgment and remanded the case for trial, holding that the trial court erred in refusing to consider extrinsic evidence that could show that the term was in fact ambiguous.[16]

Pacific Gas represents a judicial approach that is most receptive to contextual evidence to elucidate the meaning of apparently clear and unambiguous language. However, some courts are more wary of resorting to contextual evidence where there is no facial ambiguity in the language of the contract. For example, in *Wilson Arlington Co. v. Prudential Ins. Co. of America*, 912 F.2d 366 (9th Cir. 1990), the court criticized the broad definition of ambiguity in *Pacific Gas*, which it felt allowed a party too much leeway in creating ambiguity in contract language that is not reasonably understood in more than one way.

§10.5.2 Omitted Terms

If a term is omitted, it simply is not there. The agreement has a gap regarding that particular aspect of the relationship. Say that Lessor and Lessee discussed and wrote out most of the terms of the lease, but did not address the amount of the rent orally or in writing. This could mean that they failed to reach agreement on this crucial term, so that no lease came into being. However, it could also mean that the parties did not consider it necessary to articulate the amount of the rent, because they intended that the rent would be reasonable, based on the fair market rental for commercial property of this kind. In other words, the apparent gap in their agreement may indicate not a lack of consensus, but an intent to adhere to some "off-the-shelf" market or legal standard that they thought of as too obvious to need articulation. To decide which of these two possibilities is the right one, their intent must be determined by looking at the language of the agreement as a whole in light of all the circumstances of the transaction.

---

16. In the end, the admission of the evidence did not help the author. On remand, the jury heard the expert evidence on usage, but nevertheless concluded that the term covered only cash receipts. *See Wolf v. Walt Disney Pictures and Television*, 76 Cal. Rptr. 3d 585 (Cal. Ap. 2008).

§10.5.3 Terms Left for Future Determination

a. Unresolved Terms and "Agreement to Agree"

An unresolved term differs from a vague or unarticulated term in that the parties have not yet settled it, leaving it to be resolved by agreement at some later time. Where parties deliberately postpone agreement on a material term, it cannot be said that they have yet formed a contract, even if they have reached consensus on all the other terms of their relationship. Where the parties agree in principle that they will make a contract, but they have not yet settled a material term, courts sometimes describe their understanding as an "agreement to agree," which is not yet a contract and cannot be enforced. *Joseph Martin Jr. Delicatessen, Inc. v. Schumacher*, 417 N.E.2d 541 (N.Y. 1981), illustrates the approach to an "agreement to agree." A renewal option in a lease gave the tenant the right to renew the lease for an additional five-year period at "annual rental to be agreed upon." The court found this to be an unenforceable "agreement to agree" because the parties had not agreed to the rent for the renewal period and had merely postponed agreement on that term to a future date. The court noted that the parties could have entered into an enforceable contract without fixing the actual amount of the rent, had they provided some standard or formula for determining the rent in the renewal period, or if they had agreed to base the rent on a reasonable or market standard. However, they had not done this. A dissent in the case shows that it can sometimes be a difficult question of interpretation to decide whether the parties actually deferred agreement, or, instead, that they agreed to have the open term settled by a market standard. The dissent argued that because it was clear that the parties intended to create a binding renewal option, the better interpretation was that they had agreed to a renewal at a reasonable rental, to be determined by the market value of the premises at the time of renewal. On this interpretation, the parties made an enforceable contract because they did not defer agreement, but instead settled on an objective standard for fixing the future rent. Restatement, Second, §33, illustration 8 recognizes this distinction. It states that a provision for future agreement on price strongly indicates a lack of intent to be bound, but if the parties manifest intent to be bound, the court should determine a reasonable price.[17]

b. Determination by an Objective Standard

As noted above, we must distinguish an unenforceable "agreement to agree," which is not yet a contract, from a contract in which an omitted

---

17. In some circumstances, even though the court finds that deferral of a term precluded contract formation, it may conclude that the parties did make a commitment to continue to bargain in good faith. This possibility is discussed in section 10.6.

or apparently unsettled term can be resolved by a gap filler or by applying a formula or objective standard. If the parties do not actually defer agreement, but instead agree, expressly or by implication, on some means of settling the term without the need for later agreement between the parties, they have entered into an enforceable contract. The open term can be resolved under the prescribed standard. Where the parties do not make it clear whether their intent is to defer agreement or to resort to a determinate standard for fixing the term, a court must glean their intent by interpretation or construction. As *Joseph Martin Jr. Delicatessen* shows, this can be a difficult question to resolve, and different judges could reach contrary interpretations.

Say, for example, that Owner has completed the plan for a new commercial building and construction is about to begin. Owner has been negotiating with Lessee for a lease of space in the building upon its completion. The parties have reached agreement on the period of the lease, the location and size of the premises, and all other terms — except for the rent to be paid. They wish to enter the lease agreement now, even though the premises will not be ready for occupation for two years. However, neither wishes to agree to a set figure because they do not know what the rental market will be like when the building is completed. We have seen that the parties are not able to bind each other to the lease now if they simply agree to resolve the question of rent closer to the time of occupation. However, they can enter into a binding contract now, even without settling the amount of the rent, if they identify some formula or external source or standard that will allow the rent to be determined by some objective criterion at the appropriate time in the future. For example, they could provide for the rent to be calculated by applying a published economic indicator to a base figure, or they could base the rent on a market standard derived from average rent charged for comparable buildings in the area at the time of occupation, or they could provide for market-rate rent to be set by an independent arbitrator. *Feldman v. Google, Inc.*, 513 F. Supp. 2d 229 (E.D. Pa 2007), provides a good example of a valid future pricing formula. The price term in the contract for advertising on the Google site provided a pricing formula that would set the price of the advertising based on the number of clicks on the advertisement — the more people who clicked on the ad, the higher the rate charged to the advertiser. The court found this to be a practicable method of determining price with reasonable certainty, based on ascertainable objective data.

Of course, the formula or objective standard must itself be clear, so the parties must at least be able to agree now on what criterion should be used. For example, in *Walker v. Keith*, 382 S.W.2d 198 (Ky. 1964), a renewal option in a lease expressed the rent payable for the renewal period in the following exquisite prose: "[R]ental will be fixed in such amount as shall actually be agreed upon by the lessors and the lessee with the monthly rental fixed on the comparative basis of rental values as of the date of the renewal with rental values at this time reflected by the comparative business conditions of the two periods." Unsurprisingly, when the time for renewal arrived, the parties disagreed on the meaning of this language. The court held that the parties had not entered into a renewal contract because the incoherent language did not set out any kind of workable formula or objective standard for calculating the rent, and there was no basis to assume that the parties meant to contract for a reasonable rent.

c. Determination Within the Discretion of One of the Parties

The parties may decide to leave the determination of an open term to the discretion of one of them. If this is done, there is no problem with deferred agreement, because the parties have committed to this method of settling the term, and will not have to try to reach agreement on it at a future time. For example, in the above illustration involving the lease of premises, the parties could have agreed that the rent would be set by the lessor in its reasonable discretion. Of course, the lessee takes a risk in deferring to the lessor's discretion, but the lessor's obligation to act reasonably provides the lessee with some measure of control over the exercise of discretion. (We saw in section 7.9 that even in the absence of an express undertaking to set the rent reasonably, a court will readily imply either a good faith or a reasonableness standard to restrict the lessor's discretion.)

The court upheld a term allowing one of the parties to set the price in *Arbitron, Inc. v. Tralyn Broadcasting, Inc.*, 400 F.3d 130 (2d Cir. 2005). Arbitron provided listener demographics data used by radio stations to attract advertisers. It entered into an agreement with Tralyn, the owner of a radio station, under which Arbitron granted a five-year license to Tralyn to use these reports. The agreement provided that if Tralyn acquired additional radio stations or assigned the license to a successor that owned additional stations, Arbitron had the right to increase the license fee. It did not specify the amount of the increase or provide a standard for determining it. About two years later, Tralyn was bought by a corporation that owned four other stations and it assigned the license to the buyer. Arbitron increased the license fee. When neither Tralyn nor its buyer paid the increased fee, Arbitron sued. The district court granted summary judgment to Tralyn on the grounds that the agreement was unenforceably vague because it contained no basis for determining the amount of the increase in the license fee. The court of appeals reversed the summary judgment. The contract was not too indefinite because it allowed Arbitron to determine the increase, which it must do in good faith. (On remand, the district court found that Arbitron had acted in good faith in determining the fee increase. 526 F. Supp. 2d 441 (S.D.N.Y. 2007), *aff'd* 328 Fed. Appx. 755 (2d Cir. 2009).)

§10.6 IMPLICATION OF AN AGREEMENT TO NEGOTIATE IN GOOD FAITH

We saw in the discussion of an "agreement to agree" in section 10.5, that where parties have not yet resolved a material term of their agreement, the most appropriate conclusion is that they have not yet made a contract. However, even if they have not yet reached final agreement and formed a contract, it is possible that they have made an implied commitment to continue negotiating in good faith to attempt to resolve the outstanding terms.[18] Some courts refuse even to recognize the possibility of implying an obligation to bargain in good faith. They consider that just the possibility of being held to an obligation to keep negotiating could inhibit commercial interaction and could give rise to specious claims if negotiations collapse. Even those courts that are willing to recognize the concept are very slow to imply such an obligation. In most cases, parties who are negotiating understand that no promises are made unless and until they reach final agreement and make a contract. Up to that final stage when the bargain is struck, either party can break off negotiations at will for any reason. Neither has any duty to persist in negotiations or to pursue consensus. Both are free to lose interest, make unreasonable demands, or refuse reasonable offers. The only sanction for uncooperative behavior is the possible loss of the deal. However, it does sometimes happen that the facts are strong enough to imply an obligation to continue good faith negotiations.[19] If so, a court that recognizes the doctrine may find that the parties entered into a preliminary and subsidiary contract in which each gave consideration by forbearing to exercise the right to terminate negotiations at will and promising to negotiate in good faith in an effort to reach agreement on the principal contract.

One case in which the court was willing to find an implied obligation to negotiate in good faith is *Channel Home Centers v. Grossman*, 795 F.2d 291 (3d Cir. 1986). The parties had been negotiating a lease of premises to be

---

18. Section 8.9 discusses the possibility that in a rare case, a court may apply promissory estoppel to compensate a party for reliance on a promise made in negotiations. The underlying premise of the cases discussed in section 8.9 (such as *Hoffman v. Red Owl Stores*, 133 N.W.2d 267 (Wisc. 1965)), was that the promissory estoppel relief was needed to avert injustice because the promisor had violated a duty to bargain in good faith. Therefore, there is some affinity between what is discussed in section 8.9 and in this section. However, the important difference is that in section 8.9 we dealt with a promise (usually implied) by one party and reliance by the other. Here we discuss the possibility that both parties committed to continue good faith negotiations, so there is an implied contract to continue negotiations in good faith.

19. Note that we deal here only with an implied obligation. If parties expressly agree to continue negotiating in good faith, the fact that they did make such a contract is easier to establish.

purchased by the lessor. The lessee executed a letter of intent[20] setting out the proposed terms of the lease and the lessor used the letter to obtain financing for the purchase of the building. The lessee also spent $25,000 in preparations for leasing the premises, based on the lessor's assurance that agreement would be reached. The lessor then let the premises to a third party for a higher rent. The court found that the lessor had assumed and breached a duty to continue good faith bargaining. The parties had worked closely toward concluding the contract, its terms had been largely settled, the lessor had undertaken not to negotiate with others, and it had taken the benefit of using the letter of intent to secure financing. The facts of the case are particularly strong. Courts usually do not reach this conclusion and interpret a letter of intent as nothing more than a nonbinding expression of intent to work toward a contract. *See*, for example, *Burbach Broadcasting Co. of Delaware v. Elkins Radio Corp.*, 278 F.3d 401 (4th Cir. 2002).

It is one thing to recognize a duty to negotiate in good faith, but quite another to determine, once negotiations have broken down, what conduct constitutes a lack of good faith and whether the failure of agreement is attributable to a breach of the duty. In *Apothekernes Laboratorium for Specialpraeparater v. IMC Chemical Group, Inc.*, 873 F.2d 155 (7th Cir. 1989)[21] the court provided some guidance on the general standard imposed by the duty to negotiate in good faith. It said that a party is not required to abandon its interests or to make undesired concessions. Rather the standard contemplates that the party makes a genuine and sincere effort to build on what has been settled and to attempt to resolve differences. In some situations, it is easy to see that a party made no good faith attempt to negotiate. For example, in *Channel Home Centers*, it was clear that the lessor had breached the duty because it leased the premises to another and terminated negotiations. Lack of good faith may also be clear where a party does not abandon negotiations, but behaves obstructively, for example, by raising new objections to settled terms or remaining inexplicably obstinate. Bad faith is much harder to establish if the party is sneaky enough to pretend sincere negotiations with the ulterior resolve not to reach agreement.

Even if a breach of faith can be proved, the victim may have trouble showing the fact and extent of loss. If the obligation to negotiate in good faith is contractual, the victim of the breach could claim expectation damages — a monetary award designed to place him in the economic position he would have been in, had the other party not breached. A plaintiff must establish these damages with reasonable certainty. The problem here is that a promise to negotiate in good faith is not a

---

20. A letter of intent is a document executed by the parties in which they record their preliminary agreement.
21. If you can say the name of this case ten times while standing on one leg you are not too drunk to operate a vehicle.

promise that agreement will be reached, but merely a commitment to make honest efforts to reach agreement. The plaintiff therefore has no guarantee, and probably is unable to prove, that good faith negotiations would have led to a contract. Even if he can prove that, he may find it difficult to show what the ultimate contract terms would have been or what gain he would have made from the contract. As a result, in many cases, the plaintiff cannot recover expectation damages because his alleged loss caused by the breach of the duty is too speculative. However, where a party to a contract cannot prove expectation damages, reliance damages are available as an alternative. (This is discussed in sections 18.7 and 18.8.) As in the case of promissory estoppel, reliance damages for breach of contract reimburse losses and expenses incurred in reliance on the promise. The effect of this is that damages for the breach of a contract to negotiate in good faith usually turn out to be the same as promissory estoppel damages for reliance on a promise to bargain in good faith, discussed in section 8.9.

§10.7 AGREEMENTS TO RECORD IN WRITING

Say that representatives of a corporation and an advertising agency meet to negotiate a contract for the production of a promotional video. By the end of the meeting they have reached consensus on all the broad terms of the relationship. This consensus may be entirely oral, or it may be recorded in a written memorandum or letter of intent. They agree that the corporation's attorney will draw up a written contract reflecting the agreed terms and providing for matters of detail not fully addressed in the negotiations. Upon completion of the document, it will be presented to both parties for approval and signature. A couple of days later, before the writing has been prepared, the corporation changes its mind and no longer wishes to use the agency's services. Can the corporation cancel without legal liability?

If the parties had clearly stated the intended effect of their understanding, this question would be easy to answer. However, if they failed to express its intended legal significance, their purpose is unclear. They could have intended to be bound immediately upon concluding the oral or informal agreement, so the reduction of this agreement to a final writing is just a formality, and they are obliged to execute it provided that it properly reflects what they agreed. Conversely, they may not have intended to be bound by the oral or informal agreement, and did not expect any contract to come into existence until the final, formal writing has been executed and signed. (In this latter case, the parties may or may not have bound themselves to continue to negotiate any unresolved terms in good faith, as discussed in section 10.6.)

The uncertainty of the parties' intention is resolved by the process of interpretation under all the circumstances of the case. For example, in

Cochran v. Norkunas, 919 A.2d 700 (Md. 2007), the court examined the language and context of a letter of intent to sell real property and found that the parties did not intend to be bound until they had executed a formal contract. In *Janky v. Batistatos*, 559 F. Supp. 2d 923 (N.D. Ind. 2008), the parties had engaged in an e-mail exchange during the course of trying to settle protracted litigation. One of them claimed that the e-mails constituted a binding settlement agreement, but the court held that they did not. It found the e-mails to be merely an "agreement to agree" because the parties contemplated the execution of a formal agreement, and the e-mails did not fully and clearly resolve all the terms that would have to be addressed in the formal contract. By contrast, in *Texaco v. Pennzoil*, 729 S.W.2d 768 (Tex. 1987), the court found that the overall circumstances showed that the parties intended to be bound before executing a formal writing. Pennzoil had been negotiating to buy Getty Oil Company. After the parties had reached an agreement in principle, but before the sale had been formally memorialized, Texaco offered Getty stockholders a better deal and acquired the company. Pennzoil sued Texaco for the tort of interference with Pennzoil's contract rights. To succeed in that claim Pennzoil had to prove that it had already made a contract to buy Getty when Texaco intervened and bought the company itself. The court upheld the jury's finding that a contract between Pennzoil and Getty arose at the time of the agreement in principle. Although the parties did contemplate executing a formal writing, the general tone of the negotiations and the parties' public statements justified the conclusion that the parties considered themselves bound immediately, and that the writing was intended merely to memorialize their contract.

§10.8 MISUNDERSTANDING: TOTAL AMBIGUITY

As discussed in section 10.1, interpretation is based on the objective meaning of the language of an agreement, viewed in its context. We do not seek to ascertain what each party thought or believed, but what they reasonably appeared to intend. Therefore, when the parties have different understandings of their agreement, the party with the more reasonable understanding prevails.

However, it sometimes happens that while the parties have diametrically opposite understandings of a term, each of their interpretations is entirely reasonable, and there is no basis for preferring one over the other. In such cases, interpretation and construction cannot resolve the uncertainty in the apparent agreement. If the uncertainty relates to a material aspect of the agreement, the only conclusion to be reached is that no contract came into being.

The classic illustration of this problem is provided by a mid-nineteenth century English case, *Raffles v. Wichelhaus*, 159 Eng. Rep. 375 (Ex. 1864). A buyer and seller agreed to the sale of cotton on board the ship *Peerless* sailing from Bombay. It so happened that there were two ships named *Peerless* due to leave Bombay with a cargo of cotton in October and December, respectively. The seller had the later ship in mind and the buyer the earlier. Neither of them knew of the existence of the second ship. The ship contemplated by the buyer arrived in England first, but the seller did not tender delivery from that ship. In fact, he apparently did not even own that cotton. When the second ship arrived and the seller tendered delivery, the buyer refused to accept the goods, contending that he had bought the cotton on the earlier ship. The seller sued for breach of contract, but the court granted judgment in favor of the buyer on the ground that the misunderstanding prevented a contract from arising.

The doctrinal basis of the opinion is obscure, so it can be (and has been) interpreted simply as an outmoded subjectivist case, in which the court refused to find a contract in the absence of an actual meeting of the parties' minds. However, the case is now widely accepted as illustrating the kind of situation in which even an objective approach cannot resolve the misunderstanding. As each party was reasonable in believing that the agreement referred to a particular ship, and neither had any reason to know of the other's contrary understanding, there is no way to decide whose meaning should be preferred. That is, there is no objective criterion for deciding which ship must have been intended, and a contract on reasonable terms cannot be established. Hence, assuming that the date of delivery is a material term, no contract came into being.

Restatement, Second, §§20 and 201 seek to convey this principle in language so convoluted that it boggles the mind. In essence, the Restatement's rule boils down to this: A material misunderstanding precludes contract formation when the parties were equally innocent in not reasonably realizing the misunderstanding or equally guilty in realizing it but saying nothing. However, if on balancing the degree of fault of the parties, it appears that one is more accountable than the other for knowing of the misunderstanding, a contract must be found to exist on the terms understood by the more innocent party.

The *Peerless* principle may be illustrated by a more modern case involving computer accessories rather than ships sailing from Bombay. In *Konic International Corp. v. Spokane Computer Services, Inc.*, 708 P.2d 932 (Idaho 1985), a Spokane employee was instructed to investigate the purchase of a surge suppressor. After making inquiries of several sellers, in which he was quoted prices ranging from $50 to $200, he had a telephone conversation with a Konic representative, who had a product suitable for the purpose. When asked the price of the suppressor, the Konic salesman said, "fifty-six twenty," by which he meant $5,620. However, the Spokane employee, having been used to hearing prices in the $50 to $200 range, assumed he meant $56.20. The suppressor was ordered and installed before this misunderstanding was discovered. Upon realizing what had happened, Spokane tried to return the suppressor, but Konic refused to take it back. Applying "Peerless" and Restatement, Second, §20, the court held that no contract had been concluded because there had been a complete failure of communication. Each party attached a materially different but reasonable meaning to the manifestation, and neither knew or had reason to know the meaning attached by the other.

§10.9 A TRANSNATIONAL PERSPECTIVE ON INTERPRETATION

Both the UNIDROIT Principles and the CISG approach interpretation as a broad enquiry into the language and overall context of the transaction for the purpose of most accurately determining the parties' intent. Article 4.3 of the UNIDROIT Principles identifies as relevant to interpretation the parties' negotiations, their prior dealings, their conduct subsequent to contracting, and usages. Articles 8 and 9 of the CISG are to similar effect.

The CISG requires a contract to be definite, but several articles (for example, Articles 31 and 32) provide gap fillers that may be used in the absence of specific agreement on various terms. Article 55 recognizes that a reasonable price can be supplied in the absence of a stated price. The UNIDROIT Principles also include gap fillers (for example, in Articles 5.1.6 on quality of performance and 5.1.7 on price). Article 2.1.4 adopts a flexible approach to indefinite terms. It allows the court to settle indefinite terms on a reasonable basis unless it is clear that the parties did not intend a contract until they resolve the indefinite term. Article 2.1.15 of the UNIDROIT Principles generally recognizes that parties are not bound until negotiations are complete, but it does impose liability on a party who negotiates in bad faith.

Examples

1. Claire Cutter decided to remove a large oak tree in her front yard. She hired Jack Lumber, a tree remover, to cut it down. Jack has no liability insurance, so he requires his customers to sign a simple one-page written contract that includes the following standard term, drafted by his attorney: "By signing this contract, the customer assumes sole responsibility for any loss, damage, or injury caused by the performance of work under this contract and indemnifies Jack Lumber for any such claims."

   Claire read and signed the contract. Jack began work a few days later. He negligently failed to take proper precautions to ensure that the tree would fall safely. As a result, it crashed down onto Claire's driveway, pulverizing Jack's truck that was parked there. Jack says that the indemnity clause in the contract makes Claire liable to him for the cost of replacing his truck. Is he right?

2. Fairest Fowls, Inc., is a poultry supplier. Gordon Bleu is a trained chef who owns and operates a restaurant. Gordon had often ordered duck and chicken from Fairest Fowls before. Although he had always ordered the cheaper quality "regular" birds, rather than the more expensive "gourmet" quality, he had always been well satisfied.

Gordon decided to begin serving more exotic game birds at his restaurant. He found a recipe for pheasant and checked Fairest Fowls' price list to see what it cost. The list showed "regular" pheasant for $5.00 per pound, and "plump deluxe" pheasant for $12.50 per pound. Gordon ordered and received 50 pounds of the "regular" quality.[22] He prepared the birds according to his recipe. When they were cooked, he tasted them and discovered that they were tough and uneatable. He called Fairest Fowls to complain. Fairest Fowls' representative expressed surprise that Gordon did not know what was "common knowledge" in the trade — that "regular" pheasants were old, scrawny birds, sold only for making soup. The more expensive "plump deluxe" variety were intended for eating.

After being told this, Gordon asked some other chefs and wholesale poultry suppliers (eight people in all) if they knew about the distinction between "regular" and "plump deluxe" pheasants. Five of them were fully aware of it and used the same terminology in their businesses. Two did not know the terminology, but they knew that you could not buy eatable pheasant for $5.00 per pound. One had never heard the terminology and would have assumed that you could eat regular pheasant.

In light of this, did Fairest Fowls breach the contract by delivering uneatable birds to Gordon?

3. Beau Teek operates a clothing store in a shopping mall under a five-year lease. One of the terms of the lease gives Beau the option to renew the lease for a further period of five years "at a rental to be agreed at the time of renewal in light of the prevailing economic conditions."

Beau properly exercised his option to renew within the time specified in the lease. Although the parties tried to agree on rent for the renewal period, they were unable to reach consensus. The lessor called on Beau to vacate the premises, but he refused to leave and commenced

_____

22. The order was oral, but as the total price of the birds was $250, the statute of frauds is not applicable. Also, because there is no written memorial of agreement, the parol evidence rule does not apply to complicate matters. This same contract, in written form, is used in Example 4 of Chapter 12 to illustrate the impact that the parol evidence rule would have on the resolution of this interpretational issue.

suit for specific performance, requesting that the court order the lessor to extend the lease for a five-year period at a rent determined by the court to be reasonable. Should the court grant the order and determine a reasonable rent?

4. Jill Loppy agreed to sell her old car to Carr Less. They wrote out the following on a piece of paper and both signed it: "Jill Loppy agrees to sell her 1994 Chev to Carr Less for 90 percent of its retail bluebook value."

   The next day, Jill changed her mind and no longer wished to sell her car. She claims that she does not have a binding contract with Carr, and points out that the piece of writing is too skimpy to be a contract because it does not fully describe the car, has an indefinite price term, and omits many essential terms. In particular, it makes no mention of the delivery and payment obligations and warranties. Furthermore, these issues were not discussed by the parties.

   Is this a good argument?

5. Chic A. LaMode is a budding fashion designer. She entered into an agreement with Deadwood Enterprises, Inc., under which Chic granted Deadwood the exclusive right for two years to sell her fashion designs. In consideration, Deadwood promised to pay Chic half of all profits and revenues that it earned from any such sales. Chic delivered all her latest designs to Deadwood, representing well over a thousand different garments.

   Hearing nothing from Deadwood for a month, Chic called to find out how sales were going. She was told that sales were slow, but she should be patient because things would pick up soon. After waiting another month, Chic received a check for $300 from Deadwood, representing 50 percent of earnings for the sale of two designs for small garments. In a note accompanying the check, Deadwood apologized for the small return, saying that it hoped to do better in the future.

   About two weeks later Chic ran into one of her classmates from design school. The classmate told Chic that he had been approaching manufacturers directly, and had sold over $2,000 worth of designs in the last six weeks. Chic would like to dump Deadwood. Can she do so without breaching the contract?

6. Empire Building Products Co., wished to buy a sawmill. A few months ago, it heard that Woody Cutter, a lumberman, was in severe financial distress and had to sell off one of his two sawmills to pay his debts and remain in business. Empire approached Woody and negotiations for the purchase began. After several weeks of meetings, involving attorneys, accountants, and technical advisors, the parties had reached agreement on all the terms of the sale except price. They were deadlocked on this issue. Empire had refused to pay more than $2.5 million. However, Woody refused to take less than $4 million for it. The parties

therefore felt that a cooling-off period would be useful, and they agreed to meet two weeks later to see if they could resolve their differences on price. They signed a joint memorandum drafted by their attorneys, setting out the terms on which they agreed so far, and recording simply that they would meet on a stated day to continue discussions on price.

Empire's board met just before negotiations were to resume. Realizing that Woody was under pressure to sell and that he had no other prospective buyer, the board decided not to budge on the $2.5 million price. They knew that this would be a bargain because they had reliably appraised the mill at a value of $3.5 million. At about this same time, Woody, reviewing his precarious financial position, decided not to hold out for his asking price but to come down as low as $3 million (which he realized was below the mill's true value).

When the meeting took place as arranged, Woody made great efforts to persuade Empire to close the gap between the price proposals, but Empire refused to consider anything above $2.5 million. As a result, the negotiations terminated in failure.

Woody had run out of time. Before he could look for another buyer, his creditors petitioned to put him in bankruptcy so that his assets could be liquidated to pay his debts. As a result, he lost both his sawmills as well as most of his other property. He blames Empire for this calamity because its stubbornness prevented the sale of the one mill that would have allowed him to keep his creditors happy while he tried to make his other mill profitable and to turn his business around. Does Woody have any basis for holding Empire liable for his loss?

7. Molly Fido owned a profitable and successful restaurant. She decided to sell the business and she solicited inquiries by placing an advertisement in a trade journal. Faith Fullness responded and they met to discuss the possible sale. At their initial meeting, Faith examined the premises, equipment, and financial records and the parties had extensive but inconclusive discussions about price. Faith expressed strong interest in buying the business and they agreed to meet again in a week. During that week, Faith visited the restaurant several times to observe the operations, service, and customer traffic. She visited her bank to discuss financing and spoke to a couple of potential investors to see if she could raise some capital. Everything looked promising, and she became enthusiastic about buying the business.

At their next meeting, Faith and Molly discussed the sale in earnest. After some hours they had reached agreement in principle on the basic terms of the sale, which Faith wrote down on a yellow legal paid: Faith would pay Molly $300,000 for the equipment, name, goodwill, lease rights, and transferrable licenses. A third of the price would be paid upon the signing of a written agreement, and the balance would be paid in installments over two years. Faith would take over the business and receive transfer of its assets as soon as possible after the agreement was signed, and Molly would remain on as an employee of the business for six months at a salary to be mutually decided. Faith would immediately instruct her attorney to draw a written contract reflecting these terms and dealing with any necessary matters of detail that the parties had not thought of. Later that day, Faith consulted her attorney and gave her the pad with the notes of the meeting. The attorney promised to set to work as soon as possible on drafting the memorandum of agreement.

The next day, Molly received a call from Ruth Less who had also read the advertisement. Molly told Ruth that she had almost certainly sold the business already, but agreed to meet with Ruth anyhow. After a whole day's negotiations, during which Molly disclosed to Ruth the terms of the understanding with Faith, Ruth made a very attractive offer. She is willing to buy the business for $350,000 cash. Molly would like to accept the offer but is unsure if she has legally committed herself to Faith. Has she?

8. Pierre Less saw the following homemade poster on a lamppost near his home: "Lost Dog — Reward $100. If anyone sees a black poodle with the name tag "Raffles" on his collar, please bring him to 1864 Bombay St. to receive this reward." The next day Pierre came across a black poodle which was scurrying about the neighborhood in a state of distress. He looked at the poodle's collar and saw that he had a name tag showing his name as "Raffles." Pierre took Raffles to the address on the poster but the owner would not accept the dog, claiming that it was not his Raffles. It turned out, by strange coincidence unknown to both parties, that another black poodle named Raffles had wandered from his home and had become lost in the neighborhood. The poodle that Pierre found was the wrong one. Nevertheless, Pierre feels that he went to a lot of trouble on the faith of the poster and he wants his reward. Is he entitled to it?

Explanations

1. The question here is whether the indemnity clause is broad enough to impose liability on Claire for loss suffered by Jack as a result of damage he negligently inflicted on his own property in the course of his performance. Do not be too quick to scoff at Jack's claim — remember that he is handy with a chainsaw.

This Example invokes *Pacific Gas and Electric Co.* (discussed in section 10.5.1) in which the court held that extrinsic evidence must be admitted to decide whether an indemnity provision in a repair contract covered damage to machinery belonging to the owner or applied only to claims of third parties. In Jack's case, there is no similar concern about admitting extrinsic evidence of meaning because neither party offers any such evidence. Where there is no contextual evidence that bears on the meaning of contractual language, the court is necessarily confined to finding meaning within the four corners of the document.

The argument could be made that the language used in this contract is wide enough to cover damage to Jack's truck. It places on Claire "sole responsibility for . . . damage . . . caused by the performance of work under this contract. . . ." This may suggest that she is responsible for any damage that may occur during the course of performance, whatever its kind, and whoever its victim may be. However, this interpretation is overborne by other indications of reasonable intent in the contract.

The words "indemnifies . . . Jack . . . for any such claims" suggest that the contract contemplates that Claire is responsible only to protect Jack from third-party claims. This meaning makes sense in light of the purpose of the clause: work is being done on Claire's property, and she therefore assumes responsibility for any loss suffered by a third party as a result of the work. The trial court in *Pacific Gas* did make the point that "indemnifies" is capable of a broader meaning. However, that case was concerned with damage to the owner's property, not the repairer's. Even if the language can be taken to extend beyond third-party liability, it surely cannot mean that Claire should be responsible for damage caused by Jack to his own property as a result of his own negligence. Such an interpretation seems absurd, and it is most unlikely that Claire reasonably expected a generally worded indemnity provision to impose liability on her for Jack's self-inflicted injury.

In addition to being beyond Claire's reasonable expectations, such a provision is not in the public interest. Courts usually require a very specific disclaimer of liability to exclude damage caused by a party's negligence. (*See* Example 6 of Chapter 13.) A fortiori, a generally worded provision like this cannot give Jack the right to seek compensation from Claire for damage caused by his own negligence. Recall that one of the canons of interpretation is that where the meaning of language is in doubt, a court should choose an interpretation that is reasonable and in accord with public policy.

Finally, if doubt still remains over the proper interpretation of the clause, the *contra proferentum* rule may be used to resolve the doubt against Jack, who is the proponent of the indemnity.

2. This is a sale of goods under the UCC, but interpretation of the agreement is based on principles not significantly different from those applied in modern common law. UCC §1.303 recognizes the primacy of express terms but also articulates the importance of trade usage and course of dealing in the ascertainment of meaning.

This Example is loosely based on the famous chicken case, *Frigaliment Importing*, discussed in section 10.1.3. The principles set out in that case are helpful in resolving this dispute. The ordinary meaning of language is the point of departure, but "regular" has many meanings. Possibly Gordon's prior dealings would support his interpretation that a "regular" bird is eatable, but the prior contracts are not very helpful as a course of dealing because they involved different birds and distinguished "regular" quality from "gourmet," not "plump deluxe." We therefore need to go beyond the bare surface meaning of "regular" to ascribe a meaning to the word. The entire context in which it was used indicates that Fairest Fowls's meaning should prevail.

Sometimes other terms in a contract can cast light on the meaning of the term in dispute, so courts interpret language in the context of the agreement as a whole. For example, in *Frigaliment Importing*, the contract's price term was of some help in supporting the seller's argument that "chicken" was used generically, rather than more narrowly to refer only to fryers. It reflected a different price per pound for the larger and smaller chickens, and the price of the larger chickens was below the market price of fryers. We are not told of any terms in this contract that could explain what the parties meant by "regular," but price could similarly be a helpful indicator of intent.

More significantly, our preliminary information on trade usage strongly supports the meaning claimed by Fairest Fowls. (Of course, if the dispute goes to litigation, trade usage would have to be established by sworn expert testimony, but Gordon's informal survey is good enough for present purposes.) Gordon asked chefs and suppliers what they understood "regular" pheasants to mean. Although they were not unanimous in their response, there seems to be widespread recognition in the trade (defined here as the wholesale poultry market) that the word "regular" refers to pheasants that can be used only to make soup. To prove a trade usage, a party needs only establish it on the preponderance of the evidence. A severe clash of the experts could result in failure to discharge this burden, but there does not need to be unanimity to make a credible showing. As a professional chef who buys poultry from suppliers, Gordon is surely a member of this trade. Even if he did not actually know what "regular" meant, he had reason to know the usage and is bound by it.

3. The term relating to the rental for the renewal period is unquestionably vague. It suggests an "agreement to agree" but it does seek to limit the parties' discretion in negotiating by stating a standard: the economic conditions prevailing at the time of renewal. Although the rent provision in this lease is not as tortured and nonsensical as the one in *Walker v. Keith* described in section 10.5, it may not be any more workable, and a court

may refuse to give effect to the renewal agreement. However, there is a plausible argument for upholding it. After all, the rental provision was not simply an "agreement to agree," and it does refer to what could be seen as a market-based standard, albeit poorly expressed. It is not a great leap beyond their expressed intent for a court to determine and apply a reasonable market standard if they cannot reach agreement. In so doing it upholds an apparent serious intent to be bound, and conforms to the rule of interpretation that favors an effective meaning over one that renders the term ineffective.

4. No. This is a sale of goods, and the UCC is very clear on the question of omitted terms. Section 2.204(3) states that a contract for sale does not fail for indefiniteness, even though terms are left open, provided that the parties intended to make a contract and there is a reasonably certain basis for giving a remedy. In addition, Article 2 contains a number of gap fillers that apply to any agreement of sale in the absence of contrary provisions expressed by the parties. As a result, this skimpy-looking contract is much fuller than Jill suggests.

The goods sold need not be fully described in the writing. Because Jill owned only one 1994 Chev, the identity of the car is not uncertain, and it can be established by oral testimony. The parties need not fix a specific price, as long as they have indicated an objective market standard or some other reasonably certain means of determining it. Section 2.306 validates express agreement for a reasonable price and implies such agreement unless it is apparent that the parties did not intend to contract for a reasonable price. In this case, there is no need to have recourse to a reasonable price, because the parties have expressed a workable market standard. If any of the remaining terms had been settled orally by the parties and just not stated in the writing, oral evidence of their actual agreement would establish these terms. In the absence of any such agreement (and any applicable usage and course of dealing or performance), the UCC provides the following supplementary terms:

a. The seller is obliged to transfer and deliver the goods, and the buyer must accept and pay for them (§2.301).

b. The seller accomplishes her tender of delivery by holding the car available for collection by the buyer at her home at a reasonable hour and for a reasonable period (§§2.308 and 2.503). In addition, because the state requires registration of transfer of title for motor vehicles, the certificate of title must be tendered with proper endorsement.

c. The delivery must take place within a reasonable time (§2.309).

d. The buyer must pay for the goods (in cash) on receiving them (§2.310).

e. The seller warrants that she has good title to the goods (§2.312). (A full discussion of UCC warranties is beyond our scope. It is enough to note that no other warranties are implied in law. The two other implied warranties, set out in §§2.314 and 2.315, are not applicable on the facts of this case.)

5. As you may have suspected, this is a cleverly disguised ripoff of *Wood v. Lucy, Lady Duff-Gordon*, discussed in sections 10.1.1 and 10.2.2. As in *Wood*, we can easily infer from the underlying commercial purpose of the contract that Deadwood impliedly promised to make best efforts to place Chic's designs. However, this is a harder case because it requires us to give content to the obligation to use best efforts. The court did not have to do that in *Wood* because it was not Wood's duty to Lucy that had to be enforced, but Lucy's duty to Wood. (She had sold designs herself in violation of the agreement, and Wood sued her for his share of the profits.) Because the court needed to imply the obligation of best efforts only for the purpose of finding that Wood gave consideration for Lucy's promise, it did not have to decide what would have constituted best efforts. Since Chic asserts that Deadwood has fallen short of best efforts, we need to tackle the question of what level of effort would satisfy Deadwood's obligation.

To decide what constitutes best efforts, we must examine both the reasonable expectation in the trade and the scope and resources of Deadwood's operation. The standard seems to be a blend of reasonable efforts (evaluated objectively) and honest efforts (measured subjectively). We do not have enough information to make a decision on whether Deadwood's efforts would qualify. Deadwood apparently had very little success, and Chic's classmate did better without representation. But that, on its own, is not enough to prove that Deadwood breached its obligation of best efforts. The test is not one of result but of endeavor.

6. The parties clearly did not have a final contract at the end of their first set of negotiations. The price term was unresolved and there is no indication that they intended to be bound unless it was settled. This is not a case in which it would be justifiable to infer that they agreed to a sale at a reasonable or market price.

Therefore, the only basis of liability is that Empire had a duty to continue negotiating in good faith, and that it breached it by standing firm and refusing to negotiate further on the price. Negotiations are normally precursors to legal commitment, and they do not in themselves usually give rise to any legal obligations. In most cases, until the parties actually reach agreement and conclude a contract, neither assumes the legal duty to keep negotiating or to try to reach consensus. This has to be the general rule otherwise it would become difficult to distinguish negotiation from agreement, and entering into negotiations would carry too high a risk of liability. As stated in section 10.6, some courts are concerned enough about hampering negotiations that they will not countenance a legally binding implied obligation to negotiate in good faith. Even courts that do recognize the duty in principle are cautious about implying it except in the most compelling cases.

In this case, there are strong equities favoring the implication of a duty to negotiate in good faith. It would not have been enough merely that the parties had proceeded quite far in their negotiations and had agreed to meet further to try to resolve their differences over the purchase price. However, Empire knew that Woody was in trouble, he needed to sell, and his options for preserving his business were running out as time passed. It deliberately used his distress to obtain bargaining leverage. A great deal of energy had gone into negotiations already, and substantial consensus had been reached. Given Empire's apparent interest in the transaction and its willingness to meet again, Woody could reasonably have expected Empire to return to the bargaining table in a spirit of honest compromise.

If an obligation to bargain in good faith is implied in this case, what must Empire have done to satisfy it? Bad faith is easy to identify in situations where a party simply refuses to negotiate, but it is much more difficult to define in close cases where there is a thin dividing line between bad faith and acceptable commercial hardball. It would not in itself have been bad faith for Empire to make a business decision to stick to its price limit. A party should not be compelled to pay more than it desires. However, when Empire's knowledge of Woody's circumstances and its motive for the refusal to budge are taken into account, its insistence on the low price looks decidedly less wholesome. This is particularly so given Woody's concessions that considerably narrowed the price gap between them.

If Empire did breach its duty to bargain in good faith, what is Woody's remedy? If we find mutual promises to negotiate in good faith, Woody can enforce the obligation as a contract. However, if there are no reciprocal commitments, and Woody is simply claiming that he relied on Empire's promise to bargain in good faith, Woody's cause of action is promissory estoppel. Whichever theory of recovery is used, any damages Woody might recover are likely to be based on whatever reliance loss he can prove. A breach of contract would entitle Woody to expectation damages, but Woody is not likely to be able to prove his expectation interest. Woody would have to make a convincing showing of two uncertain facts to establish a link between Empire's breach and his harm: He must prove not only that a contract probably would have resulted had Empire bargained in good faith, but also that the sale of the mill would likely have enabled him to prevent the loss of his business. In addition, Woody must show the amount of the alleged loss, which is difficult where the present value of the business is in doubt and any value it may have would depend on future management and economic conditions. If such expectation damages cannot be proved, a court is able to award Woody any loss incurred in reliance on the contract to bargain in good faith. These damages would be the same as reliance damages under the theory of promissory estoppel. No reliance expenses or loss of any opportunity to sell to another are indicated in the facts, so Woody does not appear to be entitled to any compensation.

7. When parties have agreed in principle to the essential terms of a contract, but they contemplate executing a formal, signed writing, the legal effect of their oral or informal[23] agreement may be unclear if they do not specifically express the intended effect of the oral or informal understanding. They may have intended no commitment whatever until the writing is signed. Conversely, they may have concluded a contract already, subject merely to the formality of writing. As a third possibility, even if they have not yet made a final commitment, they may at least have undertaken to bargain over the unresolved issues in good faith. Their purpose must be determined from all the circumstances of their interaction.

All the usual avenues should be explored for helpful indications of intent: the language of agreement itself, statements or actions during negotiations, trade usage, and course of dealings or performance. No facts are given to suggest that there is any specific trade usage, and there is no indication of prior dealing or subsequent performance, so the only source of information is the circumstances of the transaction itself, evaluated in light of usual commercial standards. Comment c to Restatement, Second, §27 suggests some of the factors that may help in deciding if a contract was concluded orally or informally. They include considerations such as the extent of the express agreement; the nature and extent of unresolved issues; whether it is normal practice — or, stronger still, legally required — to put a contract of this kind in writing; and the value and complexity of the transaction.

There are some indications that suggest that the parties did not yet intend to be fully bound in contract. The sale of a business is a commercial exchange of a relatively complex and valuable nature, and it seems reasonable to assume that parties would normally expect to sign a written memorandum before being bound. This assumption is strengthened by the fact that a number of known or possible issues were left unresolved. Not only did they deliberately leave open the salary to be paid to Molly for

---

23. The term "oral or informal" indicates that the preliminary understanding could either be oral or in some written form short of a final contract. In this Example, the parties' agreement was oral, but it was noted down in an unsigned writing on a yellow pad. As discussed in section 10.7, an agreement in principle could be even more formal, and could be written up as a signed "letter of intent," which memorializes what has been agreed and provides a framework for further negotiation.

her work in the six months following the sale, but they also anticipated further unidentified issues to emerge when Faith's attorney drafted a comprehensive writing. Some of these may be trivial, but some could be significant and contentious. Of course, these are merely indications. They are not conclusive, and an argument can be made for the opposite result.

It is therefore conceivable that Molly and Faith had entered a binding contract of sale at the conclusion of negotiations. If so, Molly risks legal liability if she reneges. Because this is a close question, let us consider what would happen if there was no final commitment at that stage. Would this mean that there is simply no contract, or do the circumstances suggest that the parties at least agreed to bargain in good faith on unresolved issues, promising to sign unless they encounter a genuine deal breaker? The circumstances are ambiguous and may not be strong enough to deprive Molly of her normal right to abandon these negotiations in favor of a better deal. The facts do not indicate the level of trust, commitment, or reliance discussed in section 10.6 and Example 6. Nevertheless, Faith's dealings with Molly are quite far advanced, oral agreement has been reached on all apparently material terms, and Molly has at least given some implicit assurance that there are no obstacles to the completion of the transaction. It is therefore possible that a court may find that they had reached a stage that precluded Molly from walking away from the deal.

If this is so, it does not invariably mean that Faith is entitled to relief, because she has to prove economic loss. As stated in Example 6, this means that she will have to prove both that the contract probably would have resulted but for Molly's refusal to proceed further, and that following the purchase of the business, she would have been reasonably likely to have made profits in a reasonably certain amount. In the absence of this proof, she may be awarded reliance damages if any reliance loss was suffered. She may have incurred some expenses relating to her inquiries before the second meeting, but these were not incurred in reliance on any promise, and therefore not recoverable. No reliance losses are indicated following the implied promise to bargain in good faith.

8. By placing the poster on the lamppost, Raffles' owner made an offer for a unilateral contract. Pierre accepted it by the act of returning a dog called Raffles to him. (*See* section 4.12.3.) Your initial response to this Example may be that although Pierre intended to accept, he did not in fact do so because return of the wrong dog was not performance of the act required for acceptance. However, the wording of the poster simply offers the reward to anyone who "brings" to the stated address a lost black poodle with the name tag "Raffles" on his collar. Pierre performed that act

exactly as specified. Of course, Raffles' owner intended to refer to his own dog, but his subjective intent is not determinative. (Maybe it could be argued that the reasonable implication from the poster is that the offer called for the return of the dog owned by the offeror. This is a plausible argument, but the literal wording of the poster does not say that.)

However, even if Pierre prevails on the offer and acceptance issue, he is not likely to get his reward. While the objective test holds the owner to the reasonable meaning of his words, it presupposes that it is possible to determine the reasonable meaning of the disputed language. If the parties have different understandings of a word and the court cannot say which of them is more reasonable, the objective test cannot resolve the dispute and the conclusion must be that the agreement is subject to a fatal and irresoluble ambiguity. On the principle of *Raffles v. Wichelhaus*, as embodied in Restatement, Second, §20 (see section 10.8), there can be no contract, even under the objective test, if the double meaning of the name cannot be settled by recourse to its most reasonable meaning and the parties are equally blameless for the misunderstanding. Maybe Raffles' owner can be faulted for the way that he worded his poster, but can he be held accountable for not anticipating the possibility that there could be two black poodles called Raffles in the area?

The Statute of Frauds

§11.1 INTRODUCTION

As a general rule, the law gives effect to oral contracts. Although it is almost always a good idea to record a contract (whether in a physical writing or in some other retrievable form) to facilitate proof of the fact and terms of agreement, for many contracts this record is not a prerequisite to validity or enforceability. However, certain types of contract fall outside this general rule and must be written or otherwise recorded and signed to be enforceable. The requirement of a written record for specified types of contracts[1] entered the law of England just over 300 years ago, through a statutory enactment during the reign of King Charles II. As originally conceived and as applied until the advent of electronic media, the statute contemplated that writing and signature would be in tangible form on paper. The rapid advance of communications technology has required the adaptation of "writing" and "signature" to take account of communication by other, particularly electronic, media. This change is reflected both in court opinions that recognize the recording and signature of contracts in retrievable electronic form as the legal equivalent of writing and signature on paper, and in state and federal statutes that make electronic signatures effective. (This is discussed further in section 11.3.) Therefore, unless the context

---

1. The statute covered many types of transactions besides contracts. We are concerned only with its relationship to contracts.

indicates otherwise, assume that the words "written" and "writing" include other means of recording.

The original motivation for the rule was a concern over fraudulent testimony, hence the original name of the statute, "An Act for Prevention of Fraud and Perjuries," which came to be shortened to "the statute of frauds." Its principal function was to ensure that a person could not seek to enforce an obligation of the kind covered by the statute purely on the basis of unreliable and possibly perjured oral testimony, but would have to produce some adequate written record of the contract. American jurisdictions have adopted statutes modeled on the original statute of frauds, covering much the same types of contracts. Over the years, many states have enacted additional statutes requiring writing for further types of contracts. (For example, a writing is required for a contract granting a security interest in personal property under Uniform Commercial Code (UCC) Article 9. Often, consumer protection statutes require a written and signed contract for particular sales of goods and services, and may even specify that the writing must set out the terms governing certain aspects of the transaction.) Therefore, although one usually refers to "the statute of frauds" in the singular, there could be a number of statutes in existence in a jurisdiction, each prescribing writing for a different kind of contract. In this discussion, we are concerned only with the general common law statute of frauds and with that prescribed by UCC Article 2.

The basic rule of the statute of frauds (referred to from now on as "the statute") is that a contract within its scope may not be enforced unless a memorandum of it is written and signed by the party to be charged. This gives rise to a few initial observations: First, the statute does not require the entire contract to be written, but only a memorandum of it. The degree to which a writing must set out the detail and content of the contract to qualify as a sufficient memorandum is discussed below. Second, only the party who is to be charged, that is, against whom enforcement is sought, needs to have signed it. The signature of the other party is not needed. The question of what constitutes a signature is discussed below. Third, the consequence of noncompliance is usually unenforceability, not invalidity. This distinction is explained more fully in section 11.5.

The statute is intended to prevent a person from enforcing a falsely alleged contract through perjured testimony. However, when a contract was really made orally, the statute can equally be used by the party seeking to evade it. For this reason, there is some concern that the benefits of the statute are outweighed by its potential for abuse. It may be better policy to have no requirement of writing and to allow the factfinder to evaluate the credibility of the oral evidence. These considerations led to the repeal of the statute of frauds in England some time ago, but it continues to survive in U.S. jurisdictions. The principal focus of the courts has been on making it more flexible to better ensure that it efficiently achieves its purpose while cutting down on the opportunities for abuse. Sometimes this has been done by legislation (as happened when the statute of frauds relating to sales of goods was given statutory form in UCC §2.201) but more often, reforms develop in the process of judicial application of the original statutory provisions. Restatement, Second, §§110-137 seek to reflect contemporary judicial thinking on the statute.

To determine whether problems of enforcement exist under the statute, it is useful to ask three questions in the order represented in Diagram 11A.

Diagram 11A

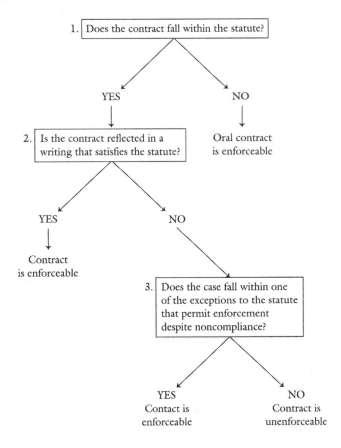

§11.2 THE FIRST INQUIRY: IS THE CONTRACT OF A TYPE THAT FALLS WITHIN THE STATUTE?

The original statute covered six types of contract. Although others have been added in different jurisdictions, these six largely continue to make up the core of modern versions of the statute. This shows remarkable durability, since the types of contract covered by the statute are more reflective of the commercial priorities of seventeenth-century Englishmen than of today's economy. The following subsections of this section describe the six categories of contracts that were included in the original statute and continue to be subject to the statute of frauds. (The categories are listed in Restatement, Second, §110, and expanded upon in subsequent sections.) The first three — contracts for the sale of land or an interest in land, contracts that cannot be performed in a year, and sales of goods — cover more common types of transactions. They are the dominant categories and are more likely to be encountered. The last three — suretyships, executors' contracts to answer for a duty of the decedent, and contracts made upon consideration of marriage, relate to a narrower range of more specialized contracts. Each of the six types of contract is explained below.

§11.2.1 Contracts for the Sale of Land or an Interest in Land

Like many rules derived from older English law, this rule reflects the importance of land as the principal means of wealth in English society at the time. The statute applies not only to a contract to sell land, but also to any other contract under which land is disposed of, as well as a transfer of an interest in land short of full ownership, such as the grant or transfer of an easement or mortgage. A lease is also an interest in land. The statute of frauds usually applies to long-term leases, but commonly is not applicable to short-term leases.

§11.2.2 Contracts That Cannot Be Performed Within a Year

Any contract, irrespective of its subject matter, must comply with the statute if it cannot be performed within a year of its execution. Note that the rule is not confined to contracts in which the performance itself will take over a year, but includes any contract — however short the period of performance may be — in which the performance will not be completed within a year of contracting. Therefore, if on July 1, 2012, a customer makes a contract with a popular resort to rent a room for July 3 and 4, 2013, the contract falls within the statute, even though the performance will last only two days.

The idea behind the one-year rule is probably to ensure that longer-term contracts are recorded. In part, this reflects the concern that parties cannot be expected to remember unrecorded terms as time passes, but it could also be motivated by the expectation that a long-term contract may involve greater economic value. Commentators have pointed out that if the rule is motivated by this goal, it does not achieve it very effectively because the one-year period does not relate to the length of performance but the period between the making of the contract and the end of performance. Therefore, the rule just as much governs a short, inexpensive transaction (such as the hotel booking used in this illustration) as a long, expensive one. Whatever the thinking behind the rule, it is obviously arbitrary and if rigidly applied, could result in absurd distinctions. For example, if an employment contract is entered into on Monday, for a year's employment beginning that day, the statute is not implicated. However, if the employment period is to begin on Tuesday, the statute applies.

While some courts are willing to apply the rule quite technically, others dislike its arbitrariness and potential to upset genuinely agreed oral contracts. Where possible, a court that dislikes the rule will do what it can to interpret the contract as performable within a year of its making. C. R. Klewin, Inc. v. Flagship Properties, Inc., 600 A.2d 772 (Conn. 1991) is an example of such a case. The developer of a major construction project (consisting of a hotel, a convention center, and a large number of commercial and residential buildings) contracted with a general contractor to manage the construction. A written contract was executed for the first phase of the construction, but the contract for the second phase was oral. The developer dismissed the contractor at the end of the first phase. When the contractor sued for breach of contract, the developer applied for summary judgment on the basis that, given the scale of the project, the contract clearly could not be performed in a year. (The contractor conceded that the project would take between three and ten years to complete.) The Supreme Court reversed the trial court's decision that the statute of frauds barred enforcement. The Supreme Court said that because the rule was difficult to justify, it should be confined as narrowly as possible. It should apply only where the contract expressly specifies that performance is required to extend more than a year beyond its execution. In the absence of such a clear contractual requirement, the contract should be treated as legally performable within a year, even if, as a matter of fact, performance cannot be completed within that period and the parties did not expect it to be.

Many courts do not treat a contract of indefinite duration as falling within the one-year rule if the contract performance could conceivably be completed within a year, or the contract could be terminated within a year, say, by the death of one of the parties, or by a notice of termination. For example, in Leon v. Kelly, 618 F. Supp. 2d 1334 (D.N.M. 2008), the court held that the statute of frauds did not apply to a partnership agreement for an indefinite term. The contract was capable of being completed in a year, even though the agreement contemplated a long-term business endeavor expected to last for several years. However, not all courts adopt this approach. Some courts do not focus on the possibility that the contract could be performed in a year, but instead base their determination on the contemplated duration of the contract according to the parties' understanding and the nature and circumstances of the contract. For example, in *Tucker v. Roman Catholic Diocese of Lafayette-In-Indiana*, 837 N.E.2d 596 (Ind. App. 2005), the plaintiff had been sexually abused as a child by a church employee. She agreed with the church not to pursue legal recourse in exchange for the church's promise that it would strip the abuser of his duties and would ensure that he had no contact with children at the parish. The church did not honor its promise and the victim sued, claiming emotional distress damages for breach of contract. The court of appeals upheld the trial court's dismissal of the complaint. The diocese could have fired the abuser within the year, but its promise to ensure that he would not have contact with parish children was an ongoing obligation with no time limit. It therefore could not be treated as performable within a year.[2]

As discussed in section 11.2.3, UCC Article 2 has its own statute of frauds in §2.201 which applies where the price of the goods sold is $500 or more. Section 2.201 does not refer to the one-year rule, so it is not clear if a contract for the sale of goods that cannot be performed within a year of its making would be subject to the common law statute as well. (Recall that under UCC §1.103(b) general principles of common law apply to sales of goods unless displaced by the provisions of the Code.) The significance of this is that if the sale agreement cannot be performed within a year, it would be subject to the common law statute, even if the price of the goods is less than $500. If the price is $500 or more, the sale agreement would have to satisfy the requirements of both §2.201 and the common law. This could make a difference if the common law requirements are more stringent.

§11.2.3 Contracts for the Sale of Goods

As mentioned above, contracts for the sale of goods are no longer covered by the traditional statute of frauds but are provided for in UCC §2.201. Section 2.201(1) requires compliance with the statute where the total price of the goods sold under the contract is $500[3] or more, so the price of all items sold

---

2. Apart from noncompliance with the statute of frauds, the court found other problems with the plaintiff's case. The contract was invalid for lack of consideration because the statute of limitations had run on the plaintiff's claim, so she suffered no legal detriment in forbearing from suit. In addition, the court held that emotional distress damages are not available for breach of contract. (*See* section 18.13.)
3. Five hundred dollars is the amount that was set in the original enactment of Article 2 about 60 years ago, and it has never been increased to account for inflation. The failed attempt to revise Article 2 in 2003 would have increased the amount to $5,000.

under the contract must be added together to determine if it is subject to the statute. If the price consists of property other than cash, the property must be valued to establish the price.

The scope of Article 2 was discussed in section 2.7.2. In many cases a contract obviously is or is not a sale of goods. However, sometimes the nature of the contract is not so clear. This could be because it is not certain if the item sold qualifies as goods (as opposed to intangible rights or real property), or it is not certain that the transaction is a sale (as opposed to, say, a lease). It could also be because the transaction is a hybrid — it consists of both a sale of goods and the rendition of services related to them. As explained in section 2.7.2, most courts apply a predominant purpose test to decide if a hybrid transaction is subject to Article 2. Article 2 applies if the sales component is dominant, but it does not apply if the central purpose of the contract is the supply of services, with goods furnished incidentally to the service.

National Historic Shrines Foundation v. Dali, 4 UCC Rep. Serv. 71 (N.Y. 1967) is a good example of how a statute of frauds argument can hang on the question of scope. Salvador Dali, the famously eccentric surrealist painter, made an oral contract with the foundation to execute a painting of the Statue of Liberty on a television show. The painting would then be sold to raise funds for a museum. Dali reneged and defended a suit for breach of contract on the basis that the oral contract was unenforceable under §2.201. He argued that the contract was for the sale of his painting which was worth considerably more than $500. The court rejected this argument. It found that the contract was for Dali's services in performing on TV. The fact that a painting would be created in the course of this performance was merely incidental to this purpose.

§11.2.4 Contracts to Answer for the Debt or Obligation of Another

This provision covers suretyship contracts. A surety is a person who promises the creditor to pay another person's debt, so that if the other person fails to pay the debt, the surety is obliged to pay it. For example, Borrower asks Lender for a loan. As a condition of lending money to Borrower, Lender requires someone else to agree to pay back the loan if Borrower defaults. Borrower persuades Mom, his mother, to promise Lender to pay Lender if Borrower fails to do so. Borrower is primarily liable on the loan, and is called the principal debtor. Mom, as surety, is secondarily liable. She is, in effect, a backup debtor who assumes the duty to pay a debt that she would not otherwise owe. The secondary nature of the surety's obligation is important to application of the statute. If the promisor is primarily liable on the debt (for example, she is a joint debtor) she is not a surety and the statute does not apply. (Sometimes the term "guaranty" is used synonymously with "suretyship." These two types of transactions both involve a commitment by a person to pay the debt of another, and they are very similar. The subtle differences between them need not concern us here. They both constitute contracts to answer for the debt of another and are subject to the statute.)

There are two justifications for subjecting a suretyship agreement to the statute of frauds. First, the formality of writing serves a cautionary function by alerting the surety that she is undertaking a serious, legally enforceable commitment. Second, it serves the usual evidentiary function of the statute of frauds by preventing the assertion of a possibly bogus claim that a person agreed to pay the debt of another.

The statute relating to suretyship has some difficult qualifications and nuances which we will not get into here. However, one of them is noted briefly: The statute presupposes that the surety undertakes the suretyship for the primary purpose of accommodating and benefiting the principal debtor. Therefore, if the main purpose of the suretyship is to serve the surety's own financial interest — that is, the surety receives a direct economic benefit — the statute does not apply and an oral undertaking is enforceable. This principle only applies if the economic interest of the surety is the main purpose of the suretyship. It is not enough that the surety has some personal stake or self-interest in undertaking liability for the debt.

§11.2.5 Contracts of Executors or Administrators to Answer for the Duty of Their Decedents

The type of contract covered here is one in which the executor or administrator of an estate assumes personal liability to a creditor of the decedent for a debt or obligation incurred by the decedent before his death. That is, the executor promises the creditor that if the estate does not have the funds to pay the debt, he will pay it himself. The statute only applies to debts that the decedent incurred, not to new debts incurred by the estate itself. This provision is really just a specialized version of the suretyship provision discussed in section 11.2.4, because the executor undertakes to answer for the debt of the decedent.

§11.2.6 Contracts upon Consideration of Marriage

This category does not cover a promise of marriage, which can be and usually is oral. (It is sometimes performed by the ritual of one of the parties going down on one knee and proffering a glittery bauble to the other, but that formality is not required by law.) Rather, it relates to a contract in consideration of marriage in which the prospective spouses agree to a marriage settlement or to financial arrangements relating to the marriage. It also covers a promise by a third person (say, a parent of one of the spouses) to settle property or money upon the spouses in consideration of their marriage. The requirement that the contract is in consideration of marriage means that the statute applies only to prenuptial contracts motivated by the impending marriage.

§11.3 THE SECOND INQUIRY: IF THE STATUTE APPLIES, IS THE CONTRACT REFLECTED IN A WRITING THAT SATISFIES ITS REQUIREMENTS?

To satisfy the general statute, the written memorial of agreement must satisfy a number of requirements. The requirements of UCC §2.201 are similar, and any significant differences are noted below. The requirements are:

§11.3.1 A Written Memorandum

As mentioned in section 11.1, although writing is traditionally the inscription of words on a tangible surface, such as paper, it is clear, in contemporary law that "writing" includes a retrievable recording in an electronic or other medium. The word is used in that sense in this chapter. There is no particular formality needed for the writing as long as it contains the statute's minimum required content and signature. For example, you may recall that the land sale contract in *Lucy v. Zehmer* (the joke case discussed in connection with the objective test in section 4.1.6) was written on the back of a restaurant guest check. The writing need not be executed with the deliberate purpose of evidencing the contract. It need not be the joint product of the parties or even delivered to the other party. It could be an internal memorandum or a document written for some other purpose than to satisfy the statute. It need not be written at the time of contracting. (Of course, the fact that it was not a purposeful contemporaneous attempt to record the agreement could affect its credibility, but this is a different issue.) Note, however, as discussed in section 11.3.3, a memorandum written and signed by just one of the parties only satisfies the statute to the extent that enforcement is sought against the party who signed it.

The written memorandum of the contract need not be in a single document, so it is possible to satisfy the statute by a series of correspondence or other linked writings. It must be clear from the face of the writings that they all refer to the same transaction and, taken together, they must contain all the content required by the statute, including a signature on at least one of them. Some courts require the signed document to refer to the others so that the signature can be attributed to the unsigned document without extrinsic evidence. Other courts are not as strict and require only that it is apparent from the writings that they refer to the same transaction. Oral testimony can then be used to prove that the signature was intended to authenticate the content of the unsigned writings. Provided that the writing was made, the statute is satisfied even if it has been lost by the time of litigation. Its prior existence and its contents can be proved by oral testimony. This may sound like a strange rule, given that the principal purpose of the statute is to require a written record to prevent a false allegation of contract. It could be just as difficult to detect perjured evidence of a lost writing as it is to expose a bogus claim that a contract was made. Nevertheless, when there is convincing evidence that a writing did exist at one time, this is one further safety valve that prevents abuse of the statute by a party who seeks to escape a genuine contract.

§11.3.2 The Content of the Memorandum

Evidentiary adequacy for the purpose of satisfying the statute is set quite low. All that is needed is enough writing to show the existence of a contract. Therefore, the writing does not have to contain every term of the contract, nor need it be completely clear and unambiguous in all respects. The common law and UCC have different standards for sufficiency of the memorandum, but, as usual, the looser UCC test tends to influence courts even in common law cases. Therefore, in some jurisdictions, the difference is fading.

At common law, it is generally required that the writing must at least identify the parties and the nature of the exchange, and it must set out all or at least most of the material terms. Provided that there is enough substance to show a contract, missing or unclear terms can be proved by oral evidence or otherwise resolved by the process of interpretation and construction discussed in Chapter 10.

UCC §2.201(1) provides for a less stringent standard. The only term that must be stated in the writing is the quantity of goods sold, so that the contract is not enforceable beyond the stated quantity. Beyond that, §2.201 demands only that "there is some writing sufficient to indicate that a contract for sale has been made between the parties." It expressly states that a writing is not insufficient merely because it omits any term other than quantity, or incorrectly states any term.

Because the level of writing needed to satisfy the statute is quite minimal, it is important to recognize that a writing sufficient for the purposes of the statute may not be clear and full enough to ultimately convince the factfinder that a contract was made on the terms alleged. Compliance with the statute is a different issue from adequate proof of the contract for the purpose of relief. If the writing is skimpy or uncertain, the statute of frauds may be only the first hurdle to be jumped by the party seeking enforcement. Thereafter, the gaps or indefiniteness in the writing will have to be supplemented or cured by interpretation and persuasive extrinsic evidence.

§11.3.3 Signature

a. The Basic Rule of Signature

It is not necessary that the enforcing party signed the writing, because the evidentiary role of the statute is satisfied as long as the party disputing the existence of the contract has signed it in person or through an agent. A signature is any mark or symbol placed by the party on the writing with the intention of authenticating it, so a full and formal signature is not needed. Initials, a logo, or even an "x" is enough. The signature does not have to be placed on the writing after the terms are written down, so a party can adopt a symbol (such as a logo at the top of the page) by writing the terms of the contract on the page. UCC §1.201(37) codifies this principle by defining "signed" to include "any symbol executed or adopted with present intention to adopt or accept a writing." Restatement, Second, §134 is to the same effect. It defines "signature" as "any symbol made or adopted with an intention, actual or apparent, to authenticate the writing as that of the signer."

When the writing consists of several pieces of paper or other records (such as a series of notes, letters, or e-mails), it is not necessary that every piece has been signed, provided that it appears from the writings themselves that they all refer to the same transaction. Some courts require that the signed writing actually makes some reference to unsigned ones, but other courts require only that the writings, on their face, relate to the same transaction.

b. Electronic Signatures

Where the writing is not in tangible form, but is recorded in an electronic or other medium, the concept of signature has been adapted by federal and state legislation to include other means of verifying authorship and adopting the recorded information. The federal statute, the Electronic Signatures in Global and National Commerce Act, 15 USC §§7001 to 7031 (called "E-Sign") applies to any transaction involving interstate or foreign commerce. States have enacted equivalent statutes, either by drafting their own statutes or by adopting a uniform statute, the Uniform Electronic Transaction Act

("UETA"). The principal focus of the federal and state statutes is to give legal effect to electronic signatures, and they declare that a signature or other record relating to a transaction may not be denied legal effect solely because it is in electronic form (15 USC §7001(a); UETA §7). This language indicates the limited scope of the statutes. They provide that to the extent that the law requires a signature, it may not deny effect to a signature in electronic form. The statutes do not purport to deal with the question of whether the signature could be denied effect for some other reason.

"Electronic signature" is defined as "an electronic sound, symbol, or process, attached to or logically associated with a contract or other record and executed or adopted by a person with the intent to sign the record" (15 USC §7006(5); The definition in UETA §2(8) is almost identical). The important point to note about this definition is that it allows a distinction to be made between an identifying symbol that is automatically generated by a computer (such as the "from" line on an e-mail or the sender's identification printed at the top of a fax message) and a deliberate placing or adoption of a signature on the communication.

While the sender's deliberate typing of his name on the e-mail is quite clearly a signature, his automatically generated name (such as in the message header) is less obviously so. However, an automatically generated name can qualify as his signature if he adopts it with intent to sign the record. If the name and message are genuine, this adoption should usually occur as a matter of course, even if the sender has no specific subjective awareness that he is "signing" the communication. For example, in *International Casings Group, Inc. v. Premium Standard Farms, Inc.*, 358 F. Supp. 863 (W.D. Mo. 2005) the court, applying UETA, found that the statute of frauds was satisfied by e-mail correspondence. The sender of the e-mails did not challenge their authenticity, and there was no question that they were forged. The court held that when the sender hit the "send" button, it intended to adopt its name in the e-mail header to authenticate the e-mail, and that the header qualified as a signature. Although the automatic generation of a name may be more commonplace in electronic communications than it is in writing on paper, this concept is not new. The general definition of signature, described in section 11.3.3a, also contemplates that signature can come about if, by writing the terms of the contract on a piece of paper with his preprinted name or identifying symbol, the writer apparently intended to adopt it to authenticate the record. Note, however, that the mere fact that a party's name appears in an e-mail does not automatically mean that the party has signed the e-mail. It must be established that in generating his name, the party reasonably intended to adopt or accept the writing. For example, in *Buckles Management, LLC v. Investordigs, LLC*, 728 F. Supp. 2d 1145 (D. Colo. 2010), the court held that a defendant's name in an e-mail string did not qualify as a signature under E-Sign, because the defendant's name was not intended as a signature. The defendant had sent an initial internal e-mail outlining terms proposed for a contract. The e-mail was then forwarded to various people, including the plaintiff, by a junior employee of the defendant (who had no authority to bind it). The court found that the mere fact that the defendant's name was on one of the e-mails in the string was not enough to constitute his signature.

With electronic signatures, as with handwritten or printed signatures on paper, a party may deny that the symbol is his signature. He may challenge the genuineness of his signature, claiming that it was forged or placed on the record by someone else without authority, or he may assert that his name or symbol on the record was not placed there with the reasonable intent to adopt or accept it. (As mentioned above, this is a particular problem where a name is automatically generated by a computer program.) In the field of electronic communications, problems of forgery and automated identification require special considerations and technological solutions. However, it is important to remember that the evidentiary issue of proving the signature exists with tangible documents as well as electronic records, and to recognize that this involves a problem of proof rather than the legal question of recognizing the validity of an electronic signature. In *International Casings* the court, in accepting an e-mail header as a signature, recognized the possibility that an e-mail message can be fraudulently generated in the name of a person who did not send it. However, the court noted that forgery is not confined to electronic communications, and this possibility should not make an e-mail header insufficient as a matter of law where the alleged sender does not successfully impugn its genuineness.

c. Article 2's Exception to the Signature Rule Where Both Parties Are Merchants

Section 2.201(2) recognizes one situation in which a writing can be enforced against the party who did not sign it. All the following requirements must be met: Both parties are merchants; within a reasonable time of the oral contract, one of the parties sends a written confirmation to the other, which is signed by the sender and otherwise satisfies the statute as against the sender; the recipient has reason to know its contents; and the recipient does not give written notice of objection to it within ten days of receipt.

In other words, although the contract could normally be enforced only against the sender, as signatory, when both parties are merchants, the non-signing recipient is also bound by the conduct of failing to protest after receiving a writing that should have been read. *Bazak International Corp. v. Tarrant Apparel Group*, 378 F. Supp. 2d 377 (S.D.N.Y. 2005) illustrates the operation of the merchant rule where the party seeking enforcement of the contract sends the confirmation by e-mail. The parties made an oral contract for the sale of a large number of pairs of jeans. When the seller failed to deliver the jeans, the buyer sued. The seller moved for summary judgment on the grounds that the oral contract did not comply with §2.201. The buyer successfully invoked the merchant exception in §2.201(2). The buyer had sent an e-mail to the seller setting out the terms of the sale and containing the buyer's typed name. The parties were clearly merchants, and the buyer's e-mail was sent within a reasonable time. The e-mail was a written confirmation containing the essential terms of the contract, signed by and sufficient against the sender. The focus of the opinion was whether §2.201(2) could be satisfied by an e-mail. The court found that it could be. Although an e-mail is an intangible form of communication, it is stored on the computer, is objectively observable, and can be rendered tangible. The court also found that the UCC definition of "signed" is broad enough to include the typed signature on the e-mail. Finally, the court found that the buyer had shown sufficiently for the purpose of overcoming the seller's application for summary judgment that the seller had received and had reason to know of the content of the e-mail, and had not objected to it.

§11.4 THE THIRD INQUIRY: IF THE STATUTE APPLIES AND IS NOT COMPLIED WITH, DOES THE ORAL CONTRACT FALL WITHIN ANY OF ITS EXCEPTIONS?

When a contract falls within the statute and fails to comply with it, the contract is unenforceable as discussed in section 11.5. However, there are a few exceptions that permit enforcement despite the lack of a sufficient signed writing. These exceptions are narrow and specific and apply only if the party seeking enforcement can establish their elements. Each of the exceptions is justified on one or both of two grounds. One is evidentiary — the circumstances recognized by the exception tend to prove that a contract was made despite the lack of writing. The other is the protection of a party who incurred a detriment in justifiable reliance on the contract.

§11.4.1 The Part Performance Exception

Following an oral contract, the parties may begin performance, which may provide reliable evidence that a contract was made. Even if the statute applies to the transaction, the performance satisfies its function, so that refusal of enforcement would be too rigid and would allow a party to renege on an established contract through a technical application of the statute. For the part performance exception to apply, the parties' performance must be unequivocally referable to the oral agreement. That is, there must be a very clear showing that the conduct does in fact refer to and demonstrate the existence of a contract. Many courts impose the additional requirement that the party seeking to enforce the oral agreement suffered some degree of prejudice in rendering performance in reliance on the agreement. The part performance exception is commonly raised in relation to contracts for the sale of land. Some courts recognize the exception in relation to other contracts subject to the statute, but others do not. For example, in *Coca Cola Co. v. Bayback's International, Inc.*, 841 N.E.2d 557 (Ind. 2006) the court, stating that this reflected the majority approach, refused to apply the exception to a contract that could not be performed within a year of its making.

Because the part performance doctrine is equitable in derivation, some courts apply it only where the plaintiff seeks the equitable remedy of specific performance, and not where the claim is for the legal remedy of damages. Some courts recognize an exception only if the party seeking enforcement has fully performed. The broad point is that at common law, part performance may allow enforcement of a contract that does not satisfy the statute, but the exception can be difficult to establish, and there are restrictions on its application.

Two subsections of §2.201 give limited recognition to the part performance exception when the contract is for the sale of goods. The two exceptions are narrow and apply only in specific circumstances. The first, in §2.201(3)(a), covers cases in which the seller has begun the manufacture of goods that are specially made for the buyer and not otherwise easily saleable. The second, in §2.201(3)(c), allows enforcement of the contract only to the extent payment for the goods has been made and accepted, or goods have been delivered and accepted. This means that if one party has performed and the other has accepted that performance, the party who performed can enforce the contract to recover the consideration due for the performance rendered. If only part performance has been made (that is, only part of the goods have been received, or only part of the price has been paid), the contract is only enforceable with respect to what has been done, but cannot be enforced with regard to the balance.

§11.4.2 The Judicial Admission Exception

As the statute is intended to guard against a fraudulent assertion of contract, it would seem logical that a party who admits the contract in pleadings or testimony should not be allowed to raise the statute as a defense. Nevertheless, the common law has been loath to embrace such a rule because of a concern of its impact on litigation. First, it has been perceived as creating an incentive for perjury because a party may choose to deny the contract to avoid losing the defense by an admission in litigation. Second, because a party can be compelled to disclose information in litigation, the admission may not be truly voluntary. These arguments have been criticized as inadequate to overcome the obvious relevance of admissions in litigation. The UCC has not followed them, and it does recognize a limited exception for judicial admissions under certain conditions.

The exception is specific and narrow. Section 2.201(3)(b) permits enforcement of a contract against a party, despite noncompliance with the statute if that party admits in "pleading, testimony or otherwise in court" that a contract was made. The contract is enforceable only to the extent of the quantity of goods admitted. Note that the admission must be made in connection with litigation, and the exception does not extend to admissions in other circumstances. (Of course, a written admission outside of litigation may itself be a memorandum satisfying the statute, but an oral admission in those circumstances has no effect.)

One of the more difficult issues that has arisen in connection with this exception is what constitutes an admission. Clearly, if the party breaks down under cross-examination and concedes the contract, an admission has been made. However, it could also be taken as an admission if a party's pleadings raise a defense on the merits (such as claiming that the other party breached by failure to deliver), rather than clearly denying the existence of a contract. There are also a number of procedural complexities, not addressed here, raised by the question of whether a party can be compelled to admit or deny the contract.

§11.4.3 The Protection of Reliance: Estoppel and Promissory Estoppel

Under some circumstances, equitable estoppel may be used to protect reliance on a false factual assertion. For example, if one of the parties represents to the other that she has made a signed written note of the contract, and the other reasonably relies on this assertion. However, as equitable estoppel is traditionally confined to an assertion of fact, it is generally only helpful in a narrow range of situations.[4] Promissory estoppel is more useful when there is no factual representation inducing reliance, but one of the parties justifiably relies on the oral contract as a promise, thereby suffering some detriment.[5]

Restatement, Second, §139, a modified version of §90, recognizes promissory estoppel in this context. The elements of promissory estoppel in this situation are similar to those in §90: A promise reasonably expected to induce reliance, the inducement of justifiable reliance on the promise by

---

4. The elements and purpose of equitable estoppel are explained in section 8.4.
5. Promissory estoppel is discussed fully in Chapter 8.

the other party, and the need to enforce the promise to prevent injustice.[6] Section 139, by its express language, appears to be stricter than §90 because it specifically stresses the need for reliance of a substantial character, reasonableness by the promisee, and foreseeability of the reliance by the promisor. Despite the articulation of these requirements, §139 is not really that different from §90 in this respect, because, as the discussion in Chapter 8 shows, these elements are implicit in §90 as well.

However, §139 does have one additional element that is unique because it relates to the evidentiary purpose of the statute. One of the factors that the court should take into account in deciding to grant promissory estoppel relief is whether the promisee's conduct in reliance or other available evidence corroborates the existence of a contract. This suggests that even where part performance does not on its own create an exception to the statute, it could be a relevant factor in deciding on whether to grant promissory estoppel relief.

Section 139 does not advocate a routine application of promissory estoppel to circumvent the statute. In most cases, a party is simply not justified in relying on an oral contract which he should reasonably have known must be in writing. Even if the reliance was justified, the detriment that he suffered in reliance may not be substantial enough to merit enforcement of the contract. The remedy of restitution can be used to restore any benefit of performance rendered under the unenforceable contract, so full enforcement of the contract usually exceeds what is needed to avert any injustice resulting from reliance on the oral contract. Some cases suggest that it may be almost impossible for a party to use promissory estoppel as the basis for enforcing an oral contract. For example, in the *Coca Cola* case cited in section 11.4.1 the court followed a line of cases that declined to apply promissory estoppel to enforce the oral contract itself, and confined relief to substantial independent detriment. It is not clear from the opinion what that independent detriment might be, because the court found that the plaintiff was seeking to enforce the very bargain that was rendered unenforceable by the statute and refused relief. Similarly in *Brown v. Branch*, 758 N.E.2d 48 (Ind. 2001) the court refused to apply promissory estoppel to enforce an oral contract to convey land. The court said it was not enough for the plaintiff to show that breach of the oral promise resulted in a denial of her rights under the contract. She must show a substantial and independent injury for which justice demands relief. As in the *Coca Cola* case, because the plaintiff's claim was for enforcement

---

6. In *Tucker v. Roman Catholic Diocese of Lafayette-In-Indiana*, discussed in relation to the one-year rule in section 11.2.2, the plaintiff also asserted the promissory estoppel exception to the statute of frauds. The court of appeals upheld the trial court's dismissal of the claim on this ground as well. Because the statute of limitations had run on the plaintiff's claim, she could not have sued anyhow, so she suffered no detriment in forbearing from suit in reliance on the promise, and there was no need to enforce the promise to prevent injustice.

of the benefit of the bargain, the court did not have occasion to explain what this other independent reliance might be.

It is not clear if promissory estoppel can be used to enforce a contract for the sale of goods that fails to comply with §2.201. As a doctrine of common law, promissory estoppel could supplement the provisions of §2.201 by virtue of §1.103(b) which recognizes general principles of common law unless they are displaced by the Code's particular provisions. There is no provision in §2.201 that specifically excludes promissory estoppel as a basis for excepting the sale from the statute. However, some courts have reasoned that an intent to exclude promissory estoppel can be inferred from the first words of §2.201, "[e]xcept as otherwise provided in this section," followed by the listing of a defined set of specific exceptions in §2.201(3).

§11.5 THE IMPACT OF NONCOMPLIANCE WITH THE STATUTE

There is some variation in the statutes of different states and some confusion in the caselaw about the effect of failure to satisfy the statute. The noncompliant contract is sometimes said to be invalid or void — that is, a legal nullity, of no force or effect. Sometimes it is called unenforceable — that is, a contract that is valid, but cannot be sued on and enforced in court. Some cases use these words interchangeably. It is more generally accepted that noncompliance with the statute does not void the contract, but merely makes it unenforceable. Although there are instances in which consequences follow from characterizing a contract as void rather than unenforceable, the distinction is not practically significant for most purposes. In either case, the plaintiff is unable to sue on the contract.

If the contract is unenforceable for noncompliance with the statute, the party seeking to rely on the statute as a defense cannot raise it by a general denial. It must be specifically pleaded as an affirmative defense, otherwise it is waived. If the defense is raised and succeeds, the contract cannot be enforced. If neither party has given or done anything under the contract, the practical effect of nonenforcement for most purposes is to put an end to any obligations that the parties might otherwise have had under the contract. However, sometimes a party may have rendered some performance before the contract was declared unenforceable. (Obviously, this partial performance could not have been sufficient to except the contract from the statute as discussed above.) Once the contract is unenforceable, the party who received the performance no longer has a right to keep it. It must therefore be returned under principles of restitution. If it was a money payment or the delivery of property still in the hands of the beneficiary, the money or the property itself must be restored. If it was services or property that has been consumed, restitution is usually measured based on its market value, but the court has the discretion to value it differently if fairness so dictates.[7]

§11.6 THE EFFECT OF THE STATUTE OF FRAUDS ON MODIFICATIONS OF A CONTRACT

Obviously, neither party can unilaterally change the terms of a contract after it has been made, but a contract can always be modified by agreement between the parties. A modification is a contract in itself, distinct from the original contract that it changes. As a separate contract, it is subject to most of the usual requirements of contract law for formation and validity.[8] As a general rule (unless the statute of a particular state provides otherwise), this means that the statute of frauds applies to modifications. Therefore, whether or not the original contract was subject to the statute, if the contract as modified falls within the statute, the modification must be recorded in a writing sufficient to satisfy it.[9] For example, under an original contract, entered into on July 1, 2012, a customer booked a room at a resort for July 3 and 4, 2013. As the contract cannot be performed in a year, it is subject to the statute. Two weeks after making the contract, the customer called the resort and the parties agreed to change the booking to December 25 and 26, 2012. The statute no longer applies to the modified contract. The opposite would occur if the original booking was for December 25 and 26, 2012, and was changed to August 3 and 4, 2013, dates more than a year after the modification. The statute did not apply to the original contract, but it does apply to the modification.

§11.7 A TRANSNATIONAL PERSPECTIVE ON THE STATUTE OF FRAUDS

Neither the CISG nor the UNIDROIT Principles contain a statute of frauds. This comports with the civilian tradition of not generally requiring the

---

7. The measurement of restitutionary benefits is discussed more fully in section 9.6.
8. As discussed in sections 7.5 and 13.9, at common law one of these requirements is that the modification must be supported by consideration. However, Article 2 dispenses with the need for consideration to support the modification of a contract for the sale of goods.
9. Even if the modification would not otherwise be subject to the statute, the contract may provide that all modifications must be in writing and signed. Such a provision can be effective as a kind of contractually created statute of frauds which prevents the enforcement of an oral modification. However, courts sometimes uphold oral modifications notwithstanding the provision. This is discussed in section 12.12.

formality of writing for the validity or enforcement of a commercial contract. CISG Article 11 states that a contract of sale is not subject to any requirements of form, and need not be evidenced by a writing. However, Article 11 is qualified by Article 12, which does allow a signatory country to opt out of Article 11 with regard to a party that has its place of business in that country. If the country exercises its power to opt out, the statute of frauds provided for in its domestic law will apply. (The United States has not exercised the power to opt out, so the Article 2 statute of frauds does not apply to a transaction governed by the CISG.) Article 1.2 of the UNIDROIT Principles follows the same approach as CISG article 11 in not requiring any writing or other formality to validate a contract. It is also worth noting that England, the country from which we derived our statute of frauds, abolished it some years ago.

Examples

1. On May 15, Viva Voce, the president of Ritten Records, Inc., interviewed Juan Annum for the position of sales manager. The parties reached agreement on a one-year period of employment, beginning on June 1 at an annual salary of $150,000. At the end of the interview, Viva tore a piece of paper from a blank pad and wrote "Call personnel dept. to enroll Juan Annum as a sales mgr. — 1-yr contract starting 6/1. Pay $150,000 p.a." She told Juan that the purpose of the note was to remind her to call the personnel department so that they would put him on the payroll from June.

   After the meeting, Juan resigned from his current employment by giving the required two weeks' notice. On May 17, he received a memo in the mail from the personnel department of Ritten Records, Inc. It was written on the company's letterhead and said simply, "We understand that you will be joining us on June 1. Please come in as soon as convenient to fill out the necessary tax forms."

   On May 23, before he had a chance to go to the personnel office, Juan received a letter in the mail from Viva on the company's letterhead. It read:

   Dear Juan,

   > I was happy to be able to extend an offer of employment to you last week. I regret, however, that since then we have reevaluated our earnings for the last quarter and find them disappointing. We have therefore decided not to hire any new employees at this time. I am sorry that we cannot use your services. I am sure that a person of your talents will have no difficulty in finding a suitable position elsewhere.

   > Sincerely,
   > Viva Voce
   > President

   Can Ritten Records, Inc., get away with this?

2. Change the facts of Example 1 as follows: Viva did not send the letter of May 23 and Ritten Records still wished to employ Juan. However, on May 23 Juan received a better job offer and is no longer interested in working for Ritten Records. Apart from this, all the facts are the same as in Example 1. Can the company enforce the contract against him?

3. Clay Potter owns a pottery in which he manufactures ceramic ovenware and crockery. Terry Cotta sells such items in his retail store. On June 1, Terry called Clay and spoke to his assistant who accepted his order of 1,000 ceramic mugs of various designs at $5.10 each, for immediate delivery. Later that day, Terry mailed the following printed form to Clay, with the blanks filled out by hand (the handwriting is denoted here by italics):

TERRY'S HOUSEWARES. Terry Cotta, Proprietor.
PURCHASE ORDER
Date *June 1, 2012*
To: *Clay Potter.*
Please ship the following goods immediately: 1,000 *assorted mugs as discussed by phone at $5.10 each*

On June 6, Terry received the following letter from Clay:

Dear Mr. Cotta,

I have received your order of June 1. I am sorry that I am out of mugs at present and cannot supply them right now. I am in the process of making a new batch and should have them in stock next month. Due to increased costs, I am going to have to raise the price to $5.50 each. If you would like me to hold your order until that time let me know. Also, tell me which designs you want. Your order refers to an assortment as discussed by phone, but no one here remembers talking to you and we have no record of your call.

Yours truly,

Clay Potter

Terry claims that he already has a contract for immediate delivery at the old price. Can he enforce it against Clay?

4. a. Fresco Fantastico is a famous, top-selling artist. Ore Alloys, Inc. (ORAL) was in the final stages of completing the construction of a new headquarters building. On March 1, 2012, it entered into an oral contract with Fresco under which it commissioned him to paint a

15 foot by 35 foot mural of its ore smelter on the wall of the building's lobby. The parties agreed that Fresco would begin the mural on May 1, 2012 (the date on which the lobby would be ready for decorative work) and would complete it by not later than June 1, 2013. ORAL would pay Fresco $100,000 on completion of the mural. On March 25, 2012, before Fresco had done any work or preparation under the contract, the president of ORAL called and told him that the corporation had changed its mind and no longer desired the mural. Does the statute of frauds preclude Fresco from enforcing his contract with ORAL?

b. Change the facts of Example 4(a) as follows: The oral contract between Fresco and ORAL on March 1, 2012, was not for a mural, but for a 15 foot by 35 foot painting of the ore smelter on canvas for $100,000. Fresco would complete the painting in his studio and deliver it to ORAL by not later than June 1, 2013. On March 15, 2012, Fresco had a large canvas made to fit the space in the lobby and he began to rough in the outlines of the painting. On March 25, the president of ORAL called and told him that the corporation had changed its mind and no longer desired the painting. Does the statute of frauds preclude Fresco from enforcing his contract with ORAL?

5. Annette X. Plorer visited the Web site of Big Browser Megastore.com and selected a Rolex watch for $10,000. She ordered it by clicking on various links; keying in her name, address, and credit card particulars; and finally clicking a "confirm order" button to confirm her order. After she did this, a message appeared on her screen thanking her for her order and stating that the goods would be shipped in 10 to 20 days. Assuming that a contract was formed through this process, does it satisfy the statute of frauds?

6. Sissy and Sybil Sibling are sisters. They were very close and made regular trips together to Atlantic City, where they played on the slot machines. About a year ago, they entered into an agreement under which they each promised that they would share any gambling winnings that either of them made. They recorded this agreement in a writing that read, "Sissy and Sybil Sibling hereby agree that for a period of two years from the date of this agreement, they will share any gambling winnings that either of them make in playing the slot machines in Atlantic City." Both sisters signed the writing. During the next eight months, the sisters visited Atlantic City three times. Each made modest winnings on the slot machines and they shared them. Eight months after signing the agreement, the sisters had a ferocious argument about a family matter and ceased speaking to each other. In a heated telephone call during the course of this argument, Sissy said "As for our agreement to share our gambling winnings, you can forget that!" Sybil replied, "That's fine with

me." A month later, Sissy went to Atlantic City on her own and won $20,000 on the slots. When Sybil heard about this, she sued Sissy for $10,000. Sissy contends that Sybil has no claim against her because they agreed to terminate their contract to share gambling winnings. Is this contention correct?

Explanations

1. Although the letter of May 23 suggests that the company is revoking an unaccepted offer, it is clear that an oral contract was made between Juan and the company, represented by its president, on May 15.

   The first question to answer is whether the contract is subject to the statute of frauds. The only applicable provision of the statute is that covering contracts not to be performed within a year. Although the performance itself will take exactly one year, it is not the length of actual performance that is crucial, but the time between making the contract and the end of performance. This period is approximately two weeks longer than a year. When there is some flexibility in the length of performance, the contract is not treated as falling within the statute if performance could conceivably be completed within the year, but this is not the case here because this is a fixed-term contract. Could it be argued that the performance could end before a year because the employee might die before that time? Although a court is more likely to accept this reasoning when the contract contemplates termination by death (for example, a lifetime employment term), it may be more hesitant to do so if death would merely be a discharge of the duty to perform. However, given the resistance to the one-year rule, it is possible that a court would be willing to entertain an argument that the mere possibility of death makes the contract performable within a year. Of course, such an interpretation would go a long way toward gutting the rule.

   If the contract is subject to the statute, the next question is whether there is a writing to satisfy it. To comply with the statute, there must, at a minimum, be a written record, signed by the party against whom enforcement is sought, identifying the parties, setting out the nature of the exchange, and containing most, if not all, of the material terms. The writing need not be contained in a single document, but can be made up of a set of linked documents. Three documents are referred to in the question: Viva's note to herself, the memo from the personnel department, and the letter from Viva. None of these documents on its own is sufficient to satisfy the statute.

   Viva's note to herself probably has enough content to show that a contract was made for a year's employment, and it seems to contain the central terms that were agreed. However, it lacks two elements needed to satisfy the statute: First, it identifies only one of the parties, Juan, and gives no indication of who the other party is — it makes no reference to Ritten Records. It is usually a requirement of the statute, in its common law version, that the writing must identify the parties. Second, the note is devoid of any kind of mark or symbol that could satisfy the requirement of a signature, even under the liberal definition of signature used in Restatement, Second §134 ("any symbol made or adopted with an intention, actual or apparent, to authenticate the writing as that of the signer"). Had the piece of paper contained the company name or logo, or had Viva signed or initialed the note, this would have satisfied the requirement of signature, but she wrote the note on a blank piece of paper and placed no mark on it that could constitute a signature.[10]

Therefore, the absence of a signature by or on behalf of Ritten Records prevents the note from being an adequate memorial of agreement. Had the note been signed, it would not have mattered that the note was intended as an internal document. The writing need not be addressed or given to the other party. The facts do not state if the note is still in existence, so it is possible that Viva may have crumpled it up and thrown it away after calling the personnel department. However, this would not necessarily be fatal to Juan's case because as long as he can prove the existence and contents of the note at an earlier time, it need not still be extant at the time of suit. (Of course, if Viva denies writing the note or disputes what it said, Juan's success in his suit will be heavily dependent on his credibility. This is not a happy situation for a plaintiff, who could easily fail to discharge his burden of proof.)

The memo from the personnel department was written on company stationery and exhibits its logo. The pre-existing printed logo should qualify as a signature because Ritten Records adopted it when using the preprinted stationery. The memo also identifies Juan and suggests the existence of a contract. However, the memo does not set out the terms of the contract. Although some degree of omission is tolerated, an indication of the central terms is usually required. In particular, there is no way to tell that this was not a contract for employment at will because of the lack of reference to the period of employment.

Viva's letter of May 23 is signed, but it is of little help to Juan because it does not in any way evidence a contract. In fact, it is written to suggest

---

10. You may be tempted to argue that Viva could be taken to have signed the note merely by writing it — after all, a handwriting expert could identify the writing as hers. However, that argument does not work. The requirement of signature — the making or adoption of a symbol to authenticate the writing — is a requirement independent of the writing itself.

just the opposite because it is phrased like the revocation of an unaccepted offer.

Although no single document sufficiently complies with the statute, taken together two of the three writings may contain all the content needed to satisfy it. As discussed in section 11.3.1, a set of writings in combination can satisfy the statute if, on their face, they refer to the same transaction and together they include all the required content. (Some courts insist that the signed document actually refers to the unsigned ones, but other courts find that test too rigorous and require only that it is apparent from the writings that they refer to the same transaction.) If Viva's note exists or can be convincingly shown to have existed, and the logo on the personnel department's memo is accepted as a signature, these two writings should be viewed in combination because they both refer to the same transaction. (Although Viva's letter of May 23 has a stronger form of signature, its implicit denial of a contract probably disqualifies it as referring to the transaction in a probative way.)

If the statute applies and Juan does not succeed in establishing compliance with it, he cannot enforce the contract unless he can fit it into one of the recognized exceptions to the statute. The only exception that might apply is promissory estoppel, based on the argument that Ritten Records made a promise in the oral contract, reasonably expecting to induce Juan's reliance, he did justifiably rely on the promise and suffered a substantial detriment in resigning from his existing job.[11] The problem with this argument is that Juan is responsible for knowing the law, and there is no apparent justification for his reliance on an oral contract. If ignorance of the need for a writing is enough to invoke promissory estoppel, the statute would be routinely circumvented.

2. Although Juan may be able to overcome the statute of frauds problem and enforce the contract against Ritten Records, the company has no corresponding right. When the writing has been signed by just one of the parties, the statute makes the contract enforceable against that party only. If the rule were otherwise, the statute would have little purpose because it would be too easy for one of the parties to write and sign a bogus document and to claim a contract binding on the other. (The UCC has a limited exception to this rule, discussed in section 11.3.4 and the next Example.) Juan has not signed anything. There is also no basis for Ritten Records to invoke promissory estoppel because it has taken no action in reliance on Juan's oral promise.

---

11. You may recall that section 8.10 discussed the problem of showing justifiable detrimental reliance on a promise of at-will employment. That issue does not arise here because the contract was for a one-year term. The issue here must be distinguished — it is whether promissory estoppel can be used as a means of enforcing an oral contract that is subject to the statute.

This means, of course, that Juan might be able to enforce a contract against Ritten, but Ritten has no basis to enforce a contract against him.[12]

3. Although the price of each item of goods is only $5.10, they are sold together in a single contract, so the price of the sale is their total price of $5,100. The contract is therefore subject to the statute of frauds in UCC §2.201. Terry's order form does not satisfy §2.201(1) as against Clay because it must be signed by the party against whom enforcement is sought. Clay's letter does have his signature ("signed" is defined in §1.201(37) as "any symbol executed or adopted by a party with present intention to authenticate a writing"), but it fails to satisfy §2.201(1) because it does not indicate that a contract has been made. In fact, phrased as a counteroffer, it suggests just the opposite.

We saw in Example 2 that under the general statute, a writing sufficient to satisfy the statute against one party does not bind the other in the absence of the other's signature. The same rule applies in many cases under the UCC, but §2.201(2) provides an exception to it. If one of the parties sends a confirmation of the oral contract to the other, the statute is satisfied as against the recipient if all the following conditions are satisfied: both parties are merchants; the writing is sufficient under §2.201(1) to satisfy the statute as against the sender; it was sent within a reasonable time; it was received by the other party who has reason to know its contents; and the recipient does not give written notice of objection to it within ten days of receipt.

Both parties are merchants under §2.104(1) because they both deal in goods of that kind. For the writing to be sufficient against Terry, the sender, it must indicate that a contract of sale has been made between the parties and must be signed by Terry. Beyond this, it need not accurately or fully state all the terms agreed, but it is not enforceable beyond the quantity stated. The order form does set out the essential terms of the contract, including the quantity of the goods. Terry's printed name at the top should qualify as his signature because it was adopted by him to authenticate the form when he filled out the blanks. The only problem is that the form is described as an order, which suggests not a contract, but an offer. It would have been clearer if the form had been headed "order confirmation." Nevertheless, this difficulty can be overcome by the reference to the telephone call that, on a reasonable interpretation, suggests a prior oral order accepted by or on behalf of Clay. This was the approach taken by the court in *Harry Rubin & Sons v. Consolidated Pipe Co.*, 153

---

12. Although Juan may be able to enforce the contract against Ritten Records, and the company has no basis to enforce the contract against him, this does not give rise to a problem of "mutuality of obligation." As discussed in section 7.9.1, provided that both parties' promises are genuine and not illusory, there is no general rule of "mutuality" that prevents one party from being bound because the other has no right of enforcement.

A.2d 472 (Pa. 1959) to a form similarly headed "order" that referred to a prior telephone call.

The form was sent on the same day as the telephone call, surely within a reasonable time, and Clay's response shows that it was received and its contents read. All is well for Terry so far, but Clay's letter could constitute a written notice of objection. To be an effective objection to the contents of the writing, the response must challenge the existence of a contract. Although the letter from Clay does not say in so many words that it denies Terry's claim of a contract, its import is clearly to that effect. It treats the order as an offer and claims no knowledge of the telephone call. It is in writing and is given within ten days of receipt of Terry's form.

4. a. The contract to paint the mural on the lobby wall is a hybrid transaction involving the supply of goods (paint) and services (applying the paint). As discussed in section 2.7.2, where a contract contains both a sale of goods and the performance of services, most courts apply a predominant purpose test to decide if the contract is subject to UCC Article 2. If the sale of goods is the more significant aspect of the transaction, Article 2 applies, but if services predominate, it does not. There can be no doubt that the parties did not intend to contract for the supply of paint, but for the skills that Fresco would employ in painting the mural. Undoubtedly, Fresco's labor predominates over the materials, both in value and scope. Because the service element is predominant, Article 2 does not apply and the contract is not subject to the statute of frauds in §2.201.

The only category of the common law statute that could apply to this contract is the one-year rule. Fresco was given 15 months from the date of the contract to complete the painting. However, there is no contractual bar to his finishing it earlier. It does not matter that the scope of the work is so large that he may not be able to get it done within a year of the contract. As shown by *C.R. Klewin, Inc. v. Flagship Properties, Inc.*, discussed in section 11.2.2, courts generally interpret the one-year rule restrictively, and do not find it applicable to a contract unless by its terms, it clearly requires the performance to continue for more than a year. The statute of frauds does not preclude Fresco from enforcing his contract with ORAL.

b. While it may seem that Fresco has contracted to perform a service by painting the picture, all his work goes into the creation of a tangible, movable end product. Where the delivery of the end product of labor is the subject matter of the contract, it is a sale of goods, even if the seller's labor in making the goods exceeds the cost of materials. Fresco's contract in this Example is therefore quite different from the contract to paint a mural in Example 4(a) and is also distinguishable from that of his colleague, Salvador Dali, whose undertaking to paint a picture on a TV show was characterized as a contract for services. (*See* section 11.2.3.)

The sale price of the painting is $100,000 so the contract is subject to the statute under §2.201. There is no writing at all, so the statute is not satisfied unless one of the exceptions in §2.201(3) applies. The only exception that has any possible relevance is the version of the part performance exception set out in §2.201(3)(a). To invoke this exception, Fresco must show that the goods are to be specially manufactured for the buyer; they are not suitable for sale to others in the ordinary course of the seller's business; before receiving notice of the buyer's repudiation, the seller made a substantial beginning on their manufacture or commitments for their procurement; and the circumstances reasonably indicate that the goods are for the buyer.

Very clearly, the exception has its basis in the principle, recognized to some extent at common law too, that the statute should not be applied to defeat relief to a party when post-formation conduct both indicates detrimental reliance on the oral contract and provides evidence of the contract's existence. By commencing performance or procurement of goods that are specific to the buyer's needs and not readily resalable, the seller incurs prejudice and his actions demonstrate the existence of a contract.

In Fresco's case, the painting is especially commissioned by and reflects a theme of particular interest to the buyer which strongly indicates that the painting is for the buyer. It is not clear if Fresco would be able to sell the painting to someone else in the ordinary course of business. There may or may not be much demand for an oversized painting of ORAL's smelter.

Fresco bought the canvas and began the painting before the repudiation. Is this a substantial enough beginning? This requirement, combined with that of difficulty of resale, is intended to confine the exception to cases in which nonenforcement would cause hardship to the seller. It is difficult to draw a definite line at which the commitment of time and materials passes from insubstantial to substantial, but Fresco could make a respectable argument that the purchase of the canvas, a major component of the materials to be used, the time spent in conceiving the painting, and the preliminary blocking work is enough to be substantial. However, as the canvas has not been consumed and could be used for another painting, this is not an overwhelming argument.

In short, the performance seems to serve the evidentiary function well, but is less compelling on the question of detriment. Fresco has a chance of success, but this is not an easy case to predict.

5. This is a sale of goods for a price of $10,000 so it falls within §2.201 and there must be a written memorandum of agreement, signed by the party against whom enforcement is sought, sufficient to show that a contract has been formed.

There is no doubt that the electronic records generated in the computers of both parties satisfy the requirement of §2.201 that there be a record sufficient to indicate a contract of sale. Annette's order, with particulars of the parties, the goods, the price, and the quantity term, accepted by Big Browser with the delivery information, surely evidences the existence of a contract. Contemporary courts interpret the word "writing" in §2.201 to include electronic records. The question of the effectiveness of the parties' signatures is settled by E-Sign and UETA, both of which require the court to give effect to the electronic signatures of the parties, provided that such electronic signatures exist and they are genuine and otherwise in conformity with the law. The facts present no question of forgery or unauthorized use of equipment, so the sole issue is whether the parties did execute or adopt a symbol associated with the contract. The facts indicate that Annette deliberately entered her name in the appropriate space on the electronic order form. Undoubtedly this qualifies as her signature.

Although the facts do not specify, Big Browser's name or symbol surely appears in its response. If an employee handled the response and typed Big Browser's name or symbol, this qualifies as its signature. Even if the employee did not actually type the name or symbol, the employee's act of sending the message under an automatically generated name or symbol likely constitutes the adoption of that name or symbol with the intent to authenticate the record. Big Browser's response may not have been made by a human at all, but could have been automatically generated by a computer program used by Big Browser. This should not make a difference to the conclusion that its name or symbol should qualify as a signature. Section 5.8 explained that a party can contract through an "electronic agent" — a computer program that is set up to initiate action or respond automatically to a communication. UETA recognizes this possibility in §14, and comment 1 to §14 points out that intention to enter into a transaction can be attributed to a party who sets up a machine to act as his agent. Therefore, attribution of signature to a party should be possible where the automatic signature is by a machine programmed to be an electronic agent.

6. The agreement to share gambling winnings is subject to the statute of frauds because it has a definite term of two years and therefore cannot be performed within a year of execution of the contract. However, the signed written agreement to share winnings satisfies the statute, so Sissy cannot claim that the original agreement is unenforceable. Instead,

she argues that the agreement was rescinded by mutual consent. The sisters did enter a termination agreement through an offer by Sissy that was accepted by Sybil. The agreement is supported by consideration because each suffers the detriment of giving up her rights under the terminated contract. If that termination agreement is enforceable, Sissy has a good defense to Sybil's suit. However, the termination agreement is oral, so the question is whether it is subject to the statute of frauds. If it is, the oral termination agreement is unenforceable, and Sybil does have a cause of action under the original contract. An agreement to terminate a contract is itself a contract. Like a modification, it is subject to all the usual rules relating to formation and validity, and it must comply with the statute of frauds if it falls within the statute. The argument could be made that it is subject to the statute of frauds because the underlying contract still had more than a year to run, so the agreement to terminate rights under the contract must last just as long and cannot be performed within a year of its making. However, that is not persuasive. It is better to view the termination agreement as taking effect immediately, and being fully performed as soon as each party commits to give up her rights under the terminated contract.

This is what the court held in *Sokaitis v. Bakaysa*, 49 Conn. L. Reptr. 812 (Conn. Super. 2010), on which this Example is based. Two octogenarian sisters enjoyed gambling at a casino and buying lottery tickets. They had made a written agreement to share their gambling winnings. Their formerly close relationship ended when they had an argument over a loan that one of the sisters made to the other. During the course of an argument over the loan, there was a heated exchange in which one of the sisters said "I don't want to be your partner anymore" and the other replied "OK." Thereafter, one of the sisters bought a Powerball lottery ticket with her brother and they won $500,000. Upon hearing of this, the other sister sued for breach of the contract to share gambling winnings. The court noted that an agreement to rescind a contract is itself a contract. An effective agreement of rescission ends the contract and waives all rights to enforce or sue on it. The court found that the sisters had entered into a valid agreement to rescind the contract. It held further that the rescission agreement was not subject to the statute of frauds because the rescission involved an instantaneous performance under which each party's duties under the original contract were immediately discharged.

12

The Parol Evidence Rule

---

§12.1 THE APPLICATION AND BASIC PURPOSE OF THE PAROL EVIDENCE RULE

§12.1.1 A Written or Recorded Agreement

The parol evidence rule applies where an agreement is recorded in writing and one of the parties proffers evidence to prove a term that is not contained in the writing or to explain or expand on a term in the writing. As noted several times before, particularly in Chapter 11, contemporary law includes in the concept of writing not just words written on paper, but also forms of recording by electronic or other means.

§12.1.2 The Relationship Between the Parol Evidence Rule and Interpretation

The parol evidence rule is closely intertwined with the process of interpretation. As you read this chapter, you will see many links to the discussion of interpretation in Chapter 10. The following general observations on the relationship between the parol evidence rule and interpretation should help to keep things straight.

Although there are some passing references to the parol evidence rule in Chapter 10, that chapter was concerned purely with the rules and principles governing the interpretation or construction of contracts to determine the parties' reasonable meaning. The central point of Chapter 10 is that unless there is no evidence of context available, the meaning of language used in the contract is not usually determined purely by reference to the dictionary meaning of the words, but by reading the words in the entire context of the transaction. This context may include the discussions between the parties in forming the contract, their previous course of dealing in prior contracts of the same kind, trade usage, and their postformation course of performing the contract. Where the agreement has been recorded in writing, the parol evidence rule qualifies what was discussed in Chapter 10 by placing controls on recourse to this extrinsic evidence. In short, it restricts the extent to which some contextual evidence may be considered in deciding what the parties intended in entering the contract.

The impact of the parol evidence rule on the contextual evidence used to interpret the contract depends both on the completeness and clarity of the written record of agreement and on the quality of the contextual evidence. The clearer and more comprehensive the writing, the higher the barrier to the admission of extrinsic evidence. On the other hand, the more compelling the extrinsic evidence, the greater the prospect of persuading the court that it should be admitted. Of course, to decide whether the writing is clear and comprehensive, the court must interpret the writing itself. The effect of this is to create a circular process that can be confounding: the parol evidence rule impacts interpretation by restricting evidence extrinsic to the written contract, but interpretation, often in the light of that very extrinsic evidence, must be used to decide whether and to what extent the writing should have the effect of excluding the extrinsic evidence. One of the most difficult tasks in understanding the parol evidence rule is to appreciate how courts navigate this circular route. As you read this chapter you will find a central theme emerging: Courts try to strike a balance between the parties' reasonable expectations that arise from the language of the written contract and their reasonable expectations that arise from the context in which that written contract was formed.

§12.2 A BASIC STATEMENT OF THE RATIONALE AND CONTENT OF THE RULE

The parol evidence rule is based on the principle that when the parties reduce their agreement to writing, they often intend the written record to be the final expression of their agreement. That is, they intend it to supersede anything that might have been proposed, discussed, or agreed to prior to execution of the writing but not ultimately recorded in the writing. Accordingly, the factfinder should not hear evidence of terms that were allegedly agreed to but are not reflected in the writing. This evidence is suspect, unreliable, and irrelevant, and is more likely to mislead and confuse than to inform the factfinder. (This rationale is taken up again and illustrated in section 12.3.)

Restatement, Second, §213 sets out the common law parol evidence rule, as it is applied by many contemporary courts. The UCC rule, in §2.202, is worded somewhat differently, but is largely similar in effect. In essence, both versions of the rule provide that to the extent that the parties execute a writing that is and is intended to be a final expression of their agreement, no parol evidence may be admitted to supplement, explain, or contradict it. However, to the extent that the writing is not a final and complete expression of agreement, consistent, but not contradictory, parol evidence may be admitted to supplement or explain those parts of it that have not been finally expressed.

§12.3 WHAT IS PAROL EVIDENCE?

§12.3.1 The Meaning of "Parol"

"Parol" is derived from the French *parole*, meaning "a word" — more particularly a spoken or oral word. It has the same etymological root as the more familiar modern English word "parole," which has now developed the specialized meaning of a prisoner's early release from jail subject to conditions. Because contract lawyers do not like in any way to be associated with criminal activity, it is a grave breach of etiquette to use that final "e" when referring to parol evidence.

Although the derivation of "parol" suggests that it refers only to oral terms, it extends to written terms as well under some circumstances. In short, the rule covers both oral and written terms allegedly agreed to prior to execution of the written contract, but not incorporated into the final written contract. It also covers terms allegedly agreed to orally at the time of the written contract, but not incorporated into the written contract.

§12.3.2 Terms Allegedly Agreed to Prior to the Written Contract

The parol evidence rule covers evidence of an alleged term not incorporated into the final written agreement, but claimed by one of the parties to have been agreed to, either in writing or orally, at some time before the execution of the written agreement. For example, Seller and Buyer sign a written agreement under which Seller sells her car to Buyer for $5,000 cash, to be paid on delivery of the car. When Seller thereafter tenders delivery of the car, Buyer refuses to pay the $5,000, claiming that on the day before the agreement was signed, Seller had orally agreed to give him 30 days' credit. If this matter should eventually be litigated, Buyer's testimony about the prior oral agreement would be parol evidence. (As we will shortly see, it most likely satisfies all the elements of the parol evidence rule, and the court would therefore refuse to allow Buyer to testify about the prior oral agreement.) The rationale for filtering such evidence through the parol evidence rule is that an allegation of prior consensus on an oral term is suspect when the oral term is not incorporated into the writing executed for the purpose of recording the agreement. Its absence from the writing suggests either that it is a complete fabrication by Buyer, or even if it was agreed to, that the parties intended to supersede it by the written term. Therefore, the evidence should be evaluated with special care by the judge before it is admitted for the factfinder's consideration.

Say that the parties had not negotiated orally, but by correspondence. Their correspondence shows agreement on a 30-day credit term, but their final written contract of sale reflects the C.O.D. term. The written evidence of prior agreement is also parol evidence. Although the presence of objectively verifiable written evidence of prior agreement reduces concern that Buyer made up the claimed agreement on the credit term, its absence from the final writing still suggests that the parties must have intended to supersede it by the cash term.

§12.3.3 Terms Allegedly Agreed to Contemporaneously with the Written Contract

Although the parol evidence rule applies to both oral and written evidence of agreement allegedly made prior to the execution of the final writing, it covers only evidence of oral agreement made contemporaneously with the final writing. The bar on evidence of contemporaneous oral agreement does not extend to evidence of contemporaneous written agreement. There are two reasons for this. First, the existence of a writing is more reliable evidence of agreement than oral testimony. Second, a contract need not be contained in a single document, so that where there are contemporaneous writings, it may not be clear that one of them was intended to supersede the other. They may simply be supplementary to each other. As a result, the parol evidence rule allows any contemporaneous writings to be admitted. (As explained more fully in section 12.6, admission of the evidence is just a preliminary matter. It allows the evidence to be placed before the factfinder.

It does not mean that the factfinder will ultimately conclude that the final agreement is reflected in both writings. It may find that one supersedes the other.)

The type of evidence of contemporaneous oral agreement that is subject to the rule can be illustrated by changing the above example involving the sale of the car. Say that Buyer wishes to testify that when the parties got together to sign the sales contract, he raised the issue of credit and Seller agreed to give him 30 days to pay for the car. However, this agreement is not reflected in the writing. Buyer's assertion is as or more suspect as his claim of a prior oral agreement and is equally subject to the rule.

§12.3.4 Evidence of Subsequent Agreement

The parol evidence rule does not affect evidence of either oral or written agreements claimed to have been made after the execution of the writing. The theory behind the parol evidence rule is that the writing is likely to have subsumed all prior understandings, and this presumption cannot have any relevance to an agreement entered into subsequent to the writing. This is in fact a modification, which is subject to its own particular rules but it is not affected by the parol evidence rule.[1]

It is usually easy to tell if an oral agreement was made after the writing because they are separated by some distance in time. However, in some situations it may not be clear if the oral agreement is contemporaneous with or subsequent to the writing. For example, in *Kehr Packages, Inc. v. Fidelity Bank*, 710 A.2d 1169 (Pa. 1998) the bank had agreed to finance the purchase of shares in a corporation. The closing of the transaction took all day. The parties signed a written loan agreement during the course of the day. After the agreement was signed, but before the closing was over, the borrowers asked the lender to increase the amount of the loan. The borrowers claimed that the lender agreed to this increase orally, but the written agreement was not changed to reflect this. The trial court admitted evidence of the oral agreement on the basis that it was subsequent to the writing and not subject to the parol evidence rule. The supreme court reversed and held that the evidence was barred by the rule. The closing was a single, continuous transaction and it was artificial to focus on the exact sequence of the signing and the alleged oral agreement. The crucial point is whether they are both within the same process of formation, and if they are, the parties (especially sophisticated parties, as in this case) should ensure that the writing is

---

1. Modifications are dealt with in sections 7.5.2 and 13.9. The written memorial of agreement may itself seek to prevent future oral modifications by requiring that all modifications must be in writing and signed by the parties. The effectiveness of such a provision is discussed in section 12.12.

changed to include any oral understandings. Because the court found the oral agreement to be contemporaneous and irreconcilable with the writing, evidence of it was excluded.

§12.3.5 Summary of the Scope of the Parol Evidence Rule

Diagram 12A summarizes the range of the parol evidence rule as discussed in the preceding subsections.

Diagram 12A

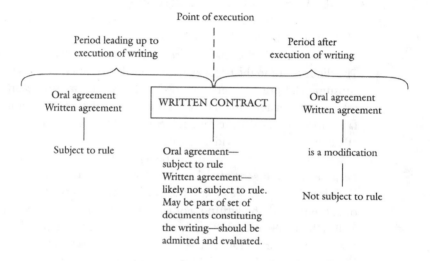

§12.4 A CLOSER LOOK AT THE PURPOSE AND PREMISE OF THE PAROL EVIDENCE RULE

The basic concept of the parol evidence rule is quite simple and its premise is grounded in common sense. Sadly, however, this basic simplicity is completely overwhelmed by the considerable difficulties that emerge when one tries to define the scope of the rule and to apply it to inconclusive facts. The complexity and confusion generated by the rule result largely from the dilemma it presents to courts: The rule serves a useful role in permitting the exclusion of evidence that is probably unreliable or dishonest, but it also has the potential of producing injustice by preventing a party from proving what was actually agreed. A firm rule is more efficient at keeping out undesirable evidence, but is also more likely to exclude legitimate evidence. A more flexible rule allows the court greater discretion in evaluating and determining the reliability of evidence, but it weakens the protection against undesirable evidence and detracts from the certainty and clarity of the law. If you think of the rule as a door to the witness box, its ideal design would keep out the perjurer and irrelevant waffler, but would admit the honest and pertinent witness. The current state of the rule aspires to that design but has not achieved it and probably cannot.

The following illustration indicates the premise of the rule: The Four Crooners is a popular troupe of tenors who sing light opera and ballads. The Four Crooners entered into a written recording contract with Integrated Recording Co., Inc. The contract provided that Integrated Recording would produce and distribute a CD of the Four Crooners' music. The Four Crooners would receive a royalty of 15 percent of gross receipts from sales of the CD. The CD was made, and 150,000 copies were sold in the first month. This resulted in a dispute between the parties and a suit by The Four Crooners for larger royalties. As the basis of the suit, The Four Crooners claim that before they signed the written contract they told Integrated Recording that they were willing to accept a 15 percent royalty on the first 100,000 CDs sold, but if sales exceeded that volume, they wanted a royalty of 18 percent on all sales beyond 100,000 copies. They allege that Integrated Recording agreed to this orally. This change does not appear in the written contract and Integrated Recording denies agreeing to it.

Because the written contract does not mention this alleged term, The Four Crooners have no case unless they are allowed to testify to the oral promise. The rule of law could simply be to admit the evidence of both parties and to leave it to the factfinder (usually the jury) to decide if such an oral agreement was reached. However, the common law has not taken this approach. Instead, it has developed the parol evidence rule, which acts as a gatekeeper by allowing the judge to determine if the jury should be allowed to hear the evidence of the oral agreement.

The primary purpose of the parol evidence rule is to control the jury's decision making. It allows the judge to restrict the information given to the jury, thereby shielding it from evidence the judge finds to be suspect and unreliable. A secondary justification for the rule is that it promotes efficiency in the conduct of litigation. By excluding suspect evidence at the outset (often at the stage of a motion for summary judgment or dismissal), the judge saves the time that would otherwise be wasted in presenting the evidence to the jury and cross-examining the witnesses. Finally, the existence of the rule may help to promote transactional efficiency. Because it exists, parties are more likely to make an effort to record their agreement fully and accurately.

As the parol evidence rule relates to the admissibility of evidence, one might be forgiven for assuming that it is a rule of evidence. However, it is generally thought of as a rule of substantive law. The distinction is subtle: If it were evidentiary, it would be an exclusionary rule based on a presumption that the writing is the best evidence of agreement. Seen as a rule of substantive contract law, it nullifies parol agreements when a writing is executed as a final expression of agreement. This rule of law then leads to the exclusion of the evidence as irrelevant. Happily, one does not usually have to worry about this distinction, because it makes no difference for most purposes. Its principal impact is on matters of procedure. For example, if a federal court deals with a contract case, it follows its own rules of evidence but is bound by the state's parol evidence rule because it is a matter of state substantive law. Similarly, if it were a rule of evidence, a party would waive it by failing to object to the evidence at trial. As a rule of substantive law, it can be raised on appeal despite the failure to object at trial.

Based on these general principles, how is the court likely to react to the Four Crooners' attempt to testify to the alleged oral term? It is quite easy to see why the parol evidence rule might be useful in a case like this. The parties went to the trouble of recording their contract in writing and the royalty provision seems definitive and clear. Surely, had the parties agreed to an 18 percent royalty on sales over 100,000 copies, this would have been in the writing. The absence of the term in the writing suggests either that The Four Crooners are mistaken in thinking that Integrated Recording agreed to it, or they were very sloppy in not making sure that the writing reflected what was actually agreed, or worse, they are making it up. Whatever the reason, the testimony is suspect and maybe it is best that the jury never gets to hear it. Because The Four Crooners' case is entirely based on the alleged oral term, the lawsuit can be dismissed summarily.

Say that the facts of the dispute were different. The written contract is as stated above, but the Four Crooners do not claim an agreement for increased royalties. Instead, they claim that Integrated Recording made an oral promise at the time of signing the contract that it would arrange a ten-city concert tour to promote the CD. It failed to do this and denies agreeing to it. The written agreement is completely silent on the question of promotional tours and concerts. If the parol evidence rule simply barred all testimony of oral agreement, it would be too blunt an instrument. Therefore, the rule is more nuanced. As this testimony does not directly contradict the writing, it may be less presumptively suspect and there may be a greater justification for admitting it. In the following sections we will explore these nuances. Before we look at the rule more closely, it is useful to articulate some of the features of the rule that have been suggested by the preceding discussion:

1. The rule only applies when a written agreement (including an agreement recorded by electronic or other means as explained in section 12.1.1) has been executed. The rule applies whether the writing is a comprehensive or incomplete record of the agreement. However, the more complete the written memorandum, the more rigorous the application of the rule.

2. The writing must have been adopted by both parties. It need not be signed by them as long as it is shown to be a mutual document. Naturally, the presence of signatures more strongly proves that it is a joint memorandum, but a letter written by one party and received by the other without objection qualifies. A memorandum written by only one of the parties and not disseminated to the other does not bring the rule into effect. To invoke the parol evidence rule, a writing must therefore have qualities beyond those needed to satisfy the statute of frauds. This is because the statute is concerned with the minimal amount of writing needed to establish the existence of a contract, while the parol evidence rule is concerned with the degree to which the writing should be used to exclude extrinsic evidence of what was agreed.

3. Remember that the word "parol" suggests that the rule is primarily concerned with oral communications between the parties before or at the time of execution of the writing. However, the rule is not confined to oral communications, and it also covers prior written communications.

4. The rule does not absolutely bar all parol evidence. If it did, our job would be much easier, but the results of the rule would be bizarre. The purpose of the rule is to exclude presumptively irrelevant or concocted testimony, but not honest and pertinent evidence of what was actually agreed. The rule must therefore be sufficiently fine-tuned to allow the court to make this distinction. Herein lies the greatest complexity and difficulty in devising and applying a rational rule.

5. The rule contemplates a two-stage process. When the parol evidence is proffered, the judge must make an initial finding of admissibility. If the judge finds that the evidence is admissible, it is presented to the factfinder (the jury unless the trial is before a judge alone) that hears the testimony and makes the ultimate finding on credibility. The judge's initial determination is characterized as a question of law, but it is not necessarily devoid of factual evaluation. This is one of the confusing aspects of the rule. Although the factfinder may eventually have to decide if the evidence is believable, the judge, in making the initial decision on admissibility, is also concerned with the plausibility of the proffered evidence, a preliminary issue of credibility.

§12.5 THE DEGREE OF FINALITY OF THE WRITING: TOTAL AND PARTIAL INTEGRATION

We begin our discussion of integration on the assumption that the written agreement is clear and unambiguous. Obviously, in many cases, this assumption is false. We saw in Chapter 10 that there are all kinds of reasons why the language chosen by the parties might be indefinite. Where the parties dispute the meaning of the writing and its terms cannot be readily ascertained, this indefiniteness or ambiguity has an impact on the way that the parol evidence rule operates. We will discuss this below in section 12.8. The first task, though, is to focus on the rule itself, which is best done if we put aside the problem of indefiniteness and ambiguity for the time being.

The impact of the parol evidence rule depends on the degree to which the writing executed by the parties constitutes a comprehensive and final written memorandum of their agreement. In short, if the writing is full, complete, unambiguous, and clear, the rule excludes all parol evidence. But to the extent that the written memorandum does not fully and unequivocally cover all of the agreed terms, parol evidence is admissible to supplement it. Even here, however, the parol evidence cannot contradict what has been written or add to those aspects of the agreement that have been fully dealt with in the writing. As discussed in section 12.6, it can be a difficult question of interpretation to determine whether and to what extent the memorandum is comprehensive and final.

If the written memorandum is a complete, final, and certain record of the parties' agreement (that is, it unambiguously and clearly expresses every term in the agreement, and it is intended to be the exclusive statement of everything that was agreed), it is said to be totally (or completely) integrated. If the writing is truly a total integration, then, by definition, no terms can exist beyond those set out in the writing. It follows that neither party should be allowed to offer parol evidence tending to prove terms extrinsic to the writing, because such evidence is irrelevant or incredible.

If the writing is not a complete and final record of the agreement, it is said to be partially integrated or unintegrated. The written agreement may fully and finally express some but not all of the terms, or it may not fully and finally express any term. If so, the parol evidence rule permits parol evidence to be admitted to supplement or explain the writing to the extent that it is not integrated. However, the parol evidence must be consistent with, and cannot contradict or vary terms that have been recorded in the writing.

§12.6 THE PROCESS OF DEALING WITH PAROL EVIDENCE

The issue of the admissibility of parol evidence could arise early in the suit if one of the parties applies for summary judgment or dismissal in response to a claim or defense based on an alleged parol term. Because the admissibility of parol evidence is a legal question, a dispute on admissibility is often appropriate for summary adjudication. If the case is not disposed of on the pleadings and it goes to trial, the admissibility of the evidence may be challenged when an attempt is made to introduce it. As noted before, the evaluation of parol evidence at trial involves two stages. In the first, the judge decides admissibility as a legal matter. If the evidence is admitted, the factfinder evaluates its credibility. We now look more closely at the process involved in each of these two stages, which may be charted as shown in Diagram 12B.

Diagram 12B

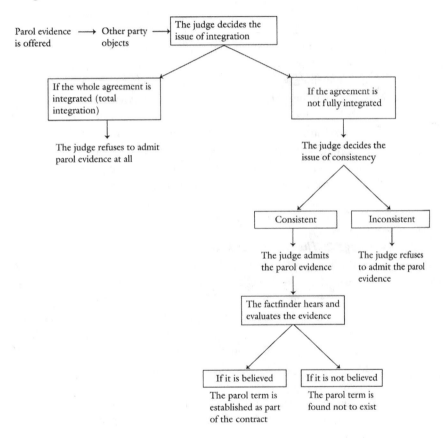

Stage 1: The judge's determination

In making the finding of admissibility, the judge conducts an inquiry that may itself be split into two sequential components:

1. Logically, the first issue to be resolved by the judge is the question of integration. Is the writing a full and final record of the agreement

as a whole (that is, a complete integration)? If so, we do not get beyond the first inquiry, because the parol evidence may not be admitted.

2. If the writing is not a complete integration, consistent supplementary parol evidence is admissible. The judge's inquiry then turns to whether the proffered parol evidence is in fact consistent with and not contradictory to what has been written. If it contradicts the writing, it may not be admitted, and it still never reaches the jury.

Having drawn this distinction between the judge's two inquiries, it is useful to express a word of caution: It is easy enough to separate the issue of integration from the issue of consistency for the purpose of theoretical analysis, and it is logical that the first must be resolved before the second is reached. However, as a practical matter, the inquiry into integration is often influenced by the question of whether the alleged parol term is consistent with the writing, and these two stages often meld into one another. That is, unless the intent to integrate is so clear that there can be no doubt on the matter, the extent to which the alleged parol term is reconcilable with the writing may affect the court's decision on whether an integration was reasonably intended by the parties. Therefore, you will see cases in which the court does not neatly proceed in the sequence that is charted here.

Stage 2: The factfinder's determination

If the judge's preliminary inquiry into the evidence leads to the determination that the subject matter covered by the alleged term has not been integrated into the writing and that the proffered parol evidence is consistent with what has been written, the judge rules the evidence admissible. It may then be presented to the factfinder, which is responsible for the ultimate decision on whether the term was agreed to. If the case is to be tried by a jury, the dichotomy between judge and factfinder is clear. However, if the parties have agreed not to try the case before a jury, the judge is the factfinder, and the dichotomy becomes quite artificial. The judge, in the role of legal arbiter, makes the initial finding as a matter of law. If she rules the evidence inadmissible, she must then exercise the professional objectivity of not being influenced by it in her role as factfinder. This is probably not as difficult as it sounds — the fact that the judge excluded it as a matter of law means that she could not have found it very convincing to begin with — as explained further below.

§12.7 DETERMINING THE QUESTION OF INTEGRATION

The determination of admissibility of evidence is the judge's function, so in the context of the parol evidence rule, intent to integrate is treated as a question of law. To decide if the parties intended the writing to be a full and final expression of their agreement, the court must interpret it. During the classical period of contract law, courts tended to emphasize the objective test of assent and to place great importance on the reasonable meaning of language. This heavy emphasis on objectivity made the question of determining integration relatively easy: If the writing, interpreted as a whole in accordance with the plain meaning of the language used, appeared to be a full and final expression of the agreement, it was deemed to be integrated. Thus, the judge decided the parties' intent to integrate their agreement in the writing purely on the basis of the "four corners" of the written document, without recourse to any extrinsic evidence. If the document appeared complete this intent was established and no parol evidence was admissible to add to or alter its reasonable meaning.

Many modern courts recognize that a strict and invariable "four corners" approach may disregard contextual evidence that is helpful in deciding intent to integrate. They realize that even when a writing appears at face value to be comprehensive, inquiry into the context in which it was written may dispel this impression. Therefore, in deciding the question of integration, a contemporary court may go beyond the face value of the writing to reach a decision on whether the parties intended an integration. As explained below, this does not mean that courts will always consider extrinsic evidence in deciding integration. Some courts are more open than others to going beyond the four corners of the document. Even courts that are generally receptive to extrinsic evidence may refuse to consider it where the intent to integrate is strongly expressed in the writing, particularly where the writing contains a merger clause that expresses the intent to integrate.[2] If the court does consider extrinsic evidence, the judge's evaluation of that evidence is preliminary. If the judge concludes that the evidence is admissible as a matter of law, the factfinder (whether a jury or the judge herself in that role) will be the final arbiter of its factual truth.

When an apparently integrated agreement does not contain the term that was allegedly agreed to, one of the key questions in determining integration under the contextual approach is to ask whether the circumstances offer an explanation of why the term may not have been included in the writing. Restatement, Second, §216(2)(b) expresses this concept by asking

---

2. Merger clauses are explained later in this section.

whether the term is such as "might naturally be omitted" from the writing. UCC §2.202, Comment 3, suggests a similar inquiry: Would the term "certainly have been included" in the document had it been agreed to? The UCC test sounds more favorable to admission because it excludes the evidence only if it clearly would have been part of the writing if the parties had agreed to it. However, in most cases, this test would not likely give a different result than the Restatement's inquiry into whether the term might naturally have been agreed separately.

It is worth stressing the caution mentioned above: Even under a contextual approach, courts pay particular attention to the scope and language of the writing. Where the writing is clear, unambiguous, and apparently complete, proffered extrinsic evidence would have to be very plausible to overcome the conclusion that the writing itself demonstrates an intent to integrate. The extrinsic evidence must both be reconcilable with the apparent intent and demonstrate a justification for going beyond the writing. It is therefore still common to find that courts rely very heavily on the "four corners" of the writing in deciding integration.

Masterson v. Sine, 436 P.2d 561 (Cal 1968) is one of the best-known cases to apply a contextual approach and to inquire whether a term absent from the agreement might naturally be omitted from the writing. Masterson and his wife sold a ranch to the Sines, his sister and her husband. The contract granted the Mastersons an option to repurchase the ranch at a price to be fixed by a formula. Masterson later became bankrupt and his trustee attempted to exercise the repurchase option to bring the property into Masterson's estate for the benefit of his creditors. The Sines claimed that the trustee could not exercise the option because the parties had orally agreed at the time of the sale that the option was personal to the Mastersons and could not be transferred to or exercised by anyone else. The majority found that such an agreement might naturally be made outside of the writing in a family transaction. The dissent disagreed with the majority's approach and resolution. It found the writing to be integrated on its face and criticized the "might naturally be omitted" test as too uncertain and open-ended. Even if that test was appropriate, the dissent did not find that this oral term would have satisfied it. A restriction on transfer of the option would not naturally be excluded from the writing if the parties had agreed to it. The option itself was granted in the writing, so surely any restriction on its exercise would be set out there too had the parties agreed to it. The dissent also commented on the credibility of the Sines' assertion: it was particularly suspicious because it was aimed at keeping the property out of Masterson's bankruptcy estate.

Myskina v. Conde Nast Publications, Inc., 386 F. Supp. 2d 409 (S.D.N.Y. 2005) is a good contrast to *Masterson*. Myskina, a Russian tennis champion, agreed with Conde Nast to pose nude for photographs to be published in a "sports" issue of GQ magazine. Immediately before the photographs were taken, Myskina signed a written release in which she irrevocably and unqualifiedly consented to the use of the photographs by Conde Nast. The first photos taken during the photo shoot portrayed Myskina as Lady Godiva. She was not entirely nude in these photos, but wore flesh-colored pants and, had long hair covering her breasts. The photos taken after that were more revealing. Myskina alleged that she had expressed discomfort over posing for them but the photographer assured her that only the Lady Godiva photos would be published.[3] GQ magazine published the Lady Godiva photos, but the photographer subsequently sold the nude photos, which were published in another magazine. Myskina sued Conde Nast and the photographer for damages and an injunction on the grounds that the nude photos were published without her authorization. Her suit did not survive summary judgment. She sought to testify to the oral undertaking to publish only the Lady Godiva photos, but the court refused to admit that evidence. The court found that the release, interpreted in its plain meaning within the context of the transaction, was an integrated document that clearly and comprehensively expressed unrestricted consent to publication. The alleged oral term imposed a fundamental condition on that consent that would not have been omitted from the writing had it been agreed to by the parties.

It is common to find a provision in a written contract to the effect that the written contract is the entire agreement between the parties, and that no representations or promises have been made save for those set out in the writing. This is called a merger clause because it signifies that all the terms of the agreement have been merged into the writing. Where the written contract appears to be complete, the inclusion of a merger clause is strong evidence of integration. As a result, a merger clause can be effective in disposing of the issue of integration and insulating the writing from parol evidence. However, a merger clause is not always conclusive. Sometimes courts will go behind a merger clause and admit parol evidence, where, under all the circumstances of the transaction, one of the parties makes a plausible argument that, despite appearances, the writing is not really integrated, and the alleged parol term can be reconciled with it. A court may be more amenable to such an argument where the merger clause is a standard term in a form contract.

To illustrate some of the difficulties in deciding the question of integration, let us return to the example of the recording contract between The Four Crooners and Integrated Recordings, introduced in section 12.4. Assume that the parties' agreement is recorded in a written contract, five pages long. The contract specifies the songs to be recorded, the date of

---

3. Myskina did not argue (and the court did not consider) that the alleged oral agreement was not subject to the parol evidence rule because it was made subsequent to the written release. This probably would not have been a good argument. Even though the oral agreement followed the writing, which was executed at the beginning of the photo shoot, they did occur during the same period of interaction and should be viewed as contemporaneous. (See the Kehr Packages case discussed in section 12.3.2.)

recording, the date of release, and the royalty of 15 percent to be paid on gross receipts. It has numerous provisions setting out the duties of The Four Crooners in the production of the recording as well as detailed provisions relating to the distribution of the CD and the accounting for and payment of royalties. It ends with a merger clause. The writing appears to be full and comprehensive. Consider the two alternative allegations of parol agreement made by the Four Crooners. One was that the parties agreed orally to a royalty of 18 percent on sales over 100,000 copies. The other was that Integrated Recording undertook to arrange a ten-city concert tour to promote the CD. On a strict "four corners" approach, the writing is unquestionably integrated, and no evidence would be admitted of either of these alleged parol terms. The Four Crooners are not likely to do any better on a contextual approach. The written contract specifies the royalty percentage, so it is not natural that the parties might agree to part of that term separately. It is hard to reconcile the parol augmentation of the royalty term with the unequivocal written term. The term relating to the concert tour is not as badly at odds with the writing, but it does not seem natural that this single term would have been omitted from an otherwise detailed written agreement. In addition, the only contextual evidence tendered is the disputed, self-serving testimony of The Four Crooners themselves about what was said at the time that the writing was signed. (As you can see, credibility issues cannot be entirely divorced from this legal inquiry, and the issues of integration and consistency, while doctrinally distinct, often intermingle in the decision on integration.)

However, say that the written contract was not as detailed as described above. It is a simple, one-page document that sets out the songs to be recorded, the date of recording, the date of release, and the royalty of 15 percent to be paid on gross receipts. It has none of the detailed provisions relating to the parties' performance set out above and no merger clause. Parol evidence on the increase in royalties is still not likely to be admissible because the royalty clause appears to be definitive and not easily reconcilable with the alleged parol agreement. However, evidence of the undertaking of a concert tour stands a better chance of admission. The absence of details about the obligations of the parties in performing the contract and the lack of a merger clause could make it more natural that an agreement about a promotional tour might be made separately from the writing.

§12.8 AMBIGUITY OR INDEFINITENESS IN AN INTEGRATED WRITING

As noted at the beginning of section 12.5, the discussion of integration up to now has assumed that the terms of the writing are clear and unambiguous. Where that is not so, a further complication arises: no matter how firmly the parties may have intended the writing to be a full and final expression of their agreement, if a term of the writing is unclear or ambiguous, the writing cannot be treated as an integration of that term. If extrinsic evidence is available to clarify the indefiniteness, that is the best means of ascertaining the parties' intended meaning. Parol evidence is therefore admissible to clarify the uncertainty or ambiguity. This does not mean that uncertainty or ambiguity allows for the admission of whatever parol evidence may be tendered on any aspect of the contract. The evidence must be pertinent to the meaning of the unclear term, and it must be reconcilable with what has been written.

As we saw in the discussion of interpretation in Chapter 10, many courts have moved away from a purely text-based approach to the question of whether a term is uncertain or ambiguous, and are receptive to available contextual evidence that casts light on the meaning of the written language. Even if the writing seems clear and unambiguous on its face, the contextual approach assumes that written words do not have a constant, immutable meaning, but that the context in which the words were used could color their meaning.

For example, recall that the written contract between The Four Crooners and Integrated Recording provided that The Four Crooners would receive a royalty of "15 percent of gross receipts from CD sales." Say that The Four Crooners do not make any allegation that the parties agreed to a higher royalty for sales over 100,000 copies. Rather, the dispute centers on the meaning of "gross receipts from CD sales." The Four Crooners say that the phrase is intended to include all income derived from sales of the recording, whether in the form of actual physical CDs, or in intangible forms, such as music files that are downloaded from Web sites. Integrated Recording argues that the clear language of the written contract intends to confine the royalties to receipts from CD sales. The Four Crooners seek to testify that this point was discussed by the parties at the time of signing the contract, and they orally agreed that "gross receipts from CD sales" meant all income from sales of the recording in any form. A literal-minded court applying a four corners approach may consider the written language to be clear in confining royalties to receipts from CD sales. However, a court that sees context as important is likely to be less confident of the face-value meaning of the writing. Provided that the written language is reasonably susceptible of the meaning alleged by The Four Crooners, it would consider this evidence as a preliminary matter to decide the question of whether the writing is unclear. The court may ultimately decide that it is not. The point though, is that the court would be reluctant to exclude the parol evidence without having the opportunity to think about the word's meaning in light of it. (It is also worth stressing again that even if the court decided to admit the evidence, the Four Crooners must still persuade the jury that the oral agreement was made.)

§12.9 DISTINGUISHING CONSISTENCY FROM CONTRADICTION

If the judge decides that the writing is a full and final expression of the parties' agreement (that is, it is totally integrated) the inquiry ends and the parol evidence is excluded. However, if the judge determines that the writing is not totally integrated, parol evidence is admissible to supplement or explain the writing, but not to contradict it. Stated differently, even where the agreement is not fully integrated, parol evidence cannot be admitted if it is inconsistent with, and cannot be reconciled with, what has been written.

It may be obvious that an alleged parol agreement contradicts the writing. For example, if a contract for the sale of a house states that the price is $500,000, evidence of a contemporaneous oral agreement that the parties agreed to a price of $475,000 cannot be reconciled with the writing. A second example of inconsistency is the illustration in section 12.7 involving the Four Crooners' proffered testimony that the parties had agreed to an 18 percent royalty on sales over 100,000 copies. It is very hard to reconcile this with the clear term in the written contract that provides for a 15 percent royalty on gross receipts. However, in some cases, the possible inconsistency is less clear and may be trickier to decide. Both *Masterson* and *Myskina*, discussed in section 12.7, involved a more subtle question of contradiction. The alleged parol term did not directly clash with a written term, but it departed from the normal legal or factual implications of the language. That is, there was no language in the written contract in *Masterson* stating that the option was assignable, and there was no language in the release in *Myskina* that expressly authorized the publication of the nude photos. However, the absence of any stated limitations on transfer or on authority to publish created the implied understanding that they did not exist.

Maday v. Grathwohl, 805 N.W.2d 285 (Minn. App. 2011), provides another example of a nuanced contradiction. The Grathwohls, owners of a pig farm, needed a means of disposing of the manure generated by their pigs. They therefore entered into a written "manure easement agreement" with Maday, the owner of neighboring farmland, under which they had the right to apply manure generated on their farm on Maday's farmland. The written agreement made it clear that this arrangement was mutually beneficial to the parties — the Grathwohls would be able to get rid of their manure, and Maday would get manure to fertilize his land. The agreement did not require any other compensation to be paid by either party. The agreement also contained no language suggesting that the Grathwohls were obligated to provide manure to Maday, and it specifically stated that they made no warranty as to the quantity or quality of the manure. For several years after this contract was executed, all the manure from the

Grathwohls' farm was applied to Maday's land. However, about seven years after the agreement was made, the Grathwohls began to sell some of the manure to third parties, thereby reducing the amount available for fertilizing Maday's land. Maday sued, claiming that by selling the manure, the Grathwohls had breached an oral agreement, made when the easement was granted, under which they had promised that Maday would receive all the manure generated by the pig farm. The trial court refused to admit this evidence of the alleged oral agreement and granted summary judgment to the Grathwohls. On appeal, Maday argued that the evidence should have been admitted because the oral agreement was separate from and consistent with the written easement. The court of appeals disagreed and affirmed the trial court's grant of summary judgment. It found that the written contract gave the Grathwohls the right, but not the duty, to spread the manure on Maday's land, and there was no provision in the contract that transferred ownership in the manure. Therefore, the court held that because the alleged oral agreement covered the same subject matter as the written agreement (the manure), and was part of the same transaction, it would not naturally be made as a separate agreement. In addition, the alleged oral term was inconsistent with the written agreement, which did not appear to contemplate that the Grathwohls made any commitment to give Maday manure.[4]

Courts do not approach the issue of conflict with implied terms uniformly. A judge who is not enthusiastic about barring parol evidence will likely be reluctant to find a conflict unless there is a very clear and express inconsistency between the writing and the parol evidence. A judge who is more favorably disposed to excluding parol evidence is likely to be more willing to look for conflict beyond what is expressly stated in the writing. It is therefore important to bear in mind that conflict may go beyond an obvious clash with an express term and may arise where the alleged parol term cannot be reconciled with the legal import of the writing.

Before leaving the subject of contradiction, it is important to express a caution about the relationship between integration and contradiction. Although it is possible, as a doctrinal matter, to separate the enquiry into integration from the question of consistency, the cases show that in practice these two concepts are often interrelated. That is, if the court considers the parol term to be at odds with the writing, this factor may influence the court in deciding whether the writing is integrated. In fact, Restatement, Second's

---

4. One odd feature of the case was that the written contract contained a merger clause, which the court found on its face to be a clear integration of the writing. However, the court's discussion of integration comes after its determination of contradiction. Logically, the court should have decided the integration question first, because once the agreement is integrated, no parol evidence comes in, even if consistent. This illustrates the point made in section 12.6, and reinforced in the next paragraph, that courts do not always neatly separate questions of contradiction and integration.

"might naturally be omitted" test and Article 2's "would certainly have been included" test speak as much to consistency as they do to finality of the writing. These two inquiries melded into each other in both the *Masterson* and *Myskina* cases. In *Masterson* the majority's conclusion that the limitation on the option might naturally be made as a separate agreement was motivated in part by its perception that the limitation did not directly contradict any express language in the written grant of the option. The dissent saw the limitation as contradictory because the usual implication of law is that an option is transferable unless the agreement clearly states otherwise. In *Myskina*, the court's conclusion that the release was integrated was based in its view that the limitation on the release would certainly have been included in the writing had the parties agreed to it. The court went on to say that, in any event, a parol term qualifying the extent of the release was inconsistent with the absolute release in the writing.

§12.10 THE EFFECT OF THE RULE ON EVIDENCE OF COURSE OF PERFORMANCE, COURSE OF DEALING, AND TRADE USAGE

In dealing with interpretation in context, section 10.1.3 explained the meaning of and the role played by course of performance, course of dealing, and trade usage. We now focus on what impact the parol evidence rule might have on the admissibility of this type of contextual evidence. In most cases course of performance can be disposed of easily because it is typically not parol evidence. Although it is conceivable that there could be a course of performance between the oral agreement and the execution of the writing, in most situations any course of performance only takes place after the written contract has been executed. However, course of dealing is, by definition, something that occurs prior to the contract and trade usage exists prior and contemporaneously with it. Therefore, a court could treat evidence of course of dealing or trade usage as a form of parol evidence and could exclude it if the agreement is integrated or, even if not, if it cannot be reconciled with the written terms. However, course of dealing and trade usage differ in an important respect from the evidence of a party on the discussions that led to the alleged parol agreement — a course of dealing or trade usage can be established by more reliable objective evidence of mutual conduct or accepted custom. Courts are therefore more likely to admit evidence of course of dealing and trade usage.

Restatement, Second, §213 provides no guidance on how a court should approach this kind of contextual evidence. It refers only to parol terms that were allegedly agreed to between the parties during their interaction leading up to the execution of the writing. By contrast, UCC §2.202(a) specifically permits an otherwise integrated agreement to be supplemented by evidence of course of dealing and trade usage. (Section 2.202(a) also specifically includes evidence of course of performance which, as noted above, typically does not even qualify as parol evidence.)

Where the written memorial of the contract is not a full and complete expression of the terms of the contract, it is easy to see why a court would be receptive to course of dealing or trade usage evidence to supplement or explain the contract's terms. For example, *Grace Label, Inc. v. Kliff*, 355 F. Supp. 2d 965 (S.D. Iowa 2005) involved a contract to supply trading cards bearing the likeness of Britney Spears, to be placed in packets of snack food. Sadly (and I am sure this is no reflection on Britney) the cards smelled bad and were unfit for inclusion in food packages. The seller sought to admit evidence of a course of dealing to establish that it had not breached the contract by supplying smelly cards. The seller offered this evidence of prior transactions to establish the parties' expectation that the seller would use the same materials in printing the cards as it had used in similar prior transactions. The seller had done so, and therefore argued that it was not responsible for the problem with the cards. The court overruled the buyer's objection to the admission of this evidence, which it held merely explained and supplemented, but did not contradict the written contract term.

However, UCC §2.202 goes beyond merely allowing evidence of course of dealing, trade usage or course of performance where the agreement is not integrated. It makes it clear that this type of contextual evidence should be admitted even where the writing is intended as a final expression of agreement.[5] That is, §2.202 presumes very strongly that the parties intend to contract in light of their own and the market's customary practices. This means that the parties could reasonably take for granted that the contract includes terms arising from these sources, and may not mention them in the writing, even where that writing is otherwise fully integrated. This strong recognition of course of dealing and trade usage compels parties to use very clear and specific language in the writing if they truly do intend to exclude a course of dealing or a trade usage from their contract.

The strength of trade usage and the likelihood that it will be found consistent with the writing in all but the most overwhelming cases of direct conflict is illustrated by *Nanakuli Paving & Rock Co. v. Shell Oil Co.*, 664 F.2d 772 (9th Cir. 1981). We first encountered this case in section 10.1.3 in connection with the role of trade usage in interpretation. Recall that the written contract under which Shell supplied asphalt to Nanakuli provided that the

---

5. Comment 1(c) to §2.202 states further that the court does not need to find that the writing is ambiguous as a precondition to admissibility of this type of evidence.

price of the asphalt was Shell's posted price at the time of delivery. The court held that this clear language was qualified by a trade usage under which the seller would "price protect" the buyer by charging the lower posted price prevailing at the time that the buyer committed itself under a paving contract with its customer. Because the contract was in writing, the court had to decide whether the evidence of trade usage was admissible. Although the price term was clear and seemed quite absolute, the court found no inconsistency between the price term and the price protection usage. *Nanakuli* may go further than other courts in its notion of consistency, but it does show that, at least where a sale of goods is involved, parties should not lightly assume that trade usage or course of dealing evidence will be barred by an apparently integrated writing that does not specifically negate the usage or course of dealing.

§12.11 THE COLLATERAL AGREEMENT RULE

The collateral agreement rule is sometimes referred to as an exception to the parol evidence rule, but it is not really an exception at all. Rather, it follows from an application of the general principles of the parol evidence rule. The collateral agreement rule developed as a means of softening a firm "four corners" approach to parol evidence at a time when courts were more inclined to determine integration by looking no further than the four corners of the writing. A court that adopts a broader contextual approach to parol evidence and uses the Restatement, Second's "might naturally be omitted" test or Article 2's "would certainly have been included" test does not need the collateral agreement rule because those tests cover the same type of situation and are less rigorous. However, the rule still features in some modern cases.

The gist of the rule is that even where a contract is integrated, if the parol agreement is sufficiently distinct from the scope of the writing, it can be seen as a different contract, related to but separate from the integrated written agreement. If so, evidence of this collateral agreement is not barred by the parol evidence rule. Stated differently, even if the alleged parol agreement relates to the same transaction as the writing, if it is self-contained and distinct enough to be seen as a collateral agreement, the parties may not have intended it to be covered by the integrated writing. Evidence of the collateral agreement may therefore be admitted. The requirement of consistency applies even where the parol agreement is found to be collateral, so evidence of a collateral agreement that contradicts the writing may not be admitted. The determination of whether an agreement is collateral can be slippery, and different courts have different views on the relationship between the writing and the parol agreement. A requirement that is regularly expressed is that both the subject matter of and the consideration for the parol agreement must be distinct and capable of being separately identified.

Mitchell v. Lath, 160 N.E. 646 (N.Y. 1928) is one of the best-known cases to deal with the collateral agreement rule. The seller of real property agreed orally to remove an unsightly ice house on land adjacent to the property sold to the buyer. This undertaking was not included in the written contract for the sale of the property. The written contract appeared comprehensive and included a number of other terms ancillary to the sale. The majority of the court refused to find that the agreement to remove the ice house was a collateral agreement — it was related closely enough to the sale of the property that one would expect to find it in the writing if it had been agreed to. The dissent felt that the oral undertaking was distinct enough that the parties could have made it as a separate ancillary contract, not intended to be integrated into the writing.

The collateral agreement rule was also considered in *Myskina v. Conde Nast Publications, Inc.,* discussed in sections 12.7. and 12.9. The court held that the oral agreement limiting the magazine's right to publish the nude photos was not collateral to, but an integral part of the release, and that it contradicted it. The close conceptual connection between the collateral agreement rule and the Restatement, Second, and UCC tests should be apparent from the account of these cases. It is even more striking in *Maday v. Grathwohl,* the case involving the manure easement agreement, also discussed in section 12.7. The court does not mention the collateral agreement rule and discusses consistency on the basis of a test equivalent to the Restatement, Second's "might naturally be omitted" test. However, in discussing the admissibility of the evidence that the Grathwohls' made an oral commitment to give all the manure to Maday, the court focused on factors associated with the collateral agreement rule: The agreements addressed the same subject matter and had the same consideration.

---

§12.12 EXCEPTIONS TO THE PAROL EVIDENCE RULE: EVIDENCE TO ESTABLISH GROUNDS FOR AVOIDANCE OR INVALIDITY, OR TO SHOW A CONDITION PRECEDENT

The primary purpose of the parol evidence rule is to keep spurious or irrelevant evidence from the factfinder, but there is always a danger that it may be used to exclude truthful evidence of genuine agreement that was, for some reason, not encompassed within the writing. If the parol evidence relates to an alleged term that was in fact agreed to but is not reflected in a completely integrated writing or is not consistent with what was written, the party seeking to present the evidence is out of luck. By failing to ensure the accuracy of the writing, that party exposed itself to the risk of not being able to prove the term.

However, in some situations, this result may be too harsh, and may play into the hands of an unscrupulous operator who has deliberately taken advantage of the other party. To cater for such situations, there is a well recognized exception to the rule that permits the introduction of parol evidence to show fraud, duress, mistake, and other bases for invalidating or avoiding the contract. For example, in *America's Directories, Inc. v. Stellhorn One Hour Photo, Inc.*, 833 N.E.2d 1059 (Ind. App. 2005) the president of America's Directories, a corporation that sold advertising in a telephone directory, used persistent hard-selling techniques to persuade Stellhorn to sign three standard form contracts under which it purchased three years' advertising in the directory. Stellhorn was reluctant to buy the ads, and only did so after being assured orally that he could cancel after one year. The standard form contracts stated unequivocally that they could not be cancelled, and they contained a merger clause excluding all verbal agreements and representations not contained in the writing. Despite that, the court admitted evidence of the oral agreement because the evidence indicated that America's Directories never intended to allow Stellhorn to cancel and it made several other false representations to induce him to enter the contracts. We will deal with the elements of fraud more fully in section 13.6. For the present, it is enough to note that relief is available for fraud if a party makes a fraudulent misrepresentation which justifiably induces the victim to enter the contract. Fraud usually involves a misrepresentation of fact. However, a misrepresentation of intent can also constitute fraud if, at the time of entering the contract, the party making the misrepresentation intends to renege on his promise.

The exception for mistake, fraud, and other forms of improper bargaining creates the risk that the parol evidence tendered to show mistake or misconduct may itself be perjured, thereby defeating the rule's purpose of protecting the integrity of a final writing. However, this risk is seen as necessary to ensure that the rule is not used as a means of defeating a party's right to avoidance.

Along similar lines, parol evidence is also admissible to show that a fact recited in a writing is false. For example, say that a contract between Archie, an architect, and Homer, a homeowner, provides, "In consideration for $1,500 paid by Homer, Archie agrees to draw plans . . . ," Archie would be permitted to introduce evidence that the money was never in fact paid. The purpose of this, of course, is to prevent Homer from using the parol evidence rule to evade payment by blocking Archie's testimony of nonpayment. That testimony would, in effect, turn the recital of payment into an implied promise to pay. (You may remember from section 7.7 that parties sometimes use a false recital of consideration in an attempt to validate gifts. That is, Archie may have agreed to draw the plans for free, and the parties merely recited the fact of payment to make it appear as if Archie received consideration for his promise. In this situation, although the parol evidence of nonpayment is admissible, it could be countered by Homer's testimony that no promise was intended.)

Another exception to the rule permits parol evidence to be admitted to show that the agreement was subject to a condition. Conditions are explained more fully in Chapter 16. For the present, it is sufficient to understand that the parties may reach agreement on an exchange of performances, but provide that one or both parties' performance obligation will take effect only if a future uncertain event occurs (or does not occur). For example, say that when Archie and Homer were negotiating their contract, Archie told Homer that he was waiting to hear if he had secured a contract to supervise the construction of an office building in another city, and if he got that contract he would have to leave town for a year and could not take on Homer's project. The parties therefore signed the memorandum subject to the oral understanding that their contract was contingent on Archie not being awarded the other contract. Archie is then awarded the other contract and seeks to escape his obligation to Homer by testifying to the oral condition.

If the court finds the writing to be an integration, the parol evidence rule would normally exclude this testimony. However, because the testimony relates to a condition precedent to Archie's performance, the rule does not apply. This exception has long been recognized by courts and is reflected in Restatement, Second, §217. Comment *b* to §217 seeks to rationalize it on the basis that if a condition exists, the writing cannot be said to be integrated. This is rather flimsy reasoning, which could just as well be applied to any other alleged term. A point of distinction could be that if a contract is subject to a condition, no obligations come into existence unless the condition is met. However, this is not a convincing rationale either, because a contract subject to a condition precedent is a contract nevertheless. There is no reason to treat the allegation of a parol condition with any less suspicion than some other term claimed to have been left out of the writing. Nevertheless, the exception is well established.

The difficulty of applying the exception is shown by *Torres v. D'Alesso*, 910 N.Y.S.2d 1 (App. Div. 2010). A written contract for the purchase of real estate had no financing contingency and included a merger clause. The buyer did not proceed with the transaction, and the seller sued him for damages. The buyer defended the suit on the basis that the sale was subject to an oral condition precedent that had not been satisfied. He sought to testify about an oral understanding that he had reached with the seller's attorney that the attorney would hold his down payment check until he notified the attorney that he had secured financing. The buyer contended that this understanding made the contract conditional on his obtaining a loan. The trial court refused to admit this testimony and granted summary judgment in favor of the seller. The majority of the Appellate Division affirmed. It acknowledged the general rule that parol evidence is admissible to prove a condition precedent to the legal effectiveness of a written agreement, provided that the condition does not contradict the express terms of the writing. However, the majority held that the exception did not apply in this case. It held that the merger clause constituted a complete integration of the writing, which barred evidence of any alleged oral condition precedent. The court indicated that even in the absence of a merger clause, evidence of the alleged oral condition would still be inadmissible as inconsistent: It contradicted terms in the writing that required the buyer to make a down payment by a "good check" that the seller's attorney was required to place in escrow immediately.[6] The dissenting judge argued that a merger clause should not preclude evidence of an oral condition precedent because the merger clause is part of a contract that only takes effect once the condition is satisfied. Therefore, the mere existence of a merger clause cannot logically preclude testimony of the oral condition precedent to its effectiveness. The dissent also did not find inconsistency between the terms of the contract and the oral condition precedent. It acknowledged that there must necessarily be some disparity between an alleged oral condition and an apparently unconditional contract, but did not consider this to amount to a contradiction. The dissent would not find inconsistency unless there was an explicit contradiction that would not allow the alleged oral condition to stand side by side with the writing.

§12.13 RESTRICTIONS ON ORAL MODIFICATION

As stated before, the parol evidence rule does not exclude testimony relating to agreements made after the writing. These are not part of the environment in which the writing was executed, and they cannot be superseded by it. However, the parties may wish to avoid disputes over possible future allegations of oral modification, and may therefore insert a "no oral modification" clause in the writing, stating that no modification will be binding unless written and signed by both parties. Such clauses are difficult to enforce because courts do not usually consider that the parties can effectively restrict in advance their right to modify orally. The parties' power to modify the contract must include the power to modify the "no oral modification" clause, and the fact that they made an oral modification in itself indicates that they did so. Therefore, although a "no oral modification" clause may make

---

6. Apart from integration and inconsistency, the majority advanced other grounds for refusing to admit the evidence: It considered that the formalities imposed on a sale of real property by the statute of frauds made it inappropriate to consider evidence of an oral condition in relation to a real estate transaction. The majority also doubted that the alleged undertaking of the seller's attorney was clear enough to constitute agreement to a condition precedent.

it more difficult for a party to succeed in asserting an oral modification, such a clause may not be a watertight exclusion. A court may be willing to admit evidence of an alleged oral modification despite the existence of the restriction in the writing, and to leave it to the jury to decide whether the modification was in fact made.

UCC §2.209(2) appears to change this approach by expressly recognizing the effectiveness of "no oral modification" clauses in sales of goods. However, the recognition is half-hearted because §2.209(4) provides that even if the later oral modification is ineffective because the original contract requires written modification, the attempt at oral modification may still operate as a waiver of rights under the original contract. Under §2.209(5) the waiver is generally effective. It can only be retracted in relation to future performance if it has not been detrimentally relied upon by the other party, and it cannot be retracted to the extent that it covers performance that has already been rendered.

§12.14 A TRANSNATIONAL PERSPECTIVE ON THE PAROL EVIDENCE RULE

As explained in section 12.4, a principal rationale for the parol evidence rule is that it keeps suspect and unreliable evidence from the factfinder, which is commonly the jury. Civilian jurisdictions do not generally have jury trials in civil cases, so there is less need for a rule that controls potentially misleading and prejudicial evidence from the factfinder. Although civilian systems may recognize a presumption in favor of the accuracy of a written contract, and some may impose restrictions on the admission of parol evidence in some cases, the general rule is that the terms of a contract may be proved by all relevant evidence. The CISG and the UNIDROIT Principles have adopted the civilian approach and do not contain a rule restricting parol evidence. However, if the parties include a clearly drafted merger clause in the written contract, the clause is likely to be given effect to exclude any alleged oral agreement that was not incorporated into the writing.

Examples

1. Ann Cestral owned a house on a large central city lot that had been in her family for four generations. When she decided to move to a smaller condo, she agreed to sell the house to her cousin, Ava Rice. They settled on the price and Ann arranged for her attorney to draw up a contract of sale. When the document was ready for signature, Ann and Ava drove together to the attorney's office. On the way Ann said to Ava, "Our family

has owned this house for a long time, and I sold it to you because I want it to remain in the family. Promise me that if you ever decide to sell the house, you will give members of our family the right of first refusal to buy it before you sell it to a stranger." Ava agreed. When Ann and Ava arrived at the attorney's office they were given a standard sales agreement which they both signed. The agreement was several pages long and had lots of details. Neither Ann nor Ava told the attorney about their discussion on the way over, so their agreement on the family's right of first refusal was not incorporated into the written contract.

Ava took transfer of the house and moved in. Over the next couple of years, large lots in the neighborhood became very valuable because of their central location. Developers were buying houses and demolishing them so the properties could be used for high-rise condominiums. Two years after she bought the house from Ann, Ava accepted a developer's offer to buy the house for an extraordinarily good price. When Ann found out that Ava had sold the property, she confronted Ava angrily. In response, Ava waved their written contract in Ann's face and yelled, "Show me where this says I can't sell the property to anyone that I please!" Does Ava have a point?

2. Klaus Merger owned two adjoining quarter-acre lots. One had a house on it and the other, overgrown and neglected, had been used by Klaus as a dumping ground for assorted bits of junk, including a couple of broken-down cars. A few months ago Klaus placed the quarter-acre with the house on the market. Andy Gration expressed interest in buying it and negotiations ensued. Andy eventually agreed to buy it for the asking price on condition that Klaus cleared up the adjacent lot and removed all the junk. Klaus agreed to do this.

Klaus then produced a standard-form agreement of sale that he had downloaded and printed from the Internet. The form had the usual provisions found in transactions of this kind, with blank spaces for details such as the property description and price. One of its standard terms was a merger clause, stating "This is the entire agreement between the parties. No agreements or representations have been made save for those stated herein." There was also a large blank space at the end of the form headed "Additional Terms." Klaus filled out all the other blanks in the form but wrote nothing in the space provided for additional terms. The form therefore did not mention the clearing of the adjacent lot. Both parties signed the form.

Klaus never cleared the lot and denies ever agreeing to do so. What are Andy's chances of proving and enforcing the oral agreement?

3. Di Aquiri owns a tavern. Margie Rita runs a small, exclusive distillery that makes a variety of health-conscious, socially responsible, nonalcoholic versions of popular liquors. Di entered into a written contract with

Margie under which Di bought 100 bottles of Margie's "fat-free, sugar-free, sodium-free,[7] nonalcoholic, non-animal-tested, all natural faux tequila." In addition to this description of the goods, the writing stated the names and addresses of the parties, the price of "$10 per bottle, subject to discount for cash," payment terms (30 days after delivery) and delivery date. It also contained a merger clause stating that the writing was intended to be "the complete, exclusive and final expression of all terms agreed to by the parties." Both parties signed the writing and Margie delivered the liquor on the due date.

Consider how the parol evidence rule would affect the following different disputes that arose after delivery.

a. Upon delivery, Di gave Margie's driver a check for $900, this being the stated contract price of $1,000 less a ten percent discount for early payment. Margie refuses to allow Di a ten percent discount. She says that the parties discussed the amount of the discount orally, and she told Di that it was five percent. Di claims that they agreed to a ten percent discount.

b. Di did not pay the driver. Five days later she sent a check for $900 in payment, less a ten percent discount. Margie's problem is not with the amount of the discount, but with Di's right to it at all. She says that "cash payment" means cash on delivery, so Di is not entitled to any discount. Di says that Margie told her orally that payment within a week of delivery qualifies as cash. Margie denies ever discussing the question.

c. After delivery Di, who is very fussy about the quality of what she serves to her customers, conducted her usual chemical analysis of the faux tequila. She found that it has traces of fat and sugar (about 0.5 percent of each). Di's tests also revealed that the faux tequila contains about 0.08 percent alcohol. She wishes to reject the goods as nonconforming to the contract and to get her money back. Margie claims that she is not entitled to do this for two reasons. First, Margie has sold liquor to Di in the past with similar small traces of fat, sugar, and alcohol, and Di has never objected before. Second, it is widely accepted in the make-believe-liquor industry that one can never completely remove the good stuff, and beverages described as free of a substance may acceptably contain up to one percent of it.

4. Gordon Bleu, a chef who owns and operates a restaurant, decided to begin serving game birds to his customers. He found a recipe for pheasant and checked the catalog of his regular supplier, Fairest Fowls, Inc., to see what it cost. The catalog showed "regular" pheasant for $5.00 per pound, and "plump deluxe" pheasant for $12.50 per

---

7. It is also taste-free, but the agreement did not specify that.

pound. Gordon decided that "regular" pheasant would be fine, and he called Fairest Fowls and placed an order for 50 birds.

A couple of days later Fairest Fowls delivered the birds, accompanied by its written delivery invoice. The invoice contained the parties' names and addresses, the date, and the statement "Delivered as per order, 50 regular pheasants @$5.00 per pound. Cash on delivery." The invoice was signed by a representative of Fairest Fowls. Gordon signed the form as requested and paid the driver.[8]

Gordon prepared the birds exactly in accordance with his recipe, but they were tough and uneatable. Gordon complained to Fairest Fowls, which explained that it used the word "regular" in its catalog to denote scrawny birds useful only for soup, and that the more expensive "plump deluxe" variety had to be used if the flesh was to be eaten. Fairest Fowls said that "everyone knew this about pheasants," and it was surprised that Gordon, as a trained chef, was unaware of the distinction.

Gordon insists that there is no reason why he should have understood "regular" in the sense used by Fairest Fowls and he points out that the dictionary meaning of "regular" is "usual, normal or customary." Fairest Fowls claims that it can produce several experts in the restaurant trade who would attest to the fact that "regular" pheasants are commonly understood to be suitable only for soup.

If Gordon and Fairest Fowls cannot settle their dispute and Gordon decides to sue Fairest Fowls for the return of his money, would Fairest Fowls be able to introduce the testimony of its expert witnesses over Gordon's objection?

5. Beverly Hill, a movie producer, offered a leading role in a new movie to Holly Wood, an actress. The parties met with their lawyers and agents and spent the full morning negotiating the terms of the contract. By noon they had reached agreement. Their attorneys spent the rest of the day drafting the written agreement.

The parties met again on the following morning and signed the agreement. After signing, the lawyers and agents left. Beverly and Holly remained in Beverly's office to celebrate making the deal. As she was sipping her champagne, Holly said, "You know, I am really unhappy about that advance of $2 million that you agreed to pay me next week.

---

8. If this Example sounds familiar, it is because it is based on Example 2 of Chapter 10. That example involved the interpretation of an oral contract. In the present Example, the contract is recorded in the invoice, which is a written memorial of agreement for parol evidence purposes. The goal of this Example is to allow you to consider the parol evidence issue that was absent from Example 2 of Chapter 10. After working through this Example, you may find it helpful to review Example 2 of Chapter 10 to compare interpretational issues in the absence of the parol evidence rule. (Note that some of the facts concerning the evidence have been changed or simplified in this Example.)

I think that it should be higher, say $2.5 million. After all, I have to live until the box office receipts come in." Beverly replied, "No problem, I'll send you a check for $2.5 million instead." The parties did not amend the figure of $2 million in the written contract, and the agreement to increase the advance was not otherwise recorded in writing. The next week, Beverly sent a check of $2 million to Holly as specified in the written agreement. She denies ever agreeing to pay more. The written agreement does not have a "no oral modification" clause.

Holly immediately sued for the additional $500,000. Beverly applied for summary judgment on the ground that the written contract clearly calls for a payment of $2 million, and no parol evidence can be tendered by Holly to support her claim for more money. Should Beverly be granted summary judgment?

6. Buffy Beefcake is a well-known football star. He was approached by Cal Candid, who asked him if he would pose for a nude photograph to be used in a "Superjocks" calendar that Cal was producing for the next year. Cal told Buffy that the calendar would feature one naked sports hero per month. Buffy would receive a modest fee of $5,000 (really just an honorarium) for posing and allowing the use of his photo, and all profits from the sales of the calendars would go to a hospital that conducted research on the prevention of sports injuries. Buffy was a bit bashful and did not like the idea of being photographed in the nude, but he felt that it was for a good cause, so he agreed. Cal produced a five-page standard form contract, which Buffy signed without reading. Had he read it, he would have seen that it said nothing at all about the donation of the profits to the hospital. Instead, it provided that apart from the payment of the $5,000 fee, Buffy had no rights or claims whatsoever, and that all profits from the sale of the calendars would be solely the property of Cal. The writing also contained a merger clause.

After the calendar was produced, Buffy discovered that Cal had not donated any of the calendar's proceeds to the hospital. He would like to institute action against Cal for an order compelling him to pay the profits to the hospital. Will the parol evidence rule prevent him from testifying about Cal's oral undertaking?

7. Mel Odorous operates a fish processing plant. To get rid of the detritus generated by his operation, he entered into a written contract with Pungent Puppy, Inc., a manufacturer of dog food, under which he agreed to "deliver" his entire output of fish waste to Pungent Puppy at the end of each week. The contract was for a term of two years. It recorded that the delivery of fish waste was mutually beneficial to the parties, and that neither was obliged to pay any additional consideration under the contract. Immediately after the contract was executed, the parties had a dispute. Mel says that Pungent Puppy must collect the waste from his

plant, but Pungent Puppy says that it's Mel's responsibility to transport the waste to its facility. Mel claims that he has been in business for 30 years. He has always disposed of waste by giving it to fertilizer and pet food manufacturers, and the manufacturers have always collected the waste from his plant. He therefore asserts that this was a term of his contract with Pungent Puppy. Pungent Puppy says that Mel's previous arrangements with other manufacturers are irrelevant, and that by using the word "deliver," the contract clearly places the duty on Mel to transport the waste to Pungent Puppy. If this dispute gets to the stage of litigation, would Mel's testimony about his prior practices be admissible?

Explanations

1. Yes, faithless Ava does have a point, because if Ann decides to sue on the basis of Ava's undertaking, she is confronted with two hurdles. She must first convince the judge to admit her evidence of the oral term that qualified the writing, and if she succeeds, she must then convince the jury that such a term was in fact agreed to. A written memorandum of agreement was executed, and Ann seeks to testify about a prior oral agreement. Ava may object to admission of the evidence under the parol evidence rule, and the judge must determine as a question of law whether the evidence is admissible. If not, it is excluded and the jury does not hear it, leaving Ann with no case. If Ann can jump this hurdle by satisfying the judge that the evidence is not barred by the rule and is admissible, she may then testify about the conversation before the jury. The next hurdle is to convince the jury that the conversation occurred. If Ava denies it, Ann will only win if the jury believes her over Ava.

   In the first stage of this process, the judge considers two questions. The first concerns the issue of integration and involves two possibilities: First, the writing may have been intended as the full and final expression of the parties' agreement (that is, a total or complete integration). If it is, parol evidence is inadmissible. If the writing is not a total integration, the judge goes to the next level of the preliminary inquiry to decide the issue of consistency. The parol evidence may be admitted to the extent that it is consistent with what has been recorded in the writing. Thus, the evidence may explain an ambiguity or vagueness, or it may fill a gap, but it may not contradict the writing.

   The parties' agreement is integrated if they intended the writing to fully express everything that they agreed, so that no additional undertakings were made. As usual, the parties' intent is gauged by objective evidence. Under the strict "four corners" test, the only objective evidence that the court uses is the written contract itself. Integration is found if the writing appears complete and unambiguous, and there is no obvious gap or inadequacy. Although the facts do not set out the terms of the contract, they were apparently detailed. At face value, it seems final and complete and would be perceived as integrated under this test.

The contextual approach to integration, which is followed by many modern courts, goes beyond the face of the writing and evaluates contextual evidence to decide the question of integration. The only contextual evidence here apart from the parol evidence itself (Ann's testimony of the conversation) is the fact that the parties were members of the family that had owned the house for generations. This has a bearing on the question of integration. If the parties were strangers, dealing at arms length, one would expect a term restricting the buyer's right to dispose freely of the property to be stated in the apparently complete writing. However, the trust and perceived mutual sentiment engendered by the family relationship might plausibly explain why the parties in this case would be happy to allow the writing to reflect only the routine legal formalities and to omit this more personal aspect of their agreement. The point, as expressed in Restatement, Second, §216(b) is whether the circumstances are such that the term might naturally be omitted from the writing.

In *Masterson v. Sine*, discussed in section 12.7, the parties' family relationship persuaded the majority that an oral agreement prohibiting the assignment of a repurchase option might naturally be made separately from the writing that granted the option. The dissent rejected the majority's test of integration and went on to say that even if that test was used, the oral agreement did not satisfy it. An agreement directly qualifying an absolute right in the written contract would not naturally be omitted from the writing. These contrary approaches show that the resolution of the question of integration largely depends on how liberal a view the court takes on this issue. It is conceivable but not assured that a court could find that the writing executed by Ann and Ava was not intended as a complete expression of the parties' agreement.

If the judge finds that the writing is not fully integrated, Ann's evidence is admissible provided that it does not contradict the writing. The oral agreement does not directly contradict an express term, but a restriction on Ava's right to transfer her property freely does contradict the normal legal assumption that an owner has the right to dispose of her property as she sees fit. This is a more subtle contradiction. A court that distrusts evidence of alleged prior oral agreement can make a good argument that this is a contradiction, but a court that is more amenable to the admission of parol evidence can make an equally good contrary argument. Again, this difference of view appears in the majority and dissenting opinions in *Masterson*. The narrower test of inconsistency would allow Ann to go to trial and to attempt to convince the jury that the oral agreement was made. A wider view would enable the court to dispose of Ann's case summarily.

2. The analysis of this problem is the same as that in Example 1, but Andy's problem is worse than Ann's. To begin with, there is a merger clause in the writing, and an unfilled blank suitable for inserting a term like this. Courts tend to be wary of standard-form merger clauses, because they may not have been conspicuous or understood, but this does not mean that such clauses are invariably treated as ineffective. A signatory has a duty to read the document before signing it, even if the document is a standard form, and one who fails to exercise that duty cannot expect relief unless the bargaining circumstances compel the conclusion of unfair imposition. (This issue is raised in sections 4.1.5 and 5.3 and is fully discussed in section 13.12.) There is nothing in the facts of this case to indicate that Andy could not be expected to read and understand the writing or that Klaus had a bargaining advantage that allowed him to impose unfairly one-sided terms.

On a "four corners" test the apparent completeness of the document, the unfilled blank space, and the merger clause will surely lead to the conclusion of integration. Even on a contextual approach, the terms of the writing, including the merger clause, are taken seriously. However, the contextual approach at least gives Andy a shot at explaining why the apparent integration was not intended as such. In other words, Andy is given the opportunity to persuade the court that despite the existence of an apparently complete and final writing, this term might naturally have been agreed to separately. On these facts, this does not seem like an easy task. One basis for making this argument is that a standard form was used which does not admit the addition of special terms tailored to the transaction. However, that will not work here because there was space for its insertion on the form. Family connection or some other relationship may explain an informal approach to some special term of a contract, as discussed in Example 1, but Andy had no prior connection with Klaus.

Section 12.11 discusses the collateral agreement rule. As you probably noticed, the facts of this Example are reminiscent of *Mitchell v. Lath* which found the rule to be inapplicable to an oral promise to remove an ice house from property adjacent to the property sold. The underlying rationale of the collateral agreement rule is similar to that of the Restatement, Second, test. In fact, the tests are really just alternative formulations of the same principle. However, the collateral agreement rule is more difficult to satisfy because it requires the parol agreement to be distinct enough from the writing to qualify as a separate but related agreement. To satisfy this standard, the subject matter of the oral and written agreements must cover different performances with identifiably separate consideration. It is hard to imagine that an oral agreement could qualify as separate if it might not naturally be agreed to separately. In addition, Andy made no promise of additional consideration for the oral promise, and there is no indication that the parties intended to allocate any portion of the property's purchase price to the clearing of the adjacent land.

3. This Example involves a sale of goods, so UCC §2.202, the Article 2 version of the parol evidence rule, applies. In general principle, it is substantially similar to the contemporary common law rule, so many courts would not answer these questions differently had this not been a sale of goods. The writing in this case is apparently intended as a complete integration. It contains all the terms essential to a sales contract and it has a merger clause. Notwithstanding, it is not a watertight final and complete memorial of agreement, so most of the parol evidence suggested by the questions should be admissible.

a. Despite the attempt at integration, the parties did not fully express their agreement. They provided for a discount but failed to specify its amount. With regard to this term, the writing cannot be a complete and final expression of their agreement, so evidence of what they agreed orally is admissible to supplement it. Note that neither denies making an oral agreement, but they argue about what was agreed. Neither party's evidence is inconsistent with the writing, so it will all be admitted and the factfinder will have to decide whose version of the discussion is correct.

b. Although the amount of the discount was omitted, the existence of that gap does not give Di license to produce parol evidence on other terms that are fully, clearly, and finally expressed in the writing. On a "four corners" test, the agreement is apparently integrated on this issue, and Di would probably prevail on the plain meaning of the word "cash." However, Comment 1 to §2.202 makes it clear that the "four corners" approach is not to be used in sales of goods, and that meaning must be determined in the commercial context in which the words were used. This does not mean that we abandon all restrictions on admissibility merely because one of the parties is willing to testify as to a meaning different from the obvious ordinary meaning of the writing. The contextual evidence must point to a meaning of which the writing is reasonably susceptible — it must persuade the court that there is some basis for going beyond the apparent clarity of the writing. If not, the evidence should not be admitted because the party offering it has not shown that the apparently integrated writing suffers from an ambiguity or vagueness that requires explanation. (Alternatively, even if there is no integration, the contended meaning does not explain, but contradicts, the writing.)

The only contextual evidence of the meaning of "cash" is the disputed parol evidence itself: Di's allegation about what was said during negotiations. This self-serving testimony is apparently not corroborated by more objective evidence, such as usage or course of dealing. In the absence of some indication that there is a common understanding or a practice between the parties that "cash" means credit of up to a week, it is difficult to reconcile Di's evidence with the word's normal meaning. Even under the more liberal rule of the UCC (and Restatement, Second), the evidence should be excluded.

c. Margie is trying to establish both a course of dealing and a trade usage to show that her faux tequila conforms to the contract even though it has traces of fat, sugar, and alcohol. Section 2.202(a) makes it clear that even if a writing appears fully integrated and has a merger clause, evidence of usage and course of dealing should always be allowed to supplement or explain the writing. However, they may not contradict it. The rationale for this more liberal rule is twofold. First, parties normally take it for granted that a transaction is subject to well-established custom or their own prior practices, so they are unlikely to trouble spelling them out in the writing. Second, the evidence to establish these facts is objective and harder to make up than an account of what was said in negotiations. Therefore, unless the parties negate usages or prior understandings by clear wording (in which case the evidence would contradict the writing), they are assumed to apply despite the silence of an apparently complete agreement.

There is nothing in the writing to indicate that the parties deliberately excluded the usage or practice claimed by Margie, so the general merger clause does not keep out the evidence, and it is admissible unless it is inconsistent with the writing. The writing unqualifiedly describes the tequila as free of fat, sugar, and alcohol, so it could be argued that the writing is contradicted by testimony that small quantities of these substances are acceptable. This again raises the difficult question of deciding whether a qualification to an absolute undertaking is a supplementation or a contradiction. There is no sure dividing line, but courts tend to favor admission of this kind of objective evidence in cases of doubt, requiring quite strong wording of negation to exclude it. A classic example is *Columbia Nitrogen Corp. v. Royster Co.*, 451 F.2d 3 (4th Cir. 1971), in which the written contract provided for the purchase of a specific minimum tonnage of phosphate. The buyer failed to take the minimum and claimed that because of market uncertainties in the industry it was accepted in the trade that quantity specifications were mere projections. Prior transactions between the parties were also alleged to support that reading of the quantity term. The court of appeals held the evidence admissible, reversing the trial court's determination that it contradicted the writing. Do not forget that the decision to admit the evidence is just the first step in the process. Margie must then convince the factfinder that the course of dealing and trade usage did exist and that they support her position.

4. The issue here is the meaning of the word "regular." Gordon contends that its plain meaning is self-evident, but Fairest Fowls argues that it is ambiguous if understood in light of trade usage. If Fairest Fowls is right, we need not be concerned about whether the parties expected the writing to be an integration. The ambiguity of the word means that, at least insofar as the quality of the pheasant is concerned, the writing did not succeed as a complete and final expression of what the parties agreed. Evidence may therefore be admitted to explain the meaning of "regular" provided that the evidence supports a meaning reconcilable with the writing.

A court adopting a "four corners" approach may be inclined to find that there is no ambiguity about "regular" in the context of the writing as a whole, and that it can only have the meaning contended by Gordon. However, such an approach is clearly not appropriate in a sale of goods, because UCC §2.202, Comment I rejects it and calls for consideration of the commercial context in establishing meaning. Section 2.202 gives very strong credence to trade usage, which is presumed to enter the contract unless the parties clearly and unequivocally indicate a contrary intent or the usage cannot be reconciled with the writing. As nothing else in the writing even remotely pertains to the quality of the pheasant, the only language that must be reconciled with the proffered evidence is the word "regular" itself. If looked at from the patterns of normal speech, it is hard to think of "regular" as meaning "old and scrawny." However, from the perspective of the trade in which the parties are engaged,[9] the evidence suggests that there is no inconsistency. That is, having decided that trade usage may support such an esoteric meaning, rendering the word ambiguous, we must necessarily conclude that the meaning is not inconsistent with the word. The expert testimony should therefore not be excluded as parol evidence, and Fairest Fowls should be able to present it to persuade the factfinder that the words mean what it contends.

5. The alleged oral term for the payment of $2.5 million directly contradicts the clear and unambiguous provision in the writing for payment of $2 million. Whether or not the agreement is fully integrated, it does definitively express the amount of the advance, and there is no way in which the written and alleged oral terms can be reconciled by interpretation. Therefore, if the oral agreement is contemporaneous with the writing, evidence of it would be barred by the parol evidence rule.

---

9. In Example 2 of Chapter 10, the issue of defining the trade and holding Gordon accountable for the usage was discussed. This issue is not duplicated here, and the facts indicate that the expert evidence covers the restaurant business, of which Gordon is a member.

However, if the oral agreement was made subsequent to the writing, the parol evidence rule does not apply, and there is no provision in the agreement barring oral modifications. This Example focuses on what is meant by a subsequent agreement for the purposes of the parol evidence rule. If we take a literal approach, the oral agreement was unquestionably made after the writing, and the evidence is admissible. However, such a technical distinction may lead to an absurd result that places too much emphasis on the sequence of events in a single interaction. The alleged amendment was made almost immediately after the execution of the writing, while the parties were still together following the meeting at which it was signed. If the parties really did agree to change the amount of the advance, it would have been easy and natural for them to alter the writing to reflect the change. The fact that the writing was not amended casts suspicion on the claim that the parties agreed to the change. A possible argument that Holly could make is that the departure of the parties' lawyers and agents terminated the stage during which the writing was executed, so that the informal agreement to increase the advance should be treated as subsequent.[10]

A timing issue similar to this arose in *Kehr Packages, Inc. v. Fidelity Bank*, discussed in section 12.3.4. The borrowers alleged that after the written agreement was signed, they made an oral agreement with the lender to increase the amount of the loan. The court found the alleged oral agreement to be contemporaneous with the writing because it was made in the course of the closing process during which the writing had been executed.

6. Buffy can obtain the order only if he can prove that Cal's undertaking to donate the profits to the hospital was a term of the contract. His problem is that this term was agreed orally before the writing was executed and it is absent from the writing. Buffy cannot claim that he did not realize at the time of signing the written contract that it failed to reflect the oral understanding. He had a duty to read it and is bound by its terms. (In *Myskina v. Conde Nast Publications, Inc.*, discussed in section 12.7, the court invoked the duty to read and firmly rejected Myskina's argument that she did not read the release because she was not fluent in English.) Although we do not have the full terms of the writing, it is compendious and is likely a fully integrated agreement. The fact that it has a merger clause adds weight to this conclusion. Even if the agreement is found not to be integrated, a prior oral promise to donate the profits to a hospital likely contradicts the express term that the profits belong to Cal alone.

---

10. Note that even if the court treats the informal agreement as a subsequent modification; the admission of this evidence may not ultimately help Holly in her claim for the extra $500,000. She apparently did not give any consideration to Beverly for the promise to increase the payment.

Although there is not much chance that the parol agreement would be admitted under the normal operation of the parol evidence rule, the facts make out a case for application of the fraud exception. As a matter of public policy, courts do not allow a party to use the parol evidence rule to mask a fraud, so parol evidence is admissible to the extent that it is offered to establish fraud. (See *America's Directories, Inc. v. Stellhorn One Hour Photo, Inc.*, discussed in section 12.12.) We will leave a detailed discussion of the elements of fraud to section 13.6. For now, it is enough to note that a victim of fraud can avoid a contract if he can show that the other party made a fraudulent misrepresentation which justifiably induced him to enter the contract. Although fraud usually involves a misrepresentation of fact, it can also arise where a person makes a contractual promise with the deliberate intention of breaking it, or where a person deliberately misrepresents the content of the document presented for signature. As we will see in section 13.6, Buffy's biggest problem in establishing fraud will be to show that he was justified in relying on an oral representation that was not included in the writing.

7. This Example seeks to surpass *Maday v. Grathwohl* in the repulsiveness of the subject matter of the contract. Unlike that case, Mel is not claiming that the parties made a prior oral agreement that speaks to the issue in dispute. Rather, it seems that the parties did not address this question at all in any negotiations or communications, and that each had a different understanding of who would be responsible for the transport of the waste. The word "deliver," used in their written contract, is ambiguous. It could mean that Mel must physically transport the waste to Pungent Puppy, or it could mean (as it is used in UCC §2.503) that Mel must hold the waste for Pungent Puppy to collect. If the term is ambiguous, there is no bar on parol evidence to establish its meaning. However, Mel's assertion about his past practices with other pet food manufacturers is not really parol evidence at all. His arrangements with previous manufacturers do not constitute a course of dealing because these transactions did not involve Pungent Puppy. Therefore, the exclusion of this evidence would be based on grounds of irrelevance, rather than under the parol evidence rule. Mel may seek to argue that his past arrangements with other manufacturers reflect a more widespread practice in the market that constitutes a trade usage, which would be admissible to clarify the meaning of the ambiguous term "deliver." However, Mel's dealings with other manufacturers in the past are not, on their own, sufficient to establish trade usage. Mel would have to go beyond his own transactions to show that collection of waste by manufacturers is a practice that is currently and widely observed in the market in which the parties operate.

CHAPTER 13

The Judicial Regulation of Improper Bargaining and of Violations of Law and Public Policy

§13.1 INTRODUCTION

This chapter and Chapter 14 deal with several related but distinct doctrines. Sections 13.2 through 13.12 cover a group of doctrines that are designed to regulate improper bargaining: misrepresentation, duress, undue influence, and unconscionability. The theme that connects these doctrines is the balance between the policy of protecting reliance that underlies the objective test of contract and the policy of freedom of contract that dictates not only that parties should have the freedom to enter contracts, but also that they should not be held to contracts to which they did not voluntarily assent. Although the objective test focuses on the manifested intent of the parties rather than on their subjective states of mind, a rigid adherence to objectivity could mask the fact that the apparent assent was not genuine, but was obtained by deceit or improper bargaining tactics. The doctrines mentioned above allow the court to go behind the manifestation of intent to decide if a party's apparent agreement is based on an acceptable degree of volition. They are regulatory in that they allow the court to regulate improper bargaining behavior. They are sometimes called policing doctrines.

Section 13.13 deals with a different kind of regulation — the policing of contracts for compliance with law and public policy. Although this form of regulation has some affinity to the improper bargaining doctrines, it is distinct. Its focus is not on whether one of the parties induced the other's manifestation of assent by deceit or improper tactics, but whether the contract violates a statute, a rule of common law, or an important public policy.

If it does, the court will not enforce it, even though the parties acted with full knowledge and deliberate intent in entering it. The possibility that a court might refuse to enforce a genuinely consensual contract creates tension between the contractual policies of freedom of contract and assent and the other public policy that is implicated in the transaction. Section 13.13 discusses how courts resolve that tension.

Chapter 14 deals with the problem of lack of contractual capacity, either as a result of minority or of mental illness. Although capacity to contract is a subject distinct from those discussed in this chapter, you will see that there are close connections because it also involves fundamental questions of reliance, assent, and public policy.

§13.2 THE OBJECTIVE TEST AND THE VIABILITY OF APPARENT ASSENT

The discussion of the objective test of assent in section 4.1 stressed that although contract is based on consensus, the law does not require a genuine subjective "meeting of the minds." The focus is on apparent assent, as it would reasonably be perceived by one party from the manifested words and actions of the other. This has to be the general rule, otherwise no one could ever rely on overt indications of assent, and the one party's reasonable expectation of agreement could be defeated by a showing that the other really did not mean what those indications reasonably conveyed.

The principal purpose of the objective test is therefore the protection of reasonable expectations. Although a consistent and unbending application of the test would have the merit of certainty, it could lead to great injustice. For example, Lilly Livered signed a memorandum of agreement to sell her casino to Attila "The Animal" Axehacker. She agreed to the sale because Attila shoved the muzzle of his revolver up her left nostril and indicated his intent to pull the trigger if a signature was not immediately forthcoming. No doubt the signature is a first-class manifestation of assent, but no judge (except for Judge "Greasy" Palmer, who was seen taking a brown paper bag from Attila the other day) would hold Lilly accountable for the reasonable import of her conduct. Not only should she not be held accountable for a manifestation of assent forced out of her, but Attila was responsible for undermining her free will and cannot legitimately claim that he relied on her assent being volitional. That is, a rigid focus on Lilly's manifested assent — her signature — would serve neither justice nor the goals of contract law. Policing doctrines allow the court to go behind the appearance of assent in cases like this, in which the process of contract formation is tainted by improper bargaining behavior. The policing doctrine applicable in this particular example is duress because Attila induced Lilly's apparent assent by illegitimate threat. Other facts may satisfy the elements of one of the other doctrines discussed below. As a general observation, it can be said that all the doctrines are safety valves for the objective test, so that it cannot be used as a tool of oppression, deceit or advantage-taking.

§13.3 GENERAL NOTE ON REMEDY: AVOIDANCE AND RESTITUTION, ADJUSTMENT OF THE CONTRACT, OR DAMAGES

The remedies available for improper bargaining are covered in the discussion of each of the separate doctrines in the following sections. This overview identifies and introduces the common remedial principles that apply to the granting of relief under the doctrines.

Avoidance and restitution

A contract induced by improper bargaining is voidable. This means that it can be avoided (rescinded) by the party who is the victim of that improper conduct. A voidable contract must be distinguished from a void contract. If a contract is void (as it would be, for example, if one party failed to give consideration), it is a legal nullity, and neither party can sue to enforce it. By contrast, a voidable contract is a valid contract that remains fully effective unless the aggrieved party elects to exercise the right to terminate it. The aggrieved party therefore has a choice — either she may sue to avoid the contract, or, if she subsequently decides that she wants to keep the contract, despite the other party's improper bargaining, she may do so. If she does not choose to avoid the contract, she may have one of the alternative remedies described below. Note that only the aggrieved party has the election to avoid the contract or keep it in force. Obviously, the party who is guilty of inducing the contract through improper bargaining cannot use his own wrongdoing as the basis of a claim that the contract should not be enforced. The aggrieved party may use the right of avoidance affirmatively, for example, by suing for a declaratory judgment terminating the contract, or defensively, by raising it as a defense when sued on the contract. When a contract is avoided, the general rule is that both parties are entitled to restitution because it would unjustly enrich a party to retain a benefit under an avoided contract. In appropriate cases, the fact that the contract was induced by improper means may affect the equities relevant to restitutionary recovery, resulting in a reduction or elimination of the restitutionary claim of the party at fault.

Adjustment of the terms of the contract to correct the consequences of improper bargaining

If the aggrieved party decides not to avoid the contract, but the other party's improper bargaining resulted in terms that are unfair, the aggrieved party may ask the court to enforce the contract after removing its unfair aspects. Offending terms may be removed entirely or may just be altered to eliminate their unfair effect. This alternative is not available in all situations and may not be possible when the problem affects the very basis of the contract. In other cases, it may be the only remedy available because the problem is not serious enough to merit avoidance.

Damages

As noted above, restitutionary damages are available where a contract is avoided. However, if the aggrieved party elects not to avoid the contract, there may be the possibility of compensatory damages to remedy the effects of the improper bargaining. Compensatory damages are not available in all cases, but courts do have remedial discretion to award such relief where appropriate. This relief may be aimed at compensating the aggrieved party for a loss in consequence of the improper bargaining, or it could compensate for tortious injury where the wrongful act is a tort as well as a bargaining impropriety.

§13.4 THE NATURE AND RELATIONSHIP OF THE DOCTRINES REGULATING BARGAINING

The doctrines considered here are regulatory in nature and are often described as policing mechanisms. They allow the court to go behind the apparent manifestation of assent to examine the bargaining conduct of one of the parties and to determine whether that conduct exceeded acceptable bounds. It is important to understand that courts apply these doctrines carefully so as not to intrude more than necessary in the process of contract formation. The contracting parties are expected to try to serve their own interests and to use their available information and resources to obtain the best deal possible. There is nothing inherently wrong in the resourceful use of superior information, clever sales techniques, and the exploitation of market advantage. Furthermore, it is to be expected that transactions routinely occur between parties having great disparity in power, sophistication and resources. Regulation aims, not at "leveling the playing field" by cutting down economic advantage, but rather at allowing the court to step in when behavior crosses the line from hard bargaining to unacceptable exploitation. In obvious cases, such as Attila's gun up Lilly's nostril, it is clear that the line has been crossed. But in more equivocal cases opinions differ on the question of when intervention is appropriate. Some courts and commentators see robust judicial regulation of bargaining practice as a crucial means of curbing abuse. Others favor policing for only the more extreme cases and see judicial regulation as leading to inefficiency and market interference.

In classical contract law the policing doctrines were very clearly distinguishable and each had relatively firm and specific elements, making it applicable to a narrow range of situations. As they have developed in more recent times (some courts having moved further away than others from the categorizations of classical law), the doctrines have become more fluid so that they have a greater tendency to meld into each other. While they still retain many of their characteristic elements, their points of connection have become more obvious. This means that although the facts of some cases may support the invocation of only one of the doctrines, others may permit alternative analyses under more than one of them. Together, the doctrines form a network of rules that permit courts to deal with a variety of sins that might be committed during the formation of a contract. As we examine the doctrines individually, we will keep an eye on their common ground and interconnections.

§13.5 MISREPRESENTATION GENERALLY: THE MEANING OF "MISREPRESENTATION" AND THE DISTINCTION BETWEEN FRAUDULENT AND NONFRAUDULENT MISREPRESENTATIONS

§13.5.1 The Distinction Between Fraudulent, Negligent, and Innocent Misrepresentations

A "misrepresentation" is defined in Restatement, Second, §159 as an assertion not in accord with the facts. It is a factually incorrect representation made by one of the parties at the time of contracting. Misrepresentations fall into one of three categories, each of which has different rules. If the assertion is made with knowledge that it is false (that is, a deliberate lie) and with the intention of inducing the other party's agreement, it is fraudulent. If the misrepresentation is not a deliberate lie, but reflects a genuine, albeit erroneous, belief by the party making the assertion, it is either negligent (the misinformation results from that party's failure to check facts that he had a duty to ascertain) or innocent.

The severity and consequences of a misrepresentation depend on the state of mind of the party making the assertion. A fraudulent misrepresentation is the most serious deviation from legal and ethical obligations, which not only violates the contractual obligation of fair dealing, but is also tortious and could have criminal sanctions, too. In addition, a party guilty of fraud cannot be said to have justifiably relied on the other's manifestation of assent. The elements of fraudulent misrepresentation reflect the law's disapprobation of deliberate falsehood: If a fraudulent assertion is proved to have been made, the remaining prerequisites for relief are comparatively lenient. The court may evaluate the consequent inducement on a more subjective standard and the perpetrator's accountability for purposeful deceit usually outweighs any culpability the victim may have for gullibility or carelessness. A negligent or innocent misrepresentation is not as morally reprehensible and may not entirely defeat the perpetrator's reliance interest. Therefore, the decision on whether or not to grant relief involves a closer balancing of the relative culpability of the parties, and a stronger focus on the objective importance (materiality) of the misrepresentation and the victim's duty to verify the facts. Obviously, a negligent misrepresentation weighs more heavily against the perpetrator than an innocent one, and negligence may give rise to tort liability, too. This is represented by Diagram 13A.

Diagram 13A

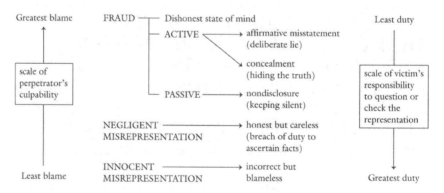

§13.5.2 The Application of the Parol Evidence Rule to Misrepresentations Made Outside a Written Contract

When a contract is recorded in writing, the misrepresentation may be in the writing itself. If so, the victim of the misrepresentation must prove the falsity of the representation by adducing evidence of facts extrinsic to the writing.

The parol evidence rule does not bar this extrinsic evidence because it is not parol evidence. It is not offered to prove a term allegedly agreed to outside the writing, but rather to prove that a fact represented in the writing is wrong.

However, the parol evidence rule does apply where the misrepresentation is not included in the writing, but was allegedly made orally before or at the time of execution of the written contract, or was made in a prior written document. The effect of the parol evidence rule differs depending on whether or not the misrepresentation was fraudulent.

We saw in section 12.12 that even where a written agreement is fully integrated, a party may not invoke the parol evidence rule to exclude proof of a fraudulent misrepresentation. The policy of shielding the factfinder from suspect and unreliable parol evidence is usually outweighed by the policy of protecting a party from dishonesty. Although the parol evidence may be admissible, it may not ultimately help the victim of the fraud. As discussed in section 13.6.6, the victim's justifiable reliance on the misrepresentation is one of the elements of fraud, so if the alleged oral misrepresentation directly contradicts an express term in the writing, the victim may not be able to show that she was justified in relying on it. This is particularly so if the written contract contains a merger clause that specifically disclaims reliance on any oral representations. This issue was addressed in *Psenicska v. Twentieth Century Fox Film Corp.*, 2008 WL 4185752 (S.D.N.Y. 2008), the case involving the *Borat* movie discussed in connection with interpretation in section 10.5.1. Recall that the plaintiffs had consented to being filmed for the movie, believing it to be a documentary. They sued the studio and filmmakers when they discovered that the movie was a satire presented in the style of a documentary. The issue was whether the plaintiffs' consent to be filmed was effective. As a matter of interpretation, the court held that the consent did cover the movie because the term "documentary-style film" unambiguously included a faux documentary. As an alternative argument, the plaintiffs sought to avoid the consent on the grounds that the defendants had fraudulently misrepresented the nature of the film in oral discussions. The court rejected that argument as well because the consent specifically stated that the plaintiffs waived reliance on any promises or statements made about the nature of the film or the identity of the other persons involved in it. In light of this language, the court said that the plaintiffs could not have justifiably relied on any such oral statements that may have been made.

A negligent or innocent misrepresentation is not as morally indefensible as a fraudulent one, and is not covered by the exception to the parol evidence rule. Therefore, the rule applies as usual. It bars evidence of a parol misrepresentation where the written contract is fully integrated (and particularly if it contains not only detailed terms but also a merger clause). If the writing is not fully integrated, evidence of a parol misrepresentation that contradicts the written terms is also inadmissible.

§13.6 FRAUDULENT MISREPRESENTATION

§13.6.1 Introduction

To qualify as fraudulent, a misrepresentation must be made with deliberate dishonest intent. The person making it must know it is false and must intend to induce the other party to enter the contract. The most common type of fraud, called fraud in the inducement, is a fraudulent misrepresentation concerning a fact that forms the basis of the contract, giving the party to whom it is made a false incentive to enter it. A less common type of fraud, fraud in the factum, is a misrepresentation relating to the nature or effect of a document to be signed (for example, persuading someone to sign an order for goods by asserting that it is merely a request for a catalog). The principal difference between them is that fraud in the inducement is generally treated as rendering the contract voidable, but fraud in the factum voids it completely. The discussion and illustrations in this section are concerned only with the more common fraud in the inducement.

For fraudulent misrepresentation to arise, a party must have made a false representation of fact with knowledge of its falsity and with intent to induce the other party to enter the contract. The other party must have relied on it justifiably to his injury. The materiality of the misrepresentation is expressed as an element by some, but not all courts. We now examine each of these elements.

§13.6.2 What Is a "Fact"? Fact, Opinion, Prediction, and Promise

We usually think of a fact as something that has existence — an objectively ascertainable reality. For example, the seller of a sofa clearly makes a representation of fact if he says "this sofa is made of leather" or "this sofa was made in the U.S.A." If the sofa is actually vinyl or it was made in China, the asserted facts are false. Fact can be distinguished from opinion ("I think this is a very beautiful sofa"), a future prediction ("this sofa will be the envy of your friends and neighbors"), or a promise of future action ("if the sofa does not look good when you put it in your living room, you can return it"). The general rule is that only a misrepresentation of fact constitutes fraud. An opinion or a prediction should be understood as nothing more than an expression of personal belief, taste, or preference, so even if it is not honest, it should not give grounds for relief for fraud. This is particularly true if the expression of opinion or the prediction should be reasonably understood as seller's hype (sometimes called "puffery"). Similarly, a promise of future action is not a representation of fact, but an undertaking. If it is breached, the proper remedy is a suit for breach of contract, not an action for fraud. However, the distinction between fact, opinion, and promise is not hard and fast. In some circumstances a dishonest opinion or a false promise can constitute a fraudulent misrepresentation.

Contemporary courts recognize that it is not always possible to make a clear distinction between fact and opinion because most opinions have a factual basis. This is not always true, of course. A seller's claim that a sofa's green and orange plaid fabric is a "fun color" is clearly just opinion. However, if the seller says "this sofa is fashionable," this suggests some familiarity with facts concerning current market trends. The fact-based opinion constitutes a misrepresentation if the party expressing it knows that it is not supported by the facts on which it is based, or if he recklessly makes the statement knowing that he has no clue about the facts on which it is based. Where the opinion of one of the parties is a decisive factor in inducing the other to enter the transaction, the misrepresentation of that opinion goes to the heart of the contract. This is particularly true where the party expressing the opinion has expertise and the other party relies on his recommendation. For example, an attorney who believes that a prospective client has a weak case on the facts makes a fraudulent misrepresentation if he expresses a contrary opinion to the prospective client with the goal of inducing him to hire the attorney to litigate the case.

Rodi v. Southern New England School of Law, 389 F.3d 5 (1st Cir. 2004) is a good illustration of fraudulent opinion. Rodi was a law student who claimed that he was induced to enroll in the law school on the basis of representations by the dean that the school was "highly confident" that it would receive American Bar Association accreditation. The school knew that accreditation was important to Rodi because he could not be admitted to practice in his state of residence if his degree was not from an accredited school. After the school failed to receive the accreditation in Rodi's first year of study, Rodi sent transfer applications to A.B.A.-accredited schools. On hearing of this, the dean (the successor to the dean who made the original representation) assured Rodi that "there was no cause for pessimism" that the school would be accredited before he graduated. It was not, and Rodi sued. The district court dismissed his claim, but the court of appeals reversed and permitted the case to go to trial on a theory of fraudulent misrepresentation. The school knew that it had substantial problems in obtaining accreditation, and Rodi had made a credible preliminary showing that the opinions expressed by school officials were not honest, given their knowledge of the A.B.A.'s criteria and the school's prospects of satisfying them. On remand, the trial court granted summary judgment to the law school on the basis that even if the deans had made false statements, Rodi had not reasonably relied on them. The court of appeals affirmed (532 F.3d 11 (1st Cir. 2008)). It turned out that Rodi had not withdrawn his transfer applications in reliance on the dean's assurance. He did not transfer because his applications had been denied. In addition, the court found that even if Rodi had relied on the deans' assurances, the reliance was not reasonable, because he knew that the school had accreditation problems and that there was a distinct possibility that the A.B.A. would not accredit the school, despite the deans' claim of optimism.

A future prediction is not a misrepresentation of an existing fact but an opinion about what might come to pass after the contract has been executed. It is really no different conceptually than an opinion, and should be approached in the same way. (In the above illustration involving the attorney's false opinion about the strength of his client's case, his assessment of his client's case is both an opinion and a prediction. The same is true of the opinions expressed by the deans in the Rodi case.) If the prediction is based on facts that are known at the time of contracting, it must be an honest assessment of how those facts will lead to the predicted result.

A promise of future performance is not a representation of fact, but an expression of intent. However, it relates to the present state of mind of the party making it and if it dishonestly represents that state of mind, it could qualify as a fraudulent misrepresentation. It can be very difficult to distinguish a mere breach of contract from a fraudulent misrepresentation of intent. To assert fraud it is not enough for the victim to show that the promise was broken. He must prove that at the time the contract was made, the party making the promise intended not to keep it. Although fraud can be proved by circumstantial evidence, so it is not necessary to have direct evidence of the promisor's state of mind in the form of an admission, it can be very difficult to establish that the promisor had already made up his mind to breach, especially if the promisor was careful to keep its intent hidden.

We saw an example of a fraudulent promise in *American Directories, Inc. v. Stellhorn One Hour Photo*, 833 N.E.2d 1059 (Ind. App. 2005), discussed in relation to the fraud exception to the parol evidence rule in section 12.12. The court held that it could qualify as fraud where a seller of advertising in a phone directory made a promise that the buyer could cancel the contract after a year, intending at the time of making the promise not to honor it. *Carey. v. FedEx Ground Package System, Inc.*, 321 F. Supp. 2d 902 (S.D. Ohio 2004), discussed in section 8.9 in relation to promissory estoppel, is another example. Recall that FedEx had kept Carey waiting for a delivery route for almost two years. During this period, it induced Carey to incur economic detriment by reiterating the assurance that he would receive the route while it took advantage of his services as a temporary driver. The court denied FedEx's motion for summary judgment and allowed Carey to proceed to trial on the basis of promissory estoppel. In addition, the court held that Carey had made out a cause of action for fraud. The court noted that although fraud is not usually predicated on a promise of future action, such a promise can qualify as fraudulent if the promisor has no intention of keeping the promise.

Sometimes it is not easy to decide if a misrepresentation related to a fact or to a promise — a representation of future intent. *Kaloti Enterprises, Inc. v. Kellogg Sales Co.*, 699 N.W.2d 205 (Wis. 2005) is a case with such an ambiguity. Kaloti and Kellogg had a longstanding arrangement under which Kaloti bought Kellogg products which it resold to large stores. Kellogg then decided to change its marketing procedures by selling some of its products directly to the same large stores that were Kaloti's customers. As a result, Kellogg would become Kaloti's competitor in that wholesale market. After it had made this decision, Kellogg accepted an order from Kaloti without telling it that Kellogg was about to devour its market. Kaloti only discovered this upon hearing from its customers that they would be buying directly from Kellogg. Kaloti sued Kellogg when it refused Kaloti's demand for cancellation of the sale and refund of the price. The issue in the case was whether Kellogg's failure to tell Kaloti about its impending change in marketing strategy constituted a fraudulent misrepresentation. The court held that Kaloti had made a sufficient case of fraud to overcome an application for dismissal. The court treated Kellogg's decision to sell its products directly to stores as a fact. However, this is not strictly correct. The real fact in issue is Kellogg's intentions, and the question is whether Kellogg had made an implied promise not to undercut Kaloti, knowing that it was about to break that promise. (The case also presents the question of whether Kellogg committed fraud by failing to disclose that it had begun to sell directly to Kaloti's customers. We will discuss this aspect of the case in section 13.6.3.)

§13.6.3 Types of Fraudulent Misrepresentation: Affirmative Statements, Concealment, and Nondisclosure

a. Affirmative False Statement

An affirmative false statement (such as the seller's assertion, mentioned in section 13.6.2, that a vinyl sofa is made of leather) is the most direct and easily identifiable type of fraudulent misrepresentation. *Rozen v. Greenberg*, 886 A.2d 924 (Md. App. 2005) illustrates fraud by affirmative misrepresentation. Greenberg was a tax preparer who specialized in preparing returns for Israeli clients. She received an e-mail from Rozen, whom she did not know, suggesting that as they were in the same business, they should enter into a cooperative arrangement. In the e-mail Rozen represented that he had "headed" a tax preparation service for Israelis for "the last few years."

He referred Greenberg to his organization's "powerful" website. On visiting the website, Greenberg read that the organization had a team of account and tax professionals headed by Rozen, who was an experienced CPA. In a subsequent phone conversation, Rozen again told Greenberg that he was very experienced and had many people working for him. Greenberg then met with Rozen who took her to show her what he claimed to be his office, which was very impressive. As a result of these representations, Greenberg agreed to sell her client list to Rozen in exchange for a share of the income that he generated from preparing her clients' returns. It turned out that at the time that he contacted Greenberg, Rozen had no business and no clients and had prepared no tax returns. He had only been a CPA for a few weeks, and the office that he showed Greenberg belonged to a tax preparation company at which he was employed. The court of appeals affirmed the trial court's decision that these misrepresentations were fraudulent. (We will return to this case shortly in relation to the other elements of fraud.)

Willen v. Hewson, 622 S.E.2d 187 (N.C. App. 2005) is another example of affirmative fraud. The seller of a large house on an estate advertised it as "peaceful" and "serene." When the buyer inspected the estate, he met the seller's niece who mentioned that there had been problems with "kids coming onto the property after high school football games around Halloween." This caused the buyer some concern and he called the seller to ask her if there had been trespass problems on the property. She assured him that such incidents occurred only once or twice and that her niece was prone to exaggeration. After the buyers bought and moved into the house they found that there was a serious and constant problem with trespass and vandalism which they could not eliminate even by installing a security system and fence. The court of appeals upheld the trial court's determination that the seller was aware of the trespass problem and had made a fraudulent misrepresentation by advertising the property as "peaceful" and "serene" and by answering the buyer's inquiry dishonestly.

b. Concealment

Deliberate conduct to hide a fact is also an affirmative act. Although it may not involve any verbal lie, it is just as dishonest and morally reprehensible. *Jablonski v. Rapalje*, 14 A.D.3d 484 (N.Y. 2005) is a good example. In contrast to *Willen*, which involved human pests, *Jablonski* was concerned with trespassing bats which inhabited the attic of the house bought by the plaintiff. The bat infestation was serious and ongoing. Over the 36 years that the sellers had lived in the house, they had tried to get rid of the bats, but they always returned. During the time that the buyer inspected the house preparatory to buying it, the sellers went to considerable trouble to conceal the bat infestation by using mothballs (which bats apparently dislike) and floodlights to keep them away and by cleaning up the telltale signs of bat presence such as bat droppings and urine. (The case also involved an affirmative misrepresentation. On one occasion the sellers did not do the best job in disposing of droppings, which the buyer noticed. The sellers asserted that they were bird droppings.) The court refused the seller's motion for summary judgment and permitted the buyer to proceed to trial on the basis of fraudulent concealment. *Weintraub v. Krobatsch*, 317 A.2d 68 (N.J. 1974) is an equally delightful case involving a cockroach infestation of nightmarish proportions. The court declined the seller's application for summary judgment and permitted the buyer of a house to proceed to trial on the theory that the seller actively concealed the presence of cockroaches by leaving all the lights on.

c. Nondisclosure (Silence)

Affirmative dishonesty, whether in the form of a false statement or active concealment of the truth, is the clearest case of fraud. However, under some circumstances, a person can commit fraud by keeping silent and failing to disclose a fact. Nondisclosure is the most difficult basis for claiming fraud because it is only fraudulent if the circumstances impose a duty on the party to disclose information. The usual assumption is that where parties contract, each is a free agent in the market, entitled to act out of self-interest. A party may use the advantage of superior information, and owes no duty to the other to reveal facts that motivate her to enter the transaction or that make it particularly attractive to her. Therefore, a buyer of property, having studied the market carefully, is not obliged to tell the seller that the property is underpriced, and the buyer of a commodity does not have to tell the seller that its research on crop yield indicates that the price will soar after the sale. Notwithstanding, a party does not have the absolute and invariable right to keep information secret. Under some circumstances honesty and fair dealing require disclosure. The difficult question is to determine when the line is crossed between facts that may fairly be kept private and those that must be revealed.

Restatement, Second, §161 provides guidelines to answer this question. It says that nondisclosure amounts to an assertion that a fact does not exist where the party knows that disclosure of that fact is necessary to correct a previous assertion, or where there is a relationship of trust between the parties. It also requires disclosure where the party knows that it is necessary to correct the other party's mistake as to a basic assumption of the contract, and nondisclosure would violate the duty of good faith and fair dealing. The concept of good faith and fair dealing is quite open-ended and fact-based, so it depends on the circumstances of each case. Two significant factors that may be relevant are whether the information should be treated as the property of the party who possesses it (for example, because that party has incurred cost and effort in conducting research or inquiry to obtain it) and whether the information is readily available on diligent inquiry.

A good illustration of the duty to disclose is provided, regrettably, by another creepy-crawly case, this time involving termites. In *Hill v. Jones*, 725 P.2d 1115 (Ariz. 1986), the sellers of a house did not tell the buyers that it had been infested with termites in the past. (The termites had been eradicated, so the problem related to damage that they had caused.) Having gone to the trouble of keeping this quiet, the sellers made the unfortunate mistake of leaving telltale brochures in the kitchen drawer which the buyers discovered after they moved in. The court refused summary judgment for the sellers and allowed the buyers to proceed to trial on the question of whether the duty of fair dealing required the seller to reveal the termite damage.[1]

Just for the sake of getting away from bugs and dealing with a more serious hidden defect in a house, it is worth mentioning everyone's favorite nondisclosure case, *Stambovsky v. Ackley*, 572 N.Y.S.2d 672 (A.D. 1991) in which the court allowed the buyer of a house to proceed to trial on the grounds that the seller failed to disclose that the house was reputed to be haunted. (Unlike the buyers in *Willen* and *Jablonski*, who actually encountered the trespassers and bats, the buyer here did not allege that he met the ghosts. It was the reputation of the house that bothered him.) The fact that the seller had widely publicized the haunting but the buyer was not aware of it and could not ascertain it by reasonable inspection persuaded the court that fair dealing imposed a disclosure duty on the seller. The court's conclusion was based on the perception that although a reasonable buyer would know, as a matter of course, that a house should be inspected for structural soundness, he would not reasonably expect the possibility of supernatural infestation. Although this may have been true in relation to the particular parties in this case, it is important to understand that the determination of the scope and nature of a buyer's reasonable inquiry should be community-based. In some communities, the possibility of spirits occupying the house may be considered realistic enough to merit inquiry.

In *Kellogg*, discussed in section 13.6.2, the court held that the facts made out a case for nondisclosure as an alternative to affirmative fraud. Although one party is not generally under a duty to disclose its business plans or marketing strategy to the other, commercial mores and the duty of fair dealing do sometimes require disclosure. This appeared to be such a case

---

1. There were some strategically placed boxes and a potted plant that covered some holes in the floor, so there was also a possibility of active concealment. In addition, the buyers had noticed rippling in the parquet floor which was consistent with termite damage and had asked the sellers about it. They had replied that it was water damage, which may or may not have been true. Accordingly, the buyers may have been able to establish a fraudulent assertion as well.

because Kellogg's action would undermine Kaloti's expectations under the contract, and the information was solely within Kellogg's knowledge, not accessible to Kaloti through diligent inquiry.

§13.6.4 Knowledge of Falsity and Intent to Induce the Contract

A guilty state of mind — knowledge of falsity and intent to mislead — is the essence of fraud. (The word "scienter" is sometimes used to describe this guilty state of mind.) Although it may be possible for one of these elements, but not the other, to exist, in most cases they go hand-in-hand. In defining knowledge of falsity, Restatement, Second, §162 covers not only an assertion made with the actual knowledge that it is not in accord with the facts, but also an assertion made without confidence in its truth or without a known basis in fact. This means that there is some blurring of the line between fraudulent and negligent misrepresentation, because reckless disregard for the truth or an extreme degree of negligence in ascertaining information before making an assertion may qualify as fraud.

For example, in Jordan v. Knafel, 880 N.E.2d 1061 (Ill. App. 2007), Michael Jordan, the basketball star, sued for a declaratory judgment avoiding a settlement agreement that he had entered into with Karla Knafel. Knafel had become pregnant after the parties had a sexual relationship. She claimed that Jordan was certainly the father of the baby. On the strength of that assertion, Jordan and Knafel entered into the settlement agreement under which Jordan promised to pay Knafel $5 million in exchange for her not initiating paternity proceedings against him. Subsequent tests revealed that the child was not Jordan's. The court of appeals affirmed the trial court's summary judgment in favor of Jordan. Although Jordan could have been the father of the child, Knafel had made a fraudulent misrepresentation by categorically stating that he was the father, thereby impliedly representing that he was her only sexual partner during the period of conception. Although she did not know that he was not the father, she did know that he might not be. She therefore made the assertion without confidence in its truth.[2] (One could also conceive of this case as involving nondisclosure because Knafel failed to disclose that Jordan was not her only sexual partner

---

2. As we saw in section 7.6, a settlement agreement that compromises a doubtful claim is valid for consideration purposes, provided that there is a good faith or reasonable basis for the dispute. Therefore, the fact that Jordan turned out not to be the father would not, in itself, have defeated the settlement agreement if the parties were unsure about the child's paternity. Knafel's problem in this case was that she concealed any doubt on this issue by categorically asserting that Jordan had to be the father, thereby inducing him to enter the settlement.

at the crucial time. However, she went beyond mere nondisclosure by asserting unequivocally that he was the father.)

§13.6.5 Materiality

A misrepresentation is material if it substantially contributes to a party's decision to enter the transaction. It must relate to a fact that is important or central enough to the bargain that it is reasonably likely to have had a significant influence on the party's decision to manifest assent to the transaction. It seems logical that materiality must be an element of fraud, because if the misrepresentation did not relate to an important aspect of the transaction, it is less likely to have induced the party to enter the transaction, and presents a less compelling case for relief. (In fact, the link between the elements of materiality and justifiable inducement is very clear and obvious.) However, there is some confusion over the role that materiality plays in the requirements for establishing fraud. Many courts specifically list materiality as one of the elements of fraud. For example, most of the cases mentioned above, *Kellogg*, *Stambovsky*, *Hill*, *Jablonski*, *Willen*, *Jordan*, and *Rozen* all assert that the misrepresentation must be material. However, Restatement, Second, §§162 and 164 and comment *c* to §162 do not require the victim of fraud to prove materiality. They confine the need to establish materiality to negligent or innocent misrepresentations. Some courts follow this approach and assert that materiality is not an element of fraud. However, even in those cases, it often appears that the materiality of the misrepresentation comes up in the court's discussion and seems to be an influential factor. As mentioned earlier, even if materiality is not identified as a separate element of fraud, the importance of the misrepresented fact inevitably features in the analysis of justifiable inducement.

In light of this confusion in the doctrine, the best approach is to recognize that materiality is commonly identified as an element of fraud, but that some courts, following the Restatement, Second, formulation, underplay it or do not articulate it as a requirement. However, even in those cases, some attention is commonly given to materiality in the opinion, either in the overall analysis or in addressing the question of justifiable inducement. The difference between recognizing and not recognizing materiality as a distinct element of fraud may influence the degree to which the court requires objective proof of materiality, beyond a more subjective focus on what was important to this particular victim. The materiality of the misrepresentation may also affect the degree to which the victim must adduce persuasive evidence to show justifiable reliance. In the *Jordan* case, the court noted that where a misrepresentation is made with regard to a material matter, inducement is more readily presumed.

§13.6.6 Justifiable Inducement

There must be a causal link between the fraud and the contract — that is, the fraud must have motivated the victim to enter the contract, or to enter it on the terms that were agreed. If the victim would have entered the contract on those terms anyway had she known the truth, or if the victim was not justified in relying on the misrepresentation, she is not entitled to relief. (As mentioned in section 13.6.2, these were the ultimate grounds for denying relief in the *Rodi* case.) The court must evaluate the impact of the false fact on the victim's state of mind. The difficult question here is whether this impact should be measured objectively (was the victim reasonable in relying on the misrepresentation) or subjectively (even if a reasonable person may not have been hoodwinked, was this victim in fact induced to enter the contract). Although, as we have seen frequently, the law tends to favor an objective test in most situations, public policy dictates a less objective standard where fraud is involved. When a court balances the fault of the perpetrator, who has deliberately lied, against the fault of the victim, who may have been unduly gullible or even careless in believing the misrepresentation, the balance usually weighs in favor of the victim. The result in most cases is a blend of objective and subjective considerations. That is, the court asks whether the victim was in fact induced, but also tests this inducement against the question of whether she would have been induced had she acted reasonably. Often, these inquiries point in the same direction because if a reasonable person would not have relied on the false fact, the victim may have trouble showing, in the absence of some special individual circumstances or attributes, that she in fact relied on it. One can also detect that courts apply a different degree of objective assessment depending on whether the misrepresentation was active (a statement or concealment) or by nondisclosure. Courts are more likely to impose a tougher standard of reasonable inquiry on the victim where the fraud lies in failure to disclose facts.

The cases discussed in section 13.6.3 illustrate the element of justifiable reliance and the blend of subjective and objective considerations that go into determining justification. *Stambovsky* considered that the buyer could justifiably have been mislead by the nondisclosure because he was not local, had no reason to know of the house's reputation, and could not have discovered the ghosts by reasonable inspection of the house. (The court may have been too generous to the buyer in concluding that the house's reputation was not easily discoverable. The haunting was quite widely publicized and was featured in both national and local publications.) In *Rozen*, the court recognized that Greenberg was not experienced in the sale of a business and was rather gullible. However, the court focused on Greenberg's subjective attributes and rejected the argument that she reasonably could and should have investigated Rozen, should have called for references, and should have noticed that the office that she was taken to did not belong to him. In *Willen*, the court approached the buyers' reliance from a reasonableness perspective but rejected the seller's argument that the buyers' reliance on her assertions was unreasonable because her niece's mention of the trespassing problem should have caused them to conduct an independent investigation. The court noted that there were no visible indicia of trespass and vandalism to place the buyers on inquiry and, in any event, even if the buyers were unreasonable, the seller cannot seek to avoid the consequences of her false representation by arguing that the buyers should not have trusted her. In *Jablonski*, the buyer visited the house many times and had it professionally inspected. The buyer observed the bat droppings on one occasion, noticed the floodlights in the attic, and also smelled the mothballs and bat urine.[3] The seller contended that the buyer's reliance was not justifiable because he had ample opportunity to discover the bats. Applying a reasonable diligence standard, the court rejected this argument because there was enough evidence to suggest that the sellers had thwarted the buyer's ability to discover the infestation.

These cases may give you the impression that courts generally treat victims leniently in evaluating justifiable reliance. That is often true, but it would be a mistake to think that it is always so. Courts do hold victims responsible for exercising due diligence in ascertaining the true facts. As noted above, Rodi ultimately lost his case because the court found his reliance unjustifiable. *Nigro v. Lee*, 882 N.Y.S. 2d 346 (App. Div. 2009), is another example of a case in which the court found a lack of justifiable reliance — in this instance because the victim failed to seek information that would have revealed the falsity of the representations. The plaintiff bought a 1995 Mercedes on an eBay auction. The seller's advertisement described the car as "gorgeous" with three minor blemishes, and stated that it was in the condition as disclosed, to the best of the seller's knowledge. The car was located in Nevada, and the buyer resided in New York, so he did not inspect the car when he bought it. After the car was delivered, the buyer discovered that it was in very poor condition. It had been damaged in an accident, its upholstery was stained, it had areas of rust and it required extensive and expensive mechanical repairs. The buyer sued the seller, claiming that the despite knowing about all the problems with the car, the seller had fraudulently misrepresented that the car was gorgeous and virtually unblemished. The Appellate Division affirmed the trial court's dismissal of the buyer's suit. The court pointed out that the description of the car as "gorgeous" was a

---

3. I hope you are not reading this case while eating. Just in case you are, it is also worth mentioning that on one occasion the buyer heard the toilet flushing repeatedly while he was waiting at the front door of the house. The buyer discovered later that the real estate agent (who was also a defendant in the case) was busy scooping up bat droppings and flushing them.

generalized expression of opinion, and mere puffery. The court recognized that the remaining misrepresentations were more substantial, but it refused relief to the buyer because they were all easily discoverable by obtaining a vehicle history report and a mechanical inspection. The court said it was no excuse that the car was located in Nevada — the buyer could have arranged for an inspection there.

§13.6.7 Injury and Remedy

Courts commonly require, as a final element of fraud, that the victim must have been injured. Injury is easy to see if misrepresentation caused the victim to overpay for the contractual performance — that is, that the performance is valueless or less valuable than it would have been had the representation been true. For example, the presence of bats, bugs, or vandals very likely diminished the market value of the houses in *Jablonski, Weintraub,* and *Willen,* or would have resulted in cost to rectify these unpleasant phenomena. In buying Kellogg products that it could not sell, Kaloti surely suffered loss of its anticipated profit, and may have been saddled with unsalable goods. However, sometimes the precise economic injury is more difficult to ascertain. For example, say that the reputed presence of ghosts had no effect on the market price of the house in *Stambovski* or that Rozen did a decent job on the tax returns of Greenberg's clients and generated the expected profits. The fact that there may be no measurable economic loss in these cases does not inevitably mean that there is no injury. The injury could lie simply in the fact that the victim finds herself in a contract that is completely different from what she expected and wanted.

The alternative remedies available for fraud allow a court to give relief whether or not actual economic loss resulted from the fraud. Even if there is no economic loss, a victim who does not desire the contract because of the misrepresentation is entitled to avoid it — to claim rescission. Upon rescission, a claim for restitution arises in favor of a party who has performed in whole or in part. In the absence of a contract, there is no basis for retaining a benefit given under the contract, so principles of unjust enrichment require that benefit to be returned. Benefit is measured by the value of property, which could be different from its contract price. This principle applies whether it is the victim or the perpetrator who has been enriched. However, the law imposes limits on the restitutionary rights of the perpetrator. Any doubts on the value of his performance are resolved against him. In addition, the victim is not obliged to return property or its value to the extent that it was worthless when received or deteriorated as a result of its own defects. (*See* Restatement, Second, §§164, 376, and 385).

As noted in section 13.3, a contract induced by fraud is voidable, not void. This means that the victim may elect to rescind it if she desires, but may choose to keep it in force. If she does so, she can claim damages to compensate for the difference between the actual value of the performance and the value that it would have had as represented. This damages claim includes such losses as reduction in market value or the costs of bringing the property into the condition as represented.

Traditionally, the remedy of rescission and restitution derives from contract law, but the remedy of damages has its roots in tort (fraud being a tort as well as a breach of contract). This could make a difference to remedy. For example, a court that applies the traditional distinction would allow a plaintiff who sues for damages to claim punitive damages as well, because the suit is based on tort. However, punitive damages are not available in contract, so a court following the traditional distinction would not award punitive damages if the plaintiff sued for rescission. This does not make a lot of sense, since the defendant's wrongful act is exactly the same, whichever form of relief is sought. Also, a rigorous focus on the tort-contract distinction would mean that if a plaintiff sues for rescission, she cannot claim any damages, even if the tort led to economic loss. This distinction between the contract and tort derivation of the alternative remedies has faded, and many modern courts do not apply it. Rather, they simply treat the remedies as available possibilities and provide the relief called for by the harm to the victim. This means that in appropriate circumstances, a court may award rescission together with damages for proven loss beyond restitution (offset by any restitution due to the perpetrator), or that it may permit punitive damages in a rescission suit.

§13.7 NEGLIGENT OR INNOCENT MISREPRESENTATION

A misrepresentation made without the deliberate intent to mislead is classified either as negligent or innocent. (As mentioned earlier, a reckless or grossly negligent misrepresentation may qualify as fraud, because knowledge of falsity could be inferred where an assertion is made without confidence in its truth or a known basis in fact.) The distinction between negligence and innocence is not always easy to make, and it depends on the circumstances of each case. A misrepresentation is negligent if the person making it failed to act with reasonable care in ascertaining and communicating the truth, but it is innocent if no such duty was breached.

Although negligent and innocent misrepresentations do not carry the same degree of disapprobation as a deliberate lie, they do permit avoidance if they are material and have induced justifiable reliance. Although Restatement, Second, §§162 and 164 do not include materiality as an element for fraudulent misrepresentation, they do specifically mention it as an element for nonfraudulent misrepresentation. Thus, an innocent or negligent misrepresentation only gives grounds for relief if it relates to a fact central to the transaction, and the party making the misrepresentation knew or had reason to know of its importance. It follows from this that the test of justifiable reliance is correspondingly strengthened, because materiality to the victim is seen from the reasonable perspective of the other. This approach accords with the general idea that some balance must be struck between the fault of the misrepresenting party and the reasonable expectations of the victim. To the extent that the party making the misrepresentation is less culpable, one would expect a stronger showing of the importance of the misrepresentation and the victim's reasonable reliance. It was also noted in section 13.5.2 that while an exception to the parol evidence rule allows the admission of parol evidence to show fraud, parol evidence relating to a nonfraudulent misrepresentation is excluded by the parol evidence rule if the writing is integrated or the term is inconsistent with a partially integrated writing.

It can be difficult to distinguish an innocent or negligent misrepresentation from a contractual promise. For example, the seller of a house, having inspected it and found no termites, informs the buyer that the house is termite-free. If termites are present this could qualify as a misrepresentation, or it could be a warranty — a contractual promise that the house does not have termites. If it is the former, the remedy of avoidance is appropriate, but if it is the latter, the failure of the house to comply with the warranty is a breach of contract, giving rise to the remedies discussed in Chapter 18. The distinction is largely factual and interpretational. It depends on whether the assertion was merely a statement inducing the contract or was actually incorporated into the contract to become one of the promises made as part of the seller's consideration for the price of the house.

§13.8 DURESS

§13.8.1 The Nature of Duress

In older contract law, duress was available as a ground of avoiding a contract only in extreme circumstances. A party claiming duress had to show that the other had induced the contract by using actual force or an unlawful threat of death or bodily harm (not merely property damage). In addition, the test of inducement was objective: The threat must have been such as would overcome the resistance of a person of "ordinary firmness." The example in section 13.2, involving Lilly Livered's sale of her casino at gunpoint to Attila "The Animal" Axehacker is a classic case of duress in this sense. Even under these strict standards, Lilly should be able to avoid the contract by showing that Attila engaged in the threatening conduct, that it was unlawful and constituted a credible threat, and that she was not being unduly wimpy in giving in to it.

During the last several decades duress has moved beyond these narrow confines. It is generally accepted that a person's free will can be undermined by unfair pressure short of physical compulsion or a threat of looming personal injury. An illegitimate threat to proprietary or economic interests (sometimes referred to as "economic duress") is well recognized in modern cases as a basis for relief. Also, the strongly objective test of "ordinary firmness" has been abandoned in favor of a less rigorous standard that combines objective and subjective factors: Did the victim have no reasonable alternative but to agree? Duress has thus become a much broader doctrine, better able to accommodate situations in which one party uses subtle threats or improper pressure to gain the other's acquiescence to a transaction. As with fraud, the basis of avoidance is consistent with, but an exception to, the general objective test of assent. The underlying rationale is that the victim should not be held accountable for her apparent assent when it is not genuine, and the other party, having improperly induced it, does not have a compelling reliance interest.

The contemporary approach to duress is set out in Restatement, Second, §§174, 175, and 176. Section 174 deals with the rare situation in which a person's manifestation of assent is physically compelled, so that the act of manifesting assent completely lacks free will. For example, instead of Attila placing his gun up Lilly's nostril, inducing her to sign, he actually clasps her fingers around a pen and forces her hand across the paper to make a signature. Because Lilly is rendered like an automaton by the physical compulsion, §174 treats such an apparent contract as void. We need not be further concerned with this unusual situation, and turn to the more common forms of duress, covered by §§175 and 176, in which an improper threat has the effect of making the contract voidable. In essence, these sections set out the following elements: One of the parties must make a threat; the threat must be improper; and it must induce the apparent assent, in that it leaves the victim no reasonable alternative but to agree.

§13.8.2 The Threat

Although the contemporary doctrine of duress still requires an improper threat, the modern concept of threat has expanded well beyond the confines of its original scope. Today, a threat may be defined as an indication of intent to do or refrain from doing something so as to inflict some harm, loss, injury, or other undesirable consequences that would have an adverse effect on the victim's person or personal or economic interests. This encompasses a wide range of behavior, including not only explicit intimidation, but also subtle or even unspoken threats. The presence of an implied threat is determined by interpretation in the usual way, taking into account the circumstances of the relationship between the parties. The transaction is examined in context to ascertain if the words or actions of the one party show a reasonable intent to make a threat, reasonably so understood by the other. The threat may be either to take positive action or to refrain from acting, and the harm may consist of any adverse consequences sufficient to overcome the victim's resistance to the contract. A threat could even be implicit in the transaction when one party knows that the other will suffer undesirable consequences if the contract is not made, and uses this knowledge to take unfair advantage of the other's need.

While this wider and more realistic scope allows courts to police less obvious forms of duress, it is less certain and stable than the earlier, more rigid approach. As a result, it presents the danger of undue judicial interference in borderline cases where the line blurs between legitimate hard bargaining and improper coercion. In this area it must be used cautiously, because duress doctrine should be used only when there has been wrongful bargaining conduct, and should not be misapplied to overturn a tough or burdensome contract simply because one of the parties has managed to use bargaining advantage effectively.

An example will illustrate how difficult it can be to distinguish legally acceptable market behavior from unfair pressure: Say that Lilly needs to sell her casino quickly because she urgently needs money to pay for an operation to cure a dangerous medical condition. Attila knows of her trouble and also knows that she will have difficulty finding a buyer quickly. He therefore offers her less than market price for her casino. Because her need for the money is desperate, she sees no alternative but to sell to Attila for that price. Clearly, Attila has taken advantage of her plight, but the only threat he has made is that unless she meets his terms, he will not contract with her. Such a threat is implicit in all contract negotiations, so it can hardly be viewed as duress. This could simply be treated as a case in which Attila has used his market position to obtain a favorable deal.[4] In this example, Lilly's bargaining weakness was caused by her need for an operation, so her case invokes easy sympathy. Some needs are less compelling and thus move away from the borderline of duress, more clearly falling into the realm of legally acceptable market interaction. Say, for example, that Attila desperately craved to own Lilly's casino, but Lilly refused to sell it unless he paid an exorbitant price. If Attila succumbs to his desires and agrees to buy at that price, he cannot claim that he acted under duress.

---

4. Although these facts do not fit comfortably into the elements of duress, if Attila's bargaining strategy is unfair and it results in unfair contract terms, the doctrine of unconscionability may provide relief to Lilly.

Because relief for duress is premised on wrongful coercion by one of the contracting parties, that party must usually be responsible for the threat. If the threat is made by a nonparty, the victim cannot normally avoid the contract unless the other party is implicated in the threat or knowingly took advantage of it. Outside pressure should not readily defeat the legitimate expectations of an innocent party who relied on the transaction in good faith and without knowledge of the threat. For example, Attila made several fair and increasingly generous offers to buy Lilly's casino but Lilly steadfastly rebuffed him every time until, one day, she received a visit from his godfather, Bull "The Butcher" Bloodbath, who threatened to smash her kneecaps unless she sold to Attila. Duress is clearly present if Attila is in some way implicated in his godfather's threat. However, if Attila's godfather acted entirely independently and without Attila's knowledge, application of the doctrine of duress would defeat Attila's honest reliance interest in the fair contract. This means that in most cases, the victim cannot raise the defense of duress. However, the protection of Attila's reliance is not absolute, and may be outweighed by the public policy of protecting people from violence. Therefore, where the conduct of the nonparty amounts to actual physical force against the victim or the threat of such force, the duress may be serious enough to render the contract void, not just voidable. The effect of this is that the contract is a nullity and cannot be enforced, even though Attila was entirely innocent and did not instigate or have knowledge of the duress. (Restatement, Second, §174 gives some recognition to this principle, but would invoke it only where the physical compulsion is so great as to render the victim a mere instrument of the perpetrator.)

Gascho v. Scheurer Hospital, 400 Fed. Appx. 978 (6th Cir. 2010), provides a good illustration of economic and third-party pressure that did not constitute duress. Gascho was a nurse and a longtime employee of the hospital. She was married to its president and CEO. There were difficulties in the marriage. Gascho claimed that her husband abused her both physically and emotionally, and that he also had an affair with a hospital vice president. Gascho was fired by her husband after a confrontation at work with him and the vice president with whom he was having the affair. When other hospital executives heard of the circumstances of Gascho's discharge, they converted it into a three-day suspension, followed by a medical leave. About a month later, the hospital offered Gascho a separation agreement under which she would receive a year's salary and benefits in exchange for her voluntary resignation and release of any claims that she may have against the hospital. The hospital's human resources director advised Gascho to consult an employment lawyer and gave her 21 days to sign the agreement, as well as a seven-day period to change her mind if she did sign it. Gascho claimed that after she was offered the separation agreement, her husband threatened and cajoled her on several occasions to accept the hospital's offer. She did seek advice about signing the agreement from various people, but did not consult an employment lawyer. She did eventually sign it. About a year later, she filed suit seeking to rescind it and to claim damages against the hospital for sexual harassment. The trial court dismissed her suit on the basis that she was bound by the release. The court of appeals affirmed. The court found that the bargaining process followed by the hospital was fair — the hospital explained the proposed agreement to her, gave her time to consider it and to seek counsel, and allowed her an opportunity to rescind after signing. The terms of the agreement were clear and she received fair consideration for the resignation and release. Gascho claimed duress on two grounds. First, she argued that if she did not accept the settlement, she would suffer economic hardship and the prospect of uncertain and lengthy litigation to vindicate her rights. The court rejected this argument: The only implicit threat that the hospital made was that if she did not accept its offer, she would not get the severance package and would have to litigate any claim she had. This is not an improper threat, but merely a normal incidence of negotiating a settlement. The fact that Gascho would suffer adverse economic consequences if she did not accept the contract is nothing more than the common form of economic pressure that people have to contend with in deciding whether to enter a contract. Gascho's second ground of duress was that she was intimidated by her husband's abuse and threats. The court recognized that the alleged threats made by her husband could amount to duress, but the hospital did not make those threats and could not be held accountable for them. (The court did not explain why the threats of the husband, who was the CEO of the hospital, could not be attributed to it. But it seems that the hospital distanced itself sufficiently from its CEO to persuade the court that he should be treated as a third party, not as an agent of the hospital.)

§13.8.3 Impropriety

When is a threat improper? In addition to the obvious threats of criminal or tortious conduct, modern law tends to take a broad view of impropriety, so that it could include any threatened behavior that goes beyond the legitimate rights of the party applying the pressure, or that constitutes an abuse of those rights. This would include, for example, a threat to engage in vexatious litigation, to withhold a performance or property to which the victim is entitled, to disclose information that would embarrass the victim, or otherwise to do something spiteful or vexatious purely for the sake of hurting the victim. It is, of course, not duress to threaten consequences, even dire ones, that may lawfully and properly be pursued in the absence of agreement. For example, at the time for renewal of an employment contract, an employee who has become indispensable may legitimately threaten to quit unless the employer agrees to a substantial raise. Similarly, a person with a colorable tort claim may justifiably threaten to sue unless the tort-feasor agrees to a settlement. As *Gascho* shows, it is also not improper to threaten (expressly or impliedly) to refuse to enter into a contract unless the other party accepts your terms. However, a threat to file criminal charges is regarded as improper, even if prosecution is warranted, because it is against public policy for a person to use the threat of criminal prosecution as a bargaining chip.

§13.8.4 Inducement

As noted earlier, the older test for inducement was objective. It required not only that the threat was credible, but also that it would have overcome the resistance of a person of "ordinary firmness." The contemporary test is not so rigorous. Although it has an objective element, it also takes the subjective attributes of the victim into account, recognizing that a bully should not be able to enforce a contract merely because his victim is easily intimidated. The inquiry is whether, under all the circumstances, the duress substantially overcame the free will of this party, leaving him no reasonable alternative but to acquiesce. Inducement is therefore considered not in the abstract, but in light of the victim's needs, personality, and circumstances.

An alternative is only reasonable if it is a feasible and practical means of evading the consequences of the threat. If it would be unduly burdensome or risky, or would not likely avoid the threatened consequences, the victim cannot be said to have had a reasonable alternative to manifesting assent. For example, say that Attila owes Lilly $1 million from a prior transaction. He threatens not to pay her unless she agrees to sell her casino to him. Lilly does have the alternative of refusing to sell and commencing suit against Attila for the debt. However, this alternative is not reasonable for Lilly if she needs the money immediately and cannot afford the cost and delay of litigating to enforce payment.

§13.8.5 Remedy

It is sometimes said that when a contract is induced by an extreme degree of duress, such as actual physical force or a threat of physical violence, the contract is void, because there has been no assent. However, because duress doctrine is designed to protect the victim, the more common and logical approach is to treat it as voidable at the victim's election. (The situations involving a physically compelled signature, mentioned in section 13.8.1, and extreme physical violence by a third party, discussed in section 13.8.2, may be narrow exceptions.) The victim may choose to abide by the contract despite the duress, or may decide to avoid it, claim restitution of any benefit conferred, and tender restoration of any benefit received. The remedy of avoidance and restitution is subject to the same general principles discussed in connection with misrepresentation.

Although in most cases the victim must choose between keeping the contract, subject to all its terms, or avoiding it entirely, there are circumstances in which courts allow a middle path — retention of the contract subject to an adjustment of its terms. For example, if a party desires to keep property purchased, but can show that she was forced to pay an excessive price for it, the court may enforce the contract, subject to a refund to the victim of the amount in excess of fair value. Although, as we will see in section 13.11, the adjustment of contract terms is a common method of curing unconscionability, it is not often employed in duress cases. However, the remedy is within the courts' discretion in granting relief for duress. If the act of duress is a tort, the victim is able to obtain damages in tort in addition to any relief under contract law.

§13.9 DURESS IN THE MODIFICATION OF AN EXISTING CONTRACT

§13.9.1 Consideration Doctrine

As explained in section 7.5, under the pre-existing duty rule a party does not suffer a legal detriment by promising to do what he is already bound to do under an existing contract. For this reason, a promise by one party to increase or enhance his performance under a contract is not binding unless it is supported by new consideration given by the other. Stated differently, under common law, an agreement to modify a contract is not valid unless both parties have suffered some new detriment under the modification. The pre-existing duty rule can serve as a means of refusing enforcement of a coerced modification. The most famous illustration of this use of consideration doctrine is *Alaska Packers Assn. v. Domenico*, 117 F. 99 (9th Cir. 1902). A cannery contracted with a group of fishermen to harvest salmon during the short Alaskan season. After the fishermen had been transported to Alaska and the season had begun, they refused to continue work unless their wages were increased. (Their demand was based on the pretext that working conditions were more burdensome than expected, but this contention was disputed by the employer and not accepted at trial.) The employer had to acquiesce because it would have been impossible to get a replacement crew to Alaska in time for the harvest, but when the fishermen claimed the extra wages at the end of the season, the employer refused to pay. The court found against the fishermen on the basis that they had incurred no new detriment in exchange for the promise of a wage increase. However, the opinion makes it clear that the true reason for nonenforcement was that the court considered the demand for more money to have been extortionate and unjustified.

§13.9.2 Common Law Duress Doctrine in Relation to Modifications

It was pointed out in section 7.5.2 that consideration doctrine is a clumsy tool for policing coerced modifications. It does not allow for easy discrimination between legitimate and improper modifications, and it can be circumvented if the party demanding the modification undertakes some new detriment of relatively small value in relation to the gain to be received, or if the parties go through the ritual of terminating the original contract and executing a new one. It is more efficient to focus directly on the problem of coerced modification by evaluating it under the rules of duress. That is, the modification should be upheld if it was fairly bargained, but it should be avoided if the one party's assent to provide increased compensation was induced by the other's improper threat to otherwise withhold his promised performance.

This is the approach adopted in another well-known case, *Austin Instrument Co. v. Loral Corp.*, 272 N.E.2d 533 (N.Y. 1971). Loral had been awarded a Navy contract to supply radar equipment. It was subject to strict delivery terms and a substantial liability for late delivery. It subcontracted with Austin for the supply of components. After performance had begun, Austin realized that it had underbid. It threatened not to deliver the parts ordered unless Loral agreed to a price increase. (The extent of the extortion was aggravated by the additional demand that Loral agree to use Austin as the subcontractor in another contract Loral had just made with the Navy.) Loral tried to find another supplier, but it could not obtain the components elsewhere in time. Faced with inevitable delay, liability for damages to the Navy, and harm to its reputation as a reliable contractor, Loral unsuccessfully tried to negotiate with Austin and eventually, under protest, gave in to its demands. After the completion of performance Loral refused to pay the extra price and Austin sued. The majority of the court held that Loral's free will was undermined by the pressure induced by Austin's threat of breach, so the modification was voidable on grounds of duress. However, a dissent expressed the view that the demand for a higher price was commercially reasonable because there had been a genuine escalation of costs, and agreements for price increases were not uncommon under such circumstances.

This difference in view shows that the distinction between a fair modification and an extortionate one is not always self-evident, but involves a careful evaluation of the motivation and business justification of the demand, the commercial expectations and practices, the force with which the demand is asserted, and the pressures to which the acquiescing party is subject. A subtle line separates opportunism and abuse of power from a fair request for an adjustment of terms.

§13.9.3 Modification Under UCC Article 2

Although *Austin Instrument* involved a sale of goods, the court did not refer to Article 2 and resolved the case under principles of common law. This shows that duress (and other common law policing doctrines) enables a court to invalidate unfair contract modifications directly without struggling with consideration issues. However, policing doctrines are only of use in avoiding an unfair modification. They do not provide a basis for upholding a fairly bargained modification that lacks consideration.

UCC §2.209 does a cleaner job of removing the issue of consideration from contract modification and focusing instead on whether the modification was in good faith. Although the duty of good faith has a broader scope than duress doctrine, Comment 2 to §2.209 makes it clear that the section covers extortion of a modification by duress. As is always true of the good faith standard, the question of what constitutes a lack of good faith can be difficult to decide where the party's conduct falls short of fraud, duress, or other clearly improper conduct. It involves an evaluation of the state of mind of the party who seeks to enforce the modification in light of the overall commercial circumstances and the business justifications or other factors motivating the parties' agreement to a change in the contract terms.

§13.9.4 The Enforcement of Modifications Despite an Absence of Consideration

Even when consideration doctrine is applied to a modification in a common law case, there are two situations recognized by Restatement, Second, §89 in which the modification may be enforced despite the absence of consideration. The first is when the party benefitted by the promise of modification has acted to her detriment in reliance on it, under circumstances in which it would be unjust to refuse enforcement. In other words, in appropriate circumstances, the doctrine of promissory estoppel may be applied to enforce a modification fully or in part. The second is when the modification was motivated by unforeseen supervening difficulties. That is, where a change in circumstances so alters a basic assumption of the contract, that the performance of the party seeking the modification becomes more burdensome than originally expected. For example, say that Loral entered into a contract with an air freight carrier to deliver the radar sets to the Navy. After the contract was executed, but before the date for shipment, the cost of air fuel skyrocketed as a result of a severe and unexpected disturbance in the market. If the carrier, without making any threat of breaching the contract, is able to persuade Loral to agree to an increase in the freight charges, this modification of the contract might be upheld under the supervening difficulties doctrine, even if the carrier suffers no new detriment in exchange for Loral's promise to pay more.[5] If the contract was for the sale of goods, rather than for the carriage of freight, we would not need the supervening difficulties rule because of §2.209. The unexpected price increase would be just one of the factors that the court would take into account in deciding whether the modification was in good faith.

§13.10 UNDUE INFLUENCE

The doctrine of undue influence was developed by courts of equity to deal with situations in which duress was not present, but one of the parties had a particularly strong influence over the other and abused this position of dominance to persuade the subservient party to enter a disadvantageous contract. Thus, while duress provides relief to one whose apparent assent has been induced by an unlawful threat, undue influence is concerned with cases of abuse of trust. Like duress, undue influence makes the contract voidable at the instance of the victim. In most jurisdictions, the doctrine has not been extended beyond its original confines and is not available to redress unfair persuasion in arms-length transactions. Restatement, Second, §177 reflects this narrow scope by confining the doctrine to relationships of dependence and trust. Although it would have been possible for courts to enlarge the scope of undue influence, making it available in all cases of unfair persuasion, the expanded concept of duress and the growing use of unconscionability provide a sufficient basis for the general regulation of bargaining, eliminating the need for a broader application of undue influence. As a result, undue influence has retained its specific character in most states.

---

5. As you will see in section 15.7, there is an affinity between the supervening difficulties doctrine and the defense of impracticability of performance. The difference, however, is that impracticability applies when the party suffering from the changed circumstances has not obtained a modification of the contract, but seeks to be excused from performance.

To obtain relief for undue influence, the victim must establish three elements: first, that a relationship of trust and dependency existed between the victim and the other party; second, that this relationship gave the other party dominance over the victim and imposed on him the duty not to act contrary to the victim's interests; and third, that the dominant party abused this position by unfairly persuading the victim to enter a contract adverse to the victim's interests.

For example, say that Lilly's father had established and built up the casino. Lilly had never been involved in the business. When her father died and left the casino to her, she had to keep this large and complex enterprise running. Because she had no clue about casino management or business in general, she turned to her father's longtime bookkeeper, Sel "The Skimmer" Short, for assistance in running it. Taking advantage of her inexperience and faith in him, Sel persuaded Lilly to sell him a large amount of stock at a bargain price.

The law does not absolutely bar contracts between a dominant party and the party who depends on him, and relief is available only if the weaker party can show that the dominant party abused his power by unfair persuasion. Unfair persuasion is an elastic concept. When the relationship of dependency is strong and the resulting contract is clearly disadvantageous to the weaker party, unfair persuasion may be inferred from those facts alone, and it may not be necessary to point to any specific underhanded bargaining strategy. However, if the degree of dependency is not as intense or the terms of the contract are not patently unfair, evidence of improper bargaining or oppressive circumstances may be needed to bolster the claim of undue influence. Unseemly bargaining can, as usual, take many forms, including the use of high-pressure tactics, the failure to disclose information, concealment of self-interest, or discouraging recourse to other advisers.

§13.11 UNCONSCIONABILITY

§13.11.1 The Role of Unconscionability

As noted earlier, duress does not cover situations in which there is no threat, express or implied. This means that it does not provide a mechanism for policing contracts that are not induced by threat, yet are the result of unfair pressure or abuse of power. Similarly, unless there is some relationship of trust between the parties, undue influence is not available in most jurisdictions to redress an imposition of terms on a weaker party. Even when imposition is accompanied by some degree of dishonesty, fraud cannot be claimed unless the misrepresentation and its consequent inducement are serious enough to satisfy the elements of fraud. Nevertheless, meaningful and genuine assent may be just as badly undermined when one party is able to impose an unfair contract on the other, using a strong bargaining position or unethical tactics to take advantage of the other's weakness, ignorance, or distress. The law therefore needs a more general doctrine under which courts may provide relief in cases that do not clearly fall within any of the more specific doctrines. The concept of unconscionability helps to cater to these situations.

Unconscionability is most commonly associated with consumer transactions in which a relatively large and powerful corporation supplies a standard form contract that is signed by a consumer with little or no opportunity to negotiate its terms. However, it is important to take note of two points. First, as the following discussion will show, a contract is not unconscionable merely because it is on standard terms drafted by an economically powerful party. Second, the doctrine is not confined to consumer transactions. It is equally applicable to commercial transactions between businesses. Bear in mind that many businesses are small, and some are operated by an individual, so there is sometimes not a clear dividing line between an individual who makes a contract as a consumer or as a business. However, the degree to which the party claiming unconscionability has economic power and business sophistication does have an impact on the finding of unconscionability. Therefore, it is often more difficult for a commercial entity to obtain relief under this doctrine.

§13.11.2 The Nature and Origins of Unconscionability

Unconscionability originated as a discretionary bar to equitable relief in a contract suit. It is the function of a court of equity[6] to do justice between the parties, and it would therefore decline relief to a plaintiff who had behaved inequitably. For example, if a party to a contract sued for equitable relief (such as specific performance) under a contract that was harsh or unfairly bargained, the court would refuse to enforce it on the ground that to do so would offend its conscience. Even after the courts of law and equity were combined, many courts did not recognize unconscionability as generally available and would only consider using the doctrine when the relief sought in the case was equitable in nature. Because most contract cases involve claims for damages or other relief at law, and claims in equity are less common, relief for unconscionability was often unavailable.

---

6. The distinction between law and equity is explained in section 2.5.

This changed dramatically when the UCC was enacted because §2.302 adopted the doctrine as a general rule, applicable to all contracts for the sale of goods. As a result of the strong influence of the UCC on the common law, courts began to apply unconscionability doctrine in cases at law involving contracts other than sales of goods. This trend was recognized and bolstered by Restatement, Second, §208, which closely follows the wording of UCC §2.302. Unconscionability is now firmly established as a general doctrine of contract law, applicable whether the basis of the suit is legal or equitable.

Unconscionability is decided by the judge, not the jury. The origin of this rule is in the equitable derivation of the doctrine, because juries have never been used in cases at equity. However, even though the doctrine is now applicable in law cases as well, the rule has not changed. Both Article 2 and the Restatement, Second, specifically state that unconscionability is a matter of law, to be decided by the judge. The main reason for preserving this rule is that a determination of unconscionability has a strong discretionary content, so it is better left in the hands of the judge.

§13.11.3 The Elements of Unconscionability

The UCC and Restatement, Second, simply acknowledge that the court has the power to refuse enforcement of an unconscionable contract or to adjust the contract by removing or modifying the unconscionable provision. Neither section attempts to say what constitutes unconscionability, but the Official Comments to §2.302, largely echoed in the comments to §208 of Restatement, Second, provide some general guidance to the court in exercising its discretion to determine whether unconscionability exists. Official Comment 1 to UCC §2.302 states that the basic test is whether, in the context of the commercial background and transactional circumstances, the contract or term is so one-sided as to be unconscionable. It expresses the aim of the doctrine as the prevention of "oppression and unfair surprise" but not the disturbance of the "allocation of risks because of superior bargaining power." Restatement, Second, Comment d to §208 makes a similar observation and expands on it by noting that gross inequality of bargaining power may satisfy the requirement of unconscionability if combined with substantively unfair terms. The Restatement comment also lists some indicia of oppressive bargaining, such as some degree of deception or compulsion, or an awareness by a dominant party of infirmity, ignorance, or lack of understanding on the part of the other. In essence, the comments point to a two-part test that examines both the process of bargaining and the resulting contract terms. *Williams v. Walker Thomas Furniture Co.*, 350 F.2d 445 (D.C. Cir. 1965), one of the earliest cases to deal with the modern approach to unconscionability, defined unconscionability as the absence of meaningful choice by the one party resulting in contract terms unreasonably favorable to the other.[7]

Over the years, as courts have worked with these vague guidelines, they have given them more content. However, because of the equitable derivation and discretionary nature of doctrine, the test for unconscionability remains quite open-ended and fluid. A very influential law review article,[8] written soon after the enactment of UCC §2.302, has given us the terminology that is now universally used to describe the two-part test of unconscionability. Unfairness in the bargaining process is called procedural unconscionability, and unfairness in the resulting contract is called substantive unconscionability. The relationship between these elements is not entirely clear. Courts generally require that both elements must be satisfied for a finding of unconscionability. That is, the court will not find a contract to be unconscionable unless the party seeking relief can demonstrate both improper conduct of the other party in the bargaining process and substantive unfairness in the resulting contract. However, there are cases in which courts have held that where one of these elements is present in a significant degree, the other need not be established. These cases suggest that if the terms of a contract are patently unfair and one-sided, the party seeking avoidance need not show procedural unconscionability. Similarly, proof of grossly improper bargaining tactics may be enough, even without a showing of substantively unfair terms. However, for the most part, this overstates the case, and it is more accurate to say that both elements are always needed, but in some transactions a powerful showing of one of the elements will allow the court to make an assumption, without much concrete proof, that the other must be present as well. For example, in a situation involving disparate bargaining power, great unfairness in the terms of the contract may itself lead to the conclusion that the party who benefits from the unfair terms has engaged in procedurally unconscionable conduct by taking unfair advantage of its dominance. Diagram 13B sketches the

---

7. Walker Thomas sold furniture and appliances on credit to low-income buyers. As security for payment of the balance of the price, Walker Thomas structured the transaction to include a "cross-collateralization" provision in the contract. This gave it a security interest in the goods bought under the new transaction as well as in all goods that the customer had ever bought from it in the past. The effect of this was that if the customer defaulted, Walker Thomas could repossess not just the goods sold in that transaction, but all other goods bought in previous transactions. Used furniture and household items do not have much value and were probably not worth enough to settle the debt. Therefore, the real purpose of the clause was to increase the stakes of default and to put pressure on the customer not to miss payments. The trial court had declined to find the cross-collateralization clause unconscionable because the UCC had not yet been enacted in the District of Columbia at that time. The court of appeals held that the doctrine did apply and it remanded the case to the district court to consider whether the contracts satisfied the test that it articulated.
8. Arthur A. Leff, *Unconscionability and the Code — The Emperor's New Clause*, 115 U. Pa. L. Rev. 485 (1967).

relationship between the two elements of unconscionability, which we examine more fully in the following sections.

Diagram 13B

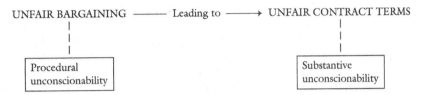

§13.11.4 Procedural Unconscionability

As noted in section 13.11.3, this element focuses on the bargaining conduct of the party who is alleged to have behaved unconscionably in the formation of the contract. As we have seen, the doctrines of duress, fraud, and undue influence are all aimed at improper bargaining conduct. However, they all have specific elements. Because the concept of procedural unconscionability is more flexible, it allows the court to deal with pressure; deception; or unfair persuasion that does not fit into the more exacting requirements of duress, fraud, or undue influence. Therefore, the principal value of unconscionability doctrine is that it expands the court's policing power, allowing it to provide relief for unfair bargaining that would not be available under the more specific policing mechanisms.

However, the flexibility of procedural unconscionability presents the risk that it could be too broadly applied. The comments to UCC §2.302 and Restatement, Second, §208 emphasize that mere disparity of bargaining power is not enough to make a contract procedurally unconscionable. It is not the doctrine's purpose to correct an imbalance between the parties in their market advantage, sophistication, or resources. Such a broad use of the doctrine would undermine the policy of protecting reliance by allowing a party dissatisfied with a contract to request relief just because the other party was smarter, bigger, wealthier, or had better lawyers. But this does not mean that the relative strength of the parties is irrelevant to the issue of unconscionability. Often it is only because of a disparity in power that a dominant party is able to behave in an unfair or oppressive manner or to insist on unfair terms. Similarly, the weaker party's lack of sophistication could make it easier to take advantage of her. Thus the key is not whether one party was more powerful, sophisticated, or knowledgeable than the other, but whether it abused its power to impose its will on the other party.

Having said this, it must be acknowledged that there are situations in which the abuse of power is quite subtle. There is no obvious dishonesty or unfair persuasion, yet it is nevertheless clear that one of the parties used its position of dominance to impose the contract or particular contract terms on the weaker. That is, one of the parties enters the transaction with such bargaining power relative to the other, that the stronger party has enough control over the transaction to leave the weaker with no choice but to enter it on the terms proposed by the dominant party. Contracts entered into under these circumstances have come to be known as contracts of adhesion because the weaker party is seen as adhering without choice to terms dictated by the stronger. Contracts of adhesion were introduced in section 5.4 and are examined more fully in section 13.12, but it is useful to anticipate and emphasize the point made in that discussion, that a contract does not become adhesive or unconscionable merely because one of the parties has greater bargaining power. Some degree of procedural impropriety — an abuse of that power — should be present as well. Nevertheless, when substantively unfair terms are present and are attributable to the bargaining dominance of the party favored by the terms, it is relatively easy to conclude that the weaker party was deprived of free choice by a degree of dominance that, in itself, amounted to procedural unfairness.

§13.11.5 Substantive Unconscionability

It should be apparent from the discussion of procedural unconscionability that there is a close relationship of cause and effect between the procedural and substantive elements: By engaging in unconscionable conduct during formation, one of the parties has been able to impose a substantively unconscionable contract or contract term on the other. It is not usually enough to show merely that the contract is disadvantageous to the complaining party or strongly favorable to the other. As we saw in the discussion of consideration doctrine in section 7.7, courts do not usually inquire into adequacy of consideration and will not normally invalidate or adjust a contract merely because one of the parties overpaid, underbid, or otherwise made a disadvantageous or unwanted deal. Unless this unfortunate state of affairs was caused by the behavior that qualifies as procedurally unconscionable, the parties should both be held to their manifested agreement. Once again, this general rule must be qualified by the caveat that the substantive and procedural elements do not have to be present to an equal degree. When the contract terms are grossly oppressive, procedural unfairness may be found simply in the opportunistic use of a position of dominance.

Most commonly, a contract is substantively unconscionable when its terms are harsh, unfair, or unduly favorable to one of the parties. One could think of endless examples of unfair terms, such as an excessive price for goods or services; exorbitant interest rates; harsh penalties in the event of default; the waiver of legal protection or of the right to seek legal redress in a proper forum, and so on. The test suggested by Comment 1 to §2.302 calls on the court to decide whether, "in the light of the general commercial background and the commercial needs of the particular trade or case, the clauses involved are so one-sided as to be unconscionable under the circumstances existing at the time of the contract." This is a hopeless circumlocution, but it does at least suggest that a contract or term is unconscionable if it favors one of the parties more than should reasonably be expected, given the commercial context in which the contract was made. The comment goes on to identify one of the goals of the doctrine as the prevention of oppression, which, while also rather vague, gives some further hint of the direction of the inquiry.

Although the conclusion that a contract is substantively unconscionable is normally based on the presence of unfair terms, it is possible for substantive unconscionability to be present even when the contract appears fair and reasonable from an objective standpoint. The unfairness could lie in the fact that the weaker party did not desire the transaction but was unfairly persuaded to enter it. For example, say that the conduct of a door-to-door sales representative is procedurally unconscionable because high-pressure techniques and smooth talk are used to bamboozle a hapless householder into buying an unneeded home appliance. Even if the price of the appliance and the other terms are reasonable, the contract as a whole may nevertheless be unconscionable, because it was unwanted by and imposed on the buyer.[9] As you can see, we are again looking at that balance between the substantive and procedural aspects of unconscionability.

§13.11.6 The Remedy for Unconscionability

As noted already, both the UCC and the Restatement, Second, leave it to the discretion of the court to devise the most appropriate response to an unconscionable contract or term. In exercising its discretion, the court is influenced, but not bound, by what relief the victim requests.

In some cases, the unconscionability so profoundly affects the quality of the victim's assent that she no longer desires the contract and should not be held to it. This is what would happen in the example of the consumer who was cajoled into buying the unwanted appliance. Here, the most appropriate remedy is for the court to refuse enforcement of the contract as a whole — that is, it avoids the contract. Upon avoidance, each party must restore any performance received under the contract under principles of unjust enrichment.

---

9. Home solicitation sales are legislatively regulated, so the buyer may have statutory grounds of avoidance as well.

In other cases (particularly where the victim would like to keep the contract with appropriate adjustments), the better remedy may be to enforce the basic bargain but to change its terms to eliminate its unconscionable aspects. This may involve either severing the unconscionable part of the contract (that is, eliminating the unconscionable provision entirely) or just altering the term to make it fair. For example, a standard form contract for the sale of goods between a large retailer and a consumer requires all disputes to be arbitrated. The court finds that although the contract as a whole is unobjectionable, the arbitration term provides for a procedure that unduly favors the retailer. The consumer does not wish to avoid the contract as a whole but would like to avoid the arbitration term. The court could sever the arbitration term in its entirety, so that there is no longer any requirement to arbitrate and the parties must litigate their dispute before a court. Alternatively, the court could remove the unfair aspects of the arbitration term, but otherwise enforce it. This would mean that the parties are still bound to arbitrate, but the terms governing the arbitration are less one-sided. In deciding whether it is appropriate to sever or alter a term, the court considers factors such as the degree to which the term was imposed without meaningful choice, the form of relief requested by the victim of unconscionability, and the impact that the change will have on the basis of the parties' bargain. Courts usually aim to interfere as little as possible with the contract's terms, and to correct the contract without fundamentally altering its purpose. Where a term cannot be severed without doing significant harm to the basis of the bargain, alteration of the term may be less intrusive. If neither severance nor alteration can cure the unconscionability, or the change in the terms fundamentally changes the nature of the agreement, avoidance of the contract is probably the only proper remedy.

The flexibility of the remedy for unconscionability often has an impact on the court's decision to find that a term is unconscionable. A court may more readily make a finding of unconscionability because it can craft a remedy that is less drastic than a total avoidance of the entire contract.

§13.11.7 A Final Note on the Temptation to Overuse Unconscionability Doctrine

Because unconscionability is such a vague and discretionary doctrine, a student may be tempted to argue it whenever the parties are not of equal bargaining power and the weaker party complains of an adverse term or contract. It therefore must be stressed that courts are careful in using the doctrine. Although we have seen that the doctrine is broad enough to make it very difficult to predict how a court might react to a claim of unconscionability, most courts do look seriously at the two elements that we have discussed and commonly require a showing of both. This is not to say that a notable discrepancy in bargaining power and sophistication is irrelevant — this often explains why the dominant party was able to take advantage of the weaker one. Bear this in mind as you read the section 13.12 on contracts of adhesion.

§13.12 UNCONSCIONABILITY AND ADHESION IN STANDARD CONTRACTS

§13.12.1 The Role of Adhesion in Unconscionability Analysis

Section 5.4 introduced the concept of adhesion in relation to standard contracts,[10] and the concept was referred to again in the discussion of procedural unconscionability in section 13.11.4. As explained in those sections, a contract is described as a contract of adhesion where one of the parties has the market power to refuse to contract except on nonnegotiable terms, and the other has no choice but to adhere to the terms if he wants the contract. It is much harder to label a contract as adhesive if the market for the desired object of the contract (such as goods, services, or employment) is competitive, and the nondrafting party is able to enter into a contract without those terms with someone else. Adhesion is more likely to be present if there is no competing provider who will contract on different terms, especially if the desired object of the contract is not a luxury.

Courts sometimes talk of adhesion in terms that suggest that it is a basis of relief independent of and separate from unconscionability. However, it would be a mistake to take this too literally, and you should not think of adhesion as divorced from unconscionability. Rather, adhesion is one of the factors that may persuade the court that the contract satisfies the elements of procedural and substantive unconscionability. That is, the fact that the dominant party had the power to insist on a contract on its own nonnegotiable terms may allow that party to take advantage of its dominance to impose an unfairly one-sided contract on the other. In effect, the abuse of the power to dictate the terms has resulted in an unfair contract. It is important to keep this perspective in mind, especially when dealing with nonnegotiable terms in standard contracts. As explained in Chapter 5, standard contracts are both widespread and necessary, whether the standard terms are in a signed paper

---

10. Adhesion is usually associated with standard contracts, and this is the focus here. However, note that an argument of adhesion could be made in any situation in which one of the parties has no choice but to accept nonnegotiable terms proffered by the other.

or are presented on a website or in software as clickwrap, browsewrap, or shrinkwrap terms. Few, if any, courts would be willing to go so far as to say that it is per se unconscionable for a party to insist on contracting on nonnegotiable standard terms that it drafted to protect its own interests. This point is illustrated by *Feldman v. Google, Inc.*, 513 F. Supp. 2d 229 (E.D. Pa 2007), cited in section 5.3. The aspect of the opinion discussed in section 5.3 was whether Feldman had assented to a clickwrap forum selection clause by clicking the "I agree" button on Google's website. The court held that the clause was easily accessible and conspicuously set out on the website, so Feldman was bound by his signification of assent. In addition to arguing that he did not assent to the term, Feldman claimed that the contract was adhesive and the term was unconscionable. The court disagreed. Although the term was a standard, nonnegotiable term, there was no procedural unconscionability because Feldman did have reasonable notice of the term, and he had not shown that a lack of alternatives in the marketplace left him with no meaningful choice. The court also held that the term was not substantively unconscionable because it was not unreasonable, unexpected, or unduly one-sided.

Although a standard nonnegotiable term is not adhesive or unconscionable by that fact alone, it could satisfy the elements of unconscionability if the dominant party crosses the line that separates acceptable self-serving terms from abusive imposition. For example, in *Mazur v. eBay, Inc.*, 2008 WL 618988 (N.D. Cal. 2008), the court found a clickwrap dispute resolution clause to be unconscionable. The clause was part of a standard agreement required by an auction house (HotJewelryAuctions .com) that operated on the eBay site. The clause required disputes to be resolved by a law firm that was nominated in the standard term, and waived all other forms of dispute resolution. The element of procedural unconscionability was satisfied because the contract was adhesive and the standard terms were laid out on the website in a manner that made them difficult to read. They were presented as a massive block of impenetrable text, without any paragraph, section, or heading breaks, and the text box allowed for only a few single-spaced lines to be read at a time. The court found substantive unconscionability in that the dispute resolution process provided for was not neutral and unduly favored the auction house. The court therefore avoided the provision and allowed the plaintiff to continue the lawsuit.

In summary, adhesion on its own, unaccompanied by any specific improper bargaining conduct, could satisfy the procedural element of unconscionability where it deprives the weaker party of meaningful choice and leads to the conclusion that the stronger party used its market power illegitimately. However, the absence of specific bargaining misbehavior would make this a borderline case of procedural unconscionability. Because the procedural and substantive elements should be balanced against each other, a strong degree of substantive unfairness must be present to compensate for the weak form of procedural unconscionability.

§13.12.2 Terms Made Available Only After the Contract Has Been Entered

Where adhesive standard terms are made available only after the contract has been entered, a court may find that the delay in transmitting the terms is procedurally unconscionable.[11] However, that is not a foregone conclusion. If the terms are reasonably to be expected and the nondrafting party had reasonable notice that the contract was subject to standard terms, the delay in transmitting the terms may not be procedurally unconscionable. If, in addition, the terms are not unfair or unduly one-sided, there may not be substantive unconscionability either. The U.S. Supreme Court considered the validity of standard terms on a cruise ticket in *Carnival Cruise Lines, Inc. v. Shute*, 499 U.S. 585 (1991). The Shutes booked a cruise and were not given a copy of the contract's standard terms until they received their cruise tickets, some time later. One of the standard terms was a forum selection clause designating the Florida courts as the agreed forum for resolving disputes. During the cruise, Ms. Shute slipped and was injured. She sued Carnival for damages in the federal district court in Washington, her home state. The district court dismissed her case on the ground that it should have been commenced in Florida. The majority of the Supreme Court agreed. It held that although a standard clause on a ticket should be carefully scrutinized for fairness, it is not presumptively invalid merely because the passenger had no opportunity to (or power to) negotiate it. The court stressed the efficiency and value of standard contracting, which should be facilitated unless it is abused. In the present case, the forum selection clause was reasonable because it centralized litigation in the courts of Carnival's

---

11. Recall that the deferred communication of contract terms was discussed in section 5.5. In that section, we considered whether standard terms that are not made available to the nondrafting party should be part of the contract. They are part of the contract if it can be interpreted as a rolling contract, in which the offeree is given the opportunity to reject the contract after receiving adequate notice of the terms. However, where the contract is not a rolling contract, standard terms not made available to the nondrafting party at the time of contracting will not be included in the contract unless the nondrafting party had a duty to ascertain what they were, or they were reasonable in content and reasonably should have been expected by the nondrafting party. Although the cases discussed in section 5.5 (*ProCD, Inc. v. Zeidenberg*, 86 F.3d 1447 (7th Cir. 1996) and *Casavant v. Norwegian Cruise Line, Ltd.*, 829 N.E.2d 1171 (Mass. App. 2005)) were concerned with the question of whether the contested terms entered the contract, and did not address the question of whether those terms were unconscionable, recognize that there is a link between these inquiries. Lack of reasonable notice of adhesive terms may satisfy the element of procedural unconscionability, and unexpected or surprising terms may be substantively unconscionable.

home state and reduced costs of litigation. The forum selected was natural, not alien, and there was no indication that it was chosen to frustrate claims. The dissent disagreed that efficiency and the reduction of Carnival's litigation costs were a good enough justification for depriving the passenger of the right to litigate in the forum that was most convenient and least expensive for her. This unfair result, combined with the likelihood that a passenger would not even notice the clause (it was one of 25 paragraphs on the ticket, not drawn to the passenger's attention at the time of contracting), led the dissent to conclude that the clause should not be enforced. *Carnival Cruise Lines* was decided under principles of federal law, and it did not mention unconscionability. However, it is not difficult to see the conceptual link between unconscionability doctrine and the principles of reasonable expectations and fairness on which the court based its conclusion.

§13.12.3 Adhesion and Unconscionability in Relation to Arbitration Provisions

In sections 4.1.5 and 5.3c we discussed standard arbitration provisions in relation to the duty to read. We noted there that arbitration provisions have become increasingly common in standard contracts (including employment contracts), and that legal challenges to those provisions have become quite common. Because there is a general public policy in favor of arbitration, as reflected in the Federal Arbitration Act, 9 USC §§1-16, a court should uphold a standard arbitration agreement unless the party challenging it can show grounds to invalidate it under principles of contract law. In sections 4.1.5 and 5.3c, we discussed the possible grounds that the party was not aware of the provision because he did not read it or consent to it. As we saw, the duty to read precludes that argument unless the party can show that the provision was not adequately brought to his notice or reasonably expected. The case of *Morales v. Sun Constructors*, 541 F.3d 218 (3rd Cir. 2008), was used as an example of how rigorous a court might be in holding a party to his duty to read: The court held that a Spanish-speaking employee, who could not read English, had a duty to read and ascertain the content and meaning of an arbitration provision written in English. However, a court is likely to react to a challenge with more sympathy where the overall circumstances show overreaching by the dominant party in the imposition of an adhesive and unfairly one-sided contract. For example, in *Samaniego v. Empire Today LLC*, 140 Cal. Rptr. 3d 492 (Cal. App. 2012), the employer required employees to sign an employment agreement that contained an arbitration provision. The agreement was dense — 11 pages long, single-spaced in a small font, and full of legal terminology. The arbitration provision was the penultimate of 37 sections.

The agreement was in English, and the employees were Spanish-speaking with little or no facility in reading English. The employer required the employees to sign the agreement as a condition of employment and gave them little or no opportunity to seek advice. The agreement stated that the arbitration was subject to the rules of the American Arbitration Association, but those rules were not provided to employees. In addition, the terms of the arbitration agreement were strongly favorable to the employer. It shortened the statute of limitations for bringing claims against the employer; it had a unilateral fee-shifting provision that allowed the employer, but not an employee, to recover attorney's fees; and while it bound the employees to arbitrate their claims, it excluded from arbitration any claims that the employer might bring against the employee to safeguard its own interests. The court found that the adhesive manner in which the agreement was presented to employees satisfied the element of procedural unconscionability, and the one-sided nature of the arbitration provision was substantively unconscionable. The court refused to sever the unconscionable provisions and to compel arbitration without them. It found the entire arbitration provision to be permeated with unconscionability — the multiple defects in the agreement showed it to be a systematic effort to impose arbitration on employees as an inferior forum that worked to the employer's advantage.

§13.13 POLICING CONTRACTS FOR ILLEGALITY OR CONTRAVENTION OF PUBLIC POLICY

§13.13.1 Illegality, Public Policy, and Freedom of Contract

It was noted in the introduction that the assent and reliance policies of contract law are not the only policies that may be implicated in the enforcement of a contract. Even when the contract is a full and genuine exercise of both parties' freedom of contract, it may break the law or so offend public policy that the court refuses to enforce it. This distinguishes regulation on grounds of illegality and public policy from the other doctrines discussed in this chapter: The issue here is not that one of the parties dealt wrongly with the other or that one party's assent is deficient (even though this factor could also be present in some cases), but that the contract is forbidden or does some damage to the public good. Therefore, the goal of policing here is different from that in cases where the only issue is bargaining impropriety. The court's concern goes beyond doing justice between the parties, to the protection of the public interest.

It is a bit artificial and sometimes quite difficult to make a firm distinction between illegality and violation of public policy. Courts do not always articulate the distinction and sometimes even use the words interchangeably. For the most part, it is not crucial to make the distinction because in many cases it would not lead to a difference in the analysis or result of the case. However, there is a conceptual distinction between a contract that is illegal and one that offends public policy, which could affect the court's approach to and resolution of a case. (This is explained in section 13.13.4.) It is therefore useful to understand it. A contract is illegal if it contravenes a statute or a rule of common law. A contract violates public policy, where there is no rule of law that forbids the contract, but the contract so harms the public interest that it should not be recognized as valid. In such a situation, the court invokes its discretionary power to refuse to enforce the contract. The principal difference between an illegal contract and one that violates public policy therefore lies in the degree to which a court uses its discretion to avoid the contract. Where a contract is not forbidden by law, the court's decision on whether to avoid it requires an exercise of discretion that comes uncomfortably close to lawmaking. Courts are generally careful in exercising this discretion and usually require a strong showing of clear harm to the public interest before finding that a contract contravenes public policy.

Although the focus here is on the public interest, it is not typically some outside agency or public body that challenges the contract. The claim of illegality or a violation of public policy is made by one of the parties who seeks to escape an obligation arising out of the contract. It is therefore important to understand that in adjudicating an issue of illegality or public policy, a court is commonly resolving a dispute between the parties. One of them is trying to enforce the contract (or sometimes trying to obtain restitution for performance under the contract) and the other is resisting. Although balancing the equities between the parties is not as dominant a consideration as the public interest, it does have an influence on the outcome.

The end result of a determination that a contract is illegal or contravenes public policy has some similarity to the remedies for improper bargaining and is in some ways analogous. (A court may decide to refuse enforcement of the improper contract in its entirety, which sounds like the equivalent to avoidance, or it may keep the contract in place and refuse enforcement of only the offending term, which approximates severance.) However, because protection of the public interest is the court's principal goal in dealing with a contract that is illegal or violates public policy, the case is conceptually different from a situation of improper bargaining. This calls for a different approach to the issue of remedy. Society is the principal victim of a contract that is illegal or in violation of public policy. Therefore, where a contract directly violates a rule of law, or its harm to society is serious enough, a court is most unlikely to enforce it under any circumstances. Such a contract is more correctly characterized as void rather than voidable. The same is often true where the parties are joint perpetrators of the offense and it cannot be said that one used the illegal contract to victimize the other. On the other hand, where one of the parties is more to blame for the transaction, the other is a member of a group which the law seeks to protect, and the contract does not involve serious illegality, the contract is more accurately described as voidable. In short, the treatment of a contract that is illegal or contrary to public policy depends on the nature and gravity of the violation, the goals of the law or public policy, and the extent to which the impropriety permeates the contract. Sometimes the best way to protect the public interest is to refuse enforcement of the contract altogether, but in other cases, enforcement of the contract, with or without the adjustment of its terms, may best serve the public good. Sometimes, as we will see in section 13.13.4, a contract's illegality or violation of public policy could even affect a restitutionary claim of one of the parties arising from nonenforcement of the contract.

§13.13.2 Illegal Contracts

Some illegal contracts are such a serious violation of the law that performance of the contract (or sometimes even making the contract) is a criminal act. This would be true, for example, of a contract under which one of the parties pays the other to murder someone. Such a contract is not enforceable and its making or performance would lead to criminal prosecution. However, there is a difference between illegality and criminality, and not all illegal contracts are criminal. A statute or the common law could forbid a contract, but provide no consequence for violation of the law other than the nonenforcement of the contract. For purposes of contract law, we are not concerned with whether the transaction attracts criminal penalties. (Although the criminal nature of the contract could affect the court's approach to the equities and the public interest when it decides on what remedy is appropriate.)

The basic rule is that a court will not enforce an illegal contract or term, even if it is clear that the parties entered the contract voluntarily and there was no improper bargaining. For example, in Parente v. Pirozzoli, 866 A.2d 629 (Conn. App. 2005), the defendant wished to buy a bar but would have had difficulty in taking transfer of the liquor license because he was a convicted felon. He therefore entered into an agreement with the plaintiff under which the plaintiff would apply for the license as a front man, and the parties would then run the bar as equal partners. The license was granted and the parties went into business. When the partnership was later dissolved, the defendant refused to pay the plaintiff his share of the profits and the plaintiff sued. The court refused to enforce the contract because it was based on the unlawful purpose of evading the liquor control laws. Similarly, in *Homani v. Iranzadi*, 211 Cal. App. 3d 1104 (1989), the court refused to enforce an agreement to pay interest on a loan where, for the purpose of evading tax on the interest, the parties had agreed orally to the payment of interest, but signed a promissory note showing the loan as interest-free.

§13.13.3 Contracts Contrary to Public Policy

If a contract is not actually illegal, but it nevertheless offends public policy, the consequence of nonenforcement is not as inevitable. A decision on whether or not to enforce the contract involves a balancing of policy concerns and of the equities between the parties. Assuming that the contract suffers from no deficiencies in assent, the regulation of contracts on the basis of broader public interest creates a tension between the policy of enforcing contracts and the other public policy that would be frustrated by enforcement. To resolve this dissonance, the countervailing policies must be balanced. If the harm to the public interest outweighs the benefit of enforcement to the public and the parties, enforcement must be refused.

How does the court identify the existence and force of a public policy affected by the contract? In the easiest case, the policy may be expressed by legislation or well-established common law precedent. Of course, if the statute or rule of common law clearly prohibits a contract in violation of a particular policy, we have a case of illegality, as discussed above. But sometimes the law does not actually forbid a particular contract, yet it is apparent that the law's policy goals are incompatible with the recognition and enforcement of a contract of this kind. Because this often amounts to judicial policymaking, most courts are cautious about identifying public policy that does not have a firm base in statute or precedent. A court may try to seek guidance in other governmental policy pronouncements and may entertain policy arguments by the parties. If it should conclude that such a policy exists, it must then weigh it against the policy of upholding contracts.

Disclaimers of liability for negligent or intentional injury (exculpatory clauses) feature frequently in the caselaw, and provide a good illustration of public policy analysis. A disclaimer of liability for wrongful conduct pits the policy of freedom of contract against the tort policy of holding a tortfeasor accountable for injury caused by his actions and of deterring wrongful conduct. The policy of freedom of contract calls for the enforcement of a freely bargained consensual agreement, but the tort policy of accountability disfavors an agreement that absolves a tortfeasor in advance from liability for future conduct. This means that the public policies of contract and tort pull in opposite directions and must be balanced. It is relatively easy to decide in favor of the tort policy where there is some problem with the way in which the disclaimer was entered into. The policy of freedom of contract is not well served by enforcing the contract unless the disclaimer is voluntary, fairly bargained, and expressed clearly and conspicuously. Therefore, as an initial matter, the court examines the disclaimer itself to decide if its enforcement serves the policies of contract law. Adhesion is a relevant consideration here, and a court is less likely to uphold a disclaimer if it was imposed on the injured party. In addition, courts insist that the language of the disclaimer must be explicit and must clearly show the intent to exonerate the party from liability. Any unclear language is interpreted restrictively to cut down the scope of or eliminate the disclaimer.

Where the provision is absolutely clear and the victim's agreement to it is not in question, the competing tort and contract policies are in the starkest opposition. To decide which policy should predominate, courts weigh all the circumstances and considerations. Courts have identified several factors that are relevant to this decision. The scope and extent of the disclaimer is important. Although it may be acceptable to exclude liability for negligence, a disclaimer will not be enforced to the extent that it exculpates gross negligence, recklessness, or intentional misconduct. Where only ordinary negligent injury is covered, the court considers the importance or necessity of the service to the public (for example, a disclaimer in a residential lease is potentially much more harmful than one in a skydiving contract); the kinds of people who are likely to execute the disclaimer (for example, whether the service is used by the public at large, or only by a specialized or qualified group); the extent to which the provider of the service has control over the person or property of the victim; and the impact that not permitting the disclaimer will have on the public's ability to obtain the service at all, or at reasonable cost. If factors such as these balance in favor of holding the service provider responsible for negligence, the court will not enforce the disclaimer, even if it is freely executed and not adhesive.

Hanks v. Power Ridge Restaurant Corp., 885 A.2d 734 (Conn. 2005) and *McCune v. Myrtle Beach Indoor Shooting Range, Inc.*, 612 S.E.2d 462 (S.C. App. 2005) show how a court might balance all these considerations. In *Hanks*, the plaintiff was injured while snowtubing and sued the operator of the ski resort for damages, claiming that it had been negligent in the way that it constructed and supervised the snowtube run. Prior to snowtubing, the plaintiff had signed a release that exculpated the operator from liability for negligent injury. The court found that the disclaimer expressed the exclusion of liability in conspicuous and unmistakable language that would alert a reasonable person to its import. The agreement was very clearly written and it unmistakably emphasized that negligent conduct was covered by the disclaimer by capitalizing the word "negligence" several times.[12] Notwithstanding this, the court avoided the disclaimer on grounds of public policy because it found that the contract was adhesive, the snowtube run was open to all members of the public who had a reasonable expectation of safety, the operator controlled the run and rented the equipment, and it would not be in the public interest to allow the operator to shift risk of liability to the customer.

By contrast, in *McCune*, the plaintiff's eye was injured while she participated in a paintball game because her mask did not fit properly. Before she began the game she signed a release that emphasized the risks of injury, acknowledged that she assumed such risks, and absolved the defendant from all liability for injury, whether caused by negligence or otherwise. The release specifically did not cover injury resulting from gross negligence or wanton misconduct. The exculpatory provisions were printed in capital letters. The court affirmed the trial court's grant of summary judgment in favor of the defendant. The release was explicit and clear, it did not seek to exclude liability for conduct more serious than negligence, and it was a voluntary assumption of risk by the plaintiff. The court pointed out that it would not serve the public good if a business could not exclude liability by a reasonable and explicit disclaimer. The risk of liability would preclude many activities and events.

§13.13.4 The Effect of Contracts That Are Illegal or Contrary to Public Policy and the *In Pari Delicto* Rule

a. Illegal Contracts

The basic rule is that where the parties share the guilt of having entered an illegal contract, the court will keep aloof from the dispute and will not intervene to help either party. This is known as the *in pari delicto* rule, an abbreviation of the maxim *in pari delicto potior est conditio defendentis*. (When the parties are in equal guilt, the defendant's position is stronger.) The rule is not as straightforward as it sounds. First, although it refers to equal guilt, it really means that the guilt of the party seeking relief must be equal to or greater than that of the other party. Second, although it is sometimes possible to assign greater fault to one of the parties, it is not always easy to do this. Third, and less obvious, the rule does not simply

---

12. The plaintiff testified that although he had read the release (and his 12-year-old son had urged him not to sign it), he did not take it seriously or believe that it would be enforceable. The court pointed out that the plaintiff's subjective opinion of the effect of the clause was irrelevant under the objective test.

depend on an evaluation of the relative guilt of the parties. It also takes into account the equities between the parties and considers whether the public interest is best served by giving or declining relief. This means that weighing the relative guilt of the parties is just one aspect of a broader inquiry into the circumstances of the transaction, the relationship of the parties and their motivations, and the public interest served by the law.

The in pari delicto rule is therefore not an absolute bar to relief where the court finds that the party requesting relief bears equal or greater guilt. Rather, it is a starting premise from which the court may depart to the extent that it considers that the equities between the parties and the public interest so demand. The weighing of these factors is illustrated by the Parente and Homani cases discussed in section 13.13.2. In Parente, the plaintiff argued that if the court refused to award him his share of the partnership profits, the defendant, who instigated the scheme to evade the liquor control laws, would be rewarded by a windfall. Although the court recognized this, it felt that the public interest was best served by refusing enforcement. Not only should the court not sanction such a contract, but the refusal of enforcement would create a disincentive for people like the plaintiff to act as front men in the future. This decision shows the difficulty of achieving the right balance. It could just as well have been argued that allowing the defendant to keep the plaintiff's share of the profits created an incentive to use a front man to deceive the liquor control authority. In Homani, the court was unpersuaded by the lender's argument that the borrower received a windfall. The court considered that the public interest was best served by removing the lender's incentive to enter such a transaction. This result makes sense. After all, it was the lender who stood to benefit from the tax evasion, and he was most guilty of breaking the law.

The effect of applying the in pari delicto rule is that the court declines to award relief and leaves the parties as it finds them. The obvious effect of this is that the court will refuse to enforce the contract where one of the parties sues for enforcement. This is what happened in both Parente and Homani. Refusal of enforcement is a natural consequence of illegality because enforcement is an affirmative recognition of the contract, and a court is understandably reluctant to play any role in upholding the improper contract. However, the in pari delicto rule also has a less obvious impact. The court may also apply it where a party does not claim enforcement of the contract, but concedes it is illegal and asks for restitution of a benefit that he conferred on the other party under the contract. The refusal of restitution is not as easily justified as nonenforcement because the grant of the remedy would not require recognition of the contract. Quite the opposite, it is based on the premise that no contract exists. Nevertheless, once the contract is found to be illegal, the in pari delicto rule covers all claims associated with it, and even a restitutionary claim could be denied if the equities and the public interest make that appropriate.

The following illustrations identify the considerations that a court weighs in deciding whether the in pari delicto rule should preclude the restitution of a benefit conferred under an illegal contract.

In contravention of a statute forbidding the ownership of casinos by mobsters, Lilly Livered sold her casino to Attila "The Animal" Axehacker, a gangster, for $10 million. Both parties knew about the prohibition. At the time of executing the agreement, Attila made a down payment of $100,000 to Lilly. A few days later she repudiated the contract. Clearly, the contract is unenforceable, and Attila cannot sue for relief on the contract, whether in the form of specific performance or damages for breach. Can he get the $100,000 back? There is no obvious answer: It could be argued that, as the mobster seeking to acquire the casino, he is more to blame than the seller. But the contrary argument could be made that people like Lilly, by deliberately violating the law, make possible the very harm that the statute seeks to avert. The determination of which of these alternatives best serves the public interest is also difficult to make: Is it better to allow her to keep a windfall profit from her deliberately wrongful transaction, or to allow the court's process to be used by a thug to recover the down payment made in an attempt to violate the law? Unless it is demonstrated that judicial intervention is the more appropriate alternative, the thrust of the in pari delicto rule is to leave the parties as they are.

As a second example, a liquor store sells a case of scotch to a 20-year-old minor, violating a statute (known to both parties) that prohibits the sale of alcohol to persons under the age of 21.[13] The buyer paid for the scotch in cash, but the seller now refuses delivery. Again, the buyer clearly cannot enforce the contract, but can he get his money back? One could argue that the buyer had no business trying to purchase the liquor and deserves no help from the court in recovering the payment. However, it seems intolerable to allow the seller to keep his money. If the whole idea of barring the sale of liquor to young people is that they do not have the maturity to use it responsibly, it would seem that this lack of maturity also diminishes blame vis-à-vis the adult seller. It is also relevant that a central purpose of the law is to protect people like the buyer, and return of the money better serves this goal.

b. Contracts That Violate Public Policy

When the contract is not illegal, but offends public policy, the same principles are generally applicable, including the evaluation under the in pari delicto rule, which takes into account the relative fault of the parties and

---

13. Although the general rule is that a person must be over 21 to buy liquor, in most states a person acquires contractual capacity at 18. The contract is therefore not avoidable for lack of capacity.

the public interest. Although such contracts are usually unenforceable, the fact that they are not actually illegal gives the court greater flexibility in tailoring relief. Therefore, in appropriate circumstances, enforcement on adjusted terms may be a better solution when the equities favor the party who seeks enforcement and the harm to the public interest can be averted or minimized by eliminating the offensive terms. If enforcement is refused, the in pari delicto rule may be applied to deny restitution, but because the wrongfulness is less grave, the equities are more likely to favor restoration of any benefit conferred.

An example based on a covenant not to compete illustrates the adjusted enforcement of a contract that offends public policy: A covenant not to compete is an undertaking by a person associated with a business that, upon leaving the business, he will not, for a specified period and in a specified area, engage in activity that competes with the business. Such covenants may be found in employment or partnership agreements or in contracts for the sale of a business. Say that a well-established pediatrician takes a newly qualified doctor into her practice as a junior partner. The established doctor is concerned that her new partner may work with her just long enough to get experience and a following among her patients, and that he will then terminate the partnership and set up practice on his own. To avoid this, she demands a provision in the partnership agreement in terms of which the junior partner undertakes that upon leaving the partnership, he will not practice medicine within a ten-mile radius of the partnership premises for a period of five years.

There is a long-established public policy against agreements that stifle competition or that restrict a person's freedom to earn a livelihood by full participation in the market. The policy against contracts that curb competition is reflected in the antitrust laws, which prohibit various kinds of anticompetitive behavior. But even in situations not covered by the antitrust legislation (such as the present case) courts apply the policy when a contract unduly hampers competition or improperly restricts the ability of a party to work. The covenant not to compete is not per se invalid, but the court will assess its impact on competition and on the interests of the party who is restrained. The court will consider all the circumstances of the case, taking into account factors including the legitimate interests (such as patient goodwill) of the established doctor, the mores of the medical profession, the hardship on the junior doctor, the patients' right to use a doctor of their choice, and the fairness of the bargaining process leading to agreement on the provision. If, on balance, the deleterious impact of the clause outweighs the interests of the established doctor, the court may refuse to enforce the clause altogether. Alternatively, it may cut down the restraint to a level that goes no further than necessary to protect those interests, reducing the time or geographic limit of the restraint or defining the prohibited activity more narrowly (for example, to cover pediatrics, rather than medical practice generally). In this case, therefore, a violation of public policy may not render the entire contract unenforceable, but more likely results in the elimination or adjustment of the offending provision.

§13.14 A TRANSNATIONAL PERSPECTIVE ON POLICING DOCTRINES

Article 4 of the CISG states that the CISG is not concerned with the validity of a contract. Because policing doctrines affect the validity of a contract, the CISG does not provide for them. Therefore, even in a transaction governed by the CISG, the policing doctrines of the governing domestic law apply to the transaction.

Article 3.1 of the UNIDROIT Principles specifically refrains from addressing questions of illegality or immorality. Apart from this, the Principles include doctrines that are equivalent to those discussed in this chapter, even though there are differences in the terminology and elements. Article 3.8 allows for the avoidance of a contract for fraud, including the nondisclosure of circumstances that should have been disclosed under principles of fair dealing. Article 3.9 allows for avoidance for an "unjustified threat" that is "imminent and serious" enough to leave the party with "no reasonable alternative." A threat is unjustified if the act is wrongful in itself or is wrongful as a means of obtaining the contract. Article 3.10 has a doctrine that covers the same ground as undue influence and unconscionability. It allows avoidance of a contract or a term of the contract if the contract or term gave the other party "an excessive advantage." Article 3.16 provides for the avoidance of the specific offending terms of a contract unless it is unreasonable to uphold the contract in the absence of those terms.

Examples

1. Cookie Racha owns a house built in 1915. The house has been plagued with chronic cockroach infestation. Although Cookie fumigated it regularly, roaches reappeared in ever-increasing numbers within a few weeks of treatment. Also, the house was slowly sinking into soft ground on one side. The sinking can only be corrected by an expensive process that requires the side of the house to be jacked up while a firm concrete foundation is laid. The sinking has caused deep cracks in the living room wall. Cookie has replastered the wall a few times, but the continuing movement reopened the cracks soon afterwards. Cookie had already become quite sick of the house when she recently read in the newspaper

that the neighboring property had been bought by the state for use as a halfway house for paroled sex offenders. This was the final straw and she decided to sell.

Acting on the advice of her real estate agent, Chic "The Snake" Canery, she fumigated the house, plastered the cracks, and repainted the wall just before the house was placed on the market. Each time that the house was shown, Chic ensured that all the lights were on. Not only did this present the house in a more attractive manner, but the brightness discouraged the regenerating population of roaches from venturing into full view. Chic brought Bugsy Crawley to see the house. On the very next day Bugsy made an offer to buy the house for the full asking price. Cookie accepted immediately. The terms of the contract of sale were set out in Bugsy's offer, made on a standard form provided by the real estate agent. The writing simply set out the basic terms of the transaction and made no representations concerning the property. The transaction closed a short while later, and Bugsy moved into his new home. It did not take very long before the roaches reappeared, the wall cracked, and the sex offenders moved in next door. Does Bugsy have grounds for avoiding the sale?

2. Tutu Tango is a 65-year-old retired tax lawyer. Her life had become quite dull since retirement, and she was looking for excitement. One day she was invited to accompany a friend to a free introductory dance lesson at the Fleece Foot Dance Studios. During the lesson, she fell into the clutches of Jig Aloe, a suave and unctuous dance instructor employed by Fleece Foot. Jig subjected Tutu to all the charm and flattery that he had perfected by taking Fleece Foot's super sales course. After observing Tutu's inept and clumsy cavortings on the dance floor, he pretended to be very impressed. He told her enthusiastically that she had a wonderful natural talent and ageless grace. He said that he was convinced that with proper training, she had the potential of becoming an elegant and alluring dancer. Tutu had been around the block a few times, so she didn't really believe a word of this. But Jig was cute and he would be her instructor, so she agreed to sign up for a month's worth of lessons at a cost of $250. Jig produced a form and asked her to sign it. He cleverly positioned his hand over the top of the form so Tutu could not see the top few lines. This little trick worked, because Tutu did not pay much attention to the form and signed it without trying to read it. Had she been more astute, she would have seen that Jig had given her a life membership contract form to sign, in which she irrevocably purchased a lifetime of lessons for a fee of $10,000, payable within seven days of signing.

A few days later Tutu went to the studio for her first lesson. She discovered that Jig had been fired and replaced by a decidedly uninteresting instructor — a pot-bellied middle-aged man. Tutu went to the manager to tell him that she wanted to cancel her month's lessons. She was shocked when the manager corrected her, showing her the contract form in which she had signed up, not for a month, but a lifetime. He told her that it was studio policy never to release customers from their commitments, and pointed out that her payment was due within the next few days.

Does the common law give her the right to cancel? (Answer on common law principles only, and disregard any consumer protection legislation of which you may have heard.)

3. Sweaty Shoppe, Inc., is a retailer of sports and fitness clothing. It sells a wide variety of all brands of merchandise. Brute Force, Inc. makes very expensive weightlifting equipment. Sweaty Shoppe considers these products overpriced and has steadfastly refused to carry them despite several requests by Brute Force.

Through contact with a disloyal employee of Sweaty Shoppe, Brute Force has come into possession of some confidential internal memoranda, written by Sweaty Shoppe's management. These memoranda show that Sweaty Shoppe's buyer routinely engaged in the practice of knowingly buying inventory at bargain prices from a criminal organization that stole it by hijacking manufacturers' delivery trucks. Brute Force told Sweaty Shoppe's president that it would publish the documents unless Sweaty Shoppe agreed to stock and vigorously promote Brute Force products. Sweaty Shoppe's president realized that if the buyer's underhanded means of acquiring inventory became public, Sweaty Shoppe's business would be badly damaged and the company might even be implicated in the buyer's crime of receiving stolen property. He therefore entered into a contract with Brute Force to purchase and promote its weightlifting equipment. The contract is on ordinary market terms, and the quantity of goods, the prices, and other aspects of the contract are fair and commercially reasonable. A week after signing the contract, and before any performance had occurred, Sweaty Shoppe's board found out about the buyer's improper purchases and the president's attempt at a cover-up. The board fired the president and it decided that it would rather deal with the consequences of exposure than buy any goods from Brute Force. Does Sweaty Shoppe have grounds to avoid the contract?

4. Lunar Tech, Inc. was awarded a contract by the Air Force to manufacture an early warning system for detecting invasions of alien spacecraft. The contract had very precise specifications. Lunar Tech was obliged to give this endeavor absolute priority and to deliver the completed system in one year. The contract provided that if delivery was late, the Air Force would be entitled to claim liquidated damages in a

horrendous amount for each day of delay. Also, it was well known in the defense industry that a contractor who has proved unreliable would have great difficulty in obtaining further government contracts in the future. Lunar Tech entered into a written one-year employment contract with Dr. Stella Starburst, a highly respected and brilliant scientist, to supervise the fabrication of the system. Dr. Starburst's contract salary for the year was $750,000. Neither party had the right to terminate the contract before the end of the one-year term, except in the case of material breach by the other.

About two months after work on the project began, Dr. Starburst approached the president of Lunar Tech and told him that she had received a very attractive job offer from a research institute and would like to resign and accept that offer. The president knew that Lunar Tech could not easily replace Dr. Starburst, and a search for a new supervisor would disrupt and delay the project. The president therefore offered to pay Dr. Starburst a $500,000 bonus at the end of the project if she stayed on until it was complete. Dr. Starburst agreed. The president had his assistant type a short memorandum headed "Contract Modification." The text of the memorandum stated, "In consideration for Dr. Stella Starburst's commitment not to leave the employ of Lunar Tech, Inc., before the end of her contractual employment period, Lunar Tech, Inc., promises to pay Dr. Starburst a bonus of $500,000 at the conclusion of her period of employment." Both parties signed the note. Dr. Starburst did remain in her position until the completion of the project. However, Lunar Tech refuses to pay her the $500,000 bonus. Can Dr. Starburst enforce Lunar Tech's commitment?

5. Add the following fact about the employment contract entered into between Lunar Tech, Inc., and Dr. Stella Starburst: The contract was on a standard form supplied by Lunar Tech. The standard contract was very detailed. It was 20 pages long, single-spaced. It consisted of 130 numbered clauses, printed in 12-point type, without any headings, boldface, or other features that distinguished any of its clauses. Clause 128 read:

> Any claim made by the employee, arising out of this employment agreement, including claims relating to discrimination, harassment, working conditions, the payment of any amounts claimed to be due under this contract, or termination of employment shall be submitted to final and binding arbitration under the rules of the American Arbitration Association. If any such claim should arise, the employee agrees to deliver a request for arbitration to the employer within six months of the date that the dispute arose. If the employee does not file a written request for arbitration within this time, such claim will be barred.

Clause 128 was the only term in the agreement relating to arbitration. There was no equivalent requirement of arbitration for any claims brought by Lunar Tech against an employee. The rules of the American Arbitration Association were not appended to the contract. Lunar Tech gave the standard contract to Dr. Starburst when it first offered to hire her, and she had it for about a week before she signed it. However, she was busy and never read beyond the first page. Quite apart from the merits of Dr. Starburst's claim, raised in Example 4, can she sue in court on that claim or is she obliged to submit it to arbitration?

6. One afternoon, Hardy Ticker developed intense chest pains while digging in his garden. His neighbor, Sam Aritan, noticed his distress and came over to see if he was all right. On being told the problem, Sam put Hardy into his car and rushed him to the nearest hospital, The Sisters of Good Conscience. The receptionist insisted that admission forms be completed before Hardy could be sent to the emergency room. Sam was concerned that Hardy needed urgent attention and begged the receptionist to admit Hardy while he completed the forms. The receptionist agreed. Sam completed as much of Hardy's biographical information as he knew and handed the form to the receptionist. She told him that he had to sign it, which he did. He noticed that the form had about half a page of printed text above the signature blank, but he did not read it. Had he done so, he would have found that he had signed a standard contract with a provision that obligated the signatory to pay all the hospital's charges for treatment administered to the patient.

Sadly, Hardy died despite the efforts of the emergency room doctors. It was then discovered that he was insolvent and there is nothing in his estate. The hospital therefore demands payment of its fees from Sam, based on his signature on the form contract. Must Sam pay?

7. Mary Maker, a resident of California, decided to go on a cruise. After studying the brochures of several cruise lines, she settled on a seven-day package from Los Angeles to Mexico on the ship S.S. Briny Binge, owned and operated by Party Lines, Inc. Party Lines has its headquarters in Miami, Florida, and operates cruises out of Miami and Los Angeles. Mary called her local travel agent and booked. A week later she received her ticket, printed on one side of a single sheet of paper. She checked to make sure that the dates and cabin booking were correct. She did not otherwise read the printed matter on the ticket, despite a warning, printed on the ticket in large red letters, that stated "PASSENGER: THIS DOCUMENT AFFECTS YOUR LEGAL RIGHTS. READ IT!" Had she read the document, she would have found the following provision:

This ticket is issued subject to the following terms and conditions:

1. Party Lines, Inc. shall not be responsible for loss or harm suffered by the passenger while on board the ship, whether or not caused by the negligence of Party Lines, Inc. or any of its employees or agents.

2. In the event of any dispute between Party Lines, Inc. and the passenger arising out of this transaction, the courts of the State of Florida shall have exclusive jurisdiction to hear and resolve such dispute.

Mary embarked on the ship. Three days into the cruise, she was injured when an inebriated entertainment director mistook her for a piñata. Upon returning home, Mary sued Party Lines in a California court, alleging that the company was liable for its employee's negligent action. She claimed medical expenses and damages for pain and suffering. Party Lines requests summary judgment on the grounds that the California court has no jurisdiction in terms of the contract and that, in any event, Mary had contractually waived any claim that she may otherwise have had. Should summary judgment be granted?

8. Hi Rate Gems, Inc., operates a retail jewelry store in a less affluent neighborhood and draws most of its customers from the local area. They are typically quite poor and do not have the means to buy jewelry for cash, nor could they qualify for credit under the usual market standards. To make sales, Hi Rate has found it necessary to provide financing to its customers under a lenient credit policy. As a result, its losses from uncollectible debt are much higher than those of more conservative lending institutions. To compensate for this, it prices its jewelry about 20 percent higher than the prevailing market and charges interest 5 percent above the market rate. To obtain credit, a customer is obliged to sign a standard contract under which Hi Rate retains a security interest in the items purchased. This means that if the customer should default in payments, Hi Rate has the right to repossess the jewelry, to credit its value against the balance owing, and to institute collection action against the customer for any remaining deficiency.

Rock Sparkler bought a diamond nose stud with matching earrings from Hi Rate for $2,000. Rock did not have the $2,000, and his terrible credit record assured that no sensible lender would advance him a penny. He therefore applied for credit from Hi Rate. One of the questions on the form asked if any judgments had been granted against the applicant. Rock knew of at least five such unsatisfied judgments, but he feared that disclosing them would be fatal to the application. He did not wish to lie, so he simply ignored the question and left the space blank. Luckily, the credit clerk did not notice the omission because he did not look at the application very carefully before approving the financing. The sales assistant then filled out the details of the items purchased and the monthly payment rate on the standard purchase agreement, and handed it to Rock for his signature. The assistant made no attempt to explain the form's printed terms to Rock, who did not read it before signing. He then took the jewelry and left.

A few weeks later, Hi Rate's credit manager was reviewing the applications and noticed that Rock had not answered the question about judgments. He checked the public record and discovered the unsatisfied judgments. Hi Rate wishes to rescind the contract and get the jewelry back. Has it the right to do so?

9. All the facts regarding the formation of the contract are the same as in Example 8. The only factual difference is as follows: Hi Rate did not check the public record. It is happy with the transaction and has no desire to avoid the contract. However, a short time after the purchase, Rock had misgivings about buying the jewelry. He would like to cancel the sale and return the jewelry. May he do so?

10. Rob Graves plundered a 3,000-year-old bronze figurine from the tomb of an ancient king. He smuggled it into the United States for the purpose of selling it. He contacted Ann Teek, a well-known collector of antiquities, to see whether she would be interested in buying the figurine. Ann did not ask Rob how he acquired the figurine, but she suspected that he had stolen it and brought it into the country illegally. She also knew that it is illegal to deal in stolen antiquities. Nevertheless, her desire to own the figurine overpowered her scruples. She entered into a contract with Rob to buy it for $5 million. In terms of the contract, Ann had to pay a deposit of $1 million in cash to Rob on signing the written agreement and would pay the balance in cash on delivery of the figurine a few days later. Ann paid the deposit to Rob, but he never delivered the figurine. What would Ann's prospects of success be if she decided to sue Rob to enforce the contract? What would her prospects of success be if she decided not to sue Rob for enforcement, but instead sued him for return of the $1 million?

Explanations

1. There are both acts and silences that could qualify as misrepresentations.

   The cockroaches and subsidence. Cookie did not make any statement asserting that the house was free of cockroaches or that it was stable. However, concealment of the truth by conduct is as much an affirmative misrepresentation as a verbal misstatement. Cookie knew the truth and intended by the act of concealment to hide it so as to induce the contract. Therefore the element of knowledge of falsity and intent to mislead is satisfied. Cookie's fumigating and performing the cosmetic repairs to the wall were not simply acceptable preparations for sale, but were deliberate steps to conceal serious problems that would have made the house less marketable.

As noted in section 13.6.5, Restatement, Second, does not require materiality for fraud, but many courts include this as an element. Even where a court follows the Restatement, Second, position, the materiality of the misrepresentation has a bearing on justifiable reliance. Materiality is a question of interpretation and the test is whether a reasonable person in Bugsy's position would have entered the transaction at all, or on these terms, had he known the truth. It is arguable that an infestation of pests and the sinking of the building would be significant to a reasonable buyer. The misrepresentation must have induced Bugsy to enter the contract on the agreed terms. When fraud is involved, the test for inducement is not purely objective, but takes into account the persuasive impact of the falsehood on the victim. Bugsy must show that the misrepresented fact was influential to him and that, given his circumstances and personal attributes, he was justified in relying on the false words or appearance. Of course, it is easier to show inducement where the misrepresentation concerns a fact that would be regarded as material and would have been relied on by a reasonable person. Although we do not know what motivated Bugsy to make the offer, the concealed facts are important even if viewed objectively, so it should not be difficult for him to show that they influenced him to make the offer. Bugsy's justification for relying on appearances is somewhat weakened because he failed to have the house inspected for structural soundness and pests, or even to ask questions beyond his inquiry into termite infestation. A court might find that his lack of diligence precludes relief for fraud. But courts do balance the neglect of the victim against the deliberate dishonesty of the perpetrator, and Cookie's purposeful concealment could outweigh Bugsy's failure to make proper inquiry. Finally, prejudice is obvious. Not only does the house have a chronic cockroach problem, but it requires expensive repairs.

The halfway house for sex offenders. Although Cookie knew about the plans to open the halfway house, she did not disclose this to Bugsy. Nondisclosure of known information can be fraud if the duty of fair dealing imposes an obligation to speak. It can be difficult to decide when disclosure is required, because the law recognizes that fair dealing does not compel a party to bare all information pertinent to the transaction. Furthermore, even if there was a duty to speak, the omission may not be as culpable as a positive act. As a result, the prerequisites for relief are not as heavily weighted against the perpetrator, and the victim is more readily held accountable for failure to make diligent inquiry. As a general guide, a party is only required to disclose information if four conditions are satisfied: She knows that the other is unaware of it; the knowledge would be reasonably likely to influence the other's decision to enter the transaction; the information is not readily accessible to the other by diligent inquiry; and the information is not fairly regarded as the party's own property, having been acquired by special efforts or study.

Given the outcry when a released sex offender takes up residence in a neighborhood, a reasonable person would assume that this information would be material to a homebuyer. The information is not proprietary, so Cookie cannot claim that she had the right to keep it to herself. However, the proposed home is a public project that has already been reported in the press. The information is freely available and for all Cookie knows, Bugsy has also read the paper. If not, it would be easy enough for him to gain access to the information. On balance, if he did not know about the halfway house, his lack of inquiry should preclude relief on this ground despite Cookie's silence.

2. This example is a factual variation of a couple of infamous Arthur Murray cases decided in the 1960s. In *Vokes v. Arthur Murray, Inc.,* 212 So. 2d 906 (Fla. 1968), and *Syester v. Banta,* 133 N.W.2d 666 (Iowa 1965), Arthur Murray franchisees employed the deliberate tactic of ongoing and excessive flattery to induce untalented elderly women to sign up for astoundingly large quantities of dance lessons at grotesque total cost. In both cases the importuning, begun at first contact, was reinforced and accelerated during a long period of continuing lessons. The courts found that the fulsome praise, unremitting sweet talk, undeserved medals and awards, and untrue claims of progress were so extreme as to pass beyond good customer relations and become outright fraud.

The fraud in these cases was not the misrepresentation of an external objective fact, but of an opinion. By pretending that they believed the victims to have talent and potential, the studio employees lied about what they thought, inducing the victims to buy copious quantities of lessons. Although false opinions do not always qualify as factual misrepresentations, a deliberate misstatement of opinion can be fraud when the party expressing it claims to have the knowledge and expertise to form a judgment and should realize that the victim is relying on an honest assessment. As the brief description of the cases suggests, the behavior of the Arthur Murray studios went far beyond the expression of a dishonest opinion. The transactions were thoroughly unsavory. Lonely and gullible elderly women were cruelly manipulated for a long period and induced to spend substantial amounts of their savings on extended courses of dance lessons that were unlikely to be used up in their lifetimes.

Fraud was the basis for relief in both cases, but the facts make an overwhelming case of unconscionability as well: As a result of the studios' slimy bargaining methods, their victims were induced to enter contracts for lessons well in excess of their needs at a ludicrous cost. Unconscionability doctrine is not needed when the elements of fraud are satisfied. However, if there is any doubt about establishing fraud, unconscionability serves as an alternative theory for avoidance. Tutu's case may be an example of this.

Fleece Foot's conduct was not as egregious as that of the Arthur Murray studios, and Tutu, being a worldly former tax lawyer, is not as sympathetic a victim as the plaintiffs in those cases. Nevertheless, there were two instances of dishonesty by Jig, acting on behalf of Fleece Foot, that could provide an argument for fraud. First, he deliberately misrepresented his opinion. However, this may not be a good basis for establishing fraud because his misrepresentation apparently did not induce Tutu to enter the contract. Tutu was not taken in by his flattery and was motivated by deeper urges. (Although he turned out not to be the instructor, there is no indication that he realized that this was an inducing factor or that he knew of and failed to disclose his impending dismissal.)

Second, he concealed the true nature of the form by placing his hands over it. If this is fraud, it would be in the factum, not in the inducement, because it relates to the document being signed rather than to a motivating fact. Note also that the misrepresentation is by concealment, not affirmative assertion. Although his intent is dishonest, Tutu is probably damned by her sophistication and training. While an illiterate or naive person may be able to convince a factfinder of having been bamboozled into unwittingly signing a lifetime contract, Tutu, a trained lawyer, should have known better than to sign something without reading it. The strategically placed hand adds no force to her case. Although the writing was concealed, it was easily discoverable (in fact, the attempt at concealment should have excited her suspicion). While inducement takes into account the victim's subjective reaction to the misrepresentation, her attributes affect the credibility of any claim that she was actually induced to sign as a result of the clumsy deception. Having said this, it must be acknowledged that an argument of fraud is not entirely inconceivable if Tutu can show an intent to defraud. Even extreme neglect may be outweighed by clear proof of the perpetrator's dishonesty.

If fraud is not a promising avenue for attack, unconscionability may be more successful. Bargaining unfairness short of actual fraud may be sufficient to show procedural unconscionability, and the facts of this Example reveal a deliberate and carefully developed process to manipulate and exploit prospective customers. It is probably safe to say, given the clear procedural unconscionability, that a court would not have too much trouble in finding that it is substantively unconscionable to sell a $10,000 lifetime dance instruction contract to a 65-year-old retiree. Unconscionability is less potent a weapon in the hands of a well-educated and commercially proficient party, but even former tax lawyers can be caught off guard by predators in the marketplace.

3. Sweaty Shoppe should be able to avoid the contract on grounds of duress because it has been induced to enter the contract by Brute Force's wrongful threat. (Although this is a sale of goods, general principles of common law apply because UCC Article 2 has no provisions relating to duress.) The exposure of the criminal conduct of Sweaty Shoppe's buyer would not itself be wrongful. In fact, the revelation of such information is in the public interest. The wrongfulness arises because Brute Force's threat is made for the purpose of blackmailing Sweaty Shoppe's president into entering the contract. Even an otherwise proper act loses its legitimacy if it is used as a threat for the purpose of extorting private advantage. It adds to the wrongfulness of the threat that the information possessed by Brute Force relates to criminal activity and it is using the information as a bargaining chip to force Sweaty Shoppe's president to enter a contract to buy its products. A person harms the public interest by withholding information of a crime from the authorities in exchange for a commercial reward. For this reason, a threat to expose the crime unless Sweaty Shoppe agrees to a contract is clearly an improper threat for duress purposes.

To show inducement, Sweaty Shoppe must establish that, under all the circumstances, its management had no reasonable alternative but to acquiesce in the contract. Sweaty Shoppe's president did have an alternative — the one that its board ultimately decided to follow. However, Sweaty Shoppe can make the plausible argument that at the time that Brute Force proposed the contract, the threatened exposure and its potentially dire impact on the company did not seem like a reasonable alternative to its president, and the threat undermined his volition in making the contract. The terms of the contract were fair and commercially reasonable, but that does not matter. Once the elements of improper threat and inducement are established, Sweaty Shoppe does not have to show that the resulting contract was substantively unfair. Because there is no substantive unfairness in the terms of the contract, duress is a better basis for avoidance than unconscionability.

Note that considerations of public policy are implicated in the determination that the threat was wrongful. If Sweaty Shoppe cannot make a convincing case of duress (say, because it cannot show that it had no reasonable alternative but to agree), could it make the argument that the contract should be avoided on the pure ground that it violates public policy? On the surface, there is nothing objectionable about this contract, which is simply the sale of goods for a price. However, if we imply into the contract a promise by Brute Force not to report a crime, the improper performance becomes part of the consideration under the contract.

This could make enforcement of the contract contrary to public policy. Under the *in pari delicto* rule, public policy analysis requires a balancing of the relative fault of the parties, but goes beyond that to consider the impact of enforcement or nonenforcement on the public good. The probable conclusion is that the equities between the parties and the public interest are best served by not enforcing the contract. By refusing enforcement, the court does not condone extortion, and it creates a disincentive to collusion to conceal a crime. In addition, the equities favor Sweaty Shoppe because its board and owners (stockholders) neither knew of nor approved of the criminal activity of the buyer and the president's attempt to cover it up.

4. This is an employment contract, not a sale of goods, so the common law applies. The parties expressly state that they intend Lunar Tech's promise of the bonus to be a modification of their existing contract. Under consideration doctrine, the modification is unenforceable unless Dr. Starburst gave new consideration to Lunar Tech. The consideration recited in the memorandum is not a new legal detriment suffered by Dr. Starburst in exchange for Lunar Tech's promise of the bonus. Dr. Starburst had a pre-existing duty to work for Lunar Tech until the end of her contract period, and had no right to terminate the contract. (For the same reason, her giving up the other job opportunity is not a detriment for consideration purposes.) Consideration doctrine therefore invalidates the modification. The problem with consideration doctrine is that it is a blunt instrument for dealing with modifications. If there is no new consideration, the modification is invalid, whether or not it was fairly obtained. Conversely, if there is some new consideration, even if slight, consideration doctrine does not invalidate a coerced modification.

   Had Dr. Starburst suffered some new detriment in exchange for the promise, the modification would be enforceable unless there was some other basis for avoiding it. Lunar Tech might be able to show that the modification should be avoided on grounds of duress. (This was the basis of policing the modification in *Austin Instrument* discussed in section 13.9.) If Dr. Starburst had threatened to breach the employment contract, that threat would be improper. However, it is not clear if she made any threat at all. The Example states merely that she told the president that she wanted to resign. It does not indicate that she made it clear (like the fishermen in *Alaska Packers*) that she would refuse to perform her contract unless Lunar Tech increased her pay. One could possibly find an implied threat here, but the basis for implication is weak in the absence of anything more aggressive than her expressing the wish to leave. This could simply be a situation in which Lunar Tech decided that the offer of a bonus was the best way to keep Dr. Starburst happy and engaged. Had Dr. Starburst made an improper threat, Lunar Tech could likely establish that it induced the contract. The stakes of delay and disruption are high, and it does not seem to have an alternative course of action that would be reasonable.[14] If Lunar Tech cannot establish the elements of duress, it is unlikely that unconscionability would be an alternative basis for relief. Unless there was some kind of coercion, there is no suggestion of procedural unconscionability, and we do not know if a $500,000 bonus for a project supervisor exceeds the bounds of substantive fairness in the in the industry.

5. There is a general public policy in favor of arbitration, and Dr. Starburst can avoid the arbitration provision only if she can show grounds for avoidance under general principles of common law. There is no basis for claiming that the contract is illegal or against public policy, or that Lunar Tech committed fraud or duress. Therefore, the only possible basis for avoidance is unconscionability. *Samaniego v. Empire Today LLC*, discussed in section 13.12.3, found an arbitration provision in an employment contract to be unconscionable where the provision had several features in common with the one in issue here. Like the clause in *Samaniego*, the clause in this contract was in a standard form proffered by the employer. The arbitration clause was near the end of a dense and lengthy contract and was not printed in a way that drew attention to it. The clause incorporated by reference the rules of the American Arbitration Association, but did not provide those rules. The clause imposes arbitration on employees, but not on the employer, and it shortens the limitation period for employees' claims, but not for the employer.

The complexity of the contract, the inconspicuousness of the clause, and the failure to specify the rules governing the arbitration may suggest procedural unconscionability. However, there is a significant factual difference between this case and *Samaniego*. The employees in *Samaniego* were not proficient in English, and the form was presented to them on a take-it-or-leave-it basis, with little or no opportunity to seek advice. Dr. Starburst is in a very different situation. She has an advanced education, is highly regarded in her field, and was being sought by Lunar Tech for an important senior position, for which they were offering her an impressive salary. She surely had the bargaining power to negotiate the terms of the contract proffered by Lunar Tech, and there is no apparent basis for thinking that contract was presented to her on a take-it-or-leave-it basis. She was given the standard contract, which she kept for a week before signing it. She had ample opportunity to read it, to consult an attorney and other

14. Had this been a sale of goods, the good faith standard of §2.209 would provide a broader basis for evaluating the modification on the good faith standard.

advisors, and to ascertain the rules of the American Arbitration Association. It is difficult to imagine that a court would find adhesion or any other grounds of procedural unconscionability in this case.

The complete absence of procedural unconscionability will probably dispose of the matter. Even if the court does not require a clear showing of procedural unconscionability where substantive unconscionability is strongly present, a sophisticated party with bargaining power is unlikely to persuade the court that relief is merited. The one-sided nature of the arbitration provision could well qualify as substantively unconscionable. Although mutuality of obligation is not required, where an arbitration provision imposes the obligation to arbitrate on only one of the parties, and additionally limits the rights of that party to pursue the arbitration, the term could be too one-sided to enforce.[15] Notwithstanding, this is probably not enough to outweigh Dr. Starburst's abject failure to read the contract and to take the opportunity to negotiate a less one-sided dispute resolution provision.

6. A similar situation occurred in *Phoenix Baptist Hospital v. Aiken*, 877 P.2d 1345 (Ariz. 1994). After rushing his wife to the hospital, a husband signed a form contract obliging him to pay the hospital's charges. In the absence of this undertaking he would not have been personally liable for his wife's medical expenses. The hospital sued him and applied for summary judgment on the basis of his signature on the form. The court refused summary judgment and held that the husband was entitled to go to trial on the question of whether the contract was unconscionable. The court said that the contract appeared adhesive, signed under traumatic and hurried circumstances in which the husband had little realistic opportunity to know what he was signing. Even if he did know, the emotional stress and the need for the hospital's immediate services would likely leave him without power to bargain, and give him no choice but to acquiesce in order to ensure that his wife received medical

---

15. Of course, even if a court finds unconscionability, it need not avoid the arbitration term entirely, but could select the intermediate remedy of enforcing the clause and adjusting it to get rid of its unconscionable aspects. However, that works only where the clause can stand without the offending aspects, and the severance of those aspects cures the unconscionability. Had the court found unconscionability here, this probably would not have been an appropriate case for adjusting the contract. Although the time limit on suit could be severed, the lack of bilaterally in the obligation to arbitrate cannot really be cured by an adjustment of the provision. In *Zullo v. Superior Court*, 127 Cal. Rptr. 3d 461 (Cal. App. 2011), the court refused to enforce an arbitration agreement in an employee handbook because it was adhesive and also lacked bilaterality — the contract imposed no restrictions on the employer's right to sue an employee, but the employee was obliged to arbitrate and lost even that means of recourse unless she gave notice of the claim to the employer almost immediately. The court refused to enforce the arbitration clause in its entirety because it found that it was permeated with unconscionability, and was drafted, not as a neutral means of dispute resolution, but merely to maximize the employer's advantage in handling disputes.

attention. The court considered that adhesion of this kind could make the contract procedurally unconscionable. In addition, substantive unconscionability could lie in the fact that he assumed liability for which he would not otherwise be responsible, and that he could not reasonably have expected to be provided for in the form that he signed. As discussed more fully in section 13.12 and Example 7, adhesion and procedural unconscionability are not present merely because the contract is a standard form drafted by the party with greater bargaining power, or because the choices of the weaker party are limited. However, when the services contracted for are desperately and urgently needed, and the party to perform the services presents a form without explanation or a reasonable opportunity to read, in circumstances that make bargaining burdensome or futile, it should not be very difficult to make a case for procedural unconscionability. It is not required that the hospital purposely used unfair bargaining methods to trick or coerce Sam into signing. The procurement of apparent assent under these circumstances should be enough. Sam's emotional stake in the rendition of the services to Hardy is not as strong as that of a spouse, but the stress and urgency of the situation are patent. Sam would not have to show that the terms were objectively unfair — for example, that the hospital charged an excessive price. The substantive unconscionability lies in the fact that Sam incurred an obligation that he would not otherwise have, for services from which he received no personal gain. In this respect, his case is stronger than that of a spouse. There is thus an adequate showing of substantive unconscionability — but even if a court may question this conclusion, the strong showing of procedural unfairness would seem to place beyond doubt the need to give Sam relief.

Unconscionability is the most appropriate basis for relief in this case. Could it also have been argued under a theory of duress? Duress doctrine has expanded enough to make this a possibility, in that the threat to withhold medical services for Hardy undermined Sam's free will and coerced him into signing. However, this strains the concept of improper threat because the hospital did nothing more than indicate intent not to enter a contract except on its own terms. This cannot be a threat unless the hospital had a duty outside of contract law (say, by statute) to render emergency services to any patient brought in.

7. Obviously, Mary is not seeking avoidance of the entire contract. Rather, to assert her tort claim, she must persuade the court that she is not bound by the forum selection clause and liability disclaimer.

Before dealing with policing doctrines, there are two preliminary questions to settle. The first is whether the disclaimer entered the contract at all. This does not appear to be a rolling contract because there is no indication that the parties intended that Mary would not be bound until she received and had a chance to review the tickets. That is, the contract was formed at the time that she booked, and the transmission of the tickets with the standard terms is not an offer. (See sections 5.5. and 13.2.) When the drafting party sends the standard terms to the other party only after the contract is formed, the terms may not be part of the contract at all. However, if the nondrafting party had reason to know that the contract was subject to standard terms and the standard terms are fair and reasonably expected, the court may find them to be part of the contract.

The second preliminary question involves interpreting the terms. If we find, as a matter of interpretation, that the forum selection clause and the disclaimer do not cover the claim in this suit, we do not need to consider whether they should be avoided or adjusted under a policing doctrine. The disclaimer's language creates some doubt about its scope. It exonerates Party Lines from "loss or harm." The provision does not expressly mention personal injury, and the juxtaposition of the words "loss" and "harm" could suggest that only economic damage is contemplated. The public policy of reading negligence disclaimers as narrowly as possible, combined with the *contra preferentum* rule could persuade a court that the clause does not cover personal injury at all. If the court accepts this interpretation, the disclaimer is simply inapplicable and we need not be concerned with avoiding it. The forum selection clause may also be subject to interpretational challenge. Mary could argue that "any dispute . . . arising out of [the] . . . transaction" is not broad enough to cover tort claims for personal injury and should be confined to disputes relating to the performance of services promised under the contract. If the court accepts this interpretation, the California suit can proceed without any determination of whether the clause is avoidable.

If the provisions are interpreted to mean what Party Lines says they mean, they are enforceable unless they can be avoided. There is no indication of fraud or duress, so unconscionability doctrine offers Mary the best hope of eliminating the provisions. This is a contract of adhesion with standard terms that Mary did not negotiate or even read. However, that is not enough to make the terms unconscionable. To establish procedural unconscionability, Mary must produce evidence of some form of underhand dealing, which she cannot do on these facts, or must at least show that the terms were imposed on her without any meaningful choice, under circumstances that make the imposition oppressive. The terms were not made available to her at the time of booking, so this is a point in her favor. However, because cruise tickets are routinely subject to standard terms, as a reasonable consumer she should have expected them. She failed in her duty to read by not requesting them before she contracted.

In addition, there is no indication that she tried to shop around to see if better terms were available from a competitor. Her case for procedural unconscionability is weak. She may have a better chance of showing substantive unconscionability, but this is not an easy case either. To establish substantive unconscionability, Mary must do more than show that the terms served Party Line's interest and were adverse to hers. She must establish that they were not justified by business realities and were so one-sided as to be oppressive. Under circumstances similar to these, *Carnival Cruise Lines*, discussed in section 13.12, found a forum selection clause to be a fair cost-saving measure that selected an appropriate forum and was not designed to suppress suit. The liability disclaimer must be analyzed similarly. It is potentially unfair, but not per se unconscionable to disclaim liability for negligent injury. In evaluating the fairness of a disclaimer the court looks at factors such as the nature of the service, the parties who are likely to avail themselves of it, the degree to which a user of the service places herself under the control of the cruise line, the scope of the disclaimer, the conspicuousness of its disclosure, the business justification for including it, the reasonableness of the clause in light of accepted commercial practice, and whether the price of the cruise would have been higher in the absence of the exclusion of liability. In short, neither procedural nor substantive unconscionability is strongly shown on these facts, and Mary's prospects of avoiding the provisions do not look very promising.

Finally, although public policy considerations have already been raised in the discussion of unconscionability, it is worth noting that even if a provision is fairly bargained, it can still be attacked as violating public policy. Where public policy outside of the area of contract is implicated, the court must balance that public policy against the policy of freedom of contract. The forum selection clause affects Mary's right to sue in a court that would otherwise have jurisdiction. It thereby impairs a strong public interest in uninhibited access to justice. The majority in *Carnival Cruise Lines* held that this policy does not absolutely invalidate an agreement restricting this right of access provided that the agreement is genuine and freely made and the selected forum is reasonable. Of course, the strong public policy of access to justice means that the clause must be scrutinized carefully. As noted in section 13.12 the clause withstood the scrutiny of the majority of the Supreme Court, but not the dissent.

As discussed in section 13.13.3, disclaimers of liability are also scrutinized carefully because public policy requires that a person is held accountable for tortious injury. Although a disclaimer of liability for intentional or reckless conduct is very likely against public policy, courts are more amenable to disclaimers of negligence. In deciding whether a disclaimer for negligence is consonant with public policy, courts consider factors similar to those listed above in relation to the inquiry into substantive unconscionability.

8. Rock's failure to disclose the judgments likely qualifies as a fraudulent misrepresentation. Even though he did not affirmatively lie, he deliberately omitted requested information, knowing that disclosure would imperil his credit application. In some situations it may be difficult to decide if a party has the duty to disclose facts pertinent to the transaction, but this is not such a case. It is generally accepted that a duty of honest response does arise if the other party asks a direct question, particularly when the information sought is not of a proprietary nature.

It is more difficult to say whether the misrepresentation induced the contract. A debtor's unreliability in other transactions is generally a crucial factor in the decision to grant credit. However, Hi Rate's cursory look at the form suggests that its standard for granting credit is very low indeed. If it really cared about the applicant's credit history or was truly interested in the answers on the application, it would have taken more trouble to read the form. Furthermore, judgments are a matter of public record, easily accessible to the prospective creditor. A creditor who regards this information as crucial would not simply rely on the applicant's disclosure and would check. Normally, when fraud is involved, the serious malfeasance of the perpetrator outweighs any lapse of care by the victim in failing to check the facts. But actual inducement must still be shown, and where the victim is sophisticated enough to know better, careless gullibility may break the chain of justified reliance.

In addition, there is some suggestion in this case that Hi Rate is not being entirely responsible or socially conscious in selling expensive luxury items to people who cannot afford them, and that it has ameliorated its risk of loss by padding its prices and interest rates. Although this does not excuse Rock's dishonesty, Hi Rate cannot comfortably don the mantle of innocent dupe. It can fairly be expected to take care of its own interests. In short, without condoning Rock's deceitful silence, a court may be indisposed to allow Hi Rate out of the contract. As long as Rock continues to make his payments as promised, Hi Rate must live with the risk of his lack of creditworthiness.

9. There is nothing to suggest that Hi Rate made any misrepresentation to Rock, or that it applied any threat to make him enter the contract. Therefore, if Rock is to have any right of avoidance, it must be based

on unconscionability.[16] Avoidance of the contract, as opposed to enforcement on adjusted terms, is within the range of relief available to Rock at the court's discretion.

Because Hi Rate seems to have a captive market and it imposes higher prices and adverse terms on its customers under standard contracts, one may jump to the conclusion that Hi Rate is a predatory mass contractor subjecting a whole section of the community to its harsh contracts of adhesion. This conclusion is even more tempting if one perceives it as socially harmful to sell luxury items on credit to people who cannot afford them. However, one cannot conclude as a matter of law that the contract is unconscionable under these circumstances. The transaction must be evaluated to see if it satisfies the two elements of unconscionability.

Hi Rate did not employ high-pressure selling techniques or deceptive practices that could lead to a clear-cut case of procedural unconscionability. However, *Williams v. Walker Thomas Furniture*, discussed in section 13.11.3, suggests that the contract could be procedurally unconscionable if Rock had no meaningful choice — the contract is adhesive because Hi Rate, the dominant party, had the power to dictate the terms, and Rock, the weaker party had no choice but to accept those terms. Under some circumstances, the mere fact of adhesion, without a demonstration of specific bargaining impropriety, could satisfy the procedural element of unconscionability. (This conclusion could be strengthened slightly if the terms were not conspicuous and drawn to Rock's attention.) However, the claim of lack of meaningful choice is tenuous in relation to a sale of luxury goods. True, this may have been the only means Rock had to acquire the jewelry, but he could have chosen not to buy it at all. In addition, there is no indication that Rock tried to buy the jewelry elsewhere or that he protested over or tried to negotiate the price or other terms. In some cases the weaker party's lack of sophistication can bolster the sense of imposition, but Rock does not appear to be particularly unsophisticated. Remember that he was sly enough to practice his own bit of deception.

Even if the basis for procedural unconscionability is shaky, a court may still find the contract to be unconscionable if the weaker party can show a strong degree of substantive unconscionability. This seems unlikely in this case. The contract terms are adverse to Rock, but the higher price and interest rate could be based on sound business practice and could conform to reasonable commercial practice in a high-risk credit market. Hi Rate's retention of a security interest to secure the

---

16. As the following discussion shows, the public policy of consumer protection is inherent in the unconscionability analysis and is one of the motivations for unconscionability doctrine. One could therefore say that the right of avoidance is based on public policy, but this is always true because all contract doctrines have a policy basis.

price is a widely accepted means of protecting a creditor from default, and the facts do not suggest that the security agreement has unusually harsh terms (for example, such as the cross-collateralization term in *Williams*).

10. The facts indicate that all aspects of this transaction — removing the figurine from the tomb, smuggling it, and selling it, are illegal. (In fact, these actions are surely criminal offenses as well. However, the question of whether the parties face criminal prosecution is not our concern here.) The facts also suggest that both parties were aware that they were entering into an illegal sale. Ann would have no chance of successfully suing Rob for enforcement of the contract. It is inconceivable that a court would abet a seriously illegal transaction by enforcing it, either by an order of specific performance or by the award of expectation damages to compensate for the loss of the bargain.

   The answer is less obvious if Ann does not seek to enforce the contract, but instead claims restitution of the $1 million that she paid to Rob under principles of unjust enrichment. By awarding restitution, the court does not uphold the illegal transaction, so there is a greater possibility that the court may be willing to intervene to remedy Rob's enrichment at Ann's expense. However, this outcome is not guaranteed because Ann's claim of restitution is also subject to the *in pari delicto* rule. The rule does not focus only on enforcement but declares that when the parties are in equal guilt, the court will not intervene to help either of them, and will leave them as it finds them. As section 13.13.4 explains, the operation of the maxim is more complicated than its language suggests. It involves a balancing of several considerations — the relative guilt of the parties, the equities between them, and the interests of society. It is difficult to choose which of these parties is more guilty — the thief-smuggler or the buyer who knowingly buys the stolen property. It seems reasonable to conclude that the parties are in equal guilt. If this was the only consideration, Ann's restitutionary claim would be dismissed. However, the balance shifts in her favor if we consider the other factors to be weighed. As between the parties, the equities favor Ann, who has been cheated of $1 million by Rob. The question of what best serves the public interest is also difficult to answer. Is the public best served by penalizing the buyer of stolen artifacts, thereby creating a disincentive to enter such transactions, or is it best served by forcing the thief to disgorge his ill-gotten gains from the transaction? This question is close, but allowing Rob to keep Ann's money seems to be more damaging to the public interest.

   This answer assumes that there is no legislative pronouncement that might assist the court in its decision. However, if transactions are made illegal by statute, the statute may provide rules or guidance on the legal rights of a party to an illegal transaction. For example, a statute that bars the sale of stolen artifacts could state that the buyer has no recourse for recovery of any sums paid. If the legislation pronounces on these matters, the resolution is clearer and obviates the need for the court to perform the balancing itself.

Incapacity

§14.1 THE SCOPE AND FOCUS OF THE DOCTRINES DISCUSSED IN THIS CHAPTER

The law generally assumes that all persons have the capacity to enter contracts. The two exceptions to this rule are minors and mentally incompetent adults. A minor's lack of contractual capacity is relatively easy to establish because it is largely based on the objective criterion of age. The determination that an adult lacks contractual capacity is more complex because it requires proof of mental illness or disturbance sufficiently serious to render the person incompetent. Although mental incapacity is necessarily based on the party's subjective state of mind, her mental condition is proved by objective evidence of her behavior observed by others, and by expert psychiatric evidence.

There are connections between incapacity and the doctrines discussed in Chapter 13, but there are also notable differences. The underlying rationale for permitting the avoidance of a contract entered into by a person who lacks mental capacity is the protection of the incapacitated person. This suggests analogies both to improper bargaining and public policy. However, there are important distinctions.

Although improper bargaining may sometimes be present in an incapacity case, especially where the other party has exploited the lack of capacity, there is no requirement that any improper bargaining be proved. Where the other party has taken advantage of the incapacitated party, this obviously has an influence on the court's decision on whether to permit avoidance of the contract on grounds of incapacity. However, the fundamental basis of incapacity is the legal status of the incapacitated party. This means that incapacity can be invoked even where there was no deception or illegitimate pressure in the formation of the contract and it is on fair terms.

Incapacity is based on the public policy of protecting an incapacitated person from assuming contractual duties to which she was not capable of assenting. However, incapacity usually does not create tension between the contract policy of freedom of contract and the more general, policy, external to contract law, of protecting mentally incapacitated people. Rather, the policies pull in the same direction because the incapacitated party's lack of mental competence means that her apparent assent to the contract is illusory. The policy of freedom of contract is not served by holding a person incapable of assent to a false manifestation of it.

Like improper bargaining, incapacity renders the contract voidable, not void. Usually, avoidance of the contract in its entirety is the only appropriate form of relief. Severance is not a proper solution because the incapacity affects the whole contract, not just a term of it. Because there has been no breach of a contract, damages are not called for unless the conduct of the other party gives rise to some other cause of action. As in other situations of avoidance, rescission of the contract is accompanied by restitution of any benefit conferred under the contract. However, in the case of a minor, there are exceptions to this.

§14.2 MINORITY

§14.2.1 The Basis and Nature of a Minor's Contractual Incapacity

a. The Minor's Right to Disaffirm

A person attains majority at the age of 18 in most states. Before that time, the minor[1] does not have the legal capacity to be bound in contract, and the contract is voidable at the minor's instance[2]. As explained in section 13.3. a voidable contract is not absolutely void, but may be avoided at the instance

---

1. The word "infant" is sometimes used in legal texts to refer to a person below the age of majority. The word sounds odd in contemporary usage, because we now take it to mean a baby.
2. As explained in section 14.2.2c, states have created some exceptions to this general rule by enacting statutes that give minors over a stated age the capacity to enter into binding contracts in relation to specific transactions.

of the party entitled to make that election. In the context of minor's contracts, it is the minor who has this power of avoidance, commonly referred to as the minor's right to disaffirm the contract. This means that the minor may disaffirm it at any time before reaching the age of majority, or within a reasonable time thereafter. Because a minor has no capacity to contract, it follows that she does not have the capacity to ratify (affirm) the contract while still a minor. This is why the right to make the election to disaffirm extends for a reasonable time past the attainment of majority. Nothing that the minor does before attaining majority, including full performance of the contract, constitutes a waiver of his right to disaffirm upon reaching majority. If the minor decides to disaffirm the contract, she must disaffirm it in its entirety. She cannot keep parts of it in force and seek to disaffirm others. For example, in *A.V. v. Iparadigms, L.L.C.*, 544 F. Supp. 2d 473 (E.D. Va. 2008), a school required its students to submit their class papers to a website that checked them for plagiarism. To use the website, students had to register on it. On registering, the students (who were minors) signified assent to a clickwrap agreement. One of its terms authorized the website to archive their work. The students later challenged terms of this agreement on several grounds[3] and also sought to disaffirm the contract as minors. The court refused disaffirmance because the minors did not entirely abandon the contract and still sought to retain the benefit of the services provided by the website.

b. Ratification

If the minor has not disaffirmed the contract by the time that he reaches the age of majority, he may ratify it as a major. Ratification can be express, or it could be by conduct if the minor takes a benefit under the contract after majority, or it could be implied if the minor fails to disaffirm the contract within a reasonable time after becoming a major. For example, in *In re The Score Board, Inc.*, 238 B.R. 585 (D.N.J. 1999) Kobe Bryant, the professional basketball player, entered into a contract at the age of 17 under which he granted rights to the use of his name and image on products. He turned 18 six weeks later. Shortly after his birthday, he deposited a check of $10,000, an initial payment under the contract, in his bank account. He continued to perform under the contract for the subsequent year and a half, and then became dissatisfied with the contract and sought to disaffirm it on the grounds that he was a minor when it was made. The court refused disaffirmance because he ratified the contract by affirmative conduct when he deposited the check. (For another case that illustrates implied ratification by

---

3. One of the grounds was that they had not assented to the clickwrap term. This aspect of the case is discussed in section 5.3.

conduct, *see State v. Bishop*, 240 P.3d 614 (Kan. App. 2010), described in section 14.2.2c.) Note, however, that some states may not treat conduct as implied ratification and may require an express or even a written ratification. For example in *Foss v. Circuit City*, 477 F. Supp. 2d 230 (D. Maine 2007), the court refused to recognize ratification by conduct because a state statute required written ratification.

c. The Objective Nature of Minors' Incapacity

The legal incapacity of minors is based on the assumption that minors lack the maturity to make reasoned judgments in the conduct of their affairs and are vulnerable to exploitation. Of course, some minors, especially those close to majority, may in fact be mature and sophisticated enough to enter a contract, and the other party may not have taken advantage of the minor's youth and inexperience. Nevertheless, the law places the risk of contracting with a minor on the other party, so the minor's physical appearance and apparent or actual competence does not matter. The test for a minor's contractual capacity is purely objective, and the other party cannot prevent avoidance by showing that the minor was sufficiently mature or that the contract was on fair terms. The purely objective test of incapacity, based on age, has the advantage of certainty and simplicity, but it has the disadvantage of inflexibility and does not take into account that some minors do have both the maturity and the need to enter into contracts. It insulates a minor from responsibility for transactions, even where the adult party has not tried to take advantage of her, and the minor did in fact have enough maturity to make a reasoned judgment about entering the contract. This is particularly true of adolescents who are not far short of the age of capacity. As a result, some courts and commentators have criticized this test as paternalistic and rigid. This bright-line test has become even more questionable in the age of the Internet because minors are now so fully engaged in electronic commerce, and in some instances, are a dominant presence in the marketplace.

d. Parental Consent

A minor might be represented by a parent in entering into a contract, or might enter the contract with express parental permission. In some situations, the parent's involvement in the contract may make it binding on the minor, but this is not the general rule, and a minor usually does not lose the power to disaffirm merely because she was represented by or had the consent of a parent. For example, in *Berg v. Traylor*, 148 Cal. App. 4th 809 (2007), the court allowed a minor, a ten-year-old child actor, to disaffirm a representation agreement with an agent, even though the minor's mother represented him in entering the agreement. Although the court recognized that there are some situations recognized in the state by statute or caselaw in which a parent can bind a minor contractually (for example, a contract for medical services or a release of liability relating to participation in school activities), this was not such a situation.[4]

§14.2.2 Situations in Which a Minor May Incur Legal Liability

There are some limited situations in which a minor can incur legal liability as a result of having entered a contract. However, this liability may not be equal to the minor's full contractual commitment and may be confined to restitution for benefits received.

a. Necessaries

The most common situation in which a minor can incur liability is if the contract is for necessaries. A necessary is not the same as a necessity, and it has a broader meaning. It includes not only the bare necessities of life, but whatever goods or services are needed for the minor's livelihood, or appropriate to his standard of living and position. However, it does not include luxuries. The question of what constitutes a necessary is factual and based on all the circumstances. As you may expect, what one court accepts as a necessary another could see as a luxury. For example, a court may or may not see a car as a necessary if it is used by the minor to drive to work or school. If the minor lives at home or is supported by her parents, even goods or services that would otherwise be required for subsistence are not likely to qualify as necessaries. For example, in *Webster St. Partnership v. Sheridan*, 368 N.W.2d 439 (Neb. 1985) the court held that an apartment leased by a minor was not a necessary. Although shelter is normally vital to an acceptable standard of living, the minor could have moved back to his parents' home whenever he wanted.

The concept of emancipation is important to the minor's liability for necessaries. *Webster St. Partnership* took the approach that unless a minor is emancipated, he has no liability for necessaries at all because his parents have a duty to support him. Other courts do not follow such a firm rule, even though they are more likely to classify goods or services as necessaries where

---

4. The adult party also argued that the contract was enforceable on the grounds that the provision of representation for a child actor was a necessary, but the court rejected that argument. Contracts for necessaries are explained in section 14.2.2.

the minor is emancipated. The exact meaning of "emancipated" is not entirely clear. Some courts define it narrowly to include only marriage or military enlistment. Other courts adopt a broader test, and find emancipation if the minor has established her own home and is independent of her parents and not supported by them.

There is also a difference of view on the enforcement of a claim for necessaries. Some courts see a contract for necessaries as an exception to the rule that the minor can avoid the contract. They therefore simply enforce it as if it was a major's contract. Other courts avoid the contract even though it involved necessaries, but hold the minor liable for restitution on the theory of unjust enrichment. This means that if the market value of the goods or services is less than the contract price, the minor is only liable for that lower value.

b. Misrepresentation of Age

The minor's ability to escape liability under a contract is weakened if she deliberately misrepresented her age and the other party, acting reasonably, was misled by the misrepresentation and gave value to the minor or otherwise suffered a detriment in reasonable reliance on it. A court may fully enforce the contract by estopping the minor from asserting minority. (See section 8.4 for an explanation of estoppel.) Alternatively, the court may deny enforcement of the contract but hold the minor liable for the tort of fraud. (Accountability for tortious conduct typically begins at an earlier age than contractual capacity.) The remedy in tort is different from that in contract and aims at restoring the other party's loss rather than giving him the benefit of his bargain. To allow grounds for relief for misrepresentation, the fact misrepresented must be the minor's age. In *Foss v. Circuit City*, cited in section 14.2.1, the minor represented that he had parental consent to enter the contract by forging his mother's signature on the written agreement. The court held that this was not enough to estop the minor from asserting minority.

c. Statutory Exceptions

Apart from any recognition of liability under these principles of common law, a state or federal statute may confer contractual capacity on a minor of a specified minimum age with regard to certain types of contract. For example, minors are usually able to enter into insurance contracts or banking transactions, and a state may validate a minor's employment contract provided that it complies with the state's regulation of child labor.

Sometimes a statute expressly lowers the age of capacity for a particular type of contract. However, the statute may not always be that clear, so the legislature's intent to lower the age of capacity for particular types of transactions has to be determined by statutory interpretation. This issue can sometimes come up in a situation outside of the ordinary commercial context of contract law, as illustrated by *State v. Bishop*, 240 P.3d 614 (Kan. App. 2010). Bishop, a 16-year-old minor, entered into a diversion agreement with the state in 2002 to avoid prosecution for the offense of driving under the influence of alcohol. Under state law, a person who avoids prosecution by entering a diversion agreement is deemed to have been convicted of the offense. Bishop became a major in 2003. She was again caught driving under the influence of alcohol in 2004 and 2007. In her sentencing for the third offense, her previous diversion agreement was treated as a prior conviction. In an attempt to avoid the more severe penalty for a third conviction, Bishop sought to avoid the diversion agreement on the grounds that she was a minor without contractual capacity when she entered it. The court acknowledged that a diversion agreement was a contract, and that a minor would normally be able to disaffirm a contract entered into during minority. Although the statute governing diversion agreements did not specifically accord minors the contractual capacity to enter such agreements, the court concluded that the overall purpose of the statute made the contract binding. A minor who is old enough to get a driver's license is subject to the same standards and has the same responsibilities as an adult driver. All persons, regardless of age, are prohibited from driving under the influence of alcohol or drugs, and the statute was silent as to any age requirements. The court also found that, even if the agreement could have been disaffirmed by Bishop, she did not seek to disaffirm for several years after becoming a major, and this would have constituted a ratification of the agreement.

§14.2.3 Restitution or Other Relief Following Disaffirmation

If the contract is purely executory — that is, neither party has performed — disaffirmance simply terminates it. However, if either party had given value to the other before disaffirmance, the effect of disaffirmance is more complicated. Where a contract between parties of full contractual capacity is avoided, each party must restore whatever she has received from the other under the avoided contract. When the avoidance concerns a minor's contract, this general rule is not as firmly followed. The major party must always restore in full the value of anything that he has received from the minor. However, the minor is generally only liable to return to the major party whatever she still has left of the major's contract performance at the time of avoidance. As part of the goal of protecting the minor from an improvident contract, the minor is shielded from liability beyond the duty to return the present and existing economic advantage that she retains at the time of avoidance. She does not have to pay the major the value of services or of property that has been consumed or lost. For example, say that the minor bought a car for $10,000. The minor paid $2,000 down and agreed to pay the balance in installments. Six months later, the car was stolen, and the minor had not bought theft insurance for it. The minor may disaffirm the contract and is entitled to restitution of the $2,000 down payment as well as the installments that she paid during the six months. As she no longer has the car, she has no obligation to restore the value of the car to the seller. She is also not obliged to compensate the seller for the value of her six months' use of the car. Similarly, if the car was not stolen but damaged in an accident, the minor's only obligation on disaffirmance is to return the damaged car to the seller.

Some courts apply this rule absolutely, but others are concerned that it is too generous to the minor. A few courts do require the minor to restore the value of what she has received, whether or not she still has it. Others courts are willing, in limited circumstances, to impose some liability on a minor beyond the bare return of what she still has. For example, if the contract was fair and did not exploit the minor, and the major was not aware of the minority, a court may allow the major party to offset (deduct) the value received by the minor against what he is obliged to refund to the minor. (That is, if the minor has paid the major party, the restitution of that payment by the major party is reduced by the value of the benefit to the minor.) Some courts limit the value of the benefit to an offset against the major's restitution, but others have granted a judgment against the minor beyond the amount of the offset. *Dodson v. Schrader*, 824 S.W.2d 545 (Tenn. 1992) is an example of the former approach. The minor had paid cash for a truck and had then caused severe damage to its engine by neglect. The court permitted the minor to avoid the contract and to recover the cash paid for the truck, but it allowed the major party to offset against his restitutionary payment the value of the minor's use of the truck and its depreciation. By contrast, in *Valencia v. White*, 654 P.2d 287 (Ariz. 1982) the court imposed liability on a minor, beyond an offset against restitution, for the cost of repairing a truck that the minor had used in his trucking business. Instead of granting restitutionary relief to the major for the value of its performance, a court may allow the major to recover in tort where the minor's fault caused the deterioration in the property. (For example, if the car accident mentioned above was caused by the minor's negligence, the court may not allow the major to recover the value of the undamaged car or the value of the minor's use, but may hold the minor liable in tort for the damage to the car.)

§14.3 MENTAL INCAPACITY

§14.3.1 The Basis and Nature of Avoidance Due to Mental Incapacity

The common law has long recognized mental incapacity as a basis for avoiding a contract. As explained in section 14.3.2, the older-established test for incapacity is strict and narrow, covering only the most severe and debilitating forms of mental disability. But in more recent times, there has been a trend toward broadening the test to include a wider range of psychological disturbances that impair a person's ability to make rational decisions. Mental incompetence is determined at the time of contracting. If it can be proved to have existed at that time, it is a basis for avoidance even if the condition was temporary or has since been cured.

a. The Subjective Nature of Mental Incapacity

In contrast to the objective incapacity of a minor, based on the fact of age alone irrespective of the minor's actual state of mind, the mental incapacity of a major is based purely on his subjective attributes. As has often been stressed, when a contracting party is of full age, the objective test of intent holds him accountable for manifested assent. The law does not excuse people from contractual obligations merely because they are of below average intelligence, misguided, or weird. However, if a party suffers from a mental disability so severe as to preclude formulation of the requisite contractual intent, he cannot be held to his apparent agreement. The policy of protecting a mentally disabled person places a limit on the law's usual emphasis on objective manifestations of assent.

Even though the person's subjective state of mind is determinative of mental incapacity, this state of mind is established by objective evidence — usually both expert testimony of psychiatric diagnosis as well as lay testimony of people who observed his conduct at or around the time of the contract. This is discussed further in section c, below.

b. The Distinction Between Mental Incapacity and Mere Incompetence

The distinction between legally recognized mental incompetence and mere infirmity is illustrated by In re Seminole Walls and Ceilings Corp., 366 B.R. 206 (Bankr. M.D. Florida 2007),[5] and Sparrow v. Demonico, 960 N.E.2d 296 (Mass.

---

5. The case was affirmed in part and reversed in part by the district court in relation to matters unconnected to the capacity issue: 388 B.R. 38 (M.D. Fla. 2008) and 412 B.R. 878 (M.D. Fla. 2008).

2012). In *Seminole Walls*, a bankruptcy court had to decide on the validity of a settlement agreement executed between a bankruptcy trustee and a photographer who claimed ownership of a collection of his photographs in the possession of the estate. The photographs were of Hollywood celebrities, including Marilyn Monroe, that had been taken by the claimant many years before and had later been acquired by the bankrupt company. The settlement agreement resolved the question of their ownership. One of the grounds raised by the claimant for avoiding the settlement agreement was that he was mentally incompetent when it was made. At the time of entering the agreement, the claimant was 87 years old and had had a mini-stroke. He was declared mentally incompetent a few months after entering the agreement. The court found that notwithstanding some degree of feebleness and considerable eccentricity at the time of contracting and the subsequent declaration of incompetence, there was insufficient evidence to show that he was incapable of entering into the settlement agreement at the time of contracting.

Sparrow involved a settlement agreement reached during mediation to resolve a family dispute over the ownership of real property. Francis Sparrow sought to enforce the settlement against her sister, Susan Demonico, and Susan's husband. The Demonicos claimed that the settlement was unenforceable because Susan had experienced a mental breakdown during the mediation and therefore lacked capacity to contract. The trial court denied enforcement of the contract on the basis of the Demonicos' testimony that Susan was very distraught and distressed at the time of the mediation. She cried most of the day, became less coherent and less in control during the course of the day, and was generally in a bad emotional state. The Supreme Court reversed. It held that the Demonicos had not sufficiently demonstrated that Susan lacked mental capacity at the time that she entered the settlement agreement. It recognized that incapacity could be present at the time of contracting, even where the party did not suffer from a permanent mental illness. However, mental incapacity cannot simply be established by lay observation of the party's emotional state, but must be proved by expert psychiatric testimony that explains the nature of the party's mental incompetence and the manner in which it affected her ability to act rationally in relation to the transaction.

c. Proving Mental Incapacity

When a person has been declared incompetent by a court and a guardian has been appointed to administer his property, the fact of incapacity is clear. However, if there has been no adjudication of incapacity prior to the contract, the presumption is that adult parties were fully capable of contracting. The burden therefore lies on the allegedly incompetent party (or those representing his interests) to prove a disabling mental condition. This requires a demonstration both that the condition existed, and that it was in nature and extent severe enough to preclude an adequate degree of assent. This is usually shown by both expert psychiatric evidence and testimony by people who observed the behavior of the party at the time of the transaction. As noted above, in *Sparrow* the court held that psychiatric diagnosis is indispensable because a lay witness is not qualified to give an opinion on mental condition. In *Gaddy v. Douglass*, 597 S.E.2d 12 (S.C. App. 2004) the dementia of the mentally incapacitated party, an elderly woman with advanced Alzheimer's disease, was convincingly established by the testimony of three neurologists who examined her and three lay people who observed her conduct and attested to her gradual mental deterioration, confusion, and forgetfulness. As a result of this testimony, the court avoided a power of attorney that the patient had executed in favor of some grasping relatives who induced her to sign it after they knew that she was suffering from the disease. In some cases, the evidence relating to mental incompetence can be complex and difficult to evaluate. For example, in *In re Jack*, 390 B.R. 307 (Bankr. S.D. Tex. 2008), the bankruptcy court had to determine whether an agreement to settle a personal injury claim, executed ten years before the case by Samuel Jack, the debtor's late husband, was voidable because of his mental incapacity at that time. Prior to entering the contract, Samuel had sustained a serious head injury while working as a longshoreman. In addition to this injury, which damaged his brain, Samuel suffered from alcoholism and had a preexisting mental disorder, known as schizoaffective disorder, which affected his judgment and reasoning ability. Around the time of entering the agreement, he was hospitalized several times, and some medical reports indicated that his thought processes were disordered and impaired. However, other expert opinion indicated that his thought processes were intact. To glean Samuel's mental capacity at the time of the contract, the court had to weigh and assess the credibility of considerable conflicting and complex evidence of medical diagnoses and observations of Samuel's conduct. It also had to take into account the nature of the contract and the degree to which a person of diminished mental capacity might be able to comprehend its purpose and effect. It ultimately determined that Samuel's wife (the debtor in bankruptcy) had not sustained the burden of proving that, at the time of contracting, Samuel was incapable of appreciating the effect of what he was doing or of understanding the nature of the transaction and the consequences of his actions.

d. The Reliance Interest of the Other Contracting Party

The protection of a mentally incompetent person from contractual commitment is balanced against the protection of the reliance interest of the other contracting party. Where the mental illness is severe and its symptoms are patent and easily observable by the other party, his reliance interest is weak.

However, where the symptoms of the illness are more subtle and harder to detect, the other party's reliance interest is stronger. In such a situation, the party seeking avoidance may have to prove not only the existence of the illness, but also that the other party knew or had reason to know of it. This is discussed further in section 14.3.2.

e. Unfair Terms

The basis of avoiding a contract for mental incompetence is lack of capacity, not harshness in the terms of the contract. Therefore, the party seeking avoidance need not show that the terms of the contract are unfair. Even a contract with perfectly reasonable terms can be avoided if mental incompetence is established. This does not mean that the existence of unfair or one-sided terms is irrelevant in cases of mental incompetence. As explained below, the decision to avoid the contract involves some degree of equitable balancing, and unfair terms or advantage-taking may influence the court in deciding to allow avoidance.

f. The Impact of a Finding of Incapacity

The purpose of permitting avoidance is the protection of the disabled person and his estate, but the benign motive of protection carries a risk of paternalism and intrusion. It could mean that a person diagnosed with or suspected of having a mental disease is deprived of his freedom to contract because others will not risk dealing with him. Even if that problem was overcome and a contract was made, a finding of incapacity might still undermine the party's autonomy. In many cases, it is not the contracting party himself who desires to escape the contract, but his friends or relatives who seek to have him declared incompetent so that the contract can be avoided. In situations like this, a court has to be particularly careful that it is truly serving his best interests and not unduly interfering with his contractual liberty.

§14.3.2 The Test for Mental Incapacity

As mentioned earlier, the older-established test for mental incapacity is strict. The contract can only be avoided if, at the time of contracting, the party was unable to understand the nature and consequences of the transaction. This standard, called the cognitive test, confines avoidance to cases in which the party was so profoundly disabled that he did not know what he was doing. Because the lack of capacity is so serious, there is a stronger likelihood that it would have been apparent to the other party, at least where the parties had personal interaction. Therefore, where incapacity is patent and observable by the other party, the equities strongly favor avoidance because the other party cannot fairly claim to have reasonably relied on the genuineness of manifested intent. For this reason, and because a narrow test is easier to apply, some courts still prefer it.

However, other courts consider it to be outdated and too rigid. Growing insight into psychology over the last several decades has shown that there are many forms of mental incapacity that fall short of cognitive disability, but that nevertheless so affect a person's judgment, self-control, and motivation, that he is incapable of genuine assent. This has led to a broader test that recognizes not only cognitive disorders, but also an illness or defect that impairs the party's ability to transact in a reasonable manner. This test is described by different names, including the motivational, affective, or volitional test. This type of incapacity may be more subtle and less apparent to the other party. Therefore, the Restatement, Second, gives greater weight to the reliance interest of the other party, and only permits avoidance if the other had reason to know of the condition.

Restatement, Second, §15(1) recognizes both tests. Section 15(1)(a) sets out the cognitive test. It allows a party to avoid a contract if he "is unable to understand in a reasonable manner the nature and consequences of the transaction." Section 15(1)(b) sets out the motivational test that allows a party to avoid the contract if "he is unable to act in a reasonable manner in relation to the transaction and the other party has reason to know of his condition." In the *Sparrow* case, discussed in section 14.3.1b, the court observed that increased understanding of the nature of mental illness has necessitated a movement away from a strict cognitive test and recognition of the motivational test. For this reason, the inquiry into incapacity should not be confined to the question of whether the person was capable of understanding the transaction, but should extend to situations in which the person's rationality in entering into the contract was affected by the illness or mental disturbance.

Davis v. Davis, 89 P.3d 1206 (Or. App. 2004) is a good illustration of the difference in approach and result between the narrower and wider tests. The parties entered into a divorce settlement in which the wife gave the husband full ownership of some stock options and of their interest in a software company. About a month later, the wife moved to avoid the settlement on the grounds that she was not mentally competent when she made it. The couple had been married for about 17 years. The husband had physically abused the wife on numerous occasions during the marriage. A social worker who treated the wife after the dissolution testified that the wife loved and feared the husband enormously. The wife was diagnosed as suffering from depression, post-traumatic stress syndrome, and battered woman's syndrome. When the parties met to negotiate the settlement, the wife was emotionally distraught and also had hopes of reconciliation. When she expressed her desire to reconcile, the husband made it clear that he was not interested and he also verbally abused her at one point during the course of the meeting. At the end of this emotional meeting, the wife told her attorney that she did not want to fight any more and wanted to get the meeting over with. Contrary to her attorney's advice, she did not press for a half share in the stock options and interest in the software company, but insisted on signing the agreement that gave the husband full ownership. The majority of the court of appeals upheld the trial court's dismissal of the wife's motion to set aside the agreement. Both courts considered themselves bound by the cognitive test, which had been adopted by the state supreme court. A concurring judge regretfully accepted this legal conclusion, but expressed the view that the affective test is more in accord with psychological theory and reflects a better understanding of human behavior.

This description of the case shows two things. First, it demonstrates the truth of the concurring judge's view that there are many situations in which a strict cognitive test disregards what could be a real and serious impairment of the capacity to make a rational and voluntary decision. Second, it suggests the hazard of the broader test. If mental incapacity is wide enough to encompass severe emotional disturbance short of cognitive disability, the test becomes less predictable and harder to apply. At the borderline, it may be difficult to distinguish incapacity that merits avoidance from eccentric, strangely motivated, ill-advised, or irrational decisionmaking that affects many transactions in the marketplace. A court that accepts the broader motivational test as a basis for avoidance can mitigate this risk by requiring persuasive expert testimony to establish a clinically recognized illness, and by adopting the qualification of Restatement, Second, §15(1)(b), which requires a showing of the other party's knowledge or reason to know of the mental condition.

§14.3.3 Avoidance and Its Consequences

Like a minor's contract, the contract of a mentally incompetent person is voidable, not void. Unlike minority, however, mental disability does not disappear on a set and certain date, after which the fact of disaffirmance or ratification can be settled. The fate of a contract by a mentally incapacitated person may therefore hang in the balance until either it is disaffirmed or the incapacity abates, and the formerly incompetent party affirms it. (Or a guardian is ultimately appointed and does so.) In the interim, there may be performance or the other party may have otherwise changed his position in reliance on the contract. If that party had not taken unfair advantage of the other's mental incapacity — that is, he contracted on fair terms without awareness of the incapacity, Restatement, Second, §15(2) acknowledges his interests. It provides for termination of the power of avoidance to the extent that the contract has been so performed, or circumstances have so changed that avoidance would be unjust.

If the contract is avoided, the parties must be restored to the status quo ante. Both must return money or property received under the contract, or the value of property consumed or dissipated, or of services rendered. However, if the other party knew of and took advantage of the incompetence, the disabled party may be excused from paying to the extent that benefits received did not ultimately enrich him.

§14.3.4 Incapacity Induced by Alcohol or Drug Abuse

Incapacity caused by intoxication is viewed less sympathetically than that resulting from age, illness, or injury, because the incapacitated party is seen as having some blame for the problem. However, courts are aware of the compulsive nature of alcoholism and drug abuse. They therefore recognize that if intoxication is severe enough, its impairing effect can be just as profound as mental illness. Furthermore, that degree of inebriation is usually obvious enough to be apparent to the other party, so a strong inference can be drawn that he deliberately took advantage of it. Therefore, despite any moral reprobation that a court may feel about the conduct of the intoxicated party, courts do generally permit avoidance on the ground of incapacity if the level of intoxication is sufficient to deprive him of understanding or of the ability to act rationally, and the other party had reason to know of this. Restatement, Second, §16 follows this approach. The case for relief is even stronger if the terms of the resulting contract are unfair or unduly favorable to the other party.

Examples

1. Hardy Culturalist, age 19, was about to leave his hometown to attend college. Up to that time, he had operated a very successful part-time yard maintenance business on weekends. As he would no longer be able to service his customers, he wished to dispose of his lawnmower, trimmer, edger, and other garden tools. Lon Mower, a 16-year-old high-school junior, who lived with his parents next door to Hardy, was interested in filling the gap that would be left by Hardy's departure. He wanted to buy the equipment and try to take over Hardy's customers. Hardy and Lon began negotiations and eventually reached agreement on the sale of all the equipment for $800. This is a fair price, somewhat below its market value. Lon did not have that much money in his savings account, so he paid $300 to Hardy and undertook to pay the balance in installments of $50 per month, which he expected would be generated from his yard

work. Lon had just taken a business law course in high school, so he knew that a sale of goods over $500 had to be recorded in writing and signed. He therefore drew up a simple document reflecting their agreement, and they both signed it. Under the state law applicable to this transaction, a person acquires contractual capacity at the age of 18.

   a. After taking delivery of the equipment and paying Hardy the $300, Lon began work. He successfully groomed about five yards in the first week, but did not enjoy the hard labor very much and began to regret having undertaken this new venture. In the second week, he had a disaster. He lost control of the lawnmower, which ran over the trimmer, completely mangling it, and then plunged off a steep embankment and exploded. This experience convinced Lon that yard work was not for him. He wishes to cancel the sale, get his $300 back, and return all the surviving equipment to Hardy. May he do this?

   b. Say that at the time he made the contract with Hardy, Lon was 17 years old and just two weeks short of his eighteenth birthday. Lon took delivery of the equipment and paid Hardy the $300. He used the garden equipment for five weeks and then decided that he no longer wished to do landscaping work. (The calamity involving the runaway lawnmower did not occur, and Lon was able to return the equipment to Hardy in much the same condition as when he bought it.) Lon would like to avoid the contract, return the equipment to Hardy, and get his money back. Does this change in the facts affect Lon's ability to disaffirm the contract?

2. Bonna Petite is a precocious 17-year-old with an appetite for *haute cuisine*. For a while she had been dying to eat lunch at Trés Cher, the most elegant and expensive restaurant in town. One day she put on her mother's best business suit and groomed herself meticulously, succeeding in making herself look like a young executive of around 25 years of age. She set off for the restaurant, where she was seated and served a magnificent lunch. At the end of the meal she announced to the waiter that she was a minor. She disaffirmed the contract and refused to pay for the lunch. The age of majority in Bonna's state is 18. Can she get away with this?

3. Price Slasher, a man of 82, had lived in his house for 45 years. During the last ten years of that period, following the death of his wife, he had lived alone. As he got older, it had become increasingly burdensome for him to maintain the house and to take care of domestic chores. He therefore decided that the time had come for him to sell it and to move to an assisted living complex. Price had always been a stubborn, impatient, and difficult man, and this had become worse as he aged. He hated asking anyone for help, and he rarely sought or listened to advice. His insistence on self-reliance had become quite worrisome to his daughter, because he did not seem to manage his affairs very well. He was constantly losing

things, could not keep his bank account balanced, forgot to pay some bills, and double-paid others without realizing it.

When he told his daughter that he planned to sell the house, she offered to help him, but he declined her assistance. She then begged him to get it appraised and to list it with a reputable real estate agent. He refused, insisting that he was fully aware of the market, knew exactly how much the house was worth, and was perfectly capable of negotiating the sale himself. In this he was quite wrong. His information about the market was years out of date, and he had never been much of a negotiator.

Price advertised the house for sale at a figure that was about 25 percent lower than its true market value. Lowe Ball saw the advertisement and came to see the house. It did not take him long to make an offer at the full asking price, which Price accepted. Lowe's contact with Price during the transaction was quite minimal. The parties had a short conversation when Lowe inspected the house, and another when the written offer was submitted and accepted. Lowe did not attempt to negotiate the price because he realized that Price's price was good (although he did not realize that it was so far below the market value of the house). His only impression about Price was that he was an elderly man of few words who seemed to know exactly what he wanted.

After the contract of sale had been signed, Price told his daughter about it. She was appalled because she knew that he had let the house go for a patently inadequate price. A long family meeting took place that evening, at which his daughter and other relatives finally convinced Price that he had sold too cheaply. He now wishes to rescind the sale. Does he have grounds to do so?

4. Clark Rapp, age 30, suffers from bipolar disorder, a psychiatric condition that causes extreme swings in mood, ranging from high periods (mania) to depressive periods. During the high periods, a patient with this disorder becomes excitable and hyperactive and experiences lack of self-control and impaired judgment. During a manic episode, Clark visited the website of an exclusive resort and booked an exorbitantly expensive and luxurious vacation. To complete and submit his online booking, Clark signified his agreement to the resort's standard terms by clicking on an "I agree" button on the website. Clark did not read the standard terms before clicking the button. One of the terms stated, "I understand that upon submission of my booking, my credit card will be debited with the full cost of the accommodation booked. This booking cannot be changed and if I cancel it I will not be entitled to a refund of this charge." A few days after booking the vacation, Clark's manic episode ended. He regretted booking the expensive vacation. When the resort refused to cancel the booking and refund his payment, Clark sued to avoid the contract and recover his payment. What are his prospects of success?

5. Change the facts of Example 4 to the following extent: Clark is not an adult suffering from bipolar disorder or any other psychiatric condition, but is a minor, age 17. Clark is intellectually gifted. He graduated from high school at the age of 16 and is a college student. He has his own credit card, which he used to book the vacation. (Under a state statute, a minor may validly contract for a credit card from the age of 16.) May Clark avoid the contract and recover his payment?

Explanations

1. a. This is a sale of goods, but apart from the statute of frauds issue, which Lon has cleverly satisfied, there are no special rules applicable in this case. UCC Article 2 does not deal with minors' contracts, which are therefore governed in sales transactions by general principles of common law.

   Because Lon is a minor, he may disaffirm the contract. It does not matter that he may have been smart and sophisticated enough to understand exactly what he was doing, that he was knowledgeable about the statute of frauds, or that he planned to use the equipment for a moneymaking venture. The protection from contractual commitment afforded a minor is based on the objective fact of age and does not take account of the subjective attributes of the minor. The objective criterion of minority also makes it irrelevant that Hardy was little over the age of minority himself, that the contract was on fair terms, or that Hardy did not exploit or take advantage of Lon. Lon's right to disaffirm does not depend on a showing of substantive unfairness or bargaining impropriety.

   When the minor elects to disaffirm the contract, each party must restore what was received from the other. However, if the minor has lost, consumed, or damaged property obtained under the contract, the established rule is that he is responsible to restore only what he has at the time of disaffirmance and need not compensate the major for any shortfall. Under this rule, Lon is entitled to his $300 back and must return the surviving equipment to Hardy. Some courts have recognized that a rigid rule to this effect may not be fair in every case, and have been willing, in proper circumstances, to hold the minor liable for more than the mere return of existing enrichment. The basis for liability could be tort where the minor has caused the loss negligently. (Liability for tort arises at a younger age than contractual capacity.) If Lon was negligent in losing control of the mower, this approach would make Lon responsible to reimburse Hardy for the value of the lost mower and trimmer, in addition to returning the other equipment. As an alternative to tort liability, some courts require the minor to restore the value of any benefit received from the use of the property. Some courts confine recovery to an offset against any restitution due to the minor, but others are willing to grant a money judgment against the minor, imposing liability on him greater than any offset against restitution. Lon was not benefited by the destruction of the mower and trimmer, so he cannot be held liable for their value. However, he did earn money by using the equipment for a week. He may therefore be responsible, in addition to restoring the remaining tools to Hardy, for payment of the rental value of all the equipment for a week.

If the court does not apply either of the above principles to compensate Hardy for the loss, he may try the argument that the mower and trimmer were necessaries, because Lon used them to earn money. This is not a strong argument because Lon was still in school and living with his parents. He did the yard work on a part-time basis, and not as a means of earning his livelihood. If the goods are classified as necessaries, some courts treat the contract as fully enforceable, so that Lon has no right of avoidance. Other courts allow avoidance but require the minor to make restitution for the value of what he received. On this basis, Lon would, in addition to returning the remaining equipment, be liable to pay for the mower and trimmer, based on the lesser rate of the contract value or fair market value at the time of sale[6]. In this case, fair value was apparently above the contract price, so the contract price of the destroyed mower and trimmer would be the proper measure of recovery.

b. The fact that Lon was almost 18, rather than 16, at the time of contracting does not affect Lon's right to avoid the contract. Minority is measured objectively, and the only question is whether or not Lon was a minor at the time of contracting, even if he was almost a major. However, once a minor reaches the age of majority, he may ratify the contract, thereby fully validating it and terminating the power to avoid it. Ratification may be express, or it could be implied where the minor fails to disaffirm the contract within a reasonable time of reaching majority or otherwise acts in a way that signifies an intent to ratify. (As noted in section 14.2.1, an argument of implied ratification would not work in a state that requires a written ratification.)

The measurement of a reasonable time for disaffirmance is a factual question, based on all the circumstances of the case. About three

---

6. Note that I argue here that if the contract is for a necessary, but the court requires the minor to restore the value of what was received instead of paying the contract price, the measure of restitution is the value of the goods themselves, not their rental value. This seems to be the more appropriate measure under these circumstances because a contract for necessaries has a stronger binding effect on the minor.

weeks have passed since Lon's eighteenth birthday and he has not yet disaffirmed. His failure to act for three weeks may in itself constitute a ratification. Even if this passive delay in disaffirming is not, in itself, enough to constitute ratification, Lon continued to use the equipment during the three-week period. This action is inconsistent with an intent to disaffirm, and likely constitutes conduct evidencing an intent to ratify.

2. A minor may disaffirm her contract at any time before or within a reasonable time after attaining majority. The general rule is that she must restore any benefits that she still retains at the time of disaffirmance, but is not accountable for the value of property that has been consumed or dissipated. (In a sense, she does still have Trés Cher's property and will retain it until the process of digestion is complete, but Trés Cher would probably not be too interested in the disgorgement of this benefit.)

The general rule places the burden on Trés Cher to inquire about the age of its youthful-looking customers, and it bears the risk of failing to do so, even if Bonna looked older than she was. On the other hand, Bonna has behaved very badly, and the law should not encourage our young citizens to do this kind of thing. There are a few possibilities for holding Bonna accountable for her conduct.

Trés Cher could argue that the meal was a necessary. Food required for sustenance could qualify as a necessary, but it is harder to so classify a sumptuous meal at a fancy restaurant, especially where the minor lives with her parents and has food available at home. Alternatively, Trés Cher could argue that Bonna should be held liable in tort for deliberately misrepresenting her age. Because responsibility for tort arises at an earlier age than contractual capacity, a finding of fraud could make Bonna liable for the loss caused by her misrepresentation. The difficulty with this argument is that courts usually require that the minor makes an affirmative lie about her age. Dressing up is probably not enough to constitute a deliberate misrepresentation of age.

In the absence of a finding of liability for a necessary or in tort, the established rule is that a minor is responsible to restore only the existing benefit received under the contract. Some courts have moved away from that absolute rule and do permit restitution of the value of a consumed benefit provided that the contract was fair and the major party was unaware of the minority. There is a stronger incentive for adopting this approach where, as here, the minor was willful in causing the major party's loss. The court may limit the minor's obligation to restore the value of his benefit to an offset against the major party's restitutionary obligation to the minor. If the court adopts this limitation in the present case and so confines the major party's recovery against the minor, Trés Cher would receive nothing because Bonna gave nothing to the restaurant and there is no restitution owed to her against which her obligation could be offset.

As a matter of policy, a rule that confines the major party's recovery to the minor's existing benefit most strongly advances the goal of protecting the minor against improvident conduct that creates liability. However, a rule that makes a minor fully accountable for the value of the benefit, even if consumed or lost, allows the court to sanction the minor's irresponsible or antisocial conduct. A rule that makes the minor accountable for a consumed or lost benefit, but only to the extent of an offset against the major party's restitutionary obligation, is a compromise solution that tries to accommodate both these goals.[7]

3. The facts concerning Price's mental capacity are deliberately vague but suggestive. It appears that he has certain character traits, such as stubbornness, resistance to advice, weak negotiating skills, and impatience, that are likely to place him at risk of entering into a disadvantageous contract. These flaws in his nature may indicate that he probably lacks skill in contracting, but do not, on their own, constitute the kind of mental incompetence that would give rise to a claim for avoidance. However, there are indications that the effect of these shortcomings have been aggravated by mental infirmity, manifested in symptoms such as loss of memory and confusion. His family has noticed a deterioration in his mental capacity, but this is not necessarily something that was obvious to Lowe.

A person is presumed to be competent to contract. If Price seeks to avoid the contract on the basis of incapacity, he must prove that he was mentally incompetent at the time of entering the contract. The degree of incompetence to be established depends on whether the jurisdiction recognizes only the older cognitive test — that he could not understand the nature and consequences of the transaction; or has extended the test to include the looser motivational standard — that his mental defect impaired his ability to transact in a reasonable manner. The motivational test is satisfied by a much less serious degree of infirmity, but for that reason it more strongly protects the reasonable reliance interest of the other party and is not a basis for avoidance unless Lowe had reason to know of Price's inability to conduct the transaction rationally.

Evidence of Price's behavior during the transaction is directly relevant to his mental state at the time. However, evidence of his conduct immediately before and after the transaction is also a pertinent indicator

---

7. Because responsibility for criminal conduct arises at an earlier age than contractual capacity, a minor who obtains goods or services under false pretenses may also face criminal prosecution. The criminal law may therefore provide a disincentive to antisocial behavior, even if contract law does not.

of his state of mind at the time of contracting. Price's daughter can testify about his confused and disoriented behavior during the period surrounding the transaction, but Lowe was the only person who observed Price during the transaction, and he claims to have found nothing amiss. Both of them could be telling the truth, because Price's condition seems to have manifested itself in lapses. The anecdotal evidence may therefore be quite inconclusive, and it may not be possible for Price to make a case for avoidance unless he can offer expert testimony by a psychiatrist who has examined him, diagnosed his condition, and can convince the factfinder that it is serious enough to have impaired his ability to contract under the applicable test.

Although evidence of Price's mental state is the most directly relevant to the decision on whether to permit avoidance on grounds of incapacity, courts are concerned with balancing the protection of the incapacitated party against the need to treat the other party fairly and to foster the security of transactions. Therefore, testimony about the transacting environment is often of great relevance, particularly when the mental incapacity falls short of a palpable cognitive disorder. Such factors as the adequacy of consideration given to the incompetent party, the fairness of the contract terms, any abuse of trust or confidence by the other party, and any other bargaining impropriety could influence the outcome of the case. In the present case, if Lowe is believed, he was guilty of no deliberate underhand dealing and had no reason to notice anything peculiar in Price's demeanor that may have alerted him to a problem. He offered what was asked for the property, and his only sin was that he made an attractive bargain. However, a 25 percent shortfall from the market price is quite extreme, and (even though Lowe may not have known how good a price it was) this could in itself be regarded as an indication to a reasonable buyer that something was wrong with Price. A person who makes a particularly favorable exchange with one who suffers from a mental disability is not in a particularly strong position.

In *Heights Realty Ltd. v. Phillips*, 749 P.2d 77 (N.M. 1988), an 84-year-old woman entered into an exclusive listing agreement with a real estate agent, and then refused to sell the property when the agent found a willing and able buyer. Although there was nothing unfair or extraordinary about the contract terms, and the agent testified that the seller was "sharp as a tack" during their negotiations, the seller had been in a gradual and subtle mental decline for some years. Her deteriorating mental condition was described by a number of family members, who had noticed erratic and confused behavior, memory lapses, and mismanagement of her affairs. A psychiatrist testified that although it could not be stated conclusively that she was mentally incompetent, this could be asserted as a matter of medical probability. He believed that she probably realized that she was contracting for the purpose of selling her property but could not have understood the detailed terms of her contract. During the course of the suit, she was in fact adjudged incompetent and was represented by a conservator. The court, applying the stricter cognitive test followed in the jurisdiction, found that the combination of psychiatric and anecdotal evidence was sufficient to satisfy the seller's burden of establishing mental incompetence under that standard.

4. In the absence of a mental condition that impairs Clark's contractual capacity, Clark would not be able to escape this contract. He signified his assent to the standard terms by clicking the "I agree" button. As explained in section 5.3, courts commonly uphold such a manifestation of assent to standard clickwrap terms. It is unlikely that any of the policing doctrines discussed in Chapter 13 would provide grounds for avoidance. The facts do not suggest any basis for claiming fraud or duress. Although the term precluding cancellation of the booking and refund may seem quite tough, it probably is not harsh and one-sided enough to be substantively unconscionable and there is no indication of procedural unconscionability.

Clark suffers from a well-recognized mental disorder, so the question is whether the disorder deprived him of the capacity to enter into this contract. Clark must establish the existence, symptoms, and effects of the disorder by expert psychiatric testimony, possibly bolstered by evidence of friends or family who observed his behavior during the manic phase of the disorder. Let's assume that he can produce this testimony. It likely will not be enough to allow avoidance in a jurisdiction that recognizes only the stricter cognitive test of mental incapacity. Although the illness impaired his judgment, motivation, and self-control, it does not appear to have disabled him from understanding and appreciating the nature and consequences of his acts when entering the transaction. In *Proctor v. Classic Automotive, Inc.*, 20 So. 3d 1281 (Ala. Civ. App. 2009), the court refused to allow avoidance of a contract to lease a car, even though the lessee suffered from bipolar disorder and had behaved impulsively and irrationally when she entered the lease transaction. (She seemed to be confused about the difference between a lease and a purchase, she had gone on a spending spree just before entering the transaction, she did not test-drive the car, and she could not afford the lease payments.) The court held that despite this, the illness failed to meet the cognitive test of incapacity, because she had enough understanding and perception to realize that she was entering into an automobile lease agreement.

A court that accepts the looser motivational test of Restatement, Second, §15(1)(b) would allow Clark to avoid the sale if he can show that a mental illness or defect affected his ability to act in a reasonable manner in the transaction and that the other party had reason to know of his condition. Although bipolar disorder likely does affect his ability to approach the transaction rationally, Clark cannot satisfy the second element of the test because there is no basis for arguing that the resort knew or had reason to know of his mental condition. This aspect of the test is particularly difficult to satisfy in an Internet transaction in which the resort had no opportunity to observe behavior that may alert it to the possibility that Clark was not approaching the transaction rationally.

5. The simpler objective test applicable to minor's contracts makes this Example much easier to answer. Clark is a minor, and he can avoid the contract. It does not matter that he is brilliant and advanced for his age. The exception relating to necessaries cannot apply here—a luxurious vacation surely cannot qualify as a necessary for a college student. Although the state has carved out a statutory exception to allow a minor to make a valid contract for a credit card, it would be a stretch, in the absence of clear statutory language, to interpret the legislation to extend to transactions in which the credit card is used. The traditional justification of the objective test for minority is that the other party should be placed on inquiry by the youthful appearance of the minor, and assumes the risk of avoidance when contracting with someone who looks young. This rationale is not very convincing in Internet transactions. The larger policy question is whether the traditional rule on minority still makes sense in the age of electronic commerce, in which minors are a significant segment of the market.

15

Mistake, Impracticability, and Frustration of Purpose

§15.1 THE COMMON THEMES AND THE DIFFERENCES BETWEEN MISTAKE, IMPRACTICABILITY, AND FRUSTRATION OF PURPOSE

The three doctrines considered in this chapter have common themes that make it useful to consider them together. They are each concerned with a situation in which the exchange between the parties turns out to be very different from what was expected. In the case of mistake, this is caused by a serious factual error made by one or both parties at the time of contracting, so that the contract is premised on incorrect information. By contrast, impracticability and frustration arise when there is no false premise at the time of contracting, but events change drastically enough after formation to belie the original expectation of the parties. An issue of mistake, impracticability, or frustration may be raised at various stages after formation of the contract and for the purpose of achieving different ends. For example, before performance is due, it may be used to excuse the prospective performance. After performance has been rendered, it could be used as a defense to a claim that the performance fell short of that called for by the contract. Most commonly, its effect is termination of the contract, but sometimes adjustment of the contract terms is the more appropriate remedy.

Each doctrine poses two central questions that will be constant themes in our discussion:

521

1. *Materiality* — *How fundamental is the discrepancy between the expected and the actual exchange?* This question is concerned with the impact of the mistake or altered circumstances on the bargain reasonably anticipated by the parties. Relief is only available when the impact is so material that it changes the very basis of their bargain.

2. *Risk* — *Which party should be made to bear the consequences of this defeat of the original expectations?* The fact that original expectations have been fundamentally upset only justifies relief if the party seeking it does not bear the risk of this upset. The allocation of risk may be clear from the terms of the contract, or it may have to be established by interpretation from the circumstances of the transaction. The determination of risk allocation is a crucial aspect of the judicial inquiry in all these cases.

Having identified common themes, it is important to stress the difference between mistake, on the one hand, and impracticability and frustration on the other. As noted earlier, the doctrine of mistake applies when the contract is based on an erroneous belief at the time of contracting that certain facts are true. The error causes one or both parties to manifest assent that would not have been given had the true facts been known. When the error is later discovered the mistaken party — or one of them, if the parties shared the mistake — may have grounds to avoid (or in a special case, to claim adjustment of) the contract. The basis of mistake is that the manifestation of assent is not genuine because it was induced by error. Although one party's error may sometimes be induced by the deception of the other, improper conduct is not an element of mistake and does not have to be shown. (Of course, if there was deception, this fact strengthens the grounds for avoidance and may give rise to an alternative claim of fraud or unconscionability.) In contrast to mistake, impracticability and frustration are concerned with the impact of supervening events on the transaction. These doctrines are not based on any defect in assent at the time of contracting, but aim to provide relief when the basis of a fully consensual transaction is profoundly altered by some external event that occurs afterwards.[1]

UCC Article 2 does not deal with the doctrine of mistake, so a mistake in a contract for the sale of goods is governed by principles of common law. As you will see in section 15.7.3, Article 2 does have a provision that deals with

---

1. Chronology is a helpful means of deciding whether a case raises an issue of impracticality or frustration rather than mistake. Impracticability and frustration should always be concerned with supervening events. This distinction is not always neatly reflected in the caselaw. Some cases have found impracticality or frustration where, unknown to the parties, the event had already occurred at the time of contracting. It seems more appropriate to treat such a case under the rules of mistake.

impracticability, written broadly enough to encompass frustration of purpose as well.

§15.2 THE MEANING OF MISTAKE AND THE DISTINCTION BETWEEN MUTUAL AND UNILATERAL MISTAKE

§15.2.1 The Legal Meaning of Mistake: An Error of Fact

In lay terms, "mistake" has quite a wide range of meaning. It could refer to a factual error, but it might also include a bad judgment, a rash decision, or simply a situation that did not work out well. For example, it may have been a real mistake to buy that ugly chair, to invest in your cousin's harebrained enterprise or to drive to town instead of taking the bus. The legal meaning of "mistake" is much narrower. It is confined to errors of fact — that is, to errors about some thing or event that actually occurred or existed and can be ascertained by objective evidence. This leads to a number of important observations on the scope of mistake doctrine:

a. An Error in Judgment Does Not Qualify as a Mistake

A party cannot escape a disadvantageous or regrettable contract resulting from poor judgment. Say, for example, that a buyer of a plot of land purchases it in the belief that it is worth more than the asking price, but then finds that this is untrue. Or a buyer of stock believes wrongly that the company is undervalued and the stock is considerably more valuable than its price. If these parties were to be allowed to avoid their obligations simply because they had judged wrongly, no transaction could be secure. Although this distinction can be drawn in principle, it is not always a simple matter to distinguish an error in judgment from a mistake of fact. Judgments are usually based on fact, and less obvious cases could require some unraveling.

A famous old case and a more modern one illustrate the subtle distinction between a mistake of fact and of judgment. In *Sherwood v. Walker*, 33 N.W. 919 (Mich. 1887) a cattle breeder, believing a highly pedigreed cow to be infertile, sold it as a beef cow for a fraction of its value. Before delivery, the seller discovered the cow to be pregnant and he refused to deliver it to the buyer. The buyer sued to compel delivery but the court allowed the seller to avoid the contract for mistake. The majority and dissenting opinions differ on whether the belief that the cow was infertile should be treated as a mistake. The majority thought that it was, but the dissent felt that the cow's ability to breed was really a question of judgment. In the dissent's view, neither party knew for sure that the cow was infertile. The seller gambled that it was, and the buyer that it was not. The buyer's judgment was right and he should not be deprived of the fruits of his successful speculation.

Firestone & Parson, Inc. v. Union League of Philadelphia, 672 F. Supp. 819 (E.D. Pa. 1987) involved the sale of a painting attributed to Albert Bierstadt, the celebrated nineteenth-century landscape painter. At the time of the sale, art experts regarded the painting as Bierstadt's and the parties had no reason to believe otherwise. As a result, it was sold for $500,000. Several years after the sale, scholarly research revealed that the painting was not by Bierstadt. As a result, it was worth only a tenth of what was paid for it. The buyer sued for avoidance of the contract. The suit was dismissed because the statute of limitations had run. However, the court discussed the claim of mistake and suggested that even had the buyer sued in time, the contract would not have been avoidable. The value and authorship of a work of art, based on expert opinion, is more a matter of judgment than of fact.

b. An Incorrect Prediction of Future Events Is Not a Mistake

A future event may one day become a fact, but until it has happened, it cannot be thought of as a fact by anyone except Nostradamus. Therefore, as a rule, it is generally accurate to say that the mistake must relate to a fact in existence at the time of contracting. A party cannot claim relief for an erroneous prediction. This is often closely related to point *a* above, because most predictions at the time of contract are speculations concerning the future value of the transaction and are therefore in the nature of judgments. For example, if a buyer of oranges purchases them in the belief that the market will rise, he cannot complain if it later turns out that he was wrong. This is not a mistake in the legal sense, but simply an erroneous prediction (or misjudgment) of profitability. Again, although the distinction between fact and prediction is easy to draw in some cases, there are situations in which a contractual assumption may have both factual and speculative elements. When that happens, it can be difficult to decide if the error should be treated as a mistake.

c. Mistake of Fact Must Be Distinguished from Mistake as to Meaning (Misunderstanding)

When the parties dispute the meaning of a contract term, this could be characterized as a type of mistake — one of the parties is mistaken as to the intention of the other. Mistake doctrine is not concerned with this type of error, which is not a mistake as to some external fact, but rather a mistake as to the meaning of a manifestation of assent. It is resolved by the process of interpretation, governed by the principles set out in Chapter 10. That is, the correct meaning of a manifestation is decided by determining the reasonable meaning of the words or conduct in context.

A court might miss this distinction, as shown by *Monarch Marketing System Co. v. Reed's Photo Mart*, 485 S.W.2d 905 (Tex. 1972). The photo store had meant to order 4,000 custom labels. The letter "M" was understood in trade usage to signify a quantity of 1,000. Instead of filling in a quantity of "4M" in its order form, the store erroneously wrote the order for "4MM" labels. When the 4 million labels were delivered, the store refused to accept them and the supplier sued for the price. The court resolved the case on the basis of mistake and found that the elements of unilateral mistake were not satisfied. (We will examine these elements shortly. In essence, the court found that the store's unilateral mistake did not merit avoidance because the store was responsible for the mistake, the supplier had no way of realizing that the order was wrong, and if the contract was not enforced, the supplier would suffer a loss which it could not recover by selling the customized labels to anyone else.) The result is doubtless correct, but the basis for reaching it is wrong. This was not a mistake as to an external fact, but an error in communication. Under the objective test, the store is held to the supplier's reasonable understanding of its manifestation of intent.

d. A Mistake of Law Could Qualify as a Fact

Courts differ in their approach to errors of law. Some courts are willing to treat the legal rules applicable to a transaction as facts — to see those legal rules as constituting an existing state of affairs that can be objectively ascertained. On this approach, a mistake of law could be the basis for relief. For example, in *Mattson v. Rachetto*, 591 N.W.2d 814 (S.D. 1999), the court held that a party to a sale of land could rescind the contract on grounds of mistake where both parties operated under the mistaken belief that a leaseback right provided for in the contract (that is, a provision in the contract that the buyer would lease the property to the seller following the sale) was lawful. The parties did not know that a state statute invalidated such leasebacks. Other courts, motivated by the rationale that parties are expected to know the law (embodied in the well-known maxim, "ignorance of the law is no excuse"), have refused to treat a mistake as to the law as a basis for relief under the doctrine of mistake. For example, the court adopted this approach in *Burggraff v. Baum*, 720 A.2d 1167 (Me. 1998), which involved a sale of seafront property. The buyers and seller both believed, based on the buyers' research of the applicable zoning ordinance, that the buyers would be able to build a cabin on the property 75 feet from the water. The buyers had erred in their research. After the sale, they discovered that they had overlooked another statute that required a 250-foot setback from the water. Upon discovering the error, the buyers sought rescission.

The court refused relief on the grounds that the mistake related to law, not fact, and the parties are presumed to know the law.[2] *See also Janusz v. Gilliam,* 947 A.2d 560 (Md. App. 2008), in which the court refused to allow avoidance of a divorce settlement agreement on the ground of mistake where the spouses had entered the agreement in the erroneous belief that federal regulations entitled the wife to a survivor's annuity under the husband's pension plan.

Even if a court does treat an error of law as a mistake of fact, the maxim "ignorance of the law is no excuse" could still have an impact on the right of avoidance. The court might deny avoidance because the party claiming avoidance should have known the law and therefore bore the risk of mistake. (Risk allocation is discussed in sections 15.3 and 15.4.)

e. Situations That Appear to Call for the Application of Mistake Doctrine May Be More Properly Treated as a Breach of a Contractual Commitment

This is not so much a new point as a reinforcement of two prior observations that merit strong emphasis: It has already been noted that many mistakes in the lay sense do not constitute mistakes in the legal sense, and that risk allocation is a crucial consideration in deciding whether a mistake should be grounds for relief. A party's responsibility for her own judgments and the parties' understanding about risk allocation may mean that a mistake does not call for application of mistake doctrine, but should be treated as the breach of a contractual promise (that is, a warranty) or as a misrepresentation.

For example, a buyer purchases a painting for $5 million, based on the seller's claim that it is a genuine Van Gogh. It turns out to be a forgery. Only by carefully examining the facts of the transaction and weighing the closely related issues of judgment and risk allocation can we decide which party must be assigned responsibility for the problem. Some of the questions to consider would be: Did the seller knowingly or unwittingly give false information to the buyer or conceal facts? If so, there may be a misrepresentation. Did the seller promise that this was a genuine Van Gogh? If so, there may be a breach of warranty. Was this an uncertain fact on which both parties gambled? If so, the buyer may be stuck with the bad judgment. Was the genuineness assumed without question by the parties, so that it was a basic premise of the contract? If so, maybe an actionable mistake was made.

---

2. The opinion made an interesting distinction. The court suggested that had the parties not known that any regulation existed, this ignorance might have been a mistake of fact. But once they knew that that the setback was regulated and they erred as to the law's provisions, this was a mistake of law. This suggests that the court may have treated complete ignorance of the law as grounds for mistake, but not an error in legal research.

The characterization is important, because the remedies are very different, ranging from no remedy at all to rescission for mistake or innocent misrepresentation, to expectation damages for breach of warranty, to expectation damages plus possible punitive damages for fraud.

§15.2.2 Mutual and Unilateral Mistake

Established doctrine draws a distinction between mutual mistake, in which the error is shared by both parties, and the unilateral mistake of only one of the parties. This sounds like a simple distinction, but it can be quite subtle and elusive. This is because a mistake is only mutual if it relates to a factual assumption so shared by the parties, that it is a joint premise of their bargain. A mistake is unilateral, not only in the obvious case where one party knows the true facts and the other does not, but also where both parties may be unaware of the truth, yet the fact in issue affects the decision of only one of the parties and is of no interest or relevance to the other. In other words, although neither knows the truth, the erroneous fact is a basic assumption of only one of the parties because the other is neutral on it. This means that the distinction between mutual and unilateral mistake is not necessarily merely a matter of deciding whether one or both parties had been misinformed. The contract must be interpreted in context to decide if it was built around the mutual assumption that a particular fact was true.

The relativity of the distinction may be illustrated by a couple of examples: A builder buys some land from a person claiming to be the owner of the land. The builder intends to build a house on it for resale. He makes a contract with an earthmover to clear and excavate the land. Immediately afterwards, and before any work is started, the builder discovers that the seller did not have title to the land. The builder therefore does not own it and cannot build on it. It could be said that the builder and earthmover entered their contract under the mutual mistake of fact that the builder owned the land. That is, the builder's ownership was a shared basic assumption of the contract. However, the better view is that the earthmover does not care who owns the property, and any mistake as to the existence of valid title is purely the builder's affair. This being so, the mistake is properly treated as unilateral on the builder's part.

Assume that the mistake does not relate to the ownership of the property. Instead, the earthmover made an arithmetical error in calculating the number of hours required to perform the excavation and accordingly submitted a bid 25 percent lower than its actual cost of doing the work. The builder, not realizing the error, accepts the earthmover's figure. Again, one could see this as a mutual erroneous assumption that the earthmover's calculations are correct. However, it is better treated as a unilateral error of the excavator. See also *Bert Allen Toyota, Inc. v. Grasz*, 909

So. 2d 763 (Miss. App. 2005) in which a car dealer's computer miscalculated the price of the car, resulting in a sale price $2,000 lower than it should have been. The dealer argued that this was a mutual mistake because both parties relied on the erroneous price calculated by the computer. The court disagreed. The buyer was interested only in the bottom line and the miscalculation that led to the final price was the dealer's unilateral mistake. These examples are not meant to suggest that there is a firm rule for distinguishing mutual and unilateral mistake. In each case the conclusion is based on assessing the relationship of the mistaken fact to the basis of the contract.

The decision on whether or not relief should be granted for the mistake is based on the considerations discussed in the following sections. When you read them you will find that unilateral and mutual mistake involve essentially the same basic inquiry—that is, their elements are the same in many respects. However, in addition to sharing the elements of mutual mistake, unilateral mistake has its own further prerequisites. This is because a party who has made a unilateral mistake must make a stronger case for relief by demonstrating that the unfairness of enforcing the contract outweighs the need to protect the reasonable reliance of the other party.

In other words, unilateral mistake calls for a stronger focus on the relative equities of enforcement or nonenforcement. In a sense, this is an additional element but, as you will see, it follows quite logically from and is really inherent in the elements held in common with mutual mistake. Thus, the difference between the elements of mutual and unilateral mistake is largely a matter of emphasis and focus. This is just as well, considering that it is sometimes difficult to decide if the error was a shared assumption or purely one-sided. Misclassification need not be fatally wrong if the elements are properly analyzed because, in the end, both types of mistake must be resolved by deciding who should suffer the consequences of the error, in light of the factual indications of contractual intent and the surrounding equities.

§15.3 THE ELEMENTS OF MUTUAL MISTAKE

According to Restatement, Second, §152 (read with §§151 and 154), a mutual mistake is avoidable by the adversely affected party if the following prerequisites are satisfied:

1. *At the time of contracting, the parties must have shared an error of fact.* As noted already, a mistake in the legal sense is an error relating to a fact. The error must be made at the time of contracting and it must relate

to a state of affairs existing at the time, rather than one predicted to occur in the future.

2. *The erroneous fact was a basic assumption on which the contract was made.* The mistaken fact must be so fundamental to the shared intent and purpose of both parties that it is reasonable to conclude that they would not have made the contract at all or on the present terms had they known the truth. For example, the seller sold a lakefront lot to the buyer for $500,000. The price was that high because this is a prime waterfront location surrounded by expensive homes in a popular vacation area. The seller knew that the buyer intended to build a luxury home on the lot and both parties believed that the lot was suitable for building. Neither party knew at the time of contracting that the lot is on porous and unstable land and it cannot support a building. Given the parties' shared understanding of the purpose of the sale, the mistake is the basis of the bargain.

3. *The mistake must have a material effect on the agreed exchange of performances.* This sounds like a repetition of the prior element, because it would seem to follow that an erroneous basic assumption of the contract will inevitably have a material effect on the exchange. This is often true, but the focus of these elements is different. The test of basic assumption examines the aggrieved party's motivation, as shared with the other party, but materiality calls for an assessment of the mistake's impact on the balance of the exchange to see if it substantially deprived the adversely affected party of the value expected. Restatement, Second, §152, Comment c, suggests that the test is whether the error creates an overall imbalance between the parties by making the exchange less desirable to the adversely affected party and more advantageous to the other. This element thus contains a component of equitable balancing, in which the court examines the effect of the mistake on both the parties to decide the fairness of enforcing the contract despite the mistake.

Sometimes, the materiality of the effect on the exchange is obvious. For example, if the land in the above illustration is worth only $25,000 because it cannot support a building, the contract price of $500,000 reflects the contrary erroneous belief. The mistake not only forms the basis of the bargain but it also has a material effect on the exchange. However, the interaction between the basis of the bargain and materiality could be more subtle. Say that the lakefront location is so desirable that the land can most likely be resold to a campground operator for $500,000 despite its unsuitability for building. The evaluation of materiality is more difficult, and it could lead to a different conclusion. Although the mistake still forms the basis of the bargain, the mistake might not have a material effect on the exchange because it did not affect the market value of the property. This is not to say that the effect of the mistake is unquestionably immaterial. After all, the buyer is deprived of the benefit of using the property as contemplated. However, this illustration shows that the considerations taken into account to decide materiality are different from those relating to the parties' basic assumption and could lead to a different conclusion.

4. *The adversely affected party must not have borne the risk of the mistake.* Although this question is commonly phrased so as to focus on the assumption of risk by the adversely affected party, the issue is to allocate the risk of error to one party or the other. There is no such thing as a neutral decision on risk because a determination that one party did not bear the risk inevitably means that the other did. (Although it is possible to find that the parties shared the risk, this does not seem to happen very often.) The allocation of risk is often the dispositive element in mistake cases. Despite everything that has been said up to now, and no matter how serious the error, if the adversely affected party bore the risk of mistake, there can be no avoidance of the contract.

How can one tell who assumed the risk of the mistake? The first place to turn for an answer to this question is the contract itself. The resolution is clearest if the contract expressly addresses the risk. Risk allocation is clear if the contract for the sale of the lakeside lot states, "While the seller believes that the lot is suitable for building, he neither represents nor warrants that this belief is correct. The buyer may not terminate this contract if this belief proves to be wrong." Even if the contract is not that clear, risk allocation may be inferred from the contract terms in context by the usual process of interpretation or construction. As always, factual interpretation is attempted first, but if no evidence of actual agreement can be found, the court must assign the risk in the way most reasonable under the circumstances, based on general expectations and practices in the market or community. That is, the court must resolve the question by construction, determining how the parties would reasonably have allocated the risk, had they thought of the issue.

Many different factors may come into play in the process of construing risk allocation. If a pertinent commercial practice exists, it is a strong indicator of the parties' reasonable expectation or risk. For example, it would be useful to know if buyers of land normally investigate its suitability for building. If so, this buyer's failure to investigate would be an assumption of the risk of error. Similarly, if loss or liability can be insured against in transactions of this type, it would be helpful to know which party normally takes out the policy. In some cases, there may be a legal rule that dictates or suggests risk allocation in the absence of contrary agreement. For example, the rule of *caveat emptor* (buyer beware) usually applies to a sale of real estate, so the buyer bears the risk of any defect in the property in the absence of an express warranty by the seller.

§15.4 THE ELEMENTS OF UNILATERAL MISTAKE

The elements of unilateral mistake are set out in Restatement, Second, §153. Relief for unilateral mistake has basically the same prerequisites as mutual mistake, with some variations to take account of the fact that the parties do not share the erroneous basic assumption. In addition, because the error affected the assent of only one of the parties, the protection of the reliance interest of the other party is emphasized more strongly. Therefore, unilateral mistake is grounds for relief only if the equities favoring release of the mistaken party outweigh the need to uphold the reasonable expectations of the nonmistaken party. (As noted in section 15.2.2, the elements of mutual mistake also take into account the reliance interests of the party against whom avoidance is sought, so this balancing of the equities is a matter of stronger emphasis, rather than an element unique to unilateral mistake.)

The elements for unilateral mistake are:

1. *The error concerns a fact.* This requirement is no different from mutual mistake.
2. *The fact is a basic assumption on which the mistaken party made the contract.* Of course, we are concerned here not with a shared assumption, but with the individual motive of only one of the parties, which has not necessarily been communicated to the other. Nevertheless, the subjectivity of this requirement is not a threat to the reliance interest of the other party, which is taken care of by the other elements.
3. *The mistake has a material effect on the exchange, adverse to the mistaken party.* As with mutual mistake, this element concerns the mistake's objectively determinable impact on the exchange of values.
4. *The mistaken party must not bear the risk of the mistake.* The allocation of risk involves issues of interpretation and construction the same as those in mutual mistake, but this element has a particular twist in unilateral mistake cases because the mistake may have resulted solely from the negligence of the mistaken party. If negligence automatically placed the risk of error on the mistaken party, unilateral mistake would rarely permit avoidance. Courts recognize this and tolerate some degree of negligence, provided that the other elements are satisfied. However, the presence and degree of negligence is relevant to the

decision on whether to grant relief. For example, in *Bert Allen Toyota, Inc. v. Grasz*, cited in section 15.2.2, the court refused the dealer's claim for avoidance of the contract where its computer miscalculated the price. The court found that the dealer failed to exercise reasonable care when it did not check the computer's calculations, especially because it was aware that the computer had made errors before. The more serious the degree of negligence — such as gross negligence, recklessness, or dereliction of a duty owed to the other party — the greater the likelihood that the court will find that the risk of mistake should be borne by the party who could have avoided the error by taking greater care. Quite apart from its role in the element of risk allocation, the carelessness of the mistaken party could have an impact on the balance of the equities discussed below. That is, even if there has not been enough sloppiness or serious negligence to dispose of the case on the question of risk allocation, the mistaken party's fault could tip the balance in favor of the other party.

5. *The equities must favor relief for the mistake.* While equitable balancing takes into account factors beyond the first four elements, it obviously cannot be performed in isolation from them. In other words, the degree to which the first four elements are satisfied forms a vital component in the overall balance. Beyond this, the court also balances the impact of avoidance on the parties. It weighs the hardship that enforcement would have on the mistaken party against the hardship of avoidance on the other party. These equitable considerations are therefore quite far ranging. They take into account not only relative innocence and fault, but also the economic consequences of avoidance on each of the parties.

Therefore, the balance weighs most heavily in favor of the nonmistaken party when the mistake involved a degree of negligence by the other, the nonmistaken party had no reason to realize the mistake, and took action in reliance on the contract. In such a situation, her good faith reliance on the apparent assent of the mistaken party has led her to incur some commitment or expense, so that avoidance would go beyond depriving her of the good bargain, but would actually cause her loss. The protection of good faith reliance is the central issue, but the principle may be articulated in different ways — for example, it is sometimes expressed as a rule to the effect that a contract cannot be avoided for unilateral mistake unless the innocent nonmistaken party can be restored to the status quo. It is sometimes stated that relief should be denied unless the mistaken party promptly notifies the other upon becoming aware of the error. This rule is aimed at ameliorating any prejudicial reliance on the mistake, and it also reflects another factor in the balance — the degree of diligence exercised by the mistaken party. At the other end of the scale, if the nonmistaken party realized the error and kept quiet in order to jump at the bargain, or worse, if the nonmistaken party actually caused the error, her reliance interest is at its weakest. Between these extremes, there are countless variations in relative fault and hardship, so that the balance may be harder to find.

To make this more concrete, refer back to *Drennan v. Star Paving*, 333 P.2d 757 (Cal. 1958), which we discussed in section 8.11 in relation to the application of promissory estoppel to validate and option. In *Drennan*, a subcontractor made an error in its bid to the prime contractor; the prime contractor then used that bid in calculating its own bid to the owner. After the owner accepted the prime contractor's bid, and the prime contractor was committed to the owner, the subcontractor discovered the error and attempted to revoke its own bid. In section 8.11 we saw that the court applied the doctrine of promissory estoppel to make the subcontractor's bid irrevocable even though it did not qualify as option with consideration and the prime contractor had not accepted it before attempted revocation. Because the bid was irrevocable, acceptance by the prime contractor within a reasonable time created a contract with the subcontractor. Viewed in the present context, you can see that this situation also presents an issue of unilateral mistake, which was raised as an alternative argument by the subcontractor in *Drennan*. The subcontractor argued that even if a contract was created by the process of offer and acceptance, it should be able to avoid the contract on the grounds that it made an error in compiling the bid. The court rejected this argument and refused relief to the subcontractor for unilateral mistake. The error was caused by the subcontractor's negligence, and because there was a considerable variation in bids for the work, the prime contractor had no reason to suspect that the subcontractor's low bid was a result of error. The prime contractor had committed itself to the owner on the strength of the bid, and the equities favored leaving the loss with the subcontractor. In *Drennan*, the balance of the relative hardship on the parties was about even. However, the result could have been different if, say, the prime contractor had such a good profit margin in its contract with the owner that the extra cost of the subcontract could have been absorbed without making the prime contract unprofitable, but the subcontractor was in such perilous financial circumstances that the loss on this job might have put it out of business.

§15.5 RELIEF FOR MISTAKE

§15.5.1 Avoidance and Restitution

The principal remedy for mistake is avoidance of the contract. If the mistake is unilateral, avoidance will be sought by the party who made the mistake. If the mistake is mutual, both parties made the mistake. The party seeking avoidance will be the one who is adversely affected by the mistake. Avoidance brings the contract to an end and both parties must restore any benefit (or its value) resulting from performance that was rendered prior to termination. Value is normally based on the market worth of the property or services (of which the contract value may be probative evidence). However, the court has some discretion in determining the basis of valuation, and it may use some other measure appropriate under the circumstances. For example, if the party who conferred the benefit was more to blame for the mistake, the value of consumed goods or services could be confined to the actual ultimate economic benefit enjoyed by the other party.

§15.5.2 Other Relief, Including Reformation

Although avoidance and mutual restitution is the standard and common remedy for mistake, the equitable derivation of mistake doctrine gives the court some flexibility in remedy, so that it could provide relief other than avoidance and restitution if the equities so dictate. For example, avoidance on the grounds of unilateral mistake could be ordered subject to the payment of reliance expenses designed to restore the nonmistaken party to the status quo.

In relatively rare cases, the court may keep the contract in force with an adjustment to its terms to counter the effect of the mistake. In the context of mistake, this remedy is known as reformation — that is, the court reforms the agreement to negate the effect of the mistake. As explained in section 15.6, reformation is more commonly used where the parties have not made a mistake of fact, but have made an error in recording the terms of their agreement. However, it is sometimes an appropriate exercise of the court's equitable discretion to use this remedy to alter the terms of the agreement so as to counteract a mistake of fact. Reformation is not a common remedy for mistake, and courts use it sparingly. It is not an appropriate remedy if the mistake is so fundamental that reformation would alter the entire character of the transaction or would defeat the contract's basic purpose. It is also seldom the best solution if the contract is entirely executory, and neither party performed or otherwise relied on it before the mistake was discovered.

However, in some cases, if avoidance would be disruptive and the error relates to an aspect of the contract that can be adjusted (say to a price calculation), an alteration of terms may be a fair remedy. For example, the court did reform the contract's price term in *Aluminum Company of America v. Essex Group, Inc.*, 499 F. Supp. 53 (W.D. Pa. 1980).[3] The parties had made a mutual mistake in adopting a particular pricing formula, believing it to be an accurate predictor of Alcoa's costs. It turned out not to be, and the price payable under the formula fell far short of Alcoa's cost of performance. The court felt that it would be unfair to allow Alcoa to avoid the contract as a whole because this would completely deprive Essex of its bargain and would give Alcoa the windfall of full release from its contractual commitment. It therefore adjusted the price term to give Alcoa a profit that accorded with the parties' reasonable expectations.

§15.6 MISTAKE IN TRANSCRIPTION

§15.6.1 Reformation to Correct Mistakes in Transcription

A mistake may relate, not to a factual premise of the agreement, but to the way in which the agreement is expressed in writing. For example, a memorandum of agreement reflects the price of a piece of land as $280,000. The buyer contends that the parties had orally agreed to a price of $250,000, and that the written price is a typographical error not noticed by the parties when signing the document. If the parties later recognize that an error occurred in transcription and they act honestly, the problem can be disposed of simply by amending the writing by agreement. However, the party who benefits from the error may claim (whether genuinely or disingenuously) that the writing is correct. If so, the other party can seek the equity-based remedy of reformation to have the court correct the writing so that it accurately reflects what was agreed. This remedy involves both a declaration by the court that the contract is on terms other than reflected in the writing, and enforcement on those terms.

A mistake in transcription is completely different in nature from a mistake of fact, discussed in the prior sections. The "fact" that is wrong did not motivate the transaction, but is in the written record of the transaction. The problem is not that the manifestation is based on a faulty

---

3. In the *Alcoa* case, the facts were ambiguous enough to be treated either under mistake or impracticability doctrine. This is explained in section 15.7.1, which contains a fuller account of the facts of the case. It is also discussed in section 15.7.3a.

premise, but that it incorrectly records the parties' agreement. Nevertheless, an error in expression has one thing in common with a mistake of underlying fact: In both cases one of the parties seeks to avoid the apparent meaning of a manifestation of assent by showing that it was induced by error. In the case of mistake as to an underlying fact, the goal is to negate assent and avoid the contract. When the mistake is in transcription, the desired relief is to have the writing changed to reflect what was actually agreed. It must be stressed that the goal of reformation in this situation is to correct the contract so that it reflects what was actually agreed, not to adjust or rewrite its terms. For example, in Sikora v. Vanderploeg, 212 S.W.3d 277 (Tenn. App. 2006), Sikora bought a chiropractic practice from Vanderploeg. Prior to the sale, the seller had a detailed financial report prepared, which included a disclosure of the earnings of the practice in the seven months prior to the sale. The buyer was given a copy of this financial report. The agreement of sale warranted the accuracy of the earnings stated in the report. However, in preparing the agreement of sale, the buyer's attorney made an error in drafting the warranty, which stated that the earnings were for a six-month period, not for seven months. After the buyer took over the practice, it deteriorated and its earnings declined. The buyer sued the seller, claiming that the contract misstated the presale earnings. The court held that since both parties intended the agreement to reflect the earnings in the report, and both had overlooked the error in the agreement, there was a mutual mistake in expression. The court therefore reformed the agreement, defeating the buyer's claim that the agreement falsely recited presale earnings.

A court will not reform a contract unless it is clear that both parties erroneously believed that the memorial of agreement embodied what they actually agreed. For example, in Silsbe v. Houston Levee Industrial Park, LLC, 165 S.W.3d 260 (Tenn. App. 2005) the last day for exercising an option turned out to be a public holiday. As a result, the option holder could not exercise it on that day, and the grantor refused to accept the exercise of the option on the following day. The option holder sought reformation of the contract on the grounds that the parties had mistakenly selected a public holiday as the deadline for exercising the option. The court refused reformation. Although the parties may not have realized that the deadline fell on a public holiday, this was the date that they intended. The option therefore correctly reflected the parties' intent and reformation would have changed the contract rather than corrected an error in expression.

Because a signed writing is usually regarded as the most reliable evidence of what was agreed, a party seeking reformation has a difficult burden. He must convincingly show that an error was indeed made in recording the terms agreed, and must also plausibly explain why the error was made and why he failed to notice it when signing the document. Because the right to reformation cannot be shown except by recourse to evidence extrinsic to the writing, the parol evidence rule does not bar the introduction of evidence for the purpose of showing a mistake in transcription. If it did, the remedy of reformation could never be used.

§15.6.2 Reformation to Rectify the Unintended Legal Effect of Language

A question of reformation could also be presented when the parties chose words in their writing that do not have the legal effect intended. For example, a written contract for the sale of a car states that it is sold "as is." This is a legal term of art that means that it is sold without any warranties. However, the buyer contends that the parties were unaware of that meaning and did not intend it at all. The seller had added a number of accessories to the car, and the words "as is" were used merely to reflect their agreement that these accessories were to be included. This kind of error in recording the agreement is more complicated than a simple error in transcription, such as the incorrect recording of the price in the illustration in section 15.6.1, because the exact nature of the problem is less clear: If the dispute centers around what the parties meant by the term "as is," the determination of its meaning is a matter of interpretation, but if they agree on what they meant, but just used the wrong words to record that agreement, reformation is the more appropriate course. Also, it is difficult to distinguish this kind of erroneous expression of agreement from a mutual mistake of law. By wrongly using the phrase "as is" the parties do, in a sense, make a legal error — but that error relates not to what the law is, but to the legal meaning of the word-symbol used in the writing.

§15.7 IMPRACTICABILITY OF PERFORMANCE

§15.7.1 The Nature of Impracticability Doctrine, Contrasted with Mistake

Mistake concerns an error of fact in existence at the time of contracting, so fundamental to the premise of the contract that it precludes the formation of true assent. Impracticability applies when events following contract formation[4] are so different from the assumptions on which the contract

---

4. As noted in footnote 1, there are cases that have applied impracticability doctrine where the facts forming the basis for the claim of relief existed at the time of contracting. Such cases are better treated under the doctrine of mistake, and impracticality is more appropriately confined to supervening events. This discussion is therefore confined to supervening impracticability.

was based, that it would be unfair to hold the adversely affected party to its commitments. Although there are close affinities between mistake and impracticability, as you will see when comparing their elements, they have an important difference in scope and purpose. A mistake causes a defect in contract formation, permitting a party to be excused from accountability for a manifestation of assent. Impracticability has nothing to do with any problem in formation and presupposes that a binding contract was made. Rather, it is concerned with whether a post-formation change of circumstances has such a serious effect on the reasonable expectations of the parties that it should be allowed to excuse performance.

An example will illustrate this difference: The owner of a beachfront cabin makes a contract to sell it. The parties execute the contract at the owner's place of business in an inland city, many miles from the cabin. Unknown to both parties at the time of contracting, a tidal wave swept the cabin into the sea just a few hours before the contract was executed. They are mutually mistaken that the cabin exists. However, if the tidal wave hits after the contract was made, but before the seller transfers and delivers the cabin to the buyer, there was no error about its existence at the time of contracting. Instead, the issue is whether this supervening event should permit the seller to escape liability for failure to deliver the cabin as promised in the otherwise valid and enforceable contract.

Although it is usually easy to distinguish mistake from impracticability, sometimes the facts are ambiguous enough to make this unclear. The case could be resolved either on grounds of mistake or impracticability, depending on the court's perspective. For example, in *Aluminum Company of America*, cited in section 15.5.2, the parties entered into a long-term contract under which Alcoa would smelt alumina for Essex. The period of the contract was 16 years, with a five-year renewal option. The parties based their pricing formula on the Wholesale Price Index-Industrial Commodities (WPI). They used the WPI because it had reliably corresponded to Alcoa's costs of production in prior years and they assumed that it would continue to do so. However, a few years after the contract had been executed, electricity prices increased steeply because of the OPEC oil embargo and the higher cost of producing electricity in compliance with pollution regulations. As a result, the WPI ceased to be an accurate predictor of Alcoa's costs, which escalated to such an extent that its costs exceeded the contract price under the formula. Had Alcoa been obliged to perform the contract on its original terms, it would have lost about $60 million over the term of the contract. The court treated this as a case of mistake because it held that the parties erroneously assumed at the time of the contract that the WPI index was an appropriate standard for achieving the goal of measuring Alcoa's future costs. However, the court discussed impracticability as an alternative basis for relief because it recognized that the case fitted equally well into that doctrine — the oil embargo and tougher environmental regulations were supervening events that overturned a basic assumption of the contract.

The issue in an impracticability case is not whether the party can be forced to perform. Clearly, in the above example of the cabin, the seller cannot deliver it because it is flotsam on the ocean. The issue is whether, by failing to perform, he has breached the contract. If failure to perform is excused on grounds of impracticability, the seller of the cabin is not in breach and is therefore not liable to pay damages to the buyer. On the facts of this example, impracticability would completely excuse the seller's performance. It follows, of course, that the buyer would not be required to perform either, so the effect of impracticability is to terminate the contract[5]. If either party has partly performed before this (say, for example, that the buyer made a down payment), the benefit of that performance must be restored under principles of unjust enrichment.

§15.7.2 The Early Form of the Doctrine: Impossibility of Performance

In older common law, once a contract had been made, the parties were absolutely bound and remained committed even if a change in circumstances made it extremely difficult or even impossible for one of them to perform. (As just noted, the party was not expected to work a miracle by performing the impossible, but the failure to perform was not excused by the supervening event and was a breach giving rise to a damages claim.) By the mid-nineteenth century, the harshness of this rule was ameliorated by judicial recognition of the doctrine of impossibility of performance. In its original form, as articulated by the English case of *Taylor v. Caldwell*, 122 Eng. Rep. 309 (Queens Bench, 1863), the doctrine was quite narrow: If, when making the contract, the parties reasonably contemplated that its performance was dependent on the continued existence of a person or thing, the post-formation death of the person or destruction of the thing, not caused by the fault of the party seeking relief, would excuse performance by that party, and hence, also the return performance, resulting in termination of the contract without liability for breach.

In *Taylor*, the contract was for the hire of a music hall that burned down after the contract was made and before the time for performance. Although the obligation to provide the hall was not qualified by any express term of

---

5. In the example of the cabin, its destruction materially affected the seller's performance, and therefore results in complete termination of the contract. However, it could happen that a supervening event has a less fundamental effect, so that performance can still be rendered, but not on the exact terms agreed. In such a case, impracticability might excuse the shortfall in performance, but might not result in complete termination of the contract.

the contract, the court found the continuing existence of the hall to have been a basic assumption of the contract. This led to the legal implication of a term that the destruction of the hall excused performance. As originally formulated, the defense of impossibility was confined to situations in which the change of circumstances made the contract objectively impossible to perform. That is, the event must have completely defeated the ability to deliver the performance, not only by this party, but by a reasonable person in his position. Say, for example, that the fire merely damaged the music hall. If a reasonable owner could have restored it sufficiently in time for the performance, this owner could not claim the defense of impossibility merely because he did not have the resources or inclination to do so.

§15.7.3 The Contemporary Doctrine of Impracticability of Performance

During the course of the twentieth century, the doctrine of impossibility came to be perceived as too restricted. There are situations in which events do not make performance absolutely impossible, yet they place such a great and unexpected burden on the party that fairness demands relief. As a result, the scope of the doctrine has broadened and has been renamed "impracticability" to reflect this change. As in so many other areas of contract law, a strong impetus for change in the doctrine came from the UCC. Section 2.615 enacted the broader concept of impracticability as the standard for sales of goods, and this has been influential in reinforcing change in common law doctrine too. By embracing a formulation based on the UCC, Restatement, Second, §§261 to 272 reinforce the common law's movement away from the stricter impossibility standard. There are a number of differences between UCC §2.615 and the provisions of the Restatement, Second, but the basic concepts are the same. This discussion focuses on general principles applicable to both.

If all of its elements are established, the excuse of impracticability is available to the party who is adversely affected by the change in circumstances. (In a sale of goods, UCC §2.615 assumes that it will always be the seller who claims impracticability, but this need not necessarily be so, and courts have recognized that a buyer can use the excuse in appropriate circumstances.) Although the following discussion identifies and discusses these elements separately, the defense of impracticability is better understood if one recognizes that they are very much interwoven and that the facts affecting one are often relevant to the others. All the elements must be satisfied for the defense to be available. As in mistake, risk allocation is usually the predominant and pervasive consideration. We now examine each of the elements:

a. After the Contract Was Made, an Event Occurred, the Nonoccurrence of Which Was a Basic Assumption of the Contract

This concept is very much like its equivalent element in mistake doctrine, except that the basic assumption relates not to an existing but to a future state of affairs. The idea here is that when the parties entered the contract they expressly or impliedly made assumptions about the future course of events and these assumptions were a central motivation of the contract. Whether or not a basic assumption is articulated, it must be patent enough from the circumstances and the apparent purpose of the contract that it is reasonable to conclude that the parties must have shared it.

Having entered the contract on this basic assumption, the parties are then faced with an event so contrary to the assumption that it changes the very basis of the exchange. Comment 1 to UCC §2.615 describes this occurrence as an "unforeseen supervening circumstance not within the contemplation of the parties at the time of contracting." This suggests that the event must be so unexpected that the parties did not think of it at the time of contracting, or if they did, that they did not consider it to be a realistic likelihood.

The comment uses the word "unforeseen," which must be distinguished from "unforeseeable." An event is unforeseen by the parties if they themselves did not contemplate it as a real likelihood. That is, although it could be imagined, the parties did not expect it to happen and contracted on the assumption that it would not. It may be a possibility, but is not treated by the parties as a probability. An event is unforeseeable if it could not have been conceived of by a reasonable person. To require unforeseeability would impose too stringent a test, making the defense of impracticability available only when the supervening event is beyond human experience. For example, it is unforeseeable that a music hall could be demolished by a rampaging dinosaur or other large beast,[6] but its destruction by fire is certainly within the range of possibility. Therefore, fire was foreseeable at the time of contracting, but it was not foreseen by the parties if, under all the circumstances, it is shown that they did not think of it at all or, even if one or both may have realized the possibility, it was not considered a strong enough likelihood to be raised and dealt with as a contingency. Of course, the fact that the event was unforeseen does not, on its own, mean that the defense of impracticability will succeed. This is only the first of the elements that must be satisfied. Often, even though the nonoccurrence of the event was a basic assumption of the contract, the risk of the occurrence may have been impliedly assumed by the party claiming impracticality. That is, if the parties foresaw the likelihood of the event, they probably allocated the risk

---

6. Of course, the fact that I (and several talented "B" movie creators) have contemplated this possibility may mean that it is indeed foreseeable.

of its happening (expressly or impliedly) in the contract. However, even if they did not foresee it, commercial practice or other surrounding circumstances may give rise to an implication of risk assumption.

Impracticability arises from the occurrence of an event, so we must identify what types of happening might constitute an event. Again, there is an analogy to mistake, in that an event is a factual situation, albeit one that arises after the contract. Most occurrences external to the contract qualify as events: war, a natural disaster, a strike, and so on. A change in the law or government regulation is also an event. Therefore, if the law changes to prohibit a performance that was lawful at the time of contracting, the change in the law defeats a basic assumption of the contract. UCC §2.615(a) and Restatement, Second, §264 expressly recognize this by providing that good faith compliance with governmental regulation excuses performance, even if the regulation is later found to be invalid. Say, for example, that the music hall did not burn down, but shortly after the contract was made, the city council strengthened its public safety regulations so that the hall no longer satisfied them and cannot be lawfully let for public performances. If the council's action was unexpected and was given no advance publicity, this would be an unforeseen contingency that defeats the basic assumption that the hall could be used lawfully for the purpose of the contract. This example highlights the development of the law from impossibility to impracticability. Although it would still be possible for the lessor to make the hall available and for the buyer to pay the rent, the contract is made impracticable because its basic assumption that the performance would be lawful has been overturned.[7]

A change in market conditions is generally not regarded as a contingency beyond the contemplation of the parties because the very purpose of setting a price or committing to a future delivery of goods or services is based on the possibility that prices or demand may change. Therefore, the basic assumption of most contracts is not that the market will remain constant, but that it might change. For example, in *Ferguson v. Ferguson*, 54 So. 3d 553 (Fla. App. 2011), the parties entered into a divorce settlement agreement under which the husband kept the marital home. In exchange, he agreed to refinance it and to pay the wife $185,000. Until that payment was made, the wife and child had the right to reside in the house. Shortly after the agreement was executed, home prices in Florida plunged. The husband claimed that because of this downturn in the market, he had not been able to

---

7. In anticipation of the discussion in section 15.8, it is also worth pointing out that these facts would support an argument that the purpose of the contract has been frustrated: Although the lessor can still deliver possession of the hall and the lessee can still pay the rent, the purpose of the hiring — the use of the hall for a public concert — has been negated by the new regulations. This illustrates the observation in section 15.8 that impracticality is broad enough to cover most, if not all, situations that would have required a separate doctrine of frustration in earlier law.

refinance the house, and it had therefore become impracticable to make payment to the wife. He sought to evict the wife, sell the house, and give her half the net sale proceeds. The court held that the impracticability doctrine did not excuse the husband from performing the settlement agreement as promised by paying the wife $185,000. The Florida real estate market is subject to periodic downward adjustment, and a market decline is not an unanticipated circumstance in a market-based economy.

This does not mean that a market disruption could never be grounds for claiming impracticability. The basic assumption of any particular contract is a factual question. It is therefore possible that a constant market was assumed in a contract, or even if not, that the market variation results from a disruption which causes changes way beyond reasonable expectations. This is particularly so if some unexpected calamity, such as a sudden war, embargo, or natural disaster is the cause of the market changes. This has happened a number of times, and there are cases arising from events such as the Suez crisis of the 1950s (when Egypt blocked the canal, making it impracticable for shipping companies to use it), the Vietnam War, and the OPEC oil embargo of the 1970s, in which the supplier of a commodity or service has claimed impracticability based on greatly added expense or burdens on performance caused by the crisis. In some of the cases, the international disturbance was found to render performance impracticable, but in others, the defense did not succeed, either because the disruption was foreseen by the parties or because one of the other elements of the defense (such as extreme hardship or risk allocation) was not satisfied.

Aluminum Company of America, discussed in sections 15.5.2 and 15.7.1, is an example of a case in which the court did recognize that severe market disruption made a contract impracticable. As stated in section 15.7.1, the parties entered into a long-term contract under which Alcoa smelted alumina for Essex. After the contract had been executed, the contract price to be paid to Alcoa for processing the alumina, calculated under the contract's WPI-based pricing formula, fell significantly below Alcoa's costs as a result of escalating electricity costs caused by the OPEC oil embargo and stricter government regulations. Although the court resolved the case in favor of Alcoa on the basis of mistake, it discussed impracticability as an alternative basis for relief. It concluded that the increase in electricity costs and the scale of the resulting loss were of such dramatic proportions that they were not foreseen by the parties and went beyond the level of risk that Alcoa had assumed.

b. The Effect of the Event Is to Render the Party's Performance "Impracticable" — That Is, Unduly Burdensome

A loss in certainty is the price paid for the law's movement away from the more discernible standard of impossibility, toward the vaguer and more relative concept of impracticability. Once a party no longer has to establish that performance is objectively incapable of being rendered, we are left with the task of deciding how extensively the performance must have changed to qualify as impracticable. If impracticability merely required a showing of inconvenience, lack of profitability, or the loss of a better opportunity, it would be too easy for a party to escape a contract that turns out to be disadvantageous because of a change in the market or commercial environment. Therefore, relief is only appropriate if the change is extreme or very burdensome. In a sense, this requirement is similar to the element of materiality in mistake. The event must have such a severe impact on the performance that it cannot be rendered without great loss, risk, or other hardship. Unfortunately, this is as vague as it sounds, but it necessarily must be so, because impracticality is relative and must be assessed on all the facts of the case.

In the easiest case, an event that creates objective impossibility also renders the performance impracticable, because the wider doctrine includes cases that would have satisfied the narrower standard. Therefore, if the parties contemplated the rental of a specific music hall, the destruction of the hall makes performance impossible and hence also impracticable. However, as the facts move beyond this clearer case, the determination becomes more difficult. Say that the music hall did not burn down, but after the contract was made, the premium payable by the lessor for liability insurance increased tenfold because of a large number of theater fires in the region over the last year. As a result, if the lessor is to permit use of the premises by the public, he must pay a huge insurance premium that will exceed the earnings he will make from renting the hall. Both parties can still perform — the lessor can make the hall available and the lessee can pay the rent — but the increase in insurance rates has imposed a financial burden (or a massive risk of liability, if the policy is not renewed) on the lessor that may make its performance impracticable.

Consider another example: The hall does burn down, but there is another hall in the same block owned by a competitor of the lessor. The hall is about the same size, is equally suitable for the performance, and it is available for the night of the concert. The lessee contends that the lessor's performance is therefore still possible, because there is nothing in the contract that makes the exact identity of the hall material, and the lessor can still provide appropriate premises by hiring the second hall and making it available to the lessee as a substitute for the destroyed hall. The problem is that the owner of the surviving hall demands a rental from the lessor far higher than that which the lessor is to be paid by the lessee under the contract, so the lessor will lose money by doing this (or by paying the rental difference to the lessee as damages if he refuses). If the lessee's contention is correct and the identity of the hall was not a central term of the contract, the lessor's performance is not impossible, so the question becomes whether the loss to be incurred in finding a substitute renders it sufficiently burdensome to constitute impracticability.

There is no definitive answer to the question in these cases. However, they point to the focus of the inquiry — the economic impact of the unforeseen supervening event. A prospective loss that is not negligible could satisfy this element. The magnitude and effect of the loss is obviously of crucial significance, and a huge loss that threatens the lessee's financial survival is more likely to be seen as making the performance impracticable, than a manageable smaller loss. This may make it sound as if the defense of impracticability can be easily invoked whenever a serious prospective loss is shown. But remember that this element is only one of several that must be satisfied, and proof of the most devastating loss is not enough to assure relief if the other elements are not also present.

c. The Party Seeking Relief Was Not at Fault in Causing the Occurrence

A person should not be able to take advantage of his own wrongful or negligent act, and a party who disables himself from performing, or makes performance more difficult, cannot expect to be excused from liability. Thus, the lessor of the music hall would have a nerve claiming impracticability if he deliberately set the fire. Similarly, a person cannot be excused from liability just because it turns out that he is incompetent and cannot perform as promised. However, the issue of fault could be more subtle. Should the lessor be denied relief if the fire was caused by an antiquated and improperly maintained electrical system in the music hall? In less obvious cases, the degree to which the party was in some way responsible for his troubles, or could have surmounted them with reasonable effort, is a relevant factor to be taken into account.

d. The Party Seeking Relief Must Not Have Borne the Risk of the Event Occurring

As with mistake, risk allocation is often the dispositive issue in impracticability cases. In many ways, the other elements foreshadow the question of risk allocation and seem to be no more than components of it. (In fact, as you may have sensed, the issue of risk allocation was constantly lurking in the discussion of the other elements and had to be restrained from jumping out.) The analysis of risk allocation is basically the same as for mistake: If the party adversely affected by the event had expressly or impliedly assumed the risk of its occurrence, the nonperformance cannot be excused even though all the other elements are satisfied.

The first place to look in determining risk allocation is the contract itself. If the parties realized that a particular future event could affect performance, the contract may have an express and specific term assigning risk. For example, a consignor of goods and a shipping company may contemplate the possibility that a war may break out along the route, requiring a diversion of the ship. If so, they may specifically state in the contract which party will bear the loss and expense of the diversion. Even if the parties do not have a particular contingency in mind, the contract may have a more general provision allocating the risk of disruptions or calamities. This is known as a force majeure clause. It may provide, for example, that the shipping company will not be responsible for any delay (or will have the right to charge for the cost of any diversion or delay) of the ship resulting from war, revolution, national disasters, governmental action, and so on.

Even in the absence of these more direct types of risk allocation clauses, the contract may impliedly place risk on a party by means of a provision such as a warranty, an undertaking to obtain insurance, or some other commitment from which the assumption of risk may be inferred. In fact, a term expressly allocating the risk of certain events to one party may give rise to the inference that the other assumed the risk of events not enumerated. For example, a clause states that the shipping company will not be responsible for delay caused by war, revolution, and governmental action. If the ship is seized by pirates and held hostage for ransom, this disruption is not apparently covered by the contract, so it could be inferred that the shipping company assumed this risk. It is good planning for the parties to consider potential risks and to provide for them clearly in the contract. This reduces the possibility of later disputes and litigation. Of course, as the last example suggests, no risk allocation provision is foolproof. It may fail to contemplate the actual event that occurs.

If the contract terms do not settle the issue, its context, including normal commercial practices and expectations, must be examined to decide where the risk should lie. For example, the facts in *Taylor v. Caldwell* satisfy all the other elements of impracticality. However, if we consider risk allocation, we could conclude that the case might come out differently if decided under the elements of impracticability. Under contemporary practice, the owner of property is the person who customarily insures it against fire and other damage. This suggests that in the absence of a contract term providing otherwise, risk of loss of the property should be borne by the owner, and not by the person who hires the premises for an event. Conversely, if the music hall did not burn down, but a sudden and unexpected recession resulted in abnormally small ticket sales, the lessee of the music hall would not likely be able to claim impracticability on this ground. Unless the contract provides otherwise, commercial practice in the entertainment industry probably places this risk on the promoter of the concert and will not allow him to foist it on the lessor of the hall by cancelling the booking if sales are weak.

§15.7.4 Relief for Impracticability

When impracticability fully defeats the feasibility of performance by a party, it is a complete defense to that party's failure to perform, relieving him of the duty of performance and liability for damages. Release of that party also discharges the contractual duties of the other. If any performance had been rendered by either party under the contract prior to the finding of impracticability, the benefit or its value must be returned, measured in accordance with the same restitutionary principles applicable to mistake.

If impracticability does not go to the entire basis of the contract, the court has the discretion to award relief short of fully excusing performance. This is recognized in general terms by Comments 6 and 7 to UCC §2.615, and in more detail by Restatement, Second, §§269 and 270. It may be more appropriate to adjust the terms of the contract, to excuse a portion of the performance (with any appropriate reciprocal reduction in counterperformance), or simply to permit a delay if this would enable the difficulties to be surmounted.

§15.8 FRUSTRATION OF PURPOSE

The doctrine of frustration of purpose developed as an extension of the original doctrine of impossibility. It was designed to provide relief when a party could not show that an unexpected supervening event rendered his performance impossible, yet it so destroyed the value of the transaction for him that the contract's underlying purpose was frustrated. The case responsible for this extension of the impossibility doctrine was *Krell v. Henry*, 2 K.B. 740 (1903). Krell owned a flat on the route to be taken by the coronation procession of Edward VII. Krell was out of the country and instructed his solicitor to attempt to let the premises while he was away. A sign was placed in the window stating that the flat was available to be let for viewing the procession. Henry responded to the sign and contracted to hire the flat on the two days of the coronation celebrations. The King became ill before the coronation and it was postponed, so Henry was left with no need for the premises on the days in question, and he did not use them. Krell sued him for the balance of the agreed rental. (Henry had made a down payment but apparently did not pursue a counterclaim for a refund of the deposit.) The court resolved the case by using an adaptation of the impossibility defense of *Taylor v. Caldwell*. Although the contract did not expressly state the purpose of the rental of the flat, both parties understood that Henry's sole purpose in making the contract was to view the coronation procession. This purpose was the very foundation of the contract. The postponement of the coronation was a supervening event that had not reasonably been contemplated by the parties at the time of contracting. Although it did not make

547

either party's performance impossible (Henry could still pay the agreed rent and Krell could give him possession of the flat), it so defeated the purpose of the contract that it should excuse Henry's performance.

Because contemporary doctrine has expanded beyond the confines of impossibility, there is probably no longer a need for a separate doctrine of frustration of purpose. Frustration could simply be treated as a class of impracticability and subsumed into that doctrine. Notwithstanding, these two closely linked defenses continue to coexist and are treated by courts (and by Restatement, Second, §265)[8] as separate but allied. It is therefore necessary to understand the difference between them. However, if you should find it difficult to decide whether a particular case involves impracticality or frustration, take comfort in the thought that misclassification probably will not make much difference in result. They involve essentially the same issues and lead to the same type of relief. The only difference between them lies in the sometimes subtle distinction between an event that makes a party's performance unduly burdensome, and one that makes it pointless.

Like impracticability, frustration is concerned with a post-formation event, the nonoccurrence of which was a basic assumption on which the contract was made. This event must not have been caused by the fault of the party whose purpose is frustrated, and that party must not have borne the risk of its occurrence. The essential difference lies in the effect of the event. It does not directly affect the performance of the adversely affected party by making it unduly burdensome. Rather, its impact is on the benefit reasonably expected by that party in exchange for the performance. The event so seriously affects the value or usefulness of that benefit that it frustrates the contract's central purpose for that party. This cannot be a secret or obscure purpose, because a party's private motivation is not relevant to the contract and cannot be the basis of disappointing the other party's reliance. Therefore, the purpose must be so patent and obvious to the other party that it can reasonably be regarded as the shared basis of the contract. *Krell v. Henry* remains one of the best illustrations of the elements of frustration. Note, however, that the court did not pay much attention to the crucial question of risk allocation. This was raised in a concurring opinion that queried whether Henry, the lessee, may have been the more appropriate party to bear the risk of the coronation's postponement. This is a fair question, and it again raises the point that when the contract does not itself provide for risk allocation, it is not always easy to know who should suffer the loss caused by the frustration. It is by no means self-evident that the court was right in imposing it on the lessor rather than the lessee.

---

8. UCC Article 2 has no doctrine of frustration of purpose, so cases of frustration in sales of goods must be dealt with either by resolving them as impracticability cases under §2.615, or by applying the common law doctrine of frustration of purpose. However, as noted before, because the basis of impracticability set out in §2.615 is broad enough to encompass frustration, it does not seem necessary to resort to common law.

The purpose of most commercial contracts is to make a profit. However, although it could be said that profit is the underlying purpose of a contract, this does not mean that a party can invoke the doctrine of frustration of purpose merely because the contract is no longer profitable to him as a result of events after contract formation. A party cannot so easily escape the performance of a contract that turns out to have been a bad deal. This distinction was made in *Karl Wendt Farm Equipment Co. v. International Harvester Co.*, 931 F.2d 1112 (6th Cir. 1991). Following losses resulting from a bad downturn in the farm equipment market, I.H. sold its farm equipment division and terminated a number of dealerships. The plaintiff, one of the terminated dealers, sued I.H. for breach of contract. I.H. raised the defense of frustration of purpose on the grounds that the loss of profit from adverse economic conditions frustrated the purpose of the contract. The court rejected the defense of frustration of purpose. It said the primary purpose of the contract was to sell farm equipment. This purpose could still be achieved, even if the desired goal of profitability could not be.[9]

§15.9 A TRANSNATIONAL PRESPECTIVE ON MISTAKE, IMPRACTICABILITY, AND FRUSTRATION

The CISG does not deal with mistake. (As noted in section 13.14, Article 4 of the CISG states that it is not concerned with the validity of a contract.) Any question of mistake would therefore be resolved under domestic law in an international sale of goods. Articles 3.4 and 3.5 of the UNIDROIT Principles cover mistake. Articles 3.17 and 3.8 are general provisions that deal with the effect of avoidance on any grounds, including mistake. Although the concepts are phrased slightly differently from the common law, the basic tenor of the doctrine is largely comparable to the common law. Article 3.4 defines a mistake as an "erroneous assumption relating to facts or to law existing when the contract was concluded." Article 3.5 sets out the elements of mistake. Unlike the common law, it does not specifically distinguish mutual and unilateral mistake. Article 3.5(1)(a) generally permits avoidance if the mistake was objectively material and the other party made the same mistake or caused the mistake, or knew or should have known of the mistake. Article 3.5(1)(b) provides an alternative basis for avoiding the contract

---

9. I.H. also raised the defense of impracticability which the court also rejected. It held that the poor market conditions were not so severe as to pass beyond the range of the normal risk that I.H. bore, and the impact of the market downturn was not grave enough to constitute undue hardship to I.H. The fact that the circumstances of the case gave rise to alternative arguments of impracticability and frustration of purpose, and that both failed, shows the close connection between the doctrines.

for mistake: if the mistake was objectively material and the other party has not yet acted in reliance on the contract. Article 3.5(2) precludes avoidance if the party bore the risk of the mistake or was grossly negligent in making the mistake. Under Article 3.17, mutual restitution is available upon avoidance of mistake. However, Article 3.18 allows for the possibility of a claim of compensatory damages if the nonmistaken party knew or had reason to know of the mistake.

Article 79(1) of the CISG contains a principle equivalent to impracticability, under which a party is not liable for a failure to perform obligations under a contract if it proves that the failure was due to an "impediment" that the party could not reasonably have been expected to take into account at the time of contracting, that was beyond its control, and that the party could not reasonably be expected to overcome or avoid. Article 7.1.7 of the UNIDROIT Principles excuses performance of a party as a result of "force majeure." (This term should be familiar, because it is used in common law to describe a general risk-allocation clause in a contract. See section 15.7.3d.) The concept of force majeure is similar to that used in Article 79(1) of the CISG: an "impediment" beyond the control of the party, which could not reasonably have been taken into account by the party at the time of contracting, and which the party could not have avoided or overcome. (In a sense, force majeure is equivalent to what we would think of as objective impossibility under common law.) Apart from this, Article 6.2 recognizes a broader concept that is more akin to the doctrine of impracticability, but more restricted in its relief. It allows excuse for "hardship," which is not as severe as force majeure, but makes performance more onerous for the party. Hardship occurs where supervening events "fundamentally alter the equilibrium of the contract," the events could not reasonably have been taken into account by the "disadvantaged party" at the time of contracting, they are beyond its control, and the disadvantaged party did not assume the risk of the events. Hardship does not necessarily result in complete excuse. It allows the disadvantaged party to request renegotiation of the contract, provided that it acts without undue delay. If the parties cannot settle the problem by negotiation, either party may ask the court to terminate or to adapt the contract to restore its equilibrium.

Examples

1. Tiffany De Canter owned an ornate silver jug. She inherited it from her grandmother who had told her that it was very valuable because it was made by Maestro Da Silva, an important nineteenth-century silversmith. Since she acquired it, Tiffany has had it examined by several experts. Although some of them thought that it might have been made by Da Silva, the prevailing view among them is that it was the product of one of

his pupils. It has therefore been appraised at $10,000. Had it been authenticated as the work of Da Silva, it would be worth $1 million.

Tiffany decided to sell the jug. She offered it to Sterling Silverman, an art collector, for $12,000. Sterling was familiar with Da Silva's work. He had a hunch that the experts may have been wrong in concluding that the jug was not made by Da Silva. He accepted Tiffany's offer to sell the jug for $12,000. The parties executed a simple written contract that set out the physical description of the jug and stated the price and delivery obligation. A few months after the sale was completed, a scholar unearthed some previously unknown notebooks and sketches by Da Silva that conclusively proved that he had made the jug.

Can Tiffany avoid the sale to Sterling?

2. Manny Lisa recently became wealthy through the exercise of his stock options. All his newfound rich friends owned portraits of themselves painted by the celebrated society portraitist Leonardo De Fancy. Although he is clueless about art, Manny decided to get hold of the divine Leonardo and commission a portrait. He looked in the yellow pages under "Painters, portrait" and found a listing for De Fancy, Leonardo. He called the number and spoke to Leonardo, who agreed to paint his portrait for $250. Manny was astounded at how reasonable this was, and he accepted. The parties arranged a date for a sitting at the end of the week.

A couple of days later, Manny discovered from a more worldly friend that the person who is listed in the yellow pages is not the Leonardo, but his father, Leonardo De Fancy the Elder, a talentless hack who ekes out a meager living by painting the children of middle-class suburbanites. Being unschooled in the ways of the art world, Manny had not known that a famous celebrity portraitist like Leonardo, the Younger, does not advertise in the yellow pages and only accepts commissions on referral. Furthermore, his charge for a portrait would be about 40 times what Manny had agreed to pay Leonardo the Elder.

Understandably, Manny no longer desires the portrait for which he contracted. Can he avoid the contract?

3. Reliabuild Contractors, Inc., was invited by the owner of property to submit a bid for the erection of a new building. Reliabuild planned to do all the work itself except for the excavation of the land. It needed to know the cost of excavation before it could complete its bid, so it sent the building plans to Bill Dozer, an earthmover whom it had used with satisfactory results on several prior projects. Bill studied the plans and calculated his own cost. Because Bill was very busy and distracted, he did not pay careful enough attention to this task and he miscalculated his cost as $500,000 instead of $800,000. He then added a 10 percent profit of $50,000 and submitted a written bid of $550,000 to Reliabuild. Reliabuild calculated its own bid on the basis of this figure and submitted it to

the owner. Reliabuild's bid was about $400,000 less than the lowest competing bid, so the owner accepted it. Reliabuild then accepted Bill's bid.

A few days before Bill was to begin his performance, he reviewed his bid and discovered his miscalculation. The error would not only deprive him of his expected profit, but would result in a loss of $250,000. He could not absorb such a loss, which would put him out of business. Bill called Reliabuild immediately, explained the error, and withdrew from the contract. Reliabuild told Bill that it regarded this as a repudiation and would hold him liable for damages. Reliabuild then sought other bids and accepted the lowest one of $900,000. As a result, Reliabuild had to pay $350,000 more than it originally expected and lost about 40 percent of the profit it had anticipated on the project.

Reliabuild claims the $350,000 from Bill as damages for breach of contract. Does Bill have a defense?

4. Change the facts of Example 3 as follows: Assume that when Bill explained the mistake, Reliabuild did not wish to drive him out of business by pressing its claim for damages. It therefore took pity on him and agreed to release him from his obligation. Reliabuild does not itself wish to assume the extra cost of employing a more expensive subcontractor, so it in turn seeks to withdraw from its contract with the owner. The owner is not so kind and threatens suit if Reliabuild does not perform as agreed. Can Reliabuild escape its contract with the owner?

5. Merlin Magnifico, Master of the Impossible, is a magician. On July 1 he entered into a contract with Showstopper Promotions, Inc., under which he agreed, for a fee of $10,000, to perform a magical extravaganza at the Pyro Palace Theater on August 30. This contract forms the basis of the separate and distinct factual variations set out in the following questions.

   a. On July 20, Merlin tried to perform the most daring escape trick ever attempted. He jumped out of a plane all trussed up like a turkey, allowing himself two minutes to free himself and pull his parachute cord. He succeeded in loosening his bonds, but in his feverish unraveling, also mistakenly untied his parachute harness. Is the estate of the late Merlin Magnifico liable to Showstopper for the substantial profits it lost as a result of having to cancel the show and refund the price of tickets sold?

   b. The sad event described in question (a) had an impact (no, I would not be so callous as to intend a pun) on a transaction between two other parties: By July 15, all the tickets to Merlin's show had been sold, and people were clamoring to buy tickets from those who had been lucky enough to get them. Buck Fast had managed to buy a ticket for $50 when they first went on sale. His friend Fanny De Voted adored Merlin and desperately wanted to see the show. She nagged Buck to sell the ticket to her, offering an increasingly higher price each time he refused. Eventually he gave in and sold it to her when her offer reached $150. When Merlin was killed, Showstopper cancelled the show and announced that ticketholders should return their tickets for a refund. Naturally, Showstopper will only refund the face value of the ticket, so Fanny demands that Buck repay her the excess of $100. Buck refuses. Is Fanny entitled to the return of her money?

c. Change the facts of (a) so that Merlin did succeed in accomplishing the parachute trick. As a result, he became an instant worldwide sensation. He is now able to command a fee of $500,000 for a booking. He does not wish to perform for Showstopper at the measly rate of $10,000. Can he escape the contract?

d. Merlin survived his parachute prank, only to be apprehended by grim-faced F.A.A. officials for failing to obtain the permits needed for exiting an aircraft in a state of physical restraint. To avoid prosecution and stern punishment, Merlin entered into a consent decree with the F.A.A. in which he undertook never again to perform magic tricks on land or sea, or in the air. When Merlin told Showstopper that he could no longer perform on August 30, Showstopper sued him for breach of contract. Does he have a defense?

e. The trick of July 20 did not happen. (In fact, Merlin is terrified of heights and can only undertake air travel under deep sedation with his seatbelt firmly fastened.) Merlin was therefore willing and able to give his show at the end of August. On August 15 the Pyro Palace burned down. Showstopper had sold almost all the tickets to the extravaganza and did not wish to cancel or postpone it. There is another theater in town that was available on August 30, and is suitable for staging the show. Showstopper proposed to change the show's venue to the other theater. Merlin refused to perform at the other theater. He argued that the parties intended the show to be performed at the Pyro Palace, and its destruction made the contract impracticable. Should Merlin be able to terminate the contract on this ground?

f. None of the above catastrophes happened. However, ticket sales for the show were appalling. Despite intensive promotion, Showstopper had filled only 30 percent of the house by August 20. It is clear that Showstopper will incur a substantial loss if the show goes on. Showstopper takes the position that, known to Merlin, its obvious purpose in entering the contract was to make a profit. The supervening lack of interest on the part of the public has frustrated this purpose, and Showstopper is therefore entitled to cancel the contract with Merlin. Is this a good argument?

6. Professor Goldbrick hates grading exams. One day he saw an advertisement by Slacker Software, Inc., in which it claimed that it could design

computer programs to meet any educational need. Goldbrick contacted Slacker and asked if they could devise a program that could grade essay exams. Slacker took full details of what Goldbrick would need and said it would consider the matter and get back to him. A few weeks later, Slacker sent him a written proposal in which it undertook to create a program of the kind he required. It was based on a complex system of identifying key words and phrases in electronically written essay answers. Because the program was so innovative, Slacker wanted the obscene price of $100,000 for producing it. Goldbrick hated grading so much that he decided it was worth it, even though it meant that he would have to sell all his assets to come up with the money. The parties entered a contract under which Slacker undertook to deliver the program within six months.

Slacker set to work on the program immediately. After struggling with it for four frustrating months, Slacker concluded that its original concept would not work. The program required considerable further research and refinement that would push Slacker's development costs to $150,000, which exceeds the contract price by $50,000. It therefore told Goldbrick that it could not produce the program and cancelled the contract. Goldbrick is deeply disappointed. He would like to contract with another programmer and hold Slacker liable for any difference in price. Would Slacker be liable?

7. Crystal Springer owns land on which a pristine spring is located. The sweet water emerges from the earth in a completely pure state. Crystal bottles her water and sells it to health food shops. Because Crystal's water is so exquisite, it is regarded as the champagne of bottled water. Although it is more expensive than other brands, it is whisked away by customers as soon as stores place it on the shelf. Holy Foods, a preeminent organic grocery store, entered into a contract with Crystal under which it bought 20,000 bottles of her water a year for five years, to be specially bottled for Holy Foods under its own "Holy Water" label. The contract provides a stated price for the water, to be adjusted at the beginning of each year in accordance with the Consumer Price Index. The contract makes no provision for changing the quantity of water supplied or terminating the contract.

The contract was performed satisfactorily for two years. Just before the third year, Crystal's spring dried up. A hydrologist has determined that this was caused by an unusual phenomenon. A subterranean tremor had blocked the channel to the surface of the land and prevents the stream from reaching it. The problem can be rectified by an expensive excavation. Crystal can obtain a mortgage on the land to pay for the excavation, but the payments under the mortgage would be so high that Crystal could not expect to make a profit from sales of her bottled water for the next

15 years. Crystal therefore decided not to do the excavation. She notified her customers, including Holy Foods, that she would not deliver the water promised for the remaining years of their contracts.

Holy Foods can obtain water of a quality equivalent to Crystal's but it has to import it from the foothills of the Himalayas at a much higher cost. Assume that Holy Foods can prove a loss of profits as a result of Crystal's failure to complete her performance under the contract. Is Crystal liable to Holy Foods for this loss?

8. Fast Fryers, a new fast-food chicken restaurant, ordered 1,000 chickens from Fairest Fowls, Inc., a poultry supplier. When the chickens were delivered, Fast Fryers found them to be tough and unusable for frying. Unknown to Fast Fryers (who is new to the chicken industry and unfamiliar with its customs) there is a well-established usage in the industry that the word "chicken" refers only to old, tough birds, suitable only for stewing or soup. A frying chicken is known in the industry as a "poulet." Can Fast Fryers avoid the contract on the basis of its mistake as to the meaning of "chicken"?

Explanations

1. This is a sale of goods, but mistake is not specifically dealt with in UCC Article 2, so it is governed by common law rules. Tiffany is a sophisticated seller who made her judgment without any reliance on a representation by Sterling or under any pressure from him. In the absence of deception or other improper bargaining, the only possible basis for avoidance is mistake. (It may be tempting to find unconscionability in the grossly inadequate price. Although there is some recognition that a gross disparity in exchange could, on its own, be grounds for unconscionability, the generally accepted view is that this substantive unfairness must have resulted from wrongful bargaining conduct or at least from an environment that would allow advantage to be taken of a vulnerable party. This is discussed in section 13.11.)

   The error in this case does not concern the actual identity of the jug itself, but of its maker. The identity of its maker is a fact, and the low price reflects an erroneous shared basic assumption (that is, a mutual mistake) about it. However, both parties were aware of the possibility of incorrect attribution, and if they were wrong, this is more a question of incorrect judgment. Tiffany gambled that she was correct in believing it to be a work of Da Silva's pupil, in which case, she obtained a good price, somewhat above its true market value. Sterling speculated that the experts might be wrong, in which case he would make a killing. When parties deal with each other in an arms-length market transaction, their respective reliance interests are entitled to protection. One of them cannot be deprived of his bargain because it later turns out that the other made a poor judgment.

Thus, the case can be disposed of quickly by treating it as a misjudgment on Tiffany's part and not an error of fact at all. However, even if, as an initial matter, it was to be conceded that there was a mistake of fact, the analysis of risk allocation leads to the same result: Tiffany must be held responsible for her own judgment. The written contract simply describes the jug without making any representation of authorship, and there is no other term that expressly allocates the risk of error. In the absence of guidance in the contract itself, risk must be allocated to the party who should most appropriately bear it under all the circumstances of the transaction. When the parties knowingly enter a contract for the sale of a work of art of uncertain attribution, the risk must lie with the party whose judgment proves to be wrong. This is the resolution suggested in *Firestone & Parson, Inc.* and the dissent in *Sherwood v. Walker* discussed in section 15.2.1.

2. There are two possible arguments that Manny could make for avoidance, but both would be difficult to establish on these facts. He could claim that Leonardo the Elder made a fraudulent misrepresentation by nondisclosure when he advertised under the name shared with his celebrated son and failed to indicate that he was not *the* Leonardo. This argument seems tenuous. Although there is some chance of confusion, and maybe a possibility that Leonardo was consciously taking advantage of his son's name recognition, the two painters operate in different spheres. Leonardo the Elder has not misrepresented his name and he made no claim to be a society painter. His advertising in the yellow pages and the modesty of his fee suggest that he may not even have imagined that there would be any reasonable confusion. Furthermore, any duty that he may have had to alert potential customers to the fact that he was not *the* Leonardo seems to be outweighed by Manny's carelessness in not making proper enquiries to obtain easily ascertainable information, especially in light of the low price.

Manny's other possible argument is that the contract was induced by unilateral mistake. A mistake as to the identity of the other party is treated as a factual error. The mistake did relate to Manny's basic assumption in entering the contract. It is harder to say whether the error materially affected the exchange of values. Manny got what he paid for, but there could still be a material impact on the exchange because this was not the portrait that Manny bargained for. Because there is probably not much of a market for hack-painted portraits of the nouveau riche, Manny does not have much chance of recouping the price by selling the painting.

Even if these elements are satisfied, Manny is likely to lose on the allocation of risk and the equities. Manny may have been untutored in the ways of the art world, but he had ready access to information and advice and should have proceeded more carefully before committing himself to ordering a painting from the wrong artist. There do not seem to be strong equities for shifting the risk to Leonardo. There is nothing to suggest that Leonardo had reason to suspect an error and exploited it, and he has a legitimate reliance interest worthy of protection.

3. This Example does not implicate the promissory estoppel issue in *Drennan v. Star Paving*, discussed in sections 8.11 and 15.4 because the offer was accepted before Bill tried to revoke it. We can therefore focus purely on the mistake analysis presented by these facts.

This mistake is not mutual, but unilateral on Bill's part. In a sense, Reliabuild has also been in error over the correct price for the earthmoving, but this does not make the mistake mutual. The calculation of Bill's price is solely within his realm and forms his individual basic assumption. Reliabuild was not involved in the determination of Bill's price. It simply reacts to the end result of Bill's calculations, which it will accept or reject. Are the requirements of unilateral mistake satisfied? Bill should not have much trouble with the first three: His cost in doing the work is a fact. It was a basic assumption on which he entered the contract. It materially effects the exchange, in that it causes him to undercharge so badly that his expected profit becomes an unbearable loss.

He is not likely to do as well with the issues of risk allocation and equitable balancing. His miscalculation is not simply a matter of conscientious error, but results from sloppy inattention to his work. Although negligence is not an absolute bar to relief for mistake, it is a factor that is taken into account in deciding whether a party assumed the risk of the error. Even if this does not dispose of the matter, the cause and nature of the mistake will weigh against him in the balance of the equities. On the other side of the balance is the hardship he will suffer if the contract is enforced. The damages may put him out of business, but shifting the loss to Reliabuild will apparently have a less devastating effect because it has a bigger profit margin and may be able to better absorb it. When the potential impact of the mistake is so severe to the mistaken party as to threaten his livelihood, and only reduces the gains of the other party, a court may be swayed by the balance of hardship.

Nevertheless, the relative economic impact on the parties, while a relevant consideration, may not be weighty enough to be the overriding factor in the decision to foist the loss onto one of them. Relative blame and innocence must be considered as well. In this case, Bill's carelessness must be weighed against Reliabuild's justifiable reliance on his contractual commitment. It could be that Reliabuild, as an experienced prime contractor, should have realized that the bid was too low, but there are no facts to indicate this. If it had no reason to have suspected the mistake, it made its own commitment to the owner in reasonable reliance on Bill's manifestation of assent. Bill cannot be released from his obligation without subjecting Reliabuild to the substantial harm of either reneging on its obligation to the owner, with the probability of ensuing litigation, loss of reputation and loss of profit, or of having to pay the additional cost of a substitute. In other words, Reliabuild cannot be restored to the status quo if Bill is allowed to escape liability under their contract.

4. If Reliabuild releases Bill from his subcontract, the question becomes whether Reliabuild itself could use mistake as the basis for seeking relief under the prime contract. That is, Reliabuild could argue that it made an error in its own cost calculations, based on having been given incorrect information by Bill. Reliabuild should not have much trouble establishing two of the elements for relief: Bill's charges are a fact forming Reliabuild's basic assumption in entering the prime contract, and the mistake has a material effect in the exchange of values. However, Reliabuild may have greater difficulty with risk allocation and the balance of the equities. If Bill's low bid did not alert Reliabuild to the error, the same might be true of Reliabuild's low bid to the owner, so both may be innocent parties with legitimate reliance interests. Although enforcement of the bid would severely diminish Reliabuild's profits, nonenforcement would deprive the owner of its bargain to the same extent. In addition, it may not be appropriate to allocate the risk of this error to the owner, who did not deal with Bill, had no means of evaluating his bid, and had no role in releasing Bill.

This Example is inspired by *Wil-Fred's Inc. v. Metropolitan Sanitary District*, 372 N.E.2d 946 (Ill. 1978), in which the court did allow the prime contractor to avoid its contract with the owner after the prime contractor released a subcontractor from a miscalculated bid. However, there was an additional fact in the case that favored relief. The subcontractor's error could have been caused in part by the owner's badly drawn specifications.

The error in this example is in the bid at the time of contracting, so it is best characterized as an issue of mistake. However, it could conceivably be treated under the doctrine of impracticability. Bill's withdrawal after formation of the contract could be seen as an unforeseen supervening event, the nonoccurrence of which was a basic assumption of the contract between Reliabuild and the owner. As a result, Reliabuild's performance becomes unduly burdensome. However, even if the case is analyzed under impracticability, the result should not change, because fault and risk allocation are again the dispositive considerations and they should be resolved in the same way.

5. All the factual variations in this example involve supervening events—occurrences after contract formation that may be grounds for a claim of impracticability or frustration of purpose.

   a. Even under the original doctrine of impossibility, performance was excused by the death of a party whose continued existence was necessary for the performance. This may seem ridiculously obvious, but remember, as the question indicates, the issue is not whether Merlin's corpse can be made to do magic tricks, but whether his estate is liable for damages. The initial two elements of impracticability are satisfied: As the contract was for Merlin's personal services, it was clearly dependent on his continued vitality. His death is a supervening event contrary to the contract's basic assumption.

      The more difficult question is who bore the risk of his death. The contract itself does not assign the risk, so the allocation must be made in light of the parties' reasonable expectations, determined from all the circumstances surrounding the transaction. These circumstances may include a particular practice in the entertainment industry that may help to determine the normal incidence of risk when an artist dies before a show. (For example, promoters may regularly insure the lives of performers who have been booked.) If not, general community expectations must be determined and any pertinent considerations of public policy must be taken into account. It is difficult to be sure what result would be reached. Many contracts do not terminate as a result of the death of a party, so that performance or damages becomes an obligation of his estate. As noted above, this may not be the reasonable expectation when the contract is for personal services. In this case, however, the risk allocation is also influenced by the circumstances of Merlin's death. Impossibility or impracticability cannot be used as a defense by a party who is at fault in causing the supervening event, and it could be argued that Merlin recklessly caused his own death. This may, in itself, be grounds for withholding relief from his estate. If not, it may tip the balance in the determination of risk.

   b. Fanny's demand for refund of the $100 is, in effect, a claim of restitution based on the implicit contention that the cancellation of the magic show frustrated the purpose of her contract with Buck. (The facts here differ from *Krell v. Henry*, but the situation is analogous.) These facts show how difficult it can be to distinguish impracticality and frustration. The latter seems more appropriate here because the contractual performance—the exchange of a ticket for $150—has not been altered by the supervening event. Rather, the goal and purpose of the exchange have been defeated. (However, it could just as plausibly be argued that the supervening event so devalued the exchange for Fanny that her performance was rendered unduly burdensome, and impracticality doctrine is applicable.)

The first three elements of frustration are clearly satisfied: Merlin's death and the ensuing cancellation of the show were supervening events that defeated a shared basic assumption of the parties entering the contract, and neither was at fault in causing the event. Therefore, once again, risk allocation becomes the determinative issue.

In the absence of any assignment of risk in the contract itself, the risk of the show's cancellation must be placed where the parties reasonably would have expected it. It is not clear what this reasonable expectation might be, but in the absence of some established practice to the contrary, the usual expectation in a sale transaction (in the absence of any express term to the contrary) is that the buyer assumes the risk that the item or service purchased will be worth less than its price, and the seller assumes the countervailing risk that it will be worth more. On this basis, Fanny would bear the risk of cancellation and partial refund, and would not be entitled to recover the $100 from Buck. This is contrary to the result in *Krell v. Henry*, but the concurring opinion in that case questioned the issue of risk allocation.

c. The only basis on which Merlin could escape the contract is to contend that his new-found fame is a supervening event that defeats the basic assumption on which the parties contracted for his services at the relatively modest sum of $10,000. As a result, his loss of the opportunity to earn 50 times that amount is such a burden as to make his performance impracticable. He should not get away with this because he does not show either that performance has become unduly burdensome or that Showstopper bears the risk of the change in circumstances. Impracticability should not be permitted as an excuse when the change in market conditions merely has the effect of making the performance more valuable than anticipated, especially when the harm to Merlin is nothing more than the loss of an opportunity to sell his services at greater advantage. In addition, the argument made in Explanation 5(b) is applicable here too: Each party made a judgment in assenting to the price of $10,000, and neither can complain if that judgment turns out to have been wrong.

d. Compliance with a change in the law or government regulation or with a judicial or administrative order is generally regarded as a basis for excusing performance on grounds of impracticability. The F.A.A.'s prohibition on Merlin's further career as a magician could fall into this category, but because the bar on his performance resulted from his violation of the law, he should be denied relief. Even had he not entered a consent decree, the event precluding his performance arises from his own fault, and he must be held to have assumed the risk of its occurrence. This resolution is made more compelling by the fact that the F.A.A. may not unilaterally have imposed the prohibition, and Merlin acquiesced in it by entering a consent decree to avoid other punishment.

These are sufficient grounds to defeat a claim of impracticability, but one further issue should be noted: We do not have to be concerned about whether the F.A.A. had the legal authority to enter the consent decree. Even if it did not, and the order was invalid, this would not in itself prevent a claim of impracticability, provided that compliance with the order is in good faith.

e. At last, we get to the fiery destruction of the Pyro Palace, but with a twist on *Taylor v. Caldwell*: It is not Showstopper, the party who is obliged to supply the hall, that raises the excuse of impracticability. Rather, Showstopper tenders a substitute performance, but it is Merlin who claims impracticability on the basis of the destruction of the hall. This may therefore not be a proper case for invoking the doctrine of impracticability, which is intended to provide a defense to the party who cannot perform as promised as a result of the supervening event. The language of Restatement, Second, §261 contemplates this by stating that where a party's performance has become impracticable, his duty to render the performance is discharged. On the facts of this Example, it is not Merlin's performance that has become impracticable, but Showstopper's. It is conceivable that Merlin could argue that the destruction of the hall renders his performance impracticable as well. He could show that there was some special reason why that venue was a basic assumption of his performance—for example, that the Pyro Palace had special facilities or characteristics essential to his performance, that were not available in the new venue. However, the facts do not suggest that he is making this claim. Therefore, unless he can show that the substitute venue defeats a basic assumption of the contract, rendering his performance unduly burdensome, Merlin cannot use the change in venue as a basis for discharging the contract.

f. Most commercial contracts are motivated by the prospect of profit, so if Showstopper's argument was taken seriously, no party could ever be held to a contract once it becomes apparent that its expectation of profit will be disappointed. Therefore, although profitmaking may, in a sense, be the purpose of a contract, the doctrine of frustration does not simply focus on this underlying "bottom line" purpose, but calls for a more penetrating examination of the parties' mutual objective in entering the contract. This shared objective must be determined in light of the contract's allocation of risk. The facts do not make it clear who bore the risk of poor sales. However, if the contract did not specifically allocate this risk to Merlin, and there is no usage to the contrary, the reasonable inference from the structure of the contract is that Showstopper assumed this risk. Merlin agreed to perform for a fixed fee, and Showstopper would keep whatever proceeds were generated from ticket sales. If Showstopper bore the risk of poor ticket sales, it follows that it was not the common purpose of the contract that Showstopper would make a profit. Rather, the common purpose was to stage a public entertainment. The prospect of making a profit may have strongly motivated Showstopper to undertake the venture, but that was its purpose, not Merlin's. Viewed this way, we can see that the purpose of staging the show has not been frustrated.

Showstopper based its argument on frustration of purpose. It could equally have argued that the supervening event of poor ticket sales rendered the contract impracticable. (A similar alternative argument was made and rejected in *Karl Wendt Equipment* discussed in section 15.8.) Because the defenses of frustration of purpose and impracticability are so closely related, we should get the same answer, whichever one is used. Again, the key to resolving an impracticability defense is to determine who bore the risk of poor ticket sales. If Showstopper bore that risk, it cannot escape the contract on grounds of impracticability.

6. This is one of those ambiguous situations that sounds like a case of impracticability, but is better characterized as a unilateral mistake. Slacker's post-contractual realization that it underestimated the complexity and cost of production is not a supervening event, but a discovery that it had underbid its price. However, because risk allocation is the key element here and it is common to both mistake and impracticability, mischaracterization should not affect the result.

Let us consider mistake first. Slacker, the expert, was approached by Goldbrick, a lay customer who desired an end product and had no idea about what may be involved in creating it. Slacker made its own evaluation of what would need to be done to create the product and then made an unqualified promise to deliver the program in six months. We may simply describe this as an error in judgment, or we could say that Slacker assumed the risk that it could not perform for the price quoted. However phrased, the point is that Goldbrick had no way of knowing that Slacker had misjudged the complexity of the project, and Slacker was foolishly overconfident in giving him an absolute promise. Because Slacker was creating an innovative custom-made product — a prototype — it would have been wiser to draw the contract so as to identify the experimental nature of the project and provide for a price increase, a delay in delivery, or a right to terminate if production difficulties are encountered. By not doing this, Slacker assumed the risk of unforeseen problems. It is therefore liable for Goldbrick's expectation damages measured as the difference between the contract price and the higher price charged by the other programmer.

It was noted earlier that this is not properly viewed as an impracticability case, but that even if it was analyzed as such, the same result would apply because Slacker assumed the risk of post-contractual difficulties in production. An impracticability defense was raised unsuccessfully in *United States v. Wegematic Corp.*, 360 F.2d 674 (2d Cir. 1966), a case with facts analogous to those here. An electronics manufacturer made a contract with the Federal Reserve Board for the supply of a computer system (touted as "revolutionary?") by a specified date. The manufacturer encountered numerous difficulties in building the system, and eventually notified the Board that it could not produce it. The Board ordered an equivalent system from another vendor and sued the manufacturer for damages. The court rejected the manufacturer's defense of impracticability on the grounds that it had assumed the risk of technical difficulties in the fabrication of the system. Although the system may have been an experimental prototype, the manufacturer's promise was simply to deliver a working computer by a specified time. (The court also found that performance was not impracticable because the element of undue hardship was not satisfied. Problems in the system could have been rectified by costly but not overwhelmingly burdensome redesign.)

7. Crystal has breached the contract and is liable for Holy Foods' damages unless she has the defense of impracticability. Bottled water satisfies the definition of "goods" under UCC article 2, so the issue of impracticability must be resolved under UCC §2.615. The analysis of impracticability under §2.615 is substantially the same as under contemporary common law.

The blockage that diverted the stream was a supervening event. Section 2.615 requires that it must have been an event "the nonoccurrence of which was a basic assumption on which the contract was made." Comment 1 to §2.615 paraphrases this by stating that the contract must have become impracticable because of unforeseen supervening circumstances not within the parties contemplation at the time of contracting. The blockage is described as an unusual phenomenon. This suggests that the parties probably did not contemplate it as a possibility. There is no indication that they discussed or provided for it in the agreement.

The supply of water is not objectively impossible because there is a means of restoring the stream. However, §2.615 (like the common law) does not require impossibility, but impracticability. Mere increase in cost, lack of profit, or even some degree of loss, is not enough to make a performance impracticable. The scale of the problem must be large enough that it makes the performance so burdensome that it cannot be rendered without devastating loss, great risk, or serious hardship. The facts here have a good chance of meeting this standard. The high cost of curing the problem is disproportionate to the value of the water. It would take Crystal 15 years of sales to pay off the cost of the work.

Although the excavation may pay for itself in the very long term, it would impose a significant burden on Crystal. She would not derive any income from her business for 15 years, even if we assume that the market for her water remains strong.

Crystal was not in any way at fault in causing the occurrence, so she is doing well so far in establishing the elements of impracticability. This leaves risk allocation as the crucial factor in deciding if she should be excused from performance. The contract makes no provision for reductions in quantity for any reason, so the parties' intent must be determined from interpretation of the contract as a whole in context. If no factual indicators of intent are available, the court must construe the parties' reasonable intent. We have no evidence of express terms or pertinent usage or custom, so are left with nothing more than the bare terms of the contract to decide if Crystal assumed this risk. The contract establishes a formula for fixing the price of the water over the five-year period. Where parties fix the price in the contract, the seller is usually assumed to undertake the risk of any increases in cost. In addition, the seller of goods assumes the risk that she may not be able to make or obtain the goods promised in the contract. However, the cost increase here was so unforeseen and so great that a court could conclude that it goes well beyond the normal level of risk assumed in a fixed price contract. If so, Crystal can escape the contract on grounds of impracticability.

It is worth making a final observation about this contract. Where parties enter into a long-term relationship, they run a greater risk of unforeseen future contingencies. Although it may be difficult to imagine all the things that could go wrong to make the contract unexpectedly burdensome to one of the parties, a generally worded clause, excusing performance in case of a force majeure could help a party like Crystal in establishing grounds for excusing performance.

8. If this Example reminds you of *Frigaliment Importing*, the cherished chicken case in section 10.1.3, that should give you a clue to its answer. Your immediate reaction may be to resolve the case on the basis of unilateral mistake because the trade usage is, after all, a fact external to the contract. However, as we saw in section 10.1.3, a trade usage, although extrinsic to the written contract, is not treated as a fact external to the contract itself, but is part of the context used to give meaning to the terms used by the parties. Unless specifically included, a usage is an implied term of the contract. Therefore, this issue is properly resolved, not as a question of mistake, but as a question of interpretation: If the usage is proved to exist, the question is whether Fast Fryers, as a new entrant to the industry, had reason to know of it. If so, as a matter of interpretation, the word "chicken" means stewing chicken and Fast Fryers is bound to a contract for the purchase of 1,000 tough old birds.

CHAPTER 16

Conditions and Promises

§16.1 THE STRUCTURE OF A CONTRACT: AN INTRODUCTION TO PROMISES AND CONDITIONS

Most terms in a contract are promises or conditions — or both. The meaning, nature, and effect of a promise is very familiar by now. The concept of promise was introduced right at the beginning of this book, and its central role in all contractual relationships has been emphasized ever since. Although conditions are just as much a fundamental component of contracts, their presence and function have not been much discussed in previous chapters. It is the purpose of this chapter to introduce the concept of conditions and to examine their functions. In doing this, we will look more carefully at the structure of a contract and explore the way in which conditions and promises interact to form the basis of the contractual relationship. We will then proceed, in this chapter and the next, to consider the performance obligations created by the network of promises and conditions, and to address the problems that are created when those obligations are violated. You will encounter some unfamiliar terminology, but this does not mean that we are entering some new and alien field of contract law. Most, if not all, of the substantive principles discussed here have been covered already, and the breakdown of a contract into promises and conditions is simply the means by which its structure is studied. As is so often the case, you will find that the key to analysis is interpretation — the determination of the parties' intent, as expressed by them in their contract or as inferred from surrounding evidence and reasonable expectations.

565

16. Conditions and Promises

We begin with a set of definitions and some simple examples to introduce terminology and to provide an initial insight into the reason for differentiating promises and conditions.

A promise (sometimes called a covenant) was defined in section 1.2.3 as an undertaking to act or refrain from acting in a specified way at some future time. As we have seen repeatedly since then, the exchange of promises (or of at least one promise for a performance) is what contracts are all about. Thus, for example, when parties make a contract for the sale of land, the buyer promises to pay the price in exchange for the seller's promise to convey title and possession of the land. Diagram 16A illustrates this in a manner similar to that used to explain the exchange element of consideration:

Diagram 16A

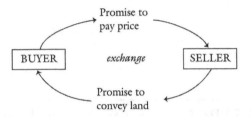

A condition is an event that is not certain to occur. A promised performance under a contract is subject to a condition if the parties agree that the performance is contingent on the occurrence of the uncertain event. That is, when making the contract, the parties agree that a particular promised performance or set of performances will not become due until and unless a particular uncertain event occurs. As this suggests, conditions commonly concern future events because, in most cases, the uncertainty no longer exists once the event has happened. However, there are situations in which a useful purpose is served by making performance conditional on a past event. Although the event in question may have occurred, the parties themselves may be uncertain about whether it took place, and it may be inconvenient or impossible for the parties to find this out at the time that they wish to execute their contract. To avoid the risk of having the agreement unravel while they delay to get the information, they could enter the contract immediately subject to the condition that their agreement — or the obligation of one of them — is contingent upon the event having occurred. (This is illustrated in section 16.2.)

The following example provides a simple illustration of the way in which conditions and promises may be combined to structure a contract in a way that binds the parties, yet allows them to deal with the risk of uncertainty: Buyer is interested in acquiring land to build a housing tract. At the time of negotiations, the land is zoned for agricultural use, but Seller has applied for rezoning for residential development. If the application succeeds, the land can be developed profitably. If not, it can be used only for farming. The parties do not know how the zoning authority will rule on the application, but neither wants to delay contracting until its outcome for fear that the other will lose interest in the transaction. Buyer does not wish to commit himself absolutely at this stage, because he does not wish to be stuck with farmland. To solve this problem, the parties can make a contract now for the sale of the land and include a provision in the contract stating: "Buyer's obligation to purchase this property is conditional upon the grant of the pending rezoning application within 60 days of the date of this agreement." The success of the rezoning application within the next 60 days — a future uncertain event — is therefore a condition of Buyer's promise to pay and take transfer of the land. (Or stated differently, Buyer's promise to pay and take transfer of the land is conditional upon the grant of the application.[1]) Until the condition occurs, Buyer's duty to perform is suspended. If it occurs, the duty becomes due and must be performed, but if the condition is not satisfied by the time that the 60 days has passed, the Buyer's obligation to perform never takes effect, and it falls away. This can be represented as shown in Diagram 16B.

Diagram 16B

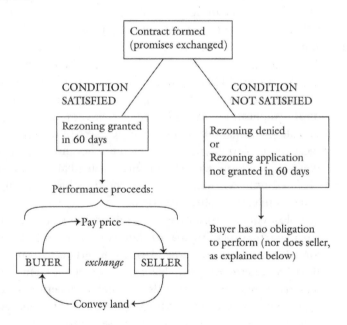

The parties' purpose in structuring the transaction in this way is to allocate the risk of the denial or inaction by the zoning authority. If

---

1. This variation in terminology can be confusing, so make a point of recognizing that these statements mean the same thing, whether made in the active voice (rezoning is a condition of Buyer's performance) or the passive voice (Buyer's performance is conditional on the rezoning).

Buyer had simply purchased the property unconditionally, he would have taken the risk of being saddled with an unwanted farm or a costly delay in the ability to develop it. Because Buyer does not wish to assume this risk, he uses a condition as an escape clause.

§16.2 THE MEANING AND SCOPE OF "UNCERTAIN EVENT"

As noted earlier, uncertainty most commonly relates to future events, but it is possible for parties to be unsure about an event that has already happened at the time of contracting. Although a past event is not uncertain in a general sense — someone probably knows that it did or did not occur and the parties themselves can find out about it — it may nevertheless be unknown to and not readily ascertainable by them at the time they are ready to form the contract. If they wish to avoid the inconvenience or risk of suspending formation until the information is obtained, they can enter the contract immediately, but make performance conditional on the event's currently unknown outcome. For example, say that Buyer and Seller know that the zoning authority made a decision late on Friday afternoon, but it is now Saturday, and the decision cannot be discovered until Monday morning. The parties would like to sign their contract before Seller leaves on vacation on Sunday morning. By making Buyer's obligation to purchase conditional on the application having been granted, they can execute the contract on Saturday without subjecting Buyer to the risk of having bought farmland incapable of development. Although this condition is based on a past event, there is still some element of futurity in that the knowledge cannot be obtained until Monday. The outcome therefore does qualify as uncertain as far as the parties are concerned.

Most conditions, however, do not relate to unknown past events, but are based on something that has not happened at the time of contracting. All future events may be thought of as uncertain to some degree, so in the broadest sense, everything that has not yet occurred must be a future uncertain event. But the law regards an event as uncertain if, in light of human experience, its occurrence is not regarded as strongly predictable. Therefore, although a pessimist may fear otherwise, it is regarded as certain that the sun will rise tomorrow morning, or that Friday will follow Thursday, or that January 1 of next year will arrive. A provision in a contract that calls for performance upon the occurrence of so certain an event is not thought of as a condition at all, but merely fixes the time for performance. The passage of time is not regarded as a condition. Or, if you prefer, it is a condition with such a strong probability of occurrence that its legal effect is insignificant. By contrast, the grant of the rezoning application is not so sure a thing. Even if it was carefully prepared, complies with the prescribed procedures, and makes a compelling case on the merits, we cannot say with the same degree of confidence that its success is inevitable. It therefore qualifies as uncertain.

Although uncertainty about the happening of the event is necessary to qualify the event as a condition, this does not invariably mean that a condition is intended merely because the contract links performance to some uncertain future event. It could be that the parties do not really contemplate the event as uncertain, assume that it will occur, and merely use it as a means of setting the time for performance. If, as a matter of interpretation, the parties do not intend the performance to be contingent upon the event, it should not be treated as a condition. For example, say that a general contractor enters into a contract with a subcontractor under which the subcontractor is to perform electrical work on a house that the general contractor is building for the owner. The subcontract states that the general contractor's payment to the subcontractor will be due "within ten days of payment for the work by the owner." This could be a condition — that is, the general contractor's obligation to pay the subcontractor is conditional on the owner paying the general contractor. However, it could also be seen merely as a term fixing the time for payment — the general contractor must pay the subcontractor ten days after the due date for the owner's payment. To resolve this question, a court would interpret the intent of the parties by examining the apparent purpose of the language in context. Because the subcontractor had no contractual relationship with the owner, did not deal with her directly, and did not have the opportunity to evaluate her creditworthiness, it seems unlikely that the subcontractor would have assumed the risk of the owner's nonpayment in the absence of very clear language assuming this risk.

Although a condition is spoken of as an event, the contingency need not be an affirmative happening. It could also be a negative contingency — a nonhappening. In the above example, the zoning authority's approval of the application is an affirmative event. But it would just as much be a condition if the buyer's performance was subject to something not taking place: Say that the zoning authority had approved the application at the time of contracting, but irate neighbors had threatened to appeal the decision. The contract of sale could provide that the buyer's obligation to purchase is conditional on the approval not being successfully appealed.

§16.3 THE INTENT TO CREATE A CONDITION: EXPRESS, IMPLIED, AND CONSTRUED CONDITIONS

Like all terms of a contract, a condition exists because the parties have agreed to it. Similarly, like all other contractual provisions, the mutual intent to create a condition and the condition's scope and meaning are matters of interpretation. Sometimes the language used by the parties to express this intent is clear, express, and unambiguous, but it could just as likely be obscure and uncertain. In some contracts, the intent to create a condition is not articulated at all, but such intent may be established by evidence extrinsic to the express words used by the parties, or it may be construed by the court. These issues are resolved by applying the general principles of interpretation discussed in Chapter 10.

§16.3.1 Express Conditions

We have already seen an example of an express condition in the land sale contract described above: The contract expressly stated that Buyer's obligation to purchase the land was contingent on approval of the zoning application within 60 days of the date of the agreement. A condition is express if the language of the contract, on its face, articulates the intent to make performance contingent on the event. Commonly, conditions are expressly denoted by using conditional language such as "on condition that," "subject to," "provided that," or "if," but no special incantation is required as long as the intention of establishing a condition arises from the language itself. For a term to be an express condition, it is not enough that the term itself is expressed. Its conditional nature must also be apparent from the language used. For example, a contract for the sale of land has two provisions. One is an undertaking by the seller to transfer title and possession of the land, and the other is an undertaking by the buyer to pay the seller $500,000 for the land. These are both express promises, but neither performance is expressly conditional on the other because there is no express language to that effect. However if, in addition to these express promises, the contract also stated expressly that each party's obligation to perform is conditional on the other performing, these express promises become express conditions as well. We will see in sections 16.3.2 and 16.3.3 that even if these conditions are not expressed, a court will read them into the contract by implication or construction. An implied or construed term is just as effective and binding as an express term, so what is the significance of deciding whether or not a condition is express? For most purposes, it makes no difference if a condition is express, implied, or construed—in any event, the condition will be part of the contract and binding on the parties. The advantage of articulating a condition expressly is that the parties make it clear that they intend a condition. Because this intent is clear, courts enforce express conditions strictly: The condition must be fulfilled exactly as stated, and cannot be satisfied by substantial compliance. For example, a contract for the sale of a house specifies that the buyer's obligation to proceed with the purchase is conditional on his obtaining a loan of $300,000, to be secured by a mortgage on the property. Although the buyer diligently tries to obtain a loan of $300,000, the best he can do is to get a loan for $298,000. Because the condition is express, it must be strictly enforced, and the court will not entertain an argument by the seller that a loan of $298,000 is close enough to constitute substantial satisfaction of the condition. Similarly, say that an insurance policy states that the insurer's duty to reimburse for loss is conditional upon the insured giving it written notice of the loss within ten days of the loss occurring. If the insured does not give notice until the morning of the eleventh day, the condition is not satisfied. Even if the few hours' delay may seem insignificant, and enforcement of the condition means that the insured loses the right of reimbursement for which she has paid a hefty premium, the rule of strict enforcement precludes an argument that there was substantial compliance with the condition of notice.

As technical as the result of strict compliance may be, it is important to recognize that the parties did go to the trouble of making the condition express, thereby manifesting the intent that it be taken literally. In some cases, the harsh results of this approach may be ameliorated by excusing the condition on one of the grounds discussed in section 16.10, but only if the facts fit into one of the narrow bases for excuse. It is also sometimes possible to avoid an unfair result by interpreting the condition so as to find that it was in fact satisfied, but this solution is available only if the language of the condition admits of such a meaning. It would not, for example, be easy to interpret the clearly stated figure "$300,000" in the above financing contingency to mean "$298,000," However, say that the condition stated that the sale was contingent on the buyer obtaining "a loan of $300,000, on market terms, to be secured by a mortgage on the property." If the buyer is able to obtain a loan of $300,000, but the dispute centers on whether the terms of the loan qualify as "market terms," the court has more leeway interpreting the express condition to avoid technical nonfulfillment.

§16.3.2 Conditions Implied in Fact

Even if there is no express language creating a condition, contextual evidence may support the inference that the parties intended a performance to be conditional. Like other terms in a contract, a condition can be implied in fact by interpreting the words used by the parties in light of the circumstances surrounding the formation of their contract. As with other terms, there is no difference in legal effect between an express and an implied condition. The difference lies in the nature of the evidence available to establish its existence. An express condition is apparent from the language of the contract itself — the actual words of the parties are the best evidence of what they intended. However, even where a condition is not ascertainable from the wording of the contract, it could be established by contextual evidence that shows that the parties did intend the condition to exist. Because the parties did not express the condition, a court may have more flexibility in interpreting the implied condition in a way that averts a rigorous strict compliance.

As with all terms implied in fact, if the agreement is recorded in writing, the parol evidence rule may preclude contextual evidence of a condition that varies an integrated term or conflicts with the writing. However, as noted in section 12.12, there is a traditionally recognized exception to the parol evidence rule when the evidence is offered to establish that the contract as a whole was subject to a condition precedent.

§16.3.3 Construed Conditions (Constructive Conditions of Exchange)

Although a condition may not be expressed or inferable from contextual evidence, it could be implied in law. The process of legal implication of conditions is the same as for any other contractual term, and is subject to the general principles discussed in Chapter 10: In essence, although there may be no evidence that the parties actually agreed to the condition, a court will imply it as a matter of law if the circumstances and nature of the contract compel the conclusion that if the parties had addressed the issue, they reasonably would have intended the condition to be part of their contract.

Construed conditions may be illustrated by returning to the example involving the sale of land subject to the express condition that the rezoning application would be granted. If you think about the exchange of performances contemplated in that contract, you will realize that while the express condition may be the only one visible, there are surely two more lurking under the surface of the express agreement: In promising to pay the price of the land, Buyer must reasonably have expected that his obligation to pay was conditional on Seller conveying the land, and Seller surely did not expect to transfer the land to Buyer without getting paid. Thus, each party's performance must reasonably be intended as a condition of the other's. Buyer's duty to pay is contingent on Seller's transfer and vice versa. (The respective performances do qualify as uncertain events, because the honoring of a contractual commitment is not inevitable and assured.)

These conditions are construed rather than implied in fact, because there is apparently no actual evidence that the parties discussed the question or expressed this intent to each other. But remember that the dividing line between factual interpretation and legal implication is not always easily discernable, and they tend to blur into each other at the edges. In other words, the conclusion that each performance is conditional upon the other could be reached as a question of fact if there is evidence (such as common commercial usage, prior dealings, or statements made during negotiations) to support it. But even in the absence of any such evidence, it may be possible to reach the same conclusion by implication of law from the nature of the exchange relationship. In an exchange transaction, unless the language of the contract or its surrounding circumstances clearly indicate a contrary intent, the parties must almost always be taken to have expected that the principal promises exchanged would be dependent on each other—that they would be what are known as constructive conditions of exchange. If they were not, this would lead to the bizarre situation in which a party could be forced to perform even when the other has failed or refused to do so.

The effect of this is that there is an initial condition that the rezoning must be approved. If it is not, Buyer has no obligation to pay and because Buyer's payment is a condition of Seller's obligation to convey, the non-fulfillment of the condition of payment releases Seller too. If the rezoning is approved, we are left with the two conditions relating to the performances, and each party must tender performance (that is, show a readiness, willingness, and ability to perform) to be entitled to performance by the other. We must therefore expand Diagram 16B in the way shown in Diagram 16C.

Diagram 16C

The standard of strict compliance, applicable to express conditions, does not apply to construed conditions because the parties have not clearly indicated, by express language, that they intend the condition to be strictly enforced. In addition, because construction is a search for the apparent intentions of the parties, measured in light of what would be reasonable, a court is unlikely to construe a condition so strictly that it would require exact technical compliance and admit of no flexibility. The issue of substantial compliance with a construed condition is discussed further in section 16.9.

So far we have identified the mutual performances as conditions of each other, but as the diagram shows, we have not dealt with the sequence in which the conditions must be satisfied, or with some other important distinctions between these two conditions and the one that relates to the rezoning. These matters will be discussed in succeeding sections.

§16.4 A CONDITION OF ONE PARTY'S PERFORMANCE, AS DISTINCT FROM A CONDITION OF THE CONTRACT AS A WHOLE

In the prior section, the success of the rezoning application was described as a condition to Buyer's obligation. Because Buyer's performance is, in turn, a condition of Seller's obligation, it follows that if the rezoning is denied and Buyer does not perform, Seller is also relieved of her obligation to perform. As a result, the entire contract falls away. This is shown by Diagram 16D.

Diagram 16D

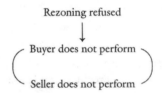

Why is this two-stage analysis necessary? Could it not simply be said that both parties' obligations are conditional on the grant of the application, as shown in Diagram 16E?

Diagram 16E

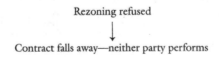

This sounds like the same thing, with one less step in the analysis, but the situations are significantly different. If the contract as a whole was conditional on the rezoning approval, this would mean that if the application is denied, neither party is bound to the transaction. Even if Buyer decided that he wanted the land despite the failure of the application, he could not disregard the condition, tender his payment, and hold Seller to the contract. This is probably not what was intended. Rather, the purpose of the condition is to affect only Buyer's obligation — it is included purely for

Buyer's protection, and not for Seller's benefit. If Buyer decides that he still wants the land with its present zoning, he should be able to waive the condition and proceed with the transaction.[2] Seller is not in any way deprived of her expected exchange and has no cause for complaint. The determination of whether a condition is purely for the benefit of one of the parties, and therefore unilaterally waivable by that party, is a matter of interpretation. The court must determine the intent of the parties in light of the contractual language in context. For example, in *Mayfield v. Koroghli*, 184 P.3d 362 (Nev. 2008), a contract for the sale of real property was subject to the condition that the buyer could obtain rezoning of the property for commercial subdivision. The parties worked together for a number of years in attempting to obtain the rezoning. They were unsuccessful, and the seller told the buyer that he would no longer sell the property to him. The buyer responded that he wished to proceed with the sale despite the failure of the rezoning efforts. When the seller refused, the buyer sued for specific performance of the contract. The court found that the condition had been included in the contract at the buyer's request, for the purpose of allowing him to abandon the transaction if he could not subdivide the property as intended. The court therefore held that the condition relating to rezoning was purely for the buyer's benefit, so that he could waive it and insist that the sale be completed.

However, if the terms or circumstances of the transaction were otherwise, we may reach a different conclusion on the intent of the condition. Say that the sale price of the land was fixed at a base amount of $100,000 (being its current market value as farmland) plus 10 percent of Buyer's profits upon selling off the subdivided lots. If the condition of rezoning is not satisfied, Buyer could not subdivide, and Seller would be deprived of her expected share of the profits. If Seller's incentive for selling the land was to share in the profit of development, and she would not have sold the property for its price as farmland, the condition can no longer be seen as merely for Buyer's benefit. It affects the contract's value to Seller as well. It must surely have been intended that neither Buyer nor Seller could unilaterally waive the condition and hold the other to the contract despite its nonfulfillment. This means that the condition was an event upon which the duties of both parties were contingent — the entire contract was subject to the condition.

---

2. The waiver of a condition is relevant in two distinct situations. Here we deal with one of them: The condition benefits only one of the parties, and that party decides that he would like performance to proceed despite nonfulfillment of the condition. The other situation, covered in section 16.10.2, occurs where one of the parties acts in a manner inconsistent with the condition, and the other party claims that the conduct constitutes a waiver by that party of its right to enforce the condition.

In short, if a condition is intended to relate only to the performance of one of the parties, that party can choose to perform despite its nonoccurrence and may fully enforce the contract against the other. But if the condition relates to the contract as a whole, its nonoccurrence discharges the right of both parties to demand performance, and neither can unilaterally waive it. To decide the intended scope of the condition, its purpose must be ascertained by the usual process of interpreting the contract's wording in context.

§16.5 PURE CONDITIONS AND PROMISSORY CONDITIONS

§16.5.1 The Distinction Between Pure and Promissory Conditions

It has already been stated that when the operative terms of a contract are analyzed, each can be classified as either a promise or a condition. Some terms may be classified as pure promises — they are not conditions at all, but merely undertakings.[3] Others may be pure conditions — they contain no promise but merely describe an event that must occur for a duty of performance to arise. However, some terms in a contract combine both these elements. They not only identify an event that must occur for performance to become due, but they also contain a promise by one of the parties that the event will take place. A term that is not only a condition, but is both a condition and a promise that the condition will occur, is called a promissory condition. This concept often confuses students on first exposure, but it is not as strange and esoteric as it sounds.

The usual process of interpretation and construction must be followed to decide if a term is a pure promise, a pure condition, or a promissory condition. If the express language of the contract does not clearly settle this question, it must be resolved with reference to any factual evidence of intent or, failing that, by construing the parties' reasonable intention. Our land sale example may be used to illustrate:

In agreeing to the sale of the land conditional upon the success of the rezoning application, the parties apparently intend to place the fate of the transaction on an event beyond their control. The application has been made, nothing more can be done by either to influence the result, and there is no indication in the contract that either of them guarantees the

---

3. The role and effect of pure promises is explained in sections 16.6 and 16.8.4.

outcome of the application. From this it must be inferred that they intended the rezoning to be a pure condition. By contrast, the conditions that make the performance of each party contingent on that of the other are promissory conditions. Each party does have control over the satisfaction of the condition that he or she will perform, and each, by committing to perform, has promised that the condition will be satisfied. The payment and conveyance of the land are not simply conditions, but promises as well. This distinction may be portrayed as shown in Diagram 16F.

Diagram 16F

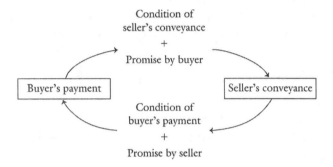

In the above example, the event constituting the condition of each party's performance is the actual performance of the other. When a party's own performance is the condition, that party has some ability to ensure that the promised condition will occur, and can make the commitment with some confidence that the condition will be satisfied. However, if the condition is some event that is beyond her control, she takes a greater risk in promising that it will occur. Therefore, in cases of doubt, it is generally assumed that a pure condition is intended when a party has no power to influence the happening of the event, but a promissory condition is intended if she can play a role in affecting the outcome. It must be stressed that this is merely an assumption — a rough guide. It is not a firm rule. The agreement could expressly or impliedly indicate that the parties intended otherwise. If she is willing to take the risk, there is no barrier to a party assuming responsibility for the happening of an event that she cannot control. For example, instead of simply making their land sale contract conditional on approval of the rezoning application, the parties could have included a warranty by Seller that the application would be granted. Although the disposition of the application is beyond her control, Seller promises that it will succeed. If it does not, there is both a failure of the condition and a breach of Seller's contractual promise.

The significance of the distinction between a pure and a promissory condition lies in the different effect of promises and conditions. If a condition is not satisfied, the performance contingent on that condition does not become due. If it is a pure condition, the performance obligation falls away and there is no basis for claiming breach of contract. However, if a contractual promise is broken, the promisor is liable for breach of contract. It follows that if a promissory condition is not fulfilled, the party whose performance was contingent on it is entitled both to withhold counter performance and to seek a remedy for breach. Therefore, in examining the language of a contract in context to interpret a term as a pure or promissory condition, it is helpful to ask two questions: First, did the parties intend a performance to be excused if the event does not occur? If the answer is yes, the event is a condition of that performance. If the answer to the first question is affirmative, the second question is whether the parties intended that one of them would be responsible for the event's occurrence and would be liable for breach of contract if it does not occur. If the answer is no, the event is a pure condition. If it is yes, it is a promissory condition.

§16.5.2 A Pure Condition Subject to an Ancillary Promise

In the land sale contract, the rezoning has been interpreted as a pure condition, so that Buyer escapes his obligation simply because the condition is not satisfied. The application has been made and is pending, so there is nothing for Buyer to do, and he has no obligation to make any effort to bring about its fulfillment. However, some pure conditions do have an ancillary promise attached to them that expressly or impliedly obliges one of the parties to take steps to try and make the event happen. If so, the party is released from performance only if the condition is unfulfilled despite his efforts to make it come about. This can be illustrated by changing the facts of the example. Say that at the time of sale, the application for rezoning had not yet been made. Buyer is willing to submit an application, but does not wish to gamble on its success. The parties could enter a contract in which Buyer undertakes to make and conscientiously pursue the application, but is excused from proceeding with the purchase if the application is declined. In this contract, Buyer makes an initial promise to apply for the rezoning, but the success of the application is a condition precedent to his obligation to buy the land. This is not completely a promissory condition, because Buyer does not promise that it will be satisfied. However, he does make a promise to take all reasonable steps in good faith to try to get it fulfilled. If he does this and fails, he escapes the contract, but if he does not make a conscientious effort to get the rezoning, Seller may ask the court to excuse the condition so that Buyer loses its protection. This means that Buyer's failure to proceed with his performance under the contract was not justified, and is a breach. This is shown in Diagram 16G.

Diagram 16G

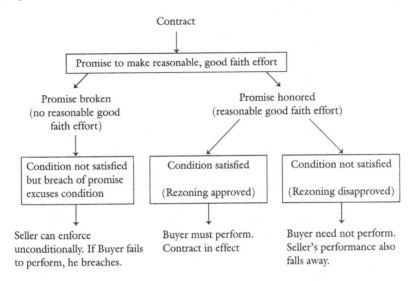

A common example of a pure condition with an ancillary promise of reasonable efforts is a contract to buy a property such as a home, with a financing contingency. The buyer commits to buy the property subject to the condition that he obtains a mortgage loan. The buyer does not promise or guarantee that he will get the loan—the grant of the loan is out of his hands because a lender must agree to give it to him. Therefore, the condition is not promissory. However, it would be a peculiar transaction (and likely would not be a contract at all for failure of consideration[4]) if he did not promise to make reasonable efforts in good faith to secure it. This promise may be expressed in the contract, but if not, it is readily implied. If the buyer breaches this promise, the condition is excused. Where the buyer makes no effort at all to obtain the financing, it is clear that he breached the promise. Where the buyer took some steps to get the loan, but was unsuccessful, the parties may dispute whether the buyer's efforts were sufficient, and the court will have to decide this question. For example, say that the buyer applies to only one lender, but his application is refused because he has a poor credit history and insufficient income to qualify for the loan. If all other lenders use the same standard, it may be futile for him to try any further, and the single application may satisfy his duty. But if other lenders have different or more lenient standards, he would fail in his obligation if he did not pursue the other opportunities to obtain financing.

Phoenix-Talent School District v. Hamilton, 210 P.3d 908 (Or. App. 2009), provides another example of a pure condition accompanied by a promise to make reasonable efforts in good faith to try to bring the condition about.

---

4. *See* section 7.9 on illusory promises.

The school district entered into a contract with the owners of land to purchase land on which it intended to build a school. The land consisted of one lot and a portion of another lot, so it was necessary for the county to approve a lot line adjustment to alter the boundaries of the property. One of the express conditions in the contract was that the county would approve a lot line adjustment by a specific date. The parties made a joint application to the county, but the county would not grant the application as submitted and required further work. As a result, the adjustment was not approved by the contract deadline. Although the school district was willing to extend the deadline, the sellers were not. The school district sued for specific performance. The court refused the claim and granted summary judgment in favor of the sellers. It found that the condition of county approval by the specified date was a pure condition, because the county's decision on the application was beyond the parties' control. The court also found that the parties had made mutual promises to cooperate in good faith in making the application, but the sellers had honored that promise by cooperating fully in trying to get the application approved.

§16.6 THE TIME SEQUENCE: CONDITIONS PRECEDENT AND CONCURRENT CONDITIONS

Another difference between the conditions in the land sale example is that the condition relating to rezoning must occur before Buyer's (and consequently, Seller's) performance becomes due. Because its fulfillment must precede the performance contingent upon it, it is known as a condition precedent. However, the contract does not indicate a sequence for fulfillment of the conditions of paying and conveyance of the land. If no such order of performance is expressed, it must be determined by interpreting the parties' intent in light of any contextual evidence or, in the absence of such evidence, by construing what must reasonably have been intended. When a contract provides for counter-performances in exchange for each other, and the contract does not prescribe a sequence of performances, the general presumption is that if the performances are capable of being rendered simultaneously, they are due at the same time. They are concurrent conditions. Thus, the promissory conditions of payment and conveyance of the land, each being capable of exchange by a single act, are concurrent conditions. Each is a condition of the other and they must be performed at the same time. This means that the parties must get together at an appointed place and perform simultaneously. If this had been the sale of goods, there could have been a physical exchange of the goods and cash, but in a real estate transaction, the funds would be deposited in escrow and released to the seller upon recording of the transfer. Because the performances are concurrent conditions of each other, both parties must show up for the exchange ready, willing, and able to tender performance. If one of them is available to tender performance but the other can or will not, the tendering party is excused from delivering his performance and may sue for breach. Our diagram now looks as shown in Diagram 16H.

Diagram 16H

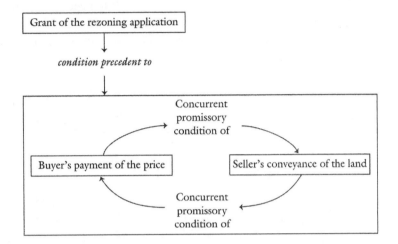

If performances are not capable of being rendered simultaneously because one of them requires a period of time to perform and the other can be rendered instantly, the general presumption, unless the contract indicates a different sequence, is that the performance that takes time must go first and must be concluded before the instantaneous one is due. That is, the completion of the longer performance is a condition precedent to the instantaneous one. For example, when Seller originally decided to make application for the rezoning of her land, she hired an attorney to prepare and submit the rezoning application for her. Unless that contract provided otherwise, the attorney's fee would only have been due after the attorney had completed the work. Her performance in handling the application takes time to complete, and it is therefore deemed to be a condition precedent to Seller's instantaneous action of paying the fee.

When one party's performance is a condition precedent to the other's, their mutual promises are still dependent in a broad sense. They are exchanged for each other, and both parties are motivated to perform by the incentive of receiving the other's performance. However, they are not mutually dependent in the same way as concurrent promissory conditions in that one of the parties — the attorney — must go first. Therefore while the client's promise of later performance is fully dependent on the attorney's earlier performance, the attorney's performance is subject to no condition at all. Her duty to perform is absolute and not contingent on the happening of any prior event.

The effect of this is that the attorney's performance is a promissory condition precedent to the client's payment, but the client's payment is not a condition of anything. It is the last performance in the chain and no further contractual duties are contingent on it. It is therefore a pure promise. In short, although the promises may still be thought of as dependent in the exchange sense (and as we will see in section 17.7.2, the attorney would not have to perform if the client repudiated his obligation in advance), the nature of the performances has the effect of making the attorney's promise a condition.[5] This is shown in Diagram 16I.

Diagram 16I

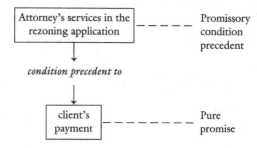

§16.7 THE CONFUSING DISTINCTION BETWEEN CONDITIONS PRECEDENT AND SUBSEQUENT

The distinction between condition precedent and subsequent is arcane and, for the most part, not particularly helpful or pertinent. It is explained here simply to clarify the confusion that it causes. First, unlike the distinction between conditions precedent and concurrent conditions, it has nothing to do with the sequence of performances. In fact, conditions precedent and subsequent have the same general effect: If the condition is not satisfied, the performance that is contingent on it does not have to be rendered. Second, the distinction is based on a semantic difference in the language of the condition. Third, the distinction has very little practical effect, and its principal relevance relates to burden of proof.

In the land sale example, we identified the rezoning as a condition precedent to the buyer's obligation to buy the land. We reached this

---

5. This is expanded upon further in section 16.8.4.

conclusion because the contract stated, "Buyer's obligation to purchase this property is conditional upon the grant of the pending rezoning application within 60 days of the date of this agreement." That is, the buyer's obligation to proceed with the purchase does not become due until the condition is satisfied. However, if the language of the contract had stated "Buyer's obligation to purchase this property will be discharged if the pending rezoning application is not granted within 60 days of the date of this agreement." This subtle change in wording turns the term into a condition subsequent. That is, if the obligation to perform the promise is suspended until the occurrence of the condition, the condition is classified as precedent, but if the performance is discharged by nonoccurrence of the condition, the condition is classified as subsequent. Stated differently, a condition precedent is a prerequisite to the duty arising, while a condition subsequent terminates a duty that came into existence when the contract was formed. As you can see, this distinction is based on a very fine difference in the way in which the provision is worded, but the ultimate effect of the condition is the same — if there is no rezoning in 60 days, Buyer does not have to proceed with the purchase of the property.

Because the impact of the condition on performance is the same, whether it is precedent or subsequent, the distinction makes no difference in most situations, and can usually be disregarded. In fact, the distinction seldom comes up in modern cases, and Restatement, Second, does not even refer to "condition subsequent" in the text of any of its sections.[6] However, there is one area in which the distinction could make a difference — with regard to the incidence of the burden of proof. The fulfillment of a condition precedent is regarded as an element of the plaintiff's case in suing on the contract and must be proved by the party seeking to enforce it. Conversely, the occurrence of a condition subsequent is a defense to nonperformance and must be proved by the party whose performance obligation has allegedly been discharged. (Therefore, if the grant of the rezoning application is a condition precedent, Seller would have to prove that rezoning was granted to enforce the contract, but if the failure of the application is a condition subsequent, Buyer would have to prove refusal of the application to escape the obligation to purchase the land.) Allocation of the burden of proof could

---

6. In defining the term "condition" in §224, the Restatement, Second confines it to an event that must occur before a performance becomes due. Although it concedes, in Comment e to §224, that a contract may provide for the discharge of a duty upon the happening of a specified event, it does not consider such a term to be a condition at all. The comment indicates a preference for interpreting contractual language as creating a condition precedent and suggests that a condition subsequent should not be found merely because the contract speaks of a duty being "discharged" or "extinguished." Section 227(3) reinforces this by stating that in cases of doubt, a condition should be interpreted as precedent.

have significant results where it is difficult to prove that the condition was fulfilled, but it has little impact in most cases, where nonfulfillment is easily shown or is conceded.

§16.8 THE PURPOSE OF USING CONDITIONS IN A CONTRACT

The preceding discussion has already provided several indications of the role played in the contract by conditions. In this section, attention is focused more directly on that subject. It is important to remember that conditions are contractual terms. Parties may choose to include conditions in their agreement if they desire them, or not to include them if they do not. By properly using conditions, they can provide for contingencies, allocate risks, and generally control the way in which their bargain is to be performed. To the extent that they can do this clearly and expressly, they are less likely to have disputes later on. However, as we have already seen, in the absence of clear provisions, unexpressed conditions may still be found by applying principles of interpretation and construction to determine what the parties had or reasonably must have intended. The following are the most common purposes achieved by conditions.

§16.8.1 The Use of a Condition as a Complete or Partial "Escape Clause"

The land sale example introduced in section 16.1 illustrates the use of a condition as an escape clause. Buyer did not wish to buy the farmland if he could not develop it for housing, so he provided in the contract that his obligation to proceed with the purchase of the land was conditional on the grant of the pending rezoning application. That is, the condition in this contract functions as an escape clause for Buyer, which allows the parties to enter the contract now, while permitting Buyer to escape his commitment to buy the land if the condition is not fulfilled. Because the rezoning application had already been submitted, its determination rested with the local authority and was out of the parties' hands. We therefore determined in section 16.5 that this was a pure condition. However, we also saw in section 16.5 that some pure conditions have an ancillary promise of reasonable good faith efforts attached to them. Therefore, if the rezoning application had not yet been submitted, and Buyer was responsible for submitting it, he would have the obligation, either expressly or by implication, to make reasonable, good faith efforts to pursue it. In this situation, the condition still functions as an escape clause, but allows Buyer to escape his commitment only if he did make the required efforts to get the rezoning application approved.

§16.8.2 Conditions of Satisfaction: The Use of a Condition to Permit the Exercise of Judgment by One of the Parties or a Third Party

One of the parties to a contract may wish to have some discretion in evaluating a future state of affairs (whether this relates to circumstances external to the contract or to the other party's performance) before rendering her own performance. To achieve this, the party could have a term included in the contract making her satisfaction (or her agent's satisfaction) with the specified state of affairs a condition precedent of her performance. This type of term, known as a condition of satisfaction, is useful to a party who does not wish to take the risk of performing until she is sure that circumstances are as desired or that the other party has properly done what the contract requires. A few examples will illustrate conditions of this kind and show how they may be employed:

A person contracts to have her portrait painted. In the contract, she undertakes to buy the portrait for $1,000 upon its completion, on condition that she likes it. The condition gives the buyer a means to escape the contract if she is not satisfied with the portrait, and places the risk of making her happy on the artist. In this illustration, the future state of affairs to be evaluated by the buyer is the adequacy of the painter's performance.

A buyer contracts to purchase an old building for the purpose of restoring it and making it into shops, but she is not sure if this kind of development would be successful. She therefore makes her promise to buy the building conditional on her determination, following a feasibility study, that it can be profitably renovated. The risk to be managed by the condition of satisfaction in this case is not related to the adequacy of the other party's performance, but to an external state of affairs — the economic environment — on which the buyer has inadequate information at the time of contracting.

In some cases, the evaluation is not to be done by the party herself, but by some expert third party. For example, a buyer may contract to buy a building subject to the condition that her engineer finds it to be structurally sound, or the owner of property may promise to pay a builder for construction work on condition that her architect certifies the work as competent.

In dealing with consideration doctrine in section 7.9.4, we saw that if a promisor reserves unrestrained discretion to perform, the apparent promise is illusory and cannot be consideration. Therefore, a promise conditional on the satisfaction of one of the parties could fail as consideration unless there is some limitation on that party's ability to claim dissatisfaction. The contract may itself express the standard by which to measure satisfaction, but if it does not, it is usually possible to imply such a standard, either as a matter of factual interpretation or legal implication. As a general rule, in the absence of the expression of a contrary intent, an objective test is used to limit discretion if, based on the underlying purpose and nature of the contract, the reason for the evaluation is to ensure that commercial or technical standards are satisfied. Under such an objective test, the question is whether the party is reasonable in being dissatisfied. In the above examples, it is a fair assumption that the market feasibility of the renovation, the soundness of the building, and the quality of the construction work would all fit into this category. Conversely, if the goal of the contract is to provide a performance that satisfies personal preference involving matters of taste or aesthetics, satisfaction is judged on a subjective standard: Is the party's dissatisfaction honest and genuine? The painting probably falls into this category, and the buyer may be able to show honest dissatisfaction with her portrait, even if art critics consider it to be a fine piece of work. Restatement, Second, §228 expresses a preference for use of the objective standard in case of doubt, because it is obviously fairer and more predictable. A party should not be taken to have subjected herself to the risk of the other's purely subjective foibles unless this is made clear in the contract or is necessarily inferred from the nature of the transaction.

A condition of satisfaction is not a promissory condition (there is no promise of satisfaction). However, it is subject to an express or implied promise to act reasonably or in good faith in judging satisfaction. It is therefore similar in nature to the conditions described in section 16.5.2 — a pure condition subject to an ancillary promise. This means that if a party refuses to perform on the basis of unreasonable or false dissatisfaction, the condition of satisfaction is excused or deemed fulfilled, and the refusal of performance is a breach.

Two cases illustrate some of the considerations that a court takes into account in deciding whether to imply a subjective or objective standard of satisfaction. In *Hutton v. Monograms Plus, Inc.*, 604 N.E.2d 200 (Ohio App. 1992), a franchise agreement permitted the franchisee to terminate the franchise and get a refund of the franchise fee if he could not obtain "financing suitable to him." The trial court held that the term "to him" signified a subjective standard. The court of appeals disagreed. The use of that language was not enough to overturn the usual assumption that the parties intend an objective standard in the evaluation of matters of commercial utility. Because it would be unusual for the parties to agree to a subjective standard in a commercial contract, much clearer language must be used to express that intent.

By contrast, in *Forman v. Benson*, 446 N.E.2d 535 (Ill. 1983) the court did find that the parties to a commercial contract intended satisfaction to be subjective. A contract of sale was conditional on the seller's satisfaction with the buyer's credit report. The seller rejected the report on the basis that it showed the buyer to be in shaky financial condition. The loan officer of a financial institution testified that his company would regard the buyer's credit as excellent on the basis of the report. The trial court applied an objective standard and held that the seller had been unreasonable in rejecting the report. The supreme court agreed that an objective test of satisfaction normally applies to matters of commercial quality and that the seller's dissatisfaction would not have met the reasonableness standard. However, it held that on the particular facts of the case, the parties intended a subjective standard. The seller was an individual, not in the business of lending money or familiar with commercial standards of evaluating credit, and the condition was included in the contract to allay his concerns about giving credit to the buyer and to induce his agreement[7]. The court need not to have applied a subjective standard. It could have accommodated the seller's individual circumstances just as well by using an objective test: His satisfaction could have been measured by the standard of a reasonable nonprofessional lender in his position, taking into account his level of expertise and his economic circumstances. It is worth reiterating a point that has been made several times before: One does not necessarily get a different result by using the more subjective good faith standard instead of the more objective reasonableness standard because it could be difficult for a party to establish that unreasonable dissatisfaction is honest and genuine.

§16.8.3 The Use of a Condition to Provide for Alternative Performances

In the example involving the sale of land subject to rezoning, the denial of the application completely released Buyer from his promise to buy the land. However, a condition need not invariably result in the total termination of a party's performance obligation. Because a condition is a contractual term, the parties can agree that some other consequence will follow its nonfulfillment. To illustrate, reconsider the land sale example with slightly changed facts: As before, at the time of contracting, Seller's application for rezoning

---

7. Although the court applied a subjective standard, it ultimately ruled against the seller. It found that the seller did not satisfy the standard of good faith because his dissatisfaction was not genuine. He claimed dissatisfaction as a pretext for terminating the agreement because the buyer refused to renegotiate the price.

was pending. If it succeeds, the land can be used for a housing development, but if not, it can only be used for farming. Buyer wishes to have the land irrespective of the outcome, but the parties recognize that its value will be very much higher if the zoning is changed. To accommodate the uncertainty of the application's outcome, they may contract for the sale, but may provide in the contract that its purchase price is $100,000 (its market value as farmland), yet if the rezoning application is successful, the price will be $300,000 (its value as a tract capable of residential development). Here, as before, the parties agree to make Buyer's performance contingent on an uncertain future event—the change in zoning. However, the condition does not operate to release Buyer, but to commit him to an alternative promise that changes the extent of his performance. The condition is used as a channeling device, not as an escape clause. This is illustrated in Diagram 16J.

Diagram 16J

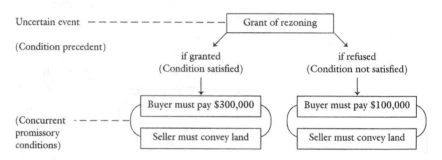

§16.8.4 The Use of a Condition to Regulate the Sequence of Performance

Conditions are routinely used to set the sequence of performances under the contract. That is, where parties structure a contract so that one performance must occur before another is due, they are, either expressly or impliedly, using conditions as a means of sequencing performances. If the parties say nothing in the contract about which performance must occur first, there are default rules that apply: If the performances are capable of being rendered simultaneously, the presumption is that the parties intended concurrent performances. However, if one of the performances is capable of being rendered instantaneously and the other needs time to be accomplished, the completion of the longer performance is deemed to be a condition precedent of the instantaneous one. This means that the party with the longer performance must go first. Of course, these are only default rules, so the parties can change them by providing differently in their contract. They can set up any sequence of performances that they think fit, and can even split up one or both parties' performances to provide for portions of each to be rendered serially.

Where parties provide for the sequencing of performances in a contract, they are in fact using conditions to achieve this end. They may do so expressly, by stating that an earlier performance is a condition precedent to a subsequent performance. However, even if they do not say this expressly, the fact that a sequence of performances is provided for readily leads to the implication that the parties intended an earlier performance to be a promissory condition precedent to a later one. To illustrate, consider the following example: The owner of property contracts with a builder to build a house on it. The builder's performance — constructing the house — will take several months, while the owner's performance — payment — could be accomplished in a single instant. If the parties do not provide for a sequencing of performances in the contract, the default rule is that the builder must fully perform before the owner has to pay. Completion of construction is therefore construed as a promissory condition precedent to payment. This requires the builder to wait for his money until he has built the house and places the entire risk of the owner's nonpayment on the builder. If the builder does not want this result, he will negotiate a different order of performance with the owner. The owner will probably not agree to pay in advance, because that shifts the whole risk of the builder's nonperformance to him. Therefore, the parties will probably agree on a sequence that allows the builder to be paid as the work progresses and that more evenly shares the risk of default. To do this, the parties use promissory conditions to break the performance into stages. For example, the contract may require the owner to pay a 10 percent deposit one week after the contract is signed; one week thereafter, the builder must begin to excavate and build the foundation; on completion the owner must pay a further 10 percent of the price; the builder must then frame the house; when that is done the owner must pay another 10 percent. This sequence of alternating performances goes on until the entire house is built and the builder has received periodic payments of 90 percent, upon which the owner must pay the final installment. Each of the incremental performances is a promise by the one party and also (whether stated so expressly or implied or construed) a condition precedent to the next stage of performance by the other. This means that if any one stage of performance is not rendered, the party entitled to that performance can refuse to render the consequent return performance and can claim breach. For instance, if the owner fails to pay after the excavation and foundation, the builder has the right to refuse to do the framing and may also sue the owner for breaching the contract.

§16.9 THE DOCTRINE OF SUBSTANTIAL COMPLIANCE IN CONSTRUED PROMISSORY CONDITIONS

Section 16.3.1 explained that if the parties have taken the trouble to create an express condition by clear language in the contract, the court will strictly enforce the express condition and unless the express condition is exactly satisfied, the conditional duty does not become due. The justification for this doctrine of strict compliance is that the parties have clearly chosen to make performance subject to the stated event, and the court should honor this intention by upholding the beneficiary party's right to demand nothing less than exact fulfillment of the condition. Therefore, even if it seems that the condition is rather technical and apparently unimportant, or even if it has been substantially satisfied, so that the shortcoming in compliance is rather unimportant or trivial, the court should not second-guess the parties by treating the condition as having been met.

Section 16.3.3 explained that the doctrine of strict enforcement does not apply to construed conditions. This difference in approach to express and construed conditions has particular importance where one of the parties has not exactly complied with a promissory condition. This may be illustrated by looking again at the example in section 16.8.4 involving the building contract under which the owner undertook to make a 10 percent down payment a week after execution of the contract, and the builder committed to begin construction a week thereafter. If the language of the contract clearly articulates that this is also a condition precedent to the builder's duty to commence performance, the owner's failure to pay the full amount of the deposit by due date constitutes nonfulfillment of the condition, so that the builder's obligation to perform does not arise. Because strict compliance is required, the owner will not be deemed to have satisfied the condition if, say, he pays the deposit one day late. However, if the promise's role as a condition is not expressly stated but is construed as a matter of reasonable intent from the way in which the contract has set out the sequence of performances, the court has more flexibility. It may employ the doctrine of substantial compliance and decide whether the delay in payment is good enough to constitute fulfillment of the condition.

Of course, we must not forget that the owner's down payment is a promissory condition. Therefore, late payment of the deposit raises not only the question of whether strict compliance with the condition is required, but also whether the owner's breach of his promise to pay at the time specified is a serious or minor breach. This issue is deferred to Chapter 17, but it is useful to note at this stage that where a promissory condition is involved, the impact of the deficiency in performance must be evaluated from both perspectives. As Chapter 17 will show, there is usually a close coordination in the results of these two enquiries, so that a minor breach that qualifies as substantial performance of the promise is likely to be also a substantial compliance with the condition, and a material breach will likely be a nonfulfillment of the condition as well. The effect of this may be illustrated by returning to our example: If late payment is a serious violation of the contract, the builder would be entitled to withhold performance and also to rescind the contract and claim the full extent of relief necessary to compensate for the lost expectation. However, if the delay is trivial, substantial compliance with the condition does not discharge the builder's duty to perform, and the minor breach does not permit rescission. The builder must perform and is confined to claiming compensation, in the form of a monetary allowance, for any loss caused by the inadequacy of performance.

§16.10 THE EXCUSE OF CONDITIONS: WRONGFUL PREVENTION, WAIVER OR ESTOPPEL, AND FORFEITURE

If a performance is subject to a condition, it does not fall due unless that condition is satisfied. However, circumstances may change after the contract is entered into, making it unfair or unreasonable to require the condition to be satisfied, or the inequitable conduct of the beneficiary of the condition may preclude his assertion of its nonfulfillment, or the impact of the condition may otherwise be so harsh that its enforcement would be unjust. To take account of this, the law recognizes certain limited and defined situations in which the condition may be excused to prevent injustice. If grounds for excuse exist, the condition falls away and the contingent obligation becomes absolute. That is, it is no longer conditional and must be performed despite the nonoccurrence of the event originally contemplated in the contract. In this section we look at three of the most common and important bases for excuse.

§16.10.1 The Party Favored by the Condition Wrongfully Prevents or Hinders Its Fulfillment

Some conditions are completely beyond the control of the promisor, and she has no power to do anything to facilitate or to hinder their occurrence. For example, if a lessor promises the lessee that she will install air conditioning in the premises next year if the average temperature for this August reaches 100 degrees, there is little that the lessor can do to manipulate the weather so as to influence the fulfillment of the condition. If a party has no capacity to influence the happening of the condition, she cannot, of course, wrongfully prevent its fulfillment. But some conditions are, to a greater or lesser extent, capable of being influenced by one or both parties.

a. When a Party Has a Duty to Take Active Steps to Facilitate Occurrence of the Condition

We saw in section 16.5.2 that even if a party does not promise that the condition will be fulfilled, she may at least have some role to play in affecting it, and may expressly or impliedly promise to make reasonable efforts in good faith to attempt to bring it about. In section 16.5.2, this was illustrated by an example involving a contract to buy a home, under which the buyer's obligation to proceed with the purchase is subject to his being able to obtain a mortgage. Although the buyer does not promise to obtain the mortgage (so the condition is not promissory), the buyer does make a promise, either express or implied, to make best efforts to secure it. If she makes adequate efforts to obtain the financing, but fails, the condition is not fulfilled and she has no duty to proceed with the purchase. However, if she does not try to get the loan, or makes only a halfhearted or token attempt, she violates her duty to deal fairly with the seller. She is therefore taken to have hindered fulfillment of the condition. This allows the seller to claim that the condition is excused, so that he can enforce her promise to purchase the house as if the condition had not existed. This means that if the buyer has refused to proceed with the purchase on grounds of nonfulfillment of the condition, that refusal is not justified and is a breach.

b. Obstructive Conduct

Even if a party has no duty to cooperate actively in the condition's fulfillment, the obligation of fair dealing may require her not to do anything to obstruct fulfillment of the condition. The example in section 16.1 involving the sale of farmland subject to rezoning may be used again to illustrate this point. Because the rezoning application had already been submitted by Seller and was awaiting disposition by the zoning authority, Buyer was not required to make active efforts to try to bring about the condition's occurrence. (That is, it is a pure condition, without any promissory elements.) Nevertheless, Buyer's general obligation of fair dealing does create an implied promise not to act in bad faith to prevent its occurrence. Therefore, the condition may be excused if its nonoccurrence resulted from some wrongful action by Buyer to negatively influence the local authority's decision. (For example, he persuaded a neighboring landowner to file an objection to the application, or he lobbied members of the board to vote against it.)

To be wrongful, Buyer's action must be a violation of his duty of good faith and fair dealing under the contract. In the above example, Buyer's attempt to influence the local authority's action clearly violates this duty because it undermines the contract's purpose. However, one should not assume, as a matter of course, that every contract imposes an implied duty not to act in a way that obstructs fulfillment of a condition. This is a matter of interpretation, dependent on the apparent intent of the parties, and some contracts may contemplate that the promisor does have the right to try to avoid satisfaction of the condition. For example, if a buyer promises to purchase goods from the seller on condition that he cannot find them cheaper elsewhere, the buyer obviously has the right to try to avoid satisfaction of the condition by seeking cheaper goods, and these efforts would not be a wrongful obstruction of the condition.

c. The Link Between Conduct and Nonfulfillment

When the promisor has wrongfully failed to make a good faith and reasonable effort to facilitate occurrence or has acted in an obstructive way, it may not be clear if that conduct was directly responsible for nonfulfillment of the condition. For example, the buyer of the house may not have obtained a mortgage, even had she made a genuine and conscientious effort, or the rezoning board may have refused the application even without Buyer's interference. Some courts have imposed a strict test of causation, excusing the condition only if it can be shown that the condition would have been fulfilled, but for the promisor's obstruction. A less rigorous test, favored by other courts, does not require the promisee to demonstrate as strong a causal link, but merely to show that the promisor's conduct played a significant role in the condition's nonfulfillment.

§16.10.2 Estoppel or Waiver

Estoppel and waiver are distinct doctrines, but they are quite muddled in the context of excuse of conditions because conduct is often ambiguous enough to be classified as giving rise to either of them. As a result, courts sometimes do not take the trouble to differentiate them, and Restatement, Second, §§84 and 230(3) combine them into a general principle of excuse. The basic idea is that after the contract is entered into, the promisor whose duty is conditional indicates by words or conduct that he will perform even if the condition does not occur. This indication of intent not to require compliance with the condition may take place either before the time on which the condition is to occur, or after that time has passed and the condition has not been satisfied. Although there are some differences in legal analysis depending on whether the condition is dispensed with before or after it is due to occur, these will not be explored here. This discussion is confined to an explanation of the basic principles applicable in either case. Although the two doctrines of estoppel and waiver are intermingled in this area, they do give rise to distinct justifications for excusing a condition, so it is useful to describe them separately and to show why they are so easily mixed up.

a. Estoppel

Estoppel, an equitable doctrine, was introduced in section 8.4. Its purpose is to prevent the unfair assertion of rights by a person who has acted inconsistently with those rights. The basic effect of the doctrine is to preclude a person from asserting a right when, by deliberate words or conduct, and with knowledge or reason to know that the words or conduct will likely be relied on by another, the actor causes the other party detriment by inducing the justifiable belief that the right does not exist or that it will not be asserted. In the context of conditions, the party who is the beneficiary of the condition may be estopped from claiming its nonfulfillment if, by her words or conduct, she induces the other party to act to his detriment by causing him justifiably to believe that the condition has been satisfied, or that compliance with it will not be required. (If, instead of misrepresenting a fact, the beneficiary party promises that she will not require compliance with the condition, the basis for relief is promissory estoppel rather than equitable estoppel, but the elements for relief are so similar, that the analysis is the same.)

To illustrate, consider again the example involving the sale of land subject to the condition that the rezoning application is granted within 60 days of execution of the contract. Fifty-five days after execution of the contract, the zoning authority tells Seller that it will not be ready to make a decision for at least two weeks. When Seller informs Buyer of this, he responds by stating that he is willing to wait an additional two weeks. On the strength of this, Seller forgoes an opportunity to sell the land to someone else. If, on the 61st day, Buyer sought to escape the contract by asserting nonfulfillment of the condition, he would likely be estopped from doing so, because he deliberately indicated to Seller that he would not insist on compliance with the 60-day provision and Seller justifiably relied on that assertion to her detriment.

b. Waiver

A waiver occurs when, after the contract has been made, the beneficiary of a condition agrees to perform even if the condition is not satisfied. In essence, the waiver is a voluntary abandonment of a contractual right. (Naturally, a party can only waive a condition that is solely for his benefit. One party cannot waive rights belonging to the other.) For example, after the rezoning application is denied, Buyer informs Seller that he wishes to proceed with the transaction despite the denial. If Buyer then refuses to perform, Seller can claim that Buyer's performance obligation became unconditional because the condition was excused by the waiver. A waiver must be distinguished from a contract modification. A modification is a contract in itself—a mutual agreement under which one party agrees to relinquish rights in return for consideration given by the other. A waiver is one-sided—one of the parties unilaterally gives up a contractual right without asking for or receiving anything in exchange. Because consideration is required for a valid modification, the general rule is that if the right to be given up is an important part of the exchange under the contract (that is, it is a material right) it cannot be validly relinquished by a unilateral waiver. Its abandonment must be exchanged for consideration in a full-fledged contractual modification. However, if the right relinquished is nonmaterial—ancillary, and not a central part of the contractual exchange—the consideration requirement is dispensed with and it can be validly waived. To decide if the grant of the rezoning application was a material part of the exchange and therefore not validly waivable without consideration, the role of the condition and its significance in the exchange must be determined by interpretation. (This is, of course, the common law rule, because UCC §2.209 does not require consideration for a modification. Therefore, even the waiver of a material part of the exchange would be valid despite a lack of consideration.)

The issue of consideration for a waiver only arises when it is the party entitled to the conditional performance who seeks to excuse the condition and to enforce the performance against the beneficiary of the condition. It does not apply when it is the beneficiary of the condition who elects to abandon his right to protection of the condition. For example, it was mentioned in section 16.4 that if the grant of the rezoning application is solely for Buyer's benefit, he can decide to proceed with the sale of the property as farmland, even if the application is denied. In such a case, Buyer is not attempting to enforce rights arising out of the excuse of a condition, but is merely enforcing his original rights for which he gave consideration under the contract. Seller cannot resist this by arguing that she gave Buyer no consideration for his waiver.

c. Distinguishing Waiver from Estoppel

As noted earlier, it can be difficult to distinguish waiver from estoppel. The estoppel example given above can be used to show just how ambiguous the distinction can be. In that example, it was stated that Buyer's conduct in indicating that he would wait a further two weeks for approval estopped him from asserting nonfulfillment of the condition on the 61st day. It could just as well be said that Buyer waived his right to have the condition fulfilled within 60 days. If the time for approval is not a central component of the exchange (which it appears not to be, but that is a question of interpretation), the waiver without consideration is valid and binding. Thus, in most situations, conduct by the party benefitted by the condition could equally well support an estoppel or waiver argument, so they should generally be regarded as alternative bases for excuse. Selection of the theory to be used would be based on the issues of reliance and materiality. Estoppel is more appropriate if detrimental reliance can be shown and there is some question about whether the right relinquished is material enough to require consideration. Waiver is a better argument if no prejudicial reliance can be established, but there is an argument that the abandoned right is ancillary, not central to the exchange.

d. Retraction of a Waiver

Although, as stated earlier, we will not go into the details of the distinction between waivers prior to and after the due date for occurrence of the condition, there is one point on which it is useful to indicate a difference in approach. If the waiver is made prior to the due date of the condition's fulfillment, it can be retracted provided that notice of retraction is received by the other party before he acts in reliance on the waiver. However, if the waiver is made after the time for occurrence of the condition has passed (so that it is clear that the condition has failed to occur), it cannot be retracted because the party benefitted by the condition is treated as having made a final election to proceed with the transaction despite nonoccurrence of the condition.

§16.10.3 Unfair Forfeiture

The doctrine of unfair forfeiture is a general principle under which the court may exercise its discretion to decline the full enforcement of one party's legal rights where doing so would have a disproportionately harsh impact on the other party. Courts use the doctrine sparingly, and only under circumstances that strongly demand the exercise of this discretion. This is particularly important to bear in mind in the area of conditions because any finding of liability under a contract, or any conclusion that a party is not entitled to performance because of the nonfulfillment of a condition, results in some forfeiture of money or expected benefits. Therefore, the doctrine of unfair forfeiture should not be applied unless enforcement of the condition would result in an inequitable windfall or benefit to one of the parties at the expense of a disproportionate and harsh consequence to the other. Thus, in deciding forfeiture, the court balances the relative hardships between the parties. It weighs the burden on the party who would suffer if the condition was enforced against the harm that excuse would do to the beneficiary of the condition.

This ground for excusing a condition is really a safety valve that ameliorates the harsh results that may follow from the rule of strict compliance with express conditions. It is therefore most useful when the condition is express and unambiguous, and is not needed when the court has flexibility in construing the terms and scope of the condition, or when ambiguous language can be interpreted in a way that avoids an unfair result. (In setting out standards of interpretation, Restatement, Second, §227 expresses a general preference in favor of interpretation that will avoid forfeiture in cases when there is doubt about the existence, scope, or nature of a condition.)

The principal purpose of the forfeiture doctrine, set out in Restatement, Second, §229, is to allow the court to disregard an express condition of a technical or procedural nature where the strict enforcement of the condition would have the unfair impact described above. It should therefore not be used if the occurrence of the condition is a material part of the exchange. To illustrate, say that an insurance policy provides two express conditions to the insurer's liability. The first is that the insured must pay the annual premium, and the second is that the insured must notify the insurer of loss within five days of its occurrence. Payment of the premium is surely a material part of the exchange — it is the entire consideration bargained for by the insurer. Therefore, if the insured suffers a loss after failing to pay the premium, he cannot claim unfair forfeiture of his right to reimbursement and ask the court to excuse the condition of payment. However, if he has paid the premium, and he does give notice of loss, but is one day late in giving it, the court is more likely to be sympathetic to an argument that the insurer's insistence on strict fulfillment is a technicality, and the insured's deprivation of his right of reimbursement would be an unfair forfeiture.

§16.11 A TRANSNATIONAL PERSPECTIVE ON CONDITIONS AND PROMISES

The common law's terminology relating to conditions and promises and its mode of analyzing the distinction developed through the judicial interpretation of contractual intent. Civilian systems do not use the same analytical framework, but general principles of interpretation usually lead to similar results. Like UCC Article 2, the CISG does not set out general rules relating to conditions and promises, which are governed by general principles of applicable law. (Article 7(2) makes general principles of law applicable in areas not specifically covered by the provisions of the CISG.) The CISG does contain some more specific provisions that comport with the common law's understanding of the distinction between conditions and promises, even though the language of the provisions is quite general and is not couched in terms of condition or promise. For example, Article 58 contains a default rule similar to UCC Article 2 that requires payment and delivery to be concurrent.

The UNIDROIT Principles likewise do not address the distinction between conditions and promises expressly or in the detail in which they have been analyzed in this chapter. However, the outcome of issues discussed in this chapter would commonly be the same in many situations because Article 4.1(1) calls for interpretation to ascertain the intent of the parties. There are a few provisions of the Principles that are somewhat more specific. For example, Article 6.1.4 deals with order of performance and contains a default rule that unless otherwise agreed, instantaneous performances are to be rendered simultaneously, but a performance that is to take time should be rendered before an instantaneous performance. Article 7.1.3 allows a party to withhold performance until it receives a performance that is to be rendered previously or simultaneously, and Article 7.3.1 allows a party to terminate performance in response to "fundamental nonperformance."

Examples

1. This first Example is an exercise in classification. Identify the promises, conditions, and promissory conditions in the following contracts. Having identified the conditions, consider whether they are express or construed and precedent or concurrent, and also identify the purpose that the condition serves in the contract.

   a. A lessor and a lessee entered into a lease of real property for a two-year term at a rent of $1,200 a month, payable in advance by the first day of each month. The lease gave the lessee the right to renew the lease for a further two years provided that she delivered written notice of renewal to the lessor not later than 30 days prior to the end of the second year of the lease. The rent for the renewal period would be $1,500 per month, but if the lessee satisfactorily repainted the premises in the first month of the renewal period, the rent would be $1,400 per month.

   b. An insurance policy provides that in consideration for an annual premium, payable in advance, the insurer will reimburse the insured for any loss by fire occurring on the insured premises, provided that the insured furnishes satisfactory proof of loss to the insurer within 30 days of the loss.

   c. On June 1, the owner of land granted an option to purchase the land. The prospective buyer had until June 30 to exercise the option. On

June 10, a second buyer expressed interest in purchasing the land, and the owner entered into a contract with him under which she agreed to sell it for $100,000 if the grantee of the option failed to exercise it by its expiration on June 30.

d. Following discussions on the possible sale of a car, the owner of the car writes to the prospective buyer, stating, "I will sell you my car for $5,000 on condition that you communicate your acceptance to me within five days of the date of this letter."

2. Wendy Vendee entered into a contract with Homer Sellar for the purchase of Homer's house for $400,000. The contract, recorded on a standard form, provided that Wendy would pay $100,000 in cash on closing and would pay the balance of the price in installments over 15 years. To secure payment of the balance, Homer would take a first mortgage in the property, to be recorded at the time of transfer. In a blank space at the end of the form, Homer wrote the sentence, "This contract is contingent on seller's approval of buyer's credit report." Both parties initialed this handwritten addition.

Shortly after the contract was signed, Homer obtained a credit report on Wendy. It showed that Wendy had gone on a credit-card spending binge five years ago and had to file a voluntary bankruptcy petition to discharge unmanageable debt. The report also showed that since obtaining her bankruptcy discharge, Wendy apparently no longer used credit cards and had not defaulted on any other debts. Homer considers bankruptcy to be shameful and thinks it immoral for a person to go on a spending spree and then file bankruptcy to get out of paying her debts in full. He no longer wished to deal with someone as unworthy as Wendy, and he certainly did not trust her enough to give her credit. Homer therefore disapproved the credit report and declared the sale to be terminated.

Wendy objected and said that Homer had no basis to reject her credit report. Wendy can show that Homer's attitude is tougher than that prevailing among financial institutions in the consumer credit industry, which would be likely to approve Wendy's credit under these circumstances. The reasoning in the industry is that a five-year-old abuse of credit and bankruptcy filing should not be held against a borrower who has behaved responsibly since then, particularly when the loan applied for is fully secured by a mortgage on real property. Did Homer have the right to disapprove the report and cancel the sale?

3. Assume that the contract between Wendy Vendee and Homer Sellar was on slightly different terms: Like the contract in Example 2, it provided for the sale of the home to Wendy for $400,000, of which $100,000 would be paid in cash on closing, and the balance would be paid to the seller over 15 years, secured by the seller's mortgage on the property.

The contract had no condition concerning a credit report. Instead, in the blank space at the end of the standard form, the parties had included the following handwritten term:

> This contract is subject to the buyer's sale of her present home for not less than $350,000 within 30 days hereof.

The reason for including this term was that at the time of the contract Wendy already owned a smaller house that she needed to sell, so that she could use the proceeds of her equity in the house to pay the $100,000 cash due on closing. Wendy's old home was subject to a mortgage of $200,000, so she had to sell it for at least $350,000 to pay the mortgage, broker's fees, and other costs and expenses, leaving at least $100,000 clear for her cash payment to Homer.

Consider the following separate and distinct factual variations:

a. After signing the contract, Wendy decided that she would save having to pay realtor's commission by marketing the house herself. She bought one of those "for sale by owner" kits, erected "for sale" signs, and placed advertisements in the paper. Unfortunately, Wendy is overbearing and insensitive and has no skill in dealing with people. Although several prospective buyers responded to her advertising, she scared all of them away with her rude and aggressive sales technique. As a result, she had not managed to sell her house by the end of the 30-day period. Wendy therefore claims that she is no longer obliged to buy Homer's house. Is she correct?

b. After signing the contract with Homer, Wendy decided that she would not sell her existing house as planned, but would keep it as rental property. To raise the down payment, she would instead borrow the $100,000 from her sister. She immediately called Homer, explained this, and told him that she waived the condition. Does Homer have any grounds for objection?

4. Consider another variation of the contract between Wendy and Homer. As before, it provided for the sale of the house to Wendy for $400,000, of which $100,000 was to be paid in cash on closing. However, unlike the prior examples, Wendy was to seek her own financing so the contract did not provide for Homer himself to extend credit for the sale on security of a mortgage. Therefore, the contract was not contingent on a satisfactory credit report. Also, Wendy did not currently own a home, so the contract was also not conditional on her selling an existing house. Instead, it contained the following provision:

> This sale is subject to the buyer obtaining a loan from a bank or other lending institution, secured by a first mortgage on the property purchased hereunder, in an amount of not less than $300,000, extending for a term of at least 15 years, and at a rate of interest not exceeding 5 percent per annum. If, after the exercise of due diligence, the buyer is unable to obtain financing

on these terms, this contract shall terminate, and neither party shall have any liability to the other.

Immediately after Wendy signed the agreement, she consulted a mortgage broker. Upon reviewing Wendy's truthful and accurate financial statement, the broker told Wendy that her income was insufficient and her indebtedness too large to qualify her for a loan of $300,000 from any lender that he knew. This made Wendy realize that she had bought a house beyond her means, and she was relieved that the financing contingency had been included in the agreement of sale. She promptly notified Homer of termination of the sale on the ground that the condition had not been satisfied. On hearing that Wendy had given up after an interview with a single broker and had done nothing more to seek financing, Homer claimed that Wendy had not exercised due diligence in trying to satisfy the condition. Is he correct?

5. Martha Tooby owned a zippy two-seater sports car. She was expecting a baby in about a month and needed to replace the sports car with a vehicle more suitable for transporting a baby. In response to an advertisement, she went to look at a minivan owned by Minnie Vann on August 3. Martha liked the minivan and wished to buy it. However, she could not afford the $15,000 price unless she first sold the sports car. Martha and Minnie therefore executed a written contract on August 3, under which Minnie sold the van to Martha for $15,000. The contract included a provision that stated, "Martha's obligation to buy the minivan is conditional on her selling her sports car for a price not less than $12,500 by not later than August 10." On August 4, Martha placed a weeklong advertisement to sell her sports car for the price of $13,000. During the course of the week, she had several inquiries in response to the advertisement, but received no offers to buy the car. On August 10, she received a response from Delia Breaker. It turned out that Delia owned a roomy SUV, but she no longer needed such a large vehicle and wanted a sports car instead. She had planned to sell the SUV, but it made more sense for the parties simply to trade the vehicles. The retail bluebook value of Delia's SUV was $12,425. Because this value was close enough to Martha's asking price for the sports car, they agreed on an even trade. Delia and Martha completed the transaction on August 10 by delivering possession of the vehicles to each other and exchanging title transfer forms. Martha no longer needs Minnie's van. She therefore informed Minnie that because she had traded the sports car, and did not sell it, the condition had not been satisfied and she was terminating the contract. Minnie disagrees. She says that Martha's barter of the car did in fact constitute a sale that satisfied the condition, so that Martha is legally obligated to buy her van or to pay damages for breach of contract. Who is correct?

6. Primo Contracting Co. is a general contractor. It was engaged in the construction of an office building under a contract with the owner of the property. Primo entered into a subcontract with Cool Conditions, Inc. (CC) for the supply and installation of the building's air conditioning unit. The subcontract between Primo and CC required the unit to be installed by July 1, and further stated: "The price due to CC under this contract shall not be payable until the project's architect has certified that the air conditioning unit has been properly installed in working order and, following such certification, Primo has received payment for this work from the owner."

   CC competently installed a fully operational air conditioning unit by June 15. On June 17, before the unit had been inspected by the architect, the owner of the property filed for bankruptcy. The owner's estate is hopelessly insolvent so no funds will be available to pay any of the debts arising from the construction. The project was abandoned and the architect resigned. Primo has not been paid for any work done during the last month, including the air conditioning.[8]

   CC has demanded payment from Primo, but Primo has refused on the grounds that neither of the two conditions of its obligation to pay — the architect's certification and the owner's payment — has been fulfilled. Is this a good argument?

7. Larson E. Grand owned an old vacant office building in a bad part of town. Because the building was unoccupied, he did not see the point of paying for burglary insurance, but he did buy an insurance policy from Equity & Fidelity Indemnity Co., Inc. (E&F) to cover damage or destruction resulting from other causes. The relevant terms of the policy stated:
   a. In consideration for the premium paid, Insurer undertakes to reimburse Insured for any loss resulting from damage to or destruction of the above-described premises caused by fire, storm, explosion, nuclear accident, civil commotion, or vandalism.
   b. For the purposes of this policy, "vandalism" is restricted to and includes only willful and malicious physical injury to the premises and excludes any loss by pilferage, theft, or burglary.
   c. No claim shall be paid under this policy unless Insured notifies Insurer of loss within seven days thereof, and submits proof of loss within a further 14 days. No action taken by Insurer to investigate such claim shall operate as a waiver of any of the terms of this policy.

---

8. You may be aware that unpaid contractors and subcontractors are entitled to a statutory lien (called a construction lien or a mechanic's lien) for unpaid labor or materials used to improve real property. This lien attaches to the real property and it arises in favor of a subcontractor even though it had no contract with the owner. Disregard these lien rights for the purposes of this Example. (Assume, say, that the lien rights are worthless because the property is fully encumbered by a pre-existing mortgage.)

The plumbing in the building was copper pipe that has some value as scrap. A few months after the policy was issued, someone broke into the building and removed all the copper pipe. To extract the pipe, the thief ripped open walls and floorboards, causing extensive damage to the building.

Larson discovered the break-in the next morning. He had to leave town on a trip that day, and did not report the loss to E&F until his return, eight days later. When he notified E&F of the loss, he told its representative that the break-in had occurred eight days previously. The E&F representative did not comment on this. E&F sent out a loss adjuster the next day. After inspecting the premises, the adjuster said "Get estimates for fixing this damage and get them to me as soon as you can. I must warn you, however, that this looks like burglary, not vandalism, and I don't think it is covered by your policy." Larson protested that it looked like vandalism of the worst kind, but the adjuster said that there was no point in their arguing about it. The claims department would make the decision, so Larson should submit the estimates and see what happens. Larson submitted the estimates a couple of days later. Shortly afterwards, he received a letter from E&F rejecting his claim on the basis that the loss resulted from burglary and was excluded from coverage. Larson sued E&F for reimbursement of his loss. E&F defended the suit on two grounds — first, that the loss was not covered by the policy and, second, that Larson had not notified it of the loss within the time prescribed by the policy. Should these defenses succeed?

8. Sue Burbanite owned a piece of land in a fast-growing suburb. Sprawling Malls, Inc., a developer of shopping malls, had some interest in building a mall on Sue's land. However, it needed to study more carefully the economic feasibility of the project, and to raise adequate funds from investors. In 2011, Sprawling Malls entered into negotiations with Sue to acquire an option to purchase the land. Sprawling Malls believed that it could conduct a comprehensive feasibility study and attract investors within a year. It therefore proposed buying a year's option to purchase the property. Sue was amenable to this, and the parties ultimately entered into an option contract on December 1, 2011, under which Sprawling Malls was given the option to purchase the land for $1.5 million. The provisions of the contract concerning the option itself were as follows: Sprawling Malls agreed to pay Sue $10,000 for the year's option, payable on the signing of the contract. If Sprawling Malls wished to exercise its option to purchase the property it was required "by not later than November 30, 2012, to deliver to Sue Burbanite written notice of its intention to exercise the option."

After the contract was signed, Sprawling Malls paid Sue the $10,000 and began its feasibility study. By June 2012 the study had been

603

completed at a cost of $300,000. It showed the shopping center development to be a viable project. Armed with the study, Sprawling Malls began to solicit investors. After some considerable effort, it finally managed to raise the necessary capital by late November 2012. On November 29, it mailed written notice to Sue, exercising its option to purchase the land. The letter was delayed in the mail and not received until December 1.

Sue had wanted to escape her contract with Sprawling Malls because the value of the property had increased since December 2011, and she would now be able to sell it for more than $1.5 million. She therefore rejected the attempted exercise of the option on the basis that it was received after the expiry of the option period. Does Sprawling Malls have a basis for challenging this?

Explanations

1. a. The lessee's payment of rent and the lessor's obligation to give the lessee use and occupation of the premises are dependent promises. That is, each party's performance is a promissory condition of the other's. Even if the conditional nature of the promises is not expressly stated in the lease, it is easily construed as being what the parties reasonably must have intended. The parties have structured the lease so that the performance of each is broken into monthly segments. The lessee's payment of the month's rent is a condition precedent to that month's tenancy, and the lessor's making the premises available for that month is in turn a condition precedent to the next rent payment. (So, if either party breaches his obligation, the other can withhold the next performance in the sequence in addition to suing for damages for breach of the lease.)

With regard to the lessee's renewal option, her delivery of notice of renewal within the prescribed time is an express condition precedent to the extension of the lease for another two years. (Its conditional nature is expressed in the language of the lease by use of the term "provided that.") It is not a promissory condition, nor even a condition subject to an implied promise to use reasonable efforts in good faith, because the lessee has no obligation to renew and need not deliver the notice unless she wishes to extend the lease. If she does want to extend, she must comply exactly with the terms of the condition. As an express condition, it will be strictly enforced.

If the lessee does exercise the renewal option, the same set of promissory conditions—payment of rent and occupation of the premises—continue through the renewal period. In addition, the lease contains another condition intended to give the lessee a choice of alternative performances: If she paints the premises in the first month of the renewal period, her rent is reduced by $100 per month. Although this condition does not use clear language of condition such as "on condition that" or "provided that," its conditional nature is clear enough to qualify it as express. It is not a promissory condition, in that the lessee has no obligation to paint the premises if she would rather pay the extra rent.

Finally, if the lessee does elect to paint the premises, she implicitly promises to do so in a workmanlike manner. The rent reduction is contingent on the paint job being satisfactory to the lessor. This condition of satisfaction is subject to a promise (implied in law, if not expressed) that the lessor will act reasonably or in good faith in assessing whether the painting is satisfactory. The preference is for an objective standard to measure satisfaction, particularly if the work is commercial or technical in nature. However, a subjective good faith standard is used if it is clear from the wording of the contract or from the nature of the performance that the parties intended satisfaction to be measured by the individual taste of the party who is to make the judgment.

b. The insurer's obligation to indemnify the insured is subject to four conditions precedent. The first is that the insured has paid the premium due under the policy. The second is that a loss by fire on the premises occurs, the third is that the insured gives proof of loss within the time specified, and the fourth is that the insurer is satisfied with the proof.

Payment of the premium appears to be a condition precedent to coverage. The language of the payment term, as suggested by the question, simply denotes the premium as consideration and does not, in so many words, expressly call it a condition of coverage. However, this does appear to be the import of the wording. The insured may or may not have promised to pay the premium. If he committed himself to pay it, it is a promissory condition. However, the application for coverage may not have obliged him to pay, but may merely have provided that coverage would not be extended unless it was paid. In that case, it is a pure condition. The purpose of this condition is to place the duty of advance payment on the insured and to suspend the insurer's contractual obligation until payment has been made.

The condition of loss does not use expressly conditional terminology, but there can be no doubt that loss must be a condition precedent to indemnity. This is so obvious that the implication of a condition is inevitable. It is also obvious that this cannot be a promissory condition. It would be a bizarre policy indeed, under which the insured committed himself to suffer a loss.

The condition of notice is express. It is also a pure condition because the insured has no obligation to submit the proof if he does not wish to claim under the policy. That is, the insurer would have no claim for breach if the insured failed to notify of loss. It would simply have no duty to indemnify. This condition is included in the policy to benefit the insurer, and its purpose is to ensure that the insurer will have no obligation to pay a claim that is not properly established within a short time of the loss.

The condition of satisfactory proof is likewise designed to protect the insurer by requiring probative proof of loss. Like the condition of satisfaction in Example 1(a), is subject to an implied promise that limits the insurer's discretion to be dissatisfied. Unquestionably, satisfaction must be measured here on an objective reasonableness standard.

c. The owner's obligation to sell the land to the buyer is subject to an express condition precedent that the option-holder does not exercise the option by June 30. This is not a promissory condition, because the seller makes no promise that the option will not be exercised. The purpose of the condition is to allow the parties to execute the sale agreement immediately, but to protect the seller from having committed to sell the property to two people. The condition enables the seller to escape the second contract if the grantee of the option (the first offeree) binds her by exercising the option. If the grantee of the option does not exercise it, the seller's obligation to convey the property becomes due, and accordingly, so does the buyer's obligation to pay for it. Even in the absence of expressly conditional language, these mutual promises of performances are construed as conditions of each other. Unless a different sequence is prescribed by the contract, they are deemed to be concurrent conditions because both are capable of instantaneous performance.

d. The letter is an offer, and one could say, broadly speaking, that the creation of the contract is conditional on acceptance within the time prescribed. However, despite the use of the word "condition" in the letter, the acceptance within five days is not a condition at all, in the sense used in this chapter. It is simply the time specified for acceptance. If the offer is accepted in time, a contract will be formed, under which the car is exchanged for $5,000. At that point, conditions in the contract will come into effect. The seller's promise to deliver the car and the buyer's promise to pay for it are dependent promises. Even if not expressly stated to be conditions of each other, they are construed promissory conditions. As in Example 1(c), they can be performed at the same time and are therefore deemed concurrent unless the contract specifies an order of performance.

2. This Example builds on *Foreman v. Benson* discussed in section 16.8.2, but provides detailed facts to allow you to apply the principles of the case. The provision concerning the credit report is a condition of satisfaction. It is an express condition precedent to Homer's obligation to sell the property to Wendy on credit. The purpose of the condition is obvious: It is intended to protect Homer from having to extend credit to Wendy if she proves to be uncreditworthy. Of course, Homer could have checked Wendy's credit before making the contract, but this would have delayed execution of the contract and risked loss of the deal. Homer avoided this risk by entering the contract immediately, subject to a satisfactory credit report.

A condition of satisfaction is not fully a promissory condition because Homer does not promise that he will be satisfied. However, this does not mean that Homer has unfettered discretion in deciding whether to be satisfied. Even if nothing is expressed in the contract to restrict his discretion, the law implies an obligation on him to exercise judgment honestly or reasonably. Unless the contract indicates differently, the objective standard is preferred, especially if the judgment involves matters of technical or commercial quality. The subjective standard of good faith is confined to contracts in which it is clearly contemplated that the performance must appeal to the party's aesthetic sense or personal taste.

The satisfaction condition simply refers to Homer's approval of the credit report and gives no indication of how his satisfaction is to be judged. Creditworthiness is quintessentially a matter of commercial utility, capable of being judged by market standards. Therefore, unless the contract clearly calls for a subjective evaluation, a buyer who submits to a credit check is not likely to have assumed the risk of subjecting herself to the seller's idiosyncrasies. Therefore, the fact that Homer has atypically strong moral qualms about bankruptcy is probably not good enough a basis for his dissatisfaction. He must judge Wendy's credit history purely on the basis of whether a person with her credit history presents a risk of default beyond a reasonably acceptable level.

However, even if we hold Homer to an objective standard, that does not automatically mean that we should apply the industry standard suggested by Wendy. Homer is not a member of the consumer financing establishment, but a simple homeowner who is selling his home on credit. A large and wealthy institution, which can distribute risks of default among many customers, is likely to be less risk-averse than a private seller. For this reason, the question is not what would constitute a reasonable credit report for the consumer credit industry, but what would be an acceptable report for a self-financing private seller. In other words, the answer suggested here is that an objective test be used, but the reasonable person evaluating the report should not be a professional lender, but a lender in Homer's position. As noted in section 18.6.2, this approach differs from the subjective standard used in *Foreman v. Benson*, but one does not need to use a subjective test to take into account the personal circumstances of the lender.

3. a. Because Wendy cannot afford to buy Homer's property without first selling her existing home, she has sensibly made her obligation to Homer contingent on selling it. That is, to avert the risk of being committed to Homer without any prospect of raising the $100,000, Wendy has agreed with Homer that her obligation to purchase his property is subject to the express condition precedent that Wendy can sell her home in 30 days. Although this is not a fully promissory condition, in that Wendy does not absolutely promise that the house will be sold, it is subject to the implied promise that Wendy will make a diligent effort to try to fulfill the condition. Diligence is not to be judged entirely subjectively, because Homer cannot be taken to have assumed the risk of idiosyncratic or irrational behavior.

   Therefore, the test is whether Wendy made an honest and genuine effort, as may reasonably be expected from a person in her position. Wendy may have tried hard to sell her house, but that does not seem good enough. Quite apart from Wendy's unfortunate personality, she was apparently not an experienced dealer in real estate. Given the short time provided in the contract for the satisfaction of the condition, she should not have attempted to sell the house on her own. This conclusion is reinforced by the fact that the price to be realized to satisfy the condition took broker's commission into account, indicating that the parties' reasonable expectation was that a broker would be used.

   If it is found that Wendy did not satisfy her implied obligation to use best efforts, this would be a ground for excusing the condition, so that the condition is deemed fulfilled. Homer can insist on her performance. If she fails to render it, she is in breach and Homer can sue for appropriate relief.

   b. Although Wendy could have abandoned this condition had it been solely for her benefit, the condition was not necessarily intended for her protection alone, and she therefore should not be able to waive it unilaterally. In addition to allowing her an escape if she cannot sell her house, the condition ensures that upon buying Homer's house, Wendy will have discharged the mortgage debt on her prior home. As the person financing Wendy's purchase of his house, Homer has an obvious stake in the level of her debt and may reasonably have taken this into account in agreeing to extend credit to her for the balance of the price. If she keeps her existing house and borrows money for the down payment, she increases her debt load, which may heighten the risk that she will default on her mortgage payments to Homer. (Although his mortgage in the property does secure his right to payment, foreclosure is inconvenient and costly, and there is always a danger that the proceeds of a foreclosure sale will not fully cover the balance of the mortgage.)

4. Like the conditions in Examples 2 and 3, the financing contingency is not fully a promissory condition, but the beneficiary party (Wendy) does commit to make best efforts to attempt its satisfaction. As long as she diligently applied for financing, she can escape the contract without liability for breach if she fails to obtain it. Unlike in the previous Example, Wendy's promise of due diligence is expressed in the contract and need not be construed. The sole question is whether her single discouraging interview with a mortgage broker was enough of an effort to qualify as due diligence.

   The question of whether a buyer used best efforts to try to have the condition satisfied is factual, to be decided under all the circumstances. If Wendy was reliably assured, on the strength of what the broker told her, that all further efforts to secure financing would be futile, her single approach to the broker may be sufficient. She should not be required to go through the motions of making doomed applications. However, she takes a risk in accepting what the broker told her. Unless she can show that the broker was correct, so that loan applications would be a pointless waste of time, she had a duty to make applications. The fact that her prospects of financing are uncertain should not dissuade her if there is any prospect that she may be successful. Wendy's decision not to make any loan applications looks especially bad in light of the fact that her desire to buy the house cooled once she realized that the house was too expensive for her. That creates the suspicion that she lost the motivation to make any further effort at all.

5. The condition that Martha sell her car for not less than $12,500 by August 10 is an express condition and must be strictly complied with. However, where an express condition contains an ambiguity, it must be interpreted to establish whether the occurrence of the event satisfied it. The ambiguity to be resolved here is whether the barter of the sports car qualifies as a "sale" as the parties used that word in their contract. The legal definition of sale is easy to discover, because it is included in UCC Article 2, which governs this sale of goods. Section 2.106(1) defines a sale as "the passing of title from the seller to the buyer for a price." Section 2.304 states that the price can be payable on money or otherwise. Clearly, a barter transaction is treated by Article 2 as a sale. The legal definition is not necessarily dispositive if it can be shown that the parties intended the word "sale" to have a narrower meaning. There

is some suggestion that they may have meant a sale for cash because the purpose of the condition was to allow Martha to realize the value of the sports car so she could apply it to the price of the minivan. However, it is not clear that the parties really focused on what they meant by "sale," so the meaning of the word must be construed. Construction probably inclines toward the statutory definition unless it can be established that the parties did not intend to use it in that sense.

Even if Minnie succeeds in her argument that barter qualifies as a sale, she has another problem. The condition was that the sports car must be sold for not less than $12,500. Because this is a barter transaction, the price of the sports car is determined by the value of the SUV that was exchanged for it. If the bluebook value is an accurate measure of value, this aspect of the condition was not satisfied, because the value of the SUV was $12,425. Under the rule that an express condition must be strictly enforced, even a small shortfall from the price stated in the condition would constitute nonfulfillment of the condition.

Minnie may also argue that the condition should be excused because, by bartering the sports car instead of selling it, Martha breached her implied promise to make reasonable efforts in good faith to try to achieve fulfillment of the condition. Although the condition is not promissory, an obligation of reasonable efforts in good faith is easily construed. Had Martha made no other efforts to sell the car, her decision to trade it for the cheaper SUV would provide a stronger basis for finding that the trade was a breach of this promise. However, the argument is less compelling because she had received no other offers for the car and the transaction occurred at the end of the weeklong period. Nevertheless, she may have had a duty to try harder to persuade Delia to pay $12,500 in cash, rather than to trade vehicles. This seems like a difficult argument on these facts, but if Minnie can establish a breach of the promise to make reasonable efforts in good faith to sell the car for $12,500, the court would excuse the condition and find Martha in breach for refusing to perform under the contract.

6. The contract expressly makes payment conditional upon the architect's certification of proper completion of CC's performance. It necessarily follows from this express condition that the proper performance itself is also a condition precedent to payment. Although the architect has not given the certificate, it is clear that the condition of proper completion of the work has been satisfied. Primo does not contend otherwise. The certification is a condition of satisfaction under which the performance must meet a standard of competence to be evaluated by a third-party expert. Although the architect was employed by the owner of the property and is its agent, her role in this contract between Primo and CC is to act on behalf of Primo.

Obviously, Primo cannot evade fulfillment of the condition simply because the architect is no longer available to inspect the work. Although it is not Primo's fault that the architect resigned, its implied duty to cooperate in the fulfillment of the condition requires it to ensure that inspection takes place within a reasonable time of completion of CC's performance. Its failure to facilitate occurrence of the condition is a wrongful hindrance of fulfillment which excuses the condition. (Alternatively, excuse could also be based on the argument that Primo waived the condition by declining to have the work inspected within a reasonable time. Another alternative is to argue excuse on grounds of unfair forfeiture because CC would surely be grievously harmed if the technicality of non-certification could be allowed to deny payment for satisfactory work. However, forfeiture is a discretionary doctrine that is not needed if there are more concrete bases for excuse.)

Primo argues that its receipt of the owner's payment for the air conditioning is a condition precedent to its obligation to pay CC. If this is so, Primo would be justified in not paying, because it has not been (and will not be) paid for the air conditioning. The parties' intent on this matter is a question of interpretation. If there is extrinsic evidence that casts light on the meaning of the clause (such as evidence of trade usage or of discussions between the parties), this would help to determine the intent of the language. If no such evidence is available, the reasonable meaning of the wording of the contract must be sought in light of the purpose of the contract as a whole. As we are told of no usage or other contextual evidence, our interpretation will be based solely on the language used in the contract.

At first sight, the language seems relatively clear. Payment from the owner does sound like an express condition precedent. It follows the condition of certification in the same sentence. This suggests that both of these events must occur before Primo's payment obligation falls due. However, courts interpreting payment provisions like this one tend to be skeptical of the argument that they are intended to be conditions. Unless the language (read in light of any contextual evidence that might be available) makes it very clear that the owner's payment was intended as a condition precedent, the assumption is that a term like this is more likely to have been intended as merely fixing a time for payment. Therefore, even if the owner does not pay the contractor, the contractor must pay the subcontractor within a reasonable time. The reasoning behind this interpretation is that, unless the parties express such an intention unequivocally, they cannot be taken to have placed the risk of the owner's nonpayment on the subcontractor, who has no contractual relationship with the owner but is employed by the prime contractor. Risk is more rationally left with the prime contractor, who has dealt with the owner and had the opportunity to evaluate its creditworthiness.

Therefore, although the language in the contract does admit of the interpretation that the owner's payment is a condition, it is not strong enough to overturn the usual assumption that the parties could not have intended to shift the risk of the owner's default to CC.

7. Two express conditions precedent are implicated in this dispute. The first is that a loss must occur of a kind covered by the policy. The second is that the insured must follow the prescribed claim procedure.

We deal first with the condition that the loss must fall within the policy's coverage. The policy covers loss by vandalism, which it defines as willful and malicious damage to the premises. However, it specifically excludes coverage for pilferage, theft or burglary. The language of the policy must be interpreted to determine if the losses are encompassed within the risk that is insured. Because this is a standard form insurance policy drafted by the insurer, the contra proferentum rule is particularly applicable. Any doubt in the meaning of a provision in it will be resolved against the insurer.

There are two separate items of loss caused by the removal of the pipe: The loss of the pipe itself and the damage caused to walls and floors in removing it. Does this loss result from vandalism? Vandalism is commonly thought of as the deliberate harming or defacement of property, purely for its own sake. However, the concept is broad enough to include purposeful damage motivated by economic gain. It is beyond doubt that the thief acted willfully (deliberately) and maliciously (with intent to violate the law and Larson's rights) in causing the loss. This applies not only to the taking of the pipe, but also to the concomitant destruction. The problem is that the policy draws a distinction between loss from vandalism and that from burglary, so when a wrongful act gives rise to injury of both kinds, the apparent conflict in terms must be reconciled. In *United States Fidelity & Guaranty Co. v. Bimco Iron & Metal Corp.*, 464 S.W.2d 353 (Tex. 1971), an insurance policy similarly distinguished vandalism, which it covered, from burglary which it excluded. Burglars entered the insured premises and stole electrical transformers and wiring, causing damage to the building. The court held that "vandalism" included any malicious damage to the building even if motivated by theft of a component of the structure. It went further and also held that the insurer was obliged to reimburse the insured not only for the damage to the structure, but also for the value of the electrical components that were removed. If this interpretation is applied to Larson's policy, it covers both the damage to the building and the value of the pipe that was removed. However, as a concurring opinion in *Bimco* pointed out, this interpretation may be too generous to the insured because once property is removed, this seems to be more a loss from burglary, which is excluded by the policy.

Even if the loss is covered by the policy, satisfying the first condition precedent, E&F is still not obliged to indemnify Larson for the loss unless the second condition — notice within seven days of loss and proof of loss 14 days thereafter — is also fulfilled. Because the condition is express, strict compliance is required. Larson's late notice failed to satisfy the condition exactly. This would preclude recovery under the policy unless there is a basis for excusing strict compliance.

Larson was about a day late in giving notice of his claim. However, E&F may have tacitly waived the condition of seven-day notice by not raising the delay during the phone call reporting the loss, and by sending an adjuster out to investigate the claim, knowing that the loss had occurred eight days before. In addition, both the adjuster and the letter rejecting the claim based the rejection on the coverage, not on the late notice. A waiver does not have to be by express words. It can be inferred from conduct if the party knows or has reason to know of noncompliance with a condition and yet acts as if the condition is satisfied. (Such conduct could also give rise to an estoppel, but waiver is a better theory because Larson has taken no detrimental action in reliance on the representation.) A waiver of rights without consideration is effective provided that the condition is ancillary and technical, rather than a material component of the exchange. Although prompt notice is important to an insurer, who needs the opportunity to investigate a claim while it is fresh, a relatively short delay in notice is likely to be interpreted as a waivable ancillary matter.

The policy states that the insurer does not waive rights under the policy by investigating a claim. Nonwaiver clauses (or nonwaiver agreements made after the loss has occurred) provide only limited protection to the insurer. They prevent an inference of waiver merely from the insurer's action in investigating or processing the claim, but they do not annul words or actions that more forcefully point to waiver. For example, in *Connecticut Fire Insurance Co. v. Fox*, 361 F.2d 1 (10th Cir. 1966), a fire damaged the aptly named Firebird Motor Hotel. Despite a nonwaiver agreement that the insured signed prior to the investigation of the loss, the court found that the insurer had waived timely proof of loss through an ongoing course of interaction with the insured. An issue of waiver also came up in the *Bimco* case. There was a similar agreement that investigation of the claim would not constitute a waiver. The insured had filed its proof of loss late, but the insurer, although denying reimbursement for the damage caused by removal of the electrical equipment, did not raise the issue of late claim submission and accepted a claim for damage to a door. The court held that although the nonwaiver agreement would have protected the insurer if it completely denied liability, it did not apply because the insurer went beyond investigating the claim and actually accepted liability for some part of the loss. In our case, E&F made no concession of liability at all, so *Bimco* is not authority for overturning the nonwaiver provision on that ground. However, failure to raise or rely on the issue of late notice in denying the claim should be enough to constitute a waiver. This argument is particularly attractive when there has been substantial compliance with the condition, the delay has caused no apparent harm to the insurer, and refusal of payment seems to be based on nothing more than a technicality.

8. The delivery of the notice by November 30, 2012, is an express condition precedent to Sue's obligation to sell the land to Sprawling Malls. It is not a promissory condition — Sprawling Malls has no commitment to ensure that it is satisfied. The purpose of the condition is to give it the discretion to send the notice if it wishes to exercise its option and purchase the land, but imposes no obligation on it to do so if it decides to allow the option to lapse.

Sprawling Malls did decide to exercise its option, but its notice of intent arrived a day late. Because the delivery of notice by November 30 is an express condition, it must be complied with strictly. If Sprawling Malls wanted the land, it had to deliver its notice to Sue within the time stated. Although the notice was mailed before November 30, the contract specified delivery — that is, receipt — by that date, and delivery occurred a day after the deadline. Although a day's delay may be a small deviation from the terms of the condition, this is not taken into account under the rule that requires strict compliance with express conditions. The rationale is that once the parties have taken the trouble to articulate and define the condition, the court should not tamper with their expressed intention. Of course, if the language used to describe the condition is unclear, the court may have some flexibility in interpreting what the condition required, but the language of this condition concerning the manner and time of exercising the option is unambiguous and provides no basis for an interpretation favorable to Sprawling Malls. Therefore, unless there is some ground for excusing exact compliance with the condition, the day's delay in delivery results in nonfulfillment of the condition, and Sprawling Malls has lost its right to buy the land.

The only possible ground for excuse presented by these facts is unfair forfeiture. Courts have the discretion to excuse exact compliance with a condition (or to excuse the condition altogether, if appropriate) when strict enforcement of the condition would result in a disproportionate and unfair forfeiture by one of the parties and a windfall gain by the other. The policy of preventing unfair forfeiture acts as a counterweight to the rule of strict compliance, allowing courts some flexibility in averting particularly harsh and unfair results where there has been a minor or technical noncompliance with a condition. This does not mean, of course, that courts routinely excuse express conditions on the basis of unfair forfeiture. Courts are wary about applying the doctrine too readily because its overuse would eliminate the rule of strict compliance. In fact, cases in which courts apply the doctrine are quite rare. For unfair forfeiture to apply as a ground for excuse, the strict enforcement of the condition must result in undue hardship to the party seeking excuse and inappropriately extensive gain to the beneficiary of the condition. The balance of hardship against unfair gain must be evaluated in light of the relationship of the condition to the exchange as a whole.

In this case, the short delay in delivery of the notice certainly results in considerable hardship to Sprawling Malls: It loses its right to buy the land, gets no benefit from the $10,000 that it paid for the option, and no chance to recoup its substantial expense in conducting the study, or to enjoy the fruits of its efforts in securing financing for the project. True, it bought an option for a year, not a year and a day, so the effect of excusing exact compliance would be to give it a longer option than it purchased. Sprawling Malls was at fault in entrusting such an important communication to the vagaries of the mails, but this was not an egregious sin. It is more the result of poor judgment than of some deliberate attempt to prolong the option period for the purpose of speculating for an additional time at Sue's expense. Looking at the delay from Sue's perspective, we must recognize that she bargained on being bound to the option until no later than November 30. The exact duration of an option is generally regarded as material, and a day's extension should not be assumed to be a trivial matter. However, the equities do not strongly favor strict compliance: She received a substantial payment for the option; the price of the land itself is apparently fair, based on its market value at the time of contracting; she has not yet taken any action in reliance on the lapse; and her motivation in refusing to accept the notice is that she can do better reselling the land. There may be enough here to tilt the balance in favor of excusing the failure of exact compliance with the condition.

This was the conclusion reached on similar facts in *Holiday Inns of America v. Knight*, 450 P.2d 42 (Cal. 1969). Holiday Inns had purchased an option to buy land. The initial period of the option was one year, but it could be extended annually for a further four years. To extend it, Holiday Inns had to pay a renewal fee of $10,000 per year, to be made by July 1 of each year. Holiday Inns had renewed the option for two years and had developed adjacent land over this period, thereby increasing the value of the property subject to the option. It intended to renew the option for a third time, and mailed its check for the renewal fee just before due date. However, the grantor did not receive it until July 2 and refused to extend the option. Holiday Inns successfully sued for a declaratory judgment that the option had been validly extended. The court excused the failure of strict compliance on the ground that it would be an unfair forfeiture for Holiday Inns to lose its option because of a short delay. The court based this conclusion on the fact that the delay did not have a material impact on the exchange, Holiday Inns had not been attempting to take advantage of the grantor by extending the option beyond the period purchased, and it would be unfair to make it sacrifice the $30,000 in option fees that it had already spent for the first three years of the option. (Although the development on the adjacent land could be seen as further justification for excusing the condition, giving Holiday Inns a stronger case on the equities than Sprawling Malls, the court did not base its determination on this fact.)

CHAPTER 17

Breach and Repudiation

---

§17.1 THE SCOPE OF THIS CHAPTER: NONFULFILLMENT OF A PROMISE

Chapter 16 drew the distinction between the nonfulfillment of a condition, which excuses the conditional performance, and the failure to honor a promise, which results in liability for breach of contract. If a term is a promissory condition — that is, one of the parties undertook that it would be satisfied — its nonfulfillment has the combined effect of entitling the other party (called the "promisee" in this chapter) both to withhold performance and to seek a remedy for breach. Chapter 16 concentrated on the effect of conditions and their nonfulfillment. This chapter considers the impact and consequences of the breach of a promise. Because promises are so often conditions as well (promissory conditions), a failure to perform often constitutes both a breach of the promise and nonfulfillment of a condition. This means that where a term of a contract is both a promise and a condition (a promissory condition), a material and total breach of the promise is also the nonfulfillment of the condition, which entitles the promisee not only to sue for damages for the breach, but also to withhold her own performance that is contingent on the promissory condition.

This concept is illustrated by the following simple contract, which we will use as an example throughout this chapter: Substantial Preforming Company, Inc. (Substantial) salvages building materials, such as brick, stone, and concrete from demolished buildings. It then has these materials crushed so that it can use them for making columns, walls, and other building components for use in new buildings. Total Material Breakers, Inc. (Total) operates a plant for crushing building materials. On July 1, Total and Substantial entered into a written contract under which Total undertook to crush a load of concrete that Substantial had hauled away from a demolition site. The contract contained the following terms:

1. Substantial agrees to pay Total $20,000 for the work. Substantial will pay $5,000 of this price to Total by 5 P.M. on July 6, and will pay the balance of $15,000 upon collecting the crushed concrete from Total.
2. Substantial will deliver the salvaged concrete to Total for crushing by 9 A.M. on July 7.
3. Total will complete the crushing and have the materials ready for collection by 5 P.M. on July 9.

Although no express language of condition has been used, it is easily inferable from the sequence set out in the contract that the parties intend Substantial's down payment on July 6 to be a promissory condition precedent — the payment is not only expressly promised, but is also impliedly a condition precedent to Total's performance. Substantial's commitment to deliver the materials to Total by 9 A.M. on July 7 is also a promissory condition precedent. Even though Substantial does not, in so many words, promise to make the delivery on time, it has to do so to enable Total to render its performance. For the same reason, it must also be seen as a condition of Total's performance. Total expressly promises that the materials will be crushed and made available for collection by 5 P.M. on July 9. The fact that final payment is to be made on completion gives rise to the inference that Total's performance is not merely a promise, but also an implied condition precedent to Substantial's final performance, the $15,000 payment. As there is no further performance contingent on this payment, it is a pure promise.

If both parties perform as undertaken, the promises are honored, the conditions are fulfilled, and the transaction ends happily. As Restatement, Second, §235(1) says (maybe somewhat self-evidently), a contractual duty is discharged by full performance. However, all kinds of things could go wrong: At some point before performance is to commence on July 6, one of the parties may renege or indicate an intention to breach the contract; or Substantial may not make the down payment at all, or in full, or on time; or it may fail to deliver the concrete as required; or Total may refuse to take the concrete, or may not process it properly or on time. The purpose of this chapter is to discuss the legal effect of breaches like this relating both to pure promises and to promissory conditions. Sections 17.2 to 17.6 deal with breach proper (that is, a violation of a promise that occurs at or after performance is due) and section 17.7 examines the particular issues that arise when a party repudiates the contract in advance of the time of his performance. The importance and extent of the breach is a crucial factor throughout this chapter, so we begin by distinguishing breaches of different degrees of gravity.

§17.2 THE NATURE OF BREACH

As intimated above, a party breaches a contract by failing, for whatever reason, to honor a promise of performance when that performance falls due. Four questions need to be resolved to establish that a breach of contract has occurred.

First, we must determine the existence and content of the contractual undertaking to ascertain the exact nature and extent of the promise that was made. This involves interpreting the contract through the process discussed in Chapter 10.

Second, we must establish the date that the promised performance fell due. Although a party can repudiate a contract before his performance is due (as discussed in section 17.1), a breach by failure to perform or improper performance cannot occur until the time arises for the party's duty to render it. If the contract does not clearly and expressly state the due date for the party's performance, this must be determined by interpretation or construction. Also, if the performance is subject to a condition precedent, it is not due until the condition is satisfied.

Third, we must decide if the performance complied with the promise. Any shortfall from the promised performance is a breach. If the party has not performed at all, noncompliance is easy to see. However, where a party has rendered a performance that is alleged to be inadequate or deficient, the question of whether it satisfies the contractual duty can be difficult to resolve.

Finally, having determined that a breach did occur, we must decide on the severity of the breach and on the promisee's rights in reacting to the breach. Some breaches are serious and fundamental enough to entitle the promisee to withhold any return performance, terminate the contract, and sue for full expectation relief. A breach of this kind is described as total and material. If the breach is less severe, or if the promisor should be given an opportunity to rectify it, the response of terminating the contract is extreme. The promisee is confined to a less drastic remedy that adjusts for the breach by allowing the promisor to cure it or to pay damages to compensate for the shortfall in performance. This final point is the subject of the following sections.

§17.3 THE SIGNIFICANCE OF A BREACH: MATERIAL BREACH OR SUBSTANTIAL PERFORMANCE, AND TOTAL OR PARTIAL BREACH

§17.3.1 Introduction to the Distinction

Any performance that falls short of that promised is a breach. However, some breaches are relatively trivial and others are serious, and not all breaches should be treated in the same way. This section introduces the nature and consequences of breaches of different degrees of severity. Each of these types of breach are expanded upon in the following sections.

a. Total and Material Breach

When a breach is profound enough to qualify as material and total, the promisee's expectations under the contract have been completely dashed, and he should therefore have the right to terminate the contract — that is, to end the transaction and to sue the breacher for whatever relief is necessary to compensate him for loss of his bargain.[1] Because most promises exchanged in a contract are dependent, as explained in section 16.3.3, each party's performance is an express, implied, or construed condition of the other's duty to perform. Therefore, if one party materially breaches his performance obligation, this is not only a breach of the promise, but also the nonfulfillment of the condition to any performance that may not yet have been rendered by the other party. For this reason, a total and material breach gives the promisee not only the right to claim damages, but also to refuse to render any part of his own performance that is still outstanding and to terminate the contract.

b. A Material Breach That Is Not Yet Total — Partial Breach and Cure

A breach that would qualify as material may be capable of rectification by the breacher. If, under the circumstances, the breacher has the ability to correct the nonconforming performance — to cure the breach — the breach does not become material and total unless the breacher fails to cure it. A material breach that is capable of cure is classified as a partial breach, rather than a total breach, because there is a possibility that the deficiency in performance

---

1. The nature and extent of these damages is considered in Chapter 18. They could include the extra cost of a substitute transaction, loss of profits, and reimbursement of costs or other losses arising as a consequence of the breach. The basic goal of the damages is to award a sum of money to place the victim in the position he would have been in had no breach occurred.

could be rectified or ameliorated by cure. When a breach is curable, the promisee does not yet have the right to terminate the contract, but must give the breacher an opportunity to cure the breach. The conditional nature of the breached promise allows the promisee to suspend his own performance until the breacher does effect a cure. In some cases, cure may completely eliminate the breach, but even if it does not, the cure may reduce the gravity of the breach so that it is no longer material and becomes substantial performance. However, if there is no cure, the breach becomes material and total, giving rise to all the rights and remedies identified in (a) above. The concepts of partial breach and cure are expanded upon in section 17.3.4.

c. Nonmaterial Breach (Substantial Performance)

The term "partial breach" is also used to describe a situation in which a party's performance falls short of what was promised, but is not so severely deficient to constitute a material breach. A partial breach of this degree is called "substantial performance" to denote that while it is a breach, it is not so serious as to defeat the promisee's reasonable expectations under the contract. Where the breacher's performance is substantially in compliance with what was promised, it would be unfairly harsh to allow the promisee to terminate, thereby depriving the breacher of all benefit of the bargain and making him liable for the whole range of damages. Therefore, the substantial performance is treated as substantial compliance with the condition, so that the promisee cannot treat the condition of his performance as unfulfilled. The promisee is obliged to stick to the contract and perform his side of the bargain. However, he is entitled to a monetary adjustment to compensate for the deficiency in the performance received from the breacher. This measure of damages is usually based on the cost of rectifying the deficiency, or possibly on the actual loss in the value of the performance, as discussed in section 17.3.3. Such damages could be substantially less than what would be awarded for a total and material breach.

§17.3.2 What Makes a Breach Material?

The gravity and extent of a breach is a matter of interpretation that can only be resolved by examining the language of the contract in context and evaluating the shortfall in performance in light of the reasonable expectations of the parties. We have encountered the concept of materiality many times before in relation to other doctrines.[2] The test for deciding whether a breach

---

2. *See*, for example, sections 6.3.2 (battle of the forms), 10.1 (indefiniteness), 13.6.5 (misrepresentation), and 15.3 (mistake).

is material is the same as that for deciding whether a term is material for other purposes. A breach is material if the failure or deficiency in performance is so central to the contract that it substantially impairs its value and deeply disappoints the reasonable expectations of the promisee. This is a rather broad and vague test, but it must be so, because materiality is a matter of interpretation that cannot be resolved in the abstract. In essence, one must consider the entirety of the exchange contemplated in the contract and decide if the defective or absent performance forms a significant part of the consideration bargained for by the promisee. Courts often use guidelines set out in Restatement, Second, §241 in deciding whether a breach is material: the extent to which the injured party will be deprived of the benefit that he reasonably expected, the extent to which the injured party can be adequately compensated for the deprivation, the extent to which the breaching party will suffer forfeiture, the likelihood that the breaching party will cure the breach, and the extent to which the behavior of the breaching party comports with standards of good faith and fair dealing. These are just guidelines, not fixed elements of materiality, so courts do not always consider all of these factors, and some may be more important in a particular case than others. Of course, the first factor — the extent to which the injured party is deprived of the reasonably expected benefit of the bargain — lies at the heart of the inquiry. However, the factors listed in §241 show that this is not the only consideration, and all the circumstances must be evaluated to judge the significance of a breach. Also, the equities between the parties are relevant here, as elsewhere, so a court may look not only at the deprivation suffered by the promisee as a result of the breach, but also at the degree of hardship (that is, forfeiture) that would be suffered by the breacher if termination was allowed. A breach does not need to be deliberate or willful to be material, and its importance is not diminished merely because it was unintended or undesired by the breacher. However, §241 indicates that in balancing the equities, courts may give some weight to the question of whether the breach was willful or innocent, or a violation of standards of fair dealing. The significance of the breach is also affected by the stage of performance at which the breach occurs. A breach at the outset of performance that affects the value of the entire exchange is patently more material than one occurring near the end of the performance and having an impact on only a small aspect of what was promised.

The importance of some breaches is so obvious that the resolution of their materiality requires no effort at probing contractual intent. In the contract between Substantial and Total for crushing the concrete, one would not need deep analysis to conclude that it would be a material breach if Substantial failed to make any down payment at all. Total's complete failure to crush the concrete likewise would be unquestionably material. In each case, the party has broken a promise that goes to the very heart of the exchange. However, the issue of materiality would be less obvious if

Substantial failed to make the down payment on July 6, but assured Total that it would bring the down payment with the concrete on July 7. To decide if that is a material breach, we would have to determine the apparent intent of the parties and ascertain if Total's contractual rights (including the security it is entitled to expect from advance payment) are seriously affected by having to wait until the next morning for the down payment. The express written terms of the contract do not indicate the purpose of the down payment. Contextual evidence may provide an explanation. If not, the court will have to construe the term to decide if a short delay in payment is material. There is no obvious reason why it should be, as long as Total receives payment before it begins work. However, the fact that the parties were so specific in providing expressly for the due date and time of the down payment may persuade a court that even this short delay is material.

Raymond Weil, S.A. v. Theron, 585 F. Supp. 2d 473 (S.D.N.Y. 2008) provides a good illustration of a court's assessment of whether a breach was material. The actress Charlize Theron entered into an endorsement contract with Raymond Weil, S.A. (RW), the watchmaker, under which RW agreed to pay Theron $3 million in exchange for the use of her image in a worldwide advertising campaign. The contract committed Theron to represent RW exclusively during its 15-month term, and she promised not to wear any watches by other manufacturers during the period of the contract. In breach of the agreement, Theron wore a Dior watch for about an hour during a panel discussion in which she participated at a film festival. Theron argued that the wearing of the watch for such a short time within a 15-month contract period did not amount to a material breach. Unfortunately, many photographs were taken of her during the panel discussion, and these photographs, showing the Dior watch, were widely distributed on the Internet. Some were sold to a prominent retailer of Dior watches, which used them for advertising purposes. The court held that the breach, however fleeting, had a material effect on Theron's promise to endorse RW products exclusively. The court considered it irrelevant that Theron was not responsible for the wide dissemination of the photographs and pointed out that, as a famous and attractive actress, she should have foreseen the likelihood that the photographs would be distributed and sold to a competitor of RW.

As noted earlier, if the breach is material, it so badly defeats the promisee's expectations that she is entitled to terminate the contract and sue for whatever relief is necessary to compensate for loss of the bargain. Although damages are discussed more fully in Chapter 18, a simple example concerning damages is helpful here to illustrate the impact of material breach. If Substantial completely fails to pay the down payment, thereby breaching materially, Total has the right to terminate the contract, to refuse to take delivery of and to crush the concrete, and to sue Substantial for the profit that it expected to make on the job, calculated by deducting its costs from the contract price. Conversely, if Substantial paid Total the $5,000 on

July 6, but Total then materially breached by refusing to accept delivery of and to crush the concrete, Substantial could terminate, withhold the payment of $15,000 that would otherwise have been due on July 9, and sue for damages. If the reasonable price of having someone else perform the work is no more than Total had charged under the contract, Substantial could at least sue Total for recovery of the $5,000 paid. But if the reasonable price of having the work done elsewhere is more than the contract price, say $22,000, Substantial could sue Total for $7,000 (the $5,000 paid to Total plus the extra $2,000 paid to the new contractor for the equivalent performance). This is how much extra Substantial ended up paying, so the award of these damages puts it into the position equivalent to full contractual performance — having the concrete crushed for $20,000.

§17.3.3 Substantial Performance

It is sometimes said that substantial performance is the opposite of material breach. This is not strictly correct because the true opposite of material breach is complete and compliant performance, and substantial performance is nevertheless a breach. However, it is a nonmaterial breach. Therefore, once it is determined that a breach is not material, it is necessarily partial, and the performance that has been rendered is substantial. This means, of course, that the question of whether substantial performance has been rendered is gauged by the same interpretive process as that used to decide materiality, and the fundamental issue is to decide the relationship of the breach to the overall exchange in values. Consider again the situation in which Substantial failed to make the down payment on July 6, but assured Total that it would bring the down payment with the concrete on July 7. Unless payment on the day before delivery of the concrete is material, the slight delay in payment is substantial performance. If so, Total has no basis for terminating and must accept the delay in payment with whatever monetary adjustment is needed to compensate for the delay. On these facts, this may be nothing, or, at most, a day's interest on the $5,000.

The best-known case involving substantial performance is *Jacob & Youngs v. Kent*, 129 N.E. 889 (N.Y. 1921). A builder had completed the construction of a grand country home for a total price of $77,000, a considerable sum when the house was built in 1914. The owner refused to pay the balance of the contract price (about $3,500) to the builder on the grounds that the builder had breached the contract by installing plumbing pipe of the wrong brand in the house. The builder had overlooked a specification in the contract that called for the pipe to be of Reading brand. As a result more than half the pipe was made by other manufacturers. There was no difference in quality between the Reading pipe and the other brands. However, the owner refused to pay the balance of the contract price on the grounds that the cost of remedying the breach far exceeded this amount. Because the pipe was already encased within the walls, the cost of removing and replacing the wrong pipe would have involved the demolition and rebuilding of a significant portion of the house. Judge Cardozo, writing for the majority of the court, found the breach to be both inadvertent[3] and trivial. Although the specification of the brand was an express promise in the contract, there was nothing in the contract to indicate that the parties considered the actual brand to be a significant term. They were more concerned about the quality of the pipe, and as the other brands were of equal quality, the breach was not material. The dissent disagreed that the breach should be treated as trivial. The owner had specified that Reading pipe be used, and the court should not deprive him of his bargain by assuming that the pipe brand was unimportant to him.

The disagreement between the majority and dissent in *Jacob & Youngs* shows that it can be difficult to decide if a breach is material. A couple of other examples illustrate how courts try to ascertain the underlying purpose of the contract in trying to resolve this question. In *Plante v. Jacobs*, 103 N.W.2d 296 (Wis. 1960), the court concluded that a builder did not materially breach a contract to build a house by making the living room a foot smaller than specified in the plan. Although this might sound like an important deviation from the contract, the house was built to stock specifications, there was no indication that the homeowners considered the exact size of the rooms to be important, and the size of the room did not affect the house's market value. By contrast, in *Lyon v. Belosky Construction*, 247 A.D.2d 730 (1998), the court found that a builder did commit a material breach by centering the roof of a house incorrectly. Although this did not affect the structural utility or soundness of the roof, it changed the aesthetic appearance of the house, which had been custom designed.

§17.3.4 Relief for Substantial Performance and Adjustment to Avoid Unfair Forfeiture

As explained above, where a breach qualifies as substantial performance, the promisee cannot withhold performance or terminate the contract, but is entitled to claim any damages suffered as a result of the breach. These damages may be offset against any payment still due to the breacher or, if no such return performance is outstanding, they form the basis of a money judgment against the breacher. The usual measure of damages is the cost to

---

3. The fact that the court found the breach to have been inadvertent, not deliberate, was important to the court's ultimate decision on the appropriate measure of relief. (The remedial aspect of the case is discussed in section 17.3.4.) The dissent disagreed with the majority's finding that the breach was not deliberate.

place the promisee in the position he would have been in had the performance been in full compliance with the contract. In most cases, this is represented by an award of the amount of money necessary to correct the shortfall in performance. For example, if work was improperly done or property supplied was defective, compensation is measured by the cost to the promisee of rectifying the work or repairing the property. If the breach lies in a failure to complete performance, the completion cost is the proper measure. If the breach involves a delay in performance, compensation is appropriately measured by determining the loss caused by the delay.

In some cases, the cost of rectifying the performance may be disproportionate to any realistic loss actually suffered by the promisee. If the court feels that damages measured by the cost of rectification are not an accurate measure of actual harm, but would provide a windfall to the promisee and impose an unfair forfeiture on the breacher, the court may adjust the damages to better represent the true harm to the promisee. This measure of damages is based on the difference in value between what was promised and what was performed. Because a determination of unfair forfeiture is not simply a matter of arithmetic, and also takes into account the balance of the equities between the parties,[4] a court is more likely to make this adjustment if the noncompliance was inadvertent and is less likely to do so if the failure to perform in accordance with the contract was deliberate.

For example, say that the contract between Substantial and Total included a term that specified that the concrete must be ground to pellets of a particular degree of fineness. On collecting the crushed concrete, Substantial found that the grind was slightly coarser than stipulated in the contract. Assume that this is not a material breach, and the slightly larger pellets are still perfectly capable of use by Substantial in the manufacture of new concrete forms, without any change in the manufacturing process or deterioration in quality. To rectify this nonmaterial breach, the concrete pellets would have to be recrushed, at considerable expense. This would impose liability on Total for damages that are so disproportionate to the actual harm suffered by Substantial that they would be an unfair forfeiture to Total.[5] When cost of rectification is not used, damages are based on loss in value. Because the larger pellets can be used for the same purpose as the

---

4. The concept of balancing the equities in the context of forfeiture is discussed in sections 16.10.3 and 18.6.6.
5. Sometimes a disproportionate award of this kind is described as economically wasteful because it would be a waste of money for the injured party to spend a disproportionate amount of money to fix a nonmaterial defect. However, that is not an accurate characterization. The victim of a breach has no obligation to use the damages to fix the defect in performance, and it could just bank the damages or spend them for some other purpose. Therefore, the basis for not awarding the cost of rectifying the defect is best described, not as economic waste, but the prevention of unfair forfeiture.

smaller ones, without any adverse consequences, there is likely no loss in value, and Substantial has suffered no damages.

Because the majority in *Jacob & Youngs* found that the contract had been substantially performed, Judge Cardozo went on to deal with the issue of unfair forfeiture. Although he recognized that the cost of rectifying the defect is the usual measure of damages, he found that a damages award calculated on the basis of the great cost of reconstruction would be grossly out of proportion to the actual loss suffered by the owner. It would confer an unfair benefit on the owner and unduly penalize the builder for a minor and inadvertent breach. (Cardozo made it clear that it was important that the breach was not willful. Had the breach been deliberate, the court would not have treated it as minor.) The court therefore limited the owner's damages to the difference in market value between a house fitted only with Reading pipe and a house fitted with pipe of the same quality made by different manufacturers. This market difference was zero. The same approach was adopted in *Plante*, in which the court found that the misplacement of the wall did not diminish the market value of the house. By contrast, in *Lyon*, the court rejected the builder's argument that loss in market value should be the basis of measuring damages. Because the appearance of the house was of great importance to the owners, who bought the house to live in, not to resell, the cost of replacing the roof, not market value reduction, was the proper measure.

Khiterer v. Bell, 800 N.Y.S.2d 348 (2005), a small claims court decision, provides a clear and succinct recent application of the doctrine in *Jacob & Youngs*. A patient sued her dentist for fitting porcelain crowns instead of crowns made of porcelain on gold. The court accepted that this was a breach of contract. However, the dentist testified that all-porcelain crowns were no less expensive and were therapeutically superior. It was also apparent that the dentist's breach was inadvertent and not deliberate. The court held that the cost of replacement would be unfairly disproportionate and confined the patient to loss in value. As the patient could show no actual injury, she was awarded nominal damages.

§17.3.5 Partial Breach and Cure

Some breaches have such an immediate, irreparable, and significant impact on the promisee's rights that they are unavoidably material as soon as they occur, and there is nothing that the promisor can do to rectify them. Other breaches are by nature so trivial that they could never result in a total breach of the contract, even if no attempt was made to remedy them. However, between these poles, there are breaches that would be material if left unrectified, but the circumstances are such that it is still possible for the breaching party to take steps to cure the defect in performance. A curable material breach is treated as partial because the breaching party can prevent total breach by taking remedial action within a reasonable time. This is shown in Diagram 17A.

Diagram 17A

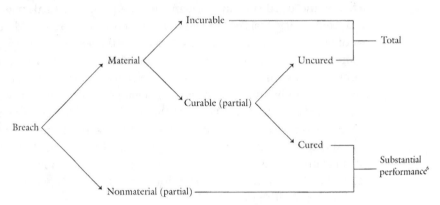

To illustrate, consider again the contract between Substantial and Total with the variation set out in section 17.3.4 — the contract specified that the concrete must be ground to pellets of a particular degree of fineness. On collecting the crushed concrete, Substantial found that the grind was slightly coarser than stipulated in the contract. Contrary to the conclusion in section 17.3.4, this is a material breach because the larger pellets cannot be used by Substantial in the manufacture of new concrete forms, and they are therefore worthless to it. Total recognizes this and offers to run the pellets through its crusher again to get them to the correct size. However, it will take a day to do that, so the conforming pellets will not be ready for collection until July 10, a day after the delivery date specified in the contract. Total's cure will rectify the material breach relating to the size of the pellets, but will place it in breach of the term that requires it to have the materials ready for collection by 5 P.M. on July 9. If the date and time of delivery is a material term, the attempt to cure one material breach would simply give rise to another, so the breach is not capable of cure. However, if the exact date of delivery — July 9 by 5 P.M. — is not material, so that delivery on July 10 would be substantial performance, the cure converts the material breach into a partial breach. As this illustration suggests, where the breacher is willing to cure the breach, there may be a dispute about whether the cure would be adequate and timely. The effectiveness of a tendered cure in averting material breach, and converting it into substantial performance is decided, as usual, with reference to the promisee's reasonable expectations under the contract.

---

6. As mentioned in section 17.3.1, it is possible that a cure could completely eliminate a breach. If so, there would be full compliance with the contract, not substantial performance.

The question of cure arose in the *Raymond Weil* case discussed in section 17.3.2. In addition to wearing the Dior watch during the panel discussion, on another occasion Theron allowed herself to be photographed holding a Montblanc necklace. Montblanc used the photograph as an advertising poster. This was also a violation of the exclusivity agreement because, apart from the promise not to wear other watches in public, Theron undertook not to endorse the jewelry of other manufacturers. She therefore breached the contract by lending her image to Montblanc for the poster. A couple of days after the poster was displayed, RW complained to Montblanc, which withdrew it. RW argued that the breach was incurable, despite the withdrawal of the poster, because people who saw the poster during the time that it was displayed could not "un-see" it. The court rejected this argument. It held that the breach was the display of the poster, not its viewing by third parties. Therefore, the breach was curable and had been effectively cured.[7]

§17.4 A SUMMARY OF THE RELATIONSHIP BETWEEN THE MATERIALITY OF BREACH AND THE NONFULFILLMENT OF A CONDITION

The previous sections have identified the relationship between material breach and the nonfulfillment of a condition. This summary encapsulates and reinforces what has been said about this relationship.

1. Where a term of a contract is both a promise and a condition (a promissory condition), a material and total breach of the promise is also the nonfulfillment of the condition. This is why the promisor can not only sue for damages for the breach, but is also entitled to withhold her own performance, which is contingent on the promissory condition.
2. If the breach is material, but not total because it can be cured, the promisee cannot immediately sue for damages for breach or terminate the contract. However, the conditional nature of the breached promise allows the promisee to suspend her own performance until such time as the condition is fulfilled by cure.

---

7. The contract itself provided for the right to cure. It stated that if there is any breach of the agreement, the injured party must give notice of the breach to the other party, who has five days to cure the breach. Montblanc withdrew the poster within the five-day period. Had the contract not contained such a provision, the court would have had to interpret the contract to decide whether withdrawal of the poster constituted an adequate cure of the breach within a reasonable time.

3. If the breach is not material so that the promissory condition is substantially performed, the doctrine of substantial compliance with the condition will also apply. This means that the promisee cannot sue for total breach and cannot suspend her own contingent performance, but must perform and seek recourse for the breach through compensation for the shortfall in performance. In *Jacob & Youngs*, Judge Cardozo couched his discussion of substantial performance in the language of conditions. Because he found that the failure to use Reading pipe was a trivial breach, he described the brand specification as an "independent promise." By this he meant that although promises in a contract are normally dependent (that is, promissory conditions of each other) a nonmaterial breach of one of those promises should not be treated as a complete failure of the condition. Therefore, the promisee's remaining obligation of performance must not be treated as conditional on exact fulfillment of the breached promissory condition. As a result, he cannot claim total breach and withhold his return performance, but remains bound to perform, subject to the offset of any damages caused by the breach. (Of course, if the breached promise is an express condition, the doctrine of substantial compliance does not apply, and failure to perform exactly as promised must be treated as a material breach.)

§17.5 SUBSTANTIAL PERFORMANCE UNDER UCC ARTICLE 2: PERFECT TENDER AND CURE

§17.5.1 Perfect Tender

Following the execution of a contract for the sale of goods, the seller is obliged to deliver the goods to the buyer at the time and place specified in the contract. Upon tender of delivery, the buyer has the right to inspect the goods to see if they conform to the contract, and if they do not, the buyer may reject them. Both the inspection and rejection must be within a reasonable time. It is beyond our scope to deal with Article 2's detailed rules concerning the tender and acceptance or rejection of goods. Our concern is with the Code's treatment of substantial performance and cure, which is notably different from the common law.

The rule was established, long before the enactment of the UCC, that the doctrine of substantial performance is not applicable to a sale of goods. The buyer is entitled to "perfect tender" of the goods ordered and has the right to reject goods that fail to conform exactly to what was called for by the contract. This rule has been retained in §2.601, which permits the buyer to reject goods that "fail in any respect to conform to the contract." This is reinforced by §2.106(2), which defines "conforming" as meaning "in accordance with the obligations under the contract."

Although the perfect tender rule provides little room for a court to recognize substantial performance, there is some scope for avoiding it under the right circumstances. For example, where the buyer's rejection of goods is clearly pretextual — that is, she rejects them on the basis of some minor nonconformity because she no longer wants them, a court may apply the general obligation of good faith and fair dealing to preclude rejection on a technicality.

Also, the rules relating to acceptance and rejection of goods sometimes give the court an opportunity to prevent a rejection of goods on trivial grounds. As noted above, it is beyond our scope to go into the intricacies of rejection, but we can note generally that the buyer must act promptly and follow the proper procedure to effectively reject goods. If the buyer delays beyond a reasonable time or slips up procedurally in rejecting, the rejection is ineffective and the buyer is deemed to have accepted the goods. If the buyer has accepted the goods, she can only thereafter revoke her acceptance if she satisfies a number of requirements, including the requirement that the nonconformity substantially impairs their value. (That is, although the rule of substantial performance does not apply where the buyer rejects the goods, it does apply where the buyer seeks to revoke its acceptance of the goods.) If the goods have been accepted and the acceptance cannot be revoked the buyer is confined by UCC §2.718 to damages based on the loss in value as a result of the nonconformity. The interaction between the perfect tender rule and the buyer's failure to reject the goods is illustrated by *Khiterer v. Bell*, the case discussed in section 17.3.4, in which a dentist fitted crowns made of porcelain instead of gold and porcelain. The court held that the dental services predominated over the sale aspect of the contract, so the common law rule of substantial performance applied. However, it went on to point out that even if this had been predominantly a sale of goods, the perfect tender rule would not have applied because the patient had accepted the crowns by not having them removed for two years after they were fitted. She could thereafter only revoke her acceptance if the nonconformity substantially impaired their value, which it did not.

§17.5.2 Cure Under UCC Article 2

Under prescribed circumstances, UCC §2.508 permits the seller to avoid final rejection of nonconforming goods by curing the deficient tender.

Where cure is possible, §2.508 mitigates the harsh effect of the perfect tender rule. The strength of the seller's right to cure depends on whether the seller would have time to complete the cure before the date due for the delivery of the goods under the contract. If the seller tenders delivery before due date, so that the buyer's rejection occurs before that date, the seller has a much greater right to cure than if the goods were delivered on or after due date. The reason for this is the perfect tender rule. Unlike the common law, which treats late performance as a material breach only if the date of performance is material, the perfect tender rule gives the buyer the right to reject late delivery even if time of delivery is not a material term. Section 2.508 takes this into account by imposing more stringent limitations on the seller's right to cure after the contractual delivery date. Section 2.508 operates as follows:

When the goods are delivered, the buyer has the right to inspect them within a reasonable time. If they are nonconforming, she has the right, within a further reasonable time, to reject them. If the seller delivered the goods in good time before the time required for delivery in the contract, the delivery date may still not have passed by the time that the buyer (having acted with the required reasonable promptness) exercises the right of rejection. If so, §2.508(1) gives the seller an unconditional right to notify the buyer seasonably of intent to cure and to affect the cure by substituting a conforming delivery before that time expires.

If the contractual delivery date has passed, this unrestricted ability to cure is no longer available, but a qualified right to cure still exists for a reasonable time. Section 2.508(2) permits the seller to notify the buyer seasonably of intent to cure and to effect the cure within a reasonable time, provided that "the seller had reasonable grounds to believe [that the tender of delivery] would be acceptable with or without money allowance. . . ." This means that if the seller had no reason to know that the goods were nonconforming, or realized that they were, but reasonably believed that the buyer would nevertheless take them if an appropriate price adjustment was made, the seller may be able to rectify the nonconformity even after the date for delivery had passed. However, the cure must be within a reasonable time, and the issue of what is reasonable depends on the nature and purpose of the sale. When delivery on the exact date specified is a material term of the contract (that is, it is clear from the contract that any delay in delivery would be a serious breach), there may be no reasonable time for cure. In other cases, the time for substituting a conforming delivery could range from a few hours to days, depending on the circumstances of the contract.

The question of whether goods conform to the contract is factual, based on an interpretation of what was called for under the contract, and an evaluation of the character of what was performed. Nonconformity may lie in the quality, quantity, or attributes of the goods themselves, or in the manner in which they are provided, such as the way in which they are packaged or delivered. It is not always easy to resolve a dispute concerning the fact and extent of an alleged nonconformity with the contract. Even if nonconformity is established or conceded, there could still be a controversy over what is appropriate to cure the deficiency.

For example, say that a consumer buys a new dining room table from a furniture store. When it arrives on the date scheduled for delivery, the buyer notices a large scratch across the top and rejects the table. The seller concedes that this is a nonconformity and gives the buyer a couple of options: She can keep the scratched table at a discount of 10 percent off the price, or the seller will take the table back, refinish it, and redeliver it in a week. The buyer, a consumer of fierce disposition, refuses to accept either option and demands delivery of another table today, failing which she threatens to terminate the sale, purchase a substitute elsewhere, and hold the seller liable for any additional cost. She points out that she bought and paid for a new table, and she neither wants a scratched one for less money nor a refinished one. Furthermore, she was promised delivery today, not next week. This dispute relates to the sufficiency of the seller's offer to cure. The buyer adopts the position that nothing short of the immediate delivery of a new table would be an adequate cure, but the seller considers it appropriate to offer a monetary allowance or the delivery of a repaired table in a week.

Both parties take the risk of breaching the contract by insisting on their positions. If the buyer is wrong, her termination is based on partial breach, which the seller was not given a reasonable opportunity to cure. She thereby commits a breach herself. If the seller is wrong, it loses the chance to rectify the breach by an effective cure within the time for delivery and converts its partial breach into a total one. To decide who is right, the judgments called for by §2.508 must be made: Was the seller justified in believing that the tender was conforming or otherwise acceptable? Is delivery by the date specified in the contract of the essence, and if not, is a week's delay reasonable? Will the table, as refinished, conform to the contract? However you may be inclined to answer these questions, recognize that each of them requires an interpretation of the contract to determine the parties' reasonable expectations.

In the above example, the contract involves a single delivery of one item. When the contract calls for the delivery of a quantity of goods in installments, the perfect tender rule is further qualified. This issue is best deferred until after the discussion of repudiation and is covered in section 17.7.8.

§17.6 THE BREACHING PARTY'S RECOVERY FOLLOWING MATERIAL BREACH AND THE CONCEPT OF DIVISIBILITY

§17.6.1 The Forfeiture of Contractual Rights by a Party Who Breaches Materially

It was noted in sections 17.3.4 and 17.4 that a party who substantially performs is entitled to return performance under the contract, subject to an offset for damages caused by the partial breach. This means that if the other party fails to render the return performance, the breacher may sue for enforcement of the contract despite the partial breach. However, if the breach is material and total, the breacher has no right to sue for enforcement of the contract. A material breach operates as a renunciation of the contract by the breacher, who thereby forfeits all rights under it and has no contractual claim to enforce. This follows naturally from the principle that a material and total breach terminates the victim's obligation to render return performance. It would be very odd if, after Substantial materially and totally breached by failing to make the down payment at all, it could sue Total for damages based on Total's failure to crush the concrete.

§17.6.2 Restitution in Favor of a Party Who Has Breached Materially

The above rule is concerned with suit on the contract and does not cover the breacher's right to claim restitution on the theory of unjust enrichment when she has performed part of her obligation before breaching, thereby giving some benefit to the other party. Once the contract has been terminated following her breach, the rationale for any benefit conferred on the other party under the contract falls away. To the extent that this benefit enriches the other party, he is unjustly enriched at her expense and should restore it. It must be stressed that a claim for restoration of the benefit is not based on the contract, but on the separate and distinct theory of unjust enrichment.

For example, say that Substantial made its down payment of $5,000 to Total on July 6. Early on July 7, Substantial decided that it did not want Total to crush the concrete, so it notified Total that it would not be delivering the concrete for processing. By repudiating its promise to deliver the concrete to Total for crushing and its obligation to pay the remainder of the contract price, Substantial has materially and totally breached the contract. Total therefore has the right to terminate and (as we shall discuss further in Chapter 18) to recover damages from Substantial to compensate for its lost profit. However, Substantial has already partially performed under the contract by making the $5,000 down payment to Total. Total no longer has a justification for keeping this payment because the premise under which it had been made — that it would crush the concrete — has fallen away. Under principles of unjust enrichment, the payment must be restored to Substantial by setting it off against Total's claim for damages. This principle is adopted by Restatement, Second, §374, which recognizes a right of restitution in favor of a material breacher to the extent that the benefit conferred on the other party exceeds his claim for damages. *See* Diagram 17B.

Diagram 17B

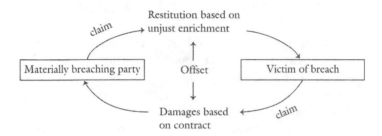

Although the Restatement's position is widely recognized by courts, it is possible that a court might continue to follow the approach more commonly seen in older cases and refuse to allow any remedy at all to a material breacher, particularly if the breach was deliberate. This punitive stance withholds even restitutionary recovery to the breacher and can have very unfair results because it disproportionally punishes a party who has rendered considerable performance before breaching. That is, the greater the value of what was performed before the breach, the greater the forfeiture.

UCC Article 2 follows an approach similar to that of Restatement, Second, in that it permits restitution in favor of a breaching party, whether or not the breach was willful. But it does impose a modest penalty on a breaching buyer. Section 2.718(2)(b) allows a defaulting buyer to obtain restitution of payments to the seller to the extent that they exceed any amount of validly agreed damages,[8] or the smaller of $500 or 20 percent of the price. Apart from this penalty, any restitutionary recovery under §2.718(2) is offset under §2.718(3) by any damages to which the seller is entitled under Article 2.

---

8. Agreed damages are explained in section 18.11.

The example concerning Substantial's restitutionary recovery from Total involved restoration of a money payment. It therefore did not present any issue of valuation of the benefit. Recognize, however, that if the breacher's performance was not the payment of money, but the rendition of a service or the transfer of property, the value of the benefit could be a matter of dispute. The general approach, reflected in Restatement, Second, §371 and §374, Comment b, is to give the breacher the lesser of the market value (quantum meruit) of the service or property, or the other party's ultimate economic enrichment (the actual increase in his economic wealth). Although the contract price may be used as evidence of value, it is not dispositive.

§17.6.3 The Enforcement Rights of a Material Breacher When the Contract Is Divisible

Divisibility is a concept of limited application, only relevant when there is some reason to break a contract into discrete units, and the contract is capable of being divided up into a set of self-standing components. Most contracts are not divisible because they contemplate the exchange of unitary performances and cannot be fragmented into a collection of independent, self-contained exchanges. However, some contracts are structured in a way that allow them to be broken up into sets of matching performances, each of which can be treated as a self-sufficient "mini-contract" within the larger contractual relationship. The determination of whether a contract is divisible is a matter of interpretation, and a court should not find a contract to be capable of division unless it is clear that this does not conflict with the apparent intent of the parties or damage the value of a performance reasonably expected by either of them.

Menorah Chapels at Millburn v. Needle, 899 A.2d 316 (N.J. Super. A.D. 2006) is a good illustration of the analysis used to determine divisibility. Needle contracted with Menorah, a funeral home, for the provision of funeral services for his father-in-law. The contract specified that the funeral services would comply with orthodox Jewish ritual. One of the requirements of orthodox ritual is that the body must be attended at all times prior to burial by watchers or *shomers* who take shifts in maintaining a constant vigil over it. Menorah's price list specifically included the provision of watchers on request and it was undisputed that Needle made such a request. In breach of this provision, Menorah provided a watcher for only three of the six shifts during the period prior to the burial. When Needle refused to pay Menorah, it sued for the contract price less a deduction of $390 for the three missed shifts. Menorah argued that the contract was divisible because each of its services was separately priced and could be ordered or declined by the customer. The trial court found the contract to be divisible, but the appellate court disagreed. The crucial question is whether it was the basis of the parties' bargain that the contract be performed in its entirety. The mere fact that the services were separately priced was not enough to make the contract divisible, especially in this case where itemization was required by state consumer protection laws. The underlying purpose of the contract was to provide a complete orthodox funeral, and Menorah could not simply fail to provide one of the services and sue under the contract for the price of what it did perform. The court remanded the case to the trial court to determine if the breach was material, and, if so, to calculate Menorah's recovery on the basis of quantum meruit.

As *Menorah Chapels* shows, division of a contract may be useful when there has been a breach or some other problem, such as illegality or impracticability, that affects only a portion of the contract, but does not taint the contract as a whole. In the context of material breach, if a contract is capable of division, splitting it into a set of relatively autonomous subparts may enable a party who has materially breached one part to isolate the breach and confine it to the affected part, so that the remainder of the contract is not sullied by the breach. This will enable him to treat the unaffected portion of the contract as if no breach had occurred and to enforce rights that have accrued in that portion. That is, if a contract is divisible, a material breach relating to only part of it is confined to that part, and the breacher can enforce the remainder without being subject to the general rule precluding action on the contract by the party who has materially breached it.

Carrig v. Gilbert Varker Corp., 50 N.E.2d 59 (Mass. 1943), remains one of the best illustrations of divisibility. Under a contract between a developer and a builder, the builder agreed to construct 35 houses for the developer. The builder repudiated the contract after completing 20 houses. Although the repudiation was material, the court allowed the builder to sue on the contract for the contract price of the 20 houses that had been completed. The court found the contract to be severable because the contract set out the price and specifications for each house individually, and each house was a self-contained economic unit. The builder's claim for the price of the completed houses was offset against the developer's claim for expectation damages — the additional cost of having the remaining 15 houses built by another contractor.

No section of UCC Article 2 speaks directly to the question of severability, so the above principles of common law are applicable. To the extent that Article 2 deals indirectly with severability, its approach is consistent with these principles. There are several provisions that recognize the concept of divisibility where the language and purpose of the contract, viewed in its commercial context, indicate that division of the goods into separate units would not impair the value of performance. Section 2.601 suggests that contracts for the sale of goods are normally divisible if the goods can be broken down into "commercial units." It contemplates that a buyer has the right to accept a commercial unit of goods that complies and to reject the rest. To constitute a commercial unit, an item or collection of goods must be regarded by commercial usage as a unit and must be capable of being traded as a unit without any impairment of value on the market. (See §2.105(6).) This approach is also reflected in the general remedy provisions in §§2.702 and 2.711 and in some of the more specific remedial provisions. For example, §2.709 allows the seller to recover the price of goods that have been accepted, even if others have been rejected, and Comment 2 to §2.612 makes it clear that when the parties apparently intended delivery in installments, a commercially reasonable fact-based interpretation must be used to break the contract into a set of self-standing exchanges, with the price apportioned among the deliveries.

§17.7 ANTICIPATORY REPUDIATION

§17.7.1 The Distinction Between Breach and Repudiation

It was stated in section 17.2 that a breach, properly speaking, can only occur when the promised performance falls due. However, it is possible for a party to breach in advance of performance—to repudiate her obligation in anticipation—if, before the time for performance, she makes it clear by words or actions that she will breach when performance falls due. A repudiation may occur between the time that the contract is made and the time due for its performance—that is, one of the parties repudiates before either party has begun performance under the contract. It may also occur after performance under the contract has begun, but before the due date of the repudiated performance.

To illustrate, recall that in the contract between Substantial and Total, executed on July 1, Substantial did not have to make its down payment of $5,000 before July 6, Total did not have to begin work until July 7, and Substantial did not have to pay the last installment of $15,000 until it collected the crushed concrete on July 9. It stands to reason that Substantial cannot be in breach for not paying until July 6, and Total cannot be in breach by failing to perform before July 7. However, if before the time due for performance, a party manifests the intent in advance that it will not perform when that date arrives, it repudiates the contract. For example, Total would be guilty of repudiation if, on July 2, it tells Substantial that it no longer intends to crush the concrete, and will refuse to accept delivery if Substantial tries to deliver it on July 7. In this case, Total has repudiated in the period before performance was due by either party. Even after performance of the contract is underway, a party might repudiate a performance due by it in the future. For example, after Substantial has made the down payment and delivered the concrete to Total, it might inform Total that it will not honor its obligation to pay the balance on July 9. Despite the fact that performance has begun, this qualifies as a repudiation rather than a breach because the final payment is not yet due and the intent to breach is communicated in advance of its due date.

§17.7.2 The Purpose and Value of the Doctrine of Anticipatory Repudiation

Older common law did not recognize the concept of anticipatory repudiation, so the promisee had no right to react to such an advance indication of breach. He had to wait until the time of performance to see if breach would in fact occur. In the interim, he had to hold himself available to tender his return performance when it fell due. Under this rule, if Substantial clearly repudiated the contract on July 2, Total could not have responded to Substantial's repudiation on July 2, but would have had to wait until July 6 to see if Substantial would in fact not make the down payment. In the interim, it would have had to hold itself available to process the concrete if Substantial repented, thereby forgoing the opportunity to mitigate its loss by allocating its facilities to a substitute contract. Under the old approach, the situation would be even worse if the victim of the repudiation had to perform first, because the law did not allow him to suspend his performance while waiting to see if the other party carried through with the threatened breach. So, if it had been Total that repudiated on July 2, Substantial would not have been allowed to react to this by withholding the down payment of $5,000 due on July 6. In these examples, the victim of the repudiation only had to wait a few days to know if a breach would occur, but the harm could be even worse if the period before the due date of performance had been longer.

During the nineteenth century, courts came to recognize that this approach was both unfair to the promisee and inefficient. The English case of *Hoechster v. De La Tour*, 118 Eng. Rep. 922 (Q.B. 1853), is generally regarded as the preeminent judicial pronouncement that when one of the parties clearly repudiates a material promise in advance, the other may treat this as a breach immediately and may seek relief for breach without delay. That is, a clear, unequivocal, and voluntary repudiation by one of the parties is recognized as the equivalent of a material and total breach, provided that the threatened action or failure to act would be a material and total breach if it happened at the time due for performance. The doctrine of anticipatory repudiation is now well established in common law and under the UCC.

Although the UCC does not define what constitutes a repudiation (thus leaving this issue to the common law, even in sales of goods), it does codify and make some refinements to the doctrine in UCC §§2.609-2.612. As in other areas, the changes brought about by the UCC have been influential in developing common law rules, and their spirit is reflected in the treatment of repudiation in Restatement, Second, §§243 and 250 to 257.

§17.7.3 The Elements of Repudiation

As stated already, for a prospective nonperformance to constitute a material and total repudiation of the contract, the promisor must clearly, unequivocally, and voluntarily communicate an intention not to render the promised performance when it falls due. This intention could be communicated by words or conduct. This definition indicates that words or conduct must satisfy a number of prerequisites to qualify as a repudiation:

a. Material and Total Repudiation

An advance repudiation does not allow the promisee to terminate and claim damages unless the threatened deviation from what was promised would constitute a material and total breach if it occurred at the time performance falls due. As with breach at the time of performance, the severity of the repudiation is determined by interpreting the contract in context. A repudiation is material and total if the promisor manifests the intent of not performing at all, or of rendering a performance that deviates in a significant way from what the contract requires.

b. Clear and Unequivocal Intent to Breach

The promisor's statement or conduct must clearly and unequivocally indicate that the promisor intends to commit a material and total breach when the time for performance arrives. The promisor's intent is interpreted objectively from the perspective of a reasonable person in the promisee's position. As we have often seen, a verbal expression of intent can be difficult to interpret. It may not be clear if the promisor is saying that she will not perform, or is merely expressing a lack of confidence in her ability to perform, or is just complaining about the terms of the contract. It could be even trickier to determine intent from conduct. To constitute a repudiation by conduct, the promisor's action must be so inconsistent with an intent to perform as promised that the only reasonable conclusion is that she has deliberately abandoned the contract. Some courts require that the conduct must make it impossible for the promisor to perform the contract.

c. Voluntary Statement or Conduct

To constitute a repudiation, the promisor's statement or conduct must be voluntary and deliberate, rather than inadvertent or beyond her control. Voluntariness is not usually an issue where repudiation is in the form of a statement of intent not to perform. However, where the alleged repudiation is by conduct, it is possible that the actions of the promisor were not deliberately intended to be a repudiation, but were compelled by circumstances beyond the promisor's control. For example, a few days before Substantial's down payment was due, Total was reliably informed that Substantial's business was struggling, it had defaulted in paying several of its debts, and some of its creditors had obtained judgments against it. This calls into question whether Substantial will be able to pay for the concrete crushing work. However, this financial adversity is neither a voluntary statement of intent not to perform nor voluntary conduct indicating such intent, so it cannot be treated as a repudiation. (As we will see in section 17.7.7, Total has a means of responding to these circumstances by requesting an assurance of performance.)

§17.7.4 The Response to a Repudiation

When a material repudiation has occurred, the other party has a choice between two alternatives. Her one option is to treat the repudiation as an immediate breach. This entitles her to refuse to render her own performance, to terminate the contract, and to sue for relief for total breach. Her other alternative is to delay responding to the repudiation to see if the repudiating party repents.

a. Treating the Repudiation as an Immediate Breach

If it is clear that the promisor has committed a total and material repudiation, the promisee may react by suspending her own performance, terminating the contract, and claiming damages for breach. However, the elements set out in section 17.7.3 make it clear that the advance manifestation of intent not to perform must be clear and serious enough to constitute a total and material repudiation. These elements impose an appropriate restraint on the promisor's ability to declare breach in advance, and prevent a premature claim of prospective breach merely because some uncertainty arises about the promisee's future performance.

In some cases there could be doubt about whether these elements are satisfied. Where it is unclear whether a party's words or conduct constitute a repudiation, neither party can be sure, until the matter is settled by litigation, if a court would agree that the promisor did in fact commit a total and material repudiation. This imposes a risk on both parties. If the court finds that there has been a total and material repudiation, the promisor will lose the benefit of the contract and will be liable for damages. If the court finds otherwise, the promisee will not have been justified in declaring a repudiation and will herself be in breach of the contract.

For example, on July 5, Total notifies Substantial that it is running behind in processing materials under other contracts and will not be able to have Substantial's concrete crushed until July 10. Substantial insists that Total must stick to the promised delivery date and threatens to cancel if it refuses to do so. If completion of the job on July 9 is a material term of the contract, Total has materially repudiated, entitling Substantial to declare breach and terminate the contract. However, if a day's delay is not material, Substantial cannot do this, and must accept the delay and may claim only such damages as are caused by it. Until a court rules on the question, neither party can be sure if Total's repudiation qualifies as material. This standoff imposes the risk of being a repudiator on both parties. If it turns out that Substantial is right, Total has repudiated the contract by indicating in advance that it will not adhere to the delivery date. However, if the delivery date is not material, Substantial will repudiate if it treats it as such and terminates the contract.

b. Encouraging Retraction of the Repudiation

A promisee is not obliged to accept a repudiation when it occurs. She can give the promisor a reasonable opportunity to retract the repudiation. (The promisee takes a risk if she waits longer than a reasonable time for a retraction. If she does, and she thereby incurs losses that could have been prevented, she may not be able to recover the aggravated damages.) Until the promisee notifies the promisor that she has accepted the repudiation, or (even without notice to the promisor) the promisee takes some substantial action in reliance on it, the promisor is generally able to retract the repudiation.

§17.7.5 Prospective Nonperformance and Assurance of Performance

The promisee's statement or conduct may not be clear and unequivocal enough to constitute a repudiation, but his words or actions, or a change in circumstances, may cast doubt on his willingness or ability to perform when his performance becomes due. Although the promisor does not have grounds to declare a repudiation, she may be entitled to react to the possible prospect of breach by demanding an assurance of performance. This right is recognized in similar terms by both UCC §2.609 and Restatement, Second, §251.

UCC §2.609 provides that if a party has reasonable grounds for insecurity regarding the other's performance, she may make a written demand for an adequate assurance of due performance. Until that assurance is received, the party requesting it may, if commercially reasonable, suspend any of her own performance for which she has not already received the agreed return. The party receiving a justified demand for assurance must provide an adequate assurance within a reasonable time, not exceeding 30 days. If he fails to do so, he has repudiated the contract. Restatement, Second, §251 differs in its wording to some extent, but is largely to similar effect. Unlike sales of goods, for which there is a statutory right to demand an assurance, the equivalent right in relation to contracts at common law must be recognized by the courts. It is generally recognized, so the ability to seek assurances is commonly available under the circumstances outlined by Restatement, Second, §251.

Although UCC §2.609 and Restatement §251 set out the broad rules under which a party who feels insecure about the prospect of receiving performance may demand an assurance of adequate and due performance, they leave many questions to the judgment of both the party demanding the assurance and the party responding to the demand. An error in judgment by either party could lead to serious consequences for that party. To begin with, the party requesting the assurance must be satisfied that her grounds for insecurity are reasonable. In making the demand, she must decide what assurance would solve the insecurity and whether it is reasonable to ask for it. When she receives the response, she must decide whether it cures the problem. If she misjudged and asked for too little, the assurance may be meaningless. If her misjudgment was to make a demand that was unjustified or went beyond her rights, she would herself commit a breach by insisting on the assurance and in suspending her own performance.

The example used in section 17.7.3c provides an illustration of circumstances giving rise to a demand for an assurance of performance: A few days before Substantial's down payment was due, Total was reliably informed that Substantial's business was shaky. It had defaulted on several of its debts, and some of its creditors had obtained judgments against it. These circumstances do not constitute a repudiation because Substantial has not indicated the intent, either by statement or by voluntary conduct, of not performing the contract. However, Substantial's financial situation may make Total insecure over whether Substantial will be able to pay for the concrete crushing work. If these circumstances give Total reasonable grounds to believe that Substantial will breach when its performance falls due, Total may demand an adequate assurance of performance from Substantial. Substantial must respond satisfactorily within a reasonable time. While Total is waiting for Substantial's response, it may suspend any performance that would otherwise be due, and if it does not get an adequate assurance in time, it may treat the contract as repudiated. This is all very well, but you can probably see immediately that there could be serious issues in dispute, some of which may be: Does Total really have reasonable grounds for feeling insecure? If not, any suspension of performance would itself be a breach. If it is justified in demanding assurance, what should it ask for? Merely asking Substantial to reaffirm that it will pay is not very helpful, because the assurance could just be a hollow promise, and Substantial may not admit that it is in financial trouble. It would be much more reassuring if Substantial would pay the full price for the job immediately, before Total begins work, but such a demand would be a unilateral revocation of the contract's payment terms and probably goes beyond what Total can legitimately demand. Maybe a demand for a verified financial statement, showing the availability of funds, would be a workable alternative to these two extremes. Once Total settles on its demand, Substantial has to decide how to respond. If it feels that Total is not justified in feeling insecure, it could refuse the assurance. If it feels that the demand is excessive, it could offer a more modest assurance. But if it is wrong, its refusal to comply with the demand crystallizes the uncertainty into a repudiation.

There are no easy answers to these fact-based questions, but this example highlights the kinds of concerns that may arise when a prospective breach is perceived. Of course, not all cases end up in a morass of uncertainty, and the ability to demand assurances can be helpful in either reinforcing the prospects of performance or in establishing a repudiation.

§17.7.6 Transactions Involving Installments

Issues of repudiation and total breach are highlighted in contracts that call for performance in installments. When a breach occurs in the performance of an earlier installment, it can be difficult to know if the breach affects only the defective installment or is so serious as to undermine the contract in its entirety, operating as a repudiation of all remaining installments.

For example, Seller, a manufacturer of machinery, contracts with Buyer for the sale of three of its machines to be used by Buyer in its factory. Under the contract, the machines are to be delivered a month apart from each other. Because Buyer is depending on prompt delivery to avoid disruption of its business, the contract requires delivery of the machines on the exact dates specified. The first machine is delivered on time and is installed. After two days of operation it breaks down as a result of a defect that cannot be repaired without removal of the machine. Because timely delivery is important in the transaction, the defect in the first machine is likely to be a material and total breach of Seller's performance obligation with respect to the first installment, but does this also constitute a material and total repudiation of the future installments and hence a breach of the contract as a whole? That is, does the delivery of a defective first installment so seriously impair Buyer's expectations concerning the remaining machines that it is a repudiation of the performance promised in the future? If so, Buyer may use the present breach as the basis for terminating the entire contract. If not, the breach does not impact future performance, so that Buyer continues to be obliged to accept and pay for the later two machines, and is confined to a remedy for breach of the current installment.

As this is a sale of goods, the principles governing these questions are set out in UCC §2.612, which qualifies the perfect tender rule of §2.601 in contracts providing for delivery in installments. Section 2.612(2) states that a nonconformity in an installment permits the buyer to reject that installment only if the nonconformity substantially impairs the value of the installment, and the nonconformity cannot be cured. For the nonconformity to impair, not just that installment, but the contract as a whole, §2.612(3) requires that the deficiency in the installment "substantially impairs the value of the whole" contract. This means that when a breach occurs in an earlier installment, it must be determined whether this is a breach so fundamental to the whole contract as to constitute not merely a partial breach, but a total and material breach of the contract as a whole. If it does, the breach operates not only as a breach of the current installment, but also as an advance breach (that is, repudiation) of the performance obligations due in the future. The question is whether it is pervasive and irreparable enough to make it clear that the promisor is incapable of rendering, or unwilling to render, substantially compliant performance in the future.

An express rule governing installment sales is particularly necessary when a sale of goods is involved because the perfect tender rule does not permit application of the doctrine of substantial performance. At common law there is less need for having a special rule for installment contracts because the result of §2.612 can be achieved by applying the general principles of substantial performance, under which the breach relating to one installment will only be a total breach if it results in an incurable material violation of the contract as a whole. This is reflected in Restatement, Second, §243(4), which, in dealing generally with total breach (and not with specific reference to installment transactions), adopts language similar to that used in UCC §2.612.

§17.8 A TRANSNATIONAL PERSPECTIVE ON BREACH AND REPUDIATION

Fundamental breach is the civilian concept equivalent to the common law concept of total and material breach. Unlike UCC article 2, the CISG does not have a perfect tender rule, but requires a fundamental breach as grounds for terminating a contract. Articles 49 and 64 of the CISG allow a buyer or seller, respectively, to terminate a contract for fundamental breach, which is defined in Article 25 as a breach that is so detrimental to the other party "as substantially to deprive him of what he is entitled to expect under the contract." Article 25 qualifies this by stating that a breach is not fundamental if the breaching party "did not foresee and a reasonable party of the same kind in the same circumstances would not have foreseen such a result." We will deal with the concept of foreseeability in relation to damages in Chapter 18, but it is interesting to note that the CISG connects foreseeability to the question of whether a breach is fundamental. Articles 47(1), 49, 63(1) and 64 recognize an exception to the rule that only fundamental breach is grounds for termination: They adopt a procedure from German law known as the *Nachfrist* exception, under which a party can make a delay in performance into a fundamental breach by giving notice to the other party fixing a reasonable additional time for performance.

Article 7.3.1 of the UNIDROIT Principles also allows the victim of fundamental breach to terminate the contract. It sets out factors to be taken into account in deciding whether a breach is fundamental. These factors are quite similar to the guidelines set out in Restatement, Second, §241 to decide whether a breach is material. They include the extent to which nonperformance substantially deprives the nonbreaching party of its entitlement under the contract, whether strict compliance with the terms of the contract was of the essence, whether nonperformance was intentional or reckless, whether the nonperformance reasonably undermines the injured party's reliance on the breacher's future performance, and whether the nonperforming party will suffer disproportionate loss if the contract is terminated. Like the CISG, Article 7.3.1 raises the concept of foreseeability in its definition of material breach by providing that a breach should not be treated as material if the breacher did not and could not reasonably foresee that the breach would substantially deprive the victim of what it was entitled to expect under the contract. Where performance is delayed, Article 7.3.1 allows the victim to terminate the contract if the delay is fundamental. If the delay is not fundamental, Article 7.3.1 adopts the same *Nachfrist* exception as the CISG, allowing a party to make delay fundamental by giving the other party notice of a reasonable extension of the time of performance. If the delay is not fundamental, Article 7.1.3 allows the victim to withhold performance until the other party performs or tenders performance.

The CISG and UNIDROIT Principles recognize the concept of repudiation and prospective inability to perform. Article 72 of the CISG allows a party to terminate a contract if it is clear that the other party will commit a fundamental breach. However, unless the repudiating party has declared that he will not perform, the victim of the repudiation should give him the opportunity to provide a reasonable assurance of performance if time allows. Article 71 deals with prospective inability to perform. It allows a party to suspend performance if it appears that the other party will not perform a substantial part of his obligations because of a "serious deficiency in his ability to perform" or "his conduct in preparing to perform or in performing the contract." The party who suspends performance must give immediate notice to the other party and must cease the suspension if the other party gives an adequate assurance of performance. The UNIDROIT Principles set out provisions very similar to those in the CISG, but in language that is even closer to the formulations of American law: Article 7.3.3 allows a party to terminate a contract where it is clear that there will be fundamental nonperformance. Under Article 7.3.4 a party who reasonably believes that there will be a fundamental nonperformance may demand adequate assurance of due performance, and if adequate assurance is not provided within a reasonable time, may terminate the contract.

Examples

1. Standard Home Construction, Inc., entered into a contract with Lofty Lanky to build a house on a lot owned by Lofty. One of the specifications in the contract and in the plans was that the ceiling height must be 9 feet. Lofty included this specification in the contract because he is 7 feet tall, and feels claustrophobic if he does not have plenty of clearance between the top of his head and the ceiling. Standard began work and building proceeded on schedule. It was not until the house was fully framed and work had begun on building the roof that Lofty first noticed that the ceilings were only 8 feet high. Standard conceded that this was not in accordance with the contract — its foreman had overlooked the contract specification and had assumed that the house would have the more common 8-foot ceiling height. The only way to correct the error is to demolish and rebuild a significant part of the existing work. This would entail considerable additional labor and the destruction and waste of materials, which would increase Standard's cost of building the house. Nevertheless, Standard accepted responsibility for fixing its mistake and was willing to incur the cost. There was enough time left before the date specified in the contract for completion of the house, so the demolition

and rebuilding would not have delayed completion beyond that date. However, Lofty was upset by Standard's error and had lost faith in its ability to build the house competently. He therefore refused to allow Standard to correct the error or to proceed with the construction. He terminated the contract and hired another contractor do the demolition and to complete the house. He then sued Standard for damages based on his additional cost. Was Lofty entitled to fire Standard and hold it liable for the extra cost?

2. As in Example 1, Standard's foreman overlooked the contract specification and failed to make the ceilings 9 feet high. However, Standard's reaction to this error was quite different. Although it conceded the mistake, it refused to dismantle the completed work and to rebuild it in conformity with the contract. It argued that this would be an economic waste because the lower ceiling height was very common and would have no impact on the value of the house. In fact, the lower ceiling might even increase its value because many people would not like the higher ceilings. Lofty refused to accept this argument and demanded that Standard correct the error. When Standard refused to do so, Lofty terminated the contract and hired another contractor to do the demolition and complete the house. He then sued Standard for damages based on his additional cost. Assume that Standard was correct in saying that the lower ceilings would not diminish the value of the house. Was Lofty entitled to fire Standard and hold it liable for the extra cost?

3. Sandy Shaw owns a small motel (called "Sandy Shaw's Motel"), a few blocks off the main strip of a seaside town. Sandy entered into a contract with Bill Board, a signwriter, under which Bill undertook to make a sign advertising the motel, which Sandy planned to be erect at the entrance to the town. The contract stipulated that the sign was to measure 6 feet long and 4 feet high. Bill delivered the sign to Sandy on time. On inspecting it, Sandy found that it was only 5 feet high and 3 feet wide. Sandy rejected the sign and refused to pay for it. Was she justified in doing that?

4. On May 1, Sandy Shaw entered into a contract with Peter Familias under which Peter booked all 15 rooms in the motel for a family reunion on the nights of June 15 and 16. Sandy gave Peter a special group rate on the understanding that the booking was firm and could not be cancelled. On May 10, Sandy received an e-mail from Peter that stated, "My family has decided that it would prefer to have its reunion in Las Vegas. I am therefore cancelling our booking and plan to find a place there. Go ahead and rent our rooms to someone else." Sandy wrote back immediately, "I received your e-mail today. Remember that when you made this

booking, we agreed that you could not cancel it. You will therefore be obliged to pay for the rooms, even if you do not use them. Think about that before you decide to change your reunion plans." On May 13, Peter responded, "OK, you are right. Besides, Las Vegas turns out to be too expensive. We'll stick to the original plan. See you on June 15." In the interim, on May 12, Sandy received an offer from a tour group to take all the rooms in her hotel at full price for a week, beginning June 13. Sandy had not yet accepted this offer when she received Peter's e-mail of May 13, but she would like to let the rooms to the tour group instead of Peter. Does she have the right to do so?

5. As in Example 3, Sandy Shore and Bill Board entered into a contract under which Bill agreed to make a sign advertising Sandy's motel. Bill made the sign satisfactorily and delivered it to Sandy, who paid for it. Sandy then realized that she needed to get a permit from the town to erect the sign. She therefore entered into a second contract with Bill under which he undertook to get the permit and erect the sign within one month of execution of the contract. Two days after the parties made the contract, Sandy read in the local newspaper that Bill's business license had been revoked by the municipality because of repeated violations of the town's signage ordinances. Sandy wrote an e-mail to Bill, immediately, saying, "I read in the paper that your business license has been revoked. This means that you will not be able to secure a permit for the sign or to erect it. Unless you can assure me by responding today that the newspaper report is wrong, and that you will be able to perform our contract on time, I will treat our contract as at an end and will hire someone else to get the permit and erect the sign." Bill sent an e-mail in reply about an hour later, saying, "Do not believe everything that you read in the newspaper. Do not worry. I will get your permit and install the sign on time." Sandy is not satisfied with Bill's response. She would like to terminate their contract and hire someone else. Is she entitled to do so?

6. In May, Cleaver Carnage, a famous chef, entered into a contract with Televicious, Inc., the owner and operator of a television network, to produce and star in a weekly cooking show, to be called "Cleaver's Critter Cookout." The show was to run for a trial season from September 1 to October 30. Each weekly installment was to begin with live video footage showing Cleaver hunting and slaughtering various woodland creatures. The scene would then change to Cleaver's well-equipped studio kitchen, in which he would prepare a delectable dish from the day's catch.

In July, Televicious came under great pressure from various consumer groups and government agencies to reduce the level of violence in its broadcasts. In attempting to respond to community concerns, it reviewed its fall programming and decided to cancel several shows that seemed unnecessarily gruesome. Cleaver's cooking show was one of them. Televicious proposed to replace it with a program entitled "Longevity with Legumes," to be hosted by Lena Lofatt, a widely published author of health-conscious recipe books. Televicious wrote to Cleaver on July 30, informing him that his services were no longer required. Cleaver responded immediately by writing a letter to Televicious, pointing out correctly that the contract gave Televicious no right to cancel unilaterally, and notifying it that he continued to hold it to the contract.

By August 10, Cleaver had heard nothing more from Televicious. On that day he received an offer to work during September as camp chef for a culinary safari of central Africa. Although he was quite attracted by the invitation, he decided that it was not nearly as beneficial to his career as a television program would be. Because he still hoped that Televicious would repent if given some time, he declined the offer of the safari and waited for its response to his letter. His optimism was in vain. A week later, he received a terse note from Televicious, stating that the decision was final. By now, it is too late for Cleaver to find anything else to replace his aborted television venture. What are his rights?

7. Hunk De Lectable is a famous actor. He entered into a contract with Matt Arial & Co. (MAC), an advertising agency, under which Hunk agreed to star in a series of six TV commercials advertising hair products manufactured by one of MAC's clients. Under the contract, Hunk was to be paid $1 million for each commercial. The commercials were to be shot over a two-week period, and Hunk would be paid the total contract price of $6 million at the end of that period. Hunk performed well in the filming of the first two commercials. When he arrived to film the third commercial he was drunk. He slurred, threw up on a producer, and eventually passed out. MAC fired Hunk immediately afterwards. Hunk concedes that MAC was justified in firing him, and he accepts that the contract is at an end. MAC has abandoned the commercials featuring Hunk, and it has found another actor to do them. Because the commercials are a set, MAC cannot use the first two in which Hunk appeared, and it must therefore redo those commercials with the new actor. MAC has decided to absorb the wasted costs itself and it does not seek damages from Hunk. However, it did not pay Hunk for the two commercials that he completed, and he claims that because he performed as required in those commercials, he is entitled to be paid the full contract price of $1 million each for them. MAC denies that he is entitled to any payment for the two commercials. What, if anything, should Hunk be able to recover?

Explanations

1. Standard breached the contract by failing to comply with the specifications. If the breach was material and total, Lofty had the right to respond by terminating the contract and claiming any expectation damages that he suffered.[9]

   Standard did not claim that it had substantially performed, and it undertook to demolish and rebuild. It, in effect, conceded that the breach was material. The only issue is whether the breach was total — that is, whether Lofty had the right to terminate immediately without giving Standard the opportunity to perform the tendered cure. Standard proposed to give Lofty his exact contractual expectations, and could have completed the house on time despite the demolition and rebuilding. Lofty rejected this offer of cure because he was angry and had lost faith in Standard.

   When the contract involves a sale of goods, the right to cure a defective performance has a clear statutory basis under UCC §2.508. This is not a sale of goods, but the common law concept of partial breach also envisages the possibility of cure when the breach is not so immediately and irrevocably material as to be incapable of reversal, and the breaching party shows a desire to remedy the defective performance within a reasonable time. The efforts at cure must produce a performance in compliance (or at least substantial compliance) with the contract. If the finished product remains significantly deficient, the failure to cure adequately will itself be a material breach. Lofty refused to give Standard an opportunity to cure. His reasons for doing so may be understandable, but they are probably not legally justifiable in the absence of some stronger indication that Standard is so incompetent that it would be incapable of properly completing performance in accordance with the contract. If cure is feasible and the will to cure is apparent, the promisee takes a risk that a court may later disagree with his prediction of inadequate performance, and may find him to have acted unreasonably in preventing rectification of the breach. If so, he could himself be the repudiator. Not only would he be denied damages, but he would be liable for any damages that Standard suffered.

---

9. We focus here on the breach issue and defer detailed discussion of damages for total breach to Chapter 18. For the present, it is enough to note that the basic measurement of damages would be the difference between the contract price and the reasonable cost to have another contractor complete the house as specified in the contract. This would include the cost of demolishing the nonconforming work and completing the house. Because Lofty has no doubt already made some periodic payments to Standard for the work done before its breach, these payments would also have to be taken into account in calculating damages.

2. Lofty did not immediately terminate the contract, but treated the breach as partial and offered Standard an opportunity to cure it by rectifying the construction to bring the house into conformity with the contract. Standard refused, claiming, in essence, that construction of a house with 8-foot-high ceilings would be substantial performance of its contract obligations. If Standard was wrong, Lofty had the right to declare total breach. If Standard was correct, Lofty had no right to terminate the contract and would have been obliged to accept the defective performance. He would then have had a claim for damages to compensate for the breach. On Standard's theory, these damages would not be the cost of rectifying the breach, but merely a reduction in the value of the house, which would be zero.

The question of whether the construction of lower ceilings was a material breach of Standard's contract obligations is a matter of interpretation to determine the parties' reasonable expectations. The term must have been so central to the bargain that its breach deprived Lofty of the value that he reasonably anticipated. The construction of a house with 8-foot-high ceilings might possibly have been substantial performance if the lower ceilings did not affect the value or salability of the house, and Lofty did not intend to live in the house but was merely building it on speculation for immediate resale. However, even here this conclusion would not be assured.[10] By contrast, in this case, Lofty was building the house for his own use and he had a particular reason for including the specification in the contract. The fact that the lower ceilings would not affect the market price should not be a significant consideration.

The facts of Lofty's case invoke *Jacob & Youngs v. Kent, Plante v. Jacobs,* and *Lyon v. Belosky Construction,* discussed in section 17.3.3. As those cases show, the court's task in deciding on the materiality of a breach is to differentiate those deviations that go to the heart of the contract from those that do not. This distinction is made by measuring the gravity of the breach in light of the contract's language, circumstances, and purpose. The circumstances of this case make the breach akin to the material breach found in *Lyon* and distinguish it from the minor breaches found in *Jacob & Youngs* and *Plante.* Lofty is therefore entitled to declare total breach, terminate the contract, and claim damages from Standard based on the difference between the contract price and the cost of completing the house to contract specifications.

---

10. It is not a foregone conclusion that the breach would have been immaterial merely because the house was being built on speculation to be sold. As the dissent in *Jacob & Youngs* pointed out, once the parties go to the trouble of specifying a term in clear and express language, the court should be slow to second-guess them and to declare the term immaterial merely because it seems unimportant to the court.

3. Bill's undertaking to make the sign is not a contract to perform a service for Sandy, but a sale of goods. The transaction involves the exchange of an end product — the completed sign — for money. (It is, of course, common for a manufacturer to sell goods that it has fabricated, and this is no less a sale because the goods are custom made.) As this is a sale of goods, the doctrine of substantial performance does not apply. Under §2.601, the buyer may reject the goods if they fail in any respect to conform to the contract.[11] This right of rejection is mitigated by the seller's right to cure under §2.508. The facts of the example do not indicate if Bill has tendered a cure, or provide enough information to determine if an effective and timely cure would be possible.

   The perfect tender rule therefore takes a very different direction from the common law. Had the common law applied to this contract, the analysis would have proceeded as follows: The first question to be decided would be whether the size of the sign was a material term of the contract. One cannot reach a definitive conclusion about the materiality of the sign's dimensions on the facts available, but as the purpose of the sign is to advertise the motel to passing motorists, size may well be material. If it was, Bill's material breach would have entitled Sandy to terminate the contract and claim any expectation damages suffered. However, if the size of the sign is not material, the otherwise competent performance may qualify as substantial. If Bill has substantially performed, Sandy may not reject the performance, but would have to accept it subject to a right to claim damages resulting from the nonconformity. If the smaller size of the sign is only a minor breach, the cost of rectification (redoing the sign) may be too harsh a remedy, so Sandy may be confined to a claim for the difference in value (if any) between what she contracted for and what she received.

4. Peter's e-mail of May 10 seems to be a clear repudiation of the entire contract. It is not simply an exploration of the possibility of cancellation, but states unequivocally that he is cancelling the booking, which he had no right to do. Sandy did not accept his repudiation, but instead wrote an e-mail to him encouraging him to retract it, which he did on May 13. Because a repudiation is a prospective breach, the promisee is able to repent and retract it before the time for performance is due, and before the promisor has accepted it or taken substantial action in reliance on it. (Action in reliance on the repudiation is enough to end the promisee's power to retract, even if the promisor has not communicated acceptance

---

11. As noted in section 17.5.1, the circumstances may allow the court some flexibility if the buyer did not reject properly or in time or there are clear grounds for finding that the buyer acted in bad faith in rejecting the goods, but no circumstances of this kind seem to be present here.

of the repudiation.) Sandy did not accept the offer from the tour group on May 12, so had not yet acted in reliance on the repudiation before Peter retracted.

5. Unlike the contract in Example 3, this is not a sale of goods, but a contract for the performance of services. It is therefore subject to the common law, not UCC Article 2. However, this would not likely make a difference to the analysis or result, because the applicable legal rules in UCC §2.609, and Restatement, Second, §251 are very similar.

   The revocation of Bill's license is not a repudiation because this is the action of a third party. Bill himself has neither made an unequivocal statement nor taken clear action to indicate an intention not to perform this contract when the time for performance becomes due. Notwithstanding, the revocation of his license does justify Sandy in feeling insecure about his ability to perform his contract obligations. She is therefore entitled to make a demand for an adequate assurance of performance, and if she does not receive it, to treat the contract as having been repudiated. The problem is that her demand is weak. It seems to ask for nothing more than an assurance that the newspaper report is false and hints vaguely at an assurance that Bill will perform on time. Bill's response seems evasive and does not offer any concrete assurance, apart from the vague statement that he will perform as promised. Sandy is right in not feeling much reassured, but she may be trapped by her inept demand, which really did not call for much more than Bill gave her. True, he did not assure her that the report was wrong, probably because it was not. However, he reaffirmed his commitment to perform, and Sandy will likely have difficulty in arguing that his failure to provide a more substantive assurance is a repudiation.

6. On July 30, Televicious unequivocally repudiated the contract. This gave Cleaver the option either of accepting the repudiation and immediately pursuing his remedy for total breach, or of declining to act on the repudiation and giving Televicious the opportunity to repent within a reasonable time. He chose the latter course. After about ten days had passed without any sign of retraction from Televicious, Cleaver was given the chance to recoup some of his potential loss by agreeing to join the African safari during September. Despite his initial decision, Cleaver has the right to change his mind and accept the repudiation at any time before retraction is communicated to him. He therefore could have accepted the offer to be a chef on the safari. He would have had no obligation to notify Televicious of this, because the repudiation cannot be retracted once Cleaver has made another commitment on the strength of it. Having accepted the repudiation, Cleaver would no longer have had to hold himself available to perform for Televicious, and could have sued immediately for damages based on the difference between what he

would have received under the contract with Televicious, and what he would have earned from the substitute employment. (We leave to Chapter 18 the question of whether someone in Cleaver's position could also have claimed any damages resulting from the loss of potential fame and fortune as a TV celebrity.)

However, Cleaver decided to pass up the opportunity in the hope that Televicious would have a change of heart. When he is eventually left with nothing to do in September, his decision to wait may be held against him. If, when he ultimately sues Televicious for damages, he is found to have acted unreasonably in continuing to await a retraction, his recovery from Televicious will be reduced to the extent that he should have acted to avoid the loss. That is, under the principle of mitigation of damages, he will not be able to hold Televicious liable for the amount that he could have recouped had he resigned himself to the repudiation and gone on the safari.

The crucial question is therefore whether Cleaver was reasonable in continuing to hold out hope for a retraction on August 10. Reasonableness is always a factual issue, to be decided in light of the nature and clarity of the repudiation and the likelihood of repentance under all the circumstances of the case. Televicious clearly and unconditionally expressed its intention to breach and completely ignored Cleaver's invitation to reconsider. He was given no reason to believe that Televicious would change its mind and was unduly optimistic in waiting further. He did not even attempt another communication before refusing the substitute employment. Under these circumstances, he would have quite a difficult task in convincing a court that he reasonably acted to cut down his loss. (Let us assume for now that the safari was indeed an appropriate substitute contract. This question will be discussed further in Chapter 18.)

7. Hunk concedes that he materially breached the contract and he does not resist MAC's termination. MAC does not claim damages for Hunk's breach. Therefore the only issue in this Example is whether Hunk is entitled to be paid the contract price, or any other amount, for the two commercials that he completed. Where a party materially breaches a contract, he cannot sue under the contract for any performance that he would have been entitled to in the absence of breach. He is, at best,[12] confined to a claim of restitution, to the extent that the other party has been enriched. Because a party who commits a material breach is at fault, enrichment is limited by the lower of the market value of the breacher's

---

12. As noted in section 17.6.2, some courts refuse to allow the breacher any recovery, even for unjust enrichment. However, most modern courts have moved away from this punitive approach.

services and the injured party's net economic gain. Because MAC has had to abandon the commercials and is redoing them with another actor,[13] it does not appear to have gained any economic benefit from Hunk's performance, so he is not entitled to any restitution.

If Hunk can show that the contract is divisible, he would be able to enforce those portions of the contract that he has fully performed and would be entitled to the payment of $2 million for the two commercials that he completed. Divisibility is a question of the parties' intent, to be decided by interpreting the contract in context. The contract is not divisible if the parties intended the exchange as an integrated whole, so that the injured party's reasonable expectations are defeated if any portion of it is eliminated. However, the contract is divisible if it can be separated into component parts, each with a distinct consideration, and the value of the components that were performed is not diminished by removing those that were not performed. This contract called for six commercials. Although we do not have enough detail to be sure, it sounds like the commercials were intended to be part of an overall campaign. (This is reinforced by the fact that MAC will not use the two commercials that Hunk made, and it is going to redo all of the commercials with another actor.) The fact that the contract identified a separate fee for each commercial could, under the right circumstances, support an argument of divisibility. However, this is not dispositive. The crucial question is whether each of the separate commercials was a self-contained and economically viable exchange. It sounds like they were not, so this contract does not appear to be divisible.

---

13. This action was apparently reasonable because MAC had to produce the commercials as a set. If there was no good reason for MAC to discard the commercials, this could complicate matters, because it may mean that MAC did get a benefit from Hunk, even if it chose not to take advantage of it.

18

Remedies for Breach of Contract

§18.1 THE SCOPE OF THIS CHAPTER

Because a contract creates obligations enforceable in law, its breach by one of the parties entitles the other to commence action to enforce it. This action may be a suit in court, or, where parties have so agreed, may be by some form of alternative dispute resolution, such as arbitration. This does not mean, of course, that the victim of a breach will inevitably take enforcement action. For most people, litigation or arbitration to enforce the contract is usually the last resort, after it becomes clear that the breach cannot be resolved by less formal means, such as a request to rectify the breach or by negotiation. Even where informal resolution fails, the victim of the breach may decide not to seek enforcement of the contract for any of a number of reasons. For example, because this may damage an important relationship between the parties, or the amount at stake is too small to justify the expense of litigation or arbitration, or it will be too difficult to prove economic injury, or the breaching party has no funds or other assets available to pay any judgment or award that may be obtained. Although these considerations should always be borne in mind, they are not addressed here. It is the concern of this chapter to set out the policies, general principles, and rules that govern the choice of remedy for breach and the measurement of compensation. We therefore focus on the judicial enforcement of the contract following its breach.

This chapter examines the remedies available for breach of contract. It presupposes that a valid and enforceable contract has been entered into and that one of the parties has breached it materially and totally.[1] If your contracts course covers remedies at or near the beginning, you will be reading this chapter before you get to questions of formation, performance, and breach. Remedial issues fall into three distinct but interrelated inquiries: First we must determine the nature and extent of the plaintiff's compensable loss, including both the harm suffered and the availability and form of the legal remedy or remedies to redress it. Second, if there is more than one means of remedying the loss, we must decide which of the available remedies most efficiently and comprehensively compensates for it. Finally, we must take into account any policies or principles that may limit the defendant's liability for the loss.

§18.2 THE BASIC GOAL OF REMEDIES FOR BREACH: ENFORCEMENT OF THE EXPECTATION INTEREST

§18.2.1 The Nature of the Expectation Interest

A valid and enforceable contract justifies a future expectation by each of the parties. They are both entitled to expect that the other will honor the contractual promise made and will perform as undertaken. If one of the parties fails to do so, thereby breaching the contract, the expectations of the other have been disappointed. Therefore, the fundamental goal of the remedy for breach is to cure that disappointment by giving the victim of the breach exactly what was promised and justifiably expected under the contract. This starkly contrasts contract damages from those for tort: While tort damages seek to compensate for something lost — to restore the victim to the pre-injury position, contract damages aim at compensating for something that was not gained — what the plaintiff should have had. This goal of enforcing contractual expectations is the beacon that guides contract remedies. The principle is described in a number of alternative ways, all of which have essentially the same meaning: Sometimes it is said that the goal is to protect the plaintiff's expectation interest; sometimes it is described as giving the plaintiff the benefit of her bargain; and sometimes it is said that the purpose of contract remedies is to place the victim of breach in the position that she would have been in had no breach occurred. This goal of damages applies both at the common law and under the UCC, which codifies it in §1.305.

---

1. Remedies for nonmaterial breach are discussed in Chapter 17. Of course, some of the principles discussed here, such as mitigation of damages and reasonable certainty of damages, are applicable to nonmaterial breach as well.

A party's expectation interest is the value of the performance to her, based on the purpose of the contract, as gleaned from its wording and the circumstances surrounding the contract's formation. However, even though the expectation interest is based on the contractual expectations of the particular party aggrieved by the breach, it is not determined on the purely subjective criterion of her privately held, subjective belief about what she would derive from the contract. Contracts are interpreted objectively, and compensation for breach is determined on the basis of objective evidence of loss. Therefore, a party's compensable expectations must be in accordance with what a reasonable person in her position would have expected as the benefit of the transaction, given the language used by the parties to express their agreement, and the circumstances surrounding it.

§18.2.2 An Introduction to the Means of Enforcement: The Primacy of Monetary Compensation over Specific Relief

The most direct and accurate way of enforcing the plaintiff's reasonable expectations under the contract would be for the court to grant an order of specific performance of the contract. This is an order to the defendant requiring him to perform as promised. For example, Harpo C. Cord owns the only extant piano known to have been used by Chopin. He entered into a contract with Nick L. Odeon under which he agreed to sell it to Nick for $25 million. Harpo breached the contract by refusing to go through with the sale. Nick's expectation is to gain the piano in exchange for depleting his bank account by $25 million, so the most accurate means for the court to ensure that he achieves that expectation is to compel Harpo to deliver the instrument against payment of its price. This seems like the most obvious solution, and on these facts — because the piano is unique — the court may see this as the most effective and desirable resolution. However, specific performance is not the norm. It is reserved for unusual cases where damages are shown to be incapable of adequately compensating the plaintiff. More commonly, the plaintiff's disappointed expectations are compensated for by an award of money.

Why does the law prefer a money equivalent of expectation over the real thing? The answer lies partly in considerations of practicality and policy, and partly in the traditional dichotomy between law and equity. The practical and policy issues may be illustrated by the following example: Sara Nade, an aspiring singer, had entered a singing competition in the hope of winning first prize, the chance to sing the national anthem at an important sports event. To give herself the best chance of winning, she contracted with Harmony R. Peggio, a voice coach, to receive an intensive period of

659

voice training in the week before the competition. Under their contract Harmony undertook, for a fee of $1,500, to give Sara four hours of coaching every day in that week. A few days before the course of instruction was to begin, Harmony notified Sara that she would be leaving town to do a last-minute concert tour, so she could not give the lessons as promised. Sara's expectation interest is to have the lessons for $1,500, and therefore the most accurate way of ensuring that Sara gets exactly what she expected would be for a court to compel Harmony to decline the tour and to give the promised lessons. However, in this situation the remedy of specific performance presents a number of problems: It would be difficult for the court to ensure that Harmony put her best efforts into a job that she is forced to do; the compulsion takes on the aspect of involuntary servitude; and the solution is not very efficient if another teacher could be found instead. For these reasons, it makes sense to allow Harmony to go on her tour, but if her breach results in a loss to Sara, to hold her liable to compensate for that loss.

As noted earlier, the preference for monetary relief is not based only on concerns of practicality, forced labor, and efficiency. Even if none of these problems exists, our legal tradition emphasizes damages as the standard remedy for breach of contract and disfavors specific relief in all but the most compelling circumstances. This is because the award of money damages was a remedy that could be granted by courts of law, whereas specific performance was granted only by a court of equity. (The distinction between law and equity is explained in section 2.5 and is discussed further in section 18.10.1.) Courts of equity were intended to intervene only when the available remedies at law were inadequate, and therefore a plaintiff who sought the equitable relief of specific performance was required to show that the nature of her expectation interest was such that the only means of achieving adequate relief was by the specific enforcement of the contract. Although courts of law and equity were merged some time ago, this ancient distinction still haunts our decisionmaking. As a result, even if it is practicable to give the plaintiff precisely what she expected, a money substitute is used in the great majority of cases: The plaintiff is awarded a sum of money that aims, as closely as possible, to put her into the economic position she would have been in had the contract been performed.

What is the basic principle on which this monetary award is calculated? To illustrate it, let us add some facts to the case of Harmony's breach of the voice-training contract: After Harmony's breach, Sara was able to find another voice coach, who was available to give her equivalent lessons for the same amount of time, but who charged $1,800 for the course. By hiring him, she got the lessons expected for $300 more, so to place her in her expected position, damages of $300 must be awarded against Harmony. Of course, this is not exactly Sara's expectation, because the teacher was different. However, we can seldom achieve the plaintiff's exact position by paying her money. The aim is to get as close possible. It should also be apparent that the concern here is only with economic loss, so if Sara could obtain the equivalent lessons at exactly the same price as Harmony charged under the contract, she has suffered no financial loss at all and is entitled to no damages for the breach.

§18.2.3 Fundamental Principles of Expectation Relief

The above examples suggest a number of important basic principles which will be recurring themes of the discussion that follows.

a. The Achievement of the Plaintiff's Expectation Is an Approximation

Contractual remedies aim to place the plaintiff in the position she would have been in had there been no breach, but because specific performance is available in only limited circumstances, the precise attainment of that expectation is seldom achieved. The best a court can do, in most cases, is to try to determine, as closely as possible, what monetary award will approximate that result.

This is already clear from the discussion of Sara's employment of a substitute trainer. The monetary award provides her with the compensation of getting the same hours of instruction for the same price, but it does not give her the less tangible benefit of being instructed by the teacher that she bargained for. The facts of the example, having been drawn with deliberate simplicity, do not illustrate some of the additional difficulties that may get in the way of an accurate measure of the value of the expectation. We will consider these later. For the present just bear in mind that the more complex the facts become, and the more uncertain the consequences of breach are, the harder it is to determine the amount of damages necessary to approximate the plaintiff's rightful position. Sometimes the amount awarded may undercompensate the plaintiff, and sometimes it may overcompensate her. It is important to remember that the burden of proving damages is on the plaintiff, who bears the ultimate risk of failing to persuade the factfinder about the fact or extent of loss. This burden is alleviated in some situations by evidentiary presumptions or inferences.

b. The Economic and Moral Dimensions of Contract Remedies

Contract law strongly emphasizes monetary compensation for the financial consequences of breach. In the discussion of Harmony's breach, no mention was made of any award for Sara's aggravation, inconvenience, or emotional distress in trying to cope with this last-minute letdown and in finding a replacement for Harmony. Unlike tort law, which is very solicitous of emotional trauma, contract law is dry-eyed and coldly commercial. It does not, except in the most unusual cases, take any account of noneconomic injury.

It is implicit in the principle that contract law compensates only for economic injury — that there is usually no sanction for a breach that causes no economic loss.[2] This may be disturbing to one who approaches this chapter after having spent so much effort learning that contractual obligations are binding and legally enforceable. Nevertheless, this is a basic truth of contractual remedies. If the contract is not one of the few that qualifies for specific enforcement, and no economic loss can be established, a breach normally results in no legal liability. (Of course, a breach may nevertheless carry some adverse nonlegal consequences, such as loss of goodwill or reputation.)

It follows naturally from this that damages measured purely by the extent of the plaintiff's loss do not generally distinguish between breaches that are inadvertent and those that are willful and purposeful. Because the focus is on rectifying harm and not on sanctioning improper conduct, punitive damages are not typically available for a breach of contract (except in unusually egregious cases), even when the violation of the contractual duty was deliberate. However, there are some rules of contract law that have particular or stricter application where a breach is willful or has an immoral dimension. In addition, there are various ways in which the court's or jury's disapprobation of the breacher's conduct might be more subtly reflected in the disposition of the case. For example, a court may use flexible rules to shift the burden of proof or otherwise give a plaintiff some advantage where the breach was purposeful, and a jury usually has enough leeway to be more generous to the plaintiff in awarding damages against a defendant whose breach was calculated and unethical.

c. The Economic Justification for Confining Damages to Financial Loss: The Concept of Efficient Breach

Although the principle of confining damages to financial loss predates the widespread resort to economics to explain, criticize, or justify legal rules, in recent times it has become popular to analyze the rule in economic terms. It is now commonly rationalized by the concept of efficient breach. A breach of contract is said to be efficient if the defendant's cost to perform would exceed the benefit that performance would give to both parties. Where this is so, the defendant makes enough gains by breaching to enable her to pay

---

2. There are limited exceptions to this rule — discussed in section 18.13 — when the defendant's conduct in breaching is also tortious or the contract is especially aimed at giving the plaintiff a noneconomic benefit.

compensatory damages to the plaintiff and still come out ahead. Provided that one looks only at the economic impact of the breach, one can say in such a case that the defendant's breach does not harm the plaintiff, who receives the financial benefit of his bargain, and yet it improves the defendant's position. In this sense, it satisfies the criterion of economic efficiency in that it makes the defendant better off without making the plaintiff worse off. If this is true, it could be argued that a rational contracting party with full information will choose to breach where circumstances make the breach efficient. This leads to the argument that the law should not discourage this because a legal rule that permits efficient breach — such as the rule that a plaintiff is entitled only to damages for economic loss — is itself efficient and thus best serves the interests of society.

Although analysis of this type is of some help in understanding and justifying the approach to contract damages, it has many limitations. The most significant is, of course, that it takes into account neither important noneconomic values (such as reliability, fair dealing, or faithfulness), nor those consequences of breach that are not measurable in economic terms (such as inconvenience, disappointment, or frustration). As a result, a conclusion that a breach imposes no harm on the plaintiff or on society may be misguided if based purely on quantifiable financial considerations.

Furthermore, economically efficient decisionmaking can only be achieved if all the conditions are right: The market must be competitive and stable, so that the relative costs and benefits of performing and breaching can be gauged. The party contemplating breach must be capable of acting voluntarily and rationally, and must have sufficiently full and reliable information to enable her to make a prediction of likely losses and gains. In addition, the transaction costs involved in terminating this contract and making substitutes must be small enough so as not to eliminate any advantage achieved by the breach.[3] Such ideal conditions are seldom likely to exist, which means that it will often be difficult to know at the time of breach whether it will turn out to have been economically efficient. Even if the party predicts an advantageous outcome at the time of the breach, economic conditions and subsequent circumstances may render it otherwise. To the extent that a theory of efficient breach is predicated on an unrealistic assumption of rational, voluntary, and informed behavior in a perfect market, with negligible transaction costs, it is likely to be unreliable, and more an academic model than a reflection of reality.

---

3. The total transaction costs incurred as a result of the breach include those costs incurred by the breaching party in entering into the more attractive transaction and the costs incurred by the victim of the breach in dealing with the breach and making any substitute transaction.

§18.2.4 The Enforcement of a Damage Award

The illustrations in section 18.2.2 do not indicate what happens after Sara gets her judgment of $300 against Harmony. The means of collecting payment on a judgment is beyond our scope, but it is useful to describe it briefly to provide an overall picture of the enforcement process. After the judgment is obtained (or if appealed, once it is affirmed on appeal),[4] Harmony may pay it voluntarily, thereby ending the matter. If she does not, Sara's only means of enforcing the judgment is to have a writ of execution issued by the clerk of the court to the sheriff (or equivalent official), calling on that official to find, seize, and sell property owned by Harmony to satisfy the judgment. The sheriff tries to execute the writ by finding property sufficient to satisfy the amount of the judgment, taking custody of it (known as levying upon it), and selling it at public auction. The proceeds of the sale are then paid to Sara, less the costs of execution. There are variations of this procedure that need not concern us here.

The point is that a judgment itself is merely a finding of liability. It does not guarantee that the plaintiff will get paid. If the defendant fails to satisfy it, and no assets can be found to execute upon, the plaintiff may never see her money. This sobering reality must be taken into account by anyone who decides to initiate litigation, and it means that being able to establish breach and damages are only part of the problem of enforcement. A judgment in law for damages is said to be in *rem* — it is enforceable only against the property of the defendant, and if the defendant has no property, the plaintiff loses in the end, having incurred substantial legal costs in the process.

§18.3 THE CALCULATION OF EXPECTATION DAMAGES

It is essential to bear in mind that the aim of expectation damages is to simulate as closely as possible the plaintiff's economic situation in the absence of breach. To determine the amount of money needed to approximate that position, a comparison must be made between what the plaintiff had the right to expect and what she actually got. Although the facts needed to calculate these two points of comparison can be very complicated and sometimes immensely difficult to prove, the basic concept of the comparison is straightforward. If one does not keep it in sight and use it constantly as a yardstick, one risks getting lost and confused.

---

4. The claim in the example is for $300. Although it is used here for the purposes of illustrating the process of collection, it should be noted that when the amount in issue is that small (or indeed, even considerably larger), very few plaintiffs would incur the legal expense of pursuing it. It would not take long for legal costs to exceed it.

Different formulas have been devised for use in making the comparison. These formulas are really just checklists to remind one of the factors to be taken into account, and they are only helpful to the extent that they do reliably cover every component of the calculation and signal clearly what figures go into each of them. A particular formula may be specific to certain kinds of cases and may not work well in others. In general, there are two essential elements to any formula, no matter how it structures the calculation: One part of it will count up the plaintiff's losses caused by the breach, and the other will take into account any savings, gains or recoupments that she has made as a result of termination of the contract. Damages consist of the losses less the savings, gains, and recoupments. Restatement, Second, §347 suggests the following general formula:

Damages =
Plaintiff's loss in value caused by the defendant's nonperformance
(This is determined by deducting the contractual value of what the plaintiff received from what she was promised)
Plus
Any **other loss**
(This includes consequential and incidental damages)
Less
Any **cost or loss** the plaintiff **avoided** by not having to perform

The principles and method of calculation are best explained by some concrete illustrations that describe some different types of situations and the various considerations that must be taken into account under each of them. Note that the actual ingredients of the calculation shift in accordance with the nature of the contract in question, but that the basic inquiry is always the same — the determination of damages always revolves around a comparison between the plaintiff's rightful position under the contract and her actual situation as a result of the breach.

a. Damages Based on a Substitute Transaction

We have already seen that in her simple contract for the purchase of voice training services, Sara's damages could be calculated by measuring the difference between what it would have cost her to receive the services under the contract, and what it ultimately cost her to obtain equivalent services elsewhere. That is, had the contract not been breached by Harmony, she would have had 28 hours of voice training for $1,500. As a result of the breach, she had 28 hours of training for $1,800, so damages of $300 puts her in the position she would have been in had the contract been performed. This is represented in Diagram 18A.

Diagram 18A

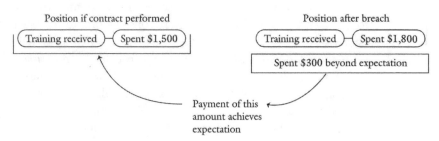

Exactly the same calculation and result would occur if, instead of purchasing lessons for $1,500, Sara had bought a car from Harmony for that price, Harmony breached by refusing to deliver, and Sara managed to find an equivalent substitute on the market for $1,800. UCC §2.712 codifies this by expressing the buyer's damages as the difference between the cover (i.e., repurchase) price and the contract price.

Change the facts: It is Sara who breached by canceling the lessons, and Harmony entered a substitute transaction by taking on a new student to fill the slot left open by Sara's breach. The same principle applies, but because the plaintiff is the provider of services, damage results only if the gains from the substitute transaction are less than those expected from the breached contract. For example, assume that Harmony could not find a replacement student at Sara's advanced level, and so she accepted a more junior student at the lower rate of $700 for the 28 hours. Harmony would be entitled to damages of $800, calculated by deducting the $700 earnings under the substitute contract from the $1,500 she expected to earn under her contract with Harmony. Similarly, a seller of goods who reasonably resells the goods at a lower price following the buyer's breach is entitled under UCC §2.706 to the difference between the contract price and the lower resale price.

b. Damages Based on the Market Value of the Promised Performance

Under both the common law and the UCC, if the aggrieved party did not enter into a substitute transaction, she is entitled to sue for loss based on a hypothetical substitute, valued at the market rate (which would have to be established by testimony, typically of an expert witness). Therefore, if, after Harmony's breach, Sara decided not to find a replacement teacher, and if the market value of the lessons is higher than what Harmony charged her, she could still sue Harmony for the difference between the market value of 28 hours of equivalent instruction and the contract price. Even though she is not actually going to pay more, because she will not have any lessons, she has nevertheless lost the benefit of a transaction below the market value, and can be compensated for this loss of benefit. The same principle applies under the UCC. Section 2.713 allows the buyer the difference between the higher market price of the goods and the contract price and §2.708(1) provides for seller's damages measured by the difference between the contract price and the lower market price of the goods.

The market price may also be used as the basis for calculating damages when the plaintiff did enter a substitute transaction, but the principle of mitigation, discussed in section 18.6.3, makes it inappropriate to award damages based on the actual cost of the substitute because the cost of the substitute transaction was higher than it needed to have been. This may happen when the market was rising and the plaintiff waited too long before making the substitute contract, or she chose an unreasonably expensive substitute. For example, following Harmony's breach, Sara hired a substitute teacher for $1,800, but that teacher charges more than the market rate of $1,600. If Sara could reasonably have found a teacher at the market rate, her damages will be confined to $100. This principle applies under the UCC as well and is reflected in UCC §§2.706 and 2.712, which require resale or cover to be without unreasonable delay and on reasonable terms.

When market value is used as the basis of determining damages, it must be decided at which place and time the value must be determined. If the parties reside in the same place and the performance was to occur in that place, there is no problem in deciding on the locality of the market, but if more than one location is connected to the contract, it must be decided which one should be used to measure market value. In addition, a market may fluctuate, so it is necessary to decide the date on which value is to be measured. There are different views on the most appropriate choice of market, and some inconsistency on this issue between the common law, the treatment of the seller under UCC §2.708, and the treatment of the buyer under UCC §2.713. Without getting into that complexity, it may simply be observed that the most sensible approach is to use the time and place that most closely approximates the market that the aggrieved party would reasonably have entered to obtain the substitute.

c. Loss of Income in a Contract for Services

Sometimes it may not be possible for the victim of a breach to find a substitute transaction. If the contract is for services, such as an employment contract in which the employee's only performance is her labor, and if the employee cannot find another job, a breach by the employer results in the employee's loss of her entire expectation under the contract. In such circumstances, the only way to compensate for the employee's disappointed expectation is to award damages equivalent to the full consideration due to her under the contract. For example, a few days before the voice training lessons are to begin, Sara reneges on her contract with Harmony because she decides that she does not need voice training. At this late date, Harmony cannot find another pupil to substitute for Sara, so she loses 28 hours of gainful employment. Sara would have come to Harmony's home for the lessons, and Harmony would not have incurred any costs in performing the service. That is, the full $1,500 would have been profit to her. Had the contract been performed she would have spent nothing and gained $1,500; now she still spends nothing, but gains nothing. Therefore, a payment of $1,500 is needed to give her the benefit of her bargain. Of course, this award really puts her in a better position than the contract would have done, because she does not have to work for it. But this is not taken into account when her savings — avoiding the act of working — have no monetary significance. *See* Diagram 18B.

Diagram 18B

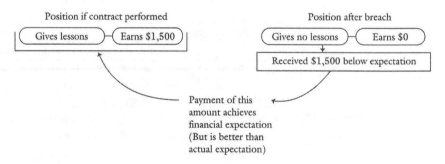

d. **Savings Resulting from the Breach Must Be Offset Against Loss**

The result in the above example would be different if Harmony would have had to incur costs to perform. Say that she would have needed to hire an accompanist for $600 to play the piano during the lessons and she is able to avoid doing so as a result of the breach. This cost, which is incurred solely in the process of and for the purpose of performing, is known as a direct or variable cost. It must be distinguished from fixed cost or overhead, such as Harmony's rent or utilities, which would have to be paid whether or not she performed this contract, and is hence not saved by the breach. Because direct costs would have reduced her expected profit had the contract been performed, it stands to reason that as they are actually saved as a result of the breach (or could have been saved if the plaintiff acted reasonably), they must be deducted from expected gains to achieve true expectation. This concept is represented by Diagram 18C.

Diagram 18C

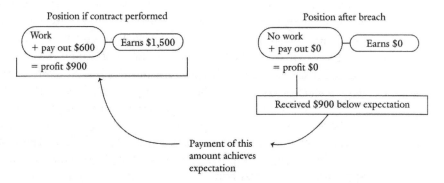

Of course, she must have been able to save the costs by reasonable action. The above example assumed that Harmony had the right to cancel her contract with the accompanist, thereby avoiding that direct cost. However, if she could not cancel without incurring liability to him for his fee (that is, she had made an irrevocable contractual commitment to him) she would not save these costs as a result of Sara's breach, and they would not be deducted. This is represented by Diagram 18D.

Diagram 18D

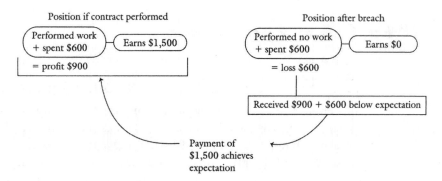

The same result would be reached if, instead of a contract for the provision of services, we were dealing with a sale of goods to be manufactured by the seller. If the buyer breached before the fabrication has begun, so that the seller avoids the direct costs of making the goods, the seller's damages are its lost profits on the sale, calculated by deducting the costs saved from the contract price.

As noted earlier, fixed costs (overhead expenses) are not saved by the breach and are not therefore deducted from damages. The above calculations therefore do not take into account costs such as the rent that Harmony paid for her studio or any other expenses that she had to incur in the course of her business, whether or not she taught Sara. Therefore, when we talk of the recovery of profit in a case like this, we mean gross, not net, profit.

In the first of the above illustrations, Harmony could avoid the direct cost of hiring the accompanist, so her damages are pure profit. But in the second, because she could not save this direct cost, her recovery includes both her expected profit and the reimbursement of the wasted expenditure that she incurred (or was committed to pay) in reliance on the contract. In a situation like this, when the plaintiff has incurred the expense of partial performance before the breach, a convenient formula for calculating expectation damages is therefore as shown in Diagram 18E.

Diagram 18E

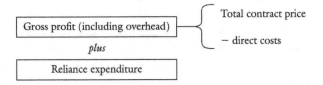

e. Offsets for Part Payment and Salvage

Any payment that the plaintiff received under the contract, as well as any loss that she may be able to salvage, is treated in the same way as costs that she has saved—these amounts must be offset against her recovery. For example, some months before the singing competition, and in anticipation of winning it and becoming an internationally renowned star, Sara decided to build a fully equipped recording studio onto the back of her house. She had the plans drawn, and entered into a contract with Ken Tractor to construct it for a total price of $75,000. The contract required Sara to make a down payment of $5,000 and to pay the remainder of the price in installments as the construction proceeded. Sara made the down payment, and Ken began work about two weeks before the competition. On the eve of the competition, he had reached the stage of completing the foundation and the framing of the new studio. Sara did not win the competition, and she immediately terminated the contract for construction of the studio. As she had no right to do this, she has breached. At that point,

Ken had received only his initial payment of $5,000. His costs in material, laborer's wages, and subcontractor charges to date were $10,000. He can show that had he completed the studio, his total direct cost would have been $60,000. The above formula leads us to a damage recovery of $20,000:

Gross profit	Contract price	$75,000
	− total direct cost	$60,000
	=	$15,000
Plus reliance expenditure	+	$10,000
Total (profit + reliance)	=	$25,000
Less payments received	−	$5,000
Recovery	=	$20,000

If you make the comparison between Ken's expected position and his position following breach, as we have done in prior illustrations, you will find that the payment of $20,000 achieves his expectation.

Consider a different case: Sara decided to have a special evening gown made for her appearance at the competition. She contracted with Cadenza La Scala, a dressmaker, for the manufacture of the dress for $1,500. Sara paid a deposit of $150 to Cadenza. After Cadenza had begun work, Sara decided that she had been profligate in ordering such an expensive outfit and decided to use an old prom dress instead. She immediately told Cadenza to stop work, thereby breaching the contract. At that stage, Cadenza had spent $200 on fabric that she had cut according to the pattern designed for Sara. In its present form, the cut fabric could be sold as scrap for $5. If Cadenza completes the dress, she will have to spend a further $50 on materials, but it would be very hard to sell the completed product because it was cut to fit Sara and it reflects her peculiar and rather eccentric fashion sense. This contract is a sale of goods, and UCC §2.708(2) codifies the formula set out above. Before looking at §2.708(2), we should note that as a manufacturer of the goods, Cadenza has the option under §2.704(2) of either scrapping the dress or of completing it and selling it to someone else. In making this choice, she must exercise commercially reasonable judgment. She would be justified in completing and attempting to resell the dress if she reasonably believed that by doing so, she could recoup all or most of the profit lost by Sara's breach, thereby reducing or eliminating her damages. As there is unlikely to be a ready market for such an idiosyncratic piece of clothing, the more reasonable judgment would be to scrap it and to seek damages under our formula, which is adopted in §2.708(2). Her recovery would be:

$$
\begin{array}{llr}
\textbf{Gross profit} & \left\{\begin{array}{l} \text{Contract price} \\ -\text{ total direct cost} \end{array}\right. & \begin{array}{r} \$1,500 \\ -\$250 \\ \hline = \$1,250 \end{array} \\
\textbf{Plus} & \text{reliance expenditure} & +\$200 \\
\textbf{Total} & (\text{profit} + \text{reliance}) & = \$1,450 \\
\textbf{Less} & \text{payments made (\$150)} & \\
& \text{and salvage (\$5)} & -\$155 \\
& \textbf{Recovery} & = \$1,295 \\
\end{array}
$$

Sara's down payment is, of course, an offset, as it was in the prior example, but the salvage must also be included in the deduction because it is, in a sense, a substitute transaction. Cadenza gains the $5 because she was able to sell the fabric — something she would not have been entitled to do in the absence of breach.

f. The Addition of Incidental and Consequential Damages

We will more fully discuss consequential damages in section 18.5 and incidental damages in section 18.12. However, it is helpful at this stage to show how they fit into the formulas that we have been working with. In short, incidental damages are expenses that the plaintiff incurs in handling the breach — the cost of taking whatever reasonable action is needed to protect and enforce the plaintiff's rights under the contract. They may include such expenses as the transaction costs of taking action to mitigate the effects of the breach and of entering into a substitute transaction. Consequential damages compensate the plaintiff for loss or injury suffered in other transactions that were dependent on this contract, or for loss or injury otherwise caused by the breach. For example, Cadenza La Scala, the dressmaker, becomes very busy during the period of the singing competition because so many of the competitors order dresses from her. To cope with the increase in demand she enters into a contract with Tex Tile, a highly skilled seamster, under which Tex agrees to work as her assistant for a month. Tex reneges at the last moment. Cadenza spends money advertising for another assistant, but she cannot find anyone with Tex's skills, so she settles for someone who is inexperienced and limited in capability. Because she does not have expert assistance, Cadenza cannot make as many dresses as she had expected and has to turn away several customers. The cost of trying to find a substitute is incidental damages, and the profit that she lost as a result of turning away the customers is consequential damages. If you look again at the formula set out at the beginning of this section, you will see that incidental and consequential damages are included in the "any other loss" category as an addition to any direct damages[5] that the plaintiff may claim to give her the benefit of the bargain, such as the difference between the contract and substitute price, or contract and market price. (On the facts of this illustration, Cadenza has not suffered any direct damages, so her claim is solely for incidental and consequential damages.)

> Plaintiff's loss in value (Direct damages)
> + any other loss (including incidental and consequential damages)
> − any cost or loss avoided

§18.4 AN OVERVIEW OF EXPECTATION DAMAGES UNDER UCC ARTICLE 2

§18.4.1 The Basic Principles

The discussion of expectation damages in section 18.3 covers both the common law and UCC Article 2, and includes illustrations concerning sales of goods. You are therefore already familiar with the pertinent Code provisions. Notwithstanding, it may be helpful to review the Article 2 provisions on expectation damages as a whole to show their organization, the symmetry between buyer's and seller's remedies, and their basis in common law principles.

The concept of expectation relief under Article 2 is essentially the same as that under the common law. Like the common law, it reserves the remedy of specific performance for special cases and treats damages as the primary remedy for breach. The award of damages is meant to achieve, as closely as possible, the economic position the plaintiff would have been in had there been no breach. This principle is strongly articulated in §1.305, which declares that UCC remedies "shall be liberally administered to the end that the aggrieved party may be put in as good a position as if the other party had fully performed." Article 2 provides statutory formulas for calculating compensation. It organizes them into seller's remedies for the buyer's breach (§§2.703-2.710) and buyer's remedies for the seller's breach (§§2.711-2.717). Although there is necessarily some variation between these two sets of remedies, they are largely mirror images of each other, providing approximately equivalent rights to buyers and sellers, but taking into account the somewhat different remedial needs of each.

---

5. The term "direct damages" is explained in section 18.5. In essence, they are the damages awarded to compensate the plaintiff for the loss of expectation under the contract itself, rather than as a result of the impact of the breach on other rights of the injured party or other transactions that are affected by the breach.

§18.4.2 The Seller's Remedies

Sections 2.706, 2.708, and 2.709 contain the core of the seller's expectation remedies. Section 2.709 is the seller's specific performance remedy for payment of the price of the goods. Like the common law, Article 2 sees specific enforcement of the contract as a limited and secondary remedy, available only when damages are inappropriate. Section 2.709 therefore allows the seller to claim the price of the goods only when the goods have been accepted by the buyer or they are incapable of being resold because they have been lost or damaged or are just not resalable.

The other two sections contain the primary remedies of the seller's expectation damages where the buyer breaches by failing to accept conforming goods tendered by the seller. Section 2.706 permits an aggrieved seller to enter a substitute transaction by reselling the goods and, provided that the resale is made in good faith and in a commercially reasonable manner, to recover the shortfall between the contract price and the resale price. Section 2.708(1) recognizes that damages may be based on a hypothetical resale as an alternative to actual resale. It allows the seller to calculate damages based on the difference between the contract price and the market price of the goods at the time and place at which delivery was to have been tendered under the contract. This may be used, for example, when the seller elects not to resell, or when the resale was not conducted reasonably, resulting in too low a resale price. Some, but not all, courts even allow it as an alternative when the seller has resold above the market price, so that the contract-market difference provides a more advantageous recovery.

When the remedy of contract-market damages does not give an adequate recovery[6] so that it is inappropriate to use the contract-market difference as a basis for measuring damages (such as cases in which the seller decides not to manufacture the goods following breach, or suffers a loss in volume of sales as explained in section 18.6.3), §2.708(2) permits recovery of the seller's gross profit plus reliance expenses, less allowance for payments or salvage received.

Nowhere in §2.706, 2.708, or 2.709 is any provision made for the seller to receive consequential damages. A few courts have found that sellers are entitled to consequential damages despite Article 2's failure to provide for them, but most courts have declined to award them. (Consequential damages are explained in section 18.5.)

---

6. Although §2.708(2) refers only to contract-market damages, lost profits should also be claimable under that section when the resale remedy under §2.706 is inadequate.

§18.4.3 The Buyer's Remedies

The buyer's specific performance remedy is set out in §2.716. It, too, is a secondary remedy, available only when damages cannot adequately compensate because the goods are fairly regarded as unique under the circumstances of the case. In other situations in which the buyer has rejected nonconforming goods or the seller has failed to deliver any goods at all, the buyer is confined to substitutionary damages, based on an actual good faith and reasonable repurchase of the goods (cover) under §2.712 or a hypothetical repurchase under 2.713, calculated as the difference between the market price at the time the buyer learned of the breach and the contract price. Note that the language identifying the buyer's hypothetical market is different from that set out for the seller in §2.708(1). This provision has caused interpretational difficulties. Briefly stated, the seller's market price is measured in §2.708(1) at the time and place of tender, whereas §2.713 requires the buyer's damages to be measured at the place of tender, or in some cases, at the place to which goods are to be shipped. The time for measuring the buyer's damages is the time that the buyer learned of the breach. This has led to some difference in interpreting the proper time and place for determining market price where the buyer claims market-contract damages, which we will not go into here.

Article 2 prefers the cover-contract difference as the more realistic measure, but the buyer is permitted not to cover, and instead use the market price of the goods as a basis of recovery. The market standard is also used if the buyer did not act reasonably in covering, so that the cover price is excessive. As in the case of sellers, there is some controversy over whether a buyer who has covered at a price lower than the market may nevertheless elect to sue for damages based on the more advantageous market-contract difference.

In some cases, a buyer may not be able to make a substitute transaction and may suffer consequential damages as a result of the breach. If so, §§2.714 and 2.715 permit their recovery. (The nature of consequential damages and the prerequisites for their recovery is discussed in section 18.5.) Finally, when the seller has breached by delivering goods that are defective or not in conformity with what was promised under the contract, but the goods have been accepted by the buyer, damages based on an actual or hypothetical repurchase are not appropriate. Section 2.714 therefore measures damages for accepted goods based on the loss suffered by the buyer as a result of the deficiency in the goods. This principle ties in with the discussion of partial breach in Chapter 17.

§18.5 THE DISTINCTION BETWEEN DIRECT AND CONSEQUENTIAL DAMAGES

The previous examples have focused on damages that are a direct result of the breach. That is, they can be readily and easily attributed to the breach and are designed to compensate for the very performance that has been promised. Thus, for example, after Harmony breached her promise to coach Sara, Sara's cost of hiring a substitute trainer does no more than substitute for the performance of the contract itself. The same is true when Ken Tractor or Cadenza La Scala seek their outlay and expected profit in their construction or manufacturing contracts. These cases are all characterized by the fact that the award of damages goes no further than the confines of the contract itself to compensate for the breach. The payment of money is designed to give nothing more than the benefit of performance, whether in the form of the costs of a substitute or the lost gains under the contract. The payment of damages thus acts as a direct equivalent for the expected performance and thereby fully cures the disappointed expectation. For this reason, the compensation paid is called direct damages.

In some cases, however, it is not enough to award only these direct damages, because the breach has had more far-ranging consequences. Not only has it disappointed the direct expectations under the contract, but it has caused further losses in other transactions or endeavors that were dependent upon the contract or has resulted in some other injury, whether physical or economic. For example, recall that Harmony had undertaken to give Sara a series of voice training lessons in the week before the competition. In our first illustration, she reneged just a few days before the lessons were to begin, but Sara was able to find another teacher. What if no other teacher was available, so that Sara could not obtain the training? As a result of being deprived of coaching in the crucial period before the competition, she was not adequately prepared for it. A whole horde of voice experts are available to testify, based on meticulous scientific tests, that Sara has talent of almost superhuman dimensions, and she would have been able to sing circles around the other competitors had she received the week's intensive training. If this can indeed be shown, a mere award of the cost of a substitute teacher comes nowhere near to compensating for her contractual expectations. Her loss consequent upon the breach is far more serious and must take account of all the opportunities for fame and fortune that would have flowed from her success in the competition. These losses, consequent on the breach, are called consequential damages.

This example graphically portrays the difference between direct and consequential damages, but it also suggests some of the particular problems that a plaintiff must deal with to obtain consequential damages. Even if she has a bevy of experts to attest to her genius and the certainty of victory that would have followed proper training, Harmony may be able to summon an equivalent phalanx of experts who will conclude differently. Even if Sara succeeds in convincing the factfinder of the important role that training would have played in her success, she must also establish the probability that Harmony's breach was the only reason why she did not win, that Harmony should reasonably have understood that this consequence was likely, and that Sara could not herself have taken some reasonable action to prevent it. Finally, Sara would also have to make a credible showing of the actual harm she suffered — that is, the opportunities that she lost, and would have to be able to place a plausible money value on her injury. All these considerations are commonly referred to as limitations on her recovery, and they are discussed more fully in the next section.

In the above example, Sara's consequential damage (if it can be proven) results from the loss of the opportunity of making gains in transactions that are dependent on the contract. However, sometimes consequential damages arise from some physical or economic injury suffered as a result of the breach. For example, a homeowner contracts with a furnace repairer to fix her gas furnace. The repairer does an incompetent job, and the furnace explodes, injuring the homeowner and destroying part of her house. Direct damages (the cost of having the job done properly) would not be adequate compensation to the homeowner. However, consequential damages would be recoverable to compensate her for her physical injury and the destruction of her property caused by the repairer's breach of contract.

The above illustrations involve common law contracts. As indicated in section 18.4.3, the buyer of goods may also suffer consequential damages as a result of the seller's breach. Sections 2.712, 2.713, and 2.714 all recognize that a buyer may suffer consequential damages apart from the direct damages covered by those sections, and §2.715(2) describes consequential damages as including "any loss resulting from general or particular requirements and needs of which the seller at the time of contracting had reason to know and which could not reasonably have been prevented by cover or otherwise." For example, say that the buyer operates a store that sells gift wrap, cards, and other such items. In July, she orders her annual stock of Christmas paper, boxes, ornaments, and cards from the seller, her major supplier, for delivery on November 1. On October 30, the seller repudiates that contract by notifying the buyer that it will not deliver the goods. The buyer tries to order substitute goods from other suppliers, but at that time all seasonal products have been sold to other stores so the buyer cannot cover. Direct damages, in the form of the difference between the cover price and the contract price, are therefore not available. The other form of direct damages — the market-contract difference — does not adequately compensate the buyer, who has lost profits as a result of the seller's breach. These lost profits are consequential damages that the buyer can claim under §2.715.

Like Sara, the buyer must establish the amount of these damages and must also prove that the seller reasonably should have contemplated that she would incur a loss of this kind as a result of the breach and that she was unable to prevent the loss.

Although Article 2 expressly provides for a buyer's consequential damages, it says nothing of a seller's right to claim them. In addition, §1.305(a) states that consequential damages are not available unless provided for in the UCC or another rule of law. It is possible that the drafters of the UCC did not mention sellers' consequential damages simply because they did not think that a seller would ever be likely to have consequential damages. Although sellers do not commonly suffer consequential damages, there have been cases in which a seller has been able to show that it suffered damages as a consequence of a buyer's breach. However, some courts have declined to allow those damages on the basis that a seller is not entitled to them under Article 2.

§18.6 LIMITATIONS ON EXPECTATION RECOVERY

§18.6.1 The Nature and Goals of the Limitations

As just intimated, a number of factors, often referred to as limitations on expectation damages, must be taken into account in reaching a final decision on the extent of the proper monetary award. Although called limitations, these factors are not, for the most part, external checks on damages, but are simply an expression of principles inherent in the goal of compensating for the loss of reasonable expectations. Each of the limitations is covered in detail below. This section just introduces them and sketches the overall values and practical considerations that they are intended to serve: The limitation of foreseeability ensures that the extent and scope of damages is consistent with what was reasonably contemplated by the parties at the time of contracting. The requirement of mitigation protects the breaching party from the unreasonable failure of the victim of the breach to control or curtail the harm resulting from the breach. The requirement of causation restricts the damages to losses that can be causally linked to the breach. The requirement of reasonable certainty places the burden on the victim of breach to prove, on the preponderance of the evidence, both the fact and the extent of loss. Finally, the doctrine of unfair forfeiture allows the court to exercise discretion to temper an award of damages that would otherwise be available on a strict application of the rules, if the award would unfairly harm the defendant and result in a windfall to the plaintiff.

§18.6.2 Foreseeability

a. The Concept of Foreseeability

An event or consequence is foreseeable when a reasonable person would realize the likelihood of its occurrence. Foreseeability is thus an objective concept, concerned not with what a particular person actually did foresee, but what she would have foreseen had she reasonably contemplated the course of likely future events. Applied in the context of liability for breach of contract, damages are foreseeable when, at the time of making the contract, the party who ultimately breached reasonably should have realized that those damages would be a likely consequence of the breach.

The reasonable foresight of probable consequences depends on the extent of information available to a party that would alert her, at the time of contracting, to the probable result of her breach. The fundamental rationale of the foreseeability principle is that a breaching party should not be held liable for a loss that she could not reasonably have anticipated as a consequence of breach when she entered the contract. The time of contracting, and not the time of breach, must necessarily be the point at which foreseeability is gauged.

The foreseeability principle is regarded as having been firmly established in the common law by the English case, *Hadley v. Baxendale*, 156 Eng. Rep. 145 (Exchequer 1864). The owners of a mill delivered a broken mill-shaft to a carrier for shipment to the manufacturer so that it could be used as a model for a new one. There was a delay in the shipment. Because this was the mill's only shaft, the delay idled the mill for longer than necessary. The owners sued the carrier for damages based on the profit that they lost when the mill could not operate during the period of delay. Although the court acknowledged that the delay did in fact directly result in the loss of profits, it declined to award those lost profits as damages. The court found the carrier not to be accountable for that loss because it was not told that this was the only shaft and had no way of knowing that a delay would cause the mill to lie idle.[7] The court enunciated the rule of foreseeability that is still current today and is reflected in modern formulations in language that deviates little from that used in the case: It held that damages for breach may only be recoverable if one of two conditions is satisfied: Either the loss must be one that may fairly and reasonably be considered to arise naturally — in the ordinary course of things — from the breach, or it must be one that may reasonably be supposed to have

---

7. *Hadley* has a famous headnote that clearly states that the clerk was told that the mill was stopped. However, the opinion itself indicates otherwise. Commentators have suggested that the headnote (written by the reporter, not the court) does not accurately reflect the facts, or that even if there was communication to the clerk, this was not sufficient to bind his employer.

679

been contemplated by the parties at the time of contract as a reasonable consequence of breach. (Although *Hadley* refers to the parties' contemplation, we are, of course, principally interested in the reasonable contemplation of the party who breached, measured objectively, not by what he actually knew and realized, but by what he reasonably should have known and realized.) In essence, the rule in *Hadley*, adopted in both Restatement, Second, §351 and UCC §2.715, treats damages as foreseeable in two situations:

1. The breaching party should reasonably have expected such damages to be a likely consequence of breach in the ordinary course of events, or
2. If, outside of the ordinary course of events, the breaching party had reason to know of special circumstances that could reasonably give rise to such damages.

b. The "Tacit Agreement" Test

The doctrine of foreseeability is based on the principle that a breaching party should not be held accountable for losses unless, at the time of making the contract, she reasonably should have conceived of those losses as a probable result of her breach. For most modern courts, reasonable contemplation of liability for loss is satisfied if it is established that the breaching party had reason to know of the probable consequences of breach, either because they would arise in the ordinary course, or because the breaching party had reason to know of special circumstances that could give rise to them. However, some courts impose a more stringent test, based upon a conception articulated by Justice Holmes in *Globe Refining Co. v. Landa Cotton Oil Co.*, 190 U.S. 540 (1903). Justice Holmes said that recovery depends on "what liability the defendant may be supposed to have assumed consciously. . . ." He required that the knowledge "must be brought home to the party . . . under such circumstances that he must know that the person he contracts with reasonably believes that he accepts the contract with the special condition attached to it." This stricter test of foreseeability, known as the "tacit agreement" test, requires not merely that the probable consequences of the breach were reasonably foreseeable by the breaching party, but that he agreed tacitly to assume liability for them. That is, had the likely consequences of the breach been brought to his attention at the time of contracting, he would have agreed that he had assumed liability for them. The tacit agreement test goes beyond an evaluation of the information available to the breaching party at the time of contracting, and also examines questions such as the nature of the contract and the extent of risk that was likely assumed, in light of the economic value earned by the breacher under the contract.

The tacit agreement test is generally regarded as too restrictive by modern courts, and it is expressly rejected by Restatement, Second, §351, Comment *a* and UCC §2.715, Comment 2. Therefore, for most modern courts, the focus of reasonable contemplation is simply on the relationship between the information available to the breacher and the loss. However, there are still some courts that follow the tacit agreement test. For example, the New Mexico Court of appeals held the test to be the law in that state in *Sunnyland Farms, Inc. v. Central New Mexico Electric Cooperative, Inc.*, 255 P.3d 324 (N.M. App. 2011).

c. Foreseeability in Relation to Direct Damages

Foreseeability is not usually an issue in a claim for direct damages. When a party enters a contract, she understands or should understand that if she breaches, the other party will suffer the loss of whatever benefit she promised under the contract, whether that benefit is a profit or the acquisition of services or property on advantageous terms. The concept of foreseeability does not require that the breaching party had to foresee the amount or exact nature of the loss or the precise way in which the other party would elect to attain his expectation, but merely that she reasonably understands that if she breaches, the other party will lose whatever value was reasonably expected.

d. Foreseeability in Relation to Consequential Damages

As discussed in section 18.5, a breach of contract could result in consequential damages if it causes losses beyond the actual deprivation of the contractual performance. This is the focus of the principle of foreseeability. It confines liability for consequential damages to those losses that a party reasonably should have contemplated as a probable result of her breach, based on information to which she had access at the time of contracting. Restatement, Second, §351 and UCC §2.715 break consequential damages into two categories: General damages are those that are foreseeable as a probable result of the breach in the ordinary course of events. Special damages are those arising out of special circumstances that the breaching party would not have reason to know unless informed of them.

i. General Consequential Damages

Damages that arise naturally, in the ordinary course, are called "general damages." They include not only all easily imaginable direct damages, but also those consequential damages that should be obvious to the breacher without any special or particular knowledge of the other party's circumstances or affairs, because such a loss would be a normal and well-accepted likelihood of the breach of a contract of this kind. Of course what is generally understood as a likely consequence of breach is not decided in the abstract, but in light of the circumstances of the case and the contracting environment.

For example, the roof of a home is damaged by a falling branch. The homeowner contracts with a roofer to repair the roof without delay, and the roofer promises to make the repair on the very day of the damage. If the roofer breaches the contract by not showing up, he must surely contemplate the probability of direct damages — that the owner may try to engage another roofer and to hold him liable for damages if the reasonable substitute is higher-priced. However, the breaching roofer must also reasonably realize that the owner may not be able to get someone else out immediately and that if it rains, there could be water damage to the interior of the house under the broken roof section. Any damage to the interior is consequential — it is not a cost of achieving the promised performance, but a loss resulting as a consequence of (I could have said "flowing from," but that sounds too much like a pun) the breach. This consequential damage would fall into the first category identified in *Hadley* because the possibility of rain damage is something that may reasonably be considered as arising naturally in the normal course of human experience. One needs no special information about the homeowner's affairs to recognize this risk of breach. (Of course, if the owner could have taken temporary measures to prevent water damage but did not do so, the owner's failure to mitigate could be a different basis for the denial of consequential damages, as discussed in section 18.6.3.)

Prutch v. Ford Motor Co., 618 P.2d 657 (Colo. 1980) provides another example of consequential damages that arise naturally and in the ordinary course from the breach. A farmer could not fully harvest his crop because his Ford farming equipment did not function properly. The court held that the farmer's resulting lost profits were foreseeable by Ford because it understood that its equipment would be used in commercial farming, and should reasonably have contemplated that the failure of the equipment could cause such a loss.

ii. Special Consequential Damages

The second category, called "special damages," can be illustrated by embellishing the facts of the last example. Say that the area beneath the broken roof happened to contain an expensive piece of electronic equipment that is affixed to the floor and cannot be moved or otherwise protected.[8] Unless the roofer was told or otherwise had reason to know about the equipment at

---

8. Again, if it could be moved, protected, or sheltered by a makeshift covering, the owner's failure to take action to safeguard it would raise issues of causation and mitigation of damages in addition to the foreseeability question.

the time that he made the contract, it would not be fair to hold him liable for damage to it because he had no basis for expecting this loss. Had he known about it, he may well have declined the contract or he may have decided to undertake it only if the owner paid a higher price to cover the cost of extra precautions or as a premium for the assumption of the greater risk of liability. By not giving the roofer the information, the homeowner deprives him of the means to make a rational decision on risk or to take additional steps to minimize the chance of breach. He therefore should not be able to hold him accountable for the unusual loss. Not only does the rule protect the roofer from surprise liability, but the fact that the rule exists is likely to be an incentive to a party in the owner's position to provide adequate information, which is likely to increase the efficiency of transacting and may even lessen the chance of breach. The foreseeability principle can therefore be justified as economically efficient as well as fair.

The concept of reasonable contemplation is central to the foreseeability of special damages, but its scope and meaning are elusive. To begin with, recognize that it does not require that a reasonable person in the breacher's position would have foreseen the exact loss with great precision and specificity. All that is required is that a loss of that nature and approximate extent could be conceived of as a probability. In requiring the contemplated loss to be probable, rather than just possible, the law does not cover every possibly imagined serendipitous or outlandish consequence, but it does cover more than those outcomes that are obvious inevitabilities. This means that it can be a subtle exercise to decide on the strength of the link between the information available to the breacher and her reasonable accountability for the ultimate consequences of her breach.

iii. The Relationship Between the Nature of the Exchange Under the Contract and the Loss

Where the consequential damages arising from a breach are very large and the consideration earned by the breacher under the contract is small, there could be a question of whether the breaching party should be liable for consequential damages so disproportionate to what it earned under the contract. This can be illustrated by facts based on *Hadley*. Say that the carrier charged $100 for transporting the broken mill shaft to the manufacturer for repair. The miller did inform the carrier that the mill could not operate until the shaft was repaired, so that the carrier did foresee the probability of loss of profits if it breached the contract. As a result of its breach, the mill was idle for several days, resulting in lost profits of $10,000. The carrier argues that because its charge under the contract was only $100, it could not possibly have assumed the risk of liability for $10,000. This argument can more readily be made under the "tacit agreement" test, which requires not merely that the breaching party should have foreseen the probability of loss, but must also have tacitly accepted liability for it. That is, the test would take into account whether the consideration given to the breacher reflected the extent of risk assumed. As noted above, most modern courts do not follow the "tacit agreement" test, so that a party could be held to have contemplated great liability despite the modest value of what she was to gain from the contract. This does not mean that the value of the consideration given to the breacher is invariably irrelevant. A court may always take the equities into account (as expressly recognized by Restatement, Second, §351(3)) and if the consequential losses are greatly disproportionate to the value of the consideration paid to the breacher, a court may exercise its equitable discretion to curtail liability for them.

§18.6.3 Mitigation

a. The Purpose and Policy of Mitigation

In most cases, a rational party, faced with a breach by the other, will naturally take whatever action is necessary to avoid or minimize loss. Unless the victim of a breach is particularly stupid, litigious, or spiteful, her self-interest will propel her in the direction of keeping her loss as small as possible, rather than aggravating it in the hope that she will ultimately be able to recover it from the breaching party. This means that it happens only rarely that the plaintiff deliberately and maliciously sets out to increase her damages, just for the satisfaction of punishing the defendant with a large claim. More commonly, the defendant's allegation that the plaintiff failed to mitigate is likely to turn on the question of whether the plaintiff's response to the breach was an unreasonable or poor judgment that aggravated damages.

The basic principle of mitigation is that if the plaintiff, through bad faith or unreasonable action (or inaction) has failed to prevent or has aggravated her damages, the defendant is not held responsible for the increase in loss caused by the plaintiff. This is often described as the plaintiff's duty to mitigate damages. Of course, this is not a duty in the normal sense, because the plaintiff owes it to no one but herself to keep her losses down. But if she fails in that duty to safeguard her own economic welfare, fairness dictates that she must be left with the added loss and the defendant should not be called on to pay it. It may be obvious from what has just been said that a failure to mitigate damages does not deprive the plaintiff of all relief, but affects recovery only to the extent that the damages were increased as a result of the plaintiff's conduct. The plaintiff is therefore still entitled to recover those damages that she could not have avoided by good faith or reasonable conduct.

It must be stressed that the question is not merely whether the plaintiff's response to the breach turned out, with hindsight, to be a wrong judgment that failed to contain or worsened the harm. Nor is it enough that a different response would have been preferable. The words "bad faith" and "unreasonable" indicate that there must be some element of fault on the plaintiff's part. It must be apparent that the plaintiff's behavior in reacting to the breach was dishonest, opportunistic, or vindictive, or that it so deviated from what would be expected, that it failed to conform to community standards of rationality. The law recognizes that the defendant has breached the contract, leaving the plaintiff in the unhappy position of having to salvage the benefit of her bargain. For this reason, the plaintiff, herself the victim of the defendant's wrong, should be given some leeway when her response is judged. It must be clear, under all the circumstances, that the plaintiff's reaction to the breach is sufficiently improper that it would be wrong to make the defendant bear the increased loss. Restatement, Second, §350 expresses this approach by stating that losses are not recoverable if the plaintiff could have avoided them without "undue risk, burden or humiliation," but the plaintiff should not be precluded from recovery to the extent that she made "reasonable but unsuccessful efforts to avoid harm."

The general principles of mitigation recognized in common law are applicable to UCC Article 2. Although there is no section specifically devoted to the principle, it is inherent in the Code by virtue of §1.103(b), which incorporates consistent common law principles, and in the general remedial principle expressed in §1.305. In addition, it is reflected throughout the remedies provisions of Article 2. Sections 2.706 and 2.712 require an aggrieved seller or buyer to act reasonably, in good faith, and within a reasonable time when making a substitute transaction; §2.715 bars a buyer from obtaining consequential damages that could have been prevented by cover or otherwise; §2.704(2) reflects the seller's duty to mitigate in deciding whether to complete the manufacture of specially ordered goods; and §2.709 requires the seller to make reasonable attempts at resale before claiming the price of the goods from the buyer.

The principle of mitigation makes perfect sense on its own merits because the defendant should not be accountable to the extent that the consequences of breach are exaggerated by the plaintiff's fault, and because a rule that encourages the plaintiff to control loss is efficient and sensible. In addition, however, it is congruent with two other limitation principles: A loss caused by the plaintiff's improper actions is not reasonably foreseeable, and the plaintiff's conduct breaks the chain of causation between the breach and the loss.

b. The Reasonableness Test for Determining Whether the Plaintiff Violated the Duty to Mitigate

As stated earlier, unless bad faith is evident, the plaintiff's accountability for aggravated loss depends upon the reasonableness of her response to breach.

As always, reasonableness is a factual matter. The plaintiff's action (or failure to act) must be evaluated by an objective standard under all the circumstances of the case: Was it reasonable for a person in the plaintiff's position to have acted as she did? This inquiry takes into account a whole range of factual questions such as what the plaintiff did or did not do; what choices were available to her; what risks, hardships, or inconveniences were involved in each choice; what her motivation was in choosing as she did; how much time she had available to respond; and how quickly she took action. All of these facts are looked at with a sympathetic eye on the plaintiff. As the breach compelled her to take action to safeguard her interests, courts are inclined to respect her judgment if it had an honest and rational basis, even if the defendant can point to a different response that may have been more effective in fully or partially preventing the loss. Because the plaintiff is the wronged party, she is not expected to take heroic or exhaustive action to keep damages at a minimum. The defendant cannot complain of a failure to mitigate if the action required to reduce loss would have been unduly burdensome, humiliating, or risky to the plaintiff. Similarly, the plaintiff cannot be expected to explore every conceivable possibility of avoiding loss or to try methods that reasonably appear to be futile.

Although the plaintiff has the burden of proving her damages, once she has established loss, the defendant has the burden of proving that the plaintiff failed to mitigate that loss. This is because the defendant's assertion that the plaintiff failed to mitigate damages is treated as an affirmative defense relating to the extent of liability. The defendant must show what reasonable actions the plaintiff should have taken to curtail her loss, and that those actions would have reduced damages by a specific amount. Once it is established that the plaintiff's reaction to the breach unjustifiably increased her loss, the next task is to calculate what the damages would have been had the proper response been made. This is also a factual issue, involving an inquiry into the causal link between the plaintiff's conduct and the loss.[9]

c. The Substitute Transaction as Mitigation

The most obvious form of mitigation is the substitute transaction. We saw an example of this right at the beginning of this chapter when, a few days before the voice training was to begin, Harmony repudiated her contract with Sara to provide the lessons for a fee of $1,500. Sara hired another voice coach for $1,800 and claimed the $300 difference as expectation damages. The decision to hire another coach is itself an act of mitigation in that it prevented any consequential loss that Sara may have suffered by entering the

---

9. *See also* section 17.7.4 in which the issue of mitigation is discussed in relation to the decision by the victim of a repudiation on whether to accept and act on the repudiation immediately, or to await the possibility of retraction.

competition without the training. (The fact that such a consequential loss may have been speculative and very difficult to prove increases Sara's incentive to avoid it.)

Although the hiring of the substitute coach prevented more serious consequential losses, the choice of the new coach is still subject to a standard of reasonableness. Sara must make reasonable and good faith efforts to find an equivalent coach at the most economic price. This does not mean that she has to use the cheapest substitute, or that she has to make exhaustive enquiries to find the best bargain available. However she will not recover the full cost of the substitute if, by the exercise of reasonable diligence, she would have been able to find an adequate substitute at a lower price. Sometimes, even with conscientious effort, the only substitute a victim can find is better than the contract performance. If this is the closest reasonable replacement for the performance, the court is likely to award the cost of it to the victim, even though it might give her more than her expectation under the contract. This may be the fairest resolution given that the breacher caused the problem and the victim has no choice but to take the more valuable substitute to approximate the performance promised by the breacher. For example, in *Handicapped Children's Education Board v. Lukaszewski*, 332 N.W.2d 774 (Wis. 1983) the defendant, a speech and language therapist, breached her employment contract by resigning. The Board sought to replace her. The only applicant for the position was more senior and had to be paid a higher salary in accordance with union rates. The Board hired that applicant and sued the defendant for the difference between what it would have paid the defendant under the contract and what it had to pay her replacement. The defendant argued that she should not be liable for this additional cost because the Board received the benefit of a more experienced therapist for the higher salary. The court rejected this argument. The Board did not need or desire a more experienced therapist, but the defendant's breach left it with no choice but to take the only available substitute.

In Sara's case, the issue of a reasonable substitute comes up in connection with her claim for damages for its added cost. However, the issue also arises when the breach releases a plaintiff from performance, so that a substitute transaction becomes available to reduce the plaintiff's loss. For example, say that a few days before the voice training lessons were to begin, Sara repudiated the contract. Harmony now finds that she has 28 hours of free time in which she will not be gainfully employed. If she does nothing about this, she will lose her full profit from the transaction — the contract price of $1,500 less any costs. However, if she is able to take another student or otherwise use this time to generate income, she will reduce or possibly eliminate completely her loss from Sara's breach. It therefore stands to reason that if Harmony sues Sara for her lost profit, she will have to deduct whatever she earned in the time freed by Sara's breach. If she failed to use the time gainfully at all, Sara may be able to reduce her liability for Harmony's loss by showing that Harmony failed to mitigate her damages by productively redeploying this time.

Assume that as soon as Sara repudiated, Harmony put up notices at local schools and colleges advertising her availability, and she also called all the people she knew who may have referrals. However, no one expressed interest in lessons for the week in question. Harmony also saw an advertisement seeking temporary, part-time help as a sales assistant in a music store. She did not pursue this possible opportunity of part-time employment. When she sues Sara for her full profit under the contract, two issues could be raised: First, were her efforts in seeking other students reasonable under the circumstances? It sounds as if she did everything reasonably possible considering the short time available to fill the slot left empty by Sara's breach. Second, should she have made an effort to recoup at least some of her loss by seeking the advertised temporary job at the music store? This is a harder question, because working in a music store is only tangentially related to her career as a voice coach, and it sounds like inferior employment that does not advance her career and could even damage her standing as a teacher. A victim of a breach is allowed reasonable discretion in declining to pursue unsuitable alternatives, and it is arguably reasonable for her to decide not to consider this prospect of generating some income to offset her loss. (Of course, as noted at the end of this section, if she did take the job at the music store, and worked there during the times that had been allocated to coaching Sara, she would have to deduct those earnings from her claim for damages.)

Parker v. Twentieth Century-Fox Film Corp., 474 P.2d 689 (Cal. 1970) is an old favorite that involved the issue of whether the victim of a breach acted reasonably in refusing to mitigate her loss by entering into an available substitute transaction. The actress Shirley MacLaine (Parker) entered into a contract with the studio to star in a musical called *Bloomer Girl* for a fee of $750,000. The studio cancelled the production, thereby breaching the contract. As a substitute, the studio offered MacLaine the leading role in another movie, a western to be filmed in Australia. MacLaine rejected the substitute and sued for the full amount of the fee for *Bloomer Girl*. The studio argued that she was not entitled to any damages because she could have avoided all loss by taking the other role offered. The court disagreed and granted summary judgment to MacLaine for her full fee. The court found that the role in the western was both different from and inferior to the lead in *Bloomer Girl* because it was a poorer vehicle for her talents and the substitute contract eliminated her rights to approve personnel and screenplay. Although the victim of a breach must take reasonable steps to mitigate her loss, she is not required to suffer undue burden or prejudice. In the employment context, the court must be particularly solicitous of the impact that the offered substitute might have on the plaintiff's career goals, professional development, and dignity. (A dissenting justice was not persuaded that the role in the western was inferior. He felt that the case should go to trial, and should not be disposed of by summary judgment.) By contrast, in *Fair v. Red Lion Inn*, 943 P.2d 431 (Colo. 1997) an employee refused her ex-employer's offer to reinstate her after she had been wrongfully dismissed. The employee sued for damages for breach of the employment contract and claimed that she was not obliged to mitigate her loss by accepting reinstatement because she feared that the employer was not sincere and would just terminate her again later. The court conceded that it was natural for her to mistrust the employer, but she could not offer any evidence to support her concerns. She therefore could not claim damages that would have been avoided had she accepted the employer's offer of mitigation. (Note that in both these cases, the plaintiff's best prospect of mitigation was to enter into a substitute transaction with the breaching party. As *Fair* suggests, the victim may find it quite unpalatable to accept mitigation from the very person who breached the contract, but this on its own is not grounds enough to refuse the substitute transaction.)

Although the victim of the breach is not required to mitigate by entering into a substitute contract that is unduly burdensome, humiliating, or harmful to her long-term interests, if she does in fact take the substitute, her earnings must be deducted from her damages. For example, in *Marshall School District v. Hill*, 939 S.W.2d 319 (Ark. App. 1997) the school district wrongfully dismissed Hill, a teacher and football coach. He found work in a shirt factory for a while before he secured employment as a teacher in another school district. The court held that because these earnings, including the earnings from his factory work, were from substitute transactions that he actually entered following his dismissal, they should be offset against his damages.

d. Postbreach Transactions That Are Not Appropriately Treated as Substitutes: The "Lost Volume" Situation

In the last example, Sara repudiated the contract for voice training a few days before the lessons were to begin. Assume that the day after Sara repudiated, Harmony took on a new student. This student would clearly be a substitute for Sara if Harmony was fully booked, and could not have taken on a new student had Sara not terminated the contract. However, if Harmony was not fully booked, and she could have accepted this student even if Sara had not breached, the new student is not a substitute for Sara. Therefore, one should not automatically assume that a similar transaction after the breach must be a substitute for the broken contract. It should only be so treated if it is clear that the plaintiff would not or could not have entered it in the absence of breach. Failure to maintain this distinction carefully could lead to an unfair and unwarranted reduction of the plaintiff's recovery by offsetting the proceeds of an entirely independent transaction.

Consider a second illustration, based on a sale of goods: A homeowner sells her used fridge for $200, but the buyer breaches the contract by failing to take delivery and pay for it. The seller then sells it to someone else for the same price. Obviously, the second sale is a substitute because the seller had only that one fridge to sell. However, if the seller was not a homeowner trying to sell a single fridge, but a huge appliance store with a whole warehouse of fridges of this exact make and model, the resale of the fridge to the second buyer is not so clearly a substitute transaction. Because the seller has a stock of identical products, it had another one to sell to the second buyer even had the first buyer not breached. It could therefore have sold two fridges instead of one, and the breach has the effect of reducing its volume of sales. If the seller can establish such a lost volume situation, the second sale is not a substitute, its proceeds should not be treated as reducing the loss from the breach, and the seller is entitled to recover its full profit expected under the breached transaction. In a sale of goods, §2.708(2) caters for lost volume. It provides in essence that when the usual measure of damages — the difference between the contract price and the market price on resale — is inadequate to fully compensate the seller, the seller's lost profit on the sale is the appropriate measure.

Rodriguez v. Learjet, Inc., 24 Kan. App. 2d 461 (1997) illustrates the application of §2.708(2). After the buyer repudiated a contract for the purchase of a jet the seller sold it to someone else. The court identified three elements that a seller must establish to be treated as a lost-volume seller and found that the seller had satisfied all three: It had shown that its plant was operating at 60 percent capacity, so it could have made and sold more planes; it proved that the additional sale would have been profitable; and it established that it probably would have made the subsequent sale even if the buyer had not breached the contract. One of the elements specified in *Rodriguez* is that the seller can show that the additional sale would have been profitable. Some commentators have argued that this should be a crucial element because additional sales may not continue to generate profits equivalent to the profit on the sale in issue. Factors such as increases in the seller's marginal costs and competition in the market from used goods may reduce and ultimately eliminate profits from successive sales. Notwithstanding, many courts do not place such a rigorous burden on the seller, who is, after all, the injured party, and who is only required to prove loss on a preponderance of the evidence. In *National Controls, Inc. v. Commodore Business Machines, Inc.*, 163 Cal. App. 3d 688 (1985) the court noted that profits might diminish as more sales are made. However, it observed that most courts do not require the seller to produce economic analysis to refute this possibility. It held that the seller had made out a sufficient case by showing merely that it had unused capacity and could have produced more units than it was able to sell.

The language of §2.708(2) is confusing because it provides that in calculating damages for lost profit, "due credit" must be given for "proceeds of resale." Taken literally, this language would eliminate the possibility of ever claiming lost profits if the seller resells the goods, even where the seller can show that the breach reduced its volume of sales. *National Controls*, adopting the approach of most courts, held that this part of the formula does not apply in a lost volume situation where the resale of the goods should not be seen as a substitute transaction and proceeds of the sale should not therefore be credited.

§18.6.4 Causation

The concept of causation is not as prominent in contract law as it is in tort because it is usually more self-evident and its function can largely be accommodated within the principles of foreseeability, mitigation, and certainty. It is therefore not given much separate attention by courts and commentators. Nevertheless, it is worth articulating as a distinct limitation on relief. A breaching party cannot be accountable for loss that was not caused by her breach. There must be a link between the breach and the loss. Causation is not usually an issue when direct damages are concerned. Unless the plaintiff has broken the chain of causation by aggravating damages, there is invariably a clear causal link between the breach and the loss of the contractual bargain. However, consequential damages are by definition more remotely connected to the breach, and when they are claimed, it must be established that they were indeed a consequence of the breach.

To illustrate, consider again one of the variations of the example concerning Harmony's breach of her contract to give voice training lessons to Sara: Harmony reneged on the contract just before the lessons were to begin, and Sara could not find a replacement teacher, so she had no choice but to sing in the competition without having had any coaching in the prior week. She lost the competition and sued Harmony for a huge amount of damages to compensate her for the loss of a career as a singing star. The theory of her suit was that Harmony's breach prevented her from winning and deprived her of the career opportunities that would have resulted. It does not take much imagination to realize that she would have great difficulty in establishing a cause and effect between the breach and her alleged loss. She may not be able to show a probable link between her failure to win and the lack of coaching because there are too many variables that could have intervened: She may not have been as talented as her competitors, she may have had a bad night, or the judges may have been wrong. Even if she could show a strong likelihood of success in the competition, she cannot go on to show that she would have had opportunities as a result, or that she would have acted successfully in pursuing them.

As you will readily recognize, some of the problems that Sara faces in proving her case may be described in terms of mitigation (did she make reasonable efforts to prevent or staunch the negative consequences of the breach?), or foreseeability (could Harmony have reasonably contemplated this huge loss?), or reasonable certainty (can Sara establish the fact and extent of loss?). Nevertheless, the question of causation is also present in the inquiry, and it is a useful adjunct to the other limitations in analyzing the issue of liability and justifying the result.

§18.6.5 Reasonable Certainty

As the party seeking to enforce the contract, the plaintiff bears the burden of proving her loss. If she is unable to show on the preponderance of the evidence the fact and extent of her loss, she will not be able to recover damages. The limitation of reasonable certainty is really nothing more than the embodiment of this principle—the evidence must be sufficient to persuade the factfinder that the loss is more likely to have occurred than not, and must give the factfinder enough basis for calculating a monetary award. As this suggests, reasonable certainty involves two inquiries: The threshold question is whether the plaintiff has proved injury. If injury is shown, the next question is whether the plaintiff has provided sufficient evidence to enable the factfinder to determine the amount of the loss.

As a general rule, the more clearly the plaintiff can demonstrate the first element (the fact that some injury was suffered), the greater effort the factfinder (court or jury) will make to come up with some kind of compensation figure. This is because it has now become clear that the plaintiff has indeed suffered some loss as a result of the defendant's wrongful violation of her rights, and the court should strive, insofar as possible, to come up with a figure to compensate for the loss. Of course, the plaintiff cannot get damages if she can present no plausible and relevant evidence of the amount of her loss, but if some helpful evidence is available, the factfinder will do the best it can to fix damages in some justifiable amount. This approach is reflected in Restatement, Second, §352, Comment a, which notes that although damages cannot be recovered for loss beyond the amount established with reasonable certainty, the policy of holding the breacher accountable for her wrongful act requires that doubts should generally be resolved against her once it is established that a significant injury has occurred. Therefore, the determination of damages is an approximation, not an exercise in mathematical precision. UCC §1.305, Comment 1, expresses a similar sentiment.

Because the injured party has the burden of proving both the fact and extent of loss, problems of certainty may affect damages of all kinds, whether direct or consequential. However, consequential damages usually present the greatest difficulties in proof. We first address reasonable certainty in relation to direct damages, and then in relation to consequential damages. Finally, we examine the particular problem of reasonable certainty where the injured party's loss arises from a new business or venture.

a. Direct Damages

Direct damages may be difficult to prove, for example, when the plaintiff seeks his expected profit from the contract, but cannot prove what that profit would have been. Say that an engineering firm enters a contract with a paper mill to design and manufacture an innovative system for the safe disposal of chemical wastes. The contract price for the system is $2 million. Before work begins, the mill reneges on the contract. The engineering firm's direct damages are its lost profits on the job, which must be established by deducting its expected costs from the contract price. However, the system would have been so revolutionary that the engineering firm has no reliable evidence of what its costs would have been. If it cannot establish those prospective costs with reasonable certainty, it will not be able to show that it expected a profit from the contract and will not recover any direct damages. Of course, if the engineering firm had done its planning properly before quoting a price for the work, it would have made a cost projection that, if it appears reasonably accurate and reliable, would likely be sufficient evidence to establish loss on the preponderance of the evidence. *Benchmark Health Care Center, Inc. v. Cain*, 912 So. 2d 175 (Miss. App. 2005) illustrates a common judicial approach to the proof of direct lost profit damages. Benchmark wrongfully terminated a contract under which Cain was to provide rehabilitation therapy services for Benchmark for one year. Cain sued Benchmark for unpaid amounts due for services that had been rendered prior to termination and also claimed the profit that it would have made for the remainder of the term of the contract had Benchmark not cancelled it. Benchmark challenged the jury's award of lost profit damages on the grounds that Cain had not proved lost profits on the preponderance of the evidence. The court upheld the jury award. The court noted that once the fact of loss has been shown, the plaintiff need not prove the amount of loss exactly or accurately. It is enough that the evidence allows the factfinder to make a fair and reasonable estimate of loss. The amount of probable lost profits over the remainder of the contract term was estimated by Cain's accountant, based on a projection from profits that Cain had made in the months prior to termination. The court said that while a future estimate necessarily involves some degree of speculation, the accountant documented and explained his methodology and his estimate was realistic.

b. Consequential Damages

Although direct damages can present problems of reasonable certainty, difficulty of proof is most commonly encountered when consequential damages are in issue. Sara's alleged loss of career opportunities, raised in the context of causation, is an extreme example of this. She would not only have trouble showing a causal link between her claimed loss and Harmony's breach of the voice training contract, but she would also have great difficulty in establishing the fact and amount of that loss. Some courts may regard those difficulties as insuperable. Others may be willing, upon being satisfied that the breach did remove all chance of her winning the competition, to allow the jury to place a value on her chance of winning.

Sara's claim is plagued with particularly troublesome issues of uncertainty. Two cases further illustrate the problem of lack of reasonable certainty where consequential damages are claimed. In *ESPN v. Office of the Commissioner of Baseball*, 76 F. Supp. 2d 416 (S.D.N.Y. 1999), the court dismissed the damages claim of the Commissioner as too speculative. ESPN breached its contract with major league baseball when it preempted games scheduled for Sunday night broadcast in favor of NFL games. The baseball commissioner claimed that as a result of this breach, the league had suffered the loss of television exposure and the associated prestige as well as opportunities for promotions and sponsorships. The problem was that the commissioner could not offer any evidence of how much the league lost. The court said that where it is clear that a breach victim has suffered damages, the court will do what it can to make an award. However, it must have some foundation for making a reasonable estimate of the loss and cannot construct a figure out of the air to compensate for speculative or intangible loss. In *Central America Health Sciences University v. Norouzian*, 236 S.W.3d 69 (Mo. App. 2007), aff'd 241 S.W.3d 255 (Mo. App. 2008), the court overturned the trial court's award of consequential damages to a medical student. The student had completed his medical studies at the medical school, but the school refused to grant him a diploma on the grounds that he had not fully paid his tuition. The amount of tuition was in dispute, and the student established at trial that the university was not justified in its claim and that its withholding of the diploma was a breach of contract. Because the student did not have the diploma, the start of his career as a doctor was delayed by about three years, and he claimed loss of income as a result. The trial court awarded him damages of about $400,000, but this award was overturned on appeal as too speculative — the student could not show that had he been given his diploma on time, he would have passed the medical boards and been hired by a hospital as a resident. The court said that his anticipated salary was subject to contingencies that made his claim too uncertain.

Many cases do not present such insurmountable difficulties of proof, and the plaintiff is able to provide enough evidence of the fact and quantum of loss to enable the trier of fact to make a consequential damages award. For example, in *Marvin Lumber and Cedar Co. v. PPG Industries, Inc.*, 401 F.3d 901 (8th Cir. 2005) PPG, a seller of wood preservative, breached its contract with Marvin by delivering preservative that did not work properly. As a result of the defective preservative, Marvin's products rotted, causing it problems with its customers and damaging its business. Marvin sued PPG for damages, including lost profits, and the jury awarded damages for lost profits. The court of appeals upheld the award. The court stated the general principle that although purely speculative and conjectural damages will not be awarded, the plaintiff does not have to prove loss with exactitude. The evidence of lost profits in this case was the testimony of Marvin executives, based on its financial records, which showed that its profits had suffered since the problems with the wood preservative and that they would likely remain flat. The court held that this was sufficient evidence to support the jury award. Marvin had also claimed damages for loss of good-will, which relates to the diminished value of the business and is distinct from lost profits. The court overturned the jury award of these damages because it found that the evidence of lost goodwill was conjectural and the loss was incapable of being quantified. In *Bollea v. World Championship Wrestling, Inc.*, 610 S.E.2d 92 (Ga. App. 2005), Bollea, professionally known as Hulk Hogan, sued WCW for damages for breach of contract. He claimed that WCW violated the terms of their contract by not making him the featured wrestler at a pay-per-view event entitled "Bash at the Beach." He alleged that as a result he had suffered significant consequential damages arising from lost bookings and reduced income from merchandising and promotions. WCW applied for summary judgment, denying that it breached the contract and arguing that any lost profits were too speculative. The court refused summary judgment and allowed Bollea to proceed to trial. It noted that he was an established wrestler with a long history of past earnings and profits. He therefore could succeed in showing lost profits with sufficient certainty to permit a jury to calculate his damages.

c. New Businesses or Ventures

Both *Marvin* and *Bollea* involved plaintiffs with established businesses and a track record of past earnings that would allow them to make projections of loss as a result of the breach. Where the defendant's breach precludes the plaintiff from making expected profits from a new business, this track record is absent and the plaintiff's prospect of proving lost profit is weaker. Some courts (particularly in older cases) are hostile to a claim of lost profits where a business is new and untested, and treat evidence of potential profit as too speculative. However, the better view, more commonly found in modern cases, is to evaluate each claim on its facts to decide if there is enough information to provide a reasonable basis for determining the fact and extent of likely loss.

Blinds To Go (U.S.), Inc. v. Times Plaza Development, L.P., 931 N.Y.S.2d 105 (A.D. 2011), illustrates how difficult it can be for a new venture to establish lost profits with reasonable certainty. Blinds To Go was not a completely new business. It was a chain with four existing stores in the New York area that sold custom-made window blinds. It planned to open a fifth store in Brooklyn and entered into a lease of retail premises. Before it opened the store, the landlord breached the lease by terminating it without justification. Blinds To Go sued the landlord for damages, including lost profits. At trial, it sought to prove those lost profits by expert evidence of the profits at its three existing stores. The jury awarded Blinds To Go about $3.75 million in lost profits. The Appellate Division overturned the jury award on the grounds that the weight of the evidence did not support it. Although Blinds To Go was not a startup business, the court treated the Brooklyn store as a new venture because it was an attempt to break into a new market. The court found that Blinds To Go had not proved with reasonable certainty that the stores in other areas were comparable — they were more suburban in nature, the customer demographics and median income were different, and there was no parking in front of the Brooklyn store. The court ordered a new trial on the issue of damages, and hinted that the lost profits might be proved with a more adequate degree of certainty by expert testimony on the profitability of comparable stores in Brooklyn. Of course, for many new businesses, a mere showing of the profitability of comparative businesses in the area will not likely be enough to establish with reasonable certainty that the new entrant into the market would achieve profits at that level. There are many variables that would have to be addressed by the plaintiff, such as the impact of a new business on the market, likely changes in the economic environment, the degree of expertise and experience of the management, the viability of the business plan, and the plausibility of income and expense projections.

§18.6.6 Unfair Forfeiture

The principle of unfair forfeiture was discussed in section 17.3.4 in relation to damages for substantial performance. Recall that the general principle, as reflected in *Jacob & Youngs v. Kent*, 129 N.E. 889 (N.Y. 1921), is that when a contract has been substantially performed and the cost of rectifying the immaterial and nonwillful breach is disproportionately large in relation to the value of the benefit that full performance will confer on the plaintiff, diminution of the ultimate value of the performance may be a more appropriate measure of damages. However, *Jacob & Youngs* confined this principle to situations in which there had been substantial performance. Where the breach is material, there is seldom a justification to limit damages merely because the amount needed to achieve the plaintiff's contractual expectations exceeds the enhancement of the ultimate objective market value of the promised performance. For example, in *American Standard, Inc. v. Schectman*, 427

N.E.2d 512 (N.Y. 1981), the owner of an industrial site sold the buildings and other movable property in exchange for $275,000 plus a promise to grade the property and to remove foundations and other structures from the property to a foot below grade level, leaving the vacant site in a reasonably attractive condition for resale. The buyer removed the property it had bought but did none of the grading and restoration work. The seller sued the buyer for $110,000, the cost of doing the work. The buyer sought to prove that its failure to restore the land reduced its market value by only $3,000, but the court refused to admit this evidence on the ground that the restoration of the land was a significant part of the consideration exchanged for the property sold and the parties intended the restoration of the property to be a material term of the contract. (In addition to this, *American Standard* is distinguishable from *Jacob & Youngs* because the breach was deliberate, not inadvertent.)

Peevyhouse v. Garland Coal & Mining Co., 382 P.2d 109 (Okla. 1963) is a famously controversial case that applied these principles where a mining company breached its contract with a landowner by failing to restore the land on completion of its strip-mining operations. The court refused to award damages to the owner based on the cost of restoring the land because that cost was greatly disproportionate to the amount by which the restoration would increase the land's market value. The court justified its decision by finding, probably incorrectly, that the restoration of the land was not a central obligation of the contract, but merely incidental to the contract's purpose of extracting coal for mutual profit. The continued validity of *Peevyhouse* was called into question by the Tenth Circuit Court of appeals in *Rock Island Improvement Co. v. Helmerich & Payne, Inc.*, 698 F.2d 1078 (10th Cir. 1983). The court concluded that changes in state environmental protection policy made *Peevyhouse* obsolete, and that rehabilitation of mined land was no longer merely an incidental purpose of the contract. Therefore, the cost of restoring the land was the proper measure of damages. The Oklahoma Supreme Court subsequently rejected this conclusion in *Schneberger v. Apache Corporation*, 890 P.2d 847 (Okla. 1995), and reaffirmed the principle that where the cost of restoration is grossly disproportionate to the diminution in value, the unfair forfeiture principle expressed in *Peevyhouse* continued to apply. In that case, the mining company breached its undertaking to clean up pollution caused by its mining operations. The court concluded that it would be gross overcompensation to award the landowner the cost of restoration, about $1.3 million, where the estimated diminution in the land's value was about $5,175. Even though environmental protection policy had changed since *Peevyhouse*, the court said that the focus should not be on state environmental regulation, but on the compensation principle of contract law. Under this principle, the court held that it was not justifiable to award damages to the landowner that were so in excess of the actual economic harm caused by the breach. The court indicated that the

697

application of the unfair forfeiture principle was not dependent on a finding that the breach — failure to perform the cleanup — was incidental to the contract's purpose. This seems wrong. If the cleanup was a material term of the contract, the cost of completing the cleanup, not the reduction in the land's value, is the actual economic loss.

§18.7 RELIANCE AND RESTITUTION AS ALTERNATIVES TO EXPECTATION

Although expectation damages are the primary remedy for breach of contract, they can only be recovered to the extent that the plaintiff can prove that the breach deprived her of an economic gain that would have resulted from the performance promised by the defendant in the contract. She must be able to show that she received less than her entitlement under the contract or was otherwise precluded from realizing an expected gain. It can happen that a breach causes no economic loss because, say, a substitute transaction can be found at the same or a lower cost, or because the contract was not profitable. If no loss can be shown, the plaintiff has no recourse for the defendant's wrongful act because there is no need for monetary compensation and contract remedies are not aimed at penalizing breaches. For example, if the seller of a house breaches the contract, but the buyer can purchase an equivalent house for the same or less money, the buyer has not suffered an economic loss in expectation and has no recourse for expectation damages against the seller.

However, the plaintiff's inability to prove expectation damages does not always end the matter of relief, because she may be able to show that she has suffered losses other than her defeated expectation. For example, it is possible that she incurred transaction costs in dealing with the breach and entering the substitute transaction. If so, she could claim this loss as incidental damages, as explained in section 18.2. Quite apart from incidental damages, the victim of the breach may have incurred expenditures or losses by partly or fully performing under, or relying upon, the contract before its breach. For example, in the above illustration involving the seller's breach of the contract to sell the house, the buyer may have partly performed before the breach by, say, paying a deposit to the seller. The buyer may also have incurred expenses in anticipation of receiving the benefits of the contract, say, by paying an architect to plan an alteration to the house. Damages of this kind may be recoverable under one or both of the alternative remedies of reliance and restitution.

The basic difference between reliance and restitution is that reliance, like expectation, is conceived of as a remedy based on affirmation of the contract — it is an enforcement of the contract, but restitution is premised on the theory of disaffirmance — it treats the breach as having caused the contract to fall away. This distinction, which will be made clearer as the remedies are discussed below, affects the aim and focus of the remedies. While the goal of expectation damages is to place the plaintiff in the position she would have been in had the contract been performed, reliance and restitutionary damages have more limited goals. Reliance damages aim to refund expenses wasted or equivalent losses by the plaintiff in reliance on the contract, thereby restoring her to the status quo ante — the position she would have been in had no contract been entered. Restitution seeks to return to the plaintiff the value of any benefit conferred on the defendant under the breached contract. It focuses not on the plaintiff's expectation or expenditure, but on the extent of the defendant's enrichment at her expense.

You should recognize, from the above description, that there is a close similarity between the reliance or restitutionary damages described here in connection with damages for breach of contract and the equivalent remedies discussed in relation to promissory estoppel (section 8.7) and unjust enrichment (section 9.6). Although the remedies are much the same, the cause of action that creates them is different. We deal with them here as possible bases of recovery for breach of contract rather than as remedies where no contract was created, but the law recognizes liability based on other grounds.

To illustrate the availability of and distinction between expectation, restitution, and reliance damages following a breach of contract, let us slightly embellish the above example of the house sale: The seller contracted to sell the house to the buyer for $150,000. After the contract was signed, the buyer paid $5,000 to the seller as a deposit. She also hired an architect to draw a plan to enlarge the living room and paid him a fee of $1,000. If, after the seller breaches, the buyer finds a reasonable replacement house for $155,000, she will claim and be entitled to expectation damages in the total amount of $11,000 because this is what she must receive to be in the position of having a house for $150,000. She gets not only the $5,000 extra cost of a substitute, but also reimbursement of her costs of $6,000 expended in reliance on the contract. Part of that reliance is the $5,000 she actually paid to the defendant — called "essential" (or sometimes "direct") reliance, and part is the $1,000 wasted in having plans drawn that are now useless to her — called "incidental" (or sometimes "consequential") reliance.[10]

However, assume that the buyer is able to purchase a replacement house for the same or less than the contract price, so she has suffered no loss in expectation. She would still be able to obtain reliance damages of $6,000 that would restore her to the status quo ante. If she chose to, she could

---

10. These terms are expanded upon below with qualifications that are not raised at this stage.

instead recover restitutionary damages, but the benefit conferred on the seller is only $5,000. (Although the plans relate to the seller's house, she is not enriched by them because she did not ask for them to be drawn and presumably does not even have them.) Therefore, the buyer has no incentive to choose restitution in preference over reliance.

Notice that some items of damage are recoverable no matter which form of relief is sought. In this case: The $5,000 deposit is both a reliance expense (and consequently also part of expectation damages) and a benefit subject to restitution. Others may be consistent with only two (here, the wasted architect's fee is counted in both expectation and reliance) or available only under one (the cost of a substitute is claimable only under expectation). Naturally, the plaintiff will select as her first choice whichever of the alternative remedies provides the widest relief. The basic distinction can be represented as shown in Diagram 18F.

Diagram 18F

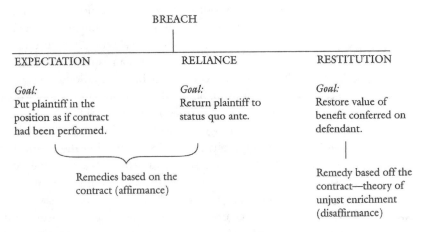

We will now proceed to a more detailed examination of reliance and restitution as alternatives to expectation and to each other.

§18.8 RELIANCE DAMAGES

§18.8.1 The Distinction Between Essential and Incidental Reliance

It was noted earlier that when a loss or expense is incurred in performing an obligation under the contract, the reliance motivating it is called "direct" or "essential" because it is directly based on the contract and essential to fulfilling the party's contractual commitment. However, if a loss or expense is incurred as a consequence of and incidentally to the contract, for the purpose of enjoying or taking advantage of the benefit expected from the contract, it is called "consequential" or "incidental." It is important not to confuse incidental reliance damages with incidental damages, which are discussed in section 18.12. Even though these two types of damages share the word "incidental," they are not related and are completely different, as you will see once you have read this section and section 18.12.

Sometimes the distinction between essential and incidental reliance is easy to draw, as in the case of the deposit and the payment for the architect's plan in the prior illustration. However, the question of whether something is essential or incidental to a party's contractual performances requires an interpretation of the party's obligations under the contract. In some cases the distinction may be harder to draw. For example, the owner of a store hires a signmaker to execute a large neon sign and to install it on the front façade of the building. In the contract, the signmaker guarantees that it will obtain approval for the sign from the city. The owner spends money in reinforcing the front of the building so that it can bear the sign, but the signwriter is unable to obtain approval for the sign. Because he promised to do this, he has breached the contract. If we interpret the owner's structural work on the building as necessary to enable the signmaker to perform, the expense incurred in doing the work is essential reliance. However, if we interpret the purpose of the reinforcement merely as a means for the owner to obtain the benefit of the signmaker's performance, then the erection costs are incidental reliance. In some cases, the distinction may not have any significant effect on the result, but as discussed below, different rules apply to these different types of reliance, and the characterization could be significant.

There is one important point to bear in mind no matter how reliance expenses are classified. The basis of awarding reliance damages is waste or loss. The plaintiff must be prejudiced in that something of value has been wasted or lost and cannot be salvaged. Thus, in the above example, the building owner's purpose in reinforcing the building was defeated when the signmaker could not get city approval of the sign. If the only function of the reinforcement was to accommodate the sign, the expense is wasted. However, if the reinforcement has other benefits — for example, it improves the structural soundness of the building, the expense may not be a waste.

§18.8.2 Essential Reliance Damages

We have already seen in section 18.3 that in many types of contracts (especially when the aggrieved party's performance consisted of the supply of work or work and materials), expectation damages are made up of expected profit on the whole contract plus expenditure already incurred in reliance on the contract. In cases like this, essential reliance expenses are therefore a component of expectation recovery. For example, a builder contracts to build a house for $150,000. After the builder has performed about half of the work and spent $60,000, the property owner breaches by terminating the project. The builder can prove that his total cost to build the house would have been $120,000. His expectation damages are $90,000, consisting of his lost profit of $30,000 as well as the reimbursement of the expenses of $60,000 already incurred. Both these components must be included to give him the benefit of his bargain — a net gain of the $30,000 profit.

On the above facts, the builder could prove that his total cost would have been less than the contract price, so he can show that he expected a profit. However, this is not always the case. A plaintiff may have no reliable evidence from which to project his total expected costs, or he may have underbid so that projected total cost exceeds the contract price. If the plaintiff cannot prove that he would have made a profit on the contract had it been fully performed, he cannot claim a loss of profit. He is nevertheless still entitled to recover the essential reliance component of his damages — the $60,000 actually spent in performing. (As these examples show, a plaintiff who can prove profit has no reason to confine his claim to reliance damages.)

When the plaintiff would have made a loss in full performance of the contract — that is, he had a negative expectation — the defendant's breach is a lucky break. It allows him to cease performance and curtail his loss. This means that if he is awarded his full reliance damages, he actually does better than he expected. For example, say that the builder agreed to build the house for $100,000, but his total cost to complete it would have been $120,000 so that he has an expected loss of $20,000. The owner breaches about halfway through the construction. At that point the builder has spent $60,000. If he is given the full $60,000, he recovers all his costs. Yet had he completed his contract performance, could only have recovered five-sixths of his cost. A convincing argument could be made that this should not be the basis of any adjustment. The defendant breached and cannot be heard to complain if the breach enabled the plaintiff to avoid expected losses. However, because the law is concerned with trying to give the plaintiff true expectation, some courts consider it appropriate to take negative expectation into account when reliance damages are claimed. However, they qualify this rule by shifting the burden of proving negative expectation to the defendant. The allocation of this burden of proof to the defendant recognizes that the defendant was in the wrong for breaching the contract. Therefore, a plaintiff seeking recovery of reliance damages need only prove his expenditure and need not show that he would not have made a loss on the contract. If the defendant seeks to reduce the award, she must show that it would have been a losing contract. This means that when projected costs are uncertain and the fact of loss unclear, the defendant's failure to sustain the burden of proof will result in the plaintiff obtaining full reimbursement of expenses.

Therefore, the general rule is that when the defendant can prove that the plaintiff would have suffered a loss in the event of complete performance, the plaintiff's reliance damages should cut back to bring his recovery into line with his expectations. Although some courts speak merely of the deduction of expected loss from the award of expenses, it is fairer and more consistent with the goal of compensation to reduce the recovery proportionally. That is, to prorate the loss and to reduce the recovery of expenses by a percentage of the total loss equal to the ratio of expenses incurred to total expenses. Thus, on our facts, the builder has incurred half the costs, so his recovery should not be reduced by the full expected loss of $20,000, but only by half the expected loss, $10,000. He therefore recovers $50,000 of the $60,000 spent. This takes into account that he did not have the expectation of recovering all his costs, but it does not undercompensate him (and reward the breacher) by diminishing his recovery by the full loss that he would have suffered had the contract been completed.

A pro rata reduction of reliance is not appropriate in every case. Even if the defendant can prove that the plaintiff will ultimately have lost money on the contract, reliance expenses should not be reduced if the purpose of the contract was not to make a profit. For example, a homeowner contracts with an artist to execute a large and colorful mosaic at the entrance to his property. After the owner has incurred expense in preparing the property for the installation of the mosaic, the artist repudiates. The owner should be able to recover his wasted expenses as reliance damages even if expert testimony from real estate brokers shows that the owner would have lost money had he installed the flashy mosaic because it would have reduced the market value of the house. This is not a proper case for reducing reliance recovery because enhancement of the property value was not the purpose of the contract, and the possibility of economic loss is not relevant to the reimbursement of the wasted costs.

§18.8.3 Incidental Reliance Damages

As stated earlier, incidental reliance expenditure or loss is incurred in consequence of having made the contract and for the purpose of using or enjoying the benefits expected under it. (Again, do not confuse incidental reliance damages with incidental damages, discussed in section 18.12.) Because incidental reliance damages are premised on the plaintiff's reliance on the contract, they must necessarily have been incurred after the contract was entered into. A loss or expense incurred in anticipation of the contract, but before it is actually formed, is therefore not included in incidental reliance damages.[11]

Incidental reliance may be illustrated and distinguished from essential reliance by the following example: Jim Nast enters into a lease of premises for the purposes of opening a gym. Jim has not run a business before, and this will be a new venture for him. At the time of signing the contract, Jim paid a deposit of $5,000 to the lessor as required under the contract. In addition, a short time before the business was due to open he spent $1,000 on flyers which he planned to distribute to advertise the opening of his gym. A few days after he had incurred this expense, the lessor breached the lease by letting the premises to someone else. Say that no other suitable premises are available, so Jim has to abandon his attempt to open the gym. Because this would have been a new business and Jim does not have credible evidence to claim lost profits as expectation damages, he decides to confine his claim to reliance damages. He has suffered both essential reliance damages — the deposit paid to the lessor as required by the contract, and incidental reliance damages — the wasted expense of the useless flyers. The former expense qualifies as essential reliance because it was incurred as part of his performance obligation. However, he had no contractual duty to have the flyers printed. He did this solely for his own purpose of attracting business. Even so, the expense was incurred in reliance on the contract, and the breach has defeated that reliance and made the expenditure useless.

Most commonly, incidental reliance takes the form illustrated above — an expenditure or outlay that is wasted as a result of the breach. But sometimes it is in the nature of a lost opportunity or other gain sacrificed. For example, after executing the lease of the premises, Jim had given up his job so that he could operate his new gym, or he had declined an offer of other premises on the strength of this lease. Lost gains and opportunities are, of course, harder to prove and quantify than wasted expenditure, but they are recoverable if properly established, subject to the qualifications discussed below.

Because incidental reliance is ancillary to the contract, there must be a limit on it to protect the breaching party from liability for expenses that it could not fairly have expected, or that were not incurred reasonably. Therefore, incidental reliance is only recoverable if the defendant foresaw or reasonably should have foreseen the possibility of the loss or expenditure being incurred, and both the amount and nature of the loss or expenditure were reasonable. The mitigation principle applies here too, but it need not

---

11. Although expenses incurred in anticipation of a contract are not recoverable as reliance damages for breach of contract, they may sometimes be recoverable under the separate theory of promissory estoppel. However, as we saw in section 8.9, it is difficult to establish justifiable reliance on precontractual promises in most situations.

be stated as a separate requirement because it is inherent in the concept of reasonable reliance. As with all other types of damage, the loss or expense must be proved with reasonable certainty. As noted before, incidental reliance is only compensable to the extent that it had been wasted. Therefore Jim could not claim wasted expenditures for the flyers if the breach occurred before they were printed and he had the ability to cancel the order. Similarly, if the loss can be salvaged or the items reused, any recoupment of the waste will limit the claim. (Again, this is consonant with the mitigation principle.) For example, say that in addition to flyers, Jim had bought some gym equipment. Unlike the flyers, the equipment can be resold and the proceeds of resale will curtail the loss.

Where the incidental reliance loss or expense would not be deducted from earnings to determine profit, the fact that the plaintiff would have made a loss upon fully performing the contract is not relevant to the reimbursement of reliance. Therefore, the incidental reliance damages are not subject to the rule of proportionate reduction. However, if the contract involves a money-making enterprise and the defendant can show that the venture as a whole would have resulted in a loss to the plaintiff, this reasonable expectation of loss could be taken into account and incidental reliance recovery could be reduced proportionately.

§18.9 RESTITUTIONARY DAMAGES

Restitutionary damages were explained in section 9.6, in which the basic premise of the remedy and measurement of relief were introduced. While the pertinent aspects of that discussion will be restated briefly in the course of this section, you should refer back to it if you want more detail. The purpose of restitutionary damages is to restore to the plaintiff the value of a benefit unjustly conferred on the defendant.[12] Section 9.6 focused on unjust enrichment as a theory of liability alternative to contract and dealt with situations in which the remedy of restitution is granted when a benefit was conferred on the defendant in the absence of contract. However, restitution is also available when a valid contract has been entered into and materially breached, because the plaintiff has the option of either suing on the contract for expectation or reliance, or of disaffirming the contract (that

---

12. This section discusses only restitution in favor of the victim of the breach. It does not consider restitution in favor of a breaching party, which is discussed in section 17.6.2. That section explains that, as a general rule, when a contract is rescinded for breach, the breaching party is also entitled to the restitution of any benefits that she conferred on the other party prior to her breach. However, the breaching party's restitution is subject to limitations and is offset by any damages due to the victim.

is, operating under the legal fiction that it does not exist) and suing in restitution for the recovery of benefits conferred under the now-defunct contract.

Stated differently, when the defendant commits a material breach, the plaintiff will, when possible, usually seek full enforcement of the contract to recover the value of her expectation. However, if the plaintiff cannot recover expectation damages either because she cannot prove them or because she has a negative expectation (that is, she would have lost money on the contract), she will be able to choose to recover in either reliance or restitution. If she claims reliance damages, she is still suing on the contract because, as explained above, reliance expense is a component of expectation damages. However, if she claims restitution, she proceeds on the theory that the breach ended the life of the contract, so that the defendant is no longer justified in retaining the benefit of any performance that the plaintiff rendered to her under it, and the value of that performance unjustly enriches her.

To understand why restitution often provides a different measure of recovery from reliance, one needs to remember their different goals, as mentioned in section 18.7: Reliance is aimed at the recovery of wasted expenses, while restitution is designed to restore the value of a benefit that the defendant has unjustly retained. Sometimes the plaintiff's expenditure may be exactly equal to the defendant's enrichment, so it would make no difference which basis of recovery was used. This is true, for example, when the benefit to the defendant is simply the payment of money. Therefore, if the seller of a house breaches the contract of sale after the buyer has paid a deposit of $5,000, the value of the benefit conferred is precisely equivalent to the plaintiff's expenditure (and interest on the money would be claimable in both restitution and reliance). However, in other situations the plaintiff's outlay could be considerably different from the value of what it produced. Say that a painter entered into a contract to paint a house, and the owner breached after the painter had stripped and primed the walls. If the painter had incurred expenses of $100 in doing this preparatory work, that is all he can recover in reliance. However, restitution based on the value of what has been done for the owner — commonly measured by the market value (quantum meruit) of the service — is likely to be more than what was actually spent. This is because it includes not only the cost of performance, but also the value of the plaintiff's labor or a reasonable profit. Conversely, restitution could be lower than reliance where the expenditure, although justifiable and reasonable, does not result in a benefit to the owner. This is particularly likely when the reliance is incidental so that nothing is actually given to the breacher.

Although market value is the preferred measure of value, the recipient's net gain is sometimes more appropriate. The factors that are taken into account in selecting the means of measurement are discussed in section

9.6 and are not repeated here. However, when restitution is based on the disaffirmance of a breached contract, there is one further question concerning the measurement of the benefit: If the market value of the benefit exceeds the value placed on it in the contract (that is, its contract price), should the contract price be an upper limit on recovery? For example, in the above contract to paint a house, say that the portion of the contract price attributable to stripping and priming the walls is $500, but the painter underbid and this price is lower than the market value of the work, which is $600. The argument against making the contract price the upper limit on recovery is that restitution, by its very nature, is based on the theory that the contract no longer exists as a result of the breach. It unduly benefits the breacher to use the price in the contract to limit his restitutionary liability. The argument in favor of limiting recovery to the contract price is that the distinction between affirmance and disaffirmance is artificial — it is a legal fiction and a contract was actually made. Because the plaintiff's expectation of loss is taken into account for reliance damages (as explained in section 18.8.2), consistency demands that the plaintiff's expectation should limit restitutionary recovery as well.

§18.10 EQUITABLE REMEDIES: SPECIFIC PERFORMANCE AND INJUNCTIONS

§18.10.1 Specific Performance

It was noted in section 18.2.2 that the remedy of specific performance — a court order commanding the defendant to perform the contract as promised — would seem to be the most precise means of achieving the plaintiff's expectation. Yet, for a number of reasons, some historical and some based on practicality and principle, damages are the primary form of relief for breach of contract, and specific performance is reserved as an extraordinary remedy. The historical basis for the primacy of the damages remedy lies in the dichotomy between law and equity. As it was originally formed, the court of equity was a court of special resort, presided over by the Lord Chancellor, acting under the sovereign's prerogative power. The Lord Chancellor would exercise his discretion to do justice only where the overall equities of the case called for this intervention and the regular courts of law had no power to provide an adequate remedy to the plaintiff.[13] Although courts of law and equity have long been combined, and the same judge decides on the alternative remedies of damages and specific performance,

---

13. *See* section 2.5 for a fuller explanation of the distinction between law and equity.

the requirement of establishing equitable grounds for the special relief of specific performance still exists in our law. These grounds are set out below.

Where a court orders specific performance, it compels the defendant to render the performance that he has promised under the contract. Unlike an award of damages, which operates in *rem* — it is a money judgment enforceable against the defendant's property[14] — an order of specific performance operates in *personam*. This means that it is a command of the court directed at the person of the defendant. If she disobeys it, she can be sanctioned for contempt of court and jailed or fined. The potential of punishment for disobedience is one of the considerations that may give a court pause in deciding if the remedy is apposite.

When an order is granted and obeyed, the defendant honors his contractual obligations. Therefore, the plaintiff must do so as well. If she has not fully performed her part of the bargain, she must render the return performance promised to the defendant, and the court may grant its order conditional on the plaintiff doing so.

Where the order for specific performance gives the plaintiff her complete expectation, there is no occasion to award her damages as well. However, when the breach has caused a loss that will not be completely averted or recouped by specific performance, it is appropriate for the court to award damages to compensate for that irretrievable loss in addition to granting specific performance. For example, if the defendant refuses to convey business premises purchased by the plaintiff, the court could decree specific performance and also award the plaintiff whatever loss in profits she can prove that she suffered for the period of delay between the date for delivery under the contract and the date on which the order is finally complied with.

a. Inadequate Remedy at Law

Because the court of equity intervenes to give a remedy only where the legal remedy of damages is inadequate, the plaintiff seeking specific performance must show that the normal legal remedy of damages would not provide adequate relief. This might occur, for example, where the contract is for the sale of unique property that cannot be substituted for on the market, or where damages would be very difficult to prove with reasonable certainty. Although it is founded on the traditional dichotomy between law and equity, the requirement that the plaintiff shows that damages would be an inadequate remedy has survived the consolidation of courts of law and equity, and is reflected in Restatement, Second, §359, UCC §2.709 (the seller's action for the price), and UCC §2.716 (the buyer's remedy for

---

14. *See* section 18.2.4 for an explanation of the enforcement of a damages award.

specific performance). The continuing vitality of the rule is not based solely on tradition, but can also be justified on grounds of efficiency. If damages are an adequate remedy, a monetary award is often a simpler, fairer, and less intrusive means of providing relief to the plaintiff.

The determination of whether damages are not an adequate remedy requires an evaluation of the purpose of the contract and the nature of the harm that will be suffered by the plaintiff as a result of its breach. Where the contract involves the sale of real property, courts tend to grant a decree of specific performance quite readily. This is because of a long-established view that real property is unique, so that monetary compensation for the cost of a substitute is not an adequate remedy. This approach may be justified in some cases — where the real property has qualities that cannot be replicated by a substitute. However, it is less supportable where there is nothing special about the property and the market price of a substitute is readily calculable. (For example, it is questionable to find the legal remedy to be inadequate where the subject of the sale is a home of standard design in a tract development in which similar homes are available.) Nevertheless, courts tend to award specific performance quite routinely in sales of real property.

In situations other than sales of real property, courts evaluate the claimed inadequacy of damages more critically. For example, in *Van Wagner Advertising Corp. v. S&M Enterprises*, 492 N.E.2d 756 (N.Y. App. 1986), the owner of a building leased space on the building's exterior wall to an advertising agency for a term of several years. The wall faced an exit ramp of the Midtown Tunnel and was therefore visible to traffic using the ramp. The lessor breached the contract by terminating the lease, and the advertising agency sued for specific performance on the grounds that the exposure of the wall to the busy exit ramp made it unique. The trial court refused summary judgment and awarded damages to the agency. The court of appeals affirmed. Although it accepted that the building wall offered advertising exposure that was, in a sense, unique, the court said that this was not enough to support the remedy of specific performance. Uniqueness must be judged in light of the difficulty or ease of measuring the cost of a substitute having the special qualities of the leased property. There is a much stronger argument for awarding specific performance if the information available to assess the financial loss resulting from the breach is scanty or unreliable, leading to a high risk of the inaccurate measure of compensation. However, in this case, the agency's loss could be calculated quite reliably because it had subleased the space for part of the time and its loss on that lease was reliably quantifiable. As to the remainder of the lease term, there was a well-established market for commercial billboard space from which the value lost by the agency could be readily calculated.

Where goods are sold, the assumption is contrary to that usually applied to sales of real property — except in special circumstances, goods are not considered unique. UCC §2.716 therefore relegates the buyer to a claim for damages, and she cannot get an order compelling the seller to perform unless she can show that the goods are unique or that the circumstances otherwise justify the order. Comment 2 to that section explains that to be unique, an item does not necessarily have to be the only one of its kind in existence. The concept is broader than that and covers any situation in which it is not commercially feasible to obtain a substitute.

b. The Balance of the Equities and Hardship to the Defendant

As in any equitable remedy, the court considers the impact on the parties of granting or denying the remedy. That is, one of the factors that it takes into account is the balance of the equities and hardships between the parties. For example, in *Kilarjian v. Vastola*, 877 A.2d 372 (N.J. Super. 2004), the Kilarjians bought the Vastolas' house. The Vastolas breached the contract by refusing to proceed with the transfer and the Kilarjians sued for specific performance. The court noted that under ordinary circumstances, specific performance would be an appropriate remedy because real property is presumed to be unique. However, the reason why the Vastolas breached was because Mrs. Vastola was suffering from a serious progressive neurological condition that disabled her and made it very difficult for the Vastolas to move. The court recognized that this was a hard case because the Kilarjians were entitled to the benefit of their bargain. However, it exercised its equitable discretion and refused specific performance on the grounds that it would be heartless and unjust to evict an ill woman from her home. Instead, the court remanded the case to the trial court to determine the Kilarjian's damages. (On the facts of the case, their damages consisted of their wasted expenditures plus any amount by which their financing costs may have increased as a result of the breach.)

In *Kilarjian*, the hardship to the defendant was profound and tragic. However, it is not always necessary to show hardship of this degree to avert an order of specific performance. In deciding whether it is appropriate to decree specific performance, a court is aware of the potential sanction for contempt of court if a defendant should disobey the order, and is likely to be sensitive to the question of the intrusiveness of the order and any difficulty a defendant may have in performing as promised. Hardship to the defendant is taken particularly seriously where the performance involves personal services. The courts' concern over forcing the performance of personal services (which is often equated to involuntary servitude) makes it most unlikely that a court will ever specifically enforce such an obligation. There is also a strong efficiency and practicality of enforcement argument against compelling the performance of personal services because of the possibility that the service would be performed grudgingly and would require careful court supervision.

c. Practicality of Enforcement

In considering whether to grant an order of specific performance, the court takes some account of the ease or difficulty in enforcing the order, and the extent to which the court will be required to supervise the performance and deal with disputes over whether performance is in accord with the contract. Some orders of performance are easy to enforce. For example, if the court orders specific performance of a contract to sell real property, the sheriff can enforce this by evicting the defendant and executing the documents transferring title to the plaintiff. However, other cases may involve a more complex performance that requires judicial monitoring to ensure that a reluctant defendant does not provide a grudging performance that falls below the reasonable standards required under the contract. This does not mean that a court will refuse an order of specific performance just because it needs supervision. But the ease or complexity of enforcement is a factor that goes into the balance. If the court concludes that specific performance is necessary to do justice, it will undertake the required supervision and may appoint a special master or some other person accountable to the court, who will evaluate performance and possibly mediate any disputes that might arise in the course of carrying it out.

d. Indefiniteness

It is a general principle of equity that a court will not make a vague order. Its command must clearly tell the defendant what he must do to obey and avoid sanctions for contempt. This principle, combined with the courts' reluctance to invent contract terms for the parties, leads to the rule that specific performance will not be decreed unless the contract is definite enough to form the basis of a clear order. In Chapter 10, it was noted that if the parties' agreement is too vague or indefinite, their arrangement may fail to qualify as a contract at all. However, even if the uncertainty is not so severe as to defeat a claim that a contract was made, it could render the contract too unclear to support an order of specific performance.

e. Public Interest and the Interests of Innocent Third Parties

As with all equitable remedies, one of the factors that the court weighs is the impact of an order of specific performance on the public interest. Because specific performance involves the enforcement of a private contractual arrangement between the parties, concerns about the general public good will not always be implicated. However, the public interest is included in the balance where an order compelling performance, or the refusal of such an order, does have some impact on that interest. For example, one can see the public interest dimension in the reference, in section b, to concerns about involuntary servitude in the compulsion of a personal services contract.

The harm that an order of specific performance may have on the rights and interests of innocent third parties may also have an impact on the court's decision on whether to grant the order. For example, the seller of a house breached a contract to sell it to the plaintiff by selling it to someone else. The second buyer entered the transaction in good faith and without knowledge that the sale was in breach of the seller's contract with the plaintiff. If the court awards specific performance to the plaintiff, this would force the seller into breaching the contract with the second buyer. A court may decide that the harm caused by the order to the second buyer outweighs the equities in favor of granting specific performance to the plaintiff.

§18.10.2 Injunctions

An injunction is an equitable remedy under which a court grants an order that either compels the defendant to perform a specified act — called a mandatory injunction — or prohibits the defendant from performing a specified act — called a prohibitory injunction. An order for specific performance is really just a form of injunction, and the standards described in section 18.10.1 for the grant of an order for specific performance apply to injunctions generally, whether mandatory or prohibitory: A court will not issue an injunction to compel or enjoin the defendant's conduct unless the plaintiff can show that the less intrusive legal remedy of damages is inadequate and that the need to protect the plaintiff's rights under the contract outweighs any hardship that the injunction might impose on the defendant, any problems of supervising the order, and any harm to the rights of innocent third parties or the public interest.

In most cases, an order of specific performance is in the form of a mandatory injunction — a court order compelling the defendant to render the performance that he promised in the contract. However, in some situations, where a contract forbids certain conduct, an order of specific performance takes the form of a prohibitory injunction. That is, the order directs the breaching party not to take action that violates the terms of the contract. For example, in *Walgreen Co. v. Sara Creek Property Co.*, 966 F.2d 273 (7th Cir. 1992) Walgreen had a long-term lease of premises in a shopping mall owned by Sara Creek. The lease provided that Sara Creek would not lease premises in the mall to another pharmacy. Sara Creek breached this term by entering into a lease with a discount store that had a pharmacy department. Walgreen sued Sara Creek, seeking an injunction prohibiting it from letting the premises to Walgreen's competitor. The court of appeals affirmed the trial court's grant of the injunction. The court noted that damages are the norm in a breach of contract case, and are usually the most efficient remedy.

Therefore, the court will not grant an injunction unless the plaintiff can justify it by showing extraordinary circumstances and a balance of the equities in favor of granting it. Walgreen had demonstrated that an injunction was the most appropriate remedy in this case because the lease term was for many years and Walgreen would have great difficulty in accurately proving its loss of profits and goodwill over the term of the lease. The injunction was a simple prohibition and would not require court supervision, and neither Sara Creek nor the competing pharmacy would be unduly harmed by it.

A prohibitory injunction may also be helpful to a plaintiff where it is not aimed directly at conduct in violation of the contract, but instead strikes at the defendant's motivation to breach. That is, if the defendant's purpose in wrongfully terminating a contract was to enter into a more advantageous contract with someone else, an injunction prohibiting the defendant from performing the other contract could eliminate the advantage of breaching and encourage the defendant to relent. For example, say that Sara Nade contracted with Smalltime, Inc. to perform a concert. Sara repudiated the contract a short time afterwards because she received a much more lucrative offer from Worldwide Promotions, Inc. to perform on the same night. The court will not grant an order of specific performance to compel Sara to perform this personal service for Smalltime, but it may be willing to enjoin Sara from performing for Worldwide. This does not help Smalltime directly, but it removes Sara's motive for breaching and encourages her to retract her repudiation.

§18.11 LIQUIDATED (AGREED) DAMAGES

§18.11.1 The Test for Enforcing a Liquidated Damages Provision

A liquidated damages (also called "agreed damages") provision is a term in a contract under which the parties agree that if a party breaches the contract, he will pay damages in a specified sum or in accordance with a prescribed formula. If such a clause is valid, it has the effect of settling in advance what damages will be due by that party in the event of a breach. It binds the breacher to pay the specified amount, even if the actual damages are less, and it limits the victim of the breach to the specified amount, even if the actual damages are more. The contract could have a liquidated damages provision that specifies the damages due by each of the parties in the event of breach by that party, or it could liquidate damages for only one of them. (If the liquidated damages clause covers breach by only one party, a breach by the other will require proof of damages in the usual way.) Unless the provision makes it clear that the liquidated damages are the plaintiff's exclusive remedy, Restatement, Second, §361 assumes that it does not prevent the plaintiff from electing to claim specific performance instead of damages.

There are a number of reasons why the parties may agree to commit themselves in advance to a set amount of damages in the event of breach: The principal one is that if damages are stipulated in the contract, it is easier and more efficient to obtain relief if a breach occurs, particularly if the transaction involves a venture that is speculative. The plaintiff avoids the problem of establishing foreseeability, mitigation, and certainty, and the defendant has a predetermined liability so that she can better predict the cost of breaching. In fact, if one of the parties is particularly concerned about protecting itself from the problem of establishing damages in the event of breach, the ability to stipulate damages in the contract may be a significant incentive to entering the contract.

However, liquidated damages have an obvious negative aspect. They are nothing more than a forecast of probable loss. Even if the parties try hard to make as precise and thoughtful a prognostication as possible, they can never prophesy exactly what the actual losses will be. If the outcome of the transaction is uncertain or speculative, reasonably accurate prediction of the impact of breach becomes more unlikely. The problem of unreliable prediction is, of course, increased to the extent that the parties are less careful in their projections. It may therefore turn out that the forecast of damage is very different from the loss that ultimately results from a breach, and that the agreed damages greatly overcompensate or undercompensate the plaintiff.

Two policies of contract law are in tension when a court is called on to enforce a fairly bargained liquidated damages provision. The policy of freedom of contract points in the direction of enforcing what the parties agreed, but the compensation policy (confining contractual relief to economic compensation) points in the direction of not enforcing a provision that goes beyond compensation to impose a penalty for breach of contract. Courts tend to give greater weight to the compensation policy. Therefore, if a party challenges a liquidated damages provision, the court will evaluate it to determine if it was a genuine attempt by the parties to settle damages in advance. If it was not, the court will characterize it as a penalty — a provision having the purpose or effect of punishing or deterring breach by imposing liability beyond reasonably anticipated loss — and will refuse to enforce it. If the court refuses to enforce the provision as a penalty, the victim of the breach must prove the actual damages that it suffered in the usual way. Note that the issue of whether to enforce a liquidated damages provision is independent of questions of bargaining unfairness, such as duress, fraud, or unconscionability. Of course, if assent to a liquidated damages clause is obtained by one of these improper means, that would in itself provide grounds for invalidating it, even if the provision is not a penalty.

In *Barrie School v. Patch*, 933 A.2d 382 (Md. App. 2007), and *National Service Industries, Inc. v. Here To Serve Restaurants, Inc.*, 695 S.E.2d 669 (Ga. App. 2010), the courts noted that because the parties agreed to the liquidated damages provision when they entered the contract, there is a presumption in favor of its validity, so the party seeking to overturn the provision bears the burden of showing that it is a penalty. However, in *National Service Industries* the court also observed that in a doubtful case, the clause should be construed as a penalty. (The facts of both of these cases are discussed in section 18.11.2.)

The distinction between enforceable liquidated damages provisions and unenforceable penalties is difficult to draw because of the uncertainty inherent in any prediction of probable loss. The mere fact that the contract stipulates that the liquidated damages are a genuine pre-estimate of harm is not in itself dispositive. In fact, it must be regarded with some skepticism because the parties, knowing that penalties are unenforceable, are not likely to call it a penalty in the contract. Therefore, the purpose of the clause must be gleaned by interpretation in context to determine its true intent and effect. Some courts look only at the circumstances existing at the time of contracting and ask only whether the liquidated damages are reasonable in light of the anticipated harm. Restatement, Second, §356 and UCC §2.718, in almost identical language, adopt a broader, two-point test that asks whether the amount fixed as damages is reasonable in light of the anticipated or actual harm caused by the breach. This formulation provides an alternative two-point test that validates the provision if it either was a reasonable forecast of harm at the time of contracting, or turned out to be reasonable in light of the actual damages suffered.

This two-point test seems to work as follows: The court should focus first on the question of whether the parties made a reasonable forecast of harm at the time of contracting. If they did, the court should defer to their genuine effort to settle damages in advance and uphold the clause, even if the actual damages suffered turn out to be higher or lower than predicted. However, even if the provision was not a very careful effort to predict damages and would fail the test of reasonable forecast, if the amount of liquidated damages ends up being reasonably close to the actual damages suffered, the provision should be upheld. (Of course if actual damages can be proved, and they are about equal to the liquidated damages, there is not much benefit in having the liquidated damages provision, but it could make it easier for the party to establish the amount of loss.) Notwithstanding that the test is formulated in the alternative, a court may decline to enforce a liquidated damages clause, even though it was a genuine effort to fix damages in advance, where it is shown that the prediction of likely damages was very wrong. That is, even if the forecast of harm was reasonable at the time of contracting, a court may balk at enforcing it if it turns out that actual harm is much less than anticipated. It is also worth noting that the two-point test cannot be applied in all cases because the comparison with actual damages is possible only in cases where actual damages can be shown with reasonable certainty. If they are too difficult to prove, there will be no information on which to base this comparison, so the court will have to focus on the test applicable to the time of contracting.

The balancing of the considerations to be weighed in deciding on the validity of a liquidated damages provision are represented in Diagram 18G.

Diagram 18G

TIME OF CONTRACTING
The issue: Was this intended as a genuine liquidation of damages?

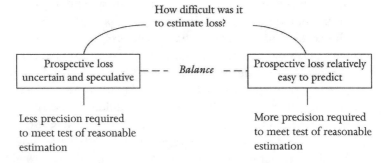

TIME OF BREACH
The issue: How does the estimate compare to the actual loss suffered?

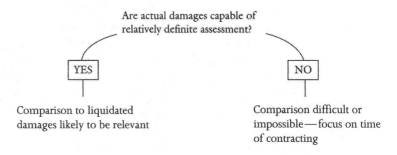

§18.11.2 The Evaluation of the Parties' Forecast of Harm

To decide the reasonableness of the anticipation of harm, the court must consider two factors: the expected difficulty of proving loss and the degree to which the estimate of harm was a reasonable advance estimate of that loss — a principled and genuine attempt to predict likely loss. On their face, these two factors appear contradictory because the more difficult it is to prove loss, the harder it must be to make any kind of reasonable pre-estimate of damages. However, the factors are not treated as rigid co-equal require-ments, but as flexible considerations to be balanced against each other. Therefore, the more uncertain and speculative the damages, the less rigorous the court will be in examining the reliability of the pre-estimate. However, if anticipated damages would be relatively mechanical and routine, the parties are held to a stricter standard in trying to estimate them. For example, if the contract relates to an innovative new business venture, it will likely be difficult to prove damages for breach with reasonable certainty, so the court should give more deference to the parties' reasonable effort to fix a plausible amount of agreed damages based on the best estimations that they can make in light of the uncertainty. However, if the contract involves the sale of property for which there is an active market, substitutionary damages are usually quite easy to prove, so the parties' means of determining the amount of agreed damages must be more rigorously examined.

Two cases illustrate how courts may go about balancing the factors of reasonable forecast and difficulty of proof. In the *Barrie School* case, cited in section 18.11.1, the parents of a student agreed, upon enrolling their child in the school, that if they withdrew her after a certain date, they would be liable to the school for the full year's tuition. When they withdrew the child after the stated date and refused to pay the year's tuition, the school sued them for the unpaid portion. The court held that the undertaking to pay the full year's tuition was a valid liquidated damages provision because it was a reasonable pre-estimate of the likely harm that would be suffered by the school as a result of the withdrawal of a student, and that, given the school's budgeting process based on student count, it would be very dif-ficult to estimate the loss of tuition in advance. The parents also argued that because the school eventually filled their daughter's place, the earnings from the substitute transaction should be deducted from damages. The court rejected this argument. It held that because the forecast of harm at the time of contracting was reasonable, it did not matter that the actual damages turned out to be less than the parties predicted. There-fore, because the valid liquidated damages provision fixed the amount of damages, the school had no duty to mitigate and the earnings need not be taken into account. A dissenting judge in this case criticized the majority for declining to take into account that the school ultimately suffered little or no damages because it admitted a student to take the place of the child who had been withdrawn. The dissent emphasized the compensation principle of contract law, and considered that it was wrong to enforce the liquidated damages provision where it manifestly overcompensated the school.

A provision in a contract to pay the balance of the contract price in the event of breach was not as well received by the court in *Lake River Corp. v. Carborundum Co.*, 769 F.2d 1284 (7th Cir. 1985). Carborundum, a manufac-turer of ferro-carbo (an abrasive powder used in steelmaking), entered into a contract with Lake River under which Lake River would provide distribution services to Carborundum by bagging the ferro-carbo and shipping it to Carborundum's customers. Lake River had to install a new bagging system to perform this work, so it insisted that the contract contain a specified minimum tonnage and a three-year term. The contract provided that Carborundum would ship a specified minimum tonnage of ferro-carbo to Lake River, and even if it did not, would pay the contract price for that minimum tonnage. A downturn in steel production led to a reduced demand for ferro-carbo, and by the end of the contract term, Carborundum had shipped just over half of the minimum quantity to Lake River. Lake River sued for the balance of the contract price as provided for in the guarantee of minimum tonnage. The court (while expressing reservations over the wisdom of interfering with contract provisions fairly negotiated by sophisticated commercial entities, but considering itself bound by precedent on the issue) invalidated the clause as a penalty. This contract involved the rendering of a service, so Lake River's damages would be its lost profit, which is normally capable of proof by arithmetical calculation. Therefore, because the formulation of agreed damages did not take into account any costs saved by the breach, it would inevitably exceed Lake River's lost profit and its actual loss. The earlier in the period that the breach occurred, the greater the cost savings would be, and the higher the disproportion between realistic and agreed damages. Accordingly, the court held that the provision was not a reasonable forecast of harm, but was an unenforceable penalty.

Even where the parties do attempt to take costs into account in estimating lost profits, a court may find that the effort did not result in a reasonable forecast of harm. In *National Service Industries, Inc.*, cited in section 18.11.1, Here To Serve Restaurants (HTS) entered onto a contract with National Service Industries (NSI) under which HTS rented linens for its restaurants from NSI. HTS breached, and NSI sought damages under a liquidated damages provision in the contract. The provision stated that if HTS breached the contract, it would pay liquidated damages to NSI "in an amount equal to forty percent (40%) of the average weekly fees charged for service prior to the date of breach . . . times the number of weeks remaining in the unexpired term." Despite the fact that the provision expressly stated that it was not a penalty, but rather a reasonable estimate of difficult-to-prove loss, the court found it to be a penalty. NSI's chief financial officer had testified that the 40 percent formula reflected its anticipated lost profits, calculated by deducting its actual historical direct costs from the contract price. However, the formula was an historical average of all NSI's contracts (and used in all its contracts), even though there were variations in the actual profitability of particular transactions. In addition, there was no evidence that NSI would be unable to secure a replacement contract to offset the profits lost as a result of the breach of this one.

§18.11.3 Damage Limitation Provisions

A term limiting damages must be distinguished from an agreed damages provision. The purpose of a damage limitation is not to forecast harm and settle the amount of the loss in advance, but to place a limit on the relief that a party may claim in the event of breach. A common example of a damage limitation is a term stating that a party will not be liable for any consequential damages arising from the breach. This provision does not anticipate the amount of damages, but rather precludes a claim for any consequential damages and confines liability to direct damages.

A provision in a contract that fixes agreed damages in an unreasonably small amount is, strictly speaking, a liquidation of damages rather than a damage limitation. It would therefore be rational to assume that it should be analyzed as described in sections 18.11.1 and 18.11.2. However both Restatement, Second, §356 and UCC §2.718 focus on the penal nature of unreasonably large liquidated damages and do not seem to encompass unreasonably small liquidated damages. (In fact, Comment d to §356 states that the section is not applicable to a term that fixes damages in an unreasonably small amount.)

If a term is classified as a damage limitation, it is treated differently from a liquidated damages provision and it is not subject to the tests discussed above. Instead, Restatement, Second, §356, Comment a, UCC §2.718, Comment 1, and UCC §2.719 indicate that damage limitation provisions are enforceable unless they are unconscionable. A limitation of remedy that grossly undercompensates the victim of a breach and deprives her of meaningful relief could, of course, be substantively unconscionable. However, as the discussion of unconscionability in section 13.11 explains, a finding of unconscionability requires more than a harsh result. There must also be some evidence that the unfair term resulted from procedural unconscionability — that it was imposed on the plaintiff by improper bargaining. In addition to avoidance on grounds of unconscionability, §2.719 permits the nonenforcement of a limitation of damages where circumstances have caused the limited remedy to fail of its essential purpose. Therefore, even if the elements of unconscionability are not satisfied, a damage limitation can be disregarded if it is clear that it badly undercompensates the plaintiff or provides for a remedy that is valueless.

§18.12 INCIDENTAL DAMAGES, ATTORNEY'S FEES, AND INTEREST

In addition to the principal remedies discussed above, there are ancillary monetary awards that are often needed to fully compensate the plaintiff for a breach of contract. They are noted briefly here.

§18.12.1 Interest

When a contract itself provides for the payment of interest on an amount due by a party, the claim of interest is simply part of the plaintiff's damage recovery and is included in the claim. For example, if a lender makes a loan and the borrower breaches the contract by failing to repay it, the lender is entitled to sue for both the principal and for the full amount of accumulated interest at the rate provided in the contract. Interest continues to accrue until the debt is paid.

Even when the contract does not provide for the payment of interest, the general rule is that a plaintiff may recover interest on a performance with a fixed or ascertainable money value from the time that the performance became due to the time that payment is ultimately made. Even when damages are uncertain until finally fixed in the judgment, interest is commonly awarded to the plaintiff from the time between when the judgment was rendered and its ultimate payment.

§18.12.2 Incidental Damages

It is worth stating again that incidental damages, as described in this section, are different from and bear no relationship to incidental reliance damages discussed in section 18.8.3. Incidental damages are those expenses reasonably incurred by the plaintiff after the breach in attempting to deal with the breach. They are essentially the administrative costs of coping with the breach and taking whatever action is necessary to protect and enforce the plaintiff's rights under the contract. They include such items as the costs incurred in making arrangements to obtain substitute performance and to mitigate damages. For example, say that the buyer of goods breaches the contract by refusing to accept the goods when the seller tenders delivery. As a result, the seller has to transport them back to a warehouse, store them, and negotiate for their resale. All the additional costs of transport, storage, and negotiation are incidental damages and may be recovered by the seller, provided that they were incurred reasonably. (As this example involves a sale of goods, incidental damages are defined in UCC §§2.710 and 2.715, but they are also available under common law.)

Although incidental damages do, in a sense, follow as a consequence of the breach, they are distinguishable from and should not be confused with consequential damages: They do not arise as a result of the impact of the breach on some other transaction or activity dependent on the contract, but are expenses directly related to the plaintiff's attempt to manage the effects of the breach.

§18.12.3 Attorney's Fees

Based on the above definition of incidental damages, one might assume that the plaintiff should be able to recover her attorney's fees incurred in suing to enforce the contract after breach. They are, after all, expenses that the plaintiff was forced to undertake in dealing with the breach and seeking to enforce her rights under the contract. Despite this, attorney's fees are not usually recoverable by the winner of a lawsuit unless the contract specifically allows them, they are authorized by statute, or the case falls within one of a few narrow categories of exception recognized at common law. The common law exceptions apply to bad faith and vexatious litigation and to other specific situations that need not concern us here. There is no statute that generally provides for the recovery of attorney's fees in contract cases (but individual states may have statutes that allow fees in certain types of contract suit). Therefore, the general rule is that attorney's fees are not recoverable by the winner of a suit on contract unless the contract itself makes provision for this.

The United States is one of the few countries in the world in which the prevailing party in litigation is not routinely entitled to recover attorney's fees from the loser. The debate over the merits of this approach is complex and beyond our scope. It is important to recognize, however, that unless one of the exceptions to the general rule applies, our system, by not reimbursing the plaintiff for the considerable expenses of litigation, does not really achieve its goal of placing the plaintiff in the position she would have been in had the contract been performed.

In tort cases, where a jury has a fairly wide discretion in deciding on the amount of noneconomic damages (such as those awarded for mental distress or pain and suffering), it has some ability to increase the plaintiff's compensatory damages to take account of attorney's fees. If the case merits punitive damages, overcompensation may go far beyond this. By contrast, because contract damages are focused on provable economic loss, the jury has much less flexibility to inflate the award to cover the plaintiff's attorney's fees. This difference in approach between contract and tort can be justified on the basis that, unlike a tort victim, a contracting party is capable of providing in the contract for the award of attorney's fees (if she has the bargaining power to do so).

§18.13 NONECONOMIC AND PUNITIVE DAMAGES

§18.13.1 Mental Distress and Other Noneconomic Loss

Because contract damages are geared to economic loss, they do not typically take account of any mental distress, inconvenience, humiliation, or other noneconomic harm caused by the breach. This principle is applied firmly, whether the aggrieved party is a corporation without heart or soul, or some poor individual who really is traumatized and distressed by the breach. For example, in *Chrum v. Charles Heating & Cooling, Inc.*, 327 N.W.2d 568 (Mich. 1982) a furnace bought from the defendant caught fire and destroyed the plaintiff's home. The court refused to award damages for mental distress because the contract was simply a commercial transaction, the breach of which led to property loss. *Valentine v. General American Credit*, 362 N.W.2d 628 (Mich. 1984) took the same approach where an employee claimed mental distress damages for wrongful discharge. The court recognized that the breach of an employment contract has a negative emotional effect on the employee, but the contract is commercial in nature, and compensation must be confined to any provable economic loss.

There are two situations in which courts have recognized exceptions to this rule. First, if the breach of contract is also a tort, the tortious nature of the breach permits compensation for whatever noneconomic damages the plaintiff suffered. However, this is not really much of an exception at all, because a tort was committed, and the noneconomic damages are linked to the tort. Courts usually require that the tort be an independent tort — that is, the breach of the contractual obligation must be one that would give rise to liability for the breach of a duty recognized as actionable under tort law. Therefore, a mere negligent (or even intentional) breach of contract is not the basis for noneconomic damages unless the plaintiff can show that the conduct of the breacher is also a violation of the duty of care required under tort law. For example, if a surgeon negligently performs an operation, thereby both breaching a contractual duty of competent performance and committing the tort of battery, the patient can recover not only any economic losses, but also damages for pain and suffering and emotional harm. The court recognized this in *Chrum*. After concluding that the contract did not involve the kind of personal interests that merited mental distress damages, the court said that the plaintiff would be able to sue in tort for mental distress if the defendant had negligently breached its duty of care in installing the furnace. It remanded the case to allow the plaintiff to pursue a tort claim.

The second exception concerns contracts whose clear and principal purpose is not to satisfy any economic or commercial goal of the plaintiff, but to give her an emotional, sentimental, or psychic benefit. It is the nature of the contract, not the nature of the breach, that is crucial.[15] Courts that recognize this exception usually apply it very narrowly to contracts that so deeply involve matters of personal concern to the plaintiff that her

---

15. Restatement, Second, §353 describes this exception as applicable to a contract or breach of a kind that makes serious emotional disturbance particularly likely. Although the text of the section appears to contemplate either a contract or a breach that is likely to cause emotional distress, the comments and caselaw indicate that the nature of the contract is the key factor.

noneconomic purpose is clear and the defendant must reasonably have realized that a breach would likely inflict serious emotional distress on her. In refusing relief for the breach of the commercial contract in *Chrum*, the court cited cases in which breach appropriately gave rise to mental distress damages — a nursing home's breach of a caregiving contract by failure to notify the plaintiff of her mother's pending death, and a funeral home's breach of a burial contract by mutilating the body of the plaintiff's daughter. Breaches of contracts for funeral services feature quite regularly as the basis for awarding mental distress damages. For example, in *Menorah Chapels at Millburn v. Needle*, 899 A.2d 316 (N.J. Super. A.D. 2006) (discussed in section 17.6.3 in relation to divisibility) the court held that the plaintiff was entitled to mental distress damages where the funeral home breached the contract to perform funeral services by failing to ensure a proper vigil over the body in accordance with orthodox Jewish ritual. Breaches of contracts for wedding services are sometimes treated as the kind of contracts that merit an award of mental distress damages. In *Dietsch v. Music Co.*, 543 N.E.2d 1302 (Ohio 1983), a band that failed to show up for a wedding was held liable for emotional distress damages. However, other courts have not allowed newlyweds to recover damages for the emotional trauma caused by a botched wedding. In *Zumwalt v. Kevin Lee Collections, Inc.* 2008 WL 5159127 (Cal. App. 2008), a wedding planner promised the plaintiffs (the bride and her mother) that he would provide a wedding that would be a "first-class dream event" and would have "elegance with a chic Hollywood vibe." The wedding, which cost $97,000, fell far short of promised expectations. Among other things, the planner did not show up to supervise the event, the food was poor and badly served, and the planner did not provide a chocolate fountain or Veuve Cliquot champagne, as promised. The court of appeals reversed the trial court's award of emotional distress damages. Although it acknowledged that a wedding has a strong emotional focus for the bride and groom, it found the production of a wedding to be nothing more than a commercial contract for food, catering, and food service. The court said that it is more closely analogous to the construction of a home than to the provision of funeral services.

When courts consider the propriety of awarding mental distress damages, they usually couch the discussion in terms of foreseeability and ask whether the nature of the contract was such that the parties reasonably contemplated that its breach would lead to mental distress. For example, in *Menorah Chapels*, the court pointed out that because a contract for funeral services is designed to bring comfort to the bereaved, the chapel could readily foresee that its breach would cause emotional distress. However, while foreseeability of the emotional damage is an important factor in deciding whether to award mental distress damages, it must be stressed that the contemplation of possible mental distress is not enough. The sentimental or emotional character of the contract performance is crucial. In *Valentine*, the court recognized that an employer can readily foresee that wrongful dismissal will cause an employee mental distress. However, because the contract is commercial in nature, that foresight is not enough to entitle the employee to mental distress damages.

§18.13.2 Punitive Damages

The purpose of punitive damages is to punish the defendant for particularly egregious conduct and to deter her from similar conduct in the future. Because the punishment of the defendant is also likely to make an example of her and thereby have a deterrent effect on others, punitive damages are also sometimes called exemplary damages. Punitive damages are principally available in tort law. They are not appropriate when the tort involves ordinary negligence and are confined to cases in which the defendant deliberately and maliciously injured the plaintiff, or sometimes when the defendant acted in callous and conscious disregard of the plaintiff's rights. Although punitive damages are aimed at punishing the defendant, they are not in the form of a fine payable to the public treasury, but are awarded to the plaintiff in addition to whatever she is entitled to as compensatory damages. They are therefore a windfall that has the effect of overcompensating her. Because punitive damage awards can be large, the degree of overcompensation can be astounding.[16] Even in the area of tort law, where the jury's discretion to award punitive damages in appropriate cases is well established, their scope and appropriateness is a matter of continuing controversy, and courts regularly reduce jury awards.

As emphasized many times in the preceding pages, the orientation of contract law is to the compensation of the plaintiff's economic loss, not to the punishment and deterrence of breach. As a result, it has long been seen as inappropriate to augment any compensatory award by punitive damages, even when the breach was deliberate and faithless. Restatement, Second, §355 reflects this attitude by taking the position that punitive damages are not recoverable for a breach of contract unless the breach consists of tortious conduct for which punitive damages would be available under tort law.

Where punitive damages are awarded for breach of contract, it is almost always because the defendant's conduct constitutes both a breach of contract and a deliberate, independent tort. This is illustrated by *America's Directories, Inc. v. Stellhorn One-Hour Photo, Inc.*, 833 N.E.2d 1059 (Ind. App. 2006), a fraud case discussed in sections 12.12 (the fraud exception to the parol evidence rule) and 13.6.2 (fraudulent promise). Recall that the seller of advertising in

---

16. The degree of overcompensation is reduced by the fact that a portion of the award will be used to pay attorney's fees and the costs of preparing for and conducting the litigation.

a phone directory made a fraudulent promise that it would permit the buyer to cancel the advertising after the first year of the three-year contract. The court upheld the jury's award to the buyer of both compensatory damages (for work and time lost in trying to deal with the fraud) and punitive damages. The court noted that in addition to violating the plaintiff's contract rights, fraud is independently recognized as a tort, and there was sufficient evidence for the jury to conclude that the seller committed the tort willfully and wantonly by intentionally misleading the buyer.

In a narrow range of cases, particularly involving an insurer's willful breach by unjustifiably failing to indemnify the insured promptly, adequately, or at all for loss covered by the policy, courts have been willing to award punitive damages even though tort law has not traditionally recognized the breach as an independent tort. (Some courts have overcome this barrier by creating a new tort, so that an egregious violation of the duty of good faith and fair dealing is recognized as a tort in itself.) Insurance policies are contracts of adhesion,[17] and the failure to indemnify the insured can have disastrous consequences for him. If an unscrupulous insurer deliberately fails to indemnify the insured until it is sued, the ultimate award of nothing more than compensatory damages is not likely to be much of a deterrent to future conduct of this kind. Therefore, punitive damages serve the purpose of increasing the risk of such behavior and may better dissuade the insurer from trying to evade its obligations. Although there are other types of contracts in which it may be appropriate to award punitive damages for bad faith breach, courts have not readily expanded this doctrine beyond the field of insurance.

§18.14 A TRANSNATIONAL PERSPECTIVE ON REMEDIES

The CISG sets out the buyer's rights generally in Articles 45 to 46 and the seller's rights generally in Articles 53 to 59. It provides for damages in Articles 74 to 77. The UNIDROIT Principles cover remedies in Articles 7.2.1 to 7.4.13. It is beyond the scope on this short note on perspective to examine in detail the remedial provisions of the CISG and the UNIDROIT Principles. In general, although there are differences, many of their remedial concepts are equivalent to those set out in this chapter. For example, they expressly or impliedly recognize that the principal purpose of damages is to give the injured party the benefit of the bargain, commonly measured by the difference between the contract price and the cost of a substitute transaction

---

17. Contracts of adhesion are discussed in section 13.12.

or the market value of the performance. They also recognize that lost profits may be the appropriate measure of damages in some cases. They require that damages be proved with reasonable certainty, be reasonably foreseeable, and be reasonably mitigated.

There are some notable differences from the common law. Neither the CISG nor the UNIDROIT Principles follow the common law's firm preference for damages over specific performance, which derives from the distinction between legal and equitable relief that is peculiar to the common law. However, Article 7.2.2 of the UNIDROIT Principles does exclude the remedy where it would be unfair or impractical — for example, where it is unreasonably burdensome or the performance is of an exclusively personal character. Article 7.4.2 of the UNIDROIT Principles deviates from the common law by allowing nonpecuniary damages for breach of contract, including damages for emotional distress. Although the CISG does not address agreed damages, Article 7.4.13 of the UNIDROIT Principles adopts a more liberal approach to agreed damages than the common law and generally upholds them irrespective of the actual damages suffered.

Examples

1. Cliff Blaster owned a piece of land on which he planned a residential development. There was a large rock outcrop on the land that was an obstacle to developing the land, and he wished to demolish it. He entered onto a contract with Dinah Mite under which Dinah agreed to demolish the outcrop for a price of $500,000, to be paid after completion of the demolition. (Following destruction of the outcrop by Dinah, Cliff would clear the rubble and use it in the construction of the development.) Shortly after the contract was executed, Dinah bought explosives at a cost of $100,000 to perform the work and she began to rig the rocks for demolition. After entering into this contract, Cliff discovered that zoning regulations precluded any development of the property. The day before Dinah was due to detonate the explosives, Cliff contacted her and terminated their contract. Dinah told Cliff that he had no legal right to back out of the contract, and she refused to accept the termination. On the next day she proceeded with the detonation and successfully demolished the outcrop. She then claimed the contract price of $500,000 from Cliff. Assume that Dinah was correct in stating that Cliff had no right to terminate the contract. By doing so, he materially repudiated it. Nevertheless, had she accepted the reality that Cliff had breached and the contract was at an end, she would have been able to return the explosives to the seller or to use them in future jobs. She had already incurred other expenses of $20,000 up to the time of Cliff's breach, but would have avoided additional costs of $5,000 involved in the process of demolition.

Can Dinah claim the contract price from Cliff? If not, what, if anything is she entitled to claim?

2. Buddy Beautiful is a celebrated supermodel, best known for his extremely seductive advertisements for men's fragrances and designer denim jeans. He decided to capitalize on his fame by becoming a movie star. Following intensive negotiations, his agent managed to secure a contract for him with Medea Mogul, an important movie producer. In terms of the contract, Buddy would be paid $10 million for taking the lead role in a movie to be called *Buddy's Big Budget Adventure*, an expensive and riotous new comedy, full of cute jokes and romantic scenes in which Buddy would have the opportunity to remove some or all of his clothing. Production of the film was to begin two months after the contract was signed, and would last for six months.

About a month after entering the contract, Medea decided not to produce the film. She wrote to Buddy, informing him of the film's cancellation and offering him the leading role in another movie called *Hamlet* that would be produced instead during the same period. Although Medea assured him that this film would do his career far more good than *Buddy's Big Budget Adventure*, Buddy was unconvinced. He read the script, which was written in strange, complicated, old-fashioned language. It was difficult to follow and would be even harder to learn. From what he understood of it, it also seemed very sleazy and definitely "R" rated. It was about this dysfunctional Danish family who are rather lacking in traditional family values and are heavily into sex and violence. The character to be played by Buddy talks too much, never has any fun, and does not conform to the sexy, but cute and wholesome image Buddy wanted to project. Furthermore, in her letter Medea described *Hamlet* as an "art film," which apparently meant that its box office draw would be small. As a result, the letter regretted to inform him, his fee for starring in it would be only $5 million.

Despite his misgivings, Buddy decided that *Hamlet* was better than nothing, so he accepted the offer. Does he have any claim for damages against Medea? If so, how much?

3. Change the facts of Example 2 as follows: Buddy did not feel that Hamlet was a suitable role, so he declined Medea's offer and insisted that she make the original movie as promised. Medea refused and their relationship broke down. Buddy put his agent to work seeking other movie opportunities. Despite a year's conscientious and persistent effort, the agent was unable to secure any film roles for Buddy. In the interim, Buddy declined several offers of modeling jobs because he felt that he should hold himself available to perform whatever new film contract his agent should find. What damages, if any, should Buddy receive?

4. How would your answer to Example 3 change if two weeks after Medea's repudiation, Buddy entered into a contract with Dee Ziner, a designer of men's fashions, to model her new line of summer clothing? Buddy's performance under the modeling contract began immediately after execution of the contract and lasted one month. Buddy earned a fee of $1 million.

5. Because Buddy's agent could not find another film contract for him, his hopes for a movie career ended in failure. Buddy is convinced that had he made the comedy for Medea, he would have established himself as a star and enjoyed unlimited opportunities for further movies. He has now sued Medea for the $10 million payable under their contract, as well as $200 million in damages for the destruction of his movie career. Should he be awarded these damages?

6. Harpo C. Chord is a young and ambitious pianist. After struggling for many months to find work, he finally received an offer to play dinner music at Trés Trendi, a fancy restaurant. This was not quite what he had in mind as a career opportunity, but his financial reserves were much depleted and he was becoming desperate. He also realized that because the restaurant was in the theater district, many of its patrons were influential in the arts, so there was a good chance that someone important might notice his talent and offer him something better. He therefore accepted the offer and on January 15 he entered into a contract with Trés Trendi under which he would play the piano during dinner from 8 P.M. to midnight every night for a month. His performances would begin on February 1, and he would be paid "the going rate" for his services. Because neither party knew at the time of contracting what the current market rate was for a dinner pianist, Trés Trendi said that it would make inquiries and tell Harpo as soon as it found out.

   Having heard nothing from Trés Trendi for a week, Harpo called the manager to find out what rate of compensation had been established by the promised market survey. He was stunned when the manager told him that inquiries had shown that the market rate for a pianist was much higher than she had anticipated, so she had decided to scrap the idea of having live music in the restaurant. This is a clear repudiation of the contract, and despite Harpo's fervent pleas, the manager refuses to relent.

   Having just gone through the agonizing process of looking for work, Harpo realizes that he has little chance of finding other employment for February. Besides, he wants to work for Trés Trendi so that he can showcase his talents to any useful diners that may be present. What recourse does he have?

7. Barney Sellers owned an acre of land in the suburbs. The land was once part of a farm that has long since been subdivided into smaller lots for housing. However, the original barn is still located on Barney's acre, which is otherwise vacant. When Barney retired last year, he decided to move from his home in the city to his suburban acre. He had plans drawn for a new house to be constructed on the eastern portion of his lot. The existing barn was on the western side of the lot, so it did not interfere with his building plans, but it was quite an unsightly structure and would occupy space that Barney wished to use as a garden. The barn was in reasonably good condition and was easily removable, so he decided to sell it instead of demolishing it. He advertised it for sale and ultimately sold it to Penny Pincher for $5,000. In terms of the contract, Penny agreed to pay all the costs of removing the barn and also to break up its concrete foundation and remove the debris.

A few weeks later, Penny removed the barn. She was going to hire someone to break up and remove the concrete foundation, but when she discovered that the cheapest quote for the job was $7,000, she decided that it was a waste of money and refused to do it. The existence of the concrete slab will spoil Barney's landscaping plans and leave him with an eyesore in his backyard. However, because suburban land is scarce and of prime value, the presence of the slab would apparently not dissuade a typical buyer from purchasing the property at its full worth. As a result, the removal of the slab would not enhance the property's market value. What damages, if any, can Barney recover for Penny's breach?

8. To satisfy the demand for its required course on professional ethics, a law school offers a summer school ethics course every year. The course is usually in great demand and attracts about 50 students each summer. Last November, the law school contracted with Bill A. Billhours, a prominent local attorney, to teach the summer ethics course for a fee of $10,000. The contract obliged him to teach four evenings a week for five weeks, beginning on June 1. On May 15, Bill was given the opportunity of advising a new client in connection with a huge international transaction. Participation in the proposed transaction promised to be both stimulating and lucrative, so Bill grabbed the chance of working on it. Unfortunately, the work required him to be out of the country for much of June and July, so it was no longer possible for him to teach. He called the dean of the law school on May 17 and told him that he could not teach summer school as planned.

   a. Not wishing to disappoint the students who were relying on taking the course that summer, the dean immediately set to work finding a replacement. After making several unsuccessful calls, she was finally put in touch with Professor Wise, a world-famous expert on legal ethics and the author of several definitive books on the subject. Professor Wise had just retired, so he had no plans for the summer, but he was unwilling to teach for less than $15,000, plus his traveling and living expenses, which amount to a further $4,000. Desperate, the dean agreed to his terms. Can the law school recover all or any of the $19,000 from Bill?

b. Assume that the dean was unable to find anyone to teach the course because it is too late to find a teacher on such short notice. The dean cannot bear to let down all those students who are relying on taking the course during the summer. Is there anything she can do to force Bill into teaching?

c. Assume that the dean can neither find a substitute teacher nor compel Bill to teach. As a result, the summer ethics course has to be canceled. Based on enrollment before cancellation, the law school can show that it would have made $75,000 in tuition from the course. In addition, the law school was sued by one of the students who had enrolled in the course. The student had been relying on the course to complete his requirements for graduation in the summer so that he could graduate in August. He had a job beginning in August, but now he cannot begin work until after he graduates at the end of December. He therefore claimed three months' salary from the law school. To avoid adverse publicity and a negative impact on alumni relations, the law school paid the student's claim. What recourse, if any, does the school have against Bill?

9. Nat Atorium hired La Goon Pool Co. to build a swimming pool in his backyard. As the yard was small, the pool had to be placed not more than five feet from the rear wall of the house. La Goon brought its excavating equipment into the yard and one of its workers began to dig the hole. After spending some hours on the job and having excavated to a depth of about six feet, the operator started to become weary and careless. As a result, he dug too close to the house, undermining its foundation and causing the rear of the house to collapse. At the time, Nat was in one of the rear rooms and he could have been severely injured or killed had he not had the presence of mind to dive out of a door just as the room began to cave in. Although he escaped physical injury, he was badly traumatized by the close call and the destruction of half his house.

This experience has removed Nat's desire for a swimming pool. La Goon concedes that it is liable for the cost of repairing Nat's house, the fair market value of all personal property lost in the collapse, and the cost of filling in the hole and restoring the yard. However, Nat says this is not enough. He demands in addition:

a. Compensation of $150,000 for the shock and distress that he suffered as a result of La Goon's incompetence.

b. Compensation of $50,000 for the loss of irreplaceable family records and photographs that were among the personal property destroyed. Although they have no economic worth, they were of immense sentimental value to Nat.

c. Punitive damages of $1 million.

Is Nat likely to succeed on any of these further claims?

10. Chic Canery has managed to train a troupe of chickens to perform amazing tricks. She has appeared on several TV shows with them and has attracted a lot of public attention. AC9 Productions, Inc., a show promoter, decided the market was ready for a live show featuring Chic and her chickens. It approached Chic with a proposal to produce such a show. Following negotiations, in January Chic and AC9 entered into a contract for the production of a show on July 4. The show was to be staged in a sports stadium with a capacity of 100,000 seats. AC9 would make all arrangements for the show and would be entitled to all proceeds from the event, save for a fee of $1 million to be paid to Chic. An advance of $100,000 on this fee would be paid to Chic on the signing of the contract, and the balance would be paid a week before the show.

Immediately after the contract was signed, AC9 paid the $100,000 to Chic and it began preparations for the show. It booked the stadium, hired a special staff to work exclusively on publicity and sales, and committed itself to the purchase of television advertising. On March 1, Chic changed her mind about doing the show and she repudiated the contract. After trying unsuccessfully to convince her to recant, AC9 had no choice but to accept the fact that Chic would not perform. As the theme and concept of the entire show were built on Chic's unique chicken act, it was too late to begin afresh by changing the theme and trying to find a new starring attraction. AC9 stopped all further work on the show and laid off its special staff. It exercised its cancellation right under the contract with the stadium and terminated its booking, forfeiting a $50,000 deposit. It had no right to cancel the television advertising slots. At the time of Chic's repudiation, AC9 had incurred the following expenses and commitments:

a. Before making a final decision to enter the contract with Chic, it had spent $30,000 on a market analysis and profit projection for the show.

b. It paid the $100,000 advance to Chic.

c. It paid $25,000 in salary and severance pay to its special staff.

d. It forfeited its $50,000 deposit on the stadium.

e. It committed itself to pay $500,000 for television advertising.

According to the market analysis and projections made by AC9 before it entered the contract with Chic, it expected the show tickets to be sold out, generating income of $5 million. It expected further earnings of $3.5 million from the sale of T-shirts, souvenirs, and food. Its projected costs, including Chic's fee, were $5.5 million, so it expected a profit of $3 million. What damages is it likely to recover from Chic?

11. Benny Fishery Co. entered into a contract with Reliant Renovations, Inc. under which Reliant agreed to build an addition to Benny Fishery's seafood processing plant. The contract required Reliant to excavate the site, build a foundation, and erect an aluminum structure on it. The total price for the project was $230,000. Reliant began work and encountered trouble immediately because the ground was much rockier than expected. As a result, it had to hire a subcontractor to blast the rock and had to use much heavier equipment than anticipated. This greatly increased its costs of excavation from an expected $50,000 to $100,000, and its total projected cost from $200,000 to $250,000. This meant that it now projected a loss of $20,000 on the contract. (Had Reliant conducted a proper inspection of the lot, it would have discovered this problem before bidding, so the underbidding is its own error in judgment. It acknowledges this and has not tried to use it as a basis for avoiding the contract for mistake or requesting a price modification.)

Soon after the excavation had been completed and before Reliant could proceed any further, Benny Fishery decided that it no longer needed the addition to its plant. It terminated the contract. As it had no right to do this, the termination was a total breach. The excavation work constitutes exactly one-quarter of Reliant's performance under the contract, and Benny Fishery has therefore offered to pay Reliant $57,500, which is exactly one-quarter of the contract price. Should Reliant accept this payment or demand more?

12. Gracie Spooner owns a busy hamburger joint. She recently decided to replace her grungy ketchup pumps with little plastic sachets of ketchup. To ensure a ready and stable supply of this vital ingredient in her cuisine, she entered into a one-year contract with Sauce Source, Inc., a wholesaler. Under the contract, Gracie committed herself to buy a minimum of ten boxes of sachets a month, at a price of $25 a box. The contract contained the following provision:

> The parties record that the pricing of the product sold under this contract is based on Buyer's commitment to take the minimum quantities specified above. Therefore if Buyer should breach this contract by failing to take the prescribed minimum quantity, Seller shall be entitled to damages based on

the difference between the amount actually paid by Buyer for purchases of the product and the total minimum price payable for the full period of this contract. The parties expressly agree that this provision does not constitute a penalty, but is a genuine attempt to estimate damages and to avoid the uncertainty and difficulties of proof.

Gracie bought and paid for the minimum quantities required by the contract for seven months, but she found that she had grossly overestimated the amount of ketchup that she needed. Unopened boxes of sachets were beginning to pile up in her small storeroom, and it was clear to her that she already had enough ketchup to last her for more than a couple of years. She therefore declined to order or accept delivery of any more ketchup from Sauce Source. When the yearlong contract period ended, Sauce Source sent an invoice to Gracie for $1,250, based on the price of the minimum quantity that she had failed to take during the last five months of the contract. Gracie protested to the manager of Sauce Source. She pointed out that ketchup had gone up in price since they made their contract, and she suggested that Sauce Source simply sell the remaining boxes at a better price to someone else. The manager told her that they had enough ketchup to keep all their customers supplied, with plenty over, so her breach actually reduced their volume of sales for the year. In any event, he reminded her that she did agree to this payment in the contract. Gracie feels that the invoice is ridiculous. Should she pay it?

Explanations

1. Cliff had no right to terminate the contract, so his termination was a material repudiation[18] that would entitle Dinah to claim expectation damages from him. Had Dina fully performed before the repudiation, it would have been appropriate to award her the full unpaid balance of the contract price. She expected to receive that price, and there would have been no deduction from it because she would not have saved any costs as a result of the repudiation. Stated differently, where a party has incurred the full cost of performing before the other party's repudiation, her contractual expectation is achieved by reimbursing the costs she expended (her reliance loss) plus her expected profit. This amounts to the contract price. However, because the repudiation occurred before Dinah had fully performed, she is not entitled to receive the full contract

---

18. This was a repudiation because it occurred in advance of Cliff's duty of performance. You may wonder if Cliff could have raised the defenses of mistake or impracticability. However, assume that neither defense would have worked to excuse his termination of the contract.

price. At the time of repudiation, Dinah had incurred costs of $20,000 in performing, but had not yet detonated the $100,000 worth of explosives or incurred the $5,000 costs of the detonation itself. Therefore, at the time of breach, Dinah's expectation damages would have been $395,000, made up of her reliance expenses of $20,000 plus her lost profit of $375,000 (the price of $500,00 less the total expected costs of $125,000). By disregarding Cliff's termination and proceeding with the demolition, Dinah aggravated her damages by using up the explosives and incurring the additional costs of demolition. The mitigation principle precludes her from holding Cliff liable for her obstinately persisting in performance after Cliff had unequivocally repudiated the contract. She must therefore be confined to her expectation before she increased her damages.

This Example is inspired by *Rockingham County v. Luten Bridge Co.*, 35 F.2d 301 (4th Cir. 1929), an old case that remains one of the best examples of obstinate damage aggravation. The county breached its contract for the construction of a bridge by terminating the project and telling the contractor to stop work. The contractor disregarded the instruction and continued to build the bridge. It was held entitled to recover its anticipated profit as well as those losses incurred up to the date of breach, but was denied any compensation for expenditures made after the breach.

2. Buddy's acceptance of the offer to star in *Hamlet* could be seen as a modification of the contract. If it was, there is no issue of breach or damages — the parties have simply changed their terms. However, when one party seeks to substitute a performance different from that originally agreed, the circumstances are also consistent with breach combined with an offer of mitigation. It is important to distinguish an agreed modification from a breach, followed by acceptance of a mitigating contract. If the parties have agreed to modify the contract, there is no claim for damages. However, if one of the parties breaches, and then offers the other a substitute contract that is accepted, the victim of the breach has a claim for damages to compensate for the difference in value of the original and substitute contracts.

In Buddy's case, the facts indicate that Medea breached and then offered a substitute in mitigation. This seems a more appropriate conclusion given Medea's attitude (she informed Buddy of her decision rather than seeking to negotiate a change) and Buddy's reluctant acquiescence. Since Medea terminated the contract before performance was due, this is an anticipatory repudiation. It is unequivocal, material, and total. (This issue is discussed in section 17.7.2.) Upon Medea's total breach, Buddy is entitled to sue for his lost profit under the contract, less any amount recovered in mitigation. (In an employment contract, lost profits are commonly equal to the full salary because employees usually do not have to incur costs to perform, but any earnings from substitute employment must be deducted from damages as mitigation.)

Hamlet is surely a substitute contract, because Buddy would not have been able to do both films, which have the same production dates. (In fact, Medea's decision to produce the second was apparently based on her decision to cancel the first.) When, as a result of the breach, the plaintiff is released from his performance so that he can undertake other work that could not have been done in the absence of breach, any earnings from that other work must be treated as a gain from the breach and offset against damages. Therefore, his earnings from *Hamlet* ($5 million) must be deducted from his lost profit damages for the breach of the initial contract ($10 million).

3. Buddy has rejected the opportunity to reduce his damages by starring in *Hamlet* for $5 million. Because he could find no other substitute film contract, he has been idle for a year. It must therefore be decided if Buddy's refusal of Medea's offer and his failure to perform other work was a violation of his duty to mitigate, resulting in aggravated loss for which Medea should not be held accountable. If so, there must be an offset against his damages of the $5 million that he could have earned from *Hamlet*, or of whatever other amount he should have earned by other substitute work in the period that would have been occupied by filming *Buddy's Big Budget Adventure*.

Buddy may have failed to mitigate by refusing the *Hamlet* role. It may seem outrageous to expect the victim of a breach to accept mitigation by dealing with the very person who breached the contract and caused the loss. However courts generally take the attitude that mitigation opportunities offered by the breacher should be evaluated under the same standards as other available means to reduce damages: If this means of mitigation is not unduly risky, burdensome, or humiliating, it does not call on the victim to waive any right to relief under the breached contract, and it provides the most reasonable means of reducing the loss, the victim must pursue it, or risk losing the right to claim any damages that could have been prevented by taking it. Because the breacher has already shown herself to be untrustworthy, the victim may have justifiable concerns about whether she will prove similarly unreliable in the substitute contract. However, the victim needs to show more than a general apprehension that the breacher might again renege. Notwithstanding, there is a different consideration that may justify Buddy in declining the *Hamlet* role. If he had the reasonable prospect of finding a more suitable movie, his decision to refuse the role and hold himself available for a better opportunity may be a rational judgment. The fact that no better offer came along does not defeat this argument. The injured party's judgment with regard to mitigation need only be reasonable, even if it later appears that it was wrong, or that a different decision would have been better.

Parker v. Twentieth Century-Fox Film Corp., discussed in section 18.6.3, held that an employee's duty of reasonable mitigation does not require her to accept work that is different and inferior to that provided for in the contract. Medea's offer of the role in *Hamlet* is clearly very different from that promised to Buddy under the contract, but is it inferior? Although *Hamlet* may be a finer piece of work than *Buddy's Big Budget Adventure*, the role of Hamlet could be inferior for Buddy's purposes. It does not have the same potential to showcase his talents, to reach his targeted audience, or to further his career goals. Note that inferiority is judged on the basis of the quality of the substitute work, and not by the mere fact that Buddy would be paid less for playing Hamlet. The difference in earnings can be compensated for by a damages award.

If Buddy's refusal of the role in Hamlet violated his duty to mitigate, he aggravated his damages by $5 million and his damages must be reduced accordingly. However, if he was justified in refusing the role, we still need to determine if he should have taken other action to reduce his loss. He did make considerable efforts to find another film role, but he may not have been reasonable in refusing to seek or consider modeling jobs. Although modeling is different from acting in a movie, this line of work is not necessarily inferior because it is a field in which he has achieved success and doing more modeling would likely not have a negative effect on his career goals. If Medea can show that Buddy could have found modeling work that would have curtailed his losses, his damages should be reduced by what he reasonably could have earned during the six-month period that became free as a result of the film's cancellation.

4. If Buddy should have accepted the Hamlet role, the answer does not change — the full $5 million that he should have earned, not just $1 million he actually earned, must be deducted from his damages. However, if his refusal of *Hamlet* was justified, the fee earned from the modeling job must be offset against the $10 million loss. The performance of the modeling job took place during the period reserved for the filming, and Buddy could not have accepted it and earned the modeling fee had Medea not breached the movie contract. It is therefore a substitute transaction and the $1 million fee is a gain that would not have been made but for the breach. (If Buddy incurred any direct costs to perform for Dee, those would be subtracted before his earnings are offset. But in the typical employment contract it is the employee's time and labor that are being contracted for, and he does not usually have to spend much in rendering that performance. As a

result, the employee's direct costs are likely to be small or even nonexistent.)

Therefore, provided that Buddy's refusal of the *Hamlet* role was justified, he can claim damages for breach in the amount of $9 million — his full contract salary of $10 million less the $1 million earned in mitigation. This has the effect of overcompensating him because he receives his full contract fee even though he worked only for a month. However, Medea cannot complain because the benefit of not having to work so hard for his money does not reduce Buddy's financial loss. As in Example 2, the issue of whether the modeling job is different or inferior does not come up where Buddy accepted the substitute work. It is only relevant if he declines a substitute transaction.

5. Buddy's claim for consequential damages is based on the theory that by losing his opportunity to star in *Buddy's Big Budget Adventure*, he was deprived of a successful movie career and lost $200 million. The mitigation issue would arise here again, because his failure to accept the Hamlet role may have precluded an opportunity to prevent this consequence. However, Buddy may argue that this consequential loss would have occurred whether or not he had accepted the Hamlet role, because *Hamlet* would not have advanced his career at all and may even have ruined it.

It is arguable that a movie producer should reasonably foresee that her failure to produce an actor's first film — especially if it is planned as an expensive blockbuster — could have an adverse impact on his career and deprive him of future opportunities. However, even if this is so, the overwhelming barrier to recovery is the highly speculative nature of the claim. It is unlikely that Buddy could prove with any degree of plausibility that the proposed movie would have been successful and would have advanced his career. There are just too many imponderables: Would he have performed well? Would good judgments have been made about publicity and promotion? Would the public have been attracted to the film and to him? Would it have made enough money to make him desirable to other producers? More uncertainties could be listed, but the point is made. Even if he could overcome this burden of showing a probability that opportunities would have been created, a further level of uncertainty would be encountered in trying to decide if he would have been lucky and clever enough to use them to advantage. In short, he cannot even prove what would have happened had the film been made, let alone establish a monetary value of the loss. The consequential damages claim must fail under the principles of certainty and causation.

The difficulty in establishing quantifiable loss when the breach results in a lost opportunity for publicity and its consequent career advancement is shown by another case springing from the entertainment industry: *Ericson v. Playgirl, Inc.*, 140 Cal. Rptr. 921 (Ct. App. 1977). *Playgirl* contracted with Ericson, one of its centerfold models and an aspiring actor, to rerun his pictures in its *"Best of Playgirl"* annual and to include him as one of the models on the annual's cover. When *Playgirl* failed to include Ericson on the cover, he sued it for consequential damages for breach of contract. He produced witnesses who testified generally on the benefits of publicity to an acting career and on the economic value of appearing on a magazine cover. The court found that *Playgirl* had breached the contract, but it awarded Ericson only nominal damages. The court accepted that as an abstract matter, exposure (forgive the double entendre) is valuable to an actor, but his evidence of loss was too generalized and nonspecific. Any economically adverse consequences of the breach were pure conjecture.

6. Although Harpo's remuneration has not been settled, this should not affect the validity of the contract, because the parties have agreed on a market standard for determining it. A contract for a reasonable fee, to be based on an objectively ascertainable standard, is sufficiently definite for enforcement.[19] If Harpo was not reasonably able to mitigate his loss by finding appropriate substitute employment, he will at a minimum be able to sue for what he would have earned under the contract (less direct costs saved, if any). To establish what this amount would have been, he would have to produce evidence of the market rate paid to a pianist of his experience for equivalent work in a restaurant of similar standing. Such evidence is apparently available. However, Harpo was expecting more than a mere month's employment. He was hoping to make contacts and to open opportunities by playing in the restaurant. Although unlike Mr. Ericson, whose case is discussed in Example 5, Harpo plans to keep his clothes on during performance, that example shows that it is difficult to establish measurable injury as a result of the loss of publicity. Therefore, an award of money damages would most likely cover only his direct damages and would fail to compensate him for speculative consequential damages.

When a plaintiff can show that a monetary award cannot adequately achieve his expectation, he establishes one of the essential grounds for the remedy of specific performance.[20] To get the order, Harpo must satisfy the court, in addition to showing the inadequacy of the damages

---

19. This issue is discussed in section 10.5.

20. Of course, had Harpo breached, Trés Trendi would not have been able to obtain an order of specific performance to compel his personal services because of the strong policy against forcing an individual to work against his will. However, this policy is not implicated where the employee sues the employer for specific performance, and orders of reinstatement are common.

remedy, that the court's burden of supervision is outweighed by the need for the remedy and that the balance of the equities favor granting the order. In addition, when there is some indefiniteness in the contract terms, even if the indefiniteness is not serious enough to invalidate the contract, the court may confine the plaintiff to damages unless the terms can be clearly established to support a precise and comprehensible order.

The indefiniteness in the fee to be paid to Harpo should not be a bar to relief because the court can establish the fee by reference to the market. There may also be some lack of detail with regard to Harpo's working conditions, which would have to be resolved, possibly also by reference to customary or reasonable standards. The primary focus of the definiteness principle in this context is to ensure that the order specifies Trés Trendi's duties precisely so that it knows what it must do to comply with the order to avoid contempt of court. By fixing the payment due to Harpo and detailing his working conditions, the court should be able to formulate a clear order. An order compelling Harpo's employment by a possibly begrudging employer does entail some burden of supervision to ensure that he is paid and that he is not mistreated or subjected to harassment. However, this supervisory task is not particularly onerous or exceptional. In a case like this the court is not likely to appoint an official to oversee the employment. It would be up to Harpo, if he alleges a breach of the order, to move for an order calling on Trés Trendi to show cause why it should not be held in contempt of court. The court would then conduct a hearing to determine if Trés Trendi violated the order and to impose a sanction if it did.

The equities of granting relief favor Harpo, not only because a damages award cannot adequately compensate him for his uncertain consequential damages, but also because Trés Trendi committed a willful breach and it suffers no undue hardship by allowing Harpo to play the piano in its restaurant for a fee that it would have to pay in any event as direct damages.

7. It is easy to identify the measure of damages required to place Barney in the position he would have been in had Penny not breached. It is the reasonable cost of demolishing the slab and removing the concrete debris, apparently $7,000. However, the facts show that although damages of $7,000 would give Barney the equivalent of performance in compliance with the contract, the breach did not actually cause him economic harm if his loss is instead measured by the diminution in the value of the property on which the work was to have been done. This raises the issue of whether the proper basis for recovery is the cost of giving him what was promised (which is $7,000) or the actual reduction in his wealth (which is zero). Stated differently, when the cost of

giving the plaintiff his contractual expectation exceeds his actual ultimate financial loss, should his damages be limited by that ultimate loss?

As discussed in sections 17.3.4 and 18.6.6, Barney is normally entitled to the full measure of his expectation damages. However, if Penny's breach was not material or willful and the cost of giving Barney his contractual expectation would be an unfair forfeiture, the court may confine relief to Barney's ultimate economic loss, measured by the diminution in market value resulting from the breach. Penny's breach was deliberate, and that on its own is enough to preclude application of the unfair forfeiture doctrine. In addition, the breach was likely material. Materiality is a question of interpretation, to be decided by assessing the importance of the breach in light of the purpose of the contract, determined by its terms and context. Had Barney intended to resell the property, Penny's failure to remove the slab may have been immaterial because it had no impact on the market value of the property. (Even under these circumstances, this outcome is not assured because the parties did stipulate for the slab's removal as part of the consideration for the barn.) However, Barney plans to live on the property, and it therefore cannot be said that the removal of the slab was merely incidental to the sale.

8. a. When, following a total breach, the plaintiff obtains a reasonable substitute performance, expectation damages are the difference between what the plaintiff had to pay for the substitute and what it would have had to pay under the contract for the equivalent performance. When the substitute is not only more expensive in itself, but also involves the plaintiff in the extra expense of having to go outside the local market, the additional cost of transportation or (as in this case, travel and living expenses) is also included in determining the replacement cost. Therefore if Professor Wise is a reasonable substitute for Bill, the law school will be able to recover substitutionary damages from Bill. These damages are not the full $19,000 paid to Wise, but rather the $9,000 difference between what it paid to Wise, $19,000, and what it would have paid Bill, $10,000.

Although it is seldom likely that a substitute performance will exactly match that promised under the contract, both the compensation and the mitigation principle require that the replacement be as close as possible. If the plaintiff is awarded the added cost of a more valuable or better-quality replacement, it is overcompensated, and its damages must be reduced to reflect the lower cost of a nearer substitute. However, this principle is not rigidly applied so that the plaintiff is invariably precluded from receiving reimbursement of the full cost of a superior replacement. As the victim of breach, the plaintiff has the burden foisted on it of finding a substitute to effectively counter the ill effects of the breach, sometimes within a very short time. When the only reasonable option open to the plaintiff under all the circumstances is to select a better replacement, it may be appropriate to hold the defendant accountable for the full cost, even if this means that the plaintiff profits somewhat by a performance superior to that expected. This is particularly so when the better substitute gives the plaintiff no realizable economic advantage.

In this case, Bill breached about two weeks before classes were to begin, and the dean had little time to find a substitute. She did make immediate efforts and only hired Professor Wise when it was apparent that she would be unlikely to find anyone else. She has no duty of exhaustive inquiry, but need only make such good faith and reasonable efforts called for by the circumstances. Even if Professor Wise is more experienced, has greater prestige, and may possibly be a better teacher, he may be the most reasonable substitute.

b. A court will not decree specific performance of personal services. Quite apart from the obvious difficulty in supervising the performance of teaching duties, the compulsion of personal services is rather too much like involuntary servitude. Therefore, even though the plaintiff may have no adequate remedy at law, the considerations disfavoring specific enforcement outweigh the plaintiff's interest in performance.

If specific performance is not available, a court may be willing to grant the plaintiff a prohibitory injunction, restraining the defendant from entering into the transaction that motivated the breach. The concerns about involuntary servitude and difficulty of supervision are not present in such a negative order. Of course, preventing Bill from participating in the international transaction does not, in itself, achieve the school's expectation, but the idea is that by removing the motivation for the breach, the order will induce Bill to perform as promised. However, even when a prohibitory injunction is sought, courts are very wary about using their power of compulsion to prevent an individual from selling his labor and earning his livelihood as he sees fit. It is therefore in only the most compelling cases that a court will issue such an order.

Like specific performance, an injunction is an equitable remedy, subject to the same general prerequisites: The plaintiff must show that the legal remedy of damages is inadequate, and that the balance of equities favors the grant of the order. In this case, given the fact that no substitute is available, the possibility of substitutionary damages does not exist. This would lead to lost profits and consequential damages that (as Explanation 8(c) discusses) could be very speculative and difficult to prove. Furthermore, no monetary award can compensate for the immeasurable harm caused by the disruption of the law school's program, its inability to provide planned educational services, and the disappointment or even hostility of its students. Overall, a good argument can be made that the school has no adequate remedy at law. If this is so, the equities of trying to protect the law school's expectation weigh heavily in the balance. They are given further weight by the fact that Bill's breach is deliberate and motivated by ambition and financial reward. Nevertheless, Bill's primary professional pursuit is legal practice and the service of his clients' needs. It may simply be too harsh on Bill to restrain him. Also, there is a strong public interest in allowing people access to an attorney of their choice, so an injunction may improperly interfere with the attorney-client relationship. This would be particularly so if Bill has already agreed to represent the client. In short, without reaching a definitive conclusion, we can recognize that an injunction may be feasible, but there may not be enough here to overcome the court's disinclination to issue such an order.

c. Because the law school is unable, after reasonable effort, to replace Bill and avert the loss resulting from cancellation of the class, its net loss is claimable as direct damages. Of course, it cannot claim the full lost earnings of $75,000. First, it must establish that its forecast of tuition income is reasonably reliable and takes into account what likely proportion of enrolled students may exercise any available right to drop the course and be excused from paying tuition. Thereafter, it must deduct its savings from the breach and any recoupment of that loss. The most obvious saving is Bill's salary of $10,000. Although the facts do not indicate them, there may be some other variable (direct) costs that are saved. Overhead expenses such as maintaining the buildings and paying support staff are likely not reduced at all by the breach and are not deducted as costs saved. In addition, there may be some recoupment of the lost earnings if some of the students decide to switch to another summer school class instead, or if the law school's fee structure is such that the students end up paying more tuition in the semester for having to take the ethics course then. Once all these savings and recoupments are calculated, the law school is entitled to claim its lost profit — expected earnings less savings and recoupment — from Bill.

The payment to the student who sued for lost salary is a consequential loss. When a breach of contract causes the plaintiff to breach a dependent contract with a third person, the plaintiff's liability to the third person could be recoverable provided that the requirements of causation, reasonable certainty, foreseeability, and mitigation are satisfied. It is not clear that the law school was legally liable to the student for the loss of salary, because the school may have had the right to cancel the course, either by express stipulation or by common usage. If so, its payment could have been purely ex gratia, and under principles of causation and mitigation, the law school is not likely to be able to hold Bill accountable for this loss. However, the law school may have committed not to cancel the course, so that Bill's repudiation forced it into a breach of its contract with the student. Even if this is so, Bill would not be liable for this loss unless he reasonably could have foreseen it. Bill will be taken to have foreseen this damage either if the school told him of its commitment to students, or if, in normal practice, this kind of commitment was common enough that Bill should have been aware of it as a practitioner and former student. Assuming that the loss was reasonably foreseeable to Bill, the school must still satisfy the requirements of mitigation and reasonable certainty. It decided to pay the student's claim in full, rather than contesting it. However, failure to challenge the student's claim would not be an aggravation of loss if the student clearly established his claim, so that litigation over it would have been costly, pointless, and damaging to the school's reputation. Although reasonable certainty can be an issue in claims for lost future earnings, it seems that in this case the student did have a job and can establish his loss for the defined three-month period. (Maybe the student's employment was also contingent on his passing the bar, which would make his loss of earnings more speculative, but the facts do not indicate that this was an issue.)

9. a./b. These Examples raise the question of whether LaGoon must compensate Nat for shock, distress, and sentimental loss. The focus of contract damages is on economic loss, so the general rule is that no compensation is claimable for emotional distress or sentimental loss resulting from the breach. In some cases, losses of this nature could be excluded simply on the basis that they were not reasonably foreseeable. But even when there may have been some basis for contemplating them as a probable consequence of breach, the policy of confining contract damages to economic loss usually outweighs any sympathy for the plaintiff's suffering. There are, however, two situations in which courts have been willing to countenance a claim for emotional or sentimental damages:

The first occurs where the purpose of the contract is clearly and purely to enhance the plaintiff's emotional well-being. It may seem, at first thought, that the construction of a swimming pool in Nat's backyard, for his own personal use and enjoyment, is such a contract. However, courts constrict this exception more narrowly. As explained in section 18.13.1, the very basis and nature of the contract must be to provide sentimental or emotional benefit to the plaintiff. It is not enough, to remove the contract from the commercial realm, that the plaintiff's desire for the performance was motivated by personal pleasure rather than profit. The reason for this rather cold-hearted approach is probably quite obvious: If the exception were extended to cases like this, it could cover almost every consumer transaction in which it is clear that the primary motivation is the use of the property or services purchased to enhance quality or enjoyment of life.

The second situation in which a court may grant the plaintiff emotional distress damages is where the breach of contract is also a tort. This is not so much an exception to the rule barring emotional distress damages in contract, as a recognition that some breaches of contract may involve conduct that is also a violation of duty under the law of torts. The noneconomic damages are therefore not really awarded for the breach of contract, but are independently compensable in tort. The damage to Nat's house was apparently caused by negligent operation of the earthmoving equipment. If this is so, the negligent performance is likely to constitute not only a breach of contract, but also a tort, allowing Nat to go forward with his claim for mental distress damages. (Whether he satisfies the requirements of tort law for award of these damages is beyond our scope.)

c. The issue in this Example is whether Nat can claim punitive damages. The compensation principle also precludes punitive damages in most contract suits unless the breach is also a tort for which such damages are appropriate. Punitive damages are not generally available in tort law unless the injury was deliberate and malicious, or was at least the result of reckless and callous disregard for the plaintiff's rights. Therefore, even if LaGoon's employee did commit a tort by damaging Nat's house, this sounds more like a case of common negligence than the kind of conduct that warrants punitive relief.

10. If AC9's projections are credible, its expectation damages are its anticipated profit of $3 million plus the reliance expenses that it has already spent or committed for which it would have been reimbursed out of its earnings under the contract. (These expenses are discussed below.) It is not clear how convincing these projections may be. To recover lost profits, a plaintiff must be able to prove the fact and amount of those profits with reasonable certainty. AC9's projections may have been made by people with great expertise and experience and based on careful and thorough research. However, it is generally very difficult to establish prospective lost profits from a canceled entertainment event. Public taste can be unpredictable and often surprises even the most seasoned promoter. The prospect of profit is even less certain

when the show centers on something as odd as a performing chicken act. Given the substantial projected costs of mounting the show, AC9 would have to do remarkably well in selling both its tickets and its associated knick-knacks. Its prediction that it could sell out a stadium of 100,000 seats shows laudable, but possibly misplaced, faith in the artistic sensibilities of the American public.

If AC9 cannot prove lost profits, what other alternatives does it have? Restitutionary relief would be available to reclaim Chic's unjust enrichment, but that would cover only the $100,000 down payment. None of the other expenditure enriched her in any way. However, a plaintiff who cannot prove lost profit may nevertheless still recover as reliance damages the expense component of its expectation claim. A claim of reliance damages would permit the recovery of not only the $100,000 down payment, which qualifies as essential reliance, but also some of the other losses incurred in reliance on the contract. Provided that they were reasonably necessary to AC9's performance under the contract and were not profligate, the forfeited stadium deposit and the staff salaries are recoverable in reliance. (They are probably best classified as essential reliance, in that they were expended in furtherance of AC9's contractual obligation to arrange and promote the show.)

The debt for television advertising would also fall into this category, but only to the extent that the expenditure is wasted and not salvageable. Although the advertising slots cannot be canceled, they may be assignable or diverted to use for other purposes. Therefore, to the extent that AC9 can recoup its expenditure by selling the slots or using them for another show, it is not claimable as a reliance loss.

The cost of the market survey and profit projection were incurred before the contract was entered into, so even though these expenses were a waste in the end, they cannot, by definition, be treated as having been incurred in reliance on the contract. This seems to be the general approach to precontractual expenses, notwithstanding that the breach cut off any prospect of earning income that may have reimbursed them.[21]

As noted above, AC9 would claim reliance only if it could not prove its larger claim of lost profit. The plaintiff does not have to prove that the contract would have made a profit to recover reliance damages. However, when the purpose of the contract was profit, and the defendant is able to prove that the plaintiff would have made a loss

---

21. There have been some situations in which courts have been willing to include precontractual expenses in reliance recovery. For example, if the defendant knew that the plaintiff was incurring the expenses in anticipation of the contract and had strongly indicated an intention to enter the contract, promissory estoppel relief may be available for the precontractual expenses. Also, the expenses take on the character of lost opportunity reliance if the plaintiff could have recouped them by entering a similar contract with a third party but gave up that chance by entering the contract with the defendant.

in the event of complete performance, the court will reduce the reliance recovery to take account of this expectation of loss. (As explained in section 18.8.2, it is fairer and more in accord with compensation principles to make a pro rata reduction in the recovery, rather than to deduct the entire anticipated loss.) In a case like this one, where profit is highly speculative, the risk of uncertainty therefore falls on the defendant. Chic probably has about as much chance of proving loss as AC9 has of proving profit, so she probably cannot satisfy her burden, and AC9's recovery is not likely to be subject to reduction.

There have been several cases in which a plaintiff who could not prove lost profits was held entitled to recover reliance expenses incurred pursuant to a contract to stage an entertainment event. For example, in *Chicago Coliseum Club v. Dempsey*, 265 Ill. App. 542 (1932) Jack Dempsey, the world-champion heavyweight boxer, repudiated a contract with the club to participate in a boxing match. The club was not able to prove its lost profit, but the court recognized its right to claim reliance damages for its post-contractual expenses reasonably and necessarily incurred in the course of organizing the match. (The club had also incurred expenses prior to the execution of the contract, but the court did not allow the recovery of these expenses, which predated and therefore could not have been incurred in reliance on the contract.) *Wartzman v. Hightower Productions, Ltd.*, 456 A.2d 82 (Md. 1983) involves an entertainment event almost as culturally significant as Chic's. A group of bright entrepreneurs embarked on an elaborate venture designed to make money out of breaking the world flagpole-sitting record. They planned to lodge an entertainer in a specially constructed perch atop a hydraulic lift mounted on a flatbed trailer, and to exhibit him around the country for about nine months, culminating in his descent from the perch in Times Square on New Year's Eve. They needed capital for this, so they contracted with an attorney to form a corporation that could solicit investments. The attorney was incompetent and failed to create an entity in compliance with securities law. This was only discovered after the promoters had incurred expenses in setting up the project. They could not proceed further without engaging in a complex and expensive procedure to remedy the violation of the securities law. The promoters could not afford the expense or the delay of the cure and the venture collapsed. The corporation was unable to prove that it would have made a profit from the venture, but the court awarded it reliance damages to compensate for the wasted expenditures incurred in reliance on the attorney's contractual commitment to incorporate the enterprise properly.

11. Had Reliant's cost been as it had estimated, it would have had a reasonable expectation of profit. Benny Fishery's material breach would

have entitled it to full expectation damages, calculated by adding its reliance expenditure, which would have been $50,000, to its anticipated profit of $30,000. However, Reliant's miscalculation of its cost has defeated its expectation of profit and its claim for expectation damages. Its only reasonable expectation from full performance is a loss of $20,000. As a result, its claim is confined to reliance or restitutionary damages. Its reliance damages are its cost of $100,000, but they may be even less than this if the defendant can make a case for reducing them, as discussed below. Restitution is measured by the market value of the work performed (quantum meruit). Unless Reliant performed inefficiently, incurring costs in excess of what would be normal on the market, the value of its performance is likely to be higher than its cost, because it would include a reasonable profit. For the sake of illustration, if the costs are indeed efficient and the industry norm is to have a 10 percent profit margin on excavation work, the market value of the performance is $110,000. This being so, Reliant would elect to sue for the higher restitutionary relief. However, the question of whether restitution turns out to be the more advantageous measure of relief depends on whether the court allows unrestricted restitutionary recovery or imposes a limit on it based on the contract value of the performance.

When the defendant can prove that the plaintiff's reasonable expectation under the contract was to lose money, the plaintiff's reliance recovery may be reduced to adjust it for that expectation of loss. Note that the burden of proving the losing expectation is placed on the breaching defendant, and the plaintiff's reliance recovery is unaffected if the defendant cannot sustain the burden. It would unfairly undercompensate the plaintiff to deduct the full amount of the expected loss from a reliance recovery that constitutes only a portion of its performance. The deduction should therefore be prorated so that it is no more than a share of the loss proportionate to the performance rendered. The most rational way of allocating the loss to completed performance is to determine its proportion of the total contractual performance based on the relationship of the cost incurred to the total cost of performance. In the present case, Reliant had incurred costs of $100,000 out of a total anticipated cost of $250,000 — that is, two-fifths of the total. Therefore (provided that Benny Fishery can prove this anticipated loss), the $100,000 reliance expenses must be reduced by two-fifths of the total expected loss of $20,000, that is $8,000, leaving a recovery of $92,000.

The possibility of prorating makes reliance damages an even less attractive alternative to restitution if no equivalent principle applies to restitutionary recovery. Some courts feel that it should not, based on the theory that if the plaintiff elects to disaffirm the contract and sue for unjust enrichment, it should not be limited to the value placed on the performance in the contract. In the present case, it would mean that by choosing restitution, Reliant could recover the full market value of its work, which we have assumed to be around $110,000. A much more advantageous choice than reliance, which would, at best, yield $100,000 and, at worst, $92,000.

Some courts, uncomfortable with the anomaly of achieving different results in reliance and restitution for exactly the same breach, do treat the contract value of the performance as a limit on restitution. In the present case, as two-fifths in value of the work was done, a court following this rule would confine Reliant to two-fifths of the contract price of $230,000. This works out to a recovery of $92,000.

12. We will first deal with the question of whether Sauce Source should be awarded agreed damages, and will then consider what relief it should receive if the agreed damages provision is held invalid.

Should Sauce Source be awarded agreed damages? Sauce Source is attempting to enforce what purports to be an agreed damages provision.[22] The agreement is on a standard form, but that in itself is not relevant unless Gracie can show that the term was unconscionable. To use unconscionability as the basis for attacking a liquidated damages clause, Gracie would have to show not only that the provision was substantively unconscionable, but also that it was adhesive or otherwise procedurally unconscionable. Although unconscionability may be an alternative basis of overturning a liquidated damages provision, we do not explore that issue here. The important point to note is that it is not necessary to show unconscionability or other bargaining unfairness to challenge a liquidated damages provision. The basis of the challenge is simply that the provision imposes a penalty for breach, which is unenforceable as a violation of the compensation principle. The compensation principle requires study of an agreed damages provision to ensure that it is a genuine attempt to liquidate damages and not an unenforceable penalty. Because this is a sale of goods, the

---

22. When a party promises to take a specified quantity of goods or to pay for that quantity even if it is not taken, the term is sometimes characterized not as an attempt to liquidate damages, but as a "take or pay" provision. As such, it is seen as a promise of the alternative performances of either taking the goods or paying for them. If so interpreted, the provision is not subject to regulation as agreed damages and is upheld even if it does not satisfy the prerequisites for a valid agreed damages provision. "Take or pay" clauses are typically found in long-term supply contracts where the supplier incurs the bulk of its costs at the outset. The buyer's commitment to pay for a minimum quantity is justified because it is needed to enable the supplier to recoup that cost. Such facts are not present in our case, and we need not concern ourselves with this ethereal distinction. The clause is both described in the contract as, and functions as, a liquidation of damages.

validity of the provision is tested under UCC §2.718(1), which employs a two-point test, later adopted for the common law by Restatement, Second, §356. The agreed damages are examined in light of both the anticipated harm at the time of contracting, and the actual loss following breach. (Both §§2.718 and 356 uphold the liquidated damages provision if the liquidated damages are reasonable in light of either "anticipated or actual" loss.) The test of anticipated loss requires that the liquidation of damages must be a genuine attempt to reasonably estimate loss at the time of contracting. The more difficult the prospect of proving loss appeared at that time, the greater leeway the parties should be given in coming up with a figure. However, if the basis of determining loss would have been reasonably straightforward at the time of contracting, the parties are held to a higher standard in calculating a figure that approximates expected loss. When actual loss is apparent following breach, the measurement against actual loss allows the court to uphold the award if it has a reasonable relationship to actual loss, even if it was not originally a reasonable estimate of loss.

We are given no facts about how the agreed damages were calculated. However, if we examine the effect of the provision, it becomes clear that the clause cannot be justified as being a realistic prognostication of harm. In most sales of goods, the seller's damages are relatively easy to predict and calculate. If the goods are resold after breach, the difference between the contract and resale price is quite easily ascertainable. If they are not resold or the resale is unreasonable, the contract-market difference can be established. If there is no substitute sale (for example, because the seller loses volume of sales), the seller's lost profit can be proved without too much difficulty. Finally, if the goods are perishable and cannot be resold, the seller is able to sue the buyer for their price. Although there could be uncertainties and disagreement on a number of issues, such as the reasonableness of resale, the market price, or the issue of lost volume, these difficulties are not comparable to, say, the problems of proving lost profits for a speculative venture. There is enough predictability to require the plaintiff to show a sensible basis for coming up with an estimate that bears some relationship to reality. Instead, Sauce Source has used a formula that assures it of full recovery of the sale price, no matter how much it actually delivers to Gracie. If there ever was a term designed as a disincentive to breach — that is, a penalty — this is it.

Furthermore, like the liquidated damages provision in *Lake River Corp. v. Carborundum Co.* (discussed in section 18.11), the amount of damages is quite random in its relationship to loss and ensures that Sauce Source is always overcompensated. To demonstrate, consider the following calculations based upon arbitrarily selected, but generous, actual damage figures: Gracie breached after taking her minimum requirements for seven months, so she is liable for agreed damages of $5 \times \$250 = \$1,250$, representing her failure to take 50 boxes of sachets.

If the ketchup can be readily resold at full price, the damages may overcompensate Sauce Source by a full $1,250 (less any incidental damages). But even if it resells at a huge loss, say at $5 a box, its actual damages would still be considerably less than what was agreed: They would be $1,000, the difference between the contract price of the 50 boxes ($1,250) and their resale price of $250.

Even if we assume that it makes no substitute transaction because it has more ketchup than it can sell, so it loses volume of sales, the agreed damages must still exceed its lost profit, no matter how big its profit margin may be. To illustrate, let's say that its total cost of selling each box is only $2, so that makes a generous profit of $23 per box. Its lost profit is still only $50 \times 23 = \$1,150$ — $100 below the agreed damages.

In fact, there seem to be only two situations in which it could have anticipated a loss equal to the damages provided. Both are highly unlikely. First, if its costs are zero and it has suffered loss of volume, its lost profit would be equal to the agreed damages. Second, if it could not resell at all and the ketchup would spoil and have to be discarded, it would lose the entire contract price. Although this could occur where perishables are sold, ketchup in sealed packages probably has a distant expiry date, which would give Sauce Source much more opportunity to sell it before it spoils.

This set of calculations is based on Gracie's breach in the seventh month of the contract. If you care to do some further arithmetic, you will see that the earlier the breach, the greater the discrepancy between the damages fixed and the reasonably likely harm. However, at no point, not even in the last month, does this disproportion entirely disappear. Our inquiry to establish that the agreement on damages was not a reasonable forecast of harm also shows that the comparison between the liquidated damages and actual damages would lead to the conclusion that the amount of liquidated damages will invariably be higher than any actual damages suffered by Sauce Source. If agreed damages are invalid what are Sauce Source's actual damages? When an agreed damages provision is invalidated, the plaintiff does not lose all remedy. It may still recover whatever actual damages it suffered. If Gracie is correct in saying that the market value of ketchup rose since the contract was entered into, Sauce Source would not be able to claim contract-market damages. Further, if it did enter a substitute transaction by reselling in a commercially reasonable way, it probably sold at the higher price and cannot claim damages based on resale. It does make the argument, however, that even if it did make a subsequent sale, this was not a substitute because it has enough ketchup in stock to satisfy all demand. As discussed in section 18.6.3d, if Sauce Source can show that the breach caused a reduction in its volume of sales and that it had unused capacity to supply all of the demand for ketchup, it should be able to claim its lost profit under §2.708(2). Despite the language in §2.708(2) that "due credit" must be given for "proceeds of resale," most courts accept that this does not apply in a lost volume situation.

Assignment, Delegation, and Third-Party Beneficiaries

§19.1 INTRODUCTION

During the entire course of this book, it has been emphasized that contract is a consensual relationship created by agreement between the parties. In dealing with the enforcement of contracts, it has been taken for granted that contractual rights and duties arise only between the parties and that the power of enforcement resides in each against the other. In the great majority of contracts, this assumption is accurate. A person who is not a party to a contract cannot be bound by it and acquires no rights under it. However, this chapter deals with two situations in which this rule is qualified. Although these situations have in common the fact that a nonparty to the contract obtains the right to enforce a promise under it, they are otherwise quite distinct and are based on very different premises:

A contract may create rights in a third party when the parties to the contract expressly or impliedly agree, at the time of making it, that the performance of one of them will be rendered to or for the benefit of a person who is not a party to the contract, and that the nonparty will have the right to enforce that commitment. The creation of the third-party rights is contemplated by the parties and occurs at the time of contract formation.

The assignment of contractual rights and the delegation of contractual duties does not involve any conferral of rights on a nonparty at the time of contracting. Rather, it is the transfer of rights or obligations by one of the parties at some time after the contract has been executed. Each party's right

753

to performance under the contract is an asset belonging to that party. As a property interest, it is generally capable (with exceptions to be noted later) of being transferred (assigned) by sale, donation, or other means of disposition. When a party assigns rights under a contract (thereby becoming the assignor), ownership of those rights passes to the recipient (assignee) who is substituted for the assignor as the person entitled to performance. Instead of, or in addition to, assigning rights under a contract, a party may wish to transfer (delegate) all or some of her obligations under the contract. Unlike assignment, delegation is not based on any concept of ownership — one cannot own a duty. Nevertheless, it is also generally permissible provided that it does not impair the reasonable expectations of the party to whom the performance is due.

§19.2 THIRD-PARTY BENEFICIARIES

§19.2.1 The Distinction Between Intended and Incidental Beneficiaries

Contracts routinely benefit people who are not parties. For example, neighbors are benefitted by the aesthetic enjoyment of a well-groomed yard, resulting from a landscape maintenance contract between a homeowner and a gardener; nearby hotels are benefitted by a contract between a property owner and builder to erect a new convention center. In fact, in a complex interactive economy, vast numbers of contracts between strangers allow people to enjoy facilities and services that would otherwise not be available. However, even though these bystanders may derive some advantage from the contract, and even have an important stake in its performance, they have no legal rights under the contract. Therefore, if the landscaper or builder breaches the contract by failing to perform, the adjacent property owners have no cause of action to enforce it. They are known as incidental beneficiaries — the benefit they anticipated was purely a fortuitous and incidental result of a transaction between others. The contracting parties may have been pleased, indifferent, or resentful to see someone else derive benefits from their contract, but they did not make the contract for the purpose of conferring those benefits.

However, in contrast to these more commonplace situations in which the positive effects of the contract on a third party occur merely by happenstance, a contract may be entered for the deliberate purpose of bestowing a benefit — and more importantly, a power to enforce that benefit — on a third party. That is, a contract is properly described as for the benefit of a third party only if it manifests the intent to give a benefit to a third party, directly enforceable by that third party against the contracting party who undertakes to perform it. It is the creation of this directly enforceable right that is the hallmark of a contract for the benefit of a third party. For example, Debbie Tor owes $20,000 to Len Der. Debbie enters into a contract with Wendy Vendee under which Debbie sells a plot of land to Wendy for $20,000, and the contract stipulates that Wendy will pay the $20,000 to Len. Debbie's purpose, of course, is to have the proceeds of the property transmitted directly to Len to settle the debt. In this case, the payment to Len does not occur as a fortuitous result of the contract but is specifically called for by it. Len's benefit is not merely incidental, but is clearly contemplated and deliberately conferred. If it is expressed or can be reasonably inferred that the parties, in contracting for the performance to be rendered to Len, also intended to give Len the right to enforce Wendy's promise of performance directly and independently of Debbie, Len acquires the status of intended beneficiary.

When a contract is intended to confer a benefit on and create enforcement rights in a third-party beneficiary, the contracting party who is to render the performance to the beneficiary (in the example above, Wendy) is usually referred to as the promisor, and the contracting party whose right to performance has been conferred on the beneficiary (in the above example, Debbie) is usually called the promisee. This nomenclature could be confusing because in a bilateral contract the terms "promisor" and "promisee" are relative — each party is both a promisor with regard to his own performance and a promisee with regard to the performance promised by the other. However, as we look at the contracting parties from the perspective of the third-party beneficiary, "promisor" means the party who has committed to perform in favor of the beneficiary. Diagram 19A illustrates the basic relationship and the terminology.

Diagram 19A

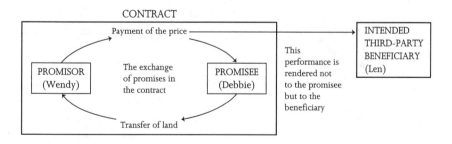

If the parties intend to confer the status of intended beneficiary on someone, that person is likely to be specifically named or identified in the contract. If this is not so, the strong inference is that the benefit is merely incidental. However, this conclusion is not inevitable. Intent to benefit is a matter of interpretation. Provided that the beneficiary will be identifiable when the time for performance falls due, it could be apparent that the parties did intend to create rights in his favor, despite the lack of specific identification at the time of contracting.

§19.2.2 The Essence of Intended Beneficiary Status: The Right of Independent Enforcement

As indicated above, when a contract confers the status of intended beneficiary on a third party, this does not mean only that performance must be rendered to or for the third party's benefit. It also means, as Restatement, Second, §304 provides, that the contract manifests the intent to grant the beneficiary an independent cause of action to enforce the promise. The grant of this enforcement right in the beneficiary is the central point of the third-party beneficiary doctrine and the distinguishing feature of a contract for the benefit of a third party. The beneficiary's direct cause of action against the promisor can be of great importance in making the benefit meaningful. He can pursue the right to performance on his own and does not have to depend on the promisee to take action on his behalf.

In the above example, if Len had no independent right of enforcement, he would not be able to sue Wendy, the promisor, if she failed to perform in his favor as promised. Debbie, the promisee, would be the only person who could sue Wendy for the payment, and Len's only claim would be against Debbie, his debtor under the loan contract. However, as an intended beneficiary, Len can sue Wendy directly if she fails to pay. He has this right of direct enforcement in addition to his right to sue Debbie under the loan contract, so he has two people against whom he can seek recourse for the unpaid loan. (Of course, he can only obtain a single satisfaction of his claim, so one of them is released from liability to him to the extent that the other pays). This is represented in Diagram 19B.

English common law did not recognize such a direct cause of action in the beneficiary unless the beneficiary could establish either that the promisee was acting as his agent, or that the contract created a trust. However, in the mid-nineteenth century, the concept of direct enforcement by the beneficiary developed in American law. *Lawrence v. Fox*, 20 N.Y. 268 (1859), is recognized as the groundbreaking case. A man named Holly lent $300 to Fox. Holly was indebted to Lawrence for the same amount, and so Holly and Fox agreed that Fox would repay the loan amount to Lawrence. When he failed to pay, Lawrence sued Fox, who defended the suit on the basis that Lawrence had no standing to sue because he was not a party to the contract—there was no privity between them. The court rejected this defense and articulated the principle that even where no agency or trust is established, the parties to a contract do have the power to create rights enforceable by a person who is not a party to a contract, and that person can sue the promisor to enforce the performance undertaken to the promisee for his benefit.

Diagram 19B

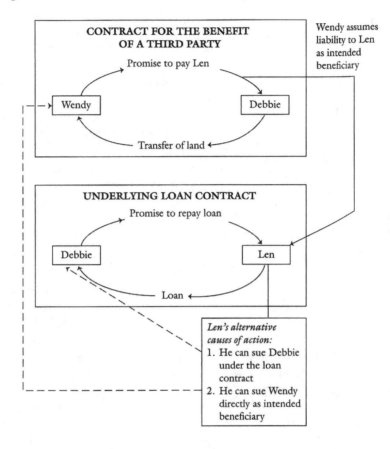

§19.2.3 The Intent to Confer an Independent Right of Enforcement

The recognition of enforcement rights in a nonparty may seem like a radical departure from the general concept of contract as a private consensual arrangement that creates rights only between those who have bound themselves to each other. However, the third-party beneficiary doctrine is consistent with that concept because the third party only acquires the right to enforce the benefit if it is apparent that the parties intended to give him that right — they have elected to create the beneficiary status as part of their agreement. As stressed already, it is not enough that the contracting parties expect or intend to benefit the third party, or even that the contract calls for performance to be rendered to the third party. It must also manifest the intention to give the third party the right to enforce the performance if it is not rendered. This is reflected in Restatement, Second, §302(1), which recognizes a "right to performance" (which means the right to enforce the performance) in the beneficiary only when it is appropriate to effectuate the intention of the parties.

Like all other contract terms, the intent to establish third-party enforcement rights is a matter of interpretation. If the contract expressly articulates the intent to confer or not to confer enforcement rights on a third party, the resolution of this question is relatively easy. If, as commonly happens, the contract does not clearly articulate the parties' intent, it must be gleaned by the normal process of interpreting the factual evidence of intent, and if that is inconclusive, by construing what the parties must reasonably have intended. As usual, an objective test is used, and it is the mutual intent of the parties that is relevant, not the uncommunicated subjective intent of just one of them. It is not enough that the promisee intends to confer the benefit on the beneficiary. The promisor must also have reasonably have understood that she was agreeing to assume an obligation to the beneficiary.

A few cases illustrate the process of interpretation where the contract does not expressly designate a third party as an intended beneficiary. *Martis v. Grinnell Mutual Reinsurance Company*, 905 N.E.2d 920 (Ill. App. 2009), involved a contract between Grinnell, an insurance company, and an employer whose workers were insured against injury. The policy stated that the insurer was "directly and primarily liable to any person entitled to benefits payable by this insurance." The plaintiff was a chiropractor who had provided medical services to one of the insured employees. He filed a class action suit against Grinnell, claiming that it had breached the contract with the employer by improperly applying a discount to the payments made to medical providers. He asserted standing to sue Grinnell on the basis that medical providers were intended beneficiaries of the insurance contract between Grinnell and the employer. The court disagreed and held that the plaintiff had not discharged the burden of showing that medical providers were intended beneficiaries of the policy. The policy language, "any person entitled to benefits," referred to the employees of the insured employer, and showed no intent to confer an independent right of action on providers, who were merely incidental beneficiaries.

In *Jackson v. American Plaza Corp.*, 2009 WL 1158829 (S.D.N.Y. 2009), the plaintiffs, who advertised room rentals on Craigslist, sued the defendant, a competitor who also advertised on the list, claiming that the defendant had violated the standard terms of use in its clickwrap agreement with Craigslist by making multiple postings of repetitive advertisements. The plaintiffs claimed that the multiple postings harmed their business, and they sought to enjoin this practice on the theory that they were intended beneficiaries of the terms of use. The court held that they were not. The terms of use did not expressly confer rights of enforcement on other list users. They made it clear that the consequence of making repetitive postings would be that Craigslist would block the postings, and that the only recourse available to a dissatisfied user was to discontinue use of the list. The court found that, interpreted as a whole, the sole purpose of the prohibition on repetitive advertisements was to prevent the overburdening of Craigslist's infrastructure.

By contrast, the court allowed the plaintiff to pursue a claim as an intended beneficiary in *Cianciotto v. Hospice Care Network*, 32 Misc. 3d 916 (N.Y. Dist. 2011). The plaintiff's terminally ill father had entered into a contract with the hospice under which the hospice would provide care for him for six months. The hospice ended the services after only a few weeks. After the father died, the plaintiff sued the hospice for breach of contract, claiming mental distress damages. The hospice sought summary judgment on the basis that it had no contract with the plaintiff. The court refused to grant the motion because it found that the plaintiff had a viable claim as an intended beneficiary of the contract between the hospice and her father. The contract recognized her by name as her father's primary caregiver and contemplated that the hospice care would relieve her of the responsibility to care for him in his declining condition. (The court also recognized that this may be a type of contract in which mental distress damages are recoverable, because its purpose was to relieve the plaintiff of mental anguish.[1])

§19.2.4 The Relevance of the Relationship Between the Promisee and the Beneficiary: Creditor and Donee Beneficiaries

As just mentioned, Restatement, Second, §302(1) sets forth a broad standard to guide the determination of whether a nonparty to the contract should be treated as an intended beneficiary: The recognition of the beneficiary's right to enforce performance must be appropriate to give effect to the parties' intent. The intent to confer the benefit is the central criterion and the focus of the inquiry. This is possibly all that needed to be said. However, motivated by a long tradition that it neither wishes to follow nor to abandon, §302(1) goes on to suggest what appears to be a second requirement: There must also be some relationship between the promisee and the beneficiary from which it can be inferred that the parties had the beneficiary's interests in mind when entering the contract. Although this seems to be set out as a prerequisite in addition to intent, it is really just a subset of the general inquiry into what the parties intended. If a relationship between the promisee and beneficiary can be identified to explain the motivation for conferring the benefit, the conclusion of intent to benefit is reinforced.

---

1. *See* section 18.13.1 for a discussion of mental distress damages.

This bipartite inquiry originates from the established conception, reflected in the first Restatement, that a beneficiary can be regarded as intended, rather than incidental, only if one of two conditions is satisfied. Either the beneficiary must be a creditor of the promisee, or it must be clear that the promisee intended to make a gift of the benefit to the beneficiary. The situation involving a creditor beneficiary has already been illustrated by both *Lawrence v. Fox* and our example involving Debbie, who made a contract with Wendy under which Wendy would render performance to Debbie's creditor, Len. This set of relationships is represented in Diagram 19C.

Diagram 19C

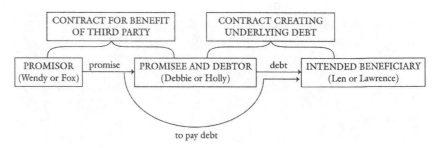

By contrast, if the promisee owes no debt to the third party, but intends to make a gift of the performance, the third party is a donee beneficiary. Although *Lawrence v. Fox* expressly dealt only with a creditor beneficiary, its basic principle was broad enough to be extended to cases in which the promisee was not indebted to the beneficiary. As a result, later cases recognized that a person could qualify as an intended beneficiary when the purpose of conferring the benefit was not to pay any debt, but to give her a gift. *Seaver v. Ransom*, 120 N.E. 639 (N.Y. 1918), is the most famous of these cases. A dying woman intended to bequeath a house to her niece. Upon being presented with a will that omitted this bequest, she agreed to sign on the strength of a promise by her husband, the residual legatee, that he would cure the omission by making provision in his own will for a bequest to the niece of equivalent value. When the husband eventually died, it was discovered that he had not made the bequest as he had promised his late wife. The niece sued his estate. The trial court gave judgment in favor of the niece on the theory that her uncle had held the house from his wife in constructive trust. Although it affirmed the judgment in favor of the niece, the court of appeals rejected the trust theory. Instead, basing its decision on *Lawrence* and subsequent cases, it found that there was no reason in principle to confine the third-party beneficiary doctrine to cases involving creditor beneficiaries. The uncle and aunt had made a contract under which the niece was an intended beneficiary, and she could enforce the promise against the uncle's estate.

As another illustration, say that Don Nation entered into a contract with Wendy Vendee under which he sold a plot of land to her for $20,000. His purpose in selling the land was not to pay a debt, as in the example involving Debbie, but to realize funds to be donated to his niece, Charity. Don therefore stipulates in the contract with Wendy that the sale price be paid directly to Charity. (Although the fact that Charity gave no consideration to Don for the benefit would preclude her from enforcing the promise against Don, the lack of consideration from Charity does not bar her suit against Wendy. The contract being enforced by Charity as an intended beneficiary is that between Don and Wendy, and consideration was exchanged between the parties to that contract.) This set of relationships is shown in Diagram 19D.

Diagram 19D

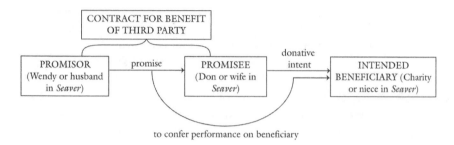

Section 302(1) attempts to move away from the creditor-donee dichotomy, which it finds too rigid and restrictive. However, it recognizes that the distinction is well ingrained in the case law and cannot be ignored. It therefore acknowledges the distinction but alters it to make it more flexible. Many courts have followed its lead. Section 302(1) identifies two types of situations in which it recognizes a relationship sufficient to bolster the conclusion that the beneficiary was intended: The first, set out in §302(1)(a), approximates the concept of creditor beneficiary by covering cases in which performance of the promise will satisfy a monetary obligation due by the promisee to the beneficiary. This is somewhat narrower than the original category, which included not only monetary obligations, but also situations in which performance of the promise would satisfy an actual, supposed, or asserted duty of the promisee to the beneficiary. The narrowing of this category is more than compensated for by the widening of the second. The second, set out in §302(1)(b) is based on, but more expansive than, the older category of donee beneficiaries. It encompasses not only situations in which gratuitous motives are apparent, but any case in which the circumstances indicate that the promisee intends to give the benefit of performance to the beneficiary. As just noted, this would include cases in which there is some supposed or asserted duty that is not clear enough to fall into §302(1)(a) as an actual liquidated monetary obligation. This sounds very vague and open-ended, but that is what is intended. The idea is to let courts decide case by case, with a strong focus on the parties' intent, as bolstered by some relationship between the promisee and the beneficiary that plausibly points to a motive for conferring the benefit.

§19.2.5 Vesting of the Benefit and the Parties' Power to Modify or Terminate It

In the same way as parties have the power to make a contract, they have the power to modify or terminate it by subsequent agreement. The alteration or discharge of a contract, like its creation, is dependent on the parties' assent.[2] It would therefore seem to follow that as the parties to the contract have created the beneficiary's rights, they could agree to change them or take them away entirely. However, if they had the unrestricted power to do this, the status of intended beneficiary would be very uncertain and unreliable. To protect the beneficiary's actual or potential reliance on the contract, the rule has been developed that at some point after the contract is made, the benefit vests in the beneficiary — it becomes irrevocably settled on her so that it cannot be changed or withdrawn by the contracting parties without her consent. If the parties do agree to modify or discharge the contract after the benefit has vested, this agreement binds the parties between themselves, but it binds only them. It does not affect the rights of the beneficiary, who can enforce the performance as it vested under the original agreement. It is therefore possible that the promisee could agree to give up her own rights of enforcement or to change them so that they are less extensive than those that have vested in the beneficiary.

Over the years, different courts have adopted various approaches to the question of when the benefit vests. Some have treated it as vesting immediately upon formation of the contract, but others have required some manifestation of acceptance or some act of reliance on it by the beneficiary. The original Restatement had different rules for vesting depending on whether the beneficiary was a donee or a creditor. Restatement, Second, §311(3) makes no such distinction. It seeks to clarify and standardize the rule for vesting, irrespective of the nature of the underlying relationship between the promisee and the beneficiary. It provides that the benefit vests in the beneficiary when she manifests assent to it at the request of one of the parties, or she sues on it, or she materially changes her position by acting in justifiable reliance on it. This formulation clearly shows the analogy between vesting and the formation of other promissory obligations. Its basis is quite akin to that for offer and acceptance or promissory estoppel: The right vests in the beneficiary either when she "accepts" it by manifesting assent to it, or when she has detrimentally relied on it. Once that has

---

2. Of course, consideration is generally required too, as discussed in sections 7.5.2 and 13.9.

occurred, the contracting parties are committed to the conferral of rights, and the beneficiary's independent cause of action on the promise is secure.

This rule is subject to a qualification: As creators of the benefit, the contracting parties can confer it subject to whatever limitations and conditions they see fit. By so stipulating in the contract, they can retain the power to modify it or take it away even after it has vested in the beneficiary. These limitations will inhere in the right created in favor of the beneficiary, and it will vest subject to them. However, the parties must clearly reserve the power to alter the rights after vesting. If they do not, their power to alter the rights, as against the beneficiary, terminates as soon as the benefit vests.

§19.2.6 The Promisee's Parallel Rights of Enforcement Against the Promisor

Notwithstanding the conferral and vesting of rights in the beneficiary, the promisee continues to be a party to the contract. As such, except to the extent that the beneficiary has enforced and obtained satisfaction of the performance, the promisee has the right to enforce the promise just as she would have had in an ordinary bilateral contract. Restatement, Second, §305(1) reflects this by stating that the promisor has a duty of performance to the promisee, even though he has a similar duty to the beneficiary. This does not mean that the promisor has to perform the obligation twice. The promisee's right against the promisor is discharged to the extent that the promisor performs in favor of the beneficiary. If full performance is not rendered to the beneficiary, the promisee may enforce the obligation to perform any remaining balance.

The nature of the relief available to the promisee depends on the circumstances. When a claim for damages is not an adequate remedy, she may request specific performance — an order compelling the promisor to render the performance to the beneficiary. Alternatively, the promisee may have a claim for damages based on her contractual expectation. This will at least consist of her direct damages, measured by the loss in value of the promised performance. In addition, if the failure to perform results in a foreseeable and unavoidable increase in the promisee's liability to the beneficiary or other consequential loss, consequential damages may also be claimed.

§19.2.7 The Promisor's Ability to Raise Defenses Against the Beneficiary

The beneficiary's rights derive from the contract, so it stands to reason that they are limited by any defense arising out of the contract. Therefore, the basic rule, as reflected in Restatement, Second, §309, is that unless the contract makes it clear that it confers rights on the beneficiary free of defenses, the beneficiary's rights are subject to any limitations inherent in the contract. The promisor may raise against the beneficiary any defense that would have been available against the promisee, arising out of a defect in the formation of the contract (such as invalidity due to lack of consideration, voidability on grounds of fraud, duress or some other bargaining defect, or unenforceability for failure to comply with the statute of frauds); or based on the promisee's breach of contract; or arising out of post-formation occurrences that affect the very basis of the contract, such as supervening impracticability and the nonoccurrence of a condition. (The beneficiary's position is very much like that of an assignee, discussed in section 19.3.3.)

Although a wrongful act of the promisee (such as breach or fraud) can be raised by the promisor as a defense against the beneficiary, it does not impose any liability on the beneficiary. He does not, by accepting the benefit, assume any responsibility for proper behavior or performance by the promisee. Any recourse that the promisor has must be pursued against the promisee.

Unless the contract expresses a contrary intent, the promisor cannot raise against the beneficiary any defense that is purely personal against the promisee, such as a defense that the promisee owes money to the promisor in another transaction. Similarly, as we saw in section 19.2.5, if the promisee and promisor make an agreement to modify or discharge the performance after vesting, this agreement would be a defense to enforcement by the promisee, but it would not avail against the beneficiary.

§19.2.8 The Beneficiary's Rights Against the Promisee in the Event of the Promisor's Nonperformance

As has been stated already, once the benefit has vested in the beneficiary, he has a direct claim against the promisor and may proceed to enforce it if the promisor fails to perform. However, it may occur that the beneficiary is unsuccessful in obtaining satisfaction of his claim against the promisor either because the promisor has no money or assets to satisfy the claim, or because she is able to raise a defense against the beneficiary. When that happens, the question is whether the beneficiary may then proceed against the promisee. The answer depends on whether the beneficiary is a creditor or donee.

If the beneficiary is a donee, his relationship with the promisee is not supported by consideration. Therefore, the beneficiary has no enforceable claim against the promisee in the event that he is unable to recover from the promisor. However, if the beneficiary is a creditor of the promisee, he may, upon being unsuccessful in pursuing his claim against the promisor, proceed against the promisee to enforce the promisee's debt.

Some courts have not allowed the creditor beneficiary to sue the promisee after unsuccessfully trying to enforce rights against the promisor. They have held that once the beneficiary elects to proceed against the promisor, the right of action against the promisor is substituted for and eliminates the cause of action on the original debt due by the promisee. (This is called novation.) However, the more common contemporary view, as expressed in Restatement, Second, §310, is that the beneficiary surrenders no rights against the promisee by seeking to enforce the benefit against the promisor. Instead, the promisee becomes a surety for the promisor, so that to the extent that the promisor fails to perform, the promisee remains liable for the outstanding amount of her undischarged debt to the beneficiary. (And, of course, the promisee may then attempt to recover from the promisor, based on the promisor's breach of her contract with the promisee.) This is shown in Diagram 19E.

Diagram 19E

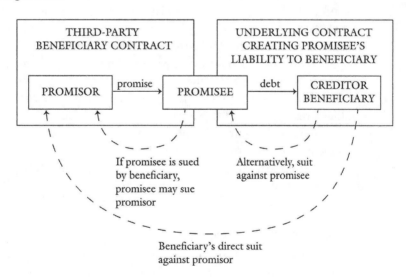

§19.2.9 Citizens' Claims as Intended Beneficiaries of Government Contracts

The government represents the public. In a broad sense, it can therefore be said that whenever the government enters a contract, it has the intention of conferring a benefit on the citizenry at large, or on a group of citizens whose interests are furthered by the contract. However, this does not mean that an individual citizen can sue to enforce the performance promised to the government. As with other contracts that result in a benefit to a nonparty, the crucial question is not simply whether there was an intent to provide the benefit, but whether there was an intent to create an independent right of enforcement in the nonparty. Therefore, as Restatement, Second, §313(1) makes clear, government contracts are to be treated the same as contracts by private parties in deciding whether a third party was an intended beneficiary: The terms of the contract must be interpreted in context to determine if it manifests the intent to confer a direct cause of action on the beneficiary. However, this is qualified by a general presumption that the government does not generally intend to confer a private right of enforcement on citizens, who are usually just incidental beneficiaries of government contracts. To overcome this presumption, a citizen must demonstrate clear intent to grant a right of enforcement to citizens in the contract, and in any legislation that authorizes the contract. Comment *a* to §313 reflects this approach by suggesting that in cases of doubt, the contract should be interpreted as not making citizens intended beneficiaries.

For example, in *Klamath Water Users Protective Ass'n. v. Patterson*, 204 F.3d 1206 (9th Cir. 1999) irrigators claimed that they were the intended beneficiaries of a government agency's contract with a power company for the management of a dam. They argued that they therefore had the independent right to enforce the power company's obligation to maintain flow levels required by the contract. Although the court recognized that one of the goals of the contract was to satisfy the government's duty to water users, it had other aims as well, and there was nothing in the contract to rebut the usual presumption that citizens who benefit from a government contract are incidental beneficiaries with no private enforcement rights. In *Edwards v. Aurora Loan Services, LLC*, 791 F. Supp. 2d 144 (D.C. 2011), the court stressed the strong general presumption that citizens are merely incidental beneficiaries of government contracts. To rebut that presumption, the language of the contract must demonstrate a clear intent to confer enforcement rights on citizens who benefit by the contract. The court held that the plaintiffs had not discharged this burden in relation to a contract entered into between the U.S. Treasury (through the agency of Fannie Mae) and loan servicers, under which the loan servicers were obliged to modify the mortgages of home-owners in danger of foreclosure.

By contrast, the court did find that citizens were intended beneficiaries of a government contract in *Zigas v. Superior Court*, 174 Cal. Rptr. 806 (Cal. App. 1981). The owner of an apartment building violated its contract with HUD to keep rentals within prescribed limits. The court decided that the sole purpose of both the contract and its authorizing legislation was to benefit tenants by keeping rents at a reasonable level and that the parties must reasonably have intended to give tenants an independent cause of action to enforce the rent limitation. The court reached this conclusion because the tenants, not the government, lost as a result of the breach, the statute provided no other procedure for tenants to seek redress, the tenants' suit did not interfere with any remedial or administrative proceedings prescribed by the statute, and there was nothing in the contract that indicated that the parties expected that the owner would be shielded from tenant suits.

§19.3 ASSIGNMENT AND DELEGATION

§19.3.1 The Basic Concept and Terminology

Section 19.2 is concerned with cases in which the parties to a contract intend, at the time of entering it, to confer an enforceable benefit on someone who is not a party to the contract. Although assignment and delegation also involve the introduction of a third party into the contract, the circumstances under which that happens and the legal relationship that arises is very different from that of a third-party beneficiary. We are not here concerned with a contract in which, at the time of contracting, the parties intend to confer rights on a third party. Rather, we deal with a decision made by one of the parties, after the contract has been entered, to transfer his rights, or his duties, or both to a third party. Because we are dealing with the transfer of contractual rights and obligations, the issue of whether transfer is permitted can arise only subsequent to the formation of the contract that created those rights and obligations. That is, assignment and delegation are only possible once a contract has been made and those rights and obligations have come into existence.[3]

It is useful to begin with the terminology used to describe such a transfer and its participants: The transfer of rights is called an assignment, and the transfer of duties is a delegation. The person who assigns a contractual right is the obligee under the contract and becomes the assignor. The person to whom it is assigned is the assignee. The other party to the contract, whose duty is transferred to the assignee by the assignment, is referred to as the obligor. A person who delegates her contractual duty is the obligor under the contract and becomes the delegator of the duty. The person who assumes the duty is called the delegate (not delegatee). The other party to the

---

3. This must be distinguished from the rule that applies in the precontract period. As noted in section 4.7, the power to accept an offer is personal to the offeree and cannot be transferred unless the offer so authorizes. This rule does not apply to a valid option — a promise exchanged for consideration not to revoke the offer. As explained in section 4.13.3, the option is a contract in itself and the right to accept the offer in the option period is a binding contractual right. It can therefore be assigned.

contract, whose right to performance has been delegated, is called the obligee. The relationships are shown in Diagram 19F, in which Party 2 is the person who decides to assign her obligations or delegate her duties.

Diagram 19F

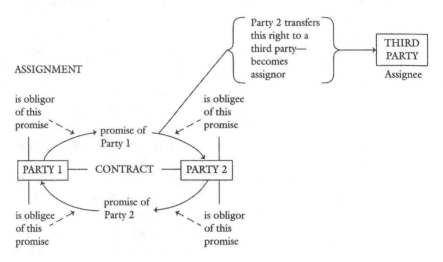

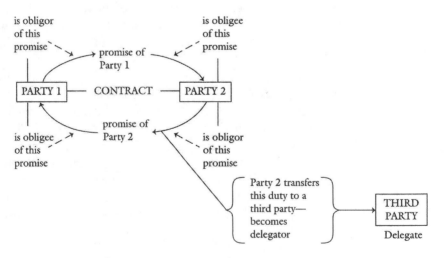

It is important to recognize that a contractual right is an asset of the obligee—an item of property with some value. Therefore, subject to some qualifications stated in section 19.3.3, the owner of a contractual right can transfer it like any other property—sell it, donate it, or use it as collateral.

The law generally presumes that contract rights can be transferred, except where the contract or public policy precludes it. By contrast, contractual obligations are not property rights of the obligor. In addition, the transfer of those duties could have a more significant impact on the rights of the obligee. Therefore, the presumption of transferability is not as strong as it is with contractual rights, and the delegation of contract duties is subject to greater restrictions than the assignment of rights. Nevertheless, if the obligor under a contract wishes to transfer the contract as a whole (including both her rights and obligations) or wishes merely to delegate her performance duties to someone else, she may usually delegate her duties, subject to the restrictions set out in section 19.3.6 and 19.3.7. We can therefore state the well-established rule, reflected in Restatement, Second, §317(2) and UCC §2.210(2), that unless a contract specifically prohibits a party from transferring her rights acquired and duties assumed under it, or the nature of the contract is such that the transfer would impair the other party's reasonable expectations or would offend public policy, a party has the power to transfer contractual rights and obligations.

§19.3.2 The Nature of an Assignment

An assignment is a voluntary manifestation of intention by the holder of an existing right to make an immediate transfer of that right to another person. This definition breaks down into two essential components: First, the assignor must voluntarily manifest intent to assign the right; second, the right must be in existence at the time of assignment, and its transfer must take effect immediately.

Although a right can be transferred without the consent of the rightholder (for example, where a judgment creditor executes on the right by the process of garnishment, or the rightholder becomes bankrupt and the right passes to the trustee of his estate), we consider here only the voluntary assignment of rights. In most cases, assignment is effected through a contract between the assignor and the assignee, but the transaction does not have to qualify as a contract. For example, a right may be transferred gratuitously so that the transfer is a gift rather than under a contract with consideration. Unless the contract creating the right forbids its assignment without the assent of the obligor, he need not be involved in the assignment.

There are some specialized types of assignment involving rights evidenced by commercial paper (such as negotiable instruments or documents) for which prescribed formalities must be satisfied. Apart from these transactions, which are beyond our scope, there are no particular formalities needed for an assignment of ordinary contract rights, but the transaction may be subject to the statute of frauds.

As section 19.3.4 explains, the effect of an assignment is to extinguish the assignor's right to performance from the obligee and to transfer it to the assignee. For such a complete transfer to occur, the right must be in existence and transferred immediately. Furthermore, the transfer must be a complete relinquishment of the right by the assignor in favor of the assignee, so that the assignor retains no control over it and no power to revoke it. This absolute and unequivocal transfer is necessary for the protection of the obligor, who must be able to rely on the fact that performance in favor of the assignee will discharge her obligation.

A right comes into existence and can be assigned as soon as the contract creating it has been formed. The right can be conditional or not yet due at the time of assignment as long as it has been created already. For example, *Speelman v. Pascal*, 10 N.Y. 2d 313 (1961) involved the assignment of rights to a percentage of profits from the hit musical *My Fair Lady*. In 1952, Pascal acquired the rights from the estate of the late George Bernard Shaw to produce a musical based on his play *Pygmalion*. Before he even wrote the musical, he assigned a share of his profits to his secretary. He died soon thereafter, and the musical was not produced and staged until after his death. The court held the assignment to be effective. Although the musical was not yet in existence at the time of the assignment, the rights to future profits did exist and could be assigned. The assignee is bound by any conditions of performance and cannot enforce the right until such conditions have been satisfied and the maturity date of the right has arrived.

The assignment of a conditional or unmatured right must be distinguished from the transfer of a right that has not yet been created, but is expected to arise in the future. This does not qualify as an assignment. It may be a valid contract between the transferor and transferee, but it lacks the hallmark of an assignment — enforceability against the obligor. Similarly, a promise to assign an existing right in the future does not constitute an assignment. To constitute an assignment effective against the obligor, the transfer of the right must actually be accomplished, so that the transferee acquires it immediately.

§19.3.3 Restrictions on Assignment

As noted in section 19.3.1, the general approach of the law is that contract rights should be freely assignable because the obligee's right to performance under the contract is his property. It is property of a nature different from, say, his car or his house, in that it has no tangible physical existence. (It is called a "chose in action.") Nevertheless, it is his property all the same, and he should be able to dispose of it if he so desires. However, this right of disposition is subject to a qualification that arises from the nature of this particular kind of property. Unlike a car or house, a contract right represents a relationship with the obligor, who also has rights under it. Therefore, the obligee's power to deal with this property is tempered by the need to assure the obligor of her contractual expectation. Accordingly, the right cannot be assigned if doing so would violate the terms of the contract or otherwise materially impair the obligor's rights under it.

a. Contractual Restrictions on Assignment

An assignment cannot be validly made if the contract prohibits it. Because the law generally favors assignment, the contractual bar must be clearly expressed. Restatement, Second, §322 and UCC §2.210(3) call for a restrictive interpretation of contract provisions that appear to preclude assignment. Any doubt or ambiguity should be resolved in favor of transferability, and a clause that prohibits "assignment of the contract" should, if possible, be taken to forbid only the delegation of duties. Even if the contract does clearly prohibit assignment, this does not necessarily mean that an assignment would be invalid. Unless the language clearly deprives the obligee of the power to assign (for example, by stating that an assignment will be void), the assignment may be a breach of the contract (giving the obligor grounds for seeking a remedy for breach), but the transfer of rights is itself effective.

Instead of absolutely forbidding assignment, a contract may prohibit it without the consent of the party whose rights are being assigned. The general approach to a provision that requires permission to assign is reflected in *Julian v. Christopher*, 575 A.2d 735 (Md. 1990). Unless the contract makes it clear that the party has complete discretion to refuse permission, he is obliged to act reasonably in refusing it. This usually means, in effect, that he cannot legitimately refuse permission unless he can show that the assignment would be unduly burdensome or risky to him or would materially affect his contract rights.

b. Restrictions on Assignment Resulting from the Nature of the Contract

Even if the contract does not, by its terms, forbid or restrict assignment, rights under the contract may not be assigned, in the absence of specific authorization in the contract, if assignment would materially change the obligor's duty, increase the burden or risk imposed by the contract, impair her prospects of getting return performance, or otherwise substantially reduce its value to her. This is recognized by Restatement, Second, §317(2) and UCC §2.210(2). Every assignment is likely to have some effect on the obligor's duty, even if that is nothing more than having to make a payment to someone other than the person she contracted with. The requirement of material impact prevents the obligor from resisting an assignment on the basis of some trivial change in her performance obligation.

To decide whether an assignment may have any of these materially adverse consequences, the contract must be interpreted in context. In many cases, especially when the performance in question is nothing more than the payment of money or the delivery of property, an assignment of rights is unlikely to have any negative impact on the obligor. It is a matter of indifference to her whether she pays or delivers to the original person with whom she contracted or to someone else designated by that person. However, in some contracts, the identity of the party who is to receive performance is important, and the obligor does have a stake in performing only for the original obligee. This may be true, for example, when performance is subject to a condition of satisfaction involving personal taste, or when the obligor reasonably expected to get some special advantage or credit by being associated with the obligee. (Cases like this may alternatively be viewed not as pure assignments, but as also involving a delegation of duty, on the ground that the obligee has a contractual duty to evaluate performance in good faith or to receive performance personally.)

c. Restrictions Based on Statute or Public Policy

Apart from any contractual barrier to assignment, the transfer of certain types of contract rights are contrary to the public interest, and therefore prohibited by statute or public policy. A common example is the statutory prohibition on the assignment of a claim for wages, intended to protect workers from disposing of earnings in advance of receiving them. Another example is a claim against an attorney for malpractice. Many courts have held the assignment of a legal malpractice claim to be contrary to public policy because of the uniquely personal nature of the attorney-client relationship, which implicates confidentiality, loyalty, and trust. Some courts consider that public policy absolutely bars assignment of a malpractice claim, while others, such as *Gurski v. Rosenblum & Filan LLC*, 885 A.2d 163 (Conn. 2005) adopt a case-by-case approach that takes into account the nature of the breach and the circumstances of the assignment. In *Gurski*, the court held the assignment to be invalid because the assignee was the adversary of the client in the very action in which the malpractice was committed. That is, to settle the action in which the attorney had committed the malpractice, the client assigned his malpractice claim to the other party to the suit.

The assignment of claims that do not arise from contract is beyond our scope. However, it is worth noting that public policy forbids the assignment of certain kinds of noncontractual claims. For example, a tort claim for personal injury cannot be assigned because the trafficking in claims harms the public interest by enabling a litigious person to purchase and aggressively prosecute personal injury claims and by encouraging a tort victim to give up a potentially more valuable claim for advance payment.[4]

---

4. This prohibition against the assignment of tort claims for personal injury has ties to the age-old common law policy against maintenance and champerty — the promotion of litigation for profit by persons who finance it in exchange for receiving part of the proceeds.

§19.3.4 The Effect of Assignment

The following simple example illustrates the basic effect and purpose of an assignment: Lender lends $10,000 to Borrower, who undertakes to repay the loan with interest in six months. After the loan is advanced, Lender no longer wishes to wait six months to get her money back. She therefore sells her contractual right of repayment to Finance Co. In this case, Lender is simply treating her contract right as a saleable asset and seeks to realize its economic worth.[5] Unless there is a term in the contract that forbids assignment, the transfer will surely be permissible, because it is not likely to have any materially adverse effect on Borrower's contractual burdens or expectations. Borrower has already received the performance of Lender's promise (advance of the loan funds) and his remaining duty is clear and not subject to any discretion or cooperation by the obligee. Borrower must simply pay a specified sum of money on a stated date. Lender falls out of the transaction and Finance Co. is substituted as the obligee. When the time for repayment comes, Borrower will pay Finance Co. Of course, Borrower must be notified of the assignment so that he knows (or reasonably should know) this. If he is not, his payment to Lender will discharge his duty. This transaction is represented in Diagram 19G.

Diagram 19G

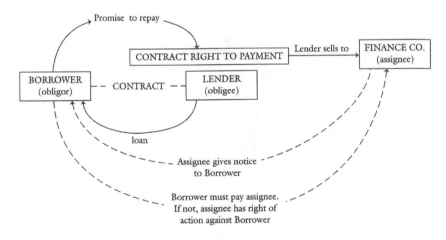

---

5. Of course, as it is an intangible right, its value is dependent on Borrower's creditworthiness. It will therefore not be sold at its face value, but its price will be discounted to take account of the risk of default. This discount, together with the prospect of earning the interest payable by Borrower under the contract, may make this an attractive purchase for a buyer like Finance Co. that is willing to take the risk of default in the hope of gaining more than it paid.

In this example, Lender assigned her contract right by sale, but sale is not the only reason for transferring rights. They may also be transferred for security — that is, used as collateral to secure a loan,[6] used to settle a preexisting debt, or simply donated as a gift. Also, Lender assigned her entire right in the example, but she could have assigned just a portion of the performance, provided that a partial assignment would not materially burden Borrower.

After a valid assignment is made, the assignee substitutes for the assignor as the person to whom performance must be rendered. It therefore follows that although the obligor need not be a party to or assent to the assignment to make it effective, she must be notified of it so that she knows the person to whom performance is now due. There is no particular formality required for the notice, provided that it coherently indicates what right has been assigned, and to whom. The notice must be received by the obligor — that is, it must either come to her attention or be delivered so that she reasonably should be aware of it. Either the assignor or the assignee may give the notice, but if it comes from the assignee, the obligor is entitled to adequate proof of the assignment.

If the obligor performs in favor of the assignor before receiving this notification, her obligation is discharged and she has no responsibility to the assignee. However, after receiving clear and adequate notification, the obligor, in effect, holds the performance in trust for the assignee and is obliged to ensure that he receives it. If the obligor disregards the assignment and performs for the assignor, she incurs personal liability to the assignee and will be obliged either to perform again or pay damages.[7] If the obligor pays the assignor after notice of assignment, he cannot defend against liability to the assignee merely on the ground that the assignor unilaterally countermanded his prior instruction to pay the assignee. For example, in Herzog v. Irace, 594 A.2d 1106 (Me. 1991), a client instructed his attorney to make payment of settlement proceeds to a creditor of the client — a doctor to whom the client owed fees for medical treatment. The client later changed his mind and told the attorney to pay

---

6. It is common for an assignment to be used for the purpose of securing a loan. While an important aspect of commercial transacting, the transfer of intangible rights as security is subject to complex and detailed rules that are beyond our scope. However, a brief description of the basic structure of such a transaction may be helpful: The owner of the contract right does not sell it outright, but instead borrows the needed funds and transfers the right to the lender as security for his promise to repay the money. In such a case, the transfer is not absolute. The secured creditor retains an interest in the contract right until such time as the loan is repaid, but has the right to foreclose on the security and collect payment of the contract performance in the event that its debtor defaults. There are variations on this format that need not concern us here.

7. Here again, there are special rules concerning the transfer of negotiable instruments and documents, for which notification alone is not enough.

the settlement to him, which the attorney did. When the doctor sued the attorney, the attorney argued that he had an ethical obligation to honor his client's instructions. The court disagreed. The attorney was aware that the client had assigned his payment right to the doctor, so the client no longer had a right to the settlement proceeds and could not validly revoke his instruction to pay the doctor.

§19.3.5 Defenses Against the Assignee

As a general rule, when rights are assigned, the assignee can get no greater right against the obligor than the assignor had. This is in accordance with the rather obvious proposition that when a person disposes of property, he cannot validly transfer more than what he owns. (Again, there are some important exceptions to this rule in the case of negotiable instruments and documents, but these are beyond our scope.) This means that the assignee takes the rights subject to any conditions and defenses that the obligor may have against the assignor arising out of the contract. For example, if the contract is avoidable by the obligor or unenforceable because of a defect in formation of the contract, or the obligor's duty is subject to an unsatisfied condition, or the assignor breached the contract, or the obligor's performance has become impracticable, these defenses can be raised against the assignee in the same way as they could have been against the assignor.

As in the case of a third-party beneficiary, the obligor may only use the assignor's breach defensively against the assignee. That is, the assignor's breach operates as a defense to the assignee's claim, and damages due to the obligor by the assignor may be offset against the assignee's claim. However, the assignee has no liability for the obligor's damages to the extent that they exceed the amount of the offset.

The obligor's right to assert defenses arising out of the contract is not cut off by the notice of assignment, so the defense is available against the assignee whether the basis for it (for example, the assignor's breach) arose before or after the obligor received notice. However, the notice does affect any claim of set off that the obligor may have against the assignor, arising out of a different transaction. The rule is that the assignee's rights are subject to any such right of set off that arose before a notice of assignment, but cannot be defeated by one that arose afterwards. For example, say that Lender lent $10,000 to Borrower. In a completely separate contract, entered into a short while later, Borrower sold her car to Lender for $5,000. Lender took delivery of the car but failed to pay Borrower. When the time comes for Borrower to repay the loan, she has the right to deduct the $5,000 owed to her by Lender — she may set off the debt due to her under the car sale transaction against the debt that she owes Lender. If Lender has assigned his rights under the loan contract, Borrower's right of set off may be asserted against the assignee provided that the right had not been assigned and notice of assignment received by her before the set off right arose. However, if she received notice of assignment before the set off right was created, the claim of set off may not be raised against the assignee.

Unless the assignment indicates an intent to the contrary, the assignor impliedly warrants to the assignee that the rights assigned are valid and not subject to any defenses. Therefore, if the obligor successfully raises a defense against the assignee, the assignee usually has a cause of action against the assignor for breach of this warranty.

§19.3.6 Delegation

Restatement, Second, §318 and UCC §2.210(1) set out the basic principles of delegation: An obligor is entitled to delegate his contractual duties unless this violates the contract or public policy. As this suggests, the law's general approach to delegation is much like that toward assignment. A party should be given the freedom to engage someone else to perform his contractual duties unless the contract prohibits this or the delegation otherwise impairs the obligee's reasonable expectations. However, delegation is not a transfer of a right, so it does not invoke the policy that protects a person's interest in dealing with her property as she desires. In addition, it stands to reason that while a mere assignment of rights will often make little difference to the other party's contractual expectations, a delegation of duty could quite likely have a direct impact on them. This is particularly true if the contract is founded on the personal attributes or skills of the obligor. For these reasons, delegation is subject to greater restriction than assignment.

Irrespective of whether the performance involves special skill or attributes, if the contract makes it clear that delegation is forbidden, this expressed intent will be given effect. A party is entitled, by so stipulating in the contract, to absolutely preclude the delegation of any duty owed to her. In the absence of a clear prohibition, delegation is allowed unless the obligee has a substantial interest in having the obligor himself perform or control the duty. This would be the case where the contract contemplates personal performance by the obligor or the obligor was chosen because of some particular attribute, skill, or talent relevant to performance. An impermissible delegation may in itself be a repudiation of the contract by the delegator, which may allow the obligee to declare advance breach and claim damages. If the obligee gives the delegator an opportunity to retract the delegation and he fails to do so in time and to render personal performance, this becomes a breach.

The effect of a permissible and effective delegation is that the delegator commits no breach of the contract by having his duty performed by the delegate, and the delegate's conforming performance discharges the delegator's contractual obligation. If a performance is properly delegated but the obligee refuses to accept it, this will be a breach by the obligee in the same way as it would have been to refuse the delegator's own performance.

Unlike assignment, delegation does not result in a complete substitution of the delegate for the delegator. Unless the obligee agrees (either in the contract or subsequently) to release the delegator from any further responsibility, he remains obligated under the contract. He cannot unilaterally release himself from his commitment to the obligee. Therefore, if the delegate fails to perform or renders a defective performance, this is as much a breach by the delegator as his own deficient performance would have been.

The delegate's nonperformance or defective performance could also render the delegate himself liable to the obligee but this is not inevitably so. It depends on whether the delegate has assumed the duty to the obligee by promising to perform it. Such a promise could be made directly to the obligee, or it could arise where the delegate has promised the delegator to perform, and this can be interpreted as a contract for the benefit of the obligee, as an intended third-party beneficiary. It is possible, therefore, that both the delegator and the delegate will be liable to the obligee in the event of the delegate's breach.

The following example illustrates how delegation may operate: Owner enters into a contract with Painter under which Painter undertakes to repaint the exterior of Owner's home for $5,000. Just before the work is due to begin, Painter decides that he does not wish to do the painting himself, so he hires Subcontractor to do it. (There is no assignment here because Painter does not transfer his payment right to Subcontractor, but makes a separate contract to pay him an hourly wage.) The delegation is established by a separate contract between Painter and Subcontractor under which Painter engages Subcontractor to do the job. (Painter may keep a profit from the transaction by paying Subcontractor less than the price to be paid by Owner.) Assuming that Owner's contract with Painter does not expressly prohibit delegation or contemplate that Painter does the work personally, Painter's delegation of the performance is likely to be permissible. However, if Painter had been engaged to paint a mural on the side of the house, there would be a strong argument that the contract is based on his individual craftsmanship, and his performance may not be delegated. Delegation is shown in Diagram 19H.

Diagram 19H

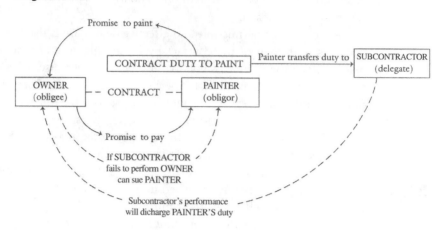

§19.3.7 "Assignment" of the Contract: The Assignment of Rights and Delegation of Duties

In the immediately preceding example involving the housepainting contract, Painter did not assign his rights against Owner. He retained his right to her contractual performance (payment of the $5,000) and made a separate arrangement to remunerate Subcontractor. However, Painter could have decided to transfer his entire package of rights and duties under the contract. This is sometimes referred to loosely as an assignment of Painter's contract. Restatement, Second, §328(1) more properly characterizes it as both an assignment of Painter's rights under the contract and a delegation of his duties. (UCC §2.210(4) provides similarly for the assignment of a contract for the sale of goods.) Painter is an obligor who delegates and an obligee who assigns. Subcontractor is the assignee of his rights and the delegate of his duties, and Owner is both the obligee as regards the delegated duty and the obligor as regards the assigned rights.

The transaction is subject to the rules governing both assignment and delegation. Where a contract is assigned as a whole, the assignment of rights may be unobjectionable, but the delegation of duties may reduce the value of the return performance reasonably expected by the original party. If so, the contract may not be assigned. This occurred in *Sally Beauty Co., Inc. v. Nexxus Products Co., Inc.*, 801 F.2d 1001 (7th Cir. 1986). Best Barber and Beauty Supply Co. was an exclusive distributor of Nexxus products. It sought to assign the exclusive distributorship to Sally which was owned by a competitor of Nexxus. Nexxus objected to the assignment of the contract on the grounds that the contract was for personal services and was based on a relationship of trust and confidence between the officers of Nexxus and Best. The court found the assignment of the contract rights was permissible.

The contract did not involve services of a special or unique nature and the relationship between the management of Nexxus and Best was irrelevant. Even in the absence of assignment, corporate officers can change and neither party had the guarantee that they would be able to deal with the same officers throughout the term of the contract. The court did find, however, that the delegation of Best's duties under the distributorship deprived Nexxus of the benefit of its bargain because the distribution of its products would be in the hands of its competitor. (The dissent felt that this was not a good reason to preclude delegation because Sally would be obliged to use best efforts in selling Nexxus products.)

§19.3.8 Grounds for Insecurity Following Assignment or Delegation

When the assignment of a right or the delegation of a duty does not clearly impair the obligee's expectation of performance, but it gives the obligee reasonable grounds for insecurity, Restatement, Second, §317, Comment d, and UCC §2.210(5) recognize the obligee's right to demand adequate assurances of performance. In an assignment, the assignor could be called upon to assure the obligor that the transfer of rights will not impair the obligor's prospect of return performance. In a delegation, the obligee may demand the assurance of proper performance, as appropriate, either from the delegator or the delegate. This process is equivalent to the demand for assurances discussed in section 17.7.5, when a promisee is concerned about the possibility of repudiation. If, following a justifiable demand, the person to whom it is addressed gives an adequate assurance that the performance will be rendered in accordance with the contract, the reasonable concern about impairment is resolved. If adequate assurances are not given, the assignment or delegation may be objected to. In some circumstances, the lack of assurance of performance may go beyond precluding effective transfer. It could amount to a repudiation by the assignor or delegator, permitting the other party to seek relief for anticipatory breach.

§19.4 A TRANSNATIONAL PERSPECTIVE ON THIRD-PARTY BENEFICIARIES, ASSIGNMENT, AND DELEGATION

The CISG does not deal with third-party rights. Therefore, in a sale of goods subject to the CISG, the question of whether a nonparty can enforce the contract as a third-party beneficiary, or whether contractual rights or duties can be assigned or delegated, must be determined by governing domestic law. The UNIDROIT Principles do cover both these areas. Third-party beneficiaries are covered by Articles 5.2.1 to 5.2.6, and assignment and delegation are covered by Articles 9.1.1 to 9.3.7.

Articles 5.2.1 to 5.2.6 of the UNIDROIT Principles are short and quite general. They recognize that the parties to a contract may expressly or impliedly confer rights on an identifiable third party, and that the beneficiary's rights are determined by the agreement of the parties. The beneficiary's rights are subject to any defense that the promisor could assert against the promisee, and the parties to the contract may not modify the rights conferred on the beneficiary after he has accepted or acted in reliance on them. Beyond this, the UNIDROIT Principles provide no detailed principles to govern the enforcement rights of the beneficiary.

Articles 9.1.2 and 9.1.3 of the UNIDROIT Principles permit either the partial or full assignment of a monetary obligation. A nonmonetary obligation may be fully assigned (or it may be assigned in part only if it is divisible) if the assignment does not render the obligation more burdensome. Under Article 9.1.7, assignment is accomplished by simple agreement between the assignor and assignee, without the obligor's consent. However, Article 9.1.10 states that until the obligor receives notice of the assignment, his duty under the contract is discharged by performing in favor of the assignor. Under Article 9.1.13, the obligor may raise against the assignee all defenses that he could have asserted against the assignor and may exercise against the assignee any setoff right that arose before notice of the assignment.

Articles 9.2.1 to 9.2.8 of the UNIDROIT Principles deal with the "transfer of obligations," which is approximately equivalent to delegation. (Articles 9.3.1 to 9.3.7 cover assignment of the contract as a whole — they essentially combine the principles relating to assignment and transfer of obligations.) Articles 9.2.1 and 9.2.3 of the UNIDROIT Principles provide for the transfer of obligations with the consent of the obligee. Unless discharged by the obligee, the original obligor remains liable for the performance. Transfer of obligations without the obligee's consent is possible under Article 9.2.6 unless the performance is essentially personal in character. The transfer does not free the original obligor from his contractual duties. Under Article 9.2.7, the new obligor acquires all the defenses that could have been asserted by the original obligor.

Examples

1. Tess Tatrix decided to leave her entire estate to Patty Third, her lifelong friend. She consulted Mel Practice, an attorney, for the purpose of making a will and instructed Mel to make Patty her heir. Mel drafted the will and Tess signed it. Tess died about a year later. It was then discovered that Mel had drafted the will so incompetently that it was invalid. As a result,

Tess was declared to have died intestate. Patty inherited nothing from her estate, which was distributed to Tess's distant relatives. Does Patty have any cause of action against Mel?

2. Every year, Fair City holds a weeklong celebration to commemorate its founding. This year it decided to set up a funfair in one of the city parks. It contracted with Meandering Merriment Co., to erect and operate the funfair for the week. Carr Parker owns a plot of vacant land a couple of blocks away from the park. When he heard that the fair was to be held so close to his property, he realized that parking would be at a premium in the area and that he could make a considerable amount of money by using his land as a parking lot. A month before the fair was due to open, he cleared the weeds and debris off the lot and leveled it so that cars could drive onto it. He painted signs and built a little booth at the entrance. Two weeks before the fair was to begin, Meandering Merriment notified Fair City that it had double-booked for the week in question and could not set up the fair as agreed. It thereby repudiated its contract with Fair City. It was too late for the city to be able to make alternative arrangements, so it canceled the funfair.

   Carr has made careful projections of his expected profits for the week of the fair, based on the anticipated attendance at the fair and the number of cars that could be accommodated on the lot on each day. Assuming that he can establish his lost profits with reasonable certainty, should he be able to recover them from Meandering Merriment?

3. After Rock Sparkler and Di Amond had been dating for about a year, they decided to become engaged. They visited the showrooms of Belle Bijoux, a jewelry dealer, to pick out a ring. After examining the selection for some time and receiving solicitous guidance from Belle, Di and Rock agreed on a diamond ring priced at $4,500. Rock purchased the ring, took delivery of it, and placed it on Di's finger.

   About six months later, Rock fell in love with another woman and broke off his engagement to Di. To assuage his guilt at abandoning her, Rock told Di that he did not want the ring back. Di no longer wished to keep the ring, and she decided to sell it. She took it to an appraiser to get an accurate assessment of its value. On examining the stone, the appraiser told her that it was not a diamond at all, but merely a piece of cut glass.

   Di is very bitter about the breakup of her engagement to Rock, and she does not want to ask for his help in making a claim against Belle. Does Di have any basis for proceeding directly against Belle?

4. Ben Derfender's car was damaged by a hit-and-run driver. He claimed the $10,000 cost of repair from his insurer, but the insurer rejected his claim because he failed to report the collision in time. Ben retained Connie Flicted to represent him in challenging the insurer's denial of liability.

The merits of Ben's claim were good, but the case was proceeding slowly and Ben needed some cash immediately. He therefore entered into a contract with Lon Shark under which Lon lent him $5,000. Ben undertook to repay the loan and interest to Lon as soon as he received payment of his pending claim against his insurer. Lon had Ben sign a letter in which he acknowledged his debt to Lon and agreed to pay the loan with interest from the proceeds of his claim. The letter ended by stating that Ben authorized his attorney, Connie Flicted, to pay Lon directly out of the proceeds. Ben gave the letter to Connie.

About a month later, Connie settled Ben's claim against the insurer for $10,000. She had forgotten about Lon's letter and Ben did not remind her that $5,000 of the proceeds plus interest had to be paid to Lon. Connie retained her fee of $3,000 and paid the balance of $7,000 to Ben. Ben immediately spent the money and cannot repay Lon. Does Lon have grounds to recover the debt from Connie?

5. Gator Deli sells kosher food to the local orthodox Jewish community. For many years it had bought all its sausages from Frumme Mentsch, a devout member of the congregation and a strictly observant kosher butcher. Frumme decided to retire and sold her business to Chazzer Food Corp., a large corporation that supplies food to the general market. As part of the sale of her business, Frumme assigned to Chazzer her two-year contract to supply sausages to Gator. Chazzer makes all its sausages in a huge plant in which it processes meat from a variety of animals. Neither the plant itself nor the meat used by Chazzer to make sausages is kosher. The contract says nothing about assignment. Can Gator object to the assignment of the contract?

6. Manny Quinn sells high-quality leather products. His store is well known for its exquisite alligator-skin purses. He buys the cured skins and gives them to his old friend Dell E. Gator, who makes them into the purses of his own design. Dell is a talented designer and is obsessively exacting in his craftsmanship. Manny has had a warm friendship with Dell for years and has relied on him for a long time to produce exceptionally fine purses. Last year, Manny and Dell entered into a five-year contract under which Dell undertook to make a stated quantity of purses for Manny each year.

A year after the contract was executed, Dell decided to retire to his cabin in the Everglades. He sold his business to Ann Phibian, his sulky and sullen apprentice. As part of the sale, Dell assigned Manny's contract to Ann. Ann has been well trained by Dell. Her designs are not as imaginative as Dell's but her craftsmanship is impeccable. However, Ann has an unpleasant nature and Manny finds her intimidating. He cannot face the thought of dealing with her over the next four years. He would prefer to terminate the contract and find someone else to make the purses. May he do so?

7. Percy Nality is a celebrity by profession. He entered into a contract with Hall Carnegie, an entertainment promoter, under which Percy would be paid $100,000 to deliver a speech as part of a special "Celebrity Lecture Series" that Hall intended to organize in the grand ballroom of a plush big-city hotel. Percy was paid his fee in advance upon signing of the contract. A few weeks before the speech was to be given, Hall decided that Percy had probably been a bad choice for his series because he was quite a boring person and had very little of consequence to say. He therefore booked another speaker for the event.

   To recover some of what he had paid Percy, Hall sold his contract with Percy to Rich X. Centric, who notified Percy that he had bought the right to Percy's performance. Rich informed Percy that instead of speaking in the "Celebrity Lecture Series," Percy was to come to Rich's home on the night set for the lecture, so that he could deliver his remarks to Rich and his wife in their living room. Percy refused and demanded that Hall allow him to speak at the event originally agreed upon. Hall declined this demand and warned Percy that if he did not deliver the speech to Rich, he would be in breach of contract. Percy did not show up at Rich's house on the evening set for delivery of the speech. What are the parties' respective rights and liabilities?

8. A lessee entered into a five-year lease of premises. The lease had a clause that provided, "The lessee may not assign this lease or any rights or interest in it without the express written permission of the lessor. Any such unauthorized assignment shall be void and shall give the lessor the right to terminate this lease immediately." A year after entering the lease, the lessee wishes to sublet the premises, but the lessor refuses to give permission. Is there anything that the lessee can do?

Explanations

1. Tess was not indebted to Patty, so Patty has no claim against the estate as a creditor and the invalid will left her with no basis for claiming testamentary rights. If she has any recourse at all for the loss of her inheritance, it will be against Mel. Mel's incompetence in drafting the will sounds like a clear case of malpractice, which would have given Tess, his client, a cause of action against him. However, Tess is dead, and her estate itself has no reason to pursue a malpractice claim against Mel — it is not the estate, but Patty who has been injured by Mel's incompetence. Patty might have a malpractice claim against Mel. Some courts do allow a nonclient to sue an attorney for malpractice on a negligence theory, provided that the

attorney's contract with the client created a duty of care towards the third party. See, for example, *Blair v. Ing*, 21 P.3d 452 (Hawaii 2001). However, other courts have held that an attorney's duty to act with reasonable competence runs only to his client, and gives no cause of action for malpractice by a nonclient who suffered economic loss as a result of the attorney's negligence in handling the client's affairs. This is based on the policy that potential malpractice liability to a nonclient could distract an attorney from focusing on the client's best interests, could undermine the attorney's loyalty to his client, and could create a conflict of interest as the attorney tries to balance his duty to his client against the need to safeguard the nonclient's interests. *See*, for example, *Guy v. Liederbach*, 459 A.2d 744 (Pa. 1983); *Noble v. Bruce*, 349 Md. 730 (1998).

However, whether or not there is a separate claim for malpractice by a nonclient, courts have recognized that the nonclient could acquire a cause of action against an attorney as an intended beneficiary of the contract between the attorney and client, provided that it is clear that the attorney and client intended to confer an independent right of enforcement on the nonclient. For example, in *Hale v. Groce*, 744 P.2d 1289 (Or. 1987), an attorney breached his contract with his client by failing to draw the client's will as instructed. As a result, a legatee was deprived of a legacy that the client had intended for him. The court found that the legatee was an intended beneficiary of the contract between the client and the attorney and therefore had an independent cause of action against the attorney for the breach. Similarly, in *Guy*, the attorney had the named beneficiary of a will sign it as a witness, thereby voiding her legacy. Although the court noted that a legatee does not become a third-party beneficiary merely because she is named in the will, it found that she was an intended beneficiary of the attorney-client contract because unless she was given a right to enforce it, there would be no one to hold the attorney accountable for his breach. The testator was dead and the estate had no incentive to sue. *Noble* took a less sympathetic approach to testamentary beneficiaries. It found no express or implied intent in the contract between the testators and their attorney to confer a direct right of enforcement on the beneficiaries, and would not imply such a right merely because they were the only persons with an incentive to enforce the contract. The court's reluctance to find a right of independent enforcement was motivated by its concern that ready recognition of third-party beneficiary rights is just as harmful to the attorney-client relationship, and raises the same policy concerns, as allowing a nonclient to sue the attorney for malpractice. The policy issue was emphasized in *Macht v. Estate of Dobkin*, 19 Mass. L. Rptr. 318 (Mass. Super. 2005), in which the client died before the attorney had complied with her instructions to draft a new will, leaving her estate to the plaintiff. The court emphasized the need not to compromise the attorney's duty of undivided loyalty to the client, and cautioned that recognition of an independent right of enforcement in a nonclient could make it difficult for an attorney to focus on the client's interests while trying to avoid possible liability to the nonclient.

2. Carr has no contract to provide parking for the fair, either with Fair City or with Meandering Merriment. His only basis for recovery against Meandering Merriment is as an intended beneficiary of its contract with Fair City. Unquestionably, Fair City's intent in organizing the fair was to benefit the public generally as well as the local economy, including nearby entrepreneurs like Carr who were in a position to reap profits from the event. Actions by government bodies are usually intended to benefit citizens, but that does not mean that they are intended to confer a private right on any individual citizen to enforce the contract. In fact the usual assumption is that a private enforcement right was not intended unless the contract or any legislation authorizing it indicates otherwise or the public interest requires recognition of private enforcement rights to give effect to the governmental purpose. In the absence of such circumstances, it is solely up to the government body to decide whether to enforce its contracts. Too ready a recognition of private enforcement rights would harm the public interest by increasing the volume of litigation and making it difficult for government to function. In Carr's case there is nothing to show that the contract, its authorizing statute, or public policy conferred the right on Carr to sue Meandering Merriment. The city had given him no commitment to hold the fair, there is no evidence that the contract contemplated any benefit to him specifically, and there is no strong public interest at stake that can only be protected by allowing Carr a right of action.

3. If Belle knew that the diamond was fake, she is guilty of fraud. Even if she honestly believed the diamond to be genuine, the delivery of a piece of cut glass was nevertheless a breach of her warranty that it was a diamond — whether such a warranty was given in so many words or arose by necessary inference from the price and description of the ring.[8] There is no doubt that Rock would have a cause of action against Belle for breach of warranty, but the issue is whether Di can proceed against her directly without relying on Rock to assert the claim. Although Di visited the showroom with Rock and helped select the ring, she was not a party to the contract for its sale. Her only basis for a direct claim against Belle (in the absence of some consumer protection statute that may extend rights to her) is as an intended beneficiary of Belle's contract with Rock.

---

8. UCC §2.313(1)(b) provides that a description of the goods that is made part of the basis of the bargain creates an express warranty that the goods conform to the description.

It is clear that Rock intended Di to have the ring. This was obviously apparent to Belle at the time of contracting because she knew Rock was buying an engagement ring and saw Di participate in its selection. Of course, this is not enough on its own, because there must also have been an understanding between the parties that Di would acquire an independent right to enforce Belle's contractual warranty. Although it is unlikely that the parties would have discussed this, or even thought of it at the time, intent to confer a right of action on the beneficiary need not be articulated if, under all the circumstances, it is, in the words of Restatement, Second, §302(1),[9] "appropriate to effectuate the intention of the parties." In this case, given Di's close involvement in the selection of the ring and the fact that she was to receive and own it, the recognition of her right to enforce Belle's warranty does seem consistent with the parties' intent.

The facts of this example are adapted from those in *Warren v. Monahan Beaches Jewelry Center, Inc.*, 548 So. 2d 870 (Fla. 1989). In that case, the plaintiff did not participate in the selection of the ring and was not known to the seller at the time of its purchase. However, the seller did know that its customer, the plaintiff's fiancé, was buying it as an engagement ring. After her fiancé gave her the ring, the plaintiff noticed a chip in it and took it back to the seller, who undertook to replace it as soon as new inventory came in. While she was waiting for the new stock, the plaintiff decided to have the ring appraised and discovered that the diamond was not genuine, but was cubic zirconia. The plaintiff then sued the seller directly. The seller responded by moving to dismiss her complaint on the basis that it did not allege sufficient facts to show that she was an intended beneficiary of the seller's contract with her fiancé. The appellate court found that the complaint did set out a cause of action. By alleging both the seller's pre-contractual discussions with the plaintiff's fiancé and its post-contractual dealings with the plaintiff herself, it adequately pleaded an intent to confer an enforceable benefit on the plaintiff. (The postcontractual dealings in *Warren* were useful bolstering evidence because they constituted a course of performance that helped to establish that the contracting parties intended to confer a right of enforcement on the beneficiary. Although no such evidence exists in Di's case, her evidence of the pre-contractual dealings is stronger than in *Warren*, and should be enough, on its own, to establish intent.)

4. Lon is clearly not an intended beneficiary of the contract in which Connie agreed to represent Ben because he was not contemplated as a beneficiary at the time that the contract was made. Also, Ben's mere sending of the

---

9. UCC Article 2 has no provisions dealing with third-party beneficiary rights in a sale of goods, which are therefore governed by general common law principles.

letter to Connie does not give rise to a contract between Lon and Connie, and Lon has no promissory estoppel claim against Connie because he did not take action in reliance on any promise by her to transmit the proceeds to him. Although Connie was negligent in disregarding the letter, Lon is not her client. Although it is conceivable that he may have a negligence claim against her, a court would likely resist recognizing such a claim because it could compromise Connie's ability to devote herself fully to the interests of Ben, her client. Lon's only basis for recovering from her is as an assignee of Ben's claim against her.

An assignment is a voluntary manifestation of intent by the owner of the right to transfer it immediately and irrevocably to another. Unless the right is embodied in a negotiable instrument or document, the assignment does not need to comply with any formalities. Nor does it need to use any particular form of words, provided that intent to assign is apparent. Ben's letter acknowledges his debt to Lon and authorizes payment to him from the fund. Its reasonable import is that Ben intends irrevocably to assign his right to the funds to the extent stated. There is nothing in Ben's contract with Connie, or in the nature of the transaction, or as a matter of policy, that would rebut the usual presumption in favor of the free assignability of Ben's contract rights.

This is the assignment of a present right, not the transfer of a future right. The contracts giving rise to the claim against the insurer and Connie were both in existence at the time of the assignment, even though the claim against the insurer was not yet liquidated at that stage and the claim against Connie was conditional on her receiving the proceeds of the claim against the insurer. An unliquidated, contingent claim can be assigned.

Ben had anticipated that his right against the insurer would exceed the amount due to Lon for principal and interest, so he contemplated a partial assignment of his right. This is permissible provided that the splitting of the right does not impose a substantial risk or burden on Connie, the obligor. Where the right simply involves payment from a fund, a partial assignment is not likely to be burdensome or risky to the obligor.

A valid assignment is binding on the obligor as soon as she receives notice of it. (If she so requests, she is also entitled to receive adequate proof of it.) At that point, the assignee is substituted for the assignor as the party entitled to performance and the obligee can only discharge her contractual duty by rendering performance to the assignee. Connie's payment to Ben was improper and does not discharge her obligation to pay Lon. (Her liability to Lon under the assignment does not raise the same concern as the recognition of a negligence cause of action, because payment to Lon would be in accordance with an undertaking to Ben.)

787

5. Upon selling her business to Chazzer Food Corp., Frumme assigned to it her entire contract with Gator Deli — she both assigned her right to payment and delegated her duty to supply sausages. Because this is a sale of goods, the rules governing the assignment of rights and the delegation of duties are set out in UCC §2.210. The contract does not mention assignment, so §2.210 allows Gator to resist the assignment and delegation only if it would materially affect its rights and obligations under the contract, or the contract gives it a substantial interest in having Frumme personally render or control the performance. Frumme is a strictly kosher butcher, and had the contract been assigned to another strictly kosher butcher, Gator would probably have had no grounds to complain. There is nothing to suggest that Frumme's skills and attributes makes it crucial that she personally performs under the contract. However, the contract was assigned to a corporation that supplies food to the general market with a centralized butchery that neither uses kosher meat nor processes it in accordance with Jewish law. It is surely a material term of the contract that the sausages are kosher, and the delegation of the duty to supply them fundamentally affects Gator's rights under the contract.

   However, this does not mean that Gator has the immediate right to refuse the delegation and to declare Frumme to be in breach. The law's presumption in favor of assignability seeks to balance the rights of Frumme to sell her assets against Gator's right to achieve its contractual expectations. Therefore, as Chazzer has not stated that it will not comply with Frumme's contractual obligation to supply sausages that are kosher, Gator has to give it the opportunity to declare its intentions with regard to performance. Under §2.210(5) Gator should treat the delegation as creating reasonable grounds for insecurity, and should clarify Chazzer's intentions by demanding an adequate assurance of performance. If Chazzer fails to provide an adequate assurance of performance, Gator has the right to refuse the delegation. In addition, because Frumme repudiates the contract by improperly delegating her duties, Gator can declare a material breach and can claim damages from her for any loss that it suffers. However, if Chazzer responds by giving the assurance that the sausages to be supplied under the contract will be processed separately from nonkosher meat in a plant and under a process that complies with Jewish law, Gator must accept the assignment and remains bound by the contract. (Remember that even if the delegation is effective, it does not release Frumme from her obligations, and she remains responsible if Chazzer fails to perform properly.)

6. Dell's contract with Manny is for services, not the sale of goods. It is therefore subject to the common law. However, the common law principles are no different from those set out for a sale of goods in Example 5.

Like the contract for the sale of sausages, this contract is assigned in its entirety and constitutes both an assignment of Dell's right to payment and his duty to make the purses. The contract is silent on assignment, so the rights are presumed to be assignable and the duties delegable unless this would violate public policy (which is not implicated here) or the nature and purpose of the contract is such that assignment would place an undue burden on Manny, would impair his prospects of return performance, or would defeat his substantial interest in having the obligor render or control the performance.

Manny's contract with Dell is highly personal in two respects. First, it is based on Dell's exceptional talent in design and craftsmanship. Second, it is grounded in a long and congenial relationship. The quality of Ann's work is equivalent to Dell's but she does not quite have his design flair. Dell's identity is clearly a significant factor in the contract, as would be true of any artist. This could be an important enough a feature of the contract to make Dell's personal performance the basis of the bargain. However, we cannot be sure of this without knowing more about the extent of the differences between his and Ann's work. The significance of the personal relationship is even more difficult to evaluate. Manny may not have entered into a long-term contract with someone with whom he did not have a good personal relationship. However, this is a commercial contract for the purpose of producing marketable products. Provided that purses of suitable quality can be produced, the parties do not have to be buddies, and their happy personal relationship may be incidental to the central purpose of the contract.[10]

In short, there is a chance that Manny could resist assignment of the contract, but this result is not assured. When the court balances Manny's reasonable contractual expectations against Dell's right to profit from the sale of his business, it could well find that Manny has not met the burden of showing this contract to be nonassignable.

7. If Hall's obligation under the contract is interpreted to be nothing more than the payment of the speaking fee, then Hall has fully performed and his sale of the contract is merely an assignment of his right to have Percy blabber for an hour or so. If this is the correct interpretation, then the performance due to Percy in return for the speech is not jeopardized because it has been paid, and unless Rich's house is substantially less accessible than the plush hotel, there seems to be little burden imposed

---

10. It was noted in section 19.3.7 that a contracting party has no right to expect that he will continue to deal with corporate officers with whom he has a special relationship because officers can change even in the absence of assignment. This consideration is inapplicable where the contracting parties are individuals. However, the personal relationship of the parties is still likely to be incidental in most contracts.

on his ability to render his performance. The assignment of the right would therefore be unobjectionable.

However, it is more than likely that Percy did not bargain only for the fee, but also had a reasonable expectation of enjoying the prestige and exposure of participating in the lecture series. This right may or may not have demonstrable economic value, but its economic worth is not the issue. Even intangible or speculative benefits can be a material part of the bargain if they are reasonably contemplated by the parties. On this interpretation, the sale of Percy's performance also entails the delegation of Hall's duty to make provision for the delivery of the speech as contemplated by the contract. (Or, to put it differently, Hall's assignment of his right to receive the speech materially reduces the value of the return performance due to Percy or impairs his chance of receiving it.)

If this is so, it follows that the assignment of the contract was a repudiation, and when Hall refused to retract before the due date for performance, he materially violated his contractual promise. This gave Percy the right to withhold his own performance and to sue Hall for damages. Presumably at that late date Percy had no opportunity to mitigate by finding another lucrative engagement, so he can at least keep the $100,000 as direct damages. (Assuming that this would have all been profit, and that he would not have had to incur costs in performing.) It may be possible for him to establish some economic loss for being deprived of the ability to speak in the lecture series, but such a loss is probably too uncertain and speculative, so consequential damages are unlikely to be provable. In addition, Hall is liable to Rich for failure to perform that contract. In transferring his right to Rich, Hall impliedly warranted the existence and validity of the right assigned. Therefore, if it was nonassignable, Rich can sue Hall for breach of this warranty. As he is unlikely to have suffered any consequential loss, his claim is probably confined to restitution of what he paid for the right.

By contrast to Percy's case, a right to the performance of personal services was held to be assignable in *Evening News Assn. v. Peterson*, 477 F. Supp. 77 (D.D.C. 1979). Peterson was employed as a news anchor at a television station. When the television station was sold, the seller assigned Peterson's employment contract to the buyer. Peterson objected to the assignment but the court upheld it. The assignment of the contract did not materially alter his working conditions, increase his burden of performance, or endanger his prospects of return performance.

8. Because the law has a general preference in favor of the assignability of rights and the delegation of duties, courts interpret clauses prohibiting or restricting assignment as narrowly as possible. The provision in the lease is clearly worded and it therefore must be taken to preclude effective transfer without the lessor's permission. As the lessee needs permission

to sublet, we must now consider if there is anything that can be done to compel the lessor to give its permission or to override its refusal. Unless the lease makes it clear that the lessor reserves absolute discretion to refuse permission, the law implies an obligation on the lessor to act reasonably in refusing it. This accords with the normal marketplace expectation of commercially reasonable conduct and is consistent with the law's general policy of requiring parties to deal with each other fairly and in good faith. Therefore, to legitimately refuse permission to sublet, the lessor must show that it has reasonable grounds for objecting to the subtenant. For example, that it is financially unstable, would use the premises improperly, or would otherwise be an unsuitable occupant.

Glossary

Accord and satisfaction. A settlement of an existing claim under which the parties agree that one of them (the debtor) will give, and the other (the creditor) will accept a lesser performance than that originally claimed by the creditor. The agreement of settlement is the accord, and its execution by rendition of the settled performance is the satisfaction. Until the settlement is satisfied by performance, it is known as an executory accord.

Actions of Assumpsit, Covenant, and Debt. *See* Assumpsit; Covenant; Debt.

Adhesion. A contract is adhesive where the party who drafts the terms of the contract has the market power to insist that the contract may be only on its terms, and the other party has no choice but to agree to the terms if he wishes to enter the contract. That is, the terms are nonnegotiable and the nondrafting party has no choice but to adhere to them if he wants the contract.

Agreed damages. *See* Liquidated damages.

Agreement to agree. Negotiating parties may have reached agreement in principle, but may not have settled all the terms of their proposed contract. They may decide to postpone resolution of those terms for later, agreeing to address them at a future date. This situation is sometimes described as an "agreement to agree." If the unresolved terms are material, no contract can come into existence until they are settled, so an "agreement to agree" is not a contract. However, the parties may have promised expressly or impliedly to continue to negotiate in good faith.

Anticipatory repudiation. A contract cannot be breached before the time of performance falls due. However, if, before his performance is due, a party makes it clear by unequivocal words or unambiguous voluntary conduct that he will not perform as promised, or will materially breach the contract when the time for performance arrives, he repudiates in anticipation of performance. The other party may react to this repudiation immediately and pursue relief for breach. *See also* Prospective nonperformance.

Arbitration. The parties may provide in the contract itself, or in a self-standing separate agreement, that any disputes relating to their contract will be resolved by a neutral third party (an arbitrator). By agreeing to arbitrate disputes, the parties forego the right to litigate, and they bind themselves to the arbitrator's disposition.

Assignment and delegation. Assignment is the transfer of a contractual right, and delegation is the transfer of a contractual duty. Sometimes "assignment" is used more loosely to mean the transfer of a contract in its entirety, which involves the transfer of both rights and duties under the contract.

Assumpsit. (Latin: "He undertook.") One of the common law forms of action under which suit was brought for damages for the breach of a contractual promise. Assumpsit, an extension of the tort action of trespass, was originally only available where the defendant performed improperly, causing harm to the plaintiff (misfeasance). It was later extended to cover situations in which the defendant broke his promise by failing to perform at all (nonfeasance). As assumpsit developed, it became the most flexible, efficient and comprehensive form of action for contract. It eventually overtook the other contractual writs of Covenant and Debt, emerging as the forebear of modern contract law.

Assurance of performance. *See* Prospective nonperformance.

Avoidable contract and **avoidance.** An avoidable contract is one that has some defect (typically resulting from improper bargaining, illegality, or incapacity) that allows one of the parties to **rescind** or **disaffirm** the contract. If that party does not elect to rescind, the contract is enforceable. An avoidable contract must be distinguished from a **void** contract, which is a nullity and cannot be enforced by either party.

Balance of the equities. *See* Equitable balancing.

Bargain theory. *See* Consideration.

Battle of the forms. A nickname given to the situation in which the buyer and seller of goods attempt to form a contract by exchanging writings with mismatching terms. Often these terms are preprinted standard provisions, designed to protect the interests of the sender.

Bilateral contract. All contracts have two or more parties, so every contract is at least bilateral (or, if not, multilateral) in the lay sense. However, in contract law, the word "bilateral" is a term of art, meaning that at the instant of contract formation, there are promises outstanding by both parties. This is in contrast to a unilateral contract, under which the offeree's act of acceptance is also her act of performance, so that at the instant of formation, the offeree has already performed, and only the offeror's promise is outstanding. Most contractual relationships involve an exchange of promises, so most contracts are bilateral. Unilateral contracts are less common. *See also* Unilateral contract.

Boilerplate. Standard provisions commonly employed in contracts of a particular kind, and often set out in preprinted standard form contract blanks.

Boxtop terms. Standard contract terms set out or referenced on a box or other container that includes a product such as goods or software.

Breach of contract. *See* Materiality; Partial breach; Substantial performance; Total breach.

Browsewrap. Standard contract terms set out on a website or other electronic medium and available to be read by the user (commonly by clicking a link to the terms) before submitting an order for the product or services purchased. Browsewrap differs from clickwrap in that it does not require the user to signify assent to the terms before completing the transaction.

Chancery. The Chancellor's Court. That is, the court of Equity. *See also* Equity.

CISG. Abbreviation for the United Nations Convention on Contracts for the International Sale of Goods. The CISG governs international sales of goods by parties whose places of business are located in signatory states. The CISG does not apply to consumer transactions or to transactions in which the parties have excluded it by agreement.

Civil law. A general term used to describe the legal system of countries that derive their legal heritage from Roman law.

Class action. Where a large group of people all have the same claim against a defendant, a small group of named plaintiffs may commence a suit against the defendant in which they represent, not only their own interests, but those of the entire class.

Classical contract law. The name used to describe the law of contracts as it existed in the period running from the late nineteenth to early twentieth century, in which modern contract law was developed and systematized.

Clickwrap. Standard contract terms contained in a website or software and set up in a way that requires the user of the site or software to access the terms and to signify assent to them, usually by action such as clicking an "I agree" button.

Common law. A term with three related but distinct meanings. It denotes:

1. The basic legal system of countries whose law derives from the common law of England.
2. The judge-made (as opposed to statutory) component of our law.
3. The process of legal analysis under which judges interpret, develop, and embellish rules of law.

Comparative law. The comparative study of the laws or legal systems of two or more nations.

Concurrent conditions. Where mutual performances under a contract are dependent on each other and the contract does not expressly or impliedly set out a sequence for performance, they must be rendered at the same time, and each performance is deemed in law to be a condition of the other. Therefore, if one of the parties fails to perform, the other is excused from doing so.

Condition. An event, not certain to occur, that must occur for the performance of a party to become due. If the parties agree that a particular performance under the contract (or the entire contract) is to be contingent on the happening of a future uncertain event, the performance (or the contract as a whole) is conditional. A condition is **express** if it is articulated in the agreement; **implied in fact** if it is inferable from interpreting the agreement in context; or **construed (or implied in law)** if the court concludes, as a matter of legal implication, that the parties reasonably intended it. Conditions are also categorized as pure or promissory. A **pure condition** is simply an event specified as a contingency on which performance is dependent, and nothing more. If the event fails to occur, the performance dependent upon it need not be rendered, and neither party incurs any liability for the nonoccurrence. However, a **promissory condition** is both a condition and a promise. That is, one of the parties promises expressly or impliedly that the condition will occur, and becomes liable for breach of contract if it does not.

Conditions precedent or subsequent. A condition precedent is one that must be fulfilled before a duty to perform comes into effect. A condition subsequent is one that discharges a duty of performance. That is, the duty to perform arises immediately upon formation of the contract, but if the condition occurs, it falls away. A condition subsequent differs from a condition precedent in that it extinguishes an existing duty, while a condition precedent is a precondition to a duty arising. As a practical matter, it is almost always impossible to tell from the language of an agreement which of these two conditions was intended by the parties, and the law's general assumption is in favor of a condition precedent. There is little practical difference between them.

Consequential damages. Losses or injuries suffered by the victim of a breach going beyond the mere loss in value of the promised performance (direct damages), and resulting from the impact of the breach on other rights, transactions, or endeavors affected by the contract.

Consideration. In its earliest formulation, "consideration" probably meant no more than that the contract was deliberately considered — that it was seriously contemplated and intended to be binding. As it has developed, it has come to mean that something of legal value (but not necessarily economic value) must be given by each party in exchange for what was promised or given by the other. Under the **bargain theory**, which prevails in modern law, a promise or performance qualifies as consideration only if it has been given in exchange for and induced the return promise or performance.

Construction/construed term. *See* Implied in law term.

Constructive conditions of exchange. Unless the contract expressly or impliedly indicates a different intent, the law generally presumes that the performances of the parties are interdependent — **dependent promises**. That is, each party's duty to perform is conditional on the other performing. *See also* Condition.

Contract of adhesion. *See* Adhesion.

Contra proferentum rule. A default rule of interpretation that where the meaning of language is unclear and cannot be resolved by contextual evidence, an interpretation is preferred that goes against the interests of the drafter, and in favor of the nondrafter.

Course of dealing/performance. Where contracting parties have entered into a number of successive transactions of a similar kind, the transactions that occurred before the contract in question are referred to as a course of dealing. Where there is some uncertainty in the meaning of a term in the current contract, evidence of the parties' course of dealing can be helpful in resolving it. The conduct of the parties in performing a contract after its execution is called a course of performance. Evidence of how the parties actually performed following the formation of the contract can likewise be useful in interpreting what they must have intended.

Covenant. In general terms, a covenant is simply an agreement, but it may also be used as a synonym for "promise." At early common law, Covenant was a form of action available to recover damages for breach of a promise under seal. Under the formalistic system of pleading in early common law, the action was not available for a contract that was not executed under seal.

Cure. A breaching party's rectification of the deficiency in performance.

Damages. A monetary award to compensate for loss or harm. See Consequential damages; Direct damages; Expectation damages; General damages; Incidental damages; Liquidated damages; Punitive or exemplary damages; Reliance damages; Special damages.

Debt. In its contemporary meaning, a debt is an obligation to pay money. (Sometimes "debt" is used even more broadly—and somewhat inaccurately—to denote any obligation of performance.) At early common law, the **Action of Debt** was a form of action that lay for recovery of a sum certain in money arising out of a contract under which money had been lent to the defendant or goods or services had been delivered to him.

Delegation. See Assignment and delegation.

Dependent promises. See Condition; Constructive conditions of exchange.

Deposited acceptance rule. See Mailbox rule.

Detriment. In law, "detriment" is sometimes used in its ordinary sense, to mean actual harm, prejudice, or injury. (Many courts require detriment in this sense before giving relief for promissory estoppel.) However, in consideration doctrine, "detriment" is used as a legal term of art. To suffer a **legal detriment**, a party must merely give up some legal right—do something that he is not obliged to do, or refrain from something that he is entitled to do. It does not matter if this legal detriment is of little or no economic value, or that it is not in fact harmful or injurious to the party suffering it.

Direct costs. See Fixed costs.

Direct damages. Losses incurred by the victim of a breach in acquiring the equivalent of the performance promised under the contract, so as to substitute for the performance that should have been rendered by the breacher.

Direct reliance. *See* Reliance damages.

Disaffirmance. Upon breach, the victim may either sue on the contract for expectation or reliance damages, or may elect to act as if no contract exists, and to sue for restitution under a theory of unjust enrichment. Disaffirmance is the plaintiff's formal abandonment of the contract in order to ground the unjust enrichment claim. Disaffirmance is also sometimes used as a synonym for **avoidance**.

Divisibility. A contract is divisible if the mutual performances promised by the parties can be split up into a number of smaller, self-sufficient exchanges. That is, the contract can be divided into independent and self-contained sets of matching performances. *See also* Severability.

Duty to read. Under the objective test of intent, a party is bound by the reasonable meaning of her manifestation of intent. Therefore, a party is usually deemed to have agreed to written or recorded terms if she manifests assent to them, even though she failed to read or comprehend them.

Economic waste. If damages for rectifying a breach are disproportionate to the victim's true loss, the court has the discretion to adjust them downwards to more accurately reflect the actual loss. It is sometimes said that the basis for this adjustment is that it would be economically wasteful to spend a large sum on curing a relatively less valuable breach, but as the plaintiff would not be obliged to waste the damages award on rectifying the breach, the true basis for the rule is that it would be an **unfair forfeiture** to compel the breacher to pay damages disproportionate to actual loss.

Efficient breach. A breach is efficient if it makes the defendant better off without making the plaintiff worse off. If the defendant's cost to perform the contract (including the cost of lost opportunity for a more lucrative transaction) would exceed the benefit that performance would give both parties, the defendant may save (or earn) enough money by breaching to pay expectation damages to the plaintiff and still come out ahead. In purely economic terms, a breach in such circumstances does not harm the plaintiff, who is compensated by the payment of damages, while it increases the defendant's wealth. A breach can only be efficient if the transaction costs of each party in making substitute transactions and of settling or litigating the plaintiff's claim do not exceed the gains to be made from the breach. Also, it must be remembered that costs of breach are often not capable of accurate calculation, and breach has implications beyond economics.

Ejusdem generis. (Latin: "of the same kind.") A rule of interpretation under which specific words limit the meaning of general words with which they are associated.

Electronic agent. A computer program or another automated means used by a party to initiate or respond to communications in the formation of a contract and intended to allow for contract formation without the intervention of a human operator.

Enforcement. A general word that denotes judicial recognition of a right. When it is said that a court enforces a contract, this means that the court will render judgment for relief upon breach of the contract. Enforcement does not necessarily take the form of a court order compelling the breaching party to perform his obligations under the contract — in fact such an order of specific performance is the exception rather than the rule. In most cases, the enforcement of a contract takes the form of a money judgment for damages. If the breaching party fails to pay the damages voluntarily, the means of compelling payment is by execution. *See also* Execution; Specific performance.

Equitable balancing. In judicial decisionmaking, the process under which the court takes into account the likely impact of countervailing resolutions, and attempts to reach a fair and balanced result by weighing the potential hardship to each party as well as their respective rights and the relative justice of their positions.

Equity. Apart from meaning "fairness" in a general sense, this word has a more technical meaning in the common law. It refers to the jurisdiction originally exercised by the Lord Chancellor, representing the monarch, for the purpose of granting discretionary relief when the more inflexible law courts were unable to provide an adequate remedy. Courts of law and equity have been combined for some time, but the distinction between suits of equitable and legal origin is still maintained.

Escrow. Money or other property delivered by a contracting party to an independent third party (the escrow agent) with instructions to deliver the money or property to the other contracting party upon the fulfillment of stated conditions. By using an escrow agent, the party with the duty to deliver the property ensures that the property is not handed over to the other party until he performs, and the other party is assured of receiving the property upon performance.

E-SIGN. The Electronic Signatures in Global and National Commerce Act, a federal statute enacted in 2000, to validate electronic signatures and records, and generally, to ensure that general principles of contract formation are applied to electronic transactions. *See also* UETA.

Essential reliance. *See* Reliance damages.

Estoppel. (Also called **equitable estoppel** or **estoppel in pais.**) A doctrine derived from equity under which a person is precluded from asserting a right where she has, by deliberate words or conduct, misled the party against whom the rights are asserted into the justifiable belief that the right does not exist or will not be asserted.

Execution. The process of enforcing a money judgment, such as a judgment of contract damages, against the judgment debtor (the party against whom the judgment has been rendered.) The judgment creditor (the party in whose favor judgment was granted) has a writ issued and delivered to the appropriate official (usually called the sheriff), who then attempts to find property belonging to the judgment debtor. If such property is found, the sheriff levies on it — that is, takes legal custody of it, and after advertising it, sells it at public auction. The proceeds of the sale are then paid over to the judgment creditor.

Executory/executed. Until a contract has been fully performed, it is executory. Once it has been fully performed on both sides, it is executed. In the case of a gift, where the gift is merely promised, but not yet given, it is executory (and hence unenforceable under consideration doctrine), but once the gift has been transferred to the donee, it is executed, and no longer subject to invalidation under consideration doctrine.

Executory accord. *See* Accord and satisfaction.

Exemplary damages. *See* Punitive damages.

Expectation damages. The standard measure of damages for breach of contract — a monetary award designed to compensate the victim of breach for her reasonable contractual expectations lost as a result of the breach. The damages are intended to place the victim in the economic position that she would have been in had the contract not been breached.

Express. Articulated or stated in words, rather than inferred from indirect language or circumstances.

Expressio unius est exclusio alterius. (Latin: "the expression of one thing excludes another.") A rule of interpretation under which the listing of a string of specific things, not followed by a general term, is taken to exclude unlisted things of the same kind.

Extrinsic evidence. Evidence of the context in which a document was executed. These facts outside the document, such as evidence of discussions, negotiations or prior dealings between the parties or trade usage, may help to cast light on what the parties meant by the language used in the document. *Compare* Four corners rule.

Fiction. *See* Legal fiction.

Firm offer. An offer that the offeror undertakes not to revoke for a stated or reasonable time. At common law, such an undertaking is not binding on the offeror unless the offer qualifies as a valid option, but under UCC Article 2, a firm offer is binding under defined circumstances.

Fixed costs (overhead). Costs that must be paid by a party whether or not she ceases performance under a contract. These overhead costs are distinguished from **variable (direct) costs**, which are costs incurred solely in the process of performance, and are saved when the party ceases performance. When the plaintiff's performance has ceased as a result of the defendant's breach, fixed costs, not being saved, are included in the plaintiff's damages, but variable costs, being saved, are not included in calculating the plaintiff's loss.

F.O.B. (Free on board.) A term in a sale of goods that identifies the seller's delivery commitment and risk of loss. The initials F.O.B. are followed by a specified place (for example, F.O.B. New York). The seller is responsible for the cost and risk of getting the goods to that place, and the buyer must accept delivery there. Upon taking delivery, the buyer assumes responsibility for the freight and risk of loss from that point.

Force majeure. (French: "superior force.") A force beyond the control of the parties, such as a natural disaster or war. A force majeure clause in a contract is one that releases a party from performance if that performance is rendered impracticable as a result of such an uncontrollable event.

Foreseen/foreseeable. An event is foreseen if the party in question recognizes the possibility of its occurrence and contemplates it as a real likelihood. However, foreseeability is based on a more objective standard: Whether or not the party in question does actually foresee the event, it is foreseeable if it can be conceived of by a reasonable person in the position of the party.

Forfeiture. *See* Unfair forfeiture.

Form of action. In older common law, different actions (for example, the contract actions of assumpsit, covenant, or debt, or the tort action of trespass) each covered a specific type of transaction or set of facts and had a particular form that had distinct features in its pleadings and in the manner in which evidence was presented and evaluated. This formalistic system no longer applies in modern law.

Forum selection clause. A term in a contract in which the parties stipulate that any litigation relating to the transaction will be commenced only in a specified court or jurisdiction.

Four corners rule. A rule of interpretation that requires the meaning of a document to be ascertained with reference only to the language used in the document itself (that is, to be found within its "four corners"), without recourse to any extrinsic evidence. *Compare* Extrinsic evidence.

Fraud. A misrepresentation of fact, opinion, or intention, made with knowledge of its falsity and intent to mislead. Most fraudulent misrepresentations are **in the inducement** — they misrepresent something that underlies and induces the contract. In rarer cases, fraud may be **in the factum** — a misrepresentation of the nature and effect of the document signed. *See also* Misrepresentation.

Frustration of purpose. A contract's purpose is frustrated where, after it is made, an unforeseen event occurs, which so changes the circumstances surrounding it, that the contract's underlying purpose — as reasonably understood by both parties — is defeated. Although it is still possible to perform as originally intended, the point of the contract has disappeared.

Under proper circumstances, the frustration of a contract's purpose is grounds for its termination.

Gap filler. A standard term recognized by law, implied as a matter of law into a contract to fill a gap in the parties' agreement.

Garnishment. A form of execution under which a writ is delivered to a person who holds property of the judgment debtor or owes money or another obligation to the judgment debtor, ordering that person to turn over the property or money to the court in satisfaction of the judgment. *See also* Execution; Writ.

General damages. In contract, damages that arise in the normal course of breach, including readily foreseeable direct damages, as well as those consequential damages that were reasonably foreseeable by the breacher at the time of contracting as a natural and probable consequence of the breach. (If the breacher could not reasonably have foreseen the damages without special information or knowledge of the victim's particular circumstances, the damages are special.)

Good faith. Actual honesty and fair dealing, with an absence of intent to act wrongfully. Despite the prevalence of an objective reasonableness standard in contract law, there are many situations in which the honesty of a party, measured subjectively by attempting to ascertain his actual state of mind, is relevant to the case.

Illusory promise. An apparent promise that is so qualified, or in respect of which such wide discretion is reserved, that the apparent promisor actually makes no binding commitment at all.

Implied in fact. A contract, term, or promise is implied in fact if it is not expressly stated, but it can be deduced as a matter of factual conclusion from other language used by the parties, or from conduct or the circumstances surrounding the transaction.

Implied–in–law contract, also known as **quasi-contract**, is not a contract at all, but a legal fiction originally created for procedural reasons — to allow the formalistic common law courts of a bygone era to use the contractual form of action as a basis for giving relief for unjust enrichment. In modern law, "quasi-contract" or "contract implied in law" is simply a term to describe one of the forms of an action for unjust enrichment.

Implied–in–law term, also known as a **construed** term, is a term found by the court to exist in a contract, even though the language of the contract does not state it, and it cannot be inferred as a matter of fact from contextual evidence. Legal implication is based on a policy judgment by the court (or by a statute or common law rule) that the term should be in the contract, even though the parties may not actually have agreed to it. The importation of the term into the contract is typically justified on the basis that the parties, as reasonable people, would have intended the term to apply had they thought about the issue.

Impracticability/impossibility. Under the older, narrower doctrine of impossibility, performance under a contract may be excused as impossible if the contract contemplated that performance to be dependent on the continued existence of a person or thing, and, without fault of the person claiming excuse, the person died or thing was destroyed after the contract's execution. The doctrine of impracticability is a modern expansion of the older impossibility doctrine. A party may be excused from performance if an unforeseen supervening event, occurring after formation of the contract, and not caused by the fault of the party claiming excuse, defeats a basic assumption on which the contract was made. To establish excuse on the basis of impracticability, the party must also show that the unforeseen event imposes a significant burden on him, beyond any risk that he expressly or impliedly assumed.

Incidental/intended beneficiary. *See* Third-party beneficiary.

Incidental damages. Costs and expenses incurred by the victim of a breach in attempting to deal with it and in taking action to seek a substitute transaction or to curtail losses.

Incidental reliance. *See* Reliance damages.

Indebitatus assumpsit. *See* Assumpsit.

Indefiniteness. Vagueness, ambiguity, or other uncertainty in an agreement.

Infancy, infant. A word commonly used in contract law to mean minority — that is, to describe any person below the age of contractual capacity (typically 18).

Injunction. An order of court compelling the performance of a specified act (called a **mandatory** injunction) or prohibiting specific action (called a **prohibitory** injunction).

In pari delicto rule. (In pari delicto potior est conditio defendantis. Latin: "where the parties are in equal guilt, the defendant's position is the stronger.") This maxim applies to contracts that are illegal or that violate public policy. If one of the parties seeks to enforce such a contract, or even to obtain restitution of performance rendered under it, the court may refuse to intervene. In making the decision on whether or not to allow relief, the court weighs the relative guilt of the parties and takes into account the equities between the parties and the public interest.

In personam/in rem. An order or command of the court directed at the defendant and compelling him to do or refrain from doing something is an in personam order, and its disobedience will result in contempt of court. By contrast, a judgment of the court that the defendant owes monetary damages is not directed against the person of the defendant, but at his property — it is in rem. If the defendant fails to pay the judgment, it can only be enforced to the extent that the sheriff can find property of the defendant on which to levy execution.

Integration/integrated writing. A written record of agreement is said to be **totally integrated** if it clearly and unambiguously expresses all the terms agreed to by the parties, and is intended by them to be a complete and final expression of all the terms of their contract. If the written record does not fully and finally incorporate all of the agreed terms, but it does set out some of them completely, clearly, and unambiguously, it is said to be **partially integrated.** That is, the writing is a final expression of agreement with regard to those terms that are fully set out.

Interpretation. The process of inferring meaning from language or from factual evidence of the context in which the language was used.

Judgment creditor/debtor. *See* Execution.

Knockout rule. A rule applied under some circumstances to resolve the "battle of the forms" under UCC §2.207. The rule provides that conflicting terms in the parties' correspondence cancel each other out, leaving an open term to be filled by the gap fillers provided by the UCC.

Last shot rule. Where the final communication in the process of offer and acceptance contains new or different terms, the recipient is deemed to have accepted those terms by conduct if she performs without objecting to them. Although the rule is followed at common law, it does not apply in the "battle of the forms" under UCC §2.207.

Legal detriment. *See* Detriment.

Legal fiction. A factual assumption, deemed to be true in law, even though the assumed fact is not established by evidence to be true, or, in some cases, even if the assumption is contrary to the actual facts. Legal fictions are used to effectuate a public policy or to achieve a just result.

Legal realism. A philosophy of law that rejects the concept of law as a set of certain, neutral legal rules, and views it in a multidisciplinary context, in which legal doctrine is part of a larger process of decisionmaking and policymaking. The Realist school moved away from the formalism of Legal Positivism, to examine not only the rules of law, but also the operation of legal rules in the broader context of the legal process, society, and social policy.

Levy. *See* Execution.

Liquidated damages. At the time of contracting, the parties may wish to avoid disputes and uncertainty over damages if a breach should occur in the future, and they may therefore include a term in the contract that fixes in advance the amount of damages to be paid if a breach occurs. A fairly bargained liquidated damages provision is enforceable provided that, at the time of contracting, it reasonably appeared to the parties that actual damages would be difficult to prove, and the parties made a genuine attempt to forecast probable loss. Many courts also evaluate the reasonableness of liquidated damages, in the alternative, in light of the actual loss ultimately suffered, and will uphold the clause if the liquidated damages are reasonably equivalent to actual loss. If a liquidated damages provision does not meet these standards, it is treated as a penalty and is unenforceable. *See also* Penalty.

Liquidated debt. A debt is liquidated when its monetary value is certain and fixed. In the context of damages for breach of contract, damages normally become liquidated once the breach has occurred and the damages can be calculated by arithmetical means. If the determination of damages cannot be made purely by arithmetical calculation (for example, because issues such as uncertainty, foreseeability, and mitigation have to be resolved), the damages only become liquidated once the factfinder has assessed them.

Lost volume. If a seller of goods or services has the capacity to supply the full demand for those goods or services, a breach by one buyer is not substituted for by a subsequent sale of the goods or services to another customer who would have bought the goods or services in any event. The breach has caused a loss in the volume of the plaintiff's sales and can only be compensated for by an award of lost profits.

Mailbox rule. (Also known as **"deposited acceptance rule."**) Where an offer expressly or impliedly authorizes acceptance through the mail or another noninstantaneous means of communication, the acceptance takes effect as soon as it is properly dispatched by the offeree.

Manifested intent. The apparent state of mind of a party, as demonstrated by her observable conduct or spoken or written words. *See also* Objective.

Material benefit rule. A doctrine that permits enforcement of a promise without present consideration where the promise is made in recognition of a substantial benefit previously conferred on the promisor by the promisee, and enforcement is needed to prevent injustice. Because this doctrine is grounded in the idea that the promisor is morally obliged to honor a promise to pay for the prior benefit, it is sometimes called **"moral obligation."** This is an ambiguous term, and can easily be confused with the different usage of "moral obligation," which means simply that the obligation in question is binding only in conscience and is not capable of being legally enforced.

Materiality/material term/material breach. A term of a contract is material if it is an important component of the contract, so central to the values exchanged that it is a fundamental basis of the bargain between the parties. A material breach is a violation of a party's obligations under the contract, so serious that it defeats the other party's reasonable expectations under the contract by substantially depriving her of the value of the transaction. Materiality cannot be decided in the abstract, but must be determined by interpreting the contract.

Merchantable. Goods are merchantable if they meet minimum acceptable trade standards, and would be regarded as of adequate quality by a reasonable member of the trade.

Merger clause. A provision in a written agreement declaring that the writing contains all the terms agreed upon by the parties, and that no terms, other than those expressed in the writing have been agreed to. Such a provision is called a "merger clause" because its purpose is to "merge" all the agreed terms into the writing, so that the writing becomes the full and complete record of what was agreed, and neither party can later allege that terms exist beyond those expressed in the writing.

Mirror image rule. (Also known as **"ribbon matching rule."**) A rule that requires an acceptance to match the offer exactly, with no alteration or qualification. Under this rule, if the acceptance deviates from the offer in any way it does not qualify as an acceptance, but is a rejection and possibly a counteroffer. Many courts no longer apply the mirror image rule, but adopt a more flexible approach under which the response to an offer may qualify as an acceptance if its divergence from the offer is not material. In sales of goods, the rule is clearly abrogated by UCC §2.207.

Misrepresentation. An assertion not in accordance with the truth. If the misrepresentation is made with **scienter** — knowledge of its falsity and intent to mislead, it is fraudulent. If it is made without scienter, it may be either negligent (the party making it would have known of its falsity had she taken reasonable care in ascertaining the truth) or innocent (the party did not breach a duty of care by failing to ascertain the truth).

Mistake. An error concerning a fact existing at the time of contracting. If the mistake relates to a common, shared assumption of the parties it is **mutual**, but if the error concerns a fact that is a basic assumption of only one of the parties, it is **unilateral.**

Mitigation of damages. The avoidance or reduction of loss following a breach of contract.

Moral obligation. *See* Material benefit rule.

Mutual mistake. *See* Mistake.

Mutuality of obligation. When consideration consists of the exchange of promises, the commitment on both sides must be real and meaningful. If the apparent promise of one of the parties is illusory — so qualified or discretionary as to be no commitment at all — that party's apparent promise does not bind him. Because only the other is bound, the transaction lacks mutuality of obligation. This is just another way of saying that the person who made the illusory promise has given no consideration, and no valid contract was formed.

Noscitur a sociis. (Latin: "known from its associates.") A rule of interpretation under which the meaning of each individual word in a series is affected by and affects the meaning of the other words in that series.

Novation. A contract under which an existing contractual duty is discharged and a completely new one is substituted. The new contract may add a party who was not a party to the original contract.

Objective. Something is objective if it is presented to the consciousness, rather than subjective — within the consciousness itself. That is, it is external to the mind rather than within it. In contract law, the word is most commonly applied to describe the legal standard for gauging the state of mind — the intent or understanding — of a party. Therefore, the **objective test** of intent is concerned, not with the party's subjective state of mind — what that party actually thinks or believes, but with what the observable, external evidence of her words or conduct indicate her intention to be. In interpreting the manifest and external **objective evidence** of intent, the law does not attempt to enter the mind of the observer, to take his subjective evidence of what he actually understood the intention to be, but evaluates it objectively by asking what a reasonable person in the position of the observer would understand it to be. *See also* Reasonableness standard; Subjective standard.

Objective value. *See* Subjective value.

Obligor/obligee. An obligor is one who owes an obligation or debt, and an obligee is one to whom it is owed. In a bilateral contract, each party is an obligor with regard to the performance promised by her, and an obligee with regard to the performance that is due to her.

Officious intermeddler. In the context of unjust enrichment, a person who imposes an unsolicited benefit on another in the absence of emergency circumstances that would have justified the conferral of an unrequested benefit.

Option. A promise, legally binding on the offeror, to keep an offer open for a period of time. A valid option eliminates the offeror's usual power to disregard her commitment to keep the offer open and to revoke it at any time before it is accepted.

Output contract. *See* Requirements and output contracts.

Overhead. *See* Fixed costs.

Pacta sunt servanda. (Latin: "agreements must be kept.") This phrase asserts the moral imperative that the law should enforce contractual promises.

Parol evidence. Evidence of alleged terms not included in the written record of agreement, but claimed by one of the parties to have been agreed to orally before or at the time of execution of the written contract, or in a prior writing.

Partial breach. A breach that is not, or has not yet become significant enough to qualify as a total and material breach. A party who has substantially performed commits a partial breach, but even where performance is not substantial and the breach is potentially material, it is a partial breach if the breaching party is able to avert it by an effective cure.

Partial integration. *See* Integration/integrated writing.

Penalty. A provision in a contract that is designed to impose, or has the effect of imposing, a burden or punishment on a party for breaching, beyond any actual or expected loss that may be suffered by the victim of the breach.

Positivism. A legal philosophy that stresses the primacy of legal rules and considers the courts' principal role as the application of settled rules to the facts of individual cases.

Precedent. *See* Stare decisis.

Pre-existing duty rule. A rule of consideration doctrine that a performance of or promise to perform an existing duty cannot qualify as consideration. Consideration consists of an exchange of legal detriments — each party must relinquish a legal right in exchange for the promise or performance received from the other. Therefore if a party already has a legal duty to do or refrain from doing something, his promise to do or refrain from that very act is no relinquishment of a right and cannot be a detriment.

Primary authority. *See* Secondary authority.

Promise. An undertaking to act or refrain from acting in a specified way at some future time.

Promisor/promisee. A promisor is one who makes a promise, and a promisee is one to whom a promise is made. In a bilateral contract, each party is both a promisor of the performance she has promised to the other party, and a promisee of the return performance promised to her by the other party. When consideration is in issue, the person whose promise is sought to be enforced (and whose consideration is not in doubt) is referred to as the promisor, and the promisee is the party whose consideration is in question. In the context of a contract for the benefit of a third party, the promisor is the party who is to perform in favor of the beneficiary, and the promisee is the other party to the contract who has called for the performance to be rendered to the beneficiary.

Promissory condition. *See* Condition.

Promissory estoppel. A doctrine, derived from equitable estoppel, under which a court has the discretion to enforce a noncontractual promise made with the intention of inducing reliance, and justifiably relied on by the promisee to her detriment. Depending on the needs of justice, The promise may be enforced fully, or only to the extent necessary to reimburse wasted costs and expenses.

Prospective nonperformance. Words or conduct by a party prior to the due date of performance, or other circumstances arising before that due date, suggesting the likelihood or possibility of breach when the time for performance arrives. Although the signs of possible future breach are not clear and strong enough to be a repudiation, they may suggest the prospect of material breach, and may give the other party reasonable grounds for feeling insecure about receiving the promised performance. If such insecurity is justified, the insecure party may demand an **adequate assurance of performance**, and if none is given, may treat the failure to furnish adequate assurance as a repudiation.

Punitive or exemplary damages. Damages awarded, not to compensate the plaintiff for established loss, but to punish the defendant and to make an example of him.

Pure condition. *See* Condition.

Quantum meruit/quantum valebant. Quantum meruit (Latin: "as much as deserved") is the term used to denote the market value of services. Quantum valebant ("as much as they are worth") signifies the market value of goods. Market value is the common means of measuring the value of goods or services either in restitutionary claims or where a contract is based on a reasonable, rather than a specified price.

Quasi. A Latin word meaning "as if." This word, when used to qualify another (such as "quasi-contract") signifies that a legal fiction is being used. Although the doctrine or fact so qualified is not the same as that represented by the qualified word, it is deemed in law to be treated the same for some purposes. (For example, although a quasi-contract is not the same as an actual contract, it is treated like a contract for some purposes.)

Quasi-contract (quasi ex contractu). *See* Implied-in-law contract.

Realism. *See* Legal realism.

Reasonable expectations. A party's expectations about the performance and benefit of a contract, evaluated not on the basis of what the party claims to have actually expected, but on the basis of what she should have expected as a reasonable person. *See also* Reasonableness standard.

Reasonableness standard. A widely used standard of contract law, under which a party is held accountable for the reasonable import of her words and actions. The meaning of a party's words, or her intention, understanding, or conduct is evaluated on the basis of what a reasonable person in her position would have meant, understood or done. The **reasonable person** is a hypothetical construct, based on a community standard, typically represented by the jury. *See also* Objective.

Reformation. Where, as a result of mistake or error in transcription, a written contract does not correctly reflect the parties' true agreement, the court may grant the equitable remedy of reformation to correct the writing so that it reflects the actual agreement between the parties.

Reliance damages. Reliance damages are those costs and expenses incurred in reliance on the contract (or, in promissory estoppel, in reliance on the promise), and wasted once the contract (or promise) is breached. If the cost or expense is incurred in performing duties required by the contract, it is **direct or essential reliance.** If the cost or expense is incurred for the purpose of enjoying or using a benefit reasonably expected from the contract, it is **incidental reliance.**

Repudiation. *See* Anticipatory repudiation.

Requirements and output contracts. A requirements contract is one in which the quantity of goods to be supplied is left flexible, and will be based on the buyer's requirements for the goods during the contract period. That is, the buyer agrees to buy all its requirements for the goods from the seller during the term of the contract, and the seller agrees to supply whatever the buyer orders. The buyer's discretion to fix quantities may be limited by a stated or customary range of demand, or if not, by an obligation to act reasonably and in good faith. An output contract is similar, but the flexible quantity is based on the seller's production rather than the buyer's requirements. That is, the seller agrees to sell and the buyer agrees to buy the seller's entire output of the goods during the contract period. Again, the seller's discretion to fix production levels may be limited by a stated or customary range, or by an obligation to act reasonably and in good faith.

Rescission. Broadly speaking, rescission is the cancellation of a contract. In its narrowest meaning, the word is confined to the cancellation of a contract by mutual consent. However, it may also be found in reference to the nullification of a contract (that is, **avoidance**) on grounds such as fraud or mistake. In its broadest usage, "rescission" could be meant as a synonym for "termination" where the victim of a material and total breach ends the contractual relationship, withholds further performance, and sues for damages.

Restitution. A judicial remedy under which the court grants judgment for the restoration of property (**specific restitution**) or its value (**monetary restitution**) to a party from whom the property was unjustly taken or has been unjustly retained.

Ribbon matching rule. *See* Mirror image rule.

Rolling contract. A contract that is not concluded at the point of purchase but becomes binding only at some later stage, after the nondrafting party has had the opportunity to review and signify assent to standard terms drafted by the other party.

Scienter. A central element of fraud, consisting of knowledge of the falsity of an assertion combined with an intent to mislead.

Seal. A wax impression or other insignia placed on paper by a person for the purpose of authenticating the document. In earlier law, a contract executed under seal did not require consideration, but this formal means of dispensing with the need for consideration has fallen away in most jurisdictions.

Secondary authority. A law review, textbook, or other commentary on the law that is not a binding source of law, but that may be persuasive to a court. Secondary authority is distinguished from **primary authority**, such as a statute or binding judicial precedent, which must be followed by a court.

Security interest. An interest in property (such as a mortgage), granted by a debtor to a creditor to secure payment of the debt. If the debtor defaults in payment, the creditor is entitled to foreclose on the property and sell it to satisfy the debt.

Security of transactions. The concept that the enforcement of individual contracts — and hence the protection of reliance in individual transactions — creates a broad sense of reliance throughout the economy, which facilitates market activity by promoting general confidence in the reliability of contractual undertakings.

Severability. A term in a contract is said to be severable if it can be removed from the contract or adjusted without significantly impairing the basis and purpose of the contract. *See also* Divisibility.

Sheriff. *See* Execution.

Shrinkwrap. Standard contract terms set out in a document included in the packaging of a product or in software. Because the terms are included with the packaged product or software, they are not likely to come to the attention of the purchaser until after the container is opened or the software is downloaded.

Signature. A mark or symbol, or an electronic means of identification, executed or adopted by a party with the intention of authenticating a writing or other record.

Special damages. In contract law, special damages are consequential losses that derive from the plaintiff's special circumstances. Because they would not flow as an obvious and natural consequence of the breach, the defendant cannot reasonably foresee them at the time of contracting, and is therefore not liable for them, unless he is informed of the special circumstances at the time of contracting.

Specific performance. An order by the court directing the defendant to render the contractual performance as promised. Specific performance is an equitable remedy, and is the exception rather than the rule, available only where damages are not an adequate remedy.

Stare decisis. (Latin: "The decision stands.") The doctrine of precedent, under which a later court is bound by the earlier decisions of a court of equal or senior rank in the same judicial hierarchy.

Standard terms/standard contract. Standard contract terms are those that are drafted in advance of contracting and are used in many transactions of the same kind. They may be set out in a written contract, in electronic form, or on an invoice, ticket, or other document. A party that enters into many similar transactions usually drafts the standard terms itself, but parties may use standard terms drafted by a nonparty (such as a trade association). A standard contract is a predrafted contract form containing standard terms.

Subjective standard. A test of intent based on what the parties actually understood, rather than on their objectively demonstrated intent — what their words or conduct reasonably indicate their intent to have been. The subjective standard is not used as a general test of intent, which has long been gauged objectively. However, the subjective standard is applied in discrete areas of contract law when a party's good faith is in issue, or her state of mind is otherwise relevant to the resolution of the case. *See also* Objective.

Subjective value. The value of property or services to the recipient personally, as opposed to **objective value**, which is measured by market worth.

Substantial performance. A performance under a contract that, while not fully in compliance with the contract (and therefore a breach), is nevertheless deficient in only a trivial way. Because the breach is not material, the plaintiff may not use it as a ground for rescinding the contract, but is confined to claiming monetary compensation for the shortfall in performance.

Surety. A person who, at the request of a debtor, enters into an undertaking with the creditor that she will pay the debtor's debt, or otherwise perform the debtor's obligations, if the debtor fails to pay or perform.

Take-or-pay provision. A term in a contract under which the buyer of goods or services commits himself to take a specified minimum quantity, and promises to pay for that minimum quantity whether or not he actually orders it. A take-or-pay provision may be interpreted as a **penalty** and could be unenforceable on that ground.

Tender. An offer of payment or performance by a party who is ready, willing, and able to render it.

Termination of contract. Where a contract has been materially and totally breached, the victim of the breach may terminate the contract, bringing the relationship to an end for purposes of any outstanding future performance, and sue for damages for breach. A contract may also terminate as a result of **rescission** in other circumstances, such as by agreement between the parties, or following mistake, fraud, or other grounds of avoidance.

Third-party beneficiary. A person who is not a party to a contract, but upon whom the parties intend to confer the benefit of performance together with an independent right to enforce that performance. A party on whom this independent right of enforcement is conferred is called an **intended beneficiary.** If a stranger to the contract fortuitously acquires an incidental benefit from the contract, without any intent of the parties to confer an enforcement right on him, he is merely an **incidental beneficiary** and has no right to sue on the contract.

"Time is of the essence." A phrase that means that performance within the time specified is a material term of the contract, and that any delay will be a total and material breach of contract.

Total breach. A breach of contract that is both material and incurable, entitling the victim to rescind the contract and claim full expectation relief.

Trade usage. *See* Usage.

Transaction costs. The costs incurred in entering a transaction. When a contract has been breached, the transaction costs resulting from the breach include expenses such as the plaintiff's costs in finding a substitute, the breacher's costs in entering the other transaction perceived as more desirable, and the costs to both parties in negotiating a settlement of the plaintiff's claim or in litigating it. To decide if the breach is efficient, these costs must be deducted from the potential gains flowing from the breach.

UETA. The Uniform Electronic Transactions Act, a uniform model law, promulgated in 1999, and subsequently adopted by most states, to validate electronic signatures and records, and generally, to ensure that general principles of contract formation are applied to electronic transactions. *See also* E-SIGN.

Unconscionable. A concept, derived from equity, but now also applicable in suits at law, under which a court may use its discretion to refuse enforcement of a term or contract that shocks its conscience. In its modern formulation, unconscionability normally consists of both a **procedural** element (unfair bargaining) and a **substantive** element (resulting unfair terms).

Unenforceable. A contract or term is unenforceable if it contains some defect that precludes its **enforcement** by a court. (For example, a contract is unenforceable if it is subject to the statute of frauds, but does not comply with it.) Strictly speaking, an unenforceable contract or term is not a legal nullity, and is not completely **void**. (For example, a contract that is unenforceable for noncompliance with the statute of frauds may be enforced if the defendant does not raise the statute of frauds as a defense.) However, in most cases, this distinction is not practically significant because the end result is that the party relying on the contract or provision will not be able to obtain a remedy for its breach.

Unfair forfeiture. A general principle of justice under which the court has the discretion to temper the enforcement of the injured party's legal rights to avoid a disproportionately harsh impact on the party against whom enforcement is sought.

Unforeseeable/unforeseen. *See* Foreseen/foreseeable.

Unilateral contract. A unilateral contract is one in which only one of the parties has a promise outstanding at the time that the contract is formed. It is distinct from a bilateral contract, in which there are promises due by both parties at the instant of formation. There can be no such thing as a "unilateral" contract as that word may be understood in a lay sense — a person cannot contract with himself, and a one-sided promise to another person does not qualify as a contract because it lacks consideration. In contract law "unilateral contract" is a term of art, used to describe a situation in which an offer prescribes or permits the act of acceptance to be the offeree's rendition of the very performance that will constitute the offeree's consideration under the contract. In this way, the act of signifying acceptance is at the same time the act of performance. The effect of this is that at the instance of acceptance, the offeree has completed the performance of his side of the transaction, and the only thing remaining is the offeror's promise of return performance. *See also* Bilateral contract.

UNIDROIT Principles of International Commercial Contracts. A compilation of general rules and common principles of contract law that are recommended as applicable to transnational commercial contracts.

Unilateral mistake. *See* Mistake.

United Nations Convention on Contracts for the International Sale of Goods. *See* CISG.

Usage. The customs and established practices in a particular trade, industry, or market.

Ut res magis valeat quam pereat. (Latin: "The thing should rather have effect than be destroyed.") A rule of interpretation under which a court resolves uncertainty in favor of a meaning that is lawful, reasonable, and congruent with public policy.

Variable costs. *See* Fixed costs.

Vesting. The irrevocable settling of rights on a person.

Void. A contract or term is void if it has no legal effect. It is a legal nullity and cannot be enforced by either party. A void contract must be distinguished from an **avoidable** contract, in which one of the parties has the election either to enforce the contract, or to **rescind** it.

Volunteer. In the context of unjust enrichment, a person who confers a benefit with gratuitous intent.

Waiver. A voluntary abandonment of a legal right.

Windfall. An unexpected and undeserved benefit. In the context of damages, an amount that exceeds what the plaintiff needs to be fully compensated for her loss.

Writ. A written order by a court, requiring or authorizing an act to be performed. A writ of execution or garnishment is an order to the sheriff or equivalent official, requiring her to seize property of the judgment debtor. (*See also* Execution.) In older common law, "writ" was also used to denote the document that commenced an action.

Table of Cases

Table of Cases

Table of Cases

820

Table of Statutes

Index

References are to sections. References to Examples and Explanations are designated by the letter "E" followed by the chapter number and the Example number (e.g., "E1-2" refers to Chapter 1, Example 2).

Index

insecurity concerning prospective
performance, 19.3.8, E19-5
notification of assignment, 19.3.4,
19.3.5, E19-4
policy favoring transferability,
10.2.3, E12-2, 19.3.1,
19.3.3, E19-5, E19-8
policy precluding certain assignments,
19.3.3
restrictions on assignment, 19.3.1, 19.3.3,
E19-6, E19-7, E19-8
restrictions on delegation, 19.3.6, E19-6,
E19-7, E19-8
transnational perspective, 19.4
Assurance of performance. *See* Anticipatory
repudiation; Assignment and
delegation
Attorney malpractice claim transfer, 19.3.3,
E19-1
Attorney's fees, 18.12.3
Automated assent. *See* Electronic,
e-mail, and Web-based contracts
Avoidance of contract
for duress, 13.8.1, 13.8.5
for fraud, 13.6.7
for impracticability, 15.7.1
by mentally incapacitated party, 14.1,
14.3.1, 14.3.3
by minor, E3-1, E3-4, 14.1, 14.2.1, 14.2.3,
E14-1, E14-2
for mistake, 15.1, 15.4, 15.5
for unconscionability, 13.11.6
for undue influence, 13.10
for unfair bargaining, generally, 13.3
voidable defined, 9.7.3, 13.3
voidable distinguished from void, 9.7.3, 13.3

Bad faith. *See* Good faith
Bankruptcy
discharged debt as moral obligation, 9.7.3
promise to refrain as consideration, E7-3
Bargain. *See* Agreement defined;
Consideration, Negotiation
Barred claim. *See* Statute of frauds; Statute of
limitations; Unenforceability
Battle of the forms. *See also* Offer and
acceptance; Sale of goods
acceptance, 6.1, 6.3.1, E6-2
acceptance by performance, 6.3.1,
6.3.3, E6-3
additional terms, 6.3.1, 6.4, E6-1,
E6-2, E6-3, E6-4

conduct, 6.3.1, 6.3.3, E6-5
confirmation, 6.1, 6.4, E6-4
counteroffer, 6.3.1, 6.3.3, E6-1,
E6-3
definite expression of acceptance,
6.3.1, E6-1, E6-2, E6-3
different terms, 6.3.1, 6.4, E6-2,
E6-4
electronic contracting, 6.1.3
expressly conditional acceptance,
6.3.1, 6.3.3, E6-1, E6-3
gap fillers, 6.3.3, E6-1, E6-3, E6-4
knockout rule, 6.3.2, E6-2, E6-3
last shot rule, 6.2, 6.3.3
limitation of acceptance to offer, 6.3.2
mailbox rule, E6-1
material alteration of offer, 6.3.2,
E6-4, E6-5
merchant, 6.3.2, E6-1, E6-2, E6-3
mirror image rule, 6.2, E6-3
offer, 6.1
performance absent written contract, 6.3.3, 6.4
proposals, 6.3.2, 6.4, E6-1, E6-3
purpose of §2.207, 6.2
seasonable acceptance, 6.3.1, E6-1
transnational perspective, 6.5
Benefit. *See* Consideration; Damages; Material
benefit rule; Restitution; Third-party
beneficiary contract
Best efforts. *See also* Gap fillers; Good faith;
Implied terms
implied, 7.9.2, 10.2.1, 10.2.2, 10.2.3, E10-5,
16.8.1, 16.10.1,
E16-3, E16-4, E16-5, E19-6
objective or subjective test, 10.2.2, E10-5
in seeking fulfillment of a condition, 16.8.1,
16.10.1, E16-3,
E16-4, E16-5
Bilateral contract
defined, 4.12.2, E1-6
noninstantaneous performance, 4.12.5,
E4-4, E4-5
offer for, 4.12.2, 4.12.4, 4.12.5,
E4-4, E4-5, E4-8
presumption in favor of, 4.12.4, E4-4
Boilerplate. *See* Adhesion; Battle of the forms;
Duty to read; Standard contracts and
terms; Unconscionability
Box-top terms. *See* Standard contracts and terms
Breach of contract
in advance of performance. *See* Anticipatory
repudiation

Index

Index